CRIME STATE RANKINGS
2002

Crime in the 50 United States

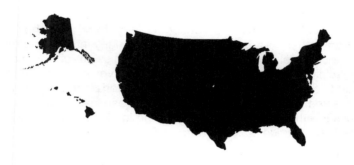

Editors:
Kathleen O'Leary Morgan and Scott Morgan

Morgan Quitno Press
© Copyright 2002, All Rights Reserved

512 East 9th Street, P.O. Box 1656
Lawrence, KS 66044-8656
USA

800-457-0742 or 785-841-3534
www.statestats.com

Ninth Edition

ISBN:
0-7401-0040-8
ISSN:
1077-4408

Crime State Rankings 2002 sells for $54.95 ($5.00 shipping) and is only available in paper binding. For those who prefer ranking information tailored to a particular state, we also offer *Crime State Perspectives*, state-specific reports for each of the 50 states. These individual guides provide information on a state's data and rank for each of the categories featured in the national *Crime State Rankings* volume. Perspectives sell for $19.00 or $9.50 if ordered with *Crime State Rankings*. If you are interested in city and metropolitan crime data, we offer *City Crime Rankings, 8th Edition* ($42.95 paper). Those interested in health statistics should check out our annual *Health Care State Rankings* ($54.95 paper). If you are interested in a general view of the states, please ask about our annual *State Rankings* ($54.95 paper) or our monthly *State Statistical Trends* ($299 a year). All of our data sets are also available in machine readable format. Shipping is $5.00 per order.

Ninth Edition
Printed in the United States of America
April 2002

PREFACE

Crime State Rankings 2002 gives you everything you need to know about crime and law enforcement in the 50 United States. This huge collection of state crime statistics reports crime numbers, rates and trends; prison statistics and corrections data; law enforcement personnel and finance; juvenile crime and delinquency; drugs and alcohol, arrests and crime clearances. Find out how your state compares in violent and property crime. How much is spent on state and local law enforcement? What percentage of murders involve handguns? Answers to these and hundreds of other crime-related questions are found in the 508 tables of *Crime State Rankings 2002*.

Important Notes About *Crime State Rankings 2002*

In publishing *Crime State Rankings,* our goal is to translate the thousands of crime statistics available through federal and state governments into meaningful state comparisons. As we review and update the book each year, we reexamine each table and ask, "Does it makes sense?" and "Is the information useful or interesting?" In this newly revised edition, most tables were updated from last year's book, while others were removed and new data of interest were added. With 508 tables of state crime comparisons, this ninth edition is a solid collection of valuable crime and law enforcement information.

While you will find a number of changes and updates, many of the organizational features that have made this book so popular with both reviewers and researchers have not changed. Data are presented in both alphabetical and rank order so that readers may quickly find information for a particular state and then just as quickly learn which states rank above and below that state. Source information and other important footnotes are clearly shown at the bottom of each page and national totals, rates and percentages are prominently displayed at the top of each table. Every other line is shaded in gray for easier reading. In addition, numerous information-finding tools are provided: a thorough table of contents, table listings at the beginning of each chapter, a detailed index and a chapter thumb index. Also included is a roster of sources showing addresses, phone numbers and websites.

For the ease of our readers, the statistics in *Crime State Rankings 2002* are "complete," meaning that no additional calculations are required to convert the numbers to thousands, millions, etc. All states are ranked on a high to low basis. Ties among states are shown alphabetically for a given ranking. Numbers reported in parentheses "( )" are negative numbers. For tables with national totals (as opposed to rates, per capita's, etc.) we include a separate column showing what percent of the national total each individual state's total represents. This column is headed by "% of USA." This percentage figure is particularly interesting when compared with a state's share of the nation's population for a particular year. The appendix contains population tables to aid in these comparisons.

For those interested in focusing on crime information for just one state, we once again are offering our *Crime State Perspective* series of publications. These 21-page, comb-bound reports feature data and ranking information for an individual state pulled from *Crime State Rankings 2002*. (For example, *New York Crime in Perspective* contains crime information about the state of New York only.) When purchased individually, *Crime State Perspectives* sell for $19. When purchased with a copy of *Crime State Rankings 2002,* these handy quick reference guides are just $9.50.

Other Books from Morgan Quitno Press

For up-to-date crime information for cities, our *City Crime Rankings* reference book compares cities of 75,000 population or more and all metropolitan areas (some as small as 65,000 population) in 40 categories of crime. Crime numbers, rates and trends are presented for all major crime categories reported by the FBI. (8th edition featuring 2000 crime statistics; 42.95 + $5 S/H; paper.)

For general state statistics or state health care information, check out *State Rankings* and *Health Care State Rankings*. *State Rankings 2002* provides statistics on a wide variety of subjects, such as agriculture, education, transportation, government finance, health, population, crime, social welfare, energy and environment. *Health Care State Rankings 2002* includes data on health care facilities, providers, insurance and finance, incidence of disease, mortality, physical fitness, natality and reproductive health. *State Rankings* and *Health Care State Rankings* sell for $54.95 each (paper; S/H $5 per order). Also available are *State Perspectives* and *Health Care State Perspectives* for each of these books, selling for $19 individually or $9.50 if purchased with their corresponding national volume. The data in all of our reference books are available on CD-ROM. These electronic editions provide a searchable PDF version of each book as well as the raw data in .dbf, Excel and ASCII formats. CD-ROM and book sets are $154.95 each.

State Statistical Trends is our popular monthly journal that compares changes in life and government for the 50 United States. Each 100-page monthly issue examines a different subject and provides a collection of tables, graphics and commentary showing state multi-year trends. For further information about *Trends* or any of our other publications, please call us toll-free at 1-800-457-0742 or check out our website at www.statestats.com.

Finally, many thanks to the many hard working librarians and government workers who help us every year with information, explanations and general support. Thanks also to you, our readers. We always welcome your thoughts and suggestions, so please give us a call, send us an e-mail or drop us a note with your ideas.

- THE EDITORS

WHICH STATE IS THE MOST DANGEROUS?

 As they say in Louisiana, "Nous somme de retour!" — "We're back!" Having been out of our awards spotlight since 1998, Louisiana is back at the top of the rankings as the nation's Most Dangerous State The Pelican State moved up from fourth place last year to reclaim the title. Florida held on to second place, while last year's Most Dangerous State, New Mexico, dropped to third. On the safer end of the ranking scale, North Dakota "owns" our Safest State Award, claiming that honor for a record sixth year in a row.

The Methodology

The Safest and Most Dangerous States rankings are determined using a four-step process. First, rates for six crime categories — murder, rape, robbery, aggravated assault, burglary and motor vehicle theft — are plugged into a formula that measures how a state compares to the national average for a given crime category.

Second, the outcome of this equation is then multiplied by a weight assigned to each crime category. For this year's award, we again gave each crime category equal weight. Thus state comparisons are based purely on crime rates and how these rates stack up to the national average for a given crime category.

Third, the weighted numbers are added together to achieve state's score ("SUM.") In the fourth and final step, these composite scores are ranked from highest to lowest to determine which states are the most dangerous and safest. Thus the farther below the national average a state's crime rate is, the lower (and safer) it ranks. The farther above the national average, the higher (and more dangerous) a state ranks in the final list.

2002 MOST DANGEROUS STATE

RANK	STATE	SUM	'01	RANK	STATE	SUM	'01
1	Louisiana	41.58	4	26	Indiana	(15.18)	24
2	Florida	39.09	2	27	Rhode Island	(15.47)	32
3	New Mexico	36.69	1	28	Hawaii	(19.03)	33
4	Maryland	33.30	6	30	Colorado	(19.45)	26
5	Arizona	28.97	7	30	Oregon	(19.45)	27
6	Tennessee	28.58	9	31	Pennsylvania	(20.02)	29
7	Nevada	27.57	3	32	Massachusetts	(23.75)	30
8	South Carolina	23.17	8	33	New Jersey	(24.03)	31
9	Michigan	19.69	12	34	Minnesota	(27.02)	36
10	Illinois	17.18	11	35	Kentucky	(29.17)	38
11	Alaska	13.50	5	36	Nebraska	(30.04)	34
12	Delaware	12.88	10	37	Connecticut	(30.96)	37
13	California	11.70	17	38	Virginia	(32.19)	35
14	Texas	11.26	15	39	Utah	(33.19)	39
15	North Carolina	9.60	14	40	Wisconsin	(40.99)	41
16	Georgia	9.56	13	41	West Virginia	(45.14)	40
17	Alabama	3.19	19	42	Montana	(46.07)	45
18	Washington	1.56	20	43	New Hampshire	(47.23)	49
19	Oklahoma	0.96	18	44	Iowa	(48.19)	43
20	Mississippi	(0.25)	16	45	Wyoming	(48.71)	46
21	Missouri	(1.55)	21	46	Idaho	(48.94)	42
22	Arkansas	(9.89)	25	47	South Dakota	(55.63)	44
23	Kansas	(10.49)	23	48	Vermont	(59.17)	47
24	New York	(12.19)	22	49	Maine	(61.44)	48
25	Ohio	(13.69)	28	50	North Dakota	(67.50)	50

FACTORS CONSIDERED (all given equal weight):
(all rates per 100,000 population)

1. Murder Rate (Table 328)
2. Rape Rate (Table 347)
3. Robbery Rate (Table 353)
4. Aggravated Assault Rate (Table 368)
5. Burglary Rate (Table 388)
6. Motor Vehicle Theft Rate (Table 398)

Morgan Quitno Press takes pride in presenting facts in a nonbiased, objective manner. While a central theme of our books is our clear presentation of data with the analysis and interpretation left to our readers, we stray from this policy once a year and issue our awards. The Safest and Most Dangerous States have been named annually since 1994. We have awarded the Most Livable State title since 1991, based on data from our *State Rankings* series. In 1993, we began the Healthiest State Award based on statistics from our *Health Care State Rankings* series. In 1994, we initiated the annual Safest and Most Dangerous City Award based on information in our *City Crime Rankings* volume.

North Dakota has earned the honor of being "stuck" as the nation's Safest State. With crime rates comparable to it's average temperature (e.g. an aggravated assault rate of 45.8 compared to the national rate of 323.6) it may be a while before another state takes away the title.

Louisiana has different issues. Its murder rate is the highest in the country, at 12.5 per 100,000 population, compared to the national rate of 5.5. Even the state with the second highest murder rate, Mississippi, is a ways back with 9.0. Still, Louisianans can takes some comfort. In the year from 1999 to 2000, their state's violent crime rate dropped 7.0%, as opposed to the national average decline of 3.2% over the same period. Here's to continued progress in the fight against crime.

— THE EDITORS

TABLE OF CONTENTS

I. Arrests

II. Corrections

TABLE OF CONTENTS (continued)

TABLE OF CONTENTS (continued)

III. Drugs and Alcohol

IV. Finance

TABLE OF CONTENTS (continued)

V. Juveniles

TABLE OF CONTENTS (continued)

VI. Law Enforcement

TABLE OF CONTENTS (continued)

VII. Offenses

TABLE OF CONTENTS (continued)

Urban/Rural Crime

TABLE OF CONTENTS (continued)

TABLE OF CONTENTS (continued)

VIII. Appendix

IX. Sources

X. Index

I. ARRESTS

Important Note Regarding Arrest Numbers

The state arrest numbers reported by the FBI and shown in tables 1 to 36 are only from those law enforcement agencies that submitted complete arrests reports for 12 months in 2000. The arrest rates were calculated by the editors using population totals provided by the FBI for those jurisdictions reporting. Reports from law enforcement agencies in Georgia, Illinois, Kentucky, Montana, New York, South Carolina and West Virginia represented less than half of their state populations. Thus rates for these states should be interpreted with caution. Reports from Delaware, Missouri, Mississippi and Ohio represented just over half of their state population. No arrest data were available for Kansas, Wisconsin and the District of Columbia.

Reported Arrests in 2000

National Total = 11,140,776 Reported Arrests*

Source: Federal Bureau of Investigation

ALPHA ORDER

RANK	STATE	ARRESTS	% of USA
24	Alabama	162,906	1.5%
41	Alaska	36,718	0.3%
10	Arizona	299,846	2.7%
19	Arkansas	206,776	1.9%
1	California	1,674,882	15.0%
18	Colorado	241,572	2.2%
28	Connecticut	132,482	1.2%
40	Delaware	36,739	0.3%
3	Florida	881,709	7.9%
15	Georgia	250,502	2.2%
37	Hawaii	57,264	0.5%
33	Idaho	79,810	0.7%
14	Illinois	253,967	2.3%
20	Indiana	206,134	1.9%
30	Iowa	113,918	1.0%
NA	Kansas**	NA	NA
46	Kentucky	15,678	0.1%
21	Louisiana	199,475	1.8%
36	Maine	61,049	0.5%
11	Maryland	292,169	2.6%
27	Massachusetts	138,649	1.2%
7	Michigan	333,591	3.0%
12	Minnesota	275,125	2.5%
29	Mississippi	124,995	1.1%
16	Missouri	246,187	2.2%
48	Montana	13,156	0.1%
31	Nebraska	105,221	0.9%
25	Nevada	156,398	1.4%
43	New Hampshire	33,622	0.3%
5	New Jersey	430,502	3.9%
35	New Mexico	78,113	0.7%
8	New York	308,480	2.8%
4	North Carolina	453,693	4.1%
45	North Dakota	26,869	0.2%
9	Ohio	301,000	2.7%
23	Oklahoma	164,613	1.5%
26	Oregon	153,693	1.4%
6	Pennsylvania	415,331	3.7%
39	Rhode Island	37,103	0.3%
34	South Carolina	78,992	0.7%
38	South Dakota	38,859	0.3%
22	Tennessee	187,110	1.7%
2	Texas	1,145,271	10.3%
32	Utah	98,038	0.9%
47	Vermont	14,101	0.1%
13	Virginia	272,656	2.4%
17	Washington	242,128	2.2%
44	West Virginia	27,275	0.2%
NA	Wisconsin**	NA	NA
42	Wyoming	36,409	0.3%

RANK ORDER

RANK	STATE	ARRESTS	% of USA
1	California	1,674,882	15.0%
2	Texas	1,145,271	10.3%
3	Florida	881,709	7.9%
4	North Carolina	453,693	4.1%
5	New Jersey	430,502	3.9%
6	Pennsylvania	415,331	3.7%
7	Michigan	333,591	3.0%
8	New York	308,480	2.8%
9	Ohio	301,000	2.7%
10	Arizona	299,846	2.7%
11	Maryland	292,169	2.6%
12	Minnesota	275,125	2.5%
13	Virginia	272,656	2.4%
14	Illinois	253,967	2.3%
15	Georgia	250,502	2.2%
16	Missouri	246,187	2.2%
17	Washington	242,128	2.2%
18	Colorado	241,572	2.2%
19	Arkansas	206,776	1.9%
20	Indiana	206,134	1.9%
21	Louisiana	199,475	1.8%
22	Tennessee	187,110	1.7%
23	Oklahoma	164,613	1.5%
24	Alabama	162,906	1.5%
25	Nevada	156,398	1.4%
26	Oregon	153,693	1.4%
27	Massachusetts	138,649	1.2%
28	Connecticut	132,482	1.2%
29	Mississippi	124,995	1.1%
30	Iowa	113,918	1.0%
31	Nebraska	105,221	0.9%
32	Utah	98,038	0.9%
33	Idaho	79,810	0.7%
34	South Carolina	78,992	0.7%
35	New Mexico	78,113	0.7%
36	Maine	61,049	0.5%
37	Hawaii	57,264	0.5%
38	South Dakota	38,859	0.3%
39	Rhode Island	37,103	0.3%
40	Delaware	36,739	0.3%
41	Alaska	36,718	0.3%
42	Wyoming	36,409	0.3%
43	New Hampshire	33,622	0.3%
44	West Virginia	27,275	0.2%
45	North Dakota	26,869	0.2%
46	Kentucky	15,678	0.1%
47	Vermont	14,101	0.1%
48	Montana	13,156	0.1%
NA	Kansas**	NA	NA
NA	Wisconsin**	NA	NA
	District of Columbia**	NA	NA

Source: Federal Bureau of Investigation
   "Crime in the United States 2000" (Uniform Crime Reports, October 22, 2001)
*By law enforcement agencies submitting complete reports to the F.B.I. for 12 months in 2000. The F.B.I. estimates 13,980,297 reported and unreported arrests occurred in 2000. See important note at beginning of this chapter.
**Not available.

Reported Arrest Rate in 2000

National Rate = 4,073.6 Reported Arrests per 100,000 Population*

ALPHA ORDER			RANK ORDER		
RANK	STATE	RATE	RANK	STATE	RATE
32	Alabama	3,659.6	1	Nevada	7,747.4
6	Alaska	5,850.5	2	Arkansas	7,721.2
7	Arizona	5,805.0	3	Wyoming	7,370.2
2	Arkansas	7,721.2	4	Nebraska	6,144.0
16	California	4,926.1	5	Idaho	6,142.7
9	Colorado	5,587.5	6	Alaska	5,850.5
30	Connecticut	3,885.0	7	Arizona	5,805.0
20	Delaware	4,672.8	8	North Carolina	5,616.8
12	Florida	5,492.0	9	Colorado	5,587.5
38	Georgia	3,043.8	10	Minnesota	5,579.4
19	Hawaii	4,723.7	11	Maryland	5,501.3
5	Idaho	6,142.7	12	Florida	5,492.0
43	Illinois	2,042.2	13	Texas	5,467.6
34	Indiana	3,384.8	14	South Dakota	5,143.4
29	Iowa	3,891.3	15	New Jersey	5,107.4
NA	Kansas**	NA	16	California	4,926.1
48	Kentucky	387.4	17	Maine	4,780.8
22	Louisiana	4,462.6	18	Oklahoma	4,766.9
17	Maine	4,780.8	19	Hawaii	4,723.7
11	Maryland	5,501.3	20	Delaware	4,672.8
42	Massachusetts	2,181.0	21	Oregon	4,481.8
36	Michigan	3,352.0	22	Louisiana	4,462.6
10	Minnesota	5,579.4	23	Missouri	4,393.4
24	Mississippi	4,387.2	24	Mississippi	4,387.2
23	Missouri	4,393.4	25	Utah	4,373.7
47	Montana	1,456.7	26	New Mexico	4,288.9
4	Nebraska	6,144.0	27	North Dakota	4,192.3
1	Nevada	7,747.4	28	Washington	4,098.0
39	New Hampshire	2,711.7	29	Iowa	3,891.3
15	New Jersey	5,107.4	30	Connecticut	3,885.0
26	New Mexico	4,288.9	31	Virginia	3,838.1
45	New York	1,624.5	32	Alabama	3,659.6
8	North Carolina	5,616.8	33	Rhode Island	3,532.8
27	North Dakota	4,192.3	34	Indiana	3,384.8
40	Ohio	2,649.7	35	Pennsylvania	3,381.5
18	Oklahoma	4,766.9	36	Michigan	3,352.0
21	Oregon	4,481.8	37	Tennessee	3,281.5
35	Pennsylvania	3,381.5	38	Georgia	3,043.8
33	Rhode Island	3,532.8	39	New Hampshire	2,711.7
44	South Carolina	1,963.3	40	Ohio	2,649.7
14	South Dakota	5,143.4	41	Vermont	2,312.7
37	Tennessee	3,281.5	42	Massachusetts	2,181.0
13	Texas	5,467.6	43	Illinois	2,042.2
25	Utah	4,373.7	44	South Carolina	1,963.3
41	Vermont	2,312.7	45	New York	1,624.5
31	Virginia	3,838.1	46	West Virginia	1,509.3
28	Washington	4,098.0	47	Montana	1,456.7
46	West Virginia	1,509.3	48	Kentucky	387.4
NA	Wisconsin**	NA	NA	Kansas**	NA
3	Wyoming	7,370.2	NA	Wisconsin**	NA
				District of Columbia**	NA

Source: Morgan Quitno Press using data from Federal Bureau of Investigation
    "Crime in the United States 2000" (Uniform Crime Reports, October 22, 2001)
*By law enforcement agencies submitting complete reports to the F.B.I. for 12 months in 2000. These rates based
on population estimates for areas under the jurisdiction of those agencies reporting. Arrest rate based on the F.B.I.
estimate of total arrests is 4,955.4 reported and unreported arrests per 100,000 population. See important note at
beginning of this chapter. **Not available.

Reported Arrests for Crime Index Offenses in 2000

National Total = 1,696,271 Reported Arrests*

ALPHA ORDER

RANK	STATE	ARRESTS	% of USA
25	Alabama	21,082	1.2%
39	Alaska	5,743	0.3%
9	Arizona	45,546	2.7%
26	Arkansas	20,895	1.2%
1	California	296,503	17.5%
19	Colorado	31,644	1.9%
28	Connecticut	19,637	1.2%
38	Delaware	7,629	0.4%
2	Florida	176,993	10.4%
13	Georgia	39,225	2.3%
37	Hawaii	7,927	0.5%
34	Idaho	9,511	0.6%
7	Illinois	51,267	3.0%
17	Indiana	32,936	1.9%
29	Iowa	17,802	1.0%
NA	Kansas**	NA	NA
47	Kentucky	2,073	0.1%
16	Louisiana	36,380	2.1%
36	Maine	8,035	0.5%
12	Maryland	40,074	2.4%
21	Massachusetts	28,292	1.7%
14	Michigan	36,937	2.2%
18	Minnesota	32,406	1.9%
31	Mississippi	15,074	0.9%
15	Missouri	36,388	2.1%
46	Montana	2,370	0.1%
32	Nebraska	12,808	0.8%
27	Nevada	20,718	1.2%
45	New Hampshire	2,437	0.1%
6	New Jersey	53,720	3.2%
35	New Mexico	9,179	0.5%
8	New York	48,489	2.9%
5	North Carolina	70,959	4.2%
44	North Dakota	2,911	0.2%
10	Ohio	43,162	2.5%
24	Oklahoma	22,908	1.4%
20	Oregon	28,717	1.7%
4	Pennsylvania	72,155	4.3%
40	Rhode Island	4,936	0.3%
33	South Carolina	10,022	0.6%
42	South Dakota	4,220	0.2%
23	Tennessee	27,699	1.6%
3	Texas	142,792	8.4%
30	Utah	16,149	1.0%
48	Vermont	1,772	0.1%
22	Virginia	28,027	1.7%
11	Washington	42,228	2.5%
41	West Virginia	4,381	0.3%
NA	Wisconsin**	NA	NA
43	Wyoming	3,513	0.2%

RANK ORDER

RANK	STATE	ARRESTS	% of USA
1	California	296,503	17.5%
2	Florida	176,993	10.4%
3	Texas	142,792	8.4%
4	Pennsylvania	72,155	4.3%
5	North Carolina	70,959	4.2%
6	New Jersey	53,720	3.2%
7	Illinois	51,267	3.0%
8	New York	48,489	2.9%
9	Arizona	45,546	2.7%
10	Ohio	43,162	2.5%
11	Washington	42,228	2.5%
12	Maryland	40,074	2.4%
13	Georgia	39,225	2.3%
14	Michigan	36,937	2.2%
15	Missouri	36,388	2.1%
16	Louisiana	36,380	2.1%
17	Indiana	32,936	1.9%
18	Minnesota	32,406	1.9%
19	Colorado	31,644	1.9%
20	Oregon	28,717	1.7%
21	Massachusetts	28,292	1.7%
22	Virginia	28,027	1.7%
23	Tennessee	27,699	1.6%
24	Oklahoma	22,908	1.4%
25	Alabama	21,082	1.2%
26	Arkansas	20,895	1.2%
27	Nevada	20,718	1.2%
28	Connecticut	19,637	1.2%
29	Iowa	17,802	1.0%
30	Utah	16,149	1.0%
31	Mississippi	15,074	0.9%
32	Nebraska	12,808	0.8%
33	South Carolina	10,022	0.6%
34	Idaho	9,511	0.6%
35	New Mexico	9,179	0.5%
36	Maine	8,035	0.5%
37	Hawaii	7,927	0.5%
38	Delaware	7,629	0.4%
39	Alaska	5,743	0.3%
40	Rhode Island	4,936	0.3%
41	West Virginia	4,381	0.3%
42	South Dakota	4,220	0.2%
43	Wyoming	3,513	0.2%
44	North Dakota	2,911	0.2%
45	New Hampshire	2,437	0.1%
46	Montana	2,370	0.1%
47	Kentucky	2,073	0.1%
48	Vermont	1,772	0.1%
NA	Kansas**	NA	NA
NA	Wisconsin**	NA	NA
	District of Columbia**	NA	NA

Source: Federal Bureau of Investigation
   "Crime in the United States 2000" (Uniform Crime Reports, October 22, 2001)
*By law enforcement agencies submitting complete reports to the F.B.I. for 12 months in 2000. The F.B.I. estimates
2,246,054 reported and unreported arrests for crime index offenses occurred in 2000. Crime index offenses consist
of murder, forcible rape, robbery, aggravated assault, burglary, larceny-theft, motor vehicle theft and arson. See
important note at beginning of this chapter. **Not available.

Reported Arrest Rate for Crime Index Offenses in 2000

National Rate = 620.2 Reported Arrests per 100,000 Population*

ALPHA ORDER			RANK ORDER		
RANK	STATE	RATE	RANK	STATE	RATE
34	Alabama	473.6	1	Florida	1,102.5
4	Alaska	915.1	2	Nevada	1,026.3
5	Arizona	881.8	3	Delaware	970.3
10	Arkansas	780.2	4	Alaska	915.1
7	California	872.1	5	Arizona	881.8
14	Colorado	731.9	6	North Carolina	878.5
27	Connecticut	575.9	7	California	872.1
3	Delaware	970.3	8	Oregon	837.4
1	Florida	1,102.5	9	Louisiana	813.9
33	Georgia	476.6	10	Arkansas	780.2
21	Hawaii	653.9	11	Maryland	754.6
13	Idaho	732.0	12	Nebraska	747.9
38	Illinois	412.2	13	Idaho	732.0
29	Indiana	540.8	14	Colorado	731.9
25	Iowa	608.1	15	Utah	720.4
NA	Kansas**	NA	16	Washington	714.7
48	Kentucky	51.2	17	Wyoming	711.1
9	Louisiana	813.9	18	Texas	681.7
24	Maine	629.2	19	Oklahoma	663.4
11	Maryland	754.6	20	Minnesota	657.2
37	Massachusetts	445.0	21	Hawaii	653.9
41	Michigan	371.2	22	Missouri	649.4
20	Minnesota	657.2	23	New Jersey	637.3
30	Mississippi	529.1	24	Maine	629.2
22	Missouri	649.4	25	Iowa	608.1
43	Montana	262.4	26	Pennsylvania	587.5
12	Nebraska	747.9	27	Connecticut	575.9
2	Nevada	1,026.3	28	South Dakota	558.6
47	New Hampshire	196.6	29	Indiana	540.8
23	New Jersey	637.3	30	Mississippi	529.1
31	New Mexico	504.0	31	New Mexico	504.0
44	New York	255.3	32	Tennessee	485.8
6	North Carolina	878.5	33	Georgia	476.6
36	North Dakota	454.2	34	Alabama	473.6
40	Ohio	379.9	35	Rhode Island	470.0
19	Oklahoma	663.4	36	North Dakota	454.2
8	Oregon	837.4	37	Massachusetts	445.0
26	Pennsylvania	587.5	38	Illinois	412.2
35	Rhode Island	470.0	39	Virginia	394.5
45	South Carolina	249.1	40	Ohio	379.9
28	South Dakota	558.6	41	Michigan	371.2
32	Tennessee	485.8	42	Vermont	290.6
18	Texas	681.7	43	Montana	262.4
15	Utah	720.4	44	New York	255.3
42	Vermont	290.6	45	South Carolina	249.1
39	Virginia	394.5	46	West Virginia	242.4
16	Washington	714.7	47	New Hampshire	196.6
46	West Virginia	242.4	48	Kentucky	51.2
NA	Wisconsin**	NA	NA	Kansas**	NA
17	Wyoming	711.1	NA	Wisconsin**	NA
				District of Columbia**	NA

Source: Morgan Quitno Press using data from Federal Bureau of Investigation
   "Crime in the United States 2000" (Uniform Crime Reports, October 22, 2001)
*By law enforcement agencies submitting complete reports to the F.B.I. for 12 months in 2000. These rates based on population estimates for areas under the jurisdiction of those agencies reporting. Arrest rate based on the F.B.I. estimate of reported and unreported arrests for crime index offenses is 796.1 arrests per 100,000 population. See important note at beginning of this chapter. **Not available.

Reported Arrests for Violent Crime in 2000

National Total = 475,521 Reported Arrests*

RANK	STATE	ARRESTS	% of USA
23	Alabama	5,851	1.2%
39	Alaska	1,204	0.3%
16	Arizona	8,187	1.7%
25	Arkansas	4,959	1.0%
1	California	129,441	27.2%
24	Colorado	5,171	1.1%
26	Connecticut	4,527	1.0%
33	Delaware	2,304	0.5%
2	Florida	53,963	11.3%
9	Georgia	11,423	2.4%
38	Hawaii	1,279	0.3%
36	Idaho	1,368	0.3%
11	Illinois	10,317	2.2%
14	Indiana	10,106	2.1%
27	Iowa	4,145	0.9%
NA	Kansas**	NA	NA
46	Kentucky	379	0.1%
12	Louisiana	10,282	2.2%
41	Maine	887	0.2%
13	Maryland	10,159	2.1%
7	Massachusetts	13,559	2.9%
15	Michigan	9,265	1.9%
20	Minnesota	6,460	1.4%
32	Mississippi	2,552	0.5%
18	Missouri	7,684	1.6%
42	Montana	691	0.1%
35	Nebraska	1,448	0.3%
29	Nevada	3,181	0.7%
45	New Hampshire	415	0.1%
6	New Jersey	15,497	3.3%
31	New Mexico	2,793	0.6%
8	New York	11,502	2.4%
5	North Carolina	20,609	4.3%
48	North Dakota	149	0.0%
10	Ohio	10,349	2.2%
22	Oklahoma	5,985	1.3%
28	Oregon	3,304	0.7%
4	Pennsylvania	23,496	4.9%
40	Rhode Island	1,048	0.2%
30	South Carolina	3,030	0.6%
44	South Dakota	570	0.1%
17	Tennessee	8,161	1.7%
3	Texas	30,624	6.4%
34	Utah	1,528	0.3%
47	Vermont	284	0.1%
21	Virginia	6,246	1.3%
19	Washington	7,192	1.5%
37	West Virginia	1,304	0.3%
NA	Wisconsin**	NA	NA
43	Wyoming	643	0.1%

RANK	STATE	ARRESTS	% of USA
1	California	129,441	27.2%
2	Florida	53,963	11.3%
3	Texas	30,624	6.4%
4	Pennsylvania	23,496	4.9%
5	North Carolina	20,609	4.3%
6	New Jersey	15,497	3.3%
7	Massachusetts	13,559	2.9%
8	New York	11,502	2.4%
9	Georgia	11,423	2.4%
10	Ohio	10,349	2.2%
11	Illinois	10,317	2.2%
12	Louisiana	10,282	2.2%
13	Maryland	10,159	2.1%
14	Indiana	10,106	2.1%
15	Michigan	9,265	1.9%
16	Arizona	8,187	1.7%
17	Tennessee	8,161	1.7%
18	Missouri	7,684	1.6%
19	Washington	7,192	1.5%
20	Minnesota	6,460	1.4%
21	Virginia	6,246	1.3%
22	Oklahoma	5,985	1.3%
23	Alabama	5,851	1.2%
24	Colorado	5,171	1.1%
25	Arkansas	4,959	1.0%
26	Connecticut	4,527	1.0%
27	Iowa	4,145	0.9%
28	Oregon	3,304	0.7%
29	Nevada	3,181	0.7%
30	South Carolina	3,030	0.6%
31	New Mexico	2,793	0.6%
32	Mississippi	2,552	0.5%
33	Delaware	2,304	0.5%
34	Utah	1,528	0.3%
35	Nebraska	1,448	0.3%
36	Idaho	1,368	0.3%
37	West Virginia	1,304	0.3%
38	Hawaii	1,279	0.3%
39	Alaska	1,204	0.3%
40	Rhode Island	1,048	0.2%
41	Maine	887	0.2%
42	Montana	691	0.1%
43	Wyoming	643	0.1%
44	South Dakota	570	0.1%
45	New Hampshire	415	0.1%
46	Kentucky	379	0.1%
47	Vermont	284	0.1%
48	North Dakota	149	0.0%
NA	Kansas**	NA	NA
NA	Wisconsin**	NA	NA
	District of Columbia**	NA	NA

Source: Federal Bureau of Investigation
   "Crime in the United States 2000" (Uniform Crime Reports, October 22, 2001)
*By law enforcement agencies submitting complete reports to the F.B.I. for 12 months in 2000. The F.B.I. estimates 625,132 reported and unreported arrests for violent crimes occurred in 2000. Violent crimes are offenses of murder, forcible rape, robbery and aggravated assault. See important note at beginning of this chapter.
**Not available.

Reported Arrest Rate for Violent Crime in 2000

National Rate = 173.9 Reported Arrests per 100,000 Population*

ALPHA ORDER

RANK	STATE	RATE
23	Alabama	131.4
7	Alaska	191.8
14	Arizona	158.5
10	Arkansas	185.2
1	California	380.7
27	Colorado	119.6
22	Connecticut	132.8
3	Delaware	293.0
2	Florida	336.1
20	Georgia	138.8
28	Hawaii	105.5
29	Idaho	105.3
37	Illinois	83.0
13	Indiana	165.9
19	Iowa	141.6
NA	Kansas**	NA
48	Kentucky	9.4
5	Louisiana	230.0
42	Maine	69.5
8	Maryland	191.3
6	Massachusetts	213.3
32	Michigan	93.1
24	Minnesota	131.0
34	Mississippi	89.6
21	Missouri	137.1
38	Montana	76.5
36	Nebraska	84.6
15	Nevada	157.6
46	New Hampshire	33.5
11	New Jersey	183.9
16	New Mexico	153.4
44	New York	60.6
4	North Carolina	255.1
47	North Dakota	23.2
33	Ohio	91.1
12	Oklahoma	173.3
31	Oregon	96.3
8	Pennsylvania	191.3
30	Rhode Island	99.8
40	South Carolina	75.3
39	South Dakota	75.4
18	Tennessee	143.1
17	Texas	146.2
43	Utah	68.2
45	Vermont	46.6
35	Virginia	87.9
26	Washington	121.7
41	West Virginia	72.2
NA	Wisconsin**	NA
25	Wyoming	130.2

RANK ORDER

RANK	STATE	RATE
1	California	380.7
2	Florida	336.1
3	Delaware	293.0
4	North Carolina	255.1
5	Louisiana	230.0
6	Massachusetts	213.3
7	Alaska	191.8
8	Maryland	191.3
8	Pennsylvania	191.3
10	Arkansas	185.2
11	New Jersey	183.9
12	Oklahoma	173.3
13	Indiana	165.9
14	Arizona	158.5
15	Nevada	157.6
16	New Mexico	153.4
17	Texas	146.2
18	Tennessee	143.1
19	Iowa	141.6
20	Georgia	138.8
21	Missouri	137.1
22	Connecticut	132.8
23	Alabama	131.4
24	Minnesota	131.0
25	Wyoming	130.2
26	Washington	121.7
27	Colorado	119.6
28	Hawaii	105.5
29	Idaho	105.3
30	Rhode Island	99.8
31	Oregon	96.3
32	Michigan	93.1
33	Ohio	91.1
34	Mississippi	89.6
35	Virginia	87.9
36	Nebraska	84.6
37	Illinois	83.0
38	Montana	76.5
39	South Dakota	75.4
40	South Carolina	75.3
41	West Virginia	72.2
42	Maine	69.5
43	Utah	68.2
44	New York	60.6
45	Vermont	46.6
46	New Hampshire	33.5
47	North Dakota	23.2
48	Kentucky	9.4
NA	Kansas**	NA
NA	Wisconsin**	NA
	District of Columbia**	NA

Source: Morgan Quitno Press using data from Federal Bureau of Investigation
   "Crime in the United States 2000" (Uniform Crime Reports, October 22, 2001)
*By law enforcement agencies submitting complete reports to the F.B.I. for 12 months in 2000. These rates based on population estimates for areas under the jurisdiction of those agencies reporting. Arrest rate based on the F.B.I. estimate of reported and unreported arrests for violent crimes is 221.6 arrests per 100,000 population. See important note at beginning of this chapter. **Not available.

Reported Arrests for Murder in 2000

National Total = 9,570 Reported Arrests*

<table>
<tr><td colspan="4">ALPHA ORDER</td><td colspan="4">RANK ORDER</td></tr>
<tr><td>RANK</td><td>STATE</td><td>ARRESTS</td><td>% of USA</td><td>RANK</td><td>STATE</td><td>ARRESTS</td><td>% of USA</td></tr>
<tr><td>9</td><td>Alabama</td><td>317</td><td>3.3%</td><td>1</td><td>California</td><td>1,635</td><td>17.1%</td></tr>
<tr><td>37</td><td>Alaska</td><td>21</td><td>0.2%</td><td>2</td><td>Texas</td><td>774</td><td>8.1%</td></tr>
<tr><td>15</td><td>Arizona</td><td>214</td><td>2.2%</td><td>3</td><td>Florida</td><td>679</td><td>7.1%</td></tr>
<tr><td>19</td><td>Arkansas</td><td>161</td><td>1.7%</td><td>4</td><td>North Carolina</td><td>621</td><td>6.5%</td></tr>
<tr><td>1</td><td>California</td><td>1,635</td><td>17.1%</td><td>5</td><td>Illinois</td><td>531</td><td>5.5%</td></tr>
<tr><td>26</td><td>Colorado</td><td>110</td><td>1.1%</td><td>6</td><td>Pennsylvania</td><td>465</td><td>4.9%</td></tr>
<tr><td>30</td><td>Connecticut</td><td>69</td><td>0.7%</td><td>7</td><td>Maryland</td><td>377</td><td>3.9%</td></tr>
<tr><td>36</td><td>Delaware</td><td>27</td><td>0.3%</td><td>8</td><td>Georgia</td><td>358</td><td>3.7%</td></tr>
<tr><td>3</td><td>Florida</td><td>679</td><td>7.1%</td><td>9</td><td>Alabama</td><td>317</td><td>3.3%</td></tr>
<tr><td>8</td><td>Georgia</td><td>358</td><td>3.7%</td><td>10</td><td>Louisiana</td><td>286</td><td>3.0%</td></tr>
<tr><td>33</td><td>Hawaii</td><td>40</td><td>0.4%</td><td>11</td><td>Missouri</td><td>239</td><td>2.5%</td></tr>
<tr><td>40</td><td>Idaho</td><td>15</td><td>0.2%</td><td>12</td><td>Virginia</td><td>238</td><td>2.5%</td></tr>
<tr><td>5</td><td>Illinois</td><td>531</td><td>5.5%</td><td>13</td><td>New Jersey</td><td>231</td><td>2.4%</td></tr>
<tr><td>16</td><td>Indiana</td><td>204</td><td>2.1%</td><td>14</td><td>New York</td><td>221</td><td>2.3%</td></tr>
<tr><td>34</td><td>Iowa</td><td>39</td><td>0.4%</td><td>15</td><td>Arizona</td><td>214</td><td>2.2%</td></tr>
<tr><td>NA</td><td>Kansas**</td><td>NA</td><td>NA</td><td>16</td><td>Indiana</td><td>204</td><td>2.1%</td></tr>
<tr><td>43</td><td>Kentucky</td><td>7</td><td>0.1%</td><td>17</td><td>Ohio</td><td>193</td><td>2.0%</td></tr>
<tr><td>10</td><td>Louisiana</td><td>286</td><td>3.0%</td><td>18</td><td>Oklahoma</td><td>182</td><td>1.9%</td></tr>
<tr><td>46</td><td>Maine</td><td>4</td><td>0.0%</td><td>19</td><td>Arkansas</td><td>161</td><td>1.7%</td></tr>
<tr><td>7</td><td>Maryland</td><td>377</td><td>3.9%</td><td>20</td><td>Tennessee</td><td>159</td><td>1.7%</td></tr>
<tr><td>31</td><td>Massachusetts</td><td>60</td><td>0.6%</td><td>21</td><td>Minnesota</td><td>149</td><td>1.6%</td></tr>
<tr><td>23</td><td>Michigan</td><td>138</td><td>1.4%</td><td>22</td><td>Mississippi</td><td>147</td><td>1.5%</td></tr>
<tr><td>21</td><td>Minnesota</td><td>149</td><td>1.6%</td><td>23</td><td>Michigan</td><td>138</td><td>1.4%</td></tr>
<tr><td>22</td><td>Mississippi</td><td>147</td><td>1.5%</td><td>23</td><td>Washington</td><td>138</td><td>1.4%</td></tr>
<tr><td>11</td><td>Missouri</td><td>239</td><td>2.5%</td><td>25</td><td>Nevada</td><td>111</td><td>1.2%</td></tr>
<tr><td>43</td><td>Montana</td><td>7</td><td>0.1%</td><td>26</td><td>Colorado</td><td>110</td><td>1.1%</td></tr>
<tr><td>32</td><td>Nebraska</td><td>48</td><td>0.5%</td><td>27</td><td>Oregon</td><td>102</td><td>1.1%</td></tr>
<tr><td>25</td><td>Nevada</td><td>111</td><td>1.2%</td><td>28</td><td>New Mexico</td><td>82</td><td>0.9%</td></tr>
<tr><td>46</td><td>New Hampshire</td><td>4</td><td>0.0%</td><td>29</td><td>South Carolina</td><td>72</td><td>0.8%</td></tr>
<tr><td>13</td><td>New Jersey</td><td>231</td><td>2.4%</td><td>30</td><td>Connecticut</td><td>69</td><td>0.7%</td></tr>
<tr><td>28</td><td>New Mexico</td><td>82</td><td>0.9%</td><td>31</td><td>Massachusetts</td><td>60</td><td>0.6%</td></tr>
<tr><td>14</td><td>New York</td><td>221</td><td>2.3%</td><td>32</td><td>Nebraska</td><td>48</td><td>0.5%</td></tr>
<tr><td>4</td><td>North Carolina</td><td>621</td><td>6.5%</td><td>33</td><td>Hawaii</td><td>40</td><td>0.4%</td></tr>
<tr><td>48</td><td>North Dakota</td><td>1</td><td>0.0%</td><td>34</td><td>Iowa</td><td>39</td><td>0.4%</td></tr>
<tr><td>17</td><td>Ohio</td><td>193</td><td>2.0%</td><td>35</td><td>Utah</td><td>31</td><td>0.3%</td></tr>
<tr><td>18</td><td>Oklahoma</td><td>182</td><td>1.9%</td><td>36</td><td>Delaware</td><td>27</td><td>0.3%</td></tr>
<tr><td>27</td><td>Oregon</td><td>102</td><td>1.1%</td><td>37</td><td>Alaska</td><td>21</td><td>0.2%</td></tr>
<tr><td>6</td><td>Pennsylvania</td><td>465</td><td>4.9%</td><td>38</td><td>West Virginia</td><td>19</td><td>0.2%</td></tr>
<tr><td>39</td><td>Rhode Island</td><td>17</td><td>0.2%</td><td>39</td><td>Rhode Island</td><td>17</td><td>0.2%</td></tr>
<tr><td>29</td><td>South Carolina</td><td>72</td><td>0.8%</td><td>40</td><td>Idaho</td><td>15</td><td>0.2%</td></tr>
<tr><td>42</td><td>South Dakota</td><td>10</td><td>0.1%</td><td>41</td><td>Wyoming</td><td>11</td><td>0.1%</td></tr>
<tr><td>20</td><td>Tennessee</td><td>159</td><td>1.7%</td><td>42</td><td>South Dakota</td><td>10</td><td>0.1%</td></tr>
<tr><td>2</td><td>Texas</td><td>774</td><td>8.1%</td><td>43</td><td>Kentucky</td><td>7</td><td>0.1%</td></tr>
<tr><td>35</td><td>Utah</td><td>31</td><td>0.3%</td><td>43</td><td>Montana</td><td>7</td><td>0.1%</td></tr>
<tr><td>45</td><td>Vermont</td><td>6</td><td>0.1%</td><td>45</td><td>Vermont</td><td>6</td><td>0.1%</td></tr>
<tr><td>12</td><td>Virginia</td><td>238</td><td>2.5%</td><td>46</td><td>Maine</td><td>4</td><td>0.0%</td></tr>
<tr><td>23</td><td>Washington</td><td>138</td><td>1.4%</td><td>46</td><td>New Hampshire</td><td>4</td><td>0.0%</td></tr>
<tr><td>38</td><td>West Virginia</td><td>19</td><td>0.2%</td><td>48</td><td>North Dakota</td><td>1</td><td>0.0%</td></tr>
<tr><td>NA</td><td>Wisconsin**</td><td>NA</td><td>NA</td><td>NA</td><td>Kansas**</td><td>NA</td><td>NA</td></tr>
<tr><td>41</td><td>Wyoming</td><td>11</td><td>0.1%</td><td>NA</td><td>Wisconsin**</td><td>NA</td><td>NA</td></tr>
<tr><td></td><td></td><td></td><td></td><td></td><td>District of Columbia**</td><td>NA</td><td>NA</td></tr>
</table>

Source: Federal Bureau of Investigation
    "Crime in the United States 2000" (Uniform Crime Reports, October 22, 2001)
*By law enforcement agencies submitting complete reports to the F.B.I. for 12 months in 2000. The F.B.I. estimates
13,227 reported and unreported arrests for murder occurred in 2000. Murder includes nonnegligent manslaughter.
See important note at beginning of this chapter.
**Not available.

Reported Arrest Rate for Murder in 2000

National Rate = 3.5 Reported Arrests per 100,000 Population*

ALPHA ORDER

RANK	STATE	RATE
2	Alabama	7.1
20	Alaska	3.3
15	Arizona	4.1
5	Arkansas	6.0
9	California	4.8
28	Colorado	2.5
31	Connecticut	2.0
18	Delaware	3.4
14	Florida	4.2
11	Georgia	4.4
20	Hawaii	3.3
39	Idaho	1.2
12	Illinois	4.3
20	Indiana	3.3
37	Iowa	1.3
NA	Kansas**	NA
47	Kentucky	0.2
4	Louisiana	6.4
45	Maine	0.3
2	Maryland	7.1
43	Massachusetts	0.9
35	Michigan	1.4
23	Minnesota	3.0
8	Mississippi	5.2
12	Missouri	4.3
44	Montana	0.8
25	Nebraska	2.8
6	Nevada	5.5
45	New Hampshire	0.3
27	New Jersey	2.7
10	New Mexico	4.5
39	New York	1.2
1	North Carolina	7.7
47	North Dakota	0.2
33	Ohio	1.7
7	Oklahoma	5.3
23	Oregon	3.0
16	Pennsylvania	3.8
34	Rhode Island	1.6
32	South Carolina	1.8
37	South Dakota	1.3
25	Tennessee	2.8
17	Texas	3.7
35	Utah	1.4
42	Vermont	1.0
18	Virginia	3.4
29	Washington	2.3
41	West Virginia	1.1
NA	Wisconsin**	NA
30	Wyoming	2.2

RANK ORDER

RANK	STATE	RATE
1	North Carolina	7.7
2	Alabama	7.1
2	Maryland	7.1
4	Louisiana	6.4
5	Arkansas	6.0
6	Nevada	5.5
7	Oklahoma	5.3
8	Mississippi	5.2
9	California	4.8
10	New Mexico	4.5
11	Georgia	4.4
12	Illinois	4.3
12	Missouri	4.3
14	Florida	4.2
15	Arizona	4.1
16	Pennsylvania	3.8
17	Texas	3.7
18	Delaware	3.4
18	Virginia	3.4
20	Alaska	3.3
20	Hawaii	3.3
20	Indiana	3.3
23	Minnesota	3.0
23	Oregon	3.0
25	Nebraska	2.8
25	Tennessee	2.8
27	New Jersey	2.7
28	Colorado	2.5
29	Washington	2.3
30	Wyoming	2.2
31	Connecticut	2.0
32	South Carolina	1.8
33	Ohio	1.7
34	Rhode Island	1.6
35	Michigan	1.4
35	Utah	1.4
37	Iowa	1.3
37	South Dakota	1.3
39	Idaho	1.2
39	New York	1.2
41	West Virginia	1.1
42	Vermont	1.0
43	Massachusetts	0.9
44	Montana	0.8
45	Maine	0.3
45	New Hampshire	0.3
47	Kentucky	0.2
47	North Dakota	0.2
NA	Kansas**	NA
NA	Wisconsin**	NA
	District of Columbia**	NA

Source: Morgan Quitno Press using data from Federal Bureau of Investigation
   "Crime in the United States 2000" (Uniform Crime Reports, October 22, 2001)
*By law enforcement agencies submitting complete reports to the F.B.I. for 12 months in 2000. These rates based on population estimates for areas under the jurisdiction of those agencies reporting. Arrest rate based on the F.B.I. estimate of reported and unreported arrests for murder is 4.7 arrests per 100,000 population. See important note at beginning of this chapter. **Not available.

Reported Arrests for Rape in 2000

National Total = 20,521 Reported Arrests*

ALPHA ORDER

RANK	STATE	ARRESTS	% of USA
20	Alabama	364	1.8%
39	Alaska	82	0.4%
28	Arizona	215	1.0%
21	Arkansas	353	1.7%
1	California	2,698	13.1%
13	Colorado	415	2.0%
29	Connecticut	214	1.0%
26	Delaware	229	1.1%
2	Florida	2,216	10.8%
14	Georgia	403	2.0%
40	Hawaii	75	0.4%
38	Idaho	96	0.5%
9	Illinois	627	3.1%
25	Indiana	242	1.2%
33	Iowa	116	0.6%
NA	Kansas**	NA	NA
47	Kentucky	19	0.1%
18	Louisiana	376	1.8%
36	Maine	107	0.5%
15	Maryland	398	1.9%
11	Massachusetts	490	2.4%
8	Michigan	650	3.2%
5	Minnesota	740	3.6%
27	Mississippi	216	1.1%
19	Missouri	375	1.8%
48	Montana	14	0.1%
32	Nebraska	152	0.7%
23	Nevada	300	1.5%
41	New Hampshire	71	0.3%
10	New Jersey	561	2.7%
37	New Mexico	97	0.5%
12	New York	476	2.3%
22	North Carolina	320	1.6%
46	North Dakota	30	0.1%
6	Ohio	680	3.3%
17	Oklahoma	391	1.9%
24	Oregon	246	1.2%
4	Pennsylvania	1,377	6.7%
35	Rhode Island	114	0.6%
33	South Carolina	116	0.6%
42	South Dakota	69	0.3%
30	Tennessee	197	1.0%
3	Texas	2,193	10.7%
31	Utah	195	1.0%
43	Vermont	48	0.2%
16	Virginia	395	1.9%
7	Washington	674	3.3%
45	West Virginia	44	0.2%
NA	Wisconsin**	NA	NA
44	Wyoming	45	0.2%

RANK ORDER

RANK	STATE	ARRESTS	% of USA
1	California	2,698	13.1%
2	Florida	2,216	10.8%
3	Texas	2,193	10.7%
4	Pennsylvania	1,377	6.7%
5	Minnesota	740	3.6%
6	Ohio	680	3.3%
7	Washington	674	3.3%
8	Michigan	650	3.2%
9	Illinois	627	3.1%
10	New Jersey	561	2.7%
11	Massachusetts	490	2.4%
12	New York	476	2.3%
13	Colorado	415	2.0%
14	Georgia	403	2.0%
15	Maryland	398	1.9%
16	Virginia	395	1.9%
17	Oklahoma	391	1.9%
18	Louisiana	376	1.8%
19	Missouri	375	1.8%
20	Alabama	364	1.8%
21	Arkansas	353	1.7%
22	North Carolina	320	1.6%
23	Nevada	300	1.5%
24	Oregon	246	1.2%
25	Indiana	242	1.2%
26	Delaware	229	1.1%
27	Mississippi	216	1.1%
28	Arizona	215	1.0%
29	Connecticut	214	1.0%
30	Tennessee	197	1.0%
31	Utah	195	1.0%
32	Nebraska	152	0.7%
33	Iowa	116	0.6%
33	South Carolina	116	0.6%
35	Rhode Island	114	0.6%
36	Maine	107	0.5%
37	New Mexico	97	0.5%
38	Idaho	96	0.5%
39	Alaska	82	0.4%
40	Hawaii	75	0.4%
41	New Hampshire	71	0.3%
42	South Dakota	69	0.3%
43	Vermont	48	0.2%
44	Wyoming	45	0.2%
45	West Virginia	44	0.2%
46	North Dakota	30	0.1%
47	Kentucky	19	0.1%
48	Montana	14	0.1%
NA	Kansas**	NA	NA
NA	Wisconsin**	NA	NA
	District of Columbia**	NA	NA

Source: Federal Bureau of Investigation
"Crime in the United States 2000" (Uniform Crime Reports, October 22, 2001)
*By law enforcement agencies submitting complete reports to the F.B.I. for 12 months in 2000. The F.B.I. estimates 27,469 reported and unreported arrests for rape occurred in 2000. Forcible rape is the carnal knowledge of a female forcibly and against her will. Assaults or attempts to commit rape by force or threat of force are included. See important note at beginning of this chapter. **Not available.**

Reported Arrest Rate for Rape in 2000

National Rate = 7.5 Reported Arrests per 100,000 Population*

ALPHA ORDER			RANK ORDER		
RANK	STATE	RATE	RANK	STATE	RATE
19	Alabama	8.2	1	Delaware	29.1
6	Alaska	13.1	2	Minnesota	15.0
39	Arizona	4.2	3	Nevada	14.9
5	Arkansas	13.2	4	Florida	13.8
20	California	7.9	5	Arkansas	13.2
12	Colorado	9.6	6	Alaska	13.1
30	Connecticut	6.3	7	Washington	11.4
1	Delaware	29.1	8	Oklahoma	11.3
4	Florida	13.8	9	Pennsylvania	11.2
37	Georgia	4.9	10	Rhode Island	10.9
31	Hawaii	6.2	11	Texas	10.5
25	Idaho	7.4	12	Colorado	9.6
36	Illinois	5.0	13	South Dakota	9.1
40	Indiana	4.0	13	Wyoming	9.1
40	Iowa	4.0	15	Nebraska	8.9
NA	Kansas**	NA	16	Utah	8.7
48	Kentucky	0.5	17	Louisiana	8.4
17	Louisiana	8.4	17	Maine	8.4
17	Maine	8.4	19	Alabama	8.2
24	Maryland	7.5	20	California	7.9
22	Massachusetts	7.7	20	Vermont	7.9
29	Michigan	6.5	22	Massachusetts	7.7
2	Minnesota	15.0	23	Mississippi	7.6
23	Mississippi	7.6	24	Maryland	7.5
27	Missouri	6.7	25	Idaho	7.4
47	Montana	1.6	26	Oregon	7.2
15	Nebraska	8.9	27	Missouri	6.7
3	Nevada	14.9	27	New Jersey	6.7
33	New Hampshire	5.7	29	Michigan	6.5
27	New Jersey	6.7	30	Connecticut	6.3
35	New Mexico	5.3	31	Hawaii	6.2
45	New York	2.5	32	Ohio	6.0
40	North Carolina	4.0	33	New Hampshire	5.7
38	North Dakota	4.7	34	Virginia	5.6
32	Ohio	6.0	35	New Mexico	5.3
8	Oklahoma	11.3	36	Illinois	5.0
26	Oregon	7.2	37	Georgia	4.9
9	Pennsylvania	11.2	38	North Dakota	4.7
10	Rhode Island	10.9	39	Arizona	4.2
44	South Carolina	2.9	40	Indiana	4.0
13	South Dakota	9.1	40	Iowa	4.0
43	Tennessee	3.5	40	North Carolina	4.0
11	Texas	10.5	43	Tennessee	3.5
16	Utah	8.7	44	South Carolina	2.9
20	Vermont	7.9	45	New York	2.5
34	Virginia	5.6	46	West Virginia	2.4
7	Washington	11.4	47	Montana	1.6
46	West Virginia	2.4	48	Kentucky	0.5
NA	Wisconsin**	NA	NA	Kansas**	NA
13	Wyoming	9.1	NA	Wisconsin**	NA
				District of Columbia**	NA

Source: Morgan Quitno Press using data from Federal Bureau of Investigation
   "Crime in the United States 2000" (Uniform Crime Reports, October 22, 2001)
*By law enforcement agencies submitting complete reports to the F.B.I. for 12 months in 2000. These rates based
on population estimates for areas under the jurisdiction of those agencies reporting. Arrest rate based on the F.B.I.
estimate of reported and unreported arrests for rape is 9.7 arrests per 100,000 population. See important note at
beginning of this chapter. **Not available.

Reported Arrests for Robbery in 2000

National Total = 82,148 Reported Arrests*

ALPHA ORDER

RANK	STATE	ARRESTS	% of USA
19	Alabama	1,154	1.4%
39	Alaska	122	0.1%
14	Arizona	1,425	1.7%
26	Arkansas	764	0.9%
1	California	17,121	20.8%
28	Colorado	671	0.8%
24	Connecticut	944	1.1%
32	Delaware	422	0.5%
2	Florida	9,147	11.1%
11	Georgia	1,979	2.4%
30	Hawaii	473	0.6%
42	Idaho	83	0.1%
7	Illinois	2,995	3.6%
13	Indiana	1,490	1.8%
35	Iowa	305	0.4%
NA	Kansas**	NA	NA
43	Kentucky	70	0.1%
20	Louisiana	1,152	1.4%
38	Maine	147	0.2%
8	Maryland	2,799	3.4%
15	Massachusetts	1,412	1.7%
23	Michigan	994	1.2%
21	Minnesota	1,065	1.3%
29	Mississippi	627	0.8%
12	Missouri	1,764	2.1%
46	Montana	25	0.0%
34	Nebraska	311	0.4%
18	Nevada	1,193	1.5%
40	New Hampshire	97	0.1%
5	New Jersey	4,083	5.0%
31	New Mexico	438	0.5%
9	New York	2,655	3.2%
6	North Carolina	3,413	4.2%
47	North Dakota	9	0.0%
10	Ohio	2,276	2.8%
27	Oklahoma	681	0.8%
22	Oregon	1,029	1.3%
3	Pennsylvania	6,209	7.6%
37	Rhode Island	209	0.3%
33	South Carolina	385	0.5%
44	South Dakota	39	0.0%
25	Tennessee	898	1.1%
4	Texas	6,073	7.4%
35	Utah	305	0.4%
48	Vermont	2	0.0%
17	Virginia	1,220	1.5%
16	Washington	1,339	1.6%
41	West Virginia	96	0.1%
NA	Wisconsin**	NA	NA
45	Wyoming	38	0.0%

RANK ORDER

RANK	STATE	ARRESTS	% of USA
1	California	17,121	20.8%
2	Florida	9,147	11.1%
3	Pennsylvania	6,209	7.6%
4	Texas	6,073	7.4%
5	New Jersey	4,083	5.0%
6	North Carolina	3,413	4.2%
7	Illinois	2,995	3.6%
8	Maryland	2,799	3.4%
9	New York	2,655	3.2%
10	Ohio	2,276	2.8%
11	Georgia	1,979	2.4%
12	Missouri	1,764	2.1%
13	Indiana	1,490	1.8%
14	Arizona	1,425	1.7%
15	Massachusetts	1,412	1.7%
16	Washington	1,339	1.6%
17	Virginia	1,220	1.5%
18	Nevada	1,193	1.5%
19	Alabama	1,154	1.4%
20	Louisiana	1,152	1.4%
21	Minnesota	1,065	1.3%
22	Oregon	1,029	1.3%
23	Michigan	994	1.2%
24	Connecticut	944	1.1%
25	Tennessee	898	1.1%
26	Arkansas	764	0.9%
27	Oklahoma	681	0.8%
28	Colorado	671	0.8%
29	Mississippi	627	0.8%
30	Hawaii	473	0.6%
31	New Mexico	438	0.5%
32	Delaware	422	0.5%
33	South Carolina	385	0.5%
34	Nebraska	311	0.4%
35	Iowa	305	0.4%
35	Utah	305	0.4%
37	Rhode Island	209	0.3%
38	Maine	147	0.2%
39	Alaska	122	0.1%
40	New Hampshire	97	0.1%
41	West Virginia	96	0.1%
42	Idaho	83	0.1%
43	Kentucky	70	0.1%
44	South Dakota	39	0.0%
45	Wyoming	38	0.0%
46	Montana	25	0.0%
47	North Dakota	9	0.0%
48	Vermont	2	0.0%
NA	Kansas**	NA	NA
NA	Wisconsin**	NA	NA
NA	District of Columbia**	NA	NA

Source: Federal Bureau of Investigation
   "Crime in the United States 2000" (Uniform Crime Reports, October 22, 2001)
*By law enforcement agencies submitting complete reports to the F.B.I. for 12 months in 2000. The F.B.I. estimates 106,130 reported and unreported arrests for robbery occurred in 2000. Robbery is the taking or attempting to take anything of value by force or threat of force. See important note at beginning of this chapter.
**Not available.

Reported Arrest Rate for Robbery in 2000

National Rate = 30.0 Reported Arrests per 100,000 Population*

<table>
<tr><td colspan="3">ALPHA ORDER</td><td colspan="3">RANK ORDER</td></tr>
<tr><td>RANK</td><td>STATE</td><td>RATE</td><td>RANK</td><td>STATE</td><td>RATE</td></tr>
<tr><td>16</td><td>Alabama</td><td>25.9</td><td>1</td><td>Nevada</td><td>59.1</td></tr>
<tr><td>29</td><td>Alaska</td><td>19.4</td><td>2</td><td>Florida</td><td>57.0</td></tr>
<tr><td>15</td><td>Arizona</td><td>27.6</td><td>3</td><td>Delaware</td><td>53.7</td></tr>
<tr><td>13</td><td>Arkansas</td><td>28.5</td><td>4</td><td>Maryland</td><td>52.7</td></tr>
<tr><td>6</td><td>California</td><td>50.4</td><td>5</td><td>Pennsylvania</td><td>50.6</td></tr>
<tr><td>33</td><td>Colorado</td><td>15.5</td><td>6</td><td>California</td><td>50.4</td></tr>
<tr><td>14</td><td>Connecticut</td><td>27.7</td><td>7</td><td>New Jersey</td><td>48.4</td></tr>
<tr><td>3</td><td>Delaware</td><td>53.7</td><td>8</td><td>North Carolina</td><td>42.3</td></tr>
<tr><td>2</td><td>Florida</td><td>57.0</td><td>9</td><td>Hawaii</td><td>39.0</td></tr>
<tr><td>20</td><td>Georgia</td><td>24.0</td><td>10</td><td>Missouri</td><td>31.5</td></tr>
<tr><td>9</td><td>Hawaii</td><td>39.0</td><td>11</td><td>Oregon</td><td>30.0</td></tr>
<tr><td>42</td><td>Idaho</td><td>6.4</td><td>12</td><td>Texas</td><td>29.0</td></tr>
<tr><td>19</td><td>Illinois</td><td>24.1</td><td>13</td><td>Arkansas</td><td>28.5</td></tr>
<tr><td>18</td><td>Indiana</td><td>24.5</td><td>14</td><td>Connecticut</td><td>27.7</td></tr>
<tr><td>37</td><td>Iowa</td><td>10.4</td><td>15</td><td>Arizona</td><td>27.6</td></tr>
<tr><td>NA</td><td>Kansas**</td><td>NA</td><td>16</td><td>Alabama</td><td>25.9</td></tr>
<tr><td>46</td><td>Kentucky</td><td>1.7</td><td>17</td><td>Louisiana</td><td>25.8</td></tr>
<tr><td>17</td><td>Louisiana</td><td>25.8</td><td>18</td><td>Indiana</td><td>24.5</td></tr>
<tr><td>36</td><td>Maine</td><td>11.5</td><td>19</td><td>Illinois</td><td>24.1</td></tr>
<tr><td>4</td><td>Maryland</td><td>52.7</td><td>20</td><td>Georgia</td><td>24.0</td></tr>
<tr><td>23</td><td>Massachusetts</td><td>22.2</td><td>20</td><td>New Mexico</td><td>24.0</td></tr>
<tr><td>38</td><td>Michigan</td><td>10.0</td><td>22</td><td>Washington</td><td>22.7</td></tr>
<tr><td>25</td><td>Minnesota</td><td>21.6</td><td>23</td><td>Massachusetts</td><td>22.2</td></tr>
<tr><td>24</td><td>Mississippi</td><td>22.0</td><td>24</td><td>Mississippi</td><td>22.0</td></tr>
<tr><td>10</td><td>Missouri</td><td>31.5</td><td>25</td><td>Minnesota</td><td>21.6</td></tr>
<tr><td>45</td><td>Montana</td><td>2.8</td><td>26</td><td>Ohio</td><td>20.0</td></tr>
<tr><td>30</td><td>Nebraska</td><td>18.2</td><td>27</td><td>Rhode Island</td><td>19.9</td></tr>
<tr><td>1</td><td>Nevada</td><td>59.1</td><td>28</td><td>Oklahoma</td><td>19.7</td></tr>
<tr><td>40</td><td>New Hampshire</td><td>7.8</td><td>29</td><td>Alaska</td><td>19.4</td></tr>
<tr><td>7</td><td>New Jersey</td><td>48.4</td><td>30</td><td>Nebraska</td><td>18.2</td></tr>
<tr><td>20</td><td>New Mexico</td><td>24.0</td><td>31</td><td>Virginia</td><td>17.2</td></tr>
<tr><td>34</td><td>New York</td><td>14.0</td><td>32</td><td>Tennessee</td><td>15.7</td></tr>
<tr><td>8</td><td>North Carolina</td><td>42.3</td><td>33</td><td>Colorado</td><td>15.5</td></tr>
<tr><td>47</td><td>North Dakota</td><td>1.4</td><td>34</td><td>New York</td><td>14.0</td></tr>
<tr><td>26</td><td>Ohio</td><td>20.0</td><td>35</td><td>Utah</td><td>13.6</td></tr>
<tr><td>28</td><td>Oklahoma</td><td>19.7</td><td>36</td><td>Maine</td><td>11.5</td></tr>
<tr><td>11</td><td>Oregon</td><td>30.0</td><td>37</td><td>Iowa</td><td>10.4</td></tr>
<tr><td>5</td><td>Pennsylvania</td><td>50.6</td><td>38</td><td>Michigan</td><td>10.0</td></tr>
<tr><td>27</td><td>Rhode Island</td><td>19.9</td><td>39</td><td>South Carolina</td><td>9.6</td></tr>
<tr><td>39</td><td>South Carolina</td><td>9.6</td><td>40</td><td>New Hampshire</td><td>7.8</td></tr>
<tr><td>44</td><td>South Dakota</td><td>5.2</td><td>41</td><td>Wyoming</td><td>7.7</td></tr>
<tr><td>32</td><td>Tennessee</td><td>15.7</td><td>42</td><td>Idaho</td><td>6.4</td></tr>
<tr><td>12</td><td>Texas</td><td>29.0</td><td>43</td><td>West Virginia</td><td>5.3</td></tr>
<tr><td>35</td><td>Utah</td><td>13.6</td><td>44</td><td>South Dakota</td><td>5.2</td></tr>
<tr><td>48</td><td>Vermont</td><td>0.3</td><td>45</td><td>Montana</td><td>2.8</td></tr>
<tr><td>31</td><td>Virginia</td><td>17.2</td><td>46</td><td>Kentucky</td><td>1.7</td></tr>
<tr><td>22</td><td>Washington</td><td>22.7</td><td>47</td><td>North Dakota</td><td>1.4</td></tr>
<tr><td>43</td><td>West Virginia</td><td>5.3</td><td>48</td><td>Vermont</td><td>0.3</td></tr>
<tr><td>NA</td><td>Wisconsin**</td><td>NA</td><td>NA</td><td>Kansas**</td><td>NA</td></tr>
<tr><td>41</td><td>Wyoming</td><td>7.7</td><td>NA</td><td>Wisconsin**</td><td>NA</td></tr>
<tr><td></td><td></td><td></td><td></td><td>District of Columbia**</td><td>NA</td></tr>
</table>

Source: Morgan Quitno Press using data from Federal Bureau of Investigation
"Crime in the United States 2000" (Uniform Crime Reports, October 22, 2001)
*By law enforcement agencies submitting complete reports to the F.B.I. for 12 months in 2000. These rates based on population estimates for areas under the jurisdiction of those agencies reporting. Arrest rate based on the F.B.I. estimate of reported and unreported arrests for robbery is 37.6 arrests per 100,000 population. See important note at beginning of this chapter. **Not available.

Reported Arrests for Aggravated Assault in 2000

National Total = 363,282 Reported Arrests*

ALPHA ORDER

RANK	STATE	ARRESTS	% of USA
23	Alabama	4,016	1.1%
37	Alaska	979	0.3%
16	Arizona	6,333	1.7%
26	Arkansas	3,681	1.0%
1	California	107,987	29.7%
24	Colorado	3,975	1.1%
27	Connecticut	3,300	0.9%
31	Delaware	1,626	0.4%
2	Florida	41,921	11.5%
8	Georgia	8,683	2.4%
40	Hawaii	691	0.2%
34	Idaho	1,174	0.3%
17	Illinois	6,164	1.7%
10	Indiana	8,170	2.2%
25	Iowa	3,685	1.0%
NA	Kansas**	NA	NA
45	Kentucky	283	0.1%
9	Louisiana	8,468	2.3%
42	Maine	629	0.2%
15	Maryland	6,585	1.8%
6	Massachusetts	11,597	3.2%
12	Michigan	7,483	2.1%
21	Minnesota	4,506	1.2%
33	Mississippi	1,562	0.4%
18	Missouri	5,306	1.5%
41	Montana	645	0.2%
38	Nebraska	937	0.3%
32	Nevada	1,577	0.4%
46	New Hampshire	243	0.1%
7	New Jersey	10,622	2.9%
29	New Mexico	2,176	0.6%
11	New York	8,150	2.2%
4	North Carolina	16,255	4.5%
48	North Dakota	109	0.0%
13	Ohio	7,200	2.0%
20	Oklahoma	4,731	1.3%
30	Oregon	1,927	0.5%
5	Pennsylvania	15,445	4.3%
39	Rhode Island	708	0.2%
28	South Carolina	2,457	0.7%
44	South Dakota	452	0.1%
14	Tennessee	6,907	1.9%
3	Texas	21,584	5.9%
36	Utah	997	0.3%
47	Vermont	228	0.1%
22	Virginia	4,393	1.2%
19	Washington	5,041	1.4%
35	West Virginia	1,145	0.3%
NA	Wisconsin**	NA	NA
43	Wyoming	549	0.2%

RANK ORDER

RANK	STATE	ARRESTS	% of USA
1	California	107,987	29.7%
2	Florida	41,921	11.5%
3	Texas	21,584	5.9%
4	North Carolina	16,255	4.5%
5	Pennsylvania	15,445	4.3%
6	Massachusetts	11,597	3.2%
7	New Jersey	10,622	2.9%
8	Georgia	8,683	2.4%
9	Louisiana	8,468	2.3%
10	Indiana	8,170	2.2%
11	New York	8,150	2.2%
12	Michigan	7,483	2.1%
13	Ohio	7,200	2.0%
14	Tennessee	6,907	1.9%
15	Maryland	6,585	1.8%
16	Arizona	6,333	1.7%
17	Illinois	6,164	1.7%
18	Missouri	5,306	1.5%
19	Washington	5,041	1.4%
20	Oklahoma	4,731	1.3%
21	Minnesota	4,506	1.2%
22	Virginia	4,393	1.2%
23	Alabama	4,016	1.1%
24	Colorado	3,975	1.1%
25	Iowa	3,685	1.0%
26	Arkansas	3,681	1.0%
27	Connecticut	3,300	0.9%
28	South Carolina	2,457	0.7%
29	New Mexico	2,176	0.6%
30	Oregon	1,927	0.5%
31	Delaware	1,626	0.4%
32	Nevada	1,577	0.4%
33	Mississippi	1,562	0.4%
34	Idaho	1,174	0.3%
35	West Virginia	1,145	0.3%
36	Utah	997	0.3%
37	Alaska	979	0.3%
38	Nebraska	937	0.3%
39	Rhode Island	708	0.2%
40	Hawaii	691	0.2%
41	Montana	645	0.2%
42	Maine	629	0.2%
43	Wyoming	549	0.2%
44	South Dakota	452	0.1%
45	Kentucky	283	0.1%
46	New Hampshire	243	0.1%
47	Vermont	228	0.1%
48	North Dakota	109	0.0%
NA	Kansas**	NA	NA
NA	Wisconsin**	NA	NA
	District of Columbia**	NA	NA

Source: Federal Bureau of Investigation
    "Crime in the United States 2000" (Uniform Crime Reports, October 22, 2001)
*By law enforcement agencies submitting complete reports to the F.B.I. for 12 months in 2000. The F.B.I. estimates 478,417 reported and unreported arrests for aggravated assault occurred in 2000. Aggravated assault is an attack for the purpose of inflicting severe bodily injury. See important note at beginning of this chapter.
**Not available.

Reported Arrest Rate for Aggravated Assault in 2000

National Rate = 132.8 Reported Arrests per 100,000 Population*

ALPHA ORDER				RANK ORDER		
RANK	STATE	RATE		RANK	STATE	RATE
26	Alabama	90.2		1	California	317.6
7	Alaska	156.0		2	Florida	261.1
15	Arizona	122.6		3	Delaware	206.8
8	Arkansas	137.5		4	North Carolina	201.2
1	California	317.6		5	Louisiana	189.4
23	Colorado	91.9		6	Massachusetts	182.4
21	Connecticut	96.8		7	Alaska	156.0
3	Delaware	206.8		8	Arkansas	137.5
2	Florida	261.1		9	Oklahoma	137.0
19	Georgia	105.5		10	Indiana	134.2
37	Hawaii	57.0		11	New Jersey	126.0
25	Idaho	90.4		12	Iowa	125.9
41	Illinois	49.6		13	Pennsylvania	125.7
10	Indiana	134.2		14	Maryland	124.0
12	Iowa	125.9		15	Arizona	122.6
NA	Kansas**	NA		16	Tennessee	121.1
48	Kentucky	7.0		17	New Mexico	119.5
5	Louisiana	189.4		18	Wyoming	111.1
42	Maine	49.3		19	Georgia	105.5
14	Maryland	124.0		20	Texas	103.0
6	Massachusetts	182.4		21	Connecticut	96.8
29	Michigan	75.2		22	Missouri	94.7
24	Minnesota	91.4		23	Colorado	91.9
39	Mississippi	54.8		24	Minnesota	91.4
22	Missouri	94.7		25	Idaho	90.4
30	Montana	71.4		26	Alabama	90.2
40	Nebraska	54.7		27	Washington	85.3
28	Nevada	78.1		28	Nevada	78.1
46	New Hampshire	19.6		29	Michigan	75.2
11	New Jersey	126.0		30	Montana	71.4
17	New Mexico	119.5		31	Rhode Island	67.4
44	New York	42.9		32	Ohio	63.4
4	North Carolina	201.2		32	West Virginia	63.4
47	North Dakota	17.0		34	Virginia	61.8
32	Ohio	63.4		35	South Carolina	61.1
9	Oklahoma	137.0		36	South Dakota	59.8
38	Oregon	56.2		37	Hawaii	57.0
13	Pennsylvania	125.7		38	Oregon	56.2
31	Rhode Island	67.4		39	Mississippi	54.8
35	South Carolina	61.1		40	Nebraska	54.7
36	South Dakota	59.8		41	Illinois	49.6
16	Tennessee	121.1		42	Maine	49.3
20	Texas	103.0		43	Utah	44.5
43	Utah	44.5		44	New York	42.9
45	Vermont	37.4		45	Vermont	37.4
34	Virginia	61.8		46	New Hampshire	19.6
27	Washington	85.3		47	North Dakota	17.0
32	West Virginia	63.4		48	Kentucky	7.0
NA	Wisconsin**	NA		NA	Kansas**	NA
18	Wyoming	111.1		NA	Wisconsin**	NA
					District of Columbia**	NA

Source: Morgan Quitno Press using data from Federal Bureau of Investigation
    "Crime in the United States 2000" (Uniform Crime Reports, October 22, 2001)
*By law enforcement agencies submitting complete reports to the F.B.I. for 12 months in 2000. These rates based on population estimates for areas under the jurisdiction of those agencies reporting. Arrest rate based on the F.B.I. estimate of reported and unreported arrests for aggravated assault is 169.6 arrests per 100,000 population. See important note at beginning of this chapter. **Not available.

14

Reported Arrests for Property Crime in 2000

National Total = 1,220,750 Reported Arrests*

ALPHA ORDER					RANK ORDER			
RANK	STATE		ARRESTS	% of USA	RANK	STATE	ARRESTS	% of USA
26	Alabama		15,231	1.2%	1	California	167,062	13.7%
39	Alaska		4,539	0.4%	2	Florida	123,030	10.1%
8	Arizona		37,359	3.1%	3	Texas	112,168	9.2%
25	Arkansas		15,936	1.3%	4	North Carolina	50,350	4.1%
1	California		167,062	13.7%	5	Pennsylvania	48,659	4.0%
16	Colorado		26,473	2.2%	6	Illinois	40,950	3.4%
27	Connecticut		15,110	1.2%	7	New Jersey	38,223	3.1%
38	Delaware		5,325	0.4%	8	Arizona	37,359	3.1%
2	Florida		123,030	10.1%	9	New York	36,987	3.0%
14	Georgia		27,802	2.3%	10	Washington	35,036	2.9%
36	Hawaii		6,648	0.5%	11	Ohio	32,813	2.7%
33	Idaho		8,143	0.7%	12	Maryland	29,915	2.5%
6	Illinois		40,950	3.4%	13	Missouri	28,704	2.4%
20	Indiana		22,830	1.9%	14	Georgia	27,802	2.3%
30	Iowa		13,657	1.1%	15	Michigan	27,672	2.3%
NA	Kansas**		NA	NA	16	Colorado	26,473	2.2%
46	Kentucky		1,694	0.1%	17	Louisiana	26,098	2.1%
17	Louisiana		26,098	2.1%	18	Minnesota	25,946	2.1%
34	Maine		7,148	0.6%	19	Oregon	25,413	2.1%
12	Maryland		29,915	2.5%	20	Indiana	22,830	1.9%
28	Massachusetts		14,733	1.2%	21	Virginia	21,781	1.8%
15	Michigan		27,672	2.3%	22	Tennessee	19,538	1.6%
18	Minnesota		25,946	2.1%	23	Nevada	17,537	1.4%
31	Mississippi		12,522	1.0%	24	Oklahoma	16,923	1.4%
13	Missouri		28,704	2.4%	25	Arkansas	15,936	1.3%
47	Montana		1,679	0.1%	26	Alabama	15,231	1.2%
32	Nebraska		11,360	0.9%	27	Connecticut	15,110	1.2%
23	Nevada		17,537	1.4%	28	Massachusetts	14,733	1.2%
45	New Hampshire		2,022	0.2%	29	Utah	14,621	1.2%
7	New Jersey		38,223	3.1%	30	Iowa	13,657	1.1%
37	New Mexico		6,386	0.5%	31	Mississippi	12,522	1.0%
9	New York		36,987	3.0%	32	Nebraska	11,360	0.9%
4	North Carolina		50,350	4.1%	33	Idaho	8,143	0.7%
44	North Dakota		2,762	0.2%	34	Maine	7,148	0.6%
11	Ohio		32,813	2.7%	35	South Carolina	6,992	0.6%
24	Oklahoma		16,923	1.4%	36	Hawaii	6,648	0.5%
19	Oregon		25,413	2.1%	37	New Mexico	6,386	0.5%
5	Pennsylvania		48,659	4.0%	38	Delaware	5,325	0.4%
40	Rhode Island		3,888	0.3%	39	Alaska	4,539	0.4%
35	South Carolina		6,992	0.6%	40	Rhode Island	3,888	0.3%
41	South Dakota		3,650	0.3%	41	South Dakota	3,650	0.3%
22	Tennessee		19,538	1.6%	42	West Virginia	3,077	0.3%
3	Texas		112,168	9.2%	43	Wyoming	2,870	0.2%
29	Utah		14,621	1.2%	44	North Dakota	2,762	0.2%
48	Vermont		1,488	0.1%	45	New Hampshire	2,022	0.2%
21	Virginia		21,781	1.8%	46	Kentucky	1,694	0.1%
10	Washington		35,036	2.9%	47	Montana	1,679	0.1%
42	West Virginia		3,077	0.3%	48	Vermont	1,488	0.1%
NA	Wisconsin**		NA	NA	NA	Kansas**	NA	NA
43	Wyoming		2,870	0.2%	NA	Wisconsin**	NA	NA
						District of Columbia**	NA	NA

Source: Federal Bureau of Investigation
"Crime in the United States 2000" (Uniform Crime Reports, October 22, 2001)
*By law enforcement agencies submitting complete reports to the F.B.I. for 12 months in 2000. The F.B.I. estimates 1,620,928 reported and unreported arrests for property crime occurred in 2000. Property crimes are offenses of burglary, larceny-theft, motor vehicle theft and arson. See important note at beginning of this chapter.
**Not available.

15

Reported Arrest Rate for Property Crime in 2000

National Rate = 446.4 Reported Arrests per 100,000 Population*

ALPHA ORDER

RANK	STATE	RATE
35	Alabama	342.2
5	Alaska	723.2
4	Arizona	723.3
12	Arkansas	595.1
22	California	491.4
11	Colorado	612.3
27	Connecticut	443.1
6	Delaware	677.3
2	Florida	766.3
36	Georgia	337.8
18	Hawaii	548.4
9	Idaho	626.7
37	Illinois	329.3
31	Indiana	374.9
25	Iowa	466.5
NA	Kansas**	NA
48	Kentucky	41.9
14	Louisiana	583.9
17	Maine	559.8
16	Maryland	563.3
42	Massachusetts	231.8
40	Michigan	278.1
20	Minnesota	526.2
28	Mississippi	439.5
21	Missouri	512.2
44	Montana	185.9
7	Nebraska	663.3
1	Nevada	868.7
47	New Hampshire	163.1
26	New Jersey	453.5
33	New Mexico	350.6
43	New York	194.8
10	North Carolina	623.3
29	North Dakota	430.9
39	Ohio	288.8
23	Oklahoma	490.1
3	Oregon	741.1
30	Pennsylvania	396.2
32	Rhode Island	370.2
45	South Carolina	173.8
24	South Dakota	483.1
34	Tennessee	342.7
19	Texas	535.5
8	Utah	652.3
41	Vermont	244.1
38	Virginia	306.6
13	Washington	593.0
46	West Virginia	170.3
NA	Wisconsin**	NA
15	Wyoming	581.0

RANK ORDER

RANK	STATE	RATE
1	Nevada	868.7
2	Florida	766.3
3	Oregon	741.1
4	Arizona	723.3
5	Alaska	723.2
6	Delaware	677.3
7	Nebraska	663.3
8	Utah	652.3
9	Idaho	626.7
10	North Carolina	623.3
11	Colorado	612.3
12	Arkansas	595.1
13	Washington	593.0
14	Louisiana	583.9
15	Wyoming	581.0
16	Maryland	563.3
17	Maine	559.8
18	Hawaii	548.4
19	Texas	535.5
20	Minnesota	526.2
21	Missouri	512.2
22	California	491.4
23	Oklahoma	490.1
24	South Dakota	483.1
25	Iowa	466.5
26	New Jersey	453.5
27	Connecticut	443.1
28	Mississippi	439.5
29	North Dakota	430.9
30	Pennsylvania	396.2
31	Indiana	374.9
32	Rhode Island	370.2
33	New Mexico	350.6
34	Tennessee	342.7
35	Alabama	342.2
36	Georgia	337.8
37	Illinois	329.3
38	Virginia	306.6
39	Ohio	288.8
40	Michigan	278.1
41	Vermont	244.1
42	Massachusetts	231.8
43	New York	194.8
44	Montana	185.9
45	South Carolina	173.8
46	West Virginia	170.3
47	New Hampshire	163.1
48	Kentucky	41.9
NA	Kansas**	NA
NA	Wisconsin**	NA
	District of Columbia**	NA

Source: Morgan Quitno Press using data from Federal Bureau of Investigation
"Crime in the United States 2000" (Uniform Crime Reports, October 22, 2001)
*By law enforcement agencies submitting complete reports to the F.B.I. for 12 months in 2000. These rates based on population estimates for areas under the jurisdiction of those agencies reporting. Arrest rate based on the F.B.I. estimate of reported and unreported arrests for property crime is 574.5 arrests per 100,000 population. See important note at beginning of this chapter. **Not available.

Reported Arrests for Burglary in 2000

National Total = 218,143 Reported Arrests*

ALPHA ORDER

RANK	STATE	ARRESTS	% of USA
27	Alabama	2,458	1.1%
40	Alaska	576	0.3%
14	Arizona	4,390	2.0%
24	Arkansas	2,720	1.2%
1	California	46,951	21.5%
26	Colorado	2,469	1.1%
30	Connecticut	2,075	1.0%
36	Delaware	1,080	0.5%
2	Florida	26,050	11.9%
12	Georgia	4,527	2.1%
38	Hawaii	798	0.4%
34	Idaho	1,182	0.5%
15	Illinois	4,119	1.9%
20	Indiana	3,154	1.4%
29	Iowa	2,145	1.0%
NA	Kansas**	NA	NA
47	Kentucky	178	0.1%
10	Louisiana	5,265	2.4%
31	Maine	1,327	0.6%
7	Maryland	6,070	2.8%
25	Massachusetts	2,517	1.2%
17	Michigan	3,690	1.7%
19	Minnesota	3,440	1.6%
28	Mississippi	2,197	1.0%
16	Missouri	3,704	1.7%
48	Montana	176	0.1%
35	Nebraska	1,135	0.5%
13	Nevada	4,512	2.1%
44	New Hampshire	296	0.1%
6	New Jersey	6,381	2.9%
37	New Mexico	1,050	0.5%
8	New York	5,827	2.7%
4	North Carolina	12,298	5.6%
45	North Dakota	285	0.1%
9	Ohio	5,304	2.4%
23	Oklahoma	2,750	1.3%
22	Oregon	2,891	1.3%
5	Pennsylvania	8,805	4.0%
39	Rhode Island	657	0.3%
32	South Carolina	1,227	0.6%
42	South Dakota	522	0.2%
21	Tennessee	2,918	1.3%
3	Texas	16,947	7.8%
33	Utah	1,216	0.6%
46	Vermont	277	0.1%
18	Virginia	3,489	1.6%
11	Washington	5,155	2.4%
41	West Virginia	547	0.3%
NA	Wisconsin**	NA	NA
43	Wyoming	396	0.2%

RANK ORDER

RANK	STATE	ARRESTS	% of USA
1	California	46,951	21.5%
2	Florida	26,050	11.9%
3	Texas	16,947	7.8%
4	North Carolina	12,298	5.6%
5	Pennsylvania	8,805	4.0%
6	New Jersey	6,381	2.9%
7	Maryland	6,070	2.8%
8	New York	5,827	2.7%
9	Ohio	5,304	2.4%
10	Louisiana	5,265	2.4%
11	Washington	5,155	2.4%
12	Georgia	4,527	2.1%
13	Nevada	4,512	2.1%
14	Arizona	4,390	2.0%
15	Illinois	4,119	1.9%
16	Missouri	3,704	1.7%
17	Michigan	3,690	1.7%
18	Virginia	3,489	1.6%
19	Minnesota	3,440	1.6%
20	Indiana	3,154	1.4%
21	Tennessee	2,918	1.3%
22	Oregon	2,891	1.3%
23	Oklahoma	2,750	1.3%
24	Arkansas	2,720	1.2%
25	Massachusetts	2,517	1.2%
26	Colorado	2,469	1.1%
27	Alabama	2,458	1.1%
28	Mississippi	2,197	1.0%
29	Iowa	2,145	1.0%
30	Connecticut	2,075	1.0%
31	Maine	1,327	0.6%
32	South Carolina	1,227	0.6%
33	Utah	1,216	0.6%
34	Idaho	1,182	0.5%
35	Nebraska	1,135	0.5%
36	Delaware	1,080	0.5%
37	New Mexico	1,050	0.5%
38	Hawaii	798	0.4%
39	Rhode Island	657	0.3%
40	Alaska	576	0.3%
41	West Virginia	547	0.3%
42	South Dakota	522	0.2%
43	Wyoming	396	0.2%
44	New Hampshire	296	0.1%
45	North Dakota	285	0.1%
46	Vermont	277	0.1%
47	Kentucky	178	0.1%
48	Montana	176	0.1%
NA	Kansas**	NA	NA
NA	Wisconsin**	NA	NA
	District of Columbia**	NA	NA

Source: Federal Bureau of Investigation
   "Crime in the United States 2000" (Uniform Crime Reports, October 22, 2001)
*By law enforcement agencies submitting complete reports to the F.B.I. for 12 months in 2000. The F.B.I. estimates 289,844 reported and unreported arrests for burglary occurred in 2000. Burglary is the unlawful entry of a structure to commit a felony or theft. Attempts are included.   See important note at beginning of this chapter.
**Not available.

Reported Arrest Rate for Burglary in 2000

National Rate = 79.8 Reported Arrests per 100,000 Population*

ALPHA ORDER

RANK	STATE	RATE
31	Alabama	55.2
10	Alaska	91.8
13	Arizona	85.0
9	Arkansas	101.6
4	California	138.1
30	Colorado	57.1
28	Connecticut	60.8
5	Delaware	137.4
2	Florida	162.3
32	Georgia	55.0
26	Hawaii	65.8
11	Idaho	91.0
42	Illinois	33.1
34	Indiana	51.8
20	Iowa	73.3
NA	Kansas**	NA
48	Kentucky	4.4
6	Louisiana	117.8
8	Maine	103.9
7	Maryland	114.3
40	Massachusetts	39.6
41	Michigan	37.1
22	Minnesota	69.8
18	Mississippi	77.1
25	Missouri	66.1
47	Montana	19.5
24	Nebraska	66.3
1	Nevada	223.5
46	New Hampshire	23.9
19	New Jersey	75.7
29	New Mexico	57.7
43	New York	30.7
3	North Carolina	152.3
39	North Dakota	44.5
37	Ohio	46.7
17	Oklahoma	79.6
14	Oregon	84.3
21	Pennsylvania	71.7
27	Rhode Island	62.6
44	South Carolina	30.5
23	South Dakota	69.1
35	Tennessee	51.2
15	Texas	80.9
33	Utah	54.2
38	Vermont	45.4
36	Virginia	49.1
12	Washington	87.2
45	West Virginia	30.3
NA	Wisconsin**	NA
16	Wyoming	80.2

RANK ORDER

RANK	STATE	RATE
1	Nevada	223.5
2	Florida	162.3
3	North Carolina	152.3
4	California	138.1
5	Delaware	137.4
6	Louisiana	117.8
7	Maryland	114.3
8	Maine	103.9
9	Arkansas	101.6
10	Alaska	91.8
11	Idaho	91.0
12	Washington	87.2
13	Arizona	85.0
14	Oregon	84.3
15	Texas	80.9
16	Wyoming	80.2
17	Oklahoma	79.6
18	Mississippi	77.1
19	New Jersey	75.7
20	Iowa	73.3
21	Pennsylvania	71.7
22	Minnesota	69.8
23	South Dakota	69.1
24	Nebraska	66.3
25	Missouri	66.1
26	Hawaii	65.8
27	Rhode Island	62.6
28	Connecticut	60.8
29	New Mexico	57.7
30	Colorado	57.1
31	Alabama	55.2
32	Georgia	55.0
33	Utah	54.2
34	Indiana	51.8
35	Tennessee	51.2
36	Virginia	49.1
37	Ohio	46.7
38	Vermont	45.4
39	North Dakota	44.5
40	Massachusetts	39.6
41	Michigan	37.1
42	Illinois	33.1
43	New York	30.7
44	South Carolina	30.5
45	West Virginia	30.3
46	New Hampshire	23.9
47	Montana	19.5
48	Kentucky	4.4
NA	Kansas**	NA
NA	Wisconsin**	NA
	District of Columbia**	NA

Source: Morgan Quitno Press using data from Federal Bureau of Investigation
    "Crime in the United States 2000" (Uniform Crime Reports, October 22, 2001)
*By law enforcement agencies submitting complete reports to the F.B.I. for 12 months in 2000. These rates based
on population estimates for areas under the jurisdiction of those agencies reporting. Arrest rate based on the F.B.I.
estimate of reported and unreported arrests for burglary is 102.7 arrests per 100,000 population. See important
note at beginning of this chapter. **Not available.

Reported Arrests for Larceny and Theft in 2000

National Total = 878,545 Reported Arrests*

ALPHA ORDER					RANK ORDER			
RANK	STATE	ARRESTS	% of USA		RANK	STATE	ARRESTS	% of USA
27	Alabama	11,762	1.3%		1	California	96,298	11.0%
39	Alaska	3,568	0.4%		2	Texas	85,555	9.7%
7	Arizona	29,041	3.3%		3	Florida	84,181	9.6%
24	Arkansas	12,621	1.4%		4	North Carolina	35,316	4.0%
1	California	96,298	11.0%		5	Pennsylvania	33,289	3.8%
13	Colorado	21,410	2.4%		6	New Jersey	30,007	3.4%
26	Connecticut	11,888	1.4%		7	Arizona	29,041	3.3%
38	Delaware	3,982	0.5%		8	New York	28,259	3.2%
3	Florida	84,181	9.6%		9	Washington	27,287	3.1%
15	Georgia	20,558	2.3%		10	Ohio	25,315	2.9%
37	Hawaii	4,780	0.5%		11	Illinois	25,309	2.9%
33	Idaho	6,474	0.7%		12	Michigan	21,740	2.5%
11	Illinois	25,309	2.9%		13	Colorado	21,410	2.4%
20	Indiana	17,559	2.0%		14	Missouri	21,283	2.4%
30	Iowa	10,747	1.2%		15	Georgia	20,558	2.3%
NA	Kansas**	NA	NA		16	Oregon	19,946	2.3%
46	Kentucky	1,465	0.2%		17	Louisiana	19,751	2.2%
17	Louisiana	19,751	2.2%		18	Minnesota	19,326	2.2%
35	Maine	5,386	0.6%		19	Maryland	19,297	2.2%
19	Maryland	19,297	2.2%		20	Indiana	17,559	2.0%
29	Massachusetts	11,171	1.3%		21	Virginia	16,516	1.9%
12	Michigan	21,740	2.5%		22	Tennessee	15,166	1.7%
18	Minnesota	19,326	2.2%		23	Utah	12,623	1.4%
32	Mississippi	9,407	1.1%		24	Arkansas	12,621	1.4%
14	Missouri	21,283	2.4%		25	Oklahoma	12,282	1.4%
47	Montana	1,374	0.2%		26	Connecticut	11,888	1.4%
31	Nebraska	9,620	1.1%		27	Alabama	11,762	1.3%
28	Nevada	11,328	1.3%		28	Nevada	11,328	1.3%
45	New Hampshire	1,566	0.2%		29	Massachusetts	11,171	1.3%
6	New Jersey	30,007	3.4%		30	Iowa	10,747	1.2%
36	New Mexico	5,035	0.6%		31	Nebraska	9,620	1.1%
8	New York	28,259	3.2%		32	Mississippi	9,407	1.1%
4	North Carolina	35,316	4.0%		33	Idaho	6,474	0.7%
44	North Dakota	2,233	0.3%		34	South Carolina	5,403	0.6%
10	Ohio	25,315	2.9%		35	Maine	5,386	0.6%
25	Oklahoma	12,282	1.4%		36	New Mexico	5,035	0.6%
16	Oregon	19,946	2.3%		37	Hawaii	4,780	0.5%
5	Pennsylvania	33,289	3.8%		38	Delaware	3,982	0.5%
41	Rhode Island	2,786	0.3%		39	Alaska	3,568	0.4%
34	South Carolina	5,403	0.6%		40	South Dakota	2,922	0.3%
40	South Dakota	2,922	0.3%		41	Rhode Island	2,786	0.3%
22	Tennessee	15,166	1.7%		42	Wyoming	2,309	0.3%
2	Texas	85,555	9.7%		43	West Virginia	2,266	0.3%
23	Utah	12,623	1.4%		44	North Dakota	2,233	0.3%
48	Vermont	1,138	0.1%		45	New Hampshire	1,566	0.2%
21	Virginia	16,516	1.9%		46	Kentucky	1,465	0.2%
9	Washington	27,287	3.1%		47	Montana	1,374	0.2%
43	West Virginia	2,266	0.3%		48	Vermont	1,138	0.1%
NA	Wisconsin**	NA	NA		NA	Kansas**	NA	NA
42	Wyoming	2,309	0.3%		NA	Wisconsin**	NA	NA
						District of Columbia**	NA	NA

Source: Federal Bureau of Investigation
  "Crime in the United States 2000" (Uniform Crime Reports, October 22, 2001)
*By law enforcement agencies submitting complete reports to the F.B.I. for 12 months in 2000. The F.B.I. estimates 1,166,362 reported and unreported arrests for larceny and theft occurred in 2000. Larceny and theft is the unlawful taking of property without use of force, violence or fraud. Attempts are included. Motor vehicle thefts are excluded. See important note at beginning of this chapter. **Not available.

19

Reported Arrest Rate for Larceny and Theft in 2000

National Rate = 321.2 Reported Arrests per 100,000 Population*

ALPHA ORDER				RANK ORDER		
RANK	STATE	RATE		RANK	STATE	RATE
35	Alabama	264.2		1	Oregon	581.6
2	Alaska	568.5		2	Alaska	568.5
4	Arizona	562.2		3	Utah	563.1
11	Arkansas	471.3		4	Arizona	562.2
30	California	283.2		5	Nebraska	561.7
10	Colorado	495.2		6	Nevada	561.1
26	Connecticut	348.6		7	Florida	524.4
8	Delaware	506.5		8	Delaware	506.5
7	Florida	524.4		9	Idaho	498.3
36	Georgia	249.8		10	Colorado	495.2
18	Hawaii	394.3		11	Arkansas	471.3
9	Idaho	498.3		12	Wyoming	467.4
40	Illinois	203.5		13	Washington	461.8
29	Indiana	288.3		14	Louisiana	441.9
22	Iowa	367.1		15	North Carolina	437.2
NA	Kansas**	NA		16	Maine	421.8
48	Kentucky	36.2		17	Texas	408.4
14	Louisiana	441.9		18	Hawaii	394.3
16	Maine	421.8		19	Minnesota	391.9
23	Maryland	363.3		20	South Dakota	386.8
42	Massachusetts	175.7		21	Missouri	379.8
39	Michigan	218.4		22	Iowa	367.1
19	Minnesota	391.9		23	Maryland	363.3
28	Mississippi	330.2		24	New Jersey	356.0
21	Missouri	379.8		25	Oklahoma	355.7
43	Montana	152.1		26	Connecticut	348.6
5	Nebraska	561.7		27	North Dakota	348.4
6	Nevada	561.1		28	Mississippi	330.2
46	New Hampshire	126.3		29	Indiana	288.3
24	New Jersey	356.0		30	California	283.2
31	New Mexico	276.5		31	New Mexico	276.5
44	New York	148.8		32	Pennsylvania	271.0
15	North Carolina	437.2		33	Tennessee	266.0
27	North Dakota	348.4		34	Rhode Island	265.3
38	Ohio	222.8		35	Alabama	264.2
25	Oklahoma	355.7		36	Georgia	249.8
1	Oregon	581.6		37	Virginia	232.5
32	Pennsylvania	271.0		38	Ohio	222.8
34	Rhode Island	265.3		39	Michigan	218.4
45	South Carolina	134.3		40	Illinois	203.5
20	South Dakota	386.8		41	Vermont	186.6
33	Tennessee	266.0		42	Massachusetts	175.7
17	Texas	408.4		43	Montana	152.1
3	Utah	563.1		44	New York	148.8
41	Vermont	186.6		45	South Carolina	134.3
37	Virginia	232.5		46	New Hampshire	126.3
13	Washington	461.8		47	West Virginia	125.4
47	West Virginia	125.4		48	Kentucky	36.2
NA	Wisconsin**	NA		NA	Kansas**	NA
12	Wyoming	467.4		NA	Wisconsin**	NA
					District of Columbia**	NA

Source: Morgan Quitno Press using data from Federal Bureau of Investigation
"Crime in the United States 2000" (Uniform Crime Reports, October 22, 2001)
*By law enforcement agencies submitting complete reports to the F.B.I. for 12 months in 2000. These rates based on population estimates for areas under the jurisdiction of those agencies reporting. Arrest rate based on the F.B.I. estimate of reported and unreported arrests for larceny and theft is 413.4 arrests per 100,000 population. See important note at beginning of this chapter. **Not available.

Reported Arrests for Motor Vehicle Theft in 2000

National Total = 112,571 Reported Arrests*

ALPHA ORDER

RANK ORDER

RANK	STATE	ARRESTS	% of USA	RANK	STATE	ARRESTS	% of USA
27	Alabama	902	0.8%	1	California	21,966	19.5%
36	Alaska	371	0.3%	2	Florida	12,260	10.9%
7	Arizona	3,658	3.2%	3	Illinois	11,301	10.0%
32	Arkansas	480	0.4%	4	Texas	8,893	7.9%
1	California	21,966	19.5%	5	Pennsylvania	5,783	5.1%
14	Colorado	2,278	2.0%	6	Maryland	4,143	3.7%
25	Connecticut	994	0.9%	7	Arizona	3,658	3.2%
43	Delaware	165	0.1%	8	Missouri	3,421	3.0%
2	Florida	12,260	10.9%	9	Minnesota	2,925	2.6%
11	Georgia	2,505	2.2%	10	New York	2,539	2.3%
24	Hawaii	1,031	0.9%	11	Georgia	2,505	2.2%
34	Idaho	399	0.4%	12	North Carolina	2,288	2.0%
3	Illinois	11,301	10.0%	13	Oregon	2,284	2.0%
16	Indiana	1,979	1.8%	14	Colorado	2,278	2.0%
30	Iowa	651	0.6%	15	Washington	2,183	1.9%
NA	Kansas**	NA	NA	16	Indiana	1,979	1.8%
48	Kentucky	37	0.0%	17	Michigan	1,943	1.7%
28	Louisiana	867	0.8%	18	Ohio	1,794	1.6%
36	Maine	371	0.3%	19	Nevada	1,625	1.4%
6	Maryland	4,143	3.7%	20	Oklahoma	1,614	1.4%
26	Massachusetts	927	0.8%	21	Virginia	1,465	1.3%
17	Michigan	1,943	1.7%	22	New Jersey	1,401	1.2%
9	Minnesota	2,925	2.6%	23	Tennessee	1,259	1.1%
29	Mississippi	771	0.7%	24	Hawaii	1,031	0.9%
8	Missouri	3,421	3.0%	25	Connecticut	994	0.9%
46	Montana	117	0.1%	26	Massachusetts	927	0.8%
33	Nebraska	460	0.4%	27	Alabama	902	0.8%
19	Nevada	1,625	1.4%	28	Louisiana	867	0.8%
45	New Hampshire	129	0.1%	29	Mississippi	771	0.7%
22	New Jersey	1,401	1.2%	30	Iowa	651	0.6%
39	New Mexico	247	0.2%	31	Utah	641	0.6%
10	New York	2,539	2.3%	32	Arkansas	480	0.4%
12	North Carolina	2,288	2.0%	33	Nebraska	460	0.4%
40	North Dakota	223	0.2%	34	Idaho	399	0.4%
18	Ohio	1,794	1.6%	35	Rhode Island	372	0.3%
20	Oklahoma	1,614	1.4%	36	Alaska	371	0.3%
13	Oregon	2,284	2.0%	36	Maine	371	0.3%
5	Pennsylvania	5,783	5.1%	38	South Carolina	309	0.3%
35	Rhode Island	372	0.3%	39	New Mexico	247	0.2%
38	South Carolina	309	0.3%	40	North Dakota	223	0.2%
42	South Dakota	181	0.2%	41	West Virginia	217	0.2%
23	Tennessee	1,259	1.1%	42	South Dakota	181	0.2%
4	Texas	8,893	7.9%	43	Delaware	165	0.1%
31	Utah	641	0.6%	44	Wyoming	136	0.1%
47	Vermont	66	0.1%	45	New Hampshire	129	0.1%
21	Virginia	1,465	1.3%	46	Montana	117	0.1%
15	Washington	2,183	1.9%	47	Vermont	66	0.1%
41	West Virginia	217	0.2%	48	Kentucky	37	0.0%
NA	Wisconsin**	NA	NA	NA	Kansas**	NA	NA
44	Wyoming	136	0.1%	NA	Wisconsin**	NA	NA
					District of Columbia**	NA	NA

Source: Federal Bureau of Investigation
  "Crime in the United States 2000" (Uniform Crime Reports, October 22, 2001)
*By law enforcement agencies submitting complete reports to the F.B.I. for 12 months in 2000. The F.B.I. estimates 148,225 reported and unreported arrests for motor vehicle theft occurred in 2000. Motor vehicle theft includes the theft or attempted theft of a self-propelled vehicle. Excludes motorboats, construction equipment, airplanes and farming equipment. See important note at beginning of this chapter. **Not available.

Reported Arrest Rate for Motor Vehicle Theft in 2000

National Rate = 41.2 Reported Arrests per 100,000 Population*

ALPHA ORDER

RANK ORDER

RANK	STATE	RATE		RANK	STATE	RATE
34	Alabama	20.3		1	Illinois	90.9
11	Alaska	59.1		2	Hawaii	85.0
6	Arizona	70.8		3	Nevada	80.5
37	Arkansas	17.9		4	Maryland	78.0
8	California	64.6		5	Florida	76.4
12	Colorado	52.7		6	Arizona	70.8
22	Connecticut	29.1		7	Oregon	66.6
32	Delaware	21.0		8	California	64.6
5	Florida	76.4		9	Missouri	61.1
21	Georgia	30.4		10	Minnesota	59.3
2	Hawaii	85.0		11	Alaska	59.1
20	Idaho	30.7		12	Colorado	52.7
1	Illinois	90.9		13	Pennsylvania	47.1
19	Indiana	32.5		14	Oklahoma	46.7
30	Iowa	22.2		15	Texas	42.5
NA	Kansas**	NA		16	Washington	36.9
48	Kentucky	0.9		17	Rhode Island	35.4
36	Louisiana	19.4		18	North Dakota	34.8
22	Maine	29.1		19	Indiana	32.5
4	Maryland	78.0		20	Idaho	30.7
40	Massachusetts	14.6		21	Georgia	30.4
35	Michigan	19.5		22	Connecticut	29.1
10	Minnesota	59.3		22	Maine	29.1
27	Mississippi	27.1		24	Utah	28.6
9	Missouri	61.1		25	North Carolina	28.3
43	Montana	13.0		26	Wyoming	27.5
28	Nebraska	26.9		27	Mississippi	27.1
3	Nevada	80.5		28	Nebraska	26.9
46	New Hampshire	10.4		29	South Dakota	24.0
38	New Jersey	16.6		30	Iowa	22.2
41	New Mexico	13.6		31	Tennessee	22.1
42	New York	13.4		32	Delaware	21.0
25	North Carolina	28.3		33	Virginia	20.6
18	North Dakota	34.8		34	Alabama	20.3
39	Ohio	15.8		35	Michigan	19.5
14	Oklahoma	46.7		36	Louisiana	19.4
7	Oregon	66.6		37	Arkansas	17.9
13	Pennsylvania	47.1		38	New Jersey	16.6
17	Rhode Island	35.4		39	Ohio	15.8
47	South Carolina	7.7		40	Massachusetts	14.6
29	South Dakota	24.0		41	New Mexico	13.6
31	Tennessee	22.1		42	New York	13.4
15	Texas	42.5		43	Montana	13.0
24	Utah	28.6		44	West Virginia	12.0
45	Vermont	10.8		45	Vermont	10.8
33	Virginia	20.6		46	New Hampshire	10.4
16	Washington	36.9		47	South Carolina	7.7
44	West Virginia	12.0		48	Kentucky	0.9
NA	Wisconsin**	NA		NA	Kansas**	NA
26	Wyoming	27.5		NA	Wisconsin**	NA
					District of Columbia**	NA

Source: Morgan Quitno Press using data from Federal Bureau of Investigation
   "Crime in the United States 2000" (Uniform Crime Reports, October 22, 2001)
*By law enforcement agencies submitting complete reports to the F.B.I. for 12 months in 2000. These rates based on population estimates for areas under the jurisdiction of those agencies reporting. Arrest rate based on the F.B.I. estimate of reported and unreported arrests for motor vehicle theft is 52.5 arrests per 100,000 population. See important note at beginning of this chapter. **Not available.

Reported Arrests for Arson in 2000

National Total = 11,491 Reported Arrests*

ALPHA ORDER

RANK ORDER

RANK	STATE	ARRESTS	% of USA		RANK	STATE	ARRESTS	% of USA
31	Alabama	109	0.9%		1	California	1,847	16.1%
44	Alaska	24	0.2%		2	Pennsylvania	782	6.8%
17	Arizona	270	2.3%		3	Texas	773	6.7%
29	Arkansas	115	1.0%		4	Florida	539	4.7%
1	California	1,847	16.1%		5	North Carolina	448	3.9%
11	Colorado	316	2.7%		6	New Jersey	434	3.8%
23	Connecticut	153	1.3%		7	Washington	411	3.6%
32	Delaware	98	0.9%		8	Maryland	405	3.5%
4	Florida	539	4.7%		9	Ohio	400	3.5%
21	Georgia	212	1.8%		10	New York	362	3.2%
40	Hawaii	39	0.3%		11	Colorado	316	2.7%
33	Idaho	88	0.8%		12	Virginia	311	2.7%
19	Illinois	221	1.9%		13	Michigan	299	2.6%
27	Indiana	138	1.2%		14	Missouri	296	2.6%
30	Iowa	114	1.0%		15	Oregon	292	2.5%
NA	Kansas**	NA	NA		16	Oklahoma	277	2.4%
46	Kentucky	14	0.1%		17	Arizona	270	2.3%
20	Louisiana	215	1.9%		18	Minnesota	255	2.2%
36	Maine	64	0.6%		19	Illinois	221	1.9%
8	Maryland	405	3.5%		20	Louisiana	215	1.9%
28	Massachusetts	118	1.0%		21	Georgia	212	1.8%
13	Michigan	299	2.6%		22	Tennessee	195	1.7%
18	Minnesota	255	2.2%		23	Connecticut	153	1.3%
24	Mississippi	147	1.3%		24	Mississippi	147	1.3%
14	Missouri	296	2.6%		25	Nebraska	145	1.3%
47	Montana	12	0.1%		26	Utah	141	1.2%
25	Nebraska	145	1.3%		27	Indiana	138	1.2%
35	Nevada	72	0.6%		28	Massachusetts	118	1.0%
41	New Hampshire	31	0.3%		29	Arkansas	115	1.0%
6	New Jersey	434	3.8%		30	Iowa	114	1.0%
37	New Mexico	54	0.5%		31	Alabama	109	0.9%
10	New York	362	3.2%		32	Delaware	98	0.9%
5	North Carolina	448	3.9%		33	Idaho	88	0.8%
45	North Dakota	21	0.2%		34	Rhode Island	73	0.6%
9	Ohio	400	3.5%		35	Nevada	72	0.6%
16	Oklahoma	277	2.4%		36	Maine	64	0.6%
15	Oregon	292	2.5%		37	New Mexico	54	0.5%
2	Pennsylvania	782	6.8%		38	South Carolina	53	0.5%
34	Rhode Island	73	0.6%		39	West Virginia	47	0.4%
38	South Carolina	53	0.5%		40	Hawaii	39	0.3%
43	South Dakota	25	0.2%		41	New Hampshire	31	0.3%
22	Tennessee	195	1.7%		42	Wyoming	29	0.3%
3	Texas	773	6.7%		43	South Dakota	25	0.2%
26	Utah	141	1.2%		44	Alaska	24	0.2%
48	Vermont	7	0.1%		45	North Dakota	21	0.2%
12	Virginia	311	2.7%		46	Kentucky	14	0.1%
7	Washington	411	3.6%		47	Montana	12	0.1%
39	West Virginia	47	0.4%		48	Vermont	7	0.1%
NA	Wisconsin**	NA	NA		NA	Kansas**	NA	NA
42	Wyoming	29	0.3%		NA	Wisconsin**	NA	NA
						District of Columbia**	NA	NA

Source: Federal Bureau of Investigation
    "Crime in the United States 2000" (Uniform Crime Reports, October 22, 2001)
*By law enforcement agencies submitting complete reports to the F.B.I. for 12 months in 2000. The F.B.I. estimates
16,530 reported and unreported arrests for arson occurred in 2000. Arson is the willful burning of or attempt to burn
a building, vehicle or another's personal property. See important note at beginning of this chapter.
**Not available.

Reported Arrest Rate for Arson in 2000

National Rate = 4.2 Reported Arrests per 100,000 Population*

ALPHA ORDER

RANK	STATE	RATE
40	Alabama	2.4
26	Alaska	3.8
16	Arizona	5.2
24	Arkansas	4.3
14	California	5.4
6	Colorado	7.3
22	Connecticut	4.5
1	Delaware	12.5
30	Florida	3.4
37	Georgia	2.6
34	Hawaii	3.2
9	Idaho	6.8
44	Illinois	1.8
41	Indiana	2.3
25	Iowa	3.9
NA	Kansas**	NA
48	Kentucky	0.3
21	Louisiana	4.8
20	Maine	5.0
5	Maryland	7.6
42	Massachusetts	1.9
35	Michigan	3.0
16	Minnesota	5.2
16	Mississippi	5.2
15	Missouri	5.3
45	Montana	1.3
2	Nebraska	8.5
28	Nevada	3.6
39	New Hampshire	2.5
19	New Jersey	5.1
35	New Mexico	3.0
42	New York	1.9
13	North Carolina	5.5
32	North Dakota	3.3
29	Ohio	3.5
4	Oklahoma	8.0
2	Oregon	8.5
10	Pennsylvania	6.4
7	Rhode Island	7.0
45	South Carolina	1.3
32	South Dakota	3.3
30	Tennessee	3.4
27	Texas	3.7
11	Utah	6.3
47	Vermont	1.1
23	Virginia	4.4
7	Washington	7.0
37	West Virginia	2.6
NA	Wisconsin**	NA
12	Wyoming	5.9

RANK ORDER

RANK	STATE	RATE
1	Delaware	12.5
2	Nebraska	8.5
2	Oregon	8.5
4	Oklahoma	8.0
5	Maryland	7.6
6	Colorado	7.3
7	Rhode Island	7.0
7	Washington	7.0
9	Idaho	6.8
10	Pennsylvania	6.4
11	Utah	6.3
12	Wyoming	5.9
13	North Carolina	5.5
14	California	5.4
15	Missouri	5.3
16	Arizona	5.2
16	Minnesota	5.2
16	Mississippi	5.2
19	New Jersey	5.1
20	Maine	5.0
21	Louisiana	4.8
22	Connecticut	4.5
23	Virginia	4.4
24	Arkansas	4.3
25	Iowa	3.9
26	Alaska	3.8
27	Texas	3.7
28	Nevada	3.6
29	Ohio	3.5
30	Florida	3.4
30	Tennessee	3.4
32	North Dakota	3.3
32	South Dakota	3.3
34	Hawaii	3.2
35	Michigan	3.0
35	New Mexico	3.0
37	Georgia	2.6
37	West Virginia	2.6
39	New Hampshire	2.5
40	Alabama	2.4
41	Indiana	2.3
42	Massachusetts	1.9
42	New York	1.9
44	Illinois	1.8
45	Montana	1.3
45	South Carolina	1.3
47	Vermont	1.1
48	Kentucky	0.3
NA	Kansas**	NA
NA	Wisconsin**	NA
	District of Columbia**	NA

Source: Morgan Quitno Press using data from Federal Bureau of Investigation
"Crime in the United States 2000" (Uniform Crime Reports, October 22, 2001)
*By law enforcement agencies submitting complete reports to the F.B.I. for 12 months in 2000. These rates based on population estimates for areas under the jurisdiction of those agencies reporting. Arrest rate based on the F.B.I. estimate of reported and unreported arrests for arson is 5.9 arrests per 100,000 population. See important note at beginning of this chapter. **Not available.

Reported Arrests for Weapons Violations in 2000

National Total = 114,429 Reported Arrests*

ALPHA ORDER

RANK	STATE	ARRESTS	% of USA
26	Alabama	1,262	1.1%
37	Alaska	444	0.4%
16	Arizona	2,740	2.4%
20	Arkansas	2,027	1.8%
1	California	21,471	18.8%
17	Colorado	2,546	2.2%
27	Connecticut	1,140	1.0%
36	Delaware	463	0.4%
3	Florida	6,573	5.7%
7	Georgia	3,432	3.0%
39	Hawaii	309	0.3%
32	Idaho	643	0.6%
5	Illinois	5,367	4.7%
24	Indiana	1,658	1.4%
34	Iowa	578	0.5%
NA	Kansas**	NA	NA
44	Kentucky	127	0.1%
25	Louisiana	1,587	1.4%
40	Maine	261	0.2%
10	Maryland	3,070	2.7%
29	Massachusetts	985	0.9%
14	Michigan	2,836	2.5%
19	Minnesota	2,219	1.9%
31	Mississippi	820	0.7%
11	Missouri	3,061	2.7%
47	Montana	48	0.0%
28	Nebraska	1,055	0.9%
21	Nevada	1,884	1.6%
43	New Hampshire	144	0.1%
6	New Jersey	5,048	4.4%
35	New Mexico	554	0.5%
13	New York	2,887	2.5%
4	North Carolina	5,547	4.8%
46	North Dakota	106	0.1%
11	Ohio	3,061	2.7%
18	Oklahoma	2,515	2.2%
23	Oregon	1,735	1.5%
9	Pennsylvania	3,362	2.9%
38	Rhode Island	357	0.3%
33	South Carolina	613	0.5%
45	South Dakota	123	0.1%
22	Tennessee	1,870	1.6%
2	Texas	10,448	9.1%
30	Utah	880	0.8%
48	Vermont	13	0.0%
8	Virginia	3,365	2.9%
15	Washington	2,813	2.5%
41	West Virginia	236	0.2%
NA	Wisconsin**	NA	NA
42	Wyoming	146	0.1%

RANK ORDER

RANK	STATE	ARRESTS	% of USA
1	California	21,471	18.8%
2	Texas	10,448	9.1%
3	Florida	6,573	5.7%
4	North Carolina	5,547	4.8%
5	Illinois	5,367	4.7%
6	New Jersey	5,048	4.4%
7	Georgia	3,432	3.0%
8	Virginia	3,365	2.9%
9	Pennsylvania	3,362	2.9%
10	Maryland	3,070	2.7%
11	Missouri	3,061	2.7%
11	Ohio	3,061	2.7%
13	New York	2,887	2.5%
14	Michigan	2,836	2.5%
15	Washington	2,813	2.5%
16	Arizona	2,740	2.4%
17	Colorado	2,546	2.2%
18	Oklahoma	2,515	2.2%
19	Minnesota	2,219	1.9%
20	Arkansas	2,027	1.8%
21	Nevada	1,884	1.6%
22	Tennessee	1,870	1.6%
23	Oregon	1,735	1.5%
24	Indiana	1,658	1.4%
25	Louisiana	1,587	1.4%
26	Alabama	1,262	1.1%
27	Connecticut	1,140	1.0%
28	Nebraska	1,055	0.9%
29	Massachusetts	985	0.9%
30	Utah	880	0.8%
31	Mississippi	820	0.7%
32	Idaho	643	0.6%
33	South Carolina	613	0.5%
34	Iowa	578	0.5%
35	New Mexico	554	0.5%
36	Delaware	463	0.4%
37	Alaska	444	0.4%
38	Rhode Island	357	0.3%
39	Hawaii	309	0.3%
40	Maine	261	0.2%
41	West Virginia	236	0.2%
42	Wyoming	146	0.1%
43	New Hampshire	144	0.1%
44	Kentucky	127	0.1%
45	South Dakota	123	0.1%
46	North Dakota	106	0.1%
47	Montana	48	0.0%
48	Vermont	13	0.0%
NA	Kansas**	NA	NA
NA	Wisconsin**	NA	NA
	District of Columbia**	NA	NA

Source: Federal Bureau of Investigation
   "Crime in the United States 2000" (Uniform Crime Reports, October 22, 2001)
*By law enforcement agencies submitting complete reports to the F.B.I. for 12 months in 2000. The F.B.I. estimates
159,181 reported and unreported arrests for weapons violations occurred in 2000. Weapons violations include
illegal carrying and possession. See important note at beginning of this chapter.
**Not available.

Reported Arrest Rate for Weapons Violations in 2000

National Rate = 41.8 Reported Arrests per 100,000 Population*

ALPHA ORDER				RANK ORDER		
RANK	STATE	RATE		RANK	STATE	RATE
32	Alabama	28.4		1	Nevada	93.3
4	Alaska	70.7		2	Arkansas	75.7
13	Arizona	53.0		3	Oklahoma	72.8
2	Arkansas	75.7		4	Alaska	70.7
6	California	63.1		5	North Carolina	68.7
9	Colorado	58.9		6	California	63.1
26	Connecticut	33.4		7	Nebraska	61.6
9	Delaware	58.9		8	New Jersey	59.9
22	Florida	40.9		9	Colorado	58.9
21	Georgia	41.7		9	Delaware	58.9
36	Hawaii	25.5		11	Maryland	57.8
16	Idaho	49.5		12	Missouri	54.6
20	Illinois	43.2		13	Arizona	53.0
34	Indiana	27.2		14	Oregon	50.6
38	Iowa	19.7		15	Texas	49.9
NA	Kansas**	NA		16	Idaho	49.5
47	Kentucky	3.1		17	Washington	47.6
24	Louisiana	35.5		18	Virginia	47.4
37	Maine	20.4		19	Minnesota	45.0
11	Maryland	57.8		20	Illinois	43.2
41	Massachusetts	15.5		21	Georgia	41.7
31	Michigan	28.5		22	Florida	40.9
19	Minnesota	45.0		23	Utah	39.3
30	Mississippi	28.8		24	Louisiana	35.5
12	Missouri	54.6		25	Rhode Island	34.0
46	Montana	5.3		26	Connecticut	33.4
7	Nebraska	61.6		27	Tennessee	32.8
1	Nevada	93.3		28	New Mexico	30.4
45	New Hampshire	11.6		29	Wyoming	29.6
8	New Jersey	59.9		30	Mississippi	28.8
28	New Mexico	30.4		31	Michigan	28.5
42	New York	15.2		32	Alabama	28.4
5	North Carolina	68.7		33	Pennsylvania	27.4
39	North Dakota	16.5		34	Indiana	27.2
35	Ohio	26.9		35	Ohio	26.9
3	Oklahoma	72.8		36	Hawaii	25.5
14	Oregon	50.6		37	Maine	20.4
33	Pennsylvania	27.4		38	Iowa	19.7
25	Rhode Island	34.0		39	North Dakota	16.5
42	South Carolina	15.2		40	South Dakota	16.3
40	South Dakota	16.3		41	Massachusetts	15.5
27	Tennessee	32.8		42	New York	15.2
15	Texas	49.9		42	South Carolina	15.2
23	Utah	39.3		44	West Virginia	13.1
48	Vermont	2.1		45	New Hampshire	11.6
18	Virginia	47.4		46	Montana	5.3
17	Washington	47.6		47	Kentucky	3.1
44	West Virginia	13.1		48	Vermont	2.1
NA	Wisconsin**	NA		NA	Kansas**	NA
29	Wyoming	29.6		NA	Wisconsin**	NA
					District of Columbia**	NA

Source: Morgan Quitno Press using data from Federal Bureau of Investigation
    "Crime in the United States 2000" (Uniform Crime Reports, October 22, 2001)
*By law enforcement agencies submitting complete reports to the F.B.I. for 12 months in 2000. These rates based on population estimates for areas under the jurisdiction of those agencies reporting. Arrest rate based on the F.B.I. estimate of reported and unreported arrests for weapons violations is 56.4 arrests per 100,000 population. See important note at beginning of this chapter. **Not available.

Reported Arrests for Driving Under the Influence in 2000

National Total = 998,186 Reported Arrests*

ALPHA ORDER

RANK	STATE	ARRESTS	% of USA
23	Alabama	13,703	1.4%
38	Alaska	4,452	0.4%
7	Arizona	32,033	3.2%
21	Arkansas	16,640	1.7%
1	California	183,267	18.4%
13	Colorado	23,725	2.4%
33	Connecticut	7,394	0.7%
47	Delaware	211	0.0%
3	Florida	60,330	6.0%
17	Georgia	21,752	2.2%
42	Hawaii	3,208	0.3%
29	Idaho	10,148	1.0%
NA	Illinois**	NA	NA
18	Indiana	19,773	2.0%
25	Iowa	12,622	1.3%
NA	Kansas**	NA	NA
44	Kentucky	2,026	0.2%
24	Louisiana	13,159	1.3%
34	Maine	7,334	0.7%
14	Maryland	22,658	2.3%
27	Massachusetts	10,722	1.1%
4	Michigan	48,962	4.9%
5	Minnesota	44,823	4.5%
28	Mississippi	10,412	1.0%
20	Missouri	16,793	1.7%
46	Montana	1,576	0.2%
26	Nebraska	11,550	1.2%
31	Nevada	8,138	0.8%
40	New Hampshire	3,857	0.4%
11	New Jersey	24,562	2.5%
30	New Mexico	8,952	0.9%
8	New York	30,993	3.1%
9	North Carolina	28,855	2.9%
41	North Dakota	3,255	0.3%
16	Ohio	21,871	2.2%
15	Oklahoma	21,925	2.2%
22	Oregon	14,549	1.5%
6	Pennsylvania	32,978	3.3%
45	Rhode Island	1,629	0.2%
32	South Carolina	7,789	0.8%
39	South Dakota	4,221	0.4%
19	Tennessee	18,628	1.9%
2	Texas	95,454	9.6%
35	Utah	6,292	0.6%
43	Vermont	2,834	0.3%
12	Virginia	24,027	2.4%
10	Washington	28,718	2.9%
36	West Virginia	4,898	0.5%
NA	Wisconsin**	NA	NA
37	Wyoming	4,488	0.4%

RANK ORDER

RANK	STATE	ARRESTS	% of USA
1	California	183,267	18.4%
2	Texas	95,454	9.6%
3	Florida	60,330	6.0%
4	Michigan	48,962	4.9%
5	Minnesota	44,823	4.5%
6	Pennsylvania	32,978	3.3%
7	Arizona	32,033	3.2%
8	New York	30,993	3.1%
9	North Carolina	28,855	2.9%
10	Washington	28,718	2.9%
11	New Jersey	24,562	2.5%
12	Virginia	24,027	2.4%
13	Colorado	23,725	2.4%
14	Maryland	22,658	2.3%
15	Oklahoma	21,925	2.2%
16	Ohio	21,871	2.2%
17	Georgia	21,752	2.2%
18	Indiana	19,773	2.0%
19	Tennessee	18,628	1.9%
20	Missouri	16,793	1.7%
21	Arkansas	16,640	1.7%
22	Oregon	14,549	1.5%
23	Alabama	13,703	1.4%
24	Louisiana	13,159	1.3%
25	Iowa	12,622	1.3%
26	Nebraska	11,550	1.2%
27	Massachusetts	10,722	1.1%
28	Mississippi	10,412	1.0%
29	Idaho	10,148	1.0%
30	New Mexico	8,952	0.9%
31	Nevada	8,138	0.8%
32	South Carolina	7,789	0.8%
33	Connecticut	7,394	0.7%
34	Maine	7,334	0.7%
35	Utah	6,292	0.6%
36	West Virginia	4,898	0.5%
37	Wyoming	4,488	0.4%
38	Alaska	4,452	0.4%
39	South Dakota	4,221	0.4%
40	New Hampshire	3,857	0.4%
41	North Dakota	3,255	0.3%
42	Hawaii	3,208	0.3%
43	Vermont	2,834	0.3%
44	Kentucky	2,026	0.2%
45	Rhode Island	1,629	0.2%
46	Montana	1,576	0.2%
47	Delaware	211	0.0%
NA	Illinois**	NA	NA
NA	Kansas**	NA	NA
NA	Wisconsin**	NA	NA
	District of Columbia**	NA	NA

Source: Federal Bureau of Investigation
   "Crime in the United States 2000" (Uniform Crime Reports, October 22, 2001)
*By law enforcement agencies submitting complete reports to the F.B.I. for 12 months in 2000. The F.B.I. estimates 1,471,289 reported and unreported arrests for driving under the influence occurred in 2000. Includes driving any vehicle while drunk or under the influence of liquor or narcotics. See important note at beginning of this chapter.
**Not available.

Reported Arrest Rate for Driving Under the Influence in 2000

National Rate = 382.4 Reported Arrests per 100,000 Population*

ALPHA ORDER

RANK ORDER

RANK	STATE	RATE		RANK	STATE	RATE
30	Alabama	307.8		1	Minnesota	909.0
4	Alaska	709.4		2	Wyoming	908.5
8	Arizona	620.2		3	Idaho	781.1
7	Arkansas	621.4		4	Alaska	709.4
12	California	539.0		5	Nebraska	674.4
11	Colorado	548.8		6	Oklahoma	634.9
39	Connecticut	216.8		7	Arkansas	621.4
47	Delaware	26.8		8	Arizona	620.2
23	Florida	375.8		9	Maine	574.3
38	Georgia	264.3		10	South Dakota	558.7
37	Hawaii	264.6		11	Colorado	548.8
3	Idaho	781.1		12	California	539.0
NA	Illinois**	NA		13	North Dakota	507.9
28	Indiana	324.7		14	Michigan	492.0
19	Iowa	431.2		15	New Mexico	491.5
NA	Kansas**	NA		16	Washington	486.1
46	Kentucky	50.1		17	Vermont	464.8
32	Louisiana	294.4		18	Texas	455.7
9	Maine	574.3		19	Iowa	431.2
20	Maryland	426.6		20	Maryland	426.6
43	Massachusetts	168.7		21	Oregon	424.3
14	Michigan	492.0		22	Nevada	403.1
1	Minnesota	909.0		23	Florida	375.8
24	Mississippi	365.4		24	Mississippi	365.4
31	Missouri	299.7		25	North Carolina	357.2
42	Montana	174.5		26	Virginia	338.2
5	Nebraska	674.4		27	Tennessee	326.7
22	Nevada	403.1		28	Indiana	324.7
29	New Hampshire	311.1		29	New Hampshire	311.1
33	New Jersey	291.4		30	Alabama	307.8
15	New Mexico	491.5		31	Missouri	299.7
44	New York	163.2		32	Louisiana	294.4
25	North Carolina	357.2		33	New Jersey	291.4
13	North Dakota	507.9		34	Utah	280.7
41	Ohio	192.5		35	West Virginia	271.0
6	Oklahoma	634.9		36	Pennsylvania	268.5
21	Oregon	424.3		37	Hawaii	264.6
36	Pennsylvania	268.5		38	Georgia	264.3
45	Rhode Island	155.1		39	Connecticut	216.8
40	South Carolina	193.6		40	South Carolina	193.6
10	South Dakota	558.7		41	Ohio	192.5
27	Tennessee	326.7		42	Montana	174.5
18	Texas	455.7		43	Massachusetts	168.7
34	Utah	280.7		44	New York	163.2
17	Vermont	464.8		45	Rhode Island	155.1
26	Virginia	338.2		46	Kentucky	50.1
16	Washington	486.1		47	Delaware	26.8
35	West Virginia	271.0		NA	Illinois**	NA
NA	Wisconsin**	NA		NA	Kansas**	NA
2	Wyoming	908.5		NA	Wisconsin**	NA
					District of Columbia**	NA

Source: Morgan Quitno Press using data from Federal Bureau of Investigation
    "Crime in the United States 2000" (Uniform Crime Reports, October 22, 2001)
*By law enforcement agencies submitting complete reports to the F.B.I. for 12 months in 2000. These rates based on population estimates for areas under the jurisdiction of those agencies reporting. Arrest rate based on the F.B.I. estimate of reported and unreported arrests for driving under the influence is 521.5 arrests per 100,000 population. See important note at beginning of this chapter. **Not available.

Reported Arrests for Drug Abuse Violations in 2000

National Total = 1,195,397 Reported Arrests*

ALPHA ORDER					RANK ORDER			
RANK	STATE	ARRESTS	% of USA		RANK	STATE	ARRESTS	% of USA
26	Alabama	12,292	1.0%		1	California	251,448	21.0%
44	Alaska	1,747	0.1%		2	Florida	131,111	11.0%
10	Arizona	28,613	2.4%		3	Texas	104,246	8.7%
27	Arkansas	12,229	1.0%		4	Illinois	58,697	4.9%
1	California	251,448	21.0%		5	New Jersey	55,527	4.6%
23	Colorado	16,080	1.3%		6	Pennsylvania	42,658	3.6%
25	Connecticut	13,915	1.2%		7	Maryland	36,150	3.0%
38	Delaware	3,419	0.3%		8	New York	35,679	3.0%
2	Florida	131,111	11.0%		9	North Carolina	34,110	2.9%
11	Georgia	26,429	2.2%		10	Arizona	28,613	2.4%
41	Hawaii	2,469	0.2%		11	Georgia	26,429	2.2%
34	Idaho	5,306	0.4%		12	Michigan	25,357	2.1%
4	Illinois	58,697	4.9%		13	Missouri	22,340	1.9%
21	Indiana	16,910	1.4%		14	Minnesota	22,268	1.9%
31	Iowa	9,205	0.8%		15	Oklahoma	21,952	1.8%
NA	Kansas**	NA	NA		16	Ohio	21,904	1.8%
45	Kentucky	1,500	0.1%		17	Washington	21,343	1.8%
19	Louisiana	18,194	1.5%		18	Virginia	21,057	1.8%
35	Maine	5,064	0.4%		19	Louisiana	18,194	1.5%
7	Maryland	36,150	3.0%		20	Tennessee	17,828	1.5%
24	Massachusetts	15,399	1.3%		21	Indiana	16,910	1.4%
12	Michigan	25,357	2.1%		22	Oregon	16,381	1.4%
14	Minnesota	22,268	1.9%		23	Colorado	16,080	1.3%
28	Mississippi	11,368	1.0%		24	Massachusetts	15,399	1.3%
13	Missouri	22,340	1.9%		25	Connecticut	13,915	1.2%
48	Montana	398	0.0%		26	Alabama	12,292	1.0%
30	Nebraska	9,995	0.8%		27	Arkansas	12,229	1.0%
29	Nevada	10,120	0.8%		28	Mississippi	11,368	1.0%
39	New Hampshire	2,943	0.2%		29	Nevada	10,120	0.8%
5	New Jersey	55,527	4.6%		30	Nebraska	9,995	0.8%
36	New Mexico	4,431	0.4%		31	Iowa	9,205	0.8%
8	New York	35,679	3.0%		32	South Carolina	7,884	0.7%
9	North Carolina	34,110	2.9%		33	Utah	6,335	0.5%
46	North Dakota	1,236	0.1%		34	Idaho	5,306	0.4%
16	Ohio	21,904	1.8%		35	Maine	5,064	0.4%
15	Oklahoma	21,952	1.8%		36	New Mexico	4,431	0.4%
22	Oregon	16,381	1.4%		37	Rhode Island	3,988	0.3%
6	Pennsylvania	42,658	3.6%		38	Delaware	3,419	0.3%
37	Rhode Island	3,988	0.3%		39	New Hampshire	2,943	0.2%
32	South Carolina	7,884	0.7%		40	South Dakota	2,608	0.2%
40	South Dakota	2,608	0.2%		41	Hawaii	2,469	0.2%
20	Tennessee	17,828	1.5%		42	Wyoming	2,310	0.2%
3	Texas	104,246	8.7%		43	West Virginia	1,918	0.2%
33	Utah	6,335	0.5%		44	Alaska	1,747	0.1%
47	Vermont	1,036	0.1%		45	Kentucky	1,500	0.1%
18	Virginia	21,057	1.8%		46	North Dakota	1,236	0.1%
17	Washington	21,343	1.8%		47	Vermont	1,036	0.1%
43	West Virginia	1,918	0.2%		48	Montana	398	0.0%
NA	Wisconsin**	NA	NA		NA	Kansas**	NA	NA
42	Wyoming	2,310	0.2%		NA	Wisconsin**	NA	NA
						District of Columbia**	NA	NA

Source: Federal Bureau of Investigation
   "Crime in the United States 2000" (Uniform Crime Reports, October 22, 2001)
*By law enforcement agencies submitting complete reports to the F.B.I. for 12 months in 2000. The F.B.I. estimates
1,579,566 reported and unreported arrests for drug abuse violations occurred in 2000. Includes offenses relating to
possession, sale, use, growing and manufacturing of narcotic drugs. See important note at beginning of this chapter.
**Not available.

Reported Arrest Rate for Drug Abuse Violations in 2000

National Rate = 437.1 Reported Arrests per 100,000 Population*

ALPHA ORDER

RANK ORDER

RANK	STATE	RATE		RANK	STATE	RATE
35	Alabama	276.1		1	Florida	816.7
33	Alaska	278.4		2	California	739.5
7	Arizona	553.9		3	Maryland	680.7
13	Arkansas	456.6		4	New Jersey	658.8
2	California	739.5		5	Oklahoma	635.7
24	Colorado	371.9		6	Nebraska	583.6
18	Connecticut	408.1		7	Arizona	553.9
15	Delaware	434.9		8	Nevada	501.3
1	Florida	816.7		9	Texas	497.7
28	Georgia	321.1		10	Oregon	477.7
40	Hawaii	203.7		11	Illinois	472.0
17	Idaho	408.4		12	Wyoming	467.6
11	Illinois	472.0		13	Arkansas	456.6
34	Indiana	277.7		14	Minnesota	451.6
29	Iowa	314.4		15	Delaware	434.9
NA	Kansas**	NA		16	North Carolina	422.3
48	Kentucky	37.1		17	Idaho	408.4
19	Louisiana	407.0		18	Connecticut	408.1
22	Maine	396.6		19	Louisiana	407.0
3	Maryland	680.7		20	Mississippi	399.0
38	Massachusetts	242.2		21	Missouri	398.7
36	Michigan	254.8		22	Maine	396.6
14	Minnesota	451.6		23	Rhode Island	379.7
20	Mississippi	399.0		24	Colorado	371.9
21	Missouri	398.7		25	Washington	361.2
47	Montana	44.1		26	Pennsylvania	347.3
6	Nebraska	583.6		27	South Dakota	345.2
8	Nevada	501.3		28	Georgia	321.1
39	New Hampshire	237.4		29	Iowa	314.4
4	New Jersey	658.8		30	Tennessee	312.7
37	New Mexico	243.3		31	Virginia	296.4
44	New York	187.9		32	Utah	282.6
16	North Carolina	422.3		33	Alaska	278.4
42	North Dakota	192.8		34	Indiana	277.7
42	Ohio	192.8		35	Alabama	276.1
5	Oklahoma	635.7		36	Michigan	254.8
10	Oregon	477.7		37	New Mexico	243.3
26	Pennsylvania	347.3		38	Massachusetts	242.2
23	Rhode Island	379.7		39	New Hampshire	237.4
41	South Carolina	196.0		40	Hawaii	203.7
27	South Dakota	345.2		41	South Carolina	196.0
30	Tennessee	312.7		42	North Dakota	192.8
9	Texas	497.7		42	Ohio	192.8
32	Utah	282.6		44	New York	187.9
45	Vermont	169.9		45	Vermont	169.9
31	Virginia	296.4		46	West Virginia	106.1
25	Washington	361.2		47	Montana	44.1
46	West Virginia	106.1		48	Kentucky	37.1
NA	Wisconsin**	NA		NA	Kansas**	NA
12	Wyoming	467.6		NA	Wisconsin**	NA
					District of Columbia**	NA

Source: Morgan Quitno Press using data from Federal Bureau of Investigation
"Crime in the United States 2000" (Uniform Crime Reports, October 22, 2001)
*By law enforcement agencies submitting complete reports to the F.B.I. for 12 months in 2000. These rates based on population estimates for areas under the jurisdiction of those agencies reporting. Arrest rate based on the F.B.I. estimate of reported and unreported arrests for drug abuse violations is 559.9 arrests per 100,000 population. See important note at beginning of this chapter. **Not available.

Reported Arrests for Sex Offenses in 2000

National Total = 66,786 Reported Arrests*

ALPHA ORDER				RANK ORDER			
RANK	STATE	ARRESTS	% of USA	RANK	STATE	ARRESTS	% of USA
34	Alabama	299	0.4%	1	California	15,354	23.0%
37	Alaska	226	0.3%	2	Texas	4,887	7.3%
11	Arizona	1,755	2.6%	3	Florida	4,721	7.1%
26	Arkansas	642	1.0%	4	New York	3,552	5.3%
1	California	15,354	23.0%	5	Pennsylvania	2,868	4.3%
16	Colorado	1,336	2.0%	6	Georgia	2,592	3.9%
28	Connecticut	566	0.8%	7	Illinois	2,472	3.7%
30	Delaware	363	0.5%	8	New Jersey	1,935	2.9%
3	Florida	4,721	7.1%	9	North Carolina	1,910	2.9%
6	Georgia	2,592	3.9%	10	Missouri	1,896	2.8%
32	Hawaii	322	0.5%	11	Arizona	1,755	2.6%
31	Idaho	345	0.5%	12	Ohio	1,723	2.6%
7	Illinois	2,472	3.7%	13	Nevada	1,454	2.2%
15	Indiana	1,389	2.1%	14	Washington	1,444	2.2%
36	Iowa	268	0.4%	15	Indiana	1,389	2.1%
NA	Kansas**	NA	NA	16	Colorado	1,336	2.0%
42	Kentucky	124	0.2%	17	Oregon	1,322	2.0%
20	Louisiana	1,192	1.8%	18	Minnesota	1,242	1.9%
35	Maine	284	0.4%	19	Maryland	1,226	1.8%
19	Maryland	1,226	1.8%	20	Louisiana	1,192	1.8%
27	Massachusetts	612	0.9%	21	Michigan	1,161	1.7%
21	Michigan	1,161	1.7%	22	Virginia	1,068	1.6%
18	Minnesota	1,242	1.9%	23	Oklahoma	893	1.3%
33	Mississippi	311	0.5%	24	Utah	775	1.2%
10	Missouri	1,896	2.8%	25	Nebraska	685	1.0%
46	Montana	64	0.1%	26	Arkansas	642	1.0%
25	Nebraska	685	1.0%	27	Massachusetts	612	0.9%
13	Nevada	1,454	2.2%	28	Connecticut	566	0.8%
43	New Hampshire	120	0.2%	29	Tennessee	384	0.6%
8	New Jersey	1,935	2.9%	30	Delaware	363	0.5%
47	New Mexico	60	0.1%	31	Idaho	345	0.5%
4	New York	3,552	5.3%	32	Hawaii	322	0.5%
9	North Carolina	1,910	2.9%	33	Mississippi	311	0.5%
45	North Dakota	80	0.1%	34	Alabama	299	0.4%
12	Ohio	1,723	2.6%	35	Maine	284	0.4%
23	Oklahoma	893	1.3%	36	Iowa	268	0.4%
17	Oregon	1,322	2.0%	37	Alaska	226	0.3%
5	Pennsylvania	2,868	4.3%	38	South Carolina	219	0.3%
44	Rhode Island	118	0.2%	39	South Dakota	216	0.3%
38	South Carolina	219	0.3%	40	Wyoming	147	0.2%
39	South Dakota	216	0.3%	41	West Virginia	132	0.2%
29	Tennessee	384	0.6%	42	Kentucky	124	0.2%
2	Texas	4,887	7.3%	43	New Hampshire	120	0.2%
24	Utah	775	1.2%	44	Rhode Island	118	0.2%
48	Vermont	32	0.0%	45	North Dakota	80	0.1%
22	Virginia	1,068	1.6%	46	Montana	64	0.1%
14	Washington	1,444	2.2%	47	New Mexico	60	0.1%
41	West Virginia	132	0.2%	48	Vermont	32	0.0%
NA	Wisconsin**	NA	NA	NA	Kansas**	NA	NA
40	Wyoming	147	0.2%	NA	Wisconsin**	NA	NA
					District of Columbia**	NA	NA

Source: Federal Bureau of Investigation
    "Crime in the United States 2000" (Uniform Crime Reports, October 22, 2001)
*By law enforcement agencies submitting complete reports to the F.B.I. for 12 months in 2000. The F.B.I. estimates
93,399 reported and unreported arrests for sex offenses occurred in 2000. Excludes forcible rape, prostitution and
commercialized vice. Includes statutory rape and offenses against chastity, common decency, morals and the like.
See important note at beginning of this chapter. **Not available.

Reported Arrest Rate for Sex Offenses in 2000

National Rate = 24.4 Reported Arrests per 100,000 Population*

ALPHA ORDER			RANK ORDER		
RANK	STATE	RATE	RANK	STATE	RATE
43	Alabama	6.7	1	Nevada	72.0
6	Alaska	36.0	2	Delaware	46.2
8	Arizona	34.0	3	California	45.2
21	Arkansas	24.0	4	Nebraska	40.0
3	California	45.2	5	Oregon	38.6
11	Colorado	30.9	6	Alaska	36.0
31	Connecticut	16.6	7	Utah	34.6
2	Delaware	46.2	8	Arizona	34.0
13	Florida	29.4	9	Missouri	33.8
10	Georgia	31.5	10	Georgia	31.5
16	Hawaii	26.6	11	Colorado	30.9
16	Idaho	26.6	12	Wyoming	29.8
29	Illinois	19.9	13	Florida	29.4
27	Indiana	22.8	14	South Dakota	28.6
40	Iowa	9.2	15	Louisiana	26.7
NA	Kansas**	NA	16	Hawaii	26.6
48	Kentucky	3.1	16	Idaho	26.6
15	Louisiana	26.7	18	Oklahoma	25.9
28	Maine	22.2	19	Minnesota	25.2
25	Maryland	23.1	20	Washington	24.4
39	Massachusetts	9.6	21	Arkansas	24.0
35	Michigan	11.7	22	North Carolina	23.6
19	Minnesota	25.2	23	Pennsylvania	23.4
37	Mississippi	10.9	24	Texas	23.3
9	Missouri	33.8	25	Maryland	23.1
42	Montana	7.1	26	New Jersey	23.0
4	Nebraska	40.0	27	Indiana	22.8
1	Nevada	72.0	28	Maine	22.2
38	New Hampshire	9.7	29	Illinois	19.9
26	New Jersey	23.0	30	New York	18.7
47	New Mexico	3.3	31	Connecticut	16.6
30	New York	18.7	32	Ohio	15.2
22	North Carolina	23.6	33	Virginia	15.0
34	North Dakota	12.5	34	North Dakota	12.5
32	Ohio	15.2	35	Michigan	11.7
18	Oklahoma	25.9	36	Rhode Island	11.2
5	Oregon	38.6	37	Mississippi	10.9
23	Pennsylvania	23.4	38	New Hampshire	9.7
36	Rhode Island	11.2	39	Massachusetts	9.6
45	South Carolina	5.4	40	Iowa	9.2
14	South Dakota	28.6	41	West Virginia	7.3
43	Tennessee	6.7	42	Montana	7.1
24	Texas	23.3	43	Alabama	6.7
7	Utah	34.6	43	Tennessee	6.7
46	Vermont	5.2	45	South Carolina	5.4
33	Virginia	15.0	46	Vermont	5.2
20	Washington	24.4	47	New Mexico	3.3
41	West Virginia	7.3	48	Kentucky	3.1
NA	Wisconsin**	NA	NA	Kansas**	NA
12	Wyoming	29.8	NA	Wisconsin**	NA
				District of Columbia**	NA

Source: Morgan Quitno Press using data from Federal Bureau of Investigation
   "Crime in the United States 2000" (Uniform Crime Reports, October 22, 2001)
*By law enforcement agencies submitting complete reports to the F.B.I. for 12 months in 2000. These rates based on population estimates for areas under the jurisdiction of those agencies reporting. Arrest rate based on the F.B.I. estimate of reported and unreported arrests for sex offenses is 33.1 arrests per 100,000 population. See important note at beginning of this chapter. **Not available.

Reported Arrests for Prostitution and Commercialized Vice in 2000

National Total = 75,477 Reported Arrests*

ALPHA ORDER

RANK	STATE	ARRESTS	% of USA
36	Alabama	138	0.2%
37	Alaska	117	0.2%
7	Arizona	2,537	3.4%
29	Arkansas	359	0.5%
2	California	12,401	16.4%
15	Colorado	1,248	1.7%
23	Connecticut	582	0.8%
35	Delaware	142	0.2%
1	Florida	13,810	18.3%
6	Georgia	3,493	4.6%
26	Hawaii	455	0.6%
43	Idaho	6	0.0%
3	Illinois	7,090	9.4%
16	Indiana	1,129	1.5%
33	Iowa	261	0.3%
NA	Kansas**	NA	NA
42	Kentucky	7	0.0%
34	Louisiana	156	0.2%
39	Maine	23	0.0%
19	Maryland	841	1.1%
13	Massachusetts	1,599	2.1%
18	Michigan	993	1.3%
10	Minnesota	2,027	2.7%
38	Mississippi	92	0.1%
12	Missouri	1,724	2.3%
46	Montana	2	0.0%
25	Nebraska	469	0.6%
5	Nevada	4,176	5.5%
45	New Hampshire	3	0.0%
11	New Jersey	1,956	2.6%
24	New Mexico	528	0.7%
14	New York	1,415	1.9%
17	North Carolina	1,053	1.4%
47	North Dakota	0	0.0%
8	Ohio	2,243	3.0%
32	Oklahoma	284	0.4%
20	Oregon	816	1.1%
9	Pennsylvania	2,136	2.8%
28	Rhode Island	382	0.5%
30	South Carolina	357	0.5%
41	South Dakota	13	0.0%
31	Tennessee	331	0.4%
4	Texas	6,308	8.4%
27	Utah	386	0.5%
47	Vermont	0	0.0%
22	Virginia	605	0.8%
21	Washington	757	1.0%
39	West Virginia	23	0.0%
NA	Wisconsin**	NA	NA
44	Wyoming	4	0.0%

RANK ORDER

RANK	STATE	ARRESTS	% of USA
1	Florida	13,810	18.3%
2	California	12,401	16.4%
3	Illinois	7,090	9.4%
4	Texas	6,308	8.4%
5	Nevada	4,176	5.5%
6	Georgia	3,493	4.6%
7	Arizona	2,537	3.4%
8	Ohio	2,243	3.0%
9	Pennsylvania	2,136	2.8%
10	Minnesota	2,027	2.7%
11	New Jersey	1,956	2.6%
12	Missouri	1,724	2.3%
13	Massachusetts	1,599	2.1%
14	New York	1,415	1.9%
15	Colorado	1,248	1.7%
16	Indiana	1,129	1.5%
17	North Carolina	1,053	1.4%
18	Michigan	993	1.3%
19	Maryland	841	1.1%
20	Oregon	816	1.1%
21	Washington	757	1.0%
22	Virginia	605	0.8%
23	Connecticut	582	0.8%
24	New Mexico	528	0.7%
25	Nebraska	469	0.6%
26	Hawaii	455	0.6%
27	Utah	386	0.5%
28	Rhode Island	382	0.5%
29	Arkansas	359	0.5%
30	South Carolina	357	0.5%
31	Tennessee	331	0.4%
32	Oklahoma	284	0.4%
33	Iowa	261	0.3%
34	Louisiana	156	0.2%
35	Delaware	142	0.2%
36	Alabama	138	0.2%
37	Alaska	117	0.2%
38	Mississippi	92	0.1%
39	Maine	23	0.0%
39	West Virginia	23	0.0%
41	South Dakota	13	0.0%
42	Kentucky	7	0.0%
43	Idaho	6	0.0%
44	Wyoming	4	0.0%
45	New Hampshire	3	0.0%
46	Montana	2	0.0%
47	North Dakota	0	0.0%
47	Vermont	0	0.0%
NA	Kansas**	NA	NA
NA	Wisconsin**	NA	NA
	District of Columbia**	NA	NA

Source: Federal Bureau of Investigation
    "Crime in the United States 2000" (Uniform Crime Reports, October 22, 2001)
*By law enforcement agencies submitting complete reports to the F.B.I. for 12 months in 2000. The F.B.I. estimates 87,620 reported and unreported arrests for prostitution and commercialized vice occurred in 2000. Includes keeping a bawdy house, procuring or transporting women for immoral purposes. Attempts are included. See important note at beginning of this chapter. **Not available.

Reported Arrest Rate for Prostitution and Commercialized Vice in 2000

National Rate = 27.6 Reported Arrests per 100,000 Population*

ALPHA ORDER

RANK ORDER

RANK	STATE	RATE	RANK	STATE	RATE
38	Alabama	3.1	1	Nevada	206.9
19	Alaska	18.6	2	Florida	86.0
4	Arizona	49.1	3	Illinois	57.0
26	Arkansas	13.4	4	Arizona	49.1
8	California	36.5	5	Georgia	42.4
13	Colorado	28.9	6	Minnesota	41.1
24	Connecticut	17.1	7	Hawaii	37.5
21	Delaware	18.1	8	California	36.5
2	Florida	86.0	9	Rhode Island	36.4
5	Georgia	42.4	10	Missouri	30.8
7	Hawaii	37.5	11	Texas	30.1
43	Idaho	0.5	12	New Mexico	29.0
3	Illinois	57.0	13	Colorado	28.9
20	Indiana	18.5	14	Nebraska	27.4
30	Iowa	8.9	15	Massachusetts	25.2
NA	Kansas**	NA	16	Oregon	23.8
44	Kentucky	0.2	17	New Jersey	23.2
36	Louisiana	3.5	18	Ohio	19.7
39	Maine	1.8	19	Alaska	18.6
25	Maryland	15.8	20	Indiana	18.5
15	Massachusetts	25.2	21	Delaware	18.1
29	Michigan	10.0	22	Pennsylvania	17.4
6	Minnesota	41.1	23	Utah	17.2
37	Mississippi	3.2	24	Connecticut	17.1
10	Missouri	30.8	25	Maryland	15.8
44	Montana	0.2	26	Arkansas	13.4
14	Nebraska	27.4	27	North Carolina	13.0
1	Nevada	206.9	28	Washington	12.8
44	New Hampshire	0.2	29	Michigan	10.0
17	New Jersey	23.2	30	Iowa	8.9
12	New Mexico	29.0	30	South Carolina	8.9
34	New York	7.5	32	Virginia	8.5
27	North Carolina	13.0	33	Oklahoma	8.2
47	North Dakota	0.0	34	New York	7.5
18	Ohio	19.7	35	Tennessee	5.8
33	Oklahoma	8.2	36	Louisiana	3.5
16	Oregon	23.8	37	Mississippi	3.2
22	Pennsylvania	17.4	38	Alabama	3.1
9	Rhode Island	36.4	39	Maine	1.8
30	South Carolina	8.9	40	South Dakota	1.7
40	South Dakota	1.7	41	West Virginia	1.3
35	Tennessee	5.8	42	Wyoming	0.8
11	Texas	30.1	43	Idaho	0.5
23	Utah	17.2	44	Kentucky	0.2
47	Vermont	0.0	44	Montana	0.2
32	Virginia	8.5	44	New Hampshire	0.2
28	Washington	12.8	47	North Dakota	0.0
41	West Virginia	1.3	47	Vermont	0.0
NA	Wisconsin**	NA	NA	Kansas**	NA
42	Wyoming	0.8	NA	Wisconsin**	NA
				District of Columbia**	NA

Source: Morgan Quitno Press using data from Federal Bureau of Investigation
"Crime in the United States 2000" (Uniform Crime Reports, October 22, 2001)
*By law enforcement agencies submitting complete reports to the F.B.I. for 12 months in 2000. These rates based on population estimates for areas under the jurisdiction of those agencies reporting. Arrest rate based on the F.B.I. estimate of reported and unreported arrests for prostitution and commercialized vice is 31.1 arrests per 100,000 population. See important note at beginning of this chapter. **Not available.

34

Reported Arrests for Offenses Against Families and Children in 2000

National Total = 92,644 Reported Arrests*

ALPHA ORDER					RANK ORDER			
RANK	STATE	ARRESTS	% of USA		RANK	STATE	ARRESTS	% of USA
21	Alabama	1,292	1.4%		1	New Jersey	16,362	17.7%
38	Alaska	372	0.4%		2	Ohio	15,729	17.0%
13	Arizona	2,131	2.3%		3	North Carolina	5,789	6.2%
12	Arkansas	2,166	2.3%		4	Texas	4,993	5.4%
30	California	629	0.7%		5	Michigan	3,707	4.0%
9	Colorado	2,578	2.8%		6	Georgia	2,975	3.2%
17	Connecticut	1,566	1.7%		7	New York	2,939	3.2%
44	Delaware	167	0.2%		8	Mississippi	2,804	3.0%
NA	Florida**	NA	NA		9	Colorado	2,578	2.8%
6	Georgia	2,975	3.2%		10	Missouri	2,513	2.7%
16	Hawaii	1,583	1.7%		11	Maryland	2,235	2.4%
36	Idaho	412	0.4%		12	Arkansas	2,166	2.3%
28	Illinois	710	0.8%		13	Arizona	2,131	2.3%
22	Indiana	1,100	1.2%		14	Massachusetts	2,049	2.2%
33	Iowa	552	0.6%		15	Louisiana	1,844	2.0%
NA	Kansas**	NA	NA		16	Hawaii	1,583	1.7%
39	Kentucky	327	0.4%		17	Connecticut	1,566	1.7%
15	Louisiana	1,844	2.0%		18	South Carolina	1,502	1.6%
35	Maine	477	0.5%		19	Nebraska	1,470	1.6%
11	Maryland	2,235	2.4%		20	Oklahoma	1,347	1.5%
14	Massachusetts	2,049	2.2%		21	Alabama	1,292	1.4%
5	Michigan	3,707	4.0%		22	Indiana	1,100	1.2%
26	Minnesota	759	0.8%		23	Nevada	1,074	1.2%
8	Mississippi	2,804	3.0%		24	Utah	987	1.1%
10	Missouri	2,513	2.7%		25	Virginia	780	0.8%
45	Montana	134	0.1%		26	Minnesota	759	0.8%
19	Nebraska	1,470	1.6%		27	Pennsylvania	754	0.8%
23	Nevada	1,074	1.2%		28	Illinois	710	0.8%
46	New Hampshire	124	0.1%		29	New Mexico	661	0.7%
1	New Jersey	16,362	17.7%		30	California	629	0.7%
29	New Mexico	661	0.7%		31	Oregon	578	0.6%
7	New York	2,939	3.2%		32	Tennessee	569	0.6%
3	North Carolina	5,789	6.2%		33	Iowa	552	0.6%
41	North Dakota	239	0.3%		34	Rhode Island	488	0.5%
2	Ohio	15,729	17.0%		35	Maine	477	0.5%
20	Oklahoma	1,347	1.5%		36	Idaho	412	0.4%
31	Oregon	578	0.6%		37	Vermont	376	0.4%
27	Pennsylvania	754	0.8%		38	Alaska	372	0.4%
34	Rhode Island	488	0.5%		39	Kentucky	327	0.4%
18	South Carolina	1,502	1.6%		40	South Dakota	323	0.3%
40	South Dakota	323	0.3%		41	North Dakota	239	0.3%
32	Tennessee	569	0.6%		42	Wyoming	210	0.2%
4	Texas	4,993	5.4%		43	Washington	185	0.2%
24	Utah	987	1.1%		44	Delaware	167	0.2%
37	Vermont	376	0.4%		45	Montana	134	0.1%
25	Virginia	780	0.8%		46	New Hampshire	124	0.1%
43	Washington	185	0.2%		47	West Virginia	83	0.1%
47	West Virginia	83	0.1%		NA	Florida**	NA	NA
NA	Wisconsin**	NA	NA		NA	Kansas**	NA	NA
42	Wyoming	210	0.2%		NA	Wisconsin**	NA	NA
						District of Columbia**	NA	NA

Source: Federal Bureau of Investigation
    "Crime in the United States 2000" (Uniform Crime Reports, October 22, 2001)
*By law enforcement agencies submitting complete reports to the F.B.I. for 12 months in 2000. The F.B.I. estimates
147,663 reported and unreported arrests for offenses against families and children occurred in 2000. Includes
nonsupport, neglect, desertion or abuse of family and children. See important note at beginning of this chapter.
**Not available.

Reported Arrest Rate for Offenses Against Families and Children in 2000

National Rate = 36.0 Reported Arrests per 100,000 Population*

ALPHA ORDER

RANK	STATE	RATE
30	Alabama	29.0
10	Alaska	59.3
19	Arizona	41.3
6	Arkansas	80.9
47	California	1.8
9	Colorado	59.6
13	Connecticut	45.9
32	Delaware	21.2
NA	Florida**	NA
27	Georgia	36.1
3	Hawaii	130.6
29	Idaho	31.7
44	Illinois	5.7
34	Indiana	18.1
33	Iowa	18.9
NA	Kansas**	NA
42	Kentucky	8.1
19	Louisiana	41.3
22	Maine	37.4
18	Maryland	42.1
28	Massachusetts	32.2
25	Michigan	37.2
37	Minnesota	15.4
4	Mississippi	98.4
14	Missouri	44.8
38	Montana	14.8
5	Nebraska	85.8
11	Nevada	53.2
40	New Hampshire	10.0
1	New Jersey	194.1
26	New Mexico	36.3
36	New York	15.5
7	North Carolina	71.7
23	North Dakota	37.3
2	Ohio	138.5
21	Oklahoma	39.0
35	Oregon	16.9
43	Pennsylvania	6.1
12	Rhode Island	46.5
23	South Carolina	37.3
16	South Dakota	42.8
40	Tennessee	10.0
31	Texas	23.8
15	Utah	44.0
8	Vermont	61.7
39	Virginia	11.0
46	Washington	3.1
45	West Virginia	4.6
NA	Wisconsin**	NA
17	Wyoming	42.5

RANK ORDER

RANK	STATE	RATE
1	New Jersey	194.1
2	Ohio	138.5
3	Hawaii	130.6
4	Mississippi	98.4
5	Nebraska	85.8
6	Arkansas	80.9
7	North Carolina	71.7
8	Vermont	61.7
9	Colorado	59.6
10	Alaska	59.3
11	Nevada	53.2
12	Rhode Island	46.5
13	Connecticut	45.9
14	Missouri	44.8
15	Utah	44.0
16	South Dakota	42.8
17	Wyoming	42.5
18	Maryland	42.1
19	Arizona	41.3
19	Louisiana	41.3
21	Oklahoma	39.0
22	Maine	37.4
23	North Dakota	37.3
23	South Carolina	37.3
25	Michigan	37.2
26	New Mexico	36.3
27	Georgia	36.1
28	Massachusetts	32.2
29	Idaho	31.7
30	Alabama	29.0
31	Texas	23.8
32	Delaware	21.2
33	Iowa	18.9
34	Indiana	18.1
35	Oregon	16.9
36	New York	15.5
37	Minnesota	15.4
38	Montana	14.8
39	Virginia	11.0
40	New Hampshire	10.0
40	Tennessee	10.0
42	Kentucky	8.1
43	Pennsylvania	6.1
44	Illinois	5.7
45	West Virginia	4.6
46	Washington	3.1
47	California	1.8
NA	Florida**	NA
NA	Kansas**	NA
NA	Wisconsin**	NA
	District of Columbia**	NA

Source: Morgan Quitno Press using data from Federal Bureau of Investigation
   "Crime in the United States 2000" (Uniform Crime Reports, October 22, 2001)
*By law enforcement agencies submitting complete reports to the F.B.I. for 12 months in 2000. These rates based on population estimates for areas under the jurisdiction of those agencies reporting. Arrest rate based on the F.B.I. estimate of reported and unreported arrests for offenses against families and children is 52.3 arrests per 100,000 population. See important note at beginning of this chapter. **Not available.

Percent of Crimes Cleared in 1999

National Percent = 21.4% Cleared*

ALPHA ORDER

RANK	STATE	PERCENT	RANK	STATE	PERCENT
27	Alabama	21.4	1	Wyoming	29.3
3	Alaska	27.1	2	Maine	29.1
43	Arizona	17.8	3	Alaska	27.1
11	Arkansas	25.2	4	Kentucky	27.0
27	California	21.4	5	New Hampshire	26.7
19	Colorado	22.6	6	Delaware	26.1
35	Connecticut	20.1	6	Pennsylvania	26.1
6	Delaware	26.1	6	South Dakota	26.1
29	Florida	21.2	9	Wisconsin	25.8
25	Georgia	21.7	10	Nebraska	25.4
46	Hawaii	15.5	11	Arkansas	25.2
21	Idaho	22.5	12	New York	24.8
NA	Illinois**	NA	13	Louisiana	24.6
33	Indiana	20.6	13	Nevada	24.6
39	Iowa	18.8	15	Maryland	24.4
NA	Kansas**	NA	16	Tennessee	22.9
4	Kentucky	27.0	17	Montana	22.8
13	Louisiana	24.6	18	Minnesota	22.7
2	Maine	29.1	19	Colorado	22.6
15	Maryland	24.4	19	Oregon	22.6
21	Massachusetts	22.5	21	Idaho	22.5
47	Michigan	14.1	21	Massachusetts	22.5
18	Minnesota	22.7	23	Mississippi	22.4
23	Mississippi	22.4	24	Virginia	22.3
26	Missouri	21.5	25	Georgia	21.7
17	Montana	22.8	26	Missouri	21.5
10	Nebraska	25.4	27	Alabama	21.4
13	Nevada	24.6	27	California	21.4
5	New Hampshire	26.7	29	Florida	21.2
34	New Jersey	20.5	30	North Carolina	21.1
44	New Mexico	16.9	31	North Dakota	21.0
12	New York	24.8	32	Utah	20.7
30	North Carolina	21.1	33	Indiana	20.6
31	North Dakota	21.0	34	New Jersey	20.5
45	Ohio	16.8	35	Connecticut	20.1
37	Oklahoma	19.6	35	Texas	20.1
19	Oregon	22.6	37	Oklahoma	19.6
6	Pennsylvania	26.1	38	Washington	19.5
39	Rhode Island	18.8	39	Iowa	18.8
41	South Carolina	18.7	39	Rhode Island	18.8
6	South Dakota	26.1	41	South Carolina	18.7
16	Tennessee	22.9	42	West Virginia	17.9
35	Texas	20.1	43	Arizona	17.8
32	Utah	20.7	44	New Mexico	16.9
48	Vermont	13.7	45	Ohio	16.8
24	Virginia	22.3	46	Hawaii	15.5
38	Washington	19.5	47	Michigan	14.1
42	West Virginia	17.9	48	Vermont	13.7
9	Wisconsin	25.8	NA	Illinois**	NA
1	Wyoming	29.3	NA	Kansas**	NA
				District of Columbia	10.1

Source: Federal Bureau of Investigation (unpublished data)
*Includes murder, rape, robbery, aggravated assault, burglary, larceny-theft and motor vehicle theft. A crime is considered cleared when at least one person is arrested, charged and turned over to the court for prosecution. Clearances recorded in 1999 may be for crimes which occurred in prior years. Several crimes may be cleared by the arrest of one person while the arrest of many persons may clear only one crime.
**Not available.

Percent of Violent Crimes Cleared in 1999

National Percent = 50.0% Cleared*

<table>
<tr><td colspan="3">ALPHA ORDER</td><td colspan="3">RANK ORDER</td></tr>
<tr><td>RANK</td><td>STATE</td><td>PERCENT</td><td>RANK</td><td>STATE</td><td>PERCENT</td></tr>
<tr><td>31</td><td>Alabama</td><td>49.8</td><td>1</td><td>Wyoming</td><td>69.1</td></tr>
<tr><td>9</td><td>Alaska</td><td>57.9</td><td>2</td><td>Vermont</td><td>67.8</td></tr>
<tr><td>44</td><td>Arizona</td><td>39.7</td><td>3</td><td>Maine</td><td>66.6</td></tr>
<tr><td>10</td><td>Arkansas</td><td>57.5</td><td>4</td><td>South Dakota</td><td>64.7</td></tr>
<tr><td>25</td><td>California</td><td>51.3</td><td>5</td><td>Nebraska</td><td>64.1</td></tr>
<tr><td>15</td><td>Colorado</td><td>54.2</td><td>6</td><td>Delaware</td><td>59.9</td></tr>
<tr><td>31</td><td>Connecticut</td><td>49.8</td><td>7</td><td>Maryland</td><td>59.7</td></tr>
<tr><td>6</td><td>Delaware</td><td>59.9</td><td>8</td><td>Idaho</td><td>58.0</td></tr>
<tr><td>35</td><td>Florida</td><td>47.9</td><td>9</td><td>Alaska</td><td>57.9</td></tr>
<tr><td>39</td><td>Georgia</td><td>46.4</td><td>10</td><td>Arkansas</td><td>57.5</td></tr>
<tr><td>43</td><td>Hawaii</td><td>41.4</td><td>11</td><td>Oregon</td><td>57.0</td></tr>
<tr><td>8</td><td>Idaho</td><td>58.0</td><td>12</td><td>Minnesota</td><td>56.8</td></tr>
<tr><td>NA</td><td>Illinois**</td><td>NA</td><td>13</td><td>Montana</td><td>56.4</td></tr>
<tr><td>28</td><td>Indiana</td><td>50.4</td><td>14</td><td>Iowa</td><td>55.5</td></tr>
<tr><td>14</td><td>Iowa</td><td>55.5</td><td>15</td><td>Colorado</td><td>54.2</td></tr>
<tr><td>NA</td><td>Kansas**</td><td>NA</td><td>16</td><td>Massachusetts</td><td>53.5</td></tr>
<tr><td>20</td><td>Kentucky</td><td>52.9</td><td>16</td><td>Virginia</td><td>53.5</td></tr>
<tr><td>20</td><td>Louisiana</td><td>52.9</td><td>16</td><td>Wisconsin</td><td>53.5</td></tr>
<tr><td>3</td><td>Maine</td><td>66.6</td><td>19</td><td>Oklahoma</td><td>53.1</td></tr>
<tr><td>7</td><td>Maryland</td><td>59.7</td><td>20</td><td>Kentucky</td><td>52.9</td></tr>
<tr><td>16</td><td>Massachusetts</td><td>53.5</td><td>20</td><td>Louisiana</td><td>52.9</td></tr>
<tr><td>48</td><td>Michigan</td><td>35.8</td><td>22</td><td>Pennsylvania</td><td>51.8</td></tr>
<tr><td>12</td><td>Minnesota</td><td>56.8</td><td>23</td><td>Utah</td><td>51.7</td></tr>
<tr><td>42</td><td>Mississippi</td><td>42.0</td><td>24</td><td>Tennessee</td><td>51.5</td></tr>
<tr><td>34</td><td>Missouri</td><td>48.3</td><td>25</td><td>California</td><td>51.3</td></tr>
<tr><td>13</td><td>Montana</td><td>56.4</td><td>26</td><td>North Carolina</td><td>51.2</td></tr>
<tr><td>5</td><td>Nebraska</td><td>64.1</td><td>27</td><td>Washington</td><td>50.8</td></tr>
<tr><td>47</td><td>Nevada</td><td>38.5</td><td>28</td><td>Indiana</td><td>50.4</td></tr>
<tr><td>40</td><td>New Hampshire</td><td>44.8</td><td>29</td><td>New York</td><td>50.2</td></tr>
<tr><td>36</td><td>New Jersey</td><td>47.7</td><td>30</td><td>West Virginia</td><td>50.0</td></tr>
<tr><td>40</td><td>New Mexico</td><td>44.8</td><td>31</td><td>Alabama</td><td>49.8</td></tr>
<tr><td>29</td><td>New York</td><td>50.2</td><td>31</td><td>Connecticut</td><td>49.8</td></tr>
<tr><td>26</td><td>North Carolina</td><td>51.2</td><td>33</td><td>Texas</td><td>49.2</td></tr>
<tr><td>45</td><td>North Dakota</td><td>39.0</td><td>34</td><td>Missouri</td><td>48.3</td></tr>
<tr><td>46</td><td>Ohio</td><td>38.9</td><td>35</td><td>Florida</td><td>47.9</td></tr>
<tr><td>19</td><td>Oklahoma</td><td>53.1</td><td>36</td><td>New Jersey</td><td>47.7</td></tr>
<tr><td>11</td><td>Oregon</td><td>57.0</td><td>37</td><td>Rhode Island</td><td>46.9</td></tr>
<tr><td>22</td><td>Pennsylvania</td><td>51.8</td><td>38</td><td>South Carolina</td><td>46.7</td></tr>
<tr><td>37</td><td>Rhode Island</td><td>46.9</td><td>39</td><td>Georgia</td><td>46.4</td></tr>
<tr><td>38</td><td>South Carolina</td><td>46.7</td><td>40</td><td>New Hampshire</td><td>44.8</td></tr>
<tr><td>4</td><td>South Dakota</td><td>64.7</td><td>40</td><td>New Mexico</td><td>44.8</td></tr>
<tr><td>24</td><td>Tennessee</td><td>51.5</td><td>42</td><td>Mississippi</td><td>42.0</td></tr>
<tr><td>33</td><td>Texas</td><td>49.2</td><td>43</td><td>Hawaii</td><td>41.4</td></tr>
<tr><td>23</td><td>Utah</td><td>51.7</td><td>44</td><td>Arizona</td><td>39.7</td></tr>
<tr><td>2</td><td>Vermont</td><td>67.8</td><td>45</td><td>North Dakota</td><td>39.0</td></tr>
<tr><td>16</td><td>Virginia</td><td>53.5</td><td>46</td><td>Ohio</td><td>38.9</td></tr>
<tr><td>27</td><td>Washington</td><td>50.8</td><td>47</td><td>Nevada</td><td>38.5</td></tr>
<tr><td>30</td><td>West Virginia</td><td>50.0</td><td>48</td><td>Michigan</td><td>35.8</td></tr>
<tr><td>16</td><td>Wisconsin</td><td>53.5</td><td>NA</td><td>Illinois**</td><td>NA</td></tr>
<tr><td>1</td><td>Wyoming</td><td>69.1</td><td>NA</td><td>Kansas**</td><td>NA</td></tr>
<tr><td></td><td></td><td></td><td></td><td>District of Columbia</td><td>28.8</td></tr>
</table>

Source: Federal Bureau of Investigation (unpublished data)

*Includes murder, rape, robbery and aggravated assault. A crime is considered cleared when at least one person is arrested, charged and turned over to the court for prosecution. Clearances recorded in 1999 may be for crimes which occurred in prior years. Several crimes may be cleared by the arrest of one person while the arrest of many persons may clear only one crime.

**Not available.

Percent of Murders Cleared in 1999

National Percent = 69.1% Cleared*

RANK	STATE	PERCENT	RANK	STATE	PERCENT
33	Alabama	62.6	1	North Dakota	100.0
5	Alaska	82.4	2	Washington	84.2
40	Arizona	59.0	3	New York	83.8
7	Arkansas	81.1	4	Oklahoma	83.5
38	California	59.7	5	Alaska	82.4
15	Colorado	75.0	6	Wyoming	81.8
31	Connecticut	64.5	7	Arkansas	81.1
44	Delaware	54.2	8	Wisconsin	81.0
32	Florida	63.4	9	Pennsylvania	80.8
10	Georgia	80.1	10	Georgia	80.1
18	Hawaii	74.4	11	North Carolina	77.8
12	Idaho	76.0	12	Idaho	76.0
NA	Illinois**	NA	12	Utah	76.0
19	Indiana	73.2	14	New Jersey	75.6
42	Iowa	56.3	15	Colorado	75.0
NA	Kansas**	NA	16	Louisiana	74.6
39	Kentucky	59.3	16	Mississippi	74.6
16	Louisiana	74.6	18	Hawaii	74.4
45	Maine	50.0	19	Indiana	73.2
20	Maryland	72.7	20	Maryland	72.7
41	Massachusetts	58.1	21	Nevada	72.1
47	Michigan	45.4	21	Texas	72.1
30	Minnesota	68.4	23	Tennessee	71.7
16	Mississippi	74.6	24	Montana	71.4
35	Missouri	60.2	25	West Virginia	71.0
24	Montana	71.4	26	South Carolina	70.5
28	Nebraska	70.0	27	New Mexico	70.2
21	Nevada	72.1	28	Nebraska	70.0
36	New Hampshire	60.0	29	Virginia	68.8
14	New Jersey	75.6	30	Minnesota	68.4
27	New Mexico	70.2	31	Connecticut	64.5
3	New York	83.8	32	Florida	63.4
11	North Carolina	77.8	33	Alabama	62.6
1	North Dakota	100.0	34	Ohio	61.6
34	Ohio	61.6	35	Missouri	60.2
4	Oklahoma	83.5	36	New Hampshire	60.0
48	Oregon	42.5	36	Vermont	60.0
9	Pennsylvania	80.8	38	California	59.7
43	Rhode Island	55.6	39	Kentucky	59.3
26	South Carolina	70.5	40	Arizona	59.0
46	South Dakota	46.2	41	Massachusetts	58.1
23	Tennessee	71.7	42	Iowa	56.3
21	Texas	72.1	43	Rhode Island	55.6
12	Utah	76.0	44	Delaware	54.2
36	Vermont	60.0	45	Maine	50.0
29	Virginia	68.8	46	South Dakota	46.2
2	Washington	84.2	47	Michigan	45.4
25	West Virginia	71.0	48	Oregon	42.5
8	Wisconsin	81.0	NA	Illinois**	NA
6	Wyoming	81.8	NA	Kansas**	NA
				District of Columbia	37.3

Source: Federal Bureau of Investigation (unpublished data)
*Includes nonnegligent manslaughter. A crime is considered cleared when at least one person is arrested, charged and turned over to the court for prosecution. Clearances recorded in 1999 may be for crimes which occurred in prior years. Several crimes may be cleared by the arrest of one person while the arrest of many persons may clear only one crime.
**Not available.

Percent of Rapes Cleared in 1999

National Percent = 49.5% Cleared*

ALPHA ORDER			RANK ORDER		
RANK	STATE	PERCENT	RANK	STATE	PERCENT
29	Alabama	45.5	1	Wisconsin	70.6
38	Alaska	38.9	2	Arkansas	62.2
45	Arizona	28.0	3	Oklahoma	61.9
2	Arkansas	62.2	4	Maryland	61.5
20	California	49.1	5	Hawaii	58.6
23	Colorado	47.3	6	Pennsylvania	58.3
31	Connecticut	45.4	7	Minnesota	58.1
NA	Delaware**	NA	8	North Carolina	57.8
18	Florida	51.4	9	Missouri	57.7
15	Georgia	52.9	9	Nebraska	57.7
5	Hawaii	58.6	11	Tennessee	55.5
36	Idaho	41.2	12	New York	55.0
NA	Illinois**	NA	13	New Jersey	54.1
33	Indiana	44.4	14	Texas	53.5
44	Iowa	28.2	15	Georgia	52.9
NA	Kansas**	NA	16	Louisiana	51.7
27	Kentucky	46.7	17	Virginia	51.6
16	Louisiana	51.7	18	Florida	51.4
26	Maine	46.8	19	New Mexico	50.4
4	Maryland	61.5	20	California	49.1
24	Massachusetts	47.2	21	Montana	48.3
42	Michigan	34.1	22	Vermont	47.9
7	Minnesota	58.1	23	Colorado	47.3
35	Mississippi	41.3	24	Massachusetts	47.2
9	Missouri	57.7	25	South Dakota	47.0
21	Montana	48.3	26	Maine	46.8
9	Nebraska	57.7	27	Kentucky	46.7
40	Nevada	35.9	28	Wyoming	46.6
43	New Hampshire	30.1	29	Alabama	45.5
13	New Jersey	54.1	29	Washington	45.5
19	New Mexico	50.4	31	Connecticut	45.4
12	New York	55.0	32	Rhode Island	45.0
8	North Carolina	57.8	33	Indiana	44.4
47	North Dakota	21.9	34	Ohio	42.2
34	Ohio	42.2	35	Mississippi	41.3
3	Oklahoma	61.9	36	Idaho	41.2
39	Oregon	38.2	37	South Carolina	41.1
6	Pennsylvania	58.3	38	Alaska	38.9
32	Rhode Island	45.0	39	Oregon	38.2
37	South Carolina	41.1	40	Nevada	35.9
25	South Dakota	47.0	41	Utah	35.0
11	Tennessee	55.5	42	Michigan	34.1
14	Texas	53.5	43	New Hampshire	30.1
41	Utah	35.0	44	Iowa	28.2
22	Vermont	47.9	45	Arizona	28.0
17	Virginia	51.6	46	West Virginia	24.3
29	Washington	45.5	47	North Dakota	21.9
46	West Virginia	24.3	NA	Delaware**	NA
1	Wisconsin	70.6	NA	Illinois**	NA
28	Wyoming	46.6	NA	Kansas**	NA
				District of Columbia	43.1

Source: Federal Bureau of Investigation (unpublished data)
*Forcible rape including attempts. However, statutory rape without force and other sex offenses are excluded. A crime is considered cleared when at least one person is arrested, charged and turned over to the court for prosecution. Clearances recorded in 1999 may be for crimes which occurred in prior years. Several crimes may be cleared by the arrest of one person while the arrest of many persons may clear only one crime.
**Not available.

Percent of Robberies Cleared in 1999

National Percent = 28.5% Cleared*

<table>
<tr><td colspan="3">ALPHA ORDER</td><td colspan="3">RANK ORDER</td></tr>
<tr><th>RANK</th><th>STATE</th><th>PERCENT</th><th>RANK</th><th>STATE</th><th>PERCENT</th></tr>
<tr><td>10</td><td>Alabama</td><td>34.6</td><td>1</td><td>Maine</td><td>55.2</td></tr>
<tr><td>23</td><td>Alaska</td><td>30.4</td><td>2</td><td>Oregon</td><td>50.4</td></tr>
<tr><td>46</td><td>Arizona</td><td>20.4</td><td>3</td><td>Wyoming</td><td>45.2</td></tr>
<tr><td>8</td><td>Arkansas</td><td>36.4</td><td>4</td><td>Montana</td><td>41.1</td></tr>
<tr><td>31</td><td>California</td><td>27.8</td><td>5</td><td>New Hampshire</td><td>39.2</td></tr>
<tr><td>29</td><td>Colorado</td><td>28.4</td><td>6</td><td>Nebraska</td><td>38.6</td></tr>
<tr><td>42</td><td>Connecticut</td><td>25.4</td><td>7</td><td>South Dakota</td><td>36.8</td></tr>
<tr><td>19</td><td>Delaware</td><td>31.4</td><td>8</td><td>Arkansas</td><td>36.4</td></tr>
<tr><td>39</td><td>Florida</td><td>26.1</td><td>9</td><td>Vermont</td><td>36.1</td></tr>
<tr><td>37</td><td>Georgia</td><td>26.3</td><td>10</td><td>Alabama</td><td>34.6</td></tr>
<tr><td>33</td><td>Hawaii</td><td>27.6</td><td>11</td><td>Tennessee</td><td>34.1</td></tr>
<tr><td>18</td><td>Idaho</td><td>31.9</td><td>12</td><td>Oklahoma</td><td>33.4</td></tr>
<tr><td>NA</td><td>Illinois**</td><td>NA</td><td>13</td><td>Maryland</td><td>33.3</td></tr>
<tr><td>22</td><td>Indiana</td><td>30.6</td><td>14</td><td>New York</td><td>33.1</td></tr>
<tr><td>25</td><td>Iowa</td><td>29.3</td><td>15</td><td>North Carolina</td><td>32.9</td></tr>
<tr><td>NA</td><td>Kansas**</td><td>NA</td><td>16</td><td>Utah</td><td>32.8</td></tr>
<tr><td>24</td><td>Kentucky</td><td>29.7</td><td>17</td><td>Minnesota</td><td>32.5</td></tr>
<tr><td>28</td><td>Louisiana</td><td>28.6</td><td>18</td><td>Idaho</td><td>31.9</td></tr>
<tr><td>1</td><td>Maine</td><td>55.2</td><td>19</td><td>Delaware</td><td>31.4</td></tr>
<tr><td>13</td><td>Maryland</td><td>33.3</td><td>20</td><td>Pennsylvania</td><td>31.0</td></tr>
<tr><td>43</td><td>Massachusetts</td><td>25.2</td><td>21</td><td>North Dakota</td><td>30.9</td></tr>
<tr><td>48</td><td>Michigan</td><td>12.6</td><td>22</td><td>Indiana</td><td>30.6</td></tr>
<tr><td>17</td><td>Minnesota</td><td>32.5</td><td>23</td><td>Alaska</td><td>30.4</td></tr>
<tr><td>35</td><td>Mississippi</td><td>27.3</td><td>24</td><td>Kentucky</td><td>29.7</td></tr>
<tr><td>37</td><td>Missouri</td><td>26.3</td><td>25</td><td>Iowa</td><td>29.3</td></tr>
<tr><td>4</td><td>Montana</td><td>41.1</td><td>26</td><td>Washington</td><td>29.2</td></tr>
<tr><td>6</td><td>Nebraska</td><td>38.6</td><td>27</td><td>Virginia</td><td>28.9</td></tr>
<tr><td>41</td><td>Nevada</td><td>25.8</td><td>28</td><td>Louisiana</td><td>28.6</td></tr>
<tr><td>5</td><td>New Hampshire</td><td>39.2</td><td>29</td><td>Colorado</td><td>28.4</td></tr>
<tr><td>34</td><td>New Jersey</td><td>27.4</td><td>30</td><td>Texas</td><td>28.2</td></tr>
<tr><td>46</td><td>New Mexico</td><td>20.4</td><td>31</td><td>California</td><td>27.8</td></tr>
<tr><td>14</td><td>New York</td><td>33.1</td><td>32</td><td>Rhode Island</td><td>27.7</td></tr>
<tr><td>15</td><td>North Carolina</td><td>32.9</td><td>33</td><td>Hawaii</td><td>27.6</td></tr>
<tr><td>21</td><td>North Dakota</td><td>30.9</td><td>34</td><td>New Jersey</td><td>27.4</td></tr>
<tr><td>44</td><td>Ohio</td><td>23.6</td><td>35</td><td>Mississippi</td><td>27.3</td></tr>
<tr><td>12</td><td>Oklahoma</td><td>33.4</td><td>36</td><td>Wisconsin</td><td>26.4</td></tr>
<tr><td>2</td><td>Oregon</td><td>50.4</td><td>37</td><td>Georgia</td><td>26.3</td></tr>
<tr><td>20</td><td>Pennsylvania</td><td>31.0</td><td>37</td><td>Missouri</td><td>26.3</td></tr>
<tr><td>32</td><td>Rhode Island</td><td>27.7</td><td>39</td><td>Florida</td><td>26.1</td></tr>
<tr><td>39</td><td>South Carolina</td><td>26.1</td><td>39</td><td>South Carolina</td><td>26.1</td></tr>
<tr><td>7</td><td>South Dakota</td><td>36.8</td><td>41</td><td>Nevada</td><td>25.8</td></tr>
<tr><td>11</td><td>Tennessee</td><td>34.1</td><td>42</td><td>Connecticut</td><td>25.4</td></tr>
<tr><td>30</td><td>Texas</td><td>28.2</td><td>43</td><td>Massachusetts</td><td>25.2</td></tr>
<tr><td>16</td><td>Utah</td><td>32.8</td><td>44</td><td>Ohio</td><td>23.6</td></tr>
<tr><td>9</td><td>Vermont</td><td>36.1</td><td>45</td><td>West Virginia</td><td>21.8</td></tr>
<tr><td>27</td><td>Virginia</td><td>28.9</td><td>46</td><td>Arizona</td><td>20.4</td></tr>
<tr><td>26</td><td>Washington</td><td>29.2</td><td>46</td><td>New Mexico</td><td>20.4</td></tr>
<tr><td>45</td><td>West Virginia</td><td>21.8</td><td>48</td><td>Michigan</td><td>12.6</td></tr>
<tr><td>36</td><td>Wisconsin</td><td>26.4</td><td>NA</td><td>Illinois**</td><td>NA</td></tr>
<tr><td>3</td><td>Wyoming</td><td>45.2</td><td>NA</td><td>Kansas**</td><td>NA</td></tr>
<tr><td></td><td></td><td></td><td></td><td>District of Columbia</td><td>11.0</td></tr>
</table>

Source: Federal Bureau of Investigation (unpublished data)
*Robbery is the taking of anything of value by force or threat of force. Attempts are included. A crime is considered cleared when at least one person is arrested, charged and turned over to the court for prosecution. Clearances recorded in 1999 may be for crimes which occurred in prior years. Several crimes may be cleared by the arrest of one person while the arrest of many persons may clear only one crime.
**Not available.

Percent of Aggravated Assaults Cleared in 1999

National Percent = 59.2% Cleared*

ALPHA ORDER				RANK ORDER		
RANK	STATE	PERCENT		RANK	STATE	PERCENT
39	Alabama	54.3		1	Vermont	79.1
8	Alaska	67.3		2	Maine	76.4
46	Arizona	48.5		3	South Dakota	76.3
21	Arkansas	62.2		4	Wyoming	74.5
22	California	61.7		5	Delaware	72.1
14	Colorado	63.9		6	Maryland	70.8
12	Connecticut	65.3		7	Nebraska	70.6
5	Delaware	72.1		8	Alaska	67.3
37	Florida	55.3		8	Wisconsin	67.3
36	Georgia	55.8		10	Virginia	66.2
47	Hawaii	47.7		11	Minnesota	65.7
17	Idaho	63.3		12	Connecticut	65.3
NA	Illinois**	NA		13	Pennsylvania	65.2
27	Indiana	60.5		14	Colorado	63.9
15	Iowa	63.7		15	Iowa	63.7
NA	Kansas**	NA		16	Oregon	63.6
19	Kentucky	62.9		17	Idaho	63.3
24	Louisiana	61.2		18	New Jersey	63.2
2	Maine	76.4		19	Kentucky	62.9
6	Maryland	70.8		20	New York	62.7
28	Massachusetts	60.1		21	Arkansas	62.2
48	Michigan	44.9		22	California	61.7
11	Minnesota	65.7		23	Montana	61.5
41	Mississippi	51.6		24	Louisiana	61.2
31	Missouri	56.8		25	Washington	61.1
23	Montana	61.5		26	Utah	60.7
7	Nebraska	70.6		27	Indiana	60.5
45	Nevada	48.6		28	Massachusetts	60.1
30	New Hampshire	57.6		29	North Carolina	58.4
18	New Jersey	63.2		30	New Hampshire	57.6
43	New Mexico	50.5		31	Missouri	56.8
20	New York	62.7		31	Texas	56.8
29	North Carolina	58.4		33	Tennessee	56.6
44	North Dakota	50.2		34	Rhode Island	56.4
40	Ohio	52.3		35	Oklahoma	55.9
35	Oklahoma	55.9		36	Georgia	55.8
16	Oregon	63.6		37	Florida	55.3
13	Pennsylvania	65.2		38	West Virginia	54.8
34	Rhode Island	56.4		39	Alabama	54.3
41	South Carolina	51.6		40	Ohio	52.3
3	South Dakota	76.3		41	Mississippi	51.6
33	Tennessee	56.6		41	South Carolina	51.6
31	Texas	56.8		43	New Mexico	50.5
26	Utah	60.7		44	North Dakota	50.2
1	Vermont	79.1		45	Nevada	48.6
10	Virginia	66.2		46	Arizona	48.5
25	Washington	61.1		47	Hawaii	47.7
38	West Virginia	54.8		48	Michigan	44.9
8	Wisconsin	67.3		NA	Illinois**	NA
4	Wyoming	74.5		NA	Kansas**	NA
				District of Columbia		40.5

Source: Federal Bureau of Investigation (unpublished data)

*Aggravated assault is an attack for the purpose of inflicting severe bodily injury. A crime is considered cleared when at least one person is arrested, charged and turned over to the court for prosecution. Clearances recorded in 1999 may be for crimes which occurred in prior years. Several crimes may be cleared by the arrest of one person while the arrest of many persons may clear only one crime.

**Not available.

Percent of Property Crimes Cleared in 1999

National Percent = 17.5% Cleared*

ALPHA ORDER			RANK ORDER		
RANK	STATE	PERCENT	RANK	STATE	PERCENT
27	Alabama	18.0	1	Maine	27.8
9	Alaska	21.9	2	Wyoming	26.4
38	Arizona	15.5	3	New Hampshire	25.7
10	Arkansas	21.3	4	Wisconsin	23.5
38	California	15.5	5	South Dakota	23.4
19	Colorado	19.7	6	Kentucky	22.8
34	Connecticut	16.7	7	Nevada	22.6
15	Delaware	20.6	8	Pennsylvania	22.0
32	Florida	16.9	9	Alaska	21.9
23	Georgia	18.9	10	Arkansas	21.3
43	Hawaii	14.2	11	Montana	21.0
20	Idaho	19.5	12	Nebraska	20.9
NA	Illinois**	NA	12	Oregon	20.9
30	Indiana	17.3	14	Mississippi	20.7
41	Iowa	15.3	15	Delaware	20.6
NA	Kansas**	NA	15	Minnesota	20.6
6	Kentucky	22.8	17	North Dakota	20.4
18	Louisiana	20.2	18	Louisiana	20.2
1	Maine	27.8	19	Colorado	19.7
21	Maryland	19.3	20	Idaho	19.5
37	Massachusetts	16.0	21	Maryland	19.3
48	Michigan	10.8	22	Virginia	19.0
15	Minnesota	20.6	23	Georgia	18.9
14	Mississippi	20.7	23	Utah	18.9
26	Missouri	18.3	25	New York	18.8
11	Montana	21.0	26	Missouri	18.3
12	Nebraska	20.9	27	Alabama	18.0
7	Nevada	22.6	28	Tennessee	17.9
3	New Hampshire	25.7	29	North Carolina	17.5
33	New Jersey	16.8	30	Indiana	17.3
46	New Mexico	12.5	31	Washington	17.1
25	New York	18.8	32	Florida	16.9
29	North Carolina	17.5	33	New Jersey	16.8
17	North Dakota	20.4	34	Connecticut	16.7
42	Ohio	14.7	35	Texas	16.4
38	Oklahoma	15.5	36	Rhode Island	16.3
12	Oregon	20.9	37	Massachusetts	16.0
8	Pennsylvania	22.0	38	Arizona	15.5
36	Rhode Island	16.3	38	California	15.5
44	South Carolina	13.4	38	Oklahoma	15.5
5	South Dakota	23.4	41	Iowa	15.3
28	Tennessee	17.9	42	Ohio	14.7
35	Texas	16.4	43	Hawaii	14.2
23	Utah	18.9	44	South Carolina	13.4
47	Vermont	11.4	45	West Virginia	13.2
22	Virginia	19.0	46	New Mexico	12.5
31	Washington	17.1	47	Vermont	11.4
45	West Virginia	13.2	48	Michigan	10.8
4	Wisconsin	23.5	NA	Illinois**	NA
2	Wyoming	26.4	NA	Kansas**	NA
				District of Columbia	5.3

Source: Federal Bureau of Investigation (unpublished data)
*Property crimes are offenses of burglary, larceny-theft and motor vehicle theft. A crime is considered cleared when at least one person is arrested, charged and turned over to the court for prosecution. Clearances recorded in 1999 may be for crimes which occurred in prior years. Several crimes may be cleared by the arrest of one person while the arrest of many persons may clear only one crime.
**Not available.

Percent of Burglaries Cleared in 1999

National Percent = 13.7% Cleared*

ALPHA ORDER			RANK ORDER		
RANK	STATE	PERCENT	RANK	STATE	PERCENT
24	Alabama	13.9	1	Nevada	22.8
6	Alaska	18.9	2	Wyoming	21.9
47	Arizona	7.6	3	Maine	21.2
12	Arkansas	17.3	4	Delaware	20.5
23	California	14.0	5	South Dakota	19.2
29	Colorado	12.8	6	Alaska	18.9
39	Connecticut	11.5	7	Kentucky	18.6
4	Delaware	20.5	8	Maryland	18.1
18	Florida	14.7	8	Virginia	18.1
21	Georgia	14.4	10	Pennsylvania	17.7
42	Hawaii	9.7	11	Wisconsin	17.5
34	Idaho	12.0	12	Arkansas	17.3
NA	Illinois**	NA	13	New Hampshire	17.2
36	Indiana	11.8	13	New York	17.2
43	Iowa	9.5	15	Mississippi	16.1
NA	Kansas**	NA	16	Louisiana	15.3
7	Kentucky	18.6	17	North Carolina	15.0
16	Louisiana	15.3	18	Florida	14.7
3	Maine	21.2	19	Massachusetts	14.5
8	Maryland	18.1	19	Minnesota	14.5
19	Massachusetts	14.5	21	Georgia	14.4
47	Michigan	7.6	22	Missouri	14.2
19	Minnesota	14.5	23	California	14.0
15	Mississippi	16.1	24	Alabama	13.9
22	Missouri	14.2	25	New Jersey	13.7
26	Montana	13.6	26	Montana	13.6
32	Nebraska	12.4	27	Oregon	13.4
1	Nevada	22.8	28	Tennessee	12.9
13	New Hampshire	17.2	29	Colorado	12.8
25	New Jersey	13.7	30	North Dakota	12.7
44	New Mexico	9.1	30	Rhode Island	12.7
13	New York	17.2	32	Nebraska	12.4
17	North Carolina	15.0	32	Utah	12.4
30	North Dakota	12.7	34	Idaho	12.0
37	Ohio	11.6	35	Texas	11.9
37	Oklahoma	11.6	36	Indiana	11.8
27	Oregon	13.4	37	Ohio	11.6
10	Pennsylvania	17.7	37	Oklahoma	11.6
30	Rhode Island	12.7	39	Connecticut	11.5
41	South Carolina	9.8	40	Washington	10.8
5	South Dakota	19.2	41	South Carolina	9.8
28	Tennessee	12.9	42	Hawaii	9.7
35	Texas	11.9	43	Iowa	9.5
32	Utah	12.4	44	New Mexico	9.1
45	Vermont	8.8	45	Vermont	8.8
8	Virginia	18.1	46	West Virginia	7.8
40	Washington	10.8	47	Arizona	7.6
46	West Virginia	7.8	47	Michigan	7.6
11	Wisconsin	17.5	NA	Illinois**	NA
2	Wyoming	21.9	NA	Kansas**	NA
				District of Columbia	10.8

Source: Federal Bureau of Investigation (unpublished data)
*Burglary is the unlawful entry of a structure to commit a felony or theft. Attempts are included. A crime is considered cleared when at least one person is arrested, charged and turned over to the court for prosecution. Clearances recorded in 1999 may be for crimes which occurred in prior years. Several crimes may be cleared by the arrest of one person while the arrest of many persons may clear only one crime.
**Not available.

Percent of Larcenies and Thefts Cleared in 1999

National Percent = 19.1% Cleared*

<table>
<tr><td colspan="3">ALPHA ORDER</td><td colspan="3">RANK ORDER</td></tr>
<tr><th>RANK</th><th>STATE</th><th>PERCENT</th><th>RANK</th><th>STATE</th><th>PERCENT</th></tr>
<tr><td>30</td><td>Alabama</td><td>18.9</td><td>1</td><td>Maine</td><td>28.8</td></tr>
<tr><td>9</td><td>Alaska</td><td>23.0</td><td>2</td><td>New Hampshire</td><td>28.4</td></tr>
<tr><td>30</td><td>Arizona</td><td>18.9</td><td>3</td><td>Wyoming</td><td>26.6</td></tr>
<tr><td>17</td><td>Arkansas</td><td>21.6</td><td>4</td><td>Nevada</td><td>25.9</td></tr>
<tr><td>39</td><td>California</td><td>17.3</td><td>5</td><td>Wisconsin</td><td>24.8</td></tr>
<tr><td>16</td><td>Colorado</td><td>21.7</td><td>6</td><td>Kentucky</td><td>24.5</td></tr>
<tr><td>29</td><td>Connecticut</td><td>19.0</td><td>7</td><td>South Dakota</td><td>24.0</td></tr>
<tr><td>14</td><td>Delaware</td><td>22.0</td><td>8</td><td>Pennsylvania</td><td>23.5</td></tr>
<tr><td>36</td><td>Florida</td><td>17.9</td><td>9</td><td>Alaska</td><td>23.0</td></tr>
<tr><td>25</td><td>Georgia</td><td>20.1</td><td>10</td><td>Nebraska</td><td>22.9</td></tr>
<tr><td>43</td><td>Hawaii</td><td>15.3</td><td>11</td><td>Mississippi</td><td>22.6</td></tr>
<tr><td>18</td><td>Idaho</td><td>21.3</td><td>11</td><td>Oregon</td><td>22.6</td></tr>
<tr><td>NA</td><td>Illinois**</td><td>NA</td><td>13</td><td>Louisiana</td><td>22.5</td></tr>
<tr><td>30</td><td>Indiana</td><td>18.9</td><td>14</td><td>Delaware</td><td>22.0</td></tr>
<tr><td>40</td><td>Iowa</td><td>16.8</td><td>15</td><td>Montana</td><td>21.8</td></tr>
<tr><td>NA</td><td>Kansas**</td><td>NA</td><td>16</td><td>Colorado</td><td>21.7</td></tr>
<tr><td>6</td><td>Kentucky</td><td>24.5</td><td>17</td><td>Arkansas</td><td>21.6</td></tr>
<tr><td>13</td><td>Louisiana</td><td>22.5</td><td>18</td><td>Idaho</td><td>21.3</td></tr>
<tr><td>1</td><td>Maine</td><td>28.8</td><td>18</td><td>Minnesota</td><td>21.3</td></tr>
<tr><td>22</td><td>Maryland</td><td>20.6</td><td>20</td><td>North Dakota</td><td>21.2</td></tr>
<tr><td>38</td><td>Massachusetts</td><td>17.4</td><td>21</td><td>New York</td><td>20.7</td></tr>
<tr><td>47</td><td>Michigan</td><td>11.8</td><td>22</td><td>Maryland</td><td>20.6</td></tr>
<tr><td>18</td><td>Minnesota</td><td>21.3</td><td>23</td><td>New Jersey</td><td>20.3</td></tr>
<tr><td>11</td><td>Mississippi</td><td>22.6</td><td>23</td><td>Tennessee</td><td>20.3</td></tr>
<tr><td>27</td><td>Missouri</td><td>19.4</td><td>25</td><td>Georgia</td><td>20.1</td></tr>
<tr><td>15</td><td>Montana</td><td>21.8</td><td>26</td><td>Utah</td><td>19.9</td></tr>
<tr><td>10</td><td>Nebraska</td><td>22.9</td><td>27</td><td>Missouri</td><td>19.4</td></tr>
<tr><td>4</td><td>Nevada</td><td>25.9</td><td>27</td><td>Washington</td><td>19.4</td></tr>
<tr><td>2</td><td>New Hampshire</td><td>28.4</td><td>29</td><td>Connecticut</td><td>19.0</td></tr>
<tr><td>23</td><td>New Jersey</td><td>20.3</td><td>30</td><td>Alabama</td><td>18.9</td></tr>
<tr><td>46</td><td>New Mexico</td><td>13.7</td><td>30</td><td>Arizona</td><td>18.9</td></tr>
<tr><td>21</td><td>New York</td><td>20.7</td><td>30</td><td>Indiana</td><td>18.9</td></tr>
<tr><td>35</td><td>North Carolina</td><td>18.0</td><td>33</td><td>Virginia</td><td>18.8</td></tr>
<tr><td>20</td><td>North Dakota</td><td>21.2</td><td>34</td><td>Rhode Island</td><td>18.3</td></tr>
<tr><td>42</td><td>Ohio</td><td>15.6</td><td>35</td><td>North Carolina</td><td>18.0</td></tr>
<tr><td>41</td><td>Oklahoma</td><td>16.5</td><td>36</td><td>Florida</td><td>17.9</td></tr>
<tr><td>11</td><td>Oregon</td><td>22.6</td><td>37</td><td>Texas</td><td>17.8</td></tr>
<tr><td>8</td><td>Pennsylvania</td><td>23.5</td><td>38</td><td>Massachusetts</td><td>17.4</td></tr>
<tr><td>34</td><td>Rhode Island</td><td>18.3</td><td>39</td><td>California</td><td>17.3</td></tr>
<tr><td>45</td><td>South Carolina</td><td>14.7</td><td>40</td><td>Iowa</td><td>16.8</td></tr>
<tr><td>7</td><td>South Dakota</td><td>24.0</td><td>41</td><td>Oklahoma</td><td>16.5</td></tr>
<tr><td>23</td><td>Tennessee</td><td>20.3</td><td>42</td><td>Ohio</td><td>15.6</td></tr>
<tr><td>37</td><td>Texas</td><td>17.8</td><td>43</td><td>Hawaii</td><td>15.3</td></tr>
<tr><td>26</td><td>Utah</td><td>19.9</td><td>44</td><td>West Virginia</td><td>15.1</td></tr>
<tr><td>47</td><td>Vermont</td><td>11.8</td><td>45</td><td>South Carolina</td><td>14.7</td></tr>
<tr><td>33</td><td>Virginia</td><td>18.8</td><td>46</td><td>New Mexico</td><td>13.7</td></tr>
<tr><td>27</td><td>Washington</td><td>19.4</td><td>47</td><td>Michigan</td><td>11.8</td></tr>
<tr><td>44</td><td>West Virginia</td><td>15.1</td><td>47</td><td>Vermont</td><td>11.8</td></tr>
<tr><td>5</td><td>Wisconsin</td><td>24.8</td><td>NA</td><td>Illinois**</td><td>NA</td></tr>
<tr><td>3</td><td>Wyoming</td><td>26.6</td><td>NA</td><td>Kansas**</td><td>NA</td></tr>
<tr><td></td><td></td><td></td><td></td><td>District of Columbia</td><td>4.4</td></tr>
</table>

Source: Federal Bureau of Investigation (unpublished data)

*Larceny and theft is the unlawful taking of property without use of force, violence or fraud. Attempts are included. Motor vehicle thefts are excluded. A crime is considered cleared when at least one person is arrested, charged and turned over to the court for prosecution. Clearances recorded in 1999 may be for crimes which occurred in prior years. Several crimes may be cleared by the arrest of one person while the arrest of many persons may clear only one crime. **Not available.

Percent of Motor Vehicle Thefts Cleared in 1999

National Percent = 14.9% Cleared*

ALPHA ORDER			RANK ORDER		
RANK	STATE	PERCENT	RANK	STATE	PERCENT
9	Alabama	23.5	1	Maine	43.6
17	Alaska	19.8	2	Wyoming	39.5
43	Arizona	11.1	3	Arkansas	30.8
3	Arkansas	30.8	4	South Dakota	29.2
47	California	10.4	5	North Dakota	28.7
26	Colorado	17.3	6	Minnesota	27.5
44	Connecticut	11.0	7	Idaho	24.5
45	Delaware	10.6	8	Montana	24.0
30	Florida	15.8	9	Alabama	23.5
19	Georgia	19.4	10	Wisconsin	23.2
36	Hawaii	12.8	11	North Carolina	23.0
7	Idaho	24.5	12	Virginia	21.9
NA	Illinois**	NA	13	Utah	21.3
24	Indiana	17.6	14	Oregon	21.2
27	Iowa	16.3	15	Kentucky	20.8
NA	Kansas**	NA	16	Mississippi	20.1
15	Kentucky	20.8	17	Alaska	19.8
28	Louisiana	16.1	17	Nebraska	19.8
1	Maine	43.6	19	Georgia	19.4
34	Maryland	13.8	19	Pennsylvania	19.4
38	Massachusetts	11.8	21	Oklahoma	18.1
46	Michigan	10.5	22	New Hampshire	17.9
6	Minnesota	27.5	22	Vermont	17.9
16	Mississippi	20.1	24	Indiana	17.6
25	Missouri	17.5	25	Missouri	17.5
8	Montana	24.0	26	Colorado	17.3
17	Nebraska	19.8	27	Iowa	16.3
39	Nevada	11.5	28	Louisiana	16.1
22	New Hampshire	17.9	29	Texas	16.0
48	New Jersey	4.7	30	Florida	15.8
37	New Mexico	12.4	31	Ohio	15.0
42	New York	11.2	32	Tennessee	14.5
11	North Carolina	23.0	33	Washington	14.0
5	North Dakota	28.7	34	Maryland	13.8
31	Ohio	15.0	35	West Virginia	13.6
21	Oklahoma	18.1	36	Hawaii	12.8
14	Oregon	21.2	37	New Mexico	12.4
19	Pennsylvania	19.4	38	Massachusetts	11.8
41	Rhode Island	11.3	39	Nevada	11.5
39	South Carolina	11.5	39	South Carolina	11.5
4	South Dakota	29.2	41	Rhode Island	11.3
32	Tennessee	14.5	42	New York	11.2
29	Texas	16.0	43	Arizona	11.1
13	Utah	21.3	44	Connecticut	11.0
22	Vermont	17.9	45	Delaware	10.6
12	Virginia	21.9	46	Michigan	10.5
33	Washington	14.0	47	California	10.4
35	West Virginia	13.6	48	New Jersey	4.7
10	Wisconsin	23.2	NA	Illinois**	NA
2	Wyoming	39.5	NA	Kansas**	NA
				District of Columbia	4.2

Source: Federal Bureau of Investigation (unpublished data)
*Motor vehicle theft includes the theft or attempted theft of a self-propelled vehicle. Excludes motorboats, construction equipment, airplanes and farming equipment. A crime is considered cleared when at least one person is arrested, charged and turned over to the court for prosecution. Clearances recorded in 1999 may be for crimes which occurred in prior years. Several crimes may be cleared by the arrest of one person while the arrest of many persons may clear only one crime. **Not available.

II. CORRECTIONS

II. CORRECTIONS (continued)

Prisoners in State Correctional Institutions: Year End 2000

National Total = 1,236,476 State Prisoners*

ALPHA ORDER

RANK ORDER

RANK	STATE	PRISONERS	% of USA		RANK	STATE	PRISONERS	% of USA
16	Alabama	26,225	2.1%		1	California	163,001	13.2%
40	Alaska	4,173	0.3%		2	Texas	157,997	12.8%
15	Arizona	26,510	2.1%		3	Florida	71,319	5.8%
28	Arkansas	11,915	1.0%		4	New York	70,198	5.7%
1	California	163,001	13.2%		5	Michigan	47,718	3.9%
25	Colorado	16,833	1.4%		6	Ohio	45,833	3.7%
24	Connecticut	18,355	1.5%		7	Illinois	45,281	3.7%
34	Delaware	6,921	0.6%		8	Georgia	44,232	3.6%
3	Florida	71,319	5.8%		9	Pennsylvania	36,847	3.0%
8	Georgia	44,232	3.6%		10	Louisiana	35,047	2.8%
39	Hawaii	5,053	0.4%		11	North Carolina	31,266	2.5%
37	Idaho	5,526	0.4%		12	Virginia	30,168	2.4%
7	Illinois	45,281	3.7%		13	New Jersey	29,784	2.4%
23	Indiana	20,125	1.6%		14	Missouri	27,323	2.2%
33	Iowa	7,955	0.6%		15	Arizona	26,510	2.1%
32	Kansas	8,344	0.7%		16	Alabama	26,225	2.1%
26	Kentucky	14,919	1.2%		17	Maryland	23,538	1.9%
10	Louisiana	35,047	2.8%		18	Oklahoma	23,181	1.9%
49	Maine	1,679	0.1%		19	Tennessee	22,166	1.8%
17	Maryland	23,538	1.9%		20	South Carolina	21,778	1.8%
29	Massachusetts	10,722	0.9%		21	Wisconsin	20,612	1.7%
5	Michigan	47,718	3.9%		22	Mississippi	20,241	1.6%
35	Minnesota	6,238	0.5%		23	Indiana	20,125	1.6%
22	Mississippi	20,241	1.6%		24	Connecticut	18,355	1.5%
14	Missouri	27,323	2.2%		25	Colorado	16,833	1.4%
44	Montana	3,105	0.3%		26	Kentucky	14,919	1.2%
41	Nebraska	3,895	0.3%		27	Washington	14,915	1.2%
31	Nevada	10,012	0.8%		28	Arkansas	11,915	1.0%
46	New Hampshire	2,257	0.2%		29	Massachusetts	10,722	0.9%
13	New Jersey	29,784	2.4%		30	Oregon	10,630	0.9%
38	New Mexico	5,342	0.4%		31	Nevada	10,012	0.8%
4	New York	70,198	5.7%		32	Kansas	8,344	0.7%
11	North Carolina	31,266	2.5%		33	Iowa	7,955	0.6%
50	North Dakota	1,076	0.1%		34	Delaware	6,921	0.6%
6	Ohio	45,833	3.7%		35	Minnesota	6,238	0.5%
18	Oklahoma	23,181	1.9%		36	Utah	5,630	0.5%
30	Oregon	10,630	0.9%		37	Idaho	5,526	0.4%
9	Pennsylvania	36,847	3.0%		38	New Mexico	5,342	0.4%
43	Rhode Island	3,286	0.3%		39	Hawaii	5,053	0.4%
20	South Carolina	21,778	1.8%		40	Alaska	4,173	0.3%
45	South Dakota	2,616	0.2%		41	Nebraska	3,895	0.3%
19	Tennessee	22,166	1.8%		42	West Virginia	3,856	0.3%
2	Texas	157,997	12.8%		43	Rhode Island	3,286	0.3%
36	Utah	5,630	0.5%		44	Montana	3,105	0.3%
47	Vermont	1,697	0.1%		45	South Dakota	2,616	0.2%
12	Virginia	30,168	2.4%		46	New Hampshire	2,257	0.2%
27	Washington	14,915	1.2%		47	Vermont	1,697	0.1%
42	West Virginia	3,856	0.3%		48	Wyoming	1,680	0.1%
21	Wisconsin	20,612	1.7%		49	Maine	1,679	0.1%
48	Wyoming	1,680	0.1%		50	North Dakota	1,076	0.1%
						District of Columbia	7,456	0.6%

Source: U.S. Department of Justice, Bureau of Justice Statistics
   "Prisoners in 2000" (August 2001, NCJ-188207)
*Advance figures as of December 31, 2000. Totals reflect all prisoners, including those sentenced to a year or less and those unsentenced. National total does not include 145,416 prisoners under federal jurisdiction. State and federal prisoners combined total 1,381,892.

Percent Change in Number of State Prisoners: 1999 to 2000

National Percent Change = 0.7% Increase*

ALPHA ORDER				RANK ORDER		
RANK	STATE	PERCENT CHANGE		RANK	STATE	PERCENT CHANGE
35	Alabama	0.0		1	Idaho	14.1
11	Alaska	5.7		1	North Dakota	14.1
28	Arizona	2.0		3	Mississippi	10.9
18	Arkansas	4.4		4	Vermont	10.5
35	California	0.0		5	Iowa	10.0
9	Colorado	7.4		6	Rhode Island	9.4
40	Connecticut	(1.5)		7	West Virginia	9.2
38	Delaware	(0.9)		8	Oregon	7.8
25	Florida	2.5		9	Colorado	7.4
15	Georgia	5.1		10	Utah	5.8
23	Hawaii	3.1		11	Alaska	5.7
1	Idaho	14.1		12	Nebraska	5.6
30	Illinois	1.4		13	Nevada	5.5
21	Indiana	4.2		14	Montana	5.2
5	Iowa	10.0		15	Georgia	5.1
45	Kansas	(2.6)		16	Minnesota	4.5
45	Kentucky	(2.6)		16	Missouri	4.5
24	Louisiana	2.9		18	Arkansas	4.4
43	Maine	(2.2)		18	South Dakota	4.4
29	Maryland	1.9		20	New Mexico	4.3
50	Massachusetts	(5.6)		21	Indiana	4.2
26	Michigan	2.4		22	Oklahoma	3.5
16	Minnesota	4.5		23	Hawaii	3.1
3	Mississippi	10.9		24	Louisiana	2.9
16	Missouri	4.5		25	Florida	2.5
14	Montana	5.2		26	Michigan	2.4
12	Nebraska	5.6		27	Washington	2.2
13	Nevada	5.5		28	Arizona	2.0
35	New Hampshire	0.0		29	Maryland	1.9
49	New Jersey	(5.4)		30	Illinois	1.4
20	New Mexico	4.3		31	Virginia	1.3
48	New York	(3.7)		32	Wisconsin	1.0
34	North Carolina	0.5		33	Pennsylvania	0.9
1	North Dakota	14.1		34	North Carolina	0.5
43	Ohio	(2.2)		35	Alabama	0.0
22	Oklahoma	3.5		35	California	0.0
8	Oregon	7.8		35	New Hampshire	0.0
33	Pennsylvania	0.9		38	Delaware	(0.9)
6	Rhode Island	9.4		39	South Carolina	(1.0)
39	South Carolina	(1.0)		40	Connecticut	(1.5)
18	South Dakota	4.4		40	Tennessee	(1.5)
40	Tennessee	(1.5)		42	Wyoming	(1.9)
47	Texas	(3.2)		43	Maine	(2.2)
10	Utah	5.8		43	Ohio	(2.2)
4	Vermont	10.5		45	Kansas	(2.6)
31	Virginia	1.3		45	Kentucky	(2.6)
27	Washington	2.2		47	Texas	(3.2)
7	West Virginia	9.2		48	New York	(3.7)
32	Wisconsin	1.0		49	New Jersey	(5.4)
42	Wyoming	(1.9)		50	Massachusetts	(5.6)
					District of Columbia	(13.8)

Source: U.S. Department of Justice, Bureau of Justice Statistics
  "Prisoners in 2000" (August 2001, NCJ-188207)
From December 31, 1999 to December 31, 2000. Includes inmates sentenced to more than one year and those sentenced to a year or less or with no sentence. The percent change in number of prisoners under federal jurisdiction during the same period was a 7.5% increase. The combined state and federal increase was 1.3%.

State Prisoners Sentenced to More than One Year in 2000

National Total = 1,196,102 State Prisoners*

ALPHA ORDER					RANK ORDER			
RANK	STATE	PRISONERS	% of USA		RANK	STATE	PRISONERS	% of USA
16	Alabama	24,123	2.0%		1	California	160,412	13.4%
45	Alaska	2,128	0.2%		2	Texas	150,107	12.5%
15	Arizona	25,412	2.1%		3	Florida	71,318	6.0%
28	Arkansas	11,851	1.0%		4	New York	70,198	5.9%
1	California	160,412	13.4%		5	Michigan	47,718	4.0%
24	Colorado	16,833	1.4%		6	Ohio	45,833	3.8%
27	Connecticut	13,155	1.1%		7	Illinois	45,281	3.8%
38	Delaware	3,937	0.3%		8	Georgia	44,141	3.7%
3	Florida	71,318	6.0%		9	Pennsylvania	36,844	3.1%
8	Georgia	44,141	3.7%		10	Louisiana	35,047	2.9%
41	Hawaii	3,553	0.3%		11	New Jersey	29,784	2.5%
35	Idaho	5,526	0.5%		12	Virginia	29,643	2.5%
7	Illinois	45,281	3.8%		13	Missouri	27,299	2.3%
21	Indiana	20,081	1.7%		14	North Carolina	27,043	2.3%
33	Iowa	7,955	0.7%		15	Arizona	25,412	2.1%
32	Kansas	8,344	0.7%		16	Alabama	24,123	2.0%
25	Kentucky	14,919	1.2%		17	Oklahoma	23,181	1.9%
10	Louisiana	35,047	2.9%		18	Maryland	22,490	1.9%
48	Maine	1,635	0.1%		19	Tennessee	22,166	1.9%
18	Maryland	22,490	1.9%		20	South Carolina	21,017	1.8%
31	Massachusetts	9,479	0.8%		21	Indiana	20,081	1.7%
5	Michigan	47,718	4.0%		22	Wisconsin	20,013	1.7%
34	Minnesota	6,238	0.5%		23	Mississippi	19,239	1.6%
23	Mississippi	19,239	1.6%		24	Colorado	16,833	1.4%
13	Missouri	27,299	2.3%		25	Kentucky	14,919	1.2%
42	Montana	3,105	0.3%		26	Washington	14,666	1.2%
39	Nebraska	3,816	0.3%		27	Connecticut	13,155	1.1%
30	Nevada	9,921	0.8%		28	Arkansas	11,851	1.0%
44	New Hampshire	2,257	0.2%		29	Oregon	10,603	0.9%
11	New Jersey	29,784	2.5%		30	Nevada	9,921	0.8%
37	New Mexico	4,887	0.4%		31	Massachusetts	9,479	0.8%
4	New York	70,198	5.9%		32	Kansas	8,344	0.7%
14	North Carolina	27,043	2.3%		33	Iowa	7,955	0.7%
50	North Dakota	994	0.1%		34	Minnesota	6,238	0.5%
6	Ohio	45,833	3.8%		35	Idaho	5,526	0.5%
17	Oklahoma	23,181	1.9%		35	Utah	5,526	0.5%
29	Oregon	10,603	0.9%		37	New Mexico	4,887	0.4%
9	Pennsylvania	36,844	3.1%		38	Delaware	3,937	0.3%
46	Rhode Island	1,966	0.2%		39	Nebraska	3,816	0.3%
20	South Carolina	21,017	1.8%		40	West Virginia	3,795	0.3%
43	South Dakota	2,613	0.2%		41	Hawaii	3,553	0.3%
19	Tennessee	22,166	1.9%		42	Montana	3,105	0.3%
2	Texas	150,107	12.5%		43	South Dakota	2,613	0.2%
35	Utah	5,526	0.5%		44	New Hampshire	2,257	0.2%
49	Vermont	1,313	0.1%		45	Alaska	2,128	0.2%
12	Virginia	29,643	2.5%		46	Rhode Island	1,966	0.2%
26	Washington	14,666	1.2%		47	Wyoming	1,680	0.1%
40	West Virginia	3,795	0.3%		48	Maine	1,635	0.1%
22	Wisconsin	20,013	1.7%		49	Vermont	1,313	0.1%
47	Wyoming	1,680	0.1%		50	North Dakota	994	0.1%
						District of Columbia	5,008	0.4%

Source: U.S. Department of Justice, Bureau of Justice Statistics
"Prisoners in 2000" (August 2001, NCJ-188207)
*Advance figures as of December 31, 2000. Does not include 125,044 prisoners under federal jurisdiction
sentenced to more than one year. State and federal prisoners sentenced to more than one year total 1,304,074.

State Prisoner Incarceration Rate in 2000

National Rate = 432 State Prisoners per 100,000 Population*

ALPHA ORDER

RANK	STATE	RATE
6	Alabama	549
32	Alaska	341
9	Arizona	515
15	Arkansas	458
13	California	474
20	Colorado	403
22	Connecticut	398
10	Delaware	513
14	Florida	462
5	Georgia	550
37	Hawaii	302
16	Idaho	430
26	Illinois	371
33	Indiana	335
39	Iowa	276
35	Kansas	312
25	Kentucky	373
1	Louisiana	801
49	Maine	129
17	Maryland	429
48	Massachusetts	152
12	Michigan	480
50	Minnesota	128
3	Mississippi	688
11	Missouri	494
30	Montana	348
42	Nebraska	228
8	Nevada	518
46	New Hampshire	185
27	New Jersey	362
38	New Mexico	279
23	New York	383
31	North Carolina	347
47	North Dakota	158
19	Ohio	406
4	Oklahoma	685
34	Oregon	316
36	Pennsylvania	307
45	Rhode Island	197
7	South Carolina	532
28	South Dakota	353
21	Tennessee	399
2	Texas	730
40	Utah	254
43	Vermont	218
18	Virginia	422
41	Washington	251
44	West Virginia	211
24	Wisconsin	376
29	Wyoming	349

RANK ORDER

RANK	STATE	RATE
1	Louisiana	801
2	Texas	730
3	Mississippi	688
4	Oklahoma	685
5	Georgia	550
6	Alabama	549
7	South Carolina	532
8	Nevada	518
9	Arizona	515
10	Delaware	513
11	Missouri	494
12	Michigan	480
13	California	474
14	Florida	462
15	Arkansas	458
16	Idaho	430
17	Maryland	429
18	Virginia	422
19	Ohio	406
20	Colorado	403
21	Tennessee	399
22	Connecticut	398
23	New York	383
24	Wisconsin	376
25	Kentucky	373
26	Illinois	371
27	New Jersey	362
28	South Dakota	353
29	Wyoming	349
30	Montana	348
31	North Carolina	347
32	Alaska	341
33	Indiana	335
34	Oregon	316
35	Kansas	312
36	Pennsylvania	307
37	Hawaii	302
38	New Mexico	279
39	Iowa	276
40	Utah	254
41	Washington	251
42	Nebraska	228
43	Vermont	218
44	West Virginia	211
45	Rhode Island	197
46	New Hampshire	185
47	North Dakota	158
48	Massachusetts	152
49	Maine	129
50	Minnesota	128
	District of Columbia	971

Source: U.S. Department of Justice, Bureau of Justice Statistics
"Prisoners in 2000" (August 2001, NCJ-188207)
*As of December 31, 2000. Includes only inmates sentenced to more than one year. Does not include federal incarceration rate of 45 prisoners per 100,000 population. State and federal combined incarceration rate is 478 prisoners per 100,000 population.

Percent Change in State Prisoner Incarceration Rate: 1999 to 2000

National Percent Change = 0.4% Decrease*

RANK	STATE	PERCENT CHANGE
33	Alabama	0.0
49	Alaska	(8.8)
12	Arizona	4.0
17	Arkansas	3.4
36	California	(1.5)
8	Colorado	5.2
31	Connecticut	0.3
10	Delaware	4.1
26	Florida	1.3
17	Georgia	3.4
48	Hawaii	(5.9)
2	Idaho	11.7
27	Illinois	0.8
17	Indiana	3.4
5	Iowa	9.5
41	Kansas	(2.8)
43	Kentucky	(3.1)
21	Louisiana	3.2
42	Maine	(3.0)
30	Maryland	0.5
50	Massachusetts	(42.9)
25	Michigan	1.7
22	Minnesota	2.4
4	Mississippi	9.9
15	Missouri	3.6
13	Montana	3.9
9	Nebraska	4.6
24	Nevada	1.8
35	New Hampshire	(1.1)
47	New Jersey	(5.7)
20	New Mexico	3.3
45	New York	(4.3)
29	North Carolina	0.6
1	North Dakota	15.3
40	Ohio	(2.6)
16	Oklahoma	3.5
6	Oregon	7.8
28	Pennsylvania	0.7
23	Rhode Island	2.1
38	South Carolina	(2.0)
10	South Dakota	4.1
39	Tennessee	(2.2)
44	Texas	(4.2)
14	Utah	3.7
3	Vermont	10.1
46	Virginia	(5.6)
33	Washington	0.0
7	West Virginia	7.7
31	Wisconsin	0.3
37	Wyoming	(1.7)

RANK	STATE	PERCENT CHANGE
1	North Dakota	15.3
2	Idaho	11.7
3	Vermont	10.1
4	Mississippi	9.9
5	Iowa	9.5
6	Oregon	7.8
7	West Virginia	7.7
8	Colorado	5.2
9	Nebraska	4.6
10	Delaware	4.1
10	South Dakota	4.1
12	Arizona	4.0
13	Montana	3.9
14	Utah	3.7
15	Missouri	3.6
16	Oklahoma	3.5
17	Arkansas	3.4
17	Georgia	3.4
17	Indiana	3.4
20	New Mexico	3.3
21	Louisiana	3.2
22	Minnesota	2.4
23	Rhode Island	2.1
24	Nevada	1.8
25	Michigan	1.7
26	Florida	1.3
27	Illinois	0.8
28	Pennsylvania	0.7
29	North Carolina	0.6
30	Maryland	0.5
31	Connecticut	0.3
31	Wisconsin	0.3
33	Alabama	0.0
33	Washington	0.0
35	New Hampshire	(1.1)
36	California	(1.5)
37	Wyoming	(1.7)
38	South Carolina	(2.0)
39	Tennessee	(2.2)
40	Ohio	(2.6)
41	Kansas	(2.8)
42	Maine	(3.0)
43	Kentucky	(3.1)
44	Texas	(4.2)
45	New York	(4.3)
46	Virginia	(5.6)
47	New Jersey	(5.7)
48	Hawaii	(5.9)
49	Alaska	(8.8)
50	Massachusetts	(42.9)

District of Columbia   (26.2)

Source: Morgan Quitno Press using data from U.S. Department of Justice, Bureau of Justice Statistics
"Prisoners in 2000" (August 2001, NCJ-188207)
*From December 31, 1999 to December 31, 2000. Includes only inmates sentenced to more than one year. The percent change in rate of prisoners under federal jurisdiction during the same period was a 7.6% increase. The combined state and federal increase was 0.3%.

State Prison Population as a Percent of Highest Capacity in 2000

National Percent = 100% of Highest Capacity*

ALPHA ORDER

RANK	STATE	PERCENT
18	Alabama	101
17	Alaska	102
13	Arizona	106
15	Arkansas	105
18	California	101
25	Colorado	98
NA	Connecticut**	NA
1	Delaware	156
49	Florida	81
45	Georgia	90
13	Hawaii	106
34	Idaho	95
3	Illinois	137
41	Indiana	91
6	Iowa	117
34	Kansas	95
28	Kentucky	96
23	Louisiana	99
20	Maine	100
23	Maryland	99
8	Massachusetts	113
26	Michigan	97
28	Minnesota	96
20	Mississippi	100
28	Missouri	96
9	Montana	112
5	Nebraska	129
41	Nevada	91
41	New Hampshire	91
2	New Jersey	141
39	New Mexico	92
15	New York	105
12	North Carolina	107
39	North Dakota	92
7	Ohio	114
34	Oklahoma	95
20	Oregon	100
10	Pennsylvania	111
47	Rhode Island	88
46	South Carolina	89
26	South Dakota	97
34	Tennessee	95
28	Texas	96
48	Utah	86
28	Vermont	96
41	Virginia	91
11	Washington	110
38	West Virginia	94
4	Wisconsin	131
28	Wyoming	96

RANK ORDER

RANK	STATE	PERCENT
1	Delaware	156
2	New Jersey	141
3	Illinois	137
4	Wisconsin	131
5	Nebraska	129
6	Iowa	117
7	Ohio	114
8	Massachusetts	113
9	Montana	112
10	Pennsylvania	111
11	Washington	110
12	North Carolina	107
13	Arizona	106
13	Hawaii	106
15	Arkansas	105
15	New York	105
17	Alaska	102
18	Alabama	101
18	California	101
20	Maine	100
20	Mississippi	100
20	Oregon	100
23	Louisiana	99
23	Maryland	99
25	Colorado	98
26	Michigan	97
26	South Dakota	97
28	Kentucky	96
28	Minnesota	96
28	Missouri	96
28	Texas	96
28	Vermont	96
28	Wyoming	96
34	Idaho	95
34	Kansas	95
34	Oklahoma	95
34	Tennessee	95
38	West Virginia	94
39	New Mexico	92
39	North Dakota	92
41	Indiana	91
41	Nevada	91
41	New Hampshire	91
41	Virginia	91
45	Georgia	90
46	South Carolina	89
47	Rhode Island	88
48	Utah	86
49	Florida	81
NA	Connecticut**	NA

District of Columbia 83

Source: U.S. Department of Justice, Bureau of Justice Statistics
"Prisoners in 2000" (August 2001, NCJ-188207)
*As of December 31, 2000. Federal prison population is at 131% of highest rated capacity. Because of a change in calculating operational capacity last year, the national figure is only comparable to last year's figure.
**Not available.

Average Annual Percent Change in
Female State Prisoner Population: 1990 to 2000
National Average Percent Change = 7.6% Annual Increase*

ALPHA ORDER

RANK	STATE	PERCENT CHANGE
39	Alabama	5.0
24	Alaska	8.3
21	Arizona	8.9
34	Arkansas	5.9
37	California	5.6
10	Colorado	11.9
30	Connecticut	7.5
15	Delaware	10.2
42	Florida	4.4
24	Georgia	8.3
9	Hawaii	12.6
2	Idaho	15.2
20	Illinois	9.2
29	Indiana	7.9
13	Iowa	10.8
34	Kansas	5.9
24	Kentucky	8.3
12	Louisiana	11.4
43	Maine	4.1
46	Maryland	3.3
50	Massachusetts	1.3
48	Michigan	2.4
22	Minnesota	8.8
6	Mississippi	14.1
18	Missouri	9.8
3	Montana	14.9
33	Nebraska	6.3
30	Nevada	7.5
14	New Hampshire	10.6
40	New Jersey	4.7
15	New Mexico	10.2
49	New York	2.0
32	North Carolina	7.3
8	North Dakota	13.0
44	Ohio	3.7
23	Oklahoma	8.4
38	Oregon	5.1
41	Pennsylvania	4.6
44	Rhode Island	3.7
47	South Carolina	3.0
17	South Dakota	10.0
7	Tennessee	13.4
1	Texas	18.7
10	Utah	11.9
24	Vermont	8.3
24	Virginia	8.3
19	Washington	9.4
4	West Virginia	14.8
5	Wisconsin	14.5
34	Wyoming	5.9

RANK ORDER

RANK	STATE	PERCENT CHANGE
1	Texas	18.7
2	Idaho	15.2
3	Montana	14.9
4	West Virginia	14.8
5	Wisconsin	14.5
6	Mississippi	14.1
7	Tennessee	13.4
8	North Dakota	13.0
9	Hawaii	12.6
10	Colorado	11.9
10	Utah	11.9
12	Louisiana	11.4
13	Iowa	10.8
14	New Hampshire	10.6
15	Delaware	10.2
15	New Mexico	10.2
17	South Dakota	10.0
18	Missouri	9.8
19	Washington	9.4
20	Illinois	9.2
21	Arizona	8.9
22	Minnesota	8.8
23	Oklahoma	8.4
24	Alaska	8.3
24	Georgia	8.3
24	Kentucky	8.3
24	Vermont	8.3
24	Virginia	8.3
29	Indiana	7.9
30	Connecticut	7.5
30	Nevada	7.5
32	North Carolina	7.3
33	Nebraska	6.3
34	Arkansas	5.9
34	Kansas	5.9
34	Wyoming	5.9
37	California	5.6
38	Oregon	5.1
39	Alabama	5.0
40	New Jersey	4.7
41	Pennsylvania	4.6
42	Florida	4.4
43	Maine	4.1
44	Ohio	3.7
44	Rhode Island	3.7
46	Maryland	3.3
47	South Carolina	3.0
48	Michigan	2.4
49	New York	2.0
50	Massachusetts	1.3

District of Columbia (5.2)

Source: U.S. Department of Justice, Bureau of Justice Statistics
   "Prisoners in 2000" (August 2001, NCJ-188207)
National rate does not include federal female inmates. Federal female inmates increased by an average annual rate of 7.4%. The combined federal and state female prison population grew at an annual average rate of 7.6%.

White Prisoners in State Correctional Institutions in 1998

National Total = 462,119 White State Prisoners*

ALPHA ORDER

RANK	STATE	PRISONERS	% of USA
22	Alabama	7,693	1.7%
43	Alaska	1,878	0.4%
6	Arizona	20,141	4.4%
30	Arkansas	4,868	1.1%
1	California	47,595	10.3%
13	Colorado	10,492	2.3%
32	Connecticut	4,691	1.0%
42	Delaware	2,028	0.4%
4	Florida	28,632	6.2%
9	Georgia	13,055	2.8%
49	Hawaii	1,039	0.2%
36	Idaho	3,327	0.7%
15	Illinois	10,371	2.2%
12	Indiana	11,016	2.4%
28	Iowa	5,117	1.1%
31	Kansas	4,853	1.1%
18	Kentucky	9,373	2.0%
23	Louisiana	7,559	1.6%
46	Maine	1,525	0.3%
29	Maryland	5,039	1.1%
26	Massachusetts	5,325	1.2%
7	Michigan	19,067	4.1%
38	Minnesota	2,619	0.6%
33	Mississippi	4,150	0.9%
8	Missouri	13,617	2.9%
40	Montana	2,108	0.5%
39	Nebraska	2,520	0.5%
27	Nevada	5,324	1.2%
41	New Hampshire	2,031	0.4%
21	New Jersey	7,880	1.7%
34	New Mexico	4,140	0.9%
3	New York	30,806	6.7%
14	North Carolina	10,419	2.3%
50	North Dakota	703	0.2%
5	Ohio	22,434	4.9%
11	Oklahoma	11,397	2.5%
25	Oregon	6,561	1.4%
10	Pennsylvania	12,287	2.7%
44	Rhode Island	1,845	0.4%
24	South Carolina	6,651	1.4%
45	South Dakota	1,826	0.4%
20	Tennessee	8,615	1.9%
2	Texas	41,383	9.0%
35	Utah	3,825	0.8%
47	Vermont	1,216	0.3%
17	Virginia	9,958	2.2%
16	Washington	10,006	2.2%
37	West Virginia	2,923	0.6%
19	Wisconsin	8,902	1.9%
48	Wyoming	1,196	0.3%

RANK ORDER

RANK	STATE	PRISONERS	% of USA
1	California	47,595	10.3%
2	Texas	41,383	9.0%
3	New York	30,806	6.7%
4	Florida	28,632	6.2%
5	Ohio	22,434	4.9%
6	Arizona	20,141	4.4%
7	Michigan	19,067	4.1%
8	Missouri	13,617	2.9%
9	Georgia	13,055	2.8%
10	Pennsylvania	12,287	2.7%
11	Oklahoma	11,397	2.5%
12	Indiana	11,016	2.4%
13	Colorado	10,492	2.3%
14	North Carolina	10,419	2.3%
15	Illinois	10,371	2.2%
16	Washington	10,006	2.2%
17	Virginia	9,958	2.2%
18	Kentucky	9,373	2.0%
19	Wisconsin	8,902	1.9%
20	Tennessee	8,615	1.9%
21	New Jersey	7,880	1.7%
22	Alabama	7,693	1.7%
23	Louisiana	7,559	1.6%
24	South Carolina	6,651	1.4%
25	Oregon	6,561	1.4%
26	Massachusetts	5,325	1.2%
27	Nevada	5,324	1.2%
28	Iowa	5,117	1.1%
29	Maryland	5,039	1.1%
30	Arkansas	4,868	1.1%
31	Kansas	4,853	1.1%
32	Connecticut	4,691	1.0%
33	Mississippi	4,150	0.9%
34	New Mexico	4,140	0.9%
35	Utah	3,825	0.8%
36	Idaho	3,327	0.7%
37	West Virginia	2,923	0.6%
38	Minnesota	2,619	0.6%
39	Nebraska	2,520	0.5%
40	Montana	2,108	0.5%
41	New Hampshire	2,031	0.4%
42	Delaware	2,028	0.4%
43	Alaska	1,878	0.4%
44	Rhode Island	1,845	0.4%
45	South Dakota	1,826	0.4%
46	Maine	1,525	0.3%
47	Vermont	1,216	0.3%
48	Wyoming	1,196	0.3%
49	Hawaii	1,039	0.2%
50	North Dakota	703	0.2%
	District of Columbia	93	0.0%

Source: U.S. Department of Justice, Bureau of Justice Statistics
"Correctional Populations in the United States, 1998"
*Preliminary data as of December 31, 1998. National total does not include 71,119 white federal prisoners.

58

White State Prisoner Incarceration Rate in 1998

National Rate = 207 White State Prisoners per 100,000 White Population*

ALPHA ORDER

RANK	STATE	RATE
19	Alabama	242
3	Alaska	406
1	Arizona	486
22	Arkansas	232
37	California	183
7	Colorado	286
41	Connecticut	163
5	Delaware	349
22	Florida	232
18	Georgia	247
11	Hawaii	263
8	Idaho	279
48	Illinois	106
28	Indiana	206
35	Iowa	185
30	Kansas	202
13	Kentucky	259
12	Louisiana	262
44	Maine	125
43	Maryland	145
49	Massachusetts	97
21	Michigan	233
50	Minnesota	59
20	Mississippi	241
6	Missouri	287
15	Montana	258
42	Nebraska	162
4	Nevada	355
39	New Hampshire	175
45	New Jersey	122
9	New Mexico	275
25	New York	222
37	North Carolina	183
46	North Dakota	117
24	Ohio	230
2	Oklahoma	410
26	Oregon	214
47	Pennsylvania	116
29	Rhode Island	203
16	South Carolina	251
10	South Dakota	273
32	Tennessee	193
17	Texas	248
34	Utah	191
27	Vermont	209
32	Virginia	193
31	Washington	198
40	West Virginia	168
35	Wisconsin	185
13	Wyoming	259

RANK ORDER

RANK	STATE	RATE
1	Arizona	486
2	Oklahoma	410
3	Alaska	406
4	Nevada	355
5	Delaware	349
6	Missouri	287
7	Colorado	286
8	Idaho	279
9	New Mexico	275
10	South Dakota	273
11	Hawaii	263
12	Louisiana	262
13	Kentucky	259
13	Wyoming	259
15	Montana	258
16	South Carolina	251
17	Texas	248
18	Georgia	247
19	Alabama	242
20	Mississippi	241
21	Michigan	233
22	Arkansas	232
22	Florida	232
24	Ohio	230
25	New York	222
26	Oregon	214
27	Vermont	209
28	Indiana	206
29	Rhode Island	203
30	Kansas	202
31	Washington	198
32	Tennessee	193
32	Virginia	193
34	Utah	191
35	Iowa	185
35	Wisconsin	185
37	California	183
37	North Carolina	183
39	New Hampshire	175
40	West Virginia	168
41	Connecticut	163
42	Nebraska	162
43	Maryland	145
44	Maine	125
45	New Jersey	122
46	North Dakota	117
47	Pennsylvania	116
48	Illinois	106
49	Massachusetts	97
50	Minnesota	59
	District of Columbia	52

Source: Morgan Quitno Press using data from U.S. Department of Justice, Bureau of Justice Statistics
    "Correctional Populations in the United States, 1998"
*Preliminary data as of December 31, 1998. National rate does not include 71,119 white federal prisoners.
Federal rate is 32 white prisoners per 100,000 white population. The combined federal/state rate is 239 white
prisoners per 100,000 white population.

White State Prisoners in State Correctional Institutions
As a Percent of All State Prisoners in 1998
National Percent = 39.3% White*

ALPHA ORDER

RANK	STATE	PERCENT
36	Alabama	33.9
29	Alaska	45.8
8	Arizona	79.6
29	Arkansas	45.8
42	California	29.7
14	Colorado	73.3
44	Connecticut	26.6
35	Delaware	36.5
33	Florida	42.6
38	Georgia	33.3
50	Hawaii	21.1
7	Idaho	81.5
47	Illinois	24.1
20	Indiana	57.4
16	Iowa	69.2
19	Kansas	59.3
18	Kentucky	62.5
48	Louisiana	23.5
3	Maine	85.6
49	Maryland	22.3
31	Massachusetts	45.1
34	Michigan	41.6
27	Minnesota	47.0
46	Mississippi	24.9
23	Missouri	54.5
9	Montana	77.1
17	Nebraska	68.6
21	Nevada	55.2
1	New Hampshire	93.6
45	New Jersey	25.3
5	New Mexico	83.0
32	New York	44.0
40	North Carolina	32.6
10	North Dakota	76.8
28	Ohio	46.3
22	Oklahoma	54.6
13	Oregon	73.5
37	Pennsylvania	33.8
24	Rhode Island	53.6
41	South Carolina	30.1
12	South Dakota	75.4
25	Tennessee	48.6
43	Texas	28.6
2	Utah	85.9
6	Vermont	82.6
39	Virginia	32.9
15	Washington	70.7
4	West Virginia	84.0
26	Wisconsin	47.8
11	Wyoming	76.1

RANK ORDER

RANK	STATE	PERCENT
1	New Hampshire	93.6
2	Utah	85.9
3	Maine	85.6
4	West Virginia	84.0
5	New Mexico	83.0
6	Vermont	82.6
7	Idaho	81.5
8	Arizona	79.6
9	Montana	77.1
10	North Dakota	76.8
11	Wyoming	76.1
12	South Dakota	75.4
13	Oregon	73.5
14	Colorado	73.3
15	Washington	70.7
16	Iowa	69.2
17	Nebraska	68.6
18	Kentucky	62.5
19	Kansas	59.3
20	Indiana	57.4
21	Nevada	55.2
22	Oklahoma	54.6
23	Missouri	54.5
24	Rhode Island	53.6
25	Tennessee	48.6
26	Wisconsin	47.8
27	Minnesota	47.0
28	Ohio	46.3
29	Alaska	45.8
29	Arkansas	45.8
31	Massachusetts	45.1
32	New York	44.0
33	Florida	42.6
34	Michigan	41.6
35	Delaware	36.5
36	Alabama	33.9
37	Pennsylvania	33.8
38	Georgia	33.3
39	Virginia	32.9
40	North Carolina	32.6
41	South Carolina	30.1
42	California	29.7
43	Texas	28.6
44	Connecticut	26.6
45	New Jersey	25.3
46	Mississippi	24.9
47	Illinois	24.1
48	Louisiana	23.5
49	Maryland	22.3
50	Hawaii	21.1
	District of Columbia	0.9

Source: Morgan Quitno Press using data from U.S. Department of Justice, Bureau of Justice Statistics "Correctional Populations in the United States, 1998"
Preliminary data as of December 31, 1998. National percent does not include white federal prisoners. Federal prison population is 57.8% white. Combined state and federal percentage is 41.0% white.

Black Prisoners in State Correctional Institutions in 1998

National Total = 568,259 Black State Prisoners*

ALPHA ORDER					RANK ORDER			
RANK	STATE	PRISONERS	% of USA		RANK	STATE	PRISONERS	% of USA
16	Alabama	14,905	2.6%		1	Texas	65,133	11.5%
39	Alaska	556	0.1%		2	California	50,052	8.8%
26	Arizona	3,739	0.7%		3	New York	38,284	6.7%
24	Arkansas	5,699	1.0%		4	Florida	37,143	6.5%
2	California	50,052	8.8%		5	Illinois	28,220	5.0%
29	Colorado	3,376	0.6%		6	Georgia	26,022	4.6%
21	Connecticut	8,290	1.5%		7	Ohio	25,798	4.5%
27	Delaware	3,521	0.6%		8	Michigan	25,336	4.5%
4	Florida	37,143	6.5%		9	Louisiana	24,621	4.3%
6	Georgia	26,022	4.6%		10	Pennsylvania	20,413	3.6%
42	Hawaii	220	0.0%		11	North Carolina	20,355	3.6%
46	Idaho	57	0.0%		12	New Jersey	20,323	3.6%
5	Illinois	28,220	5.0%		13	Virginia	20,050	3.5%
22	Indiana	8,109	1.4%		14	Maryland	17,495	3.1%
34	Iowa	1,770	0.3%		15	South Carolina	15,339	2.7%
31	Kansas	3,050	0.5%		16	Alabama	14,905	2.6%
25	Kentucky	5,574	1.0%		17	Mississippi	12,442	2.2%
9	Louisiana	24,621	4.3%		18	Missouri	11,243	2.0%
46	Maine	57	0.0%		19	Wisconsin	9,016	1.6%
14	Maryland	17,495	3.1%		20	Tennessee	8,993	1.6%
28	Massachusetts	3,384	0.6%		21	Connecticut	8,290	1.5%
8	Michigan	25,336	4.5%		22	Indiana	8,109	1.4%
33	Minnesota	2,088	0.4%		23	Oklahoma	7,119	1.3%
17	Mississippi	12,442	2.2%		24	Arkansas	5,699	1.0%
18	Missouri	11,243	2.0%		25	Kentucky	5,574	1.0%
48	Montana	49	0.0%		26	Arizona	3,739	0.7%
37	Nebraska	979	0.2%		27	Delaware	3,521	0.6%
32	Nevada	2,657	0.5%		28	Massachusetts	3,384	0.6%
43	New Hampshire	115	0.0%		29	Colorado	3,376	0.6%
12	New Jersey	20,323	3.6%		30	Washington	3,255	0.6%
38	New Mexico	560	0.1%		31	Kansas	3,050	0.5%
3	New York	38,284	6.7%		32	Nevada	2,657	0.5%
11	North Carolina	20,355	3.6%		33	Minnesota	2,088	0.4%
50	North Dakota	31	0.0%		34	Iowa	1,770	0.3%
7	Ohio	25,798	4.5%		35	Oregon	1,136	0.2%
23	Oklahoma	7,119	1.3%		36	Rhode Island	992	0.2%
35	Oregon	1,136	0.2%		37	Nebraska	979	0.2%
10	Pennsylvania	20,413	3.6%		38	New Mexico	560	0.1%
36	Rhode Island	992	0.2%		39	Alaska	556	0.1%
15	South Carolina	15,339	2.7%		40	West Virginia	552	0.1%
44	South Dakota	97	0.0%		41	Utah	346	0.1%
20	Tennessee	8,993	1.6%		42	Hawaii	220	0.0%
1	Texas	65,133	11.5%		43	New Hampshire	115	0.0%
41	Utah	346	0.1%		44	South Dakota	97	0.0%
49	Vermont	46	0.0%		45	Wyoming	78	0.0%
13	Virginia	20,050	3.5%		46	Idaho	57	0.0%
30	Washington	3,255	0.6%		46	Maine	57	0.0%
40	West Virginia	552	0.1%		48	Montana	49	0.0%
19	Wisconsin	9,016	1.6%		49	Vermont	46	0.0%
45	Wyoming	78	0.0%		50	North Dakota	31	0.0%
						District of Columbia	9,574	1.7%

Source: U.S. Department of Justice, Bureau of Justice Statistics
  "Correctional Populations in the United States, 1998"
*Preliminary data as of December 31, 1998. National total does not include 47,847 black federal prisoners.

Black State Prisoner Incarceration Rate in 1998

National Rate = 1,650 Black State Prisoners per 100,000 Black Population*

<u>ALPHA ORDER</u>

RANK	STATE	RATE
37	Alabama	1,316
7	Alaska	2,339
8	Arizona	2,210
34	Arkansas	1,398
9	California	2,038
14	Colorado	1,964
3	Connecticut	2,729
6	Delaware	2,439
27	Florida	1,638
42	Georgia	1,193
50	Hawaii	629
48	Idaho	796
28	Illinois	1,534
25	Indiana	1,653
1	Iowa	3,112
13	Kansas	1,971
15	Kentucky	1,957
22	Louisiana	1,750
46	Maine	902
40	Maryland	1,225
47	Massachusetts	857
21	Michigan	1,804
30	Minnesota	1,485
39	Mississippi	1,240
20	Missouri	1,835
29	Montana	1,522
33	Nebraska	1,457
12	Nevada	1,992
35	New Hampshire	1,352
24	New Jersey	1,710
38	New Mexico	1,241
43	New York	1,189
41	North Carolina	1,222
49	North Dakota	775
11	Ohio	2,000
4	Oklahoma	2,718
18	Oregon	1,864
22	Pennsylvania	1,750
10	Rhode Island	2,005
36	South Carolina	1,337
17	South Dakota	1,895
44	Tennessee	1,000
5	Texas	2,680
19	Utah	1,853
32	Vermont	1,470
31	Virginia	1,471
26	Washington	1,641
45	West Virginia	950
2	Wisconsin	3,103
16	Wyoming	1,911

<u>RANK ORDER</u>

RANK	STATE	RATE
1	Iowa	3,112
2	Wisconsin	3,103
3	Connecticut	2,729
4	Oklahoma	2,718
5	Texas	2,680
6	Delaware	2,439
7	Alaska	2,339
8	Arizona	2,210
9	California	2,038
10	Rhode Island	2,005
11	Ohio	2,000
12	Nevada	1,992
13	Kansas	1,971
14	Colorado	1,964
15	Kentucky	1,957
16	Wyoming	1,911
17	South Dakota	1,895
18	Oregon	1,864
19	Utah	1,853
20	Missouri	1,835
21	Michigan	1,804
22	Louisiana	1,750
22	Pennsylvania	1,750
24	New Jersey	1,710
25	Indiana	1,653
26	Washington	1,641
27	Florida	1,638
28	Illinois	1,534
29	Montana	1,522
30	Minnesota	1,485
31	Virginia	1,471
32	Vermont	1,470
33	Nebraska	1,457
34	Arkansas	1,398
35	New Hampshire	1,352
36	South Carolina	1,337
37	Alabama	1,316
38	New Mexico	1,241
39	Mississippi	1,240
40	Maryland	1,225
41	North Carolina	1,222
42	Georgia	1,193
43	New York	1,189
44	Tennessee	1,000
45	West Virginia	950
46	Maine	902
47	Massachusetts	857
48	Idaho	796
49	North Dakota	775
50	Hawaii	629
	District of Columbia	2,938

Source: Morgan Quitno Press using data from U.S. Department of Justice, Bureau of Justice Statistics
"Correctional Populations in the United States, 1998"

*Preliminary data as of December 31, 1998. National rate does not include 47,847 black federal prisoners. Federal rate is 139 black prisoners per 100,000 black population. The combined federal/state rate is 1,789 black prisoners per 100,000 black population.

Black State Prisoners in State Correctional Institutions
As a Percent of All State Prisoners in 1998
National Percent = 48.3% Black*

ALPHA ORDER

RANK ORDER

RANK	STATE	PERCENT		RANK	STATE	PERCENT
7	Alabama	65.7		1	Maryland	77.5
38	Alaska	13.6		2	Louisiana	76.4
37	Arizona	14.8		3	Mississippi	74.6
16	Arkansas	53.6		4	South Carolina	69.4
28	California	31.3		5	Georgia	66.3
34	Colorado	23.6		6	Virginia	66.2
20	Connecticut	47.1		7	Alabama	65.7
11	Delaware	63.4		8	Illinois	65.6
13	Florida	55.3		9	New Jersey	65.3
5	Georgia	66.3		10	North Carolina	63.7
44	Hawaii	4.5		11	Delaware	63.4
50	Idaho	1.4		12	Pennsylvania	56.1
8	Illinois	65.6		13	Florida	55.3
23	Indiana	42.2		14	Michigan	55.2
33	Iowa	23.9		15	New York	54.7
25	Kansas	37.3		16	Arkansas	53.6
26	Kentucky	37.2		17	Ohio	53.2
2	Louisiana	76.4		18	Tennessee	50.7
47	Maine	3.2		19	Wisconsin	48.4
1	Maryland	77.5		20	Connecticut	47.1
30	Massachusetts	28.7		21	Texas	45.1
14	Michigan	55.2		22	Missouri	45.0
24	Minnesota	37.5		23	Indiana	42.2
3	Mississippi	74.6		24	Minnesota	37.5
22	Missouri	45.0		25	Kansas	37.3
49	Montana	1.8		26	Kentucky	37.2
32	Nebraska	26.6		27	Oklahoma	34.1
31	Nevada	27.5		28	California	31.3
42	New Hampshire	5.3		29	Rhode Island	28.8
9	New Jersey	65.3		30	Massachusetts	28.7
40	New Mexico	11.2		31	Nevada	27.5
15	New York	54.7		32	Nebraska	26.6
10	North Carolina	63.7		33	Iowa	23.9
46	North Dakota	3.4		34	Colorado	23.6
17	Ohio	53.2		35	Washington	23.0
27	Oklahoma	34.1		36	West Virginia	15.9
39	Oregon	12.7		37	Arizona	14.8
12	Pennsylvania	56.1		38	Alaska	13.6
29	Rhode Island	28.8		39	Oregon	12.7
4	South Carolina	69.4		40	New Mexico	11.2
45	South Dakota	4.0		41	Utah	7.8
18	Tennessee	50.7		42	New Hampshire	5.3
21	Texas	45.1		43	Wyoming	5.0
41	Utah	7.8		44	Hawaii	4.5
48	Vermont	3.1		45	South Dakota	4.0
6	Virginia	66.2		46	North Dakota	3.4
35	Washington	23.0		47	Maine	3.2
36	West Virginia	15.9		48	Vermont	3.1
19	Wisconsin	48.4		49	Montana	1.8
43	Wyoming	5.0		50	Idaho	1.4

District of Columbia   97.4

Source: Morgan Quitno Press using data from U.S. Department of Justice, Bureau of Justice Statistics
"Correctional Populations in the United States, 1998"
*Preliminary data as of December 31, 1998. National percent does not include black federal prisoners. Federal
prison population is 38.9% black. Combined state and federal percentage is 47.4% black.

Prisoners Under Sentence of Death in 2000

National Total = 3,575 State Prisoners*

ALPHA ORDER

RANK	STATE	PRISONERS	% of USA
7	Alabama	185	5.2%
NA	Alaska**	NA	NA
11	Arizona	119	3.3%
19	Arkansas	40	1.1%
1	California	586	16.4%
33	Colorado	5	0.1%
30	Connecticut	7	0.2%
25	Delaware	15	0.4%
3	Florida	371	10.4%
10	Georgia	120	3.4%
NA	Hawaii**	NA	NA
23	Idaho	21	0.6%
8	Illinois	163	4.6%
18	Indiana	43	1.2%
NA	Iowa**	NA	NA
35	Kansas	4	0.1%
19	Kentucky	40	1.1%
13	Louisiana	90	2.5%
NA	Maine**	NA	NA
24	Maryland	16	0.4%
NA	Massachusetts**	NA	NA
NA	Michigan**	NA	NA
NA	Minnesota**	NA	NA
17	Mississippi	61	1.7%
15	Missouri	79	2.2%
31	Montana	6	0.2%
28	Nebraska	11	0.3%
14	Nevada	88	2.5%
38	New Hampshire	0	0.0%
25	New Jersey	15	0.4%
33	New Mexico	5	0.1%
31	New York	6	0.2%
5	North Carolina	215	6.0%
NA	North Dakota**	NA	NA
6	Ohio	201	5.6%
9	Oklahoma	129	3.6%
22	Oregon	25	0.7%
4	Pennsylvania	238	6.7%
NA	Rhode Island**	NA	NA
16	South Carolina	66	1.8%
36	South Dakota	3	0.1%
12	Tennessee	97	2.7%
2	Texas	450	12.6%
28	Utah	11	0.3%
NA	Vermont**	NA	NA
21	Virginia	29	0.8%
27	Washington	13	0.4%
NA	West Virginia**	NA	NA
NA	Wisconsin**	NA	NA
37	Wyoming	2	0.1%

RANK ORDER

RANK	STATE	PRISONERS	% of USA
1	California	586	16.4%
2	Texas	450	12.6%
3	Florida	371	10.4%
4	Pennsylvania	238	6.7%
5	North Carolina	215	6.0%
6	Ohio	201	5.6%
7	Alabama	185	5.2%
8	Illinois	163	4.6%
9	Oklahoma	129	3.6%
10	Georgia	120	3.4%
11	Arizona	119	3.3%
12	Tennessee	97	2.7%
13	Louisiana	90	2.5%
14	Nevada	88	2.5%
15	Missouri	79	2.2%
16	South Carolina	66	1.8%
17	Mississippi	61	1.7%
18	Indiana	43	1.2%
19	Arkansas	40	1.1%
19	Kentucky	40	1.1%
21	Virginia	29	0.8%
22	Oregon	25	0.7%
23	Idaho	21	0.6%
24	Maryland	16	0.4%
25	Delaware	15	0.4%
25	New Jersey	15	0.4%
27	Washington	13	0.4%
28	Nebraska	11	0.3%
28	Utah	11	0.3%
30	Connecticut	7	0.2%
31	Montana	6	0.2%
31	New York	6	0.2%
33	Colorado	5	0.1%
33	New Mexico	5	0.1%
35	Kansas	4	0.1%
36	South Dakota	3	0.1%
37	Wyoming	2	0.1%
38	New Hampshire	0	0.0%
NA	Alaska**	NA	NA
NA	Hawaii**	NA	NA
NA	Iowa**	NA	NA
NA	Maine**	NA	NA
NA	Massachusetts**	NA	NA
NA	Michigan**	NA	NA
NA	Minnesota**	NA	NA
NA	North Dakota**	NA	NA
NA	Rhode Island**	NA	NA
NA	Vermont**	NA	NA
NA	West Virginia**	NA	NA
NA	Wisconsin**	NA	NA
	District of Columbia**	NA	NA

Source: U.S. Department of Justice, Bureau of Justice Statistics
    "Capital Punishment 2000" (Bulletin, December 2001, NCJ-190598)
*As of December 31, 2000. Does not include 18 federal prisoners under sentence of death. There were 85 executions in 2000.
**No death penalty as of 12/31/00.

Average Number of Years Under Sentence of Death as of 2000

National Average = 8.0 Years*

ALPHA ORDER

RANK	STATE	YEARS
17	Alabama	7.3
NA	Alaska**	NA
13	Arizona	8.6
26	Arkansas	5.4
11	California	9.0
NA	Colorado***	NA
NA	Connecticut***	NA
21	Delaware	6.5
5	Florida	9.6
9	Georgia	9.1
NA	Hawaii**	NA
1	Idaho	10.6
6	Illinois	9.3
4	Indiana	9.9
NA	Iowa**	NA
NA	Kansas***	NA
6	Kentucky	9.3
24	Louisiana	5.7
NA	Maine**	NA
16	Maryland	7.4
NA	Massachusetts**	NA
NA	Michigan**	NA
NA	Minnesota**	NA
19	Mississippi	7.0
18	Missouri	7.1
NA	Montana***	NA
2	Nebraska	10.5
12	Nevada	8.9
NA	New Hampshire***	NA
23	New Jersey	5.9
NA	New Mexico***	NA
NA	New York***	NA
26	North Carolina	5.4
NA	North Dakota**	NA
9	Ohio	9.1
15	Oklahoma	7.7
26	Oregon	5.4
14	Pennsylvania	8.5
NA	Rhode Island**	NA
22	South Carolina	6.2
NA	South Dakota***	NA
3	Tennessee	10.2
20	Texas	6.9
6	Utah	9.3
NA	Vermont**	NA
29	Virginia	2.1
25	Washington	5.5
NA	West Virginia**	NA
NA	Wisconsin**	NA
NA	Wyoming***	NA

RANK ORDER

RANK	STATE	YEARS
1	Idaho	10.6
2	Nebraska	10.5
3	Tennessee	10.2
4	Indiana	9.9
5	Florida	9.6
6	Illinois	9.3
6	Kentucky	9.3
6	Utah	9.3
9	Georgia	9.1
9	Ohio	9.1
11	California	9.0
12	Nevada	8.9
13	Arizona	8.6
14	Pennsylvania	8.5
15	Oklahoma	7.7
16	Maryland	7.4
17	Alabama	7.3
18	Missouri	7.1
19	Mississippi	7.0
20	Texas	6.9
21	Delaware	6.5
22	South Carolina	6.2
23	New Jersey	5.9
24	Louisiana	5.7
25	Washington	5.5
26	Arkansas	5.4
26	North Carolina	5.4
26	Oregon	5.4
29	Virginia	2.1
NA	Alaska**	NA
NA	Colorado***	NA
NA	Connecticut***	NA
NA	Hawaii**	NA
NA	Iowa**	NA
NA	Kansas***	NA
NA	Maine**	NA
NA	Massachusetts**	NA
NA	Michigan**	NA
NA	Minnesota**	NA
NA	Montana***	NA
NA	New Hampshire***	NA
NA	New Mexico***	NA
NA	New York***	NA
NA	North Dakota**	NA
NA	Rhode Island**	NA
NA	South Dakota***	NA
NA	Vermont**	NA
NA	West Virginia**	NA
NA	Wisconsin**	NA
NA	Wyoming***	NA
	District of Columbia**	NA

Source: U.S. Department of Justice, Bureau of Justice Statistics
    "Capital Punishment 2000" (Bulletin, December 2001, NCJ-190598)
*As of December 31, 2000. Federal average is 4.2 years.
**No death penalty as of 12/31/00.
***Not available. These states had fewer than 10 prisoners under sentence of death. Averages were not calculated.

Male Prisoners Under Sentence of Death in 2000

National Total = 3,521 Male State Prisoners*

<table>
<tr><td colspan="5">ALPHA ORDER</td><td colspan="5">RANK ORDER</td></tr>
<tr><th>RANK</th><th>STATE</th><th>PRISONERS</th><th>% of USA</th><th></th><th>RANK</th><th>STATE</th><th>PRISONERS</th><th>% of USA</th></tr>
<tr><td>7</td><td>Alabama</td><td>182</td><td>5.2%</td><td></td><td>1</td><td>California</td><td>574</td><td>16.3%</td></tr>
<tr><td>NA</td><td>Alaska**</td><td>NA</td><td>NA</td><td></td><td>2</td><td>Texas</td><td>443</td><td>12.6%</td></tr>
<tr><td>11</td><td>Arizona</td><td>117</td><td>3.3%</td><td></td><td>3</td><td>Florida</td><td>368</td><td>10.5%</td></tr>
<tr><td>19</td><td>Arkansas</td><td>40</td><td>1.1%</td><td></td><td>4</td><td>Pennsylvania</td><td>234</td><td>6.6%</td></tr>
<tr><td>1</td><td>California</td><td>574</td><td>16.3%</td><td></td><td>5</td><td>North Carolina</td><td>209</td><td>5.9%</td></tr>
<tr><td>33</td><td>Colorado</td><td>5</td><td>0.1%</td><td></td><td>6</td><td>Ohio</td><td>201</td><td>5.7%</td></tr>
<tr><td>30</td><td>Connecticut</td><td>7</td><td>0.2%</td><td></td><td>7</td><td>Alabama</td><td>182</td><td>5.2%</td></tr>
<tr><td>25</td><td>Delaware</td><td>15</td><td>0.4%</td><td></td><td>8</td><td>Illinois</td><td>159</td><td>4.5%</td></tr>
<tr><td>3</td><td>Florida</td><td>368</td><td>10.5%</td><td></td><td>9</td><td>Oklahoma</td><td>126</td><td>3.6%</td></tr>
<tr><td>10</td><td>Georgia</td><td>119</td><td>3.4%</td><td></td><td>10</td><td>Georgia</td><td>119</td><td>3.4%</td></tr>
<tr><td>NA</td><td>Hawaii**</td><td>NA</td><td>NA</td><td></td><td>11</td><td>Arizona</td><td>117</td><td>3.3%</td></tr>
<tr><td>23</td><td>Idaho</td><td>20</td><td>0.6%</td><td></td><td>12</td><td>Tennessee</td><td>95</td><td>2.7%</td></tr>
<tr><td>8</td><td>Illinois</td><td>159</td><td>4.5%</td><td></td><td>13</td><td>Louisiana</td><td>89</td><td>2.5%</td></tr>
<tr><td>18</td><td>Indiana</td><td>42</td><td>1.2%</td><td></td><td>14</td><td>Nevada</td><td>87</td><td>2.5%</td></tr>
<tr><td>NA</td><td>Iowa**</td><td>NA</td><td>NA</td><td></td><td>15</td><td>Missouri</td><td>78</td><td>2.2%</td></tr>
<tr><td>35</td><td>Kansas</td><td>4</td><td>0.1%</td><td></td><td>16</td><td>South Carolina</td><td>66</td><td>1.9%</td></tr>
<tr><td>20</td><td>Kentucky</td><td>39</td><td>1.1%</td><td></td><td>17</td><td>Mississippi</td><td>60</td><td>1.7%</td></tr>
<tr><td>13</td><td>Louisiana</td><td>89</td><td>2.5%</td><td></td><td>18</td><td>Indiana</td><td>42</td><td>1.2%</td></tr>
<tr><td>NA</td><td>Maine**</td><td>NA</td><td>NA</td><td></td><td>19</td><td>Arkansas</td><td>40</td><td>1.1%</td></tr>
<tr><td>24</td><td>Maryland</td><td>16</td><td>0.5%</td><td></td><td>20</td><td>Kentucky</td><td>39</td><td>1.1%</td></tr>
<tr><td>NA</td><td>Massachusetts**</td><td>NA</td><td>NA</td><td></td><td>21</td><td>Virginia</td><td>29</td><td>0.8%</td></tr>
<tr><td>NA</td><td>Michigan**</td><td>NA</td><td>NA</td><td></td><td>22</td><td>Oregon</td><td>25</td><td>0.7%</td></tr>
<tr><td>NA</td><td>Minnesota**</td><td>NA</td><td>NA</td><td></td><td>23</td><td>Idaho</td><td>20</td><td>0.6%</td></tr>
<tr><td>17</td><td>Mississippi</td><td>60</td><td>1.7%</td><td></td><td>24</td><td>Maryland</td><td>16</td><td>0.5%</td></tr>
<tr><td>15</td><td>Missouri</td><td>78</td><td>2.2%</td><td></td><td>25</td><td>Delaware</td><td>15</td><td>0.4%</td></tr>
<tr><td>31</td><td>Montana</td><td>6</td><td>0.2%</td><td></td><td>25</td><td>New Jersey</td><td>15</td><td>0.4%</td></tr>
<tr><td>28</td><td>Nebraska</td><td>11</td><td>0.3%</td><td></td><td>27</td><td>Washington</td><td>13</td><td>0.4%</td></tr>
<tr><td>14</td><td>Nevada</td><td>87</td><td>2.5%</td><td></td><td>28</td><td>Nebraska</td><td>11</td><td>0.3%</td></tr>
<tr><td>38</td><td>New Hampshire</td><td>0</td><td>0.0%</td><td></td><td>28</td><td>Utah</td><td>11</td><td>0.3%</td></tr>
<tr><td>25</td><td>New Jersey</td><td>15</td><td>0.4%</td><td></td><td>30</td><td>Connecticut</td><td>7</td><td>0.2%</td></tr>
<tr><td>33</td><td>New Mexico</td><td>5</td><td>0.1%</td><td></td><td>31</td><td>Montana</td><td>6</td><td>0.2%</td></tr>
<tr><td>31</td><td>New York</td><td>6</td><td>0.2%</td><td></td><td>31</td><td>New York</td><td>6</td><td>0.2%</td></tr>
<tr><td>5</td><td>North Carolina</td><td>209</td><td>5.9%</td><td></td><td>33</td><td>Colorado</td><td>5</td><td>0.1%</td></tr>
<tr><td>NA</td><td>North Dakota**</td><td>NA</td><td>NA</td><td></td><td>33</td><td>New Mexico</td><td>5</td><td>0.1%</td></tr>
<tr><td>6</td><td>Ohio</td><td>201</td><td>5.7%</td><td></td><td>35</td><td>Kansas</td><td>4</td><td>0.1%</td></tr>
<tr><td>9</td><td>Oklahoma</td><td>126</td><td>3.6%</td><td></td><td>36</td><td>South Dakota</td><td>3</td><td>0.1%</td></tr>
<tr><td>22</td><td>Oregon</td><td>25</td><td>0.7%</td><td></td><td>37</td><td>Wyoming</td><td>2</td><td>0.1%</td></tr>
<tr><td>4</td><td>Pennsylvania</td><td>234</td><td>6.6%</td><td></td><td>38</td><td>New Hampshire</td><td>0</td><td>0.0%</td></tr>
<tr><td>NA</td><td>Rhode Island**</td><td>NA</td><td>NA</td><td></td><td>NA</td><td>Alaska**</td><td>NA</td><td>NA</td></tr>
<tr><td>16</td><td>South Carolina</td><td>66</td><td>1.9%</td><td></td><td>NA</td><td>Hawaii**</td><td>NA</td><td>NA</td></tr>
<tr><td>36</td><td>South Dakota</td><td>3</td><td>0.1%</td><td></td><td>NA</td><td>Iowa**</td><td>NA</td><td>NA</td></tr>
<tr><td>12</td><td>Tennessee</td><td>95</td><td>2.7%</td><td></td><td>NA</td><td>Maine**</td><td>NA</td><td>NA</td></tr>
<tr><td>2</td><td>Texas</td><td>443</td><td>12.6%</td><td></td><td>NA</td><td>Massachusetts**</td><td>NA</td><td>NA</td></tr>
<tr><td>28</td><td>Utah</td><td>11</td><td>0.3%</td><td></td><td>NA</td><td>Michigan**</td><td>NA</td><td>NA</td></tr>
<tr><td>NA</td><td>Vermont**</td><td>NA</td><td>NA</td><td></td><td>NA</td><td>Minnesota**</td><td>NA</td><td>NA</td></tr>
<tr><td>21</td><td>Virginia</td><td>29</td><td>0.8%</td><td></td><td>NA</td><td>North Dakota**</td><td>NA</td><td>NA</td></tr>
<tr><td>27</td><td>Washington</td><td>13</td><td>0.4%</td><td></td><td>NA</td><td>Rhode Island**</td><td>NA</td><td>NA</td></tr>
<tr><td>NA</td><td>West Virginia**</td><td>NA</td><td>NA</td><td></td><td>NA</td><td>Vermont**</td><td>NA</td><td>NA</td></tr>
<tr><td>NA</td><td>Wisconsin**</td><td>NA</td><td>NA</td><td></td><td>NA</td><td>West Virginia**</td><td>NA</td><td>NA</td></tr>
<tr><td>37</td><td>Wyoming</td><td>2</td><td>0.1%</td><td></td><td>NA</td><td>Wisconsin**</td><td>NA</td><td>NA</td></tr>
<tr><td></td><td></td><td></td><td></td><td></td><td></td><td>District of Columbia**</td><td>NA</td><td>NA</td></tr>
</table>

Source: Morgan Quitno Press using data from U.S. Department of Justice, Bureau of Justice Statistics
"Capital Punishment 2000" (Bulletin, December 2001, NCJ-190598)
*As of December 31, 2000. Does not include 18 male federal prisoners under sentence of death. There were 85 executions in 2000, 83 of whom were male.
**No death penalty as of 12/31/00.

Female Prisoners Under Sentence of Death in 2000

National Total = 54 Female State Prisoners*

ALPHA ORDER

RANK ORDER

RANK	STATE	PRISONERS	% of USA
6	Alabama	3	5.6%
NA	Alaska**	NA	NA
9	Arizona	2	3.7%
19	Arkansas	0	0.0%
1	California	12	22.2%
19	Colorado	0	0.0%
19	Connecticut	0	0.0%
19	Delaware	0	0.0%
6	Florida	3	5.6%
11	Georgia	1	1.9%
NA	Hawaii**	NA	NA
11	Idaho	1	1.9%
4	Illinois	4	7.4%
11	Indiana	1	1.9%
NA	Iowa**	NA	NA
19	Kansas	0	0.0%
11	Kentucky	1	1.9%
11	Louisiana	1	1.9%
NA	Maine**	NA	NA
19	Maryland	0	0.0%
NA	Massachusetts**	NA	NA
NA	Michigan**	NA	NA
NA	Minnesota**	NA	NA
11	Mississippi	1	1.9%
11	Missouri	1	1.9%
19	Montana	0	0.0%
19	Nebraska	0	0.0%
11	Nevada	1	1.9%
19	New Hampshire	0	0.0%
19	New Jersey	0	0.0%
19	New Mexico	0	0.0%
19	New York	0	0.0%
3	North Carolina	6	11.1%
NA	North Dakota**	NA	NA
19	Ohio	0	0.0%
6	Oklahoma	3	5.6%
19	Oregon	0	0.0%
4	Pennsylvania	4	7.4%
NA	Rhode Island**	NA	NA
19	South Carolina	0	0.0%
19	South Dakota	0	0.0%
9	Tennessee	2	3.7%
2	Texas	7	13.0%
19	Utah	0	0.0%
NA	Vermont**	NA	NA
19	Virginia	0	0.0%
19	Washington	0	0.0%
NA	West Virginia**	NA	NA
NA	Wisconsin**	NA	NA
19	Wyoming	0	0.0%

RANK	STATE	PRISONERS	% of USA
1	California	12	22.2%
2	Texas	7	13.0%
3	North Carolina	6	11.1%
4	Illinois	4	7.4%
4	Pennsylvania	4	7.4%
6	Alabama	3	5.6%
6	Florida	3	5.6%
6	Oklahoma	3	5.6%
9	Arizona	2	3.7%
9	Tennessee	2	3.7%
11	Georgia	1	1.9%
11	Idaho	1	1.9%
11	Indiana	1	1.9%
11	Kentucky	1	1.9%
11	Louisiana	1	1.9%
11	Mississippi	1	1.9%
11	Missouri	1	1.9%
11	Nevada	1	1.9%
19	Arkansas	0	0.0%
19	Colorado	0	0.0%
19	Connecticut	0	0.0%
19	Delaware	0	0.0%
19	Kansas	0	0.0%
19	Maryland	0	0.0%
19	Montana	0	0.0%
19	Nebraska	0	0.0%
19	New Hampshire	0	0.0%
19	New Jersey	0	0.0%
19	New Mexico	0	0.0%
19	New York	0	0.0%
19	Ohio	0	0.0%
19	Oregon	0	0.0%
19	South Carolina	0	0.0%
19	South Dakota	0	0.0%
19	Utah	0	0.0%
19	Virginia	0	0.0%
19	Washington	0	0.0%
19	Wyoming	0	0.0%
NA	Alaska**	NA	NA
NA	Hawaii**	NA	NA
NA	Iowa**	NA	NA
NA	Maine**	NA	NA
NA	Massachusetts**	NA	NA
NA	Michigan**	NA	NA
NA	Minnesota**	NA	NA
NA	North Dakota**	NA	NA
NA	Rhode Island**	NA	NA
NA	Vermont**	NA	NA
NA	West Virginia**	NA	NA
NA	Wisconsin**	NA	NA
	District of Columbia**	NA	NA

Source: U.S. Department of Justice, Bureau of Justice Statistics
   "Capital Punishment 2000" (Bulletin, December 2001, NCJ-190598)
*As of December 31, 2000. There were no federal female prisoners under sentence of death. There were 85 executions in 2000, two of whom were female.
**No death penalty as of 12/31/00.

Percent of Prisoners Under Sentence of Death Who Are Female: 2000

National Percent = 1.5% of State Death Sentence Prisoners*

ALPHA ORDER

RANK	STATE	PERCENT
11	Alabama	1.6
NA	Alaska**	NA
9	Arizona	1.7
19	Arkansas	0.0
8	California	2.0
19	Colorado	0.0
19	Connecticut	0.0
19	Delaware	0.0
17	Florida	0.8
17	Georgia	0.8
NA	Hawaii**	NA
1	Idaho	4.8
3	Illinois	2.5
5	Indiana	2.3
NA	Iowa**	NA
19	Kansas	0.0
3	Kentucky	2.5
15	Louisiana	1.1
NA	Maine**	NA
19	Maryland	0.0
NA	Massachusetts**	NA
NA	Michigan**	NA
NA	Minnesota**	NA
11	Mississippi	1.6
14	Missouri	1.3
19	Montana	0.0
19	Nebraska	0.0
15	Nevada	1.1
19	New Hampshire	0.0
19	New Jersey	0.0
19	New Mexico	0.0
19	New York	0.0
2	North Carolina	2.8
NA	North Dakota**	NA
19	Ohio	0.0
5	Oklahoma	2.3
19	Oregon	0.0
9	Pennsylvania	1.7
NA	Rhode Island**	NA
19	South Carolina	0.0
19	South Dakota	0.0
7	Tennessee	2.1
11	Texas	1.6
19	Utah	0.0
NA	Vermont**	NA
19	Virginia	0.0
19	Washington	0.0
NA	West Virginia**	NA
NA	Wisconsin**	NA
19	Wyoming	0.0

RANK ORDER

RANK	STATE	PERCENT
1	Idaho	4.8
2	North Carolina	2.8
3	Illinois	2.5
3	Kentucky	2.5
5	Indiana	2.3
5	Oklahoma	2.3
7	Tennessee	2.1
8	California	2.0
9	Arizona	1.7
9	Pennsylvania	1.7
11	Alabama	1.6
11	Mississippi	1.6
11	Texas	1.6
14	Missouri	1.3
15	Louisiana	1.1
15	Nevada	1.1
17	Florida	0.8
17	Georgia	0.8
19	Arkansas	0.0
19	Colorado	0.0
19	Connecticut	0.0
19	Delaware	0.0
19	Kansas	0.0
19	Maryland	0.0
19	Montana	0.0
19	Nebraska	0.0
19	New Hampshire	0.0
19	New Jersey	0.0
19	New Mexico	0.0
19	New York	0.0
19	Ohio	0.0
19	Oregon	0.0
19	South Carolina	0.0
19	South Dakota	0.0
19	Utah	0.0
19	Virginia	0.0
19	Washington	0.0
19	Wyoming	0.0
NA	Alaska**	NA
NA	Hawaii**	NA
NA	Iowa**	NA
NA	Maine**	NA
NA	Massachusetts**	NA
NA	Michigan**	NA
NA	Minnesota**	NA
NA	North Dakota**	NA
NA	Rhode Island**	NA
NA	Vermont**	NA
NA	West Virginia**	NA
NA	Wisconsin**	NA
	District of Columbia**	NA

Source: Morgan Quitno Press using data from U.S. Department of Justice, Bureau of Justice Statistics "Capital Punishment 2000" (Bulletin, December 2001, NCJ-190598)
*As of December 31, 2000. There were no federal female prisoners under sentence of death. There were 85 executions in 2000, two of whom were female.
**No death penalty as of 12/31/00.

White Prisoners Under Sentence of Death in 2000

National Total = 1,985 White State Prisoners*

<table>
<tr><td colspan="4">ALPHA ORDER</td><td colspan="4">RANK ORDER</td></tr>
<tr><th>RANK</th><th>STATE</th><th>PRISONERS</th><th>% of USA</th><th>RANK</th><th>STATE</th><th>PRISONERS</th><th>% of USA</th></tr>
<tr><td>6</td><td>Alabama</td><td>97</td><td>4.9%</td><td>1</td><td>California</td><td>349</td><td>17.6%</td></tr>
<tr><td>NA</td><td>Alaska**</td><td>NA</td><td>NA</td><td>2</td><td>Texas</td><td>260</td><td>13.1%</td></tr>
<tr><td>4</td><td>Arizona</td><td>103</td><td>5.2%</td><td>3</td><td>Florida</td><td>239</td><td>12.0%</td></tr>
<tr><td>23</td><td>Arkansas</td><td>16</td><td>0.8%</td><td>4</td><td>Arizona</td><td>103</td><td>5.2%</td></tr>
<tr><td>1</td><td>California</td><td>349</td><td>17.6%</td><td>5</td><td>Ohio</td><td>98</td><td>4.9%</td></tr>
<tr><td>35</td><td>Colorado</td><td>3</td><td>0.2%</td><td>6</td><td>Alabama</td><td>97</td><td>4.9%</td></tr>
<tr><td>32</td><td>Connecticut</td><td>4</td><td>0.2%</td><td>7</td><td>North Carolina</td><td>85</td><td>4.3%</td></tr>
<tr><td>26</td><td>Delaware</td><td>8</td><td>0.4%</td><td>8</td><td>Oklahoma</td><td>81</td><td>4.1%</td></tr>
<tr><td>3</td><td>Florida</td><td>239</td><td>12.0%</td><td>9</td><td>Pennsylvania</td><td>78</td><td>3.9%</td></tr>
<tr><td>10</td><td>Georgia</td><td>64</td><td>3.2%</td><td>10</td><td>Georgia</td><td>64</td><td>3.2%</td></tr>
<tr><td>NA</td><td>Hawaii**</td><td>NA</td><td>NA</td><td>11</td><td>Illinois</td><td>60</td><td>3.0%</td></tr>
<tr><td>21</td><td>Idaho</td><td>21</td><td>1.1%</td><td>12</td><td>Tennessee</td><td>59</td><td>3.0%</td></tr>
<tr><td>11</td><td>Illinois</td><td>60</td><td>3.0%</td><td>13</td><td>Nevada</td><td>52</td><td>2.6%</td></tr>
<tr><td>17</td><td>Indiana</td><td>30</td><td>1.5%</td><td>14</td><td>Missouri</td><td>46</td><td>2.3%</td></tr>
<tr><td>NA</td><td>Iowa**</td><td>NA</td><td>NA</td><td>15</td><td>South Carolina</td><td>35</td><td>1.8%</td></tr>
<tr><td>32</td><td>Kansas</td><td>4</td><td>0.2%</td><td>16</td><td>Kentucky</td><td>33</td><td>1.7%</td></tr>
<tr><td>16</td><td>Kentucky</td><td>33</td><td>1.7%</td><td>17</td><td>Indiana</td><td>30</td><td>1.5%</td></tr>
<tr><td>17</td><td>Louisiana</td><td>30</td><td>1.5%</td><td>17</td><td>Louisiana</td><td>30</td><td>1.5%</td></tr>
<tr><td>NA</td><td>Maine**</td><td>NA</td><td>NA</td><td>19</td><td>Mississippi</td><td>28</td><td>1.4%</td></tr>
<tr><td>29</td><td>Maryland</td><td>6</td><td>0.3%</td><td>20</td><td>Oregon</td><td>24</td><td>1.2%</td></tr>
<tr><td>NA</td><td>Massachusetts**</td><td>NA</td><td>NA</td><td>21</td><td>Idaho</td><td>21</td><td>1.1%</td></tr>
<tr><td>NA</td><td>Michigan**</td><td>NA</td><td>NA</td><td>22</td><td>Virginia</td><td>18</td><td>0.9%</td></tr>
<tr><td>NA</td><td>Minnesota**</td><td>NA</td><td>NA</td><td>23</td><td>Arkansas</td><td>16</td><td>0.8%</td></tr>
<tr><td>19</td><td>Mississippi</td><td>28</td><td>1.4%</td><td>24</td><td>Nebraska</td><td>10</td><td>0.5%</td></tr>
<tr><td>14</td><td>Missouri</td><td>46</td><td>2.3%</td><td>25</td><td>Washington</td><td>9</td><td>0.5%</td></tr>
<tr><td>30</td><td>Montana</td><td>5</td><td>0.3%</td><td>26</td><td>Delaware</td><td>8</td><td>0.4%</td></tr>
<tr><td>24</td><td>Nebraska</td><td>10</td><td>0.5%</td><td>26</td><td>New Jersey</td><td>8</td><td>0.4%</td></tr>
<tr><td>13</td><td>Nevada</td><td>52</td><td>2.6%</td><td>26</td><td>Utah</td><td>8</td><td>0.4%</td></tr>
<tr><td>38</td><td>New Hampshire</td><td>0</td><td>0.0%</td><td>29</td><td>Maryland</td><td>6</td><td>0.3%</td></tr>
<tr><td>26</td><td>New Jersey</td><td>8</td><td>0.4%</td><td>30</td><td>Montana</td><td>5</td><td>0.3%</td></tr>
<tr><td>30</td><td>New Mexico</td><td>5</td><td>0.3%</td><td>30</td><td>New Mexico</td><td>5</td><td>0.3%</td></tr>
<tr><td>32</td><td>New York</td><td>4</td><td>0.2%</td><td>32</td><td>Connecticut</td><td>4</td><td>0.2%</td></tr>
<tr><td>7</td><td>North Carolina</td><td>85</td><td>4.3%</td><td>32</td><td>Kansas</td><td>4</td><td>0.2%</td></tr>
<tr><td>NA</td><td>North Dakota**</td><td>NA</td><td>NA</td><td>32</td><td>New York</td><td>4</td><td>0.2%</td></tr>
<tr><td>5</td><td>Ohio</td><td>98</td><td>4.9%</td><td>35</td><td>Colorado</td><td>3</td><td>0.2%</td></tr>
<tr><td>8</td><td>Oklahoma</td><td>81</td><td>4.1%</td><td>35</td><td>South Dakota</td><td>3</td><td>0.2%</td></tr>
<tr><td>20</td><td>Oregon</td><td>24</td><td>1.2%</td><td>37</td><td>Wyoming</td><td>2</td><td>0.1%</td></tr>
<tr><td>9</td><td>Pennsylvania</td><td>78</td><td>3.9%</td><td>38</td><td>New Hampshire</td><td>0</td><td>0.0%</td></tr>
<tr><td>NA</td><td>Rhode Island**</td><td>NA</td><td>NA</td><td>NA</td><td>Alaska**</td><td>NA</td><td>NA</td></tr>
<tr><td>15</td><td>South Carolina</td><td>35</td><td>1.8%</td><td>NA</td><td>Hawaii**</td><td>NA</td><td>NA</td></tr>
<tr><td>35</td><td>South Dakota</td><td>3</td><td>0.2%</td><td>NA</td><td>Iowa**</td><td>NA</td><td>NA</td></tr>
<tr><td>12</td><td>Tennessee</td><td>59</td><td>3.0%</td><td>NA</td><td>Maine**</td><td>NA</td><td>NA</td></tr>
<tr><td>2</td><td>Texas</td><td>260</td><td>13.1%</td><td>NA</td><td>Massachusetts**</td><td>NA</td><td>NA</td></tr>
<tr><td>26</td><td>Utah</td><td>8</td><td>0.4%</td><td>NA</td><td>Michigan**</td><td>NA</td><td>NA</td></tr>
<tr><td>NA</td><td>Vermont**</td><td>NA</td><td>NA</td><td>NA</td><td>Minnesota**</td><td>NA</td><td>NA</td></tr>
<tr><td>22</td><td>Virginia</td><td>18</td><td>0.9%</td><td>NA</td><td>North Dakota**</td><td>NA</td><td>NA</td></tr>
<tr><td>25</td><td>Washington</td><td>9</td><td>0.5%</td><td>NA</td><td>Rhode Island**</td><td>NA</td><td>NA</td></tr>
<tr><td>NA</td><td>West Virginia**</td><td>NA</td><td>NA</td><td>NA</td><td>Vermont**</td><td>NA</td><td>NA</td></tr>
<tr><td>NA</td><td>Wisconsin**</td><td>NA</td><td>NA</td><td>NA</td><td>West Virginia**</td><td>NA</td><td>NA</td></tr>
<tr><td>37</td><td>Wyoming</td><td>2</td><td>0.1%</td><td>NA</td><td>Wisconsin**</td><td>NA</td><td>NA</td></tr>
<tr><td></td><td></td><td></td><td></td><td></td><td>District of Columbia**</td><td>NA</td><td>NA</td></tr>
</table>

Source: U.S. Department of Justice, Bureau of Justice Statistics
    "Capital Punishment 2000" (Bulletin, December 2001, NCJ-190598)
*As of December 31, 2000. Does not include five white federal prisoners under sentence of death. There were
85 executions in 2000, 49 of whom were white prisoners.
**No death penalty as of 12/31/00.

Percent of Prisoners Under Sentence of Death Who Are White: 2000

National Percent = 55.5% of State Death Sentence Prisoners*

<table>
<tr><td colspan="3">ALPHA ORDER</td><td colspan="3">RANK ORDER</td></tr>
<tr><th>RANK</th><th>STATE</th><th>PERCENT</th><th>RANK</th><th>STATE</th><th>PERCENT</th></tr>
<tr><td>29</td><td>Alabama</td><td>52.4</td><td>1</td><td>Idaho</td><td>100.0</td></tr>
<tr><td>NA</td><td>Alaska**</td><td>NA</td><td>1</td><td>Kansas</td><td>100.0</td></tr>
<tr><td>8</td><td>Arizona</td><td>86.6</td><td>1</td><td>New Mexico</td><td>100.0</td></tr>
<tr><td>32</td><td>Arkansas</td><td>40.0</td><td>1</td><td>South Dakota</td><td>100.0</td></tr>
<tr><td>20</td><td>California</td><td>59.6</td><td>1</td><td>Wyoming</td><td>100.0</td></tr>
<tr><td>19</td><td>Colorado</td><td>60.0</td><td>6</td><td>Oregon</td><td>96.0</td></tr>
<tr><td>24</td><td>Connecticut</td><td>57.1</td><td>7</td><td>Nebraska</td><td>90.9</td></tr>
<tr><td>25</td><td>Delaware</td><td>53.3</td><td>8</td><td>Arizona</td><td>86.6</td></tr>
<tr><td>15</td><td>Florida</td><td>64.4</td><td>9</td><td>Montana</td><td>83.3</td></tr>
<tr><td>25</td><td>Georgia</td><td>53.3</td><td>10</td><td>Kentucky</td><td>82.5</td></tr>
<tr><td>NA</td><td>Hawaii**</td><td>NA</td><td>11</td><td>Utah</td><td>72.7</td></tr>
<tr><td>1</td><td>Idaho</td><td>100.0</td><td>12</td><td>Indiana</td><td>69.8</td></tr>
<tr><td>35</td><td>Illinois</td><td>36.8</td><td>13</td><td>Washington</td><td>69.2</td></tr>
<tr><td>12</td><td>Indiana</td><td>69.8</td><td>14</td><td>New York</td><td>66.7</td></tr>
<tr><td>NA</td><td>Iowa**</td><td>NA</td><td>15</td><td>Florida</td><td>64.4</td></tr>
<tr><td>1</td><td>Kansas</td><td>100.0</td><td>16</td><td>Oklahoma</td><td>62.8</td></tr>
<tr><td>10</td><td>Kentucky</td><td>82.5</td><td>17</td><td>Virginia</td><td>62.1</td></tr>
<tr><td>36</td><td>Louisiana</td><td>33.3</td><td>18</td><td>Tennessee</td><td>60.8</td></tr>
<tr><td>NA</td><td>Maine**</td><td>NA</td><td>19</td><td>Colorado</td><td>60.0</td></tr>
<tr><td>34</td><td>Maryland</td><td>37.5</td><td>20</td><td>California</td><td>59.6</td></tr>
<tr><td>NA</td><td>Massachusetts**</td><td>NA</td><td>21</td><td>Nevada</td><td>59.1</td></tr>
<tr><td>NA</td><td>Michigan**</td><td>NA</td><td>22</td><td>Missouri</td><td>58.2</td></tr>
<tr><td>NA</td><td>Minnesota**</td><td>NA</td><td>23</td><td>Texas</td><td>57.8</td></tr>
<tr><td>31</td><td>Mississippi</td><td>45.9</td><td>24</td><td>Connecticut</td><td>57.1</td></tr>
<tr><td>22</td><td>Missouri</td><td>58.2</td><td>25</td><td>Delaware</td><td>53.3</td></tr>
<tr><td>9</td><td>Montana</td><td>83.3</td><td>25</td><td>Georgia</td><td>53.3</td></tr>
<tr><td>7</td><td>Nebraska</td><td>90.9</td><td>25</td><td>New Jersey</td><td>53.3</td></tr>
<tr><td>21</td><td>Nevada</td><td>59.1</td><td>28</td><td>South Carolina</td><td>53.0</td></tr>
<tr><td>38</td><td>New Hampshire</td><td>0.0</td><td>29</td><td>Alabama</td><td>52.4</td></tr>
<tr><td>25</td><td>New Jersey</td><td>53.3</td><td>30</td><td>Ohio</td><td>48.8</td></tr>
<tr><td>1</td><td>New Mexico</td><td>100.0</td><td>31</td><td>Mississippi</td><td>45.9</td></tr>
<tr><td>14</td><td>New York</td><td>66.7</td><td>32</td><td>Arkansas</td><td>40.0</td></tr>
<tr><td>33</td><td>North Carolina</td><td>39.5</td><td>33</td><td>North Carolina</td><td>39.5</td></tr>
<tr><td>NA</td><td>North Dakota**</td><td>NA</td><td>34</td><td>Maryland</td><td>37.5</td></tr>
<tr><td>30</td><td>Ohio</td><td>48.8</td><td>35</td><td>Illinois</td><td>36.8</td></tr>
<tr><td>16</td><td>Oklahoma</td><td>62.8</td><td>36</td><td>Louisiana</td><td>33.3</td></tr>
<tr><td>6</td><td>Oregon</td><td>96.0</td><td>37</td><td>Pennsylvania</td><td>32.8</td></tr>
<tr><td>37</td><td>Pennsylvania</td><td>32.8</td><td>38</td><td>New Hampshire</td><td>0.0</td></tr>
<tr><td>NA</td><td>Rhode Island**</td><td>NA</td><td>NA</td><td>Alaska**</td><td>NA</td></tr>
<tr><td>28</td><td>South Carolina</td><td>53.0</td><td>NA</td><td>Hawaii**</td><td>NA</td></tr>
<tr><td>1</td><td>South Dakota</td><td>100.0</td><td>NA</td><td>Iowa**</td><td>NA</td></tr>
<tr><td>18</td><td>Tennessee</td><td>60.8</td><td>NA</td><td>Maine**</td><td>NA</td></tr>
<tr><td>23</td><td>Texas</td><td>57.8</td><td>NA</td><td>Massachusetts**</td><td>NA</td></tr>
<tr><td>11</td><td>Utah</td><td>72.7</td><td>NA</td><td>Michigan**</td><td>NA</td></tr>
<tr><td>NA</td><td>Vermont**</td><td>NA</td><td>NA</td><td>Minnesota**</td><td>NA</td></tr>
<tr><td>17</td><td>Virginia</td><td>62.1</td><td>NA</td><td>North Dakota**</td><td>NA</td></tr>
<tr><td>13</td><td>Washington</td><td>69.2</td><td>NA</td><td>Rhode Island**</td><td>NA</td></tr>
<tr><td>NA</td><td>West Virginia**</td><td>NA</td><td>NA</td><td>Vermont**</td><td>NA</td></tr>
<tr><td>NA</td><td>Wisconsin**</td><td>NA</td><td>NA</td><td>West Virginia**</td><td>NA</td></tr>
<tr><td>1</td><td>Wyoming</td><td>100.0</td><td>NA</td><td>Wisconsin**</td><td>NA</td></tr>
<tr><td></td><td></td><td></td><td></td><td>District of Columbia**</td><td>NA</td></tr>
</table>

Source: Morgan Quitno Press using data from U.S. Department of Justice, Bureau of Justice Statistics
   "Capital Punishment 2000" (Bulletin, December 2001, NCJ-190598)
*As of December 31, 2000. Does not include federal prisoners under sentence of death, 27.8% of whom are white prisoners. Of the 85 executions in 2000, 57.6% were white prisoners.
**No death penalty as of 12/31/00.

Black Prisoners Under Sentence of Death in 2000

National Total = 1,522 Black State Prisoners*

RANK	STATE	PRISONERS	% of USA
8	Alabama	87	5.7%
NA	Alaska**	NA	NA
19	Arizona	12	0.8%
17	Arkansas	24	1.6%
1	California	215	14.1%
27	Colorado	2	0.1%
26	Connecticut	3	0.2%
22	Delaware	7	0.5%
4	Florida	131	8.6%
10	Georgia	55	3.6%
NA	Hawaii**	NA	NA
30	Idaho	0	0.0%
6	Illinois	103	6.8%
18	Indiana	13	0.9%
NA	Iowa**	NA	NA
30	Kansas	0	0.0%
22	Kentucky	7	0.5%
9	Louisiana	59	3.9%
NA	Maine**	NA	NA
21	Maryland	10	0.7%
NA	Massachusetts**	NA	NA
NA	Michigan**	NA	NA
NA	Minnesota**	NA	NA
14	Mississippi	33	2.2%
14	Missouri	33	2.2%
30	Montana	0	0.0%
30	Nebraska	0	0.0%
13	Nevada	35	2.3%
30	New Hampshire	0	0.0%
22	New Jersey	7	0.5%
30	New Mexico	0	0.0%
27	New York	2	0.1%
5	North Carolina	122	8.0%
NA	North Dakota**	NA	NA
7	Ohio	102	6.7%
11	Oklahoma	42	2.8%
30	Oregon	0	0.0%
3	Pennsylvania	149	9.8%
NA	Rhode Island**	NA	NA
16	South Carolina	31	2.0%
30	South Dakota	0	0.0%
12	Tennessee	36	2.4%
2	Texas	185	12.2%
27	Utah	2	0.1%
NA	Vermont**	NA	NA
20	Virginia	11	0.7%
25	Washington	4	0.3%
NA	West Virginia**	NA	NA
NA	Wisconsin**	NA	NA
30	Wyoming	0	0.0%

RANK	STATE	PRISONERS	% of USA
1	California	215	14.1%
2	Texas	185	12.2%
3	Pennsylvania	149	9.8%
4	Florida	131	8.6%
5	North Carolina	122	8.0%
6	Illinois	103	6.8%
7	Ohio	102	6.7%
8	Alabama	87	5.7%
9	Louisiana	59	3.9%
10	Georgia	55	3.6%
11	Oklahoma	42	2.8%
12	Tennessee	36	2.4%
13	Nevada	35	2.3%
14	Mississippi	33	2.2%
14	Missouri	33	2.2%
16	South Carolina	31	2.0%
17	Arkansas	24	1.6%
18	Indiana	13	0.9%
19	Arizona	12	0.8%
20	Virginia	11	0.7%
21	Maryland	10	0.7%
22	Delaware	7	0.5%
22	Kentucky	7	0.5%
22	New Jersey	7	0.5%
25	Washington	4	0.3%
26	Connecticut	3	0.2%
27	Colorado	2	0.1%
27	New York	2	0.1%
27	Utah	2	0.1%
30	Idaho	0	0.0%
30	Kansas	0	0.0%
30	Montana	0	0.0%
30	Nebraska	0	0.0%
30	New Hampshire	0	0.0%
30	New Mexico	0	0.0%
30	Oregon	0	0.0%
30	South Dakota	0	0.0%
30	Wyoming	0	0.0%
NA	Alaska**	NA	NA
NA	Hawaii**	NA	NA
NA	Iowa**	NA	NA
NA	Maine**	NA	NA
NA	Massachusetts**	NA	NA
NA	Michigan**	NA	NA
NA	Minnesota**	NA	NA
NA	North Dakota**	NA	NA
NA	Rhode Island**	NA	NA
NA	Vermont**	NA	NA
NA	West Virginia**	NA	NA
NA	Wisconsin**	NA	NA
	District of Columbia**	NA	NA

Source: U.S. Department of Justice, Bureau of Justice Statistics
    "Capital Punishment 2000" (Bulletin, December 2001, NCJ-190598)
*As of December 31, 2000. Does not include 13 black federal prisoners under sentence of death. There were
85 executions in 2000, 35 of whom were black prisoners.
**No death penalty as of 12/31/00.

Percent of Prisoners Under Sentence of Death Who Are Black: 2000

National Percent = 42.6% of State Death Sentence Prisoners*

ALPHA ORDER

RANK	STATE	PERCENT
9	Alabama	47.0
NA	Alaska**	NA
29	Arizona	10.1
5	Arkansas	60.0
21	California	36.7
17	Colorado	40.0
14	Connecticut	42.9
11	Delaware	46.7
22	Florida	35.3
13	Georgia	45.8
NA	Hawaii**	NA
30	Idaho	0.0
2	Illinois	63.2
26	Indiana	30.2
NA	Iowa**	NA
30	Kansas	0.0
28	Kentucky	17.5
1	Louisiana	65.6
NA	Maine**	NA
4	Maryland	62.5
NA	Massachusetts**	NA
NA	Michigan**	NA
NA	Minnesota**	NA
7	Mississippi	54.1
15	Missouri	41.8
30	Montana	0.0
30	Nebraska	0.0
18	Nevada	39.8
30	New Hampshire	0.0
11	New Jersey	46.7
30	New Mexico	0.0
23	New York	33.3
6	North Carolina	56.7
NA	North Dakota**	NA
8	Ohio	50.7
24	Oklahoma	32.6
30	Oregon	0.0
3	Pennsylvania	62.6
NA	Rhode Island**	NA
9	South Carolina	47.0
30	South Dakota	0.0
20	Tennessee	37.1
16	Texas	41.1
27	Utah	18.2
NA	Vermont**	NA
19	Virginia	37.9
25	Washington	30.8
NA	West Virginia**	NA
NA	Wisconsin**	NA
30	Wyoming	0.0

RANK ORDER

RANK	STATE	PERCENT
1	Louisiana	65.6
2	Illinois	63.2
3	Pennsylvania	62.6
4	Maryland	62.5
5	Arkansas	60.0
6	North Carolina	56.7
7	Mississippi	54.1
8	Ohio	50.7
9	Alabama	47.0
9	South Carolina	47.0
11	Delaware	46.7
11	New Jersey	46.7
13	Georgia	45.8
14	Connecticut	42.9
15	Missouri	41.8
16	Texas	41.1
17	Colorado	40.0
18	Nevada	39.8
19	Virginia	37.9
20	Tennessee	37.1
21	California	36.7
22	Florida	35.3
23	New York	33.3
24	Oklahoma	32.6
25	Washington	30.8
26	Indiana	30.2
27	Utah	18.2
28	Kentucky	17.5
29	Arizona	10.1
30	Idaho	0.0
30	Kansas	0.0
30	Montana	0.0
30	Nebraska	0.0
30	New Hampshire	0.0
30	New Mexico	0.0
30	Oregon	0.0
30	South Dakota	0.0
30	Wyoming	0.0
NA	Alaska**	NA
NA	Hawaii**	NA
NA	Iowa**	NA
NA	Maine**	NA
NA	Massachusetts**	NA
NA	Michigan**	NA
NA	Minnesota**	NA
NA	North Dakota**	NA
NA	Rhode Island**	NA
NA	Vermont**	NA
NA	West Virginia**	NA
NA	Wisconsin**	NA
	District of Columbia**	NA

Source: Morgan Quitno Press using data from U.S. Department of Justice, Bureau of Justice Statistics
   "Capital Punishment 2000" (Bulletin, December 2001, NCJ-190598)
*As of December 31, 2000. Does not federal prisoners under sentence of death, 72.2% of whom are black prisoners. Of the 85 executions in 2000, 41.2% were black prisoners.
**No death penalty as of 12/31/00.

Prisoners Executed in 2000

National Total = 85 Executed*

ALPHA ORDER

RANK	STATE	EXECUTED	% of USA
6	Alabama	4	4.7%
NA	Alaska**	NA	NA
7	Arizona	3	3.5%
8	Arkansas	2	2.4%
9	California	1	1.2%
15	Colorado	0	0.0%
15	Connecticut	0	0.0%
9	Delaware	1	1.2%
4	Florida	6	7.1%
15	Georgia	0	0.0%
NA	Hawaii**	NA	NA
15	Idaho	0	0.0%
15	Illinois	0	0.0%
15	Indiana	0	0.0%
NA	Iowa**	NA	NA
15	Kansas	0	0.0%
15	Kentucky	0	0.0%
9	Louisiana	1	1.2%
NA	Maine**	NA	NA
15	Maryland	0	0.0%
NA	Massachusetts**	NA	NA
NA	Michigan**	NA	NA
NA	Minnesota**	NA	NA
15	Mississippi	0	0.0%
5	Missouri	5	5.9%
15	Montana	0	0.0%
15	Nebraska	0	0.0%
15	Nevada	0	0.0%
15	New Hampshire	0	0.0%
15	New Jersey	0	0.0%
15	New Mexico	0	0.0%
15	New York	0	0.0%
9	North Carolina	1	1.2%
NA	North Dakota**	NA	NA
15	Ohio	0	0.0%
2	Oklahoma	11	12.9%
15	Oregon	0	0.0%
15	Pennsylvania	0	0.0%
NA	Rhode Island**	NA	NA
9	South Carolina	1	1.2%
15	South Dakota	0	0.0%
9	Tennessee	1	1.2%
1	Texas	40	47.1%
15	Utah	0	0.0%
NA	Vermont**	NA	NA
3	Virginia	8	9.4%
15	Washington	0	0.0%
NA	West Virginia**	NA	NA
NA	Wisconsin**	NA	NA
15	Wyoming	0	0.0%

RANK ORDER

RANK	STATE	EXECUTED	% of USA
1	Texas	40	47.1%
2	Oklahoma	11	12.9%
3	Virginia	8	9.4%
4	Florida	6	7.1%
5	Missouri	5	5.9%
6	Alabama	4	4.7%
7	Arizona	3	3.5%
8	Arkansas	2	2.4%
9	California	1	1.2%
9	Delaware	1	1.2%
9	Louisiana	1	1.2%
9	North Carolina	1	1.2%
9	South Carolina	1	1.2%
9	Tennessee	1	1.2%
15	Colorado	0	0.0%
15	Connecticut	0	0.0%
15	Georgia	0	0.0%
15	Idaho	0	0.0%
15	Illinois	0	0.0%
15	Indiana	0	0.0%
15	Kansas	0	0.0%
15	Kentucky	0	0.0%
15	Maryland	0	0.0%
15	Mississippi	0	0.0%
15	Montana	0	0.0%
15	Nebraska	0	0.0%
15	Nevada	0	0.0%
15	New Hampshire	0	0.0%
15	New Jersey	0	0.0%
15	New Mexico	0	0.0%
15	New York	0	0.0%
15	Ohio	0	0.0%
15	Oregon	0	0.0%
15	Pennsylvania	0	0.0%
15	South Dakota	0	0.0%
15	Utah	0	0.0%
15	Washington	0	0.0%
15	Wyoming	0	0.0%
NA	Alaska**	NA	NA
NA	Hawaii**	NA	NA
NA	Iowa**	NA	NA
NA	Maine**	NA	NA
NA	Massachusetts**	NA	NA
NA	Michigan**	NA	NA
NA	Minnesota**	NA	NA
NA	North Dakota**	NA	NA
NA	Rhode Island**	NA	NA
NA	Vermont**	NA	NA
NA	West Virginia**	NA	NA
NA	Wisconsin**	NA	NA
	District of Columbia**	NA	NA

Source: U.S. Department of Justice, Bureau of Justice Statistics
  "Capital Punishment 2000" (Bulletin, December 2001, NCJ-190598)
*No federal prisoners were executed in 2000
**No death penalty as of 12/31/00.

Prisoners Executed: 1930 to 2000

National Total = 4,542 Prisoners*

ALPHA ORDER

RANK ORDER

RANK	STATE	PRISONERS	% of USA
11	Alabama	158	3.5%
43	Alaska	0	0.0%
22	Arizona	60	1.3%
14	Arkansas	141	3.1%
4	California	300	6.6%
24	Colorado	48	1.1%
30	Connecticut	21	0.5%
29	Delaware	23	0.5%
6	Florida	220	4.8%
2	Georgia	389	8.6%
43	Hawaii	0	0.0%
39	Idaho	4	0.1%
17	Illinois	102	2.2%
24	Indiana	48	1.1%
33	Iowa	18	0.4%
34	Kansas	15	0.3%
16	Kentucky	105	2.3%
10	Louisiana	159	3.5%
43	Maine	0	0.0%
21	Maryland	71	1.6%
28	Massachusetts	27	0.6%
43	Michigan	0	0.0%
43	Minnesota	0	0.0%
11	Mississippi	158	3.5%
15	Missouri	108	2.4%
35	Montana	8	0.2%
38	Nebraska	7	0.2%
27	Nevada	37	0.8%
41	New Hampshire	1	0.0%
20	New Jersey	74	1.6%
35	New Mexico	8	0.2%
3	New York	329	7.2%
5	North Carolina	279	6.1%
43	North Dakota	0	0.0%
8	Ohio	173	3.8%
19	Oklahoma	90	2.0%
30	Oregon	21	0.5%
13	Pennsylvania	155	3.4%
43	Rhode Island	0	0.0%
7	South Carolina	187	4.1%
41	South Dakota	1	0.0%
18	Tennessee	94	2.1%
1	Texas	536	11.8%
32	Utah	19	0.4%
39	Vermont	4	0.1%
8	Virginia	173	3.8%
23	Washington	50	1.1%
26	West Virginia	40	0.9%
43	Wisconsin	0	0.0%
35	Wyoming	8	0.2%

RANK	STATE	PRISONERS	% of USA
1	Texas	536	11.8%
2	Georgia	389	8.6%
3	New York	329	7.2%
4	California	300	6.6%
5	North Carolina	279	6.1%
6	Florida	220	4.8%
7	South Carolina	187	4.1%
8	Ohio	173	3.8%
8	Virginia	173	3.8%
10	Louisiana	159	3.5%
11	Alabama	158	3.5%
11	Mississippi	158	3.5%
13	Pennsylvania	155	3.4%
14	Arkansas	141	3.1%
15	Missouri	108	2.4%
16	Kentucky	105	2.3%
17	Illinois	102	2.2%
18	Tennessee	94	2.1%
19	Oklahoma	90	2.0%
20	New Jersey	74	1.6%
21	Maryland	71	1.6%
22	Arizona	60	1.3%
23	Washington	50	1.1%
24	Colorado	48	1.1%
24	Indiana	48	1.1%
26	West Virginia	40	0.9%
27	Nevada	37	0.8%
28	Massachusetts	27	0.6%
29	Delaware	23	0.5%
30	Connecticut	21	0.5%
30	Oregon	21	0.5%
32	Utah	19	0.4%
33	Iowa	18	0.4%
34	Kansas	15	0.3%
35	Montana	8	0.2%
35	New Mexico	8	0.2%
35	Wyoming	8	0.2%
38	Nebraska	7	0.2%
39	Idaho	4	0.1%
39	Vermont	4	0.1%
41	New Hampshire	1	0.0%
41	South Dakota	1	0.0%
43	Alaska	0	0.0%
43	Hawaii	0	0.0%
43	Maine	0	0.0%
43	Michigan	0	0.0%
43	Minnesota	0	0.0%
43	North Dakota	0	0.0%
43	Rhode Island	0	0.0%
43	Wisconsin	0	0.0%
	District of Columbia	40	0.9%

Source: U.S. Department of Justice, Bureau of Justice Statistics
    "Capital Punishment 2000" (Bulletin, December 2001, NCJ-190598)
*Includes 33 executions by the federal government. Does not include 160 executions carried out under military authority. There were no executions from 1968 to 1976.

Prisoners Executed: 1977 to 2000

National Total = 683 Prisoners*

ALPHA ORDER				RANK ORDER			
RANK	STATE	PRISONERS	% of USA	RANK	STATE	PRISONERS	% of USA
8	Alabama	23	3.4%	1	Texas	239	35.0%
32	Alaska	0	0.0%	2	Virginia	81	11.9%
11	Arizona	22	3.2%	3	Florida	50	7.3%
8	Arkansas	23	3.4%	4	Missouri	46	6.7%
15	California	8	1.2%	5	Oklahoma	30	4.4%
27	Colorado	1	0.1%	6	Louisiana	26	3.8%
32	Connecticut	0	0.0%	7	South Carolina	25	3.7%
14	Delaware	11	1.6%	8	Alabama	23	3.4%
3	Florida	50	7.3%	8	Arkansas	23	3.4%
8	Georgia	23	3.4%	8	Georgia	23	3.4%
32	Hawaii	0	0.0%	11	Arizona	22	3.2%
27	Idaho	1	0.1%	12	North Carolina	16	2.3%
13	Illinois	12	1.8%	13	Illinois	12	1.8%
17	Indiana	7	1.0%	14	Delaware	11	1.6%
32	Iowa	0	0.0%	15	California	8	1.2%
32	Kansas	0	0.0%	15	Nevada	8	1.2%
24	Kentucky	2	0.3%	17	Indiana	7	1.0%
6	Louisiana	26	3.8%	18	Utah	6	0.9%
32	Maine	0	0.0%	19	Mississippi	4	0.6%
20	Maryland	3	0.4%	20	Maryland	3	0.4%
32	Massachusetts	0	0.0%	20	Nebraska	3	0.4%
32	Michigan	0	0.0%	20	Pennsylvania	3	0.4%
32	Minnesota	0	0.0%	20	Washington	3	0.4%
19	Mississippi	4	0.6%	24	Kentucky	2	0.3%
4	Missouri	46	6.7%	24	Montana	2	0.3%
24	Montana	2	0.3%	24	Oregon	2	0.3%
20	Nebraska	3	0.4%	27	Colorado	1	0.1%
15	Nevada	8	1.2%	27	Idaho	1	0.1%
32	New Hampshire	0	0.0%	27	Ohio	1	0.1%
32	New Jersey	0	0.0%	27	Tennessee	1	0.1%
32	New Mexico	0	0.0%	27	Wyoming	1	0.1%
32	New York	0	0.0%	32	Alaska	0	0.0%
12	North Carolina	16	2.3%	32	Connecticut	0	0.0%
32	North Dakota	0	0.0%	32	Hawaii	0	0.0%
27	Ohio	1	0.1%	32	Iowa	0	0.0%
5	Oklahoma	30	4.4%	32	Kansas	0	0.0%
24	Oregon	2	0.3%	32	Maine	0	0.0%
20	Pennsylvania	3	0.4%	32	Massachusetts	0	0.0%
32	Rhode Island	0	0.0%	32	Michigan	0	0.0%
7	South Carolina	25	3.7%	32	Minnesota	0	0.0%
32	South Dakota	0	0.0%	32	New Hampshire	0	0.0%
27	Tennessee	1	0.1%	32	New Jersey	0	0.0%
1	Texas	239	35.0%	32	New Mexico	0	0.0%
18	Utah	6	0.9%	32	New York	0	0.0%
32	Vermont	0	0.0%	32	North Dakota	0	0.0%
2	Virginia	81	11.9%	32	Rhode Island	0	0.0%
20	Washington	3	0.4%	32	South Dakota	0	0.0%
32	West Virginia	0	0.0%	32	Vermont	0	0.0%
32	Wisconsin	0	0.0%	32	West Virginia	0	0.0%
27	Wyoming	1	0.1%	32	Wisconsin	0	0.0%
					District of Columbia	0	0.0%

Source: U.S. Department of Justice, Bureau of Justice Statistics
    "Capital Punishment 2000" (Bulletin, December 2001, NCJ-190598)
*As of December 31, 2000. All executions since 1977 have been for murder. In this time period, there have been
no executions by the federal government. The most common method of executions was lethal injection (518)
followed by electrocution (149), lethal gas (11), hanging (3) and firing squad (2).

Prisoners Sentenced to Death: 1973 to 2000

National Total = 6,906 State Death Sentences*

ALPHA ORDER

RANK	STATE	SENTENCES	% of USA
7	Alabama	325	4.7%
40	Alaska	0	0.0%
11	Arizona	231	3.3%
19	Arkansas	97	1.4%
3	California	753	10.9%
31	Colorado	18	0.3%
35	Connecticut	8	0.1%
25	Delaware	41	0.6%
2	Florida	847	12.3%
9	Georgia	294	4.3%
40	Hawaii	0	0.0%
26	Idaho	37	0.5%
10	Illinois	284	4.1%
20	Indiana	93	1.3%
40	Iowa	0	0.0%
36	Kansas	4	0.1%
21	Kentucky	74	1.1%
12	Louisiana	205	3.0%
40	Maine	0	0.0%
22	Maryland	50	0.7%
36	Massachusetts	4	0.1%
40	Michigan	0	0.0%
40	Minnesota	0	0.0%
15	Mississippi	165	2.4%
16	Missouri	160	2.3%
32	Montana	15	0.2%
29	Nebraska	26	0.4%
17	Nevada	133	1.9%
40	New Hampshire	0	0.0%
23	New Jersey	49	0.7%
28	New Mexico	27	0.4%
34	New York	9	0.1%
4	North Carolina	485	7.0%
40	North Dakota	0	0.0%
5	Ohio	354	5.1%
8	Oklahoma	303	4.4%
24	Oregon	46	0.7%
6	Pennsylvania	336	4.9%
39	Rhode Island	2	0.0%
14	South Carolina	167	2.4%
38	South Dakota	3	0.0%
13	Tennessee	196	2.8%
1	Texas	863	12.5%
29	Utah	26	0.4%
40	Vermont	0	0.0%
18	Virginia	131	1.9%
27	Washington	34	0.5%
40	West Virginia	0	0.0%
40	Wisconsin	0	0.0%
33	Wyoming	11	0.2%

RANK ORDER

RANK	STATE	SENTENCES	% of USA
1	Texas	863	12.5%
2	Florida	847	12.3%
3	California	753	10.9%
4	North Carolina	485	7.0%
5	Ohio	354	5.1%
6	Pennsylvania	336	4.9%
7	Alabama	325	4.7%
8	Oklahoma	303	4.4%
9	Georgia	294	4.3%
10	Illinois	284	4.1%
11	Arizona	231	3.3%
12	Louisiana	205	3.0%
13	Tennessee	196	2.8%
14	South Carolina	167	2.4%
15	Mississippi	165	2.4%
16	Missouri	160	2.3%
17	Nevada	133	1.9%
18	Virginia	131	1.9%
19	Arkansas	97	1.4%
20	Indiana	93	1.3%
21	Kentucky	74	1.1%
22	Maryland	50	0.7%
23	New Jersey	49	0.7%
24	Oregon	46	0.7%
25	Delaware	41	0.6%
26	Idaho	37	0.5%
27	Washington	34	0.5%
28	New Mexico	27	0.4%
29	Nebraska	26	0.4%
29	Utah	26	0.4%
31	Colorado	18	0.3%
32	Montana	15	0.2%
33	Wyoming	11	0.2%
34	New York	9	0.1%
35	Connecticut	8	0.1%
36	Kansas	4	0.1%
36	Massachusetts	4	0.1%
38	South Dakota	3	0.0%
39	Rhode Island	2	0.0%
40	Alaska	0	0.0%
40	Hawaii	0	0.0%
40	Iowa	0	0.0%
40	Maine	0	0.0%
40	Michigan	0	0.0%
40	Minnesota	0	0.0%
40	New Hampshire	0	0.0%
40	North Dakota	0	0.0%
40	Vermont	0	0.0%
40	West Virginia	0	0.0%
40	Wisconsin	0	0.0%
	District of Columbia	0	0.0%

Source: U.S. Department of Justice, Bureau of Justice Statistics
   "Capital Punishment 2000" (Bulletin, December 2001, NCJ-190598)
*As of December 31, 2000. Does not include 24 federal prisoners sentenced to death. For those sentenced to death more than once, the numbers are based on the most recent death sentence.

Death Sentences Overturned or Commuted: 1973 to 2000

National Total = 2,395 Sentences*

ALPHA ORDER

RANK	STATE	SENTENCES	% of USA
8	Alabama	103	4.3%
NA	Alaska**	NA	NA
14	Arizona	79	3.3%
17	Arkansas	32	1.3%
7	California	128	5.3%
29	Colorado	11	0.5%
37	Connecticut	1	0.0%
27	Delaware	15	0.6%
1	Florida	393	16.4%
5	Georgia	141	5.9%
NA	Hawaii**	NA	NA
28	Idaho	14	0.6%
10	Illinois	91	3.8%
16	Indiana	40	1.7%
NA	Iowa**	NA	NA
38	Kansas	0	0.0%
18	Kentucky	30	1.3%
12	Louisiana	85	3.5%
NA	Maine**	NA	NA
18	Maryland	30	1.3%
34	Massachusetts	4	0.2%
NA	Michigan**	NA	NA
NA	Minnesota**	NA	NA
9	Mississippi	94	3.9%
21	Missouri	27	1.1%
32	Montana	7	0.3%
30	Nebraska	10	0.4%
18	Nevada	30	1.3%
NA	New Hampshire**	NA	NA
22	New Jersey	23	1.0%
23	New Mexico	21	0.9%
35	New York	3	0.1%
2	North Carolina	244	10.2%
NA	North Dakota**	NA	NA
4	Ohio	142	5.9%
6	Oklahoma	136	5.7%
24	Oregon	18	0.8%
13	Pennsylvania	83	3.5%
36	Rhode Island	2	0.1%
15	South Carolina	72	3.0%
38	South Dakota	0	0.0%
11	Tennessee	86	3.6%
3	Texas	150	6.3%
31	Utah	9	0.4%
NA	Vermont**	NA	NA
25	Virginia	17	0.7%
25	Washington	17	0.7%
NA	West Virginia**	NA	NA
NA	Wisconsin**	NA	NA
32	Wyoming	7	0.3%

RANK ORDER

RANK	STATE	SENTENCES	% of USA
1	Florida	393	16.4%
2	North Carolina	244	10.2%
3	Texas	150	6.3%
4	Ohio	142	5.9%
5	Georgia	141	5.9%
6	Oklahoma	136	5.7%
7	California	128	5.3%
8	Alabama	103	4.3%
9	Mississippi	94	3.9%
10	Illinois	91	3.8%
11	Tennessee	86	3.6%
12	Louisiana	85	3.5%
13	Pennsylvania	83	3.5%
14	Arizona	79	3.3%
15	South Carolina	72	3.0%
16	Indiana	40	1.7%
17	Arkansas	32	1.3%
18	Kentucky	30	1.3%
18	Maryland	30	1.3%
18	Nevada	30	1.3%
21	Missouri	27	1.1%
22	New Jersey	23	1.0%
23	New Mexico	21	0.9%
24	Oregon	18	0.8%
25	Virginia	17	0.7%
25	Washington	17	0.7%
27	Delaware	15	0.6%
28	Idaho	14	0.6%
29	Colorado	11	0.5%
30	Nebraska	10	0.4%
31	Utah	9	0.4%
32	Montana	7	0.3%
32	Wyoming	7	0.3%
34	Massachusetts	4	0.2%
35	New York	3	0.1%
36	Rhode Island	2	0.1%
37	Connecticut	1	0.0%
38	Kansas	0	0.0%
38	South Dakota	0	0.0%
NA	Alaska**	NA	NA
NA	Hawaii**	NA	NA
NA	Iowa**	NA	NA
NA	Maine**	NA	NA
NA	Michigan**	NA	NA
NA	Minnesota**	NA	NA
NA	New Hampshire**	NA	NA
NA	North Dakota**	NA	NA
NA	Vermont**	NA	NA
NA	West Virginia**	NA	NA
NA	Wisconsin**	NA	NA
	District of Columbia**	NA	NA

Source: U.S. Department of Justice, Bureau of Justice Statistics
"Capital Punishment 2000" (Bulletin, December 2001, NCJ-190598)
As of December 31, 2000. Does not include six federal prisoners whose sentences were overturned.
**Not applicable.*

Percent of Death Penalty Sentences Overturned or Commuted: 1973 to 2000

National Percent = 34.7% of Sentences*

ALPHA ORDER

RANK	STATE	PERCENT
30	Alabama	31.7
NA	Alaska**	NA
26	Arizona	34.2
28	Arkansas	33.0
34	California	17.0
5	Colorado	61.1
37	Connecticut	12.5
24	Delaware	36.6
13	Florida	46.4
10	Georgia	48.0
NA	Hawaii**	NA
23	Idaho	37.8
29	Illinois	32.0
17	Indiana	43.0
NA	Iowa**	NA
38	Kansas	0.0
19	Kentucky	40.5
18	Louisiana	41.5
NA	Maine**	NA
6	Maryland	60.0
1	Massachusetts	100.0
NA	Michigan**	NA
NA	Minnesota**	NA
7	Mississippi	57.0
35	Missouri	16.9
12	Montana	46.7
22	Nebraska	38.5
32	Nevada	22.6
NA	New Hampshire**	NA
11	New Jersey	46.9
3	New Mexico	77.8
27	New York	33.3
8	North Carolina	50.3
NA	North Dakota**	NA
20	Ohio	40.1
14	Oklahoma	44.9
21	Oregon	39.1
31	Pennsylvania	24.7
1	Rhode Island	100.0
16	South Carolina	43.1
38	South Dakota	0.0
15	Tennessee	43.9
33	Texas	17.4
25	Utah	34.6
NA	Vermont**	NA
36	Virginia	13.0
9	Washington	50.0
NA	West Virginia**	NA
NA	Wisconsin**	NA
4	Wyoming	63.6

RANK ORDER

RANK	STATE	PERCENT
1	Massachusetts	100.0
1	Rhode Island	100.0
3	New Mexico	77.8
4	Wyoming	63.6
5	Colorado	61.1
6	Maryland	60.0
7	Mississippi	57.0
8	North Carolina	50.3
9	Washington	50.0
10	Georgia	48.0
11	New Jersey	46.9
12	Montana	46.7
13	Florida	46.4
14	Oklahoma	44.9
15	Tennessee	43.9
16	South Carolina	43.1
17	Indiana	43.0
18	Louisiana	41.5
19	Kentucky	40.5
20	Ohio	40.1
21	Oregon	39.1
22	Nebraska	38.5
23	Idaho	37.8
24	Delaware	36.6
25	Utah	34.6
26	Arizona	34.2
27	New York	33.3
28	Arkansas	33.0
29	Illinois	32.0
30	Alabama	31.7
31	Pennsylvania	24.7
32	Nevada	22.6
33	Texas	17.4
34	California	17.0
35	Missouri	16.9
36	Virginia	13.0
37	Connecticut	12.5
38	Kansas	0.0
38	South Dakota	0.0
NA	Alaska**	NA
NA	Hawaii**	NA
NA	Iowa**	NA
NA	Maine**	NA
NA	Michigan**	NA
NA	Minnesota**	NA
NA	New Hampshire**	NA
NA	North Dakota**	NA
NA	Vermont**	NA
NA	West Virginia**	NA
NA	Wisconsin**	NA
	District of Columbia**	NA

Source: Morgan Quitno Press using data from U.S. Department of Justice, Bureau of Justice Statistics "Capital Punishment 2000" (Bulletin, December 2001, NCJ-190598)
As of December 31, 2000. National percent does not include federal sentences or prisoners whose sentences were overturned. Six of 24 federal death penalty sentences have been overturned.
**Not applicable.*

Sentenced Prisoners Admitted to State Correctional Institutions in 1998

National Total = 576,038 Prisoners Admitted*

ALPHA ORDER

RANK	STATE	ADMISSIONS	% of USA
22	Alabama	7,750	1.3%
36	Alaska	2,647	0.5%
16	Arizona	10,175	1.8%
27	Arkansas	6,204	1.1%
1	California	134,485	23.3%
25	Colorado	6,881	1.2%
39	Connecticut	1,933	0.3%
40	Delaware	1,888	0.3%
5	Florida	25,524	4.4%
9	Georgia	15,471	2.7%
33	Hawaii	3,481	0.6%
37	Idaho	2,621	0.5%
4	Illinois	27,362	4.8%
15	Indiana	10,566	1.8%
28	Iowa	4,798	0.8%
30	Kansas	4,517	0.8%
21	Kentucky	7,989	1.4%
7	Louisiana	17,079	3.0%
48	Maine	795	0.1%
13	Maryland	11,078	1.9%
34	Massachusetts	3,227	0.6%
10	Michigan	14,435	2.5%
31	Minnesota	4,307	0.7%
26	Mississippi	6,670	1.2%
11	Missouri	13,660	2.4%
44	Montana	1,289	0.2%
41	Nebraska	1,791	0.3%
29	Nevada	4,773	0.8%
45	New Hampshire	1,000	0.2%
8	New Jersey	16,801	2.9%
38	New Mexico	2,347	0.4%
3	New York	28,871	5.0%
12	North Carolina	11,403	2.0%
49	North Dakota	765	0.1%
6	Ohio	20,637	3.6%
23	Oklahoma	7,297	1.3%
32	Oregon	3,688	0.6%
14	Pennsylvania	10,679	1.9%
46	Rhode Island	991	0.2%
18	South Carolina	8,914	1.5%
43	South Dakota	1,337	0.2%
20	Tennessee	8,770	1.5%
2	Texas	59,340	10.3%
35	Utah	3,076	0.5%
47	Vermont	824	0.1%
17	Virginia	10,152	1.8%
24	Washington	7,151	1.2%
42	West Virginia	1,444	0.3%
19	Wisconsin	8,785	1.5%
50	Wyoming	757	0.1%

RANK ORDER

RANK	STATE	ADMISSIONS	% of USA
1	California	134,485	23.3%
2	Texas	59,340	10.3%
3	New York	28,871	5.0%
4	Illinois	27,362	4.8%
5	Florida	25,524	4.4%
6	Ohio	20,637	3.6%
7	Louisiana	17,079	3.0%
8	New Jersey	16,801	2.9%
9	Georgia	15,471	2.7%
10	Michigan	14,435	2.5%
11	Missouri	13,660	2.4%
12	North Carolina	11,403	2.0%
13	Maryland	11,078	1.9%
14	Pennsylvania	10,679	1.9%
15	Indiana	10,566	1.8%
16	Arizona	10,175	1.8%
17	Virginia	10,152	1.8%
18	South Carolina	8,914	1.5%
19	Wisconsin	8,785	1.5%
20	Tennessee	8,770	1.5%
21	Kentucky	7,989	1.4%
22	Alabama	7,750	1.3%
23	Oklahoma	7,297	1.3%
24	Washington	7,151	1.2%
25	Colorado	6,881	1.2%
26	Mississippi	6,670	1.2%
27	Arkansas	6,204	1.1%
28	Iowa	4,798	0.8%
29	Nevada	4,773	0.8%
30	Kansas	4,517	0.8%
31	Minnesota	4,307	0.7%
32	Oregon	3,688	0.6%
33	Hawaii	3,481	0.6%
34	Massachusetts	3,227	0.6%
35	Utah	3,076	0.5%
36	Alaska	2,647	0.5%
37	Idaho	2,621	0.5%
38	New Mexico	2,347	0.4%
39	Connecticut	1,933	0.3%
40	Delaware	1,888	0.3%
41	Nebraska	1,791	0.3%
42	West Virginia	1,444	0.3%
43	South Dakota	1,337	0.2%
44	Montana	1,289	0.2%
45	New Hampshire	1,000	0.2%
46	Rhode Island	991	0.2%
47	Vermont	824	0.1%
48	Maine	795	0.1%
49	North Dakota	765	0.1%
50	Wyoming	757	0.1%
	District of Columbia	7,613	1.3%

Source: U.S. Department of Justice, Bureau of Justice Statistics
    "Correctional Populations in the United States, 1998"
*Preliminary data. Includes sentenced prisoners admitted because of new court commitments, parole violators
returned, escapees returned and others. Does not include 39,188 new federal admissions.

Sentenced Prisoners Admitted to State Correctional Institutions
Through New Court Commitments in 1998
National Total = 347,270 New Prisoners*

<u>ALPHA ORDER</u>

RANK	STATE	PRISONERS	% of USA
17	Alabama	6,664	1.9%
36	Alaska	1,612	0.5%
14	Arizona	7,709	2.2%
27	Arkansas	3,732	1.1%
1	California	46,529	13.4%
26	Colorado	4,585	1.3%
43	Connecticut	947	0.3%
41	Delaware	1,118	0.3%
3	Florida	21,937	6.3%
7	Georgia	11,329	3.3%
34	Hawaii	2,003	0.6%
39	Idaho	1,331	0.4%
4	Illinois	19,655	5.7%
10	Indiana	9,495	2.7%
29	Iowa	3,312	1.0%
31	Kansas	2,886	0.8%
22	Kentucky	6,171	1.8%
16	Louisiana	7,367	2.1%
49	Maine	449	0.1%
15	Maryland	7,552	2.2%
33	Massachusetts	2,154	0.6%
12	Michigan	8,024	2.3%
30	Minnesota	3,001	0.9%
23	Mississippi	5,301	1.5%
13	Missouri	7,822	2.3%
45	Montana	638	0.2%
37	Nebraska	1,462	0.4%
28	Nevada	3,617	1.0%
46	New Hampshire	629	0.2%
8	New Jersey	9,938	2.9%
35	New Mexico	1,631	0.5%
5	New York	19,497	5.6%
9	North Carolina	9,582	2.8%
47	North Dakota	613	0.2%
6	Ohio	17,652	5.1%
20	Oklahoma	6,302	1.8%
32	Oregon	2,267	0.7%
18	Pennsylvania	6,650	1.9%
44	Rhode Island	700	0.2%
19	South Carolina	6,521	1.9%
42	South Dakota	1,087	0.3%
24	Tennessee	4,855	1.4%
2	Texas	34,876	10.0%
38	Utah	1,378	0.4%
50	Vermont	211	0.1%
11	Virginia	8,659	2.5%
21	Washington	6,211	1.8%
40	West Virginia	1,259	0.4%
25	Wisconsin	4,790	1.4%
48	Wyoming	461	0.1%

<u>RANK ORDER</u>

RANK	STATE	PRISONERS	% of USA
1	California	46,529	13.4%
2	Texas	34,876	10.0%
3	Florida	21,937	6.3%
4	Illinois	19,655	5.7%
5	New York	19,497	5.6%
6	Ohio	17,652	5.1%
7	Georgia	11,329	3.3%
8	New Jersey	9,938	2.9%
9	North Carolina	9,582	2.8%
10	Indiana	9,495	2.7%
11	Virginia	8,659	2.5%
12	Michigan	8,024	2.3%
13	Missouri	7,822	2.3%
14	Arizona	7,709	2.2%
15	Maryland	7,552	2.2%
16	Louisiana	7,367	2.1%
17	Alabama	6,664	1.9%
18	Pennsylvania	6,650	1.9%
19	South Carolina	6,521	1.9%
20	Oklahoma	6,302	1.8%
21	Washington	6,211	1.8%
22	Kentucky	6,171	1.8%
23	Mississippi	5,301	1.5%
24	Tennessee	4,855	1.4%
25	Wisconsin	4,790	1.4%
26	Colorado	4,585	1.3%
27	Arkansas	3,732	1.1%
28	Nevada	3,617	1.0%
29	Iowa	3,312	1.0%
30	Minnesota	3,001	0.9%
31	Kansas	2,886	0.8%
32	Oregon	2,267	0.7%
33	Massachusetts	2,154	0.6%
34	Hawaii	2,003	0.6%
35	New Mexico	1,631	0.5%
36	Alaska	1,612	0.5%
37	Nebraska	1,462	0.4%
38	Utah	1,378	0.4%
39	Idaho	1,331	0.4%
40	West Virginia	1,259	0.4%
41	Delaware	1,118	0.3%
42	South Dakota	1,087	0.3%
43	Connecticut	947	0.3%
44	Rhode Island	700	0.2%
45	Montana	638	0.2%
46	New Hampshire	629	0.2%
47	North Dakota	613	0.2%
48	Wyoming	461	0.1%
49	Maine	449	0.1%
50	Vermont	211	0.1%
	District of Columbia	3,099	0.9%

Source: U.S. Department of Justice, Bureau of Justice Statistics
"Correctional Populations in the United States, 1998"
Preliminary data. Does not include 34,376 new federal court commitments.

Parole Violators Returned to State Prisons in 1998

National Total = 206,152 Prisoners*

ALPHA ORDER					RANK ORDER			
RANK	STATE	PRISONERS	% of USA		RANK	STATE	PRISONERS	% of USA
34	Alabama	700	0.3%		1	California	87,539	42.5%
29	Alaska	993	0.5%		2	Texas	23,784	11.5%
14	Arizona	2,398	1.2%		3	Louisiana	8,853	4.3%
19	Arkansas	1,694	0.8%		4	New York	7,613	3.7%
1	California	87,539	42.5%		5	New Jersey	6,822	3.3%
17	Colorado	1,951	0.9%		6	Illinois	6,802	3.3%
31	Connecticut	849	0.4%		7	Michigan	4,453	2.2%
39	Delaware	513	0.2%		8	Georgia	4,078	2.0%
15	Florida	2,362	1.1%		9	Missouri	3,965	1.9%
8	Georgia	4,078	2.0%		10	Tennessee	3,836	1.9%
25	Hawaii	1,408	0.7%		11	Pennsylvania	3,665	1.8%
NA	Idaho**	NA	NA		12	Maryland	3,408	1.7%
6	Illinois	6,802	3.3%		13	Ohio	2,961	1.4%
28	Indiana	1,052	0.5%		14	Arizona	2,398	1.2%
37	Iowa	660	0.3%		15	Florida	2,362	1.1%
22	Kansas	1,595	0.8%		16	South Carolina	2,140	1.0%
18	Kentucky	1,700	0.8%		17	Colorado	1,951	0.9%
3	Louisiana	8,853	4.3%		18	Kentucky	1,700	0.8%
43	Maine	303	0.1%		19	Arkansas	1,694	0.8%
12	Maryland	3,408	1.7%		20	Utah	1,683	0.8%
35	Massachusetts	682	0.3%		21	North Carolina	1,681	0.8%
7	Michigan	4,453	2.2%		22	Kansas	1,595	0.8%
26	Minnesota	1,306	0.6%		23	Wisconsin	1,567	0.8%
40	Mississippi	454	0.2%		24	Virginia	1,493	0.7%
9	Missouri	3,965	1.9%		25	Hawaii	1,408	0.7%
38	Montana	616	0.3%		26	Minnesota	1,306	0.6%
42	Nebraska	309	0.1%		27	Oregon	1,271	0.6%
32	Nevada	794	0.4%		28	Indiana	1,052	0.5%
41	New Hampshire	358	0.2%		29	Alaska	993	0.5%
5	New Jersey	6,822	3.3%		30	Oklahoma	879	0.4%
36	New Mexico	671	0.3%		31	Connecticut	849	0.4%
4	New York	7,613	3.7%		32	Nevada	794	0.4%
21	North Carolina	1,681	0.8%		33	Washington	788	0.4%
48	North Dakota	150	0.1%		34	Alabama	700	0.3%
13	Ohio	2,961	1.4%		35	Massachusetts	682	0.3%
30	Oklahoma	879	0.4%		36	New Mexico	671	0.3%
27	Oregon	1,271	0.6%		37	Iowa	660	0.3%
11	Pennsylvania	3,665	1.8%		38	Montana	616	0.3%
45	Rhode Island	270	0.1%		39	Delaware	513	0.2%
16	South Carolina	2,140	1.0%		40	Mississippi	454	0.2%
46	South Dakota	208	0.1%		41	New Hampshire	358	0.2%
10	Tennessee	3,836	1.9%		42	Nebraska	309	0.1%
2	Texas	23,784	11.5%		43	Maine	303	0.1%
20	Utah	1,683	0.8%		44	Wyoming	287	0.1%
49	Vermont	122	0.1%		45	Rhode Island	270	0.1%
24	Virginia	1,493	0.7%		46	South Dakota	208	0.1%
33	Washington	788	0.4%		47	West Virginia	181	0.1%
47	West Virginia	181	0.1%		48	North Dakota	150	0.1%
23	Wisconsin	1,567	0.8%		49	Vermont	122	0.1%
44	Wyoming	287	0.1%		NA	Idaho**	NA	NA
					District of Columbia		2,285	1.1%

Source: U.S. Department of Justice, Bureau of Justice Statistics
    "Correctional Populations in the United States, 1998"
*Preliminary data. Includes other conditional release violators. Does not include 3,630 federal parole violators returned to prison.
**Not available.

Escapees Returned to State Prisons in 1998

National Total = 7,175 Prisoners*

ALPHA ORDER

RANK	STATE	PRISONERS	% of USA
7	Alabama	217	3.0%
24	Alaska	40	0.6%
31	Arizona	15	0.2%
32	Arkansas	14	0.2%
8	California	209	2.9%
6	Colorado	322	4.5%
11	Connecticut	131	1.8%
25	Delaware	33	0.5%
9	Florida	167	2.3%
20	Georgia	51	0.7%
27	Hawaii	26	0.4%
44	Idaho	0	0.0%
3	Illinois	892	12.4%
29	Indiana	17	0.2%
5	Iowa	618	8.6%
36	Kansas	8	0.1%
17	Kentucky	88	1.2%
15	Louisiana	97	1.4%
36	Maine	8	0.1%
14	Maryland	102	1.4%
30	Massachusetts	16	0.2%
2	Michigan	1,067	14.9%
44	Minnesota	0	0.0%
23	Mississippi	44	0.6%
4	Missouri	760	10.6%
25	Montana	33	0.5%
28	Nebraska	20	0.3%
44	Nevada	0	0.0%
33	New Hampshire	13	0.2%
44	New Jersey	0	0.0%
34	New Mexico	10	0.1%
1	New York	1,092	15.2%
13	North Carolina	111	1.5%
43	North Dakota	1	0.0%
39	Ohio	6	0.1%
12	Oklahoma	116	1.6%
20	Oregon	51	0.7%
18	Pennsylvania	72	1.0%
34	Rhode Island	10	0.1%
22	South Carolina	48	0.7%
40	South Dakota	5	0.1%
19	Tennessee	53	0.7%
44	Texas	0	0.0%
38	Utah	7	0.1%
16	Vermont	94	1.3%
44	Virginia	0	0.0%
10	Washington	139	1.9%
42	West Virginia	2	0.0%
44	Wisconsin	0	0.0%
41	Wyoming	3	0.0%

RANK ORDER

RANK	STATE	PRISONERS	% of USA
1	New York	1,092	15.2%
2	Michigan	1,067	14.9%
3	Illinois	892	12.4%
4	Missouri	760	10.6%
5	Iowa	618	8.6%
6	Colorado	322	4.5%
7	Alabama	217	3.0%
8	California	209	2.9%
9	Florida	167	2.3%
10	Washington	139	1.9%
11	Connecticut	131	1.8%
12	Oklahoma	116	1.6%
13	North Carolina	111	1.5%
14	Maryland	102	1.4%
15	Louisiana	97	1.4%
16	Vermont	94	1.3%
17	Kentucky	88	1.2%
18	Pennsylvania	72	1.0%
19	Tennessee	53	0.7%
20	Georgia	51	0.7%
20	Oregon	51	0.7%
22	South Carolina	48	0.7%
23	Mississippi	44	0.6%
24	Alaska	40	0.6%
25	Delaware	33	0.5%
25	Montana	33	0.5%
27	Hawaii	26	0.4%
28	Nebraska	20	0.3%
29	Indiana	17	0.2%
30	Massachusetts	16	0.2%
31	Arizona	15	0.2%
32	Arkansas	14	0.2%
33	New Hampshire	13	0.2%
34	New Mexico	10	0.1%
34	Rhode Island	10	0.1%
36	Kansas	8	0.1%
36	Maine	8	0.1%
38	Utah	7	0.1%
39	Ohio	6	0.1%
40	South Dakota	5	0.1%
41	Wyoming	3	0.0%
42	West Virginia	2	0.0%
43	North Dakota	1	0.0%
44	Idaho	0	0.0%
44	Minnesota	0	0.0%
44	Nevada	0	0.0%
44	New Jersey	0	0.0%
44	Texas	0	0.0%
44	Virginia	0	0.0%
44	Wisconsin	0	0.0%
	District of Columbia	347	4.8%

Source: U.S. Department of Justice, Bureau of Justice Statistics
"Correctional Populations in the United States, 1998"
*Preliminary data. Includes AWOLs returned. Federal data were not reported.

Prisoners Released from State Correctional Institutions in 1998

National Total = 531,312 Prisoners*

ALPHA ORDER

RANK	STATE	PRISONERS	% of USA	RANK	STATE	PRISONERS	% of USA
21	Alabama	7,280	1.4%	1	California	129,800	24.4%
35	Alaska	2,677	0.5%	2	Texas	55,181	10.4%
17	Arizona	8,573	1.6%	3	New York	27,978	5.3%
26	Arkansas	5,579	1.1%	4	Illinois	25,099	4.7%
1	California	129,800	24.4%	5	Florida	22,905	4.3%
25	Colorado	6,030	1.1%	6	Ohio	20,203	3.8%
40	Connecticut	1,660	0.3%	7	Louisiana	14,116	2.7%
39	Delaware	1,941	0.4%	8	New Jersey	14,041	2.6%
5	Florida	22,905	4.3%	9	Michigan	13,327	2.5%
10	Georgia	12,607	2.4%	10	Georgia	12,607	2.4%
33	Hawaii	3,259	0.6%	11	Missouri	12,374	2.3%
37	Idaho	2,486	0.5%	12	North Carolina	11,726	2.2%
4	Illinois	25,099	4.7%	13	Maryland	10,626	2.0%
14	Indiana	9,280	1.7%	14	Indiana	9,280	1.7%
28	Iowa	4,342	0.8%	15	Pennsylvania	9,270	1.7%
29	Kansas	4,245	0.8%	16	Virginia	9,004	1.7%
20	Kentucky	7,602	1.4%	17	Arizona	8,573	1.6%
7	Louisiana	14,116	2.7%	18	South Carolina	7,942	1.5%
50	Maine	606	0.1%	19	Tennessee	7,691	1.4%
13	Maryland	10,626	2.0%	20	Kentucky	7,602	1.4%
32	Massachusetts	3,330	0.6%	21	Alabama	7,280	1.4%
9	Michigan	13,327	2.5%	22	Oklahoma	6,947	1.3%
31	Minnesota	4,056	0.8%	23	Wisconsin	6,464	1.2%
27	Mississippi	4,491	0.8%	24	Washington	6,204	1.2%
11	Missouri	12,374	2.3%	25	Colorado	6,030	1.1%
44	Montana	1,096	0.2%	26	Arkansas	5,579	1.1%
41	Nebraska	1,532	0.3%	27	Mississippi	4,491	0.8%
30	Nevada	4,146	0.8%	28	Iowa	4,342	0.8%
45	New Hampshire	999	0.2%	29	Kansas	4,245	0.8%
8	New Jersey	14,041	2.6%	30	Nevada	4,146	0.8%
38	New Mexico	2,264	0.4%	31	Minnesota	4,056	0.8%
3	New York	27,978	5.3%	32	Massachusetts	3,330	0.6%
12	North Carolina	11,726	2.2%	33	Hawaii	3,259	0.6%
49	North Dakota	646	0.1%	34	Utah	2,954	0.6%
6	Ohio	20,203	3.8%	35	Alaska	2,677	0.5%
22	Oklahoma	6,947	1.3%	35	Oregon	2,677	0.5%
35	Oregon	2,677	0.5%	37	Idaho	2,486	0.5%
15	Pennsylvania	9,270	1.7%	38	New Mexico	2,264	0.4%
46	Rhode Island	916	0.2%	39	Delaware	1,941	0.4%
18	South Carolina	7,942	1.5%	40	Connecticut	1,660	0.3%
42	South Dakota	1,162	0.2%	41	Nebraska	1,532	0.3%
19	Tennessee	7,691	1.4%	42	South Dakota	1,162	0.2%
2	Texas	55,181	10.4%	43	West Virginia	1,114	0.2%
34	Utah	2,954	0.6%	44	Montana	1,096	0.2%
48	Vermont	695	0.1%	45	New Hampshire	999	0.2%
16	Virginia	9,004	1.7%	46	Rhode Island	916	0.2%
24	Washington	6,204	1.2%	47	Wyoming	735	0.1%
43	West Virginia	1,114	0.2%	48	Vermont	695	0.1%
23	Wisconsin	6,464	1.2%	49	North Dakota	646	0.1%
47	Wyoming	735	0.1%	50	Maine	606	0.1%
					District of Columbia	9,434	1.8%

RANK ORDER

Source: U.S. Department of Justice, Bureau of Justice Statistics
   "Correctional Populations in the United States, 1998"
*Preliminary data. Includes conditional releases, unconditional releases, escapees, out on appeal, deaths and
other releases. Does not include 29,708 federal prisoners released.

State Prisoners Released with Conditions in 1998

National Total = 403,902 Prisoners*

ALPHA ORDER				RANK ORDER			
RANK	STATE	PRISONERS	% of USA	RANK	STATE	PRISONERS	% of USA
20	Alabama	4,420	1.1%	1	California	122,094	30.2%
36	Alaska	1,862	0.5%	2	Texas	40,550	10.0%
15	Arizona	6,917	1.7%	3	New York	24,197	6.0%
18	Arkansas	4,854	1.2%	4	Illinois	22,662	5.6%
1	California	122,094	30.2%	5	Louisiana	13,179	3.3%
21	Colorado	4,387	1.1%	6	Ohio	11,643	2.9%
38	Connecticut	1,104	0.3%	7	Missouri	10,636	2.6%
48	Delaware	454	0.1%	8	Michigan	10,500	2.6%
11	Florida	8,674	2.1%	9	New Jersey	9,654	2.4%
13	Georgia	8,602	2.1%	10	Maryland	9,205	2.3%
35	Hawaii	2,042	0.5%	11	Florida	8,674	2.1%
34	Idaho	2,127	0.5%	12	Indiana	8,603	2.1%
4	Illinois	22,662	5.6%	13	Georgia	8,602	2.1%
12	Indiana	8,603	2.1%	14	Pennsylvania	7,285	1.8%
28	Iowa	3,366	0.8%	15	Arizona	6,917	1.7%
25	Kansas	3,910	1.0%	16	North Carolina	6,560	1.6%
26	Kentucky	3,739	0.9%	17	Tennessee	5,288	1.3%
5	Louisiana	13,179	3.3%	18	Arkansas	4,854	1.2%
50	Maine	352	0.1%	19	Wisconsin	4,523	1.1%
10	Maryland	9,205	2.3%	20	Alabama	4,420	1.1%
39	Massachusetts	953	0.2%	21	Colorado	4,387	1.1%
8	Michigan	10,500	2.6%	22	Virginia	4,193	1.0%
27	Minnesota	3,544	0.9%	23	South Carolina	4,134	1.0%
33	Mississippi	2,193	0.5%	24	Washington	3,983	1.0%
7	Missouri	10,636	2.6%	25	Kansas	3,910	1.0%
41	Montana	839	0.2%	26	Kentucky	3,739	0.9%
44	Nebraska	702	0.2%	27	Minnesota	3,544	0.9%
32	Nevada	2,255	0.6%	28	Iowa	3,366	0.8%
43	New Hampshire	768	0.2%	29	Oklahoma	3,104	0.8%
9	New Jersey	9,654	2.4%	30	Utah	2,673	0.7%
37	New Mexico	1,421	0.4%	31	Oregon	2,584	0.6%
3	New York	24,197	6.0%	32	Nevada	2,255	0.6%
16	North Carolina	6,560	1.6%	33	Mississippi	2,193	0.5%
47	North Dakota	499	0.1%	34	Idaho	2,127	0.5%
6	Ohio	11,643	2.9%	35	Hawaii	2,042	0.5%
29	Oklahoma	3,104	0.8%	36	Alaska	1,862	0.5%
31	Oregon	2,584	0.6%	37	New Mexico	1,421	0.4%
14	Pennsylvania	7,285	1.8%	38	Connecticut	1,104	0.3%
40	Rhode Island	877	0.2%	39	Massachusetts	953	0.2%
23	South Carolina	4,134	1.0%	40	Rhode Island	877	0.2%
42	South Dakota	793	0.2%	41	Montana	839	0.2%
17	Tennessee	5,288	1.3%	42	South Dakota	793	0.2%
2	Texas	40,550	10.0%	43	New Hampshire	768	0.2%
30	Utah	2,673	0.7%	44	Nebraska	702	0.2%
46	Vermont	608	0.2%	45	West Virginia	686	0.2%
22	Virginia	4,193	1.0%	46	Vermont	608	0.2%
24	Washington	3,983	1.0%	47	North Dakota	499	0.1%
45	West Virginia	686	0.2%	48	Delaware	454	0.1%
19	Wisconsin	4,523	1.1%	49	Wyoming	420	0.1%
49	Wyoming	420	0.1%	50	Maine	352	0.1%
					District of Columbia	3,284	0.8%

Source: U.S. Department of Justice, Bureau of Justice Statistics
"Correctional Populations in the United States, 1998"
*Preliminary data. Released on parole, probation, supervised mandatory release or other conditions. Does not include 2,148 federal prisoners released with conditions.

State Prisoners Released Conditionally as a Percent of All Releases in 1998

National Percent = 76.0% of Prisoners Released*

ALPHA ORDER

RANK	STATE	PERCENT
36	Alabama	60.7
26	Alaska	69.6
16	Arizona	80.7
11	Arkansas	87.0
3	California	94.1
24	Colorado	72.8
31	Connecticut	66.5
50	Delaware	23.4
48	Florida	37.9
29	Georgia	68.2
34	Hawaii	62.7
15	Idaho	85.6
8	Illinois	90.3
5	Indiana	92.7
19	Iowa	77.5
6	Kansas	92.1
43	Kentucky	49.2
4	Louisiana	93.4
37	Maine	58.1
12	Maryland	86.6
49	Massachusetts	28.6
17	Michigan	78.8
10	Minnesota	87.4
44	Mississippi	48.8
14	Missouri	86.0
22	Montana	76.6
46	Nebraska	45.8
41	Nevada	54.4
21	New Hampshire	76.9
27	New Jersey	68.8
33	New Mexico	62.8
13	New York	86.5
40	North Carolina	55.9
20	North Dakota	77.2
38	Ohio	57.6
47	Oklahoma	44.7
1	Oregon	96.5
18	Pennsylvania	78.6
2	Rhode Island	95.7
42	South Carolina	52.1
29	South Dakota	68.2
27	Tennessee	68.8
23	Texas	73.5
7	Utah	90.5
9	Vermont	87.5
45	Virginia	46.6
32	Washington	64.2
35	West Virginia	61.6
25	Wisconsin	70.0
39	Wyoming	57.1

RANK ORDER

RANK	STATE	PERCENT
1	Oregon	96.5
2	Rhode Island	95.7
3	California	94.1
4	Louisiana	93.4
5	Indiana	92.7
6	Kansas	92.1
7	Utah	90.5
8	Illinois	90.3
9	Vermont	87.5
10	Minnesota	87.4
11	Arkansas	87.0
12	Maryland	86.6
13	New York	86.5
14	Missouri	86.0
15	Idaho	85.6
16	Arizona	80.7
17	Michigan	78.8
18	Pennsylvania	78.6
19	Iowa	77.5
20	North Dakota	77.2
21	New Hampshire	76.9
22	Montana	76.6
23	Texas	73.5
24	Colorado	72.8
25	Wisconsin	70.0
26	Alaska	69.6
27	New Jersey	68.8
27	Tennessee	68.8
29	Georgia	68.2
29	South Dakota	68.2
31	Connecticut	66.5
32	Washington	64.2
33	New Mexico	62.8
34	Hawaii	62.7
35	West Virginia	61.6
36	Alabama	60.7
37	Maine	58.1
38	Ohio	57.6
39	Wyoming	57.1
40	North Carolina	55.9
41	Nevada	54.4
42	South Carolina	52.1
43	Kentucky	49.2
44	Mississippi	48.8
45	Virginia	46.6
46	Nebraska	45.8
47	Oklahoma	44.7
48	Florida	37.9
49	Massachusetts	28.6
50	Delaware	23.4

District of Columbia 34.8

Source: Morgan Quitno Press using data from U.S. Department of Justice, Bureau of Justice Statistics
"Correctional Populations in the United States, 1998"
*Preliminary data. Released on parole, probation, supervised mandatory release or other conditions. Does not include federal prisoners released with conditions. Federal percent is 7.2% of releases. The combined state and federal percent is 72.4% of prisoners released are released with conditions.

State Prisoners Released on Parole in 1998

National Total = 135,138 Prisoners*

ALPHA ORDER				RANK ORDER			
RANK	STATE	PRISONERS	% of USA	RANK	STATE	PRISONERS	% of USA
14	Alabama	2,688	2.0%	1	New York	18,367	13.6%
43	Alaska	80	0.1%	2	Texas	13,037	9.6%
35	Arizona	600	0.4%	3	Michigan	10,500	7.8%
10	Arkansas	4,428	3.3%	4	New Jersey	8,821	6.5%
49	California	0	0.0%	5	Pennsylvania	7,285	5.4%
13	Colorado	3,011	2.2%	6	Georgia	7,195	5.3%
41	Connecticut	211	0.2%	7	North Carolina	6,560	4.9%
46	Delaware	26	0.0%	8	Ohio	5,656	4.2%
42	Florida	160	0.1%	9	Missouri	4,828	3.6%
6	Georgia	7,195	5.3%	10	Arkansas	4,428	3.3%
29	Hawaii	852	0.6%	11	Kansas	3,691	2.7%
26	Idaho	988	0.7%	12	Maryland	3,352	2.5%
45	Illinois	32	0.0%	13	Colorado	3,011	2.2%
49	Indiana	0	0.0%	14	Alabama	2,688	2.0%
22	Iowa	1,729	1.3%	15	South Carolina	2,687	2.0%
11	Kansas	3,691	2.7%	16	Utah	2,673	2.0%
18	Kentucky	2,611	1.9%	17	Tennessee	2,626	1.9%
27	Louisiana	978	0.7%	18	Kentucky	2,611	1.9%
48	Maine	3	0.0%	19	Wisconsin	2,609	1.9%
12	Maryland	3,352	2.5%	20	Oregon	2,386	1.8%
28	Massachusetts	953	0.7%	21	Nevada	2,255	1.7%
3	Michigan	10,500	7.8%	22	Iowa	1,729	1.3%
47	Minnesota	10	0.0%	23	New Mexico	1,420	1.1%
25	Mississippi	1,084	0.8%	24	Virginia	1,356	1.0%
9	Missouri	4,828	3.6%	25	Mississippi	1,084	0.8%
34	Montana	634	0.5%	26	Idaho	988	0.7%
30	Nebraska	702	0.5%	27	Louisiana	978	0.7%
21	Nevada	2,255	1.7%	28	Massachusetts	953	0.7%
33	New Hampshire	636	0.5%	29	Hawaii	852	0.6%
4	New Jersey	8,821	6.5%	30	Nebraska	702	0.5%
23	New Mexico	1,420	1.1%	31	South Dakota	688	0.5%
1	New York	18,367	13.6%	32	West Virginia	664	0.5%
7	North Carolina	6,560	4.9%	33	New Hampshire	636	0.5%
39	North Dakota	285	0.2%	34	Montana	634	0.5%
8	Ohio	5,656	4.2%	35	Arizona	600	0.4%
37	Oklahoma	317	0.2%	36	Rhode Island	427	0.3%
20	Oregon	2,386	1.8%	37	Oklahoma	317	0.2%
5	Pennsylvania	7,285	5.4%	38	Wyoming	311	0.2%
36	Rhode Island	427	0.3%	39	North Dakota	285	0.2%
15	South Carolina	2,687	2.0%	40	Vermont	231	0.2%
31	South Dakota	688	0.5%	41	Connecticut	211	0.2%
17	Tennessee	2,626	1.9%	42	Florida	160	0.1%
2	Texas	13,037	9.6%	43	Alaska	80	0.1%
16	Utah	2,673	2.0%	44	Washington	63	0.0%
40	Vermont	231	0.2%	45	Illinois	32	0.0%
24	Virginia	1,356	1.0%	46	Delaware	26	0.0%
44	Washington	63	0.0%	47	Minnesota	10	0.0%
32	West Virginia	664	0.5%	48	Maine	3	0.0%
19	Wisconsin	2,609	1.9%	49	California	0	0.0%
38	Wyoming	311	0.2%	49	Indiana	0	0.0%
					District of Columbia	2,432	1.8%

Source: U.S. Department of Justice, Bureau of Justice Statistics
   "Correctional Populations in the United States, 1998"
*Preliminary data. Does not include 1,328 federal prisoners released on parole.

State Prisoners Released on Probation in 1998

National Total = 37,085 Prisoners*

ALPHA ORDER					RANK ORDER			
RANK	STATE	PRISONERS	% of USA		RANK	STATE	PRISONERS	% of USA
8	Alabama	1,644	4.4%		1	Texas	7,649	20.6%
11	Alaska	1,156	3.1%		2	Indiana	4,290	11.6%
27	Arizona	30	0.1%		3	Florida	3,898	10.5%
30	Arkansas	0	0.0%		4	Missouri	3,647	9.8%
30	California	0	0.0%		5	Oklahoma	2,532	6.8%
18	Colorado	215	0.6%		6	Ohio	1,990	5.4%
30	Connecticut	0	0.0%		7	Tennessee	1,791	4.8%
30	Delaware	0	0.0%		8	Alabama	1,644	4.4%
3	Florida	3,898	10.5%		9	South Carolina	1,424	3.8%
25	Georgia	42	0.1%		10	Hawaii	1,186	3.2%
10	Hawaii	1,186	3.2%		11	Alaska	1,156	3.1%
12	Idaho	1,139	3.1%		12	Idaho	1,139	3.1%
30	Illinois	0	0.0%		13	Kentucky	1,128	3.0%
2	Indiana	4,290	11.6%		14	Mississippi	1,109	3.0%
15	Iowa	694	1.9%		15	Iowa	694	1.9%
23	Kansas	59	0.2%		16	Rhode Island	444	1.2%
13	Kentucky	1,128	3.0%		17	Maine	311	0.8%
24	Louisiana	43	0.1%		18	Colorado	215	0.6%
17	Maine	311	0.8%		19	North Dakota	206	0.6%
30	Maryland	0	0.0%		20	Montana	205	0.6%
30	Massachusetts	0	0.0%		21	Wyoming	109	0.3%
30	Michigan	0	0.0%		22	New Hampshire	89	0.2%
30	Minnesota	0	0.0%		23	Kansas	59	0.2%
14	Mississippi	1,109	3.0%		24	Louisiana	43	0.1%
4	Missouri	3,647	9.8%		25	Georgia	42	0.1%
20	Montana	205	0.6%		26	Vermont	32	0.1%
30	Nebraska	0	0.0%		27	Arizona	30	0.1%
30	Nevada	0	0.0%		28	West Virginia	22	0.1%
22	New Hampshire	89	0.2%		29	New Mexico	1	0.0%
30	New Jersey	0	0.0%		30	Arkansas	0	0.0%
29	New Mexico	1	0.0%		30	California	0	0.0%
30	New York	0	0.0%		30	Connecticut	0	0.0%
30	North Carolina	0	0.0%		30	Delaware	0	0.0%
19	North Dakota	206	0.6%		30	Illinois	0	0.0%
6	Ohio	1,990	5.4%		30	Maryland	0	0.0%
5	Oklahoma	2,532	6.8%		30	Massachusetts	0	0.0%
30	Oregon	0	0.0%		30	Michigan	0	0.0%
30	Pennsylvania	0	0.0%		30	Minnesota	0	0.0%
16	Rhode Island	444	1.2%		30	Nebraska	0	0.0%
9	South Carolina	1,424	3.8%		30	Nevada	0	0.0%
30	South Dakota	0	0.0%		30	New Jersey	0	0.0%
7	Tennessee	1,791	4.8%		30	New York	0	0.0%
1	Texas	7,649	20.6%		30	North Carolina	0	0.0%
30	Utah	0	0.0%		30	Oregon	0	0.0%
26	Vermont	32	0.1%		30	Pennsylvania	0	0.0%
30	Virginia	0	0.0%		30	South Dakota	0	0.0%
30	Washington	0	0.0%		30	Utah	0	0.0%
28	West Virginia	22	0.1%		30	Virginia	0	0.0%
30	Wisconsin	0	0.0%		30	Washington	0	0.0%
21	Wyoming	109	0.3%		30	Wisconsin	0	0.0%
						District of Columbia	0	0.0%

Source: U.S. Department of Justice, Bureau of Justice Statistics
   "Correctional Populations in the United States, 1998"
*Preliminary data. Does not include 79 federal prisoners released on probation.

State Prisoners Released on Supervised Mandatory Release in 1998

National Total = 210,394 Prisoners*

ALPHA ORDER

RANK	STATE	PRISONERS	% of USA
18	Alabama	0	0.0%
15	Alaska	327	0.2%
17	Arizona	65	0.0%
18	Arkansas	0	0.0%
1	California	122,094	58.0%
13	Colorado	1,161	0.6%
18	Connecticut	0	0.0%
14	Delaware	428	0.2%
18	Florida	0	0.0%
18	Georgia	0	0.0%
18	Hawaii	0	0.0%
18	Idaho	0	0.0%
2	Illinois	22,630	10.8%
7	Indiana	4,313	2.0%
18	Iowa	0	0.0%
18	Kansas	0	0.0%
18	Kentucky	0	0.0%
4	Louisiana	12,158	5.8%
18	Maine	0	0.0%
5	Maryland	5,845	2.8%
18	Massachusetts	0	0.0%
18	Michigan	0	0.0%
11	Minnesota	2,738	1.3%
18	Mississippi	0	0.0%
18	Missouri	0	0.0%
18	Montana	0	0.0%
18	Nebraska	0	0.0%
18	Nevada	0	0.0%
18	New Hampshire	0	0.0%
18	New Jersey	0	0.0%
18	New Mexico	0	0.0%
6	New York	5,830	2.8%
18	North Carolina	0	0.0%
18	North Dakota	0	0.0%
8	Ohio	3,997	1.9%
18	Oklahoma	0	0.0%
18	Oregon	0	0.0%
18	Pennsylvania	0	0.0%
18	Rhode Island	0	0.0%
18	South Carolina	0	0.0%
16	South Dakota	105	0.0%
18	Tennessee	0	0.0%
3	Texas	19,864	9.4%
18	Utah	0	0.0%
18	Vermont	0	0.0%
10	Virginia	2,837	1.3%
9	Washington	3,920	1.9%
18	West Virginia	0	0.0%
12	Wisconsin	1,913	0.9%
18	Wyoming	0	0.0%

RANK ORDER

RANK	STATE	PRISONERS	% of USA
1	California	122,094	58.0%
2	Illinois	22,630	10.8%
3	Texas	19,864	9.4%
4	Louisiana	12,158	5.8%
5	Maryland	5,845	2.8%
6	New York	5,830	2.8%
7	Indiana	4,313	2.0%
8	Ohio	3,997	1.9%
9	Washington	3,920	1.9%
10	Virginia	2,837	1.3%
11	Minnesota	2,738	1.3%
12	Wisconsin	1,913	0.9%
13	Colorado	1,161	0.6%
14	Delaware	428	0.2%
15	Alaska	327	0.2%
16	South Dakota	105	0.0%
17	Arizona	65	0.0%
18	Alabama	0	0.0%
18	Arkansas	0	0.0%
18	Connecticut	0	0.0%
18	Florida	0	0.0%
18	Georgia	0	0.0%
18	Hawaii	0	0.0%
18	Idaho	0	0.0%
18	Iowa	0	0.0%
18	Kansas	0	0.0%
18	Kentucky	0	0.0%
18	Maine	0	0.0%
18	Massachusetts	0	0.0%
18	Michigan	0	0.0%
18	Mississippi	0	0.0%
18	Missouri	0	0.0%
18	Montana	0	0.0%
18	Nebraska	0	0.0%
18	Nevada	0	0.0%
18	New Hampshire	0	0.0%
18	New Jersey	0	0.0%
18	New Mexico	0	0.0%
18	North Carolina	0	0.0%
18	North Dakota	0	0.0%
18	Oklahoma	0	0.0%
18	Oregon	0	0.0%
18	Pennsylvania	0	0.0%
18	Rhode Island	0	0.0%
18	South Carolina	0	0.0%
18	Tennessee	0	0.0%
18	Utah	0	0.0%
18	Vermont	0	0.0%
18	West Virginia	0	0.0%
18	Wyoming	0	0.0%
	District of Columbia	169	0.1%

Source: U.S. Department of Justice, Bureau of Justice Statistics
"Correctional Populations in the United States, 1998"
*Preliminary data. Does not include 741 federal prisoners released on supervised mandatory release.

State Prisoners Released Unconditionally in 1998

National Total = 102,147 Prisoners*

ALPHA ORDER					RANK ORDER			
RANK	STATE	PRISONERS	% of USA		RANK	STATE	PRISONERS	% of USA
12	Alabama	2,375	2.3%		1	Florida	13,504	13.2%
29	Alaska	746	0.7%		2	Texas	12,922	12.7%
21	Arizona	1,268	1.2%		3	Ohio	8,372	8.2%
33	Arkansas	584	0.6%		4	North Carolina	5,007	4.9%
11	California	2,603	2.5%		5	Virginia	4,743	4.6%
24	Colorado	1,103	1.1%		6	New Jersey	4,116	4.0%
41	Connecticut	238	0.2%		7	Oklahoma	3,685	3.6%
26	Delaware	911	0.9%		8	Kentucky	3,629	3.6%
1	Florida	13,504	13.2%		9	South Carolina	3,488	3.4%
10	Georgia	3,431	3.4%		10	Georgia	3,431	3.4%
45	Hawaii	205	0.2%		11	California	2,603	2.5%
37	Idaho	331	0.3%		12	Alabama	2,375	2.3%
20	Illinois	1,409	1.4%		13	Mississippi	2,170	2.1%
32	Indiana	614	0.6%		14	Tennessee	2,168	2.1%
28	Iowa	748	0.7%		15	Washington	2,037	2.0%
38	Kansas	301	0.3%		16	Massachusetts	1,923	1.9%
8	Kentucky	3,629	3.6%		17	Nevada	1,862	1.8%
31	Louisiana	671	0.7%		18	New York	1,648	1.6%
42	Maine	229	0.2%		19	Pennsylvania	1,608	1.6%
22	Maryland	1,225	1.2%		20	Illinois	1,409	1.4%
16	Massachusetts	1,923	1.9%		21	Arizona	1,268	1.2%
23	Michigan	1,174	1.1%		22	Maryland	1,225	1.2%
34	Minnesota	504	0.5%		23	Michigan	1,174	1.1%
13	Mississippi	2,170	2.1%		24	Colorado	1,103	1.1%
25	Missouri	1,036	1.0%		25	Missouri	1,036	1.0%
43	Montana	216	0.2%		26	Delaware	911	0.9%
27	Nebraska	809	0.8%		27	Nebraska	809	0.8%
17	Nevada	1,862	1.8%		28	Iowa	748	0.7%
44	New Hampshire	206	0.2%		29	Alaska	746	0.7%
6	New Jersey	4,116	4.0%		30	New Mexico	712	0.7%
30	New Mexico	712	0.7%		31	Louisiana	671	0.7%
18	New York	1,648	1.6%		32	Indiana	614	0.6%
4	North Carolina	5,007	4.9%		33	Arkansas	584	0.6%
47	North Dakota	140	0.1%		34	Minnesota	504	0.5%
3	Ohio	8,372	8.2%		35	West Virginia	410	0.4%
7	Oklahoma	3,685	3.6%		36	South Dakota	356	0.3%
50	Oregon	4	0.0%		37	Idaho	331	0.3%
19	Pennsylvania	1,608	1.6%		38	Kansas	301	0.3%
49	Rhode Island	6	0.0%		39	Wyoming	277	0.3%
9	South Carolina	3,488	3.4%		40	Utah	253	0.2%
36	South Dakota	356	0.3%		41	Connecticut	238	0.2%
14	Tennessee	2,168	2.1%		42	Maine	229	0.2%
2	Texas	12,922	12.7%		43	Montana	216	0.2%
40	Utah	253	0.2%		44	New Hampshire	206	0.2%
48	Vermont	81	0.1%		45	Hawaii	205	0.2%
5	Virginia	4,743	4.6%		46	Wisconsin	195	0.2%
15	Washington	2,037	2.0%		47	North Dakota	140	0.1%
35	West Virginia	410	0.4%		48	Vermont	81	0.1%
46	Wisconsin	195	0.2%		49	Rhode Island	6	0.0%
39	Wyoming	277	0.3%		50	Oregon	4	0.0%
						District of Columbia	3,894	3.8%

Source: U.S. Department of Justice, Bureau of Justice Statistics
   "Correctional Populations in the United States, 1998"
*Preliminary data. Does not include 23,939 federal prisoners released without conditions.

State Prisoners Released Unconditionally as a Percent of All Releases in 1998

National Percent = 19.2% of Released Prisoners*

RANK	STATE (Alpha Order)	PERCENT		RANK	STATE (Rank Order)	PERCENT
17	Alabama	32.6		1	Florida	59.0
22	Alaska	27.9		2	Massachusetts	57.7
31	Arizona	14.8		3	Oklahoma	53.0
37	Arkansas	10.5		4	Nebraska	52.8
48	California	2.0		5	Virginia	52.7
28	Colorado	18.3		6	Mississippi	48.3
32	Connecticut	14.3		7	Kentucky	47.7
8	Delaware	46.9		8	Delaware	46.9
1	Florida	59.0		9	Nevada	44.9
23	Georgia	27.2		10	South Carolina	43.9
43	Hawaii	6.3		11	North Carolina	42.7
33	Idaho	13.3		12	Ohio	41.4
45	Illinois	5.6		13	Maine	37.8
42	Indiana	6.6		14	Wyoming	37.7
30	Iowa	17.2		15	West Virginia	36.8
41	Kansas	7.1		16	Washington	32.8
7	Kentucky	47.7		17	Alabama	32.6
46	Louisiana	4.8		18	New Mexico	31.4
13	Maine	37.8		19	South Dakota	30.6
36	Maryland	11.5		20	New Jersey	29.3
2	Massachusetts	57.7		21	Tennessee	28.2
38	Michigan	8.8		22	Alaska	27.9
34	Minnesota	12.4		23	Georgia	27.2
6	Mississippi	48.3		24	Texas	23.4
40	Missouri	8.4		25	North Dakota	21.7
27	Montana	19.7		26	New Hampshire	20.6
4	Nebraska	52.8		27	Montana	19.7
9	Nevada	44.9		28	Colorado	18.3
26	New Hampshire	20.6		29	Pennsylvania	17.3
20	New Jersey	29.3		30	Iowa	17.2
18	New Mexico	31.4		31	Arizona	14.8
44	New York	5.9		32	Connecticut	14.3
11	North Carolina	42.7		33	Idaho	13.3
25	North Dakota	21.7		34	Minnesota	12.4
12	Ohio	41.4		35	Vermont	11.7
3	Oklahoma	53.0		36	Maryland	11.5
50	Oregon	0.1		37	Arkansas	10.5
29	Pennsylvania	17.3		38	Michigan	8.8
49	Rhode Island	0.7		39	Utah	8.6
10	South Carolina	43.9		40	Missouri	8.4
19	South Dakota	30.6		41	Kansas	7.1
21	Tennessee	28.2		42	Indiana	6.6
24	Texas	23.4		43	Hawaii	6.3
39	Utah	8.6		44	New York	5.9
35	Vermont	11.7		45	Illinois	5.6
5	Virginia	52.7		46	Louisiana	4.8
16	Washington	32.8		47	Wisconsin	3.0
15	West Virginia	36.8		48	California	2.0
47	Wisconsin	3.0		49	Rhode Island	0.7
14	Wyoming	37.7		50	Oregon	0.1
					District of Columbia	41.3

Source: Morgan Quitno Press using data from U.S. Department of Justice, Bureau of Justice Statistics
"Correctional Populations in the United States, 1998"
*Preliminary data. Does not include federal prisoners released without conditions. Federal percent is 80.6% of releases. The combined state and federal percent is 22.5% of prisoners released are released without conditions.

State Prisoners Released on Appeal or Bond in 1998

National Total = 797 Prisoners*

ALPHA ORDER

RANK ORDER

RANK	STATE	PRISONERS	% of USA
5	Alabama	86	10.8%
21	Alaska	3	0.4%
30	Arizona	0	0.0%
8	Arkansas	40	5.0%
30	California	0	0.0%
12	Colorado	14	1.8%
26	Connecticut	1	0.1%
30	Delaware	0	0.0%
26	Florida	1	0.1%
30	Georgia	0	0.0%
1	Hawaii	125	15.7%
30	Idaho	0	0.0%
13	Illinois	11	1.4%
30	Indiana	0	0.0%
6	Iowa	56	7.0%
15	Kansas	7	0.9%
30	Kentucky	0	0.0%
30	Louisiana	0	0.0%
18	Maine	4	0.5%
30	Maryland	0	0.0%
30	Massachusetts	0	0.0%
2	Michigan	105	13.2%
30	Minnesota	0	0.0%
30	Mississippi	0	0.0%
9	Missouri	20	2.5%
18	Montana	4	0.5%
30	Nebraska	0	0.0%
24	Nevada	2	0.3%
30	New Hampshire	0	0.0%
4	New Jersey	102	12.8%
26	New Mexico	1	0.1%
2	New York	105	13.2%
30	North Carolina	0	0.0%
17	North Dakota	5	0.6%
7	Ohio	43	5.4%
30	Oklahoma	0	0.0%
15	Oregon	7	0.9%
18	Pennsylvania	4	0.5%
21	Rhode Island	3	0.4%
13	South Carolina	11	1.4%
26	South Dakota	1	0.1%
30	Tennessee	0	0.0%
30	Texas	0	0.0%
10	Utah	16	2.0%
30	Vermont	0	0.0%
30	Virginia	0	0.0%
11	Washington	15	1.9%
24	West Virginia	2	0.3%
30	Wisconsin	0	0.0%
21	Wyoming	3	0.4%

RANK	STATE	PRISONERS	% of USA
1	Hawaii	125	15.7%
2	Michigan	105	13.2%
2	New York	105	13.2%
4	New Jersey	102	12.8%
5	Alabama	86	10.8%
6	Iowa	56	7.0%
7	Ohio	43	5.4%
8	Arkansas	40	5.0%
9	Missouri	20	2.5%
10	Utah	16	2.0%
11	Washington	15	1.9%
12	Colorado	14	1.8%
13	Illinois	11	1.4%
13	South Carolina	11	1.4%
15	Kansas	7	0.9%
15	Oregon	7	0.9%
17	North Dakota	5	0.6%
18	Maine	4	0.5%
18	Montana	4	0.5%
18	Pennsylvania	4	0.5%
21	Alaska	3	0.4%
21	Rhode Island	3	0.4%
21	Wyoming	3	0.4%
24	Nevada	2	0.3%
24	West Virginia	2	0.3%
26	Connecticut	1	0.1%
26	Florida	1	0.1%
26	New Mexico	1	0.1%
26	South Dakota	1	0.1%
30	Arizona	0	0.0%
30	California	0	0.0%
30	Delaware	0	0.0%
30	Georgia	0	0.0%
30	Idaho	0	0.0%
30	Indiana	0	0.0%
30	Kentucky	0	0.0%
30	Louisiana	0	0.0%
30	Maryland	0	0.0%
30	Massachusetts	0	0.0%
30	Minnesota	0	0.0%
30	Mississippi	0	0.0%
30	Nebraska	0	0.0%
30	New Hampshire	0	0.0%
30	North Carolina	0	0.0%
30	Oklahoma	0	0.0%
30	Tennessee	0	0.0%
30	Texas	0	0.0%
30	Vermont	0	0.0%
30	Virginia	0	0.0%
30	Wisconsin	0	0.0%
	District of Columbia	0	0.0%

Source: U.S. Department of Justice, Bureau of Justice Statistics
"Correctional Populations in the United States, 1998"
Preliminary data. Numbers of federal prisoners released on appeal or bond were not available.

State Prisoners Escaped in 1998

National Total = 6,530 Prisoners*

ALPHA ORDER					RANK ORDER			
RANK	STATE	PRISONERS	% of USA		RANK	STATE	PRISONERS	% of USA
7	Alabama	221	3.4%		1	Michigan	1,249	19.1%
21	Alaska	41	0.6%		2	New York	1,117	17.1%
32	Arizona	10	0.2%		3	Illinois	894	13.7%
29	Arkansas	13	0.2%		4	Missouri	622	9.5%
6	California	319	4.9%		5	Colorado	347	5.3%
5	Colorado	347	5.3%		6	California	319	4.9%
14	Connecticut	94	1.4%		7	Alabama	221	3.4%
44	Delaware	0	0.0%		8	Florida	144	2.2%
8	Florida	144	2.2%		9	Washington	123	1.9%
20	Georgia	47	0.7%		10	Maryland	118	1.8%
23	Hawaii	27	0.4%		11	North Carolina	111	1.7%
25	Idaho	17	0.3%		12	Louisiana	103	1.6%
3	Illinois	894	13.7%		13	Oklahoma	101	1.5%
25	Indiana	17	0.3%		14	Connecticut	94	1.4%
39	Iowa	3	0.0%		15	Kentucky	93	1.4%
34	Kansas	6	0.1%		16	Mississippi	73	1.1%
15	Kentucky	93	1.4%		17	Pennsylvania	72	1.1%
12	Louisiana	103	1.6%		18	Oregon	64	1.0%
34	Maine	6	0.1%		19	Tennessee	63	1.0%
10	Maryland	118	1.8%		20	Georgia	47	0.7%
27	Massachusetts	16	0.2%		21	Alaska	41	0.6%
1	Michigan	1,249	19.1%		22	South Carolina	39	0.6%
44	Minnesota	0	0.0%		23	Hawaii	27	0.4%
16	Mississippi	73	1.1%		24	Montana	20	0.3%
4	Missouri	622	9.5%		25	Idaho	17	0.3%
24	Montana	20	0.3%		25	Indiana	17	0.3%
27	Nebraska	16	0.2%		27	Massachusetts	16	0.2%
44	Nevada	0	0.0%		27	Nebraska	16	0.2%
29	New Hampshire	13	0.2%		29	Arkansas	13	0.2%
44	New Jersey	0	0.0%		29	New Hampshire	13	0.2%
42	New Mexico	1	0.0%		31	West Virginia	11	0.2%
2	New York	1,117	17.1%		32	Arizona	10	0.2%
11	North Carolina	111	1.7%		33	Utah	7	0.1%
42	North Dakota	1	0.0%		34	Kansas	6	0.1%
38	Ohio	4	0.1%		34	Maine	6	0.1%
13	Oklahoma	101	1.5%		34	Rhode Island	6	0.1%
18	Oregon	64	1.0%		34	South Dakota	6	0.1%
17	Pennsylvania	72	1.1%		38	Ohio	4	0.1%
34	Rhode Island	6	0.1%		39	Iowa	3	0.0%
22	South Carolina	39	0.6%		39	Virginia	3	0.0%
34	South Dakota	6	0.1%		39	Wyoming	3	0.0%
19	Tennessee	63	1.0%		42	New Mexico	1	0.0%
44	Texas	0	0.0%		42	North Dakota	1	0.0%
33	Utah	7	0.1%		44	Delaware	0	0.0%
44	Vermont	0	0.0%		44	Minnesota	0	0.0%
39	Virginia	3	0.0%		44	Nevada	0	0.0%
9	Washington	123	1.9%		44	New Jersey	0	0.0%
31	West Virginia	11	0.2%		44	Texas	0	0.0%
44	Wisconsin	0	0.0%		44	Vermont	0	0.0%
39	Wyoming	3	0.0%		44	Wisconsin	0	0.0%
						District of Columbia	269	4.1%

Source: U.S. Department of Justice, Bureau of Justice Statistics
"Correctional Populations in the United States, 1998"
*Preliminary data. Includes AWOLs. Numbers of escaped federal prisoners were not available.

State Prisoner Deaths in 1999

National Total = 2,923 Deaths*

RANK	STATE	DEATHS	% of USA		RANK	STATE	DEATHS	% of USA
19	Alabama	53	1.8%		1	Texas	444	15.2%
42	Alaska	6	0.2%		2	California	304	10.4%
15	Arizona	67	2.3%		3	New York	194	6.6%
26	Arkansas	31	1.1%		4	Florida	177	6.1%
2	California	304	10.4%		5	Ohio	129	4.4%
23	Colorado	36	1.2%		6	Pennsylvania	115	3.9%
28	Connecticut	30	1.0%		7	Michigan	114	3.9%
36	Delaware	13	0.4%		8	Illinois	93	3.2%
4	Florida	177	6.1%		9	New Jersey	92	3.1%
12	Georgia	82	2.8%		10	Virginia	85	2.9%
34	Hawaii	14	0.5%		11	Oklahoma	83	2.8%
32	Idaho	15	0.5%		12	Georgia	82	2.8%
8	Illinois	93	3.2%		12	Louisiana	82	2.8%
21	Indiana	47	1.6%		14	Tennessee	72	2.5%
32	Iowa	15	0.5%		15	Arizona	67	2.3%
34	Kansas	14	0.5%		16	North Carolina	61	2.1%
24	Kentucky	35	1.2%		17	Missouri	55	1.9%
12	Louisiana	82	2.8%		17	South Carolina	55	1.9%
42	Maine	6	0.2%		19	Alabama	53	1.8%
20	Maryland	50	1.7%		20	Maryland	50	1.7%
29	Massachusetts	21	0.7%		21	Indiana	47	1.6%
7	Michigan	114	3.9%		22	Nevada	38	1.3%
39	Minnesota	9	0.3%		23	Colorado	36	1.2%
25	Mississippi	34	1.2%		24	Kentucky	35	1.2%
17	Missouri	55	1.9%		25	Mississippi	34	1.2%
44	Montana	5	0.2%		26	Arkansas	31	1.1%
37	Nebraska	10	0.3%		26	Washington	31	1.1%
22	Nevada	38	1.3%		28	Connecticut	30	1.0%
48	New Hampshire	1	0.0%		29	Massachusetts	21	0.7%
9	New Jersey	92	3.1%		29	Wisconsin	21	0.7%
37	New Mexico	10	0.3%		31	Oregon	20	0.7%
3	New York	194	6.6%		32	Idaho	15	0.5%
16	North Carolina	61	2.1%		32	Iowa	15	0.5%
50	North Dakota	0	0.0%		34	Hawaii	14	0.5%
5	Ohio	129	4.4%		34	Kansas	14	0.5%
11	Oklahoma	83	2.8%		36	Delaware	13	0.4%
31	Oregon	20	0.7%		37	Nebraska	10	0.3%
6	Pennsylvania	115	3.9%		37	New Mexico	10	0.3%
48	Rhode Island	1	0.0%		39	Minnesota	9	0.3%
17	South Carolina	55	1.9%		39	Utah	9	0.3%
47	South Dakota	2	0.1%		41	West Virginia	7	0.2%
14	Tennessee	72	2.5%		42	Alaska	6	0.2%
1	Texas	444	15.2%		42	Maine	6	0.2%
39	Utah	9	0.3%		44	Montana	5	0.2%
44	Vermont	5	0.2%		44	Vermont	5	0.2%
10	Virginia	85	2.9%		46	Wyoming	3	0.1%
26	Washington	31	1.1%		47	South Dakota	2	0.1%
41	West Virginia	7	0.2%		48	New Hampshire	1	0.0%
29	Wisconsin	21	0.7%		48	Rhode Island	1	0.0%
46	Wyoming	3	0.1%		50	North Dakota	0	0.0%
						District of Columbia	27	0.9%

Source: U.S. Department of Justice, Bureau of Justice Statistics
"HIV in Prisons and Jails, 1999" (Bulletin, July 2001, NCJ-187456)
*Does not include 268 deaths of federal prisoners.

Death Rate of State Prisoners in 1999

National Rate = 239 State Prisoner Deaths per 100,000 Inmates*

ALPHA ORDER

RANK	STATE	RATE
24	Alabama	218
45	Alaska	142
17	Arizona	257
10	Arkansas	284
37	California	185
21	Colorado	239
43	Connecticut	163
30	Delaware	208
16	Florida	258
32	Georgia	197
11	Hawaii	283
6	Idaho	323
28	Illinois	210
21	Indiana	239
31	Iowa	207
42	Kansas	165
23	Kentucky	232
20	Louisiana	245
3	Maine	348
25	Maryland	217
39	Massachusetts	179
19	Michigan	246
44	Minnesota	155
35	Mississippi	190
26	Missouri	216
41	Montana	175
13	Nebraska	273
1	Nevada	400
48	New Hampshire	44
8	New Jersey	288
34	New Mexico	193
15	New York	262
33	North Carolina	194
50	North Dakota	0
12	Ohio	274
2	Oklahoma	377
28	Oregon	210
7	Pennsylvania	315
49	Rhode Island	31
18	South Carolina	247
47	South Dakota	79
5	Tennessee	325
13	Texas	273
40	Utah	178
4	Vermont	332
9	Virginia	286
27	Washington	213
36	West Virginia	189
46	Wisconsin	109
38	Wyoming	184

RANK ORDER

RANK	STATE	RATE
1	Nevada	400
2	Oklahoma	377
3	Maine	348
4	Vermont	332
5	Tennessee	325
6	Idaho	323
7	Pennsylvania	315
8	New Jersey	288
9	Virginia	286
10	Arkansas	284
11	Hawaii	283
12	Ohio	274
13	Nebraska	273
13	Texas	273
15	New York	262
16	Florida	258
17	Arizona	257
18	South Carolina	247
19	Michigan	246
20	Louisiana	245
21	Colorado	239
21	Indiana	239
23	Kentucky	232
24	Alabama	218
25	Maryland	217
26	Missouri	216
27	Washington	213
28	Illinois	210
28	Oregon	210
30	Delaware	208
31	Iowa	207
32	Georgia	197
33	North Carolina	194
34	New Mexico	193
35	Mississippi	190
36	West Virginia	189
37	California	185
38	Wyoming	184
39	Massachusetts	179
40	Utah	178
41	Montana	175
42	Kansas	165
43	Connecticut	163
44	Minnesota	155
45	Alaska	142
46	Wisconsin	109
47	South Dakota	79
48	New Hampshire	44
49	Rhode Island	31
50	North Dakota	0
	District of Columbia	281

Source: U.S. Department of Justice, Bureau of Justice Statistics
   "HIV in Prisons and Jails, 1999" (Bulletin, July 2001, NCJ-187456)
*Does not include deaths of federal prisoners. Federal death rate is 206 deaths per 100,000 federal inmates. The combined federal and state rate is 236 prisoner deaths per 100,000 inmates.

State Prisoner Deaths by Illness or Other Natural Causes in 1998

National Total = 1,831 Deaths*

ALPHA ORDER

RANK	STATE	DEATHS	% of USA
NA	Alabama**	NA	NA
40	Alaska	4	0.2%
10	Arizona	50	2.7%
21	Arkansas	30	1.6%
1	California	208	11.4%
28	Colorado	18	1.0%
29	Connecticut	16	0.9%
30	Delaware	8	0.4%
4	Florida	130	7.1%
8	Georgia	70	3.8%
30	Hawaii	8	0.4%
30	Idaho	8	0.4%
9	Illinois	63	3.4%
13	Indiana	45	2.5%
34	Iowa	6	0.3%
26	Kansas	19	1.0%
21	Kentucky	30	1.6%
NA	Louisiana**	NA	NA
44	Maine	1	0.1%
23	Maryland	25	1.4%
25	Massachusetts	20	1.1%
7	Michigan	80	4.4%
34	Minnesota	6	0.3%
14	Mississippi	44	2.4%
20	Missouri	31	1.7%
36	Montana	5	0.3%
36	Nebraska	5	0.3%
26	Nevada	19	1.0%
36	New Hampshire	5	0.3%
18	New Jersey	36	2.0%
NA	New Mexico**	NA	NA
3	New York	158	8.6%
16	North Carolina	37	2.0%
44	North Dakota	1	0.1%
5	Ohio	124	6.8%
11	Oklahoma	47	2.6%
33	Oregon	7	0.4%
6	Pennsylvania	89	4.9%
43	Rhode Island	2	0.1%
12	South Carolina	46	2.5%
47	South Dakota	0	0.0%
15	Tennessee	38	2.1%
2	Texas	170	9.3%
41	Utah	3	0.2%
44	Vermont	1	0.1%
16	Virginia	37	2.0%
19	Washington	34	1.9%
36	West Virginia	5	0.3%
24	Wisconsin	24	1.3%
41	Wyoming	3	0.2%

RANK ORDER

RANK	STATE	DEATHS	% of USA
1	California	208	11.4%
2	Texas	170	9.3%
3	New York	158	8.6%
4	Florida	130	7.1%
5	Ohio	124	6.8%
6	Pennsylvania	89	4.9%
7	Michigan	80	4.4%
8	Georgia	70	3.8%
9	Illinois	63	3.4%
10	Arizona	50	2.7%
11	Oklahoma	47	2.6%
12	South Carolina	46	2.5%
13	Indiana	45	2.5%
14	Mississippi	44	2.4%
15	Tennessee	38	2.1%
16	North Carolina	37	2.0%
16	Virginia	37	2.0%
18	New Jersey	36	2.0%
19	Washington	34	1.9%
20	Missouri	31	1.7%
21	Arkansas	30	1.6%
21	Kentucky	30	1.6%
23	Maryland	25	1.4%
24	Wisconsin	24	1.3%
25	Massachusetts	20	1.1%
26	Kansas	19	1.0%
26	Nevada	19	1.0%
28	Colorado	18	1.0%
29	Connecticut	16	0.9%
30	Delaware	8	0.4%
30	Hawaii	8	0.4%
30	Idaho	8	0.4%
33	Oregon	7	0.4%
34	Iowa	6	0.3%
34	Minnesota	6	0.3%
36	Montana	5	0.3%
36	Nebraska	5	0.3%
36	New Hampshire	5	0.3%
36	West Virginia	5	0.3%
40	Alaska	4	0.2%
41	Utah	3	0.2%
41	Wyoming	3	0.2%
43	Rhode Island	2	0.1%
44	Maine	1	0.1%
44	North Dakota	1	0.1%
44	Vermont	1	0.1%
47	South Dakota	0	0.0%
NA	Alabama**	NA	NA
NA	Louisiana**	NA	NA
NA	New Mexico**	NA	NA
	District of Columbia	15	0.8%

Source: U.S. Department of Justice, Bureau of Justice Statistics
    "Correctional Populations in the United States, 1998"
*Preliminary data. Excludes AIDS. Federal data were not reported.
**Not available.

Deaths of State Prisoners by Illness or Other Natural Causes
As a Percent of All State Prison Deaths in 1998
National Percent = 65.5% of Deaths*

ALPHA ORDER

RANK ORDER

RANK	STATE	PERCENT		RANK	STATE	PERCENT
NA	Alabama**	NA		1	Alaska	100.0
1	Alaska	100.0		1	Kentucky	100.0
19	Arizona	80.6		1	Nebraska	100.0
13	Arkansas	85.7		1	North Dakota	100.0
26	California	73.2		1	Utah	100.0
34	Colorado	69.2		1	Vermont	100.0
44	Connecticut	48.5		1	West Virginia	100.0
11	Delaware	88.9		8	Indiana	97.8
37	Florida	62.8		9	Kansas	90.5
29	Georgia	71.4		10	Mississippi	89.8
27	Hawaii	72.7		11	Delaware	88.9
27	Idaho	72.7		12	Ohio	88.6
36	Illinois	63.6		13	Arkansas	85.7
8	Indiana	97.8		13	Iowa	85.7
13	Iowa	85.7		15	Massachusetts	83.3
9	Kansas	90.5		15	Michigan	83.3
1	Kentucky	100.0		17	Washington	82.9
NA	Louisiana**	NA		18	Oklahoma	82.5
43	Maine	50.0		19	Arizona	80.6
40	Maryland	54.3		20	Tennessee	79.2
15	Massachusetts	83.3		21	North Carolina	77.1
15	Michigan	83.3		22	Minnesota	75.0
22	Minnesota	75.0		22	Wyoming	75.0
10	Mississippi	89.8		24	New York	74.2
25	Missouri	73.8		25	Missouri	73.8
29	Montana	71.4		26	California	73.2
1	Nebraska	100.0		27	Hawaii	72.7
32	Nevada	70.4		27	Idaho	72.7
38	New Hampshire	62.5		29	Georgia	71.4
42	New Jersey	52.2		29	Montana	71.4
NA	New Mexico**	NA		31	Wisconsin	70.6
24	New York	74.2		32	Nevada	70.4
21	North Carolina	77.1		33	Pennsylvania	70.1
1	North Dakota	100.0		34	Colorado	69.2
12	Ohio	88.6		35	South Carolina	65.7
18	Oklahoma	82.5		36	Illinois	63.6
41	Oregon	53.8		37	Florida	62.8
33	Pennsylvania	70.1		38	New Hampshire	62.5
46	Rhode Island	33.3		39	Virginia	56.9
35	South Carolina	65.7		40	Maryland	54.3
47	South Dakota	0.0		41	Oregon	53.8
20	Tennessee	79.2		42	New Jersey	52.2
45	Texas	45.6		43	Maine	50.0
1	Utah	100.0		44	Connecticut	48.5
1	Vermont	100.0		45	Texas	45.6
39	Virginia	56.9		46	Rhode Island	33.3
17	Washington	82.9		47	South Dakota	0.0
1	West Virginia	100.0		NA	Alabama**	NA
31	Wisconsin	70.6		NA	Louisiana**	NA
22	Wyoming	75.0		NA	New Mexico**	NA
					District of Columbia	75.0

Source: Morgan Quitno Press using data from U.S. Department of Justice, Bureau of Justice Statistics "Correctional Populations in the United States, 1998"

*Preliminary data. Excludes AIDS. Federal data were not reported.
**Not available.

Deaths of State Prisoners by AIDS in 1999

Reporting States Total = 242 Deaths*

<u>ALPHA ORDER</u>

RANK	STATE	DEATHS	% of USA
NA	Alabama**	NA	NA
24	Alaska	0	0.0%
17	Arizona	4	1.7%
24	Arkansas	0	0.0%
2	California	32	13.2%
24	Colorado	0	0.0%
11	Connecticut	6	2.5%
10	Delaware	8	3.3%
1	Florida	52	21.5%
5	Georgia	13	5.4%
24	Hawaii	0	0.0%
24	Idaho	0	0.0%
13	Illinois	5	2.1%
NA	Indiana**	NA	NA
24	Iowa	0	0.0%
24	Kansas	0	0.0%
24	Kentucky	0	0.0%
NA	Louisiana**	NA	NA
24	Maine	0	0.0%
18	Maryland	2	0.8%
11	Massachusetts	6	2.5%
13	Michigan	5	2.1%
24	Minnesota	0	0.0%
21	Mississippi	1	0.4%
13	Missouri	5	2.1%
24	Montana	0	0.0%
24	Nebraska	0	0.0%
9	Nevada	10	4.1%
24	New Hampshire	0	0.0%
4	New Jersey	14	5.8%
24	New Mexico	0	0.0%
3	New York	26	10.7%
13	North Carolina	5	2.1%
24	North Dakota	0	0.0%
NA	Ohio**	NA	NA
18	Oklahoma	2	0.8%
24	Oregon	0	0.0%
6	Pennsylvania	12	5.0%
24	Rhode Island	0	0.0%
6	South Carolina	12	5.0%
24	South Dakota	0	0.0%
18	Tennessee	2	0.8%
NA	Texas**	NA	NA
24	Utah	0	0.0%
24	Vermont	0	0.0%
8	Virginia	11	4.5%
21	Washington	1	0.4%
24	West Virginia	0	0.0%
21	Wisconsin	1	0.4%
24	Wyoming	0	0.0%

<u>RANK ORDER</u>

RANK	STATE	DEATHS	% of USA
1	Florida	52	21.5%
2	California	32	13.2%
3	New York	26	10.7%
4	New Jersey	14	5.8%
5	Georgia	13	5.4%
6	Pennsylvania	12	5.0%
6	South Carolina	12	5.0%
8	Virginia	11	4.5%
9	Nevada	10	4.1%
10	Delaware	8	3.3%
11	Connecticut	6	2.5%
11	Massachusetts	6	2.5%
13	Illinois	5	2.1%
13	Michigan	5	2.1%
13	Missouri	5	2.1%
13	North Carolina	5	2.1%
17	Arizona	4	1.7%
18	Maryland	2	0.8%
18	Oklahoma	2	0.8%
18	Tennessee	2	0.8%
21	Mississippi	1	0.4%
21	Washington	1	0.4%
21	Wisconsin	1	0.4%
24	Alaska	0	0.0%
24	Arkansas	0	0.0%
24	Colorado	0	0.0%
24	Hawaii	0	0.0%
24	Idaho	0	0.0%
24	Iowa	0	0.0%
24	Kansas	0	0.0%
24	Kentucky	0	0.0%
24	Maine	0	0.0%
24	Minnesota	0	0.0%
24	Montana	0	0.0%
24	Nebraska	0	0.0%
24	New Hampshire	0	0.0%
24	New Mexico	0	0.0%
24	North Dakota	0	0.0%
24	Oregon	0	0.0%
24	Rhode Island	0	0.0%
24	South Dakota	0	0.0%
24	Utah	0	0.0%
24	Vermont	0	0.0%
24	West Virginia	0	0.0%
24	Wyoming	0	0.0%
NA	Alabama**	NA	NA
NA	Indiana**	NA	NA
NA	Louisiana**	NA	NA
NA	Ohio**	NA	NA
NA	Texas**	NA	NA
	District of Columbia	7	2.9%

Source: U.S. Department of Justice, Bureau of Justice Statistics
   "HIV in Prisons and Jails, 1999" (Bulletin, July 2001, NCJ-187456)
*National total is for reporting states only. Does not include 16 deaths of federal prisoners.
**Not reported.

AIDS-Related Death Rate for State Prisoners in 1999

National Rate = 20 State Prisoner Deaths per 100,000 Prison Population*

ALPHA ORDER				RANK ORDER		
RANK	STATE	RATE		RANK	STATE	RATE
NA	Alabama**	NA		1	Delaware	128
24	Alaska	0		2	Nevada	105
15	Arizona	15		3	Florida	76
24	Arkansas	0		4	South Carolina	54
13	California	19		5	Massachusetts	51
24	Colorado	0		6	New Jersey	44
9	Connecticut	33		7	Virginia	37
1	Delaware	128		8	New York	35
3	Florida	76		9	Connecticut	33
11	Georgia	31		9	Pennsylvania	33
24	Hawaii	0		11	Georgia	31
24	Idaho	0		12	Missouri	20
16	Illinois	11		13	California	19
NA	Indiana**	NA		14	North Carolina	16
24	Iowa	0		15	Arizona	15
24	Kansas	0		16	Illinois	11
24	Kentucky	0		16	Michigan	11
NA	Louisiana**	NA		18	Maryland	9
24	Maine	0		18	Oklahoma	9
18	Maryland	9		18	Tennessee	9
5	Massachusetts	51		21	Washington	7
16	Michigan	11		22	Mississippi	6
24	Minnesota	0		23	Wisconsin	5
22	Mississippi	6		24	Alaska	0
12	Missouri	20		24	Arkansas	0
24	Montana	0		24	Colorado	0
24	Nebraska	0		24	Hawaii	0
2	Nevada	105		24	Idaho	0
24	New Hampshire	0		24	Iowa	0
6	New Jersey	44		24	Kansas	0
24	New Mexico	0		24	Kentucky	0
8	New York	35		24	Maine	0
14	North Carolina	16		24	Minnesota	0
24	North Dakota	0		24	Montana	0
NA	Ohio**	NA		24	Nebraska	0
18	Oklahoma	9		24	New Hampshire	0
24	Oregon	0		24	New Mexico	0
9	Pennsylvania	33		24	North Dakota	0
24	Rhode Island	0		24	Oregon	0
4	South Carolina	54		24	Rhode Island	0
24	South Dakota	0		24	South Dakota	0
18	Tennessee	9		24	Utah	0
NA	Texas**	NA		24	Vermont	0
24	Utah	0		24	West Virginia	0
24	Vermont	0		24	Wyoming	0
7	Virginia	37		NA	Alabama**	NA
21	Washington	7		NA	Indiana**	NA
24	West Virginia	0		NA	Louisiana**	NA
23	Wisconsin	5		NA	Ohio**	NA
24	Wyoming	0		NA	Texas**	NA

District of Columbia   73

Source: U.S. Department of Justice, Bureau of Justice Statistics
    "HIV in Prisons and Jails, 1999" (Bulletin, July 2001, NCJ-187456)
*National rate is for reporting states only. Federal rate is 12 deaths per 100,000 federal prisoners.
**Not reported.

Deaths of State Prisoners by AIDS as a Percent of All Prison Deaths in 1999

National Percent = 11.2% of Deaths*

ALPHA ORDER

RANK	STATE	PERCENT
NA	Alabama**	NA
24	Alaska	0.0
15	Arizona	6.0
24	Arkansas	0.0
11	California	10.5
24	Colorado	0.0
6	Connecticut	20.0
1	Delaware	61.5
2	Florida	29.4
7	Georgia	15.9
24	Hawaii	0.0
24	Idaho	0.0
16	Illinois	5.4
NA	Indiana**	NA
24	Iowa	0.0
24	Kansas	0.0
24	Kentucky	0.0
NA	Louisiana**	NA
24	Maine	0.0
19	Maryland	4.0
3	Massachusetts	28.6
18	Michigan	4.4
24	Minnesota	0.0
21	Mississippi	2.9
13	Missouri	9.1
24	Montana	0.0
24	Nebraska	0.0
4	Nevada	26.3
24	New Hampshire	0.0
8	New Jersey	15.2
24	New Mexico	0.0
9	New York	13.4
14	North Carolina	8.2
24	North Dakota	0.0
NA	Ohio**	NA
23	Oklahoma	2.4
24	Oregon	0.0
12	Pennsylvania	10.4
24	Rhode Island	0.0
5	South Carolina	21.8
24	South Dakota	0.0
22	Tennessee	2.8
NA	Texas**	NA
24	Utah	0.0
24	Vermont	0.0
10	Virginia	12.9
20	Washington	3.2
24	West Virginia	0.0
17	Wisconsin	4.8
24	Wyoming	0.0

RANK ORDER

RANK	STATE	PERCENT
1	Delaware	61.5
2	Florida	29.4
3	Massachusetts	28.6
4	Nevada	26.3
5	South Carolina	21.8
6	Connecticut	20.0
7	Georgia	15.9
8	New Jersey	15.2
9	New York	13.4
10	Virginia	12.9
11	California	10.5
12	Pennsylvania	10.4
13	Missouri	9.1
14	North Carolina	8.2
15	Arizona	6.0
16	Illinois	5.4
17	Wisconsin	4.8
18	Michigan	4.4
19	Maryland	4.0
20	Washington	3.2
21	Mississippi	2.9
22	Tennessee	2.8
23	Oklahoma	2.4
24	Alaska	0.0
24	Arkansas	0.0
24	Colorado	0.0
24	Hawaii	0.0
24	Idaho	0.0
24	Iowa	0.0
24	Kansas	0.0
24	Kentucky	0.0
24	Maine	0.0
24	Minnesota	0.0
24	Montana	0.0
24	Nebraska	0.0
24	New Hampshire	0.0
24	New Mexico	0.0
24	North Dakota	0.0
24	Oregon	0.0
24	Rhode Island	0.0
24	South Dakota	0.0
24	Utah	0.0
24	Vermont	0.0
24	West Virginia	0.0
24	Wyoming	0.0
NA	Alabama**	NA
NA	Indiana**	NA
NA	Louisiana**	NA
NA	Ohio**	NA
NA	Texas**	NA

District of Columbia   25.9

Source: U.S. Department of Justice, Bureau of Justice Statistics
    "HIV in Prisons and Jails, 1999" (Bulletin, July 2001, NCJ-187456)
*National percent is for reporting states only. Federal percent is 6.0% of deaths.
**Not reported.

State Prisoners Known to be Positive for HIV Infection/AIDS in 1999

National Total = 24,607 Inmates*

ALPHA ORDER

RANK	STATE	INMATES	% of USA
19	Alabama	283	1.2%
41	Alaska	16	0.1%
25	Arizona	144	0.6%
29	Arkansas	99	0.4%
4	California	1,570	6.4%
26	Colorado	131	0.5%
10	Connecticut	632	2.6%
23	Delaware	170	0.7%
2	Florida	2,633	10.7%
7	Georgia	846	3.4%
35	Hawaii	30	0.1%
42	Idaho	15	0.1%
9	Illinois	635	2.6%
NA	Indiana**	NA	NA
35	Iowa	30	0.1%
32	Kansas	41	0.2%
30	Kentucky	78	0.3%
15	Louisiana	381	1.5%
46	Maine	9	0.0%
8	Maryland	820	3.3%
16	Massachusetts	346	1.4%
12	Michigan	578	2.3%
34	Minnesota	32	0.1%
21	Mississippi	192	0.8%
18	Missouri	290	1.2%
44	Montana	10	0.0%
39	Nebraska	20	0.1%
27	Nevada	125	0.5%
40	New Hampshire	17	0.1%
6	New Jersey	869	3.5%
37	New Mexico	26	0.1%
1	New York	7,000	28.4%
13	North Carolina	554	2.3%
49	North Dakota	2	0.0%
14	Ohio	391	1.6%
28	Oklahoma	122	0.5%
38	Oregon	23	0.1%
5	Pennsylvania	939	3.8%
20	Rhode Island	203	0.8%
11	South Carolina	617	2.5%
48	South Dakota	5	0.0%
22	Tennessee	185	0.8%
3	Texas	2,520	10.2%
33	Utah	34	0.1%
42	Vermont	15	0.1%
17	Virginia	330	1.3%
31	Washington	75	0.3%
44	West Virginia	10	0.0%
24	Wisconsin	147	0.6%
47	Wyoming	8	0.0%

RANK ORDER

RANK	STATE	INMATES	% of USA
1	New York	7,000	28.4%
2	Florida	2,633	10.7%
3	Texas	2,520	10.2%
4	California	1,570	6.4%
5	Pennsylvania	939	3.8%
6	New Jersey	869	3.5%
7	Georgia	846	3.4%
8	Maryland	820	3.3%
9	Illinois	635	2.6%
10	Connecticut	632	2.6%
11	South Carolina	617	2.5%
12	Michigan	578	2.3%
13	North Carolina	554	2.3%
14	Ohio	391	1.6%
15	Louisiana	381	1.5%
16	Massachusetts	346	1.4%
17	Virginia	330	1.3%
18	Missouri	290	1.2%
19	Alabama	283	1.2%
20	Rhode Island	203	0.8%
21	Mississippi	192	0.8%
22	Tennessee	185	0.8%
23	Delaware	170	0.7%
24	Wisconsin	147	0.6%
25	Arizona	144	0.6%
26	Colorado	131	0.5%
27	Nevada	125	0.5%
28	Oklahoma	122	0.5%
29	Arkansas	99	0.4%
30	Kentucky	78	0.3%
31	Washington	75	0.3%
32	Kansas	41	0.2%
33	Utah	34	0.1%
34	Minnesota	32	0.1%
35	Hawaii	30	0.1%
35	Iowa	30	0.1%
37	New Mexico	26	0.1%
38	Oregon	23	0.1%
39	Nebraska	20	0.1%
40	New Hampshire	17	0.1%
41	Alaska	16	0.1%
42	Idaho	15	0.1%
42	Vermont	15	0.1%
44	Montana	10	0.0%
44	West Virginia	10	0.0%
46	Maine	9	0.0%
47	Wyoming	8	0.0%
48	South Dakota	5	0.0%
49	North Dakota	2	0.0%
NA	Indiana**	NA	NA
	District of Columbia	359	1.5%

Source: U.S. Department of Justice, Bureau of Justice Statistics
   "HIV in Prisons and Jails, 1999" (Bulletin, July 2001, NCJ-187456)
*Does not include 1,150 positive federal inmates.
**Not available.

State Prisoners Known to Be Positive for HIV Infection/AIDS As a Percent of Total Prison Population in 1999
National Percent = 2.3% of State Prisoners*

ALPHA ORDER

RANK	STATE	PERCENT
19	Alabama	1.3
34	Alaska	0.6
34	Arizona	0.6
24	Arkansas	1.0
24	California	1.0
24	Colorado	1.0
4	Connecticut	3.7
9	Delaware	2.6
3	Florida	3.8
12	Georgia	2.0
28	Hawaii	0.9
44	Idaho	0.4
16	Illinois	1.4
NA	Indiana**	NA
44	Iowa	0.4
40	Kansas	0.5
32	Kentucky	0.7
11	Louisiana	2.1
40	Maine	0.5
5	Maryland	3.6
7	Massachusetts	3.3
19	Michigan	1.3
34	Minnesota	0.6
13	Mississippi	1.9
23	Missouri	1.1
32	Montana	0.7
34	Nebraska	0.6
16	Nevada	1.4
29	New Hampshire	0.8
6	New Jersey	3.5
40	New Mexico	0.5
1	New York	9.7
13	North Carolina	1.9
47	North Dakota	0.2
29	Ohio	0.8
29	Oklahoma	0.8
47	Oregon	0.2
9	Pennsylvania	2.6
2	Rhode Island	6.9
8	South Carolina	2.9
47	South Dakota	0.2
16	Tennessee	1.4
15	Texas	1.8
34	Utah	0.6
19	Vermont	1.3
19	Virginia	1.3
40	Washington	0.5
46	West Virginia	0.3
24	Wisconsin	1.0
34	Wyoming	0.6

RANK ORDER

RANK	STATE	PERCENT
1	New York	9.7
2	Rhode Island	6.9
3	Florida	3.8
4	Connecticut	3.7
5	Maryland	3.6
6	New Jersey	3.5
7	Massachusetts	3.3
8	South Carolina	2.9
9	Delaware	2.6
9	Pennsylvania	2.6
11	Louisiana	2.1
12	Georgia	2.0
13	Mississippi	1.9
13	North Carolina	1.9
15	Texas	1.8
16	Illinois	1.4
16	Nevada	1.4
16	Tennessee	1.4
19	Alabama	1.3
19	Michigan	1.3
19	Vermont	1.3
19	Virginia	1.3
23	Missouri	1.1
24	Arkansas	1.0
24	California	1.0
24	Colorado	1.0
24	Wisconsin	1.0
28	Hawaii	0.9
29	New Hampshire	0.8
29	Ohio	0.8
29	Oklahoma	0.8
32	Kentucky	0.7
32	Montana	0.7
34	Alaska	0.6
34	Arizona	0.6
34	Minnesota	0.6
34	Nebraska	0.6
34	Utah	0.6
34	Wyoming	0.6
40	Kansas	0.5
40	Maine	0.5
40	New Mexico	0.5
40	Washington	0.5
44	Idaho	0.4
44	Iowa	0.4
46	West Virginia	0.3
47	North Dakota	0.2
47	Oregon	0.2
47	South Dakota	0.2
NA	Indiana**	NA
	District of Columbia	7.8

Source: U.S. Department of Justice, Bureau of Justice Statistics
    "HIV in Prisons and Jails, 1999" (Bulletin, July 2001, NCJ-187456)
*Federal rate is 0.9%, combined state and federal rate is 2.1%.
**Not available.

Deaths of State Prisoners by Suicide in 1998

National Total = 176 Suicides*

<u>ALPHA ORDER</u>

RANK	STATE	SUICIDES	% of USA
NA	Alabama**	NA	NA
39	Alaska	0	0.0%
10	Arizona	5	2.8%
16	Arkansas	3	1.7%
2	California	21	11.9%
10	Colorado	5	2.8%
27	Connecticut	1	0.6%
27	Delaware	1	0.6%
9	Florida	6	3.4%
10	Georgia	5	2.8%
27	Hawaii	1	0.6%
27	Idaho	1	0.6%
4	Illinois	12	6.8%
NA	Indiana**	NA	NA
27	Iowa	1	0.6%
27	Kansas	1	0.6%
39	Kentucky	0	0.0%
NA	Louisiana**	NA	NA
27	Maine	1	0.6%
19	Maryland	2	1.1%
27	Massachusetts	1	0.6%
6	Michigan	7	4.0%
27	Minnesota	1	0.6%
19	Mississippi	2	1.1%
6	Missouri	7	4.0%
27	Montana	1	0.6%
39	Nebraska	0	0.0%
19	Nevada	2	1.1%
27	New Hampshire	1	0.6%
19	New Jersey	2	1.1%
NA	New Mexico**	NA	NA
3	New York	14	8.0%
19	North Carolina	2	1.1%
39	North Dakota	0	0.0%
6	Ohio	7	4.0%
19	Oklahoma	2	1.1%
10	Oregon	5	2.8%
5	Pennsylvania	11	6.3%
39	Rhode Island	0	0.0%
16	South Carolina	3	1.7%
19	South Dakota	2	1.1%
10	Tennessee	5	2.8%
1	Texas	22	12.5%
39	Utah	0	0.0%
39	Vermont	0	0.0%
19	Virginia	2	1.1%
16	Washington	3	1.7%
39	West Virginia	0	0.0%
10	Wisconsin	5	2.8%
27	Wyoming	1	0.6%

<u>RANK ORDER</u>

RANK	STATE	SUICIDES	% of USA
1	Texas	22	12.5%
2	California	21	11.9%
3	New York	14	8.0%
4	Illinois	12	6.8%
5	Pennsylvania	11	6.3%
6	Michigan	7	4.0%
6	Missouri	7	4.0%
6	Ohio	7	4.0%
9	Florida	6	3.4%
10	Arizona	5	2.8%
10	Colorado	5	2.8%
10	Georgia	5	2.8%
10	Oregon	5	2.8%
10	Tennessee	5	2.8%
10	Wisconsin	5	2.8%
16	Arkansas	3	1.7%
16	South Carolina	3	1.7%
16	Washington	3	1.7%
19	Maryland	2	1.1%
19	Mississippi	2	1.1%
19	Nevada	2	1.1%
19	New Jersey	2	1.1%
19	North Carolina	2	1.1%
19	Oklahoma	2	1.1%
19	South Dakota	2	1.1%
19	Virginia	2	1.1%
27	Connecticut	1	0.6%
27	Delaware	1	0.6%
27	Hawaii	1	0.6%
27	Idaho	1	0.6%
27	Iowa	1	0.6%
27	Kansas	1	0.6%
27	Maine	1	0.6%
27	Massachusetts	1	0.6%
27	Minnesota	1	0.6%
27	Montana	1	0.6%
27	New Hampshire	1	0.6%
27	Wyoming	1	0.6%
39	Alaska	0	0.0%
39	Kentucky	0	0.0%
39	Nebraska	0	0.0%
39	North Dakota	0	0.0%
39	Rhode Island	0	0.0%
39	Utah	0	0.0%
39	Vermont	0	0.0%
39	West Virginia	0	0.0%
NA	Alabama**	NA	NA
NA	Indiana**	NA	NA
NA	Louisiana**	NA	NA
NA	New Mexico**	NA	NA
	District of Columbia	2	1.1%

Source: U.S. Department of Justice, Bureau of Justice Statistics
   "Correctional Populations in the United States, 1998"
*Preliminary data. Federal data were not reported.
**Not available.

Deaths of State Prisoners by Suicide as a Percent of All Prison Deaths in 1998

National Percent = 6.3% of Deaths*

ALPHA ORDER

RANK	STATE	PERCENT
NA	Alabama**	NA
39	Alaska	0.0
19	Arizona	8.1
18	Arkansas	8.6
20	California	7.4
5	Colorado	19.2
36	Connecticut	3.0
13	Delaware	11.1
37	Florida	2.9
26	Georgia	5.1
15	Hawaii	9.1
15	Idaho	9.1
12	Illinois	12.1
NA	Indiana**	NA
8	Iowa	14.3
28	Kansas	4.8
39	Kentucky	0.0
NA	Louisiana**	NA
2	Maine	50.0
29	Maryland	4.3
31	Massachusetts	4.2
22	Michigan	7.3
10	Minnesota	12.5
33	Mississippi	4.1
6	Missouri	16.7
8	Montana	14.3
39	Nebraska	0.0
20	Nevada	7.4
10	New Hampshire	12.5
37	New Jersey	2.9
NA	New Mexico**	NA
24	New York	6.6
31	North Carolina	4.2
39	North Dakota	0.0
27	Ohio	5.0
34	Oklahoma	3.5
3	Oregon	38.5
17	Pennsylvania	8.7
39	Rhode Island	0.0
29	South Carolina	4.3
1	South Dakota	100.0
14	Tennessee	10.4
25	Texas	5.9
39	Utah	0.0
39	Vermont	0.0
35	Virginia	3.1
22	Washington	7.3
39	West Virginia	0.0
7	Wisconsin	14.7
4	Wyoming	25.0

RANK ORDER

RANK	STATE	PERCENT
1	South Dakota	100.0
2	Maine	50.0
3	Oregon	38.5
4	Wyoming	25.0
5	Colorado	19.2
6	Missouri	16.7
7	Wisconsin	14.7
8	Iowa	14.3
8	Montana	14.3
10	Minnesota	12.5
10	New Hampshire	12.5
12	Illinois	12.1
13	Delaware	11.1
14	Tennessee	10.4
15	Hawaii	9.1
15	Idaho	9.1
17	Pennsylvania	8.7
18	Arkansas	8.6
19	Arizona	8.1
20	California	7.4
20	Nevada	7.4
22	Michigan	7.3
22	Washington	7.3
24	New York	6.6
25	Texas	5.9
26	Georgia	5.1
27	Ohio	5.0
28	Kansas	4.8
29	Maryland	4.3
29	South Carolina	4.3
31	Massachusetts	4.2
31	North Carolina	4.2
33	Mississippi	4.1
34	Oklahoma	3.5
35	Virginia	3.1
36	Connecticut	3.0
37	Florida	2.9
37	New Jersey	2.9
39	Alaska	0.0
39	Kentucky	0.0
39	Nebraska	0.0
39	North Dakota	0.0
39	Rhode Island	0.0
39	Utah	0.0
39	Vermont	0.0
39	West Virginia	0.0
NA	Alabama**	NA
NA	Indiana**	NA
NA	Louisiana**	NA
NA	New Mexico**	NA

District of Columbia — 10.0

Source: Morgan Quitno Press using data from U.S. Department of Justice, Bureau of Justice Statistics
     "Correctional Populations in the United States, 1998"
*Preliminary data. Federal data were not reported.
**Not available.

Adults Under State Correctional Supervision in 2000

National Total = 6,228,400 Adults*

ALPHA ORDER

RANK	STATE	ADULTS	% of USA
23	Alabama	79,500	1.3%
46	Alaska	9,500	0.2%
17	Arizona	101,100	1.6%
29	Arkansas	55,300	0.9%
2	California	698,600	11.2%
26	Colorado	70,600	1.1%
25	Connecticut	73,600	1.2%
37	Delaware	27,200	0.4%
3	Florida	422,600	6.8%
4	Georgia	406,800	6.5%
39	Hawaii	22,800	0.4%
31	Idaho	45,500	0.7%
9	Illinois	231,400	3.7%
13	Indiana	144,300	2.3%
33	Iowa	34,900	0.6%
34	Kansas	32,600	0.5%
30	Kentucky	46,900	0.8%
16	Louisiana	103,800	1.7%
45	Maine	10,600	0.2%
14	Maryland	132,500	2.1%
27	Massachusetts	70,000	1.1%
8	Michigan	251,900	4.0%
15	Minnesota	128,600	2.1%
32	Mississippi	39,900	0.6%
18	Missouri	96,600	1.6%
44	Montana	10,700	0.2%
36	Nebraska	27,800	0.4%
35	Nevada	30,700	0.5%
48	New Hampshire	8,400	0.1%
10	New Jersey	188,900	3.0%
40	New Mexico	22,700	0.4%
5	New York	353,700	5.7%
12	North Carolina	151,200	2.4%
50	North Dakota	4,500	0.1%
6	Ohio	272,500	4.4%
28	Oklahoma	61,400	1.0%
22	Oregon	79,800	1.3%
7	Pennsylvania	266,800	4.3%
38	Rhode Island	26,700	0.4%
24	South Carolina	76,800	1.2%
47	South Dakota	9,400	0.2%
21	Tennessee	84,600	1.4%
1	Texas	755,700	12.1%
41	Utah	20,000	0.3%
43	Vermont	11,500	0.2%
20	Virginia	88,100	1.4%
11	Washington	183,100	2.9%
42	West Virginia	12,700	0.2%
19	Wisconsin	96,000	1.5%
49	Wyoming	7,200	0.1%

RANK ORDER

RANK	STATE	ADULTS	% of USA
1	Texas	755,700	12.1%
2	California	698,600	11.2%
3	Florida	422,600	6.8%
4	Georgia	406,800	6.5%
5	New York	353,700	5.7%
6	Ohio	272,500	4.4%
7	Pennsylvania	266,800	4.3%
8	Michigan	251,900	4.0%
9	Illinois	231,400	3.7%
10	New Jersey	188,900	3.0%
11	Washington	183,100	2.9%
12	North Carolina	151,200	2.4%
13	Indiana	144,300	2.3%
14	Maryland	132,500	2.1%
15	Minnesota	128,600	2.1%
16	Louisiana	103,800	1.7%
17	Arizona	101,100	1.6%
18	Missouri	96,600	1.6%
19	Wisconsin	96,000	1.5%
20	Virginia	88,100	1.4%
21	Tennessee	84,600	1.4%
22	Oregon	79,800	1.3%
23	Alabama	79,500	1.3%
24	South Carolina	76,800	1.2%
25	Connecticut	73,600	1.2%
26	Colorado	70,600	1.1%
27	Massachusetts	70,000	1.1%
28	Oklahoma	61,400	1.0%
29	Arkansas	55,300	0.9%
30	Kentucky	46,900	0.8%
31	Idaho	45,500	0.7%
32	Mississippi	39,900	0.6%
33	Iowa	34,900	0.6%
34	Kansas	32,600	0.5%
35	Nevada	30,700	0.5%
36	Nebraska	27,800	0.4%
37	Delaware	27,200	0.4%
38	Rhode Island	26,700	0.4%
39	Hawaii	22,800	0.4%
40	New Mexico	22,700	0.4%
41	Utah	20,000	0.3%
42	West Virginia	12,700	0.2%
43	Vermont	11,500	0.2%
44	Montana	10,700	0.2%
45	Maine	10,600	0.2%
46	Alaska	9,500	0.2%
47	South Dakota	9,400	0.2%
48	New Hampshire	8,400	0.1%
49	Wyoming	7,200	0.1%
50	North Dakota	4,500	0.1%
	District of Columbia	25,500	0.4%

Source: U.S. Department of Justice, Bureau of Justice Statistics
"Probation and Parole in the United States, 2000" (Press Release, August 2001, NCJ-188208)
*Includes adults in prison or jail, on probation or parole. Does not include 238,000 adults under federal correctional supervision. Figures are as of December 31, 2000 except for state jail counts, which are as of June 30, 1999.

Rate of Adults Under State Correctional Supervision in 2000

National Rate = 2,978 Adults per 100,000 Adult Population*

RANK	STATE	RATE
29	Alabama	2,391
33	Alaska	2,172
20	Arizona	2,685
19	Arkansas	2,773
18	California	2,837
31	Colorado	2,205
16	Connecticut	2,871
4	Delaware	4,618
8	Florida	3,426
1	Georgia	6,760
24	Hawaii	2,492
3	Idaho	4,917
22	Illinois	2,522
12	Indiana	3,203
43	Iowa	1,590
41	Kansas	1,648
44	Kentucky	1,539
13	Louisiana	3,194
47	Maine	1,086
9	Maryland	3,363
45	Massachusetts	1,445
7	Michigan	3,431
6	Minnesota	3,540
37	Mississippi	1,929
30	Missouri	2,318
42	Montana	1,597
32	Nebraska	2,201
34	Nevada	2,062
49	New Hampshire	911
15	New Jersey	2,986
38	New Mexico	1,735
26	New York	2,476
25	North Carolina	2,485
48	North Dakota	938
11	Ohio	3,219
28	Oklahoma	2,399
14	Oregon	3,098
17	Pennsylvania	2,851
10	Rhode Island	3,341
21	South Carolina	2,557
39	South Dakota	1,693
35	Tennessee	1,972
2	Texas	5,049
46	Utah	1,318
23	Vermont	2,496
40	Virginia	1,649
5	Washington	4,180
50	West Virginia	905
27	Wisconsin	2,403
36	Wyoming	1,967

RANK ORDER

RANK	STATE	RATE
1	Georgia	6,760
2	Texas	5,049
3	Idaho	4,917
4	Delaware	4,618
5	Washington	4,180
6	Minnesota	3,540
7	Michigan	3,431
8	Florida	3,426
9	Maryland	3,363
10	Rhode Island	3,341
11	Ohio	3,219
12	Indiana	3,203
13	Louisiana	3,194
14	Oregon	3,098
15	New Jersey	2,986
16	Connecticut	2,871
17	Pennsylvania	2,851
18	California	2,837
19	Arkansas	2,773
20	Arizona	2,685
21	South Carolina	2,557
22	Illinois	2,522
23	Vermont	2,496
24	Hawaii	2,492
25	North Carolina	2,485
26	New York	2,476
27	Wisconsin	2,403
28	Oklahoma	2,399
29	Alabama	2,391
30	Missouri	2,318
31	Colorado	2,205
32	Nebraska	2,201
33	Alaska	2,172
34	Nevada	2,062
35	Tennessee	1,972
36	Wyoming	1,967
37	Mississippi	1,929
38	New Mexico	1,735
39	South Dakota	1,693
40	Virginia	1,649
41	Kansas	1,648
42	Montana	1,597
43	Iowa	1,590
44	Kentucky	1,539
45	Massachusetts	1,445
46	Utah	1,318
47	Maine	1,086
48	North Dakota	938
49	New Hampshire	911
50	West Virginia	905
	District of Columbia	5,585

Source: U.S. Department of Justice, Bureau of Justice Statistics
"Probation and Parole in the United States, 2000" (Press Release, August 2001, NCJ-188208)
*Includes adults in prison or jail, on probation or parole. Figures are as of December 31, 2000 except for state jail counts, which are as of June 30, 1999. Does not include adults under federal correctional supervision. Federal rate is 114 per 100,000 adult population. The combined state and federal figure is 3,092 per 100,000 adult population.

Percent of Population Under State Correctional Supervision in 2000

National Percent = 3.0% of Adult Population*

<table>
<tr><td colspan="3">ALPHA ORDER</td><td colspan="3">RANK ORDER</td></tr>
<tr><td>RANK</td><td>STATE</td><td>PERCENT</td><td>RANK</td><td>STATE</td><td>PERCENT</td></tr>
<tr><td>27</td><td>Alabama</td><td>2.4</td><td>1</td><td>Georgia</td><td>6.8</td></tr>
<tr><td>31</td><td>Alaska</td><td>2.2</td><td>2</td><td>Texas</td><td>5.0</td></tr>
<tr><td>20</td><td>Arizona</td><td>2.7</td><td>3</td><td>Idaho</td><td>4.9</td></tr>
<tr><td>18</td><td>Arkansas</td><td>2.8</td><td>4</td><td>Delaware</td><td>4.6</td></tr>
<tr><td>18</td><td>California</td><td>2.8</td><td>5</td><td>Washington</td><td>4.2</td></tr>
<tr><td>31</td><td>Colorado</td><td>2.2</td><td>6</td><td>Minnesota</td><td>3.5</td></tr>
<tr><td>16</td><td>Connecticut</td><td>2.9</td><td>7</td><td>Florida</td><td>3.4</td></tr>
<tr><td>4</td><td>Delaware</td><td>4.6</td><td>7</td><td>Maryland</td><td>3.4</td></tr>
<tr><td>7</td><td>Florida</td><td>3.4</td><td>7</td><td>Michigan</td><td>3.4</td></tr>
<tr><td>1</td><td>Georgia</td><td>6.8</td><td>10</td><td>Rhode Island</td><td>3.3</td></tr>
<tr><td>22</td><td>Hawaii</td><td>2.5</td><td>11</td><td>Indiana</td><td>3.2</td></tr>
<tr><td>3</td><td>Idaho</td><td>4.9</td><td>11</td><td>Louisiana</td><td>3.2</td></tr>
<tr><td>22</td><td>Illinois</td><td>2.5</td><td>11</td><td>Ohio</td><td>3.2</td></tr>
<tr><td>11</td><td>Indiana</td><td>3.2</td><td>14</td><td>Oregon</td><td>3.1</td></tr>
<tr><td>41</td><td>Iowa</td><td>1.6</td><td>15</td><td>New Jersey</td><td>3.0</td></tr>
<tr><td>38</td><td>Kansas</td><td>1.7</td><td>16</td><td>Connecticut</td><td>2.9</td></tr>
<tr><td>44</td><td>Kentucky</td><td>1.5</td><td>16</td><td>Pennsylvania</td><td>2.9</td></tr>
<tr><td>11</td><td>Louisiana</td><td>3.2</td><td>18</td><td>Arkansas</td><td>2.8</td></tr>
<tr><td>47</td><td>Maine</td><td>1.1</td><td>18</td><td>California</td><td>2.8</td></tr>
<tr><td>7</td><td>Maryland</td><td>3.4</td><td>20</td><td>Arizona</td><td>2.7</td></tr>
<tr><td>45</td><td>Massachusetts</td><td>1.4</td><td>21</td><td>South Carolina</td><td>2.6</td></tr>
<tr><td>7</td><td>Michigan</td><td>3.4</td><td>22</td><td>Hawaii</td><td>2.5</td></tr>
<tr><td>6</td><td>Minnesota</td><td>3.5</td><td>22</td><td>Illinois</td><td>2.5</td></tr>
<tr><td>37</td><td>Mississippi</td><td>1.9</td><td>22</td><td>New York</td><td>2.5</td></tr>
<tr><td>30</td><td>Missouri</td><td>2.3</td><td>22</td><td>North Carolina</td><td>2.5</td></tr>
<tr><td>41</td><td>Montana</td><td>1.6</td><td>22</td><td>Vermont</td><td>2.5</td></tr>
<tr><td>31</td><td>Nebraska</td><td>2.2</td><td>27</td><td>Alabama</td><td>2.4</td></tr>
<tr><td>34</td><td>Nevada</td><td>2.1</td><td>27</td><td>Oklahoma</td><td>2.4</td></tr>
<tr><td>48</td><td>New Hampshire</td><td>0.9</td><td>27</td><td>Wisconsin</td><td>2.4</td></tr>
<tr><td>15</td><td>New Jersey</td><td>3.0</td><td>30</td><td>Missouri</td><td>2.3</td></tr>
<tr><td>38</td><td>New Mexico</td><td>1.7</td><td>31</td><td>Alaska</td><td>2.2</td></tr>
<tr><td>22</td><td>New York</td><td>2.5</td><td>31</td><td>Colorado</td><td>2.2</td></tr>
<tr><td>22</td><td>North Carolina</td><td>2.5</td><td>31</td><td>Nebraska</td><td>2.2</td></tr>
<tr><td>48</td><td>North Dakota</td><td>0.9</td><td>34</td><td>Nevada</td><td>2.1</td></tr>
<tr><td>11</td><td>Ohio</td><td>3.2</td><td>35</td><td>Tennessee</td><td>2.0</td></tr>
<tr><td>27</td><td>Oklahoma</td><td>2.4</td><td>35</td><td>Wyoming</td><td>2.0</td></tr>
<tr><td>14</td><td>Oregon</td><td>3.1</td><td>37</td><td>Mississippi</td><td>1.9</td></tr>
<tr><td>16</td><td>Pennsylvania</td><td>2.9</td><td>38</td><td>Kansas</td><td>1.7</td></tr>
<tr><td>10</td><td>Rhode Island</td><td>3.3</td><td>38</td><td>New Mexico</td><td>1.7</td></tr>
<tr><td>21</td><td>South Carolina</td><td>2.6</td><td>38</td><td>South Dakota</td><td>1.7</td></tr>
<tr><td>38</td><td>South Dakota</td><td>1.7</td><td>41</td><td>Iowa</td><td>1.6</td></tr>
<tr><td>35</td><td>Tennessee</td><td>2.0</td><td>41</td><td>Montana</td><td>1.6</td></tr>
<tr><td>2</td><td>Texas</td><td>5.0</td><td>41</td><td>Virginia</td><td>1.6</td></tr>
<tr><td>46</td><td>Utah</td><td>1.3</td><td>44</td><td>Kentucky</td><td>1.5</td></tr>
<tr><td>22</td><td>Vermont</td><td>2.5</td><td>45</td><td>Massachusetts</td><td>1.4</td></tr>
<tr><td>41</td><td>Virginia</td><td>1.6</td><td>46</td><td>Utah</td><td>1.3</td></tr>
<tr><td>5</td><td>Washington</td><td>4.2</td><td>47</td><td>Maine</td><td>1.1</td></tr>
<tr><td>48</td><td>West Virginia</td><td>0.9</td><td>48</td><td>New Hampshire</td><td>0.9</td></tr>
<tr><td>27</td><td>Wisconsin</td><td>2.4</td><td>48</td><td>North Dakota</td><td>0.9</td></tr>
<tr><td>35</td><td>Wyoming</td><td>2.0</td><td>48</td><td>West Virginia</td><td>0.9</td></tr>
<tr><td></td><td></td><td></td><td></td><td>District of Columbia</td><td>5.6</td></tr>
</table>

Source: Morgan Quitno Press using data from U.S. Department of Justice, Bureau of Justice Statistics "Probation and Parole in the United States, 2000" (Press Release, August 2001, NCJ-188208)
*Population 18 years old and older. Includes adults in prison or jail, on probation or parole. Does not include adults under federal correctional supervision. Federal percent is 0.1% making a combined state and federal percent of 3.1% of adult population is under state or federal correctional supervision.

Percent of Adults Under State Correctional Supervision
Who Are Incarcerated: 2000
National Percent = 28.9% Incarcerated*

ALPHA ORDER

RANK	STATE	PERCENT
11	Alabama	43.4
8	Alaska	44.4
18	Arizona	36.4
30	Arkansas	28.9
22	California	34.0
25	Colorado	30.6
40	Connecticut	22.6
36	Delaware	24.2
29	Florida	29.0
46	Georgia	18.9
43	Hawaii	21.0
45	Idaho	19.7
32	Illinois	26.9
41	Indiana	22.0
24	Iowa	31.4
14	Kansas	39.1
7	Kentucky	45.6
10	Louisiana	43.4
33	Maine	26.1
34	Maryland	26.1
26	Massachusetts	30.1
35	Michigan	25.1
50	Minnesota	8.6
1	Mississippi	58.1
21	Missouri	35.5
17	Montana	38.0
42	Nebraska	21.6
3	Nevada	47.6
6	New Hampshire	45.8
38	New Jersey	23.0
5	New Mexico	46.4
28	New York	29.4
27	North Carolina	29.6
19	North Dakota	35.7
39	Ohio	22.8
4	Oklahoma	46.7
44	Oregon	20.6
37	Pennsylvania	23.9
48	Rhode Island	12.8
16	South Carolina	38.6
15	South Dakota	39.1
12	Tennessee	43.3
31	Texas	28.2
13	Utah	42.3
49	Vermont	11.4
2	Virginia	55.6
47	Washington	13.9
9	West Virginia	43.6
23	Wisconsin	33.6
20	Wyoming	35.5

RANK ORDER

RANK	STATE	PERCENT
1	Mississippi	58.1
2	Virginia	55.6
3	Nevada	47.6
4	Oklahoma	46.7
5	New Mexico	46.4
6	New Hampshire	45.8
7	Kentucky	45.6
8	Alaska	44.4
9	West Virginia	43.6
10	Louisiana	43.4
11	Alabama	43.4
12	Tennessee	43.3
13	Utah	42.3
14	Kansas	39.1
15	South Dakota	39.1
16	South Carolina	38.6
17	Montana	38.0
18	Arizona	36.4
19	North Dakota	35.7
20	Wyoming	35.5
21	Missouri	35.5
22	California	34.0
23	Wisconsin	33.6
24	Iowa	31.4
25	Colorado	30.6
26	Massachusetts	30.1
27	North Carolina	29.6
28	New York	29.4
29	Florida	29.0
30	Arkansas	28.9
31	Texas	28.2
32	Illinois	26.9
33	Maine	26.1
34	Maryland	26.1
35	Michigan	25.1
36	Delaware	24.2
37	Pennsylvania	23.9
38	New Jersey	23.0
39	Ohio	22.8
40	Connecticut	22.6
41	Indiana	22.0
42	Nebraska	21.6
43	Hawaii	21.0
44	Oregon	20.6
45	Idaho	19.7
46	Georgia	18.9
47	Washington	13.9
48	Rhode Island	12.8
49	Vermont	11.4
50	Minnesota	8.6
	District of Columbia	30.5

Source: U.S. Department of Justice, Bureau of Justice Statistics
  "Probation and Parole in the United States, 2000" (Press Release, August 2001, NCJ-188208)
*Includes adults in prison or jail, on probation or parole. Figures are as of December 31, 2000 except for state jail counts, which are as of June 30, 1999. Does not include adults under federal correctional supervision. Federal figure is 56.1% incarcerated. The combined state and federal figure is 29.9% incarcerated.

Adults on State Probation in 2000

National Total = 3,807,993 Adults*

ALPHA ORDER

RANK	STATE	ADULTS	% of USA
25	Alabama	40,627	1.1%
46	Alaska	4,760	0.1%
16	Arizona	60,751	1.6%
30	Arkansas	30,353	0.8%
2	California	343,145	9.0%
20	Colorado	47,084	1.2%
17	Connecticut	55,070	1.4%
35	Delaware	20,052	0.5%
4	Florida	294,786	7.7%
3	Georgia	308,344	8.1%
37	Hawaii	15,525	0.4%
27	Idaho	35,091	0.9%
9	Illinois	139,029	3.7%
13	Indiana	107,673	2.8%
33	Iowa	21,147	0.6%
36	Kansas	15,996	0.4%
34	Kentucky	20,610	0.5%
26	Louisiana	35,854	0.9%
43	Maine	7,788	0.2%
15	Maryland	83,852	2.2%
22	Massachusetts	45,233	1.2%
7	Michigan	173,676	4.6%
12	Minnesota	114,468	3.0%
38	Mississippi	15,118	0.4%
19	Missouri	49,975	1.3%
45	Montana	6,043	0.2%
32	Nebraska	21,483	0.6%
39	Nevada	12,189	0.3%
49	New Hampshire	3,629	0.1%
10	New Jersey	130,610	3.4%
40	New Mexico	10,512	0.3%
6	New York	191,970	5.0%
14	North Carolina	105,949	2.8%
50	North Dakota	2,789	0.1%
5	Ohio	194,875	5.1%
29	Oklahoma	30,994	0.8%
21	Oregon	46,199	1.2%
11	Pennsylvania	121,034	3.2%
31	Rhode Island	22,964	0.6%
23	South Carolina	42,883	1.1%
47	South Dakota	4,214	0.1%
24	Tennessee	40,829	1.1%
1	Texas	442,251	11.6%
41	Utah	9,828	0.3%
42	Vermont	9,303	0.2%
28	Virginia	33,955	0.9%
8	Washington	160,977	4.2%
44	West Virginia	6,058	0.2%
18	Wisconsin	54,272	1.4%
48	Wyoming	4,115	0.1%

RANK ORDER

RANK	STATE	ADULTS	% of USA
1	Texas	442,251	11.6%
2	California	343,145	9.0%
3	Georgia	308,344	8.1%
4	Florida	294,786	7.7%
5	Ohio	194,875	5.1%
6	New York	191,970	5.0%
7	Michigan	173,676	4.6%
8	Washington	160,977	4.2%
9	Illinois	139,029	3.7%
10	New Jersey	130,610	3.4%
11	Pennsylvania	121,034	3.2%
12	Minnesota	114,468	3.0%
13	Indiana	107,673	2.8%
14	North Carolina	105,949	2.8%
15	Maryland	83,852	2.2%
16	Arizona	60,751	1.6%
17	Connecticut	55,070	1.4%
18	Wisconsin	54,272	1.4%
19	Missouri	49,975	1.3%
20	Colorado	47,084	1.2%
21	Oregon	46,199	1.2%
22	Massachusetts	45,233	1.2%
23	South Carolina	42,883	1.1%
24	Tennessee	40,829	1.1%
25	Alabama	40,627	1.1%
26	Louisiana	35,854	0.9%
27	Idaho	35,091	0.9%
28	Virginia	33,955	0.9%
29	Oklahoma	30,994	0.8%
30	Arkansas	30,353	0.8%
31	Rhode Island	22,964	0.6%
32	Nebraska	21,483	0.6%
33	Iowa	21,147	0.6%
34	Kentucky	20,610	0.5%
35	Delaware	20,052	0.5%
36	Kansas	15,996	0.4%
37	Hawaii	15,525	0.4%
38	Mississippi	15,118	0.4%
39	Nevada	12,189	0.3%
40	New Mexico	10,512	0.3%
41	Utah	9,828	0.3%
42	Vermont	9,303	0.2%
43	Maine	7,788	0.2%
44	West Virginia	6,058	0.2%
45	Montana	6,043	0.2%
46	Alaska	4,760	0.1%
47	South Dakota	4,214	0.1%
48	Wyoming	4,115	0.1%
49	New Hampshire	3,629	0.1%
50	North Dakota	2,789	0.1%
	District of Columbia	12,061	0.3%

Source: U.S. Department of Justice, Bureau of Justice Statistics
"Probation and Parole in the United States, 2000" (Press Release, August 2001, NCJ-188208)
*As of December 31, 2000. Does not include 31,539 adults on federal probation.

Rate of Adults on State Probation in 2000

National Rate = 1,821 Adults on State Probation per 100,000 Adult Population*

ALPHA ORDER			RANK ORDER		
RANK	STATE	RATE	RANK	STATE	RATE
29	Alabama	1,222	1	Georgia	5,124
34	Alaska	1,091	2	Idaho	3,794
20	Arizona	1,614	3	Washington	3,675
21	Arkansas	1,523	4	Delaware	3,404
25	California	1,394	5	Minnesota	3,151
23	Colorado	1,471	6	Texas	2,955
12	Connecticut	2,148	7	Rhode Island	2,869
4	Delaware	3,404	8	Florida	2,390
8	Florida	2,390	8	Indiana	2,390
1	Georgia	5,124	10	Michigan	2,365
19	Hawaii	1,695	11	Ohio	2,302
2	Idaho	3,794	12	Connecticut	2,148
22	Illinois	1,515	13	Maryland	2,128
8	Indiana	2,390	14	New Jersey	2,064
35	Iowa	964	15	Vermont	2,017
40	Kansas	810	16	Oregon	1,794
45	Kentucky	676	17	North Carolina	1,741
33	Louisiana	1,103	18	Nebraska	1,704
42	Maine	800	19	Hawaii	1,695
13	Maryland	2,128	20	Arizona	1,614
37	Massachusetts	933	21	Arkansas	1,523
10	Michigan	2,365	22	Illinois	1,515
5	Minnesota	3,151	23	Colorado	1,471
44	Mississippi	731	24	South Carolina	1,428
31	Missouri	1,199	25	California	1,394
38	Montana	899	26	Wisconsin	1,359
18	Nebraska	1,704	27	New York	1,344
39	Nevada	820	28	Pennsylvania	1,293
50	New Hampshire	392	29	Alabama	1,222
14	New Jersey	2,064	30	Oklahoma	1,212
41	New Mexico	802	31	Missouri	1,199
27	New York	1,344	32	Wyoming	1,128
17	North Carolina	1,741	33	Louisiana	1,103
48	North Dakota	579	34	Alaska	1,091
11	Ohio	2,302	35	Iowa	964
30	Oklahoma	1,212	36	Tennessee	952
16	Oregon	1,794	37	Massachusetts	933
28	Pennsylvania	1,293	38	Montana	899
7	Rhode Island	2,869	39	Nevada	820
24	South Carolina	1,428	40	Kansas	810
43	South Dakota	763	41	New Mexico	802
36	Tennessee	952	42	Maine	800
6	Texas	2,955	43	South Dakota	763
46	Utah	649	44	Mississippi	731
15	Vermont	2,017	45	Kentucky	676
47	Virginia	636	46	Utah	649
3	Washington	3,675	47	Virginia	636
49	West Virginia	431	48	North Dakota	579
26	Wisconsin	1,359	49	West Virginia	431
32	Wyoming	1,128	50	New Hampshire	392
				District of Columbia	2,639

Source: U.S. Department of Justice, Bureau of Justice Statistics
   "Probation and Parole in the United States, 2000" (Press Release, August 2001, NCJ-188208)
*As of December 31, 2000. Federal rate is 15 adults on federal probation per 100,000 adult population.

Adults on State Parole in 2000

National Total = 652,199 Adults*

RANK	STATE	ADULTS	% of USA
19	Alabama	5,494	0.8%
45	Alaska	507	0.1%
27	Arizona	3,474	0.5%
14	Arkansas	9,453	1.4%
1	California	117,647	18.0%
18	Colorado	5,500	0.8%
33	Connecticut	1,868	0.3%
43	Delaware	579	0.1%
17	Florida	6,046	0.9%
7	Georgia	21,556	3.3%
32	Hawaii	2,504	0.4%
38	Idaho	1,443	0.2%
5	Illinois	30,199	4.6%
21	Indiana	4,917	0.8%
31	Iowa	2,763	0.4%
25	Kansas	3,829	0.6%
22	Kentucky	4,909	0.8%
6	Louisiana	22,860	3.5%
50	Maine	28	0.0%
12	Maryland	14,143	2.2%
26	Massachusetts	3,703	0.6%
10	Michigan	15,753	2.4%
30	Minnesota	3,072	0.5%
36	Mississippi	1,596	0.2%
13	Missouri	12,357	1.9%
42	Montana	621	0.1%
46	Nebraska	473	0.1%
24	Nevada	4,056	0.6%
40	New Hampshire	944	0.1%
11	New Jersey	14,899	2.3%
35	New Mexico	1,670	0.3%
4	New York	57,858	8.9%
28	North Carolina	3,352	0.5%
49	North Dakota	116	0.0%
8	Ohio	18,248	2.8%
34	Oklahoma	1,825	0.3%
9	Oregon	17,832	2.7%
3	Pennsylvania	82,002	12.6%
47	Rhode Island	353	0.1%
23	South Carolina	4,240	0.7%
37	South Dakota	1,481	0.2%
16	Tennessee	8,094	1.2%
2	Texas	111,719	17.1%
29	Utah	3,266	0.5%
41	Vermont	902	0.1%
20	Virginia	5,148	0.8%
48	Washington	160	0.0%
39	West Virginia	1,112	0.2%
15	Wisconsin	9,430	1.4%
44	Wyoming	514	0.1%

RANK	STATE	ADULTS	% of USA
1	California	117,647	18.0%
2	Texas	111,719	17.1%
3	Pennsylvania	82,002	12.6%
4	New York	57,858	8.9%
5	Illinois	30,199	4.6%
6	Louisiana	22,860	3.5%
7	Georgia	21,556	3.3%
8	Ohio	18,248	2.8%
9	Oregon	17,832	2.7%
10	Michigan	15,753	2.4%
11	New Jersey	14,899	2.3%
12	Maryland	14,143	2.2%
13	Missouri	12,357	1.9%
14	Arkansas	9,453	1.4%
15	Wisconsin	9,430	1.4%
16	Tennessee	8,094	1.2%
17	Florida	6,046	0.9%
18	Colorado	5,500	0.8%
19	Alabama	5,494	0.8%
20	Virginia	5,148	0.8%
21	Indiana	4,917	0.8%
22	Kentucky	4,909	0.8%
23	South Carolina	4,240	0.7%
24	Nevada	4,056	0.6%
25	Kansas	3,829	0.6%
26	Massachusetts	3,703	0.6%
27	Arizona	3,474	0.5%
28	North Carolina	3,352	0.5%
29	Utah	3,266	0.5%
30	Minnesota	3,072	0.5%
31	Iowa	2,763	0.4%
32	Hawaii	2,504	0.4%
33	Connecticut	1,868	0.3%
34	Oklahoma	1,825	0.3%
35	New Mexico	1,670	0.3%
36	Mississippi	1,596	0.2%
37	South Dakota	1,481	0.2%
38	Idaho	1,443	0.2%
39	West Virginia	1,112	0.2%
40	New Hampshire	944	0.1%
41	Vermont	902	0.1%
42	Montana	621	0.1%
43	Delaware	579	0.1%
44	Wyoming	514	0.1%
45	Alaska	507	0.1%
46	Nebraska	473	0.1%
47	Rhode Island	353	0.1%
48	Washington	160	0.0%
49	North Dakota	116	0.0%
50	Maine	28	0.0%
	District of Columbia	5,684	0.9%

Source: U.S. Department of Justice, Bureau of Justice Statistics
"Probation and Parole in the United States, 2000" (Press Release, August 2001, NCJ-188208)
*As of December 31, 2000. Does not include 73,328 adults on federal parole.

Rate of Adults on State Parole in 2000

National Rate = 312 Adults on State Parole per 100,000 Adult Population*

ALPHA ORDER

RANK ORDER

RANK	STATE	RATE
24	Alabama	165
31	Alaska	116
36	Arizona	92
6	Arkansas	474
5	California	478
23	Colorado	172
42	Connecticut	73
34	Delaware	98
45	Florida	49
9	Georgia	358
12	Hawaii	273
26	Idaho	156
10	Illinois	329
32	Indiana	109
30	Iowa	126
21	Kansas	194
25	Kentucky	161
3	Louisiana	704
50	Maine	3
8	Maryland	359
41	Massachusetts	76
19	Michigan	215
38	Minnesota	85
40	Mississippi	77
11	Missouri	297
36	Montana	92
47	Nebraska	38
12	Nevada	273
33	New Hampshire	102
16	New Jersey	235
29	New Mexico	127
7	New York	405
44	North Carolina	55
48	North Dakota	24
17	Ohio	216
43	Oklahoma	71
4	Oregon	693
1	Pennsylvania	876
46	Rhode Island	44
27	South Carolina	141
14	South Dakota	268
22	Tennessee	189
2	Texas	747
17	Utah	216
20	Vermont	196
35	Virginia	96
49	Washington	4
39	West Virginia	79
15	Wisconsin	236
27	Wyoming	141

RANK	STATE	RATE
1	Pennsylvania	876
2	Texas	747
3	Louisiana	704
4	Oregon	693
5	California	478
6	Arkansas	474
7	New York	405
8	Maryland	359
9	Georgia	358
10	Illinois	329
11	Missouri	297
12	Hawaii	273
12	Nevada	273
14	South Dakota	268
15	Wisconsin	236
16	New Jersey	235
17	Ohio	216
17	Utah	216
19	Michigan	215
20	Vermont	196
21	Kansas	194
22	Tennessee	189
23	Colorado	172
24	Alabama	165
25	Kentucky	161
26	Idaho	156
27	South Carolina	141
27	Wyoming	141
29	New Mexico	127
30	Iowa	126
31	Alaska	116
32	Indiana	109
33	New Hampshire	102
34	Delaware	98
35	Virginia	96
36	Arizona	92
36	Montana	92
38	Minnesota	85
39	West Virginia	79
40	Mississippi	77
41	Massachusetts	76
42	Connecticut	73
43	Oklahoma	71
44	North Carolina	55
45	Florida	49
46	Rhode Island	44
47	Nebraska	38
48	North Dakota	24
49	Washington	4
50	Maine	3
	District of Columbia	1,244

Source: U.S. Department of Justice, Bureau of Justice Statistics
   "Probation and Parole in the United States, 2000" (Press Release, August 2001, NCJ-188208)
*As of December 31, 2000. Federal rate is 35 adults on federal parole per 100,000 adult population.

State and Local Government Employees in Corrections in 2000

National Total = 683,475 Employees*

ALPHA ORDER

RANK	STATE	EMPLOYEES	% of USA
28	Alabama	7,103	1.0%
44	Alaska	1,713	0.3%
15	Arizona	13,556	2.0%
33	Arkansas	5,345	0.8%
1	California	77,838	11.4%
23	Colorado	9,410	1.4%
24	Connecticut	9,003	1.3%
39	Delaware	2,423	0.4%
4	Florida	42,666	6.2%
5	Georgia	26,595	3.9%
40	Hawaii	2,396	0.4%
38	Idaho	2,627	0.4%
8	Illinois	25,178	3.7%
20	Indiana	11,278	1.7%
35	Iowa	4,418	0.6%
31	Kansas	6,137	0.9%
29	Kentucky	6,682	1.0%
16	Louisiana	13,412	2.0%
42	Maine	1,767	0.3%
13	Maryland	14,365	2.1%
22	Massachusetts	10,364	1.5%
9	Michigan	23,749	3.5%
26	Minnesota	7,867	1.2%
30	Mississippi	6,254	0.9%
14	Missouri	13,811	2.0%
45	Montana	1,619	0.2%
37	Nebraska	2,998	0.4%
34	Nevada	4,536	0.7%
43	New Hampshire	1,740	0.3%
12	New Jersey	15,899	2.3%
32	New Mexico	5,498	0.8%
3	New York	61,377	9.0%
10	North Carolina	22,892	3.3%
50	North Dakota	804	0.1%
6	Ohio	26,386	3.9%
27	Oklahoma	7,131	1.0%
25	Oregon	8,159	1.2%
7	Pennsylvania	26,321	3.9%
41	Rhode Island	1,822	0.3%
19	South Carolina	11,366	1.7%
47	South Dakota	1,354	0.2%
21	Tennessee	10,733	1.6%
2	Texas	69,116	10.1%
36	Utah	4,292	0.6%
49	Vermont	988	0.1%
11	Virginia	22,180	3.2%
18	Washington	12,379	1.8%
46	West Virginia	1,597	0.2%
17	Wisconsin	12,857	1.9%
48	Wyoming	1,109	0.2%

RANK ORDER

RANK	STATE	EMPLOYEES	% of USA
1	California	77,838	11.4%
2	Texas	69,116	10.1%
3	New York	61,377	9.0%
4	Florida	42,666	6.2%
5	Georgia	26,595	3.9%
6	Ohio	26,386	3.9%
7	Pennsylvania	26,321	3.9%
8	Illinois	25,178	3.7%
9	Michigan	23,749	3.5%
10	North Carolina	22,892	3.3%
11	Virginia	22,180	3.2%
12	New Jersey	15,899	2.3%
13	Maryland	14,365	2.1%
14	Missouri	13,811	2.0%
15	Arizona	13,556	2.0%
16	Louisiana	13,412	2.0%
17	Wisconsin	12,857	1.9%
18	Washington	12,379	1.8%
19	South Carolina	11,366	1.7%
20	Indiana	11,278	1.7%
21	Tennessee	10,733	1.6%
22	Massachusetts	10,364	1.5%
23	Colorado	9,410	1.4%
24	Connecticut	9,003	1.3%
25	Oregon	8,159	1.2%
26	Minnesota	7,867	1.2%
27	Oklahoma	7,131	1.0%
28	Alabama	7,103	1.0%
29	Kentucky	6,682	1.0%
30	Mississippi	6,254	0.9%
31	Kansas	6,137	0.9%
32	New Mexico	5,498	0.8%
33	Arkansas	5,345	0.8%
34	Nevada	4,536	0.7%
35	Iowa	4,418	0.6%
36	Utah	4,292	0.6%
37	Nebraska	2,998	0.4%
38	Idaho	2,627	0.4%
39	Delaware	2,423	0.4%
40	Hawaii	2,396	0.4%
41	Rhode Island	1,822	0.3%
42	Maine	1,767	0.3%
43	New Hampshire	1,740	0.3%
44	Alaska	1,713	0.3%
45	Montana	1,619	0.2%
46	West Virginia	1,597	0.2%
47	South Dakota	1,354	0.2%
48	Wyoming	1,109	0.2%
49	Vermont	988	0.1%
50	North Dakota	804	0.1%
	District of Columbia	2,365	0.3%

Source: U.S. Bureau of the Census, Governments Division
"State and Local Employment and Payroll - March 2000" (http://www.census.gov/govs/www/apesstl00.html)
*Full-time equivalent as of March 2000.

State and Local Government Employees in Corrections as a Percent of All State and Local Government Employees in 2000
National Percent = 4.5% of Employees*

ALPHA ORDER

RANK	STATE	PERCENT
44	Alabama	2.7
26	Alaska	3.6
5	Arizona	5.5
25	Arkansas	3.7
17	California	4.6
22	Colorado	4.1
10	Connecticut	5.1
6	Delaware	5.4
4	Florida	5.6
1	Georgia	5.9
32	Hawaii	3.5
26	Idaho	3.6
22	Illinois	4.1
26	Indiana	3.6
47	Iowa	2.5
26	Kansas	3.6
40	Kentucky	3.0
14	Louisiana	4.8
47	Maine	2.5
8	Maryland	5.2
38	Massachusetts	3.2
14	Michigan	4.8
41	Minnesota	2.8
35	Mississippi	3.3
17	Missouri	4.6
39	Montana	3.1
41	Nebraska	2.8
6	Nevada	5.4
44	New Hampshire	2.7
32	New Jersey	3.5
16	New Mexico	4.7
8	New York	5.2
10	North Carolina	5.1
49	North Dakota	2.1
21	Ohio	4.4
26	Oklahoma	3.6
17	Oregon	4.6
12	Pennsylvania	4.9
35	Rhode Island	3.3
12	South Carolina	4.9
35	South Dakota	3.3
26	Tennessee	3.6
1	Texas	5.9
32	Utah	3.5
44	Vermont	2.7
3	Virginia	5.7
22	Washington	4.1
50	West Virginia	1.7
20	Wisconsin	4.5
41	Wyoming	2.8

RANK ORDER

RANK	STATE	PERCENT
1	Georgia	5.9
1	Texas	5.9
3	Virginia	5.7
4	Florida	5.6
5	Arizona	5.5
6	Delaware	5.4
6	Nevada	5.4
8	Maryland	5.2
8	New York	5.2
10	Connecticut	5.1
10	North Carolina	5.1
12	Pennsylvania	4.9
12	South Carolina	4.9
14	Louisiana	4.8
14	Michigan	4.8
16	New Mexico	4.7
17	California	4.6
17	Missouri	4.6
17	Oregon	4.6
20	Wisconsin	4.5
21	Ohio	4.4
22	Colorado	4.1
22	Illinois	4.1
22	Washington	4.1
25	Arkansas	3.7
26	Alaska	3.6
26	Idaho	3.6
26	Indiana	3.6
26	Kansas	3.6
26	Oklahoma	3.6
26	Tennessee	3.6
32	Hawaii	3.5
32	New Jersey	3.5
32	Utah	3.5
35	Mississippi	3.3
35	Rhode Island	3.3
35	South Dakota	3.3
38	Massachusetts	3.2
39	Montana	3.1
40	Kentucky	3.0
41	Minnesota	2.8
41	Nebraska	2.8
41	Wyoming	2.8
44	Alabama	2.7
44	New Hampshire	2.7
44	Vermont	2.7
47	Iowa	2.5
47	Maine	2.5
49	North Dakota	2.1
50	West Virginia	1.7

	District of Columbia	5.2

Source: Morgan Quitno Press using data from U.S. Bureau of the Census, Governments Division
    "State and Local Employment and Payroll - March 2000" (http://www.census.gov/govs/www/apesstl00.html)
*Full-time equivalent as of March 2000.

State Government Employees in Corrections in 2000

National Total = 450,751 Employees*

RANK	STATE	EMPLOYEES	% of USA
26	Alabama	4,368	1.0%
41	Alaska	1,583	0.4%
14	Arizona	9,524	2.1%
30	Arkansas	3,752	0.8%
2	California	45,244	10.0%
24	Colorado	6,043	1.3%
17	Connecticut	8,953	2.0%
38	Delaware	2,307	0.5%
4	Florida	28,255	6.3%
6	Georgia	18,994	4.2%
37	Hawaii	2,383	0.5%
42	Idaho	1,578	0.4%
9	Illinois	15,751	3.5%
22	Indiana	6,481	1.4%
34	Iowa	3,286	0.7%
33	Kansas	3,582	0.8%
31	Kentucky	3,643	0.8%
19	Louisiana	7,427	1.6%
45	Maine	1,164	0.3%
13	Maryland	11,124	2.5%
20	Massachusetts	6,970	1.5%
7	Michigan	18,295	4.1%
32	Minnesota	3,612	0.8%
28	Mississippi	4,227	0.9%
12	Missouri	11,376	2.5%
46	Montana	1,032	0.2%
39	Nebraska	1,962	0.4%
35	Nevada	2,913	0.6%
44	New Hampshire	1,215	0.3%
15	New Jersey	9,465	2.1%
29	New Mexico	3,972	0.9%
3	New York	35,386	7.9%
5	North Carolina	19,087	4.2%
50	North Dakota	551	0.1%
8	Ohio	18,085	4.0%
25	Oklahoma	5,930	1.3%
27	Oregon	4,334	1.0%
11	Pennsylvania	14,714	3.3%
40	Rhode Island	1,822	0.4%
16	South Carolina	9,092	2.0%
48	South Dakota	847	0.2%
23	Tennessee	6,187	1.4%
1	Texas	47,392	10.5%
36	Utah	2,811	0.6%
47	Vermont	974	0.2%
10	Virginia	15,440	3.4%
21	Washington	6,737	1.5%
43	West Virginia	1,263	0.3%
18	Wisconsin	8,817	2.0%
49	Wyoming	801	0.2%

RANK	STATE	EMPLOYEES	% of USA
1	Texas	47,392	10.5%
2	California	45,244	10.0%
3	New York	35,386	7.9%
4	Florida	28,255	6.3%
5	North Carolina	19,087	4.2%
6	Georgia	18,994	4.2%
7	Michigan	18,295	4.1%
8	Ohio	18,085	4.0%
9	Illinois	15,751	3.5%
10	Virginia	15,440	3.4%
11	Pennsylvania	14,714	3.3%
12	Missouri	11,376	2.5%
13	Maryland	11,124	2.5%
14	Arizona	9,524	2.1%
15	New Jersey	9,465	2.1%
16	South Carolina	9,092	2.0%
17	Connecticut	8,953	2.0%
18	Wisconsin	8,817	2.0%
19	Louisiana	7,427	1.6%
20	Massachusetts	6,970	1.5%
21	Washington	6,737	1.5%
22	Indiana	6,481	1.4%
23	Tennessee	6,187	1.4%
24	Colorado	6,043	1.3%
25	Oklahoma	5,930	1.3%
26	Alabama	4,368	1.0%
27	Oregon	4,334	1.0%
28	Mississippi	4,227	0.9%
29	New Mexico	3,972	0.9%
30	Arkansas	3,752	0.8%
31	Kentucky	3,643	0.8%
32	Minnesota	3,612	0.8%
33	Kansas	3,582	0.8%
34	Iowa	3,286	0.7%
35	Nevada	2,913	0.6%
36	Utah	2,811	0.6%
37	Hawaii	2,383	0.5%
38	Delaware	2,307	0.5%
39	Nebraska	1,962	0.4%
40	Rhode Island	1,822	0.4%
41	Alaska	1,583	0.4%
42	Idaho	1,578	0.4%
43	West Virginia	1,263	0.3%
44	New Hampshire	1,215	0.3%
45	Maine	1,164	0.3%
46	Montana	1,032	0.2%
47	Vermont	974	0.2%
48	South Dakota	847	0.2%
49	Wyoming	801	0.2%
50	North Dakota	551	0.1%
	District of Columbia**	NA	NA

Source: U.S. Bureau of the Census, Governments Division

"State Government Employment and Payroll - March 2000" (http://www.census.gov/govs/www/apesst00.html)
*Full-time equivalent as of March 2000.
**Not applicable.

State Government Employees in Corrections
As a Percent of All State Government Employees in 2000
National Percent = 12.6% of Employees*

ALPHA ORDER

RANK	STATE	PERCENT
45	Alabama	6.2
38	Alaska	7.5
3	Arizona	17.1
30	Arkansas	8.4
13	California	14.9
17	Colorado	13.2
9	Connecticut	15.4
20	Delaware	11.0
4	Florida	17.0
2	Georgia	18.2
48	Hawaii	4.9
28	Idaho	8.7
14	Illinois	14.3
26	Indiana	9.2
34	Iowa	7.7
23	Kansas	9.8
47	Kentucky	5.6
29	Louisiana	8.6
44	Maine	6.5
16	Maryland	13.6
32	Massachusetts	8.1
7	Michigan	16.4
46	Minnesota	6.1
30	Mississippi	8.4
15	Missouri	13.8
42	Montana	6.7
38	Nebraska	7.5
12	Nevada	15.0
34	New Hampshire	7.7
37	New Jersey	7.6
25	New Mexico	9.4
11	New York	15.1
4	North Carolina	17.0
50	North Dakota	4.2
8	Ohio	15.9
21	Oklahoma	10.5
24	Oregon	9.6
19	Pennsylvania	11.1
22	Rhode Island	10.3
18	South Carolina	12.5
41	South Dakota	7.3
27	Tennessee	8.8
1	Texas	19.5
43	Utah	6.6
34	Vermont	7.7
10	Virginia	15.3
40	Washington	7.4
49	West Virginia	4.3
6	Wisconsin	16.6
33	Wyoming	8.0

RANK ORDER

RANK	STATE	PERCENT
1	Texas	19.5
2	Georgia	18.2
3	Arizona	17.1
4	Florida	17.0
4	North Carolina	17.0
6	Wisconsin	16.6
7	Michigan	16.4
8	Ohio	15.9
9	Connecticut	15.4
10	Virginia	15.3
11	New York	15.1
12	Nevada	15.0
13	California	14.9
14	Illinois	14.3
15	Missouri	13.8
16	Maryland	13.6
17	Colorado	13.2
18	South Carolina	12.5
19	Pennsylvania	11.1
20	Delaware	11.0
21	Oklahoma	10.5
22	Rhode Island	10.3
23	Kansas	9.8
24	Oregon	9.6
25	New Mexico	9.4
26	Indiana	9.2
27	Tennessee	8.8
28	Idaho	8.7
29	Louisiana	8.6
30	Arkansas	8.4
30	Mississippi	8.4
32	Massachusetts	8.1
33	Wyoming	8.0
34	Iowa	7.7
34	New Hampshire	7.7
34	Vermont	7.7
37	New Jersey	7.6
38	Alaska	7.5
38	Nebraska	7.5
40	Washington	7.4
41	South Dakota	7.3
42	Montana	6.7
43	Utah	6.6
44	Maine	6.5
45	Alabama	6.2
46	Minnesota	6.1
47	Kentucky	5.6
48	Hawaii	4.9
49	West Virginia	4.3
50	North Dakota	4.2
	District of Columbia**	NA

Source: Morgan Quitno Press using data from U.S. Bureau of the Census, Governments Division
"State Government Employment and Payroll - March 2000" (http://www.census.gov/govs/www/apesst00.html)
*Full-time equivalent as of March 2000.
**Not applicable.

Jail and Detention Centers in 1999

National Total = 3,365 Jails*

RANK	STATE	JAILS	% of USA
3	Alabama	155	4.6%
43	Alaska	15	0.4%
36	Arizona	28	0.8%
18	Arkansas	87	2.6%
4	California	145	4.3%
27	Colorado	61	1.8%
NA	Connecticut**	NA	NA
NA	Delaware**	NA	NA
6	Florida	108	3.2%
2	Georgia	204	6.1%
NA	Hawaii**	NA	NA
30	Idaho	41	1.2%
15	Illinois	93	2.8%
15	Indiana	93	2.8%
14	Iowa	94	2.8%
13	Kansas	97	2.9%
19	Kentucky	82	2.4%
9	Louisiana	107	3.2%
43	Maine	15	0.4%
34	Maryland	29	0.9%
41	Massachusetts	21	0.6%
15	Michigan	93	2.8%
22	Minnesota	78	2.3%
11	Mississippi	102	3.0%
5	Missouri	129	3.8%
29	Montana	42	1.2%
25	Nebraska	65	1.9%
41	Nevada	21	0.6%
45	New Hampshire	10	0.3%
38	New Jersey	24	0.7%
32	New Mexico	34	1.0%
21	New York	81	2.4%
10	North Carolina	104	3.1%
39	North Dakota	23	0.7%
6	Ohio	108	3.2%
11	Oklahoma	102	3.0%
30	Oregon	41	1.2%
23	Pennsylvania	76	2.3%
NA	Rhode Island**	NA	NA
28	South Carolina	52	1.5%
33	South Dakota	31	0.9%
6	Tennessee	108	3.2%
1	Texas	271	8.1%
37	Utah	26	0.8%
NA	Vermont**	NA	NA
19	Virginia	82	2.4%
26	Washington	62	1.8%
34	West Virginia	29	0.9%
24	Wisconsin	73	2.2%
40	Wyoming	22	0.7%

RANK	STATE	JAILS	% of USA
1	Texas	271	8.1%
2	Georgia	204	6.1%
3	Alabama	155	4.6%
4	California	145	4.3%
5	Missouri	129	3.8%
6	Florida	108	3.2%
6	Ohio	108	3.2%
6	Tennessee	108	3.2%
9	Louisiana	107	3.2%
10	North Carolina	104	3.1%
11	Mississippi	102	3.0%
11	Oklahoma	102	3.0%
13	Kansas	97	2.9%
14	Iowa	94	2.8%
15	Illinois	93	2.8%
15	Indiana	93	2.8%
15	Michigan	93	2.8%
18	Arkansas	87	2.6%
19	Kentucky	82	2.4%
19	Virginia	82	2.4%
21	New York	81	2.4%
22	Minnesota	78	2.3%
23	Pennsylvania	76	2.3%
24	Wisconsin	73	2.2%
25	Nebraska	65	1.9%
26	Washington	62	1.8%
27	Colorado	61	1.8%
28	South Carolina	52	1.5%
29	Montana	42	1.2%
30	Idaho	41	1.2%
30	Oregon	41	1.2%
32	New Mexico	34	1.0%
33	South Dakota	31	0.9%
34	Maryland	29	0.9%
34	West Virginia	29	0.9%
36	Arizona	28	0.8%
37	Utah	26	0.8%
38	New Jersey	24	0.7%
39	North Dakota	23	0.7%
40	Wyoming	22	0.7%
41	Massachusetts	21	0.6%
41	Nevada	21	0.6%
43	Alaska	15	0.4%
43	Maine	15	0.4%
45	New Hampshire	10	0.3%
NA	Connecticut**	NA	NA
NA	Delaware**	NA	NA
NA	Hawaii**	NA	NA
NA	Rhode Island**	NA	NA
NA	Vermont**	NA	NA
	District of Columbia	1	0.0%

Source: U.S. Department of Justice, Bureau of Justice Statistics
"Census of Jails, 1999" (August 2001, NCJ-186633)
As of July 1, 1999. Jails are locally operated correctional facilities that confine persons before or after adjudication. Inmates sentenced to jail usually have a sentence of a year or less.
**These states have combined state and local jail systems and are excluded from this count.*

Inmates in Local Jails in 1999

National Total = 605,943 Inmates*

ALPHA ORDER

RANK	STATE	INMATES	% of USA
17	Alabama	11,418	1.9%
45	Alaska	68	0.0%
22	Arizona	10,320	1.7%
32	Arkansas	4,832	0.8%
1	California	77,142	12.7%
23	Colorado	9,004	1.5%
NA	Connecticut**	NA	NA
NA	Delaware**	NA	NA
3	Florida	51,080	8.4%
5	Georgia	32,835	5.4%
NA	Hawaii**	NA	NA
36	Idaho	2,809	0.5%
10	Illinois	16,880	2.8%
15	Indiana	12,787	2.1%
35	Iowa	2,998	0.5%
33	Kansas	4,378	0.7%
21	Kentucky	10,373	1.7%
7	Louisiana	25,631	4.2%
41	Maine	1,113	0.2%
18	Maryland	10,945	1.8%
19	Massachusetts	10,774	1.8%
13	Michigan	15,629	2.6%
30	Minnesota	5,002	0.8%
24	Mississippi	8,886	1.5%
26	Missouri	6,940	1.1%
40	Montana	1,521	0.3%
38	Nebraska	2,189	0.4%
31	Nevada	4,898	0.8%
39	New Hampshire	1,592	0.3%
11	New Jersey	16,830	2.8%
29	New Mexico	5,217	0.9%
4	New York	33,411	5.5%
14	North Carolina	13,279	2.2%
44	North Dakota	588	0.1%
12	Ohio	16,638	2.7%
27	Oklahoma	6,743	1.1%
28	Oregon	6,283	1.0%
6	Pennsylvania	26,996	4.5%
NA	Rhode Island**	NA	NA
25	South Carolina	8,780	1.4%
42	South Dakota	1,064	0.2%
8	Tennessee	19,629	3.2%
2	Texas	57,930	9.6%
34	Utah	4,024	0.7%
NA	Vermont**	NA	NA
9	Virginia	18,235	3.0%
20	Washington	10,542	1.7%
37	West Virginia	2,493	0.4%
16	Wisconsin	12,559	2.1%
43	Wyoming	1,005	0.2%

RANK ORDER

RANK	STATE	INMATES	% of USA
1	California	77,142	12.7%
2	Texas	57,930	9.6%
3	Florida	51,080	8.4%
4	New York	33,411	5.5%
5	Georgia	32,835	5.4%
6	Pennsylvania	26,996	4.5%
7	Louisiana	25,631	4.2%
8	Tennessee	19,629	3.2%
9	Virginia	18,235	3.0%
10	Illinois	16,880	2.8%
11	New Jersey	16,830	2.8%
12	Ohio	16,638	2.7%
13	Michigan	15,629	2.6%
14	North Carolina	13,279	2.2%
15	Indiana	12,787	2.1%
16	Wisconsin	12,559	2.1%
17	Alabama	11,418	1.9%
18	Maryland	10,945	1.8%
19	Massachusetts	10,774	1.8%
20	Washington	10,542	1.7%
21	Kentucky	10,373	1.7%
22	Arizona	10,320	1.7%
23	Colorado	9,004	1.5%
24	Mississippi	8,886	1.5%
25	South Carolina	8,780	1.4%
26	Missouri	6,940	1.1%
27	Oklahoma	6,743	1.1%
28	Oregon	6,283	1.0%
29	New Mexico	5,217	0.9%
30	Minnesota	5,002	0.8%
31	Nevada	4,898	0.8%
32	Arkansas	4,832	0.8%
33	Kansas	4,378	0.7%
34	Utah	4,024	0.7%
35	Iowa	2,998	0.5%
36	Idaho	2,809	0.5%
37	West Virginia	2,493	0.4%
38	Nebraska	2,189	0.4%
39	New Hampshire	1,592	0.3%
40	Montana	1,521	0.3%
41	Maine	1,113	0.2%
42	South Dakota	1,064	0.2%
43	Wyoming	1,005	0.2%
44	North Dakota	588	0.1%
45	Alaska	68	0.0%
NA	Connecticut**	NA	NA
NA	Delaware**	NA	NA
NA	Hawaii**	NA	NA
NA	Rhode Island**	NA	NA
NA	Vermont**	NA	NA
	District of Columbia	1,653	0.3%

Source: U.S. Department of Justice, Bureau of Justice Statistics
    "Census of Jails, 1999" (August 2001, NCJ-186633)
*As of July 1, 1999. Jails are locally operated correctional facilities that confine persons before or after
adjudication. Inmates sentenced to jail usually have a sentence of a year or less.
**These states have combined state and local jail systems and are excluded from this count.

Rate of Inmates in Local Jails in 1999

National Rate = 222 Inmates per 100,000 Population*

<table>
<tr><td colspan="3">ALPHA ORDER</td><td colspan="3">RANK ORDER</td></tr>
<tr><td>RANK</td><td>STATE</td><td>RATE</td><td>RANK</td><td>STATE</td><td>RATE</td></tr>
<tr><td>11</td><td>Alabama</td><td>261</td><td>1</td><td>Louisiana</td><td>585</td></tr>
<tr><td>NA</td><td>Alaska**</td><td>NA</td><td>2</td><td>Georgia</td><td>421</td></tr>
<tr><td>18</td><td>Arizona</td><td>216</td><td>3</td><td>Tennessee</td><td>358</td></tr>
<tr><td>24</td><td>Arkansas</td><td>189</td><td>4</td><td>Florida</td><td>337</td></tr>
<tr><td>13</td><td>California</td><td>233</td><td>5</td><td>Mississippi</td><td>320</td></tr>
<tr><td>17</td><td>Colorado</td><td>222</td><td>6</td><td>New Mexico</td><td>298</td></tr>
<tr><td>NA</td><td>Connecticut**</td><td>NA</td><td>7</td><td>Texas</td><td>288</td></tr>
<tr><td>NA</td><td>Delaware**</td><td>NA</td><td>8</td><td>Nevada</td><td>270</td></tr>
<tr><td>4</td><td>Florida</td><td>337</td><td>9</td><td>Virginia</td><td>266</td></tr>
<tr><td>2</td><td>Georgia</td><td>421</td><td>10</td><td>Kentucky</td><td>262</td></tr>
<tr><td>NA</td><td>Hawaii**</td><td>NA</td><td>11</td><td>Alabama</td><td>261</td></tr>
<tr><td>15</td><td>Idaho</td><td>225</td><td>12</td><td>Wisconsin</td><td>239</td></tr>
<tr><td>36</td><td>Illinois</td><td>139</td><td>13</td><td>California</td><td>233</td></tr>
<tr><td>19</td><td>Indiana</td><td>215</td><td>14</td><td>South Carolina</td><td>226</td></tr>
<tr><td>42</td><td>Iowa</td><td>104</td><td>15</td><td>Idaho</td><td>225</td></tr>
<tr><td>32</td><td>Kansas</td><td>165</td><td>15</td><td>Pennsylvania</td><td>225</td></tr>
<tr><td>10</td><td>Kentucky</td><td>262</td><td>17</td><td>Colorado</td><td>222</td></tr>
<tr><td>1</td><td>Louisiana</td><td>585</td><td>18</td><td>Arizona</td><td>216</td></tr>
<tr><td>44</td><td>Maine</td><td>89</td><td>19</td><td>Indiana</td><td>215</td></tr>
<tr><td>20</td><td>Maryland</td><td>211</td><td>20</td><td>Maryland</td><td>211</td></tr>
<tr><td>29</td><td>Massachusetts</td><td>174</td><td>21</td><td>Wyoming</td><td>209</td></tr>
<tr><td>33</td><td>Michigan</td><td>159</td><td>22</td><td>New Jersey</td><td>206</td></tr>
<tr><td>41</td><td>Minnesota</td><td>105</td><td>23</td><td>Oklahoma</td><td>200</td></tr>
<tr><td>5</td><td>Mississippi</td><td>320</td><td>24</td><td>Arkansas</td><td>189</td></tr>
<tr><td>40</td><td>Missouri</td><td>127</td><td>24</td><td>Oregon</td><td>189</td></tr>
<tr><td>31</td><td>Montana</td><td>172</td><td>26</td><td>Utah</td><td>188</td></tr>
<tr><td>39</td><td>Nebraska</td><td>131</td><td>27</td><td>New York</td><td>184</td></tr>
<tr><td>8</td><td>Nevada</td><td>270</td><td>28</td><td>Washington</td><td>183</td></tr>
<tr><td>38</td><td>New Hampshire</td><td>133</td><td>29</td><td>Massachusetts</td><td>174</td></tr>
<tr><td>22</td><td>New Jersey</td><td>206</td><td>30</td><td>North Carolina</td><td>173</td></tr>
<tr><td>6</td><td>New Mexico</td><td>298</td><td>31</td><td>Montana</td><td>172</td></tr>
<tr><td>27</td><td>New York</td><td>184</td><td>32</td><td>Kansas</td><td>165</td></tr>
<tr><td>30</td><td>North Carolina</td><td>173</td><td>33</td><td>Michigan</td><td>159</td></tr>
<tr><td>43</td><td>North Dakota</td><td>92</td><td>34</td><td>Ohio</td><td>148</td></tr>
<tr><td>34</td><td>Ohio</td><td>148</td><td>35</td><td>South Dakota</td><td>144</td></tr>
<tr><td>23</td><td>Oklahoma</td><td>200</td><td>36</td><td>Illinois</td><td>139</td></tr>
<tr><td>24</td><td>Oregon</td><td>189</td><td>37</td><td>West Virginia</td><td>138</td></tr>
<tr><td>15</td><td>Pennsylvania</td><td>225</td><td>38</td><td>New Hampshire</td><td>133</td></tr>
<tr><td>NA</td><td>Rhode Island**</td><td>NA</td><td>39</td><td>Nebraska</td><td>131</td></tr>
<tr><td>14</td><td>South Carolina</td><td>226</td><td>40</td><td>Missouri</td><td>127</td></tr>
<tr><td>35</td><td>South Dakota</td><td>144</td><td>41</td><td>Minnesota</td><td>105</td></tr>
<tr><td>3</td><td>Tennessee</td><td>358</td><td>42</td><td>Iowa</td><td>104</td></tr>
<tr><td>7</td><td>Texas</td><td>288</td><td>43</td><td>North Dakota</td><td>92</td></tr>
<tr><td>26</td><td>Utah</td><td>188</td><td>44</td><td>Maine</td><td>89</td></tr>
<tr><td>NA</td><td>Vermont**</td><td>NA</td><td>NA</td><td>Alaska**</td><td>NA</td></tr>
<tr><td>9</td><td>Virginia</td><td>266</td><td>NA</td><td>Connecticut**</td><td>NA</td></tr>
<tr><td>28</td><td>Washington</td><td>183</td><td>NA</td><td>Delaware**</td><td>NA</td></tr>
<tr><td>37</td><td>West Virginia</td><td>138</td><td>NA</td><td>Hawaii**</td><td>NA</td></tr>
<tr><td>12</td><td>Wisconsin</td><td>239</td><td>NA</td><td>Rhode Island**</td><td>NA</td></tr>
<tr><td>21</td><td>Wyoming</td><td>209</td><td>NA</td><td>Vermont**</td><td>NA</td></tr>
<tr><td></td><td></td><td></td><td></td><td>District of Columbia</td><td>320</td></tr>
</table>

Source: U.S. Department of Justice, Bureau of Justice Statistics
   "Census of Jails, 1999" (August 2001, NCJ-186633)
*As of July 1, 1999.   Jails are locally operated correctional facilities that confine persons before or after
adjudication. Inmates sentenced to jail usually have a sentence of a year or less.
**These states, except for Alaska, have combined state and local jail systems and are excluded from this count.
Alaska's rate would be less than one.

Average Daily Population in Local Jails in 1999

National Daily Average = 607,978 Inmates*

ALPHA ORDER					RANK ORDER			
RANK	STATE	INMATES	% of USA		RANK	STATE	INMATES	% of USA
19	Alabama	11,121	1.8%		1	California	77,851	12.8%
45	Alaska	67	0.0%		2	Texas	56,683	9.3%
21	Arizona	10,620	1.7%		3	Florida	50,863	8.4%
32	Arkansas	4,864	0.8%		4	New York	34,397	5.7%
1	California	77,851	12.8%		5	Georgia	34,039	5.6%
23	Colorado	8,879	1.5%		6	Pennsylvania	26,627	4.4%
NA	Connecticut**	NA	NA		7	Louisiana	25,569	4.2%
NA	Delaware**	NA	NA		8	Tennessee	20,536	3.4%
3	Florida	50,863	8.4%		9	Virginia	18,371	3.0%
5	Georgia	34,039	5.6%		10	Illinois	17,176	2.8%
NA	Hawaii**	NA	NA		11	New Jersey	16,543	2.7%
36	Idaho	2,586	0.4%		12	Ohio	16,526	2.7%
10	Illinois	17,176	2.8%		13	Michigan	15,770	2.6%
15	Indiana	12,014	2.0%		14	North Carolina	13,413	2.2%
35	Iowa	2,958	0.5%		15	Indiana	12,014	2.0%
33	Kansas	4,545	0.7%		16	Wisconsin	11,765	1.9%
22	Kentucky	10,512	1.7%		17	Maryland	11,370	1.9%
7	Louisiana	25,569	4.2%		18	Massachusetts	11,140	1.8%
42	Maine	1,132	0.2%		19	Alabama	11,121	1.8%
17	Maryland	11,370	1.9%		20	Washington	10,656	1.8%
18	Massachusetts	11,140	1.8%		21	Arizona	10,620	1.7%
13	Michigan	15,770	2.6%		22	Kentucky	10,512	1.7%
30	Minnesota	5,510	0.9%		23	Colorado	8,879	1.5%
24	Mississippi	8,878	1.5%		24	Mississippi	8,878	1.5%
26	Missouri	6,941	1.1%		25	South Carolina	8,792	1.4%
40	Montana	1,432	0.2%		26	Missouri	6,941	1.1%
38	Nebraska	1,528	0.3%		27	Oklahoma	6,700	1.1%
31	Nevada	5,194	0.9%		28	Oregon	6,320	1.0%
39	New Hampshire	1,513	0.2%		29	New Mexico	5,518	0.9%
11	New Jersey	16,543	2.7%		30	Minnesota	5,510	0.9%
29	New Mexico	5,518	0.9%		31	Nevada	5,194	0.9%
4	New York	34,397	5.7%		32	Arkansas	4,864	0.8%
14	North Carolina	13,413	2.2%		33	Kansas	4,545	0.7%
44	North Dakota	585	0.1%		34	Utah	4,159	0.7%
12	Ohio	16,526	2.7%		35	Iowa	2,958	0.5%
27	Oklahoma	6,700	1.1%		36	Idaho	2,586	0.4%
28	Oregon	6,320	1.0%		37	West Virginia	2,478	0.4%
6	Pennsylvania	26,627	4.4%		38	Nebraska	1,528	0.3%
NA	Rhode Island**	NA	NA		39	New Hampshire	1,513	0.2%
25	South Carolina	8,792	1.4%		40	Montana	1,432	0.2%
41	South Dakota	1,200	0.2%		41	South Dakota	1,200	0.2%
8	Tennessee	20,536	3.4%		42	Maine	1,132	0.2%
2	Texas	56,683	9.3%		43	Wyoming	977	0.2%
34	Utah	4,159	0.7%		44	North Dakota	585	0.1%
NA	Vermont**	NA	NA		45	Alaska	67	0.0%
9	Virginia	18,371	3.0%		NA	Connecticut**	NA	NA
20	Washington	10,656	1.8%		NA	Delaware**	NA	NA
37	West Virginia	2,478	0.4%		NA	Hawaii**	NA	NA
16	Wisconsin	11,765	1.9%		NA	Rhode Island**	NA	NA
43	Wyoming	977	0.2%		NA	Vermont**	NA	NA
						District of Columbia	1,660	0.3%

Source: U.S. Department of Justice, Bureau of Justice Statistics
   "Census of Jails, 1999" (August 2001, NCJ-186633)
*As of July 1, 1999. Jails are locally operated correctional facilities that confine persons before or after adjudication. Inmates sentenced to jail usually have a sentence of a year or less. This average is the sum of the number of inmates in a jail each day for a year divided by 365.
**These states have combined state and local jail systems and are excluded from this count.

Local Jail Inmates per Correctional Officer in 1999

National Rate = 4.3 Inmates per Officer*

ALPHA ORDER

RANK	STATE	RATE
9	Alabama	5.6
44	Alaska	1.8
15	Arizona	4.7
30	Arkansas	3.5
3	California	7.2
34	Colorado	3.2
NA	Connecticut**	NA
NA	Delaware**	NA
16	Florida	4.6
10	Georgia	5.3
NA	Hawaii**	NA
8	Idaho	5.7
1	Illinois	8.1
5	Indiana	5.9
41	Iowa	2.5
37	Kansas	3.1
12	Kentucky	4.9
4	Louisiana	6.0
44	Maine	1.8
28	Maryland	3.6
28	Massachusetts	3.6
12	Michigan	4.9
39	Minnesota	2.8
5	Mississippi	5.9
34	Missouri	3.2
34	Montana	3.2
40	Nebraska	2.6
24	Nevada	4.2
25	New Hampshire	3.8
27	New Jersey	3.7
5	New Mexico	5.9
43	New York	2.0
22	North Carolina	4.3
42	North Dakota	2.2
32	Ohio	3.3
16	Oklahoma	4.6
25	Oregon	3.8
18	Pennsylvania	4.5
NA	Rhode Island**	NA
20	South Carolina	4.4
37	South Dakota	3.1
20	Tennessee	4.4
18	Texas	4.5
2	Utah	7.3
NA	Vermont**	NA
32	Virginia	3.3
11	Washington	5.1
22	West Virginia	4.3
14	Wisconsin	4.8
31	Wyoming	3.4

RANK ORDER

RANK	STATE	RATE
1	Illinois	8.1
2	Utah	7.3
3	California	7.2
4	Louisiana	6.0
5	Indiana	5.9
5	Mississippi	5.9
5	New Mexico	5.9
8	Idaho	5.7
9	Alabama	5.6
10	Georgia	5.3
11	Washington	5.1
12	Kentucky	4.9
12	Michigan	4.9
14	Wisconsin	4.8
15	Arizona	4.7
16	Florida	4.6
16	Oklahoma	4.6
18	Pennsylvania	4.5
18	Texas	4.5
20	South Carolina	4.4
20	Tennessee	4.4
22	North Carolina	4.3
22	West Virginia	4.3
24	Nevada	4.2
25	New Hampshire	3.8
25	Oregon	3.8
27	New Jersey	3.7
28	Maryland	3.6
28	Massachusetts	3.6
30	Arkansas	3.5
31	Wyoming	3.4
32	Ohio	3.3
32	Virginia	3.3
34	Colorado	3.2
34	Missouri	3.2
34	Montana	3.2
37	Kansas	3.1
37	South Dakota	3.1
39	Minnesota	2.8
40	Nebraska	2.6
41	Iowa	2.5
42	North Dakota	2.2
43	New York	2.0
44	Alaska	1.8
44	Maine	1.8
NA	Connecticut**	NA
NA	Delaware**	NA
NA	Hawaii**	NA
NA	Rhode Island**	NA
NA	Vermont**	NA
	District of Columbia	2.8

Source: U.S. Department of Justice, Bureau of Justice Statistics
   "Census of Jails, 1999" (August 2001, NCJ-186633)
*As of July 1, 1999. Jails are locally operated correctional facilities that confine persons before or after adjudication. Inmates sentenced to jail usually have a sentence of a year or less.
**These states have combined state and local jail systems and are excluded from this count.

III. DRUGS AND ALCOHOL

Drug Laboratory Seizures in 1999

National Total = 7,528 Laboratories*

RANK	STATE	LABORATORIES	% of USA
23	Alabama	30	0.4%
26	Alaska	20	0.3%
5	Arizona	383	5.1%
7	Arkansas	334	4.4%
1	California	2,691	35.7%
17	Colorado	105	1.4%
44	Connecticut	0	0.0%
44	Delaware	0	0.0%
25	Florida	23	0.3%
22	Georgia	34	0.5%
33	Hawaii	6	0.1%
14	Idaho	133	1.8%
15	Illinois	128	1.7%
13	Indiana	160	2.1%
6	Iowa	356	4.7%
11	Kansas	210	2.8%
19	Kentucky	68	0.9%
31	Louisiana	8	0.1%
44	Maine	0	0.0%
42	Maryland	1	0.0%
44	Massachusetts	0	0.0%
30	Michigan	10	0.1%
18	Minnesota	102	1.4%
20	Mississippi	59	0.8%
3	Missouri	438	5.8%
24	Montana	26	0.3%
29	Nebraska	14	0.2%
8	Nevada	292	3.9%
44	New Hampshire	0	0.0%
39	New Jersey	2	0.0%
21	New Mexico	47	0.6%
42	New York	1	0.0%
33	North Carolina	6	0.1%
33	North Dakota	6	0.1%
28	Ohio	16	0.2%
4	Oklahoma	396	5.3%
9	Oregon	251	3.3%
39	Pennsylvania	2	0.0%
44	Rhode Island	0	0.0%
36	South Carolina	5	0.1%
39	South Dakota	2	0.0%
16	Tennessee	106	1.4%
12	Texas	181	2.4%
10	Utah	242	3.2%
44	Vermont	0	0.0%
31	Virginia	8	0.1%
2	Washington	597	7.9%
36	West Virginia	5	0.1%
36	Wisconsin	5	0.1%
27	Wyoming	19	0.3%

RANK	STATE	LABORATORIES	% of USA
1	California	2,691	35.7%
2	Washington	597	7.9%
3	Missouri	438	5.8%
4	Oklahoma	396	5.3%
5	Arizona	383	5.1%
6	Iowa	356	4.7%
7	Arkansas	334	4.4%
8	Nevada	292	3.9%
9	Oregon	251	3.3%
10	Utah	242	3.2%
11	Kansas	210	2.8%
12	Texas	181	2.4%
13	Indiana	160	2.1%
14	Idaho	133	1.8%
15	Illinois	128	1.7%
16	Tennessee	106	1.4%
17	Colorado	105	1.4%
18	Minnesota	102	1.4%
19	Kentucky	68	0.9%
20	Mississippi	59	0.8%
21	New Mexico	47	0.6%
22	Georgia	34	0.5%
23	Alabama	30	0.4%
24	Montana	26	0.3%
25	Florida	23	0.3%
26	Alaska	20	0.3%
27	Wyoming	19	0.3%
28	Ohio	16	0.2%
29	Nebraska	14	0.2%
30	Michigan	10	0.1%
31	Louisiana	8	0.1%
31	Virginia	8	0.1%
33	Hawaii	6	0.1%
33	North Carolina	6	0.1%
33	North Dakota	6	0.1%
36	South Carolina	5	0.1%
36	West Virginia	5	0.1%
36	Wisconsin	5	0.1%
39	New Jersey	2	0.0%
39	Pennsylvania	2	0.0%
39	South Dakota	2	0.0%
42	Maryland	1	0.0%
42	New York	1	0.0%
44	Connecticut	0	0.0%
44	Delaware	0	0.0%
44	Maine	0	0.0%
44	Massachusetts	0	0.0%
44	New Hampshire	0	0.0%
44	Rhode Island	0	0.0%
44	Vermont	0	0.0%
	District of Columbia**	NA	NA

Source: Drug Enforcement Administration
"Methamphetamine" (http://www.dea.gov/concern/meth.htm)
*More than 97 percent of lab seizures were methamphetamine labs.

Percent of Population Who are Illicit Drug Users: 1999

National Percent = 6.9% of Population*

ALPHA ORDER

RANK	STATE	PERCENT
46	Alabama	5.1
1	Alaska	10.7
17	Arizona	7.1
49	Arkansas	5.0
9	California	8.3
4	Colorado	9.3
11	Connecticut	7.7
7	Delaware	8.5
25	Florida	6.8
36	Georgia	5.8
17	Hawaii	7.1
30	Idaho	6.4
24	Illinois	6.9
15	Indiana	7.5
40	Iowa	5.5
35	Kansas	5.9
33	Kentucky	6.0
38	Louisiana	5.7
17	Maine	7.1
45	Maryland	5.3
2	Massachusetts	10.1
10	Michigan	8.0
27	Minnesota	6.7
36	Mississippi	5.8
28	Missouri	6.6
11	Montana	7.7
39	Nebraska	5.6
3	Nevada	9.6
20	New Hampshire	7.0
11	New Jersey	7.7
5	New Mexico	8.9
20	New York	7.0
31	North Carolina	6.3
42	North Dakota	5.4
29	Ohio	6.5
46	Oklahoma	5.1
11	Oregon	7.7
20	Pennsylvania	7.0
6	Rhode Island	8.7
42	South Carolina	5.4
33	South Dakota	6.0
40	Tennessee	5.5
42	Texas	5.4
32	Utah	6.2
25	Vermont	6.8
50	Virginia	4.7
8	Washington	8.4
46	West Virginia	5.1
20	Wisconsin	7.0
16	Wyoming	7.3

RANK ORDER

RANK	STATE	PERCENT
1	Alaska	10.7
2	Massachusetts	10.1
3	Nevada	9.6
4	Colorado	9.3
5	New Mexico	8.9
6	Rhode Island	8.7
7	Delaware	8.5
8	Washington	8.4
9	California	8.3
10	Michigan	8.0
11	Connecticut	7.7
11	Montana	7.7
11	New Jersey	7.7
11	Oregon	7.7
15	Indiana	7.5
16	Wyoming	7.3
17	Arizona	7.1
17	Hawaii	7.1
17	Maine	7.1
20	New Hampshire	7.0
20	New York	7.0
20	Pennsylvania	7.0
20	Wisconsin	7.0
24	Illinois	6.9
25	Florida	6.8
25	Vermont	6.8
27	Minnesota	6.7
28	Missouri	6.6
29	Ohio	6.5
30	Idaho	6.4
31	North Carolina	6.3
32	Utah	6.2
33	Kentucky	6.0
33	South Dakota	6.0
35	Kansas	5.9
36	Georgia	5.8
36	Mississippi	5.8
38	Louisiana	5.7
39	Nebraska	5.6
40	Iowa	5.5
40	Tennessee	5.5
42	North Dakota	5.4
42	South Carolina	5.4
42	Texas	5.4
45	Maryland	5.3
46	Alabama	5.1
46	Oklahoma	5.1
46	West Virginia	5.1
49	Arkansas	5.0
50	Virginia	4.7
	District of Columbia	7.6

Source: U.S. Department of Health and Human Services, Substance Abuse and Mental Health Services Administration
"National Household Survey on Drug Abuse, 1999"
*Population 12 years old and over who used any illicit drug at least once within month of survey.

Alcohol and Other Drug Treatment Units in 1999

National Total = 6,389 Units*

ALPHA ORDER

RANK	STATE	UNITS	% of USA
31	Alabama	39	0.6%
34	Alaska	38	0.6%
16	Arizona	119	1.9%
42	Arkansas	26	0.4%
1	California	911	14.3%
35	Colorado	37	0.6%
10	Connecticut	175	2.7%
38	Delaware	35	0.5%
12	Florida	132	2.1%
35	Georgia	37	0.6%
44	Hawaii	18	0.3%
NA	Idaho**	NA	NA
5	Illinois	358	5.6%
38	Indiana	35	0.5%
41	Iowa	32	0.5%
24	Kansas	53	0.8%
8	Kentucky	220	3.4%
14	Louisiana	129	2.0%
25	Maine	51	0.8%
13	Maryland	130	2.0%
46	Massachusetts	0	0.0%
7	Michigan	302	4.7%
NA	Minnesota**	NA	NA
19	Mississippi	76	1.2%
18	Missouri	84	1.3%
NA	Montana**	NA	NA
20	Nebraska	63	1.0%
27	Nevada	41	0.6%
28	New Hampshire	40	0.6%
11	New Jersey	134	2.1%
35	New Mexico	37	0.6%
2	New York	763	11.9%
31	North Carolina	39	0.6%
45	North Dakota	9	0.1%
3	Ohio	583	9.1%
22	Oklahoma	60	0.9%
16	Oregon	119	1.9%
4	Pennsylvania	499	7.8%
21	Rhode Island	62	1.0%
40	South Carolina	34	0.5%
22	South Dakota	60	0.9%
26	Tennessee	49	0.8%
9	Texas	192	3.0%
28	Utah	40	0.6%
43	Vermont	19	0.3%
28	Virginia	40	0.6%
6	Washington	310	4.9%
31	West Virginia	39	0.6%
15	Wisconsin	120	1.9%
NA	Wyoming**	NA	NA

RANK ORDER

RANK	STATE	UNITS	% of USA
1	California	911	14.3%
2	New York	763	11.9%
3	Ohio	583	9.1%
4	Pennsylvania	499	7.8%
5	Illinois	358	5.6%
6	Washington	310	4.9%
7	Michigan	302	4.7%
8	Kentucky	220	3.4%
9	Texas	192	3.0%
10	Connecticut	175	2.7%
11	New Jersey	134	2.1%
12	Florida	132	2.1%
13	Maryland	130	2.0%
14	Louisiana	129	2.0%
15	Wisconsin	120	1.9%
16	Arizona	119	1.9%
16	Oregon	119	1.9%
18	Missouri	84	1.3%
19	Mississippi	76	1.2%
20	Nebraska	63	1.0%
21	Rhode Island	62	1.0%
22	Oklahoma	60	0.9%
22	South Dakota	60	0.9%
24	Kansas	53	0.8%
25	Maine	51	0.8%
26	Tennessee	49	0.8%
27	Nevada	41	0.6%
28	New Hampshire	40	0.6%
28	Utah	40	0.6%
28	Virginia	40	0.6%
31	Alabama	39	0.6%
31	North Carolina	39	0.6%
31	West Virginia	39	0.6%
34	Alaska	38	0.6%
35	Colorado	37	0.6%
35	Georgia	37	0.6%
35	New Mexico	37	0.6%
38	Delaware	35	0.5%
38	Indiana	35	0.5%
40	South Carolina	34	0.5%
41	Iowa	32	0.5%
42	Arkansas	26	0.4%
43	Vermont	19	0.3%
44	Hawaii	18	0.3%
45	North Dakota	9	0.1%
46	Massachusetts	0	0.0%
NA	Idaho**	NA	NA
NA	Minnesota**	NA	NA
NA	Montana**	NA	NA
NA	Wyoming**	NA	NA
	District of Columbia**	NA	NA

Source: National Association of State Alcohol and Drug Abuse Directors
"State Resources and Services Related to Alcohol and Other Drug Problems-Fiscal Year 1998-1999" (July 2001)
*Data are only from treatment units that received at least some funds administered by a state's alcohol/drug agency in fiscal year 1999. National total is only for reporting states.
**Not available.

Alcohol and Other Drug Treatment Admissions in 1999

National Total = 1,823,276 Admissions*

RANK	STATE	ADMISSIONS	% of USA
29	Alabama	16,602	0.9%
42	Alaska	5,948	0.3%
8	Arizona	66,006	3.6%
33	Arkansas	13,337	0.7%
1	California	216,727	11.9%
12	Colorado	64,485	3.5%
18	Connecticut	37,639	2.1%
39	Delaware	7,283	0.4%
6	Florida	75,237	4.1%
28	Georgia	16,626	0.9%
43	Hawaii	5,629	0.3%
NA	Idaho**	NA	NA
3	Illinois	124,966	6.9%
25	Indiana	19,713	1.1%
24	Iowa	24,502	1.3%
34	Kansas	13,117	0.7%
22	Kentucky	26,314	1.4%
20	Louisiana	28,664	1.6%
37	Maine	10,328	0.6%
21	Maryland	27,737	1.5%
5	Massachusetts	94,378	5.2%
7	Michigan	70,320	3.9%
NA	Minnesota**	NA	NA
26	Mississippi	18,782	1.0%
17	Missouri	40,263	2.2%
NA	Montana**	NA	NA
45	Nebraska	2,946	0.2%
36	Nevada	10,474	0.6%
40	New Hampshire	6,574	0.4%
16	New Jersey	40,296	2.2%
31	New Mexico	15,725	0.9%
2	New York	145,892	8.0%
14	North Carolina	46,610	2.6%
46	North Dakota	2,286	0.1%
4	Ohio	97,007	5.3%
44	Oklahoma	5,413	0.3%
11	Oregon	64,720	3.5%
9	Pennsylvania	65,791	3.6%
35	Rhode Island	12,137	0.7%
19	South Carolina	30,627	1.7%
32	South Dakota	14,456	0.8%
41	Tennessee	6,220	0.3%
15	Texas	44,788	2.5%
27	Utah	17,535	1.0%
38	Vermont	7,658	0.4%
10	Virginia	64,899	3.6%
13	Washington	54,963	3.0%
30	West Virginia	15,793	0.9%
23	Wisconsin	25,863	1.4%
NA	Wyoming**	NA	NA

RANK	STATE	ADMISSIONS	% of USA
1	California	216,727	11.9%
2	New York	145,892	8.0%
3	Illinois	124,966	6.9%
4	Ohio	97,007	5.3%
5	Massachusetts	94,378	5.2%
6	Florida	75,237	4.1%
7	Michigan	70,320	3.9%
8	Arizona	66,006	3.6%
9	Pennsylvania	65,791	3.6%
10	Virginia	64,899	3.6%
11	Oregon	64,720	3.5%
12	Colorado	64,485	3.5%
13	Washington	54,963	3.0%
14	North Carolina	46,610	2.6%
15	Texas	44,788	2.5%
16	New Jersey	40,296	2.2%
17	Missouri	40,263	2.2%
18	Connecticut	37,639	2.1%
19	South Carolina	30,627	1.7%
20	Louisiana	28,664	1.6%
21	Maryland	27,737	1.5%
22	Kentucky	26,314	1.4%
23	Wisconsin	25,863	1.4%
24	Iowa	24,502	1.3%
25	Indiana	19,713	1.1%
26	Mississippi	18,782	1.0%
27	Utah	17,535	1.0%
28	Georgia	16,626	0.9%
29	Alabama	16,602	0.9%
30	West Virginia	15,793	0.9%
31	New Mexico	15,725	0.9%
32	South Dakota	14,456	0.8%
33	Arkansas	13,337	0.7%
34	Kansas	13,117	0.7%
35	Rhode Island	12,137	0.7%
36	Nevada	10,474	0.6%
37	Maine	10,328	0.6%
38	Vermont	7,658	0.4%
39	Delaware	7,283	0.4%
40	New Hampshire	6,574	0.4%
41	Tennessee	6,220	0.3%
42	Alaska	5,948	0.3%
43	Hawaii	5,629	0.3%
44	Oklahoma	5,413	0.3%
45	Nebraska	2,946	0.2%
46	North Dakota	2,286	0.1%
NA	Idaho**	NA	NA
NA	Minnesota**	NA	NA
NA	Montana**	NA	NA
NA	Wyoming**	NA	NA
	District of Columbia**	NA	NA

Source: National Association of State Alcohol and Drug Abuse Directors
    "State Resources and Services Related to Alcohol and Other Drug Problems-Fiscal Year 1998-1999" (July 2001)
*Data are only from treatment units that received at least some funds administered by a state's alcohol/drug agency
in fiscal year 1999. National total is only for reporting states.*
**Not available.*

Male Admissions to Alcohol and Other Drug Treatment Programs in 1999

National Total = 1,195,115 Male Admissions*

RANK	STATE	ADMISSIONS	% of USA	RANK	STATE	ADMISSIONS	% of USA
26	Alabama	12,238	1.0%	1	California	137,851	11.5%
40	Alaska	3,928	0.3%	2	New York	109,924	9.2%
NA	Arizona**	NA	NA	3	Illinois	79,516	6.7%
31	Arkansas	10,318	0.9%	4	Ohio	67,069	5.6%
1	California	137,851	11.5%	5	Massachusetts	66,982	5.6%
7	Colorado	48,610	4.1%	6	Florida	52,728	4.4%
16	Connecticut	27,614	2.3%	7	Colorado	48,610	4.1%
38	Delaware	5,332	0.4%	8	Michigan	47,743	4.0%
6	Florida	52,728	4.4%	9	Pennsylvania	46,056	3.9%
29	Georgia	11,352	0.9%	10	Oregon	44,207	3.7%
41	Hawaii	3,712	0.3%	11	Virginia	44,159	3.7%
NA	Idaho**	NA	NA	12	North Carolina	33,636	2.8%
3	Illinois	79,516	6.7%	13	Texas	29,147	2.4%
24	Indiana	13,765	1.2%	14	Missouri	28,633	2.4%
22	Iowa	17,636	1.5%	15	New Jersey	27,881	2.3%
33	Kansas	9,223	0.8%	16	Connecticut	27,614	2.3%
21	Kentucky	17,854	1.5%	17	South Carolina	22,683	1.9%
18	Louisiana	20,925	1.8%	18	Louisiana	20,925	1.8%
36	Maine	7,031	0.6%	19	Wisconsin	19,656	1.6%
20	Maryland	19,327	1.6%	20	Maryland	19,327	1.6%
5	Massachusetts	66,982	5.6%	21	Kentucky	17,854	1.5%
8	Michigan	47,743	4.0%	22	Iowa	17,636	1.5%
NA	Minnesota**	NA	NA	23	Washington	16,161	1.4%
25	Mississippi	13,568	1.1%	24	Indiana	13,765	1.2%
14	Missouri	28,633	2.4%	25	Mississippi	13,568	1.1%
NA	Montana**	NA	NA	26	Alabama	12,238	1.0%
43	Nebraska	2,146	0.2%	27	Utah	12,074	1.0%
35	Nevada	7,170	0.6%	28	West Virginia	11,613	1.0%
44	New Hampshire	1,820	0.2%	29	Georgia	11,352	0.9%
15	New Jersey	27,881	2.3%	30	South Dakota	10,335	0.9%
32	New Mexico	10,187	0.9%	31	Arkansas	10,318	0.9%
2	New York	109,924	9.2%	32	New Mexico	10,187	0.9%
12	North Carolina	33,636	2.8%	33	Kansas	9,223	0.8%
45	North Dakota	1,623	0.1%	34	Rhode Island	8,527	0.7%
4	Ohio	67,069	5.6%	35	Nevada	7,170	0.6%
42	Oklahoma	3,510	0.3%	36	Maine	7,031	0.6%
10	Oregon	44,207	3.7%	37	Vermont	5,398	0.5%
9	Pennsylvania	46,056	3.9%	38	Delaware	5,332	0.4%
34	Rhode Island	8,527	0.7%	39	Tennessee	4,247	0.4%
17	South Carolina	22,683	1.9%	40	Alaska	3,928	0.3%
30	South Dakota	10,335	0.9%	41	Hawaii	3,712	0.3%
39	Tennessee	4,247	0.4%	42	Oklahoma	3,510	0.3%
13	Texas	29,147	2.4%	43	Nebraska	2,146	0.2%
27	Utah	12,074	1.0%	44	New Hampshire	1,820	0.2%
37	Vermont	5,398	0.5%	45	North Dakota	1,623	0.1%
11	Virginia	44,159	3.7%	NA	Arizona**	NA	NA
23	Washington	16,161	1.4%	NA	Idaho**	NA	NA
28	West Virginia	11,613	1.0%	NA	Minnesota**	NA	NA
19	Wisconsin	19,656	1.6%	NA	Montana**	NA	NA
NA	Wyoming**	NA	NA	NA	Wyoming**	NA	NA
					District of Columbia**	NA	NA

Source: National Association of State Alcohol and Drug Abuse Directors
    "State Resources and Services Related to Alcohol and Other Drug Problems-Fiscal Year 1998-1999" (July 2001)
*Data are only from treatment units that received at least some funds administered by a state's alcohol/drug agency in fiscal year 1999. An additional 83,973 admissions were not reported by sex. National total is only for reporting states.
**Not available.

Male Admissions to Alcohol and Drug Treatment Programs
As a Percent of All Admissions in 1999
National Percent = 68.7% Males*

ALPHA ORDER				RANK ORDER		
RANK	STATE	PERCENT		RANK	STATE	PERCENT
6	Alabama	73.7		1	Colorado	79.5
39	Alaska	66.0		2	Arkansas	77.4
NA	Arizona**	NA		3	Wisconsin	76.0
2	Arkansas	77.4		4	New York	75.3
43	California	63.6		5	South Carolina	74.3
1	Colorado	79.5		6	Alabama	73.7
8	Connecticut	73.4		7	West Virginia	73.5
9	Delaware	73.2		8	Connecticut	73.4
20	Florida	70.5		9	Delaware	73.2
31	Georgia	68.3		10	Louisiana	73.0
40	Hawaii	65.9		10	Nebraska	73.0
NA	Idaho**	NA		12	New Mexico	72.7
38	Illinois	66.1		13	Mississippi	72.2
25	Indiana	69.8		13	North Carolina	72.2
15	Iowa	72.0		15	Iowa	72.0
22	Kansas	70.3		16	South Dakota	71.5
37	Kentucky	67.8		17	Missouri	71.1
10	Louisiana	73.0		18	Massachusetts	71.0
34	Maine	68.1		18	North Dakota	71.0
26	Maryland	69.7		20	Florida	70.5
18	Massachusetts	71.0		20	Vermont	70.5
36	Michigan	67.9		22	Kansas	70.3
NA	Minnesota**	NA		22	Rhode Island	70.3
13	Mississippi	72.2		24	Pennsylvania	70.0
17	Missouri	71.1		25	Indiana	69.8
NA	Montana**	NA		26	Maryland	69.7
10	Nebraska	73.0		27	New Jersey	69.3
30	Nevada	68.5		28	Ohio	69.1
NA	New Hampshire**	NA		29	Utah	68.9
27	New Jersey	69.3		30	Nevada	68.5
12	New Mexico	72.7		31	Georgia	68.3
4	New York	75.3		31	Oregon	68.3
13	North Carolina	72.2		31	Tennessee	68.3
18	North Dakota	71.0		34	Maine	68.1
28	Ohio	69.1		34	Virginia	68.1
42	Oklahoma	64.8		36	Michigan	67.9
31	Oregon	68.3		37	Kentucky	67.8
24	Pennsylvania	70.0		38	Illinois	66.1
22	Rhode Island	70.3		39	Alaska	66.0
5	South Carolina	74.3		40	Hawaii	65.9
16	South Dakota	71.5		41	Texas	65.1
31	Tennessee	68.3		42	Oklahoma	64.8
41	Texas	65.1		43	California	63.6
29	Utah	68.9		NA	Arizona**	NA
20	Vermont	70.5		NA	Idaho**	NA
34	Virginia	68.1		NA	Minnesota**	NA
NA	Washington**	NA		NA	Montana**	NA
7	West Virginia	73.5		NA	New Hampshire**	NA
3	Wisconsin	76.0		NA	Washington**	NA
NA	Wyoming**	NA		NA	Wyoming**	NA
				NA	District of Columbia**	NA

Source: Morgan Quitno Press using data from National Association of State Alcohol and Drug Abuse Directors
"State Resources and Services Related to Alcohol and Other Drug Problems-Fiscal Year 1998-1999" (July 2001)
Data are only from treatment units that received at least some funds administered by a state's alcohol/drug agency in fiscal year 1999. Percentages reflect admissions reported by sex. An additional 83,973 admissions were not reported by sex. National rate is only for reporting states.
**Not available.*

Female Admissions to Alcohol and Other Drug Treatment Programs in 1999

National Total = 544,188 Female Admissions*

ALPHA ORDER

RANK	STATE	ADMISSIONS	% of USA
29	Alabama	4,364	0.8%
39	Alaska	2,020	0.4%
NA	Arizona**	NA	NA
37	Arkansas	3,019	0.6%
1	California	78,876	14.5%
14	Colorado	12,530	2.3%
17	Connecticut	10,025	1.8%
41	Delaware	1,951	0.4%
8	Florida	22,115	4.1%
26	Georgia	5,274	1.0%
42	Hawaii	1,917	0.4%
NA	Idaho**	NA	NA
2	Illinois	40,733	7.5%
24	Indiana	5,948	1.1%
22	Iowa	6,866	1.3%
32	Kansas	3,894	0.7%
18	Kentucky	8,460	1.6%
21	Louisiana	7,739	1.4%
36	Maine	3,296	0.6%
19	Maryland	8,400	1.5%
6	Massachusetts	27,396	5.0%
7	Michigan	22,563	4.1%
NA	Minnesota**	NA	NA
27	Mississippi	5,214	1.0%
16	Missouri	11,630	2.1%
NA	Montana**	NA	NA
44	Nebraska	793	0.1%
35	Nevada	3,304	0.6%
28	New Hampshire	4,754	0.9%
15	New Jersey	12,339	2.3%
33	New Mexico	3,821	0.7%
3	New York	35,968	6.6%
13	North Carolina	12,940	2.4%
45	North Dakota	663	0.1%
5	Ohio	29,938	5.5%
43	Oklahoma	1,903	0.3%
10	Oregon	20,513	3.8%
11	Pennsylvania	19,735	3.6%
34	Rhode Island	3,610	0.7%
20	South Carolina	7,845	1.4%
31	South Dakota	4,121	0.8%
40	Tennessee	1,973	0.4%
12	Texas	15,639	2.9%
25	Utah	5,461	1.0%
38	Vermont	2,256	0.4%
9	Virginia	20,687	3.8%
4	Washington	31,308	5.8%
30	West Virginia	4,180	0.8%
23	Wisconsin	6,207	1.1%
NA	Wyoming**	NA	NA

RANK ORDER

RANK	STATE	ADMISSIONS	% of USA
1	California	78,876	14.5%
2	Illinois	40,733	7.5%
3	New York	35,968	6.6%
4	Washington	31,308	5.8%
5	Ohio	29,938	5.5%
6	Massachusetts	27,396	5.0%
7	Michigan	22,563	4.1%
8	Florida	22,115	4.1%
9	Virginia	20,687	3.8%
10	Oregon	20,513	3.8%
11	Pennsylvania	19,735	3.6%
12	Texas	15,639	2.9%
13	North Carolina	12,940	2.4%
14	Colorado	12,530	2.3%
15	New Jersey	12,339	2.3%
16	Missouri	11,630	2.1%
17	Connecticut	10,025	1.8%
18	Kentucky	8,460	1.6%
19	Maryland	8,400	1.5%
20	South Carolina	7,845	1.4%
21	Louisiana	7,739	1.4%
22	Iowa	6,866	1.3%
23	Wisconsin	6,207	1.1%
24	Indiana	5,948	1.1%
25	Utah	5,461	1.0%
26	Georgia	5,274	1.0%
27	Mississippi	5,214	1.0%
28	New Hampshire	4,754	0.9%
29	Alabama	4,364	0.8%
30	West Virginia	4,180	0.8%
31	South Dakota	4,121	0.8%
32	Kansas	3,894	0.7%
33	New Mexico	3,821	0.7%
34	Rhode Island	3,610	0.7%
35	Nevada	3,304	0.6%
36	Maine	3,296	0.6%
37	Arkansas	3,019	0.6%
38	Vermont	2,256	0.4%
39	Alaska	2,020	0.4%
40	Tennessee	1,973	0.4%
41	Delaware	1,951	0.4%
42	Hawaii	1,917	0.4%
43	Oklahoma	1,903	0.3%
44	Nebraska	793	0.1%
45	North Dakota	663	0.1%
NA	Arizona**	NA	NA
NA	Idaho**	NA	NA
NA	Minnesota**	NA	NA
NA	Montana**	NA	NA
NA	Wyoming**	NA	NA
	District of Columbia**	NA	NA

Source: National Association of State Alcohol and Drug Abuse Directors
"State Resources and Services Related to Alcohol and Other Drug Problems-Fiscal Year 1998-1999" (July 2001)
*Data are only from treatment units that received at least some funds administered by a state's alcohol/drug agency in fiscal year 1999. An additional 83,973 admissions were not reported by sex. National total is only for reporting states.
**Not available.

Female Admissions to Alcohol and Drug Treatment Programs
As a Percent of All Admissions in 1999
National Percent = 31.3% Females*

ALPHA ORDER

RANK	STATE	PERCENT
38	Alabama	26.3
5	Alaska	34.0
NA	Arizona**	NA
42	Arkansas	22.6
1	California	36.4
43	Colorado	20.5
36	Connecticut	26.6
35	Delaware	26.8
23	Florida	29.5
11	Georgia	31.7
4	Hawaii	34.1
NA	Idaho**	NA
6	Illinois	33.9
19	Indiana	30.2
29	Iowa	28.0
21	Kansas	29.7
7	Kentucky	32.2
33	Louisiana	27.0
9	Maine	31.9
18	Maryland	30.3
25	Massachusetts	29.0
8	Michigan	32.1
NA	Minnesota**	NA
30	Mississippi	27.8
27	Missouri	28.9
NA	Montana**	NA
33	Nebraska	27.0
14	Nevada	31.5
NA	New Hampshire**	NA
17	New Jersey	30.7
32	New Mexico	27.3
40	New York	24.7
30	North Carolina	27.8
25	North Dakota	29.0
16	Ohio	30.9
2	Oklahoma	35.2
11	Oregon	31.7
20	Pennsylvania	30.0
21	Rhode Island	29.7
39	South Carolina	25.7
28	South Dakota	28.5
11	Tennessee	31.7
3	Texas	34.9
15	Utah	31.1
23	Vermont	29.5
9	Virginia	31.9
NA	Washington**	NA
37	West Virginia	26.5
41	Wisconsin	24.0
NA	Wyoming**	NA

RANK ORDER

RANK	STATE	PERCENT
1	California	36.4
2	Oklahoma	35.2
3	Texas	34.9
4	Hawaii	34.1
5	Alaska	34.0
6	Illinois	33.9
7	Kentucky	32.2
8	Michigan	32.1
9	Maine	31.9
9	Virginia	31.9
11	Georgia	31.7
11	Oregon	31.7
11	Tennessee	31.7
14	Nevada	31.5
15	Utah	31.1
16	Ohio	30.9
17	New Jersey	30.7
18	Maryland	30.3
19	Indiana	30.2
20	Pennsylvania	30.0
21	Kansas	29.7
21	Rhode Island	29.7
23	Florida	29.5
23	Vermont	29.5
25	Massachusetts	29.0
25	North Dakota	29.0
27	Missouri	28.9
28	South Dakota	28.5
29	Iowa	28.0
30	Mississippi	27.8
30	North Carolina	27.8
32	New Mexico	27.3
33	Louisiana	27.0
33	Nebraska	27.0
35	Delaware	26.8
36	Connecticut	26.6
37	West Virginia	26.5
38	Alabama	26.3
39	South Carolina	25.7
40	New York	24.7
41	Wisconsin	24.0
42	Arkansas	22.6
43	Colorado	20.5
NA	Arizona**	NA
NA	Idaho**	NA
NA	Minnesota**	NA
NA	Montana**	NA
NA	New Hampshire**	NA
NA	Washington**	NA
NA	Wyoming**	NA
	District of Columbia**	NA

Source: Morgan Quitno Press using data from National Association of State Alcohol and Drug Abuse Directors
   "State Resources and Services Related to Alcohol and Other Drug Problems-Fiscal Year 1998-1999" (July 2001)
Data are only from treatment units that received at least some funds administered by a state's alcohol/drug agency in fiscal year 1999. Percentages reflect admissions reported by sex. An additional 83,973 admissions were not reported by sex. National rate is only for reporting states.
**Not available.*

White Admissions to Alcohol and Other Drug Treatment Programs in 1999

National Total = 1,023,641 White Admissions*

ALPHA ORDER

RANK	STATE	ADMISSIONS	% of USA
34	Alabama	8,868	0.9%
42	Alaska	2,530	0.2%
NA	Arizona**	NA	NA
30	Arkansas	9,660	0.9%
1	California	105,556	10.3%
12	Colorado	31,610	3.1%
20	Connecticut	20,067	2.0%
39	Delaware	4,429	0.4%
7	Florida	46,535	4.5%
28	Georgia	9,784	1.0%
44	Hawaii	1,840	0.2%
NA	Idaho**	NA	NA
6	Illinois	49,476	4.8%
23	Indiana	14,426	1.4%
18	Iowa	21,152	2.1%
33	Kansas	8,980	0.9%
17	Kentucky	21,801	2.1%
24	Louisiana	14,229	1.4%
29	Maine	9,783	1.0%
25	Maryland	13,785	1.3%
2	Massachusetts	65,392	6.4%
9	Michigan	42,154	4.1%
NA	Minnesota**	NA	NA
32	Mississippi	8,990	0.9%
13	Missouri	27,207	2.7%
NA	Montana**	NA	NA
43	Nebraska	2,043	0.2%
35	Nevada	7,533	0.7%
37	New Hampshire	6,199	0.6%
19	New Jersey	21,016	2.1%
38	New Mexico	4,431	0.4%
4	New York	58,809	5.7%
14	North Carolina	25,876	2.5%
45	North Dakota	1,647	0.2%
3	Ohio	61,133	6.0%
41	Oklahoma	3,833	0.4%
5	Oregon	51,463	5.0%
8	Pennsylvania	45,729	4.5%
31	Rhode Island	9,128	0.9%
21	South Carolina	18,309	1.8%
27	South Dakota	9,978	1.0%
40	Tennessee	3,971	0.4%
16	Texas	21,990	2.1%
26	Utah	13,545	1.3%
36	Vermont	7,113	0.7%
11	Virginia	34,872	3.4%
10	Washington	38,569	3.8%
22	West Virginia	14,484	1.4%
15	Wisconsin	23,716	2.3%
NA	Wyoming**	NA	NA

RANK ORDER

RANK	STATE	ADMISSIONS	% of USA
1	California	105,556	10.3%
2	Massachusetts	65,392	6.4%
3	Ohio	61,133	6.0%
4	New York	58,809	5.7%
5	Oregon	51,463	5.0%
6	Illinois	49,476	4.8%
7	Florida	46,535	4.5%
8	Pennsylvania	45,729	4.5%
9	Michigan	42,154	4.1%
10	Washington	38,569	3.8%
11	Virginia	34,872	3.4%
12	Colorado	31,610	3.1%
13	Missouri	27,207	2.7%
14	North Carolina	25,876	2.5%
15	Wisconsin	23,716	2.3%
16	Texas	21,990	2.1%
17	Kentucky	21,801	2.1%
18	Iowa	21,152	2.1%
19	New Jersey	21,016	2.1%
20	Connecticut	20,067	2.0%
21	South Carolina	18,309	1.8%
22	West Virginia	14,484	1.4%
23	Indiana	14,426	1.4%
24	Louisiana	14,229	1.4%
25	Maryland	13,785	1.3%
26	Utah	13,545	1.3%
27	South Dakota	9,978	1.0%
28	Georgia	9,784	1.0%
29	Maine	9,783	1.0%
30	Arkansas	9,660	0.9%
31	Rhode Island	9,128	0.9%
32	Mississippi	8,990	0.9%
33	Kansas	8,980	0.9%
34	Alabama	8,868	0.9%
35	Nevada	7,533	0.7%
36	Vermont	7,113	0.7%
37	New Hampshire	6,199	0.6%
38	New Mexico	4,431	0.4%
39	Delaware	4,429	0.4%
40	Tennessee	3,971	0.4%
41	Oklahoma	3,833	0.4%
42	Alaska	2,530	0.2%
43	Nebraska	2,043	0.2%
44	Hawaii	1,840	0.2%
45	North Dakota	1,647	0.2%
NA	Arizona**	NA	NA
NA	Idaho**	NA	NA
NA	Minnesota**	NA	NA
NA	Montana**	NA	NA
NA	Wyoming**	NA	NA
	District of Columbia**	NA	NA

Source: National Association of State Alcohol and Drug Abuse Directors
 "State Resources and Services Related to Alcohol and Other Drug Problems-Fiscal Year 1998-1999" (July 2001)
*Data are only from treatment units that received at least some funds administered by a state's alcohol/drug agency in fiscal year 1999. An additional 96,652 admissions were not reported by race. National total is only for reporting states.
**Not available.

White Admissions to Alcohol and Other Drug Treatment Programs
As a Percent of All Admissions in 1999
National Percent = 59.3% of Admissions*

ALPHA ORDER

RANK	STATE	PERCENT
29	Alabama	59.9
41	Alaska	42.6
NA	Arizona**	NA
12	Arkansas	72.4
36	California	49.8
33	Colorado	55.6
34	Connecticut	53.4
28	Delaware	60.8
26	Florida	62.1
24	Georgia	63.0
44	Hawaii	32.9
NA	Idaho**	NA
42	Illinois	41.1
11	Indiana	73.2
6	Iowa	86.3
21	Kansas	68.5
7	Kentucky	83.6
38	Louisiana	49.6
2	Maine	94.8
37	Maryland	49.7
19	Massachusetts	69.4
27	Michigan	61.0
NA	Minnesota**	NA
40	Mississippi	47.9
22	Missouri	67.6
NA	Montana**	NA
18	Nebraska	69.7
14	Nevada	71.9
3	New Hampshire	94.3
35	New Jersey	52.2
45	New Mexico	31.9
43	New York	40.3
32	North Carolina	55.9
13	North Dakota	72.1
24	Ohio	63.0
16	Oklahoma	70.8
8	Oregon	79.5
15	Pennsylvania	71.7
10	Rhode Island	75.2
29	South Carolina	59.9
19	South Dakota	69.4
23	Tennessee	64.6
39	Texas	49.2
9	Utah	78.6
1	Vermont	94.9
31	Virginia	56.7
17	Washington	70.3
4	West Virginia	92.1
5	Wisconsin	91.7
NA	Wyoming**	NA

RANK ORDER

RANK	STATE	PERCENT
1	Vermont	94.9
2	Maine	94.8
3	New Hampshire	94.3
4	West Virginia	92.1
5	Wisconsin	91.7
6	Iowa	86.3
7	Kentucky	83.6
8	Oregon	79.5
9	Utah	78.6
10	Rhode Island	75.2
11	Indiana	73.2
12	Arkansas	72.4
13	North Dakota	72.1
14	Nevada	71.9
15	Pennsylvania	71.7
16	Oklahoma	70.8
17	Washington	70.3
18	Nebraska	69.7
19	Massachusetts	69.4
19	South Dakota	69.4
21	Kansas	68.5
22	Missouri	67.6
23	Tennessee	64.6
24	Georgia	63.0
24	Ohio	63.0
26	Florida	62.1
27	Michigan	61.0
28	Delaware	60.8
29	Alabama	59.9
29	South Carolina	59.9
31	Virginia	56.7
32	North Carolina	55.9
33	Colorado	55.6
34	Connecticut	53.4
35	New Jersey	52.2
36	California	49.8
37	Maryland	49.7
38	Louisiana	49.6
39	Texas	49.2
40	Mississippi	47.9
41	Alaska	42.6
42	Illinois	41.1
43	New York	40.3
44	Hawaii	32.9
45	New Mexico	31.9
NA	Arizona**	NA
NA	Idaho**	NA
NA	Minnesota**	NA
NA	Montana**	NA
NA	Wyoming**	NA
	District of Columbia**	NA

Source: Morgan Quitno Press using data from National Association of State Alcohol and Drug Abuse Directors
"State Resources and Services Related to Alcohol and Other Drug Problems-Fiscal Year 1998-1999" (July 2001)
*Data are only from treatment units that received at least some funds administered by a state's alcohol/drug agency in fiscal year 1999. Percentages reflect admissions reported by race. An additional 96,652 admissions were not reported by race. National rate is only for reporting states.
**Not available.

Black Admissions to Alcohol and Other Drug Treatment Programs in 1999

National Total = 439,934 Black Admissions*

ALPHA ORDER

RANK	STATE	ADMISSIONS	% of USA
19	Alabama	5,889	1.3%
40	Alaska	217	0.0%
NA	Arizona**	NA	NA
25	Arkansas	3,431	0.8%
3	California	39,965	9.1%
22	Colorado	4,722	1.1%
18	Connecticut	9,302	2.1%
27	Delaware	2,494	0.6%
7	Florida	19,349	4.4%
20	Georgia	5,679	1.3%
42	Hawaii	128	0.0%
NA	Idaho**	NA	NA
1	Illinois	57,206	13.0%
23	Indiana	4,112	0.9%
30	Iowa	2,013	0.5%
28	Kansas	2,478	0.6%
24	Kentucky	3,739	0.8%
9	Louisiana	14,100	3.2%
43	Maine	96	0.0%
10	Maryland	13,127	3.0%
13	Massachusetts	12,675	2.9%
6	Michigan	21,008	4.8%
NA	Minnesota**	NA	NA
17	Mississippi	9,506	2.2%
14	Missouri	12,308	2.8%
NA	Montana**	NA	NA
37	Nebraska	425	0.1%
31	Nevada	1,393	0.3%
41	New Hampshire	147	0.0%
12	New Jersey	12,821	2.9%
38	New Mexico	286	0.1%
2	New York	56,396	12.8%
8	North Carolina	18,664	4.2%
45	North Dakota	20	0.0%
4	Ohio	32,165	7.3%
34	Oklahoma	783	0.2%
26	Oregon	3,107	0.7%
11	Pennsylvania	12,986	3.0%
32	Rhode Island	1,268	0.3%
15	South Carolina	11,666	2.7%
39	South Dakota	221	0.1%
29	Tennessee	2,125	0.5%
16	Texas	10,234	2.3%
36	Utah	564	0.1%
44	Vermont	94	0.0%
5	Virginia	23,909	5.4%
21	Washington	5,162	1.2%
33	West Virginia	1,178	0.3%
35	Wisconsin	776	0.2%
NA	Wyoming**	NA	NA

RANK ORDER

RANK	STATE	ADMISSIONS	% of USA
1	Illinois	57,206	13.0%
2	New York	56,396	12.8%
3	California	39,965	9.1%
4	Ohio	32,165	7.3%
5	Virginia	23,909	5.4%
6	Michigan	21,008	4.8%
7	Florida	19,349	4.4%
8	North Carolina	18,664	4.2%
9	Louisiana	14,100	3.2%
10	Maryland	13,127	3.0%
11	Pennsylvania	12,986	3.0%
12	New Jersey	12,821	2.9%
13	Massachusetts	12,675	2.9%
14	Missouri	12,308	2.8%
15	South Carolina	11,666	2.7%
16	Texas	10,234	2.3%
17	Mississippi	9,506	2.2%
18	Connecticut	9,302	2.1%
19	Alabama	5,889	1.3%
20	Georgia	5,679	1.3%
21	Washington	5,162	1.2%
22	Colorado	4,722	1.1%
23	Indiana	4,112	0.9%
24	Kentucky	3,739	0.8%
25	Arkansas	3,431	0.8%
26	Oregon	3,107	0.7%
27	Delaware	2,494	0.6%
28	Kansas	2,478	0.6%
29	Tennessee	2,125	0.5%
30	Iowa	2,013	0.5%
31	Nevada	1,393	0.3%
32	Rhode Island	1,268	0.3%
33	West Virginia	1,178	0.3%
34	Oklahoma	783	0.2%
35	Wisconsin	776	0.2%
36	Utah	564	0.1%
37	Nebraska	425	0.1%
38	New Mexico	286	0.1%
39	South Dakota	221	0.1%
40	Alaska	217	0.0%
41	New Hampshire	147	0.0%
42	Hawaii	128	0.0%
43	Maine	96	0.0%
44	Vermont	94	0.0%
45	North Dakota	20	0.0%
NA	Arizona**	NA	NA
NA	Idaho**	NA	NA
NA	Minnesota**	NA	NA
NA	Montana**	NA	NA
NA	Wyoming**	NA	NA
	District of Columbia**	NA	NA

Source: National Association of State Alcohol and Drug Abuse Directors
    "State Resources and Services Related to Alcohol and Other Drug Problems-Fiscal Year 1998-1999" (July 2001)
*Data are only from treatment units that received at least some funds administered by a state's alcohol/drug agency in fiscal year 1999. An additional 96,652 admissions were not reported by race. National total is only for reporting states.
**Not available.

131

Black Admissions to Alcohol and Other Drug Treatment Programs
As a Percent of All Admissions in 1999
National Percent = 25.5% of Admissions*

ALPHA ORDER

RANK ORDER

RANK	STATE	PERCENT	RANK	STATE	PERCENT
6	Alabama	39.7	1	Mississippi	50.6
36	Alaska	3.7	2	Louisiana	49.2
NA	Arizona**	NA	3	Illinois	47.6
18	Arkansas	25.7	4	Maryland	47.3
23	California	18.9	5	North Carolina	40.4
32	Colorado	8.3	6	Alabama	39.7
19	Connecticut	24.8	7	Virginia	38.9
12	Delaware	34.3	8	New York	38.7
17	Florida	25.8	9	South Carolina	38.1
10	Georgia	36.5	10	Georgia	36.5
39	Hawaii	2.3	11	Tennessee	34.6
NA	Idaho**	NA	12	Delaware	34.3
3	Illinois	47.6	13	Ohio	33.2
21	Indiana	20.9	14	New Jersey	31.8
33	Iowa	8.2	15	Missouri	30.6
23	Kansas	18.9	16	Michigan	30.4
27	Kentucky	14.3	17	Florida	25.8
2	Louisiana	49.2	18	Arkansas	25.7
44	Maine	0.9	19	Connecticut	24.8
4	Maryland	47.3	20	Texas	22.9
28	Massachusetts	13.4	21	Indiana	20.9
16	Michigan	30.4	22	Pennsylvania	20.4
NA	Minnesota**	NA	23	California	18.9
1	Mississippi	50.6	23	Kansas	18.9
15	Missouri	30.6	25	Nebraska	14.5
NA	Montana**	NA	25	Oklahoma	14.5
25	Nebraska	14.5	27	Kentucky	14.3
29	Nevada	13.3	28	Massachusetts	13.4
40	New Hampshire	2.2	29	Nevada	13.3
14	New Jersey	31.8	30	Rhode Island	10.4
41	New Mexico	2.1	31	Washington	9.4
8	New York	38.7	32	Colorado	8.3
5	North Carolina	40.4	33	Iowa	8.2
44	North Dakota	0.9	34	West Virginia	7.5
13	Ohio	33.2	35	Oregon	4.8
25	Oklahoma	14.5	36	Alaska	3.7
35	Oregon	4.8	37	Utah	3.3
22	Pennsylvania	20.4	38	Wisconsin	3.0
30	Rhode Island	10.4	39	Hawaii	2.3
9	South Carolina	38.1	40	New Hampshire	2.2
42	South Dakota	1.5	41	New Mexico	2.1
11	Tennessee	34.6	42	South Dakota	1.5
20	Texas	22.9	43	Vermont	1.3
37	Utah	3.3	44	Maine	0.9
43	Vermont	1.3	44	North Dakota	0.9
7	Virginia	38.9	NA	Arizona**	NA
31	Washington	9.4	NA	Idaho**	NA
34	West Virginia	7.5	NA	Minnesota**	NA
38	Wisconsin	3.0	NA	Montana**	NA
NA	Wyoming**	NA	NA	Wyoming**	NA
				District of Columbia**	NA

Source: Morgan Quitno Press using data from National Association of State Alcohol and Drug Abuse Directors
"State Resources and Services Related to Alcohol and Other Drug Problems-Fiscal Year 1998-1999" (July 2001)
*Data are only from treatment units that received at least some funds administered by a state's alcohol/drug agency in fiscal year 1999. Percentages reflect admissions reported by race. An additional 96,652 admissions were not reported by race. National rate is only for reporting states.
**Not available.

Hispanic Admissions to Alcohol and Other Drug Treatment Programs in 1999

National Total = 192,778 Hispanic Admissions*

ALPHA ORDER

RANK	STATE	ADMISSIONS	% of USA
42	Alabama	0	0.0%
32	Alaska	134	0.1%
NA	Arizona**	NA	NA
36	Arkansas	82	0.0%
1	California	58,178	30.2%
3	Colorado	16,476	8.5%
7	Connecticut	7,870	4.1%
25	Delaware	315	0.2%
8	Florida	7,232	3.8%
38	Georgia	48	0.0%
26	Hawaii	268	0.1%
NA	Idaho**	NA	NA
6	Illinois	8,908	4.6%
20	Indiana	931	0.5%
21	Iowa	838	0.4%
18	Kansas	1,071	0.6%
23	Kentucky	461	0.2%
42	Louisiana	0	0.0%
35	Maine	117	0.1%
22	Maryland	557	0.3%
4	Massachusetts	12,912	6.7%
14	Michigan	3,384	1.8%
NA	Minnesota**	NA	NA
42	Mississippi	0	0.0%
28	Missouri	230	0.1%
NA	Montana**	NA	NA
29	Nebraska	190	0.1%
19	Nevada	1,000	0.5%
33	New Hampshire	131	0.1%
10	New Jersey	5,659	2.9%
11	New Mexico	5,148	2.7%
2	New York	27,445	14.2%
36	North Carolina	82	0.0%
40	North Dakota	26	0.0%
15	Ohio	2,436	1.3%
34	Oklahoma	127	0.1%
9	Oregon	5,686	2.9%
12	Pennsylvania	4,344	2.3%
17	Rhode Island	1,299	0.7%
24	South Carolina	348	0.2%
30	South Dakota	153	0.1%
39	Tennessee	34	0.0%
5	Texas	12,027	6.2%
16	Utah	1,933	1.0%
31	Vermont	135	0.1%
NA	Virginia**	NA	NA
13	Washington	4,295	2.2%
41	West Virginia	9	0.0%
27	Wisconsin	259	0.1%
NA	Wyoming**	NA	NA

RANK ORDER

RANK	STATE	ADMISSIONS	% of USA
1	California	58,178	30.2%
2	New York	27,445	14.2%
3	Colorado	16,476	8.5%
4	Massachusetts	12,912	6.7%
5	Texas	12,027	6.2%
6	Illinois	8,908	4.6%
7	Connecticut	7,870	4.1%
8	Florida	7,232	3.8%
9	Oregon	5,686	2.9%
10	New Jersey	5,659	2.9%
11	New Mexico	5,148	2.7%
12	Pennsylvania	4,344	2.3%
13	Washington	4,295	2.2%
14	Michigan	3,384	1.8%
15	Ohio	2,436	1.3%
16	Utah	1,933	1.0%
17	Rhode Island	1,299	0.7%
18	Kansas	1,071	0.6%
19	Nevada	1,000	0.5%
20	Indiana	931	0.5%
21	Iowa	838	0.4%
22	Maryland	557	0.3%
23	Kentucky	461	0.2%
24	South Carolina	348	0.2%
25	Delaware	315	0.2%
26	Hawaii	268	0.1%
27	Wisconsin	259	0.1%
28	Missouri	230	0.1%
29	Nebraska	190	0.1%
30	South Dakota	153	0.1%
31	Vermont	135	0.1%
32	Alaska	134	0.1%
33	New Hampshire	131	0.1%
34	Oklahoma	127	0.1%
35	Maine	117	0.1%
36	Arkansas	82	0.0%
36	North Carolina	82	0.0%
38	Georgia	48	0.0%
39	Tennessee	34	0.0%
40	North Dakota	26	0.0%
41	West Virginia	9	0.0%
42	Alabama	0	0.0%
42	Louisiana	0	0.0%
42	Mississippi	0	0.0%
NA	Arizona**	NA	NA
NA	Idaho**	NA	NA
NA	Minnesota**	NA	NA
NA	Montana**	NA	NA
NA	Virginia**	NA	NA
NA	Wyoming**	NA	NA
	District of Columbia**	NA	NA

Source: National Association of State Alcohol and Drug Abuse Directors
   "State Resources and Services Related to Alcohol and Other Drug Problems-Fiscal Year 1998-1999" (July 2001)
*Data are only from treatment units that received at least some funds administered by a state's alcohol/drug agency in fiscal year 1999. An additional 96,652 admissions were not reported by race. National total is only for reporting states.
**Not available.

133

Hispanic Admissions to Alcohol and Other Drug Treatment Programs
As a Percent of All Admissions in 1999
National Percent = 11.2% of Admissions*

ALPHA ORDER

RANK	STATE	PERCENT
42	Alabama	0.0
25	Alaska	2.3
NA	Arizona**	NA
36	Arkansas	0.6
3	California	27.5
2	Colorado	29.0
5	Connecticut	20.9
22	Delaware	4.3
11	Florida	9.7
39	Georgia	0.3
20	Hawaii	4.8
NA	Idaho**	NA
16	Illinois	7.4
21	Indiana	4.7
23	Iowa	3.4
14	Kansas	8.2
29	Kentucky	1.8
42	Louisiana	0.0
31	Maine	1.1
27	Maryland	2.0
8	Massachusetts	13.7
19	Michigan	4.9
NA	Minnesota**	NA
42	Mississippi	0.0
36	Missouri	0.6
NA	Montana**	NA
18	Nebraska	6.5
12	Nevada	9.5
27	New Hampshire	2.0
7	New Jersey	14.0
1	New Mexico	37.0
6	New York	18.8
40	North Carolina	0.2
31	North Dakota	1.1
24	Ohio	2.5
25	Oklahoma	2.3
13	Oregon	8.8
17	Pennsylvania	6.8
10	Rhode Island	10.7
31	South Carolina	1.1
31	South Dakota	1.1
36	Tennessee	0.6
4	Texas	26.9
9	Utah	11.2
29	Vermont	1.8
NA	Virginia**	NA
15	Washington	7.8
41	West Virginia	0.1
35	Wisconsin	1.0
NA	Wyoming**	NA

RANK ORDER

RANK	STATE	PERCENT
1	New Mexico	37.0
2	Colorado	29.0
3	California	27.5
4	Texas	26.9
5	Connecticut	20.9
6	New York	18.8
7	New Jersey	14.0
8	Massachusetts	13.7
9	Utah	11.2
10	Rhode Island	10.7
11	Florida	9.7
12	Nevada	9.5
13	Oregon	8.8
14	Kansas	8.2
15	Washington	7.8
16	Illinois	7.4
17	Pennsylvania	6.8
18	Nebraska	6.5
19	Michigan	4.9
20	Hawaii	4.8
21	Indiana	4.7
22	Delaware	4.3
23	Iowa	3.4
24	Ohio	2.5
25	Alaska	2.3
25	Oklahoma	2.3
27	Maryland	2.0
27	New Hampshire	2.0
29	Kentucky	1.8
29	Vermont	1.8
31	Maine	1.1
31	North Dakota	1.1
31	South Carolina	1.1
31	South Dakota	1.1
35	Wisconsin	1.0
36	Arkansas	0.6
36	Missouri	0.6
36	Tennessee	0.6
39	Georgia	0.3
40	North Carolina	0.2
41	West Virginia	0.1
42	Alabama	0.0
42	Louisiana	0.0
42	Mississippi	0.0
NA	Arizona**	NA
NA	Idaho**	NA
NA	Minnesota**	NA
NA	Montana**	NA
NA	Virginia**	NA
NA	Wyoming**	NA
	District of Columbia**	NA

Source: Morgan Quitno Press using data from National Association of State Alcohol and Drug Abuse Directors
    "State Resources and Services Related to Alcohol and Other Drug Problems-Fiscal Year 1998-1999" (July 2001)
*Data are only from treatment units that received at least some funds administered by a state's alcohol/drug agency
in fiscal year 1999. Percentages reflect admissions reported by race. An additional 96,652 admissions were not
reported by race. National rate is only for reporting states.
**Not available.

Expenditures for State-Supported Alcohol and Other Drug Abuse Services: 1999

National Total = $4,458,499,261*

ALPHA ORDER

RANK	STATE	EXPENDITURES	% of USA
29	Alabama	$26,445,127	0.6%
33	Alaska	21,653,700	0.5%
22	Arizona	49,743,917	1.1%
35	Arkansas	17,467,261	0.4%
2	California	610,936,800	13.7%
20	Colorado	61,024,378	1.4%
8	Connecticut	151,084,202	3.4%
38	Delaware	15,487,181	0.3%
4	Florida	277,919,335	6.2%
14	Georgia	91,526,367	2.1%
41	Hawaii	13,277,010	0.3%
NA	Idaho**	NA	NA
6	Illinois	181,590,033	4.1%
21	Indiana	57,908,582	1.3%
31	Iowa	22,957,079	0.5%
30	Kansas	24,147,823	0.5%
27	Kentucky	31,540,881	0.7%
23	Louisiana	47,815,896	1.1%
37	Maine	16,287,432	0.4%
15	Maryland	90,316,960	2.0%
16	Massachusetts	83,936,000	1.9%
10	Michigan	106,463,847	2.4%
NA	Minnesota**	NA	NA
34	Mississippi	18,298,496	0.4%
19	Missouri	64,438,137	1.4%
NA	Montana**	NA	NA
36	Nebraska	16,619,072	0.4%
43	Nevada	11,936,658	0.3%
45	New Hampshire	9,639,268	0.2%
9	New Jersey	115,695,281	2.6%
39	New Mexico	15,205,431	0.3%
1	New York	817,434,167	18.3%
17	North Carolina	80,874,423	1.8%
44	North Dakota	10,495,761	0.2%
3	Ohio	357,187,274	8.0%
28	Oklahoma	27,171,005	0.6%
13	Oregon	98,001,660	2.2%
7	Pennsylvania	165,151,693	3.7%
32	Rhode Island	21,778,492	0.5%
26	South Carolina	32,920,339	0.7%
46	South Dakota	7,109,929	0.2%
25	Tennessee	35,397,300	0.8%
5	Texas	210,313,860	4.7%
24	Utah	42,682,349	1.0%
42	Vermont	12,135,884	0.3%
12	Virginia	98,644,801	2.2%
11	Washington	101,517,659	2.3%
40	West Virginia	13,734,718	0.3%
18	Wisconsin	74,585,793	1.7%
NA	Wyoming**	NA	NA

RANK ORDER

RANK	STATE	EXPENDITURES	% of USA
1	New York	$817,434,167	18.3%
2	California	610,936,800	13.7%
3	Ohio	357,187,274	8.0%
4	Florida	277,919,335	6.2%
5	Texas	210,313,860	4.7%
6	Illinois	181,590,033	4.1%
7	Pennsylvania	165,151,693	3.7%
8	Connecticut	151,084,202	3.4%
9	New Jersey	115,695,281	2.6%
10	Michigan	106,463,847	2.4%
11	Washington	101,517,659	2.3%
12	Virginia	98,644,801	2.2%
13	Oregon	98,001,660	2.2%
14	Georgia	91,526,367	2.1%
15	Maryland	90,316,960	2.0%
16	Massachusetts	83,936,000	1.9%
17	North Carolina	80,874,423	1.8%
18	Wisconsin	74,585,793	1.7%
19	Missouri	64,438,137	1.4%
20	Colorado	61,024,378	1.4%
21	Indiana	57,908,582	1.3%
22	Arizona	49,743,917	1.1%
23	Louisiana	47,815,896	1.1%
24	Utah	42,682,349	1.0%
25	Tennessee	35,397,300	0.8%
26	South Carolina	32,920,339	0.7%
27	Kentucky	31,540,881	0.7%
28	Oklahoma	27,171,005	0.6%
29	Alabama	26,445,127	0.6%
30	Kansas	24,147,823	0.5%
31	Iowa	22,957,079	0.5%
32	Rhode Island	21,778,492	0.5%
33	Alaska	21,653,700	0.5%
34	Mississippi	18,298,496	0.4%
35	Arkansas	17,467,261	0.4%
36	Nebraska	16,619,072	0.4%
37	Maine	16,287,432	0.4%
38	Delaware	15,487,181	0.3%
39	New Mexico	15,205,431	0.3%
40	West Virginia	13,734,718	0.3%
41	Hawaii	13,277,010	0.3%
42	Vermont	12,135,884	0.3%
43	Nevada	11,936,658	0.3%
44	North Dakota	10,495,761	0.2%
45	New Hampshire	9,639,268	0.2%
46	South Dakota	7,109,929	0.2%
NA	Idaho**	NA	NA
NA	Minnesota**	NA	NA
NA	Montana**	NA	NA
NA	Wyoming**	NA	NA
	District of Columbia**	NA	NA

Source: National Association of State Alcohol and Drug Abuse Directors
   "State Resources and Services Related to Alcohol and Other Drug Problems-Fiscal Year 1998-1999" (July 2001)
*Funds for treatment and prevention programs as well as "other" costs (e.g. administration, capital construction and research.) National total is only for reporting states. Data are only from treatment units that received at least some funds administered by a state's alcohol/drug agency in fiscal year 1999.
**Not available.

Per Capita Expenditures for State-Supported Alcohol and Other Drug Abuse Services in 1999
National Per Capita = $16.78*

ALPHA ORDER

RANK	STATE	PER CAPITA
46	Alabama	$6.05
3	Alaska	34.95
30	Arizona	10.41
42	Arkansas	6.85
10	California	18.43
15	Colorado	15.04
1	Connecticut	46.03
7	Delaware	20.55
11	Florida	18.39
24	Georgia	11.75
25	Hawaii	11.20
NA	Idaho**	NA
16	Illinois	14.97
32	Indiana	9.74
39	Iowa	8.00
34	Kansas	9.10
40	Kentucky	7.96
26	Louisiana	10.94
22	Maine	13.00
13	Maryland	17.46
21	Massachusetts	13.59
27	Michigan	10.79
NA	Minnesota**	NA
43	Mississippi	6.61
23	Missouri	11.78
NA	Montana**	NA
31	Nebraska	9.98
44	Nevada	6.60
38	New Hampshire	8.03
18	New Jersey	14.21
35	New Mexico	8.74
2	New York	44.92
28	North Carolina	10.57
14	North Dakota	16.56
4	Ohio	31.73
37	Oklahoma	8.09
5	Oregon	29.55
20	Pennsylvania	13.77
6	Rhode Island	21.98
36	South Carolina	8.47
33	South Dakota	9.70
45	Tennessee	6.46
29	Texas	10.49
9	Utah	20.04
8	Vermont	20.44
17	Virginia	14.35
12	Washington	17.64
41	West Virginia	7.60
18	Wisconsin	14.21
NA	Wyoming**	NA

RANK ORDER

RANK	STATE	PER CAPITA
1	Connecticut	$46.03
2	New York	44.92
3	Alaska	34.95
4	Ohio	31.73
5	Oregon	29.55
6	Rhode Island	21.98
7	Delaware	20.55
8	Vermont	20.44
9	Utah	20.04
10	California	18.43
11	Florida	18.39
12	Washington	17.64
13	Maryland	17.46
14	North Dakota	16.56
15	Colorado	15.04
16	Illinois	14.97
17	Virginia	14.35
18	New Jersey	14.21
18	Wisconsin	14.21
20	Pennsylvania	13.77
21	Massachusetts	13.59
22	Maine	13.00
23	Missouri	11.78
24	Georgia	11.75
25	Hawaii	11.20
26	Louisiana	10.94
27	Michigan	10.79
28	North Carolina	10.57
29	Texas	10.49
30	Arizona	10.41
31	Nebraska	9.98
32	Indiana	9.74
33	South Dakota	9.70
34	Kansas	9.10
35	New Mexico	8.74
36	South Carolina	8.47
37	Oklahoma	8.09
38	New Hampshire	8.03
39	Iowa	8.00
40	Kentucky	7.96
41	West Virginia	7.60
42	Arkansas	6.85
43	Mississippi	6.61
44	Nevada	6.60
45	Tennessee	6.46
46	Alabama	6.05
NA	Idaho**	NA
NA	Minnesota**	NA
NA	Montana**	NA
NA	Wyoming**	NA
	District of Columbia**	NA

*Source: Morgan Quitno Press using data from National Association of State Alcohol and Drug Abuse Directors
"State Resources and Services Related to Alcohol and Other Drug Problems-Fiscal Year 1998-1999" (July 2001)*
*Funds for treatment and prevention programs as well as "other" costs (e.g. administration, capital construction and research.) National per capita is only for reporting states' expenditures and population. Data are only from treatment units that received at least some funds administered by a state's alcohol/drug agency in fiscal year 1999.
**Not available.

Expenditures for State-Supported Alcohol and Other Drug Abuse Treatment Programs in 1999
National Total = $3,498,137,678*

ALPHA ORDER

RANK	STATE	EXPENDITURES	% of USA
29	Alabama	$19,973,325	0.6%
31	Alaska	17,065,700	0.5%
23	Arizona	38,112,492	1.1%
38	Arkansas	12,327,520	0.4%
2	California	429,361,500	12.3%
19	Colorado	52,484,556	1.5%
8	Connecticut	131,466,043	3.8%
36	Delaware	12,900,461	0.4%
4	Florida	236,169,048	6.8%
16	Georgia	66,892,677	1.9%
41	Hawaii	9,673,579	0.3%
NA	Idaho**	NA	NA
6	Illinois	160,868,533	4.6%
20	Indiana	46,860,354	1.3%
32	Iowa	16,479,248	0.5%
30	Kansas	19,836,670	0.6%
27	Kentucky	21,480,780	0.6%
22	Louisiana	40,312,582	1.2%
40	Maine	10,567,537	0.3%
12	Maryland	78,433,877	2.2%
13	Massachusetts	71,872,000	2.1%
14	Michigan	71,052,474	2.0%
NA	Minnesota**	NA	NA
33	Mississippi	15,066,733	0.4%
18	Missouri	55,539,865	1.6%
NA	Montana**	NA	NA
35	Nebraska	12,939,208	0.4%
43	Nevada	8,135,442	0.2%
44	New Hampshire	6,865,912	0.2%
9	New Jersey	95,809,777	2.7%
37	New Mexico	12,827,293	0.4%
1	New York	649,225,726	18.6%
15	North Carolina	69,370,230	2.0%
42	North Dakota	9,427,963	0.3%
3	Ohio	293,189,616	8.4%
28	Oklahoma	20,343,017	0.6%
21	Oregon	43,681,075	1.2%
7	Pennsylvania	132,004,425	3.8%
34	Rhode Island	14,238,905	0.4%
25	South Carolina	24,566,568	0.7%
46	South Dakota	5,071,930	0.1%
26	Tennessee	23,799,800	0.7%
5	Texas	161,201,069	4.6%
24	Utah	33,660,570	1.0%
45	Vermont	6,753,262	0.2%
10	Virginia	85,780,971	2.5%
11	Washington	82,786,703	2.4%
39	West Virginia	11,561,153	0.3%
17	Wisconsin	60,099,509	1.7%
NA	Wyoming**	NA	NA

RANK ORDER

RANK	STATE	EXPENDITURES	% of USA
1	New York	$649,225,726	18.6%
2	California	429,361,500	12.3%
3	Ohio	293,189,616	8.4%
4	Florida	236,169,048	6.8%
5	Texas	161,201,069	4.6%
6	Illinois	160,868,533	4.6%
7	Pennsylvania	132,004,425	3.8%
8	Connecticut	131,466,043	3.8%
9	New Jersey	95,809,777	2.7%
10	Virginia	85,780,971	2.5%
11	Washington	82,786,703	2.4%
12	Maryland	78,433,877	2.2%
13	Massachusetts	71,872,000	2.1%
14	Michigan	71,052,474	2.0%
15	North Carolina	69,370,230	2.0%
16	Georgia	66,892,677	1.9%
17	Wisconsin	60,099,509	1.7%
18	Missouri	55,539,865	1.6%
19	Colorado	52,484,556	1.5%
20	Indiana	46,860,354	1.3%
21	Oregon	43,681,075	1.2%
22	Louisiana	40,312,582	1.2%
23	Arizona	38,112,492	1.1%
24	Utah	33,660,570	1.0%
25	South Carolina	24,566,568	0.7%
26	Tennessee	23,799,800	0.7%
27	Kentucky	21,480,780	0.6%
28	Oklahoma	20,343,017	0.6%
29	Alabama	19,973,325	0.6%
30	Kansas	19,836,670	0.6%
31	Alaska	17,065,700	0.5%
32	Iowa	16,479,248	0.5%
33	Mississippi	15,066,733	0.4%
34	Rhode Island	14,238,905	0.4%
35	Nebraska	12,939,208	0.4%
36	Delaware	12,900,461	0.4%
37	New Mexico	12,827,293	0.4%
38	Arkansas	12,327,520	0.4%
39	West Virginia	11,561,153	0.3%
40	Maine	10,567,537	0.3%
41	Hawaii	9,673,579	0.3%
42	North Dakota	9,427,963	0.3%
43	Nevada	8,135,442	0.2%
44	New Hampshire	6,865,912	0.2%
45	Vermont	6,753,262	0.2%
46	South Dakota	5,071,930	0.1%
NA	Idaho**	NA	NA
NA	Minnesota**	NA	NA
NA	Montana**	NA	NA
NA	Wyoming**	NA	NA
	District of Columbia**	NA	NA

Source: National Association of State Alcohol and Drug Abuse Directors
"State Resources and Services Related to Alcohol and Other Drug Problems-Fiscal Year 1998-1999" (July 2001)
*National total is only for reporting states. Data are only from treatment units that received at least some funds administered by a state's alcohol/drug agency in fiscal year 1999.
**Not available.

Expenditures per Alcohol and Other Drug Treatment Admission in 1999

National Rate = $1,919 in Treatment Expenditures per Admission*

<table>
<tr><td colspan="3">ALPHA ORDER</td><td colspan="3">RANK ORDER</td></tr>
<tr><td>RANK</td><td>STATE</td><td>RATE</td><td>RANK</td><td>STATE</td><td>RATE</td></tr>
<tr><td>28</td><td>Alabama</td><td>$1,203</td><td>1</td><td>New York</td><td>$4,450</td></tr>
<tr><td>11</td><td>Alaska</td><td>2,869</td><td>2</td><td>Nebraska</td><td>4,392</td></tr>
<tr><td>45</td><td>Arizona</td><td>577</td><td>3</td><td>North Dakota</td><td>4,124</td></tr>
<tr><td>33</td><td>Arkansas</td><td>924</td><td>4</td><td>Georgia</td><td>4,023</td></tr>
<tr><td>17</td><td>California</td><td>1,981</td><td>5</td><td>Tennessee</td><td>3,826</td></tr>
<tr><td>37</td><td>Colorado</td><td>814</td><td>6</td><td>Oklahoma</td><td>3,758</td></tr>
<tr><td>8</td><td>Connecticut</td><td>3,493</td><td>7</td><td>Texas</td><td>3,599</td></tr>
<tr><td>19</td><td>Delaware</td><td>1,771</td><td>8</td><td>Connecticut</td><td>3,493</td></tr>
<tr><td>9</td><td>Florida</td><td>3,139</td><td>9</td><td>Florida</td><td>3,139</td></tr>
<tr><td>4</td><td>Georgia</td><td>4,023</td><td>10</td><td>Ohio</td><td>3,022</td></tr>
<tr><td>20</td><td>Hawaii</td><td>1,719</td><td>11</td><td>Alaska</td><td>2,869</td></tr>
<tr><td>NA</td><td>Idaho**</td><td>NA</td><td>12</td><td>Maryland</td><td>2,828</td></tr>
<tr><td>27</td><td>Illinois</td><td>1,287</td><td>13</td><td>New Jersey</td><td>2,378</td></tr>
<tr><td>14</td><td>Indiana</td><td>2,377</td><td>14</td><td>Indiana</td><td>2,377</td></tr>
<tr><td>44</td><td>Iowa</td><td>673</td><td>15</td><td>Wisconsin</td><td>2,324</td></tr>
<tr><td>21</td><td>Kansas</td><td>1,512</td><td>16</td><td>Pennsylvania</td><td>2,006</td></tr>
<tr><td>35</td><td>Kentucky</td><td>816</td><td>17</td><td>California</td><td>1,981</td></tr>
<tr><td>24</td><td>Louisiana</td><td>1,406</td><td>18</td><td>Utah</td><td>1,920</td></tr>
<tr><td>31</td><td>Maine</td><td>1,023</td><td>19</td><td>Delaware</td><td>1,771</td></tr>
<tr><td>12</td><td>Maryland</td><td>2,828</td><td>20</td><td>Hawaii</td><td>1,719</td></tr>
<tr><td>41</td><td>Massachusetts</td><td>762</td><td>21</td><td>Kansas</td><td>1,512</td></tr>
<tr><td>32</td><td>Michigan</td><td>1,010</td><td>22</td><td>Washington</td><td>1,506</td></tr>
<tr><td>NA</td><td>Minnesota**</td><td>NA</td><td>23</td><td>North Carolina</td><td>1,488</td></tr>
<tr><td>38</td><td>Mississippi</td><td>802</td><td>24</td><td>Louisiana</td><td>1,406</td></tr>
<tr><td>25</td><td>Missouri</td><td>1,379</td><td>25</td><td>Missouri</td><td>1,379</td></tr>
<tr><td>NA</td><td>Montana**</td><td>NA</td><td>26</td><td>Virginia</td><td>1,322</td></tr>
<tr><td>2</td><td>Nebraska</td><td>4,392</td><td>27</td><td>Illinois</td><td>1,287</td></tr>
<tr><td>40</td><td>Nevada</td><td>777</td><td>28</td><td>Alabama</td><td>1,203</td></tr>
<tr><td>30</td><td>New Hampshire</td><td>1,044</td><td>29</td><td>Rhode Island</td><td>1,173</td></tr>
<tr><td>13</td><td>New Jersey</td><td>2,378</td><td>30</td><td>New Hampshire</td><td>1,044</td></tr>
<tr><td>35</td><td>New Mexico</td><td>816</td><td>31</td><td>Maine</td><td>1,023</td></tr>
<tr><td>1</td><td>New York</td><td>4,450</td><td>32</td><td>Michigan</td><td>1,010</td></tr>
<tr><td>23</td><td>North Carolina</td><td>1,488</td><td>33</td><td>Arkansas</td><td>924</td></tr>
<tr><td>3</td><td>North Dakota</td><td>4,124</td><td>34</td><td>Vermont</td><td>882</td></tr>
<tr><td>10</td><td>Ohio</td><td>3,022</td><td>35</td><td>Kentucky</td><td>816</td></tr>
<tr><td>6</td><td>Oklahoma</td><td>3,758</td><td>35</td><td>New Mexico</td><td>816</td></tr>
<tr><td>43</td><td>Oregon</td><td>675</td><td>37</td><td>Colorado</td><td>814</td></tr>
<tr><td>16</td><td>Pennsylvania</td><td>2,006</td><td>38</td><td>Mississippi</td><td>802</td></tr>
<tr><td>29</td><td>Rhode Island</td><td>1,173</td><td>38</td><td>South Carolina</td><td>802</td></tr>
<tr><td>38</td><td>South Carolina</td><td>802</td><td>40</td><td>Nevada</td><td>777</td></tr>
<tr><td>46</td><td>South Dakota</td><td>351</td><td>41</td><td>Massachusetts</td><td>762</td></tr>
<tr><td>5</td><td>Tennessee</td><td>3,826</td><td>42</td><td>West Virginia</td><td>732</td></tr>
<tr><td>7</td><td>Texas</td><td>3,599</td><td>43</td><td>Oregon</td><td>675</td></tr>
<tr><td>18</td><td>Utah</td><td>1,920</td><td>44</td><td>Iowa</td><td>673</td></tr>
<tr><td>34</td><td>Vermont</td><td>882</td><td>45</td><td>Arizona</td><td>577</td></tr>
<tr><td>26</td><td>Virginia</td><td>1,322</td><td>46</td><td>South Dakota</td><td>351</td></tr>
<tr><td>22</td><td>Washington</td><td>1,506</td><td>NA</td><td>Idaho**</td><td>NA</td></tr>
<tr><td>42</td><td>West Virginia</td><td>732</td><td>NA</td><td>Minnesota**</td><td>NA</td></tr>
<tr><td>15</td><td>Wisconsin</td><td>2,324</td><td>NA</td><td>Montana**</td><td>NA</td></tr>
<tr><td>NA</td><td>Wyoming**</td><td>NA</td><td>NA</td><td>Wyoming**</td><td>NA</td></tr>
<tr><td></td><td></td><td></td><td></td><td>District of Columbia**</td><td>NA</td></tr>
</table>

Source: Morgan Quitno Press using data from National Association of State Alcohol and Drug Abuse Directors
    "State Resources and Services Related to Alcohol and Other Drug Problems-Fiscal Year 1998-1999" (July 2001)
*National rate is only for reporting states' expenditures and admissions. Data are only from treatment units that
received at least some funds administered by a state's alcohol/drug agency in fiscal year 1999.
**Not available.

Per Capita Expenditures for State-Supported Alcohol and Other Drug Abuse Treatment Programs in 1999
National Per Capita = $13.17*

ALPHA ORDER

RANK	STATE	PER CAPITA
44	Alabama	$4.57
3	Alaska	27.55
29	Arizona	7.98
43	Arkansas	4.83
14	California	12.95
15	Colorado	12.94
1	Connecticut	40.06
5	Delaware	17.12
7	Florida	15.63
25	Georgia	8.59
27	Hawaii	8.16
NA	Idaho**	NA
12	Illinois	13.26
30	Indiana	7.89
39	Iowa	5.74
32	Kansas	7.47
42	Kentucky	5.42
23	Louisiana	9.22
26	Maine	8.43
8	Maryland	15.17
18	Massachusetts	11.64
34	Michigan	7.20
NA	Minnesota**	NA
41	Mississippi	5.44
22	Missouri	10.16
NA	Montana**	NA
31	Nebraska	7.77
45	Nevada	4.50
40	New Hampshire	5.72
17	New Jersey	11.77
33	New Mexico	7.37
2	New York	35.68
24	North Carolina	9.07
9	North Dakota	14.88
4	Ohio	26.05
38	Oklahoma	6.06
13	Oregon	13.17
21	Pennsylvania	11.01
11	Rhode Island	14.37
37	South Carolina	6.32
35	South Dakota	6.92
46	Tennessee	4.34
28	Texas	8.04
6	Utah	15.80
20	Vermont	11.37
16	Virginia	12.48
10	Washington	14.38
36	West Virginia	6.40
19	Wisconsin	11.45
NA	Wyoming**	NA

RANK ORDER

RANK	STATE	PER CAPITA
1	Connecticut	$40.06
2	New York	35.68
3	Alaska	27.55
4	Ohio	26.05
5	Delaware	17.12
6	Utah	15.80
7	Florida	15.63
8	Maryland	15.17
9	North Dakota	14.88
10	Washington	14.38
11	Rhode Island	14.37
12	Illinois	13.26
13	Oregon	13.17
14	California	12.95
15	Colorado	12.94
16	Virginia	12.48
17	New Jersey	11.77
18	Massachusetts	11.64
19	Wisconsin	11.45
20	Vermont	11.37
21	Pennsylvania	11.01
22	Missouri	10.16
23	Louisiana	9.22
24	North Carolina	9.07
25	Georgia	8.59
26	Maine	8.43
27	Hawaii	8.16
28	Texas	8.04
29	Arizona	7.98
30	Indiana	7.89
31	Nebraska	7.77
32	Kansas	7.47
33	New Mexico	7.37
34	Michigan	7.20
35	South Dakota	6.92
36	West Virginia	6.40
37	South Carolina	6.32
38	Oklahoma	6.06
39	Iowa	5.74
40	New Hampshire	5.72
41	Mississippi	5.44
42	Kentucky	5.42
43	Arkansas	4.83
44	Alabama	4.57
45	Nevada	4.50
46	Tennessee	4.34
NA	Idaho**	NA
NA	Minnesota**	NA
NA	Montana**	NA
NA	Wyoming**	NA
	District of Columbia**	NA

Source: Morgan Quitno Press using data from National Association of State Alcohol and Drug Abuse Directors
    "State Resources and Services Related to Alcohol and Other Drug Problems-Fiscal Year 1998-1999" (July 2001)
*Data are only from treatment units that received at least some funds administered by a state's alcohol/drug agency
in fiscal year 1999. National per capita is only for reporting states' expenditures and population.
**Not available.

Expenditures for State-Supported Alcohol and Other Drug Abuse Prevention Programs in 1999
National Total = $599,107,352*

ALPHA ORDER

RANK	STATE	EXPENDITURES	% of USA
25	Alabama	$5,484,679	0.9%
37	Alaska	2,817,300	0.5%
17	Arizona	10,201,503	1.7%
35	Arkansas	3,180,813	0.5%
2	California	71,931,100	12.0%
22	Colorado	7,972,114	1.3%
10	Connecticut	18,099,290	3.0%
46	Delaware	565,672	0.1%
3	Florida	38,629,678	6.4%
8	Georgia	22,204,185	3.7%
43	Hawaii	1,575,763	0.3%
NA	Idaho**	NA	NA
9	Illinois	20,721,500	3.5%
18	Indiana	9,854,989	1.6%
28	Iowa	4,730,709	0.8%
34	Kansas	3,868,896	0.6%
24	Kentucky	7,369,634	1.2%
27	Louisiana	4,817,596	0.8%
30	Maine	4,347,428	0.7%
21	Maryland	8,181,468	1.4%
16	Massachusetts	10,804,000	1.8%
7	Michigan	22,701,088	3.8%
NA	Minnesota**	NA	NA
38	Mississippi	2,628,483	0.4%
26	Missouri	5,393,261	0.9%
NA	Montana**	NA	NA
36	Nebraska	2,884,886	0.5%
40	Nevada	2,182,417	0.4%
41	New Hampshire	1,973,661	0.3%
12	New Jersey	15,233,572	2.5%
39	New Mexico	2,378,138	0.4%
1	New York	98,877,105	16.5%
19	North Carolina	9,484,683	1.6%
45	North Dakota	1,067,798	0.2%
4	Ohio	36,610,936	6.1%
29	Oklahoma	4,649,905	0.8%
6	Oregon	23,212,713	3.9%
11	Pennsylvania	17,338,569	2.9%
31	Rhode Island	4,217,299	0.7%
33	South Carolina	3,957,974	0.7%
44	South Dakota	1,511,051	0.3%
20	Tennessee	8,283,400	1.4%
5	Texas	28,295,181	4.7%
23	Utah	7,754,732	1.3%
32	Vermont	3,962,103	0.7%
15	Virginia	11,587,390	1.9%
14	Washington	11,843,176	2.0%
42	West Virginia	1,771,100	0.3%
13	Wisconsin	11,948,414	2.0%
NA	Wyoming**	NA	NA

RANK ORDER

RANK	STATE	EXPENDITURES	% of USA
1	New York	$98,877,105	16.5%
2	California	71,931,100	12.0%
3	Florida	38,629,678	6.4%
4	Ohio	36,610,936	6.1%
5	Texas	28,295,181	4.7%
6	Oregon	23,212,713	3.9%
7	Michigan	22,701,088	3.8%
8	Georgia	22,204,185	3.7%
9	Illinois	20,721,500	3.5%
10	Connecticut	18,099,290	3.0%
11	Pennsylvania	17,338,569	2.9%
12	New Jersey	15,233,572	2.5%
13	Wisconsin	11,948,414	2.0%
14	Washington	11,843,176	2.0%
15	Virginia	11,587,390	1.9%
16	Massachusetts	10,804,000	1.8%
17	Arizona	10,201,503	1.7%
18	Indiana	9,854,989	1.6%
19	North Carolina	9,484,683	1.6%
20	Tennessee	8,283,400	1.4%
21	Maryland	8,181,468	1.4%
22	Colorado	7,972,114	1.3%
23	Utah	7,754,732	1.3%
24	Kentucky	7,369,634	1.2%
25	Alabama	5,484,679	0.9%
26	Missouri	5,393,261	0.9%
27	Louisiana	4,817,596	0.8%
28	Iowa	4,730,709	0.8%
29	Oklahoma	4,649,905	0.8%
30	Maine	4,347,428	0.7%
31	Rhode Island	4,217,299	0.7%
32	Vermont	3,962,103	0.7%
33	South Carolina	3,957,974	0.7%
34	Kansas	3,868,896	0.6%
35	Arkansas	3,180,813	0.5%
36	Nebraska	2,884,886	0.5%
37	Alaska	2,817,300	0.5%
38	Mississippi	2,628,483	0.4%
39	New Mexico	2,378,138	0.4%
40	Nevada	2,182,417	0.4%
41	New Hampshire	1,973,661	0.3%
42	West Virginia	1,771,100	0.3%
43	Hawaii	1,575,763	0.3%
44	South Dakota	1,511,051	0.3%
45	North Dakota	1,067,798	0.2%
46	Delaware	565,672	0.1%
NA	Idaho**	NA	NA
NA	Minnesota**	NA	NA
NA	Montana**	NA	NA
NA	Wyoming**	NA	NA
	District of Columbia**	NA	NA

Source: National Association of State Alcohol and Drug Abuse Directors
    "State Resources and Services Related to Alcohol and Other Drug Problems-Fiscal Year 1998-1999" (July 2001)
*National total is only for reporting states. Data are only from treatment units that received at least some funds administered by a state's alcohol/drug agency in fiscal year 1999.
**Not available.

Per Capita Expenditures for State-Supported Alcohol and Other Drug Abuse Prevention Programs in 1999
National Per Capita = $2.26*

ALPHA ORDER

RANK	STATE	PER CAPITA
37	Alabama	$1.26
5	Alaska	4.55
15	Arizona	2.13
38	Arkansas	1.25
14	California	2.17
18	Colorado	1.97
3	Connecticut	5.51
46	Delaware	0.75
11	Florida	2.56
10	Georgia	2.85
36	Hawaii	1.33
NA	Idaho**	NA
23	Illinois	1.71
26	Indiana	1.66
27	Iowa	1.65
31	Kansas	1.46
20	Kentucky	1.86
41	Louisiana	1.10
8	Maine	3.47
29	Maryland	1.58
21	Massachusetts	1.75
12	Michigan	2.30
NA	Minnesota**	NA
45	Mississippi	0.95
43	Missouri	0.99
NA	Montana**	NA
22	Nebraska	1.73
40	Nevada	1.21
28	New Hampshire	1.64
19	New Jersey	1.87
35	New Mexico	1.37
4	New York	5.43
39	North Carolina	1.24
24	North Dakota	1.69
9	Ohio	3.25
34	Oklahoma	1.38
1	Oregon	7.00
32	Pennsylvania	1.45
6	Rhode Island	4.26
42	South Carolina	1.02
16	South Dakota	2.06
30	Tennessee	1.51
33	Texas	1.41
7	Utah	3.64
2	Vermont	6.67
24	Virginia	1.69
16	Washington	2.06
44	West Virginia	0.98
13	Wisconsin	2.28
NA	Wyoming**	NA

RANK ORDER

RANK	STATE	PER CAPITA
1	Oregon	$7.00
2	Vermont	6.67
3	Connecticut	5.51
4	New York	5.43
5	Alaska	4.55
6	Rhode Island	4.26
7	Utah	3.64
8	Maine	3.47
9	Ohio	3.25
10	Georgia	2.85
11	Florida	2.56
12	Michigan	2.30
13	Wisconsin	2.28
14	California	2.17
15	Arizona	2.13
16	South Dakota	2.06
16	Washington	2.06
18	Colorado	1.97
19	New Jersey	1.87
20	Kentucky	1.86
21	Massachusetts	1.75
22	Nebraska	1.73
23	Illinois	1.71
24	North Dakota	1.69
24	Virginia	1.69
26	Indiana	1.66
27	Iowa	1.65
28	New Hampshire	1.64
29	Maryland	1.58
30	Tennessee	1.51
31	Kansas	1.46
32	Pennsylvania	1.45
33	Texas	1.41
34	Oklahoma	1.38
35	New Mexico	1.37
36	Hawaii	1.33
37	Alabama	1.26
38	Arkansas	1.25
39	North Carolina	1.24
40	Nevada	1.21
41	Louisiana	1.10
42	South Carolina	1.02
43	Missouri	0.99
44	West Virginia	0.98
45	Mississippi	0.95
46	Delaware	0.75
NA	Idaho**	NA
NA	Minnesota**	NA
NA	Montana**	NA
NA	Wyoming**	NA
	District of Columbia**	NA

Source: Morgan Quitno Press using data from National Association of State Alcohol and Drug Abuse Directors
"State Resources and Services Related to Alcohol and Other Drug Problems-Fiscal Year 1998-1999" (July 2001)
*Data are only from treatment units that received at least some funds administered by a state's alcohol/drug agency in fiscal year 1999. National per capita is only for reporting states' expenditures and population.
**Not available.

IV. FINANCE

State and Local Government Expenditures for Justice Activities in 1999

National Total = $124,280,885,000*

ALPHA ORDER

RANK	STATE	EXPENDITURES	% of USA
27	Alabama	$1,311,879,000	1.1%
40	Alaska	454,514,000	0.4%
15	Arizona	2,424,089,000	2.0%
36	Arkansas	747,519,000	0.6%
1	California	20,391,918,000	16.4%
18	Colorado	1,885,175,000	1.5%
25	Connecticut	1,569,325,000	1.3%
41	Delaware	439,930,000	0.4%
4	Florida	8,041,064,000	6.5%
10	Georgia	2,986,249,000	2.4%
37	Hawaii	520,767,000	0.4%
38	Idaho	497,103,000	0.4%
6	Illinois	5,194,122,000	4.2%
23	Indiana	1,721,947,000	1.4%
32	Iowa	920,733,000	0.7%
31	Kansas	938,780,000	0.8%
28	Kentucky	1,224,080,000	1.0%
20	Louisiana	1,835,825,000	1.5%
45	Maine	328,139,000	0.3%
17	Maryland	2,388,972,000	1.9%
11	Massachusetts	2,830,286,000	2.3%
8	Michigan	4,365,594,000	3.5%
22	Minnesota	1,788,617,000	1.4%
34	Mississippi	831,994,000	0.7%
21	Missouri	1,815,547,000	1.5%
46	Montana	306,222,000	0.2%
39	Nebraska	485,915,000	0.4%
29	Nevada	1,084,395,000	0.9%
44	New Hampshire	369,550,000	0.3%
9	New Jersey	4,356,722,000	3.5%
35	New Mexico	801,453,000	0.6%
2	New York	11,955,972,000	9.6%
12	North Carolina	2,824,785,000	2.3%
49	North Dakota	156,228,000	0.1%
7	Ohio	4,816,462,000	3.9%
30	Oklahoma	1,035,481,000	0.8%
24	Oregon	1,585,644,000	1.3%
5	Pennsylvania	5,212,148,000	4.2%
42	Rhode Island	427,686,000	0.3%
26	South Carolina	1,327,561,000	1.1%
48	South Dakota	202,328,000	0.2%
19	Tennessee	1,839,514,000	1.5%
3	Texas	8,081,539,000	6.5%
33	Utah	894,190,000	0.7%
50	Vermont	150,909,000	0.1%
13	Virginia	2,748,453,000	2.2%
14	Washington	2,465,249,000	2.0%
43	West Virginia	412,143,000	0.3%
16	Wisconsin	2,406,478,000	1.9%
47	Wyoming	238,399,000	0.2%

RANK ORDER

RANK	STATE	EXPENDITURES	% of USA
1	California	$20,391,918,000	16.4%
2	New York	11,955,972,000	9.6%
3	Texas	8,081,539,000	6.5%
4	Florida	8,041,064,000	6.5%
5	Pennsylvania	5,212,148,000	4.2%
6	Illinois	5,194,122,000	4.2%
7	Ohio	4,816,462,000	3.9%
8	Michigan	4,365,594,000	3.5%
9	New Jersey	4,356,722,000	3.5%
10	Georgia	2,986,249,000	2.4%
11	Massachusetts	2,830,286,000	2.3%
12	North Carolina	2,824,785,000	2.3%
13	Virginia	2,748,453,000	2.2%
14	Washington	2,465,249,000	2.0%
15	Arizona	2,424,089,000	2.0%
16	Wisconsin	2,406,478,000	1.9%
17	Maryland	2,388,972,000	1.9%
18	Colorado	1,885,175,000	1.5%
19	Tennessee	1,839,514,000	1.5%
20	Louisiana	1,835,825,000	1.5%
21	Missouri	1,815,547,000	1.5%
22	Minnesota	1,788,617,000	1.4%
23	Indiana	1,721,947,000	1.4%
24	Oregon	1,585,644,000	1.3%
25	Connecticut	1,569,325,000	1.3%
26	South Carolina	1,327,561,000	1.1%
27	Alabama	1,311,879,000	1.1%
28	Kentucky	1,224,080,000	1.0%
29	Nevada	1,084,395,000	0.9%
30	Oklahoma	1,035,481,000	0.8%
31	Kansas	938,780,000	0.8%
32	Iowa	920,733,000	0.7%
33	Utah	894,190,000	0.7%
34	Mississippi	831,994,000	0.7%
35	New Mexico	801,453,000	0.6%
36	Arkansas	747,519,000	0.6%
37	Hawaii	520,767,000	0.4%
38	Idaho	497,103,000	0.4%
39	Nebraska	485,915,000	0.4%
40	Alaska	454,514,000	0.4%
41	Delaware	439,930,000	0.4%
42	Rhode Island	427,686,000	0.3%
43	West Virginia	412,143,000	0.3%
44	New Hampshire	369,550,000	0.3%
45	Maine	328,139,000	0.3%
46	Montana	306,222,000	0.2%
47	Wyoming	238,399,000	0.2%
48	South Dakota	202,328,000	0.2%
49	North Dakota	156,228,000	0.1%
50	Vermont	150,909,000	0.1%
	District of Columbia	641,291,000	0.5%

Source: Morgan Quitno Press using data from U.S. Bureau of the Census
"Government Finances 1998-99" (http://www.census.gov/govs/estimate/99allpub.pdf, September 2001)
*Direct general expenditures. Includes Police Protection, Corrections and Judicial and Legal Services.

Per Capita State & Local Government Expenditures for Justice Activities: 1999

National Per Capita = $456*

ALPHA ORDER

RANK	STATE	PER CAPITA
42	Alabama	$300
1	Alaska	734
8	Arizona	507
43	Arkansas	293
3	California	615
12	Colorado	465
10	Connecticut	478
5	Delaware	584
7	Florida	532
29	Georgia	383
18	Hawaii	439
28	Idaho	397
21	Illinois	428
45	Indiana	290
37	Iowa	321
32	Kansas	354
38	Kentucky	309
24	Louisiana	420
47	Maine	262
13	Maryland	462
15	Massachusetts	458
17	Michigan	443
30	Minnesota	375
41	Mississippi	301
36	Missouri	332
33	Montana	347
44	Nebraska	292
4	Nevada	599
39	New Hampshire	308
6	New Jersey	535
14	New Mexico	461
2	New York	657
31	North Carolina	369
49	North Dakota	247
21	Ohio	428
39	Oklahoma	308
10	Oregon	478
19	Pennsylvania	435
20	Rhode Island	432
34	South Carolina	342
46	South Dakota	276
35	Tennessee	335
26	Texas	403
24	Utah	420
48	Vermont	254
27	Virginia	400
21	Washington	428
50	West Virginia	228
15	Wisconsin	458
9	Wyoming	497

RANK ORDER

RANK	STATE	PER CAPITA
1	Alaska	$734
2	New York	657
3	California	615
4	Nevada	599
5	Delaware	584
6	New Jersey	535
7	Florida	532
8	Arizona	507
9	Wyoming	497
10	Connecticut	478
10	Oregon	478
12	Colorado	465
13	Maryland	462
14	New Mexico	461
15	Massachusetts	458
15	Wisconsin	458
17	Michigan	443
18	Hawaii	439
19	Pennsylvania	435
20	Rhode Island	432
21	Illinois	428
21	Ohio	428
21	Washington	428
24	Louisiana	420
24	Utah	420
26	Texas	403
27	Virginia	400
28	Idaho	397
29	Georgia	383
30	Minnesota	375
31	North Carolina	369
32	Kansas	354
33	Montana	347
34	South Carolina	342
35	Tennessee	335
36	Missouri	332
37	Iowa	321
38	Kentucky	309
39	New Hampshire	308
39	Oklahoma	308
41	Mississippi	301
42	Alabama	300
43	Arkansas	293
44	Nebraska	292
45	Indiana	290
46	South Dakota	276
47	Maine	262
48	Vermont	254
49	North Dakota	247
50	West Virginia	228

| | District of Columbia | 1,236 |

Source: Morgan Quitno Press using data from Morgan Quitno Press using data from U.S. Bureau of the Census "Government Finances 1998-99" (http://www.census.gov/govs/estimate/99allpub.pdf, September 2001)
*Direct general expenditures. Includes Police Protection, Corrections and Judicial and Legal Services.

State and Local Government Expenditures for Justice Activities
As a Percent of All Direct General Expenditures in 1999
National Percent = 8.9% of Direct General Expenditures*

ALPHA ORDER

RANK ORDER

RANK	STATE	PERCENT		RANK	STATE	PERCENT
39	Alabama	6.5		1	Arizona	11.9
41	Alaska	6.4		2	Nevada	11.7
1	Arizona	11.9		3	California	11.3
36	Arkansas	7.0		4	Florida	11.2
3	California	11.3		5	Delaware	9.8
8	Colorado	9.4		5	New Jersey	9.8
25	Connecticut	8.0		7	Maryland	9.6
5	Delaware	9.8		8	Colorado	9.4
4	Florida	11.2		9	Texas	9.2
22	Georgia	8.3		10	Ohio	9.1
28	Hawaii	7.6		11	Idaho	8.9
11	Idaho	8.9		11	New York	8.9
13	Illinois	8.7		13	Illinois	8.7
39	Indiana	6.5		13	Louisiana	8.7
44	Iowa	6.3		13	Oregon	8.7
26	Kansas	7.8		16	Michigan	8.6
38	Kentucky	6.8		16	Utah	8.6
13	Louisiana	8.7		16	Wisconsin	8.6
47	Maine	5.1		19	New Mexico	8.5
7	Maryland	9.6		19	Pennsylvania	8.5
23	Massachusetts	8.1		19	Virginia	8.5
16	Michigan	8.6		22	Georgia	8.3
41	Minnesota	6.4		23	Massachusetts	8.1
41	Mississippi	6.4		23	Rhode Island	8.1
28	Missouri	7.6		25	Connecticut	8.0
35	Montana	7.1		26	Kansas	7.8
44	Nebraska	6.3		27	North Carolina	7.7
2	Nevada	11.7		28	Hawaii	7.6
37	New Hampshire	6.9		28	Missouri	7.6
5	New Jersey	9.8		28	Oklahoma	7.6
19	New Mexico	8.5		28	Tennessee	7.6
11	New York	8.9		28	Washington	7.6
27	North Carolina	7.7		28	Wyoming	7.6
50	North Dakota	4.5		34	South Carolina	7.3
10	Ohio	9.1		35	Montana	7.1
28	Oklahoma	7.6		36	Arkansas	7.0
13	Oregon	8.7		37	New Hampshire	6.9
19	Pennsylvania	8.5		38	Kentucky	6.8
23	Rhode Island	8.1		39	Alabama	6.5
34	South Carolina	7.3		39	Indiana	6.5
46	South Dakota	6.2		41	Alaska	6.4
28	Tennessee	7.6		41	Minnesota	6.4
9	Texas	9.2		41	Mississippi	6.4
16	Utah	8.6		44	Iowa	6.3
48	Vermont	5.0		44	Nebraska	6.3
19	Virginia	8.5		46	South Dakota	6.2
28	Washington	7.6		47	Maine	5.1
48	West Virginia	5.0		48	Vermont	5.0
16	Wisconsin	8.6		48	West Virginia	5.0
28	Wyoming	7.6		50	North Dakota	4.5

| | District of Columbia | 13.9 |

Source: Morgan Quitno Press using data from Morgan Quitno Press using data from U.S. Bureau of the Census "Government Finances 1998-99" (http://www.census.gov/govs/estimate/99allpub.pdf, September 2001)
*Includes Police Protection, Corrections and Judicial and Legal Services.

State Government Expenditures for Justice Activities in 1999

National Total = $49,964,923,000*

ALPHA ORDER

RANK	STATE	EXPENDITURES	% of USA
29	Alabama	$534,801,000	1.1%
37	Alaska	316,489,000	0.6%
16	Arizona	942,083,000	1.9%
34	Arkansas	355,787,000	0.7%
1	California	6,827,407,000	13.7%
19	Colorado	827,478,000	1.7%
15	Connecticut	989,983,000	2.0%
36	Delaware	340,993,000	0.7%
4	Florida	3,062,353,000	6.1%
14	Georgia	1,176,542,000	2.4%
39	Hawaii	274,060,000	0.5%
41	Idaho	252,483,000	0.5%
9	Illinois	1,674,360,000	3.4%
21	Indiana	742,824,000	1.5%
30	Iowa	468,490,000	0.9%
33	Kansas	398,793,000	0.8%
23	Kentucky	685,295,000	1.4%
24	Louisiana	675,970,000	1.4%
45	Maine	176,879,000	0.4%
12	Maryland	1,232,607,000	2.5%
11	Massachusetts	1,549,947,000	3.1%
6	Michigan	1,855,824,000	3.7%
28	Minnesota	557,963,000	1.1%
35	Mississippi	345,400,000	0.7%
20	Missouri	776,671,000	1.6%
46	Montana	142,297,000	0.3%
43	Nebraska	208,756,000	0.4%
38	Nevada	298,282,000	0.6%
44	New Hampshire	182,480,000	0.4%
7	New Jersey	1,792,521,000	3.6%
31	New Mexico	412,826,000	0.8%
2	New York	3,956,242,000	7.9%
10	North Carolina	1,604,136,000	3.2%
50	North Dakota	77,963,000	0.2%
8	Ohio	1,696,010,000	3.4%
27	Oklahoma	586,213,000	1.2%
22	Oregon	718,080,000	1.4%
5	Pennsylvania	2,401,478,000	4.8%
40	Rhode Island	262,892,000	0.5%
25	South Carolina	665,887,000	1.3%
48	South Dakota	97,335,000	0.2%
26	Tennessee	640,774,000	1.3%
3	Texas	3,286,674,000	6.6%
32	Utah	402,098,000	0.8%
49	Vermont	94,921,000	0.2%
13	Virginia	1,216,452,000	2.4%
18	Washington	878,919,000	1.8%
42	West Virginia	235,583,000	0.5%
17	Wisconsin	940,498,000	1.9%
47	Wyoming	124,124,000	0.2%

RANK ORDER

RANK	STATE	EXPENDITURES	% of USA
1	California	$6,827,407,000	13.7%
2	New York	3,956,242,000	7.9%
3	Texas	3,286,674,000	6.6%
4	Florida	3,062,353,000	6.1%
5	Pennsylvania	2,401,478,000	4.8%
6	Michigan	1,855,824,000	3.7%
7	New Jersey	1,792,521,000	3.6%
8	Ohio	1,696,010,000	3.4%
9	Illinois	1,674,360,000	3.4%
10	North Carolina	1,604,136,000	3.2%
11	Massachusetts	1,549,947,000	3.1%
12	Maryland	1,232,607,000	2.5%
13	Virginia	1,216,452,000	2.4%
14	Georgia	1,176,542,000	2.4%
15	Connecticut	989,983,000	2.0%
16	Arizona	942,083,000	1.9%
17	Wisconsin	940,498,000	1.9%
18	Washington	878,919,000	1.8%
19	Colorado	827,478,000	1.7%
20	Missouri	776,671,000	1.6%
21	Indiana	742,824,000	1.5%
22	Oregon	718,080,000	1.4%
23	Kentucky	685,295,000	1.4%
24	Louisiana	675,970,000	1.4%
25	South Carolina	665,887,000	1.3%
26	Tennessee	640,774,000	1.3%
27	Oklahoma	586,213,000	1.2%
28	Minnesota	557,963,000	1.1%
29	Alabama	534,801,000	1.1%
30	Iowa	468,490,000	0.9%
31	New Mexico	412,826,000	0.8%
32	Utah	402,098,000	0.8%
33	Kansas	398,793,000	0.8%
34	Arkansas	355,787,000	0.7%
35	Mississippi	345,400,000	0.7%
36	Delaware	340,993,000	0.7%
37	Alaska	316,489,000	0.6%
38	Nevada	298,282,000	0.6%
39	Hawaii	274,060,000	0.5%
40	Rhode Island	262,892,000	0.5%
41	Idaho	252,483,000	0.5%
42	West Virginia	235,583,000	0.5%
43	Nebraska	208,756,000	0.4%
44	New Hampshire	182,480,000	0.4%
45	Maine	176,879,000	0.4%
46	Montana	142,297,000	0.3%
47	Wyoming	124,124,000	0.2%
48	South Dakota	97,335,000	0.2%
49	Vermont	94,921,000	0.2%
50	North Dakota	77,963,000	0.2%
	District of Columbia**	NA	NA

Source: Morgan Quitno Press using data from Morgan Quitno Press using data from U.S. Bureau of the Census
"Government Finances 1998-99" (http://www.census.gov/govs/estimate/99allpub.pdf, September 2001)
*Direct general expenditures. Includes Police Protection, Corrections and Judicial and Legal Services.
**Not applicable.

Per Capita State Government Expenditures for Justice Activities in 1999

National Per Capita = $183*

ALPHA ORDER				RANK ORDER		
RANK	STATE	PER CAPITA		RANK	STATE	PER CAPITA
48	Alabama	$122		1	Alaska	$511
1	Alaska	511		2	Delaware	453
19	Arizona	197		3	Connecticut	302
40	Arkansas	139		4	Rhode Island	265
14	California	206		5	Wyoming	259
15	Colorado	204		6	Massachusetts	251
3	Connecticut	302		7	Maryland	238
2	Delaware	453		8	New Mexico	237
16	Florida	203		9	Hawaii	231
35	Georgia	151		10	New Jersey	220
9	Hawaii	231		11	New York	217
17	Idaho	202		11	Oregon	217
41	Illinois	138		13	North Carolina	210
44	Indiana	125		14	California	206
29	Iowa	163		15	Colorado	204
37	Kansas	150		16	Florida	203
25	Kentucky	173		17	Idaho	202
32	Louisiana	155		18	Pennsylvania	200
39	Maine	141		19	Arizona	197
7	Maryland	238		20	Utah	189
6	Massachusetts	251		21	Michigan	188
21	Michigan	188		22	Wisconsin	179
49	Minnesota	117		23	Virginia	177
44	Mississippi	125		24	Oklahoma	175
38	Missouri	142		25	Kentucky	173
30	Montana	161		26	South Carolina	171
44	Nebraska	125		27	Nevada	165
27	Nevada	165		28	Texas	164
34	New Hampshire	152		29	Iowa	163
10	New Jersey	220		30	Montana	161
8	New Mexico	237		31	Vermont	160
11	New York	217		32	Louisiana	155
13	North Carolina	210		33	Washington	153
47	North Dakota	123		34	New Hampshire	152
35	Ohio	151		35	Georgia	151
24	Oklahoma	175		35	Ohio	151
11	Oregon	217		37	Kansas	150
18	Pennsylvania	200		38	Missouri	142
4	Rhode Island	265		39	Maine	141
26	South Carolina	171		40	Arkansas	139
42	South Dakota	133		41	Illinois	138
49	Tennessee	117		42	South Dakota	133
28	Texas	164		43	West Virginia	130
20	Utah	189		44	Indiana	125
31	Vermont	160		44	Mississippi	125
23	Virginia	177		44	Nebraska	125
33	Washington	153		47	North Dakota	123
43	West Virginia	130		48	Alabama	122
22	Wisconsin	179		49	Minnesota	117
5	Wyoming	259		49	Tennessee	117
					District of Columbia**	NA

Source: Morgan Quitno Press using data from Morgan Quitno Press using data from U.S. Bureau of the Census
"Government Finances 1998-99" (http://www.census.gov/govs/estimate/99allpub.pdf, September 2001)
*Direct general expenditures. Includes Police Protection, Corrections and Judicial and Legal Services.
**Not applicable.

State Government Expenditures for Justice Activities
As a Percent of All Direct General Expenditures for 1999
National Percent = 8.5% of Direct General Expenditures*

ALPHA ORDER

RANK ORDER

RANK	STATE	PERCENT
44	Alabama	5.5
31	Alaska	7.0
1	Arizona	13.1
37	Arkansas	6.2
4	California	11.0
6	Colorado	10.1
12	Connecticut	9.4
2	Delaware	11.6
2	Florida	11.6
26	Georgia	7.9
46	Hawaii	5.0
9	Idaho	9.8
29	Illinois	7.1
35	Indiana	6.6
31	Iowa	7.0
21	Kansas	8.2
34	Kentucky	6.8
36	Louisiana	6.5
46	Maine	5.0
5	Maryland	10.7
23	Massachusetts	8.1
10	Michigan	9.7
48	Minnesota	4.9
43	Mississippi	5.7
29	Missouri	7.1
42	Montana	5.9
39	Nebraska	6.0
14	Nevada	9.3
31	New Hampshire	7.0
8	New Jersey	9.9
23	New Mexico	8.1
21	New York	8.2
7	North Carolina	10.0
50	North Dakota	4.1
25	Ohio	8.0
12	Oklahoma	9.4
16	Oregon	9.0
18	Pennsylvania	8.7
19	Rhode Island	8.4
28	South Carolina	7.2
39	South Dakota	6.0
39	Tennessee	6.0
11	Texas	9.5
27	Utah	7.4
45	Vermont	5.4
20	Virginia	8.3
38	Washington	6.1
48	West Virginia	4.9
16	Wisconsin	9.0
15	Wyoming	9.2

RANK	STATE	PERCENT
1	Arizona	13.1
2	Delaware	11.6
2	Florida	11.6
4	California	11.0
5	Maryland	10.7
6	Colorado	10.1
7	North Carolina	10.0
8	New Jersey	9.9
9	Idaho	9.8
10	Michigan	9.7
11	Texas	9.5
12	Connecticut	9.4
12	Oklahoma	9.4
14	Nevada	9.3
15	Wyoming	9.2
16	Oregon	9.0
16	Wisconsin	9.0
18	Pennsylvania	8.7
19	Rhode Island	8.4
20	Virginia	8.3
21	Kansas	8.2
21	New York	8.2
23	Massachusetts	8.1
23	New Mexico	8.1
25	Ohio	8.0
26	Georgia	7.9
27	Utah	7.4
28	South Carolina	7.2
29	Illinois	7.1
29	Missouri	7.1
31	Alaska	7.0
31	Iowa	7.0
31	New Hampshire	7.0
34	Kentucky	6.8
35	Indiana	6.6
36	Louisiana	6.5
37	Arkansas	6.2
38	Washington	6.1
39	Nebraska	6.0
39	South Dakota	6.0
39	Tennessee	6.0
42	Montana	5.9
43	Mississippi	5.7
44	Alabama	5.5
45	Vermont	5.4
46	Hawaii	5.0
46	Maine	5.0
48	Minnesota	4.9
48	West Virginia	4.9
50	North Dakota	4.1

District of Columbia** NA

Source: Morgan Quitno Press using data from Morgan Quitno Press using data from U.S. Bureau of the Census "Government Finances 1998-99" (http://www.census.gov/govs/estimate/99allpub.pdf, September 2001)
*Includes Police Protection, Corrections and Judicial and Legal Services.
**Not applicable.

Local Government Expenditures for Justice Activities in 1999

National Total = $74,315,962,000*

ALPHA ORDER

RANK	STATE	EXPENDITURES	% of USA
26	Alabama	$777,078,000	1.0%
45	Alaska	138,025,000	0.2%
13	Arizona	1,482,006,000	2.0%
35	Arkansas	391,732,000	0.5%
1	California	13,564,511,000	18.3%
21	Colorado	1,057,697,000	1.4%
28	Connecticut	579,342,000	0.8%
48	Delaware	98,937,000	0.1%
3	Florida	4,978,711,000	6.7%
10	Georgia	1,809,707,000	2.4%
38	Hawaii	246,707,000	0.3%
39	Idaho	244,620,000	0.3%
5	Illinois	3,519,762,000	4.7%
23	Indiana	979,123,000	1.3%
33	Iowa	452,243,000	0.6%
29	Kansas	539,987,000	0.7%
30	Kentucky	538,785,000	0.7%
19	Louisiana	1,159,855,000	1.6%
44	Maine	151,260,000	0.2%
20	Maryland	1,156,365,000	1.6%
15	Massachusetts	1,280,339,000	1.7%
9	Michigan	2,509,770,000	3.4%
16	Minnesota	1,230,654,000	1.7%
32	Mississippi	486,594,000	0.7%
22	Missouri	1,038,876,000	1.4%
43	Montana	163,925,000	0.2%
37	Nebraska	277,159,000	0.4%
25	Nevada	786,113,000	1.1%
40	New Hampshire	187,070,000	0.3%
8	New Jersey	2,564,201,000	3.5%
36	New Mexico	388,627,000	0.5%
2	New York	7,999,730,000	10.8%
17	North Carolina	1,220,649,000	1.6%
49	North Dakota	78,265,000	0.1%
6	Ohio	3,120,452,000	4.2%
34	Oklahoma	449,268,000	0.6%
24	Oregon	867,564,000	1.2%
7	Pennsylvania	2,810,670,000	3.8%
42	Rhode Island	164,794,000	0.2%
27	South Carolina	661,674,000	0.9%
47	South Dakota	104,993,000	0.1%
18	Tennessee	1,198,740,000	1.6%
4	Texas	4,794,865,000	6.5%
31	Utah	492,092,000	0.7%
50	Vermont	55,988,000	0.1%
12	Virginia	1,532,001,000	2.1%
11	Washington	1,586,330,000	2.1%
41	West Virginia	176,560,000	0.2%
14	Wisconsin	1,465,980,000	2.0%
46	Wyoming	114,275,000	0.2%

RANK ORDER

RANK	STATE	EXPENDITURES	% of USA
1	California	$13,564,511,000	18.3%
2	New York	7,999,730,000	10.8%
3	Florida	4,978,711,000	6.7%
4	Texas	4,794,865,000	6.5%
5	Illinois	3,519,762,000	4.7%
6	Ohio	3,120,452,000	4.2%
7	Pennsylvania	2,810,670,000	3.8%
8	New Jersey	2,564,201,000	3.5%
9	Michigan	2,509,770,000	3.4%
10	Georgia	1,809,707,000	2.4%
11	Washington	1,586,330,000	2.1%
12	Virginia	1,532,001,000	2.1%
13	Arizona	1,482,006,000	2.0%
14	Wisconsin	1,465,980,000	2.0%
15	Massachusetts	1,280,339,000	1.7%
16	Minnesota	1,230,654,000	1.7%
17	North Carolina	1,220,649,000	1.6%
18	Tennessee	1,198,740,000	1.6%
19	Louisiana	1,159,855,000	1.6%
20	Maryland	1,156,365,000	1.6%
21	Colorado	1,057,697,000	1.4%
22	Missouri	1,038,876,000	1.4%
23	Indiana	979,123,000	1.3%
24	Oregon	867,564,000	1.2%
25	Nevada	786,113,000	1.1%
26	Alabama	777,078,000	1.0%
27	South Carolina	661,674,000	0.9%
28	Connecticut	579,342,000	0.8%
29	Kansas	539,987,000	0.7%
30	Kentucky	538,785,000	0.7%
31	Utah	492,092,000	0.7%
32	Mississippi	486,594,000	0.7%
33	Iowa	452,243,000	0.6%
34	Oklahoma	449,268,000	0.6%
35	Arkansas	391,732,000	0.5%
36	New Mexico	388,627,000	0.5%
37	Nebraska	277,159,000	0.4%
38	Hawaii	246,707,000	0.3%
39	Idaho	244,620,000	0.3%
40	New Hampshire	187,070,000	0.3%
41	West Virginia	176,560,000	0.2%
42	Rhode Island	164,794,000	0.2%
43	Montana	163,925,000	0.2%
44	Maine	151,260,000	0.2%
45	Alaska	138,025,000	0.2%
46	Wyoming	114,275,000	0.2%
47	South Dakota	104,993,000	0.1%
48	Delaware	98,937,000	0.1%
49	North Dakota	78,265,000	0.1%
50	Vermont	55,988,000	0.1%
	District of Columbia	641,291,000	0.9%

Source: Morgan Quitno Press using data from Morgan Quitno Press using data from U.S. Bureau of the Census
"Government Finances 1998-99" (http://www.census.gov/govs/estimate/99allpub.pdf, September 2001)
*Direct general expenditures. Includes Police Protection, Corrections and Judicial and Legal Services.

Per Capita Local Government Expenditures for Justice Activities in 1999

National Per Capita = $273*

ALPHA ORDER

RANK	STATE	PER CAPITA
32	Alabama	$178
22	Alaska	223
6	Arizona	310
42	Arkansas	154
3	California	409
13	Colorado	261
33	Connecticut	177
46	Delaware	131
4	Florida	329
19	Georgia	232
26	Hawaii	208
29	Idaho	195
7	Illinois	290
38	Indiana	165
40	Iowa	158
28	Kansas	203
44	Kentucky	136
11	Louisiana	265
48	Maine	121
21	Maryland	224
27	Massachusetts	207
15	Michigan	254
14	Minnesota	258
34	Mississippi	176
30	Missouri	190
31	Montana	186
36	Nebraska	166
2	Nevada	434
41	New Hampshire	156
5	New Jersey	315
22	New Mexico	223
1	New York	440
39	North Carolina	160
47	North Dakota	124
9	Ohio	277
45	Oklahoma	134
12	Oregon	262
18	Pennsylvania	234
36	Rhode Island	166
35	South Carolina	170
43	South Dakota	143
25	Tennessee	219
16	Texas	239
20	Utah	231
50	Vermont	94
22	Virginia	223
10	Washington	276
49	West Virginia	98
8	Wisconsin	279
17	Wyoming	238

RANK ORDER

RANK	STATE	PER CAPITA
1	New York	$440
2	Nevada	434
3	California	409
4	Florida	329
5	New Jersey	315
6	Arizona	310
7	Illinois	290
8	Wisconsin	279
9	Ohio	277
10	Washington	276
11	Louisiana	265
12	Oregon	262
13	Colorado	261
14	Minnesota	258
15	Michigan	254
16	Texas	239
17	Wyoming	238
18	Pennsylvania	234
19	Georgia	232
20	Utah	231
21	Maryland	224
22	Alaska	223
22	New Mexico	223
22	Virginia	223
25	Tennessee	219
26	Hawaii	208
27	Massachusetts	207
28	Kansas	203
29	Idaho	195
30	Missouri	190
31	Montana	186
32	Alabama	178
33	Connecticut	177
34	Mississippi	176
35	South Carolina	170
36	Nebraska	166
36	Rhode Island	166
38	Indiana	165
39	North Carolina	160
40	Iowa	158
41	New Hampshire	156
42	Arkansas	154
43	South Dakota	143
44	Kentucky	136
45	Oklahoma	134
46	Delaware	131
47	North Dakota	124
48	Maine	121
49	West Virginia	98
50	Vermont	94

District of Columbia — 1,236

Source: Morgan Quitno Press using data from Morgan Quitno Press using data from U.S. Bureau of the Census "Government Finances 1998-99" (http://www.census.gov/govs/estimate/99allpub.pdf, September 2001)
*Direct general expenditures. Includes Police Protection, Corrections and Judicial and Legal Services.

Local Government Expenditures for Justice Activities
As a Percent of All Direct General Expenditures in 1999
National Percent = 9.1% of Direct General Expenditures*

ALPHA ORDER

RANK	STATE	PERCENT
31	Alabama	7.4
46	Alaska	5.3
4	Arizona	11.3
28	Arkansas	7.9
3	California	11.4
13	Colorado	8.9
40	Connecticut	6.3
37	Delaware	6.5
5	Florida	11.0
19	Georgia	8.6
1	Hawaii	17.7
24	Idaho	8.0
10	Illinois	9.7
40	Indiana	6.3
45	Iowa	5.6
30	Kansas	7.5
36	Kentucky	6.7
6	Louisiana	10.8
46	Maine	5.3
19	Maryland	8.6
24	Massachusetts	8.0
24	Michigan	8.0
33	Minnesota	7.3
34	Mississippi	7.1
24	Missouri	8.0
16	Montana	8.8
37	Nebraska	6.5
2	Nevada	12.9
35	New Hampshire	6.9
7	New Jersey	9.8
16	New Mexico	8.8
11	New York	9.4
44	North Carolina	5.9
49	North Dakota	4.9
7	Ohio	9.8
43	Oklahoma	6.2
21	Oregon	8.4
21	Pennsylvania	8.4
29	Rhode Island	7.7
31	South Carolina	7.4
37	South Dakota	6.5
13	Tennessee	8.9
12	Texas	9.1
7	Utah	9.8
50	Vermont	4.4
18	Virginia	8.7
13	Washington	8.9
48	West Virginia	5.1
23	Wisconsin	8.3
40	Wyoming	6.3

RANK ORDER

RANK	STATE	PERCENT
1	Hawaii	17.7
2	Nevada	12.9
3	California	11.4
4	Arizona	11.3
5	Florida	11.0
6	Louisiana	10.8
7	New Jersey	9.8
7	Ohio	9.8
7	Utah	9.8
10	Illinois	9.7
11	New York	9.4
12	Texas	9.1
13	Colorado	8.9
13	Tennessee	8.9
13	Washington	8.9
16	Montana	8.8
16	New Mexico	8.8
18	Virginia	8.7
19	Georgia	8.6
19	Maryland	8.6
21	Oregon	8.4
21	Pennsylvania	8.4
23	Wisconsin	8.3
24	Idaho	8.0
24	Massachusetts	8.0
24	Michigan	8.0
24	Missouri	8.0
28	Arkansas	7.9
29	Rhode Island	7.7
30	Kansas	7.5
31	Alabama	7.4
31	South Carolina	7.4
33	Minnesota	7.3
34	Mississippi	7.1
35	New Hampshire	6.9
36	Kentucky	6.7
37	Delaware	6.5
37	Nebraska	6.5
37	South Dakota	6.5
40	Connecticut	6.3
40	Indiana	6.3
40	Wyoming	6.3
43	Oklahoma	6.2
44	North Carolina	5.9
45	Iowa	5.6
46	Alaska	5.3
46	Maine	5.3
48	West Virginia	5.1
49	North Dakota	4.9
50	Vermont	4.4

District of Columbia		13.9

Source: Morgan Quitno Press using data from Morgan Quitno Press using data from U.S. Bureau of the Census "Government Finances 1998-99" (http://www.census.gov/govs/estimate/99allpub.pdf, September 2001)
*Includes Police Protection, Corrections and Judicial and Legal Services.

State and Local Government Expenditures for Police Protection in 1999

National Total = $53,366,526,000*

ALPHA ORDER

RANK	STATE	EXPENDITURES	% of USA
25	Alabama	$646,298,000	1.2%
41	Alaska	177,696,000	0.3%
15	Arizona	1,035,267,000	1.9%
36	Arkansas	337,363,000	0.6%
1	California	8,130,654,000	15.2%
22	Colorado	777,886,000	1.5%
24	Connecticut	659,432,000	1.2%
45	Delaware	152,110,000	0.3%
3	Florida	3,583,096,000	6.7%
12	Georgia	1,183,464,000	2.2%
37	Hawaii	221,151,000	0.4%
39	Idaho	192,939,000	0.4%
5	Illinois	2,786,607,000	5.2%
23	Indiana	757,079,000	1.4%
32	Iowa	397,350,000	0.7%
30	Kansas	428,514,000	0.8%
29	Kentucky	443,166,000	0.8%
21	Louisiana	819,511,000	1.5%
44	Maine	156,210,000	0.3%
16	Maryland	1,012,564,000	1.9%
10	Massachusetts	1,388,748,000	2.6%
9	Michigan	1,712,787,000	3.2%
20	Minnesota	820,700,000	1.5%
33	Mississippi	394,047,000	0.7%
18	Missouri	860,847,000	1.6%
46	Montana	121,339,000	0.2%
38	Nebraska	220,340,000	0.4%
28	Nevada	462,973,000	0.9%
42	New Hampshire	175,312,000	0.3%
8	New Jersey	1,984,430,000	3.7%
35	New Mexico	353,017,000	0.7%
2	New York	5,549,130,000	10.4%
11	North Carolina	1,251,050,000	2.3%
49	North Dakota	66,074,000	0.1%
7	Ohio	2,036,448,000	3.8%
31	Oklahoma	413,775,000	0.8%
26	Oregon	630,463,000	1.2%
6	Pennsylvania	2,102,439,000	3.9%
40	Rhode Island	187,804,000	0.4%
27	South Carolina	589,893,000	1.1%
48	South Dakota	87,027,000	0.2%
19	Tennessee	858,935,000	1.6%
4	Texas	3,095,682,000	5.8%
34	Utah	360,317,000	0.7%
50	Vermont	62,233,000	0.1%
13	Virginia	1,108,587,000	2.1%
17	Washington	954,647,000	1.8%
43	West Virginia	157,923,000	0.3%
14	Wisconsin	1,054,501,000	2.0%
47	Wyoming	93,477,000	0.2%

RANK ORDER

RANK	STATE	EXPENDITURES	% of USA
1	California	$8,130,654,000	15.2%
2	New York	5,549,130,000	10.4%
3	Florida	3,583,096,000	6.7%
4	Texas	3,095,682,000	5.8%
5	Illinois	2,786,607,000	5.2%
6	Pennsylvania	2,102,439,000	3.9%
7	Ohio	2,036,448,000	3.8%
8	New Jersey	1,984,430,000	3.7%
9	Michigan	1,712,787,000	3.2%
10	Massachusetts	1,388,748,000	2.6%
11	North Carolina	1,251,050,000	2.3%
12	Georgia	1,183,464,000	2.2%
13	Virginia	1,108,587,000	2.1%
14	Wisconsin	1,054,501,000	2.0%
15	Arizona	1,035,267,000	1.9%
16	Maryland	1,012,564,000	1.9%
17	Washington	954,647,000	1.8%
18	Missouri	860,847,000	1.6%
19	Tennessee	858,935,000	1.6%
20	Minnesota	820,700,000	1.5%
21	Louisiana	819,511,000	1.5%
22	Colorado	777,886,000	1.5%
23	Indiana	757,079,000	1.4%
24	Connecticut	659,432,000	1.2%
25	Alabama	646,298,000	1.2%
26	Oregon	630,463,000	1.2%
27	South Carolina	589,893,000	1.1%
28	Nevada	462,973,000	0.9%
29	Kentucky	443,166,000	0.8%
30	Kansas	428,514,000	0.8%
31	Oklahoma	413,775,000	0.8%
32	Iowa	397,350,000	0.7%
33	Mississippi	394,047,000	0.7%
34	Utah	360,317,000	0.7%
35	New Mexico	353,017,000	0.7%
36	Arkansas	337,363,000	0.6%
37	Hawaii	221,151,000	0.4%
38	Nebraska	220,340,000	0.4%
39	Idaho	192,939,000	0.4%
40	Rhode Island	187,804,000	0.4%
41	Alaska	177,696,000	0.3%
42	New Hampshire	175,312,000	0.3%
43	West Virginia	157,923,000	0.3%
44	Maine	156,210,000	0.3%
45	Delaware	152,110,000	0.3%
46	Montana	121,339,000	0.2%
47	Wyoming	93,477,000	0.2%
48	South Dakota	87,027,000	0.2%
49	North Dakota	66,074,000	0.1%
50	Vermont	62,233,000	0.1%
	District of Columbia	313,224,000	0.6%

Source: Morgan Quitno Press using data from Morgan Quitno Press using data from U.S. Bureau of the Census "Government Finances 1998-99" (http://www.census.gov/govs/estimate/99allpub.pdf, September 2001)
Direct general expenditures.

Per Capita State & Local Government Expenditures for Police Protection: 1999

National Per Capita = $196*

ALPHA ORDER

RANK	STATE	PER CAPITA
36	Alabama	$148
2	Alaska	287
9	Arizona	217
41	Arkansas	132
4	California	245
16	Colorado	192
12	Connecticut	201
11	Delaware	202
6	Florida	237
34	Georgia	152
19	Hawaii	187
32	Idaho	154
7	Illinois	230
43	Indiana	127
39	Iowa	138
28	Kansas	161
47	Kentucky	112
19	Louisiana	187
44	Maine	125
14	Maryland	196
8	Massachusetts	225
23	Michigan	174
24	Minnesota	172
38	Mississippi	142
30	Missouri	157
40	Montana	137
41	Nebraska	132
3	Nevada	256
37	New Hampshire	146
5	New Jersey	244
10	New Mexico	203
1	New York	305
27	North Carolina	164
49	North Dakota	104
21	Ohio	181
45	Oklahoma	123
17	Oregon	190
22	Pennsylvania	175
17	Rhode Island	190
34	South Carolina	152
46	South Dakota	119
30	Tennessee	157
32	Texas	154
25	Utah	169
48	Vermont	105
28	Virginia	161
26	Washington	166
50	West Virginia	87
12	Wisconsin	201
15	Wyoming	195

RANK ORDER

RANK	STATE	PER CAPITA
1	New York	$305
2	Alaska	287
3	Nevada	256
4	California	245
5	New Jersey	244
6	Florida	237
7	Illinois	230
8	Massachusetts	225
9	Arizona	217
10	New Mexico	203
11	Delaware	202
12	Connecticut	201
12	Wisconsin	201
14	Maryland	196
15	Wyoming	195
16	Colorado	192
17	Oregon	190
17	Rhode Island	190
19	Hawaii	187
19	Louisiana	187
21	Ohio	181
22	Pennsylvania	175
23	Michigan	174
24	Minnesota	172
25	Utah	169
26	Washington	166
27	North Carolina	164
28	Kansas	161
28	Virginia	161
30	Missouri	157
30	Tennessee	157
32	Idaho	154
32	Texas	154
34	Georgia	152
34	South Carolina	152
36	Alabama	148
37	New Hampshire	146
38	Mississippi	142
39	Iowa	138
40	Montana	137
41	Arkansas	132
41	Nebraska	132
43	Indiana	127
44	Maine	125
45	Oklahoma	123
46	South Dakota	119
47	Kentucky	112
48	Vermont	105
49	North Dakota	104
50	West Virginia	87

District of Columbia 604

Source: Morgan Quitno Press using data from Morgan Quitno Press using data from U.S. Bureau of the Census "Government Finances 1998-99" (http://www.census.gov/govs/estimate/99allpub.pdf, September 2001)
*Direct general expenditures.

State and Local Government Expenditures for Police Protection
As a Percent of All Direct General Expenditures in 1999
National Percent = 3.8% of Direct General Expenditures

ALPHA ORDER

RANK	STATE	PERCENT
31	Alabama	3.2
45	Alaska	2.5
1	Arizona	5.1
31	Arkansas	3.2
5	California	4.5
10	Colorado	3.9
28	Connecticut	3.3
21	Delaware	3.4
2	Florida	5.0
28	Georgia	3.3
31	Hawaii	3.2
21	Idaho	3.4
4	Illinois	4.7
41	Indiana	2.8
43	Iowa	2.7
15	Kansas	3.6
45	Kentucky	2.5
10	Louisiana	3.9
47	Maine	2.4
7	Maryland	4.1
9	Massachusetts	4.0
21	Michigan	3.4
39	Minnesota	2.9
36	Mississippi	3.0
15	Missouri	3.6
41	Montana	2.8
39	Nebraska	2.9
2	Nevada	5.0
28	New Hampshire	3.3
5	New Jersey	4.5
14	New Mexico	3.7
7	New York	4.1
21	North Carolina	3.4
49	North Dakota	1.9
12	Ohio	3.8
35	Oklahoma	3.1
21	Oregon	3.4
21	Pennsylvania	3.4
15	Rhode Island	3.6
31	South Carolina	3.2
43	South Dakota	2.7
15	Tennessee	3.6
19	Texas	3.5
19	Utah	3.5
48	Vermont	2.1
21	Virginia	3.4
36	Washington	3.0
49	West Virginia	1.9
12	Wisconsin	3.8
36	Wyoming	3.0

RANK ORDER

RANK	STATE	PERCENT
1	Arizona	5.1
2	Florida	5.0
2	Nevada	5.0
4	Illinois	4.7
5	California	4.5
5	New Jersey	4.5
7	Maryland	4.1
7	New York	4.1
9	Massachusetts	4.0
10	Colorado	3.9
10	Louisiana	3.9
12	Ohio	3.8
12	Wisconsin	3.8
14	New Mexico	3.7
15	Kansas	3.6
15	Missouri	3.6
15	Rhode Island	3.6
15	Tennessee	3.6
19	Texas	3.5
19	Utah	3.5
21	Delaware	3.4
21	Idaho	3.4
21	Michigan	3.4
21	North Carolina	3.4
21	Oregon	3.4
21	Pennsylvania	3.4
21	Virginia	3.4
28	Connecticut	3.3
28	Georgia	3.3
28	New Hampshire	3.3
31	Alabama	3.2
31	Arkansas	3.2
31	Hawaii	3.2
31	South Carolina	3.2
35	Oklahoma	3.1
36	Mississippi	3.0
36	Washington	3.0
36	Wyoming	3.0
39	Minnesota	2.9
39	Nebraska	2.9
41	Indiana	2.8
41	Montana	2.8
43	Iowa	2.7
43	South Dakota	2.7
45	Alaska	2.5
45	Kentucky	2.5
47	Maine	2.4
48	Vermont	2.1
49	North Dakota	1.9
49	West Virginia	1.9

District of Columbia	6.8

Source: Morgan Quitno Press using data from Morgan Quitno Press using data from U.S. Bureau of the Census
"Government Finances 1998-99" (http://www.census.gov/govs/estimate/99allpub.pdf, September 2001)

State Government Expenditures for Police Protection in 1999

National Total = $7,809,838,000*

ALPHA ORDER

RANK	STATE	EXPENDITURES	% of USA
27	Alabama	$89,432,000	1.1%
35	Alaska	52,196,000	0.7%
19	Arizona	139,775,000	1.8%
32	Arkansas	66,083,000	0.8%
1	California	932,482,000	11.9%
29	Colorado	70,165,000	0.9%
21	Connecticut	128,226,000	1.6%
33	Delaware	60,754,000	0.8%
5	Florida	340,037,000	4.4%
17	Georgia	165,912,000	2.1%
50	Hawaii	4,928,000	0.1%
41	Idaho	35,248,000	0.5%
8	Illinois	313,397,000	4.0%
14	Indiana	179,236,000	2.3%
28	Iowa	75,189,000	1.0%
37	Kansas	46,278,000	0.6%
22	Kentucky	126,228,000	1.6%
15	Louisiana	177,339,000	2.3%
39	Maine	43,057,000	0.6%
11	Maryland	211,081,000	2.7%
4	Massachusetts	376,959,000	4.8%
10	Michigan	263,582,000	3.4%
25	Minnesota	105,611,000	1.4%
34	Mississippi	56,909,000	0.7%
20	Missouri	132,868,000	1.7%
45	Montana	24,860,000	0.3%
38	Nebraska	45,764,000	0.6%
36	Nevada	47,974,000	0.6%
42	New Hampshire	34,336,000	0.4%
9	New Jersey	298,215,000	3.8%
30	New Mexico	70,074,000	0.9%
3	New York	421,067,000	5.4%
7	North Carolina	316,795,000	4.1%
49	North Dakota	13,117,000	0.2%
12	Ohio	203,281,000	2.6%
44	Oklahoma	30,728,000	0.4%
23	Oregon	117,354,000	1.5%
2	Pennsylvania	752,123,000	9.6%
43	Rhode Island	31,905,000	0.4%
16	South Carolina	173,978,000	2.2%
47	South Dakota	18,074,000	0.2%
24	Tennessee	114,349,000	1.5%
6	Texas	318,884,000	4.1%
31	Utah	68,621,000	0.9%
46	Vermont	24,035,000	0.3%
13	Virginia	188,846,000	2.4%
18	Washington	143,381,000	1.8%
40	West Virginia	41,922,000	0.5%
26	Wisconsin	99,303,000	1.3%
48	Wyoming	17,880,000	0.2%

RANK ORDER

RANK	STATE	EXPENDITURES	% of USA
1	California	$932,482,000	11.9%
2	Pennsylvania	752,123,000	9.6%
3	New York	421,067,000	5.4%
4	Massachusetts	376,959,000	4.8%
5	Florida	340,037,000	4.4%
6	Texas	318,884,000	4.1%
7	North Carolina	316,795,000	4.1%
8	Illinois	313,397,000	4.0%
9	New Jersey	298,215,000	3.8%
10	Michigan	263,582,000	3.4%
11	Maryland	211,081,000	2.7%
12	Ohio	203,281,000	2.6%
13	Virginia	188,846,000	2.4%
14	Indiana	179,236,000	2.3%
15	Louisiana	177,339,000	2.3%
16	South Carolina	173,978,000	2.2%
17	Georgia	165,912,000	2.1%
18	Washington	143,381,000	1.8%
19	Arizona	139,775,000	1.8%
20	Missouri	132,868,000	1.7%
21	Connecticut	128,226,000	1.6%
22	Kentucky	126,228,000	1.6%
23	Oregon	117,354,000	1.5%
24	Tennessee	114,349,000	1.5%
25	Minnesota	105,611,000	1.4%
26	Wisconsin	99,303,000	1.3%
27	Alabama	89,432,000	1.1%
28	Iowa	75,189,000	1.0%
29	Colorado	70,165,000	0.9%
30	New Mexico	70,074,000	0.9%
31	Utah	68,621,000	0.9%
32	Arkansas	66,083,000	0.8%
33	Delaware	60,754,000	0.8%
34	Mississippi	56,909,000	0.7%
35	Alaska	52,196,000	0.7%
36	Nevada	47,974,000	0.6%
37	Kansas	46,278,000	0.6%
38	Nebraska	45,764,000	0.6%
39	Maine	43,057,000	0.6%
40	West Virginia	41,922,000	0.5%
41	Idaho	35,248,000	0.5%
42	New Hampshire	34,336,000	0.4%
43	Rhode Island	31,905,000	0.4%
44	Oklahoma	30,728,000	0.4%
45	Montana	24,860,000	0.3%
46	Vermont	24,035,000	0.3%
47	South Dakota	18,074,000	0.2%
48	Wyoming	17,880,000	0.2%
49	North Dakota	13,117,000	0.2%
50	Hawaii	4,928,000	0.1%
	District of Columbia**	NA	NA

Source: Morgan Quitno Press using data from Morgan Quitno Press using data from U.S. Bureau of the Census "Government Finances 1998-99" (http://www.census.gov/govs/estimate/99allpub.pdf, September 2001)
Direct general expenditures.
**Not applicable.*

Per Capita State Government Expenditures for Police Protection in 1999

National Per Capita = $28.64*

ALPHA ORDER				RANK ORDER		
RANK	STATE	PER CAPITA		RANK	STATE	PER CAPITA
43	Alabama	$20.47		1	Alaska	$84.26
1	Alaska	84.26		2	Delaware	80.62
20	Arizona	29.25		3	Pennsylvania	62.71
30	Arkansas	25.90		4	Massachusetts	61.04
24	California	28.13		5	South Carolina	44.77
47	Colorado	17.30		6	North Carolina	41.41
11	Connecticut	39.07		7	Maryland	40.82
2	Delaware	80.62		8	Louisiana	40.56
37	Florida	22.50		9	Vermont	40.48
39	Georgia	21.30		10	New Mexico	40.28
50	Hawaii	4.16		11	Connecticut	39.07
22	Idaho	28.16		12	Wyoming	37.28
31	Illinois	25.84		13	New Jersey	36.62
19	Indiana	30.16		14	Oregon	35.39
29	Iowa	26.20		15	Maine	34.36
46	Kansas	17.44		16	Utah	32.22
18	Kentucky	31.87		17	Rhode Island	32.20
8	Louisiana	40.56		18	Kentucky	31.87
15	Maine	34.36		19	Indiana	30.16
7	Maryland	40.82		20	Arizona	29.25
4	Massachusetts	61.04		21	New Hampshire	28.59
27	Michigan	26.72		22	Idaho	28.16
38	Minnesota	22.12		22	Montana	28.16
42	Mississippi	20.56		24	California	28.13
34	Missouri	24.30		25	Virginia	27.48
22	Montana	28.16		26	Nebraska	27.47
26	Nebraska	27.47		27	Michigan	26.72
28	Nevada	26.52		28	Nevada	26.52
21	New Hampshire	28.59		29	Iowa	26.20
13	New Jersey	36.62		30	Arkansas	25.90
10	New Mexico	40.28		31	Illinois	25.84
36	New York	23.14		32	Washington	24.91
6	North Carolina	41.41		33	South Dakota	24.65
41	North Dakota	20.70		34	Missouri	24.30
45	Ohio	18.06		35	West Virginia	23.20
49	Oklahoma	9.15		36	New York	23.14
14	Oregon	35.39		37	Florida	22.50
3	Pennsylvania	62.71		38	Minnesota	22.12
17	Rhode Island	32.20		39	Georgia	21.30
5	South Carolina	44.77		40	Tennessee	20.85
33	South Dakota	24.65		41	North Dakota	20.70
40	Tennessee	20.85		42	Mississippi	20.56
48	Texas	15.91		43	Alabama	20.47
16	Utah	32.22		44	Wisconsin	18.91
9	Vermont	40.48		45	Ohio	18.06
25	Virginia	27.48		46	Kansas	17.44
32	Washington	24.91		47	Colorado	17.30
35	West Virginia	23.20		48	Texas	15.91
44	Wisconsin	18.91		49	Oklahoma	9.15
12	Wyoming	37.28		50	Hawaii	4.16
					District of Columbia**	NA

Source: Morgan Quitno Press using data from Morgan Quitno Press using data from U.S. Bureau of the Census
"Government Finances 1998-99" (http://www.census.gov/govs/estimate/99allpub.pdf, September 2001)
*Direct general expenditures.
**Not applicable.

State Government Expenditures for Police Protection
As a Percent of All Direct General Expenditures in 1999
National Percent = 1.3% of Direct General Expenditures

ALPHA ORDER

RANK	STATE	PERCENT
40	Alabama	0.9
30	Alaska	1.1
5	Arizona	1.9
26	Arkansas	1.2
11	California	1.5
40	Colorado	0.9
26	Connecticut	1.2
2	Delaware	2.1
18	Florida	1.3
30	Georgia	1.1
50	Hawaii	0.1
14	Idaho	1.4
18	Illinois	1.3
10	Indiana	1.6
30	Iowa	1.1
40	Kansas	0.9
18	Kentucky	1.3
8	Louisiana	1.7
26	Maine	1.2
7	Maryland	1.8
3	Massachusetts	2.0
14	Michigan	1.4
40	Minnesota	0.9
40	Mississippi	0.9
26	Missouri	1.2
35	Montana	1.0
18	Nebraska	1.3
11	Nevada	1.5
18	New Hampshire	1.3
8	New Jersey	1.7
14	New Mexico	1.4
40	New York	0.9
3	North Carolina	2.0
48	North Dakota	0.7
35	Ohio	1.0
49	Oklahoma	0.5
11	Oregon	1.5
1	Pennsylvania	2.7
35	Rhode Island	1.0
5	South Carolina	1.9
30	South Dakota	1.1
30	Tennessee	1.1
40	Texas	0.9
18	Utah	1.3
14	Vermont	1.4
18	Virginia	1.3
35	Washington	1.0
40	West Virginia	0.9
35	Wisconsin	1.0
18	Wyoming	1.3

RANK ORDER

RANK	STATE	PERCENT
1	Pennsylvania	2.7
2	Delaware	2.1
3	Massachusetts	2.0
3	North Carolina	2.0
5	Arizona	1.9
5	South Carolina	1.9
7	Maryland	1.8
8	Louisiana	1.7
8	New Jersey	1.7
10	Indiana	1.6
11	California	1.5
11	Nevada	1.5
11	Oregon	1.5
14	Idaho	1.4
14	Michigan	1.4
14	New Mexico	1.4
14	Vermont	1.4
18	Florida	1.3
18	Illinois	1.3
18	Kentucky	1.3
18	Nebraska	1.3
18	New Hampshire	1.3
18	Utah	1.3
18	Virginia	1.3
18	Wyoming	1.3
26	Arkansas	1.2
26	Connecticut	1.2
26	Maine	1.2
26	Missouri	1.2
30	Alaska	1.1
30	Georgia	1.1
30	Iowa	1.1
30	South Dakota	1.1
30	Tennessee	1.1
35	Montana	1.0
35	Ohio	1.0
35	Rhode Island	1.0
35	Washington	1.0
35	Wisconsin	1.0
40	Alabama	0.9
40	Colorado	0.9
40	Kansas	0.9
40	Minnesota	0.9
40	Mississippi	0.9
40	New York	0.9
40	Texas	0.9
40	West Virginia	0.9
48	North Dakota	0.7
49	Oklahoma	0.5
50	Hawaii	0.1

District of Columbia*   NA

Source: Morgan Quitno Press using data from Morgan Quitno Press using data from U.S. Bureau of the Census "Government Finances 1998-99" (http://www.census.gov/govs/estimate/99allpub.pdf, September 2001)
*Not applicable.

Local Government Expenditures for Police Protection in 1999

National Total = $45,556,688,000*

ALPHA ORDER

RANK	STATE	EXPENDITURES	% of USA
24	Alabama	$556,866,000	1.2%
42	Alaska	125,500,000	0.3%
15	Arizona	895,492,000	2.0%
36	Arkansas	271,280,000	0.6%
1	California	7,198,172,000	15.8%
21	Colorado	707,721,000	1.6%
25	Connecticut	531,206,000	1.2%
46	Delaware	91,356,000	0.2%
3	Florida	3,243,059,000	7.1%
10	Georgia	1,017,552,000	2.2%
37	Hawaii	216,223,000	0.5%
39	Idaho	157,691,000	0.3%
5	Illinois	2,473,210,000	5.4%
23	Indiana	577,843,000	1.3%
32	Iowa	322,161,000	0.7%
30	Kansas	382,236,000	0.8%
33	Kentucky	316,938,000	0.7%
22	Louisiana	642,172,000	1.4%
44	Maine	113,153,000	0.2%
17	Maryland	801,483,000	1.8%
11	Massachusetts	1,011,789,000	2.2%
8	Michigan	1,449,205,000	3.2%
20	Minnesota	715,089,000	1.6%
31	Mississippi	337,138,000	0.7%
19	Missouri	727,979,000	1.6%
45	Montana	96,479,000	0.2%
38	Nebraska	174,576,000	0.4%
28	Nevada	414,999,000	0.9%
41	New Hampshire	140,976,000	0.3%
7	New Jersey	1,686,215,000	3.7%
35	New Mexico	282,943,000	0.6%
2	New York	5,128,063,000	11.3%
13	North Carolina	934,255,000	2.1%
49	North Dakota	52,957,000	0.1%
6	Ohio	1,833,167,000	4.0%
29	Oklahoma	383,047,000	0.8%
26	Oregon	513,109,000	1.1%
9	Pennsylvania	1,350,316,000	3.0%
40	Rhode Island	155,899,000	0.3%
27	South Carolina	415,915,000	0.9%
48	South Dakota	68,953,000	0.2%
18	Tennessee	744,586,000	1.6%
4	Texas	2,776,798,000	6.1%
34	Utah	291,696,000	0.6%
50	Vermont	38,198,000	0.1%
14	Virginia	919,741,000	2.0%
16	Washington	811,266,000	1.8%
43	West Virginia	116,001,000	0.3%
12	Wisconsin	955,198,000	2.1%
47	Wyoming	75,597,000	0.2%

RANK ORDER

RANK	STATE	EXPENDITURES	% of USA
1	California	$7,198,172,000	15.8%
2	New York	5,128,063,000	11.3%
3	Florida	3,243,059,000	7.1%
4	Texas	2,776,798,000	6.1%
5	Illinois	2,473,210,000	5.4%
6	Ohio	1,833,167,000	4.0%
7	New Jersey	1,686,215,000	3.7%
8	Michigan	1,449,205,000	3.2%
9	Pennsylvania	1,350,316,000	3.0%
10	Georgia	1,017,552,000	2.2%
11	Massachusetts	1,011,789,000	2.2%
12	Wisconsin	955,198,000	2.1%
13	North Carolina	934,255,000	2.1%
14	Virginia	919,741,000	2.0%
15	Arizona	895,492,000	2.0%
16	Washington	811,266,000	1.8%
17	Maryland	801,483,000	1.8%
18	Tennessee	744,586,000	1.6%
19	Missouri	727,979,000	1.6%
20	Minnesota	715,089,000	1.6%
21	Colorado	707,721,000	1.6%
22	Louisiana	642,172,000	1.4%
23	Indiana	577,843,000	1.3%
24	Alabama	556,866,000	1.2%
25	Connecticut	531,206,000	1.2%
26	Oregon	513,109,000	1.1%
27	South Carolina	415,915,000	0.9%
28	Nevada	414,999,000	0.9%
29	Oklahoma	383,047,000	0.8%
30	Kansas	382,236,000	0.8%
31	Mississippi	337,138,000	0.7%
32	Iowa	322,161,000	0.7%
33	Kentucky	316,938,000	0.7%
34	Utah	291,696,000	0.6%
35	New Mexico	282,943,000	0.6%
36	Arkansas	271,280,000	0.6%
37	Hawaii	216,223,000	0.5%
38	Nebraska	174,576,000	0.4%
39	Idaho	157,691,000	0.3%
40	Rhode Island	155,899,000	0.3%
41	New Hampshire	140,976,000	0.3%
42	Alaska	125,500,000	0.3%
43	West Virginia	116,001,000	0.3%
44	Maine	113,153,000	0.2%
45	Montana	96,479,000	0.2%
46	Delaware	91,356,000	0.2%
47	Wyoming	75,597,000	0.2%
48	South Dakota	68,953,000	0.2%
49	North Dakota	52,957,000	0.1%
50	Vermont	38,198,000	0.1%
	District of Columbia	313,224,000	0.7%

Source: Morgan Quitno Press using data from Morgan Quitno Press using data from U.S. Bureau of the Census "Government Finances 1998-99" (http://www.census.gov/govs/estimate/99allpub.pdf, September 2001)
Direct general expenditures.

Per Capita Local Government Expenditures for Police Protection in 1999

National Per Capita = $167*

ALPHA ORDER

ALPHA ORDER

RANK	STATE	PER CAPITA
31	Alabama	$127
7	Alaska	203
8	Arizona	187
42	Arkansas	106
3	California	217
11	Colorado	174
15	Connecticut	162
35	Delaware	121
4	Florida	215
30	Georgia	131
9	Hawaii	182
32	Idaho	126
6	Illinois	204
44	Indiana	97
39	Iowa	112
23	Kansas	144
48	Kentucky	80
21	Louisiana	147
46	Maine	90
18	Maryland	155
12	Massachusetts	164
21	Michigan	147
20	Minnesota	150
33	Mississippi	122
29	Missouri	133
40	Montana	109
43	Nebraska	105
2	Nevada	229
36	New Hampshire	117
5	New Jersey	207
13	New Mexico	163
1	New York	282
33	North Carolina	122
47	North Dakota	84
13	Ohio	163
37	Oklahoma	114
18	Oregon	155
38	Pennsylvania	113
17	Rhode Island	157
41	South Carolina	107
45	South Dakota	94
27	Tennessee	136
25	Texas	139
26	Utah	137
49	Vermont	64
28	Virginia	134
24	Washington	141
49	West Virginia	64
9	Wisconsin	182
16	Wyoming	158

RANK ORDER

RANK	STATE	PER CAPITA
1	New York	$282
2	Nevada	229
3	California	217
4	Florida	215
5	New Jersey	207
6	Illinois	204
7	Alaska	203
8	Arizona	187
9	Hawaii	182
9	Wisconsin	182
11	Colorado	174
12	Massachusetts	164
13	New Mexico	163
13	Ohio	163
15	Connecticut	162
16	Wyoming	158
17	Rhode Island	157
18	Maryland	155
18	Oregon	155
20	Minnesota	150
21	Louisiana	147
21	Michigan	147
23	Kansas	144
24	Washington	141
25	Texas	139
26	Utah	137
27	Tennessee	136
28	Virginia	134
29	Missouri	133
30	Georgia	131
31	Alabama	127
32	Idaho	126
33	Mississippi	122
33	North Carolina	122
35	Delaware	121
36	New Hampshire	117
37	Oklahoma	114
38	Pennsylvania	113
39	Iowa	112
40	Montana	109
41	South Carolina	107
42	Arkansas	106
43	Nebraska	105
44	Indiana	97
45	South Dakota	94
46	Maine	90
47	North Dakota	84
48	Kentucky	80
49	Vermont	64
49	West Virginia	64

District of Columbia 604

Source: Morgan Quitno Press using data from Morgan Quitno Press using data from U.S. Bureau of the Census "Government Finances 1998-99" (http://www.census.gov/govs/estimate/99allpub.pdf, September 2001)
Direct general expenditures.

Local Government Expenditures for Police Protection
As a Percent of All Direct General Expenditures in 1999
National Percent = 5.6% of Direct General Expenditures

ALPHA ORDER

RANK	STATE	PERCENT
23	Alabama	5.3
34	Alaska	4.8
4	Arizona	6.8
20	Arkansas	5.5
10	California	6.0
10	Colorado	6.0
16	Connecticut	5.8
10	Delaware	6.0
3	Florida	7.2
32	Georgia	4.9
1	Hawaii	15.5
27	Idaho	5.2
4	Illinois	6.8
47	Indiana	3.7
43	Iowa	4.0
23	Kansas	5.3
43	Kentucky	4.0
10	Louisiana	6.0
43	Maine	4.0
10	Maryland	6.0
7	Massachusetts	6.4
35	Michigan	4.6
39	Minnesota	4.3
32	Mississippi	4.9
19	Missouri	5.6
27	Montana	5.2
42	Nebraska	4.1
4	Nevada	6.8
27	New Hampshire	5.2
7	New Jersey	6.4
7	New Mexico	6.4
10	New York	6.0
37	North Carolina	4.5
49	North Dakota	3.3
16	Ohio	5.8
23	Oklahoma	5.3
31	Oregon	5.0
43	Pennsylvania	4.0
2	Rhode Island	7.3
35	South Carolina	4.6
39	South Dakota	4.3
20	Tennessee	5.5
23	Texas	5.3
16	Utah	5.8
50	Vermont	3.0
27	Virginia	5.2
37	Washington	4.5
48	West Virginia	3.4
22	Wisconsin	5.4
41	Wyoming	4.2

RANK ORDER

RANK	STATE	PERCENT
1	Hawaii	15.5
2	Rhode Island	7.3
3	Florida	7.2
4	Arizona	6.8
4	Illinois	6.8
4	Nevada	6.8
7	Massachusetts	6.4
7	New Jersey	6.4
7	New Mexico	6.4
10	California	6.0
10	Colorado	6.0
10	Delaware	6.0
10	Louisiana	6.0
10	Maryland	6.0
10	New York	6.0
16	Connecticut	5.8
16	Ohio	5.8
16	Utah	5.8
19	Missouri	5.6
20	Arkansas	5.5
20	Tennessee	5.5
22	Wisconsin	5.4
23	Alabama	5.3
23	Kansas	5.3
23	Oklahoma	5.3
23	Texas	5.3
27	Idaho	5.2
27	Montana	5.2
27	New Hampshire	5.2
27	Virginia	5.2
31	Oregon	5.0
32	Georgia	4.9
32	Mississippi	4.9
34	Alaska	4.8
35	Michigan	4.6
35	South Carolina	4.6
37	North Carolina	4.5
37	Washington	4.5
39	Minnesota	4.3
39	South Dakota	4.3
41	Wyoming	4.2
42	Nebraska	4.1
43	Iowa	4.0
43	Kentucky	4.0
43	Maine	4.0
43	Pennsylvania	4.0
47	Indiana	3.7
48	West Virginia	3.4
49	North Dakota	3.3
50	Vermont	3.0

District of Columbia   6.8

Source: Morgan Quitno Press using data from Morgan Quitno Press using data from U.S. Bureau of the Census
"Government Finances 1998-99" (http://www.census.gov/govs/estimate/99allpub.pdf, September 2001)

State and Local Government Expenditures for Corrections in 1999

National Total = $45,598,065,000*

ALPHA ORDER

RANK	STATE	EXPENDITURES	% of USA
29	Alabama	$407,973,000	0.9%
40	Alaska	154,514,000	0.3%
16	Arizona	849,835,000	1.9%
36	Arkansas	280,903,000	0.6%
1	California	6,530,580,000	14.3%
18	Colorado	787,586,000	1.7%
26	Connecticut	523,219,000	1.1%
38	Delaware	201,753,000	0.4%
4	Florida	3,115,566,000	6.8%
10	Georgia	1,286,453,000	2.8%
43	Hawaii	134,302,000	0.3%
37	Idaho	206,183,000	0.5%
8	Illinois	1,531,028,000	3.4%
21	Indiana	660,944,000	1.4%
35	Iowa	281,543,000	0.6%
32	Kansas	314,590,000	0.7%
27	Kentucky	501,230,000	1.1%
20	Louisiana	675,511,000	1.5%
46	Maine	107,056,000	0.2%
15	Maryland	911,185,000	2.0%
17	Massachusetts	807,946,000	1.8%
6	Michigan	1,825,673,000	4.0%
25	Minnesota	548,865,000	1.2%
34	Mississippi	284,544,000	0.6%
22	Missouri	640,288,000	1.4%
44	Montana	120,856,000	0.3%
39	Nebraska	172,626,000	0.4%
30	Nevada	405,993,000	0.9%
45	New Hampshire	108,051,000	0.2%
9	New Jersey	1,413,071,000	3.1%
33	New Mexico	293,448,000	0.6%
2	New York	4,254,175,000	9.3%
12	North Carolina	1,106,341,000	2.4%
49	North Dakota	47,672,000	0.1%
7	Ohio	1,694,553,000	3.7%
28	Oklahoma	445,426,000	1.0%
19	Oregon	700,093,000	1.5%
5	Pennsylvania	2,132,626,000	4.7%
42	Rhode Island	140,655,000	0.3%
24	South Carolina	561,623,000	1.2%
48	South Dakota	78,137,000	0.2%
23	Tennessee	580,928,000	1.3%
3	Texas	3,735,722,000	8.2%
31	Utah	353,746,000	0.8%
50	Vermont	39,254,000	0.1%
11	Virginia	1,159,203,000	2.5%
13	Washington	1,016,487,000	2.2%
41	West Virginia	153,593,000	0.3%
14	Wisconsin	926,721,000	2.0%
47	Wyoming	95,071,000	0.2%

RANK ORDER

RANK	STATE	EXPENDITURES	% of USA
1	California	$6,530,580,000	14.3%
2	New York	4,254,175,000	9.3%
3	Texas	3,735,722,000	8.2%
4	Florida	3,115,566,000	6.8%
5	Pennsylvania	2,132,626,000	4.7%
6	Michigan	1,825,673,000	4.0%
7	Ohio	1,694,553,000	3.7%
8	Illinois	1,531,028,000	3.4%
9	New Jersey	1,413,071,000	3.1%
10	Georgia	1,286,453,000	2.8%
11	Virginia	1,159,203,000	2.5%
12	North Carolina	1,106,341,000	2.4%
13	Washington	1,016,487,000	2.2%
14	Wisconsin	926,721,000	2.0%
15	Maryland	911,185,000	2.0%
16	Arizona	849,835,000	1.9%
17	Massachusetts	807,946,000	1.8%
18	Colorado	787,586,000	1.7%
19	Oregon	700,093,000	1.5%
20	Louisiana	675,511,000	1.5%
21	Indiana	660,944,000	1.4%
22	Missouri	640,288,000	1.4%
23	Tennessee	580,928,000	1.3%
24	South Carolina	561,623,000	1.2%
25	Minnesota	548,865,000	1.2%
26	Connecticut	523,219,000	1.1%
27	Kentucky	501,230,000	1.1%
28	Oklahoma	445,426,000	1.0%
29	Alabama	407,973,000	0.9%
30	Nevada	405,993,000	0.9%
31	Utah	353,746,000	0.8%
32	Kansas	314,590,000	0.7%
33	New Mexico	293,448,000	0.6%
34	Mississippi	284,544,000	0.6%
35	Iowa	281,543,000	0.6%
36	Arkansas	280,903,000	0.6%
37	Idaho	206,183,000	0.5%
38	Delaware	201,753,000	0.4%
39	Nebraska	172,626,000	0.4%
40	Alaska	154,514,000	0.3%
41	West Virginia	153,593,000	0.3%
42	Rhode Island	140,655,000	0.3%
43	Hawaii	134,302,000	0.3%
44	Montana	120,856,000	0.3%
45	New Hampshire	108,051,000	0.2%
46	Maine	107,056,000	0.2%
47	Wyoming	95,071,000	0.2%
48	South Dakota	78,137,000	0.2%
49	North Dakota	47,672,000	0.1%
50	Vermont	39,254,000	0.1%
	District of Columbia	292,724,000	0.6%

*Source: Morgan Quitno Press using data from Morgan Quitno Press using data from U.S. Bureau of the Census
"Government Finances 1998-99" (http://www.census.gov/govs/estimate/99allpub.pdf, September 2001)
Direct general expenditures.

Per Capita State and Local Government Expenditures for Corrections in 1999

National Per Capita = $167*

ALPHA ORDER				RANK ORDER		
RANK	STATE	PER CAPITA		RANK	STATE	PER CAPITA
45	Alabama	$93		1	Delaware	$268
2	Alaska	249		2	Alaska	249
12	Arizona	178		3	New York	234
39	Arkansas	110		4	Nevada	224
8	California	197		5	Oregon	211
9	Colorado	194		6	Florida	206
23	Connecticut	159		7	Wyoming	198
1	Delaware	268		8	California	197
6	Florida	206		9	Colorado	194
21	Georgia	165		10	Texas	186
37	Hawaii	113		11	Michigan	185
21	Idaho	165		12	Arizona	178
33	Illinois	126		12	Pennsylvania	178
38	Indiana	111		14	Washington	177
44	Iowa	98		14	Wisconsin	177
34	Kansas	119		16	Maryland	176
32	Kentucky	127		17	New Jersey	174
24	Louisiana	155		18	New Mexico	169
47	Maine	85		18	Virginia	169
16	Maryland	176		20	Utah	166
31	Massachusetts	131		21	Georgia	165
11	Michigan	185		21	Idaho	165
36	Minnesota	115		23	Connecticut	159
43	Mississippi	103		24	Louisiana	155
35	Missouri	117		25	Ohio	151
29	Montana	137		26	North Carolina	145
42	Nebraska	104		26	South Carolina	145
4	Nevada	224		28	Rhode Island	142
46	New Hampshire	90		29	Montana	137
17	New Jersey	174		30	Oklahoma	133
18	New Mexico	169		31	Massachusetts	131
3	New York	234		32	Kentucky	127
26	North Carolina	145		33	Illinois	126
49	North Dakota	75		34	Kansas	119
25	Ohio	151		35	Missouri	117
30	Oklahoma	133		36	Minnesota	115
5	Oregon	211		37	Hawaii	113
12	Pennsylvania	178		38	Indiana	111
28	Rhode Island	142		39	Arkansas	110
26	South Carolina	145		40	South Dakota	107
40	South Dakota	107		41	Tennessee	106
41	Tennessee	106		42	Nebraska	104
10	Texas	186		43	Mississippi	103
20	Utah	166		44	Iowa	98
50	Vermont	66		45	Alabama	93
18	Virginia	169		46	New Hampshire	90
14	Washington	177		47	Maine	85
47	West Virginia	85		47	West Virginia	85
14	Wisconsin	177		49	North Dakota	75
7	Wyoming	198		50	Vermont	66
					District of Columbia	564

Source: Morgan Quitno Press using data from Morgan Quitno Press using data from U.S. Bureau of the Census "Government Finances 1998-99" (http://www.census.gov/govs/estimate/99allpub.pdf, September 2001)
*Direct general expenditures.

State and Local Government Expenditures for Corrections
As a Percent of All Direct General Expenditures in 1999
National Percent = 3.3% of Direct General Expenditures

ALPHA ORDER

RANK ORDER

RANK	STATE	PERCENT		RANK	STATE	PERCENT
42	Alabama	2.0		1	Delaware	4.5
39	Alaska	2.2		2	Nevada	4.4
5	Arizona	4.2		3	Florida	4.3
32	Arkansas	2.6		3	Texas	4.3
10	California	3.6		5	Arizona	4.2
6	Colorado	3.9		6	Colorado	3.9
29	Connecticut	2.7		7	Oregon	3.8
1	Delaware	4.5		8	Idaho	3.7
3	Florida	4.3		8	Maryland	3.7
10	Georgia	3.6		10	California	3.6
44	Hawaii	1.9		10	Georgia	3.6
8	Idaho	3.7		10	Michigan	3.6
32	Illinois	2.6		10	Virginia	3.6
35	Indiana	2.5		14	Pennsylvania	3.5
44	Iowa	1.9		15	Utah	3.4
32	Kansas	2.6		16	Oklahoma	3.3
27	Kentucky	2.8		16	Wisconsin	3.3
18	Louisiana	3.2		18	Louisiana	3.2
48	Maine	1.7		18	New Jersey	3.2
8	Maryland	3.7		18	New York	3.2
38	Massachusetts	2.3		18	Ohio	3.2
10	Michigan	3.6		22	New Mexico	3.1
44	Minnesota	1.9		22	South Carolina	3.1
39	Mississippi	2.2		22	Washington	3.1
29	Missouri	2.7		25	North Carolina	3.0
27	Montana	2.8		25	Wyoming	3.0
39	Nebraska	2.2		27	Kentucky	2.8
2	Nevada	4.4		27	Montana	2.8
42	New Hampshire	2.0		29	Connecticut	2.7
18	New Jersey	3.2		29	Missouri	2.7
22	New Mexico	3.1		29	Rhode Island	2.7
18	New York	3.2		32	Arkansas	2.6
25	North Carolina	3.0		32	Illinois	2.6
49	North Dakota	1.4		32	Kansas	2.6
18	Ohio	3.2		35	Indiana	2.5
16	Oklahoma	3.3		36	South Dakota	2.4
7	Oregon	3.8		36	Tennessee	2.4
14	Pennsylvania	3.5		38	Massachusetts	2.3
29	Rhode Island	2.7		39	Alaska	2.2
22	South Carolina	3.1		39	Mississippi	2.2
36	South Dakota	2.4		39	Nebraska	2.2
36	Tennessee	2.4		42	Alabama	2.0
3	Texas	4.3		42	New Hampshire	2.0
15	Utah	3.4		44	Hawaii	1.9
50	Vermont	1.3		44	Iowa	1.9
10	Virginia	3.6		44	Minnesota	1.9
22	Washington	3.1		44	West Virginia	1.9
44	West Virginia	1.9		48	Maine	1.7
16	Wisconsin	3.3		49	North Dakota	1.4
25	Wyoming	3.0		50	Vermont	1.3

District of Columbia 6.3

Source: Morgan Quitno Press using data from Morgan Quitno Press using data from U.S. Bureau of the Census "Government Finances 1998-99" (http://www.census.gov/govs/estimate/99allpub.pdf, September 2001)

State Government Expenditures for Corrections in 1999

National Total = $30,769,786,000*

RANK	STATE	EXPENDITURES	% of USA
	ALPHA ORDER		
29	Alabama	$276,694,000	0.9%
39	Alaska	153,161,000	0.5%
14	Arizona	675,644,000	2.2%
31	Arkansas	221,310,000	0.7%
1	California	3,733,689,000	12.1%
18	Colorado	588,941,000	1.9%
19	Connecticut	523,219,000	1.7%
37	Delaware	201,753,000	0.7%
4	Florida	2,105,295,000	6.8%
11	Georgia	883,523,000	2.9%
41	Hawaii	134,302,000	0.4%
38	Idaho	167,170,000	0.5%
8	Illinois	1,110,434,000	3.6%
21	Indiana	472,702,000	1.5%
36	Iowa	206,126,000	0.7%
30	Kansas	232,093,000	0.8%
27	Kentucky	330,489,000	1.1%
25	Louisiana	381,011,000	1.2%
45	Maine	78,446,000	0.3%
13	Maryland	731,500,000	2.4%
17	Massachusetts	591,601,000	1.9%
5	Michigan	1,464,701,000	4.8%
28	Minnesota	276,783,000	0.9%
32	Mississippi	220,683,000	0.7%
20	Missouri	486,262,000	1.6%
44	Montana	94,084,000	0.3%
43	Nebraska	124,459,000	0.4%
34	Nevada	215,172,000	0.7%
46	New Hampshire	77,878,000	0.3%
9	New Jersey	999,688,000	3.2%
35	New Mexico	207,767,000	0.7%
3	New York	2,199,904,000	7.1%
10	North Carolina	895,951,000	2.9%
50	North Dakota	36,678,000	0.1%
7	Ohio	1,311,505,000	4.3%
24	Oklahoma	423,350,000	1.4%
22	Oregon	445,144,000	1.4%
6	Pennsylvania	1,359,417,000	4.4%
40	Rhode Island	140,655,000	0.5%
23	South Carolina	436,680,000	1.4%
48	South Dakota	58,292,000	0.2%
26	Tennessee	347,345,000	1.1%
2	Texas	2,577,114,000	8.4%
33	Utah	217,280,000	0.7%
49	Vermont	38,993,000	0.1%
12	Virginia	808,494,000	2.6%
15	Washington	662,984,000	2.2%
42	West Virginia	124,779,000	0.4%
16	Wisconsin	643,354,000	2.1%
47	Wyoming	75,287,000	0.2%

RANK	STATE	EXPENDITURES	% of USA
	RANK ORDER		
1	California	$3,733,689,000	12.1%
2	Texas	2,577,114,000	8.4%
3	New York	2,199,904,000	7.1%
4	Florida	2,105,295,000	6.8%
5	Michigan	1,464,701,000	4.8%
6	Pennsylvania	1,359,417,000	4.4%
7	Ohio	1,311,505,000	4.3%
8	Illinois	1,110,434,000	3.6%
9	New Jersey	999,688,000	3.2%
10	North Carolina	895,951,000	2.9%
11	Georgia	883,523,000	2.9%
12	Virginia	808,494,000	2.6%
13	Maryland	731,500,000	2.4%
14	Arizona	675,644,000	2.2%
15	Washington	662,984,000	2.2%
16	Wisconsin	643,354,000	2.1%
17	Massachusetts	591,601,000	1.9%
18	Colorado	588,941,000	1.9%
19	Connecticut	523,219,000	1.7%
20	Missouri	486,262,000	1.6%
21	Indiana	472,702,000	1.5%
22	Oregon	445,144,000	1.4%
23	South Carolina	436,680,000	1.4%
24	Oklahoma	423,350,000	1.4%
25	Louisiana	381,011,000	1.2%
26	Tennessee	347,345,000	1.1%
27	Kentucky	330,489,000	1.1%
28	Minnesota	276,783,000	0.9%
29	Alabama	276,694,000	0.9%
30	Kansas	232,093,000	0.8%
31	Arkansas	221,310,000	0.7%
32	Mississippi	220,683,000	0.7%
33	Utah	217,280,000	0.7%
34	Nevada	215,172,000	0.7%
35	New Mexico	207,767,000	0.7%
36	Iowa	206,126,000	0.7%
37	Delaware	201,753,000	0.7%
38	Idaho	167,170,000	0.5%
39	Alaska	153,161,000	0.5%
40	Rhode Island	140,655,000	0.5%
41	Hawaii	134,302,000	0.4%
42	West Virginia	124,779,000	0.4%
43	Nebraska	124,459,000	0.4%
44	Montana	94,084,000	0.3%
45	Maine	78,446,000	0.3%
46	New Hampshire	77,878,000	0.3%
47	Wyoming	75,287,000	0.2%
48	South Dakota	58,292,000	0.2%
49	Vermont	38,993,000	0.1%
50	North Dakota	36,678,000	0.1%
	District of Columbia**	NA	NA

Source: Morgan Quitno Press using data from Morgan Quitno Press using data from U.S. Bureau of the Census "Government Finances 1998-99" (http://www.census.gov/govs/estimate/99allpub.pdf, September 2001)
*Direct general expenditures.
**Not applicable.

Per Capita State Government Expenditures for Corrections in 1999

National Per Capita = $113*

ALPHA ORDER

RANK	STATE	PER CAPITA
46	Alabama	$63
2	Alaska	247
8	Arizona	141
34	Arkansas	87
24	California	113
6	Colorado	145
3	Connecticut	159
1	Delaware	268
10	Florida	139
24	Georgia	113
24	Hawaii	113
11	Idaho	134
32	Illinois	92
38	Indiana	80
42	Iowa	72
34	Kansas	87
37	Kentucky	83
34	Louisiana	87
46	Maine	63
8	Maryland	141
31	Massachusetts	96
5	Michigan	148
49	Minnesota	58
38	Mississippi	80
33	Missouri	89
29	Montana	107
41	Nebraska	75
18	Nevada	119
45	New Hampshire	65
15	New Jersey	123
18	New Mexico	119
17	New York	121
21	North Carolina	117
49	North Dakota	58
21	Ohio	117
14	Oklahoma	126
11	Oregon	134
24	Pennsylvania	113
7	Rhode Island	142
28	South Carolina	112
38	South Dakota	80
46	Tennessee	63
13	Texas	129
30	Utah	102
44	Vermont	66
20	Virginia	118
23	Washington	115
43	West Virginia	69
15	Wisconsin	123
4	Wyoming	157

RANK ORDER

RANK	STATE	PER CAPITA
1	Delaware	$268
2	Alaska	247
3	Connecticut	159
4	Wyoming	157
5	Michigan	148
6	Colorado	145
7	Rhode Island	142
8	Arizona	141
8	Maryland	141
10	Florida	139
11	Idaho	134
11	Oregon	134
13	Texas	129
14	Oklahoma	126
15	New Jersey	123
15	Wisconsin	123
17	New York	121
18	Nevada	119
18	New Mexico	119
20	Virginia	118
21	North Carolina	117
21	Ohio	117
23	Washington	115
24	California	113
24	Georgia	113
24	Hawaii	113
24	Pennsylvania	113
28	South Carolina	112
29	Montana	107
30	Utah	102
31	Massachusetts	96
32	Illinois	92
33	Missouri	89
34	Arkansas	87
34	Kansas	87
34	Louisiana	87
37	Kentucky	83
38	Indiana	80
38	Mississippi	80
38	South Dakota	80
41	Nebraska	75
42	Iowa	72
43	West Virginia	69
44	Vermont	66
45	New Hampshire	65
46	Alabama	63
46	Maine	63
46	Tennessee	63
49	Minnesota	58
49	North Dakota	58
	District of Columbia**	NA

Source: Morgan Quitno Press using data from Morgan Quitno Press using data from U.S. Bureau of the Census
"Government Finances 1998-99" (http://www.census.gov/govs/estimate/99allpub.pdf, September 2001)
*Direct general expenditures.
**Not applicable.

State Government Expenditures for Corrections
As a Percent of All Direct General Expenditures in 1999
National Percent = 5.3% of Direct General Expenditures

ALPHA ORDER

RANK	STATE	PERCENT
44	Alabama	2.9
38	Alaska	3.4
1	Arizona	9.4
32	Arkansas	3.9
13	California	6.0
5	Colorado	7.2
20	Connecticut	5.0
6	Delaware	6.8
2	Florida	8.0
14	Georgia	5.9
46	Hawaii	2.4
9	Idaho	6.5
23	Illinois	4.7
29	Indiana	4.2
41	Iowa	3.1
22	Kansas	4.8
39	Kentucky	3.3
34	Louisiana	3.7
48	Maine	2.2
10	Maryland	6.4
41	Massachusetts	3.1
3	Michigan	7.7
46	Minnesota	2.4
35	Mississippi	3.6
27	Missouri	4.5
32	Montana	3.9
35	Nebraska	3.6
8	Nevada	6.7
43	New Hampshire	3.0
18	New Jersey	5.5
30	New Mexico	4.1
25	New York	4.6
15	North Carolina	5.6
50	North Dakota	1.9
11	Ohio	6.2
6	Oklahoma	6.8
15	Oregon	5.6
21	Pennsylvania	4.9
27	Rhode Island	4.5
23	South Carolina	4.7
35	South Dakota	3.6
40	Tennessee	3.2
4	Texas	7.5
31	Utah	4.0
48	Vermont	2.2
18	Virginia	5.5
25	Washington	4.6
45	West Virginia	2.6
11	Wisconsin	6.2
15	Wyoming	5.6

RANK ORDER

RANK	STATE	PERCENT
1	Arizona	9.4
2	Florida	8.0
3	Michigan	7.7
4	Texas	7.5
5	Colorado	7.2
6	Delaware	6.8
6	Oklahoma	6.8
8	Nevada	6.7
9	Idaho	6.5
10	Maryland	6.4
11	Ohio	6.2
11	Wisconsin	6.2
13	California	6.0
14	Georgia	5.9
15	North Carolina	5.6
15	Oregon	5.6
15	Wyoming	5.6
18	New Jersey	5.5
18	Virginia	5.5
20	Connecticut	5.0
21	Pennsylvania	4.9
22	Kansas	4.8
23	Illinois	4.7
23	South Carolina	4.7
25	New York	4.6
25	Washington	4.6
27	Missouri	4.5
27	Rhode Island	4.5
29	Indiana	4.2
30	New Mexico	4.1
31	Utah	4.0
32	Arkansas	3.9
32	Montana	3.9
34	Louisiana	3.7
35	Mississippi	3.6
35	Nebraska	3.6
35	South Dakota	3.6
38	Alaska	3.4
39	Kentucky	3.3
40	Tennessee	3.2
41	Iowa	3.1
41	Massachusetts	3.1
43	New Hampshire	3.0
44	Alabama	2.9
45	West Virginia	2.6
46	Hawaii	2.4
46	Minnesota	2.4
48	Maine	2.2
48	Vermont	2.2
50	North Dakota	1.9

District of Columbia*   NA

Source: Morgan Quitno Press using data from Morgan Quitno Press using data from U.S. Bureau of the Census "Government Finances 1998-99" (http://www.census.gov/govs/estimate/99allpub.pdf, September 2001)
*Not applicable.

Expenditures for State Prisons in 1996

National Total = $22,033,214,000*

RANK	STATE	EXPENDITURES	% of USA
30	Alabama	$168,989,000	0.8%
36	Alaska	116,664,000	0.5%
15	Arizona	418,094,000	1.9%
33	Arkansas	133,729,000	0.6%
1	California	3,031,047,000	13.8%
25	Colorado	249,833,000	1.1%
13	Connecticut	497,838,000	2.3%
39	Delaware	87,961,000	0.4%
4	Florida	1,224,933,000	5.6%
11	Georgia	560,358,000	2.5%
40	Hawaii	87,417,000	0.4%
42	Idaho	56,957,000	0.3%
10	Illinois	740,423,000	3.4%
19	Indiana	338,195,000	1.5%
32	Iowa	146,069,000	0.7%
29	Kansas	170,848,000	0.8%
26	Kentucky	208,706,000	0.9%
20	Louisiana	316,245,000	1.4%
43	Maine	51,713,000	0.2%
12	Maryland	520,263,000	2.4%
22	Massachusetts	309,674,000	1.4%
5	Michigan	1,167,610,000	5.3%
28	Minnesota	185,983,000	0.8%
31	Mississippi	148,852,000	0.7%
23	Missouri	262,787,000	1.2%
46	Montana	42,448,000	0.2%
41	Nebraska	69,867,000	0.3%
35	Nevada	121,960,000	0.6%
45	New Hampshire	42,970,000	0.2%
8	New Jersey	839,308,000	3.8%
34	New Mexico	125,602,000	0.6%
2	New York	2,220,586,000	10.1%
9	North Carolina	756,829,000	3.4%
50	North Dakota	10,749,000	0.0%
6	Ohio	1,014,917,000	4.6%
27	Oklahoma	198,290,000	0.9%
24	Oregon	254,330,000	1.2%
7	Pennsylvania	978,769,000	4.4%
38	Rhode Island	109,596,000	0.5%
21	South Carolina	315,539,000	1.4%
47	South Dakota	34,152,000	0.2%
18	Tennessee	350,575,000	1.6%
3	Texas	1,713,935,000	7.8%
37	Utah	113,394,000	0.5%
48	Vermont	33,505,000	0.2%
14	Virginia	476,715,000	2.2%
17	Washington	357,862,000	1.6%
44	West Virginia	46,949,000	0.2%
16	Wisconsin	360,439,000	1.6%
49	Wyoming	29,025,000	0.1%

RANK	STATE	EXPENDITURES	% of USA
1	California	$3,031,047,000	13.8%
2	New York	2,220,586,000	10.1%
3	Texas	1,713,935,000	7.8%
4	Florida	1,224,933,000	5.6%
5	Michigan	1,167,610,000	5.3%
6	Ohio	1,014,917,000	4.6%
7	Pennsylvania	978,769,000	4.4%
8	New Jersey	839,308,000	3.8%
9	North Carolina	756,829,000	3.4%
10	Illinois	740,423,000	3.4%
11	Georgia	560,358,000	2.5%
12	Maryland	520,263,000	2.4%
13	Connecticut	497,838,000	2.3%
14	Virginia	476,715,000	2.2%
15	Arizona	418,094,000	1.9%
16	Wisconsin	360,439,000	1.6%
17	Washington	357,862,000	1.6%
18	Tennessee	350,575,000	1.6%
19	Indiana	338,195,000	1.5%
20	Louisiana	316,245,000	1.4%
21	South Carolina	315,539,000	1.4%
22	Massachusetts	309,674,000	1.4%
23	Missouri	262,787,000	1.2%
24	Oregon	254,330,000	1.2%
25	Colorado	249,833,000	1.1%
26	Kentucky	208,706,000	0.9%
27	Oklahoma	198,290,000	0.9%
28	Minnesota	185,983,000	0.8%
29	Kansas	170,848,000	0.8%
30	Alabama	168,989,000	0.8%
31	Mississippi	148,852,000	0.7%
32	Iowa	146,069,000	0.7%
33	Arkansas	133,729,000	0.6%
34	New Mexico	125,602,000	0.6%
35	Nevada	121,960,000	0.6%
36	Alaska	116,664,000	0.5%
37	Utah	113,394,000	0.5%
38	Rhode Island	109,596,000	0.5%
39	Delaware	87,961,000	0.4%
40	Hawaii	87,417,000	0.4%
41	Nebraska	69,867,000	0.3%
42	Idaho	56,957,000	0.3%
43	Maine	51,713,000	0.2%
44	West Virginia	46,949,000	0.2%
45	New Hampshire	42,970,000	0.2%
46	Montana	42,448,000	0.2%
47	South Dakota	34,152,000	0.2%
48	Vermont	33,505,000	0.2%
49	Wyoming	29,025,000	0.1%
50	North Dakota	10,749,000	0.0%
	District of Columbia	213,716,000	1.0%

Source: U.S. Department of Justice, Bureau of Justice Statistics
    "State Prison Expenditures, 1996" (August 1999, NCJ-172211)
*State government expenditures, including adult prison operations and capital outlays. They do not include state juvenile justice activities, probation and parole services or nonresidential community corrections. Expenditures are net amounts after deductions for revenue from prison farms, industries and services.

Operating Expenditures for State Prisons in 1996

National Total = $20,737,888,000*

Source: U.S. Department of Justice, Bureau of Justice Statistics
"State Prison Expenditures, 1996" (August 1999, NCJ-172211)
*State government expenditures, including adult prison operations but not capital outlays. They do not include
state juvenile justice activities, probation and parole services or nonresidential community corrections.
Expenditures are net amounts after deductions for revenue from prison farms, industries and services.

Annual Operating Expenditures per Inmate in 1996

National Annual Average = $20,142 per Inmate*

ALPHA ORDER				RANK ORDER		
RANK	STATE	PER INMATE		RANK	STATE	PER INMATE
50	Alabama	$7,987		1	Minnesota	$37,825
4	Alaska	32,415		2	Rhode Island	35,739
32	Arizona	19,091		3	Maine	33,711
44	Arkansas	13,341		4	Alaska	32,415
24	California	21,385		5	Utah	32,361
25	Colorado	21,020		6	Connecticut	31,912
6	Connecticut	31,912		7	Oregon	31,837
33	Delaware	17,987		8	Vermont	31,094
35	Florida	17,327		9	New Jersey	30,773
41	Georgia	15,933		10	New Mexico	29,491
19	Hawaii	23,318		11	New York	28,426
40	Idaho	16,277		12	Michigan	28,067
31	Illinois	19,351		13	Pennsylvania	28,063
28	Indiana	20,188		14	Wisconsin	27,771
18	Iowa	24,286		15	Washington	26,662
23	Kansas	22,242		16	Massachusetts	26,002
38	Kentucky	16,320		17	North Carolina	25,303
46	Louisiana	12,304		18	Iowa	24,286
3	Maine	33,711		19	Hawaii	23,318
22	Maryland	22,247		20	Tennessee	22,904
16	Massachusetts	26,002		21	Nebraska	22,271
12	Michigan	28,067		22	Maryland	22,247
1	Minnesota	37,825		23	Kansas	22,242
48	Mississippi	11,156		24	California	21,385
45	Missouri	12,832		25	Colorado	21,020
27	Montana	20,782		26	New Hampshire	20,839
21	Nebraska	22,271		27	Montana	20,782
42	Nevada	15,370		28	Indiana	20,188
26	New Hampshire	20,839		29	Ohio	19,613
9	New Jersey	30,773		30	Wyoming	19,456
10	New Mexico	29,491		31	Illinois	19,351
11	New York	28,426		32	Arizona	19,091
17	North Carolina	25,303		33	Delaware	17,987
37	North Dakota	17,154		34	South Dakota	17,787
29	Ohio	19,613		35	Florida	17,327
49	Oklahoma	10,601		36	West Virginia	17,245
7	Oregon	31,837		37	North Dakota	17,154
13	Pennsylvania	28,063		38	Kentucky	16,320
2	Rhode Island	35,739		39	Virginia	16,306
43	South Carolina	13,977		40	Idaho	16,277
34	South Dakota	17,787		41	Georgia	15,933
20	Tennessee	22,904		42	Nevada	15,370
47	Texas	12,215		43	South Carolina	13,977
5	Utah	32,361		44	Arkansas	13,341
8	Vermont	31,094		45	Missouri	12,832
39	Virginia	16,306		46	Louisiana	12,304
15	Washington	26,662		47	Texas	12,215
36	West Virginia	17,245		48	Mississippi	11,156
14	Wisconsin	27,771		49	Oklahoma	10,601
30	Wyoming	19,456		50	Alabama	7,987
					District of Columbia	21,296

Source: U.S. Department of Justice, Bureau of Justice Statistics
   "State Prison Expenditures, 1996" (August 1999, NCJ-172211)
*Based on estimated average daily number of inmates, June 1995 to June 1996. State government expenditures, including adult prison operations but not capital outlays. They do not include state juvenile justice activities, probation and parole services or nonresidential community corrections. Expenditures are net amounts after deductions for revenue from prison farms, industries and services.

Daily Operating Expenditures per Inmate in 1996

National Daily Average = $55.18 per Inmate*

ALPHA ORDER			RANK ORDER		
RANK	STATE	PER INMATE	RANK	STATE	PER INMATE
50	Alabama	$21.88	1	Minnesota	$103.63
4	Alaska	88.81	2	Rhode Island	97.92
32	Arizona	52.30	3	Maine	92.36
44	Arkansas	36.55	4	Alaska	88.81
24	California	58.59	5	Utah	88.66
25	Colorado	57.59	6	Connecticut	87.43
6	Connecticut	87.43	7	Oregon	87.22
33	Delaware	49.28	8	Vermont	85.19
35	Florida	47.47	9	New Jersey	84.31
41	Georgia	43.65	10	New Mexico	80.80
19	Hawaii	63.88	11	New York	77.88
40	Idaho	44.60	12	Michigan	76.89
31	Illinois	53.02	13	Pennsylvania	76.88
28	Indiana	55.31	14	Wisconsin	76.08
18	Iowa	66.54	15	Washington	73.05
23	Kansas	60.94	16	Massachusetts	71.24
38	Kentucky	44.71	17	North Carolina	69.32
46	Louisiana	33.71	18	Iowa	66.54
3	Maine	92.36	19	Hawaii	63.88
22	Maryland	60.95	20	Tennessee	62.75
16	Massachusetts	71.24	21	Nebraska	61.02
12	Michigan	76.89	22	Maryland	60.95
1	Minnesota	103.63	23	Kansas	60.94
48	Mississippi	30.56	24	California	58.59
45	Missouri	35.16	25	Colorado	57.59
27	Montana	56.94	26	New Hampshire	57.09
21	Nebraska	61.02	27	Montana	56.94
42	Nevada	42.11	28	Indiana	55.31
26	New Hampshire	57.09	29	Ohio	53.74
9	New Jersey	84.31	30	Wyoming	53.30
10	New Mexico	80.80	31	Illinois	53.02
11	New York	77.88	32	Arizona	52.30
17	North Carolina	69.32	33	Delaware	49.28
37	North Dakota	47.00	34	South Dakota	48.73
29	Ohio	53.74	35	Florida	47.47
49	Oklahoma	29.04	36	West Virginia	47.25
7	Oregon	87.22	37	North Dakota	47.00
13	Pennsylvania	76.88	38	Kentucky	44.71
2	Rhode Island	97.92	39	Virginia	44.67
43	South Carolina	38.29	40	Idaho	44.60
34	South Dakota	48.73	41	Georgia	43.65
20	Tennessee	62.75	42	Nevada	42.11
47	Texas	33.47	43	South Carolina	38.29
5	Utah	88.66	44	Arkansas	36.55
8	Vermont	85.19	45	Missouri	35.16
39	Virginia	44.67	46	Louisiana	33.71
15	Washington	73.05	47	Texas	33.47
36	West Virginia	47.25	48	Mississippi	30.56
14	Wisconsin	76.08	49	Oklahoma	29.04
30	Wyoming	53.30	50	Alabama	21.88
				District of Columbia	58.34

Source: U.S. Department of Justice, Bureau of Justice Statistics
"State Prison Expenditures, 1996" (August 1999, NCJ-172211)
*Based on estimated average daily number of inmates, June 1995 to June 1996. State government expenditures, including adult prison operations but not capital outlays. They do not include state juvenile justice activities, probation and parole services or nonresidential community corrections. Expenditures are net amounts after deductions for revenue from prison farms, industries and services.

Local Government Expenditures for Corrections in 1999

National Total = $14,828,279,000*

ALPHA ORDER

ALPHA ORDER

RANK	STATE	EXPENDITURES	% of USA
28	Alabama	$131,279,000	0.9%
45	Alaska	1,353,000	0.0%
24	Arizona	174,191,000	1.2%
34	Arkansas	59,593,000	0.4%
1	California	2,796,891,000	18.9%
20	Colorado	198,645,000	1.3%
47	Connecticut	0	0.0%
47	Delaware	0	0.0%
4	Florida	1,010,271,000	6.8%
8	Georgia	402,930,000	2.7%
47	Hawaii	0	0.0%
36	Idaho	39,013,000	0.3%
6	Illinois	420,594,000	2.8%
22	Indiana	188,242,000	1.3%
32	Iowa	75,417,000	0.5%
31	Kansas	82,497,000	0.6%
25	Kentucky	170,741,000	1.2%
13	Louisiana	294,500,000	2.0%
39	Maine	28,610,000	0.2%
23	Maryland	179,685,000	1.2%
18	Massachusetts	216,345,000	1.5%
10	Michigan	360,972,000	2.4%
15	Minnesota	272,082,000	1.8%
33	Mississippi	63,861,000	0.4%
26	Missouri	154,026,000	1.0%
40	Montana	26,772,000	0.2%
35	Nebraska	48,167,000	0.3%
21	Nevada	190,821,000	1.3%
37	New Hampshire	30,173,000	0.2%
7	New Jersey	413,383,000	2.8%
30	New Mexico	85,681,000	0.6%
2	New York	2,054,271,000	13.9%
19	North Carolina	210,390,000	1.4%
44	North Dakota	10,994,000	0.1%
9	Ohio	383,048,000	2.6%
41	Oklahoma	22,076,000	0.1%
16	Oregon	254,949,000	1.7%
5	Pennsylvania	773,209,000	5.2%
47	Rhode Island	0	0.0%
29	South Carolina	124,943,000	0.8%
42	South Dakota	19,845,000	0.1%
17	Tennessee	233,583,000	1.6%
3	Texas	1,158,608,000	7.8%
27	Utah	136,466,000	0.9%
46	Vermont	261,000	0.0%
12	Virginia	350,709,000	2.4%
11	Washington	353,503,000	2.4%
38	West Virginia	28,814,000	0.2%
14	Wisconsin	283,367,000	1.9%
43	Wyoming	19,784,000	0.1%

RANK ORDER

RANK	STATE	EXPENDITURES	% of USA
1	California	$2,796,891,000	18.9%
2	New York	2,054,271,000	13.9%
3	Texas	1,158,608,000	7.8%
4	Florida	1,010,271,000	6.8%
5	Pennsylvania	773,209,000	5.2%
6	Illinois	420,594,000	2.8%
7	New Jersey	413,383,000	2.8%
8	Georgia	402,930,000	2.7%
9	Ohio	383,048,000	2.6%
10	Michigan	360,972,000	2.4%
11	Washington	353,503,000	2.4%
12	Virginia	350,709,000	2.4%
13	Louisiana	294,500,000	2.0%
14	Wisconsin	283,367,000	1.9%
15	Minnesota	272,082,000	1.8%
16	Oregon	254,949,000	1.7%
17	Tennessee	233,583,000	1.6%
18	Massachusetts	216,345,000	1.5%
19	North Carolina	210,390,000	1.4%
20	Colorado	198,645,000	1.3%
21	Nevada	190,821,000	1.3%
22	Indiana	188,242,000	1.3%
23	Maryland	179,685,000	1.2%
24	Arizona	174,191,000	1.2%
25	Kentucky	170,741,000	1.2%
26	Missouri	154,026,000	1.0%
27	Utah	136,466,000	0.9%
28	Alabama	131,279,000	0.9%
29	South Carolina	124,943,000	0.8%
30	New Mexico	85,681,000	0.6%
31	Kansas	82,497,000	0.6%
32	Iowa	75,417,000	0.5%
33	Mississippi	63,861,000	0.4%
34	Arkansas	59,593,000	0.4%
35	Nebraska	48,167,000	0.3%
36	Idaho	39,013,000	0.3%
37	New Hampshire	30,173,000	0.2%
38	West Virginia	28,814,000	0.2%
39	Maine	28,610,000	0.2%
40	Montana	26,772,000	0.2%
41	Oklahoma	22,076,000	0.1%
42	South Dakota	19,845,000	0.1%
43	Wyoming	19,784,000	0.1%
44	North Dakota	10,994,000	0.1%
45	Alaska	1,353,000	0.0%
46	Vermont	261,000	0.0%
47	Connecticut	0	0.0%
47	Delaware	0	0.0%
47	Hawaii	0	0.0%
47	Rhode Island	0	0.0%
	District of Columbia	292,724,000	2.0%

Source: Morgan Quitno Press using data from Morgan Quitno Press using data from U.S. Bureau of the Census "Government Finances 1998-99" (http://www.census.gov/govs/estimate/99allpub.pdf, September 2001)
*Direct general expenditures.

Per Capita Local Government Expenditures for Corrections in 1999

National Per Capita = $54.38*

ALPHA ORDER

RANK	STATE	PER CAPITA
32	Alabama	$30.04
45	Alaska	2.18
22	Arizona	36.45
39	Arkansas	23.36
3	California	84.38
17	Colorado	48.97
47	Connecticut	0.00
47	Delaware	0.00
6	Florida	66.86
13	Georgia	51.74
47	Hawaii	0.00
29	Idaho	31.17
25	Illinois	34.68
28	Indiana	31.68
37	Iowa	26.28
30	Kansas	31.08
18	Kentucky	43.11
5	Louisiana	67.36
41	Maine	22.83
24	Maryland	34.74
23	Massachusetts	35.03
21	Michigan	36.60
11	Minnesota	56.97
40	Mississippi	23.07
34	Missouri	28.17
31	Montana	30.33
33	Nebraska	28.91
2	Nevada	105.47
38	New Hampshire	25.12
15	New Jersey	50.76
16	New Mexico	49.25
1	New York	112.89
35	North Carolina	27.50
42	North Dakota	17.35
26	Ohio	34.03
44	Oklahoma	6.57
4	Oregon	76.88
7	Pennsylvania	64.47
47	Rhode Island	0.00
27	South Carolina	32.15
36	South Dakota	27.07
19	Tennessee	42.60
10	Texas	57.80
8	Utah	64.07
46	Vermont	0.44
14	Virginia	51.03
9	Washington	61.41
43	West Virginia	15.95
12	Wisconsin	53.97
20	Wyoming	41.25

RANK ORDER

RANK	STATE	PER CAPITA
1	New York	$112.89
2	Nevada	105.47
3	California	84.38
4	Oregon	76.88
5	Louisiana	67.36
6	Florida	66.86
7	Pennsylvania	64.47
8	Utah	64.07
9	Washington	61.41
10	Texas	57.80
11	Minnesota	56.97
12	Wisconsin	53.97
13	Georgia	51.74
14	Virginia	51.03
15	New Jersey	50.76
16	New Mexico	49.25
17	Colorado	48.97
18	Kentucky	43.11
19	Tennessee	42.60
20	Wyoming	41.25
21	Michigan	36.60
22	Arizona	36.45
23	Massachusetts	35.03
24	Maryland	34.74
25	Illinois	34.68
26	Ohio	34.03
27	South Carolina	32.15
28	Indiana	31.68
29	Idaho	31.17
30	Kansas	31.08
31	Montana	30.33
32	Alabama	30.04
33	Nebraska	28.91
34	Missouri	28.17
35	North Carolina	27.50
36	South Dakota	27.07
37	Iowa	26.28
38	New Hampshire	25.12
39	Arkansas	23.36
40	Mississippi	23.07
41	Maine	22.83
42	North Dakota	17.35
43	West Virginia	15.95
44	Oklahoma	6.57
45	Alaska	2.18
46	Vermont	0.44
47	Connecticut	0.00
47	Delaware	0.00
47	Hawaii	0.00
47	Rhode Island	0.00

District of Columbia   564.02

Source: Morgan Quitno Press using data from Morgan Quitno Press using data from U.S. Bureau of the Census "Government Finances 1998-99" (http://www.census.gov/govs/estimate/99allpub.pdf, September 2001)
*Direct general expenditures.

Local Government Expenditures for Corrections
As a Percent of All Direct General Expenditures in 1999
National Percent = 1.8% of Direct General Expenditures

ALPHA ORDER

RANK	STATE	PERCENT
23	Alabama	1.3
45	Alaska	0.1
23	Arizona	1.3
27	Arkansas	1.2
6	California	2.3
15	Colorado	1.7
46	Connecticut	0.0
46	Delaware	0.0
8	Florida	2.2
13	Georgia	1.9
46	Hawaii	0.0
23	Idaho	1.3
27	Illinois	1.2
27	Indiana	1.2
40	Iowa	0.9
33	Kansas	1.1
10	Kentucky	2.1
2	Louisiana	2.7
38	Maine	1.0
23	Maryland	1.3
20	Massachusetts	1.4
33	Michigan	1.1
17	Minnesota	1.6
40	Mississippi	0.9
27	Missouri	1.2
20	Montana	1.4
33	Nebraska	1.1
1	Nevada	3.1
33	New Hampshire	1.1
17	New Jersey	1.6
13	New Mexico	1.9
5	New York	2.4
38	North Carolina	1.0
43	North Dakota	0.7
27	Ohio	1.2
44	Oklahoma	0.3
4	Oregon	2.5
6	Pennsylvania	2.3
46	Rhode Island	0.0
20	South Carolina	1.4
27	South Dakota	1.2
15	Tennessee	1.7
8	Texas	2.2
2	Utah	2.7
46	Vermont	0.0
11	Virginia	2.0
11	Washington	2.0
42	West Virginia	0.8
17	Wisconsin	1.6
33	Wyoming	1.1

RANK ORDER

RANK	STATE	PERCENT
1	Nevada	3.1
2	Louisiana	2.7
2	Utah	2.7
4	Oregon	2.5
5	New York	2.4
6	California	2.3
6	Pennsylvania	2.3
8	Florida	2.2
8	Texas	2.2
10	Kentucky	2.1
11	Virginia	2.0
11	Washington	2.0
13	Georgia	1.9
13	New Mexico	1.9
15	Colorado	1.7
15	Tennessee	1.7
17	Minnesota	1.6
17	New Jersey	1.6
17	Wisconsin	1.6
20	Massachusetts	1.4
20	Montana	1.4
20	South Carolina	1.4
23	Alabama	1.3
23	Arizona	1.3
23	Idaho	1.3
23	Maryland	1.3
27	Arkansas	1.2
27	Illinois	1.2
27	Indiana	1.2
27	Missouri	1.2
27	Ohio	1.2
27	South Dakota	1.2
33	Kansas	1.1
33	Michigan	1.1
33	Nebraska	1.1
33	New Hampshire	1.1
33	Wyoming	1.1
38	Maine	1.0
38	North Carolina	1.0
40	Iowa	0.9
40	Mississippi	0.9
42	West Virginia	0.8
43	North Dakota	0.7
44	Oklahoma	0.3
45	Alaska	0.1
46	Connecticut	0.0
46	Delaware	0.0
46	Hawaii	0.0
46	Rhode Island	0.0
46	Vermont	0.0

District of Columbia	6.3

Source: Morgan Quitno Press using data from Morgan Quitno Press using data from U.S. Bureau of the Census
"Government Finances 1998-99" (http://www.census.gov/govs/estimate/99allpub.pdf, September 2001)

State and Local Government Expenditures for Judicial and Legal Services: 1999

National Total = $25,316,294,000*

ALPHA ORDER				RANK ORDER			
RANK	STATE	EXPENDITURES	% of USA	RANK	STATE	EXPENDITURES	% of USA
26	Alabama	$257,608,000	1.0%	1	California	$5,730,684,000	22.6%
38	Alaska	122,304,000	0.5%	2	New York	2,152,667,000	8.5%
11	Arizona	538,987,000	2.1%	3	Florida	1,342,402,000	5.3%
37	Arkansas	129,253,000	0.5%	4	Texas	1,250,135,000	4.9%
1	California	5,730,684,000	22.6%	5	Ohio	1,085,461,000	4.3%
22	Colorado	319,703,000	1.3%	6	Pennsylvania	977,083,000	3.9%
20	Connecticut	386,674,000	1.5%	7	New Jersey	959,221,000	3.8%
44	Delaware	86,067,000	0.3%	8	Illinois	876,487,000	3.5%
3	Florida	1,342,402,000	5.3%	9	Michigan	827,134,000	3.3%
12	Georgia	516,332,000	2.0%	10	Massachusetts	633,592,000	2.5%
34	Hawaii	165,314,000	0.7%	11	Arizona	538,987,000	2.1%
41	Idaho	97,981,000	0.4%	12	Georgia	516,332,000	2.0%
8	Illinois	876,487,000	3.5%	13	Washington	494,115,000	2.0%
24	Indiana	303,924,000	1.2%	14	Virginia	480,663,000	1.9%
28	Iowa	241,840,000	1.0%	15	North Carolina	467,394,000	1.8%
30	Kansas	195,676,000	0.8%	16	Maryland	465,223,000	1.8%
25	Kentucky	279,684,000	1.1%	17	Wisconsin	425,256,000	1.7%
21	Louisiana	340,803,000	1.3%	18	Minnesota	419,052,000	1.7%
45	Maine	64,873,000	0.3%	19	Tennessee	399,651,000	1.6%
16	Maryland	465,223,000	1.8%	20	Connecticut	386,674,000	1.5%
10	Massachusetts	633,592,000	2.5%	21	Louisiana	340,803,000	1.3%
9	Michigan	827,134,000	3.3%	22	Colorado	319,703,000	1.3%
18	Minnesota	419,052,000	1.7%	23	Missouri	314,412,000	1.2%
36	Mississippi	153,403,000	0.6%	24	Indiana	303,924,000	1.2%
23	Missouri	314,412,000	1.2%	25	Kentucky	279,684,000	1.1%
46	Montana	64,027,000	0.3%	26	Alabama	257,608,000	1.0%
42	Nebraska	92,949,000	0.4%	27	Oregon	255,088,000	1.0%
29	Nevada	215,429,000	0.9%	28	Iowa	241,840,000	1.0%
43	New Hampshire	86,187,000	0.3%	29	Nevada	215,429,000	0.9%
7	New Jersey	959,221,000	3.8%	30	Kansas	195,676,000	0.8%
35	New Mexico	154,988,000	0.6%	31	Utah	180,127,000	0.7%
2	New York	2,152,667,000	8.5%	32	Oklahoma	176,280,000	0.7%
15	North Carolina	467,394,000	1.8%	33	South Carolina	176,045,000	0.7%
49	North Dakota	42,482,000	0.2%	34	Hawaii	165,314,000	0.7%
5	Ohio	1,085,461,000	4.3%	35	New Mexico	154,988,000	0.6%
32	Oklahoma	176,280,000	0.7%	36	Mississippi	153,403,000	0.6%
27	Oregon	255,088,000	1.0%	37	Arkansas	129,253,000	0.5%
6	Pennsylvania	977,083,000	3.9%	38	Alaska	122,304,000	0.5%
40	Rhode Island	99,227,000	0.4%	39	West Virginia	100,627,000	0.4%
33	South Carolina	176,045,000	0.7%	40	Rhode Island	99,227,000	0.4%
50	South Dakota	37,164,000	0.1%	41	Idaho	97,981,000	0.4%
19	Tennessee	399,651,000	1.6%	42	Nebraska	92,949,000	0.4%
4	Texas	1,250,135,000	4.9%	43	New Hampshire	86,187,000	0.3%
31	Utah	180,127,000	0.7%	44	Delaware	86,067,000	0.3%
48	Vermont	49,422,000	0.2%	45	Maine	64,873,000	0.3%
14	Virginia	480,663,000	1.9%	46	Montana	64,027,000	0.3%
13	Washington	494,115,000	2.0%	47	Wyoming	49,851,000	0.2%
39	West Virginia	100,627,000	0.4%	48	Vermont	49,422,000	0.2%
17	Wisconsin	425,256,000	1.7%	49	North Dakota	42,482,000	0.2%
47	Wyoming	49,851,000	0.2%	50	South Dakota	37,164,000	0.1%
					District of Columbia	35,343,000	0.1%

Source: Morgan Quitno Press using data from Morgan Quitno Press using data from U.S. Bureau of the Census
"Government Finances 1998-99" (http://www.census.gov/govs/estimate/99allpub.pdf, September 2001)
*Direct general expenditures. Includes Courts, Prosecution and Legal Services and Public Defense.

Per Capita State and Local Government Expenditures
for Judicial and Legal Services in 1999
National Per Capita = $92.84*

ALPHA ORDER

RANK	STATE	PER CAPITA
40	Alabama	$58.95
1	Alaska	197.42
9	Arizona	112.80
49	Arkansas	50.66
2	California	172.90
25	Colorado	78.82
6	Connecticut	117.82
8	Delaware	114.22
16	Florida	88.83
37	Georgia	66.30
3	Hawaii	139.45
26	Idaho	78.28
32	Illinois	72.27
47	Indiana	51.14
20	Iowa	84.28
29	Kansas	73.73
34	Kentucky	70.61
27	Louisiana	77.95
46	Maine	51.77
14	Maryland	89.96
11	Massachusetts	102.60
21	Michigan	83.86
17	Minnesota	87.75
44	Mississippi	55.41
41	Missouri	57.50
31	Montana	72.53
42	Nebraska	55.79
4	Nevada	119.07
33	New Hampshire	71.75
7	New Jersey	117.79
15	New Mexico	89.08
5	New York	118.30
39	North Carolina	61.09
36	North Dakota	67.04
13	Ohio	96.43
45	Oklahoma	52.49
28	Oregon	76.92
23	Pennsylvania	81.46
12	Rhode Island	100.15
50	South Carolina	45.31
48	South Dakota	50.69
30	Tennessee	72.88
38	Texas	62.37
19	Utah	84.57
22	Vermont	83.24
35	Virginia	69.94
18	Washington	85.84
43	West Virginia	55.69
24	Wisconsin	80.99
10	Wyoming	103.94

RANK ORDER

RANK	STATE	PER CAPITA
1	Alaska	$197.42
2	California	172.90
3	Hawaii	139.45
4	Nevada	119.07
5	New York	118.30
6	Connecticut	117.82
7	New Jersey	117.79
8	Delaware	114.22
9	Arizona	112.80
10	Wyoming	103.94
11	Massachusetts	102.60
12	Rhode Island	100.15
13	Ohio	96.43
14	Maryland	89.96
15	New Mexico	89.08
16	Florida	88.83
17	Minnesota	87.75
18	Washington	85.84
19	Utah	84.57
20	Iowa	84.28
21	Michigan	83.86
22	Vermont	83.24
23	Pennsylvania	81.46
24	Wisconsin	80.99
25	Colorado	78.82
26	Idaho	78.28
27	Louisiana	77.95
28	Oregon	76.92
29	Kansas	73.73
30	Tennessee	72.88
31	Montana	72.53
32	Illinois	72.27
33	New Hampshire	71.75
34	Kentucky	70.61
35	Virginia	69.94
36	North Dakota	67.04
37	Georgia	66.30
38	Texas	62.37
39	North Carolina	61.09
40	Alabama	58.95
41	Missouri	57.50
42	Nebraska	55.79
43	West Virginia	55.69
44	Mississippi	55.41
45	Oklahoma	52.49
46	Maine	51.77
47	Indiana	51.14
48	South Dakota	50.69
49	Arkansas	50.66
50	South Carolina	45.31
	District of Columbia	68.10

Source: Morgan Quitno Press using data from Morgan Quitno Press using data from U.S. Bureau of the Census "Government Finances 1998-99" (http://www.census.gov/govs/estimate/99allpub.pdf, September 2001)
*Direct general expenditures. Includes Courts, Prosecution and Legal Services and Public Defense.

State and Local Government Expenditures for Judicial and Legal Services As a Percent of All Direct General Expenditures in 1999
National Percent = 1.8% of Direct General Expenditures*

ALPHA ORDER

RANK	STATE	PERCENT
38	Alabama	1.3
13	Alaska	1.7
2	Arizona	2.7
42	Arkansas	1.2
1	California	3.2
17	Colorado	1.6
6	Connecticut	2.0
8	Delaware	1.9
8	Florida	1.9
35	Georgia	1.4
3	Hawaii	2.4
13	Idaho	1.7
28	Illinois	1.5
47	Indiana	1.1
17	Iowa	1.6
17	Kansas	1.6
28	Kentucky	1.5
17	Louisiana	1.6
49	Maine	1.0
8	Maryland	1.9
12	Massachusetts	1.8
17	Michigan	1.6
28	Minnesota	1.5
42	Mississippi	1.2
38	Missouri	1.3
28	Montana	1.5
42	Nebraska	1.2
4	Nevada	2.3
17	New Hampshire	1.6
5	New Jersey	2.2
17	New Mexico	1.6
17	New York	1.6
38	North Carolina	1.3
42	North Dakota	1.2
6	Ohio	2.0
38	Oklahoma	1.3
35	Oregon	1.4
17	Pennsylvania	1.6
8	Rhode Island	1.9
49	South Carolina	1.0
47	South Dakota	1.1
13	Tennessee	1.7
35	Texas	1.4
13	Utah	1.7
17	Vermont	1.6
28	Virginia	1.5
28	Washington	1.5
42	West Virginia	1.2
28	Wisconsin	1.5
17	Wyoming	1.6

RANK ORDER

RANK	STATE	PERCENT
1	California	3.2
2	Arizona	2.7
3	Hawaii	2.4
4	Nevada	2.3
5	New Jersey	2.2
6	Connecticut	2.0
6	Ohio	2.0
8	Delaware	1.9
8	Florida	1.9
8	Maryland	1.9
8	Rhode Island	1.9
12	Massachusetts	1.8
13	Alaska	1.7
13	Idaho	1.7
13	Tennessee	1.7
13	Utah	1.7
17	Colorado	1.6
17	Iowa	1.6
17	Kansas	1.6
17	Louisiana	1.6
17	Michigan	1.6
17	New Hampshire	1.6
17	New Mexico	1.6
17	New York	1.6
17	Pennsylvania	1.6
17	Vermont	1.6
17	Wyoming	1.6
28	Illinois	1.5
28	Kentucky	1.5
28	Minnesota	1.5
28	Montana	1.5
28	Virginia	1.5
28	Washington	1.5
28	Wisconsin	1.5
35	Georgia	1.4
35	Oregon	1.4
35	Texas	1.4
38	Alabama	1.3
38	Missouri	1.3
38	North Carolina	1.3
38	Oklahoma	1.3
42	Arkansas	1.2
42	Mississippi	1.2
42	Nebraska	1.2
42	North Dakota	1.2
42	West Virginia	1.2
47	Indiana	1.1
47	South Dakota	1.1
49	Maine	1.0
49	South Carolina	1.0

District of Columbia 0.8

Source: Morgan Quitno Press using data from Morgan Quitno Press using data from U.S. Bureau of the Census "Government Finances 1998-99" (http://www.census.gov/govs/estimate/99allpub.pdf, September 2001)
*Includes Courts, Prosecution and Legal Services and Public Defense.

State Government Expenditures for Judicial and Legal Services in 1999

National Total = $11,385,299,000*

ALPHA ORDER

RANK	STATE	EXPENDITURES	% of USA
19	Alabama	$168,675,000	1.5%
32	Alaska	111,132,000	1.0%
28	Arizona	126,664,000	1.1%
39	Arkansas	68,394,000	0.6%
1	California	2,161,236,000	19.0%
20	Colorado	168,372,000	1.5%
8	Connecticut	338,538,000	3.0%
35	Delaware	78,486,000	0.7%
3	Florida	617,021,000	5.4%
27	Georgia	127,107,000	1.1%
24	Hawaii	134,830,000	1.2%
43	Idaho	50,065,000	0.4%
11	Illinois	250,529,000	2.2%
33	Indiana	90,886,000	0.8%
15	Iowa	187,175,000	1.6%
29	Kansas	120,422,000	1.1%
12	Kentucky	228,578,000	2.0%
30	Louisiana	117,620,000	1.0%
41	Maine	55,376,000	0.5%
9	Maryland	290,026,000	2.5%
4	Massachusetts	581,387,000	5.1%
26	Michigan	127,541,000	1.1%
18	Minnesota	175,569,000	1.5%
40	Mississippi	67,808,000	0.6%
21	Missouri	157,541,000	1.4%
49	Montana	23,353,000	0.2%
44	Nebraska	38,533,000	0.3%
45	Nevada	35,136,000	0.3%
37	New Hampshire	70,266,000	0.6%
5	New Jersey	494,618,000	4.3%
23	New Mexico	134,985,000	1.2%
2	New York	1,335,271,000	11.7%
6	North Carolina	391,390,000	3.4%
48	North Dakota	28,168,000	0.2%
16	Ohio	181,224,000	1.6%
25	Oklahoma	132,135,000	1.2%
22	Oregon	155,582,000	1.4%
10	Pennsylvania	289,938,000	2.5%
34	Rhode Island	90,332,000	0.8%
42	South Carolina	55,229,000	0.5%
50	South Dakota	20,969,000	0.2%
17	Tennessee	179,080,000	1.6%
7	Texas	390,676,000	3.4%
31	Utah	116,197,000	1.0%
46	Vermont	31,893,000	0.3%
13	Virginia	219,112,000	1.9%
36	Washington	72,554,000	0.6%
38	West Virginia	68,882,000	0.6%
14	Wisconsin	197,841,000	1.7%
47	Wyoming	30,957,000	0.3%

RANK ORDER

RANK	STATE	EXPENDITURES	% of USA
1	California	$2,161,236,000	19.0%
2	New York	1,335,271,000	11.7%
3	Florida	617,021,000	5.4%
4	Massachusetts	581,387,000	5.1%
5	New Jersey	494,618,000	4.3%
6	North Carolina	391,390,000	3.4%
7	Texas	390,676,000	3.4%
8	Connecticut	338,538,000	3.0%
9	Maryland	290,026,000	2.5%
10	Pennsylvania	289,938,000	2.5%
11	Illinois	250,529,000	2.2%
12	Kentucky	228,578,000	2.0%
13	Virginia	219,112,000	1.9%
14	Wisconsin	197,841,000	1.7%
15	Iowa	187,175,000	1.6%
16	Ohio	181,224,000	1.6%
17	Tennessee	179,080,000	1.6%
18	Minnesota	175,569,000	1.5%
19	Alabama	168,675,000	1.5%
20	Colorado	168,372,000	1.5%
21	Missouri	157,541,000	1.4%
22	Oregon	155,582,000	1.4%
23	New Mexico	134,985,000	1.2%
24	Hawaii	134,830,000	1.2%
25	Oklahoma	132,135,000	1.2%
26	Michigan	127,541,000	1.1%
27	Georgia	127,107,000	1.1%
28	Arizona	126,664,000	1.1%
29	Kansas	120,422,000	1.1%
30	Louisiana	117,620,000	1.0%
31	Utah	116,197,000	1.0%
32	Alaska	111,132,000	1.0%
33	Indiana	90,886,000	0.8%
34	Rhode Island	90,332,000	0.8%
35	Delaware	78,486,000	0.7%
36	Washington	72,554,000	0.6%
37	New Hampshire	70,266,000	0.6%
38	West Virginia	68,882,000	0.6%
39	Arkansas	68,394,000	0.6%
40	Mississippi	67,808,000	0.6%
41	Maine	55,376,000	0.5%
42	South Carolina	55,229,000	0.5%
43	Idaho	50,065,000	0.4%
44	Nebraska	38,533,000	0.3%
45	Nevada	35,136,000	0.3%
46	Vermont	31,893,000	0.3%
47	Wyoming	30,957,000	0.3%
48	North Dakota	28,168,000	0.2%
49	Montana	23,353,000	0.2%
50	South Dakota	20,969,000	0.2%

District of Columbia**   NA   NA

Source: Morgan Quitno Press using data from Morgan Quitno Press using data from U.S. Bureau of the Census "Government Finances 1998-99" (http://www.census.gov/govs/estimate/99allpub.pdf, September 2001)
*Direct general expenditures. Includes Courts, Prosecution and Legal Services and Public Defense.
**Not applicable.

Per Capita State Government Expenditures for Judicial and Legal Services: 1999

National Per Capita = $41.75*

ALPHA ORDER				RANK ORDER		
RANK	STATE	PER CAPITA		RANK	STATE	PER CAPITA
27	Alabama	$38.60		1	Alaska	$179.39
1	Alaska	179.39		2	Hawaii	113.73
37	Arizona	26.51		3	Delaware	104.16
36	Arkansas	26.81		4	Connecticut	103.15
10	California	65.21		5	Massachusetts	94.15
23	Colorado	41.51		6	Rhode Island	91.17
4	Connecticut	103.15		7	New Mexico	77.58
3	Delaware	104.16		8	New York	73.38
24	Florida	40.83		9	Iowa	65.23
45	Georgia	16.32		10	California	65.21
2	Hawaii	113.73		11	Wyoming	64.55
25	Idaho	40.00		12	New Jersey	60.74
42	Illinois	20.66		13	New Hampshire	58.50
47	Indiana	15.29		14	Kentucky	57.71
9	Iowa	65.23		15	Maryland	56.08
20	Kansas	45.37		16	Utah	54.56
14	Kentucky	57.71		17	Vermont	53.72
35	Louisiana	26.90		18	North Carolina	51.16
22	Maine	44.19		19	Oregon	46.92
15	Maryland	56.08		20	Kansas	45.37
5	Massachusetts	94.15		21	North Dakota	44.45
49	Michigan	12.93		22	Maine	44.19
30	Minnesota	36.76		23	Colorado	41.51
39	Mississippi	24.49		24	Florida	40.83
33	Missouri	28.81		25	Idaho	40.00
38	Montana	26.45		26	Oklahoma	39.35
41	Nebraska	23.13		27	Alabama	38.60
44	Nevada	19.42		28	West Virginia	38.12
13	New Hampshire	58.50		29	Wisconsin	37.68
12	New Jersey	60.74		30	Minnesota	36.76
7	New Mexico	77.58		31	Tennessee	32.66
8	New York	73.38		32	Virginia	31.88
18	North Carolina	51.16		33	Missouri	28.81
21	North Dakota	44.45		34	South Dakota	28.60
46	Ohio	16.10		35	Louisiana	26.90
26	Oklahoma	39.35		36	Arkansas	26.81
19	Oregon	46.92		37	Arizona	26.51
40	Pennsylvania	24.17		38	Montana	26.45
6	Rhode Island	91.17		39	Mississippi	24.49
48	South Carolina	14.21		40	Pennsylvania	24.17
34	South Dakota	28.60		41	Nebraska	23.13
31	Tennessee	32.66		42	Illinois	20.66
43	Texas	19.49		43	Texas	19.49
16	Utah	54.56		44	Nevada	19.42
17	Vermont	53.72		45	Georgia	16.32
32	Virginia	31.88		46	Ohio	16.10
50	Washington	12.60		47	Indiana	15.29
28	West Virginia	38.12		48	South Carolina	14.21
29	Wisconsin	37.68		49	Michigan	12.93
11	Wyoming	64.55		50	Washington	12.60
					District of Columbia**	NA

Source: Morgan Quitno Press using data from Morgan Quitno Press using data from U.S. Bureau of the Census
"Government Finances 1998-99" (http://www.census.gov/govs/estimate/99allpub.pdf, September 2001)
*Direct general expenditures. Includes Courts, Prosecution and Legal Services and Public Defense.
**Not applicable.

State Government Expenditures for Judicial and Legal Services
As a Percent of All Direct General Expenditures in 1999
National Percent = 1.9% of Direct General Expenditures*

ALPHA ORDER

RANK	STATE	PERCENT
27	Alabama	1.7
14	Alaska	2.4
25	Arizona	1.8
36	Arkansas	1.2
1	California	3.5
20	Colorado	2.1
2	Connecticut	3.2
7	Delaware	2.7
16	Florida	2.3
45	Georgia	0.9
11	Hawaii	2.5
22	Idaho	2.0
37	Illinois	1.1
47	Indiana	0.8
5	Iowa	2.8
11	Kansas	2.5
16	Kentucky	2.3
37	Louisiana	1.1
29	Maine	1.6
11	Maryland	2.5
3	Massachusetts	3.0
48	Michigan	0.7
30	Minnesota	1.5
37	Mississippi	1.1
33	Missouri	1.4
44	Montana	1.0
37	Nebraska	1.1
37	Nevada	1.1
7	New Hampshire	2.7
7	New Jersey	2.7
7	New Mexico	2.7
5	New York	2.8
14	North Carolina	2.4
30	North Dakota	1.5
45	Ohio	0.9
20	Oklahoma	2.1
22	Oregon	2.0
37	Pennsylvania	1.1
4	Rhode Island	2.9
49	South Carolina	0.6
35	South Dakota	1.3
27	Tennessee	1.7
37	Texas	1.1
19	Utah	2.2
25	Vermont	1.8
30	Virginia	1.5
50	Washington	0.5
33	West Virginia	1.4
24	Wisconsin	1.9
16	Wyoming	2.3

RANK ORDER

RANK	STATE	PERCENT
1	California	3.5
2	Connecticut	3.2
3	Massachusetts	3.0
4	Rhode Island	2.9
5	Iowa	2.8
5	New York	2.8
7	Delaware	2.7
7	New Hampshire	2.7
7	New Jersey	2.7
7	New Mexico	2.7
11	Hawaii	2.5
11	Kansas	2.5
11	Maryland	2.5
14	Alaska	2.4
14	North Carolina	2.4
16	Florida	2.3
16	Kentucky	2.3
16	Wyoming	2.3
19	Utah	2.2
20	Colorado	2.1
20	Oklahoma	2.1
22	Idaho	2.0
22	Oregon	2.0
24	Wisconsin	1.9
25	Arizona	1.8
25	Vermont	1.8
27	Alabama	1.7
27	Tennessee	1.7
29	Maine	1.6
30	Minnesota	1.5
30	North Dakota	1.5
30	Virginia	1.5
33	Missouri	1.4
33	West Virginia	1.4
35	South Dakota	1.3
36	Arkansas	1.2
37	Illinois	1.1
37	Louisiana	1.1
37	Mississippi	1.1
37	Nebraska	1.1
37	Nevada	1.1
37	Pennsylvania	1.1
37	Texas	1.1
44	Montana	1.0
45	Georgia	0.9
45	Ohio	0.9
47	Indiana	0.8
48	Michigan	0.7
49	South Carolina	0.6
50	Washington	0.5

District of Columbia**   NA

Source: Morgan Quitno Press using data from Morgan Quitno Press using data from U.S. Bureau of the Census
"Government Finances 1998-99" (http://www.census.gov/govs/estimate/99allpub.pdf, September 2001)
*Includes Courts, Prosecution and Legal Services and Public Defense.
**Not applicable.

Local Government Expenditures for Judicial and Legal Services in 1999

National Total = 13,930,995,000*

ALPHA ORDER

RANK	STATE	EXPENDITURES	% of USA
25	Alabama	$88,933,000	0.6%
47	Alaska	11,172,000	0.1%
11	Arizona	412,323,000	3.0%
30	Arkansas	60,859,000	0.4%
1	California	3,569,448,000	25.6%
22	Colorado	151,331,000	1.1%
35	Connecticut	48,136,000	0.3%
50	Delaware	7,581,000	0.1%
5	Florida	725,381,000	5.2%
12	Georgia	389,225,000	2.8%
40	Hawaii	30,484,000	0.2%
36	Idaho	47,916,000	0.3%
8	Illinois	625,958,000	4.5%
18	Indiana	213,038,000	1.5%
31	Iowa	54,665,000	0.4%
28	Kansas	75,254,000	0.5%
34	Kentucky	51,106,000	0.4%
16	Louisiana	223,183,000	1.6%
48	Maine	9,497,000	0.1%
20	Maryland	175,197,000	1.3%
33	Massachusetts	52,205,000	0.4%
6	Michigan	699,593,000	5.0%
14	Minnesota	243,483,000	1.7%
26	Mississippi	85,595,000	0.6%
21	Missouri	156,871,000	1.1%
38	Montana	40,674,000	0.3%
32	Nebraska	54,416,000	0.4%
19	Nevada	180,293,000	1.3%
45	New Hampshire	15,921,000	0.1%
9	New Jersey	464,603,000	3.3%
41	New Mexico	20,003,000	0.1%
4	New York	817,396,000	5.9%
27	North Carolina	76,004,000	0.5%
46	North Dakota	14,314,000	0.1%
2	Ohio	904,237,000	6.5%
37	Oklahoma	44,145,000	0.3%
24	Oregon	99,506,000	0.7%
7	Pennsylvania	687,145,000	4.9%
49	Rhode Island	8,895,000	0.1%
23	South Carolina	120,816,000	0.9%
44	South Dakota	16,195,000	0.1%
17	Tennessee	220,571,000	1.6%
3	Texas	859,459,000	6.2%
29	Utah	63,930,000	0.5%
43	Vermont	17,529,000	0.1%
13	Virginia	261,551,000	1.9%
10	Washington	421,561,000	3.0%
39	West Virginia	31,745,000	0.2%
15	Wisconsin	227,415,000	1.6%
42	Wyoming	18,894,000	0.1%

RANK ORDER

RANK	STATE	EXPENDITURES	% of USA
1	California	$3,569,448,000	25.6%
2	Ohio	904,237,000	6.5%
3	Texas	859,459,000	6.2%
4	New York	817,396,000	5.9%
5	Florida	725,381,000	5.2%
6	Michigan	699,593,000	5.0%
7	Pennsylvania	687,145,000	4.9%
8	Illinois	625,958,000	4.5%
9	New Jersey	464,603,000	3.3%
10	Washington	421,561,000	3.0%
11	Arizona	412,323,000	3.0%
12	Georgia	389,225,000	2.8%
13	Virginia	261,551,000	1.9%
14	Minnesota	243,483,000	1.7%
15	Wisconsin	227,415,000	1.6%
16	Louisiana	223,183,000	1.6%
17	Tennessee	220,571,000	1.6%
18	Indiana	213,038,000	1.5%
19	Nevada	180,293,000	1.3%
20	Maryland	175,197,000	1.3%
21	Missouri	156,871,000	1.1%
22	Colorado	151,331,000	1.1%
23	South Carolina	120,816,000	0.9%
24	Oregon	99,506,000	0.7%
25	Alabama	88,933,000	0.6%
26	Mississippi	85,595,000	0.6%
27	North Carolina	76,004,000	0.5%
28	Kansas	75,254,000	0.5%
29	Utah	63,930,000	0.5%
30	Arkansas	60,859,000	0.4%
31	Iowa	54,665,000	0.4%
32	Nebraska	54,416,000	0.4%
33	Massachusetts	52,205,000	0.4%
34	Kentucky	51,106,000	0.4%
35	Connecticut	48,136,000	0.3%
36	Idaho	47,916,000	0.3%
37	Oklahoma	44,145,000	0.3%
38	Montana	40,674,000	0.3%
39	West Virginia	31,745,000	0.2%
40	Hawaii	30,484,000	0.2%
41	New Mexico	20,003,000	0.1%
42	Wyoming	18,894,000	0.1%
43	Vermont	17,529,000	0.1%
44	South Dakota	16,195,000	0.1%
45	New Hampshire	15,921,000	0.1%
46	North Dakota	14,314,000	0.1%
47	Alaska	11,172,000	0.1%
48	Maine	9,497,000	0.1%
49	Rhode Island	8,895,000	0.1%
50	Delaware	7,581,000	0.1%
	District of Columbia	35,343,000	0.3%

Source: Morgan Quitno Press using data from Morgan Quitno Press using data from U.S. Bureau of the Census
"Government Finances 1998-99" (http://www.census.gov/govs/estimate/99allpub.pdf, September 2001)
*Direct general expenditures. Includes Courts, Prosecution and Legal Services and Public Defense.

Per Capita Local Government Expenditures for Judicial & Legal Services: 1999

National Per Capita = $51.09*

ALPHA ORDER

RANK	STATE	PER CAPITA
37	Alabama	$20.35
39	Alaska	18.03
3	Arizona	86.29
34	Arkansas	23.85
1	California	107.69
22	Colorado	37.31
41	Connecticut	14.67
46	Delaware	10.06
13	Florida	48.00
12	Georgia	49.98
33	Hawaii	25.71
20	Idaho	38.28
9	Illinois	51.61
23	Indiana	35.85
38	Iowa	19.05
32	Kansas	28.35
44	Kentucky	12.90
10	Louisiana	51.05
50	Maine	7.58
24	Maryland	33.88
49	Massachusetts	8.45
6	Michigan	70.93
11	Minnesota	50.99
27	Mississippi	30.92
31	Missouri	28.69
14	Montana	46.07
25	Nebraska	32.66
2	Nevada	99.65
42	New Hampshire	13.25
8	New Jersey	57.05
45	New Mexico	11.50
15	New York	44.92
47	North Carolina	9.93
35	North Dakota	22.59
4	Ohio	80.33
43	Oklahoma	13.15
29	Oregon	30.01
7	Pennsylvania	57.29
48	Rhode Island	8.98
26	South Carolina	31.09
36	South Dakota	22.09
18	Tennessee	40.22
17	Texas	42.88
28	Utah	30.02
30	Vermont	29.52
21	Virginia	38.06
5	Washington	73.23
40	West Virginia	17.57
16	Wisconsin	43.31
19	Wyoming	39.40

RANK ORDER

RANK	STATE	PER CAPITA
1	California	$107.69
2	Nevada	99.65
3	Arizona	86.29
4	Ohio	80.33
5	Washington	73.23
6	Michigan	70.93
7	Pennsylvania	57.29
8	New Jersey	57.05
9	Illinois	51.61
10	Louisiana	51.05
11	Minnesota	50.99
12	Georgia	49.98
13	Florida	48.00
14	Montana	46.07
15	New York	44.92
16	Wisconsin	43.31
17	Texas	42.88
18	Tennessee	40.22
19	Wyoming	39.40
20	Idaho	38.28
21	Virginia	38.06
22	Colorado	37.31
23	Indiana	35.85
24	Maryland	33.88
25	Nebraska	32.66
26	South Carolina	31.09
27	Mississippi	30.92
28	Utah	30.02
29	Oregon	30.01
30	Vermont	29.52
31	Missouri	28.69
32	Kansas	28.35
33	Hawaii	25.71
34	Arkansas	23.85
35	North Dakota	22.59
36	South Dakota	22.09
37	Alabama	20.35
38	Iowa	19.05
39	Alaska	18.03
40	West Virginia	17.57
41	Connecticut	14.67
42	New Hampshire	13.25
43	Oklahoma	13.15
44	Kentucky	12.90
45	New Mexico	11.50
46	Delaware	10.06
47	North Carolina	9.93
48	Rhode Island	8.98
49	Massachusetts	8.45
50	Maine	7.58

District of Columbia 68.10

Source: Morgan Quitno Press using data from Morgan Quitno Press using data from U.S. Bureau of the Census "Government Finances 1998-99" (http://www.census.gov/govs/estimate/99allpub.pdf, September 2001)
*Direct general expenditures. Includes Courts, Prosecution and Legal Services and Public Defense.

Local Government Expenditures for Judicial and Legal Services
As a Percent of All Direct General Expenditures in 1999
National Percent = 1.7% of Direct General Expenditures*

ALPHA ORDER

RANK	STATE	PERCENT
36	Alabama	0.9
46	Alaska	0.4
1	Arizona	3.1
28	Arkansas	1.2
2	California	3.0
23	Colorado	1.3
43	Connecticut	0.5
43	Delaware	0.5
14	Florida	1.6
11	Georgia	1.9
6	Hawaii	2.2
14	Idaho	1.6
13	Illinois	1.7
20	Indiana	1.4
39	Iowa	0.7
31	Kansas	1.0
40	Kentucky	0.6
9	Louisiana	2.1
49	Maine	0.3
23	Maryland	1.3
49	Massachusetts	0.3
6	Michigan	2.2
18	Minnesota	1.5
28	Mississippi	1.2
28	Missouri	1.2
6	Montana	2.2
23	Nebraska	1.3
2	Nevada	3.0
40	New Hampshire	0.6
12	New Jersey	1.8
43	New Mexico	0.5
31	New York	1.0
46	North Carolina	0.4
36	North Dakota	0.9
4	Ohio	2.8
40	Oklahoma	0.6
31	Oregon	1.0
10	Pennsylvania	2.0
46	Rhode Island	0.4
20	South Carolina	1.4
31	South Dakota	1.0
14	Tennessee	1.6
14	Texas	1.6
23	Utah	1.3
20	Vermont	1.4
18	Virginia	1.5
5	Washington	2.4
36	West Virginia	0.9
23	Wisconsin	1.3
31	Wyoming	1.0

RANK ORDER

RANK	STATE	PERCENT
1	Arizona	3.1
2	California	3.0
2	Nevada	3.0
4	Ohio	2.8
5	Washington	2.4
6	Hawaii	2.2
6	Michigan	2.2
6	Montana	2.2
9	Louisiana	2.1
10	Pennsylvania	2.0
11	Georgia	1.9
12	New Jersey	1.8
13	Illinois	1.7
14	Florida	1.6
14	Idaho	1.6
14	Tennessee	1.6
14	Texas	1.6
18	Minnesota	1.5
18	Virginia	1.5
20	Indiana	1.4
20	South Carolina	1.4
20	Vermont	1.4
23	Colorado	1.3
23	Maryland	1.3
23	Nebraska	1.3
23	Utah	1.3
23	Wisconsin	1.3
28	Arkansas	1.2
28	Mississippi	1.2
28	Missouri	1.2
31	Kansas	1.0
31	New York	1.0
31	Oregon	1.0
31	South Dakota	1.0
31	Wyoming	1.0
36	Alabama	0.9
36	North Dakota	0.9
36	West Virginia	0.9
39	Iowa	0.7
40	Kentucky	0.6
40	New Hampshire	0.6
40	Oklahoma	0.6
43	Connecticut	0.5
43	Delaware	0.5
43	New Mexico	0.5
46	Alaska	0.4
46	North Carolina	0.4
46	Rhode Island	0.4
49	Maine	0.3
49	Massachusetts	0.3
	District of Columbia	0.8

Source: Morgan Quitno Press using data from Morgan Quitno Press using data from U.S. Bureau of the Census
"Government Finances 1998-99" (http://www.census.gov/govs/estimate/99allpub.pdf, September 2001)
*Includes Courts, Prosecution and Legal Services and Public Defense.

State and Local Government Judicial and Legal Payroll in 2000

National Total = $16,398,254,352*

ALPHA ORDER

RANK	STATE	PAYROLL	% of USA
27	Alabama	$178,713,480	1.1%
38	Alaska	65,542,296	0.4%
12	Arizona	373,681,740	2.3%
40	Arkansas	59,418,840	0.4%
1	California	2,796,643,980	17.1%
19	Colorado	246,621,780	1.5%
24	Connecticut	196,467,996	1.2%
41	Delaware	57,644,568	0.4%
3	Florida	1,111,069,980	6.8%
13	Georgia	362,060,208	2.2%
34	Hawaii	109,236,696	0.7%
43	Idaho	53,658,456	0.3%
6	Illinois	731,673,420	4.5%
23	Indiana	205,999,020	1.3%
30	Iowa	137,357,616	0.8%
31	Kansas	126,726,876	0.8%
25	Kentucky	194,389,944	1.2%
21	Louisiana	218,494,932	1.3%
46	Maine	30,537,684	0.2%
15	Maryland	279,570,828	1.7%
10	Massachusetts	454,676,928	2.8%
9	Michigan	501,595,836	3.1%
16	Minnesota	271,413,624	1.7%
36	Mississippi	91,139,280	0.6%
18	Missouri	257,424,360	1.6%
45	Montana	34,118,460	0.2%
39	Nebraska	64,532,052	0.4%
28	Nevada	168,072,192	1.0%
44	New Hampshire	45,702,576	0.3%
4	New Jersey	943,864,608	5.8%
32	New Mexico	114,319,740	0.7%
2	New York	1,567,700,592	9.6%
17	North Carolina	261,722,664	1.6%
48	North Dakota	27,090,024	0.2%
7	Ohio	691,479,756	4.2%
29	Oklahoma	145,186,884	0.9%
26	Oregon	186,567,300	1.1%
8	Pennsylvania	608,276,244	3.7%
42	Rhode Island	56,498,592	0.3%
33	South Carolina	111,429,108	0.7%
47	South Dakota	27,167,016	0.2%
22	Tennessee	207,803,868	1.3%
5	Texas	854,477,244	5.2%
35	Utah	102,095,916	0.6%
49	Vermont	26,207,424	0.2%
14	Virginia	310,374,168	1.9%
11	Washington	374,760,588	2.3%
37	West Virginia	66,448,212	0.4%
20	Wisconsin	245,519,832	1.5%
50	Wyoming	22,854,924	0.1%

RANK ORDER

RANK	STATE	PAYROLL	% of USA
1	California	$2,796,643,980	17.1%
2	New York	1,567,700,592	9.6%
3	Florida	1,111,069,980	6.8%
4	New Jersey	943,864,608	5.8%
5	Texas	854,477,244	5.2%
6	Illinois	731,673,420	4.5%
7	Ohio	691,479,756	4.2%
8	Pennsylvania	608,276,244	3.7%
9	Michigan	501,595,836	3.1%
10	Massachusetts	454,676,928	2.8%
11	Washington	374,760,588	2.3%
12	Arizona	373,681,740	2.3%
13	Georgia	362,060,208	2.2%
14	Virginia	310,374,168	1.9%
15	Maryland	279,570,828	1.7%
16	Minnesota	271,413,624	1.7%
17	North Carolina	261,722,664	1.6%
18	Missouri	257,424,360	1.6%
19	Colorado	246,621,780	1.5%
20	Wisconsin	245,519,832	1.5%
21	Louisiana	218,494,932	1.3%
22	Tennessee	207,803,868	1.3%
23	Indiana	205,999,020	1.3%
24	Connecticut	196,467,996	1.2%
25	Kentucky	194,389,944	1.2%
26	Oregon	186,567,300	1.1%
27	Alabama	178,713,480	1.1%
28	Nevada	168,072,192	1.0%
29	Oklahoma	145,186,884	0.9%
30	Iowa	137,357,616	0.8%
31	Kansas	126,726,876	0.8%
32	New Mexico	114,319,740	0.7%
33	South Carolina	111,429,108	0.7%
34	Hawaii	109,236,696	0.7%
35	Utah	102,095,916	0.6%
36	Mississippi	91,139,280	0.6%
37	West Virginia	66,448,212	0.4%
38	Alaska	65,542,296	0.4%
39	Nebraska	64,532,052	0.4%
40	Arkansas	59,418,840	0.4%
41	Delaware	57,644,568	0.4%
42	Rhode Island	56,498,592	0.3%
43	Idaho	53,658,456	0.3%
44	New Hampshire	45,702,576	0.3%
45	Montana	34,118,460	0.2%
46	Maine	30,537,684	0.2%
47	South Dakota	27,167,016	0.2%
48	North Dakota	27,090,024	0.2%
49	Vermont	26,207,424	0.2%
50	Wyoming	22,854,924	0.1%
	District of Columbia	22,224,000	0.1%

Source: U.S. Bureau of the Census, Governments Division
    "State and Local Employment and Payroll - March 2000" (http://www.census.gov/govs/www/apesstl00.html)
*Twelve times the March 2000 full-time equivalent payroll. Includes court and court related activities (except
probation and parole which are part of corrections), court activities of sheriffs' offices, prosecuting attorneys' and
public defenders' offices, legal departments and attorneys providing government-wide legal service.*

State and Local Government Police Protection Payroll in 2000

National Total = $38,695,562,724*

ALPHA ORDER

RANK ORDER

RANK	STATE	PAYROLL	% of USA		RANK	STATE	PAYROLL	% of USA
26	Alabama	$408,539,052	1.1%		1	California	$5,728,756,176	14.8%
45	Alaska	90,310,956	0.2%		2	New York	5,214,751,344	13.5%
16	Arizona	708,311,820	1.8%		3	Florida	2,272,088,124	5.9%
34	Arkansas	217,854,972	0.6%		4	Texas	2,194,062,684	5.7%
1	California	5,728,756,176	14.8%		5	Illinois	2,047,864,740	5.3%
19	Colorado	590,772,180	1.5%		6	New Jersey	1,844,826,072	4.8%
22	Connecticut	539,109,528	1.4%		7	Pennsylvania	1,409,981,604	3.6%
44	Delaware	103,713,444	0.3%		8	Ohio	1,359,908,268	3.5%
3	Florida	2,272,088,124	5.9%		9	Massachusetts	1,140,158,928	2.9%
13	Georgia	779,836,296	2.0%		10	Michigan	1,121,799,768	2.9%
38	Hawaii	163,602,552	0.4%		11	North Carolina	786,311,196	2.0%
41	Idaho	116,027,184	0.3%		12	Maryland	785,296,044	2.0%
5	Illinois	2,047,864,740	5.3%		13	Georgia	779,836,296	2.0%
21	Indiana	553,566,744	1.4%		14	Virginia	745,797,264	1.9%
32	Iowa	266,209,440	0.7%		15	Washington	736,425,636	1.9%
31	Kansas	321,776,100	0.8%		16	Arizona	708,311,820	1.8%
29	Kentucky	331,439,988	0.9%		17	Wisconsin	643,588,380	1.7%
24	Louisiana	467,242,428	1.2%		18	Missouri	596,405,748	1.5%
42	Maine	108,088,464	0.3%		19	Colorado	590,772,180	1.5%
12	Maryland	785,296,044	2.0%		20	Tennessee	579,735,336	1.5%
9	Massachusetts	1,140,158,928	2.9%		21	Indiana	553,566,744	1.4%
10	Michigan	1,121,799,768	2.9%		22	Connecticut	539,109,528	1.4%
23	Minnesota	509,875,656	1.3%		23	Minnesota	509,875,656	1.3%
33	Mississippi	236,867,940	0.6%		24	Louisiana	467,242,428	1.2%
18	Missouri	596,405,748	1.5%		25	South Carolina	418,145,880	1.1%
46	Montana	72,080,028	0.2%		26	Alabama	408,539,052	1.1%
37	Nebraska	165,385,056	0.4%		27	Oregon	393,578,820	1.0%
30	Nevada	328,967,844	0.9%		28	Oklahoma	347,967,924	0.9%
40	New Hampshire	150,447,084	0.4%		29	Kentucky	331,439,988	0.9%
6	New Jersey	1,844,826,072	4.8%		30	Nevada	328,967,844	0.9%
36	New Mexico	185,336,880	0.5%		31	Kansas	321,776,100	0.8%
2	New York	5,214,751,344	13.5%		32	Iowa	266,209,440	0.7%
11	North Carolina	786,311,196	2.0%		33	Mississippi	236,867,940	0.6%
50	North Dakota	46,118,112	0.1%		34	Arkansas	217,854,972	0.6%
8	Ohio	1,359,908,268	3.5%		35	Utah	201,512,604	0.5%
28	Oklahoma	347,967,924	0.9%		36	New Mexico	185,336,880	0.5%
27	Oregon	393,578,820	1.0%		37	Nebraska	165,385,056	0.4%
7	Pennsylvania	1,409,981,604	3.6%		38	Hawaii	163,602,552	0.4%
39	Rhode Island	152,876,592	0.4%		39	Rhode Island	152,876,592	0.4%
25	South Carolina	418,145,880	1.1%		40	New Hampshire	150,447,084	0.4%
48	South Dakota	54,473,784	0.1%		41	Idaho	116,027,184	0.3%
20	Tennessee	579,735,336	1.5%		42	Maine	108,088,464	0.3%
4	Texas	2,194,062,684	5.7%		43	West Virginia	106,425,588	0.3%
35	Utah	201,512,604	0.5%		44	Delaware	103,713,444	0.3%
49	Vermont	52,233,024	0.1%		45	Alaska	90,310,956	0.2%
14	Virginia	745,797,264	1.9%		46	Montana	72,080,028	0.2%
15	Washington	736,425,636	1.9%		47	Wyoming	58,487,544	0.2%
43	West Virginia	106,425,588	0.3%		48	South Dakota	54,473,784	0.1%
17	Wisconsin	643,588,380	1.7%		49	Vermont	52,233,024	0.1%
47	Wyoming	58,487,544	0.2%		50	North Dakota	46,118,112	0.1%
						District of Columbia	240,623,904	0.6%

Source: U.S. Bureau of the Census, Governments Division
   "State and Local Employment and Payroll - March 2000" (http://www.census.gov/govs/www/apesstl00.html)
*Twelve times the March 2000 full-time equivalent payroll. Includes all activities concerned with the enforcement of
law and order, including coroners' offices, police training academies, investigation bureaus and local jails.

State and Local Government Corrections Payroll in 2000

National Total = $25,098,243,792*

ALPHA ORDER

RANK	STATE	PAYROLL	% of USA
27	Alabama	$211,442,436	0.8%
40	Alaska	80,285,760	0.3%
17	Arizona	435,807,228	1.7%
36	Arkansas	128,403,900	0.5%
1	California	3,869,825,736	15.4%
20	Colorado	373,697,808	1.5%
18	Connecticut	386,011,392	1.5%
39	Delaware	86,322,912	0.3%
4	Florida	1,657,797,756	6.6%
9	Georgia	764,395,176	3.0%
42	Hawaii	77,528,400	0.3%
41	Idaho	78,324,060	0.3%
6	Illinois	977,221,308	3.9%
24	Indiana	313,424,076	1.2%
33	Iowa	155,367,624	0.6%
30	Kansas	181,511,652	0.7%
31	Kentucky	174,904,116	0.7%
19	Louisiana	381,317,844	1.5%
44	Maine	49,122,864	0.2%
13	Maryland	546,228,012	2.2%
15	Massachusetts	472,600,692	1.9%
5	Michigan	1,005,234,072	4.0%
22	Minnesota	326,919,660	1.3%
35	Mississippi	135,278,304	0.5%
21	Missouri	351,400,332	1.4%
45	Montana	45,447,156	0.2%
38	Nebraska	86,820,732	0.3%
28	Nevada	202,426,572	0.8%
43	New Hampshire	58,749,504	0.2%
10	New Jersey	731,967,780	2.9%
32	New Mexico	164,436,096	0.7%
2	New York	2,830,973,436	11.3%
11	North Carolina	718,065,204	2.9%
50	North Dakota	21,213,840	0.1%
8	Ohio	948,759,768	3.8%
29	Oklahoma	194,615,892	0.8%
23	Oregon	319,566,792	1.3%
7	Pennsylvania	951,241,248	3.8%
37	Rhode Island	89,970,972	0.4%
25	South Carolina	311,925,636	1.2%
47	South Dakota	35,463,372	0.1%
26	Tennessee	287,923,164	1.1%
3	Texas	1,913,757,984	7.6%
34	Utah	144,008,268	0.6%
48	Vermont	34,366,236	0.1%
12	Virginia	659,178,816	2.6%
14	Washington	497,686,704	2.0%
46	West Virginia	36,649,596	0.1%
16	Wisconsin	455,339,784	1.8%
49	Wyoming	28,289,184	0.1%

RANK ORDER

RANK	STATE	PAYROLL	% of USA
1	California	$3,869,825,736	15.4%
2	New York	2,830,973,436	11.3%
3	Texas	1,913,757,984	7.6%
4	Florida	1,657,797,756	6.6%
5	Michigan	1,005,234,072	4.0%
6	Illinois	977,221,308	3.9%
7	Pennsylvania	951,241,248	3.8%
8	Ohio	948,759,768	3.8%
9	Georgia	764,395,176	3.0%
10	New Jersey	731,967,780	2.9%
11	North Carolina	718,065,204	2.9%
12	Virginia	659,178,816	2.6%
13	Maryland	546,228,012	2.2%
14	Washington	497,686,704	2.0%
15	Massachusetts	472,600,692	1.9%
16	Wisconsin	455,339,784	1.8%
17	Arizona	435,807,228	1.7%
18	Connecticut	386,011,392	1.5%
19	Louisiana	381,317,844	1.5%
20	Colorado	373,697,808	1.5%
21	Missouri	351,400,332	1.4%
22	Minnesota	326,919,660	1.3%
23	Oregon	319,566,792	1.3%
24	Indiana	313,424,076	1.2%
25	South Carolina	311,925,636	1.2%
26	Tennessee	287,923,164	1.1%
27	Alabama	211,442,436	0.8%
28	Nevada	202,426,572	0.8%
29	Oklahoma	194,615,892	0.8%
30	Kansas	181,511,652	0.7%
31	Kentucky	174,904,116	0.7%
32	New Mexico	164,436,096	0.7%
33	Iowa	155,367,624	0.6%
34	Utah	144,008,268	0.6%
35	Mississippi	135,278,304	0.5%
36	Arkansas	128,403,900	0.5%
37	Rhode Island	89,970,972	0.4%
38	Nebraska	86,820,732	0.3%
39	Delaware	86,322,912	0.3%
40	Alaska	80,285,760	0.3%
41	Idaho	78,324,060	0.3%
42	Hawaii	77,528,400	0.3%
43	New Hampshire	58,749,504	0.2%
44	Maine	49,122,864	0.2%
45	Montana	45,447,156	0.2%
46	West Virginia	36,649,596	0.1%
47	South Dakota	35,463,372	0.1%
48	Vermont	34,366,236	0.1%
49	Wyoming	28,289,184	0.1%
50	North Dakota	21,213,840	0.1%
	District of Columbia	109,026,936	0.4%

Source: U.S. Bureau of the Census, Governments Division
"State and Local Employment and Payroll - March 2000" (http://www.census.gov/govs/www/apesstl00.html)
*Twelve times the March 2000 full-time equivalent payroll. Includes all activities pertaining to the confinement and correction of adults and minors accused or convicted of criminal offenses. Includes any pardon, probation or parole activity.

Base Salary for Justices of States' Highest Courts in 2001

National Average = $119,343

ALPHA ORDER				RANK ORDER		
RANK	STATE	SALARY		RANK	STATE	SALARY
9	Alabama	$140,580		1	California	$162,409
32	Alaska	112,224		2	Michigan	159,960
16	Arizona	126,525		3	Illinois	153,052
21	Arkansas	120,346		4	New Jersey	152,191
1	California	162,409		5	New York	151,200
36	Colorado	107,808		6	Florida	150,000
12	Connecticut	129,404		7	Georgia	147,909
8	Delaware	141,300		8	Delaware	141,300
6	Florida	150,000		9	Alabama	140,580
7	Georgia	147,909		10	Pennsylvania	133,643
26	Hawaii	115,547		11	Virginia	132,523
44	Idaho	97,727		12	Connecticut	129,404
3	Illinois	153,052		13	Nevada	128,044
28	Indiana	115,000		14	Rhode Island	127,098
30	Iowa	113,200		15	Massachusetts	126,943
33	Kansas	111,402		16	Arizona	126,525
22	Kentucky	120,092		17	Maryland	126,500
40	Louisiana	103,336		18	Washington	123,600
39	Maine	103,584		19	Missouri	123,000
17	Maryland	126,500		20	Ohio	120,750
15	Massachusetts	126,943		21	Arkansas	120,346
2	Michigan	159,960		22	Kentucky	120,092
35	Minnesota	110,998		23	Wisconsin	118,824
41	Mississippi	102,300		24	Tennessee	118,428
19	Missouri	123,000		25	South Carolina	117,167
50	Montana	89,381		26	Hawaii	115,547
34	Nebraska	111,003		27	North Carolina	115,336
13	Nevada	128,044		28	Indiana	115,000
38	New Hampshire	106,518		29	Utah	114,036
4	New Jersey	152,191		30	Iowa	113,200
49	New Mexico	90,407		31	Texas	113,000
5	New York	151,200		32	Alaska	112,224
27	North Carolina	115,336		33	Kansas	111,402
48	North Dakota	92,289		34	Nebraska	111,003
20	Ohio	120,750		35	Minnesota	110,998
37	Oklahoma	106,706		36	Colorado	107,808
46	Oregon	93,600		37	Oklahoma	106,706
10	Pennsylvania	133,643		38	New Hampshire	106,518
14	Rhode Island	127,098		39	Maine	103,584
25	South Carolina	117,167		40	Louisiana	103,336
43	South Dakota	97,735		41	Mississippi	102,300
24	Tennessee	118,428		42	Vermont	99,489
31	Texas	113,000		43	South Dakota	97,735
29	Utah	114,036		44	Idaho	97,727
42	Vermont	99,489		45	West Virginia	95,000
11	Virginia	132,523		46	Oregon	93,600
18	Washington	123,600		47	Wyoming	93,000
45	West Virginia	95,000		48	North Dakota	92,289
23	Wisconsin	118,824		49	New Mexico	90,407
47	Wyoming	93,000		50	Montana	89,381
					District of Columbia	153,900

Source: National Center for State Courts
"Survey of Judicial Salaries-Summer 2001" (Volume 26, Number 2)

Base Salary for Judges of Intermediate Appellate Courts in 2001

National Average = $117,130

ALPHA ORDER

RANK	STATE	SALARY
7	Alabama	$139,580
30	Alaska	106,020
11	Arizona	123,900
16	Arkansas	116,539
1	California	152,260
33	Colorado	103,308
12	Connecticut	120,988
NA	Delaware**	NA
8	Florida	138,500
3	Georgia	146,994
23	Hawaii	110,618
36	Idaho	96,727
5	Illinois	144,049
25	Indiana	110,000
26	Iowa	108,900
28	Kansas	107,544
17	Kentucky	115,190
35	Louisiana	97,928
NA	Maine**	NA
13	Maryland	119,000
14	Massachusetts	117,467
2	Michigan	147,163
32	Minnesota	104,589
37	Mississippi	95,500
18	Missouri	115,000
NA	Montana**	NA
31	Nebraska	105,452
NA	Nevada**	NA
NA	New Hampshire**	NA
4	New Jersey	145,588
39	New Mexico	85,887
6	New York	144,000
24	North Carolina	110,530
NA	North Dakota**	NA
21	Ohio	112,550
34	Oklahoma	101,714
38	Oregon	91,500
9	Pennsylvania	129,458
NA	Rhode Island**	NA
19	South Carolina	114,237
NA	South Dakota**	NA
20	Tennessee	112,908
29	Texas	107,350
27	Utah	108,888
NA	Vermont**	NA
10	Virginia	125,899
15	Washington	117,420
NA	West Virginia**	NA
22	Wisconsin	112,180
NA	Wyoming**	NA

RANK ORDER

RANK	STATE	SALARY
1	California	$152,260
2	Michigan	147,163
3	Georgia	146,994
4	New Jersey	145,588
5	Illinois	144,049
6	New York	144,000
7	Alabama	139,580
8	Florida	138,500
9	Pennsylvania	129,458
10	Virginia	125,899
11	Arizona	123,900
12	Connecticut	120,988
13	Maryland	119,000
14	Massachusetts	117,467
15	Washington	117,420
16	Arkansas	116,539
17	Kentucky	115,190
18	Missouri	115,000
19	South Carolina	114,237
20	Tennessee	112,908
21	Ohio	112,550
22	Wisconsin	112,180
23	Hawaii	110,618
24	North Carolina	110,530
25	Indiana	110,000
26	Iowa	108,900
27	Utah	108,888
28	Kansas	107,544
29	Texas	107,350
30	Alaska	106,020
31	Nebraska	105,452
32	Minnesota	104,589
33	Colorado	103,308
34	Oklahoma	101,714
35	Louisiana	97,928
36	Idaho	96,727
37	Mississippi	95,500
38	Oregon	91,500
39	New Mexico	85,887
NA	Delaware**	NA
NA	Maine**	NA
NA	Montana**	NA
NA	Nevada**	NA
NA	New Hampshire**	NA
NA	North Dakota**	NA
NA	Rhode Island**	NA
NA	South Dakota**	NA
NA	Vermont**	NA
NA	West Virginia**	NA
NA	Wyoming**	NA
	District of Columbia**	NA

Source: National Center for State Courts
   "Survey of Judicial Salaries-Summer 2001" (Volume 26, Number 2)
*No intermediate court.

Base Salary for Judges of General Trial Courts in 2001

National Average = $106,656

ALPHA ORDER

RANK	STATE	SALARY
32	Alabama	$100,526
26	Alaska	103,776
10	Arizona	120,750
16	Arkansas	112,728
5	California	133,052
34	Colorado	98,808
12	Connecticut	116,000
4	Delaware	134,700
7	Florida	130,000
9	Georgia	121,769
23	Hawaii	106,922
42	Idaho	91,596
6	Illinois	132,184
44	Indiana	90,000
28	Iowa	103,500
36	Kansas	97,285
19	Kentucky	110,288
41	Louisiana	92,520
37	Maine	97,110
13	Maryland	115,000
15	Massachusetts	112,777
3	Michigan	135,966
35	Minnesota	98,180
39	Mississippi	94,700
22	Missouri	108,000
49	Montana	82,606
30	Nebraska	102,677
20	Nevada	110,000
33	New Hampshire	99,861
1	New Jersey	137,165
50	New Mexico	81,593
2	New York	136,700
25	North Carolina	104,523
47	North Dakota	84,765
28	Ohio	103,500
38	Oklahoma	95,898
46	Oregon	85,300
11	Pennsylvania	116,065
14	Rhode Island	114,430
18	South Carolina	111,309
43	South Dakota	91,286
21	Tennessee	108,036
31	Texas	101,700
27	Utah	103,688
40	Vermont	94,504
8	Virginia	123,027
17	Washington	111,549
44	West Virginia	90,000
24	Wisconsin	105,755
48	Wyoming	83,700

RANK ORDER

RANK	STATE	SALARY
1	New Jersey	$137,165
2	New York	136,700
3	Michigan	135,966
4	Delaware	134,700
5	California	133,052
6	Illinois	132,184
7	Florida	130,000
8	Virginia	123,027
9	Georgia	121,769
10	Arizona	120,750
11	Pennsylvania	116,065
12	Connecticut	116,000
13	Maryland	115,000
14	Rhode Island	114,430
15	Massachusetts	112,777
16	Arkansas	112,728
17	Washington	111,549
18	South Carolina	111,309
19	Kentucky	110,288
20	Nevada	110,000
21	Tennessee	108,036
22	Missouri	108,000
23	Hawaii	106,922
24	Wisconsin	105,755
25	North Carolina	104,523
26	Alaska	103,776
27	Utah	103,688
28	Iowa	103,500
28	Ohio	103,500
30	Nebraska	102,677
31	Texas	101,700
32	Alabama	100,526
33	New Hampshire	99,861
34	Colorado	98,808
35	Minnesota	98,180
36	Kansas	97,285
37	Maine	97,110
38	Oklahoma	95,898
39	Mississippi	94,700
40	Vermont	94,504
41	Louisiana	92,520
42	Idaho	91,596
43	South Dakota	91,286
44	Indiana	90,000
44	West Virginia	90,000
46	Oregon	85,300
47	North Dakota	84,765
48	Wyoming	83,700
49	Montana	82,606
50	New Mexico	81,593
	District of Columbia	145,600

Source: National Center for State Courts
"Survey of Judicial Salaries-Summer 2001" (Volume 26, Number 2)

V. JUVENILES

V. JUVENILES (continued)

Important Note Regarding Juvenile Arrest Rates

The juvenile arrest rates shown in tables 188 to 241 were calculated by the editors as follows:

The state arrest numbers reported by the FBI are only from those law enforcement agencies that submitted complete arrests reports for 12 months in 2000. Included in the FBI report are population totals of these reporting jurisdictions by state. Using these FBI population figures, we first determined what percentage the FBI numbers represented of each state's total resident population. Next, using 2000 Census state counts for 10 to 17-year-olds, we multiplied the percentages derived from the FBI population figures into the Census Bureau's total juvenile population counts. The resulting juvenile population is the base that was used to determine juvenile arrests per 100,000 juvenile population. The national rate was calculated in the same manner.

Reports from law enforcement agencies in Georgia, Illinois, Kentucky, Montana, New York, South Carolina and West Virginia represented less than half of their state populations. Thus rates for these states should be interpreted with caution. Reports from Delaware, Missouri, Mississippi and Ohio represented just over half of their state population. No arrest data were available for Kansas, Wisconsin and the District of Columbia.

Reported Arrests of Juveniles in 2000

National Total = 1,835,103 Reported Arrests*

ALPHA ORDER

RANK	STATE	ARRESTS	% of USA
33	Alabama	11,684	0.6%
44	Alaska	5,953	0.3%
7	Arizona	57,491	3.1%
31	Arkansas	17,153	0.9%
1	California	265,978	14.5%
11	Colorado	48,636	2.7%
26	Connecticut	20,983	1.1%
41	Delaware	7,374	0.4%
3	Florida	124,845	6.8%
21	Georgia	28,235	1.5%
34	Hawaii	11,407	0.6%
30	Idaho	19,491	1.1%
15	Illinois	45,896	2.5%
16	Indiana	37,124	2.0%
25	Iowa	23,042	1.3%
NA	Kansas**	NA	NA
48	Kentucky	1,831	0.1%
17	Louisiana	34,440	1.9%
35	Maine	10,885	0.6%
14	Maryland	46,630	2.5%
27	Massachusetts	19,933	1.1%
13	Michigan	47,165	2.6%
5	Minnesota	74,282	4.0%
32	Mississippi	15,741	0.9%
20	Missouri	31,553	1.7%
45	Montana	4,663	0.3%
29	Nebraska	19,509	1.1%
22	Nevada	26,966	1.5%
43	New Hampshire	6,898	0.4%
6	New Jersey	73,582	4.0%
36	New Mexico	10,611	0.6%
9	New York	50,003	2.7%
10	North Carolina	48,857	2.7%
40	North Dakota	8,085	0.4%
8	Ohio	56,887	3.1%
24	Oklahoma	25,618	1.4%
18	Oregon	34,061	1.9%
4	Pennsylvania	94,702	5.2%
42	Rhode Island	7,300	0.4%
37	South Carolina	9,154	0.5%
38	South Dakota	9,111	0.5%
28	Tennessee	19,846	1.1%
2	Texas	202,504	11.0%
23	Utah	25,824	1.4%
47	Vermont	2,343	0.1%
19	Virginia	32,759	1.8%
12	Washington	47,404	2.6%
46	West Virginia	2,508	0.1%
NA	Wisconsin**	NA	NA
39	Wyoming	8,156	0.4%

RANK ORDER

RANK	STATE	ARRESTS	% of USA
1	California	265,978	14.5%
2	Texas	202,504	11.0%
3	Florida	124,845	6.8%
4	Pennsylvania	94,702	5.2%
5	Minnesota	74,282	4.0%
6	New Jersey	73,582	4.0%
7	Arizona	57,491	3.1%
8	Ohio	56,887	3.1%
9	New York	50,003	2.7%
10	North Carolina	48,857	2.7%
11	Colorado	48,636	2.7%
12	Washington	47,404	2.6%
13	Michigan	47,165	2.6%
14	Maryland	46,630	2.5%
15	Illinois	45,896	2.5%
16	Indiana	37,124	2.0%
17	Louisiana	34,440	1.9%
18	Oregon	34,061	1.9%
19	Virginia	32,759	1.8%
20	Missouri	31,553	1.7%
21	Georgia	28,235	1.5%
22	Nevada	26,966	1.5%
23	Utah	25,824	1.4%
24	Oklahoma	25,618	1.4%
25	Iowa	23,042	1.3%
26	Connecticut	20,983	1.1%
27	Massachusetts	19,933	1.1%
28	Tennessee	19,846	1.1%
29	Nebraska	19,509	1.1%
30	Idaho	19,491	1.1%
31	Arkansas	17,153	0.9%
32	Mississippi	15,741	0.9%
33	Alabama	11,684	0.6%
34	Hawaii	11,407	0.6%
35	Maine	10,885	0.6%
36	New Mexico	10,611	0.6%
37	South Carolina	9,154	0.5%
38	South Dakota	9,111	0.5%
39	Wyoming	8,156	0.4%
40	North Dakota	8,085	0.4%
41	Delaware	7,374	0.4%
42	Rhode Island	7,300	0.4%
43	New Hampshire	6,898	0.4%
44	Alaska	5,953	0.3%
45	Montana	4,663	0.3%
46	West Virginia	2,508	0.1%
47	Vermont	2,343	0.1%
48	Kentucky	1,831	0.1%
NA	Kansas**	NA	NA
NA	Wisconsin**	NA	NA
	District of Columbia**	NA	NA

Source: Federal Bureau of Investigation
    "Crime in the United States 2000" (Uniform Crime Reports, October 22, 2001)
*Arrests of youths 17 years and younger by law enforcement agencies submitting complete reports to the F.B.I. for 12 months in 2000. See important note at beginning of this chapter.
**Not available.

Reported Juvenile Arrest Rate in 2000

National Rate = 7,861.5 Reported Arrests per 100,000 Juvenile Population*

ALPHA ORDER

RANK	STATE	RATE
47	Alabama	3,202.1
31	Alaska	7,308.6
13	Arizona	10,662.5
39	Arkansas	6,354.0
38	California	6,619.5
4	Colorado	12,999.2
30	Connecticut	7,414.1
1	Delaware	16,822.9
27	Florida	7,651.0
41	Georgia	6,141.7
16	Hawaii	9,817.0
10	Idaho	11,562.4
2	Illinois	13,804.2
24	Indiana	8,243.9
28	Iowa	7,607.4
NA	Kansas**	NA
35	Kentucky	7,017.2
21	Louisiana	8,798.2
29	Maine	7,511.0
19	Maryland	9,088.1
46	Massachusetts	3,892.4
43	Michigan	4,700.1
3	Minnesota	13,203.7
20	Mississippi	8,916.4
18	Missouri	9,240.2
11	Montana	10,746.0
14	Nebraska	10,215.0
6	Nevada	12,767.4
26	New Hampshire	7,973.6
23	New Jersey	8,271.1
34	New Mexico	7,113.2
36	New York	6,846.5
32	North Carolina	7,140.4
9	North Dakota	11,640.3
22	Ohio	8,308.6
40	Oklahoma	6,238.7
12	Oregon	10,725.1
17	Pennsylvania	9,323.7
37	Rhode Island	6,826.9
33	South Carolina	7,124.3
7	South Dakota	11,837.8
44	Tennessee	4,599.6
25	Texas	8,103.6
8	Utah	11,706.5
45	Vermont	4,015.1
42	Virginia	5,758.2
15	Washington	9,846.4
48	West Virginia	2,705.2
NA	Wisconsin**	NA
5	Wyoming	12,856.9

RANK ORDER

RANK	STATE	RATE
1	Delaware	16,822.9
2	Illinois	13,804.2
3	Minnesota	13,203.7
4	Colorado	12,999.2
5	Wyoming	12,856.9
6	Nevada	12,767.4
7	South Dakota	11,837.8
8	Utah	11,706.5
9	North Dakota	11,640.3
10	Idaho	11,562.4
11	Montana	10,746.0
12	Oregon	10,725.1
13	Arizona	10,662.5
14	Nebraska	10,215.0
15	Washington	9,846.4
16	Hawaii	9,817.0
17	Pennsylvania	9,323.7
18	Missouri	9,240.2
19	Maryland	9,088.1
20	Mississippi	8,916.4
21	Louisiana	8,798.2
22	Ohio	8,308.6
23	New Jersey	8,271.1
24	Indiana	8,243.9
25	Texas	8,103.6
26	New Hampshire	7,973.6
27	Florida	7,651.0
28	Iowa	7,607.4
29	Maine	7,511.0
30	Connecticut	7,414.1
31	Alaska	7,308.6
32	North Carolina	7,140.4
33	South Carolina	7,124.3
34	New Mexico	7,113.2
35	Kentucky	7,017.2
36	New York	6,846.5
37	Rhode Island	6,826.9
38	California	6,619.5
39	Arkansas	6,354.0
40	Oklahoma	6,238.7
41	Georgia	6,141.7
42	Virginia	5,758.2
43	Michigan	4,700.1
44	Tennessee	4,599.6
45	Vermont	4,015.1
46	Massachusetts	3,892.4
47	Alabama	3,202.1
48	West Virginia	2,705.2
NA	Kansas**	NA
NA	Wisconsin**	NA
	District of Columbia**	NA

Source: Morgan Quitno Press using data from Federal Bureau of Investigation
"Crime in the United States 2000" (Uniform Crime Reports, October 22, 2001)
*By law enforcement agencies submitting complete reports to the F.B.I. for 12 months in 2000. Arrests of youths 17 years and younger divided into population of 10 to 17 year olds. See important note at beginning of this chapter.
**Not available.

Reported Arrests of Juveniles as a Percent of All Arrests in 2000

National Percent = 16.5% of Reported Arrests*

RANK	STATE	PERCENT
48	Alabama	7.2
28	Alaska	16.2
17	Arizona	19.2
47	Arkansas	8.3
31	California	15.9
12	Colorado	20.1
32	Connecticut	15.8
12	Delaware	20.1
35	Florida	14.2
43	Georgia	11.3
14	Hawaii	19.9
5	Idaho	24.4
20	Illinois	18.1
21	Indiana	18.0
11	Iowa	20.2
NA	Kansas**	NA
41	Kentucky	11.7
24	Louisiana	17.3
22	Maine	17.8
30	Maryland	16.0
34	Massachusetts	14.4
36	Michigan	14.1
3	Minnesota	27.0
39	Mississippi	12.6
38	Missouri	12.8
1	Montana	35.4
19	Nebraska	18.5
25	Nevada	17.2
10	New Hampshire	20.5
26	New Jersey	17.1
37	New Mexico	13.6
28	New York	16.2
44	North Carolina	10.8
2	North Dakota	30.1
18	Ohio	18.9
33	Oklahoma	15.6
9	Oregon	22.2
7	Pennsylvania	22.8
15	Rhode Island	19.7
42	South Carolina	11.6
6	South Dakota	23.4
45	Tennessee	10.6
23	Texas	17.7
4	Utah	26.3
27	Vermont	16.6
40	Virginia	12.0
16	Washington	19.6
46	West Virginia	9.2
NA	Wisconsin**	NA
8	Wyoming	22.4

RANK	STATE	PERCENT
1	Montana	35.4
2	North Dakota	30.1
3	Minnesota	27.0
4	Utah	26.3
5	Idaho	24.4
6	South Dakota	23.4
7	Pennsylvania	22.8
8	Wyoming	22.4
9	Oregon	22.2
10	New Hampshire	20.5
11	Iowa	20.2
12	Colorado	20.1
12	Delaware	20.1
14	Hawaii	19.9
15	Rhode Island	19.7
16	Washington	19.6
17	Arizona	19.2
18	Ohio	18.9
19	Nebraska	18.5
20	Illinois	18.1
21	Indiana	18.0
22	Maine	17.8
23	Texas	17.7
24	Louisiana	17.3
25	Nevada	17.2
26	New Jersey	17.1
27	Vermont	16.6
28	Alaska	16.2
28	New York	16.2
30	Maryland	16.0
31	California	15.9
32	Connecticut	15.8
33	Oklahoma	15.6
34	Massachusetts	14.4
35	Florida	14.2
36	Michigan	14.1
37	New Mexico	13.6
38	Missouri	12.8
39	Mississippi	12.6
40	Virginia	12.0
41	Kentucky	11.7
42	South Carolina	11.6
43	Georgia	11.3
44	North Carolina	10.8
45	Tennessee	10.6
46	West Virginia	9.2
47	Arkansas	8.3
48	Alabama	7.2
NA	Kansas**	NA
NA	Wisconsin**	NA
	District of Columbia**	NA

*Source: Morgan Quitno Press using data from Federal Bureau of Investigation
"Crime in the United States 2000" (Uniform Crime Reports, October 22, 2001)*
*Arrests of youths 17 years and younger by law enforcement agencies submitting complete reports to the F.B.I. for 12 months in 2000.
**Not available.

Reported Arrests of Juveniles for Crime Index Offenses in 2000

National Total = 469,598 Reported Arrests*

ALPHA ORDER

RANK	STATE	ARRESTS	% of USA
33	Alabama	3,550	0.8%
38	Alaska	2,279	0.5%
9	Arizona	13,357	2.8%
30	Arkansas	4,464	1.0%
1	California	73,108	15.6%
15	Colorado	10,729	2.3%
28	Connecticut	5,183	1.1%
39	Delaware	2,033	0.4%
2	Florida	50,042	10.7%
21	Georgia	7,604	1.6%
37	Hawaii	2,323	0.5%
31	Idaho	4,441	0.9%
13	Illinois	12,297	2.6%
16	Indiana	9,361	2.0%
24	Iowa	6,630	1.4%
NA	Kansas**	NA	NA
47	Kentucky	573	0.1%
18	Louisiana	8,652	1.8%
34	Maine	2,931	0.6%
11	Maryland	12,526	2.7%
25	Massachusetts	5,803	1.2%
12	Michigan	12,408	2.6%
7	Minnesota	13,851	2.9%
32	Mississippi	3,706	0.8%
17	Missouri	8,717	1.9%
44	Montana	978	0.2%
29	Nebraska	4,949	1.1%
26	Nevada	5,646	1.2%
45	New Hampshire	964	0.2%
6	New Jersey	14,523	3.1%
35	New Mexico	2,610	0.6%
10	New York	12,750	2.7%
8	North Carolina	13,791	2.9%
42	North Dakota	1,566	0.3%
14	Ohio	11,681	2.5%
20	Oklahoma	7,915	1.7%
19	Oregon	8,566	1.8%
4	Pennsylvania	19,477	4.1%
40	Rhode Island	1,820	0.4%
36	South Carolina	2,589	0.6%
41	South Dakota	1,810	0.4%
27	Tennessee	5,280	1.1%
3	Texas	44,220	9.4%
22	Utah	6,823	1.5%
47	Vermont	573	0.1%
23	Virginia	6,642	1.4%
5	Washington	15,655	3.3%
46	West Virginia	897	0.2%
NA	Wisconsin**	NA	NA
43	Wyoming	1,305	0.3%

RANK ORDER

RANK	STATE	ARRESTS	% of USA
1	California	73,108	15.6%
2	Florida	50,042	10.7%
3	Texas	44,220	9.4%
4	Pennsylvania	19,477	4.1%
5	Washington	15,655	3.3%
6	New Jersey	14,523	3.1%
7	Minnesota	13,851	2.9%
8	North Carolina	13,791	2.9%
9	Arizona	13,357	2.8%
10	New York	12,750	2.7%
11	Maryland	12,526	2.7%
12	Michigan	12,408	2.6%
13	Illinois	12,297	2.6%
14	Ohio	11,681	2.5%
15	Colorado	10,729	2.3%
16	Indiana	9,361	2.0%
17	Missouri	8,717	1.9%
18	Louisiana	8,652	1.8%
19	Oregon	8,566	1.8%
20	Oklahoma	7,915	1.7%
21	Georgia	7,604	1.6%
22	Utah	6,823	1.5%
23	Virginia	6,642	1.4%
24	Iowa	6,630	1.4%
25	Massachusetts	5,803	1.2%
26	Nevada	5,646	1.2%
27	Tennessee	5,280	1.1%
28	Connecticut	5,183	1.1%
29	Nebraska	4,949	1.1%
30	Arkansas	4,464	1.0%
31	Idaho	4,441	0.9%
32	Mississippi	3,706	0.8%
33	Alabama	3,550	0.8%
34	Maine	2,931	0.6%
35	New Mexico	2,610	0.6%
36	South Carolina	2,589	0.6%
37	Hawaii	2,323	0.5%
38	Alaska	2,279	0.5%
39	Delaware	2,033	0.4%
40	Rhode Island	1,820	0.4%
41	South Dakota	1,810	0.4%
42	North Dakota	1,566	0.3%
43	Wyoming	1,305	0.3%
44	Montana	978	0.2%
45	New Hampshire	964	0.2%
46	West Virginia	897	0.2%
47	Kentucky	573	0.1%
47	Vermont	573	0.1%
NA	Kansas**	NA	NA
NA	Wisconsin**	NA	NA
NA	District of Columbia**	NA	NA

Source: Federal Bureau of Investigation
    "Crime in the United States 2000" (Uniform Crime Reports, October 22, 2001)
*Arrests of youths 17 years and younger by law enforcement agencies submitting complete reports to the F.B.I. for
12 months in 2000. Crime index offenses consist of murder, forcible rape, robbery, aggravated assault, burglary,
larceny-theft, motor vehicle theft and arson. See important note at beginning of this chapter.
**Not available.

Reported Juvenile Arrest Rate for Crime Index Offenses in 2000

National Rate = 2,011.7 Reported Arrests per 100,000 Juvenile Population*

ALPHA ORDER

RANK ORDER

RANK	STATE	RATE		RANK	STATE	RATE
47	Alabama	972.9		1	Delaware	4,638.1
7	Alaska	2,798.0		2	Illinois	3,698.6
13	Arizona	2,477.2		3	Washington	3,251.7
39	Arkansas	1,653.6		4	Utah	3,093.0
32	California	1,819.5		5	Florida	3,066.8
6	Colorado	2,867.6		6	Colorado	2,867.6
31	Connecticut	1,831.4		7	Alaska	2,798.0
1	Delaware	4,638.1		8	Oregon	2,697.3
5	Florida	3,066.8		9	Nevada	2,673.2
38	Georgia	1,654.0		10	Idaho	2,634.5
28	Hawaii	1,999.2		11	Nebraska	2,591.3
10	Idaho	2,634.5		12	Missouri	2,552.7
2	Illinois	3,698.6		13	Arizona	2,477.2
23	Indiana	2,078.7		14	Minnesota	2,462.0
21	Iowa	2,188.9		15	Maryland	2,441.3
NA	Kansas**	NA		16	South Dakota	2,351.7
20	Kentucky	2,196.0		17	North Dakota	2,254.6
19	Louisiana	2,210.3		18	Montana	2,253.8
25	Maine	2,022.5		19	Louisiana	2,210.3
15	Maryland	2,441.3		20	Kentucky	2,196.0
44	Massachusetts	1,133.2		21	Iowa	2,188.9
41	Michigan	1,236.5		22	Mississippi	2,099.2
14	Minnesota	2,462.0		23	Indiana	2,078.7
22	Mississippi	2,099.2		24	Wyoming	2,057.2
12	Missouri	2,552.7		25	Maine	2,022.5
18	Montana	2,253.8		26	North Carolina	2,015.5
11	Nebraska	2,591.3		27	South Carolina	2,015.0
9	Nevada	2,673.2		28	Hawaii	1,999.2
45	New Hampshire	1,114.3		29	Oklahoma	1,927.5
40	New Jersey	1,632.5		30	Pennsylvania	1,917.6
34	New Mexico	1,749.6		31	Connecticut	1,831.4
35	New York	1,745.8		32	California	1,819.5
26	North Carolina	2,015.5		33	Texas	1,769.6
17	North Dakota	2,254.6		34	New Mexico	1,749.6
36	Ohio	1,706.1		35	New York	1,745.8
29	Oklahoma	1,927.5		36	Ohio	1,706.1
8	Oregon	2,697.3		37	Rhode Island	1,702.0
30	Pennsylvania	1,917.6		38	Georgia	1,654.0
37	Rhode Island	1,702.0		39	Arkansas	1,653.6
27	South Carolina	2,015.0		40	New Jersey	1,632.5
16	South Dakota	2,351.7		41	Michigan	1,236.5
42	Tennessee	1,223.7		42	Tennessee	1,223.7
33	Texas	1,769.6		43	Virginia	1,167.5
4	Utah	3,093.0		44	Massachusetts	1,133.2
46	Vermont	981.9		45	New Hampshire	1,114.3
43	Virginia	1,167.5		46	Vermont	981.9
3	Washington	3,251.7		47	Alabama	972.9
48	West Virginia	967.5		48	West Virginia	967.5
NA	Wisconsin**	NA		NA	Kansas**	NA
24	Wyoming	2,057.2		NA	Wisconsin**	NA
					District of Columbia**	NA

Source: Morgan Quitno Press using data from Federal Bureau of Investigation
   "Crime in the United States 2000" (Uniform Crime Reports, October 22, 2001)
*By law enforcement agencies submitting complete reports to the F.B.I. for 12 months in 2000. Arrests of youths 17 years and younger divided into population of 10 to 17 year olds. See important note at beginning of this chapter. Crime index offenses consist of murder, forcible rape, robbery, aggravated assault, burglary, larceny-theft, motor vehicle theft and arson.   **Not available.

Reported Arrests of Juveniles for Crime Index Offenses
As a Percent of All Such Arrests in 2000
National Percent = 27.7% of Reported Crime Index Offense Arrests*

ALPHA ORDER

RANK ORDER

RANK	STATE	PERCENT	RANK	STATE	PERCENT
48	Alabama	16.8	1	North Dakota	53.8
7	Alaska	39.7	2	Idaho	46.7
22	Arizona	29.3	3	South Dakota	42.9
42	Arkansas	21.4	4	Minnesota	42.7
36	California	24.7	5	Utah	42.3
16	Colorado	33.9	6	Montana	41.3
33	Connecticut	26.4	7	Alaska	39.7
32	Delaware	26.6	8	New Hampshire	39.6
26	Florida	28.3	9	Nebraska	38.6
45	Georgia	19.4	10	Iowa	37.2
22	Hawaii	29.3	11	Washington	37.1
2	Idaho	46.7	11	Wyoming	37.1
38	Illinois	24.0	13	Rhode Island	36.9
24	Indiana	28.4	14	Maine	36.5
10	Iowa	37.2	15	Oklahoma	34.6
NA	Kansas**	NA	16	Colorado	33.9
27	Kentucky	27.6	17	Michigan	33.6
40	Louisiana	23.8	18	Vermont	32.3
14	Maine	36.5	19	Maryland	31.3
19	Maryland	31.3	20	Texas	31.0
43	Massachusetts	20.5	21	Oregon	29.8
17	Michigan	33.6	22	Arizona	29.3
4	Minnesota	42.7	22	Hawaii	29.3
37	Mississippi	24.6	24	Indiana	28.4
38	Missouri	24.0	24	New Mexico	28.4
6	Montana	41.3	26	Florida	28.3
9	Nebraska	38.6	27	Kentucky	27.6
28	Nevada	27.3	28	Nevada	27.3
8	New Hampshire	39.6	29	Ohio	27.1
30	New Jersey	27.0	30	New Jersey	27.0
24	New Mexico	28.4	30	Pennsylvania	27.0
34	New York	26.3	32	Delaware	26.6
45	North Carolina	19.4	33	Connecticut	26.4
1	North Dakota	53.8	34	New York	26.3
29	Ohio	27.1	35	South Carolina	25.8
15	Oklahoma	34.6	36	California	24.7
21	Oregon	29.8	37	Mississippi	24.6
30	Pennsylvania	27.0	38	Illinois	24.0
13	Rhode Island	36.9	38	Missouri	24.0
35	South Carolina	25.8	40	Louisiana	23.8
3	South Dakota	42.9	41	Virginia	23.7
47	Tennessee	19.1	42	Arkansas	21.4
20	Texas	31.0	43	Massachusetts	20.5
5	Utah	42.3	43	West Virginia	20.5
18	Vermont	32.3	45	Georgia	19.4
41	Virginia	23.7	45	North Carolina	19.4
11	Washington	37.1	47	Tennessee	19.1
43	West Virginia	20.5	48	Alabama	16.8
NA	Wisconsin**	NA	NA	Kansas**	NA
11	Wyoming	37.1	NA	Wisconsin**	NA
				District of Columbia**	NA

Source: Morgan Quitno Press using data from Federal Bureau of Investigation
   "Crime in the United States 2000" (Uniform Crime Reports, October 22, 2001)
*Arrests of youths 17 years and younger by law enforcement agencies submitting complete reports to the F.B.I. for 12 months in 2000. Crime index offenses consist of murder, forcible rape, robbery, aggravated assault, burglary, larceny-theft, motor vehicle theft and arson.
**Not available.

193

Reported Arrests of Juveniles for Violent Crime in 2000

National Total = 76,957 Reported Arrests*

ALPHA ORDER

RANK	STATE	ARRESTS	% of USA
27	Alabama	546	0.7%
39	Alaska	197	0.3%
13	Arizona	1,586	2.1%
29	Arkansas	492	0.6%
1	California	16,315	21.2%
22	Colorado	891	1.2%
23	Connecticut	788	1.0%
31	Delaware	463	0.6%
2	Florida	10,025	13.0%
18	Georgia	1,250	1.6%
36	Hawaii	288	0.4%
34	Idaho	296	0.4%
6	Illinois	3,120	4.1%
14	Indiana	1,580	2.1%
25	Iowa	740	1.0%
NA	Kansas**	NA	NA
46	Kentucky	54	0.1%
12	Louisiana	1,592	2.1%
40	Maine	175	0.2%
7	Maryland	2,721	3.5%
8	Massachusetts	2,295	3.0%
16	Michigan	1,490	1.9%
11	Minnesota	1,593	2.1%
37	Mississippi	261	0.3%
19	Missouri	1,121	1.5%
41	Montana	164	0.2%
38	Nebraska	224	0.3%
28	Nevada	538	0.7%
44	New Hampshire	83	0.1%
5	New Jersey	3,209	4.2%
32	New Mexico	419	0.5%
9	New York	2,289	3.0%
10	North Carolina	2,169	2.8%
48	North Dakota	22	0.0%
16	Ohio	1,490	1.9%
20	Oklahoma	1,022	1.3%
26	Oregon	636	0.8%
4	Pennsylvania	4,699	6.1%
35	Rhode Island	293	0.4%
33	South Carolina	412	0.5%
42	South Dakota	106	0.1%
24	Tennessee	760	1.0%
3	Texas	5,385	7.0%
30	Utah	469	0.6%
47	Vermont	33	0.0%
21	Virginia	901	1.2%
15	Washington	1,575	2.0%
45	West Virginia	79	0.1%
NA	Wisconsin**	NA	NA
43	Wyoming	101	0.1%

RANK ORDER

RANK	STATE	ARRESTS	% of USA
1	California	16,315	21.2%
2	Florida	10,025	13.0%
3	Texas	5,385	7.0%
4	Pennsylvania	4,699	6.1%
5	New Jersey	3,209	4.2%
6	Illinois	3,120	4.1%
7	Maryland	2,721	3.5%
8	Massachusetts	2,295	3.0%
9	New York	2,289	3.0%
10	North Carolina	2,169	2.8%
11	Minnesota	1,593	2.1%
12	Louisiana	1,592	2.1%
13	Arizona	1,586	2.1%
14	Indiana	1,580	2.1%
15	Washington	1,575	2.0%
16	Michigan	1,490	1.9%
16	Ohio	1,490	1.9%
18	Georgia	1,250	1.6%
19	Missouri	1,121	1.5%
20	Oklahoma	1,022	1.3%
21	Virginia	901	1.2%
22	Colorado	891	1.2%
23	Connecticut	788	1.0%
24	Tennessee	760	1.0%
25	Iowa	740	1.0%
26	Oregon	636	0.8%
27	Alabama	546	0.7%
28	Nevada	538	0.7%
29	Arkansas	492	0.6%
30	Utah	469	0.6%
31	Delaware	463	0.6%
32	New Mexico	419	0.5%
33	South Carolina	412	0.5%
34	Idaho	296	0.4%
35	Rhode Island	293	0.4%
36	Hawaii	288	0.4%
37	Mississippi	261	0.3%
38	Nebraska	224	0.3%
39	Alaska	197	0.3%
40	Maine	175	0.2%
41	Montana	164	0.2%
42	South Dakota	106	0.1%
43	Wyoming	101	0.1%
44	New Hampshire	83	0.1%
45	West Virginia	79	0.1%
46	Kentucky	54	0.1%
47	Vermont	33	0.0%
48	North Dakota	22	0.0%
NA	Kansas**	NA	NA
NA	Wisconsin**	NA	NA
	District of Columbia**	NA	NA

Source: Federal Bureau of Investigation
  "Crime in the United States 2000" (Uniform Crime Reports, October 22, 2001)
*Arrests of youths 17 years and younger by law enforcement agencies submitting complete reports to the F.B.I. for 12 months in 2000. Violent crimes are offenses of murder, forcible rape, robbery and aggravated assault. See important note at beginning of this chapter.
**Not available.

Reported Juvenile Arrest Rate for Violent Crime in 2000

National Rate = 329.7 Reported Arrests per 100,000 Juvenile Population*

ALPHA ORDER

RANK	STATE	RATE
39	Alabama	149.6
27	Alaska	241.9
17	Arizona	294.1
34	Arkansas	182.3
8	California	406.0
28	Colorado	238.1
20	Connecticut	278.4
1	Delaware	1,056.3
3	Florida	614.4
22	Georgia	271.9
25	Hawaii	247.9
36	Idaho	175.6
2	Illinois	938.4
11	Indiana	350.9
26	Iowa	244.3
NA	Kansas**	NA
32	Kentucky	207.0
7	Louisiana	406.7
43	Maine	120.8
4	Maryland	530.3
6	Massachusetts	448.2
40	Michigan	148.5
18	Minnesota	283.2
41	Mississippi	147.8
12	Missouri	328.3
9	Montana	377.9
44	Nebraska	117.3
23	Nevada	254.7
45	New Hampshire	95.9
10	New Jersey	360.7
19	New Mexico	280.9
16	New York	313.4
15	North Carolina	317.0
48	North Dakota	31.7
29	Ohio	217.6
24	Oklahoma	248.9
33	Oregon	200.3
5	Pennsylvania	462.6
21	Rhode Island	274.0
14	South Carolina	320.7
42	South Dakota	137.7
35	Tennessee	176.1
30	Texas	215.5
31	Utah	212.6
47	Vermont	56.6
38	Virginia	158.4
13	Washington	327.1
46	West Virginia	85.2
NA	Wisconsin**	NA
37	Wyoming	159.2

RANK ORDER

RANK	STATE	RATE
1	Delaware	1,056.3
2	Illinois	938.4
3	Florida	614.4
4	Maryland	530.3
5	Pennsylvania	462.6
6	Massachusetts	448.2
7	Louisiana	406.7
8	California	406.0
9	Montana	377.9
10	New Jersey	360.7
11	Indiana	350.9
12	Missouri	328.3
13	Washington	327.1
14	South Carolina	320.7
15	North Carolina	317.0
16	New York	313.4
17	Arizona	294.1
18	Minnesota	283.2
19	New Mexico	280.9
20	Connecticut	278.4
21	Rhode Island	274.0
22	Georgia	271.9
23	Nevada	254.7
24	Oklahoma	248.9
25	Hawaii	247.9
26	Iowa	244.3
27	Alaska	241.9
28	Colorado	238.1
29	Ohio	217.6
30	Texas	215.5
31	Utah	212.6
32	Kentucky	207.0
33	Oregon	200.3
34	Arkansas	182.3
35	Tennessee	176.1
36	Idaho	175.6
37	Wyoming	159.2
38	Virginia	158.4
39	Alabama	149.6
40	Michigan	148.5
41	Mississippi	147.8
42	South Dakota	137.7
43	Maine	120.8
44	Nebraska	117.3
45	New Hampshire	95.9
46	West Virginia	85.2
47	Vermont	56.6
48	North Dakota	31.7
NA	Kansas**	NA
NA	Wisconsin**	NA
	District of Columbia**	NA

Source: Morgan Quitno Press using data from Federal Bureau of Investigation
"Crime in the United States 2000" (Uniform Crime Reports, October 22, 2001)
*By law enforcement agencies submitting complete reports to the F.B.I. for 12 months in 2000. Arrests of youths 17 years and younger divided into population of 10 to 17 year olds. See important note at beginning of this chapter. Violent crimes are offenses of murder, forcible rape, robbery and aggravated assault.
**Not available.

195

Reported Arrests of Juveniles for Violent Crime
As a Percent of All Such Arrests in 2000
National Percent = 16.2% of Reported Violent Crime Arrests*

ALPHA ORDER

RANK	STATE	PERCENT
46	Alabama	9.3
27	Alaska	16.4
16	Arizona	19.4
45	Arkansas	9.9
40	California	12.6
23	Colorado	17.2
22	Connecticut	17.4
11	Delaware	20.1
18	Florida	18.6
42	Georgia	10.9
7	Hawaii	22.5
9	Idaho	21.6
2	Illinois	30.2
30	Indiana	15.6
20	Iowa	17.9
NA	Kansas**	NA
38	Kentucky	14.2
31	Louisiana	15.5
15	Maine	19.7
4	Maryland	26.8
25	Massachusetts	16.9
28	Michigan	16.1
5	Minnesota	24.7
44	Mississippi	10.2
35	Missouri	14.6
6	Montana	23.7
31	Nebraska	15.5
25	Nevada	16.9
12	New Hampshire	20.0
10	New Jersey	20.7
33	New Mexico	15.0
14	New York	19.9
43	North Carolina	10.5
34	North Dakota	14.8
36	Ohio	14.4
24	Oklahoma	17.1
17	Oregon	19.2
12	Pennsylvania	20.0
3	Rhode Island	28.0
39	South Carolina	13.6
18	South Dakota	18.6
46	Tennessee	9.3
21	Texas	17.6
1	Utah	30.7
41	Vermont	11.6
36	Virginia	14.4
8	Washington	21.9
48	West Virginia	6.1
NA	Wisconsin**	NA
29	Wyoming	15.7

RANK ORDER

RANK	STATE	PERCENT
1	Utah	30.7
2	Illinois	30.2
3	Rhode Island	28.0
4	Maryland	26.8
5	Minnesota	24.7
6	Montana	23.7
7	Hawaii	22.5
8	Washington	21.9
9	Idaho	21.6
10	New Jersey	20.7
11	Delaware	20.1
12	New Hampshire	20.0
12	Pennsylvania	20.0
14	New York	19.9
15	Maine	19.7
16	Arizona	19.4
17	Oregon	19.2
18	Florida	18.6
18	South Dakota	18.6
20	Iowa	17.9
21	Texas	17.6
22	Connecticut	17.4
23	Colorado	17.2
24	Oklahoma	17.1
25	Massachusetts	16.9
25	Nevada	16.9
27	Alaska	16.4
28	Michigan	16.1
29	Wyoming	15.7
30	Indiana	15.6
31	Louisiana	15.5
31	Nebraska	15.5
33	New Mexico	15.0
34	North Dakota	14.8
35	Missouri	14.6
36	Ohio	14.4
36	Virginia	14.4
38	Kentucky	14.2
39	South Carolina	13.6
40	California	12.6
41	Vermont	11.6
42	Georgia	10.9
43	North Carolina	10.5
44	Mississippi	10.2
45	Arkansas	9.9
46	Alabama	9.3
46	Tennessee	9.3
48	West Virginia	6.1
NA	Kansas**	NA
NA	Wisconsin**	NA
	District of Columbia**	NA

Source: Morgan Quitno Press using data from Federal Bureau of Investigation
  "Crime in the United States 2000" (Uniform Crime Reports, October 22, 2001)
*Arrests of youths 17 years and younger by law enforcement agencies submitting complete reports to the F.B.I. for 12 months in 2000. Violent crimes are offenses of murder, forcible rape, robbery and aggravated assault.
**Not available.

Reported Arrests of Juveniles for Murder in 2000

National Total = 875 Reported Arrests*

ALPHA ORDER   RANK ORDER

RANK	STATE	ARRESTS	% of USA		RANK	STATE	ARRESTS	% of USA
10	Alabama	22	2.5%		1	California	160	18.3%
37	Alaska	2	0.2%		2	Texas	87	9.9%
16	Arizona	16	1.8%		3	Illinois	67	7.7%
14	Arkansas	18	2.1%		4	Georgia	62	7.1%
1	California	160	18.3%		5	Florida	50	5.7%
26	Colorado	6	0.7%		6	North Carolina	45	5.1%
31	Connecticut	3	0.3%		7	Maryland	44	5.0%
31	Delaware	3	0.3%		8	Missouri	39	4.5%
5	Florida	50	5.7%		9	Pennsylvania	36	4.1%
4	Georgia	62	7.1%		10	Alabama	22	2.5%
30	Hawaii	4	0.5%		11	Louisiana	20	2.3%
31	Idaho	3	0.3%		12	Oklahoma	19	2.2%
3	Illinois	67	7.7%		12	Washington	19	2.2%
26	Indiana	6	0.7%		14	Arkansas	18	2.1%
31	Iowa	3	0.3%		14	New Jersey	18	2.1%
NA	Kansas**	NA	NA		16	Arizona	16	1.8%
39	Kentucky	1	0.1%		17	Nevada	15	1.7%
11	Louisiana	20	2.3%		18	Minnesota	13	1.5%
39	Maine	1	0.1%		18	Virginia	13	1.5%
7	Maryland	44	5.0%		20	New York	11	1.3%
29	Massachusetts	5	0.6%		21	Michigan	10	1.1%
21	Michigan	10	1.1%		21	Mississippi	10	1.1%
18	Minnesota	13	1.5%		21	Ohio	10	1.1%
21	Mississippi	10	1.1%		24	Oregon	9	1.0%
8	Missouri	39	4.5%		25	Tennessee	8	0.9%
39	Montana	1	0.1%		26	Colorado	6	0.7%
31	Nebraska	3	0.3%		26	Indiana	6	0.7%
17	Nevada	15	1.7%		26	New Mexico	6	0.7%
44	New Hampshire	0	0.0%		29	Massachusetts	5	0.6%
14	New Jersey	18	2.1%		30	Hawaii	4	0.5%
26	New Mexico	6	0.7%		31	Connecticut	3	0.3%
20	New York	11	1.3%		31	Delaware	3	0.3%
6	North Carolina	45	5.1%		31	Idaho	3	0.3%
44	North Dakota	0	0.0%		31	Iowa	3	0.3%
21	Ohio	10	1.1%		31	Nebraska	3	0.3%
12	Oklahoma	19	2.2%		31	South Carolina	3	0.3%
24	Oregon	9	1.0%		37	Alaska	2	0.2%
9	Pennsylvania	36	4.1%		37	West Virginia	2	0.2%
44	Rhode Island	0	0.0%		39	Kentucky	1	0.1%
31	South Carolina	3	0.3%		39	Maine	1	0.1%
39	South Dakota	1	0.1%		39	Montana	1	0.1%
25	Tennessee	8	0.9%		39	South Dakota	1	0.1%
2	Texas	87	9.9%		39	Vermont	1	0.1%
44	Utah	0	0.0%		44	New Hampshire	0	0.0%
39	Vermont	1	0.1%		44	North Dakota	0	0.0%
18	Virginia	13	1.5%		44	Rhode Island	0	0.0%
12	Washington	19	2.2%		44	Utah	0	0.0%
37	West Virginia	2	0.2%		44	Wyoming	0	0.0%
NA	Wisconsin**	NA	NA		NA	Kansas**	NA	NA
44	Wyoming	0	0.0%		NA	Wisconsin**	NA	NA
						District of Columbia**	NA	NA

Source: Federal Bureau of Investigation
   "Crime in the United States 2000" (Uniform Crime Reports, October 22, 2001)
*Arrests of youths 17 years and younger by law enforcement agencies submitting complete reports to the F.B.I. for 12 months in 2000. Includes nonnegligent manslaughter. See important note at beginning of this chapter.
**Not available.

Reported Juvenile Arrest Rate for Murder in 2000

National Rate = 3.7 Reported Arrests per 100,000 Juvenile Population*

ALPHA ORDER

RANK	STATE	RATE
9	Alabama	6.0
23	Alaska	2.5
21	Arizona	3.0
7	Arkansas	6.7
13	California	4.0
33	Colorado	1.6
39	Connecticut	1.1
6	Delaware	6.8
20	Florida	3.1
2	Georgia	13.5
19	Hawaii	3.4
31	Idaho	1.8
1	Illinois	20.2
37	Indiana	1.3
40	Iowa	1.0
NA	Kansas**	NA
16	Kentucky	3.8
11	Louisiana	5.1
43	Maine	0.7
4	Maryland	8.6
40	Massachusetts	1.0
40	Michigan	1.0
24	Minnesota	2.3
10	Mississippi	5.7
3	Missouri	11.4
24	Montana	2.3
33	Nebraska	1.6
5	Nevada	7.1
44	New Hampshire	0.0
29	New Jersey	2.0
13	New Mexico	4.0
35	New York	1.5
8	North Carolina	6.6
44	North Dakota	0.0
35	Ohio	1.5
12	Oklahoma	4.6
22	Oregon	2.8
17	Pennsylvania	3.5
44	Rhode Island	0.0
24	South Carolina	2.3
37	South Dakota	1.3
30	Tennessee	1.9
17	Texas	3.5
44	Utah	0.0
32	Vermont	1.7
24	Virginia	2.3
15	Washington	3.9
28	West Virginia	2.2
NA	Wisconsin**	NA
44	Wyoming	0.0

RANK ORDER

RANK	STATE	RATE
1	Illinois	20.2
2	Georgia	13.5
3	Missouri	11.4
4	Maryland	8.6
5	Nevada	7.1
6	Delaware	6.8
7	Arkansas	6.7
8	North Carolina	6.6
9	Alabama	6.0
10	Mississippi	5.7
11	Louisiana	5.1
12	Oklahoma	4.6
13	California	4.0
13	New Mexico	4.0
15	Washington	3.9
16	Kentucky	3.8
17	Pennsylvania	3.5
17	Texas	3.5
19	Hawaii	3.4
20	Florida	3.1
21	Arizona	3.0
22	Oregon	2.8
23	Alaska	2.5
24	Minnesota	2.3
24	Montana	2.3
24	South Carolina	2.3
24	Virginia	2.3
28	West Virginia	2.2
29	New Jersey	2.0
30	Tennessee	1.9
31	Idaho	1.8
32	Vermont	1.7
33	Colorado	1.6
33	Nebraska	1.6
35	New York	1.5
35	Ohio	1.5
37	Indiana	1.3
37	South Dakota	1.3
39	Connecticut	1.1
40	Iowa	1.0
40	Massachusetts	1.0
40	Michigan	1.0
43	Maine	0.7
44	New Hampshire	0.0
44	North Dakota	0.0
44	Rhode Island	0.0
44	Utah	0.0
44	Wyoming	0.0
NA	Kansas**	NA
NA	Wisconsin**	NA
	District of Columbia**	NA

Source: Morgan Quitno Press using data from Federal Bureau of Investigation
    "Crime in the United States 2000" (Uniform Crime Reports, October 22, 2001)
*By law enforcement agencies submitting complete reports to the F.B.I. for 12 months in 2000. Includes
nonnegligent manslaughter. Arrests of youths 17 years and younger divided into population of 10 to 17 year olds.
See important note at beginning of this chapter.
**Not available.

Reported Arrests of Juveniles for Murder
As a Percent of All Such Arrests in 2000
National Percent = 9.1% of Reported Murder Arrests*

ALPHA ORDER

RANK	STATE	PERCENT
33	Alabama	6.9
20	Alaska	9.5
27	Arizona	7.5
12	Arkansas	11.2
19	California	9.8
36	Colorado	5.5
41	Connecticut	4.3
14	Delaware	11.1
28	Florida	7.4
3	Georgia	17.3
17	Hawaii	10.0
2	Idaho	20.0
10	Illinois	12.6
43	Indiana	2.9
25	Iowa	7.7
NA	Kansas**	NA
6	Kentucky	14.3
32	Louisiana	7.0
1	Maine	25.0
11	Maryland	11.7
23	Massachusetts	8.3
30	Michigan	7.2
22	Minnesota	8.7
34	Mississippi	6.8
5	Missouri	16.3
6	Montana	14.3
35	Nebraska	6.3
9	Nevada	13.5
44	New Hampshire	0.0
24	New Jersey	7.8
29	New Mexico	7.3
39	New York	5.0
30	North Carolina	7.2
44	North Dakota	0.0
38	Ohio	5.2
16	Oklahoma	10.4
21	Oregon	8.8
25	Pennsylvania	7.7
44	Rhode Island	0.0
42	South Carolina	4.2
17	South Dakota	10.0
39	Tennessee	5.0
12	Texas	11.2
44	Utah	0.0
4	Vermont	16.7
36	Virginia	5.5
8	Washington	13.8
15	West Virginia	10.5
NA	Wisconsin**	NA
44	Wyoming	0.0

RANK ORDER

RANK	STATE	PERCENT
1	Maine	25.0
2	Idaho	20.0
3	Georgia	17.3
4	Vermont	16.7
5	Missouri	16.3
6	Kentucky	14.3
6	Montana	14.3
8	Washington	13.8
9	Nevada	13.5
10	Illinois	12.6
11	Maryland	11.7
12	Arkansas	11.2
12	Texas	11.2
14	Delaware	11.1
15	West Virginia	10.5
16	Oklahoma	10.4
17	Hawaii	10.0
17	South Dakota	10.0
19	California	9.8
20	Alaska	9.5
21	Oregon	8.8
22	Minnesota	8.7
23	Massachusetts	8.3
24	New Jersey	7.8
25	Iowa	7.7
25	Pennsylvania	7.7
27	Arizona	7.5
28	Florida	7.4
29	New Mexico	7.3
30	Michigan	7.2
30	North Carolina	7.2
32	Louisiana	7.0
33	Alabama	6.9
34	Mississippi	6.8
35	Nebraska	6.3
36	Colorado	5.5
36	Virginia	5.5
38	Ohio	5.2
39	New York	5.0
39	Tennessee	5.0
41	Connecticut	4.3
42	South Carolina	4.2
43	Indiana	2.9
44	New Hampshire	0.0
44	North Dakota	0.0
44	Rhode Island	0.0
44	Utah	0.0
44	Wyoming	0.0
NA	Kansas**	NA
NA	Wisconsin**	NA
	District of Columbia**	NA

Source: Morgan Quitno Press using data from Federal Bureau of Investigation
"Crime in the United States 2000" (Uniform Crime Reports, October 22, 2001)
*Arrests of youths 17 years and younger by law enforcement agencies submitting complete reports to the F.B.I. for 12 months in 2000. Includes nonnegligent manslaughter.
**Not available.

Reported Arrests of Juveniles for Rape in 2000

National Total = 3,382 Reported Arrests*

ALPHA ORDER

RANK	STATE	ARRESTS	% of USA
25	Alabama	37	1.1%
38	Alaska	16	0.5%
35	Arizona	20	0.6%
24	Arkansas	38	1.1%
3	California	347	10.3%
12	Colorado	74	2.2%
26	Connecticut	35	1.0%
21	Delaware	44	1.3%
2	Florida	368	10.9%
20	Georgia	46	1.4%
43	Hawaii	7	0.2%
33	Idaho	22	0.7%
8	Illinois	140	4.1%
17	Indiana	50	1.5%
31	Iowa	27	0.8%
NA	Kansas**	NA	NA
46	Kentucky	2	0.1%
22	Louisiana	43	1.3%
39	Maine	15	0.4%
13	Maryland	60	1.8%
19	Massachusetts	47	1.4%
9	Michigan	135	4.0%
5	Minnesota	187	5.5%
32	Mississippi	23	0.7%
14	Missouri	58	1.7%
46	Montana	2	0.1%
33	Nebraska	22	0.7%
23	Nevada	42	1.2%
41	New Hampshire	12	0.4%
10	New Jersey	77	2.3%
36	New Mexico	17	0.5%
15	New York	53	1.6%
27	North Carolina	32	0.9%
42	North Dakota	10	0.3%
6	Ohio	159	4.7%
10	Oklahoma	77	2.3%
27	Oregon	32	0.9%
4	Pennsylvania	256	7.6%
30	Rhode Island	30	0.9%
36	South Carolina	17	0.5%
39	South Dakota	15	0.4%
27	Tennessee	32	0.9%
1	Texas	394	11.6%
16	Utah	51	1.5%
46	Vermont	2	0.1%
18	Virginia	49	1.4%
7	Washington	152	4.5%
45	West Virginia	3	0.1%
NA	Wisconsin**	NA	NA
44	Wyoming	5	0.1%

RANK ORDER

RANK	STATE	ARRESTS	% of USA
1	Texas	394	11.6%
2	Florida	368	10.9%
3	California	347	10.3%
4	Pennsylvania	256	7.6%
5	Minnesota	187	5.5%
6	Ohio	159	4.7%
7	Washington	152	4.5%
8	Illinois	140	4.1%
9	Michigan	135	4.0%
10	New Jersey	77	2.3%
10	Oklahoma	77	2.3%
12	Colorado	74	2.2%
13	Maryland	60	1.8%
14	Missouri	58	1.7%
15	New York	53	1.6%
16	Utah	51	1.5%
17	Indiana	50	1.5%
18	Virginia	49	1.4%
19	Massachusetts	47	1.4%
20	Georgia	46	1.4%
21	Delaware	44	1.3%
22	Louisiana	43	1.3%
23	Nevada	42	1.2%
24	Arkansas	38	1.1%
25	Alabama	37	1.1%
26	Connecticut	35	1.0%
27	North Carolina	32	0.9%
27	Oregon	32	0.9%
27	Tennessee	32	0.9%
30	Rhode Island	30	0.9%
31	Iowa	27	0.8%
32	Mississippi	23	0.7%
33	Idaho	22	0.7%
33	Nebraska	22	0.7%
35	Arizona	20	0.6%
36	New Mexico	17	0.5%
36	South Carolina	17	0.5%
38	Alaska	16	0.5%
39	Maine	15	0.4%
39	South Dakota	15	0.4%
41	New Hampshire	12	0.4%
42	North Dakota	10	0.3%
43	Hawaii	7	0.2%
44	Wyoming	5	0.1%
45	West Virginia	3	0.1%
46	Kentucky	2	0.1%
46	Montana	2	0.1%
46	Vermont	2	0.1%
NA	Kansas**	NA	NA
NA	Wisconsin**	NA	NA
	District of Columbia**	NA	NA

Source: Federal Bureau of Investigation
   "Crime in the United States 2000" (Uniform Crime Reports, October 22, 2001)
*Arrests of youths 17 years and younger by law enforcement agencies submitting complete reports to the F.B.I. for 12 months in 2000. Forcible rape is the carnal knowledge of a female forcibly and against her will. Assaults or attempts to commit rape by force or threat of force are included. However, statutory rape without force and other sex offenses are excluded. See important note at beginning of this chapter. **Not available.

Reported Juvenile Arrest Rate for Rape in 2000

National Rate = 14.5 Reported Arrests per 100,000 Juvenile Population*

ALPHA ORDER

RANK	STATE	RATE
31	Alabama	10.1
12	Alaska	19.6
46	Arizona	3.7
18	Arkansas	14.1
37	California	8.6
11	Colorado	19.8
24	Connecticut	12.4
1	Delaware	100.4
9	Florida	22.6
33	Georgia	10.0
43	Hawaii	6.0
22	Idaho	13.1
2	Illinois	42.1
28	Indiana	11.1
35	Iowa	8.9
NA	Kansas**	NA
40	Kentucky	7.7
29	Louisiana	11.0
30	Maine	10.4
25	Maryland	11.7
34	Massachusetts	9.2
20	Michigan	13.5
3	Minnesota	33.2
23	Mississippi	13.0
15	Missouri	17.0
45	Montana	4.6
26	Nebraska	11.5
10	Nevada	19.9
19	New Hampshire	13.9
36	New Jersey	8.7
27	New Mexico	11.4
42	New York	7.3
44	North Carolina	4.7
17	North Dakota	14.4
7	Ohio	23.2
14	Oklahoma	18.8
31	Oregon	10.1
6	Pennsylvania	25.2
5	Rhode Island	28.1
21	South Carolina	13.2
13	South Dakota	19.5
41	Tennessee	7.4
16	Texas	15.8
8	Utah	23.1
47	Vermont	3.4
37	Virginia	8.6
4	Washington	31.6
48	West Virginia	3.2
NA	Wisconsin**	NA
39	Wyoming	7.9

RANK ORDER

RANK	STATE	RATE
1	Delaware	100.4
2	Illinois	42.1
3	Minnesota	33.2
4	Washington	31.6
5	Rhode Island	28.1
6	Pennsylvania	25.2
7	Ohio	23.2
8	Utah	23.1
9	Florida	22.6
10	Nevada	19.9
11	Colorado	19.8
12	Alaska	19.6
13	South Dakota	19.5
14	Oklahoma	18.8
15	Missouri	17.0
16	Texas	15.8
17	North Dakota	14.4
18	Arkansas	14.1
19	New Hampshire	13.9
20	Michigan	13.5
21	South Carolina	13.2
22	Idaho	13.1
23	Mississippi	13.0
24	Connecticut	12.4
25	Maryland	11.7
26	Nebraska	11.5
27	New Mexico	11.4
28	Indiana	11.1
29	Louisiana	11.0
30	Maine	10.4
31	Alabama	10.1
31	Oregon	10.1
33	Georgia	10.0
34	Massachusetts	9.2
35	Iowa	8.9
36	New Jersey	8.7
37	California	8.6
37	Virginia	8.6
39	Wyoming	7.9
40	Kentucky	7.7
41	Tennessee	7.4
42	New York	7.3
43	Hawaii	6.0
44	North Carolina	4.7
45	Montana	4.6
46	Arizona	3.7
47	Vermont	3.4
48	West Virginia	3.2
NA	Kansas**	NA
NA	Wisconsin**	NA
	District of Columbia**	NA

Source: Morgan Quitno Press using data from Federal Bureau of Investigation
    "Crime in the United States 2000" (Uniform Crime Reports, October 22, 2001)
*By law enforcement agencies submitting complete reports to the F.B.I. for 12 months in 2000. Arrests of youths 17 years and younger divided into population of 10 to 17 year olds. See important note at beginning of this chapter. Forcible rape is the carnal knowledge of a female forcibly and against her will. Assaults or attempts to commit rape by force or threat of force are included. **Not available.

201

Reported Arrests of Juveniles for Rape
As a Percent of All Such Arrests in 2000
National Percent = 16.5% of Reported Rape Arrests*

ALPHA ORDER

RANK	STATE	PERCENT
42	Alabama	10.2
14	Alaska	19.5
45	Arizona	9.3
39	Arkansas	10.8
33	California	12.9
18	Colorado	17.8
22	Connecticut	16.4
15	Delaware	19.2
21	Florida	16.6
35	Georgia	11.4
45	Hawaii	9.3
7	Idaho	22.9
9	Illinois	22.3
12	Indiana	20.7
6	Iowa	23.3
NA	Kansas**	NA
41	Kentucky	10.5
35	Louisiana	11.4
29	Maine	14.0
25	Maryland	15.1
44	Massachusetts	9.6
11	Michigan	20.8
4	Minnesota	25.3
40	Mississippi	10.6
24	Missouri	15.5
28	Montana	14.3
27	Nebraska	14.5
29	Nevada	14.0
20	New Hampshire	16.9
31	New Jersey	13.7
19	New Mexico	17.5
37	New York	11.1
43	North Carolina	10.0
1	North Dakota	33.3
5	Ohio	23.4
13	Oklahoma	19.7
32	Oregon	13.0
16	Pennsylvania	18.6
2	Rhode Island	26.3
26	South Carolina	14.7
10	South Dakota	21.7
23	Tennessee	16.2
17	Texas	18.0
3	Utah	26.2
48	Vermont	4.2
34	Virginia	12.4
8	Washington	22.6
47	West Virginia	6.8
NA	Wisconsin**	NA
37	Wyoming	11.1

RANK ORDER

RANK	STATE	PERCENT
1	North Dakota	33.3
2	Rhode Island	26.3
3	Utah	26.2
4	Minnesota	25.3
5	Ohio	23.4
6	Iowa	23.3
7	Idaho	22.9
8	Washington	22.6
9	Illinois	22.3
10	South Dakota	21.7
11	Michigan	20.8
12	Indiana	20.7
13	Oklahoma	19.7
14	Alaska	19.5
15	Delaware	19.2
16	Pennsylvania	18.6
17	Texas	18.0
18	Colorado	17.8
19	New Mexico	17.5
20	New Hampshire	16.9
21	Florida	16.6
22	Connecticut	16.4
23	Tennessee	16.2
24	Missouri	15.5
25	Maryland	15.1
26	South Carolina	14.7
27	Nebraska	14.5
28	Montana	14.3
29	Maine	14.0
29	Nevada	14.0
31	New Jersey	13.7
32	Oregon	13.0
33	California	12.9
34	Virginia	12.4
35	Georgia	11.4
35	Louisiana	11.4
37	New York	11.1
37	Wyoming	11.1
39	Arkansas	10.8
40	Mississippi	10.6
41	Kentucky	10.5
42	Alabama	10.2
43	North Carolina	10.0
44	Massachusetts	9.6
45	Arizona	9.3
45	Hawaii	9.3
47	West Virginia	6.8
48	Vermont	4.2
NA	Kansas**	NA
NA	Wisconsin**	NA

District of Columbia**   NA

Source: Morgan Quitno Press using data from Federal Bureau of Investigation
"Crime in the United States 2000" (Uniform Crime Reports, October 22, 2001)
*Arrests of youths 17 years and younger by law enforcement agencies submitting complete reports to the F.B.I. for
12 months in 2000. Forcible rape is the carnal knowledge of a female forcibly and against her will. Assaults or
attempts to commit rape by force or threat of force are included. However, statutory rape without force and other sex
offenses are excluded. **Not available.

Reported Arrests of Juveniles for Robbery in 2000

National Total = 20,718 Reported Arrests*

ALPHA ORDER

RANK	STATE	ARRESTS	% of USA
26	Alabama	185	0.9%
39	Alaska	36	0.2%
17	Arizona	277	1.3%
30	Arkansas	104	0.5%
1	California	4,965	24.0%
24	Colorado	205	1.0%
21	Connecticut	209	1.0%
32	Delaware	90	0.4%
2	Florida	2,222	10.7%
15	Georgia	304	1.5%
27	Hawaii	148	0.7%
41	Idaho	15	0.1%
6	Illinois	1,091	5.3%
18	Indiana	253	1.2%
35	Iowa	78	0.4%
NA	Kansas**	NA	NA
42	Kentucky	12	0.1%
25	Louisiana	203	1.0%
38	Maine	37	0.2%
7	Maryland	1,039	5.0%
12	Massachusetts	384	1.9%
23	Michigan	207	1.0%
14	Minnesota	339	1.6%
29	Mississippi	106	0.5%
13	Missouri	365	1.8%
42	Montana	12	0.1%
34	Nebraska	81	0.4%
20	Nevada	220	1.1%
40	New Hampshire	30	0.1%
5	New Jersey	1,195	5.8%
33	New Mexico	83	0.4%
8	New York	781	3.8%
9	North Carolina	560	2.7%
47	North Dakota	0	0.0%
10	Ohio	427	2.1%
22	Oklahoma	208	1.0%
19	Oregon	228	1.1%
3	Pennsylvania	1,540	7.4%
31	Rhode Island	101	0.5%
37	South Carolina	56	0.3%
44	South Dakota	11	0.1%
28	Tennessee	120	0.6%
4	Texas	1,439	6.9%
36	Utah	62	0.3%
47	Vermont	0	0.0%
16	Virginia	284	1.4%
11	Washington	386	1.9%
44	West Virginia	11	0.1%
NA	Wisconsin**	NA	NA
46	Wyoming	9	0.0%

RANK ORDER

RANK	STATE	ARRESTS	% of USA
1	California	4,965	24.0%
2	Florida	2,222	10.7%
3	Pennsylvania	1,540	7.4%
4	Texas	1,439	6.9%
5	New Jersey	1,195	5.8%
6	Illinois	1,091	5.3%
7	Maryland	1,039	5.0%
8	New York	781	3.8%
9	North Carolina	560	2.7%
10	Ohio	427	2.1%
11	Washington	386	1.9%
12	Massachusetts	384	1.9%
13	Missouri	365	1.8%
14	Minnesota	339	1.6%
15	Georgia	304	1.5%
16	Virginia	284	1.4%
17	Arizona	277	1.3%
18	Indiana	253	1.2%
19	Oregon	228	1.1%
20	Nevada	220	1.1%
21	Connecticut	209	1.0%
22	Oklahoma	208	1.0%
23	Michigan	207	1.0%
24	Colorado	205	1.0%
25	Louisiana	203	1.0%
26	Alabama	185	0.9%
27	Hawaii	148	0.7%
28	Tennessee	120	0.6%
29	Mississippi	106	0.5%
30	Arkansas	104	0.5%
31	Rhode Island	101	0.5%
32	Delaware	90	0.4%
33	New Mexico	83	0.4%
34	Nebraska	81	0.4%
35	Iowa	78	0.4%
36	Utah	62	0.3%
37	South Carolina	56	0.3%
38	Maine	37	0.2%
39	Alaska	36	0.2%
40	New Hampshire	30	0.1%
41	Idaho	15	0.1%
42	Kentucky	12	0.1%
42	Montana	12	0.1%
44	South Dakota	11	0.1%
44	West Virginia	11	0.1%
46	Wyoming	9	0.0%
47	North Dakota	0	0.0%
47	Vermont	0	0.0%
NA	Kansas**	NA	NA
NA	Wisconsin**	NA	NA
	District of Columbia**	NA	NA

Source: Federal Bureau of Investigation
   "Crime in the United States 2000" (Uniform Crime Reports, October 22, 2001)
*Arrests of youths 17 years and younger by law enforcement agencies submitting complete reports to the F.B.I. for 12 months in 2000. Robbery is the taking or attempting to take anything of value by force or threat of force. See important note at beginning of this chapter. **Not available.

Reported Juvenile Arrest Rate for Robbery in 2000

National Rate = 88.8 Reported Arrests per 100,000 Juvenile Population*

ALPHA ORDER

RANK	STATE	RATE
28	Alabama	50.7
32	Alaska	44.2
27	Arizona	51.4
35	Arkansas	38.5
8	California	123.6
25	Colorado	54.8
16	Connecticut	73.8
2	Delaware	205.3
5	Florida	136.2
18	Georgia	66.1
7	Hawaii	127.4
46	Idaho	8.9
1	Illinois	328.1
23	Indiana	56.2
40	Iowa	25.8
NA	Kansas**	NA
31	Kentucky	46.0
26	Louisiana	51.9
41	Maine	25.5
3	Maryland	202.5
15	Massachusetts	75.0
42	Michigan	20.6
20	Minnesota	60.3
21	Mississippi	60.0
9	Missouri	106.9
39	Montana	27.7
34	Nebraska	42.4
11	Nevada	104.2
36	New Hampshire	34.7
6	New Jersey	134.3
24	New Mexico	55.6
9	New York	106.9
13	North Carolina	81.8
47	North Dakota	0.0
19	Ohio	62.4
28	Oklahoma	50.7
17	Oregon	71.8
4	Pennsylvania	151.6
12	Rhode Island	94.5
33	South Carolina	43.6
43	South Dakota	14.3
38	Tennessee	27.8
22	Texas	57.6
37	Utah	28.1
47	Vermont	0.0
30	Virginia	49.9
14	Washington	80.2
45	West Virginia	11.9
NA	Wisconsin**	NA
44	Wyoming	14.2

RANK ORDER

RANK	STATE	RATE
1	Illinois	328.1
2	Delaware	205.3
3	Maryland	202.5
4	Pennsylvania	151.6
5	Florida	136.2
6	New Jersey	134.3
7	Hawaii	127.4
8	California	123.6
9	Missouri	106.9
9	New York	106.9
11	Nevada	104.2
12	Rhode Island	94.5
13	North Carolina	81.8
14	Washington	80.2
15	Massachusetts	75.0
16	Connecticut	73.8
17	Oregon	71.8
18	Georgia	66.1
19	Ohio	62.4
20	Minnesota	60.3
21	Mississippi	60.0
22	Texas	57.6
23	Indiana	56.2
24	New Mexico	55.6
25	Colorado	54.8
26	Louisiana	51.9
27	Arizona	51.4
28	Alabama	50.7
28	Oklahoma	50.7
30	Virginia	49.9
31	Kentucky	46.0
32	Alaska	44.2
33	South Carolina	43.6
34	Nebraska	42.4
35	Arkansas	38.5
36	New Hampshire	34.7
37	Utah	28.1
38	Tennessee	27.8
39	Montana	27.7
40	Iowa	25.8
41	Maine	25.5
42	Michigan	20.6
43	South Dakota	14.3
44	Wyoming	14.2
45	West Virginia	11.9
46	Idaho	8.9
47	North Dakota	0.0
47	Vermont	0.0
NA	Kansas**	NA
NA	Wisconsin**	NA
	District of Columbia**	NA

Source: Morgan Quitno Press using data from Federal Bureau of Investigation
    "Crime in the United States 2000" (Uniform Crime Reports, October 22, 2001)
*By law enforcement agencies submitting complete reports to the F.B.I. for 12 months in 2000. Arrests of youths 17 years and younger divided into population of 10 to 17 year olds. See important note at beginning of this chapter. Robbery is the taking or attempting to take anything of value by force or threat of force.
**Not available.

Reported Arrests of Juveniles for Robbery
As a Percent of All Such Arrests in 2000
National Percent = 25.2% of Reported Robbery Arrests*

ALPHA ORDER

RANK	STATE	PERCENT
41	Alabama	16.0
10	Alaska	29.5
31	Arizona	19.4
44	Arkansas	13.6
13	California	29.0
8	Colorado	30.6
26	Connecticut	22.1
27	Delaware	21.3
21	Florida	24.3
42	Georgia	15.4
6	Hawaii	31.3
35	Idaho	18.1
4	Illinois	36.4
38	Indiana	17.0
18	Iowa	25.6
NA	Kansas**	NA
37	Kentucky	17.1
36	Louisiana	17.6
19	Maine	25.2
3	Maryland	37.1
16	Massachusetts	27.2
28	Michigan	20.8
5	Minnesota	31.8
39	Mississippi	16.9
29	Missouri	20.7
2	Montana	48.0
17	Nebraska	26.0
34	Nevada	18.4
7	New Hampshire	30.9
12	New Jersey	29.3
32	New Mexico	18.9
11	New York	29.4
40	North Carolina	16.4
47	North Dakota	0.0
33	Ohio	18.8
9	Oklahoma	30.5
25	Oregon	22.2
20	Pennsylvania	24.8
1	Rhode Island	48.3
43	South Carolina	14.5
15	South Dakota	28.2
45	Tennessee	13.4
22	Texas	23.7
30	Utah	20.3
47	Vermont	0.0
24	Virginia	23.3
14	Washington	28.8
46	West Virginia	11.5
NA	Wisconsin**	NA
22	Wyoming	23.7

RANK ORDER

RANK	STATE	PERCENT
1	Rhode Island	48.3
2	Montana	48.0
3	Maryland	37.1
4	Illinois	36.4
5	Minnesota	31.8
6	Hawaii	31.3
7	New Hampshire	30.9
8	Colorado	30.6
9	Oklahoma	30.5
10	Alaska	29.5
11	New York	29.4
12	New Jersey	29.3
13	California	29.0
14	Washington	28.8
15	South Dakota	28.2
16	Massachusetts	27.2
17	Nebraska	26.0
18	Iowa	25.6
19	Maine	25.2
20	Pennsylvania	24.8
21	Florida	24.3
22	Texas	23.7
22	Wyoming	23.7
24	Virginia	23.3
25	Oregon	22.2
26	Connecticut	22.1
27	Delaware	21.3
28	Michigan	20.8
29	Missouri	20.7
30	Utah	20.3
31	Arizona	19.4
32	New Mexico	18.9
33	Ohio	18.8
34	Nevada	18.4
35	Idaho	18.1
36	Louisiana	17.6
37	Kentucky	17.1
38	Indiana	17.0
39	Mississippi	16.9
40	North Carolina	16.4
41	Alabama	16.0
42	Georgia	15.4
43	South Carolina	14.5
44	Arkansas	13.6
45	Tennessee	13.4
46	West Virginia	11.5
47	North Dakota	0.0
47	Vermont	0.0
NA	Kansas**	NA
NA	Wisconsin**	NA
	District of Columbia**	NA

Source: Morgan Quitno Press using data from Federal Bureau of Investigation
   "Crime in the United States 2000" (Uniform Crime Reports, October 22, 2001)
*Arrests of youths 17 years and younger by law enforcement agencies submitting complete reports to the F.B.I. for 12 months in 2000. Robbery is the taking or attempting to take anything of value by force or threat of force.
**Not available.

Reported Arrests of Juveniles for Aggravated Assault in 2000

National Total = 51,982 Reported Arrests*

ALPHA ORDER

RANK	STATE	ARRESTS	% of USA
32	Alabama	302	0.6%
37	Alaska	143	0.3%
12	Arizona	1,273	2.4%
29	Arkansas	332	0.6%
1	California	10,843	20.9%
22	Colorado	606	1.2%
25	Connecticut	541	1.0%
30	Delaware	326	0.6%
2	Florida	7,385	14.2%
18	Georgia	838	1.6%
38	Hawaii	129	0.2%
34	Idaho	256	0.5%
7	Illinois	1,822	3.5%
13	Indiana	1,271	2.4%
21	Iowa	632	1.2%
NA	Kansas**	NA	NA
46	Kentucky	39	0.1%
11	Louisiana	1,326	2.6%
39	Maine	122	0.2%
8	Maryland	1,578	3.0%
6	Massachusetts	1,859	3.6%
14	Michigan	1,138	2.2%
15	Minnesota	1,054	2.0%
39	Mississippi	122	0.2%
20	Missouri	659	1.3%
36	Montana	149	0.3%
41	Nebraska	118	0.2%
33	Nevada	261	0.5%
45	New Hampshire	41	0.1%
5	New Jersey	1,919	3.7%
31	New Mexico	313	0.6%
10	New York	1,444	2.8%
9	North Carolina	1,532	2.9%
48	North Dakota	12	0.0%
17	Ohio	894	1.7%
19	Oklahoma	718	1.4%
26	Oregon	367	0.7%
4	Pennsylvania	2,867	5.5%
35	Rhode Island	162	0.3%
28	South Carolina	336	0.6%
43	South Dakota	79	0.2%
23	Tennessee	600	1.2%
3	Texas	3,465	6.7%
27	Utah	356	0.7%
47	Vermont	30	0.1%
24	Virginia	555	1.1%
16	Washington	1,018	2.0%
44	West Virginia	63	0.1%
NA	Wisconsin**	NA	NA
42	Wyoming	87	0.2%

RANK ORDER

RANK	STATE	ARRESTS	% of USA
1	California	10,843	20.9%
2	Florida	7,385	14.2%
3	Texas	3,465	6.7%
4	Pennsylvania	2,867	5.5%
5	New Jersey	1,919	3.7%
6	Massachusetts	1,859	3.6%
7	Illinois	1,822	3.5%
8	Maryland	1,578	3.0%
9	North Carolina	1,532	2.9%
10	New York	1,444	2.8%
11	Louisiana	1,326	2.6%
12	Arizona	1,273	2.4%
13	Indiana	1,271	2.4%
14	Michigan	1,138	2.2%
15	Minnesota	1,054	2.0%
16	Washington	1,018	2.0%
17	Ohio	894	1.7%
18	Georgia	838	1.6%
19	Oklahoma	718	1.4%
20	Missouri	659	1.3%
21	Iowa	632	1.2%
22	Colorado	606	1.2%
23	Tennessee	600	1.2%
24	Virginia	555	1.1%
25	Connecticut	541	1.0%
26	Oregon	367	0.7%
27	Utah	356	0.7%
28	South Carolina	336	0.6%
29	Arkansas	332	0.6%
30	Delaware	326	0.6%
31	New Mexico	313	0.6%
32	Alabama	302	0.6%
33	Nevada	261	0.5%
34	Idaho	256	0.5%
35	Rhode Island	162	0.3%
36	Montana	149	0.3%
37	Alaska	143	0.3%
38	Hawaii	129	0.2%
39	Maine	122	0.2%
39	Mississippi	122	0.2%
41	Nebraska	118	0.2%
42	Wyoming	87	0.2%
43	South Dakota	79	0.2%
44	West Virginia	63	0.1%
45	New Hampshire	41	0.1%
46	Kentucky	39	0.1%
47	Vermont	30	0.1%
48	North Dakota	12	0.0%
NA	Kansas**	NA	NA
NA	Wisconsin**	NA	NA
	District of Columbia**	NA	NA

Source: Federal Bureau of Investigation
    "Crime in the United States 2000" (Uniform Crime Reports, October 22, 2001)
*Arrests of youths 17 years and younger by law enforcement agencies submitting complete reports to the F.B.I. for 12 months in 2000. Aggravated assault is an attack for the purpose of inflicting severe bodily injury. See important note at beginning of this chapter.
**Not available.

Reported Juvenile Arrest Rate for Aggravated Assault in 2000

National Rate = 222.7 Reported Arrests per 100,000 Population*

ALPHA ORDER

RANK	STATE	RATE
42	Alabama	82.8
23	Alaska	175.6
12	Arizona	236.1
35	Arkansas	123.0
10	California	269.9
25	Colorado	162.0
20	Connecticut	191.2
1	Delaware	743.7
3	Florida	452.6
22	Georgia	182.3
38	Hawaii	111.0
27	Idaho	151.9
2	Illinois	548.0
9	Indiana	282.2
17	Iowa	208.7
NA	Kansas**	NA
29	Kentucky	149.5
6	Louisiana	338.7
41	Maine	84.2
7	Maryland	307.5
4	Massachusetts	363.0
37	Michigan	113.4
21	Minnesota	187.4
43	Mississippi	69.1
19	Missouri	193.0
5	Montana	343.4
45	Nebraska	61.8
34	Nevada	123.6
47	New Hampshire	47.4
14	New Jersey	215.7
16	New Mexico	209.8
18	New York	197.7
13	North Carolina	223.9
48	North Dakota	17.3
33	Ohio	130.6
24	Oklahoma	174.9
36	Oregon	115.6
8	Pennsylvania	282.3
28	Rhode Island	151.5
11	South Carolina	261.5
39	South Dakota	102.6
30	Tennessee	139.1
31	Texas	138.7
26	Utah	161.4
46	Vermont	51.4
40	Virginia	97.6
15	Washington	211.5
44	West Virginia	68.0
NA	Wisconsin**	NA
32	Wyoming	137.1

RANK ORDER

RANK	STATE	RATE
1	Delaware	743.7
2	Illinois	548.0
3	Florida	452.6
4	Massachusetts	363.0
5	Montana	343.4
6	Louisiana	338.7
7	Maryland	307.5
8	Pennsylvania	282.3
9	Indiana	282.2
10	California	269.9
11	South Carolina	261.5
12	Arizona	236.1
13	North Carolina	223.9
14	New Jersey	215.7
15	Washington	211.5
16	New Mexico	209.8
17	Iowa	208.7
18	New York	197.7
19	Missouri	193.0
20	Connecticut	191.2
21	Minnesota	187.4
22	Georgia	182.3
23	Alaska	175.6
24	Oklahoma	174.9
25	Colorado	162.0
26	Utah	161.4
27	Idaho	151.9
28	Rhode Island	151.5
29	Kentucky	149.5
30	Tennessee	139.1
31	Texas	138.7
32	Wyoming	137.1
33	Ohio	130.6
34	Nevada	123.6
35	Arkansas	123.0
36	Oregon	115.6
37	Michigan	113.4
38	Hawaii	111.0
39	South Dakota	102.6
40	Virginia	97.6
41	Maine	84.2
42	Alabama	82.8
43	Mississippi	69.1
44	West Virginia	68.0
45	Nebraska	61.8
46	Vermont	51.4
47	New Hampshire	47.4
48	North Dakota	17.3
NA	Kansas**	NA
NA	Wisconsin**	NA
	District of Columbia**	NA

Source: Morgan Quitno Press using data from Federal Bureau of Investigation
"Crime in the United States 2000" (Uniform Crime Reports, October 22, 2001)
*By law enforcement agencies submitting complete reports to the F.B.I. for 12 months in 2000. Arrests of youths 17 years and younger divided into population of 10 to 17 year olds. See important note at beginning of this chapter. Aggravated assault is an attack for the purpose of inflicting severe bodily injury.
**Not available.

Reported Arrests of Juveniles for Aggravated Assault
As a Percent of All Such Arrests in 2000
National Percent = 14.3% of Reported Aggravated Assault Arrests*

ALPHA ORDER

RANK	STATE	PERCENT
47	Alabama	7.5
31	Alaska	14.6
9	Arizona	20.1
44	Arkansas	9.0
41	California	10.0
28	Colorado	15.2
22	Connecticut	16.4
10	Delaware	20.0
17	Florida	17.6
42	Georgia	9.7
13	Hawaii	18.7
7	Idaho	21.8
2	Illinois	29.6
27	Indiana	15.6
19	Iowa	17.2
NA	Kansas**	NA
33	Kentucky	13.8
26	Louisiana	15.7
11	Maine	19.4
3	Maryland	24.0
24	Massachusetts	16.0
28	Michigan	15.2
4	Minnesota	23.4
46	Mississippi	7.8
38	Missouri	12.4
5	Montana	23.1
36	Nebraska	12.6
21	Nevada	16.6
20	New Hampshire	16.9
15	New Jersey	18.1
32	New Mexico	14.4
16	New York	17.7
43	North Carolina	9.4
40	North Dakota	11.0
38	Ohio	12.4
28	Oklahoma	15.2
12	Oregon	19.0
14	Pennsylvania	18.6
6	Rhode Island	22.9
34	South Carolina	13.7
18	South Dakota	17.5
45	Tennessee	8.7
23	Texas	16.1
1	Utah	35.7
35	Vermont	13.2
36	Virginia	12.6
8	Washington	20.2
48	West Virginia	5.5
NA	Wisconsin**	NA
25	Wyoming	15.8

RANK ORDER

RANK	STATE	PERCENT
1	Utah	35.7
2	Illinois	29.6
3	Maryland	24.0
4	Minnesota	23.4
5	Montana	23.1
6	Rhode Island	22.9
7	Idaho	21.8
8	Washington	20.2
9	Arizona	20.1
10	Delaware	20.0
11	Maine	19.4
12	Oregon	19.0
13	Hawaii	18.7
14	Pennsylvania	18.6
15	New Jersey	18.1
16	New York	17.7
17	Florida	17.6
18	South Dakota	17.5
19	Iowa	17.2
20	New Hampshire	16.9
21	Nevada	16.6
22	Connecticut	16.4
23	Texas	16.1
24	Massachusetts	16.0
25	Wyoming	15.8
26	Louisiana	15.7
27	Indiana	15.6
28	Colorado	15.2
28	Michigan	15.2
28	Oklahoma	15.2
31	Alaska	14.6
32	New Mexico	14.4
33	Kentucky	13.8
34	South Carolina	13.7
35	Vermont	13.2
36	Nebraska	12.6
36	Virginia	12.6
38	Missouri	12.4
38	Ohio	12.4
40	North Dakota	11.0
41	California	10.0
42	Georgia	9.7
43	North Carolina	9.4
44	Arkansas	9.0
45	Tennessee	8.7
46	Mississippi	7.8
47	Alabama	7.5
48	West Virginia	5.5
NA	Kansas**	NA
NA	Wisconsin**	NA
	District of Columbia**	NA

Source: Morgan Quitno Press using data from Federal Bureau of Investigation
"Crime in the United States 2000" (Uniform Crime Reports, October 22, 2001)
*Arrests of youths 17 years and younger by law enforcement agencies submitting complete reports to the F.B.I. for 12 months in 2000. Aggravated assault is an attack for the purpose of inflicting severe bodily injury.
**Not available.

Reported Arrests of Juveniles for Property Crimes in 2000

National Total = 392,641 Reported Arrests*

ALPHA ORDER

RANK	STATE	ARRESTS	% of USA
33	Alabama	3,004	0.8%
37	Alaska	2,082	0.5%
7	Arizona	11,771	3.0%
30	Arkansas	3,972	1.0%
1	California	56,793	14.5%
13	Colorado	9,838	2.5%
28	Connecticut	4,395	1.1%
40	Delaware	1,570	0.4%
2	Florida	40,017	10.2%
21	Georgia	6,354	1.6%
38	Hawaii	2,035	0.5%
29	Idaho	4,145	1.1%
15	Illinois	9,177	2.3%
17	Indiana	7,781	2.0%
23	Iowa	5,890	1.5%
NA	Kansas**	NA	NA
48	Kentucky	519	0.1%
19	Louisiana	7,060	1.8%
34	Maine	2,756	0.7%
14	Maryland	9,805	2.5%
31	Massachusetts	3,508	0.9%
10	Michigan	10,918	2.8%
6	Minnesota	12,258	3.1%
32	Mississippi	3,445	0.9%
18	Missouri	7,596	1.9%
46	Montana	814	0.2%
26	Nebraska	4,725	1.2%
25	Nevada	5,108	1.3%
44	New Hampshire	881	0.2%
9	New Jersey	11,314	2.9%
35	New Mexico	2,191	0.6%
11	New York	10,461	2.7%
8	North Carolina	11,622	3.0%
41	North Dakota	1,544	0.4%
12	Ohio	10,191	2.6%
20	Oklahoma	6,893	1.8%
16	Oregon	7,930	2.0%
4	Pennsylvania	14,778	3.8%
42	Rhode Island	1,527	0.4%
36	South Carolina	2,177	0.6%
39	South Dakota	1,704	0.4%
27	Tennessee	4,520	1.2%
3	Texas	38,835	9.9%
21	Utah	6,354	1.6%
47	Vermont	540	0.1%
24	Virginia	5,741	1.5%
5	Washington	14,080	3.6%
45	West Virginia	818	0.2%
NA	Wisconsin**	NA	NA
43	Wyoming	1,204	0.3%

RANK ORDER

RANK	STATE	ARRESTS	% of USA
1	California	56,793	14.5%
2	Florida	40,017	10.2%
3	Texas	38,835	9.9%
4	Pennsylvania	14,778	3.8%
5	Washington	14,080	3.6%
6	Minnesota	12,258	3.1%
7	Arizona	11,771	3.0%
8	North Carolina	11,622	3.0%
9	New Jersey	11,314	2.9%
10	Michigan	10,918	2.8%
11	New York	10,461	2.7%
12	Ohio	10,191	2.6%
13	Colorado	9,838	2.5%
14	Maryland	9,805	2.5%
15	Illinois	9,177	2.3%
16	Oregon	7,930	2.0%
17	Indiana	7,781	2.0%
18	Missouri	7,596	1.9%
19	Louisiana	7,060	1.8%
20	Oklahoma	6,893	1.8%
21	Georgia	6,354	1.6%
21	Utah	6,354	1.6%
23	Iowa	5,890	1.5%
24	Virginia	5,741	1.5%
25	Nevada	5,108	1.3%
26	Nebraska	4,725	1.2%
27	Tennessee	4,520	1.2%
28	Connecticut	4,395	1.1%
29	Idaho	4,145	1.1%
30	Arkansas	3,972	1.0%
31	Massachusetts	3,508	0.9%
32	Mississippi	3,445	0.9%
33	Alabama	3,004	0.8%
34	Maine	2,756	0.7%
35	New Mexico	2,191	0.6%
36	South Carolina	2,177	0.6%
37	Alaska	2,082	0.5%
38	Hawaii	2,035	0.5%
39	South Dakota	1,704	0.4%
40	Delaware	1,570	0.4%
41	North Dakota	1,544	0.4%
42	Rhode Island	1,527	0.4%
43	Wyoming	1,204	0.3%
44	New Hampshire	881	0.2%
45	West Virginia	818	0.2%
46	Montana	814	0.2%
47	Vermont	540	0.1%
48	Kentucky	519	0.1%
NA	Kansas**	NA	NA
NA	Wisconsin**	NA	NA
	District of Columbia**	NA	NA

Source: Federal Bureau of Investigation
   "Crime in the United States 2000" (Uniform Crime Reports, October 22, 2001)
*Arrests of youths 17 years and younger by law enforcement agencies submitting complete reports to the F.B.I. for 12 months in 2000. Property crimes are offenses of burglary, larceny-theft, motor vehicle theft and arson. See important note at beginning of this chapter.
**Not available.

Reported Juvenile Arrest Rate for Property Crime in 2000

National Rate = 1,682.1 Reported Arrests per 100,000 Juvenile Population*

ALPHA ORDER

RANK	STATE	RATE
47	Alabama	823.3
6	Alaska	2,556.1
15	Arizona	2,183.1
33	Arkansas	1,471.3
38	California	1,413.4
5	Colorado	2,629.4
31	Connecticut	1,552.9
1	Delaware	3,581.8
10	Florida	2,452.4
39	Georgia	1,382.1
25	Hawaii	1,751.4
9	Idaho	2,458.9
4	Illinois	2,760.2
26	Indiana	1,727.9
19	Iowa	1,944.6
NA	Kansas**	NA
17	Kentucky	1,989.0
24	Louisiana	1,803.6
21	Maine	1,901.7
20	Maryland	1,911.0
48	Massachusetts	685.0
41	Michigan	1,088.0
16	Minnesota	2,178.9
18	Mississippi	1,951.4
12	Missouri	2,224.5
23	Montana	1,875.9
8	Nebraska	2,474.0
11	Nevada	2,418.5
43	New Hampshire	1,018.4
40	New Jersey	1,271.8
34	New Mexico	1,468.8
36	New York	1,432.3
27	North Carolina	1,698.5
13	North Dakota	2,223.0
32	Ohio	1,488.4
29	Oklahoma	1,678.6
7	Oregon	2,497.0
35	Pennsylvania	1,454.9
37	Rhode Island	1,428.0
28	South Carolina	1,694.3
14	South Dakota	2,214.0
42	Tennessee	1,047.6
30	Texas	1,554.1
3	Utah	2,880.4
45	Vermont	925.4
44	Virginia	1,009.1
2	Washington	2,924.6
46	West Virginia	882.3
NA	Wisconsin**	NA
22	Wyoming	1,897.9

RANK ORDER

RANK	STATE	RATE
1	Delaware	3,581.8
2	Washington	2,924.6
3	Utah	2,880.4
4	Illinois	2,760.2
5	Colorado	2,629.4
6	Alaska	2,556.1
7	Oregon	2,497.0
8	Nebraska	2,474.0
9	Idaho	2,458.9
10	Florida	2,452.4
11	Nevada	2,418.5
12	Missouri	2,224.5
13	North Dakota	2,223.0
14	South Dakota	2,214.0
15	Arizona	2,183.1
16	Minnesota	2,178.9
17	Kentucky	1,989.0
18	Mississippi	1,951.4
19	Iowa	1,944.6
20	Maryland	1,911.0
21	Maine	1,901.7
22	Wyoming	1,897.9
23	Montana	1,875.9
24	Louisiana	1,803.6
25	Hawaii	1,751.4
26	Indiana	1,727.9
27	North Carolina	1,698.5
28	South Carolina	1,694.3
29	Oklahoma	1,678.6
30	Texas	1,554.1
31	Connecticut	1,552.9
32	Ohio	1,488.4
33	Arkansas	1,471.3
34	New Mexico	1,468.8
35	Pennsylvania	1,454.9
36	New York	1,432.3
37	Rhode Island	1,428.0
38	California	1,413.4
39	Georgia	1,382.1
40	New Jersey	1,271.8
41	Michigan	1,088.0
42	Tennessee	1,047.6
43	New Hampshire	1,018.4
44	Virginia	1,009.1
45	Vermont	925.4
46	West Virginia	882.3
47	Alabama	823.3
48	Massachusetts	685.0
NA	Kansas**	NA
NA	Wisconsin**	NA
	District of Columbia**	NA

Source: Morgan Quitno Press using data from Federal Bureau of Investigation
"Crime in the United States 2000" (Uniform Crime Reports, October 22, 2001)
*By law enforcement agencies submitting complete reports to the F.B.I. for 12 months in 2000. Arrests of youths 17 years and younger divided into population of 10 to 17 year olds. See important note at beginning of this chapter. Property crimes are offenses of burglary, larceny-theft, motor vehicle theft and arson.
**Not available.

Reported Arrests of Juveniles for Property Crime
As a Percent of All Such Arrests in 2000
National Percent = 32.2% of Reported Property Crime Arrests*

ALPHA ORDER

RANK	STATE	PERCENT
48	Alabama	19.7
6	Alaska	45.9
25	Arizona	31.5
42	Arkansas	24.9
22	California	34.0
17	Colorado	37.2
34	Connecticut	29.1
33	Delaware	29.5
24	Florida	32.5
46	Georgia	22.9
29	Hawaii	30.6
2	Idaho	50.9
47	Illinois	22.4
21	Indiana	34.1
9	Iowa	43.1
NA	Kansas**	NA
29	Kentucky	30.6
38	Louisiana	27.1
16	Maine	38.6
23	Maryland	32.8
43	Massachusetts	23.8
14	Michigan	39.5
4	Minnesota	47.2
37	Mississippi	27.5
40	Missouri	26.5
3	Montana	48.5
11	Nebraska	41.6
34	Nevada	29.1
7	New Hampshire	43.6
32	New Jersey	29.6
20	New Mexico	34.3
36	New York	28.3
44	North Carolina	23.1
1	North Dakota	55.9
27	Ohio	31.1
12	Oklahoma	40.7
26	Oregon	31.2
31	Pennsylvania	30.4
15	Rhode Island	39.3
27	South Carolina	31.1
5	South Dakota	46.7
44	Tennessee	23.1
19	Texas	34.6
8	Utah	43.5
18	Vermont	36.3
41	Virginia	26.4
13	Washington	40.2
39	West Virginia	26.6
NA	Wisconsin**	NA
10	Wyoming	42.0

RANK ORDER

RANK	STATE	PERCENT
1	North Dakota	55.9
2	Idaho	50.9
3	Montana	48.5
4	Minnesota	47.2
5	South Dakota	46.7
6	Alaska	45.9
7	New Hampshire	43.6
8	Utah	43.5
9	Iowa	43.1
10	Wyoming	42.0
11	Nebraska	41.6
12	Oklahoma	40.7
13	Washington	40.2
14	Michigan	39.5
15	Rhode Island	39.3
16	Maine	38.6
17	Colorado	37.2
18	Vermont	36.3
19	Texas	34.6
20	New Mexico	34.3
21	Indiana	34.1
22	California	34.0
23	Maryland	32.8
24	Florida	32.5
25	Arizona	31.5
26	Oregon	31.2
27	Ohio	31.1
27	South Carolina	31.1
29	Hawaii	30.6
29	Kentucky	30.6
31	Pennsylvania	30.4
32	New Jersey	29.6
33	Delaware	29.5
34	Connecticut	29.1
34	Nevada	29.1
36	New York	28.3
37	Mississippi	27.5
38	Louisiana	27.1
39	West Virginia	26.6
40	Missouri	26.5
41	Virginia	26.4
42	Arkansas	24.9
43	Massachusetts	23.8
44	North Carolina	23.1
44	Tennessee	23.1
46	Georgia	22.9
47	Illinois	22.4
48	Alabama	19.7
NA	Kansas**	NA
NA	Wisconsin**	NA
	District of Columbia**	NA

Source: Morgan Quitno Press using data from Federal Bureau of Investigation
"Crime in the United States 2000" (Uniform Crime Reports, October 22, 2001)
*Arrests of youths 17 years and younger by law enforcement agencies submitting complete reports to the F.B.I. for 12 months in 2000. Property crimes are offenses of burglary, larceny-theft, motor vehicle theft and arson.
**Not available.

Reported Arrests of Juveniles for Burglary in 2000

National Total = 73,207 Reported Arrests*

ALPHA ORDER

RANK	STATE	ARRESTS	% of USA
31	Alabama	554	0.8%
37	Alaska	344	0.5%
10	Arizona	1,819	2.5%
25	Arkansas	780	1.1%
1	California	15,938	21.8%
20	Colorado	991	1.4%
29	Connecticut	615	0.8%
38	Delaware	332	0.5%
2	Florida	9,648	13.2%
22	Georgia	969	1.3%
39	Hawaii	277	0.4%
30	Idaho	602	0.8%
15	Illinois	1,351	1.8%
24	Indiana	902	1.2%
23	Iowa	914	1.2%
NA	Kansas**	NA	NA
48	Kentucky	54	0.1%
12	Louisiana	1,684	2.3%
32	Maine	514	0.7%
8	Maryland	1,954	2.7%
26	Massachusetts	704	1.0%
13	Michigan	1,479	2.0%
14	Minnesota	1,451	2.0%
28	Mississippi	650	0.9%
18	Missouri	1,042	1.4%
47	Montana	77	0.1%
34	Nebraska	419	0.6%
17	Nevada	1,044	1.4%
44	New Hampshire	132	0.2%
9	New Jersey	1,848	2.5%
36	New Mexico	350	0.5%
7	New York	2,045	2.8%
5	North Carolina	2,721	3.7%
45	North Dakota	131	0.2%
11	Ohio	1,778	2.4%
19	Oklahoma	1,002	1.4%
16	Oregon	1,051	1.4%
4	Pennsylvania	2,819	3.9%
40	Rhode Island	260	0.4%
35	South Carolina	410	0.6%
41	South Dakota	237	0.3%
27	Tennessee	651	0.9%
3	Texas	6,658	9.1%
33	Utah	501	0.7%
46	Vermont	117	0.2%
21	Virginia	984	1.3%
6	Washington	2,072	2.8%
42	West Virginia	171	0.2%
NA	Wisconsin**	NA	NA
43	Wyoming	161	0.2%

RANK ORDER

RANK	STATE	ARRESTS	% of USA
1	California	15,938	21.8%
2	Florida	9,648	13.2%
3	Texas	6,658	9.1%
4	Pennsylvania	2,819	3.9%
5	North Carolina	2,721	3.7%
6	Washington	2,072	2.8%
7	New York	2,045	2.8%
8	Maryland	1,954	2.7%
9	New Jersey	1,848	2.5%
10	Arizona	1,819	2.5%
11	Ohio	1,778	2.4%
12	Louisiana	1,684	2.3%
13	Michigan	1,479	2.0%
14	Minnesota	1,451	2.0%
15	Illinois	1,351	1.8%
16	Oregon	1,051	1.4%
17	Nevada	1,044	1.4%
18	Missouri	1,042	1.4%
19	Oklahoma	1,002	1.4%
20	Colorado	991	1.4%
21	Virginia	984	1.3%
22	Georgia	969	1.3%
23	Iowa	914	1.2%
24	Indiana	902	1.2%
25	Arkansas	780	1.1%
26	Massachusetts	704	1.0%
27	Tennessee	651	0.9%
28	Mississippi	650	0.9%
29	Connecticut	615	0.8%
30	Idaho	602	0.8%
31	Alabama	554	0.8%
32	Maine	514	0.7%
33	Utah	501	0.7%
34	Nebraska	419	0.6%
35	South Carolina	410	0.6%
36	New Mexico	350	0.5%
37	Alaska	344	0.5%
38	Delaware	332	0.5%
39	Hawaii	277	0.4%
40	Rhode Island	260	0.4%
41	South Dakota	237	0.3%
42	West Virginia	171	0.2%
43	Wyoming	161	0.2%
44	New Hampshire	132	0.2%
45	North Dakota	131	0.2%
46	Vermont	117	0.2%
47	Montana	77	0.1%
48	Kentucky	54	0.1%
NA	Kansas**	NA	NA
NA	Wisconsin**	NA	NA
	District of Columbia**	NA	NA

Source: Federal Bureau of Investigation
    "Crime in the United States 2000" (Uniform Crime Reports, October 22, 2001)
*Arrests of youths 17 years and younger by law enforcement agencies submitting complete reports to the F.B.I. for 12 months in 2000. Burglary is the unlawful entry of a structure to commit a felony or theft. Attempts are included. See important note at beginning of this chapter.
**Not available.

Reported Juvenile Arrest Rate for Burglary in 2000

National Rate = 313.6 Reported Arrests per 100,000 Juvenile Population*

ALPHA ORDER

RANK	STATE	RATE
45	Alabama	151.8
6	Alaska	422.3
14	Arizona	337.4
20	Arkansas	288.9
9	California	396.7
24	Colorado	264.9
34	Connecticut	217.3
1	Delaware	757.4
2	Florida	591.3
35	Georgia	210.8
30	Hawaii	238.4
12	Idaho	357.1
7	Illinois	406.3
39	Indiana	200.3
19	Iowa	301.8
NA	Kansas**	NA
37	Kentucky	207.0
5	Louisiana	430.2
13	Maine	354.7
10	Maryland	380.8
48	Massachusetts	137.5
47	Michigan	147.4
26	Minnesota	257.9
11	Mississippi	368.2
18	Missouri	305.1
42	Montana	177.4
33	Nebraska	219.4
3	Nevada	494.3
44	New Hampshire	152.6
36	New Jersey	207.7
31	New Mexico	234.6
21	New York	280.0
8	North Carolina	397.7
40	North Dakota	188.6
25	Ohio	259.7
28	Oklahoma	244.0
15	Oregon	330.9
22	Pennsylvania	277.5
29	Rhode Island	243.1
16	South Carolina	319.1
17	South Dakota	307.9
46	Tennessee	150.9
23	Texas	266.4
32	Utah	227.1
38	Vermont	200.5
43	Virginia	173.0
4	Washington	430.4
41	West Virginia	184.4
NA	Wisconsin**	NA
27	Wyoming	253.8

RANK ORDER

RANK	STATE	RATE
1	Delaware	757.4
2	Florida	591.3
3	Nevada	494.3
4	Washington	430.4
5	Louisiana	430.2
6	Alaska	422.3
7	Illinois	406.3
8	North Carolina	397.7
9	California	396.7
10	Maryland	380.8
11	Mississippi	368.2
12	Idaho	357.1
13	Maine	354.7
14	Arizona	337.4
15	Oregon	330.9
16	South Carolina	319.1
17	South Dakota	307.9
18	Missouri	305.1
19	Iowa	301.8
20	Arkansas	288.9
21	New York	280.0
22	Pennsylvania	277.5
23	Texas	266.4
24	Colorado	264.9
25	Ohio	259.7
26	Minnesota	257.9
27	Wyoming	253.8
28	Oklahoma	244.0
29	Rhode Island	243.1
30	Hawaii	238.4
31	New Mexico	234.6
32	Utah	227.1
33	Nebraska	219.4
34	Connecticut	217.3
35	Georgia	210.8
36	New Jersey	207.7
37	Kentucky	207.0
38	Vermont	200.5
39	Indiana	200.3
40	North Dakota	188.6
41	West Virginia	184.4
42	Montana	177.4
43	Virginia	173.0
44	New Hampshire	152.6
45	Alabama	151.8
46	Tennessee	150.9
47	Michigan	147.4
48	Massachusetts	137.5
NA	Kansas**	NA
NA	Wisconsin**	NA
	District of Columbia**	NA

Source: Morgan Quitno Press using data from Federal Bureau of Investigation
 "Crime in the United States 2000" (Uniform Crime Reports, October 22, 2001)
*By law enforcement agencies submitting complete reports to the F.B.I. for 12 months in 2000. Arrests of youths 17 years and younger divided into population of 10 to 17 year olds. See important note at beginning of this chapter. Burglary is the unlawful entry of a structure to commit a felony or theft. Attempts are included.
**Not available.

Reported Arrests of Juveniles for Burglary
As a Percent of All Such Arrests in 2000
National Percent = 33.6% of Reported Burglary Arrests*

RANK	STATE	PERCENT
45	Alabama	22.5
1	Alaska	59.7
10	Arizona	41.4
39	Arkansas	28.7
25	California	33.9
14	Colorado	40.1
36	Connecticut	29.6
34	Delaware	30.7
19	Florida	37.0
48	Georgia	21.4
24	Hawaii	34.7
2	Idaho	50.9
29	Illinois	32.8
40	Indiana	28.6
7	Iowa	42.6
NA	Kansas**	NA
35	Kentucky	30.3
31	Louisiana	32.0
18	Maine	38.7
30	Maryland	32.2
43	Massachusetts	28.0
14	Michigan	40.1
8	Minnesota	42.2
36	Mississippi	29.6
42	Missouri	28.1
6	Montana	43.8
20	Nebraska	36.9
44	Nevada	23.1
5	New Hampshire	44.6
38	New Jersey	29.0
28	New Mexico	33.3
23	New York	35.1
47	North Carolina	22.1
3	North Dakota	46.0
26	Ohio	33.5
21	Oklahoma	36.4
21	Oregon	36.4
31	Pennsylvania	32.0
16	Rhode Island	39.6
27	South Carolina	33.4
4	South Dakota	45.4
46	Tennessee	22.3
17	Texas	39.3
11	Utah	41.2
8	Vermont	42.2
41	Virginia	28.2
13	Washington	40.2
33	West Virginia	31.3
NA	Wisconsin**	NA
12	Wyoming	40.7

RANK	STATE	PERCENT
1	Alaska	59.7
2	Idaho	50.9
3	North Dakota	46.0
4	South Dakota	45.4
5	New Hampshire	44.6
6	Montana	43.8
7	Iowa	42.6
8	Minnesota	42.2
8	Vermont	42.2
10	Arizona	41.4
11	Utah	41.2
12	Wyoming	40.7
13	Washington	40.2
14	Colorado	40.1
14	Michigan	40.1
16	Rhode Island	39.6
17	Texas	39.3
18	Maine	38.7
19	Florida	37.0
20	Nebraska	36.9
21	Oklahoma	36.4
21	Oregon	36.4
23	New York	35.1
24	Hawaii	34.7
25	California	33.9
26	Ohio	33.5
27	South Carolina	33.4
28	New Mexico	33.3
29	Illinois	32.8
30	Maryland	32.2
31	Louisiana	32.0
31	Pennsylvania	32.0
33	West Virginia	31.3
34	Delaware	30.7
35	Kentucky	30.3
36	Connecticut	29.6
36	Mississippi	29.6
38	New Jersey	29.0
39	Arkansas	28.7
40	Indiana	28.6
41	Virginia	28.2
42	Missouri	28.1
43	Massachusetts	28.0
44	Nevada	23.1
45	Alabama	22.5
46	Tennessee	22.3
47	North Carolina	22.1
48	Georgia	21.4
NA	Kansas**	NA
NA	Wisconsin**	NA
	District of Columbia**	NA

Source: Morgan Quitno Press using data from Federal Bureau of Investigation
   "Crime in the United States 2000" (Uniform Crime Reports, October 22, 2001)
*Arrests of youths 17 years and younger by law enforcement agencies submitting complete reports to the F.B.I. for 12 months in 2000. Burglary is the unlawful entry of a structure to commit a felony or theft. Attempts are included.
**Not available.

Reported Arrests of Juveniles for Larceny and Theft in 2000

National Total = 274,616 Reported Arrests*

ALPHA ORDER

RANK ORDER

RANK	STATE	ARRESTS	% of USA		RANK	STATE	ARRESTS	% of USA
33	Alabama	2,268	0.8%		1	California	33,109	12.1%
37	Alaska	1,543	0.6%		2	Texas	28,978	10.6%
8	Arizona	8,664	3.2%		3	Florida	25,763	9.4%
30	Arkansas	3,034	1.1%		4	Washington	10,844	3.9%
1	California	33,109	12.1%		5	Pennsylvania	9,439	3.4%
11	Colorado	7,570	2.8%		6	Minnesota	9,243	3.4%
29	Connecticut	3,300	1.2%		7	New Jersey	8,685	3.2%
41	Delaware	1,129	0.4%		8	Arizona	8,664	3.2%
3	Florida	25,763	9.4%		9	Michigan	8,445	3.1%
21	Georgia	4,780	1.7%		10	North Carolina	8,046	2.9%
38	Hawaii	1,539	0.6%		11	Colorado	7,570	2.8%
28	Idaho	3,314	1.2%		12	Ohio	7,362	2.7%
25	Illinois	3,864	1.4%		13	New York	7,349	2.7%
14	Indiana	6,083	2.2%		14	Indiana	6,083	2.2%
22	Iowa	4,594	1.7%		15	Oregon	6,076	2.2%
NA	Kansas**	NA	NA		16	Maryland	5,805	2.1%
47	Kentucky	447	0.2%		17	Missouri	5,469	2.0%
20	Louisiana	4,963	1.8%		18	Utah	5,455	2.0%
34	Maine	2,055	0.7%		19	Oklahoma	5,130	1.9%
16	Maryland	5,805	2.1%		20	Louisiana	4,963	1.8%
32	Massachusetts	2,446	0.9%		21	Georgia	4,780	1.7%
9	Michigan	8,445	3.1%		22	Iowa	4,594	1.7%
6	Minnesota	9,243	3.4%		23	Virginia	4,137	1.5%
31	Mississippi	2,532	0.9%		24	Nebraska	3,979	1.4%
17	Missouri	5,469	2.0%		25	Illinois	3,864	1.4%
45	Montana	658	0.2%		26	Tennessee	3,483	1.3%
24	Nebraska	3,979	1.4%		27	Nevada	3,482	1.3%
27	Nevada	3,482	1.3%		28	Idaho	3,314	1.2%
44	New Hampshire	662	0.2%		29	Connecticut	3,300	1.2%
7	New Jersey	8,685	3.2%		30	Arkansas	3,034	1.1%
35	New Mexico	1,711	0.6%		31	Mississippi	2,532	0.9%
13	New York	7,349	2.7%		32	Massachusetts	2,446	0.9%
10	North Carolina	8,046	2.9%		33	Alabama	2,268	0.8%
40	North Dakota	1,265	0.5%		34	Maine	2,055	0.7%
12	Ohio	7,362	2.7%		35	New Mexico	1,711	0.6%
19	Oklahoma	5,130	1.9%		36	South Carolina	1,646	0.6%
15	Oregon	6,076	2.2%		37	Alaska	1,543	0.6%
5	Pennsylvania	9,439	3.4%		38	Hawaii	1,539	0.6%
42	Rhode Island	996	0.4%		39	South Dakota	1,356	0.5%
36	South Carolina	1,646	0.6%		40	North Dakota	1,265	0.5%
39	South Dakota	1,356	0.5%		41	Delaware	1,129	0.4%
26	Tennessee	3,483	1.3%		42	Rhode Island	996	0.4%
2	Texas	28,978	10.6%		43	Wyoming	964	0.4%
18	Utah	5,455	2.0%		44	New Hampshire	662	0.2%
48	Vermont	392	0.1%		45	Montana	658	0.2%
23	Virginia	4,137	1.5%		46	West Virginia	562	0.2%
4	Washington	10,844	3.9%		47	Kentucky	447	0.2%
46	West Virginia	562	0.2%		48	Vermont	392	0.1%
NA	Wisconsin**	NA	NA		NA	Kansas**	NA	NA
43	Wyoming	964	0.4%		NA	Wisconsin**	NA	NA
					NA	District of Columbia**	NA	NA

Source: Federal Bureau of Investigation
   "Crime in the United States 2000" (Uniform Crime Reports, October 22, 2001)
*Arrests of youths 17 years and younger by law enforcement agencies submitting complete reports to the F.B.I. for
12 months in 2000. Larceny and theft is the unlawful taking of property without use of force, violence or fraud.
Attempts are included. Motor vehicle thefts are excluded. See important note at beginning of this chapter.
**Not available.

Reported Juvenile Arrest Rate for Larceny and Theft in 2000

National Rate = 1,176.4 Reported Arrests per 100,000 Juvenile Population*

ALPHA ORDER				RANK ORDER		
RANK	STATE	RATE		RANK	STATE	RATE
46	Alabama	621.6		1	Delaware	2,575.7
8	Alaska	1,894.4		2	Utah	2,472.8
14	Arizona	1,606.9		3	Washington	2,252.4
33	Arkansas	1,123.9		4	Nebraska	2,083.4
41	California	824.0		5	Colorado	2,023.3
5	Colorado	2,023.3		6	Idaho	1,965.9
28	Connecticut	1,166.0		7	Oregon	1,913.2
1	Delaware	2,575.7		8	Alaska	1,894.4
16	Florida	1,578.9		9	North Dakota	1,821.3
35	Georgia	1,039.8		10	South Dakota	1,761.8
23	Hawaii	1,324.5		11	Kentucky	1,713.1
6	Idaho	1,965.9		12	Nevada	1,648.6
29	Illinois	1,162.2		13	Minnesota	1,643.0
22	Indiana	1,350.8		14	Arizona	1,606.9
18	Iowa	1,516.7		15	Missouri	1,601.6
NA	Kansas**	NA		16	Florida	1,578.9
11	Kentucky	1,713.1		17	Wyoming	1,519.6
25	Louisiana	1,267.9		18	Iowa	1,516.7
21	Maine	1,418.0		19	Montana	1,516.4
32	Maryland	1,131.4		20	Mississippi	1,434.2
48	Massachusetts	477.6		21	Maine	1,418.0
40	Michigan	841.6		22	Indiana	1,350.8
13	Minnesota	1,643.0		23	Hawaii	1,324.5
20	Mississippi	1,434.2		24	South Carolina	1,281.0
15	Missouri	1,601.6		25	Louisiana	1,267.9
19	Montana	1,516.4		26	Oklahoma	1,249.3
4	Nebraska	2,083.4		27	North Carolina	1,175.9
12	Nevada	1,648.6		28	Connecticut	1,166.0
43	New Hampshire	765.2		29	Illinois	1,162.2
37	New Jersey	976.2		30	Texas	1,159.6
31	New Mexico	1,147.0		31	New Mexico	1,147.0
36	New York	1,006.2		32	Maryland	1,131.4
27	North Carolina	1,175.9		33	Arkansas	1,123.9
9	North Dakota	1,821.3		34	Ohio	1,075.2
34	Ohio	1,075.2		35	Georgia	1,039.8
26	Oklahoma	1,249.3		36	New York	1,006.2
7	Oregon	1,913.2		37	New Jersey	976.2
39	Pennsylvania	929.3		38	Rhode Island	931.5
38	Rhode Island	931.5		39	Pennsylvania	929.3
24	South Carolina	1,281.0		40	Michigan	841.6
10	South Dakota	1,761.8		41	California	824.0
42	Tennessee	807.2		42	Tennessee	807.2
30	Texas	1,159.6		43	New Hampshire	765.2
2	Utah	2,472.8		44	Virginia	727.2
45	Vermont	671.8		45	Vermont	671.8
44	Virginia	727.2		46	Alabama	621.6
3	Washington	2,252.4		47	West Virginia	606.2
47	West Virginia	606.2		48	Massachusetts	477.6
NA	Wisconsin**	NA		NA	Kansas**	NA
17	Wyoming	1,519.6		NA	Wisconsin**	NA
				NA	District of Columbia**	NA

Source: Morgan Quitno Press using data from Federal Bureau of Investigation
    "Crime in the United States 2000" (Uniform Crime Reports, October 22, 2001)
*By law enforcement agencies submitting complete reports to the F.B.I. for 12 months in 2000. Arrests of youths 17 years and younger divided into population of 10 to 17 year olds. See important note at beginning of this chapter. Larceny and theft is the unlawful taking of property without use of force, violence or fraud. Attempts are included. Motor vehicle thefts are excluded. **Not available.

Reported Arrests of Juveniles for Larceny and Theft
As a Percent of All Such Arrests in 2000
National Percent = 31.3% of Reported Larceny and Theft Arrests*

ALPHA ORDER

RANK	STATE	PERCENT
47	Alabama	19.3
6	Alaska	43.2
30	Arizona	29.8
42	Arkansas	24.0
19	California	34.4
17	Colorado	35.4
35	Connecticut	27.8
33	Delaware	28.4
25	Florida	30.6
43	Georgia	23.3
23	Hawaii	32.2
2	Idaho	51.2
48	Illinois	15.3
18	Indiana	34.6
8	Iowa	42.7
NA	Kansas**	NA
26	Kentucky	30.5
39	Louisiana	25.1
15	Maine	38.2
29	Maryland	30.1
46	Massachusetts	21.9
14	Michigan	38.8
4	Minnesota	47.8
36	Mississippi	26.9
38	Missouri	25.7
3	Montana	47.9
12	Nebraska	41.4
24	Nevada	30.7
9	New Hampshire	42.3
32	New Jersey	28.9
21	New Mexico	34.0
37	New York	26.0
45	North Carolina	22.8
1	North Dakota	56.7
31	Ohio	29.1
10	Oklahoma	41.8
26	Oregon	30.5
33	Pennsylvania	28.4
16	Rhode Island	35.8
26	South Carolina	30.5
5	South Dakota	46.4
44	Tennessee	23.0
22	Texas	33.9
6	Utah	43.2
19	Vermont	34.4
40	Virginia	25.0
13	Washington	39.7
41	West Virginia	24.8
NA	Wisconsin**	NA
11	Wyoming	41.7

RANK ORDER

RANK	STATE	PERCENT
1	North Dakota	56.7
2	Idaho	51.2
3	Montana	47.9
4	Minnesota	47.8
5	South Dakota	46.4
6	Alaska	43.2
6	Utah	43.2
8	Iowa	42.7
9	New Hampshire	42.3
10	Oklahoma	41.8
11	Wyoming	41.7
12	Nebraska	41.4
13	Washington	39.7
14	Michigan	38.8
15	Maine	38.2
16	Rhode Island	35.8
17	Colorado	35.4
18	Indiana	34.6
19	California	34.4
19	Vermont	34.4
21	New Mexico	34.0
22	Texas	33.9
23	Hawaii	32.2
24	Nevada	30.7
25	Florida	30.6
26	Kentucky	30.5
26	Oregon	30.5
26	South Carolina	30.5
29	Maryland	30.1
30	Arizona	29.8
31	Ohio	29.1
32	New Jersey	28.9
33	Delaware	28.4
33	Pennsylvania	28.4
35	Connecticut	27.8
36	Mississippi	26.9
37	New York	26.0
38	Missouri	25.7
39	Louisiana	25.1
40	Virginia	25.0
41	West Virginia	24.8
42	Arkansas	24.0
43	Georgia	23.3
44	Tennessee	23.0
45	North Carolina	22.8
46	Massachusetts	21.9
47	Alabama	19.3
48	Illinois	15.3
NA	Kansas**	NA
NA	Wisconsin**	NA
	District of Columbia**	NA

Source: Morgan Quitno Press using data from Federal Bureau of Investigation
"Crime in the United States 2000" (Uniform Crime Reports, October 22, 2001)
*Arrests of youths 17 years and younger by law enforcement agencies submitting complete reports to the F.B.I. for 12 months in 2000. Larceny and theft is the unlawful taking of property without use of force, violence or fraud. Attempts are included. Motor vehicle thefts are excluded.
**Not available.

Reported Arrests of Juveniles for Motor Vehicle Theft in 2000

National Total = 38,784 Reported Arrests*

ALPHA ORDER

RANK	STATE	ARRESTS	% of USA
36	Alabama	155	0.4%
33	Alaska	188	0.5%
8	Arizona	1,107	2.9%
37	Arkansas	134	0.3%
1	California	6,615	17.1%
9	Colorado	1,074	2.8%
23	Connecticut	418	1.1%
45	Delaware	66	0.2%
2	Florida	4,358	11.2%
19	Georgia	549	1.4%
32	Hawaii	205	0.5%
34	Idaho	180	0.5%
3	Illinois	3,876	10.0%
15	Indiana	727	1.9%
26	Iowa	308	0.8%
NA	Kansas**	NA	NA
48	Kentucky	11	0.0%
25	Louisiana	318	0.8%
35	Maine	163	0.4%
6	Maryland	1,851	4.8%
28	Massachusetts	304	0.8%
12	Michigan	847	2.2%
7	Minnesota	1,392	3.6%
29	Mississippi	226	0.6%
10	Missouri	985	2.5%
44	Montana	68	0.2%
31	Nebraska	208	0.5%
20	Nevada	527	1.4%
42	New Hampshire	70	0.2%
21	New Jersey	507	1.3%
39	New Mexico	110	0.3%
13	New York	844	2.2%
16	North Carolina	668	1.7%
37	North Dakota	134	0.3%
14	Ohio	802	2.1%
17	Oklahoma	610	1.6%
18	Oregon	602	1.6%
5	Pennsylvania	2,167	5.6%
30	Rhode Island	219	0.6%
40	South Carolina	98	0.3%
41	South Dakota	90	0.2%
24	Tennessee	350	0.9%
4	Texas	2,833	7.3%
27	Utah	306	0.8%
47	Vermont	30	0.1%
22	Virginia	442	1.1%
11	Washington	912	2.4%
42	West Virginia	70	0.2%
NA	Wisconsin**	NA	NA
46	Wyoming	60	0.2%

RANK ORDER

RANK	STATE	ARRESTS	% of USA
1	California	6,615	17.1%
2	Florida	4,358	11.2%
3	Illinois	3,876	10.0%
4	Texas	2,833	7.3%
5	Pennsylvania	2,167	5.6%
6	Maryland	1,851	4.8%
7	Minnesota	1,392	3.6%
8	Arizona	1,107	2.9%
9	Colorado	1,074	2.8%
10	Missouri	985	2.5%
11	Washington	912	2.4%
12	Michigan	847	2.2%
13	New York	844	2.2%
14	Ohio	802	2.1%
15	Indiana	727	1.9%
16	North Carolina	668	1.7%
17	Oklahoma	610	1.6%
18	Oregon	602	1.6%
19	Georgia	549	1.4%
20	Nevada	527	1.4%
21	New Jersey	507	1.3%
22	Virginia	442	1.1%
23	Connecticut	418	1.1%
24	Tennessee	350	0.9%
25	Louisiana	318	0.8%
26	Iowa	308	0.8%
27	Utah	306	0.8%
28	Massachusetts	304	0.8%
29	Mississippi	226	0.6%
30	Rhode Island	219	0.6%
31	Nebraska	208	0.5%
32	Hawaii	205	0.5%
33	Alaska	188	0.5%
34	Idaho	180	0.5%
35	Maine	163	0.4%
36	Alabama	155	0.4%
37	Arkansas	134	0.3%
37	North Dakota	134	0.3%
39	New Mexico	110	0.3%
40	South Carolina	98	0.3%
41	South Dakota	90	0.2%
42	New Hampshire	70	0.2%
42	West Virginia	70	0.2%
44	Montana	68	0.2%
45	Delaware	66	0.2%
46	Wyoming	60	0.2%
47	Vermont	30	0.1%
48	Kentucky	11	0.0%
NA	Kansas**	NA	NA
NA	Wisconsin**	NA	NA
	District of Columbia**	NA	NA

Source: Federal Bureau of Investigation
   "Crime in the United States 2000" (Uniform Crime Reports, October 22, 2001)
*Arrests of youths 17 years and younger by law enforcement agencies submitting complete reports to the F.B.I. for 12 months in 2000. Motor vehicle theft includes the theft or attempted theft of a self-propelled vehicle. Excludes motorboats, construction equipment, airplanes and farming equipment. See important note at beginning of this chapter. **Not available.

Reported Juvenile Arrest Rate for Motor Vehicle Theft in 2000

National Rate = 166.1 Reported Arrests per 100,000 Juvenile Population*

ALPHA ORDER

RANK ORDER

RANK	STATE	RATE
47	Alabama	42.5
8	Alaska	230.8
10	Arizona	205.3
46	Arkansas	49.6
16	California	164.6
4	Colorado	287.1
21	Connecticut	147.7
19	Delaware	150.6
5	Florida	267.1
24	Georgia	119.4
15	Hawaii	176.4
31	Idaho	106.8
1	Illinois	1,165.8
17	Indiana	161.4
32	Iowa	101.7
NA	Kansas**	NA
48	Kentucky	42.2
36	Louisiana	81.2
29	Maine	112.5
2	Maryland	360.8
43	Massachusetts	59.4
35	Michigan	84.4
7	Minnesota	247.4
23	Mississippi	128.0
3	Missouri	288.5
18	Montana	156.7
30	Nebraska	108.9
6	Nevada	249.5
38	New Hampshire	80.9
44	New Jersey	57.0
42	New Mexico	73.7
27	New York	115.6
33	North Carolina	97.6
12	North Dakota	192.9
25	Ohio	117.1
20	Oklahoma	148.6
13	Oregon	189.6
9	Pennsylvania	213.3
11	Rhode Island	204.8
40	South Carolina	76.3
26	South Dakota	116.9
37	Tennessee	81.1
28	Texas	113.4
22	Utah	138.7
45	Vermont	51.4
39	Virginia	77.7
14	Washington	189.4
41	West Virginia	75.5
NA	Wisconsin**	NA
34	Wyoming	94.6

RANK	STATE	RATE
1	Illinois	1,165.8
2	Maryland	360.8
3	Missouri	288.5
4	Colorado	287.1
5	Florida	267.1
6	Nevada	249.5
7	Minnesota	247.4
8	Alaska	230.8
9	Pennsylvania	213.3
10	Arizona	205.3
11	Rhode Island	204.8
12	North Dakota	192.9
13	Oregon	189.6
14	Washington	189.4
15	Hawaii	176.4
16	California	164.6
17	Indiana	161.4
18	Montana	156.7
19	Delaware	150.6
20	Oklahoma	148.6
21	Connecticut	147.7
22	Utah	138.7
23	Mississippi	128.0
24	Georgia	119.4
25	Ohio	117.1
26	South Dakota	116.9
27	New York	115.6
28	Texas	113.4
29	Maine	112.5
30	Nebraska	108.9
31	Idaho	106.8
32	Iowa	101.7
33	North Carolina	97.6
34	Wyoming	94.6
35	Michigan	84.4
36	Louisiana	81.2
37	Tennessee	81.1
38	New Hampshire	80.9
39	Virginia	77.7
40	South Carolina	76.3
41	West Virginia	75.5
42	New Mexico	73.7
43	Massachusetts	59.4
44	New Jersey	57.0
45	Vermont	51.4
46	Arkansas	49.6
47	Alabama	42.5
48	Kentucky	42.2
NA	Kansas**	NA
NA	Wisconsin**	NA
	District of Columbia**	NA

Source: Morgan Quitno Press using data from Federal Bureau of Investigation
"Crime in the United States 2000" (Uniform Crime Reports, October 22, 2001)
*By law enforcement agencies submitting complete reports to the F.B.I. for 12 months in 2000. Arrests of youths 17 years and younger divided into population of 10 to 17 year olds. See important note at beginning of this chapter. Motor vehicle theft includes the theft or attempted theft of a self-propelled vehicle. Excludes motorboats, construction equipment, airplanes and farming equipment. **Not available.

Reported Arrests of Juveniles for Motor Vehicle Theft
As a Percent of All Such Arrests in 2000
National Percent = 34.5% of Reported Motor Vehicle Theft Arrests*

ALPHA ORDER

RANK ORDER

RANK	STATE	PERCENT		RANK	STATE	PERCENT
48	Alabama	17.2		1	North Dakota	60.1
5	Alaska	50.7		2	Rhode Island	58.9
36	Arizona	30.3		3	Montana	58.1
43	Arkansas	27.9		4	New Hampshire	54.3
38	California	30.1		5	Alaska	50.7
10	Colorado	47.1		6	South Dakota	49.7
20	Connecticut	42.1		7	Utah	47.7
22	Delaware	40.0		8	Minnesota	47.6
28	Florida	35.5		9	Iowa	47.3
46	Georgia	21.9		10	Colorado	47.1
47	Hawaii	19.9		11	Vermont	45.5
13	Idaho	45.1		12	Nebraska	45.2
29	Illinois	34.3		13	Idaho	45.1
25	Indiana	36.7		14	Maryland	44.7
9	Iowa	47.3		14	Ohio	44.7
NA	Kansas**	NA		16	New Mexico	44.5
39	Kentucky	29.7		17	Wyoming	44.1
25	Louisiana	36.7		18	Maine	43.9
18	Maine	43.9		19	Michigan	43.6
14	Maryland	44.7		20	Connecticut	42.1
31	Massachusetts	32.8		21	Washington	41.8
19	Michigan	43.6		22	Delaware	40.0
8	Minnesota	47.6		23	Oklahoma	37.8
40	Mississippi	29.3		24	Pennsylvania	37.5
42	Missouri	28.8		25	Indiana	36.7
3	Montana	58.1		25	Louisiana	36.7
12	Nebraska	45.2		27	New Jersey	36.2
32	Nevada	32.4		28	Florida	35.5
4	New Hampshire	54.3		29	Illinois	34.3
27	New Jersey	36.2		30	New York	33.2
16	New Mexico	44.5		31	Massachusetts	32.8
30	New York	33.2		32	Nevada	32.4
41	North Carolina	29.2		33	West Virginia	32.3
1	North Dakota	60.1		34	Texas	31.9
14	Ohio	44.7		35	South Carolina	31.7
23	Oklahoma	37.8		36	Arizona	30.3
45	Oregon	26.4		37	Virginia	30.2
24	Pennsylvania	37.5		38	California	30.1
2	Rhode Island	58.9		39	Kentucky	29.7
35	South Carolina	31.7		40	Mississippi	29.3
6	South Dakota	49.7		41	North Carolina	29.2
44	Tennessee	27.8		42	Missouri	28.8
34	Texas	31.9		43	Arkansas	27.9
7	Utah	47.7		44	Tennessee	27.8
11	Vermont	45.5		45	Oregon	26.4
37	Virginia	30.2		46	Georgia	21.9
21	Washington	41.8		47	Hawaii	19.9
33	West Virginia	32.3		48	Alabama	17.2
NA	Wisconsin**	NA		NA	Kansas**	NA
17	Wyoming	44.1		NA	Wisconsin**	NA
				NA	District of Columbia**	NA

Source: Morgan Quitno Press using data from Federal Bureau of Investigation
  "Crime in the United States 2000" (Uniform Crime Reports, October 22, 2001)
*Arrests of youths 17 years and younger by law enforcement agencies submitting complete reports to the F.B.I. for 12 months in 2000. Motor vehicle theft includes the theft or attempted theft of a self-propelled vehicle. Excludes motorboats, construction equipment, airplanes and farming equipment.
**Not available.

Reported Arrests of Juveniles for Arson in 2000

National Total = 6,034 Reported Arrests*

ALPHA ORDER

RANK ORDER

RANK	STATE	ARRESTS	% of USA	RANK	STATE	ARRESTS	% of USA
34	Alabama	27	0.4%	1	California	1,131	18.7%
46	Alaska	7	0.1%	2	Texas	366	6.1%
13	Arizona	181	3.0%	3	Pennsylvania	353	5.9%
35	Arkansas	24	0.4%	4	New Jersey	274	4.5%
1	California	1,131	18.7%	5	Washington	252	4.2%
9	Colorado	203	3.4%	6	Ohio	249	4.1%
25	Connecticut	62	1.0%	7	Florida	248	4.1%
31	Delaware	43	0.7%	8	New York	223	3.7%
7	Florida	248	4.1%	9	Colorado	203	3.4%
26	Georgia	56	0.9%	10	Oregon	201	3.3%
43	Hawaii	14	0.2%	11	Maryland	195	3.2%
30	Idaho	49	0.8%	12	North Carolina	187	3.1%
22	Illinois	86	1.4%	13	Arizona	181	3.0%
24	Indiana	69	1.1%	14	Virginia	178	2.9%
23	Iowa	74	1.2%	15	Minnesota	172	2.9%
NA	Kansas**	NA	NA	16	Oklahoma	151	2.5%
46	Kentucky	7	0.1%	17	Michigan	147	2.4%
20	Louisiana	95	1.6%	18	Nebraska	119	2.0%
35	Maine	24	0.4%	19	Missouri	100	1.7%
11	Maryland	195	3.2%	20	Louisiana	95	1.6%
28	Massachusetts	54	0.9%	21	Utah	92	1.5%
17	Michigan	147	2.4%	22	Illinois	86	1.4%
15	Minnesota	172	2.9%	23	Iowa	74	1.2%
32	Mississippi	37	0.6%	24	Indiana	69	1.1%
19	Missouri	100	1.7%	25	Connecticut	62	1.0%
45	Montana	11	0.2%	26	Georgia	56	0.9%
18	Nebraska	119	2.0%	27	Nevada	55	0.9%
27	Nevada	55	0.9%	28	Massachusetts	54	0.9%
41	New Hampshire	17	0.3%	29	Rhode Island	52	0.9%
4	New Jersey	274	4.5%	30	Idaho	49	0.8%
39	New Mexico	20	0.3%	31	Delaware	43	0.7%
8	New York	223	3.7%	32	Mississippi	37	0.6%
12	North Carolina	187	3.1%	33	Tennessee	36	0.6%
43	North Dakota	14	0.2%	34	Alabama	27	0.4%
6	Ohio	249	4.1%	35	Arkansas	24	0.4%
16	Oklahoma	151	2.5%	35	Maine	24	0.4%
10	Oregon	201	3.3%	37	South Carolina	23	0.4%
3	Pennsylvania	353	5.9%	38	South Dakota	21	0.3%
29	Rhode Island	52	0.9%	39	New Mexico	20	0.3%
37	South Carolina	23	0.4%	40	Wyoming	19	0.3%
38	South Dakota	21	0.3%	41	New Hampshire	17	0.3%
33	Tennessee	36	0.6%	42	West Virginia	15	0.2%
2	Texas	366	6.1%	43	Hawaii	14	0.2%
21	Utah	92	1.5%	43	North Dakota	14	0.2%
48	Vermont	1	0.0%	45	Montana	11	0.2%
14	Virginia	178	2.9%	46	Alaska	7	0.1%
5	Washington	252	4.2%	46	Kentucky	7	0.1%
42	West Virginia	15	0.2%	48	Vermont	1	0.0%
NA	Wisconsin**	NA	NA	NA	Kansas**	NA	NA
40	Wyoming	19	0.3%	NA	Wisconsin**	NA	NA
					District of Columbia**	NA	NA

Source: Federal Bureau of Investigation
"Crime in the United States 2000" (Uniform Crime Reports, October 22, 2001)
*Arrests of youths 17 years and younger by law enforcement agencies submitting complete reports to the F.B.I. for 12 months in 2000. Arson is the willful burning of or attempt to burn a building, vehicle or another's personal property. See important note at beginning of this chapter.
**Not available.

Reported Juvenile Arrest Rate for Arson in 2000

National Rate = 25.8 Reported Arrests per 100,000 Population*

ALPHA ORDER

RANK	STATE	RATE
47	Alabama	7.4
45	Alaska	8.6
12	Arizona	33.6
44	Arkansas	8.9
20	California	28.1
4	Colorado	54.3
29	Connecticut	21.9
1	Delaware	98.1
37	Florida	15.2
41	Georgia	12.2
42	Hawaii	12.0
19	Idaho	29.1
25	Illinois	25.9
36	Indiana	15.3
27	Iowa	24.4
NA	Kansas**	NA
23	Kentucky	26.8
28	Louisiana	24.3
34	Maine	16.6
8	Maryland	38.0
43	Massachusetts	10.5
38	Michigan	14.6
15	Minnesota	30.6
30	Mississippi	21.0
18	Missouri	29.3
26	Montana	25.3
3	Nebraska	62.3
24	Nevada	26.0
32	New Hampshire	19.7
14	New Jersey	30.8
40	New Mexico	13.4
16	New York	30.5
21	North Carolina	27.3
31	North Dakota	20.2
10	Ohio	36.4
9	Oklahoma	36.8
2	Oregon	63.3
11	Pennsylvania	34.8
6	Rhode Island	48.6
33	South Carolina	17.9
21	South Dakota	27.3
46	Tennessee	8.3
38	Texas	14.6
7	Utah	41.7
48	Vermont	1.7
13	Virginia	31.3
5	Washington	52.3
35	West Virginia	16.2
NA	Wisconsin**	NA
17	Wyoming	30.0

RANK ORDER

RANK	STATE	RATE
1	Delaware	98.1
2	Oregon	63.3
3	Nebraska	62.3
4	Colorado	54.3
5	Washington	52.3
6	Rhode Island	48.6
7	Utah	41.7
8	Maryland	38.0
9	Oklahoma	36.8
10	Ohio	36.4
11	Pennsylvania	34.8
12	Arizona	33.6
13	Virginia	31.3
14	New Jersey	30.8
15	Minnesota	30.6
16	New York	30.5
17	Wyoming	30.0
18	Missouri	29.3
19	Idaho	29.1
20	California	28.1
21	North Carolina	27.3
21	South Dakota	27.3
23	Kentucky	26.8
24	Nevada	26.0
25	Illinois	25.9
26	Montana	25.3
27	Iowa	24.4
28	Louisiana	24.3
29	Connecticut	21.9
30	Mississippi	21.0
31	North Dakota	20.2
32	New Hampshire	19.7
33	South Carolina	17.9
34	Maine	16.6
35	West Virginia	16.2
36	Indiana	15.3
37	Florida	15.2
38	Michigan	14.6
38	Texas	14.6
40	New Mexico	13.4
41	Georgia	12.2
42	Hawaii	12.0
43	Massachusetts	10.5
44	Arkansas	8.9
45	Alaska	8.6
46	Tennessee	8.3
47	Alabama	7.4
48	Vermont	1.7
NA	Kansas**	NA
NA	Wisconsin**	NA
NA	District of Columbia**	NA

Source: Morgan Quitno Press using data from Federal Bureau of Investigation
"Crime in the United States 2000" (Uniform Crime Reports, October 22, 2001)
*By law enforcement agencies submitting complete reports to the F.B.I. for 12 months in 2000. Arrests of youths 17 years and younger divided into population of 10 to 17 year olds. See important note at beginning of this chapter. Arson is the willful burning of or attempt to burn a building, vehicle or another's personal property.
**Not available.

Reported Arrests of Juveniles for Arson
As a Percent of All Such Arrests in 2000
National Percent = 52.5% of Reported Arson Arrests*

ALPHA ORDER

RANK	STATE	PERCENT
45	Alabama	24.8
42	Alaska	29.2
8	Arizona	67.0
46	Arkansas	20.9
18	California	61.2
13	Colorado	64.2
35	Connecticut	40.5
32	Delaware	43.9
28	Florida	46.0
43	Georgia	26.4
39	Hawaii	35.9
20	Idaho	55.7
36	Illinois	38.9
23	Indiana	50.0
12	Iowa	64.9
NA	Kansas**	NA
23	Kentucky	50.0
31	Louisiana	44.2
37	Maine	37.5
26	Maryland	48.1
29	Massachusetts	45.8
25	Michigan	49.2
7	Minnesota	67.5
44	Mississippi	25.2
40	Missouri	33.8
1	Montana	91.7
3	Nebraska	82.1
4	Nevada	76.4
21	New Hampshire	54.8
14	New Jersey	63.1
38	New Mexico	37.0
16	New York	61.6
34	North Carolina	41.7
9	North Dakota	66.7
15	Ohio	62.3
22	Oklahoma	54.5
6	Oregon	68.8
30	Pennsylvania	45.1
5	Rhode Island	71.2
33	South Carolina	43.4
2	South Dakota	84.0
47	Tennessee	18.5
27	Texas	47.3
11	Utah	65.2
48	Vermont	14.3
19	Virginia	57.2
17	Washington	61.3
41	West Virginia	31.9
NA	Wisconsin**	NA
10	Wyoming	65.5

RANK ORDER

RANK	STATE	PERCENT
1	Montana	91.7
2	South Dakota	84.0
3	Nebraska	82.1
4	Nevada	76.4
5	Rhode Island	71.2
6	Oregon	68.8
7	Minnesota	67.5
8	Arizona	67.0
9	North Dakota	66.7
10	Wyoming	65.5
11	Utah	65.2
12	Iowa	64.9
13	Colorado	64.2
14	New Jersey	63.1
15	Ohio	62.3
16	New York	61.6
17	Washington	61.3
18	California	61.2
19	Virginia	57.2
20	Idaho	55.7
21	New Hampshire	54.8
22	Oklahoma	54.5
23	Indiana	50.0
23	Kentucky	50.0
25	Michigan	49.2
26	Maryland	48.1
27	Texas	47.3
28	Florida	46.0
29	Massachusetts	45.8
30	Pennsylvania	45.1
31	Louisiana	44.2
32	Delaware	43.9
33	South Carolina	43.4
34	North Carolina	41.7
35	Connecticut	40.5
36	Illinois	38.9
37	Maine	37.5
38	New Mexico	37.0
39	Hawaii	35.9
40	Missouri	33.8
41	West Virginia	31.9
42	Alaska	29.2
43	Georgia	26.4
44	Mississippi	25.2
45	Alabama	24.8
46	Arkansas	20.9
47	Tennessee	18.5
48	Vermont	14.3
NA	Kansas**	NA
NA	Wisconsin**	NA
	District of Columbia**	NA

Source: Morgan Quitno Press using data from Federal Bureau of Investigation
   "Crime in the United States 2000" (Uniform Crime Reports, October 22, 2001)
*Arrests of youths 17 years and younger by law enforcement agencies submitting complete reports to the F.B.I. for
12 months in 2000. Arson is the willful burning of or attempt to burn a building, vehicle or another's personal
property.
**Not available.

Reported Arrests of Juveniles for Weapons Violations in 2000

National Total = 27,029 Reported Arrests*

ALPHA ORDER

RANK	STATE	ARRESTS	% of USA
28	Alabama	216	0.8%
38	Alaska	82	0.3%
17	Arizona	437	1.6%
26	Arkansas	229	0.8%
1	California	6,424	23.8%
11	Colorado	705	2.6%
23	Connecticut	301	1.1%
36	Delaware	115	0.4%
2	Florida	1,780	6.6%
16	Georgia	529	2.0%
41	Hawaii	53	0.2%
27	Idaho	222	0.8%
5	Illinois	1,419	5.2%
31	Indiana	200	0.7%
35	Iowa	143	0.5%
NA	Kansas**	NA	NA
47	Kentucky	19	0.1%
21	Louisiana	349	1.3%
42	Maine	40	0.1%
8	Maryland	968	3.6%
32	Massachusetts	198	0.7%
15	Michigan	563	2.1%
9	Minnesota	864	3.2%
33	Mississippi	164	0.6%
18	Missouri	427	1.6%
45	Montana	25	0.1%
30	Nebraska	202	0.7%
19	Nevada	405	1.5%
43	New Hampshire	29	0.1%
4	New Jersey	1,537	5.7%
29	New Mexico	213	0.8%
12	New York	695	2.6%
6	North Carolina	1,087	4.0%
44	North Dakota	28	0.1%
13	Ohio	592	2.2%
20	Oklahoma	372	1.4%
24	Oregon	298	1.1%
7	Pennsylvania	1,023	3.8%
36	Rhode Island	115	0.4%
34	South Carolina	151	0.6%
39	South Dakota	71	0.3%
25	Tennessee	283	1.0%
3	Texas	1,735	6.4%
22	Utah	314	1.2%
48	Vermont	9	0.0%
14	Virginia	580	2.1%
10	Washington	737	2.7%
45	West Virginia	25	0.1%
NA	Wisconsin**	NA	NA
40	Wyoming	56	0.2%

RANK ORDER

RANK	STATE	ARRESTS	% of USA
1	California	6,424	23.8%
2	Florida	1,780	6.6%
3	Texas	1,735	6.4%
4	New Jersey	1,537	5.7%
5	Illinois	1,419	5.2%
6	North Carolina	1,087	4.0%
7	Pennsylvania	1,023	3.8%
8	Maryland	968	3.6%
9	Minnesota	864	3.2%
10	Washington	737	2.7%
11	Colorado	705	2.6%
12	New York	695	2.6%
13	Ohio	592	2.2%
14	Virginia	580	2.1%
15	Michigan	563	2.1%
16	Georgia	529	2.0%
17	Arizona	437	1.6%
18	Missouri	427	1.6%
19	Nevada	405	1.5%
20	Oklahoma	372	1.4%
21	Louisiana	349	1.3%
22	Utah	314	1.2%
23	Connecticut	301	1.1%
24	Oregon	298	1.1%
25	Tennessee	283	1.0%
26	Arkansas	229	0.8%
27	Idaho	222	0.8%
28	Alabama	216	0.8%
29	New Mexico	213	0.8%
30	Nebraska	202	0.7%
31	Indiana	200	0.7%
32	Massachusetts	198	0.7%
33	Mississippi	164	0.6%
34	South Carolina	151	0.6%
35	Iowa	143	0.5%
36	Delaware	115	0.4%
36	Rhode Island	115	0.4%
38	Alaska	82	0.3%
39	South Dakota	71	0.3%
40	Wyoming	56	0.2%
41	Hawaii	53	0.2%
42	Maine	40	0.1%
43	New Hampshire	29	0.1%
44	North Dakota	28	0.1%
45	Montana	25	0.1%
45	West Virginia	25	0.1%
47	Kentucky	19	0.1%
48	Vermont	9	0.0%
NA	Kansas**	NA	NA
NA	Wisconsin**	NA	NA
	District of Columbia**	NA	NA

Source: Federal Bureau of Investigation
 "Crime in the United States 2000" (Uniform Crime Reports, October 22, 2001)
*Arrests of youths 17 years and younger by law enforcement agencies submitting complete reports to the F.B.I. for 12 months in 2000. Weapons violations include illegal carrying and possession. See important note at beginning of this chapter.
**Not available.

Reported Juvenile Arrest Rate for Weapons Violations in 2000

National Rate = 115.8 Reported Arrests per 100,000 Juvenile Population*

ALPHA ORDER

RANK ORDER

RANK	STATE	RATE		RANK	STATE	RATE
37	Alabama	59.2		1	Illinois	426.8
22	Alaska	100.7		2	Delaware	262.4
33	Arizona	81.0		3	Nevada	191.8
32	Arkansas	84.8		4	Maryland	188.7
7	California	159.9		5	Colorado	188.4
5	Colorado	188.4		6	New Jersey	172.8
19	Connecticut	106.4		7	California	159.9
2	Delaware	262.4		8	North Carolina	158.9
17	Florida	109.1		9	Minnesota	153.6
16	Georgia	115.1		10	Washington	153.1
41	Hawaii	45.6		11	New Mexico	142.8
13	Idaho	131.7		12	Utah	142.3
1	Illinois	426.8		13	Idaho	131.7
42	Indiana	44.4		14	Missouri	125.0
40	Iowa	47.2		15	South Carolina	117.5
NA	Kansas**	NA		16	Georgia	115.1
34	Kentucky	72.8		17	Florida	109.1
29	Louisiana	89.2		18	Rhode Island	107.5
46	Maine	27.6		19	Connecticut	106.4
4	Maryland	188.7		20	Nebraska	105.8
44	Massachusetts	38.7		21	Virginia	101.9
39	Michigan	56.1		22	Alaska	100.7
9	Minnesota	153.6		22	Pennsylvania	100.7
26	Mississippi	92.9		24	New York	95.2
14	Missouri	125.0		25	Oregon	93.8
38	Montana	57.6		26	Mississippi	92.9
20	Nebraska	105.8		27	South Dakota	92.2
3	Nevada	191.8		28	Oklahoma	90.6
45	New Hampshire	33.5		29	Louisiana	89.2
6	New Jersey	172.8		30	Wyoming	88.3
11	New Mexico	142.8		31	Ohio	86.5
24	New York	95.2		32	Arkansas	84.8
8	North Carolina	158.9		33	Arizona	81.0
43	North Dakota	40.3		34	Kentucky	72.8
31	Ohio	86.5		35	Texas	69.4
28	Oklahoma	90.6		36	Tennessee	65.6
25	Oregon	93.8		37	Alabama	59.2
22	Pennsylvania	100.7		38	Montana	57.6
18	Rhode Island	107.5		39	Michigan	56.1
15	South Carolina	117.5		40	Iowa	47.2
27	South Dakota	92.2		41	Hawaii	45.6
36	Tennessee	65.6		42	Indiana	44.4
35	Texas	69.4		43	North Dakota	40.3
12	Utah	142.3		44	Massachusetts	38.7
48	Vermont	15.4		45	New Hampshire	33.5
21	Virginia	101.9		46	Maine	27.6
10	Washington	153.1		47	West Virginia	27.0
47	West Virginia	27.0		48	Vermont	15.4
NA	Wisconsin**	NA		NA	Kansas**	NA
30	Wyoming	88.3		NA	Wisconsin**	NA
				NA	District of Columbia**	NA

Source: Morgan Quitno Press using data from Federal Bureau of Investigation
   "Crime in the United States 2000" (Uniform Crime Reports, October 22, 2001)
*By law enforcement agencies submitting complete reports to the F.B.I. for 12 months in 2000. Arrests of youths 17 years and younger divided into population of 10 to 17 year olds. See important note at beginning of this chapter. Weapons violations include illegal carrying and possession.
**Not available.

Reported Arrests of Juveniles for Weapons Violations
As a Percent of All Such Arrests in 2000
National Percent = 23.6% of Reported Weapons Violations Arrests*

ALPHA ORDER

RANK	STATE	PERCENT
37	Alabama	17.1
33	Alaska	18.5
39	Arizona	15.9
47	Arkansas	11.3
13	California	29.9
14	Colorado	27.7
16	Connecticut	26.4
20	Delaware	24.8
15	Florida	27.1
40	Georgia	15.4
34	Hawaii	17.2
8	Idaho	34.5
16	Illinois	26.4
46	Indiana	12.1
21	Iowa	24.7
NA	Kansas**	NA
43	Kentucky	15.0
24	Louisiana	22.0
41	Maine	15.3
10	Maryland	31.5
26	Massachusetts	20.1
29	Michigan	19.9
4	Minnesota	38.9
28	Mississippi	20.0
45	Missouri	13.9
3	Montana	52.1
32	Nebraska	19.1
25	Nevada	21.5
26	New Hampshire	20.1
11	New Jersey	30.4
5	New Mexico	38.4
23	New York	24.1
30	North Carolina	19.6
16	North Dakota	26.4
31	Ohio	19.3
44	Oklahoma	14.8
34	Oregon	17.2
11	Pennsylvania	30.4
9	Rhode Island	32.2
22	South Carolina	24.6
2	South Dakota	57.7
42	Tennessee	15.1
38	Texas	16.6
7	Utah	35.7
1	Vermont	69.2
34	Virginia	17.2
19	Washington	26.2
48	West Virginia	10.6
NA	Wisconsin**	NA
5	Wyoming	38.4

RANK ORDER

RANK	STATE	PERCENT
1	Vermont	69.2
2	South Dakota	57.7
3	Montana	52.1
4	Minnesota	38.9
5	New Mexico	38.4
5	Wyoming	38.4
7	Utah	35.7
8	Idaho	34.5
9	Rhode Island	32.2
10	Maryland	31.5
11	New Jersey	30.4
11	Pennsylvania	30.4
13	California	29.9
14	Colorado	27.7
15	Florida	27.1
16	Connecticut	26.4
16	Illinois	26.4
16	North Dakota	26.4
19	Washington	26.2
20	Delaware	24.8
21	Iowa	24.7
22	South Carolina	24.6
23	New York	24.1
24	Louisiana	22.0
25	Nevada	21.5
26	Massachusetts	20.1
26	New Hampshire	20.1
28	Mississippi	20.0
29	Michigan	19.9
30	North Carolina	19.6
31	Ohio	19.3
32	Nebraska	19.1
33	Alaska	18.5
34	Hawaii	17.2
34	Oregon	17.2
34	Virginia	17.2
37	Alabama	17.1
38	Texas	16.6
39	Arizona	15.9
40	Georgia	15.4
41	Maine	15.3
42	Tennessee	15.1
43	Kentucky	15.0
44	Oklahoma	14.8
45	Missouri	13.9
46	Indiana	12.1
47	Arkansas	11.3
48	West Virginia	10.6
NA	Kansas**	NA
NA	Wisconsin**	NA
	District of Columbia**	NA

Source: Morgan Quitno Press using data from Federal Bureau of Investigation
       "Crime in the United States 2000" (Uniform Crime Reports, October 22, 2001)
*Arrests of youths 17 years and younger by law enforcement agencies submitting complete reports to the F.B.I. for 12 months in 2000.   Weapons violations include illegal carrying and possession.
**Not available.

Reported Arrests of Juveniles for Driving Under the Influence in 2000

National Total = 14,074 Reported Arrests*

ALPHA ORDER

RANK	STATE	ARRESTS	% of USA
31	Alabama	153	1.1%
35	Alaska	86	0.6%
9	Arizona	472	3.4%
22	Arkansas	252	1.8%
1	California	1,542	11.0%
8	Colorado	486	3.5%
34	Connecticut	87	0.6%
47	Delaware	0	0.0%
10	Florida	468	3.3%
23	Georgia	247	1.8%
39	Hawaii	69	0.5%
19	Idaho	284	2.0%
NA	Illinois**	NA	NA
25	Indiana	175	1.2%
18	Iowa	286	2.0%
NA	Kansas**	NA	NA
44	Kentucky	29	0.2%
25	Louisiana	175	1.2%
29	Maine	160	1.1%
16	Maryland	309	2.2%
28	Massachusetts	161	1.1%
4	Michigan	556	4.0%
3	Minnesota	1,095	7.8%
24	Mississippi	207	1.5%
19	Missouri	284	2.0%
43	Montana	38	0.3%
12	Nebraska	398	2.8%
36	Nevada	85	0.6%
40	New Hampshire	64	0.5%
13	New Jersey	351	2.5%
21	New Mexico	268	1.9%
14	New York	333	2.4%
11	North Carolina	467	3.3%
41	North Dakota	52	0.4%
15	Ohio	318	2.3%
6	Oklahoma	525	3.7%
25	Oregon	175	1.2%
5	Pennsylvania	536	3.8%
46	Rhode Island	14	0.1%
38	South Carolina	72	0.5%
36	South Dakota	85	0.6%
32	Tennessee	147	1.0%
2	Texas	1,434	10.2%
29	Utah	160	1.1%
45	Vermont	23	0.2%
17	Virginia	308	2.2%
7	Washington	500	3.6%
42	West Virginia	50	0.4%
NA	Wisconsin**	NA	NA
33	Wyoming	88	0.6%

RANK ORDER

RANK	STATE	ARRESTS	% of USA
1	California	1,542	11.0%
2	Texas	1,434	10.2%
3	Minnesota	1,095	7.8%
4	Michigan	556	4.0%
5	Pennsylvania	536	3.8%
6	Oklahoma	525	3.7%
7	Washington	500	3.6%
8	Colorado	486	3.5%
9	Arizona	472	3.4%
10	Florida	468	3.3%
11	North Carolina	467	3.3%
12	Nebraska	398	2.8%
13	New Jersey	351	2.5%
14	New York	333	2.4%
15	Ohio	318	2.3%
16	Maryland	309	2.2%
17	Virginia	308	2.2%
18	Iowa	286	2.0%
19	Idaho	284	2.0%
19	Missouri	284	2.0%
21	New Mexico	268	1.9%
22	Arkansas	252	1.8%
23	Georgia	247	1.8%
24	Mississippi	207	1.5%
25	Indiana	175	1.2%
25	Louisiana	175	1.2%
25	Oregon	175	1.2%
28	Massachusetts	161	1.1%
29	Maine	160	1.1%
29	Utah	160	1.1%
31	Alabama	153	1.1%
32	Tennessee	147	1.0%
33	Wyoming	88	0.6%
34	Connecticut	87	0.6%
35	Alaska	86	0.6%
36	Nevada	85	0.6%
36	South Dakota	85	0.6%
38	South Carolina	72	0.5%
39	Hawaii	69	0.5%
40	New Hampshire	64	0.5%
41	North Dakota	52	0.4%
42	West Virginia	50	0.4%
43	Montana	38	0.3%
44	Kentucky	29	0.2%
45	Vermont	23	0.2%
46	Rhode Island	14	0.1%
47	Delaware	0	0.0%
NA	Illinois**	NA	NA
NA	Kansas**	NA	NA
NA	Wisconsin**	NA	NA
	District of Columbia**	NA	NA

Source: Federal Bureau of Investigation
   "Crime in the United States 2000" (Uniform Crime Reports, October 22, 2001)
*Arrests of youths 17 years and younger by law enforcement agencies submitting complete reports to the F.B.I. for 12 months in 2000. Includes driving any vehicle while drunk or under the influence of liquor or narcotics. See important note at beginning of this chapter.
**Not available.

Reported Juvenile Arrest Rate for Driving Under the Influence in 2000

National Rate = 61.2 Reported Arrests per 100,000 Juvenile Population*

ALPHA ORDER

RANK ORDER

RANK	STATE	RATE	RANK	STATE	RATE
36	Alabama	41.9	1	Nebraska	208.4
12	Alaska	105.6	2	Minnesota	194.6
17	Arizona	87.5	3	New Mexico	179.7
15	Arkansas	93.3	4	Idaho	168.5
41	California	38.4	5	Wyoming	138.7
6	Colorado	129.9	6	Colorado	129.9
44	Connecticut	30.7	7	Oklahoma	127.9
47	Delaware	0.0	8	Mississippi	117.3
45	Florida	28.7	9	Kentucky	111.1
31	Georgia	53.7	10	Maine	110.4
24	Hawaii	59.4	10	South Dakota	110.4
4	Idaho	168.5	12	Alaska	105.6
NA	Illinois**	NA	13	Washington	103.9
40	Indiana	38.9	14	Iowa	94.4
14	Iowa	94.4	15	Arkansas	93.3
NA	Kansas**	NA	16	Montana	87.6
9	Kentucky	111.1	17	Arizona	87.5
35	Louisiana	44.7	18	Missouri	83.2
10	Maine	110.4	19	North Dakota	74.9
23	Maryland	60.2	20	New Hampshire	74.0
43	Massachusetts	31.4	21	Utah	72.5
27	Michigan	55.4	22	North Carolina	68.3
2	Minnesota	194.6	23	Maryland	60.2
8	Mississippi	117.3	24	Hawaii	59.4
18	Missouri	83.2	25	Texas	57.4
16	Montana	87.6	26	South Carolina	56.0
1	Nebraska	208.4	27	Michigan	55.4
37	Nevada	40.2	28	Oregon	55.1
20	New Hampshire	74.0	29	Virginia	54.1
38	New Jersey	39.5	30	West Virginia	53.9
3	New Mexico	179.7	31	Georgia	53.7
34	New York	45.6	32	Pennsylvania	52.8
22	North Carolina	68.3	33	Ohio	46.4
19	North Dakota	74.9	34	New York	45.6
33	Ohio	46.4	35	Louisiana	44.7
7	Oklahoma	127.9	36	Alabama	41.9
28	Oregon	55.1	37	Nevada	40.2
32	Pennsylvania	52.8	38	New Jersey	39.5
46	Rhode Island	13.1	39	Vermont	39.4
26	South Carolina	56.0	40	Indiana	38.9
10	South Dakota	110.4	41	California	38.4
42	Tennessee	34.1	42	Tennessee	34.1
25	Texas	57.4	43	Massachusetts	31.4
21	Utah	72.5	44	Connecticut	30.7
39	Vermont	39.4	45	Florida	28.7
29	Virginia	54.1	46	Rhode Island	13.1
13	Washington	103.9	47	Delaware	0.0
30	West Virginia	53.9	NA	Illinois**	NA
NA	Wisconsin**	NA	NA	Kansas**	NA
5	Wyoming	138.7	NA	Wisconsin**	NA
				District of Columbia**	NA

Source: Morgan Quitno Press using data from Federal Bureau of Investigation
   "Crime in the United States 2000" (Uniform Crime Reports, October 22, 2001)
*By law enforcement agencies submitting complete reports to the F.B.I. for 12 months in 2000. Arrests of youths 17 years and younger divided into population of 10 to 17 year olds. See important note at beginning of this chapter. Includes driving any vehicle while drunk or under the influence of liquor or narcotics.
**Not available.

Reported Arrests of Juveniles for Driving Under the Influence
As a Percent of All Such Arrests in 2000
National Percent = 1.4% of Reported Driving Under the Influence Arrests*

ALPHA ORDER

RANK ORDER

RANK	STATE	PERCENT		RANK	STATE	PERCENT
34	Alabama	1.1		1	Nebraska	3.4
15	Alaska	1.9		2	New Mexico	3.0
22	Arizona	1.5		3	Idaho	2.8
22	Arkansas	1.5		4	Utah	2.5
43	California	0.8		5	Minnesota	2.4
11	Colorado	2.0		5	Montana	2.4
32	Connecticut	1.2		5	Oklahoma	2.4
47	Delaware	0.0		8	Iowa	2.3
43	Florida	0.8		9	Hawaii	2.2
34	Georgia	1.1		9	Maine	2.2
9	Hawaii	2.2		11	Colorado	2.0
3	Idaho	2.8		11	Mississippi	2.0
NA	Illinois**	NA		11	South Dakota	2.0
40	Indiana	0.9		11	Wyoming	2.0
8	Iowa	2.3		15	Alaska	1.9
NA	Kansas**	NA		16	Missouri	1.7
27	Kentucky	1.4		16	New Hampshire	1.7
30	Louisiana	1.3		16	Washington	1.7
9	Maine	2.2		19	North Carolina	1.6
27	Maryland	1.4		19	North Dakota	1.6
22	Massachusetts	1.5		19	Pennsylvania	1.6
34	Michigan	1.1		22	Arizona	1.5
5	Minnesota	2.4		22	Arkansas	1.5
11	Mississippi	2.0		22	Massachusetts	1.5
16	Missouri	1.7		22	Ohio	1.5
5	Montana	2.4		22	Texas	1.5
1	Nebraska	3.4		27	Kentucky	1.4
38	Nevada	1.0		27	Maryland	1.4
16	New Hampshire	1.7		27	New Jersey	1.4
27	New Jersey	1.4		30	Louisiana	1.3
2	New Mexico	3.0		30	Virginia	1.3
34	New York	1.1		32	Connecticut	1.2
19	North Carolina	1.6		32	Oregon	1.2
19	North Dakota	1.6		34	Alabama	1.1
22	Ohio	1.5		34	Georgia	1.1
5	Oklahoma	2.4		34	Michigan	1.1
32	Oregon	1.2		34	New York	1.1
19	Pennsylvania	1.6		38	Nevada	1.0
40	Rhode Island	0.9		38	West Virginia	1.0
40	South Carolina	0.9		40	Indiana	0.9
11	South Dakota	2.0		40	Rhode Island	0.9
43	Tennessee	0.8		40	South Carolina	0.9
22	Texas	1.5		43	California	0.8
4	Utah	2.5		43	Florida	0.8
43	Vermont	0.8		43	Tennessee	0.8
30	Virginia	1.3		43	Vermont	0.8
16	Washington	1.7		47	Delaware	0.0
38	West Virginia	1.0		NA	Illinois**	NA
NA	Wisconsin**	NA		NA	Kansas**	NA
11	Wyoming	2.0		NA	Wisconsin**	NA
					District of Columbia**	NA

Source: Morgan Quitno Press using data from Federal Bureau of Investigation
   "Crime in the United States 2000" (Uniform Crime Reports, October 22, 2001)
*Arrests of youths 17 years and younger by law enforcement agencies submitting complete reports to the F.B.I. for
12 months in 2000. Includes driving any vehicle while drunk or under the influence of liquor or narcotics.
**Not available.

Reported Arrests of Juveniles for Drug Abuse Violations in 2000

National Total = 151,111 Reported Arrests*

ALPHA ORDER					RANK ORDER			
RANK	STATE		ARRESTS	% of USA	RANK	STATE	ARRESTS	% of USA
31	Alabama		963	0.6%	1	California	23,481	15.5%
43	Alaska		420	0.3%	2	Texas	15,024	9.9%
9	Arizona		4,817	3.2%	3	Florida	14,475	9.6%
35	Arkansas		863	0.6%	4	Illinois	9,526	6.3%
1	California		23,481	15.5%	5	New Jersey	7,812	5.2%
13	Colorado		3,014	2.0%	6	Maryland	6,600	4.4%
24	Connecticut		1,897	1.3%	7	Pennsylvania	5,672	3.8%
38	Delaware		610	0.4%	8	Minnesota	5,012	3.3%
3	Florida		14,475	9.6%	9	Arizona	4,817	3.2%
19	Georgia		2,253	1.5%	10	New York	4,623	3.1%
41	Hawaii		492	0.3%	11	North Carolina	3,470	2.3%
36	Idaho		813	0.5%	12	Michigan	3,423	2.3%
4	Illinois		9,526	6.3%	13	Colorado	3,014	2.0%
17	Indiana		2,362	1.6%	14	Ohio	2,887	1.9%
29	Iowa		1,251	0.8%	15	Washington	2,870	1.9%
NA	Kansas**		NA	NA	16	Missouri	2,688	1.8%
47	Kentucky		163	0.1%	17	Indiana	2,362	1.6%
20	Louisiana		2,215	1.5%	18	Virginia	2,271	1.5%
32	Maine		895	0.6%	19	Georgia	2,253	1.5%
6	Maryland		6,600	4.4%	20	Louisiana	2,215	1.5%
21	Massachusetts		2,144	1.4%	21	Massachusetts	2,144	1.4%
12	Michigan		3,423	2.3%	22	Oregon	2,067	1.4%
8	Minnesota		5,012	3.3%	23	Oklahoma	2,056	1.4%
30	Mississippi		1,093	0.7%	24	Connecticut	1,897	1.3%
16	Missouri		2,688	1.8%	25	Tennessee	1,830	1.2%
48	Montana		144	0.1%	26	Nevada	1,647	1.1%
27	Nebraska		1,368	0.9%	27	Nebraska	1,368	0.9%
26	Nevada		1,647	1.1%	28	Utah	1,277	0.8%
39	New Hampshire		595	0.4%	29	Iowa	1,251	0.8%
5	New Jersey		7,812	5.2%	30	Mississippi	1,093	0.7%
34	New Mexico		868	0.6%	31	Alabama	963	0.6%
10	New York		4,623	3.1%	32	Maine	895	0.6%
11	North Carolina		3,470	2.3%	33	South Carolina	873	0.6%
44	North Dakota		246	0.2%	34	New Mexico	868	0.6%
14	Ohio		2,887	1.9%	35	Arkansas	863	0.6%
23	Oklahoma		2,056	1.4%	36	Idaho	813	0.5%
22	Oregon		2,067	1.4%	37	Rhode Island	684	0.5%
7	Pennsylvania		5,672	3.8%	38	Delaware	610	0.4%
37	Rhode Island		684	0.5%	39	New Hampshire	595	0.4%
33	South Carolina		873	0.6%	40	South Dakota	518	0.3%
40	South Dakota		518	0.3%	41	Hawaii	492	0.3%
25	Tennessee		1,830	1.2%	42	Wyoming	486	0.3%
2	Texas		15,024	9.9%	43	Alaska	420	0.3%
28	Utah		1,277	0.8%	44	North Dakota	246	0.2%
45	Vermont		182	0.1%	45	Vermont	182	0.1%
18	Virginia		2,271	1.5%	46	West Virginia	171	0.1%
15	Washington		2,870	1.9%	47	Kentucky	163	0.1%
46	West Virginia		171	0.1%	48	Montana	144	0.1%
NA	Wisconsin**		NA	NA	NA	Kansas**	NA	NA
42	Wyoming		486	0.3%	NA	Wisconsin**	NA	NA
						District of Columbia**	NA	NA

Source: Federal Bureau of Investigation
   "Crime in the United States 2000" (Uniform Crime Reports, October 22, 2001)
*Arrests of youths 17 years and younger by law enforcement agencies submitting complete reports to the F.B.I. for
12 months in 2000. Includes offenses relating to possession, sale, use, growing and manufacturing of narcotic
drugs. See important note at beginning of this chapter.
**Not available.

Reported Juvenile Arrest Rate for Drug Abuse Violations in 2000

National Rate = 647.4 Reported Arrests per 100,000 Juvenile Population*

ALPHA ORDER

RANK	STATE	RATE
47	Alabama	263.9
31	Alaska	515.6
4	Arizona	893.4
45	Arkansas	319.7
25	California	584.4
8	Colorado	805.6
16	Connecticut	670.3
2	Delaware	1,391.6
6	Florida	887.1
34	Georgia	490.1
37	Hawaii	423.4
35	Idaho	482.3
1	Illinois	2,865.2
30	Indiana	524.5
40	Iowa	413.0
NA	Kansas**	NA
20	Kentucky	624.7
28	Louisiana	565.9
22	Maine	617.6
3	Maryland	1,286.3
39	Massachusetts	418.7
43	Michigan	341.1
5	Minnesota	890.9
21	Mississippi	619.1
9	Missouri	787.2
44	Montana	331.9
12	Nebraska	716.3
10	Nevada	779.8
13	New Hampshire	687.8
7	New Jersey	878.1
26	New Mexico	581.9
19	New York	633.0
32	North Carolina	507.1
42	North Dakota	354.2
38	Ohio	421.7
33	Oklahoma	500.7
17	Oregon	650.9
29	Pennsylvania	558.4
18	Rhode Island	639.7
14	South Carolina	679.4
15	South Dakota	673.0
36	Tennessee	424.1
23	Texas	601.2
27	Utah	578.9
46	Vermont	311.9
41	Virginia	399.2
24	Washington	596.1
48	West Virginia	184.4
NA	Wisconsin**	NA
11	Wyoming	766.1

RANK ORDER

RANK	STATE	RATE
1	Illinois	2,865.2
2	Delaware	1,391.6
3	Maryland	1,286.3
4	Arizona	893.4
5	Minnesota	890.9
6	Florida	887.1
7	New Jersey	878.1
8	Colorado	805.6
9	Missouri	787.2
10	Nevada	779.8
11	Wyoming	766.1
12	Nebraska	716.3
13	New Hampshire	687.8
14	South Carolina	679.4
15	South Dakota	673.0
16	Connecticut	670.3
17	Oregon	650.9
18	Rhode Island	639.7
19	New York	633.0
20	Kentucky	624.7
21	Mississippi	619.1
22	Maine	617.6
23	Texas	601.2
24	Washington	596.1
25	California	584.4
26	New Mexico	581.9
27	Utah	578.9
28	Louisiana	565.9
29	Pennsylvania	558.4
30	Indiana	524.5
31	Alaska	515.6
32	North Carolina	507.1
33	Oklahoma	500.7
34	Georgia	490.1
35	Idaho	482.3
36	Tennessee	424.1
37	Hawaii	423.4
38	Ohio	421.7
39	Massachusetts	418.7
40	Iowa	413.0
41	Virginia	399.2
42	North Dakota	354.2
43	Michigan	341.1
44	Montana	331.9
45	Arkansas	319.7
46	Vermont	311.9
47	Alabama	263.9
48	West Virginia	184.4
NA	Kansas**	NA
NA	Wisconsin**	NA
	District of Columbia**	NA

Source: Morgan Quitno Press using data from Federal Bureau of Investigation
    "Crime in the United States 2000" (Uniform Crime Reports, October 22, 2001)
*By law enforcement agencies submitting complete reports to the F.B.I. for 12 months in 2000. Arrests of youths 17
years and younger divided into population of 10 to 17 year olds. See important note at beginning of this chapter.
Includes offenses relating to possession, sale, use, growing and manufacturing of narcotic drugs.
**Not available.

Reported Arrests of Juveniles for Drug Abuse Violations
As a Percent of All Such Arrests in 2000
National Percent = 12.6% of Reported Drug Abuse Violation Arrests*

RANK	STATE	PERCENT	RANK	STATE	PERCENT
47	Alabama	7.8	1	Montana	36.2
2	Alaska	24.0	2	Alaska	24.0
17	Arizona	16.8	3	Minnesota	22.5
48	Arkansas	7.1	4	Wyoming	21.0
44	California	9.3	5	New Hampshire	20.2
11	Colorado	18.7	5	Utah	20.2
26	Connecticut	13.6	7	Hawaii	19.9
13	Delaware	17.8	7	North Dakota	19.9
37	Florida	11.0	7	South Dakota	19.9
46	Georgia	8.5	10	New Mexico	19.6
7	Hawaii	19.9	11	Colorado	18.7
20	Idaho	15.3	12	Maryland	18.3
19	Illinois	16.2	13	Delaware	17.8
23	Indiana	14.0	14	Maine	17.7
26	Iowa	13.6	15	Vermont	17.6
NA	Kansas**	NA	16	Rhode Island	17.2
38	Kentucky	10.9	17	Arizona	16.8
34	Louisiana	12.2	18	Nevada	16.3
14	Maine	17.7	19	Illinois	16.2
12	Maryland	18.3	20	Idaho	15.3
24	Massachusetts	13.9	21	Texas	14.4
28	Michigan	13.5	22	New Jersey	14.1
3	Minnesota	22.5	23	Indiana	14.0
42	Mississippi	9.6	24	Massachusetts	13.9
35	Missouri	12.0	25	Nebraska	13.7
1	Montana	36.2	26	Connecticut	13.6
25	Nebraska	13.7	26	Iowa	13.6
18	Nevada	16.3	28	Michigan	13.5
5	New Hampshire	20.2	29	Washington	13.4
22	New Jersey	14.1	30	Pennsylvania	13.3
10	New Mexico	19.6	31	Ohio	13.2
32	New York	13.0	32	New York	13.0
41	North Carolina	10.2	33	Oregon	12.6
7	North Dakota	19.9	34	Louisiana	12.2
31	Ohio	13.2	35	Missouri	12.0
43	Oklahoma	9.4	36	South Carolina	11.1
33	Oregon	12.6	37	Florida	11.0
30	Pennsylvania	13.3	38	Kentucky	10.9
16	Rhode Island	17.2	39	Virginia	10.8
36	South Carolina	11.1	40	Tennessee	10.3
7	South Dakota	19.9	41	North Carolina	10.2
40	Tennessee	10.3	42	Mississippi	9.6
21	Texas	14.4	43	Oklahoma	9.4
5	Utah	20.2	44	California	9.3
15	Vermont	17.6	45	West Virginia	8.9
39	Virginia	10.8	46	Georgia	8.5
29	Washington	13.4	47	Alabama	7.8
45	West Virginia	8.9	48	Arkansas	7.1
NA	Wisconsin**	NA	NA	Kansas**	NA
4	Wyoming	21.0	NA	Wisconsin**	NA
				District of Columbia**	NA

Source: Morgan Quitno Press using data from Federal Bureau of Investigation
"Crime in the United States 2000" (Uniform Crime Reports, October 22, 2001)
*Arrests of youths 17 years and younger by law enforcement agencies submitting complete reports to the F.B.I. for 12 months in 2000. Includes offenses relating to possession, sale, use, growing and manufacturing of narcotic drugs.
**Not available.

232

Reported Arrests of Juveniles for Sex Offenses in 2000

National Total = 11,933 Reported Arrests*

<table>
<tr><td colspan="5">ALPHA ORDER</td><td colspan="5">RANK ORDER</td></tr>
<tr><th>RANK</th><th>STATE</th><th>ARRESTS</th><th>% of USA</th><th>RANK</th><th>STATE</th><th>ARRESTS</th><th>% of USA</th></tr>
<tr><td>42</td><td>Alabama</td><td>25</td><td>0.2%</td><td>1</td><td>California</td><td>2,588</td><td>21.7%</td></tr>
<tr><td>36</td><td>Alaska</td><td>49</td><td>0.4%</td><td>2</td><td>Texas</td><td>933</td><td>7.8%</td></tr>
<tr><td>14</td><td>Arizona</td><td>284</td><td>2.4%</td><td>3</td><td>New York</td><td>735</td><td>6.2%</td></tr>
<tr><td>28</td><td>Arkansas</td><td>89</td><td>0.7%</td><td>4</td><td>Pennsylvania</td><td>670</td><td>5.6%</td></tr>
<tr><td>1</td><td>California</td><td>2,588</td><td>21.7%</td><td>5</td><td>New Jersey</td><td>460</td><td>3.9%</td></tr>
<tr><td>10</td><td>Colorado</td><td>313</td><td>2.6%</td><td>6</td><td>Florida</td><td>450</td><td>3.8%</td></tr>
<tr><td>23</td><td>Connecticut</td><td>152</td><td>1.3%</td><td>7</td><td>Maryland</td><td>404</td><td>3.4%</td></tr>
<tr><td>31</td><td>Delaware</td><td>70</td><td>0.6%</td><td>8</td><td>Georgia</td><td>363</td><td>3.0%</td></tr>
<tr><td>6</td><td>Florida</td><td>450</td><td>3.8%</td><td>9</td><td>Michigan</td><td>336</td><td>2.8%</td></tr>
<tr><td>8</td><td>Georgia</td><td>363</td><td>3.0%</td><td>10</td><td>Colorado</td><td>313</td><td>2.6%</td></tr>
<tr><td>27</td><td>Hawaii</td><td>103</td><td>0.9%</td><td>10</td><td>Utah</td><td>313</td><td>2.6%</td></tr>
<tr><td>26</td><td>Idaho</td><td>120</td><td>1.0%</td><td>12</td><td>Minnesota</td><td>297</td><td>2.5%</td></tr>
<tr><td>16</td><td>Illinois</td><td>258</td><td>2.2%</td><td>13</td><td>Washington</td><td>291</td><td>2.4%</td></tr>
<tr><td>22</td><td>Indiana</td><td>200</td><td>1.7%</td><td>14</td><td>Arizona</td><td>284</td><td>2.4%</td></tr>
<tr><td>30</td><td>Iowa</td><td>74</td><td>0.6%</td><td>15</td><td>Oregon</td><td>281</td><td>2.4%</td></tr>
<tr><td>NA</td><td>Kansas**</td><td>NA</td><td>NA</td><td>16</td><td>Illinois</td><td>258</td><td>2.2%</td></tr>
<tr><td>46</td><td>Kentucky</td><td>14</td><td>0.1%</td><td>17</td><td>Louisiana</td><td>255</td><td>2.1%</td></tr>
<tr><td>17</td><td>Louisiana</td><td>255</td><td>2.1%</td><td>18</td><td>Virginia</td><td>254</td><td>2.1%</td></tr>
<tr><td>37</td><td>Maine</td><td>47</td><td>0.4%</td><td>19</td><td>Missouri</td><td>252</td><td>2.1%</td></tr>
<tr><td>7</td><td>Maryland</td><td>404</td><td>3.4%</td><td>20</td><td>Ohio</td><td>226</td><td>1.9%</td></tr>
<tr><td>33</td><td>Massachusetts</td><td>61</td><td>0.5%</td><td>21</td><td>North Carolina</td><td>218</td><td>1.8%</td></tr>
<tr><td>9</td><td>Michigan</td><td>336</td><td>2.8%</td><td>22</td><td>Indiana</td><td>200</td><td>1.7%</td></tr>
<tr><td>12</td><td>Minnesota</td><td>297</td><td>2.5%</td><td>23</td><td>Connecticut</td><td>152</td><td>1.3%</td></tr>
<tr><td>35</td><td>Mississippi</td><td>50</td><td>0.4%</td><td>24</td><td>Nevada</td><td>151</td><td>1.3%</td></tr>
<tr><td>19</td><td>Missouri</td><td>252</td><td>2.1%</td><td>25</td><td>Nebraska</td><td>141</td><td>1.2%</td></tr>
<tr><td>38</td><td>Montana</td><td>32</td><td>0.3%</td><td>26</td><td>Idaho</td><td>120</td><td>1.0%</td></tr>
<tr><td>25</td><td>Nebraska</td><td>141</td><td>1.2%</td><td>27</td><td>Hawaii</td><td>103</td><td>0.9%</td></tr>
<tr><td>24</td><td>Nevada</td><td>151</td><td>1.3%</td><td>28</td><td>Arkansas</td><td>89</td><td>0.7%</td></tr>
<tr><td>44</td><td>New Hampshire</td><td>16</td><td>0.1%</td><td>29</td><td>Oklahoma</td><td>84</td><td>0.7%</td></tr>
<tr><td>5</td><td>New Jersey</td><td>460</td><td>3.9%</td><td>30</td><td>Iowa</td><td>74</td><td>0.6%</td></tr>
<tr><td>47</td><td>New Mexico</td><td>13</td><td>0.1%</td><td>31</td><td>Delaware</td><td>70</td><td>0.6%</td></tr>
<tr><td>3</td><td>New York</td><td>735</td><td>6.2%</td><td>32</td><td>Tennessee</td><td>68</td><td>0.6%</td></tr>
<tr><td>21</td><td>North Carolina</td><td>218</td><td>1.8%</td><td>33</td><td>Massachusetts</td><td>61</td><td>0.5%</td></tr>
<tr><td>38</td><td>North Dakota</td><td>32</td><td>0.3%</td><td>34</td><td>South Carolina</td><td>58</td><td>0.5%</td></tr>
<tr><td>20</td><td>Ohio</td><td>226</td><td>1.9%</td><td>35</td><td>Mississippi</td><td>50</td><td>0.4%</td></tr>
<tr><td>29</td><td>Oklahoma</td><td>84</td><td>0.7%</td><td>36</td><td>Alaska</td><td>49</td><td>0.4%</td></tr>
<tr><td>15</td><td>Oregon</td><td>281</td><td>2.4%</td><td>37</td><td>Maine</td><td>47</td><td>0.4%</td></tr>
<tr><td>4</td><td>Pennsylvania</td><td>670</td><td>5.6%</td><td>38</td><td>Montana</td><td>32</td><td>0.3%</td></tr>
<tr><td>40</td><td>Rhode Island</td><td>29</td><td>0.2%</td><td>38</td><td>North Dakota</td><td>32</td><td>0.3%</td></tr>
<tr><td>34</td><td>South Carolina</td><td>58</td><td>0.5%</td><td>40</td><td>Rhode Island</td><td>29</td><td>0.2%</td></tr>
<tr><td>40</td><td>South Dakota</td><td>29</td><td>0.2%</td><td>40</td><td>South Dakota</td><td>29</td><td>0.2%</td></tr>
<tr><td>32</td><td>Tennessee</td><td>68</td><td>0.6%</td><td>42</td><td>Alabama</td><td>25</td><td>0.2%</td></tr>
<tr><td>2</td><td>Texas</td><td>933</td><td>7.8%</td><td>43</td><td>Wyoming</td><td>23</td><td>0.2%</td></tr>
<tr><td>10</td><td>Utah</td><td>313</td><td>2.6%</td><td>44</td><td>New Hampshire</td><td>16</td><td>0.1%</td></tr>
<tr><td>48</td><td>Vermont</td><td>6</td><td>0.1%</td><td>44</td><td>West Virginia</td><td>16</td><td>0.1%</td></tr>
<tr><td>18</td><td>Virginia</td><td>254</td><td>2.1%</td><td>46</td><td>Kentucky</td><td>14</td><td>0.1%</td></tr>
<tr><td>13</td><td>Washington</td><td>291</td><td>2.4%</td><td>47</td><td>New Mexico</td><td>13</td><td>0.1%</td></tr>
<tr><td>44</td><td>West Virginia</td><td>16</td><td>0.1%</td><td>48</td><td>Vermont</td><td>6</td><td>0.1%</td></tr>
<tr><td>NA</td><td>Wisconsin**</td><td>NA</td><td>NA</td><td>NA</td><td>Kansas**</td><td>NA</td><td>NA</td></tr>
<tr><td>43</td><td>Wyoming</td><td>23</td><td>0.2%</td><td>NA</td><td>Wisconsin**</td><td>NA</td><td>NA</td></tr>
<tr><td></td><td></td><td></td><td></td><td>NA</td><td>District of Columbia**</td><td>NA</td><td>NA</td></tr>
</table>

Source: Federal Bureau of Investigation
    "Crime in the United States 2000" (Uniform Crime Reports, October 22, 2001)
*Arrests of youths 17 years and younger by law enforcement agencies submitting complete reports to the F.B.I. for 12 months in 2000. Excludes forcible rape, prostitution and commercialized vice. Includes statutory rape and offenses against chastity, common decency, morals and the like. See important note at beginning of this chapter.
**Not available.

233

Reported Juvenile Arrest Rate for Sex Offenses in 2000

National Rate = 51.1 Reported Arrests per 100,000 Juvenile Population*

ALPHA ORDER

RANK ORDER

RANK	STATE	RATE
48	Alabama	6.9
19	Alaska	60.2
23	Arizona	52.7
33	Arkansas	33.0
17	California	64.4
6	Colorado	83.7
20	Connecticut	53.7
1	Delaware	159.7
38	Florida	27.6
7	Georgia	79.0
4	Hawaii	88.6
14	Idaho	71.2
9	Illinois	77.6
28	Indiana	44.4
40	Iowa	24.4
NA	Kansas**	NA
20	Kentucky	53.7
16	Louisiana	65.1
35	Maine	32.4
8	Maryland	78.7
45	Massachusetts	11.9
32	Michigan	33.5
22	Minnesota	52.8
37	Mississippi	28.3
10	Missouri	73.8
12	Montana	73.7
10	Nebraska	73.8
13	Nevada	71.5
42	New Hampshire	18.5
24	New Jersey	51.7
47	New Mexico	8.7
3	New York	100.6
36	North Carolina	31.9
25	North Dakota	46.1
33	Ohio	33.0
41	Oklahoma	20.5
5	Oregon	88.5
15	Pennsylvania	66.0
39	Rhode Island	27.1
26	South Carolina	45.1
29	South Dakota	37.7
44	Tennessee	15.8
30	Texas	37.3
2	Utah	141.9
46	Vermont	10.3
27	Virginia	44.6
18	Washington	60.4
43	West Virginia	17.3
NA	Wisconsin**	NA
31	Wyoming	36.3

RANK	STATE	RATE
1	Delaware	159.7
2	Utah	141.9
3	New York	100.6
4	Hawaii	88.6
5	Oregon	88.5
6	Colorado	83.7
7	Georgia	79.0
8	Maryland	78.7
9	Illinois	77.6
10	Missouri	73.8
10	Nebraska	73.8
12	Montana	73.7
13	Nevada	71.5
14	Idaho	71.2
15	Pennsylvania	66.0
16	Louisiana	65.1
17	California	64.4
18	Washington	60.4
19	Alaska	60.2
20	Connecticut	53.7
20	Kentucky	53.7
22	Minnesota	52.8
23	Arizona	52.7
24	New Jersey	51.7
25	North Dakota	46.1
26	South Carolina	45.1
27	Virginia	44.6
28	Indiana	44.4
29	South Dakota	37.7
30	Texas	37.3
31	Wyoming	36.3
32	Michigan	33.5
33	Arkansas	33.0
33	Ohio	33.0
35	Maine	32.4
36	North Carolina	31.9
37	Mississippi	28.3
38	Florida	27.6
39	Rhode Island	27.1
40	Iowa	24.4
41	Oklahoma	20.5
42	New Hampshire	18.5
43	West Virginia	17.3
44	Tennessee	15.8
45	Massachusetts	11.9
46	Vermont	10.3
47	New Mexico	8.7
48	Alabama	6.9
NA	Kansas**	NA
NA	Wisconsin**	NA
	District of Columbia**	NA

Source: Morgan Quitno Press using data from Federal Bureau of Investigation
   "Crime in the United States 2000" (Uniform Crime Reports, October 22, 2001)
*By law enforcement agencies submitting complete reports to the F.B.I. for 12 months in 2000. Arrests of youths 17 years and younger divided into population of 10 to 17 year olds. See important note at beginning of this chapter. Excludes forcible rape, prostitution and commercialized vice. Includes statutory rape and offenses against chastity, common decency, morals and the like. **Not available.

Reported Arrests of Juveniles for Sex Offenses
As a Percent of All Such Arrests in 2000
National Percent = 17.9% of Reported Sex Offenses Arrests*

ALPHA ORDER

RANK	STATE	PERCENT
48	Alabama	8.4
17	Alaska	21.7
30	Arizona	16.2
35	Arkansas	13.9
28	California	16.9
15	Colorado	23.4
9	Connecticut	26.9
24	Delaware	19.3
46	Florida	9.5
34	Georgia	14.0
6	Hawaii	32.0
4	Idaho	34.8
43	Illinois	10.4
33	Indiana	14.4
8	Iowa	27.6
NA	Kansas**	NA
42	Kentucky	11.3
19	Louisiana	21.4
29	Maine	16.5
5	Maryland	33.0
45	Massachusetts	10.0
7	Michigan	28.9
12	Minnesota	23.9
31	Mississippi	16.1
37	Missouri	13.3
1	Montana	50.0
22	Nebraska	20.6
43	Nevada	10.4
37	New Hampshire	13.3
13	New Jersey	23.8
17	New Mexico	21.7
21	New York	20.7
41	North Carolina	11.4
3	North Dakota	40.0
39	Ohio	13.1
47	Oklahoma	9.4
20	Oregon	21.3
15	Pennsylvania	23.4
11	Rhode Island	24.6
10	South Carolina	26.5
36	South Dakota	13.4
27	Tennessee	17.7
25	Texas	19.1
2	Utah	40.4
26	Vermont	18.8
13	Virginia	23.8
23	Washington	20.2
40	West Virginia	12.1
NA	Wisconsin**	NA
32	Wyoming	15.6

RANK ORDER

RANK	STATE	PERCENT
1	Montana	50.0
2	Utah	40.4
3	North Dakota	40.0
4	Idaho	34.8
5	Maryland	33.0
6	Hawaii	32.0
7	Michigan	28.9
8	Iowa	27.6
9	Connecticut	26.9
10	South Carolina	26.5
11	Rhode Island	24.6
12	Minnesota	23.9
13	New Jersey	23.8
13	Virginia	23.8
15	Colorado	23.4
15	Pennsylvania	23.4
17	Alaska	21.7
17	New Mexico	21.7
19	Louisiana	21.4
20	Oregon	21.3
21	New York	20.7
22	Nebraska	20.6
23	Washington	20.2
24	Delaware	19.3
25	Texas	19.1
26	Vermont	18.8
27	Tennessee	17.7
28	California	16.9
29	Maine	16.5
30	Arizona	16.2
31	Mississippi	16.1
32	Wyoming	15.6
33	Indiana	14.4
34	Georgia	14.0
35	Arkansas	13.9
36	South Dakota	13.4
37	Missouri	13.3
37	New Hampshire	13.3
39	Ohio	13.1
40	West Virginia	12.1
41	North Carolina	11.4
42	Kentucky	11.3
43	Illinois	10.4
43	Nevada	10.4
45	Massachusetts	10.0
46	Florida	9.5
47	Oklahoma	9.4
48	Alabama	8.4
NA	Kansas**	NA
NA	Wisconsin**	NA
	District of Columbia**	NA

Source: Morgan Quitno Press using data from Federal Bureau of Investigation
   "Crime in the United States 2000" (Uniform Crime Reports, October 22, 2001)
*Arrests of youths 17 years and younger by law enforcement agencies submitting complete reports to the F.B.I. for
12 months in 2000. Excludes forcible rape, prostitution and commercialized vice. Includes statutory rape and
offenses against chastity, common decency, morals and the like.*
**Not available.*

Reported Arrests of Juveniles for Prostitution and Commercialized Vice in 2000

National Total = 1,134 Reported Arrests*

ALPHA ORDER					RANK ORDER			
RANK	STATE		ARRESTS	% of USA	RANK	STATE	ARRESTS	% of USA
37	Alabama		0	0.0%	1	California	266	23.5%
30	Alaska		1	0.1%	2	Florida	196	17.3%
6	Arizona		46	4.1%	3	Texas	115	10.1%
26	Arkansas		2	0.2%	4	Illinois	84	7.4%
1	California		266	23.5%	5	Minnesota	75	6.6%
20	Colorado		11	1.0%	6	Arizona	46	4.1%
23	Connecticut		5	0.4%	7	Georgia	45	4.0%
37	Delaware		0	0.0%	8	Nevada	34	3.0%
2	Florida		196	17.3%	9	Pennsylvania	33	2.9%
7	Georgia		45	4.0%	10	Maryland	29	2.6%
20	Hawaii		11	1.0%	11	Massachusetts	25	2.2%
37	Idaho		0	0.0%	12	New Jersey	24	2.1%
4	Illinois		84	7.4%	13	Ohio	21	1.9%
24	Indiana		4	0.4%	14	New York	16	1.4%
37	Iowa		0	0.0%	15	Missouri	14	1.2%
NA	Kansas**		NA	NA	15	Oklahoma	14	1.2%
37	Kentucky		0	0.0%	17	Oregon	13	1.1%
30	Louisiana		1	0.1%	17	Washington	13	1.1%
37	Maine		0	0.0%	19	North Carolina	12	1.1%
10	Maryland		29	2.6%	20	Colorado	11	1.0%
11	Massachusetts		25	2.2%	20	Hawaii	11	1.0%
30	Michigan		1	0.1%	22	Nebraska	9	0.8%
5	Minnesota		75	6.6%	23	Connecticut	5	0.4%
30	Mississippi		1	0.1%	24	Indiana	4	0.4%
15	Missouri		14	1.2%	24	South Carolina	4	0.4%
37	Montana		0	0.0%	26	Arkansas	2	0.2%
22	Nebraska		9	0.8%	26	New Mexico	2	0.2%
8	Nevada		34	3.0%	26	Rhode Island	2	0.2%
30	New Hampshire		1	0.1%	26	Virginia	2	0.2%
12	New Jersey		24	2.1%	30	Alaska	1	0.1%
26	New Mexico		2	0.2%	30	Louisiana	1	0.1%
14	New York		16	1.4%	30	Michigan	1	0.1%
19	North Carolina		12	1.1%	30	Mississippi	1	0.1%
37	North Dakota		0	0.0%	30	New Hampshire	1	0.1%
13	Ohio		21	1.9%	30	Tennessee	1	0.1%
15	Oklahoma		14	1.2%	30	Utah	1	0.1%
17	Oregon		13	1.1%	37	Alabama	0	0.0%
9	Pennsylvania		33	2.9%	37	Delaware	0	0.0%
26	Rhode Island		2	0.2%	37	Idaho	0	0.0%
24	South Carolina		4	0.4%	37	Iowa	0	0.0%
37	South Dakota		0	0.0%	37	Kentucky	0	0.0%
30	Tennessee		1	0.1%	37	Maine	0	0.0%
3	Texas		115	10.1%	37	Montana	0	0.0%
30	Utah		1	0.1%	37	North Dakota	0	0.0%
37	Vermont		0	0.0%	37	South Dakota	0	0.0%
26	Virginia		2	0.2%	37	Vermont	0	0.0%
17	Washington		13	1.1%	37	West Virginia	0	0.0%
37	West Virginia		0	0.0%	37	Wyoming	0	0.0%
NA	Wisconsin**		NA	NA	NA	Kansas**	NA	NA
37	Wyoming		0	0.0%	NA	Wisconsin**	NA	NA
						District of Columbia**	NA	NA

Source: Federal Bureau of Investigation
   "Crime in the United States 2000" (Uniform Crime Reports, October 22, 2001)
*Arrests of youths 17 years and younger by law enforcement agencies submitting complete reports to the F.B.I. for 12 months in 2000. Includes keeping a bawdy house, procuring or transporting women for immoral purposes. Attempts are included. See important note at beginning of this chapter.
**Not available.

Reported Juvenile Arrest Rate for Prostitution and Commercialized Vice in 2000

National Rate = 4.9 Reported Arrests per 100,000 Juvenile Population*

ALPHA ORDER

RANK	STATE	RATE
37	Alabama	0.0
27	Alaska	1.2
7	Arizona	8.5
30	Arkansas	0.7
8	California	6.6
19	Colorado	2.9
24	Connecticut	1.8
37	Delaware	0.0
4	Florida	12.0
5	Georgia	9.8
6	Hawaii	9.5
37	Idaho	0.0
1	Illinois	25.3
29	Indiana	0.9
37	Iowa	0.0
NA	Kansas**	NA
37	Kentucky	0.0
34	Louisiana	0.3
37	Maine	0.0
9	Maryland	5.7
10	Massachusetts	4.9
36	Michigan	0.1
3	Minnesota	13.3
31	Mississippi	0.6
13	Missouri	4.1
37	Montana	0.0
11	Nebraska	4.7
2	Nevada	16.1
27	New Hampshire	1.2
20	New Jersey	2.7
26	New Mexico	1.3
22	New York	2.2
24	North Carolina	1.8
37	North Dakota	0.0
17	Ohio	3.1
15	Oklahoma	3.4
13	Oregon	4.1
16	Pennsylvania	3.2
23	Rhode Island	1.9
17	South Carolina	3.1
37	South Dakota	0.0
35	Tennessee	0.2
12	Texas	4.6
32	Utah	0.5
37	Vermont	0.0
33	Virginia	0.4
20	Washington	2.7
37	West Virginia	0.0
NA	Wisconsin**	NA
37	Wyoming	0.0

RANK ORDER

RANK	STATE	RATE
1	Illinois	25.3
2	Nevada	16.1
3	Minnesota	13.3
4	Florida	12.0
5	Georgia	9.8
6	Hawaii	9.5
7	Arizona	8.5
8	California	6.6
9	Maryland	5.7
10	Massachusetts	4.9
11	Nebraska	4.7
12	Texas	4.6
13	Missouri	4.1
13	Oregon	4.1
15	Oklahoma	3.4
16	Pennsylvania	3.2
17	Ohio	3.1
17	South Carolina	3.1
19	Colorado	2.9
20	New Jersey	2.7
20	Washington	2.7
22	New York	2.2
23	Rhode Island	1.9
24	Connecticut	1.8
24	North Carolina	1.8
26	New Mexico	1.3
27	Alaska	1.2
27	New Hampshire	1.2
29	Indiana	0.9
30	Arkansas	0.7
31	Mississippi	0.6
32	Utah	0.5
33	Virginia	0.4
34	Louisiana	0.3
35	Tennessee	0.2
36	Michigan	0.1
37	Alabama	0.0
37	Delaware	0.0
37	Idaho	0.0
37	Iowa	0.0
37	Kentucky	0.0
37	Maine	0.0
37	Montana	0.0
37	North Dakota	0.0
37	South Dakota	0.0
37	Vermont	0.0
37	West Virginia	0.0
37	Wyoming	0.0
NA	Kansas**	NA
NA	Wisconsin**	NA
	District of Columbia**	NA

Source: Morgan Quitno Press using data from Federal Bureau of Investigation
   "Crime in the United States 2000" (Uniform Crime Reports, October 22, 2001)
*By law enforcement agencies submitting complete reports to the F.B.I. for 12 months in 2000. Arrests of youths 17
years and younger divided into population of 10 to 17 year olds. See important note at beginning of this chapter.
Includes keeping a bawdy house, procuring or transporting women for immoral purposes. Attempts are included.
**Not available.

237

Reported Arrests of Juveniles for Prostitution and Commercialized Vice
As a Percent of All Such Arrests in 2000
National Percent = 1.5% of Reported Prostitution/Commercialized Vice Arrests*

ALPHA ORDER

RANK ORDER

RANK	STATE	PERCENT
37	Alabama	0.0
22	Alaska	0.9
8	Arizona	1.8
28	Arkansas	0.6
6	California	2.1
22	Colorado	0.9
22	Connecticut	0.9
37	Delaware	0.0
14	Florida	1.4
15	Georgia	1.3
5	Hawaii	2.4
37	Idaho	0.0
16	Illinois	1.2
31	Indiana	0.4
37	Iowa	0.0
NA	Kansas**	NA
37	Kentucky	0.0
28	Louisiana	0.6
37	Maine	0.0
4	Maryland	3.4
11	Massachusetts	1.6
36	Michigan	0.1
3	Minnesota	3.7
18	Mississippi	1.1
26	Missouri	0.8
37	Montana	0.0
7	Nebraska	1.9
26	Nevada	0.8
1	New Hampshire	33.3
16	New Jersey	1.2
31	New Mexico	0.4
18	New York	1.1
18	North Carolina	1.1
37	North Dakota	0.0
22	Ohio	0.9
2	Oklahoma	4.9
11	Oregon	1.6
13	Pennsylvania	1.5
30	Rhode Island	0.5
18	South Carolina	1.1
37	South Dakota	0.0
33	Tennessee	0.3
8	Texas	1.8
33	Utah	0.3
37	Vermont	0.0
33	Virginia	0.3
10	Washington	1.7
37	West Virginia	0.0
NA	Wisconsin**	NA
37	Wyoming	0.0

RANK	STATE	PERCENT
1	New Hampshire	33.3
2	Oklahoma	4.9
3	Minnesota	3.7
4	Maryland	3.4
5	Hawaii	2.4
6	California	2.1
7	Nebraska	1.9
8	Arizona	1.8
8	Texas	1.8
10	Washington	1.7
11	Massachusetts	1.6
11	Oregon	1.6
13	Pennsylvania	1.5
14	Florida	1.4
15	Georgia	1.3
16	Illinois	1.2
16	New Jersey	1.2
18	Mississippi	1.1
18	New York	1.1
18	North Carolina	1.1
18	South Carolina	1.1
22	Alaska	0.9
22	Colorado	0.9
22	Connecticut	0.9
22	Ohio	0.9
26	Missouri	0.8
26	Nevada	0.8
28	Arkansas	0.6
28	Louisiana	0.6
30	Rhode Island	0.5
31	Indiana	0.4
31	New Mexico	0.4
33	Tennessee	0.3
33	Utah	0.3
33	Virginia	0.3
36	Michigan	0.1
37	Alabama	0.0
37	Delaware	0.0
37	Idaho	0.0
37	Iowa	0.0
37	Kentucky	0.0
37	Maine	0.0
37	Montana	0.0
37	North Dakota	0.0
37	South Dakota	0.0
37	Vermont	0.0
37	West Virginia	0.0
37	Wyoming	0.0
NA	Kansas**	NA
NA	Wisconsin**	NA
	District of Columbia**	NA

Source: Morgan Quitno Press using data from Federal Bureau of Investigation
    "Crime in the United States 2000" (Uniform Crime Reports, October 22, 2001)
**Arrests of youths 17 years and younger by law enforcement agencies submitting complete reports to the F.B.I. for
12 months in 2000. Includes keeping a bawdy house, procuring or transporting women for immoral purposes.
Attempts are included.*
**Not available.

Reported Arrests of Juveniles for Offenses Against Families & Children in 2000

National Total = 5,858 Reported Arrests*

<u>ALPHA ORDER</u>

RANK	STATE	ARRESTS	% of USA
19	Alabama	60	1.0%
28	Alaska	29	0.5%
6	Arizona	245	4.2%
12	Arkansas	111	1.9%
31	California	20	0.3%
15	Colorado	94	1.6%
14	Connecticut	100	1.7%
43	Delaware	4	0.1%
NA	Florida**	NA	NA
16	Georgia	80	1.4%
10	Hawaii	117	2.0%
30	Idaho	24	0.4%
22	Illinois	51	0.9%
7	Indiana	204	3.5%
40	Iowa	6	0.1%
NA	Kansas**	NA	NA
43	Kentucky	4	0.1%
4	Louisiana	416	7.1%
36	Maine	14	0.2%
21	Maryland	53	0.9%
13	Massachusetts	104	1.8%
34	Michigan	17	0.3%
32	Minnesota	18	0.3%
8	Mississippi	150	2.6%
10	Missouri	117	2.0%
41	Montana	5	0.1%
27	Nebraska	30	0.5%
46	Nevada	0	0.0%
36	New Hampshire	14	0.2%
24	New Jersey	34	0.6%
38	New Mexico	12	0.2%
3	New York	481	8.2%
9	North Carolina	126	2.2%
18	North Dakota	66	1.1%
1	Ohio	1,826	31.2%
19	Oklahoma	60	1.0%
32	Oregon	18	0.3%
23	Pennsylvania	48	0.8%
5	Rhode Island	273	4.7%
39	South Carolina	8	0.1%
17	South Dakota	78	1.3%
28	Tennessee	29	0.5%
2	Texas	619	10.6%
24	Utah	34	0.6%
41	Vermont	5	0.1%
24	Virginia	34	0.6%
45	Washington	3	0.1%
46	West Virginia	0	0.0%
NA	Wisconsin**	NA	NA
34	Wyoming	17	0.3%

<u>RANK ORDER</u>

RANK	STATE	ARRESTS	% of USA
1	Ohio	1,826	31.2%
2	Texas	619	10.6%
3	New York	481	8.2%
4	Louisiana	416	7.1%
5	Rhode Island	273	4.7%
6	Arizona	245	4.2%
7	Indiana	204	3.5%
8	Mississippi	150	2.6%
9	North Carolina	126	2.2%
10	Hawaii	117	2.0%
10	Missouri	117	2.0%
12	Arkansas	111	1.9%
13	Massachusetts	104	1.8%
14	Connecticut	100	1.7%
15	Colorado	94	1.6%
16	Georgia	80	1.4%
17	South Dakota	78	1.3%
18	North Dakota	66	1.1%
19	Alabama	60	1.0%
19	Oklahoma	60	1.0%
21	Maryland	53	0.9%
22	Illinois	51	0.9%
23	Pennsylvania	48	0.8%
24	New Jersey	34	0.6%
24	Utah	34	0.6%
24	Virginia	34	0.6%
27	Nebraska	30	0.5%
28	Alaska	29	0.5%
28	Tennessee	29	0.5%
30	Idaho	24	0.4%
31	California	20	0.3%
32	Minnesota	18	0.3%
32	Oregon	18	0.3%
34	Michigan	17	0.3%
34	Wyoming	17	0.3%
36	Maine	14	0.2%
36	New Hampshire	14	0.2%
38	New Mexico	12	0.2%
39	South Carolina	8	0.1%
40	Iowa	6	0.1%
41	Montana	5	0.1%
41	Vermont	5	0.1%
43	Delaware	4	0.1%
43	Kentucky	4	0.1%
45	Washington	3	0.1%
46	Nevada	0	0.0%
46	West Virginia	0	0.0%
NA	Florida**	NA	NA
NA	Kansas**	NA	NA
NA	Wisconsin**	NA	NA
	District of Columbia**	NA	NA

Source: Federal Bureau of Investigation
    "Crime in the United States 2000" (Uniform Crime Reports, October 22, 2001)

Arrests of youths 17 years and younger by law enforcement agencies submitting complete reports to the F.B.I. for 12 months in 2000. Includes nonsupport, neglect, desertion or abuse of family and children. See important note at beginning of this chapter.
*Not available.

Reported Juvenile Arrest Rate for Offenses Against Families & Children in 2000

National Rate = 27.0 Reported Arrests per 100,000 Juvenile Population*

ALPHA ORDER

RANK ORDER

RANK	STATE	RATE		RANK	STATE	RATE
21	Alabama	16.4		1	Ohio	266.7
12	Alaska	35.6		2	Rhode Island	255.3
9	Arizona	45.4		3	Louisiana	106.3
11	Arkansas	41.1		4	South Dakota	101.3
45	California	0.5		5	Hawaii	100.7
16	Colorado	25.1		6	North Dakota	95.0
13	Connecticut	35.3		7	Mississippi	85.0
32	Delaware	9.1		8	New York	65.9
NA	Florida**	NA		9	Arizona	45.4
20	Georgia	17.4		10	Indiana	45.3
5	Hawaii	100.7		11	Arkansas	41.1
28	Idaho	14.2		12	Alaska	35.6
25	Illinois	15.3		13	Connecticut	35.3
10	Indiana	45.3		14	Missouri	34.3
42	Iowa	2.0		15	Wyoming	26.8
NA	Kansas**	NA		16	Colorado	25.1
25	Kentucky	15.3		17	Texas	24.8
3	Louisiana	106.3		18	Massachusetts	20.3
31	Maine	9.7		19	North Carolina	18.4
30	Maryland	10.3		20	Georgia	17.4
18	Massachusetts	20.3		21	Alabama	16.4
43	Michigan	1.7		22	New Hampshire	16.2
41	Minnesota	3.2		23	Nebraska	15.7
7	Mississippi	85.0		24	Utah	15.4
14	Missouri	34.3		25	Illinois	15.3
29	Montana	11.5		25	Kentucky	15.3
23	Nebraska	15.7		27	Oklahoma	14.6
46	Nevada	0.0		28	Idaho	14.2
22	New Hampshire	16.2		29	Montana	11.5
40	New Jersey	3.8		30	Maryland	10.3
34	New Mexico	8.0		31	Maine	9.7
8	New York	65.9		32	Delaware	9.1
19	North Carolina	18.4		33	Vermont	8.6
6	North Dakota	95.0		34	New Mexico	8.0
1	Ohio	266.7		35	Tennessee	6.7
27	Oklahoma	14.6		36	South Carolina	6.2
38	Oregon	5.7		37	Virginia	6.0
39	Pennsylvania	4.7		38	Oregon	5.7
2	Rhode Island	255.3		39	Pennsylvania	4.7
36	South Carolina	6.2		40	New Jersey	3.8
4	South Dakota	101.3		41	Minnesota	3.2
35	Tennessee	6.7		42	Iowa	2.0
17	Texas	24.8		43	Michigan	1.7
24	Utah	15.4		44	Washington	0.6
33	Vermont	8.6		45	California	0.5
37	Virginia	6.0		46	Nevada	0.0
44	Washington	0.6		46	West Virginia	0.0
46	West Virginia	0.0		NA	Florida**	NA
NA	Wisconsin**	NA		NA	Kansas**	NA
15	Wyoming	26.8		NA	Wisconsin**	NA
					District of Columbia**	NA

Source: Morgan Quitno Press using data from Federal Bureau of Investigation
"Crime in the United States 2000" (Uniform Crime Reports, October 22, 2001)
By law enforcement agencies submitting complete reports to the F.B.I. for 12 months in 2000. Arrests of youths 17 years and younger divided into population of 10 to 17 year olds. See important note at beginning of this chapter. Includes nonsupport, neglect, desertion or abuse of family and children.
***Not available.*

240

Reported Arrests of Juveniles for Offenses Against Families and Children As a Percent of All Such Arrests in 2000

National Percent = 6.3% of Offenses Against Families and Children Arrests*

RANK	STATE	PERCENT		RANK	STATE	PERCENT
ALPHA ORDER				RANK ORDER		
23	Alabama	4.6		1	Rhode Island	55.9
12	Alaska	7.8		2	North Dakota	27.6
9	Arizona	11.5		3	South Dakota	24.1
19	Arkansas	5.1		4	Louisiana	22.6
29	California	3.2		5	Indiana	18.5
27	Colorado	3.6		6	New York	16.4
15	Connecticut	6.4		7	Texas	12.4
33	Delaware	2.4		8	Ohio	11.6
NA	Florida**	NA		9	Arizona	11.5
32	Georgia	2.7		10	New Hampshire	11.3
13	Hawaii	7.4		11	Wyoming	8.1
17	Idaho	5.8		12	Alaska	7.8
14	Illinois	7.2		13	Hawaii	7.4
5	Indiana	18.5		14	Illinois	7.2
42	Iowa	1.1		15	Connecticut	6.4
NA	Kansas**	NA		15	Pennsylvania	6.4
41	Kentucky	1.2		17	Idaho	5.8
4	Louisiana	22.6		18	Mississippi	5.3
31	Maine	2.9		19	Arkansas	5.1
33	Maryland	2.4		19	Massachusetts	5.1
19	Massachusetts	5.1		19	Tennessee	5.1
43	Michigan	0.5		22	Missouri	4.7
33	Minnesota	2.4		23	Alabama	4.6
18	Mississippi	5.3		24	Oklahoma	4.5
22	Missouri	4.7		25	Virginia	4.4
26	Montana	3.7		26	Montana	3.7
37	Nebraska	2.0		27	Colorado	3.6
46	Nevada	0.0		28	Utah	3.4
10	New Hampshire	11.3		29	California	3.2
45	New Jersey	0.2		30	Oregon	3.1
38	New Mexico	1.8		31	Maine	2.9
6	New York	16.4		32	Georgia	2.7
36	North Carolina	2.2		33	Delaware	2.4
2	North Dakota	27.6		33	Maryland	2.4
8	Ohio	11.6		33	Minnesota	2.4
24	Oklahoma	4.5		36	North Carolina	2.2
30	Oregon	3.1		37	Nebraska	2.0
15	Pennsylvania	6.4		38	New Mexico	1.8
1	Rhode Island	55.9		39	Washington	1.6
43	South Carolina	0.5		40	Vermont	1.3
3	South Dakota	24.1		41	Kentucky	1.2
19	Tennessee	5.1		42	Iowa	1.1
7	Texas	12.4		43	Michigan	0.5
28	Utah	3.4		43	South Carolina	0.5
40	Vermont	1.3		45	New Jersey	0.2
25	Virginia	4.4		46	Nevada	0.0
39	Washington	1.6		46	West Virginia	0.0
46	West Virginia	0.0		NA	Florida**	NA
NA	Wisconsin**	NA		NA	Kansas**	NA
11	Wyoming	8.1		NA	Wisconsin**	NA
					District of Columbia**	NA

Source: Morgan Quitno Press using data from Federal Bureau of Investigation
    "Crime in the United States 2000" (Uniform Crime Reports, October 22, 2001)
*Arrests of youths 17 years and younger by law enforcement agencies submitting complete reports to the F.B.I. for
12 months in 2000. Includes nonsupport, neglect, desertion or abuse of family and children.
**Not available.

Juvenile Death Sentences: 1973 to 2000

National Total = 182 Juveniles Sentenced to Death*

ALPHA ORDER

RANK ORDER

RANK	STATE	JUVENILES	% of USA
3	Alabama	20	11.0%
NA	Alaska***	NA	NA
12	Arizona	5	2.7%
17	Arkansas	2	1.1%
23	California	0	0.0%
23	Colorado	0	0.0%
23	Connecticut	0	0.0%
23	Delaware	0	0.0%
2	Florida	25	13.7%
6	Georgia	7	3.8%
NA	Hawaii***	NA	NA
23	Idaho	0	0.0%
23	Illinois	0	0.0%
15	Indiana	3	1.6%
NA	Iowa***	NA	NA
23	Kansas	0	0.0%
15	Kentucky	3	1.6%
4	Louisiana	11	6.0%
NA	Maine***	NA	NA
17	Maryland**	2	1.1%
NA	Massachusetts***	NA	NA
NA	Michigan***	NA	NA
NA	Minnesota***	NA	NA
4	Mississippi	11	6.0%
14	Missouri	4	2.2%
23	Montana	0	0.0%
20	Nebraska**	1	0.5%
17	Nevada	2	1.1%
23	New Hampshire	0	0.0%
20	New Jersey**	1	0.5%
23	New Mexico	0	0.0%
23	New York	0	0.0%
8	North Carolina	6	3.3%
NA	North Dakota***	NA	NA
8	Ohio**	6	3.3%
8	Oklahoma	6	3.3%
23	Oregon	0	0.0%
8	Pennsylvania	6	3.3%
NA	Rhode Island***	NA	NA
6	South Carolina	7	3.8%
23	South Dakota	0	0.0%
23	Tennessee	0	0.0%
1	Texas	48	26.4%
23	Utah	0	0.0%
NA	Vermont***	NA	NA
12	Virginia	5	2.7%
20	Washington**	1	0.5%
NA	West Virginia***	NA	NA
NA	Wisconsin***	NA	NA
23	Wyoming	0	0.0%

RANK	STATE	JUVENILES	% of USA
1	Texas	48	26.4%
2	Florida	25	13.7%
3	Alabama	20	11.0%
4	Louisiana	11	6.0%
4	Mississippi	11	6.0%
6	Georgia	7	3.8%
6	South Carolina	7	3.8%
8	North Carolina	6	3.3%
8	Ohio**	6	3.3%
8	Oklahoma	6	3.3%
8	Pennsylvania	6	3.3%
12	Arizona	5	2.7%
12	Virginia	5	2.7%
14	Missouri	4	2.2%
15	Indiana	3	1.6%
15	Kentucky	3	1.6%
17	Arkansas	2	1.1%
17	Maryland**	2	1.1%
17	Nevada	2	1.1%
20	Nebraska**	1	0.5%
20	New Jersey**	1	0.5%
20	Washington**	1	0.5%
23	California	0	0.0%
23	Colorado	0	0.0%
23	Connecticut	0	0.0%
23	Delaware	0	0.0%
23	Idaho	0	0.0%
23	Illinois	0	0.0%
23	Kansas	0	0.0%
23	Montana	0	0.0%
23	New Hampshire	0	0.0%
23	New Mexico	0	0.0%
23	New York	0	0.0%
23	Oregon	0	0.0%
23	South Dakota	0	0.0%
23	Tennessee	0	0.0%
23	Utah	0	0.0%
23	Wyoming	0	0.0%
NA	Alaska***	NA	NA
NA	Hawaii***	NA	NA
NA	Iowa***	NA	NA
NA	Maine***	NA	NA
NA	Massachusetts***	NA	NA
NA	Michigan***	NA	NA
NA	Minnesota***	NA	NA
NA	North Dakota***	NA	NA
NA	Rhode Island***	NA	NA
NA	Vermont***	NA	NA
NA	West Virginia***	NA	NA
NA	Wisconsin***	NA	NA
	District of Columbia***	NA	NA

Source: U.S. Department of Justice, Office of Juvenile Justice and Delinquency Prevention
    "Juveniles and the Death Penalty" (November 2000)
*These are juveniles 15 to 17 at the time of their crime. There were 196 sentences for these 182 juveniles.
**These states no longer allow the death penalty for offenders who commit crimes before age 18.
***No death penalty.

Juveniles in Custody in 1997

National Total = 105,790 Juveniles*

ALPHA ORDER

RANK	STATE	JUVENILES	% of USA
19	Alabama	1,685	1.6%
41	Alaska	352	0.3%
17	Arizona	1,868	1.8%
37	Arkansas	603	0.6%
1	California	19,899	18.8%
18	Colorado	1,748	1.7%
25	Connecticut	1,326	1.3%
44	Delaware	311	0.3%
3	Florida	5,975	5.6%
8	Georgia	3,622	3.4%
49	Hawaii	134	0.1%
47	Idaho	242	0.2%
9	Illinois	3,425	3.2%
12	Indiana	2,485	2.3%
30	Iowa	1,064	1.0%
26	Kansas	1,242	1.2%
28	Kentucky	1,079	1.0%
11	Louisiana	2,776	2.6%
43	Maine	318	0.3%
22	Maryland	1,498	1.4%
29	Massachusetts	1,065	1.0%
7	Michigan	3,710	3.5%
21	Minnesota	1,522	1.4%
35	Mississippi	756	0.7%
24	Missouri	1,401	1.3%
45	Montana	302	0.3%
36	Nebraska	741	0.7%
31	Nevada	857	0.8%
48	New Hampshire	186	0.2%
13	New Jersey	2,251	2.1%
33	New Mexico	778	0.7%
4	New York	4,661	4.4%
27	North Carolina	1,204	1.1%
46	North Dakota	272	0.3%
5	Ohio	4,318	4.1%
32	Oklahoma	808	0.8%
23	Oregon	1,462	1.4%
6	Pennsylvania	3,962	3.7%
39	Rhode Island	426	0.4%
20	South Carolina	1,583	1.5%
38	South Dakota	528	0.5%
15	Tennessee	2,118	2.0%
2	Texas	6,898	6.5%
34	Utah	768	0.7%
50	Vermont	49	0.0%
10	Virginia	2,879	2.7%
14	Washington	2,216	2.1%
40	West Virginia	398	0.4%
16	Wisconsin	2,013	1.9%
42	Wyoming	340	0.3%

RANK ORDER

RANK	STATE	JUVENILES	% of USA
1	California	19,899	18.8%
2	Texas	6,898	6.5%
3	Florida	5,975	5.6%
4	New York	4,661	4.4%
5	Ohio	4,318	4.1%
6	Pennsylvania	3,962	3.7%
7	Michigan	3,710	3.5%
8	Georgia	3,622	3.4%
9	Illinois	3,425	3.2%
10	Virginia	2,879	2.7%
11	Louisiana	2,776	2.6%
12	Indiana	2,485	2.3%
13	New Jersey	2,251	2.1%
14	Washington	2,216	2.1%
15	Tennessee	2,118	2.0%
16	Wisconsin	2,013	1.9%
17	Arizona	1,868	1.8%
18	Colorado	1,748	1.7%
19	Alabama	1,685	1.6%
20	South Carolina	1,583	1.5%
21	Minnesota	1,522	1.4%
22	Maryland	1,498	1.4%
23	Oregon	1,462	1.4%
24	Missouri	1,401	1.3%
25	Connecticut	1,326	1.3%
26	Kansas	1,242	1.2%
27	North Carolina	1,204	1.1%
28	Kentucky	1,079	1.0%
29	Massachusetts	1,065	1.0%
30	Iowa	1,064	1.0%
31	Nevada	857	0.8%
32	Oklahoma	808	0.8%
33	New Mexico	778	0.7%
34	Utah	768	0.7%
35	Mississippi	756	0.7%
36	Nebraska	741	0.7%
37	Arkansas	603	0.6%
38	South Dakota	528	0.5%
39	Rhode Island	426	0.4%
40	West Virginia	398	0.4%
41	Alaska	352	0.3%
42	Wyoming	340	0.3%
43	Maine	318	0.3%
44	Delaware	311	0.3%
45	Montana	302	0.3%
46	North Dakota	272	0.3%
47	Idaho	242	0.2%
48	New Hampshire	186	0.2%
49	Hawaii	134	0.1%
50	Vermont	49	0.0%
	District of Columbia	265	0.3%

Source: U.S. Department of Justice, Office of Juvenile Justice and Delinquency Prevention "Juvenile Offenders and Victims: 1999 National Report" (NCJ 178257)

*National total includes 3,401 juveniles in private facilities for whom state was not reported. All states are for ages through 17 except Georgia, Illinois, Louisiana, Massachusetts, Michigan, Missouri, New Hampshire, South Carolina, Texas and Wisconsin which are through age 16 and Connecticut, New York and North Carolina which are through age 15.

Rate of Juveniles in Custody in 1997

National Rate = 368 per 100,000 Juvenile Population*

ALPHA ORDER				RANK ORDER		
RANK	STATE	RATE		RANK	STATE	RATE
22	Alabama	348		1	Louisiana	582
9	Alaska	418		2	South Dakota	556
23	Arizona	344		3	California	549
43	Arkansas	198		4	Wyoming	511
3	California	549		5	Connecticut	508
16	Colorado	379		6	Georgia	480
5	Connecticut	508		7	Nevada	460
11	Delaware	402		8	South Carolina	427
13	Florida	394		9	Alaska	418
6	Georgia	480		10	Rhode Island	412
49	Hawaii	106		11	Delaware	402
48	Idaho	145		12	Virginia	399
32	Illinois	286		13	Florida	394
18	Indiana	366		14	Oregon	389
30	Iowa	307		15	Kansas	386
15	Kansas	386		16	Colorado	379
39	Kentucky	243		17	Michigan	375
1	Louisiana	582		18	Indiana	366
40	Maine	220		19	Wisconsin	359
33	Maryland	273		20	Tennessee	358
46	Massachusetts	194		21	Nebraska	353
17	Michigan	375		22	Alabama	348
36	Minnesota	258		23	Arizona	344
41	Mississippi	218		24	New Mexico	342
37	Missouri	248		25	North Dakota	336
34	Montana	266		26	Washington	335
21	Nebraska	353		27	Ohio	332
7	Nevada	460		28	Texas	327
47	New Hampshire	154		29	New York	323
34	New Jersey	266		30	Iowa	307
24	New Mexico	342		31	Pennsylvania	302
29	New York	323		32	Illinois	286
44	North Carolina	196		33	Maryland	273
25	North Dakota	336		34	Montana	266
27	Ohio	332		34	New Jersey	266
44	Oklahoma	196		36	Minnesota	258
14	Oregon	389		37	Missouri	248
31	Pennsylvania	302		38	Utah	247
10	Rhode Island	412		39	Kentucky	243
8	South Carolina	427		40	Maine	220
2	South Dakota	556		41	Mississippi	218
20	Tennessee	358		42	West Virginia	200
28	Texas	327		43	Arkansas	198
38	Utah	247		44	North Carolina	196
50	Vermont	70		44	Oklahoma	196
12	Virginia	399		46	Massachusetts	194
26	Washington	335		47	New Hampshire	154
42	West Virginia	200		48	Idaho	145
19	Wisconsin	359		49	Hawaii	106
4	Wyoming	511		50	Vermont	70
					District of Columbia	662

Source: U.S. Department of Justice, Office of Juvenile Justice and Delinquency Prevention
"Juvenile Offenders and Victims: 1999 National Report" (NCJ 178257)
*Includes committed and detained. Based on population age 10 through upper age of juvenile as defined by each state. All states are for ages through 17 except Georgia, Illinois, Louisiana, Massachusetts, Michigan, Missouri, New Hampshire, South Carolina, Texas and Wisconsin which are through age 16 and Connecticut, New York and North Carolina which are through age 15.

White Juvenile Custody Rate in 1997

National Rate = 204 White Juveniles in Custody per 100,000 White Juveniles*

ALPHA ORDER

RANK	STATE	RATE
27	Alabama	202
6	Alaska	289
11	Arizona	244
46	Arkansas	106
5	California	299
15	Colorado	238
32	Connecticut	160
40	Delaware	132
12	Florida	243
13	Georgia	240
50	Hawaii	65
38	Idaho	139
42	Illinois	127
7	Indiana	268
14	Iowa	239
9	Kansas	249
29	Kentucky	174
18	Louisiana	231
22	Maine	210
43	Maryland	123
47	Massachusetts	96
24	Michigan	205
34	Minnesota	155
41	Mississippi	129
31	Missouri	168
20	Montana	221
17	Nebraska	234
2	Nevada	382
37	New Hampshire	143
48	New Jersey	71
30	New Mexico	169
36	New York	152
45	North Carolina	108
8	North Dakota	261
24	Ohio	205
43	Oklahoma	123
4	Oregon	326
39	Pennsylvania	137
21	Rhode Island	220
15	South Carolina	238
3	South Dakota	356
19	Tennessee	226
34	Texas	155
28	Utah	188
49	Vermont	66
26	Virginia	204
10	Washington	246
33	West Virginia	156
23	Wisconsin	206
1	Wyoming	454

RANK ORDER

RANK	STATE	RATE
1	Wyoming	454
2	Nevada	382
3	South Dakota	356
4	Oregon	326
5	California	299
6	Alaska	289
7	Indiana	268
8	North Dakota	261
9	Kansas	249
10	Washington	246
11	Arizona	244
12	Florida	243
13	Georgia	240
14	Iowa	239
15	Colorado	238
15	South Carolina	238
17	Nebraska	234
18	Louisiana	231
19	Tennessee	226
20	Montana	221
21	Rhode Island	220
22	Maine	210
23	Wisconsin	206
24	Michigan	205
24	Ohio	205
26	Virginia	204
27	Alabama	202
28	Utah	188
29	Kentucky	174
30	New Mexico	169
31	Missouri	168
32	Connecticut	160
33	West Virginia	156
34	Minnesota	155
34	Texas	155
36	New York	152
37	New Hampshire	143
38	Idaho	139
39	Pennsylvania	137
40	Delaware	132
41	Mississippi	129
42	Illinois	127
43	Maryland	123
43	Oklahoma	123
45	North Carolina	108
46	Arkansas	106
47	Massachusetts	96
48	New Jersey	71
49	Vermont	66
50	Hawaii	65
	District of Columbia	0

Source: U.S. Department of Justice, Office of Juvenile Justice and Delinquency Prevention
"Juvenile Offenders and Victims: 1999 National Report" (NCJ 178257)
*Juveniles in residential placement. National rate includes juveniles in private facilities for whom state of offense was not reported. Does not include Hispanic juveniles. Based on population age 10 through upper age of juvenile as defined by each state. All states are for ages through 17 except Georgia, Illinois, Louisiana, Massachusetts, Michigan, Missouri, New Hampshire, South Carolina, Texas and Wisconsin which are through age 16 and Connecticut, New York and North Carolina which are through age 15.

Black Juvenile Custody Rate in 1997

National Rate = 1,018 Black Juveniles in Custody per 100,000 Black Juveniles*

ALPHA ORDER

RANK ORDER

RANK	STATE	RATE
37	Alabama	650
20	Alaska	1,055
24	Arizona	975
39	Arkansas	533
3	California	1,819
12	Colorado	1,397
2	Connecticut	2,225
15	Delaware	1,195
23	Florida	980
26	Georgia	952
42	Hawaii	212
NA	Idaho**	NA
27	Illinois	943
17	Indiana	1,168
1	Iowa	2,250
5	Kansas	1,767
25	Kentucky	967
18	Louisiana	1,140
NA	Maine**	NA
38	Maryland	592
33	Massachusetts	804
16	Michigan	1,171
8	Minnesota	1,676
41	Mississippi	319
35	Missouri	741
NA	Montana**	NA
7	Nebraska	1,754
28	Nevada	942
NA	New Hampshire**	NA
21	New Jersey	1,007
29	New Mexico	905
30	New York	886
40	North Carolina	435
NA	North Dakota**	NA
19	Ohio	1,105
36	Oklahoma	688
10	Oregon	1,505
13	Pennsylvania	1,348
4	Rhode Island	1,799
34	South Carolina	753
NA	South Dakota**	NA
32	Tennessee	843
31	Texas	853
11	Utah	1,400
NA	Vermont**	NA
22	Virginia	997
9	Washington	1,592
14	West Virginia	1,230
6	Wisconsin	1,756
NA	Wyoming**	NA

RANK	STATE	RATE
1	Iowa	2,250
2	Connecticut	2,225
3	California	1,819
4	Rhode Island	1,799
5	Kansas	1,767
6	Wisconsin	1,756
7	Nebraska	1,754
8	Minnesota	1,676
9	Washington	1,592
10	Oregon	1,505
11	Utah	1,400
12	Colorado	1,397
13	Pennsylvania	1,348
14	West Virginia	1,230
15	Delaware	1,195
16	Michigan	1,171
17	Indiana	1,168
18	Louisiana	1,140
19	Ohio	1,105
20	Alaska	1,055
21	New Jersey	1,007
22	Virginia	997
23	Florida	980
24	Arizona	975
25	Kentucky	967
26	Georgia	952
27	Illinois	943
28	Nevada	942
29	New Mexico	905
30	New York	886
31	Texas	853
32	Tennessee	843
33	Massachusetts	804
34	South Carolina	753
35	Missouri	741
36	Oklahoma	688
37	Alabama	650
38	Maryland	592
39	Arkansas	533
40	North Carolina	435
41	Mississippi	319
42	Hawaii	212
NA	Idaho**	NA
NA	Maine**	NA
NA	Montana**	NA
NA	New Hampshire**	NA
NA	North Dakota**	NA
NA	South Dakota**	NA
NA	Vermont**	NA
NA	Wyoming**	NA

District of Columbia   855

Source: U.S. Department of Justice, Office of Juvenile Justice and Delinquency Prevention
    "Juvenile Offenders and Victims: 1999 National Report" (NCJ 178257)
*Juveniles in residential placement. National rate includes juveniles in private facilities for whom state of offense was not reported. Does not include Hispanic juveniles. Based on population age 10 through upper age of juvenile as defined by each state. See note on preceding table for individual state upper ages.
**Too few black juveniles to calculate a reliable rate.

High School Dropout Rate in 1999

National Rate = 5.0%*

ALPHA ORDER

RANK	STATE	RATE
25	Alabama	4.4
10	Alaska	5.3
2	Arizona	8.4
9	Arkansas	6.0
NA	California**	NA
NA	Colorado**	NA
32	Connecticut	3.3
28	Delaware	4.1
NA	Florida**	NA
4	Georgia	7.4
NA	Hawaii**	NA
6	Idaho	6.9
7	Illinois	6.5
NA	Indiana**	NA
36	Iowa	2.5
NA	Kansas**	NA
14	Kentucky	4.9
1	Louisiana	10.0
32	Maine	3.3
25	Maryland	4.4
31	Massachusetts	3.6
NA	Michigan**	NA
20	Minnesota	4.5
11	Mississippi	5.2
16	Missouri	4.8
20	Montana	4.5
27	Nebraska	4.2
3	Nevada	7.9
NA	New Hampshire**	NA
34	New Jersey	3.1
5	New Mexico	7.0
NA	New York**	NA
NA	North Carolina**	NA
37	North Dakota	2.4
29	Ohio	3.9
11	Oklahoma	5.2
7	Oregon	6.5
30	Pennsylvania	3.8
20	Rhode Island	4.5
NA	South Carolina**	NA
20	South Dakota	4.5
18	Tennessee	4.6
NA	Texas**	NA
17	Utah	4.7
18	Vermont	4.6
20	Virginia	4.5
NA	Washington**	NA
14	West Virginia	4.9
35	Wisconsin	2.6
11	Wyoming	5.2

RANK ORDER

RANK	STATE	RATE
1	Louisiana	10.0
2	Arizona	8.4
3	Nevada	7.9
4	Georgia	7.4
5	New Mexico	7.0
6	Idaho	6.9
7	Illinois	6.5
7	Oregon	6.5
9	Arkansas	6.0
10	Alaska	5.3
11	Mississippi	5.2
11	Oklahoma	5.2
11	Wyoming	5.2
14	Kentucky	4.9
14	West Virginia	4.9
16	Missouri	4.8
17	Utah	4.7
18	Tennessee	4.6
18	Vermont	4.6
20	Minnesota	4.5
20	Montana	4.5
20	Rhode Island	4.5
20	South Dakota	4.5
20	Virginia	4.5
25	Alabama	4.4
25	Maryland	4.4
27	Nebraska	4.2
28	Delaware	4.1
29	Ohio	3.9
30	Pennsylvania	3.8
31	Massachusetts	3.6
32	Connecticut	3.3
32	Maine	3.3
34	New Jersey	3.1
35	Wisconsin	2.6
36	Iowa	2.5
37	North Dakota	2.4
NA	California**	NA
NA	Colorado**	NA
NA	Florida**	NA
NA	Hawaii**	NA
NA	Indiana**	NA
NA	Kansas**	NA
NA	Michigan**	NA
NA	New Hampshire**	NA
NA	New York**	NA
NA	North Carolina**	NA
NA	South Carolina**	NA
NA	Texas**	NA
NA	Washington**	NA

| | District of Columbia | 8.2 |

Source: U.S. Department of Education, National Center for Educational Statistics
    "Dropout Rates in the United States: 2000" (NCES 2002-114, November 2001)
*"Event" dropout rates showing the proportion of youth, ages 15-24 who dropped out of grades 10-12 in the 12
months preceding October 1999.
**Not available.

Percent of High School Students Who Carried a Weapon On School Property in the Previous Month: 1999
National Percent = 6.9% of High School Students*

ALPHA ORDER

RANK	STATE	PERCENT
7	Alabama	9.6
3	Alaska	11.4
NA	Arizona**	NA
5	Arkansas	10.4
NA	California**	NA
NA	Colorado**	NA
18	Connecticut	7.2
26	Delaware	6.2
20	Florida	7.1
NA	Georgia**	NA
27	Hawaii	6.0
NA	Idaho**	NA
24	Illinois	6.5
NA	Indiana**	NA
28	Iowa	5.7
NA	Kansas**	NA
7	Kentucky	9.6
33	Louisiana	4.3
22	Maine	6.9
NA	Maryland**	NA
17	Massachusetts	7.3
14	Michigan	7.5
NA	Minnesota**	NA
21	Mississippi	7.0
10	Missouri	8.5
9	Montana	9.2
31	Nebraska	5.1
12	Nevada	8.1
14	New Hampshire	7.5
32	New Jersey	4.5
4	New Mexico	11.0
11	New York	8.2
NA	North Carolina**	NA
14	North Dakota	7.5
29	Ohio	5.6
NA	Oklahoma**	NA
NA	Oregon**	NA
NA	Pennsylvania**	NA
NA	Rhode Island**	NA
18	South Carolina	7.2
24	South Dakota	6.5
12	Tennessee	8.1
NA	Texas**	NA
23	Utah	6.7
1	Vermont	11.9
NA	Virginia**	NA
NA	Washington**	NA
6	West Virginia	9.8
30	Wisconsin	5.5
2	Wyoming	11.8

RANK ORDER

RANK	STATE	PERCENT
1	Vermont	11.9
2	Wyoming	11.8
3	Alaska	11.4
4	New Mexico	11.0
5	Arkansas	10.4
6	West Virginia	9.8
7	Alabama	9.6
7	Kentucky	9.6
9	Montana	9.2
10	Missouri	8.5
11	New York	8.2
12	Nevada	8.1
12	Tennessee	8.1
14	Michigan	7.5
14	New Hampshire	7.5
14	North Dakota	7.5
17	Massachusetts	7.3
18	Connecticut	7.2
18	South Carolina	7.2
20	Florida	7.1
21	Mississippi	7.0
22	Maine	6.9
23	Utah	6.7
24	Illinois	6.5
24	South Dakota	6.5
26	Delaware	6.2
27	Hawaii	6.0
28	Iowa	5.7
29	Ohio	5.6
30	Wisconsin	5.5
31	Nebraska	5.1
32	New Jersey	4.5
33	Louisiana	4.3
NA	Arizona**	NA
NA	California**	NA
NA	Colorado**	NA
NA	Georgia**	NA
NA	Idaho**	NA
NA	Indiana**	NA
NA	Kansas**	NA
NA	Maryland**	NA
NA	Minnesota**	NA
NA	North Carolina**	NA
NA	Oklahoma**	NA
NA	Oregon**	NA
NA	Pennsylvania**	NA
NA	Rhode Island**	NA
NA	Texas**	NA
NA	Virginia**	NA
NA	Washington**	NA
	District of Columbia**	NA

Source: U.S. Department of Health and Human Services, Centers for Disease Control and Prevention
"Youth Risk Behavior Surveillance, United States 1999" (June 9, 2000)
(http://www.cdc.gov/mmwr/preview/mmwrhtml/ss4905a1.htm)
*Grades 9 through 12.
**Not available.

Percent of High School Students Threatened or Injured
With a Weapon on School Property in 1999
National Percent = 7.7% of High School Students*

ALPHA ORDER

RANK	STATE	PERCENT
26	Alabama	7.5
10	Alaska	9.2
NA	Arizona**	NA
4	Arkansas	9.8
NA	California**	NA
NA	Colorado**	NA
12	Connecticut	9.1
18	Delaware	8.2
1	Florida	10.9
NA	Georgia**	NA
31	Hawaii	6.7
NA	Idaho**	NA
27	Illinois	7.4
NA	Indiana**	NA
14	Iowa	8.8
NA	Kansas**	NA
7	Kentucky	9.5
2	Louisiana	10.0
3	Maine	9.9
NA	Maryland**	NA
15	Massachusetts	8.6
10	Michigan	9.2
NA	Minnesota**	NA
19	Mississippi	8.1
13	Missouri	8.9
32	Montana	6.5
33	Nebraska	5.5
8	Nevada	9.4
24	New Hampshire	7.6
6	New Jersey	9.6
5	New Mexico	9.7
9	New York	9.3
NA	North Carolina**	NA
22	North Dakota	8.0
19	Ohio	8.1
NA	Oklahoma**	NA
NA	Oregon**	NA
NA	Pennsylvania**	NA
NA	Rhode Island**	NA
15	South Carolina	8.6
30	South Dakota	6.8
15	Tennessee	8.6
NA	Texas**	NA
28	Utah	7.2
29	Vermont	7.0
NA	Virginia**	NA
NA	Washington**	NA
23	West Virginia	7.7
24	Wisconsin	7.6
19	Wyoming	8.1

RANK ORDER

RANK	STATE	PERCENT
1	Florida	10.9
2	Louisiana	10.0
3	Maine	9.9
4	Arkansas	9.8
5	New Mexico	9.7
6	New Jersey	9.6
7	Kentucky	9.5
8	Nevada	9.4
9	New York	9.3
10	Alaska	9.2
10	Michigan	9.2
12	Connecticut	9.1
13	Missouri	8.9
14	Iowa	8.8
15	Massachusetts	8.6
15	South Carolina	8.6
15	Tennessee	8.6
18	Delaware	8.2
19	Mississippi	8.1
19	Ohio	8.1
19	Wyoming	8.1
22	North Dakota	8.0
23	West Virginia	7.7
24	New Hampshire	7.6
24	Wisconsin	7.6
26	Alabama	7.5
27	Illinois	7.4
28	Utah	7.2
29	Vermont	7.0
30	South Dakota	6.8
31	Hawaii	6.7
32	Montana	6.5
33	Nebraska	5.5
NA	Arizona**	NA
NA	California**	NA
NA	Colorado**	NA
NA	Georgia**	NA
NA	Idaho**	NA
NA	Indiana**	NA
NA	Kansas**	NA
NA	Maryland**	NA
NA	Minnesota**	NA
NA	North Carolina**	NA
NA	Oklahoma**	NA
NA	Oregon**	NA
NA	Pennsylvania**	NA
NA	Rhode Island**	NA
NA	Texas**	NA
NA	Virginia**	NA
NA	Washington**	NA
	District of Columbia**	NA

Source: U.S. Department of Health and Human Services, Centers for Disease Control and Prevention
   "Youth Risk Behavior Surveillance, United States 1999" (June 9, 2000)
      (http://www.cdc.gov/mmwr/preview/mmwrhtml/ss4905a1.htm)
*Grades 9 through 12.
**Not available.

Percent of Teens Who Drink Alcohol: 1999

National Percent = 50.0% of Teenagers*

	ALPHA ORDER			RANK ORDER	
RANK	STATE	PERCENT	RANK	STATE	PERCENT
28	Alabama	45.4	1	North Dakota	60.5
26	Alaska	46.9	2	South Dakota	59.2
NA	Arizona**	NA	3	Montana	57.6
24	Arkansas	48.3	4	Nebraska	55.8
NA	California**	NA	5	Ohio	55.5
NA	Colorado**	NA	6	Iowa	55.0
19	Connecticut	49.6	7	Wyoming	54.8
26	Delaware	46.9	8	Louisiana	53.7
25	Florida	48.1	9	Nevada	53.0
NA	Georgia**	NA	9	New Mexico	53.0
31	Hawaii	44.6	11	Maine	52.5
NA	Idaho**	NA	11	New Hampshire	52.5
18	Illinois	49.7	13	Massachusetts	51.8
NA	Indiana**	NA	13	Wisconsin	51.8
6	Iowa	55.0	15	New Jersey	50.0
NA	Kansas**	NA	16	Missouri	49.9
17	Kentucky	49.8	17	Kentucky	49.8
8	Louisiana	53.7	18	Illinois	49.7
11	Maine	52.5	19	Connecticut	49.6
NA	Maryland**	NA	19	New York	49.6
13	Massachusetts	51.8	21	Vermont	49.5
23	Michigan	48.5	22	West Virginia	48.6
NA	Minnesota**	NA	23	Michigan	48.5
32	Mississippi	42.5	24	Arkansas	48.3
16	Missouri	49.9	25	Florida	48.1
3	Montana	57.6	26	Alaska	46.9
4	Nebraska	55.8	26	Delaware	46.9
9	Nevada	53.0	28	Alabama	45.4
11	New Hampshire	52.5	28	South Carolina	45.4
15	New Jersey	50.0	30	Tennessee	45.2
9	New Mexico	53.0	31	Hawaii	44.6
19	New York	49.6	32	Mississippi	42.5
NA	North Carolina**	NA	33	Utah	22.7
1	North Dakota	60.5	NA	Arizona**	NA
5	Ohio	55.5	NA	California**	NA
NA	Oklahoma**	NA	NA	Colorado**	NA
NA	Oregon**	NA	NA	Georgia**	NA
NA	Pennsylvania**	NA	NA	Idaho**	NA
NA	Rhode Island**	NA	NA	Indiana**	NA
28	South Carolina	45.4	NA	Kansas**	NA
2	South Dakota	59.2	NA	Maryland**	NA
30	Tennessee	45.2	NA	Minnesota**	NA
NA	Texas**	NA	NA	North Carolina**	NA
33	Utah	22.7	NA	Oklahoma**	NA
21	Vermont	49.5	NA	Oregon**	NA
NA	Virginia**	NA	NA	Pennsylvania**	NA
NA	Washington**	NA	NA	Rhode Island**	NA
22	West Virginia	48.6	NA	Texas**	NA
13	Wisconsin	51.8	NA	Virginia**	NA
7	Wyoming	54.8	NA	Washington**	NA
				District of Columbia**	NA

Source: U.S. Department of Health and Human Services, Centers for Disease Control and Prevention
"Youth Risk Behavior Surveillance, United States 1999" (June 9, 2000)
*Percentage of students (grades 9-12) who had at least one drink of alcohol on one or more of the past 30 days.
**Not available.

Percent of Teens Who Use Marijuana: 1999

National Percent = 26.7% of Teenagers*

RANK	STATE	PERCENT
23	Alabama	22.2
4	Alaska	30.7
NA	Arizona**	NA
18	Arkansas	24.4
NA	California**	NA
NA	Colorado**	NA
9	Connecticut	27.8
8	Delaware	29.0
21	Florida	23.1
NA	Georgia**	NA
16	Hawaii	24.7
NA	Idaho**	NA
24	Illinois	21.5
NA	Indiana**	NA
31	Iowa	18.5
NA	Kansas**	NA
19	Kentucky	23.6
28	Louisiana	20.2
3	Maine	30.9
NA	Maryland**	NA
5	Massachusetts	30.6
12	Michigan	25.9
NA	Minnesota**	NA
29	Mississippi	18.9
14	Missouri	25.6
15	Montana	25.5
32	Nebraska	15.6
12	Nevada	25.9
6	New Hampshire	30.3
22	New Jersey	22.7
2	New Mexico	31.2
20	New York	23.4
NA	North Carolina**	NA
30	North Dakota	18.8
11	Ohio	26.1
NA	Oklahoma**	NA
NA	Oregon**	NA
NA	Pennsylvania**	NA
NA	Rhode Island**	NA
17	South Carolina	24.5
27	South Dakota	20.7
10	Tennessee	26.6
NA	Texas**	NA
33	Utah	10.6
1	Vermont	33.7
NA	Virginia**	NA
NA	Washington**	NA
7	West Virginia	29.3
24	Wisconsin	21.5
26	Wyoming	21.4

RANK	STATE	PERCENT
1	Vermont	33.7
2	New Mexico	31.2
3	Maine	30.9
4	Alaska	30.7
5	Massachusetts	30.6
6	New Hampshire	30.3
7	West Virginia	29.3
8	Delaware	29.0
9	Connecticut	27.8
10	Tennessee	26.6
11	Ohio	26.1
12	Michigan	25.9
12	Nevada	25.9
14	Missouri	25.6
15	Montana	25.5
16	Hawaii	24.7
17	South Carolina	24.5
18	Arkansas	24.4
19	Kentucky	23.6
20	New York	23.4
21	Florida	23.1
22	New Jersey	22.7
23	Alabama	22.2
24	Illinois	21.5
24	Wisconsin	21.5
26	Wyoming	21.4
27	South Dakota	20.7
28	Louisiana	20.2
29	Mississippi	18.9
30	North Dakota	18.8
31	Iowa	18.5
32	Nebraska	15.6
33	Utah	10.6
NA	Arizona**	NA
NA	California**	NA
NA	Colorado**	NA
NA	Georgia**	NA
NA	Idaho**	NA
NA	Indiana**	NA
NA	Kansas**	NA
NA	Maryland**	NA
NA	Minnesota**	NA
NA	North Carolina**	NA
NA	Oklahoma**	NA
NA	Oregon**	NA
NA	Pennsylvania**	NA
NA	Rhode Island**	NA
NA	Texas**	NA
NA	Virginia**	NA
NA	Washington**	NA
	District of Columbia**	NA

Source: U.S. Department of Health and Human Services, Centers for Disease Control and Prevention
"Youth Risk Behavior Surveillance, United States 1999" (June 9, 2000)
*Percentage of students (grades 9-12) who used marijuana at least one or more times during the past 30 days.
**Not available.

Admissions of Juveniles to Alcohol and Other Drug Treatment Programs in 1999

National Total = 134,147 Juvenile Admissions*

ALPHA ORDER

RANK	STATE	ADMISSIONS	% of USA
23	Alabama	1,491	1.1%
36	Alaska	469	0.3%
NA	Arizona**	NA	NA
37	Arkansas	362	0.3%
1	California	13,798	10.3%
12	Colorado	3,525	2.6%
39	Connecticut	281	0.2%
43	Delaware	22	0.0%
6	Florida	8,255	6.2%
33	Georgia	740	0.6%
24	Hawaii	1,419	1.1%
NA	Idaho**	NA	NA
3	Illinois	11,648	8.7%
29	Indiana	891	0.7%
13	Iowa	3,376	2.5%
22	Kansas	1,635	1.2%
26	Kentucky	1,273	0.9%
18	Louisiana	2,365	1.8%
NA	Maine**	NA	NA
14	Maryland	3,183	2.4%
21	Massachusetts	2,181	1.6%
9	Michigan	4,821	3.6%
NA	Minnesota**	NA	NA
31	Mississippi	795	0.6%
20	Missouri	2,227	1.7%
NA	Montana**	NA	NA
42	Nebraska	72	0.1%
30	Nevada	842	0.6%
32	New Hampshire	768	0.6%
19	New Jersey	2,341	1.7%
41	New Mexico	125	0.1%
4	New York	9,690	7.2%
11	North Carolina	3,550	2.6%
38	North Dakota	327	0.2%
2	Ohio	12,416	9.3%
40	Oklahoma	226	0.2%
5	Oregon	8,492	6.3%
9	Pennsylvania	4,821	3.6%
34	Rhode Island	629	0.5%
16	South Carolina	2,808	2.1%
15	South Dakota	3,034	2.3%
35	Tennessee	576	0.4%
8	Texas	5,288	3.9%
17	Utah	2,524	1.9%
28	Vermont	967	0.7%
NA	Virginia**	NA	NA
7	Washington	7,450	5.6%
25	West Virginia	1,307	1.0%
27	Wisconsin	1,137	0.8%
NA	Wyoming**	NA	NA

RANK ORDER

RANK	STATE	ADMISSIONS	% of USA
1	California	13,798	10.3%
2	Ohio	12,416	9.3%
3	Illinois	11,648	8.7%
4	New York	9,690	7.2%
5	Oregon	8,492	6.3%
6	Florida	8,255	6.2%
7	Washington	7,450	5.6%
8	Texas	5,288	3.9%
9	Michigan	4,821	3.6%
9	Pennsylvania	4,821	3.6%
11	North Carolina	3,550	2.6%
12	Colorado	3,525	2.6%
13	Iowa	3,376	2.5%
14	Maryland	3,183	2.4%
15	South Dakota	3,034	2.3%
16	South Carolina	2,808	2.1%
17	Utah	2,524	1.9%
18	Louisiana	2,365	1.8%
19	New Jersey	2,341	1.7%
20	Missouri	2,227	1.7%
21	Massachusetts	2,181	1.6%
22	Kansas	1,635	1.2%
23	Alabama	1,491	1.1%
24	Hawaii	1,419	1.1%
25	West Virginia	1,307	1.0%
26	Kentucky	1,273	0.9%
27	Wisconsin	1,137	0.8%
28	Vermont	967	0.7%
29	Indiana	891	0.7%
30	Nevada	842	0.6%
31	Mississippi	795	0.6%
32	New Hampshire	768	0.6%
33	Georgia	740	0.6%
34	Rhode Island	629	0.5%
35	Tennessee	576	0.4%
36	Alaska	469	0.3%
37	Arkansas	362	0.3%
38	North Dakota	327	0.2%
39	Connecticut	281	0.2%
40	Oklahoma	226	0.2%
41	New Mexico	125	0.1%
42	Nebraska	72	0.1%
43	Delaware	22	0.0%
NA	Arizona**	NA	NA
NA	Idaho**	NA	NA
NA	Maine**	NA	NA
NA	Minnesota**	NA	NA
NA	Montana**	NA	NA
NA	Virginia**	NA	NA
NA	Wyoming**	NA	NA
	District of Columbia**	NA	NA

Source: National Association of State Alcohol and Drug Abuse Directors
    "State Resources and Services Related to Alcohol and Other Drug Problems-Fiscal Year 1998-1999" (July 2001)
*Youths 17 years and younger. National total is only for reporting states. Data are only from treatment units that received at least some funds administered by a state's alcohol/drug agency in fiscal year 1999. An additional 152,048 admissions were not reported by age.
**Not available.

Admissions of Juveniles to Alcohol and Other Drug Treatment Programs
As a Percent of All Admissions in 1999
National Percent = 8.0% of Admissions*

ALPHA ORDER

RANK STATE   PERCENT

RANK ORDER

RANK STATE   PERCENT

RANK	STATE	PERCENT		RANK	STATE	PERCENT
18	Alabama	9.0		1	Hawaii	25.2
22	Alaska	7.9		2	South Dakota	21.0
NA	Arizona**	NA		3	Utah	14.4
38	Arkansas	2.7		4	North Dakota	14.3
27	California	6.4		5	Iowa	13.8
28	Colorado	5.8		6	Washington	13.6
42	Connecticut	0.7		7	Oregon	13.1
43	Delaware	0.3		8	Ohio	12.8
14	Florida	11.0		9	Vermont	12.6
33	Georgia	4.5		10	Kansas	12.5
1	Hawaii	25.2		11	Texas	11.8
NA	Idaho**	NA		12	New Hampshire	11.7
15	Illinois	9.7		13	Maryland	11.5
33	Indiana	4.5		14	Florida	11.0
5	Iowa	13.8		15	Illinois	9.7
10	Kansas	12.5		16	Tennessee	9.4
32	Kentucky	4.8		17	South Carolina	9.2
19	Louisiana	8.3		18	Alabama	9.0
NA	Maine**	NA		19	Louisiana	8.3
13	Maryland	11.5		19	West Virginia	8.3
40	Massachusetts	2.3		21	Nevada	8.0
25	Michigan	6.9		22	Alaska	7.9
NA	Minnesota**	NA		23	North Carolina	7.6
36	Mississippi	4.2		24	Pennsylvania	7.3
30	Missouri	5.5		25	Michigan	6.9
NA	Montana**	NA		26	New York	6.6
39	Nebraska	2.5		27	California	6.4
21	Nevada	8.0		28	Colorado	5.8
12	New Hampshire	11.7		28	New Jersey	5.8
28	New Jersey	5.8		30	Missouri	5.5
41	New Mexico	0.9		31	Rhode Island	5.2
26	New York	6.6		32	Kentucky	4.8
23	North Carolina	7.6		33	Georgia	4.5
4	North Dakota	14.3		33	Indiana	4.5
8	Ohio	12.8		35	Wisconsin	4.4
36	Oklahoma	4.2		36	Mississippi	4.2
7	Oregon	13.1		36	Oklahoma	4.2
24	Pennsylvania	7.3		38	Arkansas	2.7
31	Rhode Island	5.2		39	Nebraska	2.5
17	South Carolina	9.2		40	Massachusetts	2.3
2	South Dakota	21.0		41	New Mexico	0.9
16	Tennessee	9.4		42	Connecticut	0.7
11	Texas	11.8		43	Delaware	0.3
3	Utah	14.4		NA	Arizona**	NA
9	Vermont	12.6		NA	Idaho**	NA
NA	Virginia**	NA		NA	Maine**	NA
6	Washington	13.6		NA	Minnesota**	NA
19	West Virginia	8.3		NA	Montana**	NA
35	Wisconsin	4.4		NA	Virginia**	NA
NA	Wyoming**	NA		NA	Wyoming**	NA
				NA	District of Columbia**	NA

Source: Morgan Quitno Press using data from National Association of State Alcohol and Drug Abuse Directors
"State Resources and Services Related to Alcohol and Other Drug Problems-Fiscal Year 1998-1999" (July 2001)
*Youths 17 years and younger. Data are only from treatment units that received at least some funds administered by
a state's alcohol/drug agency in fiscal year 1999. Percentages reflect admissions reported by age. An additional
152,048 admissions were not reported by age.
**Not available.

Victims of Child Abuse and Neglect in 1999

National Total = 826,162 Children*

ALPHA ORDER

RANK	STATE	CHILDREN	% of USA
16	Alabama	13,773	1.7%
36	Alaska	6,032	0.7%
25	Arizona	9,205	1.1%
33	Arkansas	7,564	0.9%
1	California	130,510	15.8%
34	Colorado	6,989	0.8%
15	Connecticut	14,514	1.8%
46	Delaware	2,111	0.3%
2	Florida	67,530	8.2%
9	Georgia	26,888	3.3%
44	Hawaii	2,669	0.3%
43	Idaho	2,928	0.4%
7	Illinois	33,125	4.0%
11	Indiana	21,608	2.6%
22	Iowa	9,763	1.2%
29	Kansas	8,452	1.0%
12	Kentucky	18,650	2.3%
17	Louisiana	12,614	1.5%
38	Maine	4,154	0.5%
14	Maryland	15,451	1.9%
8	Massachusetts	29,633	3.6%
10	Michigan	24,505	3.0%
19	Minnesota	11,113	1.3%
35	Mississippi	6,523	0.8%
26	Missouri	9,079	1.1%
42	Montana	3,414	0.4%
41	Nebraska	3,474	0.4%
30	Nevada	8,238	1.0%
50	New Hampshire	926	0.1%
24	New Jersey	9,222	1.1%
39	New Mexico	3,730	0.5%
3	New York	64,045	7.8%
6	North Carolina	36,976	4.5%
47	North Dakota	1,284	0.2%
4	Ohio	53,311	6.5%
13	Oklahoma	16,210	2.0%
18	Oregon	11,241	1.4%
37	Pennsylvania	5,076	0.6%
40	Rhode Island	3,485	0.4%
23	South Carolina	9,580	1.2%
45	South Dakota	2,561	0.3%
20	Tennessee	10,611	1.3%
5	Texas	39,488	4.8%
27	Utah	8,660	1.0%
49	Vermont	1,080	0.1%
31	Virginia	8,199	1.0%
32	Washington	8,039	1.0%
28	West Virginia	8,609	1.0%
21	Wisconsin	9,791	1.2%
48	Wyoming	1,221	0.1%

RANK ORDER

RANK	STATE	CHILDREN	% of USA
1	California	130,510	15.8%
2	Florida	67,530	8.2%
3	New York	64,045	7.8%
4	Ohio	53,311	6.5%
5	Texas	39,488	4.8%
6	North Carolina	36,976	4.5%
7	Illinois	33,125	4.0%
8	Massachusetts	29,633	3.6%
9	Georgia	26,888	3.3%
10	Michigan	24,505	3.0%
11	Indiana	21,608	2.6%
12	Kentucky	18,650	2.3%
13	Oklahoma	16,210	2.0%
14	Maryland	15,451	1.9%
15	Connecticut	14,514	1.8%
16	Alabama	13,773	1.7%
17	Louisiana	12,614	1.5%
18	Oregon	11,241	1.4%
19	Minnesota	11,113	1.3%
20	Tennessee	10,611	1.3%
21	Wisconsin	9,791	1.2%
22	Iowa	9,763	1.2%
23	South Carolina	9,580	1.2%
24	New Jersey	9,222	1.1%
25	Arizona	9,205	1.1%
26	Missouri	9,079	1.1%
27	Utah	8,660	1.0%
28	West Virginia	8,609	1.0%
29	Kansas	8,452	1.0%
30	Nevada	8,238	1.0%
31	Virginia	8,199	1.0%
32	Washington	8,039	1.0%
33	Arkansas	7,564	0.9%
34	Colorado	6,989	0.8%
35	Mississippi	6,523	0.8%
36	Alaska	6,032	0.7%
37	Pennsylvania	5,076	0.6%
38	Maine	4,154	0.5%
39	New Mexico	3,730	0.5%
40	Rhode Island	3,485	0.4%
41	Nebraska	3,474	0.4%
42	Montana	3,414	0.4%
43	Idaho	2,928	0.4%
44	Hawaii	2,669	0.3%
45	South Dakota	2,561	0.3%
46	Delaware	2,111	0.3%
47	North Dakota	1,284	0.2%
48	Wyoming	1,221	0.1%
49	Vermont	1,080	0.1%
50	New Hampshire	926	0.1%
	District of Columbia	2,308	0.3%

Source: U.S. Department of Health and Human Services, Children's Bureau
"Child Maltreatment 1999: 10 Years of Reporting"
State-substantiated or indicated incidents. Some children may be counted twice if they were victims of multiple types of abuse. Fifty-eight percent of maltreated children suffered neglect, 21% physical abuse, 11% sexual abuse, and the remainder suffered emotional maltreatment, medical neglect or other forms of maltreatment.

Rate of Child Abuse and Neglect in 1999

National Rate = 11.8 Abused Children per 1,000 Population Under 18*

ALPHA ORDER

RANK ORDER

RANK	STATE	RATE		RANK	STATE	RATE
20	Alabama	12.9		1	Alaska	30.7
1	Alaska	30.7		2	West Virginia	21.3
42	Arizona	6.9		3	Massachusetts	20.2
26	Arkansas	11.5		4	Kentucky	19.3
12	California	14.6		5	North Carolina	19.1
44	Colorado	6.6		6	Florida	18.9
9	Connecticut	17.5		7	Ohio	18.7
25	Delaware	11.6		8	Oklahoma	18.4
6	Florida	18.9		9	Connecticut	17.5
19	Georgia	13.1		10	Nevada	16.8
32	Hawaii	9.2		11	Montana	15.3
35	Idaho	8.4		12	California	14.6
28	Illinois	10.4		13	Rhode Island	14.5
16	Indiana	14.1		14	New York	14.4
17	Iowa	13.6		15	Maine	14.3
23	Kansas	12.1		16	Indiana	14.1
4	Kentucky	19.3		17	Iowa	13.6
27	Louisiana	10.6		17	Oregon	13.6
15	Maine	14.3		19	Georgia	13.1
24	Maryland	11.8		20	Alabama	12.9
3	Massachusetts	20.2		20	South Dakota	12.9
30	Michigan	9.6		22	Utah	12.2
33	Minnesota	8.7		23	Kansas	12.1
33	Mississippi	8.7		24	Maryland	11.8
45	Missouri	6.5		25	Delaware	11.6
11	Montana	15.3		26	Arkansas	11.5
38	Nebraska	7.8		27	Louisiana	10.6
10	Nevada	16.8		28	Illinois	10.4
49	New Hampshire	3.0		29	South Carolina	10.0
48	New Jersey	4.6		30	Michigan	9.6
40	New Mexico	7.5		30	Wyoming	9.6
14	New York	14.4		32	Hawaii	9.2
5	North Carolina	19.1		33	Minnesota	8.7
36	North Dakota	8.0		33	Mississippi	8.7
7	Ohio	18.7		35	Idaho	8.4
8	Oklahoma	18.4		36	North Dakota	8.0
17	Oregon	13.6		37	Tennessee	7.9
50	Pennsylvania	1.8		38	Nebraska	7.8
13	Rhode Island	14.5		38	Vermont	7.8
29	South Carolina	10.0		40	New Mexico	7.5
20	South Dakota	12.9		41	Wisconsin	7.3
37	Tennessee	7.9		42	Arizona	6.9
42	Texas	6.9		42	Texas	6.9
22	Utah	12.2		44	Colorado	6.6
38	Vermont	7.8		45	Missouri	6.5
47	Virginia	4.9		46	Washington	5.4
46	Washington	5.4		47	Virginia	4.9
2	West Virginia	21.3		48	New Jersey	4.6
41	Wisconsin	7.3		49	New Hampshire	3.0
30	Wyoming	9.6		50	Pennsylvania	1.8

District of Columbia   24.2

Source: Morgan Quitno Press using data from U.S. Department of Health and Human Services, Children's Bureau
     "Child Maltreatment 1999: 10 Years of Reporting"
*State-substantiated or indicated incidents.

Physically Abused Children in 1999

National Reporting States' Total = 166,626 Children*

RANK	STATE	CHILDREN	% of USA
7	Alabama	5,631	3.4%
32	Alaska	1,430	0.9%
20	Arizona	2,279	1.4%
27	Arkansas	2,055	1.2%
1	California	22,775	13.7%
28	Colorado	1,930	1.2%
19	Connecticut	2,357	1.4%
42	Delaware	534	0.3%
4	Florida	12,004	7.2%
12	Georgia	3,593	2.2%
47	Hawaii	173	0.1%
38	Idaho	848	0.5%
11	Illinois	3,724	2.2%
6	Indiana	6,725	4.0%
18	Iowa	2,460	1.5%
16	Kansas	2,604	1.6%
8	Kentucky	5,154	3.1%
15	Louisiana	2,641	1.6%
33	Maine	1,427	0.9%
NA	Maryland**	NA	NA
NA	Massachusetts**	NA	NA
9	Michigan	5,124	3.1%
14	Minnesota	2,758	1.7%
29	Mississippi	1,736	1.0%
21	Missouri	2,192	1.3%
44	Montana	315	0.2%
40	Nebraska	752	0.5%
36	Nevada	1,204	0.7%
45	New Hampshire	255	0.2%
24	New Jersey	2,149	1.3%
39	New Mexico	830	0.5%
2	New York	15,913	9.6%
34	North Carolina	1,327	0.8%
48	North Dakota	160	0.1%
3	Ohio	14,930	9.0%
10	Oklahoma	4,033	2.4%
30	Oregon	1,479	0.9%
13	Pennsylvania	3,151	1.9%
37	Rhode Island	928	0.6%
35	South Carolina	1,310	0.8%
41	South Dakota	643	0.4%
26	Tennessee	2,124	1.3%
5	Texas	11,567	6.9%
31	Utah	1,434	0.9%
46	Vermont	238	0.1%
17	Virginia	2,548	1.5%
22	Washington	2,180	1.3%
23	West Virginia	2,165	1.3%
25	Wisconsin	2,146	1.3%
43	Wyoming	359	0.2%

RANK ORDER

RANK	STATE	CHILDREN	% of USA
1	California	22,775	13.7%
2	New York	15,913	9.6%
3	Ohio	14,930	9.0%
4	Florida	12,004	7.2%
5	Texas	11,567	6.9%
6	Indiana	6,725	4.0%
7	Alabama	5,631	3.4%
8	Kentucky	5,154	3.1%
9	Michigan	5,124	3.1%
10	Oklahoma	4,033	2.4%
11	Illinois	3,724	2.2%
12	Georgia	3,593	2.2%
13	Pennsylvania	3,151	1.9%
14	Minnesota	2,758	1.7%
15	Louisiana	2,641	1.6%
16	Kansas	2,604	1.6%
17	Virginia	2,548	1.5%
18	Iowa	2,460	1.5%
19	Connecticut	2,357	1.4%
20	Arizona	2,279	1.4%
21	Missouri	2,192	1.3%
22	Washington	2,180	1.3%
23	West Virginia	2,165	1.3%
24	New Jersey	2,149	1.3%
25	Wisconsin	2,146	1.3%
26	Tennessee	2,124	1.3%
27	Arkansas	2,055	1.2%
28	Colorado	1,930	1.2%
29	Mississippi	1,736	1.0%
30	Oregon	1,479	0.9%
31	Utah	1,434	0.9%
32	Alaska	1,430	0.9%
33	Maine	1,427	0.9%
34	North Carolina	1,327	0.8%
35	South Carolina	1,310	0.8%
36	Nevada	1,204	0.7%
37	Rhode Island	928	0.6%
38	Idaho	848	0.5%
39	New Mexico	830	0.5%
40	Nebraska	752	0.5%
41	South Dakota	643	0.4%
42	Delaware	534	0.3%
43	Wyoming	359	0.2%
44	Montana	315	0.2%
45	New Hampshire	255	0.2%
46	Vermont	238	0.1%
47	Hawaii	173	0.1%
48	North Dakota	160	0.1%
NA	Maryland**	NA	NA
NA	Massachusetts**	NA	NA
	District of Columbia	332	0.2%

Source: U.S. Department of Health and Human Services, Children's Bureau
"Child Maltreatment 1999: 10 Years of Reporting"
*State-substantiated or indicated incidents. Some children may be counted twice if they were victims of multiple types of abuse. Fifty-eight percent of maltreated children suffered neglect, 21% physical abuse, 11% sexual abuse, and the remainder suffered emotional maltreatment, medical neglect or other forms of maltreatment.
**Not available.

Rate of Physically Abused Children in 1999

National Rate = 2.4 Physically Abused Children per 1,000 Population Under 18*

ALPHA ORDER

RANK	STATE	RATE
3	Alabama	5.3
1	Alaska	7.3
30	Arizona	1.7
15	Arkansas	3.1
19	California	2.6
28	Colorado	1.8
17	Connecticut	2.8
16	Delaware	2.9
12	Florida	3.4
30	Georgia	1.7
48	Hawaii	0.6
20	Idaho	2.4
42	Illinois	1.2
8	Indiana	4.4
12	Iowa	3.4
10	Kansas	3.7
3	Kentucky	5.3
23	Louisiana	2.2
6	Maine	4.9
NA	Maryland**	NA
NA	Massachusetts**	NA
25	Michigan	2.0
23	Minnesota	2.2
22	Mississippi	2.3
35	Missouri	1.6
40	Montana	1.4
30	Nebraska	1.7
20	Nevada	2.4
46	New Hampshire	0.8
43	New Jersey	1.1
30	New Mexico	1.7
11	New York	3.6
47	North Carolina	0.7
45	North Dakota	1.0
5	Ohio	5.2
7	Oklahoma	4.6
28	Oregon	1.8
43	Pennsylvania	1.1
9	Rhode Island	3.8
40	South Carolina	1.4
14	South Dakota	3.2
35	Tennessee	1.6
25	Texas	2.0
25	Utah	2.0
30	Vermont	1.7
38	Virginia	1.5
38	Washington	1.5
2	West Virginia	5.4
35	Wisconsin	1.6
17	Wyoming	2.8

RANK ORDER

RANK	STATE	RATE
1	Alaska	7.3
2	West Virginia	5.4
3	Alabama	5.3
3	Kentucky	5.3
5	Ohio	5.2
6	Maine	4.9
7	Oklahoma	4.6
8	Indiana	4.4
9	Rhode Island	3.8
10	Kansas	3.7
11	New York	3.6
12	Florida	3.4
12	Iowa	3.4
14	South Dakota	3.2
15	Arkansas	3.1
16	Delaware	2.9
17	Connecticut	2.8
17	Wyoming	2.8
19	California	2.6
20	Idaho	2.4
20	Nevada	2.4
22	Mississippi	2.3
23	Louisiana	2.2
23	Minnesota	2.2
25	Michigan	2.0
25	Texas	2.0
25	Utah	2.0
28	Colorado	1.8
28	Oregon	1.8
30	Arizona	1.7
30	Georgia	1.7
30	Nebraska	1.7
30	New Mexico	1.7
30	Vermont	1.7
35	Missouri	1.6
35	Tennessee	1.6
35	Wisconsin	1.6
38	Virginia	1.5
38	Washington	1.5
40	Montana	1.4
40	South Carolina	1.4
42	Illinois	1.2
43	New Jersey	1.1
43	Pennsylvania	1.1
45	North Dakota	1.0
46	New Hampshire	0.8
47	North Carolina	0.7
48	Hawaii	0.6
NA	Maryland**	NA
NA	Massachusetts**	NA

District of Columbia 3.5

Source: Morgan Quitno Press using data from U.S. Department of Health and Human Services, Children's Bureau
   "Child Maltreatment 1999: 10 Years of Reporting"
*State-substantiated or indicated incidents. National rate is for reporting states only. Some children may be counted twice if they were victims of multiple types of abuse. Fifty-eight percent of maltreated children suffered neglect, 21% physical abuse, 11% sexual abuse, and the remainder suffered emotional maltreatment, medical neglect or other forms of maltreatment. **Not available.

Sexually Abused Children in 1999

National Reporting States' Total = 88,238 Children*

ALPHA ORDER				RANK ORDER			
RANK	STATE	CHILDREN	% of USA	RANK	STATE	CHILDREN	% of USA
10	Alabama	3,181	3.6%	1	California	11,895	13.5%
32	Alaska	686	0.8%	2	Ohio	7,548	8.6%
35	Arizona	516	0.6%	3	Texas	5,901	6.7%
11	Arkansas	2,800	3.2%	4	Indiana	5,521	6.3%
1	California	11,895	13.5%	5	Florida	4,407	5.0%
25	Colorado	1,053	1.2%	6	Pennsylvania	4,079	4.6%
34	Connecticut	597	0.7%	7	Wisconsin	3,707	4.2%
43	Delaware	234	0.3%	8	New York	3,591	4.1%
5	Florida	4,407	5.0%	9	Illinois	3,363	3.8%
13	Georgia	2,265	2.6%	10	Alabama	3,181	3.6%
46	Hawaii	142	0.2%	11	Arkansas	2,800	3.2%
37	Idaho	383	0.4%	12	Missouri	2,363	2.7%
9	Illinois	3,363	3.8%	13	Georgia	2,265	2.6%
4	Indiana	5,521	6.3%	14	Tennessee	2,230	2.5%
24	Iowa	1,084	1.2%	15	Utah	1,891	2.1%
20	Kansas	1,327	1.5%	16	Michigan	1,589	1.8%
17	Kentucky	1,436	1.6%	17	Kentucky	1,436	1.6%
27	Louisiana	824	0.9%	18	Mississippi	1,379	1.6%
26	Maine	895	1.0%	19	North Carolina	1,353	1.5%
NA	Maryland**	NA	NA	20	Kansas	1,327	1.5%
NA	Massachusetts**	NA	NA	21	Oregon	1,325	1.5%
16	Michigan	1,589	1.8%	22	Oklahoma	1,294	1.5%
28	Minnesota	806	0.9%	23	Virginia	1,179	1.3%
18	Mississippi	1,379	1.6%	24	Iowa	1,084	1.2%
12	Missouri	2,363	2.7%	25	Colorado	1,053	1.2%
39	Montana	314	0.4%	26	Maine	895	1.0%
38	Nebraska	340	0.4%	27	Louisiana	824	0.9%
44	Nevada	227	0.3%	28	Minnesota	806	0.9%
42	New Hampshire	238	0.3%	29	West Virginia	743	0.8%
30	New Jersey	740	0.8%	30	New Jersey	740	0.8%
45	New Mexico	223	0.3%	31	Washington	724	0.8%
8	New York	3,591	4.1%	32	Alaska	686	0.8%
19	North Carolina	1,353	1.5%	33	South Carolina	599	0.7%
48	North Dakota	93	0.1%	34	Connecticut	597	0.7%
2	Ohio	7,548	8.6%	35	Arizona	516	0.6%
22	Oklahoma	1,294	1.5%	36	Vermont	436	0.5%
21	Oregon	1,325	1.5%	37	Idaho	383	0.4%
6	Pennsylvania	4,079	4.6%	38	Nebraska	340	0.4%
40	Rhode Island	310	0.4%	39	Montana	314	0.4%
33	South Carolina	599	0.7%	40	Rhode Island	310	0.4%
41	South Dakota	257	0.3%	41	South Dakota	257	0.3%
14	Tennessee	2,230	2.5%	42	New Hampshire	238	0.3%
3	Texas	5,901	6.7%	43	Delaware	234	0.3%
15	Utah	1,891	2.1%	44	Nevada	227	0.3%
36	Vermont	436	0.5%	45	New Mexico	223	0.3%
23	Virginia	1,179	1.3%	46	Hawaii	142	0.2%
31	Washington	724	0.8%	47	Wyoming	110	0.1%
29	West Virginia	743	0.8%	48	North Dakota	93	0.1%
7	Wisconsin	3,707	4.2%	NA	Maryland**	NA	NA
47	Wyoming	110	0.1%	NA	Massachusetts**	NA	NA
					District of Columbia	40	0.0%

Source: U.S. Department of Health and Human Services, Children's Bureau
    "Child Maltreatment 1999: 10 Years of Reporting"
*State-substantiated or indicated incidents. Some children may be counted twice if they were victims of multiple types of abuse. Fifty-eight percent of maltreated children suffered neglect, 21% physical abuse, 11% sexual abuse, and the remainder suffered emotional maltreatment, medical neglect or other forms of maltreatment.
**Not available.

Rate of Sexually Abused Children in 1999

National Rate = 1.3 Sexually Abused Children per 1,000 Population Under 18*

<table>
<tr><td colspan="3">ALPHA ORDER</td><td colspan="3">RANK ORDER</td></tr>
<tr><th>RANK</th><th>STATE</th><th>RATE</th><th>RANK</th><th>STATE</th><th>RATE</th></tr>
<tr><td>6</td><td>Alabama</td><td>3.0</td><td>1</td><td>Arkansas</td><td>4.2</td></tr>
<tr><td>3</td><td>Alaska</td><td>3.5</td><td>2</td><td>Indiana</td><td>3.6</td></tr>
<tr><td>46</td><td>Arizona</td><td>0.4</td><td>3</td><td>Alaska</td><td>3.5</td></tr>
<tr><td>1</td><td>Arkansas</td><td>4.2</td><td>4</td><td>Maine</td><td>3.1</td></tr>
<tr><td>21</td><td>California</td><td>1.3</td><td>4</td><td>Vermont</td><td>3.1</td></tr>
<tr><td>29</td><td>Colorado</td><td>1.0</td><td>6</td><td>Alabama</td><td>3.0</td></tr>
<tr><td>35</td><td>Connecticut</td><td>0.7</td><td>7</td><td>Ohio</td><td>2.7</td></tr>
<tr><td>21</td><td>Delaware</td><td>1.3</td><td>7</td><td>Utah</td><td>2.7</td></tr>
<tr><td>25</td><td>Florida</td><td>1.2</td><td>7</td><td>Wisconsin</td><td>2.7</td></tr>
<tr><td>26</td><td>Georgia</td><td>1.1</td><td>10</td><td>Kansas</td><td>1.9</td></tr>
<tr><td>43</td><td>Hawaii</td><td>0.5</td><td>11</td><td>Mississippi</td><td>1.8</td></tr>
<tr><td>26</td><td>Idaho</td><td>1.1</td><td>11</td><td>West Virginia</td><td>1.8</td></tr>
<tr><td>26</td><td>Illinois</td><td>1.1</td><td>13</td><td>Missouri</td><td>1.7</td></tr>
<tr><td>2</td><td>Indiana</td><td>3.6</td><td>13</td><td>Tennessee</td><td>1.7</td></tr>
<tr><td>16</td><td>Iowa</td><td>1.5</td><td>15</td><td>Oregon</td><td>1.6</td></tr>
<tr><td>10</td><td>Kansas</td><td>1.9</td><td>16</td><td>Iowa</td><td>1.5</td></tr>
<tr><td>16</td><td>Kentucky</td><td>1.5</td><td>16</td><td>Kentucky</td><td>1.5</td></tr>
<tr><td>35</td><td>Louisiana</td><td>0.7</td><td>16</td><td>Oklahoma</td><td>1.5</td></tr>
<tr><td>4</td><td>Maine</td><td>3.1</td><td>19</td><td>Montana</td><td>1.4</td></tr>
<tr><td>NA</td><td>Maryland**</td><td>NA</td><td>19</td><td>Pennsylvania</td><td>1.4</td></tr>
<tr><td>NA</td><td>Massachusetts**</td><td>NA</td><td>21</td><td>California</td><td>1.3</td></tr>
<tr><td>39</td><td>Michigan</td><td>0.6</td><td>21</td><td>Delaware</td><td>1.3</td></tr>
<tr><td>39</td><td>Minnesota</td><td>0.6</td><td>21</td><td>Rhode Island</td><td>1.3</td></tr>
<tr><td>11</td><td>Mississippi</td><td>1.8</td><td>21</td><td>South Dakota</td><td>1.3</td></tr>
<tr><td>13</td><td>Missouri</td><td>1.7</td><td>25</td><td>Florida</td><td>1.2</td></tr>
<tr><td>19</td><td>Montana</td><td>1.4</td><td>26</td><td>Georgia</td><td>1.1</td></tr>
<tr><td>32</td><td>Nebraska</td><td>0.8</td><td>26</td><td>Idaho</td><td>1.1</td></tr>
<tr><td>43</td><td>Nevada</td><td>0.5</td><td>26</td><td>Illinois</td><td>1.1</td></tr>
<tr><td>32</td><td>New Hampshire</td><td>0.8</td><td>29</td><td>Colorado</td><td>1.0</td></tr>
<tr><td>46</td><td>New Jersey</td><td>0.4</td><td>29</td><td>Texas</td><td>1.0</td></tr>
<tr><td>46</td><td>New Mexico</td><td>0.4</td><td>31</td><td>Wyoming</td><td>0.9</td></tr>
<tr><td>32</td><td>New York</td><td>0.8</td><td>32</td><td>Nebraska</td><td>0.8</td></tr>
<tr><td>35</td><td>North Carolina</td><td>0.7</td><td>32</td><td>New Hampshire</td><td>0.8</td></tr>
<tr><td>39</td><td>North Dakota</td><td>0.6</td><td>32</td><td>New York</td><td>0.8</td></tr>
<tr><td>7</td><td>Ohio</td><td>2.7</td><td>35</td><td>Connecticut</td><td>0.7</td></tr>
<tr><td>16</td><td>Oklahoma</td><td>1.5</td><td>35</td><td>Louisiana</td><td>0.7</td></tr>
<tr><td>15</td><td>Oregon</td><td>1.6</td><td>35</td><td>North Carolina</td><td>0.7</td></tr>
<tr><td>19</td><td>Pennsylvania</td><td>1.4</td><td>35</td><td>Virginia</td><td>0.7</td></tr>
<tr><td>21</td><td>Rhode Island</td><td>1.3</td><td>39</td><td>Michigan</td><td>0.6</td></tr>
<tr><td>39</td><td>South Carolina</td><td>0.6</td><td>39</td><td>Minnesota</td><td>0.6</td></tr>
<tr><td>21</td><td>South Dakota</td><td>1.3</td><td>39</td><td>North Dakota</td><td>0.6</td></tr>
<tr><td>13</td><td>Tennessee</td><td>1.7</td><td>39</td><td>South Carolina</td><td>0.6</td></tr>
<tr><td>29</td><td>Texas</td><td>1.0</td><td>43</td><td>Hawaii</td><td>0.5</td></tr>
<tr><td>7</td><td>Utah</td><td>2.7</td><td>43</td><td>Nevada</td><td>0.5</td></tr>
<tr><td>4</td><td>Vermont</td><td>3.1</td><td>43</td><td>Washington</td><td>0.5</td></tr>
<tr><td>35</td><td>Virginia</td><td>0.7</td><td>46</td><td>Arizona</td><td>0.4</td></tr>
<tr><td>43</td><td>Washington</td><td>0.5</td><td>46</td><td>New Jersey</td><td>0.4</td></tr>
<tr><td>11</td><td>West Virginia</td><td>1.8</td><td>46</td><td>New Mexico</td><td>0.4</td></tr>
<tr><td>7</td><td>Wisconsin</td><td>2.7</td><td>NA</td><td>Maryland**</td><td>NA</td></tr>
<tr><td>31</td><td>Wyoming</td><td>0.9</td><td>NA</td><td>Massachusetts**</td><td>NA</td></tr>
<tr><td></td><td></td><td></td><td></td><td>District of Columbia</td><td>0.4</td></tr>
</table>

Source: Morgan Quitno Press using data from U.S. Department of Health and Human Services, Children's Bureau
"Child Maltreatment 1999: 10 Years of Reporting"
*State-substantiated or indicated incidents. National rate is for reporting states only. Some children may be counted twice if they were victims of multiple types of abuse. Fifty-eight percent of maltreated children suffered neglect, 21% physical abuse, 11% sexual abuse, and the remainder suffered emotional maltreatment, medical neglect or other forms of maltreatment. **Not available.

Emotionally Abused Children in 1999

National Reporting States' Total = 59,846 Children*

ALPHA ORDER

RANK	STATE	CHILDREN	% of USA
18	Alabama	677	1.1%
22	Alaska	488	0.8%
36	Arizona	115	0.2%
42	Arkansas	44	0.1%
1	California	23,190	38.7%
13	Colorado	1,020	1.7%
2	Connecticut	7,229	12.1%
25	Delaware	327	0.5%
6	Florida	2,031	3.4%
12	Georgia	1,059	1.8%
42	Hawaii	44	0.1%
46	Idaho	10	0.0%
24	Illinois	399	0.7%
NA	Indiana**	NA	NA
34	Iowa	119	0.2%
10	Kansas	1,184	2.0%
16	Kentucky	769	1.3%
21	Louisiana	527	0.9%
4	Maine	2,263	3.8%
NA	Maryland**	NA	NA
NA	Massachusetts**	NA	NA
8	Michigan	1,690	2.8%
37	Minnesota	109	0.2%
30	Mississippi	174	0.3%
31	Missouri	139	0.2%
23	Montana	418	0.7%
32	Nebraska	134	0.2%
26	Nevada	302	0.5%
41	New Hampshire	49	0.1%
29	New Jersey	256	0.4%
20	New Mexico	615	1.0%
11	New York	1,116	1.9%
35	North Carolina	118	0.2%
19	North Dakota	620	1.0%
5	Ohio	2,252	3.8%
7	Oklahoma	1,851	3.1%
17	Oregon	749	1.3%
38	Pennsylvania	102	0.2%
44	Rhode Island	21	0.0%
40	South Carolina	50	0.1%
27	South Dakota	293	0.5%
33	Tennessee	130	0.2%
9	Texas	1,392	2.3%
3	Utah	3,583	6.0%
46	Vermont	10	0.0%
28	Virginia	275	0.5%
14	Washington	877	1.5%
15	West Virginia	853	1.4%
39	Wisconsin	66	0.1%
45	Wyoming	19	0.0%

RANK ORDER

RANK	STATE	CHILDREN	% of USA
1	California	23,190	38.7%
2	Connecticut	7,229	12.1%
3	Utah	3,583	6.0%
4	Maine	2,263	3.8%
5	Ohio	2,252	3.8%
6	Florida	2,031	3.4%
7	Oklahoma	1,851	3.1%
8	Michigan	1,690	2.8%
9	Texas	1,392	2.3%
10	Kansas	1,184	2.0%
11	New York	1,116	1.9%
12	Georgia	1,059	1.8%
13	Colorado	1,020	1.7%
14	Washington	877	1.5%
15	West Virginia	853	1.4%
16	Kentucky	769	1.3%
17	Oregon	749	1.3%
18	Alabama	677	1.1%
19	North Dakota	620	1.0%
20	New Mexico	615	1.0%
21	Louisiana	527	0.9%
22	Alaska	488	0.8%
23	Montana	418	0.7%
24	Illinois	399	0.7%
25	Delaware	327	0.5%
26	Nevada	302	0.5%
27	South Dakota	293	0.5%
28	Virginia	275	0.5%
29	New Jersey	256	0.4%
30	Mississippi	174	0.3%
31	Missouri	139	0.2%
32	Nebraska	134	0.2%
33	Tennessee	130	0.2%
34	Iowa	119	0.2%
35	North Carolina	118	0.2%
36	Arizona	115	0.2%
37	Minnesota	109	0.2%
38	Pennsylvania	102	0.2%
39	Wisconsin	66	0.1%
40	South Carolina	50	0.1%
41	New Hampshire	49	0.1%
42	Arkansas	44	0.1%
42	Hawaii	44	0.1%
44	Rhode Island	21	0.0%
45	Wyoming	19	0.0%
46	Idaho	10	0.0%
46	Vermont	10	0.0%
NA	Indiana**	NA	NA
NA	Maryland**	NA	NA
NA	Massachusetts**	NA	NA
	District of Columbia	88	0.1%

Source: U.S. Department of Health and Human Services, Children's Bureau
"Child Maltreatment 1999: 10 Years of Reporting"
*State-substantiated or indicated incidents. Some children may be counted twice if they were victims of multiple types of abuse. Fifty-eight percent of maltreated children suffered neglect, 21% physical abuse, 11% sexual abuse, and the remainder suffered emotional maltreatment, medical neglect or other forms of maltreatment.
**Not available.

Rate of Emotionally Abused Children in 1999

National Rate = 0.9 Emotionally Abused Children per 1,000 Population Under 18*

ALPHA ORDER

RANK ORDER

RANK	STATE	RATE		RANK	STATE	RATE
19	Alabama	0.6		1	Connecticut	8.7
6	Alaska	2.5		2	Maine	7.8
33	Arizona	0.1		3	Utah	5.1
33	Arkansas	0.1		4	North Dakota	3.9
5	California	2.6		5	California	2.6
14	Colorado	1.0		6	Alaska	2.5
1	Connecticut	8.7		7	Oklahoma	2.1
10	Delaware	1.8		7	West Virginia	2.1
19	Florida	0.6		9	Montana	1.9
23	Georgia	0.5		10	Delaware	1.8
27	Hawaii	0.2		11	Kansas	1.7
45	Idaho	0.0		12	South Dakota	1.5
33	Illinois	0.1		13	New Mexico	1.2
NA	Indiana**	NA		14	Colorado	1.0
27	Iowa	0.2		15	Oregon	0.9
11	Kansas	1.7		16	Kentucky	0.8
16	Kentucky	0.8		16	Ohio	0.8
24	Louisiana	0.4		18	Michigan	0.7
2	Maine	7.8		19	Alabama	0.6
NA	Maryland**	NA		19	Florida	0.6
NA	Massachusetts**	NA		19	Nevada	0.6
18	Michigan	0.7		19	Washington	0.6
33	Minnesota	0.1		23	Georgia	0.5
27	Mississippi	0.2		24	Louisiana	0.4
33	Missouri	0.1		25	Nebraska	0.3
9	Montana	1.9		25	New York	0.3
25	Nebraska	0.3		27	Hawaii	0.2
19	Nevada	0.6		27	Iowa	0.2
27	New Hampshire	0.2		27	Mississippi	0.2
33	New Jersey	0.1		27	New Hampshire	0.2
13	New Mexico	1.2		27	Texas	0.2
25	New York	0.3		27	Virginia	0.2
33	North Carolina	0.1		33	Arizona	0.1
4	North Dakota	3.9		33	Arkansas	0.1
16	Ohio	0.8		33	Illinois	0.1
7	Oklahoma	2.1		33	Minnesota	0.1
15	Oregon	0.9		33	Missouri	0.1
45	Pennsylvania	0.0		33	New Jersey	0.1
33	Rhode Island	0.1		33	North Carolina	0.1
33	South Carolina	0.1		33	Rhode Island	0.1
12	South Dakota	1.5		33	South Carolina	0.1
33	Tennessee	0.1		33	Tennessee	0.1
27	Texas	0.2		33	Vermont	0.1
3	Utah	5.1		33	Wyoming	0.1
33	Vermont	0.1		45	Idaho	0.0
27	Virginia	0.2		45	Pennsylvania	0.0
19	Washington	0.6		45	Wisconsin	0.0
7	West Virginia	2.1		NA	Indiana**	NA
45	Wisconsin	0.0		NA	Maryland**	NA
33	Wyoming	0.1		NA	Massachusetts**	NA

	District of Columbia	0.9

Source: Morgan Quitno Press using data from U.S. Department of Health and Human Services, Children's Bureau
"Child Maltreatment 1999: 10 Years of Reporting"
*State-substantiated or indicated incidents. National rate is for reporting states only. Some children may be counted twice if they were victims of multiple types of abuse. Fifty-eight percent of maltreated children suffered neglect, 21% physical abuse, 11% sexual abuse, and the remainder suffered emotional maltreatment, medical neglect or other forms of maltreatment. **Not available.

Neglected Children in 1999

National Reporting States' Total = 437,540 Children*

ALPHA ORDER

RANK	STATE	CHILDREN	% of USA
16	Alabama	6,335	1.4%
30	Alaska	3,418	0.8%
20	Arizona	5,376	1.2%
23	Arkansas	5,213	1.2%
1	California	73,470	16.8%
24	Colorado	4,939	1.1%
12	Connecticut	13,097	3.0%
43	Delaware	791	0.2%
5	Florida	26,887	6.1%
8	Georgia	16,978	3.9%
47	Hawaii	216	0.0%
41	Idaho	1,448	0.3%
11	Illinois	13,435	3.1%
4	Indiana	26,999	6.2%
17	Iowa	6,163	1.4%
27	Kansas	4,184	1.0%
13	Kentucky	11,887	2.7%
15	Louisiana	8,584	2.0%
34	Maine	2,457	0.6%
NA	Maryland**	NA	NA
NA	Massachusetts**	NA	NA
7	Michigan	17,342	4.0%
14	Minnesota	8,600	2.0%
31	Mississippi	3,066	0.7%
26	Missouri	4,500	1.0%
37	Montana	2,116	0.5%
36	Nebraska	2,241	0.5%
39	Nevada	1,823	0.4%
45	New Hampshire	604	0.1%
18	New Jersey	5,779	1.3%
38	New Mexico	1,956	0.4%
10	New York	14,952	3.4%
2	North Carolina	32,482	7.4%
42	North Dakota	822	0.2%
3	Ohio	28,467	6.5%
9	Oklahoma	15,893	3.6%
35	Oregon	2,368	0.5%
48	Pennsylvania	194	0.0%
32	Rhode Island	2,949	0.7%
22	South Carolina	5,246	1.2%
40	South Dakota	1,816	0.4%
25	Tennessee	4,612	1.1%
6	Texas	23,529	5.4%
33	Utah	2,494	0.6%
46	Vermont	472	0.1%
21	Virginia	5,306	1.2%
19	Washington	5,692	1.3%
29	West Virginia	3,774	0.9%
28	Wisconsin	4,132	0.9%
44	Wyoming	780	0.2%

RANK ORDER

RANK	STATE	CHILDREN	% of USA
1	California	73,470	16.8%
2	North Carolina	32,482	7.4%
3	Ohio	28,467	6.5%
4	Indiana	26,999	6.2%
5	Florida	26,887	6.1%
6	Texas	23,529	5.4%
7	Michigan	17,342	4.0%
8	Georgia	16,978	3.9%
9	Oklahoma	15,893	3.6%
10	New York	14,952	3.4%
11	Illinois	13,435	3.1%
12	Connecticut	13,097	3.0%
13	Kentucky	11,887	2.7%
14	Minnesota	8,600	2.0%
15	Louisiana	8,584	2.0%
16	Alabama	6,335	1.4%
17	Iowa	6,163	1.4%
18	New Jersey	5,779	1.3%
19	Washington	5,692	1.3%
20	Arizona	5,376	1.2%
21	Virginia	5,306	1.2%
22	South Carolina	5,246	1.2%
23	Arkansas	5,213	1.2%
24	Colorado	4,939	1.1%
25	Tennessee	4,612	1.1%
26	Missouri	4,500	1.0%
27	Kansas	4,184	1.0%
28	Wisconsin	4,132	0.9%
29	West Virginia	3,774	0.9%
30	Alaska	3,418	0.8%
31	Mississippi	3,066	0.7%
32	Rhode Island	2,949	0.7%
33	Utah	2,494	0.6%
34	Maine	2,457	0.6%
35	Oregon	2,368	0.5%
36	Nebraska	2,241	0.5%
37	Montana	2,116	0.5%
38	New Mexico	1,956	0.4%
39	Nevada	1,823	0.4%
40	South Dakota	1,816	0.4%
41	Idaho	1,448	0.3%
42	North Dakota	822	0.2%
43	Delaware	791	0.2%
44	Wyoming	780	0.2%
45	New Hampshire	604	0.1%
46	Vermont	472	0.1%
47	Hawaii	216	0.0%
48	Pennsylvania	194	0.0%
NA	Maryland**	NA	NA
NA	Massachusetts**	NA	NA
	District of Columbia	1,656	0.4%

Source: U.S. Department of Health and Human Services, Children's Bureau
   "Child Maltreatment 1999: 10 Years of Reporting"
State-substantiated or indicated incidents. Some children may be counted twice if they were victims of multiple types of abuse. Fifty-eight percent of maltreated children suffered neglect, 21% physical abuse, 11% sexual abuse, and the remainder suffered emotional maltreatment, medical neglect or other forms of maltreatment.
**Not available.*

Rate of Neglected Children in 1999

National Rate = 6.2 Neglected Children per 1,000 Population Under 18*

<u>ALPHA ORDER</u>

RANK	STATE	RATE
23	Alabama	5.9
3	Alaska	17.4
33	Arizona	4.0
16	Arkansas	7.9
15	California	8.2
27	Colorado	4.6
5	Connecticut	15.8
28	Delaware	4.3
17	Florida	7.5
14	Georgia	8.3
47	Hawaii	0.7
30	Idaho	4.1
29	Illinois	4.2
2	Indiana	17.7
12	Iowa	8.6
22	Kansas	6.0
6	Kentucky	12.3
18	Louisiana	7.2
13	Maine	8.5
NA	Maryland**	NA
NA	Massachusetts**	NA
19	Michigan	6.8
19	Minnesota	6.8
30	Mississippi	4.1
41	Missouri	3.2
9	Montana	9.5
26	Nebraska	5.0
36	Nevada	3.7
46	New Hampshire	2.0
44	New Jersey	2.9
34	New Mexico	3.9
38	New York	3.4
4	North Carolina	16.7
25	North Dakota	5.1
8	Ohio	10.0
1	Oklahoma	18.0
44	Oregon	2.9
48	Pennsylvania	0.1
7	Rhode Island	12.2
24	South Carolina	5.5
11	South Dakota	9.2
38	Tennessee	3.4
30	Texas	4.1
37	Utah	3.5
38	Vermont	3.4
41	Virginia	3.2
35	Washington	3.8
10	West Virginia	9.4
43	Wisconsin	3.1
21	Wyoming	6.2

<u>RANK ORDER</u>

RANK	STATE	RATE
1	Oklahoma	18.0
2	Indiana	17.7
3	Alaska	17.4
4	North Carolina	16.7
5	Connecticut	15.8
6	Kentucky	12.3
7	Rhode Island	12.2
8	Ohio	10.0
9	Montana	9.5
10	West Virginia	9.4
11	South Dakota	9.2
12	Iowa	8.6
13	Maine	8.5
14	Georgia	8.3
15	California	8.2
16	Arkansas	7.9
17	Florida	7.5
18	Louisiana	7.2
19	Michigan	6.8
19	Minnesota	6.8
21	Wyoming	6.2
22	Kansas	6.0
23	Alabama	5.9
24	South Carolina	5.5
25	North Dakota	5.1
26	Nebraska	5.0
27	Colorado	4.6
28	Delaware	4.3
29	Illinois	4.2
30	Idaho	4.1
30	Mississippi	4.1
30	Texas	4.1
33	Arizona	4.0
34	New Mexico	3.9
35	Washington	3.8
36	Nevada	3.7
37	Utah	3.5
38	New York	3.4
38	Tennessee	3.4
38	Vermont	3.4
41	Missouri	3.2
41	Virginia	3.2
43	Wisconsin	3.1
44	New Jersey	2.9
44	Oregon	2.9
46	New Hampshire	2.0
47	Hawaii	0.7
48	Pennsylvania	0.1
NA	Maryland**	NA
NA	Massachusetts**	NA

District of Columbia   17.4

Source: Morgan Quitno Press using data from U.S. Department of Health and Human Services, Children's Bureau
   "Child Maltreatment 1999: 10 Years of Reporting"
*State-substantiated or indicated incidents. National rate is for reporting states only. Some children may be counted twice if they were victims of multiple types of abuse. Fifty-eight percent of maltreated children suffered neglect, 21% physical abuse, 11% sexual abuse, and the remainder suffered emotional maltreatment, medical neglect or other forms of maltreatment. **Not available.

Child Abuse and Neglect Fatalities in 1999

National Total = 1,100 Fatalities*

ALPHA ORDER

RANK	STATE	FATALITIES	% of USA
15	Alabama	29	2.6%
35	Alaska	4	0.4%
26	Arizona	8	0.7%
24	Arkansas	9	0.8%
13	California	33	3.0%
14	Colorado	32	2.9%
40	Connecticut	3	0.3%
40	Delaware	3	0.3%
4	Florida	57	5.2%
9	Georgia	42	3.8%
33	Hawaii	5	0.5%
35	Idaho	4	0.4%
2	Illinois	80	7.3%
10	Indiana	41	3.7%
23	Iowa	11	1.0%
31	Kansas	6	0.5%
33	Kentucky	5	0.5%
18	Louisiana	21	1.9%
40	Maine	3	0.3%
NA	Maryland**	NA	NA
NA	Massachusetts**	NA	NA
7	Michigan	48	4.4%
17	Minnesota	28	2.5%
27	Mississippi	7	0.6%
11	Missouri	36	3.3%
35	Montana	4	0.4%
NA	Nebraska**	NA	NA
27	Nevada	7	0.6%
40	New Hampshire	3	0.3%
15	New Jersey	29	2.6%
27	New Mexico	7	0.6%
3	New York	79	7.2%
18	North Carolina	21	1.9%
47	North Dakota	0	0.0%
5	Ohio	54	4.9%
8	Oklahoma	47	4.3%
20	Oregon	18	1.6%
6	Pennsylvania	50	4.5%
35	Rhode Island	4	0.4%
22	South Carolina	13	1.2%
40	South Dakota	3	0.3%
21	Tennessee	16	1.5%
1	Texas	143	13.0%
27	Utah	7	0.6%
35	Vermont	4	0.4%
11	Virginia	36	3.3%
31	Washington	6	0.5%
45	West Virginia	1	0.1%
24	Wisconsin	9	0.8%
45	Wyoming	1	0.1%

RANK ORDER

RANK	STATE	FATALITIES	% of USA
1	Texas	143	13.0%
2	Illinois	80	7.3%
3	New York	79	7.2%
4	Florida	57	5.2%
5	Ohio	54	4.9%
6	Pennsylvania	50	4.5%
7	Michigan	48	4.4%
8	Oklahoma	47	4.3%
9	Georgia	42	3.8%
10	Indiana	41	3.7%
11	Missouri	36	3.3%
11	Virginia	36	3.3%
13	California	33	3.0%
14	Colorado	32	2.9%
15	Alabama	29	2.6%
15	New Jersey	29	2.6%
17	Minnesota	28	2.5%
18	Louisiana	21	1.9%
18	North Carolina	21	1.9%
20	Oregon	18	1.6%
21	Tennessee	16	1.5%
22	South Carolina	13	1.2%
23	Iowa	11	1.0%
24	Arkansas	9	0.8%
24	Wisconsin	9	0.8%
26	Arizona	8	0.7%
27	Mississippi	7	0.6%
27	Nevada	7	0.6%
27	New Mexico	7	0.6%
27	Utah	7	0.6%
31	Kansas	6	0.5%
31	Washington	6	0.5%
33	Hawaii	5	0.5%
33	Kentucky	5	0.5%
35	Alaska	4	0.4%
35	Idaho	4	0.4%
35	Montana	4	0.4%
35	Rhode Island	4	0.4%
35	Vermont	4	0.4%
40	Connecticut	3	0.3%
40	Delaware	3	0.3%
40	Maine	3	0.3%
40	New Hampshire	3	0.3%
40	South Dakota	3	0.3%
45	West Virginia	1	0.1%
45	Wyoming	1	0.1%
47	North Dakota	0	0.0%
NA	Maryland**	NA	NA
NA	Massachusetts**	NA	NA
NA	Nebraska**	NA	NA
	District of Columbia	5	0.5%

Source: U.S. Department of Health and Human Services, Children's Bureau
"Child Maltreatment 1999: 10 Years of Reporting"
*National total is an estimate. State-substantiated or indicated incidents. Some children may be counted twice if they were victims of multiple types of abuse. Fifty-eight percent of maltreated children suffered neglect, 21% physical abuse, 11% sexual abuse, and the remainder suffered emotional maltreatment, medical neglect or other forms of maltreatment. **Not available.*

Rate of Child Abuse and Neglect Fatalities in 1999

National Rate = 1.62 Fatalities per 100,000 Population Under 18*

ALPHA ORDER

RANK	STATE	RATE
4	Alabama	2.72
13	Alaska	2.03
41	Arizona	0.60
29	Arkansas	1.36
44	California	0.37
2	Colorado	3.00
45	Connecticut	0.36
22	Delaware	1.64
23	Florida	1.60
12	Georgia	2.04
20	Hawaii	1.73
32	Idaho	1.14
7	Illinois	2.51
5	Indiana	2.68
24	Iowa	1.53
38	Kansas	0.86
42	Kentucky	0.52
18	Louisiana	1.76
34	Maine	1.03
NA	Maryland**	NA
NA	Massachusetts**	NA
15	Michigan	1.87
9	Minnesota	2.20
37	Mississippi	0.93
6	Missouri	2.57
16	Montana	1.79
NA	Nebraska**	NA
27	Nevada	1.42
35	New Hampshire	0.99
26	New Jersey	1.45
28	New Mexico	1.41
17	New York	1.78
33	North Carolina	1.08
47	North Dakota	0.00
14	Ohio	1.90
1	Oklahoma	5.33
10	Oregon	2.18
19	Pennsylvania	1.75
21	Rhode Island	1.66
29	South Carolina	1.36
25	South Dakota	1.51
31	Tennessee	1.19
8	Texas	2.50
35	Utah	0.99
3	Vermont	2.87
11	Virginia	2.16
43	Washington	0.40
46	West Virginia	0.25
40	Wisconsin	0.67
39	Wyoming	0.79

RANK ORDER

RANK	STATE	RATE
1	Oklahoma	5.33
2	Colorado	3.00
3	Vermont	2.87
4	Alabama	2.72
5	Indiana	2.68
6	Missouri	2.57
7	Illinois	2.51
8	Texas	2.50
9	Minnesota	2.20
10	Oregon	2.18
11	Virginia	2.16
12	Georgia	2.04
13	Alaska	2.03
14	Ohio	1.90
15	Michigan	1.87
16	Montana	1.79
17	New York	1.78
18	Louisiana	1.76
19	Pennsylvania	1.75
20	Hawaii	1.73
21	Rhode Island	1.66
22	Delaware	1.64
23	Florida	1.60
24	Iowa	1.53
25	South Dakota	1.51
26	New Jersey	1.45
27	Nevada	1.42
28	New Mexico	1.41
29	Arkansas	1.36
29	South Carolina	1.36
31	Tennessee	1.19
32	Idaho	1.14
33	North Carolina	1.08
34	Maine	1.03
35	New Hampshire	0.99
35	Utah	0.99
37	Mississippi	0.93
38	Kansas	0.86
39	Wyoming	0.79
40	Wisconsin	0.67
41	Arizona	0.60
42	Kentucky	0.52
43	Washington	0.40
44	California	0.37
45	Connecticut	0.36
46	West Virginia	0.25
47	North Dakota	0.00
NA	Maryland**	NA
NA	Massachusetts**	NA
NA	Nebraska**	NA

District of Columbia   5.25

Source: Morgan Quitno Press using data from U.S. Department of Health and Human Services, Children's Bureau
"Child Maltreatment 1999: 10 Years of Reporting"
*State-substantiated or indicated incidents. National rate is an estimate of all states including states not reporting.
Some children may be counted twice if they were victims of multiple types of abuse. Fifty-eight percent of
maltreated children suffered neglect, 21% physical abuse, 11% sexual abuse, and the remainder suffered
emotional maltreatment, medical neglect or other forms of maltreatment. **Not available.

VI. LAW ENFORCEMENT

Federal Law Enforcement Officers in 2000

National Total = 88,496 Officers*

ALPHA ORDER

RANK ORDER

RANK	STATE	OFFICERS	% of USA
26	Alabama	723	0.8%
40	Alaska	338	0.4%
5	Arizona	3,912	4.4%
34	Arkansas	439	0.5%
2	California	12,074	13.6%
12	Colorado	1,489	1.7%
35	Connecticut	431	0.5%
49	Delaware	104	0.1%
4	Florida	5,532	6.3%
10	Georgia	2,164	2.4%
30	Hawaii	515	0.6%
41	Idaho	297	0.3%
7	Illinois	2,713	3.1%
28	Indiana	651	0.7%
45	Iowa	207	0.2%
33	Kansas	456	0.5%
22	Kentucky	941	1.1%
14	Louisiana	1,285	1.5%
37	Maine	367	0.4%
15	Maryland	1,274	1.4%
16	Massachusetts	1,268	1.4%
11	Michigan	1,555	1.8%
23	Minnesota	915	1.0%
32	Mississippi	472	0.5%
18	Missouri	1,163	1.3%
39	Montana	356	0.4%
44	Nebraska	208	0.2%
31	Nevada	479	0.5%
50	New Hampshire	84	0.1%
9	New Jersey	2,274	2.6%
17	New Mexico	1,249	1.4%
3	New York	7,183	8.1%
20	North Carolina	1,103	1.2%
43	North Dakota	278	0.3%
19	Ohio	1,137	1.3%
24	Oklahoma	779	0.9%
27	Oregon	664	0.8%
6	Pennsylvania	3,184	3.6%
48	Rhode Island	130	0.1%
25	South Carolina	769	0.9%
46	South Dakota	204	0.2%
21	Tennessee	975	1.1%
1	Texas	12,225	13.8%
38	Utah	361	0.4%
42	Vermont	286	0.3%
8	Virginia	2,712	3.1%
13	Washington	1,394	1.6%
29	West Virginia	583	0.7%
36	Wisconsin	424	0.5%
47	Wyoming	180	0.2%

RANK	STATE	OFFICERS	% of USA
1	Texas	12,225	13.8%
2	California	12,074	13.6%
3	New York	7,183	8.1%
4	Florida	5,532	6.3%
5	Arizona	3,912	4.4%
6	Pennsylvania	3,184	3.6%
7	Illinois	2,713	3.1%
8	Virginia	2,712	3.1%
9	New Jersey	2,274	2.6%
10	Georgia	2,164	2.4%
11	Michigan	1,555	1.8%
12	Colorado	1,489	1.7%
13	Washington	1,394	1.6%
14	Louisiana	1,285	1.5%
15	Maryland	1,274	1.4%
16	Massachusetts	1,268	1.4%
17	New Mexico	1,249	1.4%
18	Missouri	1,163	1.3%
19	Ohio	1,137	1.3%
20	North Carolina	1,103	1.2%
21	Tennessee	975	1.1%
22	Kentucky	941	1.1%
23	Minnesota	915	1.0%
24	Oklahoma	779	0.9%
25	South Carolina	769	0.9%
26	Alabama	723	0.8%
27	Oregon	664	0.8%
28	Indiana	651	0.7%
29	West Virginia	583	0.7%
30	Hawaii	515	0.6%
31	Nevada	479	0.5%
32	Mississippi	472	0.5%
33	Kansas	456	0.5%
34	Arkansas	439	0.5%
35	Connecticut	431	0.5%
36	Wisconsin	424	0.5%
37	Maine	367	0.4%
38	Utah	361	0.4%
39	Montana	356	0.4%
40	Alaska	338	0.4%
41	Idaho	297	0.3%
42	Vermont	286	0.3%
43	North Dakota	278	0.3%
44	Nebraska	208	0.2%
45	Iowa	207	0.2%
46	South Dakota	204	0.2%
47	Wyoming	180	0.2%
48	Rhode Island	130	0.1%
49	Delaware	104	0.1%
50	New Hampshire	84	0.1%
	District of Columbia	7,991	9.0%

Source: U.S. Department of Justice, Bureau of Justice Statistics
    "Federal Law Enforcement Officers, 2000" (NCJ-187231, July 2001)
*Full-time officers authorized to carry firearms and make arrests. Includes F.B.I., Customs Service, Immigration and
Naturalization Service, I.R.S., Postal Inspection, Drug Enforcement Administration, Secret Service, National Park
Service, Bureau of Alcohol, Tobacco and Firearms, Capitol Police, U.S. Courts, Federal Bureau of Prisons,
Tennessee Valley Authority, and U.S. Forest Service.

Rate of Federal Law Enforcement Officers in 2000

National Rate = 31 Officers per 100,000 Population*

ALPHA ORDER			RANK ORDER		
RANK	STATE	RATE	RANK	STATE	RATE
37	Alabama	16	1	Arizona	76
4	Alaska	54	2	New Mexico	69
1	Arizona	76	3	Texas	59
37	Arkansas	16	4	Alaska	54
11	California	36	5	Vermont	47
13	Colorado	35	6	Hawaii	43
42	Connecticut	13	6	North Dakota	43
42	Delaware	13	8	Montana	39
13	Florida	35	9	New York	38
20	Georgia	26	9	Virginia	38
6	Hawaii	43	11	California	36
25	Idaho	23	11	Wyoming	36
28	Illinois	22	13	Colorado	35
46	Indiana	11	13	Florida	35
49	Iowa	7	15	West Virginia	32
34	Kansas	17	16	Louisiana	29
25	Kentucky	23	16	Maine	29
16	Louisiana	29	18	New Jersey	27
16	Maine	29	18	South Dakota	27
22	Maryland	24	20	Georgia	26
30	Massachusetts	20	20	Pennsylvania	26
37	Michigan	16	22	Maryland	24
31	Minnesota	19	22	Nevada	24
34	Mississippi	17	22	Washington	24
29	Missouri	21	25	Idaho	23
8	Montana	39	25	Kentucky	23
44	Nebraska	12	25	Oklahoma	23
22	Nevada	24	28	Illinois	22
49	New Hampshire	7	29	Missouri	21
18	New Jersey	27	30	Massachusetts	20
2	New Mexico	69	31	Minnesota	19
9	New York	38	31	Oregon	19
41	North Carolina	14	31	South Carolina	19
6	North Dakota	43	34	Kansas	17
47	Ohio	10	34	Mississippi	17
25	Oklahoma	23	34	Tennessee	17
31	Oregon	19	37	Alabama	16
20	Pennsylvania	26	37	Arkansas	16
44	Rhode Island	12	37	Michigan	16
31	South Carolina	19	37	Utah	16
18	South Dakota	27	41	North Carolina	14
34	Tennessee	17	42	Connecticut	13
3	Texas	59	42	Delaware	13
37	Utah	16	44	Nebraska	12
5	Vermont	47	44	Rhode Island	12
9	Virginia	38	46	Indiana	11
22	Washington	24	47	Ohio	10
15	West Virginia	32	48	Wisconsin	8
48	Wisconsin	8	49	Iowa	7
11	Wyoming	36	49	New Hampshire	7
				District of Columbia	1,397

Source: U.S. Department of Justice, Bureau of Justice Statistics
   "Federal Law Enforcement Officers, 2000" (NCJ-187231, July 2001)
*Full-time officers authorized to carry firearms and make arrests. Includes F.B.I., Customs Service, Immigration and Naturalization Service, I.R.S., Postal Inspection, Drug Enforcement Administration, Secret Service, National Park Service, Bureau of Alcohol, Tobacco and Firearms, Capitol Police, U.S. Courts, Federal Bureau of Prisons, Tennessee Valley Authority, and U.S. Forest Service.

State and Local Justice System Employment in 2000

National Total = 1,940,456 Employees*

ALPHA ORDER					RANK ORDER			

RANK	STATE	EMPLOYEES	% of USA		RANK	STATE	EMPLOYEES	% of USA
24	Alabama	25,298	1.3%		1	California	226,448	11.7%
46	Alaska	4,693	0.2%		2	New York	177,474	9.1%
14	Arizona	39,345	2.0%		3	Texas	150,718	7.8%
32	Arkansas	15,172	0.8%		4	Florida	127,600	6.6%
1	California	226,448	11.7%		5	Illinois	86,729	4.5%
23	Colorado	26,869	1.4%		6	Ohio	80,117	4.1%
26	Connecticut	23,845	1.2%		7	Pennsylvania	74,927	3.9%
43	Delaware	6,353	0.3%		8	New Jersey	69,960	3.6%
4	Florida	127,600	6.6%		9	Michigan	61,474	3.2%
10	Georgia	60,195	3.1%		10	Georgia	60,195	3.1%
38	Hawaii	8,701	0.4%		11	North Carolina	52,656	2.7%
40	Idaho	7,365	0.4%		12	Virginia	48,070	2.5%
5	Illinois	86,729	4.5%		13	Massachusetts	44,731	2.3%
21	Indiana	33,189	1.7%		14	Arizona	39,345	2.0%
33	Iowa	14,919	0.8%		15	Missouri	38,349	2.0%
30	Kansas	18,906	1.0%		16	Maryland	37,870	2.0%
27	Kentucky	22,371	1.2%		17	Louisiana	36,601	1.9%
17	Louisiana	36,601	1.9%		18	Tennessee	34,375	1.8%
44	Maine	5,725	0.3%		19	Washington	34,250	1.8%
16	Maryland	37,870	2.0%		20	Wisconsin	34,030	1.8%
13	Massachusetts	44,731	2.3%		21	Indiana	33,189	1.7%
9	Michigan	61,474	3.2%		22	South Carolina	28,447	1.5%
25	Minnesota	24,272	1.3%		23	Colorado	26,869	1.4%
31	Mississippi	17,786	0.9%		24	Alabama	25,298	1.3%
15	Missouri	38,349	2.0%		25	Minnesota	24,272	1.3%
45	Montana	4,841	0.2%		26	Connecticut	23,845	1.2%
37	Nebraska	9,309	0.5%		27	Kentucky	22,371	1.2%
34	Nevada	14,702	0.8%		28	Oklahoma	22,213	1.1%
41	New Hampshire	7,146	0.4%		29	Oregon	21,554	1.1%
8	New Jersey	69,960	3.6%		30	Kansas	18,906	1.0%
35	New Mexico	14,096	0.7%		31	Mississippi	17,786	0.9%
2	New York	177,474	9.1%		32	Arkansas	15,172	0.8%
11	North Carolina	52,656	2.7%		33	Iowa	14,919	0.8%
49	North Dakota	3,019	0.2%		34	Nevada	14,702	0.8%
6	Ohio	80,117	4.1%		35	New Mexico	14,096	0.7%
28	Oklahoma	22,213	1.1%		36	Utah	12,318	0.6%
29	Oregon	21,554	1.1%		37	Nebraska	9,309	0.5%
7	Pennsylvania	74,927	3.9%		38	Hawaii	8,701	0.4%
42	Rhode Island	6,427	0.3%		39	West Virginia	7,519	0.4%
22	South Carolina	28,447	1.5%		40	Idaho	7,365	0.4%
47	South Dakota	3,813	0.2%		41	New Hampshire	7,146	0.4%
18	Tennessee	34,375	1.8%		42	Rhode Island	6,427	0.3%
3	Texas	150,718	7.8%		43	Delaware	6,353	0.3%
36	Utah	12,318	0.6%		44	Maine	5,725	0.3%
50	Vermont	2,935	0.2%		45	Montana	4,841	0.2%
12	Virginia	48,070	2.5%		46	Alaska	4,693	0.2%
19	Washington	34,250	1.8%		47	South Dakota	3,813	0.2%
39	West Virginia	7,519	0.4%		48	Wyoming	3,499	0.2%
20	Wisconsin	34,030	1.8%		49	North Dakota	3,019	0.2%
48	Wyoming	3,499	0.2%		50	Vermont	2,935	0.2%
						District of Columbia	7,235	0.4%

Source: Morgan Quitno Press using data from U.S. Bureau of the Census, Governments Division
"State and Local Employment and Payroll - March 2000" (http://www.census.gov/govs/www/apesstl00.html)
*Full-time equivalent as of March 2000. Includes police, courts, prosecution, public defense and corrections.

Rate of State and Local Justice System Employment in 2000

National Rate = 69.0 Employees per 10,000 Population*

ALPHA ORDER				RANK ORDER		
RANK	STATE	RATE		RANK	STATE	RATE
36	Alabama	56.9		1	New York	93.5
8	Alaska	74.9		2	New Jersey	83.1
7	Arizona	76.7		3	Louisiana	81.9
38	Arkansas	56.8		4	Delaware	81.1
23	California	66.9		5	Florida	79.8
28	Colorado	62.5		6	New Mexico	77.5
19	Connecticut	70.0		7	Arizona	76.7
4	Delaware	81.1		8	Alaska	74.9
5	Florida	79.8		9	Nevada	73.6
10	Georgia	73.5		10	Georgia	73.5
12	Hawaii	71.8		11	Texas	72.3
36	Idaho	56.9		12	Hawaii	71.8
20	Illinois	69.8		13	Maryland	71.5
41	Indiana	54.6		14	South Carolina	70.9
44	Iowa	51.0		14	Wyoming	70.9
18	Kansas	70.3		16	Ohio	70.6
39	Kentucky	55.3		17	Massachusetts	70.5
3	Louisiana	81.9		18	Kansas	70.3
49	Maine	44.9		19	Connecticut	70.0
13	Maryland	71.5		20	Illinois	69.8
17	Massachusetts	70.5		21	Missouri	68.5
30	Michigan	61.9		22	Virginia	67.9
46	Minnesota	49.3		23	California	66.9
28	Mississippi	62.5		24	North Carolina	65.4
21	Missouri	68.5		25	Oklahoma	64.4
43	Montana	53.7		26	Wisconsin	63.4
42	Nebraska	54.4		27	Oregon	63.0
9	Nevada	73.6		28	Colorado	62.5
35	New Hampshire	57.8		28	Mississippi	62.5
2	New Jersey	83.1		30	Michigan	61.9
6	New Mexico	77.5		31	Rhode Island	61.3
1	New York	93.5		32	Pennsylvania	61.0
24	North Carolina	65.4		33	Tennessee	60.4
48	North Dakota	47.0		34	Washington	58.1
16	Ohio	70.6		35	New Hampshire	57.8
25	Oklahoma	64.4		36	Alabama	56.9
27	Oregon	63.0		36	Idaho	56.9
32	Pennsylvania	61.0		38	Arkansas	56.8
31	Rhode Island	61.3		39	Kentucky	55.3
14	South Carolina	70.9		40	Utah	55.2
45	South Dakota	50.5		41	Indiana	54.6
33	Tennessee	60.4		42	Nebraska	54.4
11	Texas	72.3		43	Montana	53.7
40	Utah	55.2		44	Iowa	51.0
47	Vermont	48.2		45	South Dakota	50.5
22	Virginia	67.9		46	Minnesota	49.3
34	Washington	58.1		47	Vermont	48.2
50	West Virginia	41.6		48	North Dakota	47.0
26	Wisconsin	63.4		49	Maine	44.9
14	Wyoming	70.9		50	West Virginia	41.6
					District of Columbia	126.5

Source: Morgan Quitno Press using data from U.S. Bureau of the Census, Governments Division
   "State and Local Employment and Payroll - March 2000" (http://www.census.gov/govs/www/apesstl00.html)
*Full-time equivalent as of March 2000. Includes police, courts, prosecution, public defense and corrections.

State and Local Judicial and Legal Employment in 2000

National Total = 389,756 Employees*

ALPHA ORDER					RANK ORDER			
RANK	STATE	EMPLOYEES	% of USA		RANK	STATE	EMPLOYEES	% of USA
25	Alabama	5,072	1.3%		1	California	51,752	13.3%
42	Alaska	1,352	0.3%		2	New York	29,841	7.7%
11	Arizona	9,648	2.5%		3	Florida	29,771	7.6%
38	Arkansas	1,956	0.5%		4	Texas	22,748	5.8%
1	California	51,752	13.3%		5	New Jersey	20,620	5.3%
24	Colorado	5,417	1.4%		6	Ohio	20,255	5.2%
27	Connecticut	4,340	1.1%		7	Illinois	17,459	4.5%
40	Delaware	1,552	0.4%		8	Pennsylvania	17,159	4.4%
3	Florida	29,771	7.6%		9	Michigan	11,911	3.1%
12	Georgia	9,339	2.4%		10	Massachusetts	10,499	2.7%
35	Hawaii	2,693	0.7%		11	Arizona	9,648	2.5%
41	Idaho	1,392	0.4%		12	Georgia	9,339	2.4%
7	Illinois	17,459	4.5%		13	Washington	7,734	2.0%
19	Indiana	6,132	1.6%		14	Missouri	7,455	1.9%
32	Iowa	3,250	0.8%		15	Virginia	7,140	1.8%
29	Kansas	3,785	1.0%		16	Louisiana	7,131	1.8%
20	Kentucky	5,905	1.5%		17	Maryland	6,877	1.8%
16	Louisiana	7,131	1.8%		18	North Carolina	6,711	1.7%
46	Maine	848	0.2%		19	Indiana	6,132	1.6%
17	Maryland	6,877	1.8%		20	Kentucky	5,905	1.5%
10	Massachusetts	10,499	2.7%		21	Minnesota	5,769	1.5%
9	Michigan	11,911	3.1%		22	Tennessee	5,585	1.4%
21	Minnesota	5,769	1.5%		23	Wisconsin	5,558	1.4%
34	Mississippi	2,905	0.7%		24	Colorado	5,417	1.4%
14	Missouri	7,455	1.9%		25	Alabama	5,072	1.3%
45	Montana	1,006	0.3%		26	Oregon	4,768	1.2%
39	Nebraska	1,816	0.5%		27	Connecticut	4,340	1.1%
31	Nevada	3,415	0.9%		28	Oklahoma	4,034	1.0%
44	New Hampshire	1,179	0.3%		29	Kansas	3,785	1.0%
5	New Jersey	20,620	5.3%		30	South Carolina	3,483	0.9%
33	New Mexico	3,181	0.8%		31	Nevada	3,415	0.9%
2	New York	29,841	7.7%		32	Iowa	3,250	0.8%
18	North Carolina	6,711	1.7%		33	New Mexico	3,181	0.8%
47	North Dakota	775	0.2%		34	Mississippi	2,905	0.7%
6	Ohio	20,255	5.2%		35	Hawaii	2,693	0.7%
28	Oklahoma	4,034	1.0%		36	Utah	2,626	0.7%
26	Oregon	4,768	1.2%		37	West Virginia	2,155	0.6%
8	Pennsylvania	17,159	4.4%		38	Arkansas	1,956	0.5%
43	Rhode Island	1,247	0.3%		39	Nebraska	1,816	0.5%
30	South Carolina	3,483	0.9%		40	Delaware	1,552	0.4%
48	South Dakota	759	0.2%		41	Idaho	1,392	0.4%
22	Tennessee	5,585	1.4%		42	Alaska	1,352	0.3%
4	Texas	22,748	5.8%		43	Rhode Island	1,247	0.3%
36	Utah	2,626	0.7%		44	New Hampshire	1,179	0.3%
50	Vermont	644	0.2%		45	Montana	1,006	0.3%
15	Virginia	7,140	1.8%		46	Maine	848	0.2%
13	Washington	7,734	2.0%		47	North Dakota	775	0.2%
37	West Virginia	2,155	0.6%		48	South Dakota	759	0.2%
23	Wisconsin	5,558	1.4%		49	Wyoming	695	0.2%
49	Wyoming	695	0.2%		50	Vermont	644	0.2%
						District of Columbia	412	0.1%

Source: Morgan Quitno Press using data from U.S. Bureau of the Census, Governments Division
"State and Local Employment and Payroll - March 2000" (http://www.census.gov/govs/www/apesstl00.html)
*Full-time equivalent as of March 2000. Includes courts, prosecution and public defense.

Rate of State and Local Judicial and Legal Employment in 2000

National Rate = 13.8 Employees per 10,000 Population*

ALPHA ORDER

RANK	STATE	RATE
32	Alabama	11.4
3	Alaska	21.6
5	Arizona	18.8
49	Arkansas	7.3
13	California	15.3
24	Colorado	12.6
23	Connecticut	12.7
4	Delaware	19.8
6	Florida	18.6
32	Georgia	11.4
2	Hawaii	22.2
37	Idaho	10.8
15	Illinois	14.1
42	Indiana	10.1
35	Iowa	11.1
15	Kansas	14.1
14	Kentucky	14.6
11	Louisiana	16.0
50	Maine	6.7
22	Maryland	13.0
10	Massachusetts	16.5
26	Michigan	12.0
30	Minnesota	11.7
41	Mississippi	10.2
20	Missouri	13.3
34	Montana	11.2
38	Nebraska	10.6
9	Nevada	17.1
46	New Hampshire	9.5
1	New Jersey	24.5
8	New Mexico	17.5
12	New York	15.7
48	North Carolina	8.3
25	North Dakota	12.1
7	Ohio	17.8
30	Oklahoma	11.7
19	Oregon	13.9
18	Pennsylvania	14.0
27	Rhode Island	11.9
47	South Carolina	8.7
42	South Dakota	10.1
45	Tennessee	9.8
36	Texas	10.9
29	Utah	11.8
38	Vermont	10.6
42	Virginia	10.1
21	Washington	13.1
27	West Virginia	11.9
40	Wisconsin	10.4
15	Wyoming	14.1

RANK ORDER

RANK	STATE	RATE
1	New Jersey	24.5
2	Hawaii	22.2
3	Alaska	21.6
4	Delaware	19.8
5	Arizona	18.8
6	Florida	18.6
7	Ohio	17.8
8	New Mexico	17.5
9	Nevada	17.1
10	Massachusetts	16.5
11	Louisiana	16.0
12	New York	15.7
13	California	15.3
14	Kentucky	14.6
15	Illinois	14.1
15	Kansas	14.1
15	Wyoming	14.1
18	Pennsylvania	14.0
19	Oregon	13.9
20	Missouri	13.3
21	Washington	13.1
22	Maryland	13.0
23	Connecticut	12.7
24	Colorado	12.6
25	North Dakota	12.1
26	Michigan	12.0
27	Rhode Island	11.9
27	West Virginia	11.9
29	Utah	11.8
30	Minnesota	11.7
30	Oklahoma	11.7
32	Alabama	11.4
32	Georgia	11.4
34	Montana	11.2
35	Iowa	11.1
36	Texas	10.9
37	Idaho	10.8
38	Nebraska	10.6
38	Vermont	10.6
40	Wisconsin	10.4
41	Mississippi	10.2
42	Indiana	10.1
42	South Dakota	10.1
42	Virginia	10.1
45	Tennessee	9.8
46	New Hampshire	9.5
47	South Carolina	8.7
48	North Carolina	8.3
49	Arkansas	7.3
50	Maine	6.7

District of Columbia   7.2

Source: Morgan Quitno Press using data from U.S. Bureau of the Census, Governments Division
"State and Local Employment and Payroll - March 2000" (http://www.census.gov/govs/www/apesstl00.html)
*Full-time equivalent as of March 2000. Includes courts, prosecution and public defense.

State and Local Police Officers in 2000

National Total = 651,480 Officers*

ALPHA ORDER

RANK	STATE	OFFICERS	% of USA
21	Alabama	10,188	1.6%
48	Alaska	1,127	0.2%
16	Arizona	12,258	1.9%
32	Arkansas	5,938	0.9%
2	California	64,675	9.9%
24	Colorado	8,783	1.3%
26	Connecticut	8,125	1.2%
44	Delaware	1,683	0.3%
4	Florida	36,655	5.6%
11	Georgia	19,350	3.0%
40	Hawaii	2,788	0.4%
43	Idaho	2,391	0.4%
5	Illinois	34,301	5.3%
20	Indiana	11,440	1.8%
33	Iowa	5,378	0.8%
29	Kansas	6,716	1.0%
28	Kentucky	7,144	1.1%
18	Louisiana	11,961	1.8%
41	Maine	2,481	0.4%
15	Maryland	12,580	1.9%
10	Massachusetts	19,516	3.0%
9	Michigan	20,034	3.1%
27	Minnesota	7,840	1.2%
30	Mississippi	6,163	0.9%
17	Missouri	12,109	1.9%
45	Montana	1,495	0.2%
38	Nebraska	3,278	0.5%
34	Nevada	4,022	0.6%
37	New Hampshire	3,411	0.5%
8	New Jersey	24,625	3.8%
35	New Mexico	3,927	0.6%
1	New York	74,310	11.4%
12	North Carolina	18,157	2.8%
49	North Dakota	1,108	0.2%
7	Ohio	25,652	3.9%
25	Oklahoma	8,207	1.3%
31	Oregon	6,148	0.9%
6	Pennsylvania	25,820	4.0%
42	Rhode Island	2,432	0.4%
22	South Carolina	10,055	1.5%
46	South Dakota	1,271	0.2%
14	Tennessee	13,805	2.1%
3	Texas	43,629	6.7%
36	Utah	3,735	0.6%
50	Vermont	933	0.1%
13	Virginia	14,467	2.2%
23	Washington	9,923	1.5%
39	West Virginia	2,965	0.5%
19	Wisconsin	11,753	1.8%
47	Wyoming	1,143	0.2%

RANK ORDER

RANK	STATE	OFFICERS	% of USA
1	New York	74,310	11.4%
2	California	64,675	9.9%
3	Texas	43,629	6.7%
4	Florida	36,655	5.6%
5	Illinois	34,301	5.3%
6	Pennsylvania	25,820	4.0%
7	Ohio	25,652	3.9%
8	New Jersey	24,625	3.8%
9	Michigan	20,034	3.1%
10	Massachusetts	19,516	3.0%
11	Georgia	19,350	3.0%
12	North Carolina	18,157	2.8%
13	Virginia	14,467	2.2%
14	Tennessee	13,805	2.1%
15	Maryland	12,580	1.9%
16	Arizona	12,258	1.9%
17	Missouri	12,109	1.9%
18	Louisiana	11,961	1.8%
19	Wisconsin	11,753	1.8%
20	Indiana	11,440	1.8%
21	Alabama	10,188	1.6%
22	South Carolina	10,055	1.5%
23	Washington	9,923	1.5%
24	Colorado	8,783	1.3%
25	Oklahoma	8,207	1.3%
26	Connecticut	8,125	1.2%
27	Minnesota	7,840	1.2%
28	Kentucky	7,144	1.1%
29	Kansas	6,716	1.0%
30	Mississippi	6,163	0.9%
31	Oregon	6,148	0.9%
32	Arkansas	5,938	0.9%
33	Iowa	5,378	0.8%
34	Nevada	4,022	0.6%
35	New Mexico	3,927	0.6%
36	Utah	3,735	0.6%
37	New Hampshire	3,411	0.5%
38	Nebraska	3,278	0.5%
39	West Virginia	2,965	0.5%
40	Hawaii	2,788	0.4%
41	Maine	2,481	0.4%
42	Rhode Island	2,432	0.4%
43	Idaho	2,391	0.4%
44	Delaware	1,683	0.3%
45	Montana	1,495	0.2%
46	South Dakota	1,271	0.2%
47	Wyoming	1,143	0.2%
48	Alaska	1,127	0.2%
49	North Dakota	1,108	0.2%
50	Vermont	933	0.1%
	District of Columbia	3,585	0.6%

Source: U.S. Bureau of the Census, Governments Division
    "State and Local Employment and Payroll - March 2000" (http://www.census.gov/govs/www/apesstl00.html)
Full-time equivalent as of March 2000. Does not include employees of police departments who are not officers.

Rate of State and Local Police Officers in 2000

National Rate = 23.1 Officers per 10,000 Population*

ALPHA ORDER

RANK	STATE	RATE
18	Alabama	22.9
40	Alaska	18.0
10	Arizona	23.9
22	Arkansas	22.2
36	California	19.1
30	Colorado	20.4
10	Connecticut	23.9
27	Delaware	21.5
18	Florida	22.9
14	Georgia	23.6
17	Hawaii	23.0
38	Idaho	18.5
4	Illinois	27.6
37	Indiana	18.8
39	Iowa	18.4
8	Kansas	25.0
42	Kentucky	17.7
6	Louisiana	26.8
34	Maine	19.5
12	Maryland	23.8
2	Massachusetts	30.7
32	Michigan	20.2
49	Minnesota	15.9
24	Mississippi	21.7
25	Missouri	21.6
47	Montana	16.6
35	Nebraska	19.2
33	Nevada	20.1
4	New Hampshire	27.6
3	New Jersey	29.3
25	New Mexico	21.6
1	New York	39.2
20	North Carolina	22.6
43	North Dakota	17.3
20	Ohio	22.6
12	Oklahoma	23.8
40	Oregon	18.0
28	Pennsylvania	21.0
15	Rhode Island	23.2
7	South Carolina	25.1
44	South Dakota	16.8
9	Tennessee	24.3
29	Texas	20.9
46	Utah	16.7
50	Vermont	15.3
30	Virginia	20.4
44	Washington	16.8
48	West Virginia	16.4
23	Wisconsin	21.9
16	Wyoming	23.1

RANK ORDER

RANK	STATE	RATE
1	New York	39.2
2	Massachusetts	30.7
3	New Jersey	29.3
4	Illinois	27.6
4	New Hampshire	27.6
6	Louisiana	26.8
7	South Carolina	25.1
8	Kansas	25.0
9	Tennessee	24.3
10	Arizona	23.9
10	Connecticut	23.9
12	Maryland	23.8
12	Oklahoma	23.8
14	Georgia	23.6
15	Rhode Island	23.2
16	Wyoming	23.1
17	Hawaii	23.0
18	Alabama	22.9
18	Florida	22.9
20	North Carolina	22.6
20	Ohio	22.6
22	Arkansas	22.2
23	Wisconsin	21.9
24	Mississippi	21.7
25	Missouri	21.6
25	New Mexico	21.6
27	Delaware	21.5
28	Pennsylvania	21.0
29	Texas	20.9
30	Colorado	20.4
30	Virginia	20.4
32	Michigan	20.2
33	Nevada	20.1
34	Maine	19.5
35	Nebraska	19.2
36	California	19.1
37	Indiana	18.8
38	Idaho	18.5
39	Iowa	18.4
40	Alaska	18.0
40	Oregon	18.0
42	Kentucky	17.7
43	North Dakota	17.3
44	South Dakota	16.8
44	Washington	16.8
46	Utah	16.7
47	Montana	16.6
48	West Virginia	16.4
49	Minnesota	15.9
50	Vermont	15.3
	District of Columbia	62.7

Source: Morgan Quitno Press using data from U.S. Bureau of the Census, Governments Division
    "State and Local Employment and Payroll - March 2000" (http://www.census.gov/govs/www/apesstl00.html)
*Full-time equivalent as of March 2000. Does not include employees of police departments who are not officers.

Law Enforcement Agencies in 1996

National Total = 18,769 Agencies*

ALPHA ORDER					RANK ORDER			
RANK	STATE		AGENCIES	% of USA	RANK	STATE	AGENCIES	% of USA
16	Alabama		432	2.3%	1	Texas	1,861	9.9%
45	Alaska		69	0.4%	2	Pennsylvania	1,298	6.9%
40	Arizona		130	0.7%	3	Illinois	963	5.1%
24	Arkansas		360	1.9%	4	Ohio	938	5.0%
12	California		524	2.8%	5	Missouri	647	3.4%
31	Colorado		247	1.3%	6	New York	598	3.2%
41	Connecticut		129	0.7%	7	Michigan	588	3.1%
49	Delaware		45	0.2%	8	Georgia	581	3.1%
20	Florida		385	2.1%	9	Wisconsin	567	3.0%
8	Georgia		581	3.1%	10	New Jersey	554	3.0%
50	Hawaii		7	0.0%	11	Indiana	547	2.9%
43	Idaho		124	0.7%	12	California	524	2.8%
3	Illinois		963	5.1%	13	North Carolina	503	2.7%
11	Indiana		547	2.9%	14	Minnesota	486	2.6%
17	Iowa		426	2.3%	15	Oklahoma	459	2.4%
22	Kansas		369	2.0%	16	Alabama	432	2.3%
18	Kentucky		391	2.1%	17	Iowa	426	2.3%
23	Louisiana		365	1.9%	18	Kentucky	391	2.1%
37	Maine		141	0.8%	19	Massachusetts	390	2.1%
35	Maryland		147	0.8%	20	Florida	385	2.1%
19	Massachusetts		390	2.1%	21	Tennessee	374	2.0%
7	Michigan		588	3.1%	22	Kansas	369	2.0%
14	Minnesota		486	2.6%	23	Louisiana	365	1.9%
26	Mississippi		317	1.7%	24	Arkansas	360	1.9%
5	Missouri		647	3.4%	25	Virginia	330	1.8%
41	Montana		129	0.7%	26	Mississippi	317	1.7%
28	Nebraska		266	1.4%	27	Washington	277	1.5%
47	Nevada		58	0.3%	28	Nebraska	266	1.4%
32	New Hampshire		233	1.2%	29	South Carolina	264	1.4%
10	New Jersey		554	3.0%	30	West Virginia	250	1.3%
38	New Mexico		140	0.7%	31	Colorado	247	1.3%
6	New York		598	3.2%	32	New Hampshire	233	1.2%
13	North Carolina		503	2.7%	33	South Dakota	191	1.0%
36	North Dakota		142	0.8%	34	Oregon	184	1.0%
4	Ohio		938	5.0%	35	Maryland	147	0.8%
15	Oklahoma		459	2.4%	36	North Dakota	142	0.8%
34	Oregon		184	1.0%	37	Maine	141	0.8%
2	Pennsylvania		1,298	6.9%	38	New Mexico	140	0.7%
48	Rhode Island		51	0.3%	39	Utah	138	0.7%
29	South Carolina		264	1.4%	40	Arizona	130	0.7%
33	South Dakota		191	1.0%	41	Connecticut	129	0.7%
21	Tennessee		374	2.0%	41	Montana	129	0.7%
1	Texas		1,861	9.9%	43	Idaho	124	0.7%
39	Utah		138	0.7%	44	Wyoming	82	0.4%
45	Vermont		69	0.4%	45	Alaska	69	0.4%
25	Virginia		330	1.8%	45	Vermont	69	0.4%
27	Washington		277	1.5%	47	Nevada	58	0.3%
30	West Virginia		250	1.3%	48	Rhode Island	51	0.3%
9	Wisconsin		567	3.0%	49	Delaware	45	0.2%
44	Wyoming		82	0.4%	50	Hawaii	7	0.0%
						District of Columbia	3	0.0%

Source: U.S. Department of Justice, Bureau of Justice Statistics
   "Census of State and Local Law Enforcement Agencies, 1996" (Bulletin, June 1998, NCJ-164618)
*Includes state and local police, sheriffs' departments and special police agencies.

Population per Law Enforcement Agency in 1996

National Rate = 14,134 Population per Agency*

ALPHA ORDER

RANK ORDER

RANK	STATE	RATE	RANK	STATE	RATE
30	Alabama	9,891	1	Hawaii	169,103
36	Alaska	8,797	2	California	60,836
5	Arizona	34,062	3	Florida	37,403
42	Arkansas	6,972	4	Maryland	34,501
2	California	60,836	5	Arizona	34,062
16	Colorado	15,476	6	New York	30,409
8	Connecticut	25,382	7	Nevada	27,641
14	Delaware	16,108	8	Connecticut	25,382
3	Florida	37,403	9	Virginia	20,229
22	Georgia	12,656	10	Washington	19,975
1	Hawaii	169,103	11	Rhode Island	19,416
31	Idaho	9,591	12	Oregon	17,412
23	Illinois	12,302	13	Michigan	16,317
27	Indiana	10,677	14	Delaware	16,108
45	Iowa	6,694	15	Massachusetts	15,621
43	Kansas	6,971	16	Colorado	15,476
29	Kentucky	9,933	17	North Carolina	14,558
25	Louisiana	11,919	18	Utah	14,496
35	Maine	8,818	19	New Jersey	14,419
4	Maryland	34,501	20	Tennessee	14,224
15	Massachusetts	15,621	21	South Carolina	14,010
13	Michigan	16,317	22	Georgia	12,656
32	Minnesota	9,584	23	Illinois	12,302
37	Mississippi	8,568	24	New Mexico	12,239
39	Missouri	8,282	25	Louisiana	11,919
44	Montana	6,817	26	Ohio	11,911
46	Nebraska	6,211	27	Indiana	10,677
7	Nevada	27,641	28	Texas	10,278
48	New Hampshire	4,989	29	Kentucky	9,933
19	New Jersey	14,419	30	Alabama	9,891
24	New Mexico	12,239	31	Idaho	9,591
6	New York	30,409	32	Minnesota	9,584
17	North Carolina	14,558	33	Pennsylvania	9,288
49	North Dakota	4,532	34	Wisconsin	9,100
26	Ohio	11,911	35	Maine	8,818
41	Oklahoma	7,192	36	Alaska	8,797
12	Oregon	17,412	37	Mississippi	8,568
33	Pennsylvania	9,288	38	Vermont	8,531
11	Rhode Island	19,416	39	Missouri	8,282
21	South Carolina	14,010	40	West Virginia	7,303
50	South Dakota	3,835	41	Oklahoma	7,192
20	Tennessee	14,224	42	Arkansas	6,972
28	Texas	10,278	43	Kansas	6,971
18	Utah	14,496	44	Montana	6,817
38	Vermont	8,531	45	Iowa	6,694
9	Virginia	20,229	46	Nebraska	6,211
10	Washington	19,975	47	Wyoming	5,871
40	West Virginia	7,303	48	New Hampshire	4,989
34	Wisconsin	9,100	49	North Dakota	4,532
47	Wyoming	5,871	50	South Dakota	3,835
				District of Columbia	181,071

Source: Morgan Quitno Press using data from U.S. Department of Justice, Bureau of Justice Statistics
"Census of State and Local Law Enforcement Agencies, 1996" (Bulletin, June 1998, NCJ-164618)
*Includes state and local police, sheriffs' departments and special police agencies.

Law Enforcement Agencies per 1,000 Square Miles in 1996

National Rate = 5.0 Agencies per 1,000 Square Miles*

ALPHA ORDER			RANK ORDER		
RANK	**STATE**	**RATE**	**RANK**	**STATE**	**RATE**
21	Alabama	8.3	1	New Jersey	67.4
50	Alaska	0.1	2	Massachusetts	42.2
45	Arizona	1.1	3	Rhode Island	41.4
27	Arkansas	6.8	4	Pennsylvania	28.2
37	California	3.3	5	New Hampshire	25.1
39	Colorado	2.4	6	Connecticut	23.3
6	Connecticut	23.3	7	Ohio	20.9
8	Delaware	18.8	8	Delaware	18.8
30	Florida	6.4	9	Illinois	16.6
14	Georgia	9.9	10	Indiana	15.0
45	Hawaii	1.1	11	Maryland	12.0
43	Idaho	1.5	12	New York	11.1
9	Illinois	16.6	13	West Virginia	10.3
10	Indiana	15.0	14	Georgia	9.9
23	Iowa	7.6	15	Kentucky	9.7
33	Kansas	4.5	16	North Carolina	9.5
15	Kentucky	9.7	17	Missouri	9.3
24	Louisiana	7.4	18	Tennessee	8.9
34	Maine	4.2	19	Wisconsin	8.7
11	Maryland	12.0	20	South Carolina	8.5
2	Massachusetts	42.2	21	Alabama	8.3
31	Michigan	6.1	22	Virginia	7.8
32	Minnesota	5.6	23	Iowa	7.6
28	Mississippi	6.6	24	Louisiana	7.4
17	Missouri	9.3	25	Vermont	7.2
47	Montana	0.9	26	Texas	7.0
36	Nebraska	3.4	27	Arkansas	6.8
49	Nevada	0.5	28	Mississippi	6.6
5	New Hampshire	25.1	28	Oklahoma	6.6
1	New Jersey	67.4	30	Florida	6.4
44	New Mexico	1.2	31	Michigan	6.1
12	New York	11.1	32	Minnesota	5.6
16	North Carolina	9.5	33	Kansas	4.5
40	North Dakota	2.0	34	Maine	4.2
7	Ohio	20.9	35	Washington	3.9
28	Oklahoma	6.6	36	Nebraska	3.4
41	Oregon	1.9	37	California	3.3
4	Pennsylvania	28.2	38	South Dakota	2.5
3	Rhode Island	41.4	39	Colorado	2.4
20	South Carolina	8.5	40	North Dakota	2.0
38	South Dakota	2.5	41	Oregon	1.9
18	Tennessee	8.9	42	Utah	1.6
26	Texas	7.0	43	Idaho	1.5
42	Utah	1.6	44	New Mexico	1.2
25	Vermont	7.2	45	Arizona	1.1
22	Virginia	7.8	45	Hawaii	1.1
35	Washington	3.9	47	Montana	0.9
13	West Virginia	10.3	48	Wyoming	0.8
19	Wisconsin	8.7	49	Nevada	0.5
48	Wyoming	0.8	50	Alaska	0.1
				District of Columbia**	NA

Source: Morgan Quitno Press using data from U.S. Department of Justice, Bureau of Justice Statistics
"Census of State and Local Law Enforcement Agencies, 1996" (Bulletin, June 1998, NCJ-164618)
*Includes state and local police, sheriffs' departments and special police agencies.
**The District of Columbia has three agencies for its 68 square miles.

Full-Time Sworn Officers in Law Enforcement Agencies in 1996

National Total = 663,535 Officers*

<u>ALPHA ORDER</u>

RANK	STATE	OFFICERS	% of USA
22	Alabama	9,767	1.5%
48	Alaska	1,254	0.2%
20	Arizona	10,088	1.5%
31	Arkansas	5,819	0.9%
2	California	69,134	10.4%
21	Colorado	9,896	1.5%
25	Connecticut	8,525	1.3%
45	Delaware	1,660	0.3%
5	Florida	37,395	5.6%
10	Georgia	19,115	2.9%
38	Hawaii	2,989	0.5%
40	Idaho	2,524	0.4%
4	Illinois	38,192	5.8%
19	Indiana	10,931	1.6%
33	Iowa	5,043	0.8%
29	Kansas	6,183	0.9%
28	Kentucky	6,466	1.0%
14	Louisiana	16,125	2.4%
42	Maine	2,318	0.3%
15	Maryland	13,828	2.1%
12	Massachusetts	17,935	2.7%
9	Michigan	20,568	3.1%
26	Minnesota	7,994	1.2%
32	Mississippi	5,813	0.9%
16	Missouri	12,998	2.0%
44	Montana	1,682	0.3%
37	Nebraska	3,297	0.5%
34	Nevada	4,363	0.7%
43	New Hampshire	2,305	0.3%
6	New Jersey	28,058	4.2%
35	New Mexico	4,134	0.6%
1	New York	71,221	10.7%
13	North Carolina	16,953	2.6%
49	North Dakota	1,141	0.2%
8	Ohio	23,811	3.6%
27	Oklahoma	7,232	1.1%
30	Oregon	6,064	0.9%
7	Pennsylvania	24,873	3.7%
41	Rhode Island	2,422	0.4%
24	South Carolina	8,675	1.3%
46	South Dakota	1,464	0.2%
18	Tennessee	12,152	1.8%
3	Texas	47,767	7.2%
36	Utah	3,699	0.6%
50	Vermont	981	0.1%
11	Virginia	18,448	2.8%
23	Washington	9,292	1.4%
39	West Virginia	2,977	0.4%
17	Wisconsin	12,678	1.9%
47	Wyoming	1,377	0.2%

<u>RANK ORDER</u>

RANK	STATE	OFFICERS	% of USA
1	New York	71,221	10.7%
2	California	69,134	10.4%
3	Texas	47,767	7.2%
4	Illinois	38,192	5.8%
5	Florida	37,395	5.6%
6	New Jersey	28,058	4.2%
7	Pennsylvania	24,873	3.7%
8	Ohio	23,811	3.6%
9	Michigan	20,568	3.1%
10	Georgia	19,115	2.9%
11	Virginia	18,448	2.8%
12	Massachusetts	17,935	2.7%
13	North Carolina	16,953	2.6%
14	Louisiana	16,125	2.4%
15	Maryland	13,828	2.1%
16	Missouri	12,998	2.0%
17	Wisconsin	12,678	1.9%
18	Tennessee	12,152	1.8%
19	Indiana	10,931	1.6%
20	Arizona	10,088	1.5%
21	Colorado	9,896	1.5%
22	Alabama	9,767	1.5%
23	Washington	9,292	1.4%
24	South Carolina	8,675	1.3%
25	Connecticut	8,525	1.3%
26	Minnesota	7,994	1.2%
27	Oklahoma	7,232	1.1%
28	Kentucky	6,466	1.0%
29	Kansas	6,183	0.9%
30	Oregon	6,064	0.9%
31	Arkansas	5,819	0.9%
32	Mississippi	5,813	0.9%
33	Iowa	5,043	0.8%
34	Nevada	4,363	0.7%
35	New Mexico	4,134	0.6%
36	Utah	3,699	0.6%
37	Nebraska	3,297	0.5%
38	Hawaii	2,989	0.5%
39	West Virginia	2,977	0.4%
40	Idaho	2,524	0.4%
41	Rhode Island	2,422	0.4%
42	Maine	2,318	0.3%
43	New Hampshire	2,305	0.3%
44	Montana	1,682	0.3%
45	Delaware	1,660	0.3%
46	South Dakota	1,464	0.2%
47	Wyoming	1,377	0.2%
48	Alaska	1,254	0.2%
49	North Dakota	1,141	0.2%
50	Vermont	981	0.1%
	District of Columbia	3,909	0.6%

Source: U.S. Department of Justice, Bureau of Justice Statistics
  "Census of State and Local Law Enforcement Agencies, 1996" (Bulletin, June 1998, NCJ-164618)
*Includes state and local police, sheriffs' departments and special police agencies.

Percent of Full-Time Law Enforcement Agency Employees Who are Sworn Officers: 1996
National Percent = 72.0% of Employees are Sworn Officers*

ALPHA ORDER

RANK	STATE	PERCENT
34	Alabama	67.9
40	Alaska	66.6
50	Arizona	59.9
22	Arkansas	73.1
41	California	66.5
29	Colorado	70.7
2	Connecticut	82.6
10	Delaware	77.8
49	Florida	61.5
36	Georgia	67.8
6	Hawaii	79.8
33	Idaho	68.7
12	Illinois	76.0
39	Indiana	66.7
17	Iowa	74.2
28	Kansas	70.8
13	Kentucky	75.7
3	Louisiana	81.4
44	Maine	65.6
15	Maryland	75.2
19	Massachusetts	73.4
16	Michigan	74.8
30	Minnesota	70.6
37	Mississippi	67.7
27	Missouri	72.7
42	Montana	66.2
25	Nebraska	72.8
31	Nevada	70.0
9	New Hampshire	78.0
5	New Jersey	80.3
38	New Mexico	66.9
4	New York	80.6
24	North Carolina	72.9
17	North Dakota	74.2
25	Ohio	72.8
32	Oklahoma	68.9
34	Oregon	67.9
1	Pennsylvania	84.3
8	Rhode Island	78.2
14	South Carolina	75.5
48	South Dakota	62.0
46	Tennessee	64.8
45	Texas	65.3
21	Utah	73.2
19	Vermont	73.4
6	Virginia	79.8
43	Washington	66.1
22	West Virginia	73.1
11	Wisconsin	76.9
47	Wyoming	64.1

RANK ORDER

RANK	STATE	PERCENT
1	Pennsylvania	84.3
2	Connecticut	82.6
3	Louisiana	81.4
4	New York	80.6
5	New Jersey	80.3
6	Hawaii	79.8
6	Virginia	79.8
8	Rhode Island	78.2
9	New Hampshire	78.0
10	Delaware	77.8
11	Wisconsin	76.9
12	Illinois	76.0
13	Kentucky	75.7
14	South Carolina	75.5
15	Maryland	75.2
16	Michigan	74.8
17	Iowa	74.2
17	North Dakota	74.2
19	Massachusetts	73.4
19	Vermont	73.4
21	Utah	73.2
22	Arkansas	73.1
22	West Virginia	73.1
24	North Carolina	72.9
25	Nebraska	72.8
25	Ohio	72.8
27	Missouri	72.7
28	Kansas	70.8
29	Colorado	70.7
30	Minnesota	70.6
31	Nevada	70.0
32	Oklahoma	68.9
33	Idaho	68.7
34	Alabama	67.9
34	Oregon	67.9
36	Georgia	67.8
37	Mississippi	67.7
38	New Mexico	66.9
39	Indiana	66.7
40	Alaska	66.6
41	California	66.5
42	Montana	66.2
43	Washington	66.1
44	Maine	65.6
45	Texas	65.3
46	Tennessee	64.8
47	Wyoming	64.1
48	South Dakota	62.0
49	Florida	61.5
50	Arizona	59.9

	District of Columbia	84.0

Source: Morgan Quitno Press using data from U.S. Department of Justice, Bureau of Justice Statistics "Census of State and Local Law Enforcement Agencies, 1996" (Bulletin, June 1998, NCJ-164618)
*Includes state and local police, sheriffs' departments and special police agencies.

Rate of Full-Time Sworn Officers in Law Enforcement Agencies in 1996

National Rate = 25 Officers per 10,000 Population*

ALPHA ORDER

RANK	STATE	RATE
21	Alabama	23
30	Alaska	21
21	Arizona	23
21	Arkansas	23
28	California	22
10	Colorado	26
10	Connecticut	26
21	Delaware	23
10	Florida	26
10	Georgia	26
14	Hawaii	25
30	Idaho	21
4	Illinois	32
39	Indiana	19
43	Iowa	18
17	Kansas	24
46	Kentucky	17
2	Louisiana	37
39	Maine	19
8	Maryland	27
5	Massachusetts	29
30	Michigan	21
46	Minnesota	17
30	Mississippi	21
17	Missouri	24
39	Montana	19
36	Nebraska	20
8	Nevada	27
36	New Hampshire	20
3	New Jersey	35
17	New Mexico	24
1	New York	39
21	North Carolina	23
43	North Dakota	18
30	Ohio	21
28	Oklahoma	22
39	Oregon	19
30	Pennsylvania	21
17	Rhode Island	24
21	South Carolina	23
36	South Dakota	20
21	Tennessee	23
14	Texas	25
43	Utah	18
46	Vermont	17
7	Virginia	28
46	Washington	17
50	West Virginia	16
14	Wisconsin	25
5	Wyoming	29

RANK ORDER

RANK	STATE	RATE
1	New York	39
2	Louisiana	37
3	New Jersey	35
4	Illinois	32
5	Massachusetts	29
5	Wyoming	29
7	Virginia	28
8	Maryland	27
8	Nevada	27
10	Colorado	26
10	Connecticut	26
10	Florida	26
10	Georgia	26
14	Hawaii	25
14	Texas	25
14	Wisconsin	25
17	Kansas	24
17	Missouri	24
17	New Mexico	24
17	Rhode Island	24
21	Alabama	23
21	Arizona	23
21	Arkansas	23
21	Delaware	23
21	North Carolina	23
21	South Carolina	23
21	Tennessee	23
28	California	22
28	Oklahoma	22
30	Alaska	21
30	Idaho	21
30	Michigan	21
30	Mississippi	21
30	Ohio	21
30	Pennsylvania	21
36	Nebraska	20
36	New Hampshire	20
36	South Dakota	20
39	Indiana	19
39	Maine	19
39	Montana	19
39	Oregon	19
43	Iowa	18
43	North Dakota	18
43	Utah	18
46	Kentucky	17
46	Minnesota	17
46	Vermont	17
46	Washington	17
50	West Virginia	16

| | District of Columbia | 72 |

Source: Morgan Quitno Press using data from U.S. Department of Justice, Bureau of Justice Statistics
    "Census of State and Local Law Enforcement Agencies, 1996" (Bulletin, June 1998, NCJ-164618)
*Includes state and local police, sheriffs' departments and special police agencies.

Full-Time Sworn Law Enforcement Officers per 1,000 Square Miles in 1996

National Rate = 178 Officers per 1,000 Square Miles*

ALPHA ORDER

RANK	STATE	RATE
24	Alabama	187
50	Alaska	2
37	Arizona	88
31	Arkansas	109
14	California	435
34	Colorado	95
4	Connecticut	1,538
7	Delaware	693
9	Florida	624
16	Georgia	324
12	Hawaii	463
45	Idaho	30
8	Illinois	659
18	Indiana	300
36	Iowa	90
38	Kansas	75
27	Kentucky	160
15	Louisiana	325
39	Maine	69
6	Maryland	1,125
3	Massachusetts	1,941
22	Michigan	213
35	Minnesota	92
30	Mississippi	120
25	Missouri	186
49	Montana	11
42	Nebraska	43
43	Nevada	39
21	New Hampshire	248
1	New Jersey	3,415
44	New Mexico	34
5	New York	1,319
17	North Carolina	322
47	North Dakota	16
11	Ohio	531
32	Oklahoma	103
40	Oregon	62
10	Pennsylvania	540
2	Rhode Island	1,968
20	South Carolina	278
46	South Dakota	19
19	Tennessee	288
26	Texas	179
41	Utah	44
33	Vermont	102
13	Virginia	436
28	Washington	132
29	West Virginia	123
23	Wisconsin	194
48	Wyoming	14

RANK ORDER

RANK	STATE	RATE
1	New Jersey	3,415
2	Rhode Island	1,968
3	Massachusetts	1,941
4	Connecticut	1,538
5	New York	1,319
6	Maryland	1,125
7	Delaware	693
8	Illinois	659
9	Florida	624
10	Pennsylvania	540
11	Ohio	531
12	Hawaii	463
13	Virginia	436
14	California	435
15	Louisiana	325
16	Georgia	324
17	North Carolina	322
18	Indiana	300
19	Tennessee	288
20	South Carolina	278
21	New Hampshire	248
22	Michigan	213
23	Wisconsin	194
24	Alabama	187
25	Missouri	186
26	Texas	179
27	Kentucky	160
28	Washington	132
29	West Virginia	123
30	Mississippi	120
31	Arkansas	109
32	Oklahoma	103
33	Vermont	102
34	Colorado	95
35	Minnesota	92
36	Iowa	90
37	Arizona	88
38	Kansas	75
39	Maine	69
40	Oregon	62
41	Utah	44
42	Nebraska	43
43	Nevada	39
44	New Mexico	34
45	Idaho	30
46	South Dakota	19
47	North Dakota	16
48	Wyoming	14
49	Montana	11
50	Alaska	2
	District of Columbia**	NA

*Source: Morgan Quitno Press using data from U.S. Department of Justice, Bureau of Justice Statistics
"Census of State and Local Law Enforcement Agencies, 1996" (Bulletin, June 1998, NCJ-164618)
*Includes state and local police, sheriffs' departments and special police agencies.
**The District of Columbia has 3,909 sworn officers for its 68 square miles.*

Full-Time Employees in Law Enforcement Agencies in 1996

National Total = 921,978 Employees*

ALPHA ORDER

RANK	STATE	EMPLOYEES	% of USA
21	Alabama	14,389	1.6%
48	Alaska	1,884	0.2%
18	Arizona	16,828	1.8%
32	Arkansas	7,958	0.9%
1	California	103,967	11.3%
23	Colorado	14,002	1.5%
27	Connecticut	10,319	1.1%
47	Delaware	2,134	0.2%
4	Florida	60,808	6.6%
9	Georgia	28,204	3.1%
39	Hawaii	3,745	0.4%
40	Idaho	3,674	0.4%
5	Illinois	50,255	5.5%
20	Indiana	16,378	1.8%
33	Iowa	6,799	0.7%
29	Kansas	8,736	0.9%
31	Kentucky	8,544	0.9%
14	Louisiana	19,817	2.1%
41	Maine	3,534	0.4%
16	Maryland	18,382	2.0%
11	Massachusetts	24,434	2.7%
10	Michigan	27,490	3.0%
25	Minnesota	11,317	1.2%
30	Mississippi	8,583	0.9%
17	Missouri	17,889	1.9%
44	Montana	2,541	0.3%
37	Nebraska	4,529	0.5%
34	Nevada	6,231	0.7%
43	New Hampshire	2,957	0.3%
6	New Jersey	34,940	3.8%
35	New Mexico	6,182	0.7%
2	New York	88,348	9.6%
12	North Carolina	23,263	2.5%
49	North Dakota	1,537	0.2%
7	Ohio	32,719	3.5%
26	Oklahoma	10,491	1.1%
28	Oregon	8,933	1.0%
8	Pennsylvania	29,506	3.2%
42	Rhode Island	3,098	0.3%
24	South Carolina	11,494	1.2%
45	South Dakota	2,360	0.3%
15	Tennessee	18,746	2.0%
3	Texas	73,112	7.9%
36	Utah	5,052	0.5%
50	Vermont	1,336	0.1%
13	Virginia	23,108	2.5%
22	Washington	14,061	1.5%
38	West Virginia	4,074	0.4%
19	Wisconsin	16,490	1.8%
46	Wyoming	2,149	0.2%

RANK ORDER

RANK	STATE	EMPLOYEES	% of USA
1	California	103,967	11.3%
2	New York	88,348	9.6%
3	Texas	73,112	7.9%
4	Florida	60,808	6.6%
5	Illinois	50,255	5.5%
6	New Jersey	34,940	3.8%
7	Ohio	32,719	3.5%
8	Pennsylvania	29,506	3.2%
9	Georgia	28,204	3.1%
10	Michigan	27,490	3.0%
11	Massachusetts	24,434	2.7%
12	North Carolina	23,263	2.5%
13	Virginia	23,108	2.5%
14	Louisiana	19,817	2.1%
15	Tennessee	18,746	2.0%
16	Maryland	18,382	2.0%
17	Missouri	17,889	1.9%
18	Arizona	16,828	1.8%
19	Wisconsin	16,490	1.8%
20	Indiana	16,378	1.8%
21	Alabama	14,389	1.6%
22	Washington	14,061	1.5%
23	Colorado	14,002	1.5%
24	South Carolina	11,494	1.2%
25	Minnesota	11,317	1.2%
26	Oklahoma	10,491	1.1%
27	Connecticut	10,319	1.1%
28	Oregon	8,933	1.0%
29	Kansas	8,736	0.9%
30	Mississippi	8,583	0.9%
31	Kentucky	8,544	0.9%
32	Arkansas	7,958	0.9%
33	Iowa	6,799	0.7%
34	Nevada	6,231	0.7%
35	New Mexico	6,182	0.7%
36	Utah	5,052	0.5%
37	Nebraska	4,529	0.5%
38	West Virginia	4,074	0.4%
39	Hawaii	3,745	0.4%
40	Idaho	3,674	0.4%
41	Maine	3,534	0.4%
42	Rhode Island	3,098	0.3%
43	New Hampshire	2,957	0.3%
44	Montana	2,541	0.3%
45	South Dakota	2,360	0.3%
46	Wyoming	2,149	0.2%
47	Delaware	2,134	0.2%
48	Alaska	1,884	0.2%
49	North Dakota	1,537	0.2%
50	Vermont	1,336	0.1%
	District of Columbia	4,651	0.5%

Source: U.S. Department of Justice, Bureau of Justice Statistics
   "Census of State and Local Law Enforcement Agencies, 1996" (Bulletin, June 1998, NCJ-164618)
*Includes state and local police, sheriffs' departments and special police agencies.

Rate of Full-Time Employees in Law Enforcement Agencies in 1996

National Rate = 35 Employees per 10,000 Population*

ALPHA ORDER				RANK ORDER		
RANK	STATE	RATE		RANK	STATE	RATE
17	Alabama	34		1	New York	49
29	Alaska	31		2	Louisiana	46
9	Arizona	38		3	Wyoming	45
21	Arkansas	32		4	New Jersey	44
19	California	33		5	Florida	42
12	Colorado	37		5	Illinois	42
21	Connecticut	32		7	Massachusetts	40
33	Delaware	29		8	Nevada	39
5	Florida	42		9	Arizona	38
9	Georgia	38		9	Georgia	38
21	Hawaii	32		9	Texas	38
29	Idaho	31		12	Colorado	37
5	Illinois	42		13	Maryland	36
37	Indiana	28		13	New Mexico	36
44	Iowa	24		15	Tennessee	35
17	Kansas	34		15	Virginia	35
49	Kentucky	22		17	Alabama	34
2	Louisiana	46		17	Kansas	34
37	Maine	28		19	California	33
13	Maryland	36		19	Missouri	33
7	Massachusetts	40		21	Arkansas	32
33	Michigan	29		21	Connecticut	32
44	Minnesota	24		21	Hawaii	32
21	Mississippi	32		21	Mississippi	32
19	Missouri	33		21	North Carolina	32
33	Montana	29		21	Oklahoma	32
40	Nebraska	27		21	South Dakota	32
8	Nevada	39		21	Wisconsin	32
41	New Hampshire	25		29	Alaska	31
4	New Jersey	44		29	Idaho	31
13	New Mexico	36		29	Rhode Island	31
1	New York	49		29	South Carolina	31
21	North Carolina	32		33	Delaware	29
44	North Dakota	24		33	Michigan	29
33	Ohio	29		33	Montana	29
21	Oklahoma	32		33	Ohio	29
37	Oregon	28		37	Indiana	28
44	Pennsylvania	24		37	Maine	28
29	Rhode Island	31		37	Oregon	28
29	South Carolina	31		40	Nebraska	27
21	South Dakota	32		41	New Hampshire	25
15	Tennessee	35		41	Utah	25
9	Texas	38		41	Washington	25
41	Utah	25		44	Iowa	24
48	Vermont	23		44	Minnesota	24
15	Virginia	35		44	North Dakota	24
41	Washington	25		44	Pennsylvania	24
49	West Virginia	22		48	Vermont	23
21	Wisconsin	32		49	Kentucky	22
3	Wyoming	45		49	West Virginia	22
					District of Columbia	86

Source: U.S. Department of Justice, Bureau of Justice Statistics
"Census of State and Local Law Enforcement Agencies, 1996" (Bulletin, June 1998, NCJ-164618)
*Includes state and local police, sheriffs' departments and special police agencies.

Full-Time Sworn Officers in State Police Departments in 1996

National Total = 54,587 Officers*

ALPHA ORDER

RANK	STATE	OFFICERS	% of USA
27	Alabama	581	1.1%
41	Alaska	290	0.5%
18	Arizona	952	1.7%
32	Arkansas	522	1.0%
1	California	6,219	11.4%
27	Colorado	581	1.1%
15	Connecticut	1,022	1.9%
30	Delaware	540	1.0%
9	Florida	1,740	3.2%
21	Georgia	878	1.6%
50	Hawaii	0	0.0%
46	Idaho	192	0.4%
8	Illinois	1,988	3.6%
14	Indiana	1,207	2.2%
37	Iowa	433	0.8%
29	Kansas	552	1.0%
17	Kentucky	984	1.8%
22	Louisiana	873	1.6%
40	Maine	337	0.6%
11	Maryland	1,625	3.0%
6	Massachusetts	2,565	4.7%
7	Michigan	2,164	4.0%
34	Minnesota	484	0.9%
31	Mississippi	535	1.0%
16	Missouri	996	1.8%
44	Montana	212	0.4%
35	Nebraska	464	0.9%
38	Nevada	375	0.7%
43	New Hampshire	245	0.4%
5	New Jersey	2,702	4.9%
36	New Mexico	435	0.8%
3	New York	3,972	7.3%
13	North Carolina	1,380	2.5%
49	North Dakota	120	0.2%
12	Ohio	1,391	2.5%
25	Oklahoma	756	1.4%
23	Oregon	824	1.5%
2	Pennsylvania	4,114	7.5%
45	Rhode Island	193	0.4%
20	South Carolina	892	1.6%
47	South Dakota	155	0.3%
24	Tennessee	768	1.4%
4	Texas	2,873	5.3%
39	Utah	355	0.7%
41	Vermont	290	0.5%
10	Virginia	1,662	3.0%
19	Washington	906	1.7%
26	West Virginia	595	1.1%
33	Wisconsin	497	0.9%
48	Wyoming	151	0.3%

RANK ORDER

RANK	STATE	OFFICERS	% of USA
1	California	6,219	11.4%
2	Pennsylvania	4,114	7.5%
3	New York	3,972	7.3%
4	Texas	2,873	5.3%
5	New Jersey	2,702	4.9%
6	Massachusetts	2,565	4.7%
7	Michigan	2,164	4.0%
8	Illinois	1,988	3.6%
9	Florida	1,740	3.2%
10	Virginia	1,662	3.0%
11	Maryland	1,625	3.0%
12	Ohio	1,391	2.5%
13	North Carolina	1,380	2.5%
14	Indiana	1,207	2.2%
15	Connecticut	1,022	1.9%
16	Missouri	996	1.8%
17	Kentucky	984	1.8%
18	Arizona	952	1.7%
19	Washington	906	1.7%
20	South Carolina	892	1.6%
21	Georgia	878	1.6%
22	Louisiana	873	1.6%
23	Oregon	824	1.5%
24	Tennessee	768	1.4%
25	Oklahoma	756	1.4%
26	West Virginia	595	1.1%
27	Alabama	581	1.1%
27	Colorado	581	1.1%
29	Kansas	552	1.0%
30	Delaware	540	1.0%
31	Mississippi	535	1.0%
32	Arkansas	522	1.0%
33	Wisconsin	497	0.9%
34	Minnesota	484	0.9%
35	Nebraska	464	0.9%
36	New Mexico	435	0.8%
37	Iowa	433	0.8%
38	Nevada	375	0.7%
39	Utah	355	0.7%
40	Maine	337	0.6%
41	Alaska	290	0.5%
41	Vermont	290	0.5%
43	New Hampshire	245	0.4%
44	Montana	212	0.4%
45	Rhode Island	193	0.4%
46	Idaho	192	0.4%
47	South Dakota	155	0.3%
48	Wyoming	151	0.3%
49	North Dakota	120	0.2%
50	Hawaii	0	0.0%
	District of Columbia	0	0.0%

Source: U.S. Department of Justice, Bureau of Justice Statistics
"Census of State and Local Law Enforcement Agencies, 1996" (Bulletin, June 1998, NCJ-164618)
*All states except Hawaii and the District of Columbia have a state police department.

Percent of Full-Time State Police Department Employees
Who are Sworn Officers: 1996
National Percent = 65.2% of Employees*

ALPHA ORDER

RANK	STATE	PERCENT
45	Alabama	48.9
34	Alaska	64.7
39	Arizona	56.8
14	Arkansas	73.3
27	California	68.1
19	Colorado	71.9
31	Connecticut	66.1
22	Delaware	71.1
7	Florida	78.8
49	Georgia	30.5
NA	Hawaii**	NA
17	Idaho	73.0
41	Illinois	55.5
36	Indiana	64.0
1	Iowa	92.5
15	Kansas	73.2
37	Kentucky	58.4
21	Louisiana	71.2
22	Maine	71.1
29	Maryland	67.0
2	Massachusetts	88.9
24	Michigan	69.0
25	Minnesota	68.8
26	Mississippi	68.4
46	Missouri	47.8
10	Montana	76.5
18	Nebraska	72.7
20	Nevada	71.4
13	New Hampshire	73.6
11	New Jersey	74.1
42	New Mexico	52.6
4	New York	85.2
8	North Carolina	78.7
35	North Dakota	64.5
38	Ohio	58.2
40	Oklahoma	56.6
30	Oregon	66.2
9	Pennsylvania	77.6
5	Rhode Island	81.8
6	South Carolina	80.9
28	South Dakota	67.7
44	Tennessee	49.3
48	Texas	42.6
3	Utah	88.3
33	Vermont	65.2
12	Virginia	73.9
47	Washington	43.9
32	West Virginia	65.4
16	Wisconsin	73.1
43	Wyoming	50.2

RANK ORDER

RANK	STATE	PERCENT
1	Iowa	92.5
2	Massachusetts	88.9
3	Utah	88.3
4	New York	85.2
5	Rhode Island	81.8
6	South Carolina	80.9
7	Florida	78.8
8	North Carolina	78.7
9	Pennsylvania	77.6
10	Montana	76.5
11	New Jersey	74.1
12	Virginia	73.9
13	New Hampshire	73.6
14	Arkansas	73.3
15	Kansas	73.2
16	Wisconsin	73.1
17	Idaho	73.0
18	Nebraska	72.7
19	Colorado	71.9
20	Nevada	71.4
21	Louisiana	71.2
22	Delaware	71.1
22	Maine	71.1
24	Michigan	69.0
25	Minnesota	68.8
26	Mississippi	68.4
27	California	68.1
28	South Dakota	67.7
29	Maryland	67.0
30	Oregon	66.2
31	Connecticut	66.1
32	West Virginia	65.4
33	Vermont	65.2
34	Alaska	64.7
35	North Dakota	64.5
36	Indiana	64.0
37	Kentucky	58.4
38	Ohio	58.2
39	Arizona	56.8
40	Oklahoma	56.6
41	Illinois	55.5
42	New Mexico	52.6
43	Wyoming	50.2
44	Tennessee	49.3
45	Alabama	48.9
46	Missouri	47.8
47	Washington	43.9
48	Texas	42.6
49	Georgia	30.5
NA	Hawaii**	NA
	District of Columbia**	NA

Source: Morgan Quitno Press using data from U.S. Department of Justice, Bureau of Justice Statistics
    "Census of State and Local Law Enforcement Agencies, 1996" (Bulletin, June 1998, NCJ-164618)
*All states except Hawaii and the District of Columbia have a state police department.
**Not applicable.

Rate of Full-Time Sworn Officers in State Police Departments in 1996

National Rate = 2.1 Officers per 10,000 Population*

ALPHA ORDER

RANK ORDER

RANK	STATE	RATE		RANK	STATE	RATE
43	Alabama	1.4		1	Delaware	7.4
3	Alaska	4.8		2	Vermont	4.9
23	Arizona	2.1		3	Alaska	4.8
23	Arkansas	2.1		4	Massachusetts	4.2
29	California	2.0		5	New Jersey	3.4
40	Colorado	1.5		5	Pennsylvania	3.4
9	Connecticut	3.1		7	West Virginia	3.3
1	Delaware	7.4		8	Maryland	3.2
45	Florida	1.2		9	Connecticut	3.1
45	Georgia	1.2		9	Wyoming	3.1
50	Hawaii*	0.0		11	Nebraska	2.8
38	Idaho	1.6		12	Maine	2.7
37	Illinois	1.7		13	Oregon	2.6
23	Indiana	2.1		14	Kentucky	2.5
40	Iowa	1.5		14	New Mexico	2.5
23	Kansas	2.1		14	Virginia	2.5
14	Kentucky	2.5		17	Montana	2.4
29	Louisiana	2.0		17	South Carolina	2.4
12	Maine	2.7		19	Michigan	2.3
8	Maryland	3.2		19	Nevada	2.3
4	Massachusetts	4.2		19	Oklahoma	2.3
19	Michigan	2.3		22	New York	2.2
48	Minnesota	1.0		23	Arizona	2.1
29	Mississippi	2.0		23	Arkansas	2.1
32	Missouri	1.9		23	Indiana	2.1
17	Montana	2.4		23	Kansas	2.1
11	Nebraska	2.8		23	New Hampshire	2.1
19	Nevada	2.3		23	South Dakota	2.1
23	New Hampshire	2.1		29	California	2.0
5	New Jersey	3.4		29	Louisiana	2.0
14	New Mexico	2.5		29	Mississippi	2.0
22	New York	2.2		32	Missouri	1.9
32	North Carolina	1.9		32	North Carolina	1.9
32	North Dakota	1.9		32	North Dakota	1.9
45	Ohio	1.2		32	Rhode Island	1.9
19	Oklahoma	2.3		36	Utah	1.8
13	Oregon	2.6		37	Illinois	1.7
5	Pennsylvania	3.4		38	Idaho	1.6
32	Rhode Island	1.9		38	Washington	1.6
17	South Carolina	2.4		40	Colorado	1.5
23	South Dakota	2.1		40	Iowa	1.5
43	Tennessee	1.4		40	Texas	1.5
40	Texas	1.5		43	Alabama	1.4
36	Utah	1.8		43	Tennessee	1.4
2	Vermont	4.9		45	Florida	1.2
14	Virginia	2.5		45	Georgia	1.2
38	Washington	1.6		45	Ohio	1.2
7	West Virginia	3.3		48	Minnesota	1.0
48	Wisconsin	1.0		48	Wisconsin	1.0
9	Wyoming	3.1		50	Hawaii*	0.0
					District of Columbia*	0.0

Source: Morgan Quitno Press using data from U.S. Department of Justice, Bureau of Justice Statistics
    "Census of State and Local Law Enforcement Agencies, 1996" (Bulletin, June 1998, NCJ-164618)
*All states except Hawaii and the District of Columbia have a state police department.

State Government Law Enforcement Officers in 2000

National Total = 67,235 Officers*

ALPHA ORDER

ALPHA ORDER

RANK	STATE	OFFICERS	% of USA
26	Alabama	857	1.3%
41	Alaska	323	0.5%
22	Arizona	1,034	1.5%
NA	Arkansas**	NA	NA
1	California	7,203	10.7%
31	Colorado	688	1.0%
21	Connecticut	1,084	1.6%
24	Delaware	930	1.4%
9	Florida	2,280	3.4%
18	Georgia	1,148	1.7%
49	Hawaii	0	0.0%
44	Idaho	255	0.4%
7	Illinois	2,638	3.9%
17	Indiana	1,262	1.9%
32	Iowa	666	1.0%
30	Kansas	708	1.1%
15	Kentucky	1,525	2.3%
19	Louisiana	1,115	1.7%
38	Maine	420	0.6%
6	Maryland	2,717	4.0%
11	Massachusetts	2,212	3.3%
12	Michigan	2,083	3.1%
34	Minnesota	542	0.8%
35	Mississippi	528	0.8%
20	Missouri	1,089	1.6%
45	Montana	197	0.3%
37	Nebraska	456	0.7%
39	Nevada	381	0.6%
40	New Hampshire	329	0.5%
4	New Jersey	3,200	4.8%
36	New Mexico	524	0.8%
2	New York	5,863	8.7%
10	North Carolina	2,226	3.3%
48	North Dakota	124	0.2%
14	Ohio	1,881	2.8%
25	Oklahoma	867	1.3%
27	Oregon	805	1.2%
3	Pennsylvania	4,104	6.1%
43	Rhode Island	257	0.4%
13	South Carolina	2,025	3.0%
46	South Dakota	150	0.2%
16	Tennessee	1,511	2.2%
5	Texas	3,065	4.6%
33	Utah	598	0.9%
42	Vermont	290	0.4%
8	Virginia	2,361	3.5%
23	Washington	1,018	1.5%
28	West Virginia	792	1.2%
29	Wisconsin	756	1.1%
47	Wyoming	148	0.2%

RANK ORDER

RANK	STATE	OFFICERS	% of USA
1	California	7,203	10.7%
2	New York	5,863	8.7%
3	Pennsylvania	4,104	6.1%
4	New Jersey	3,200	4.8%
5	Texas	3,065	4.6%
6	Maryland	2,717	4.0%
7	Illinois	2,638	3.9%
8	Virginia	2,361	3.5%
9	Florida	2,280	3.4%
10	North Carolina	2,226	3.3%
11	Massachusetts	2,212	3.3%
12	Michigan	2,083	3.1%
13	South Carolina	2,025	3.0%
14	Ohio	1,881	2.8%
15	Kentucky	1,525	2.3%
16	Tennessee	1,511	2.2%
17	Indiana	1,262	1.9%
18	Georgia	1,148	1.7%
19	Louisiana	1,115	1.7%
20	Missouri	1,089	1.6%
21	Connecticut	1,084	1.6%
22	Arizona	1,034	1.5%
23	Washington	1,018	1.5%
24	Delaware	930	1.4%
25	Oklahoma	867	1.3%
26	Alabama	857	1.3%
27	Oregon	805	1.2%
28	West Virginia	792	1.2%
29	Wisconsin	756	1.1%
30	Kansas	708	1.1%
31	Colorado	688	1.0%
32	Iowa	666	1.0%
33	Utah	598	0.9%
34	Minnesota	542	0.8%
35	Mississippi	528	0.8%
36	New Mexico	524	0.8%
37	Nebraska	456	0.7%
38	Maine	420	0.6%
39	Nevada	381	0.6%
40	New Hampshire	329	0.5%
41	Alaska	323	0.5%
42	Vermont	290	0.4%
43	Rhode Island	257	0.4%
44	Idaho	255	0.4%
45	Montana	197	0.3%
46	South Dakota	150	0.2%
47	Wyoming	148	0.2%
48	North Dakota	124	0.2%
49	Hawaii	0	0.0%
NA	Arkansas**	NA	NA
	District of Columbia	0	0.0%

Source: Morgan Quitno Press using data from Federal Bureau of Investigation
   "Crime in the United States 2000" (Uniform Crime Reports, October 22, 2001)
*Includes state police agencies and other agencies with law enforcement powers. Hawaii and the District of Columbia do not have a state police agency.
**Not available.

Male State Government Law Enforcement Officers in 2000

National Total = 62,430 Male Officers*

ALPHA ORDER

RANK ORDER

RANK	STATE	OFFICERS	% of USA	RANK	STATE	OFFICERS	% of USA
25	Alabama	834	1.3%	1	California	6,485	10.4%
40	Alaska	304	0.5%	2	New York	5,434	8.7%
22	Arizona	955	1.5%	3	Pennsylvania	3,937	6.3%
NA	Arkansas**	NA	NA	4	New Jersey	3,074	4.9%
1	California	6,485	10.4%	5	Texas	2,904	4.7%
31	Colorado	659	1.1%	6	Illinois	2,400	3.8%
21	Connecticut	1,012	1.6%	7	Maryland	2,389	3.8%
26	Delaware	794	1.3%	8	Virginia	2,235	3.6%
10	Florida	2,081	3.3%	9	North Carolina	2,082	3.3%
19	Georgia	1,071	1.7%	10	Florida	2,081	3.3%
49	Hawaii	0	0.0%	11	Massachusetts	1,996	3.2%
43	Idaho	241	0.4%	12	South Carolina	1,866	3.0%
6	Illinois	2,400	3.8%	13	Michigan	1,824	2.9%
17	Indiana	1,194	1.9%	14	Ohio	1,720	2.8%
32	Iowa	626	1.0%	15	Kentucky	1,461	2.3%
29	Kansas	681	1.1%	16	Tennessee	1,401	2.2%
15	Kentucky	1,461	2.3%	17	Indiana	1,194	1.9%
18	Louisiana	1,080	1.7%	18	Louisiana	1,080	1.7%
38	Maine	394	0.6%	19	Georgia	1,071	1.7%
7	Maryland	2,389	3.8%	20	Missouri	1,046	1.7%
11	Massachusetts	1,996	3.2%	21	Connecticut	1,012	1.6%
13	Michigan	1,824	2.9%	22	Arizona	955	1.5%
36	Minnesota	495	0.8%	23	Washington	949	1.5%
34	Mississippi	520	0.8%	24	Oklahoma	844	1.4%
20	Missouri	1,046	1.7%	25	Alabama	834	1.3%
45	Montana	184	0.3%	26	Delaware	794	1.3%
37	Nebraska	436	0.7%	27	West Virginia	775	1.2%
39	Nevada	358	0.6%	28	Oregon	731	1.2%
41	New Hampshire	299	0.5%	29	Kansas	681	1.1%
4	New Jersey	3,074	4.9%	30	Wisconsin	666	1.1%
35	New Mexico	506	0.8%	31	Colorado	659	1.1%
2	New York	5,434	8.7%	32	Iowa	626	1.0%
9	North Carolina	2,082	3.3%	33	Utah	574	0.9%
48	North Dakota	118	0.2%	34	Mississippi	520	0.8%
14	Ohio	1,720	2.8%	35	New Mexico	506	0.8%
24	Oklahoma	844	1.4%	36	Minnesota	495	0.8%
28	Oregon	731	1.2%	37	Nebraska	436	0.7%
3	Pennsylvania	3,937	6.3%	38	Maine	394	0.6%
44	Rhode Island	234	0.4%	39	Nevada	358	0.6%
12	South Carolina	1,866	3.0%	40	Alaska	304	0.5%
46	South Dakota	148	0.2%	41	New Hampshire	299	0.5%
16	Tennessee	1,401	2.2%	42	Vermont	268	0.4%
5	Texas	2,904	4.7%	43	Idaho	241	0.4%
33	Utah	574	0.9%	44	Rhode Island	234	0.4%
42	Vermont	268	0.4%	45	Montana	184	0.3%
8	Virginia	2,235	3.6%	46	South Dakota	148	0.2%
23	Washington	949	1.5%	47	Wyoming	145	0.2%
27	West Virginia	775	1.2%	48	North Dakota	118	0.2%
30	Wisconsin	666	1.1%	49	Hawaii	0	0.0%
47	Wyoming	145	0.2%	NA	Arkansas**	NA	NA
					District of Columbia	0	0.0%

Source: Morgan Quitno Press using data from Federal Bureau of Investigation
    "Crime in the United States 2000" (Uniform Crime Reports, October 22, 2001)
*Includes state police agencies and other agencies with law enforcement powers. Hawaii and the District of
Columbia do not have a state police agency.
**Not available.

Female State Government Law Enforcement Officers in 2000

National Total = 4,805 Female Officers*

ALPHA ORDER					RANK ORDER			
RANK	STATE		OFFICERS	% of USA	RANK	STATE		OFFICERS	% of USA
34	Alabama		23	0.5%	1	California		718	14.9%
40	Alaska		19	0.4%	2	New York		429	8.9%
18	Arizona		79	1.6%	3	Maryland		328	6.8%
NA	Arkansas**		NA	NA	4	Michigan		259	5.4%
1	California		718	14.9%	5	Illinois		238	5.0%
30	Colorado		29	0.6%	6	Massachusetts		216	4.5%
21	Connecticut		72	1.5%	7	Florida		199	4.1%
13	Delaware		136	2.8%	8	Pennsylvania		167	3.5%
7	Florida		199	4.1%	9	Ohio		161	3.4%
19	Georgia		77	1.6%	9	Texas		161	3.4%
49	Hawaii		0	0.0%	11	South Carolina		159	3.3%
43	Idaho		14	0.3%	12	North Carolina		144	3.0%
5	Illinois		238	5.0%	13	Delaware		136	2.8%
23	Indiana		68	1.4%	14	New Jersey		126	2.6%
27	Iowa		40	0.8%	14	Virginia		126	2.6%
31	Kansas		27	0.6%	16	Tennessee		110	2.3%
24	Kentucky		64	1.3%	17	Wisconsin		90	1.9%
28	Louisiana		35	0.7%	18	Arizona		79	1.6%
32	Maine		26	0.5%	19	Georgia		77	1.6%
3	Maryland		328	6.8%	20	Oregon		74	1.5%
6	Massachusetts		216	4.5%	21	Connecticut		72	1.5%
4	Michigan		259	5.4%	22	Washington		69	1.4%
25	Minnesota		47	1.0%	23	Indiana		68	1.4%
45	Mississippi		8	0.2%	24	Kentucky		64	1.3%
26	Missouri		43	0.9%	25	Minnesota		47	1.0%
44	Montana		13	0.3%	26	Missouri		43	0.9%
39	Nebraska		20	0.4%	27	Iowa		40	0.8%
34	Nevada		23	0.5%	28	Louisiana		35	0.7%
29	New Hampshire		30	0.6%	29	New Hampshire		30	0.6%
14	New Jersey		126	2.6%	30	Colorado		29	0.6%
41	New Mexico		18	0.4%	31	Kansas		27	0.6%
2	New York		429	8.9%	32	Maine		26	0.5%
12	North Carolina		144	3.0%	33	Utah		24	0.5%
46	North Dakota		6	0.1%	34	Alabama		23	0.5%
9	Ohio		161	3.4%	34	Nevada		23	0.5%
34	Oklahoma		23	0.5%	34	Oklahoma		23	0.5%
20	Oregon		74	1.5%	34	Rhode Island		23	0.5%
8	Pennsylvania		167	3.5%	38	Vermont		22	0.5%
34	Rhode Island		23	0.5%	39	Nebraska		20	0.4%
11	South Carolina		159	3.3%	40	Alaska		19	0.4%
48	South Dakota		2	0.0%	41	New Mexico		18	0.4%
16	Tennessee		110	2.3%	42	West Virginia		17	0.4%
9	Texas		161	3.4%	43	Idaho		14	0.3%
33	Utah		24	0.5%	44	Montana		13	0.3%
38	Vermont		22	0.5%	45	Mississippi		8	0.2%
14	Virginia		126	2.6%	46	North Dakota		6	0.1%
22	Washington		69	1.4%	47	Wyoming		3	0.1%
42	West Virginia		17	0.4%	48	South Dakota		2	0.0%
17	Wisconsin		90	1.9%	49	Hawaii		0	0.0%
47	Wyoming		3	0.1%	NA	Arkansas**		NA	NA
						District of Columbia		0	0.0%

Source: Morgan Quitno Press using data from Federal Bureau of Investigation
    "Crime in the United States 2000" (Uniform Crime Reports, October 22, 2001)
*Includes state police agencies and other agencies with law enforcement powers. Hawaii and the District of Columbia do not have a state police agency.
**Not available.

288

Female State Government Law Enforcement Officers
As a Percent of All Officers: 2000
National Percent = 7.1% of Officers*

ALPHA ORDER

RANK ORDER

RANK	STATE	PERCENT		RANK	STATE	PERCENT
43	Alabama	2.7		1	Delaware	14.6
27	Alaska	5.9		2	Michigan	12.4
15	Arizona	7.6		3	Maryland	12.1
NA	Arkansas**	NA		4	Wisconsin	11.9
5	California	10.0		5	California	10.0
34	Colorado	4.2		6	Massachusetts	9.8
21	Connecticut	6.6		7	Oregon	9.2
1	Delaware	14.6		8	New Hampshire	9.1
11	Florida	8.7		9	Illinois	9.0
20	Georgia	6.7		10	Rhode Island	8.9
NA	Hawaii**	NA		11	Florida	8.7
28	Idaho	5.5		11	Minnesota	8.7
9	Illinois	9.0		13	Ohio	8.6
29	Indiana	5.4		14	South Carolina	7.9
25	Iowa	6.0		15	Arizona	7.6
40	Kansas	3.8		15	Vermont	7.6
34	Kentucky	4.2		17	New York	7.3
42	Louisiana	3.1		17	Tennessee	7.3
24	Maine	6.2		19	Washington	6.8
3	Maryland	12.1		20	Georgia	6.7
6	Massachusetts	9.8		21	Connecticut	6.6
2	Michigan	12.4		21	Montana	6.6
11	Minnesota	8.7		23	North Carolina	6.5
47	Mississippi	1.5		24	Maine	6.2
38	Missouri	3.9		25	Iowa	6.0
21	Montana	6.6		25	Nevada	6.0
33	Nebraska	4.4		27	Alaska	5.9
25	Nevada	6.0		28	Idaho	5.5
8	New Hampshire	9.1		29	Indiana	5.4
38	New Jersey	3.9		30	Texas	5.3
41	New Mexico	3.4		30	Virginia	5.3
17	New York	7.3		32	North Dakota	4.8
23	North Carolina	6.5		33	Nebraska	4.4
32	North Dakota	4.8		34	Colorado	4.2
13	Ohio	8.6		34	Kentucky	4.2
43	Oklahoma	2.7		36	Pennsylvania	4.1
7	Oregon	9.2		37	Utah	4.0
36	Pennsylvania	4.1		38	Missouri	3.9
10	Rhode Island	8.9		38	New Jersey	3.9
14	South Carolina	7.9		40	Kansas	3.8
48	South Dakota	1.3		41	New Mexico	3.4
17	Tennessee	7.3		42	Louisiana	3.1
30	Texas	5.3		43	Alabama	2.7
37	Utah	4.0		43	Oklahoma	2.7
15	Vermont	7.6		45	West Virginia	2.1
30	Virginia	5.3		46	Wyoming	2.0
19	Washington	6.8		47	Mississippi	1.5
45	West Virginia	2.1		48	South Dakota	1.3
4	Wisconsin	11.9		NA	Arkansas**	NA
46	Wyoming	2.0		NA	Hawaii**	NA
					District of Columbia**	NA

Source: Morgan Quitno Press using data from Federal Bureau of Investigation
   "Crime in the United States 2000" (Uniform Crime Reports, October 22, 2001)
*Includes state police agencies and other agencies with law enforcement powers.
**Hawaii and the District of Columbia do not have a state police agency. Arkansas' information is not available.

Local Police Departments in 1996

National Total = 13,578 Departments*

RANK	STATE	DEPARTMENTS	% of USA
17	Alabama	331	2.4%
44	Alaska	61	0.4%
39	Arizona	88	0.6%
21	Arkansas	261	1.9%
15	California	344	2.5%
32	Colorado	163	1.2%
36	Connecticut	107	0.8%
48	Delaware	35	0.3%
19	Florida	289	2.1%
12	Georgia	377	2.8%
50	Hawaii	4	0.0%
42	Idaho	76	0.6%
2	Illinois	809	6.0%
10	Indiana	432	3.2%
18	Iowa	318	2.3%
24	Kansas	245	1.8%
23	Kentucky	254	1.9%
20	Louisiana	271	2.0%
35	Maine	115	0.8%
41	Maryland	78	0.6%
16	Massachusetts	341	2.5%
8	Michigan	475	3.5%
11	Minnesota	384	2.8%
27	Mississippi	205	1.5%
5	Missouri	509	3.7%
43	Montana	65	0.5%
31	Nebraska	168	1.2%
49	Nevada	26	0.2%
26	New Hampshire	219	1.6%
6	New Jersey	487	3.6%
38	New Mexico	91	0.7%
7	New York	476	3.5%
13	North Carolina	370	2.7%
40	North Dakota	81	0.6%
3	Ohio	808	6.0%
14	Oklahoma	347	2.6%
33	Oregon	142	1.0%
1	Pennsylvania	1,141	8.4%
47	Rhode Island	40	0.3%
28	South Carolina	192	1.4%
34	South Dakota	119	0.9%
22	Tennessee	255	1.9%
4	Texas	735	5.4%
37	Utah	95	0.7%
46	Vermont	52	0.4%
30	Virginia	170	1.3%
25	Washington	223	1.6%
29	West Virginia	179	1.3%
9	Wisconsin	471	3.5%
45	Wyoming	53	0.4%

RANK	STATE	DEPARTMENTS	% of USA
1	Pennsylvania	1,141	8.4%
2	Illinois	809	6.0%
3	Ohio	808	6.0%
4	Texas	735	5.4%
5	Missouri	509	3.7%
6	New Jersey	487	3.6%
7	New York	476	3.5%
8	Michigan	475	3.5%
9	Wisconsin	471	3.5%
10	Indiana	432	3.2%
11	Minnesota	384	2.8%
12	Georgia	377	2.8%
13	North Carolina	370	2.7%
14	Oklahoma	347	2.6%
15	California	344	2.5%
16	Massachusetts	341	2.5%
17	Alabama	331	2.4%
18	Iowa	318	2.3%
19	Florida	289	2.1%
20	Louisiana	271	2.0%
21	Arkansas	261	1.9%
22	Tennessee	255	1.9%
23	Kentucky	254	1.9%
24	Kansas	245	1.8%
25	Washington	223	1.6%
26	New Hampshire	219	1.6%
27	Mississippi	205	1.5%
28	South Carolina	192	1.4%
29	West Virginia	179	1.3%
30	Virginia	170	1.3%
31	Nebraska	168	1.2%
32	Colorado	163	1.2%
33	Oregon	142	1.0%
34	South Dakota	119	0.9%
35	Maine	115	0.8%
36	Connecticut	107	0.8%
37	Utah	95	0.7%
38	New Mexico	91	0.7%
39	Arizona	88	0.6%
40	North Dakota	81	0.6%
41	Maryland	78	0.6%
42	Idaho	76	0.6%
43	Montana	65	0.5%
44	Alaska	61	0.4%
45	Wyoming	53	0.4%
46	Vermont	52	0.4%
47	Rhode Island	40	0.3%
48	Delaware	35	0.3%
49	Nevada	26	0.2%
50	Hawaii	4	0.0%
	District of Columbia	1	0.0%

Source: U.S. Department of Justice, Bureau of Justice Statistics
"Census of State and Local Law Enforcement Agencies, 1996" (Bulletin, June 1998, NCJ-164618)
Includes consolidated police-sheriffs' departments.

Full-Time Officers in Local Police Departments in 1996

National Total = 410,956 Officers*

ALPHA ORDER

RANK	STATE	OFFICERS	% of USA
19	Alabama	6,484	1.6%
46	Alaska	740	0.2%
18	Arizona	6,967	1.7%
32	Arkansas	3,244	0.8%
2	California	35,939	8.7%
23	Colorado	5,451	1.3%
21	Connecticut	6,411	1.6%
44	Delaware	923	0.2%
6	Florida	19,652	4.8%
11	Georgia	10,241	2.5%
34	Hawaii	2,746	0.7%
43	Idaho	1,142	0.3%
4	Illinois	26,151	6.4%
20	Indiana	6,426	1.6%
33	Iowa	3,037	0.7%
29	Kansas	3,616	0.9%
27	Kentucky	4,089	1.0%
22	Louisiana	5,733	1.4%
41	Maine	1,426	0.3%
13	Maryland	8,923	2.2%
10	Massachusetts	13,068	3.2%
9	Michigan	13,288	3.2%
25	Minnesota	5,006	1.2%
30	Mississippi	3,326	0.8%
15	Missouri	8,836	2.2%
47	Montana	690	0.2%
38	Nebraska	1,929	0.5%
35	Nevada	2,565	0.6%
40	New Hampshire	1,862	0.5%
5	New Jersey	19,891	4.8%
36	New Mexico	2,462	0.6%
1	New York	54,657	13.3%
12	North Carolina	9,505	2.3%
49	North Dakota	561	0.1%
8	Ohio	15,932	3.9%
26	Oklahoma	4,951	1.2%
31	Oregon	3,245	0.8%
7	Pennsylvania	17,655	4.3%
37	Rhode Island	1,958	0.5%
28	South Carolina	4,004	1.0%
45	South Dakota	847	0.2%
17	Tennessee	7,076	1.7%
3	Texas	28,269	6.9%
39	Utah	1,882	0.5%
50	Vermont	548	0.1%
14	Virginia	8,911	2.2%
24	Washington	5,430	1.3%
42	West Virginia	1,416	0.3%
16	Wisconsin	7,640	1.9%
48	Wyoming	618	0.2%

RANK ORDER

RANK	STATE	OFFICERS	% of USA
1	New York	54,657	13.3%
2	California	35,939	8.7%
3	Texas	28,269	6.9%
4	Illinois	26,151	6.4%
5	New Jersey	19,891	4.8%
6	Florida	19,652	4.8%
7	Pennsylvania	17,655	4.3%
8	Ohio	15,932	3.9%
9	Michigan	13,288	3.2%
10	Massachusetts	13,068	3.2%
11	Georgia	10,241	2.5%
12	North Carolina	9,505	2.3%
13	Maryland	8,923	2.2%
14	Virginia	8,911	2.2%
15	Missouri	8,836	2.2%
16	Wisconsin	7,640	1.9%
17	Tennessee	7,076	1.7%
18	Arizona	6,967	1.7%
19	Alabama	6,484	1.6%
20	Indiana	6,426	1.6%
21	Connecticut	6,411	1.6%
22	Louisiana	5,733	1.4%
23	Colorado	5,451	1.3%
24	Washington	5,430	1.3%
25	Minnesota	5,006	1.2%
26	Oklahoma	4,951	1.2%
27	Kentucky	4,089	1.0%
28	South Carolina	4,004	1.0%
29	Kansas	3,616	0.9%
30	Mississippi	3,326	0.8%
31	Oregon	3,245	0.8%
32	Arkansas	3,244	0.8%
33	Iowa	3,037	0.7%
34	Hawaii	2,746	0.7%
35	Nevada	2,565	0.6%
36	New Mexico	2,462	0.6%
37	Rhode Island	1,958	0.5%
38	Nebraska	1,929	0.5%
39	Utah	1,882	0.5%
40	New Hampshire	1,862	0.5%
41	Maine	1,426	0.3%
42	West Virginia	1,416	0.3%
43	Idaho	1,142	0.3%
44	Delaware	923	0.2%
45	South Dakota	847	0.2%
46	Alaska	740	0.2%
47	Montana	690	0.2%
48	Wyoming	618	0.2%
49	North Dakota	561	0.1%
50	Vermont	548	0.1%
	District of Columbia	3,587	0.9%

Source: U.S. Department of Justice, Bureau of Justice Statistics
    "Census of State and Local Law Enforcement Agencies, 1996" (Bulletin, June 1998, NCJ-164618)
*Includes consolidated police-sheriffs' departments.

Percent of Full-Time Local Police Department Employees
Who Are Sworn Officers: 1996
National Percent = 78.7% of Employees*

ALPHA ORDER

RANK ORDER

RANK	STATE	PERCENT		RANK	STATE	PERCENT
35	Alabama	76.7		1	Pennsylvania	86.4
50	Alaska	63.9		2	Delaware	86.1
45	Arizona	71.9		3	West Virginia	85.7
27	Arkansas	78.7		4	Michigan	84.4
46	California	71.2		5	Massachusetts	84.3
42	Colorado	74.8		6	Connecticut	84.1
6	Connecticut	84.1		7	New Jersey	83.5
2	Delaware	86.1		8	New York	83.0
47	Florida	70.0		9	Iowa	82.9
25	Georgia	79.1		10	Minnesota	82.7
25	Hawaii	79.1		11	North Carolina	82.3
21	Idaho	80.0		12	Wisconsin	82.2
19	Illinois	80.4		13	South Carolina	82.0
17	Indiana	80.7		14	Louisiana	81.9
9	Iowa	82.9		15	North Dakota	81.8
36	Kansas	76.4		16	Maryland	81.0
23	Kentucky	79.3		17	Indiana	80.7
14	Louisiana	81.9		18	Ohio	80.5
29	Maine	78.1		19	Illinois	80.4
16	Maryland	81.0		20	Nebraska	80.1
5	Massachusetts	84.3		21	Idaho	80.0
4	Michigan	84.4		22	Utah	79.6
10	Minnesota	82.7		23	Kentucky	79.3
44	Mississippi	73.7		24	New Hampshire	79.2
37	Missouri	76.2		25	Georgia	79.1
31	Montana	77.9		25	Hawaii	79.1
20	Nebraska	80.1		27	Arkansas	78.7
49	Nevada	67.3		28	Vermont	78.3
24	New Hampshire	79.2		29	Maine	78.1
7	New Jersey	83.5		30	Oklahoma	78.0
48	New Mexico	68.5		31	Montana	77.9
8	New York	83.0		32	Rhode Island	77.5
11	North Carolina	82.3		32	Virginia	77.5
15	North Dakota	81.8		34	Tennessee	76.9
18	Ohio	80.5		35	Alabama	76.7
30	Oklahoma	78.0		36	Kansas	76.4
38	Oregon	75.4		37	Missouri	76.2
1	Pennsylvania	86.4		38	Oregon	75.4
32	Rhode Island	77.5		38	Texas	75.4
13	South Carolina	82.0		40	Wyoming	75.2
43	South Dakota	74.0		41	Washington	74.9
34	Tennessee	76.9		42	Colorado	74.8
38	Texas	75.4		43	South Dakota	74.0
22	Utah	79.6		44	Mississippi	73.7
28	Vermont	78.3		45	Arizona	71.9
32	Virginia	77.5		46	California	71.2
41	Washington	74.9		47	Florida	70.0
3	West Virginia	85.7		48	New Mexico	68.5
12	Wisconsin	82.2		49	Nevada	67.3
40	Wyoming	75.2		50	Alaska	63.9
					District of Columbia	84.9

Source: Morgan Quitno Press using data from U.S. Department of Justice, Bureau of Justice Statistics
"Census of State and Local Law Enforcement Agencies, 1996" (Bulletin, June 1998, NCJ-164618)
*Includes consolidated police-sheriffs' departments.

Rate of Full-Time Officers in Local Police Departments in 1996

National Rate = 15 Officers per 10,000 Population*

ALPHA ORDER

RANK	STATE	RATE
13	Alabama	15
32	Alaska	12
9	Arizona	16
25	Arkansas	13
36	California	11
18	Colorado	14
6	Connecticut	20
25	Delaware	13
18	Florida	14
18	Georgia	14
3	Hawaii	23
43	Idaho	10
4	Illinois	22
36	Indiana	11
36	Iowa	11
18	Kansas	14
36	Kentucky	11
25	Louisiana	13
36	Maine	11
8	Maryland	18
5	Massachusetts	21
18	Michigan	14
36	Minnesota	11
32	Mississippi	12
9	Missouri	16
49	Montana	8
32	Nebraska	12
9	Nevada	16
9	New Hampshire	16
2	New Jersey	25
18	New Mexico	14
1	New York	30
25	North Carolina	13
46	North Dakota	9
18	Ohio	14
13	Oklahoma	15
43	Oregon	10
13	Pennsylvania	15
6	Rhode Island	20
36	South Carolina	11
32	South Dakota	12
25	Tennessee	13
13	Texas	15
46	Utah	9
46	Vermont	9
25	Virginia	13
43	Washington	10
49	West Virginia	8
13	Wisconsin	15
25	Wyoming	13

RANK ORDER

RANK	STATE	RATE
1	New York	30
2	New Jersey	25
3	Hawaii	23
4	Illinois	22
5	Massachusetts	21
6	Connecticut	20
6	Rhode Island	20
8	Maryland	18
9	Arizona	16
9	Missouri	16
9	Nevada	16
9	New Hampshire	16
13	Alabama	15
13	Oklahoma	15
13	Pennsylvania	15
13	Texas	15
13	Wisconsin	15
18	Colorado	14
18	Florida	14
18	Georgia	14
18	Kansas	14
18	Michigan	14
18	New Mexico	14
18	Ohio	14
25	Arkansas	13
25	Delaware	13
25	Louisiana	13
25	North Carolina	13
25	Tennessee	13
25	Virginia	13
25	Wyoming	13
32	Alaska	12
32	Mississippi	12
32	Nebraska	12
32	South Dakota	12
36	California	11
36	Indiana	11
36	Iowa	11
36	Kentucky	11
36	Maine	11
36	Minnesota	11
36	South Carolina	11
43	Idaho	10
43	Oregon	10
43	Washington	10
46	North Dakota	9
46	Utah	9
46	Vermont	9
49	Montana	8
49	West Virginia	8
	District of Columbia	66

Source: U.S. Department of Justice, Bureau of Justice Statistics
    "Census of State and Local Law Enforcement Agencies, 1996" (Bulletin, June 1998, NCJ-164618)
*Includes consolidated police-sheriffs' departments.

Full-Time Employees in Local Police Departments in 1996

National Total = 521,985 Employees*

ALPHA ORDER					RANK ORDER			
RANK	STATE	EMPLOYEES	% of USA		RANK	STATE	EMPLOYEES	% of USA
19	Alabama	8,454	1.6%		1	New York	65,854	12.6%
44	Alaska	1,158	0.2%		2	California	50,491	9.7%
16	Arizona	9,686	1.9%		3	Texas	37,472	7.2%
32	Arkansas	4,124	0.8%		4	Illinois	32,522	6.2%
2	California	50,491	9.7%		5	Florida	28,075	5.4%
22	Colorado	7,283	1.4%		6	New Jersey	23,829	4.6%
21	Connecticut	7,625	1.5%		7	Pennsylvania	20,427	3.9%
46	Delaware	1,072	0.2%		8	Ohio	19,799	3.8%
5	Florida	28,075	5.4%		9	Michigan	15,735	3.0%
11	Georgia	12,954	2.5%		10	Massachusetts	15,506	3.0%
36	Hawaii	3,471	0.7%		11	Georgia	12,954	2.5%
43	Idaho	1,428	0.3%		12	Missouri	11,594	2.2%
4	Illinois	32,522	6.2%		13	North Carolina	11,546	2.2%
20	Indiana	7,965	1.5%		14	Virginia	11,502	2.2%
34	Iowa	3,664	0.7%		15	Maryland	11,015	2.1%
29	Kansas	4,732	0.9%		16	Arizona	9,686	1.9%
27	Kentucky	5,157	1.0%		17	Wisconsin	9,298	1.8%
24	Louisiana	7,001	1.3%		18	Tennessee	9,206	1.8%
41	Maine	1,826	0.3%		19	Alabama	8,454	1.6%
15	Maryland	11,015	2.1%		20	Indiana	7,965	1.5%
10	Massachusetts	15,506	3.0%		21	Connecticut	7,625	1.5%
9	Michigan	15,735	3.0%		22	Colorado	7,283	1.4%
26	Minnesota	6,053	1.2%		23	Washington	7,246	1.4%
30	Mississippi	4,511	0.9%		24	Louisiana	7,001	1.3%
12	Missouri	11,594	2.2%		25	Oklahoma	6,348	1.2%
47	Montana	886	0.2%		26	Minnesota	6,053	1.2%
38	Nebraska	2,409	0.5%		27	Kentucky	5,157	1.0%
33	Nevada	3,809	0.7%		28	South Carolina	4,884	0.9%
40	New Hampshire	2,351	0.5%		29	Kansas	4,732	0.9%
6	New Jersey	23,829	4.6%		30	Mississippi	4,511	0.9%
35	New Mexico	3,593	0.7%		31	Oregon	4,305	0.8%
1	New York	65,854	12.6%		32	Arkansas	4,124	0.8%
13	North Carolina	11,546	2.2%		33	Nevada	3,809	0.7%
50	North Dakota	686	0.1%		34	Iowa	3,664	0.7%
8	Ohio	19,799	3.8%		35	New Mexico	3,593	0.7%
25	Oklahoma	6,348	1.2%		36	Hawaii	3,471	0.7%
31	Oregon	4,305	0.8%		37	Rhode Island	2,527	0.5%
7	Pennsylvania	20,427	3.9%		38	Nebraska	2,409	0.5%
37	Rhode Island	2,527	0.5%		39	Utah	2,363	0.5%
28	South Carolina	4,884	0.9%		40	New Hampshire	2,351	0.5%
45	South Dakota	1,144	0.2%		41	Maine	1,826	0.3%
18	Tennessee	9,206	1.8%		42	West Virginia	1,652	0.3%
3	Texas	37,472	7.2%		43	Idaho	1,428	0.3%
39	Utah	2,363	0.5%		44	Alaska	1,158	0.2%
49	Vermont	700	0.1%		45	South Dakota	1,144	0.2%
14	Virginia	11,502	2.2%		46	Delaware	1,072	0.2%
23	Washington	7,246	1.4%		47	Montana	886	0.2%
42	West Virginia	1,652	0.3%		48	Wyoming	822	0.2%
17	Wisconsin	9,298	1.8%		49	Vermont	700	0.1%
48	Wyoming	822	0.2%		50	North Dakota	686	0.1%
						District of Columbia	4,225	0.8%

Source: U.S. Department of Justice, Bureau of Justice Statistics
"Census of State and Local Law Enforcement Agencies, 1996" (Bulletin, June 1998, NCJ-164618)
*Includes consolidated police-sheriffs' departments.

Sheriffs' Departments in 1996

National Total = 3,088 Departments*

ALPHA ORDER

RANK	STATE	DEPARTMENTS	% of USA
20	Alabama	67	2.2%
49	Alaska	0	0.0%
42	Arizona	15	0.5%
18	Arkansas	75	2.4%
26	California	58	1.9%
25	Colorado	63	2.0%
46	Connecticut	8	0.3%
48	Delaware	3	0.1%
23	Florida	65	2.1%
2	Georgia	159	5.1%
49	Hawaii	0	0.0%
32	Idaho	44	1.4%
7	Illinois	102	3.3%
12	Indiana	92	3.0%
9	Iowa	99	3.2%
6	Kansas	104	3.4%
4	Kentucky	120	3.9%
24	Louisiana	64	2.1%
40	Maine	16	0.5%
37	Maryland	24	0.8%
43	Massachusetts	14	0.5%
15	Michigan	83	2.7%
14	Minnesota	87	2.8%
16	Mississippi	82	2.7%
5	Missouri	115	3.7%
28	Montana	55	1.8%
11	Nebraska	93	3.0%
40	Nevada	16	0.5%
45	New Hampshire	10	0.3%
39	New Jersey	21	0.7%
35	New Mexico	33	1.1%
27	New York	57	1.8%
8	North Carolina	100	3.2%
30	North Dakota	53	1.7%
13	Ohio	88	2.8%
17	Oklahoma	77	2.5%
34	Oregon	36	1.2%
20	Pennsylvania	67	2.2%
47	Rhode Island	5	0.2%
31	South Carolina	46	1.5%
22	South Dakota	66	2.1%
10	Tennessee	95	3.1%
1	Texas	254	8.2%
36	Utah	29	0.9%
43	Vermont	14	0.5%
3	Virginia	125	4.0%
33	Washington	39	1.3%
28	West Virginia	55	1.8%
19	Wisconsin	72	2.3%
38	Wyoming	23	0.7%

RANK ORDER

RANK	STATE	DEPARTMENTS	% of USA
1	Texas	254	8.2%
2	Georgia	159	5.1%
3	Virginia	125	4.0%
4	Kentucky	120	3.9%
5	Missouri	115	3.7%
6	Kansas	104	3.4%
7	Illinois	102	3.3%
8	North Carolina	100	3.2%
9	Iowa	99	3.2%
10	Tennessee	95	3.1%
11	Nebraska	93	3.0%
12	Indiana	92	3.0%
13	Ohio	88	2.8%
14	Minnesota	87	2.8%
15	Michigan	83	2.7%
16	Mississippi	82	2.7%
17	Oklahoma	77	2.5%
18	Arkansas	75	2.4%
19	Wisconsin	72	2.3%
20	Alabama	67	2.2%
20	Pennsylvania	67	2.2%
22	South Dakota	66	2.1%
23	Florida	65	2.1%
24	Louisiana	64	2.1%
25	Colorado	63	2.0%
26	California	58	1.9%
27	New York	57	1.8%
28	Montana	55	1.8%
28	West Virginia	55	1.8%
30	North Dakota	53	1.7%
31	South Carolina	46	1.5%
32	Idaho	44	1.4%
33	Washington	39	1.3%
34	Oregon	36	1.2%
35	New Mexico	33	1.1%
36	Utah	29	0.9%
37	Maryland	24	0.8%
38	Wyoming	23	0.7%
39	New Jersey	21	0.7%
40	Maine	16	0.5%
40	Nevada	16	0.5%
42	Arizona	15	0.5%
43	Massachusetts	14	0.5%
43	Vermont	14	0.5%
45	New Hampshire	10	0.3%
46	Connecticut	8	0.3%
47	Rhode Island	5	0.2%
48	Delaware	3	0.1%
49	Alaska	0	0.0%
49	Hawaii	0	0.0%
	District of Columbia	0	0.0%

Source: U.S. Department of Justice, Bureau of Justice Statistics
   "Census of State and Local Law Enforcement Agencies, 1996" (Bulletin, June 1998, NCJ-164618)
*Sheriffs' departments generally operate at the county level.

Full-Time Officers in Sheriffs' Departments in 1996

National Total = 152,922 Officers*

ALPHA ORDER

ALPHA ORDER

RANK	STATE	OFFICERS	% of USA
21	Alabama	1,963	1.3%
49	Alaska	0	0.0%
24	Arizona	1,563	1.0%
28	Arkansas	1,410	0.9%
1	California	22,869	15.0%
14	Colorado	3,324	2.2%
37	Connecticut	886	0.6%
48	Delaware	24	0.0%
2	Florida	14,124	9.2%
6	Georgia	6,752	4.4%
49	Hawaii	0	0.0%
33	Idaho	1,053	0.7%
5	Illinois	8,426	5.5%
17	Indiana	2,618	1.7%
29	Iowa	1,343	0.9%
23	Kansas	1,683	1.1%
32	Kentucky	1,113	0.7%
4	Louisiana	8,720	5.7%
44	Maine	321	0.2%
27	Maryland	1,438	0.9%
25	Massachusetts	1,540	1.0%
11	Michigan	4,435	2.9%
20	Minnesota	2,139	1.4%
26	Mississippi	1,474	1.0%
19	Missouri	2,421	1.6%
40	Montana	616	0.4%
38	Nebraska	794	0.5%
35	Nevada	935	0.6%
46	New Hampshire	129	0.1%
15	New Jersey	3,145	2.1%
36	New Mexico	889	0.6%
8	New York	5,852	3.8%
9	North Carolina	5,264	3.4%
42	North Dakota	364	0.2%
10	Ohio	5,179	3.4%
34	Oklahoma	1,014	0.7%
22	Oregon	1,921	1.3%
30	Pennsylvania	1,239	0.8%
45	Rhode Island	153	0.1%
16	South Carolina	3,037	2.0%
43	South Dakota	344	0.2%
13	Tennessee	3,520	2.3%
3	Texas	11,326	7.4%
31	Utah	1,198	0.8%
47	Vermont	87	0.1%
7	Virginia	6,605	4.3%
18	Washington	2,553	1.7%
39	West Virginia	726	0.5%
12	Wisconsin	3,886	2.5%
41	Wyoming	507	0.3%

RANK ORDER

RANK	STATE	OFFICERS	% of USA
1	California	22,869	15.0%
2	Florida	14,124	9.2%
3	Texas	11,326	7.4%
4	Louisiana	8,720	5.7%
5	Illinois	8,426	5.5%
6	Georgia	6,752	4.4%
7	Virginia	6,605	4.3%
8	New York	5,852	3.8%
9	North Carolina	5,264	3.4%
10	Ohio	5,179	3.4%
11	Michigan	4,435	2.9%
12	Wisconsin	3,886	2.5%
13	Tennessee	3,520	2.3%
14	Colorado	3,324	2.2%
15	New Jersey	3,145	2.1%
16	South Carolina	3,037	2.0%
17	Indiana	2,618	1.7%
18	Washington	2,553	1.7%
19	Missouri	2,421	1.6%
20	Minnesota	2,139	1.4%
21	Alabama	1,963	1.3%
22	Oregon	1,921	1.3%
23	Kansas	1,683	1.1%
24	Arizona	1,563	1.0%
25	Massachusetts	1,540	1.0%
26	Mississippi	1,474	1.0%
27	Maryland	1,438	0.9%
28	Arkansas	1,410	0.9%
29	Iowa	1,343	0.9%
30	Pennsylvania	1,239	0.8%
31	Utah	1,198	0.8%
32	Kentucky	1,113	0.7%
33	Idaho	1,053	0.7%
34	Oklahoma	1,014	0.7%
35	Nevada	935	0.6%
36	New Mexico	889	0.6%
37	Connecticut	886	0.6%
38	Nebraska	794	0.5%
39	West Virginia	726	0.5%
40	Montana	616	0.4%
41	Wyoming	507	0.3%
42	North Dakota	364	0.2%
43	South Dakota	344	0.2%
44	Maine	321	0.2%
45	Rhode Island	153	0.1%
46	New Hampshire	129	0.1%
47	Vermont	87	0.1%
48	Delaware	24	0.0%
49	Alaska	0	0.0%
49	Hawaii	0	0.0%
	District of Columbia	0	0.0%

Source: U.S. Department of Justice, Bureau of Justice Statistics
"Census of State and Local Law Enforcement Agencies, 1996" (Bulletin, June 1998, NCJ-164618)
*Sheriffs' departments generally operate at the county level.

Percent of Full-Time Sheriffs' Department Employees
Who Are Sworn Officers: 1996
National Percent = 59.3% of Employees*

RANK	STATE	PERCENT
39	Alabama	51.7
NA	Alaska**	NA
47	Arizona	33.9
22	Arkansas	59.5
23	California	59.2
17	Colorado	64.3
1	Connecticut	99.7
43	Delaware	46.2
40	Florida	50.6
18	Georgia	64.1
NA	Hawaii**	NA
31	Idaho	57.9
13	Illinois	69.0
44	Indiana	45.8
33	Iowa	56.8
21	Kansas	59.7
3	Kentucky	87.6
5	Louisiana	81.9
46	Maine	34.2
25	Maryland	58.8
48	Massachusetts	30.5
24	Michigan	59.1
38	Minnesota	52.0
34	Mississippi	55.5
7	Missouri	74.5
36	Montana	54.0
25	Nebraska	58.8
8	Nevada	74.1
11	New Hampshire	70.5
10	New Jersey	70.7
16	New Mexico	66.2
32	New York	57.7
25	North Carolina	58.8
15	North Dakota	67.7
28	Ohio	58.5
42	Oklahoma	47.4
28	Oregon	58.5
6	Pennsylvania	77.6
2	Rhode Island	99.4
9	South Carolina	72.9
45	South Dakota	40.4
41	Tennessee	50.4
37	Texas	52.6
19	Utah	61.0
12	Vermont	69.6
4	Virginia	84.5
20	Washington	60.5
28	West Virginia	58.5
14	Wisconsin	67.9
34	Wyoming	55.5

RANK	STATE	PERCENT
1	Connecticut	99.7
2	Rhode Island	99.4
3	Kentucky	87.6
4	Virginia	84.5
5	Louisiana	81.9
6	Pennsylvania	77.6
7	Missouri	74.5
8	Nevada	74.1
9	South Carolina	72.9
10	New Jersey	70.7
11	New Hampshire	70.5
12	Vermont	69.6
13	Illinois	69.0
14	Wisconsin	67.9
15	North Dakota	67.7
16	New Mexico	66.2
17	Colorado	64.3
18	Georgia	64.1
19	Utah	61.0
20	Washington	60.5
21	Kansas	59.7
22	Arkansas	59.5
23	California	59.2
24	Michigan	59.1
25	Maryland	58.8
25	Nebraska	58.8
25	North Carolina	58.8
28	Ohio	58.5
28	Oregon	58.5
28	West Virginia	58.5
31	Idaho	57.9
32	New York	57.7
33	Iowa	56.8
34	Mississippi	55.5
34	Wyoming	55.5
36	Montana	54.0
37	Texas	52.6
38	Minnesota	52.0
39	Alabama	51.7
40	Florida	50.6
41	Tennessee	50.4
42	Oklahoma	47.4
43	Delaware	46.2
44	Indiana	45.8
45	South Dakota	40.4
46	Maine	34.2
47	Arizona	33.9
48	Massachusetts	30.5
NA	Alaska**	NA
NA	Hawaii**	NA
	District of Columbia**	NA

Source: Morgan Quitno Press using data from U.S. Department of Justice, Bureau of Justice Statistics
"Census of State and Local Law Enforcement Agencies, 1996" (Bulletin, June 1998, NCJ-164618)
*Sheriffs' departments generally operate at the county level.
**Not applicable.

Rate of Full-Time Sworn Officers in Sheriffs' Departments in 1996

National Rate = 5.8 Officers per 10,000 Population*

ALPHA ORDER

RANK	STATE	RATE
27	Alabama	4.6
49	Alaska	0.0
36	Arizona	3.5
21	Arkansas	5.6
10	California	7.2
7	Colorado	8.7
41	Connecticut	2.7
48	Delaware	0.3
4	Florida	9.8
5	Georgia	9.2
49	Hawaii	0.0
6	Idaho	8.9
12	Illinois	7.1
32	Indiana	4.5
25	Iowa	4.7
15	Kansas	6.5
39	Kentucky	2.9
1	Louisiana	20.0
42	Maine	2.6
40	Maryland	2.8
43	Massachusetts	2.5
27	Michigan	4.6
27	Minnesota	4.6
22	Mississippi	5.4
32	Missouri	4.5
13	Montana	7.0
24	Nebraska	4.8
19	Nevada	5.8
46	New Hampshire	1.1
35	New Jersey	3.9
23	New Mexico	5.2
37	New York	3.2
10	North Carolina	7.2
20	North Dakota	5.7
27	Ohio	4.6
38	Oklahoma	3.1
16	Oregon	6.0
47	Pennsylvania	1.0
44	Rhode Island	1.5
8	South Carolina	8.2
25	South Dakota	4.7
14	Tennessee	6.6
18	Texas	5.9
16	Utah	6.0
44	Vermont	1.5
3	Virginia	9.9
27	Washington	4.6
34	West Virginia	4.0
9	Wisconsin	7.5
2	Wyoming	10.5

RANK ORDER

RANK	STATE	RATE
1	Louisiana	20.0
2	Wyoming	10.5
3	Virginia	9.9
4	Florida	9.8
5	Georgia	9.2
6	Idaho	8.9
7	Colorado	8.7
8	South Carolina	8.2
9	Wisconsin	7.5
10	California	7.2
10	North Carolina	7.2
12	Illinois	7.1
13	Montana	7.0
14	Tennessee	6.6
15	Kansas	6.5
16	Oregon	6.0
16	Utah	6.0
18	Texas	5.9
19	Nevada	5.8
20	North Dakota	5.7
21	Arkansas	5.6
22	Mississippi	5.4
23	New Mexico	5.2
24	Nebraska	4.8
25	Iowa	4.7
25	South Dakota	4.7
27	Alabama	4.6
27	Michigan	4.6
27	Minnesota	4.6
27	Ohio	4.6
27	Washington	4.6
32	Indiana	4.5
32	Missouri	4.5
34	West Virginia	4.0
35	New Jersey	3.9
36	Arizona	3.5
37	New York	3.2
38	Oklahoma	3.1
39	Kentucky	2.9
40	Maryland	2.8
41	Connecticut	2.7
42	Maine	2.6
43	Massachusetts	2.5
44	Rhode Island	1.5
44	Vermont	1.5
46	New Hampshire	1.1
47	Pennsylvania	1.0
48	Delaware	0.3
49	Alaska	0.0
49	Hawaii	0.0
	District of Columbia	0.0

Source: U.S. Department of Justice, Bureau of Justice Statistics
"Census of State and Local Law Enforcement Agencies, 1996" (Bulletin, June 1998, NCJ-164618)
*Sheriffs' departments generally operate at the county level.

Full-Time Employees in Sheriffs' Departments in 1996

National Total = 257,712 Employees*

ALPHA ORDER

RANK	STATE	EMPLOYEES	% of USA
22	Alabama	3,796	1.5%
49	Alaska	0	0.0%
17	Arizona	4,604	1.8%
28	Arkansas	2,370	0.9%
1	California	38,603	15.0%
15	Colorado	5,168	2.0%
42	Connecticut	889	0.3%
48	Delaware	52	0.0%
2	Florida	27,928	10.8%
6	Georgia	10,537	4.1%
49	Hawaii	0	0.0%
32	Idaho	1,820	0.7%
4	Illinois	12,212	4.7%
14	Indiana	5,721	2.2%
29	Iowa	2,364	0.9%
25	Kansas	2,817	1.1%
36	Kentucky	1,270	0.5%
5	Louisiana	10,652	4.1%
40	Maine	939	0.4%
27	Maryland	2,445	0.9%
16	Massachusetts	5,047	2.0%
11	Michigan	7,508	2.9%
21	Minnesota	4,115	1.6%
26	Mississippi	2,657	1.0%
24	Missouri	3,250	1.3%
39	Montana	1,141	0.4%
34	Nebraska	1,351	0.5%
37	Nevada	1,261	0.5%
45	New Hampshire	183	0.1%
18	New Jersey	4,451	1.7%
35	New Mexico	1,343	0.5%
7	New York	10,150	3.9%
8	North Carolina	8,948	3.5%
44	North Dakota	538	0.2%
9	Ohio	8,855	3.4%
30	Oklahoma	2,138	0.8%
23	Oregon	3,285	1.3%
33	Pennsylvania	1,596	0.6%
46	Rhode Island	154	0.1%
20	South Carolina	4,167	1.6%
43	South Dakota	851	0.3%
12	Tennessee	6,981	2.7%
3	Texas	21,548	8.4%
31	Utah	1,965	0.8%
47	Vermont	125	0.0%
10	Virginia	7,816	3.0%
19	Washington	4,223	1.6%
38	West Virginia	1,242	0.5%
13	Wisconsin	5,723	2.2%
41	Wyoming	913	0.4%

RANK ORDER

RANK	STATE	EMPLOYEES	% of USA
1	California	38,603	15.0%
2	Florida	27,928	10.8%
3	Texas	21,548	8.4%
4	Illinois	12,212	4.7%
5	Louisiana	10,652	4.1%
6	Georgia	10,537	4.1%
7	New York	10,150	3.9%
8	North Carolina	8,948	3.5%
9	Ohio	8,855	3.4%
10	Virginia	7,816	3.0%
11	Michigan	7,508	2.9%
12	Tennessee	6,981	2.7%
13	Wisconsin	5,723	2.2%
14	Indiana	5,721	2.2%
15	Colorado	5,168	2.0%
16	Massachusetts	5,047	2.0%
17	Arizona	4,604	1.8%
18	New Jersey	4,451	1.7%
19	Washington	4,223	1.6%
20	South Carolina	4,167	1.6%
21	Minnesota	4,115	1.6%
22	Alabama	3,796	1.5%
23	Oregon	3,285	1.3%
24	Missouri	3,250	1.3%
25	Kansas	2,817	1.1%
26	Mississippi	2,657	1.0%
27	Maryland	2,445	0.9%
28	Arkansas	2,370	0.9%
29	Iowa	2,364	0.9%
30	Oklahoma	2,138	0.8%
31	Utah	1,965	0.8%
32	Idaho	1,820	0.7%
33	Pennsylvania	1,596	0.6%
34	Nebraska	1,351	0.5%
35	New Mexico	1,343	0.5%
36	Kentucky	1,270	0.5%
37	Nevada	1,261	0.5%
38	West Virginia	1,242	0.5%
39	Montana	1,141	0.4%
40	Maine	939	0.4%
41	Wyoming	913	0.4%
42	Connecticut	889	0.3%
43	South Dakota	851	0.3%
44	North Dakota	538	0.2%
45	New Hampshire	183	0.1%
46	Rhode Island	154	0.1%
47	Vermont	125	0.0%
48	Delaware	52	0.0%
49	Alaska	0	0.0%
49	Hawaii	0	0.0%
	District of Columbia	0	0.0%

Source: U.S. Department of Justice, Bureau of Justice Statistics
"Census of State and Local Law Enforcement Agencies, 1996" (Bulletin, June 1998, NCJ-164618)
*Sheriffs' departments generally operate at the county level.

Special Police Agencies in 1996

National Total = 1,316 Agencies*

ALPHA ORDER					RANK ORDER			
RANK	STATE		AGENCIES	% of USA	RANK	STATE	AGENCIES	% of USA
13	Alabama		33	2.5%	1	Texas	133	10.1%
39	Alaska		7	0.5%	2	California	121	9.2%
19	Arizona		26	2.0%	3	Pennsylvania	89	6.8%
21	Arkansas		23	1.7%	4	New York	64	4.9%
2	California		121	9.2%	5	Illinois	51	3.9%
26	Colorado		20	1.5%	6	New Jersey	45	3.4%
34	Connecticut		13	1.0%	7	Georgia	44	3.3%
41	Delaware		6	0.5%	7	Maryland	44	3.3%
15	Florida		30	2.3%	9	Ohio	41	3.1%
7	Georgia		44	3.3%	10	Massachusetts	34	2.6%
47	Hawaii		3	0.2%	10	Oklahoma	34	2.6%
47	Idaho		3	0.2%	10	Virginia	34	2.6%
5	Illinois		51	3.9%	13	Alabama	33	2.5%
24	Indiana		22	1.7%	14	North Carolina	32	2.4%
37	Iowa		8	0.6%	15	Florida	30	2.3%
27	Kansas		19	1.4%	16	Louisiana	29	2.2%
28	Kentucky		16	1.2%	16	Michigan	29	2.2%
16	Louisiana		29	2.2%	16	Mississippi	29	2.2%
36	Maine		9	0.7%	19	Arizona	26	2.0%
7	Maryland		44	3.3%	20	South Carolina	25	1.9%
10	Massachusetts		34	2.6%	21	Arkansas	23	1.7%
16	Michigan		29	2.2%	21	Tennessee	23	1.7%
32	Minnesota		14	1.1%	21	Wisconsin	23	1.7%
16	Mississippi		29	2.2%	24	Indiana	22	1.7%
24	Missouri		22	1.7%	24	Missouri	22	1.7%
37	Montana		8	0.6%	26	Colorado	20	1.5%
46	Nebraska		4	0.3%	27	Kansas	19	1.4%
29	Nevada		15	1.1%	28	Kentucky	16	1.2%
47	New Hampshire		3	0.2%	29	Nevada	15	1.1%
6	New Jersey		45	3.4%	29	New Mexico	15	1.1%
29	New Mexico		15	1.1%	29	West Virginia	15	1.1%
4	New York		64	4.9%	32	Minnesota	14	1.1%
14	North Carolina		32	2.4%	32	Washington	14	1.1%
39	North Dakota		7	0.5%	34	Connecticut	13	1.0%
9	Ohio		41	3.1%	34	Utah	13	1.0%
10	Oklahoma		34	2.6%	36	Maine	9	0.7%
42	Oregon		5	0.4%	37	Iowa	8	0.6%
3	Pennsylvania		89	6.8%	37	Montana	8	0.6%
42	Rhode Island		5	0.4%	39	Alaska	7	0.5%
20	South Carolina		25	1.9%	39	North Dakota	7	0.5%
42	South Dakota		5	0.4%	41	Delaware	6	0.5%
21	Tennessee		23	1.7%	42	Oregon	5	0.4%
1	Texas		133	10.1%	42	Rhode Island	5	0.4%
34	Utah		13	1.0%	42	South Dakota	5	0.4%
50	Vermont		2	0.2%	42	Wyoming	5	0.4%
10	Virginia		34	2.6%	46	Nebraska	4	0.3%
32	Washington		14	1.1%	47	Hawaii	3	0.2%
29	West Virginia		15	1.1%	47	Idaho	3	0.2%
21	Wisconsin		23	1.7%	47	New Hampshire	3	0.2%
42	Wyoming		5	0.4%	50	Vermont	2	0.2%
						District of Columbia	2	0.2%

Source: U.S. Department of Justice, Bureau of Justice Statistics
   "Census of State and Local Law Enforcement Agencies, 1996" (Bulletin, June 1998, NCJ-164618)
*Agencies with special jurisdictions or special enforcement responsibilities.

Full-Time Sworn Officers in Special Police Departments in 1996

National Total = 43,082 Officers*

ALPHA ORDER

ALPHA ORDER

RANK	STATE	OFFICERS	% of USA
18	Alabama	739	1.7%
38	Alaska	224	0.5%
23	Arizona	606	1.4%
22	Arkansas	643	1.5%
2	California	4,107	9.5%
24	Colorado	540	1.3%
39	Connecticut	206	0.5%
40	Delaware	173	0.4%
5	Florida	1,879	4.4%
11	Georgia	1,244	2.9%
34	Hawaii	243	0.6%
42	Idaho	137	0.3%
8	Illinois	1,627	3.8%
20	Indiana	680	1.6%
37	Iowa	230	0.5%
31	Kansas	332	0.8%
32	Kentucky	280	0.6%
13	Louisiana	799	1.9%
36	Maine	234	0.5%
7	Maryland	1,842	4.3%
15	Massachusetts	762	1.8%
19	Michigan	681	1.6%
29	Minnesota	365	0.8%
27	Mississippi	478	1.1%
16	Missouri	745	1.7%
41	Montana	164	0.4%
45	Nebraska	110	0.3%
26	Nevada	488	1.1%
49	New Hampshire	69	0.2%
4	New Jersey	2,320	5.4%
30	New Mexico	348	0.8%
1	New York	6,740	15.6%
12	North Carolina	804	1.9%
47	North Dakota	96	0.2%
9	Ohio	1,309	3.0%
25	Oklahoma	511	1.2%
48	Oregon	74	0.2%
6	Pennsylvania	1,865	4.3%
43	Rhode Island	118	0.3%
17	South Carolina	742	1.7%
43	South Dakota	118	0.3%
14	Tennessee	788	1.8%
3	Texas	3,311	7.7%
33	Utah	264	0.6%
50	Vermont	56	0.1%
10	Virginia	1,270	2.9%
28	Washington	403	0.9%
35	West Virginia	240	0.6%
21	Wisconsin	655	1.5%
46	Wyoming	101	0.2%

RANK ORDER

RANK	STATE	OFFICERS	% of USA
1	New York	6,740	15.6%
2	California	4,107	9.5%
3	Texas	3,311	7.7%
4	New Jersey	2,320	5.4%
5	Florida	1,879	4.4%
6	Pennsylvania	1,865	4.3%
7	Maryland	1,842	4.3%
8	Illinois	1,627	3.8%
9	Ohio	1,309	3.0%
10	Virginia	1,270	2.9%
11	Georgia	1,244	2.9%
12	North Carolina	804	1.9%
13	Louisiana	799	1.9%
14	Tennessee	788	1.8%
15	Massachusetts	762	1.8%
16	Missouri	745	1.7%
17	South Carolina	742	1.7%
18	Alabama	739	1.7%
19	Michigan	681	1.6%
20	Indiana	680	1.6%
21	Wisconsin	655	1.5%
22	Arkansas	643	1.5%
23	Arizona	606	1.4%
24	Colorado	540	1.3%
25	Oklahoma	511	1.2%
26	Nevada	488	1.1%
27	Mississippi	478	1.1%
28	Washington	403	0.9%
29	Minnesota	365	0.8%
30	New Mexico	348	0.8%
31	Kansas	332	0.8%
32	Kentucky	280	0.6%
33	Utah	264	0.6%
34	Hawaii	243	0.6%
35	West Virginia	240	0.6%
36	Maine	234	0.5%
37	Iowa	230	0.5%
38	Alaska	224	0.5%
39	Connecticut	206	0.5%
40	Delaware	173	0.4%
41	Montana	164	0.4%
42	Idaho	137	0.3%
43	Rhode Island	118	0.3%
43	South Dakota	118	0.3%
45	Nebraska	110	0.3%
46	Wyoming	101	0.2%
47	North Dakota	96	0.2%
48	Oregon	74	0.2%
49	New Hampshire	69	0.2%
50	Vermont	56	0.1%
	District of Columbia	322	0.7%

Source: U.S. Department of Justice, Bureau of Justice Statistics
"Census of State and Local Law Enforcement Agencies, 1996" (Bulletin, June 1998, NCJ-164618)
*Agencies with special jurisdictions or special enforcement responsibilities.

Percent of Full-Time Special Police Department Employees
Who Are Sworn Officers: 1996
National Percent = 76.6% of Employees*

ALPHA ORDER

RANK ORDER

RANK	STATE	PERCENT
25	Alabama	77.7
19	Alaska	80.6
42	Arizona	70.2
6	Arkansas	85.5
41	California	71.5
39	Colorado	72.7
20	Connecticut	79.8
43	Delaware	69.2
40	Florida	72.3
45	Georgia	67.8
3	Hawaii	88.7
11	Idaho	84.0
13	Illinois	83.8
10	Indiana	84.4
34	Iowa	75.9
28	Kansas	76.7
48	Kentucky	64.8
8	Louisiana	85.2
21	Maine	79.3
38	Maryland	73.7
31	Massachusetts	76.6
49	Michigan	61.2
18	Minnesota	81.8
36	Mississippi	75.5
26	Missouri	77.4
43	Montana	69.2
11	Nebraska	84.0
28	Nevada	76.7
28	New Hampshire	76.7
27	New Jersey	76.9
14	New Mexico	83.1
4	New York	87.7
22	North Carolina	79.1
35	North Dakota	75.6
24	Ohio	78.1
33	Oklahoma	76.4
37	Oregon	74.7
6	Pennsylvania	85.5
47	Rhode Island	65.2
50	South Carolina	55.4
5	South Dakota	86.8
23	Tennessee	78.7
46	Texas	65.7
17	Utah	82.0
9	Vermont	84.8
16	Virginia	82.4
32	Washington	76.5
2	West Virginia	88.9
15	Wisconsin	83.0
1	Wyoming	89.4

RANK	STATE	PERCENT
1	Wyoming	89.4
2	West Virginia	88.9
3	Hawaii	88.7
4	New York	87.7
5	South Dakota	86.8
6	Arkansas	85.5
6	Pennsylvania	85.5
8	Louisiana	85.2
9	Vermont	84.8
10	Indiana	84.4
11	Idaho	84.0
11	Nebraska	84.0
13	Illinois	83.8
14	New Mexico	83.1
15	Wisconsin	83.0
16	Virginia	82.4
17	Utah	82.0
18	Minnesota	81.8
19	Alaska	80.6
20	Connecticut	79.8
21	Maine	79.3
22	North Carolina	79.1
23	Tennessee	78.7
24	Ohio	78.1
25	Alabama	77.7
26	Missouri	77.4
27	New Jersey	76.9
28	Kansas	76.7
28	Nevada	76.7
28	New Hampshire	76.7
31	Massachusetts	76.6
32	Washington	76.5
33	Oklahoma	76.4
34	Iowa	75.9
35	North Dakota	75.6
36	Mississippi	75.5
37	Oregon	74.7
38	Maryland	73.7
39	Colorado	72.7
40	Florida	72.3
41	California	71.5
42	Arizona	70.2
43	Delaware	69.2
43	Montana	69.2
45	Georgia	67.8
46	Texas	65.7
47	Rhode Island	65.2
48	Kentucky	64.8
49	Michigan	61.2
50	South Carolina	55.4

District of Columbia 75.6

Source: Morgan Quitno Press using data from U.S. Department of Justice, Bureau of Justice Statistics
"Census of State and Local Law Enforcement Agencies, 1996" (Bulletin, June 1998, NCJ-164618)
*Agencies with special jurisdictions or special enforcement responsibilities.

Rate of Full-Time Sworn Officers in Special Police Departments in 1996

National Rate = 1.6 Officers per 10,000 Population*

ALPHA ORDER

RANK ORDER

RANK	STATE	RATE
17	Alabama	1.7
1	Alaska	3.7
25	Arizona	1.4
6	Arkansas	2.6
29	California	1.3
25	Colorado	1.4
48	Connecticut	0.6
7	Delaware	2.4
29	Florida	1.3
17	Georgia	1.7
8	Hawaii	2.1
36	Idaho	1.2
25	Illinois	1.4
36	Indiana	1.2
42	Iowa	0.8
29	Kansas	1.3
44	Kentucky	0.7
15	Louisiana	1.8
12	Maine	1.9
3	Maryland	3.6
29	Massachusetts	1.3
44	Michigan	0.7
42	Minnesota	0.8
15	Mississippi	1.8
25	Missouri	1.4
12	Montana	1.9
44	Nebraska	0.7
4	Nevada	3.0
48	New Hampshire	0.6
5	New Jersey	2.9
10	New Mexico	2.0
1	New York	3.7
40	North Carolina	1.1
21	North Dakota	1.5
36	Ohio	1.2
21	Oklahoma	1.5
50	Oregon	0.2
21	Pennsylvania	1.5
36	Rhode Island	1.2
10	South Carolina	2.0
20	South Dakota	1.6
21	Tennessee	1.5
17	Texas	1.7
29	Utah	1.3
41	Vermont	1.0
12	Virginia	1.9
44	Washington	0.7
29	West Virginia	1.3
29	Wisconsin	1.3
8	Wyoming	2.1

RANK	STATE	RATE
1	Alaska	3.7
1	New York	3.7
3	Maryland	3.6
4	Nevada	3.0
5	New Jersey	2.9
6	Arkansas	2.6
7	Delaware	2.4
8	Hawaii	2.1
8	Wyoming	2.1
10	New Mexico	2.0
10	South Carolina	2.0
12	Maine	1.9
12	Montana	1.9
12	Virginia	1.9
15	Louisiana	1.8
15	Mississippi	1.8
17	Alabama	1.7
17	Georgia	1.7
17	Texas	1.7
20	South Dakota	1.6
21	North Dakota	1.5
21	Oklahoma	1.5
21	Pennsylvania	1.5
21	Tennessee	1.5
25	Arizona	1.4
25	Colorado	1.4
25	Illinois	1.4
25	Missouri	1.4
29	California	1.3
29	Florida	1.3
29	Kansas	1.3
29	Massachusetts	1.3
29	Utah	1.3
29	West Virginia	1.3
29	Wisconsin	1.3
36	Idaho	1.2
36	Indiana	1.2
36	Ohio	1.2
36	Rhode Island	1.2
40	North Carolina	1.1
41	Vermont	1.0
42	Iowa	0.8
42	Minnesota	0.8
44	Kentucky	0.7
44	Michigan	0.7
44	Nebraska	0.7
44	Washington	0.7
48	Connecticut	0.6
48	New Hampshire	0.6
50	Oregon	0.2
	District of Columbia	5.9

Source: U.S. Department of Justice, Bureau of Justice Statistics
   "Census of State and Local Law Enforcement Agencies, 1996" (Bulletin, June 1998, NCJ-164618)
*Agencies with special jurisdictions or special enforcement responsibilities.

Full-Time Employees in Special Police Departments in 1996

National Total = 56,229 Employees*

ALPHA ORDER

RANK	STATE	EMPLOYEES	% of USA
18	Alabama	951	1.7%
36	Alaska	278	0.5%
20	Arizona	863	1.5%
23	Arkansas	752	1.3%
2	California	5,741	10.2%
24	Colorado	743	1.3%
39	Connecticut	258	0.5%
40	Delaware	250	0.4%
5	Florida	2,598	4.6%
9	Georgia	1,835	3.3%
37	Hawaii	274	0.5%
43	Idaho	163	0.3%
8	Illinois	1,942	3.5%
21	Indiana	806	1.4%
34	Iowa	303	0.5%
30	Kansas	433	0.8%
31	Kentucky	432	0.8%
19	Louisiana	938	1.7%
35	Maine	295	0.5%
6	Maryland	2,498	4.4%
16	Massachusetts	995	1.8%
13	Michigan	1,113	2.0%
29	Minnesota	446	0.8%
27	Mississippi	633	1.1%
17	Missouri	962	1.7%
41	Montana	237	0.4%
45	Nebraska	131	0.2%
26	Nevada	636	1.1%
49	New Hampshire	90	0.2%
4	New Jersey	3,016	5.4%
32	New Mexico	419	0.7%
1	New York	7,681	13.7%
14	North Carolina	1,016	1.8%
46	North Dakota	127	0.2%
10	Ohio	1,675	3.0%
25	Oklahoma	669	1.2%
48	Oregon	99	0.2%
7	Pennsylvania	2,182	3.9%
42	Rhode Island	181	0.3%
12	South Carolina	1,340	2.4%
44	South Dakota	136	0.2%
15	Tennessee	1,001	1.8%
3	Texas	5,037	9.0%
33	Utah	322	0.6%
50	Vermont	66	0.1%
11	Virginia	1,541	2.7%
28	Washington	527	0.9%
38	West Virginia	270	0.5%
22	Wisconsin	789	1.4%
47	Wyoming	113	0.2%

RANK ORDER

RANK	STATE	EMPLOYEES	% of USA
1	New York	7,681	13.7%
2	California	5,741	10.2%
3	Texas	5,037	9.0%
4	New Jersey	3,016	5.4%
5	Florida	2,598	4.6%
6	Maryland	2,498	4.4%
7	Pennsylvania	2,182	3.9%
8	Illinois	1,942	3.5%
9	Georgia	1,835	3.3%
10	Ohio	1,675	3.0%
11	Virginia	1,541	2.7%
12	South Carolina	1,340	2.4%
13	Michigan	1,113	2.0%
14	North Carolina	1,016	1.8%
15	Tennessee	1,001	1.8%
16	Massachusetts	995	1.8%
17	Missouri	962	1.7%
18	Alabama	951	1.7%
19	Louisiana	938	1.7%
20	Arizona	863	1.5%
21	Indiana	806	1.4%
22	Wisconsin	789	1.4%
23	Arkansas	752	1.3%
24	Colorado	743	1.3%
25	Oklahoma	669	1.2%
26	Nevada	636	1.1%
27	Mississippi	633	1.1%
28	Washington	527	0.9%
29	Minnesota	446	0.8%
30	Kansas	433	0.8%
31	Kentucky	432	0.8%
32	New Mexico	419	0.7%
33	Utah	322	0.6%
34	Iowa	303	0.5%
35	Maine	295	0.5%
36	Alaska	278	0.5%
37	Hawaii	274	0.5%
38	West Virginia	270	0.5%
39	Connecticut	258	0.5%
40	Delaware	250	0.4%
41	Montana	237	0.4%
42	Rhode Island	181	0.3%
43	Idaho	163	0.3%
44	South Dakota	136	0.2%
45	Nebraska	131	0.2%
46	North Dakota	127	0.2%
47	Wyoming	113	0.2%
48	Oregon	99	0.2%
49	New Hampshire	90	0.2%
50	Vermont	66	0.1%
	District of Columbia	426	0.8%

Source: U.S. Department of Justice, Bureau of Justice Statistics
"Census of State and Local Law Enforcement Agencies, 1996" (Bulletin, June 1998, NCJ-164618)
*Agencies with special jurisdictions or special enforcement responsibilities.

Law Enforcement Officers Feloniously Killed in 2000

National Total = 49 Officers*

ALPHA ORDER

RANK	STATE	OFFICERS	% of USA
22	Alabama	0	0.0%
22	Alaska	0	0.0%
13	Arizona	1	2.0%
13	Arkansas	1	2.0%
7	California	2	4.1%
22	Colorado	0	0.0%
22	Connecticut	0	0.0%
22	Delaware	0	0.0%
13	Florida	1	2.0%
2	Georgia	6	12.2%
22	Hawaii	0	0.0%
22	Idaho	0	0.0%
13	Illinois	1	2.0%
7	Indiana	2	4.1%
22	Iowa	0	0.0%
13	Kansas	1	2.0%
22	Kentucky	0	0.0%
3	Louisiana	3	6.1%
22	Maine	0	0.0%
3	Maryland	3	6.1%
22	Massachusetts	0	0.0%
7	Michigan	2	4.1%
13	Minnesota	1	2.0%
22	Mississippi	0	0.0%
3	Missouri	3	6.1%
22	Montana	0	0.0%
22	Nebraska	0	0.0%
22	Nevada	0	0.0%
22	New Hampshire	0	0.0%
22	New Jersey	0	0.0%
22	New Mexico	0	0.0%
22	New York	0	0.0%
7	North Carolina	2	4.1%
22	North Dakota	0	0.0%
7	Ohio	2	4.1%
22	Oklahoma	0	0.0%
22	Oregon	0	0.0%
22	Pennsylvania	0	0.0%
22	Rhode Island	0	0.0%
7	South Carolina	2	4.1%
22	South Dakota	0	0.0%
3	Tennessee	3	6.1%
1	Texas	10	20.4%
22	Utah	0	0.0%
22	Vermont	0	0.0%
22	Virginia	0	0.0%
13	Washington	1	2.0%
13	West Virginia	1	2.0%
13	Wisconsin	1	2.0%
22	Wyoming	0	0.0%

RANK ORDER

RANK	STATE	OFFICERS	% of USA
1	Texas	10	20.4%
2	Georgia	6	12.2%
3	Louisiana	3	6.1%
3	Maryland	3	6.1%
3	Missouri	3	6.1%
3	Tennessee	3	6.1%
7	California	2	4.1%
7	Indiana	2	4.1%
7	Michigan	2	4.1%
7	North Carolina	2	4.1%
7	Ohio	2	4.1%
7	South Carolina	2	4.1%
13	Arizona	1	2.0%
13	Arkansas	1	2.0%
13	Florida	1	2.0%
13	Illinois	1	2.0%
13	Kansas	1	2.0%
13	Minnesota	1	2.0%
13	Washington	1	2.0%
13	West Virginia	1	2.0%
13	Wisconsin	1	2.0%
22	Alabama	0	0.0%
22	Alaska	0	0.0%
22	Colorado	0	0.0%
22	Connecticut	0	0.0%
22	Delaware	0	0.0%
22	Hawaii	0	0.0%
22	Idaho	0	0.0%
22	Iowa	0	0.0%
22	Kentucky	0	0.0%
22	Maine	0	0.0%
22	Massachusetts	0	0.0%
22	Mississippi	0	0.0%
22	Montana	0	0.0%
22	Nebraska	0	0.0%
22	Nevada	0	0.0%
22	New Hampshire	0	0.0%
22	New Jersey	0	0.0%
22	New Mexico	0	0.0%
22	New York	0	0.0%
22	North Dakota	0	0.0%
22	Oklahoma	0	0.0%
22	Oregon	0	0.0%
22	Pennsylvania	0	0.0%
22	Rhode Island	0	0.0%
22	South Dakota	0	0.0%
22	Utah	0	0.0%
22	Vermont	0	0.0%
22	Virginia	0	0.0%
22	Wyoming	0	0.0%
	District of Columbia	0	0.0%

Source: Federal Bureau of Investigation
   "Law Enforcement Officers Killed and Assaulted 2000" (http://www.fbi.gov/ucr/killed/00leoka.pdf)
*Total does not include two officers killed in Puerto Rico.

Law Enforcement Officers Feloniously Killed: 1991 to 2000

National Total = 591 Officers*

ALPHA ORDER

RANK	STATE	OFFICERS	% of USA
18	Alabama	12	2.0%
32	Alaska	5	0.8%
9	Arizona	17	2.9%
18	Arkansas	12	2.0%
1	California	60	10.2%
26	Colorado	9	1.5%
37	Connecticut	3	0.5%
46	Delaware	0	0.0%
6	Florida	21	3.6%
3	Georgia	30	5.1%
42	Hawaii	1	0.2%
34	Idaho	4	0.7%
7	Illinois	18	3.0%
17	Indiana	15	2.5%
46	Iowa	0	0.0%
28	Kansas	8	1.4%
22	Kentucky	10	1.7%
13	Louisiana	16	2.7%
46	Maine	0	0.0%
26	Maryland	9	1.5%
28	Massachusetts	8	1.4%
9	Michigan	17	2.9%
22	Minnesota	10	1.7%
9	Mississippi	17	2.9%
13	Missouri	16	2.7%
42	Montana	1	0.2%
39	Nebraska	2	0.3%
32	Nevada	5	0.8%
34	New Hampshire	4	0.7%
22	New Jersey	10	1.7%
31	New Mexico	6	1.0%
5	New York	27	4.6%
4	North Carolina	29	4.9%
39	North Dakota	2	0.3%
7	Ohio	18	3.0%
18	Oklahoma	12	2.0%
34	Oregon	4	0.7%
9	Pennsylvania	17	2.9%
42	Rhode Island	1	0.2%
13	South Carolina	16	2.7%
46	South Dakota	0	0.0%
13	Tennessee	16	2.7%
2	Texas	56	9.5%
39	Utah	2	0.3%
46	Vermont	0	0.0%
22	Virginia	10	1.7%
30	Washington	7	1.2%
37	West Virginia	3	0.5%
18	Wisconsin	12	2.0%
42	Wyoming	1	0.2%

RANK ORDER

RANK	STATE	OFFICERS	% of USA
1	California	60	10.2%
2	Texas	56	9.5%
3	Georgia	30	5.1%
4	North Carolina	29	4.9%
5	New York	27	4.6%
6	Florida	21	3.6%
7	Illinois	18	3.0%
7	Ohio	18	3.0%
9	Arizona	17	2.9%
9	Michigan	17	2.9%
9	Mississippi	17	2.9%
9	Pennsylvania	17	2.9%
13	Louisiana	16	2.7%
13	Missouri	16	2.7%
13	South Carolina	16	2.7%
13	Tennessee	16	2.7%
17	Indiana	15	2.5%
18	Alabama	12	2.0%
18	Arkansas	12	2.0%
18	Oklahoma	12	2.0%
18	Wisconsin	12	2.0%
22	Kentucky	10	1.7%
22	Minnesota	10	1.7%
22	New Jersey	10	1.7%
22	Virginia	10	1.7%
26	Colorado	9	1.5%
26	Maryland	9	1.5%
28	Kansas	8	1.4%
28	Massachusetts	8	1.4%
30	Washington	7	1.2%
31	New Mexico	6	1.0%
32	Alaska	5	0.8%
32	Nevada	5	0.8%
34	Idaho	4	0.7%
34	New Hampshire	4	0.7%
34	Oregon	4	0.7%
37	Connecticut	3	0.5%
37	West Virginia	3	0.5%
39	Nebraska	2	0.3%
39	North Dakota	2	0.3%
39	Utah	2	0.3%
42	Hawaii	1	0.2%
42	Montana	1	0.2%
42	Rhode Island	1	0.2%
42	Wyoming	1	0.2%
46	Delaware	0	0.0%
46	Iowa	0	0.0%
46	Maine	0	0.0%
46	South Dakota	0	0.0%
46	Vermont	0	0.0%
	District of Columbia	12	2.0%

Source: Federal Bureau of Investigation
"Law Enforcement Officers Killed and Assaulted 2000" (http://www.fbi.gov/ucr/killed/00leoka.pdf)
*Total does not include 53 officers killed in U.S. territories (51 officers killed in Puerto Rico, one in the U.S. Virgin Islands and one in the Mariana Islands).

U.S. District Court Judges in 2000

National Total = 655 Judges*

RANK	STATE	JUDGES	% of USA
15	Alabama	13	2.0%
41	Alaska	3	0.5%
17	Arizona	11	1.7%
26	Arkansas	8	1.2%
1	California	56	8.5%
29	Colorado	7	1.1%
26	Connecticut	8	1.2%
38	Delaware	4	0.6%
5	Florida	35	5.3%
10	Georgia	18	2.7%
38	Hawaii	4	0.6%
48	Idaho	2	0.3%
6	Illinois	30	4.6%
21	Indiana	10	1.5%
35	Iowa	5	0.8%
31	Kansas	6	0.9%
23	Kentucky	9	1.4%
7	Louisiana	22	3.4%
41	Maine	3	0.5%
21	Maryland	10	1.5%
15	Massachusetts	13	2.0%
9	Michigan	19	2.9%
29	Minnesota	7	1.1%
23	Mississippi	9	1.4%
12	Missouri	14	2.1%
41	Montana	3	0.5%
38	Nebraska	4	0.6%
31	Nevada	6	0.9%
41	New Hampshire	3	0.5%
11	New Jersey	17	2.6%
35	New Mexico	5	0.8%
2	New York	52	7.9%
17	North Carolina	11	1.7%
48	North Dakota	2	0.3%
8	Ohio	20	3.1%
17	Oklahoma	11	1.7%
31	Oregon	6	0.9%
4	Pennsylvania	38	5.8%
41	Rhode Island	3	0.5%
23	South Carolina	9	1.4%
41	South Dakota	3	0.5%
12	Tennessee	14	2.1%
3	Texas	47	7.2%
35	Utah	5	0.8%
48	Vermont	2	0.3%
12	Virginia	14	2.1%
17	Washington	11	1.7%
26	West Virginia	8	1.2%
31	Wisconsin	6	0.9%
41	Wyoming	3	0.5%

RANK	STATE	JUDGES	% of USA
1	California	56	8.5%
2	New York	52	7.9%
3	Texas	47	7.2%
4	Pennsylvania	38	5.8%
5	Florida	35	5.3%
6	Illinois	30	4.6%
7	Louisiana	22	3.4%
8	Ohio	20	3.1%
9	Michigan	19	2.9%
10	Georgia	18	2.7%
11	New Jersey	17	2.6%
12	Missouri	14	2.1%
12	Tennessee	14	2.1%
12	Virginia	14	2.1%
15	Alabama	13	2.0%
15	Massachusetts	13	2.0%
17	Arizona	11	1.7%
17	North Carolina	11	1.7%
17	Oklahoma	11	1.7%
17	Washington	11	1.7%
21	Indiana	10	1.5%
21	Maryland	10	1.5%
23	Kentucky	9	1.4%
23	Mississippi	9	1.4%
23	South Carolina	9	1.4%
26	Arkansas	8	1.2%
26	Connecticut	8	1.2%
26	West Virginia	8	1.2%
29	Colorado	7	1.1%
29	Minnesota	7	1.1%
31	Kansas	6	0.9%
31	Nevada	6	0.9%
31	Oregon	6	0.9%
31	Wisconsin	6	0.9%
35	Iowa	5	0.8%
35	New Mexico	5	0.8%
35	Utah	5	0.8%
38	Delaware	4	0.6%
38	Hawaii	4	0.6%
38	Nebraska	4	0.6%
41	Alaska	3	0.5%
41	Maine	3	0.5%
41	Montana	3	0.5%
41	New Hampshire	3	0.5%
41	Rhode Island	3	0.5%
41	South Dakota	3	0.5%
41	Wyoming	3	0.5%
48	Idaho	2	0.3%
48	North Dakota	2	0.3%
48	Vermont	2	0.3%
	District of Columbia	15	2.3%

Source: Administrative Office of the United States Courts
   "2000 Federal Court Management Statistics"
*Total includes 11 judgeships in U.S. territories.

Population per U.S. District Court Judge in 2000

National Average = 438,082 People per U.S. District Judge*

ALPHA ORDER				RANK ORDER		
RANK	**STATE**	**RATE**		**RANK**	**STATE**	**RATE**
35	Alabama	342,423		1	Wisconsin	895,374
47	Alaska	209,200		2	North Carolina	734,306
17	Arizona	469,570		3	Minnesota	704,442
37	Arkansas	334,754		4	Idaho	649,629
7	California	607,151		5	Colorado	617,630
5	Colorado	617,630		6	Indiana	608,995
26	Connecticut	426,260		7	California	607,151
49	Delaware	196,559		8	Iowa	585,502
18	Florida	458,695		9	Oregon	571,549
19	Georgia	457,212		10	Ohio	567,998
43	Hawaii	303,070		11	Washington	537,125
4	Idaho	649,629		12	Maryland	531,091
28	Illinois	414,532		13	Michigan	523,790
6	Indiana	608,995		14	Virginia	507,430
8	Iowa	585,502		15	New Jersey	495,824
21	Kansas	448,625		16	Massachusetts	489,006
20	Kentucky	449,714		17	Arizona	469,570
48	Louisiana	203,180		18	Florida	458,695
27	Maine	425,654		19	Georgia	457,212
12	Maryland	531,091		20	Kentucky	449,714
16	Massachusetts	489,006		21	Kansas	448,625
13	Michigan	523,790		22	Utah	448,311
3	Minnesota	704,442		23	South Carolina	447,049
40	Mississippi	316,567		24	Texas	445,670
31	Missouri	400,254		25	Nebraska	428,144
44	Montana	301,052		26	Connecticut	426,260
25	Nebraska	428,144		27	Maine	425,654
36	Nevada	336,454		28	Illinois	414,532
29	New Hampshire	413,294		29	New Hampshire	413,294
15	New Jersey	495,824		30	Tennessee	407,288
33	New Mexico	364,256		31	Missouri	400,254
32	New York	365,179		32	New York	365,179
2	North Carolina	734,306		33	New Mexico	364,256
39	North Dakota	320,460		34	Rhode Island	350,079
10	Ohio	567,998		35	Alabama	342,423
41	Oklahoma	313,932		36	Nevada	336,454
9	Oregon	571,549		37	Arkansas	334,754
38	Pennsylvania	323,226		38	Pennsylvania	323,226
34	Rhode Island	350,079		39	North Dakota	320,460
23	South Carolina	447,049		40	Mississippi	316,567
45	South Dakota	251,836		41	Oklahoma	313,932
30	Tennessee	407,288		42	Vermont	304,855
24	Texas	445,670		43	Hawaii	303,070
22	Utah	448,311		44	Montana	301,052
42	Vermont	304,855		45	South Dakota	251,836
14	Virginia	507,430		46	West Virginia	225,887
11	Washington	537,125		47	Alaska	209,200
46	West Virginia	225,887		48	Louisiana	203,180
1	Wisconsin	895,374		49	Delaware	196,559
50	Wyoming	164,667		50	Wyoming	164,667
					District of Columbia	38,071

Source: Morgan Quitno Press using data from Administrative Office of the United States Courts
"2000 Federal Court Management Statistics"
*National rate does not include judgeships or population in U.S. territories.

Authorized Wiretaps in 2000

National Total = 711 State Authorized Wiretaps*

ALPHA ORDER

RANK	STATE	WIRETAPS	% of USA
NA	Alabama**	NA	NA
26	Alaska	0	0.0%
8	Arizona	18	2.5%
NA	Arkansas**	NA	NA
2	California	88	12.4%
11	Colorado	5	0.7%
13	Connecticut	4	0.6%
26	Delaware	0	0.0%
4	Florida	43	6.0%
16	Georgia	3	0.4%
26	Hawaii	0	0.0%
19	Idaho	1	0.1%
6	Illinois	41	5.8%
26	Indiana	0	0.0%
19	Iowa	1	0.1%
19	Kansas	1	0.1%
NA	Kentucky**	NA	NA
19	Louisiana	1	0.1%
NA	Maine**	NA	NA
7	Maryland	31	4.4%
11	Massachusetts	5	0.7%
NA	Michigan**	NA	NA
26	Minnesota	0	0.0%
26	Mississippi	0	0.0%
26	Missouri	0	0.0%
NA	Montana**	NA	NA
26	Nebraska	0	0.0%
9	Nevada	10	1.4%
26	New Hampshire	0	0.0%
3	New Jersey	45	6.3%
13	New Mexico	4	0.6%
1	New York	349	49.1%
26	North Carolina	0	0.0%
26	North Dakota	0	0.0%
10	Ohio	6	0.8%
13	Oklahoma	4	0.6%
19	Oregon	1	0.1%
4	Pennsylvania	43	6.0%
26	Rhode Island	0	0.0%
NA	South Carolina**	NA	NA
26	South Dakota	0	0.0%
19	Tennessee	1	0.1%
26	Texas	0	0.0%
16	Utah	3	0.4%
NA	Vermont**	NA	NA
26	Virginia	0	0.0%
18	Washington	2	0.3%
26	West Virginia	0	0.0%
19	Wisconsin	1	0.1%
26	Wyoming	0	0.0%

RANK ORDER

RANK	STATE	WIRETAPS	% of USA
1	New York	349	49.1%
2	California	88	12.4%
3	New Jersey	45	6.3%
4	Florida	43	6.0%
4	Pennsylvania	43	6.0%
6	Illinois	41	5.8%
7	Maryland	31	4.4%
8	Arizona	18	2.5%
9	Nevada	10	1.4%
10	Ohio	6	0.8%
11	Colorado	5	0.7%
11	Massachusetts	5	0.7%
13	Connecticut	4	0.6%
13	New Mexico	4	0.6%
13	Oklahoma	4	0.6%
16	Georgia	3	0.4%
16	Utah	3	0.4%
18	Washington	2	0.3%
19	Idaho	1	0.1%
19	Iowa	1	0.1%
19	Kansas	1	0.1%
19	Louisiana	1	0.1%
19	Oregon	1	0.1%
19	Tennessee	1	0.1%
19	Wisconsin	1	0.1%
26	Alaska	0	0.0%
26	Delaware	0	0.0%
26	Hawaii	0	0.0%
26	Indiana	0	0.0%
26	Minnesota	0	0.0%
26	Mississippi	0	0.0%
26	Missouri	0	0.0%
26	Nebraska	0	0.0%
26	New Hampshire	0	0.0%
26	North Carolina	0	0.0%
26	North Dakota	0	0.0%
26	Rhode Island	0	0.0%
26	South Dakota	0	0.0%
26	Texas	0	0.0%
26	Virginia	0	0.0%
26	West Virginia	0	0.0%
26	Wyoming	0	0.0%
NA	Alabama**	NA	NA
NA	Arkansas**	NA	NA
NA	Kentucky**	NA	NA
NA	Maine**	NA	NA
NA	Michigan**	NA	NA
NA	Montana**	NA	NA
NA	South Carolina**	NA	NA
NA	Vermont**	NA	NA
	District of Columbia	0	0.0%

Source: Administrative Office of the United States Courts
  "2000 Wiretap Report" (2001)
*Total does not include 479 wiretaps authorized under federal statute.
**No state statute authorizing wiretaps.

VII. OFFENSES

VII. OFFENSES (continued)

372 Percent of Aggravated Assaults Involving Firearms in 2000
373 Aggravated Assaults with Knives or Cutting Instruments in 2000
374 Percent of Aggravated Assaults Involving Knives or Cutting Instruments in 2000
375 Aggravated Assaults with Blunt Objects and Other Dangerous Weapons in 2000
376 Percent of Aggravated Assaults Involving Blunt Objects and Other Dangerous Weapons in 2000
377 Aggravated Assaults Committed with Hands, Fists or Feet in 2000
378 Percent of Aggravated Assaults Committed with Hands, Fists or Feet in 2000
379 Property Crimes in 2000
380 Average Time Between Property Crimes in 2000
381 Property Crimes per Square Mile in 2000
382 Percent Change in Number of Property Crimes: 1999 to 2000
383 Property Crime Rate in 2000
384 Percent Change in Property Crime Rate: 1999 to 2000
385 Burglaries in 2000
386 Average Time Between Burglaries in 2000
387 Percent Change in Number of Burglaries: 1999 to 2000
388 Burglary Rate in 2000
389 Percent Change in Burglary Rate: 1999 to 2000
390 Larcenies and Thefts in 2000
391 Average Time Between Larcenies and Thefts in 2000
392 Percent Change in Number of Larcenies and Thefts: 1999 to 2000
393 Larceny and Theft Rate in 2000
394 Percent Change in Larceny and Theft Rate: 1999 to 2000
395 Motor Vehicle Thefts in 2000
396 Average Time Between Motor Vehicle Thefts in 2000
397 Percent Change in Number of Motor Vehicle Thefts: 1999 to 2000
398 Motor Vehicle Theft Rate in 2000
399 Percent Change in Motor Vehicle Theft Rate: 1999 to 2000

Urban/Rural Crime

400 Crimes in Urban Areas in 2000
401 Urban Crime Rate in 2000
402 Percent of Crimes Occurring in Urban Areas in 2000
403 Crimes in Rural Areas in 2000
404 Rural Crime Rate in 2000
405 Percent of Crimes Occurring in Rural Areas in 2000
406 Violent Crimes in Urban Areas in 2000
407 Urban Violent Crime Rate in 2000
408 Percent of Violent Crimes Occurring in Urban Areas in 2000
409 Violent Crimes in Rural Areas in 2000
410 Rural Violent Crime Rate in 2000
411 Percent of Violent Crimes Occurring in Rural Areas in 2000
412 Murders in Urban Areas in 2000
413 Urban Murder Rate in 2000
414 Percent of Murders Occurring in Urban Areas in 2000
415 Murders in Rural Areas in 2000
416 Rural Murder Rate in 2000
417 Percent of Murders Occurring in Rural Areas in 2000
418 Rapes in Urban Areas in 2000
419 Urban Rape Rate in 2000
420 Percent of Rapes Occurring in Urban Areas in 2000
421 Rapes in Rural Areas in 2000
422 Rural Rape Rate in 2000
423 Percent of Rapes Occurring in Rural Areas in 2000
424 Robberies in Urban Areas in 2000
425 Urban Robbery Rate in 2000
426 Percent of Robberies Occurring in Urban Areas in 2000
427 Robberies in Rural Areas in 2000
428 Rural Robbery Rate in 2000
429 Percent of Robberies Occurring in Rural Areas in 2000
430 Aggravated Assaults in Urban Areas in 2000

VII. OFFENSES (continued)

1996 Crimes

VII. OFFENSES (continued)

Crimes in 2000

National Total = 11,605,751 Crimes*

ALPHA ORDER					RANK ORDER			
RANK	STATE	CRIMES	% of USA		RANK	STATE	CRIMES	% of USA
21	Alabama	202,159	1.7%		1	California	1,266,714	10.9%
46	Alaska	26,641	0.2%		2	Texas	1,033,311	8.9%
12	Arizona	299,092	2.6%		3	Florida	910,154	7.8%
32	Arkansas	110,019	0.9%		4	New York	588,189	5.1%
1	California	1,266,714	10.9%		5	Illinois	532,315	4.6%
25	Colorado	171,304	1.5%		6	Ohio	458,874	4.0%
31	Connecticut	110,091	0.9%		7	Michigan	408,456	3.5%
42	Delaware	35,090	0.3%		8	North Carolina	395,972	3.4%
3	Florida	910,154	7.8%		9	Georgia	388,949	3.4%
9	Georgia	388,949	3.4%		10	Pennsylvania	367,858	3.2%
38	Hawaii	62,987	0.5%		11	Washington	300,932	2.6%
40	Idaho	41,228	0.4%		12	Arizona	299,092	2.6%
5	Illinois	532,315	4.6%		13	Tennessee	278,218	2.4%
18	Indiana	228,135	2.0%		14	New Jersey	265,935	2.3%
35	Iowa	94,630	0.8%		15	Maryland	255,085	2.2%
29	Kansas	118,527	1.0%		16	Missouri	253,338	2.2%
28	Kentucky	119,626	1.0%		17	Louisiana	242,344	2.1%
17	Louisiana	242,344	2.1%		18	Indiana	228,135	2.0%
43	Maine	33,400	0.3%		19	Virginia	214,348	1.8%
15	Maryland	255,085	2.2%		20	South Carolina	209,482	1.8%
22	Massachusetts	192,131	1.7%		21	Alabama	202,159	1.7%
7	Michigan	408,456	3.5%		22	Massachusetts	192,131	1.7%
24	Minnesota	171,611	1.5%		23	Wisconsin	172,124	1.5%
30	Mississippi	113,911	1.0%		24	Minnesota	171,611	1.5%
16	Missouri	253,338	2.2%		25	Colorado	171,304	1.5%
44	Montana	31,878	0.3%		26	Oregon	165,780	1.4%
37	Nebraska	70,085	0.6%		27	Oklahoma	157,302	1.4%
36	Nevada	85,297	0.7%		28	Kentucky	119,626	1.0%
45	New Hampshire	30,068	0.3%		29	Kansas	118,527	1.0%
14	New Jersey	265,935	2.3%		30	Mississippi	113,911	1.0%
33	New Mexico	100,391	0.9%		31	Connecticut	110,091	0.9%
4	New York	588,189	5.1%		32	Arkansas	110,019	0.9%
8	North Carolina	395,972	3.4%		33	New Mexico	100,391	0.9%
50	North Dakota	14,694	0.1%		34	Utah	99,958	0.9%
6	Ohio	458,874	4.0%		35	Iowa	94,630	0.8%
27	Oklahoma	157,302	1.4%		36	Nevada	85,297	0.7%
26	Oregon	165,780	1.4%		37	Nebraska	70,085	0.6%
10	Pennsylvania	367,858	3.2%		38	Hawaii	62,987	0.5%
41	Rhode Island	36,444	0.3%		39	West Virginia	47,067	0.4%
20	South Carolina	209,482	1.8%		40	Idaho	41,228	0.4%
48	South Dakota	17,511	0.2%		41	Rhode Island	36,444	0.3%
13	Tennessee	278,218	2.4%		42	Delaware	35,090	0.3%
2	Texas	1,033,311	8.9%		43	Maine	33,400	0.3%
34	Utah	99,958	0.9%		44	Montana	31,878	0.3%
47	Vermont	18,185	0.2%		45	New Hampshire	30,068	0.3%
19	Virginia	214,348	1.8%		46	Alaska	26,641	0.2%
11	Washington	300,932	2.6%		47	Vermont	18,185	0.2%
39	West Virginia	47,067	0.4%		48	South Dakota	17,511	0.2%
23	Wisconsin	172,124	1.5%		49	Wyoming	16,285	0.1%
49	Wyoming	16,285	0.1%		50	North Dakota	14,694	0.1%
						District of Columbia	41,626	0.4%

Source: Federal Bureau of Investigation
"Crime in the United States 2000" (Uniform Crime Reports, October 22, 2001)
Includes murder, rape, robbery, aggravated assault, burglary, larceny-theft and motor vehicle theft.

Average Time Between Crimes in 2000

National Rate = A Crime Occurs Every 2.7 Seconds*

ALPHA ORDER

RANK	STATE	MINUTES.SECONDS
30	Alabama	2.36
5	Alaska	19.44
39	Arizona	1.46
19	Arkansas	4.47
50	California	0.25
26	Colorado	3.04
20	Connecticut	4.46
9	Delaware	14.59
48	Florida	0.35
42	Georgia	1.21
13	Hawaii	8.20
11	Idaho	12.45
46	Illinois	0.59
33	Indiana	2.18
16	Iowa	5.33
22	Kansas	4.26
23	Kentucky	4.23
34	Louisiana	2.10
8	Maine	15.44
35	Maryland	2.04
29	Massachusetts	2.44
44	Michigan	1.17
26	Minnesota	3.04
21	Mississippi	4.37
35	Missouri	2.04
7	Montana	16.29
14	Nebraska	7.30
15	Nevada	6.10
6	New Hampshire	17.29
37	New Jersey	1.59
18	New Mexico	5.14
47	New York	0.53
43	North Carolina	1.20
1	North Dakota	35.46
45	Ohio	1.09
24	Oklahoma	3.20
25	Oregon	3.10
41	Pennsylvania	1.26
10	Rhode Island	14.25
31	South Carolina	2.31
3	South Dakota	30.01
38	Tennessee	1.53
49	Texas	0.31
17	Utah	5.16
4	Vermont	28.54
32	Virginia	2.27
40	Washington	1.45
12	West Virginia	11.10
28	Wisconsin	3.03
2	Wyoming	32.17

RANK ORDER

RANK	STATE	MINUTES.SECONDS
1	North Dakota	35.46
2	Wyoming	32.17
3	South Dakota	30.01
4	Vermont	28.54
5	Alaska	19.44
6	New Hampshire	17.29
7	Montana	16.29
8	Maine	15.44
9	Delaware	14.59
10	Rhode Island	14.25
11	Idaho	12.45
12	West Virginia	11.10
13	Hawaii	8.20
14	Nebraska	7.30
15	Nevada	6.10
16	Iowa	5.33
17	Utah	5.16
18	New Mexico	5.14
19	Arkansas	4.47
20	Connecticut	4.46
21	Mississippi	4.37
22	Kansas	4.26
23	Kentucky	4.23
24	Oklahoma	3.20
25	Oregon	3.10
26	Colorado	3.04
26	Minnesota	3.04
28	Wisconsin	3.03
29	Massachusetts	2.44
30	Alabama	2.36
31	South Carolina	2.31
32	Virginia	2.27
33	Indiana	2.18
34	Louisiana	2.10
35	Maryland	2.04
35	Missouri	2.04
37	New Jersey	1.59
38	Tennessee	1.53
39	Arizona	1.46
40	Washington	1.45
41	Pennsylvania	1.26
42	Georgia	1.21
43	North Carolina	1.20
44	Michigan	1.17
45	Ohio	1.09
46	Illinois	0.59
47	New York	0.53
48	Florida	0.35
49	Texas	0.31
50	California	0.25

District of Columbia	12.38

Source: Morgan Quitno Press using data from Federal Bureau of Investigation
   "Crime in the United States 2000" (Uniform Crime Reports, October 22, 2001)
*Includes murder, rape, robbery, aggravated assault, burglary, larceny-theft and motor vehicle theft.

Crimes per Square Mile in 2000

National Rate = 3.1 Crimes per Square Mile*

RANK	STATE	RATE		RANK	STATE	RATE
23	Alabama	3.9		1	New Jersey	32.4
50	Alaska	0.0		2	Rhode Island	29.6
28	Arizona	2.6		3	Massachusetts	20.8
32	Arkansas	2.1		4	Maryland	20.7
12	California	8.0		5	Connecticut	19.9
38	Colorado	1.6		6	Florida	15.2
5	Connecticut	19.9		7	Delaware	14.6
7	Delaware	14.6		8	New York	10.9
6	Florida	15.2		9	Ohio	10.2
16	Georgia	6.6		10	Hawaii	9.8
10	Hawaii	9.8		11	Illinois	9.2
45	Idaho	0.5		12	California	8.0
11	Illinois	9.2		12	Pennsylvania	8.0
18	Indiana	6.3		14	North Carolina	7.5
36	Iowa	1.7		15	South Carolina	6.7
39	Kansas	1.4		16	Georgia	6.6
27	Kentucky	3.0		16	Tennessee	6.6
20	Louisiana	4.9		18	Indiana	6.3
41	Maine	1.0		19	Virginia	5.1
4	Maryland	20.7		20	Louisiana	4.9
3	Massachusetts	20.8		21	Washington	4.3
22	Michigan	4.2		22	Michigan	4.2
33	Minnesota	2.0		23	Alabama	3.9
30	Mississippi	2.4		23	Texas	3.9
25	Missouri	3.6		25	Missouri	3.6
46	Montana	0.2		26	New Hampshire	3.2
42	Nebraska	0.9		27	Kentucky	3.0
43	Nevada	0.8		28	Arizona	2.6
26	New Hampshire	3.2		28	Wisconsin	2.6
1	New Jersey	32.4		30	Mississippi	2.4
43	New Mexico	0.8		31	Oklahoma	2.3
8	New York	10.9		32	Arkansas	2.1
14	North Carolina	7.5		33	Minnesota	2.0
46	North Dakota	0.2		34	Vermont	1.9
9	Ohio	10.2		34	West Virginia	1.9
31	Oklahoma	2.3		36	Iowa	1.7
36	Oregon	1.7		36	Oregon	1.7
12	Pennsylvania	8.0		38	Colorado	1.6
2	Rhode Island	29.6		39	Kansas	1.4
15	South Carolina	6.7		40	Utah	1.2
46	South Dakota	0.2		41	Maine	1.0
16	Tennessee	6.6		42	Nebraska	0.9
23	Texas	3.9		43	Nevada	0.8
40	Utah	1.2		43	New Mexico	0.8
34	Vermont	1.9		45	Idaho	0.5
19	Virginia	5.1		46	Montana	0.2
21	Washington	4.3		46	North Dakota	0.2
34	West Virginia	1.9		46	South Dakota	0.2
28	Wisconsin	2.6		46	Wyoming	0.2
46	Wyoming	0.2		50	Alaska	0.0
					District of Columbia	612.1

Source: Morgan Quitno Press using data from Federal Bureau of Investigation
   "Crime in the United States 2000" (Uniform Crime Reports, October 22, 2001)
*Includes murder, rape, robbery, aggravated assault, burglary, larceny-theft and motor vehicle theft. "Square miles"
includes total land and water area.

Percent Change in Number of Crimes: 1999 to 2000

National Percent Change = 0.2% Decrease*

ALPHA ORDER				RANK ORDER		
RANK	STATE	PERCENT CHANGE		RANK	STATE	PERCENT CHANGE
6	Alabama	4.8		1	Hawaii	9.9
30	Alaska	(1.4)		2	Vermont	8.7
5	Arizona	6.2		3	Tennessee	8.1
4	Arkansas	6.7		4	Arkansas	6.7
21	California	0.4		5	Arizona	6.2
8	Colorado	3.9		6	Alabama	4.8
29	Connecticut	(1.0)		7	Idaho	4.6
40	Delaware	(3.7)		8	Colorado	3.9
35	Florida	(2.9)		9	Rhode Island	2.7
36	Georgia	(3.0)		10	Texas	2.5
1	Hawaii	9.9		11	Nebraska	2.4
7	Idaho	4.6		12	Iowa	2.3
34	Illinois	(2.8)		12	Kentucky	2.3
16	Indiana	1.9		14	Montana	2.2
12	Iowa	2.3		15	Ohio	2.0
20	Kansas	0.6		16	Indiana	1.9
12	Kentucky	2.3		17	Nevada	1.3
39	Louisiana	(3.5)		18	Missouri	1.2
47	Maine	(7.3)		18	South Carolina	1.2
22	Maryland	0.3		20	Kansas	0.6
45	Massachusetts	(4.6)		21	California	0.4
43	Michigan	(4.3)		22	Maryland	0.3
25	Minnesota	(0.1)		23	North Carolina	0.0
40	Mississippi	(3.7)		23	Oklahoma	0.0
18	Missouri	1.2		25	Minnesota	(0.1)
14	Montana	2.2		25	Oregon	(0.1)
11	Nebraska	2.4		27	Washington	(0.5)
17	Nevada	1.3		27	Wisconsin	(0.5)
NA	New Hampshire**	NA		29	Connecticut	(1.0)
42	New Jersey	(4.0)		30	Alaska	(1.4)
37	New Mexico	(3.2)		30	New York	(1.4)
30	New York	(1.4)		32	Pennsylvania	(1.5)
23	North Carolina	0.0		33	Wyoming	(1.8)
37	North Dakota	(3.2)		34	Illinois	(2.8)
15	Ohio	2.0		35	Florida	(2.9)
23	Oklahoma	0.0		36	Georgia	(3.0)
25	Oregon	(0.1)		37	New Mexico	(3.2)
32	Pennsylvania	(1.5)		37	North Dakota	(3.2)
9	Rhode Island	2.7		39	Louisiana	(3.5)
18	South Carolina	1.2		40	Delaware	(3.7)
49	South Dakota	(9.7)		40	Mississippi	(3.7)
3	Tennessee	8.1		42	New Jersey	(4.0)
10	Texas	2.5		43	Michigan	(4.3)
46	Utah	(5.7)		43	West Virginia	(4.3)
2	Vermont	8.7		45	Massachusetts	(4.6)
48	Virginia	(7.6)		46	Utah	(5.7)
27	Washington	(0.5)		47	Maine	(7.3)
43	West Virginia	(4.3)		48	Virginia	(7.6)
27	Wisconsin	(0.5)		49	South Dakota	(9.7)
33	Wyoming	(1.8)		NA	New Hampshire**	NA
					District of Columbia	(0.6)

Source: Federal Bureau of Investigation
    "Crime in the United States 2000" (Uniform Crime Reports, October 22, 2001)
*Includes murder, rape, robbery, aggravated assault, burglary, larceny-theft and motor vehicle theft.
**Not available.

Crime Rate in 2000

National Rate = 4,124.0 Crimes per 100,000 Population*

ALPHA ORDER

RANK	STATE	RATE
15	Alabama	4,545.9
22	Alaska	4,249.4
1	Arizona	5,829.5
23	Arkansas	4,115.3
30	California	3,739.7
28	Colorado	3,982.6
36	Connecticut	3,232.7
17	Delaware	4,478.1
2	Florida	5,694.7
13	Georgia	4,751.1
6	Hawaii	5,198.9
38	Idaho	3,186.2
20	Illinois	4,286.2
29	Indiana	3,751.9
35	Iowa	3,233.7
19	Kansas	4,408.8
45	Kentucky	2,959.7
4	Louisiana	5,422.8
46	Maine	2,619.8
12	Maryland	4,816.1
42	Massachusetts	3,026.1
24	Michigan	4,109.9
32	Minnesota	3,488.4
27	Mississippi	4,004.4
16	Missouri	4,527.8
31	Montana	3,533.4
25	Nebraska	4,095.5
21	Nevada	4,268.6
48	New Hampshire	2,433.1
39	New Jersey	3,160.5
3	New Mexico	5,518.9
40	New York	3,099.6
9	North Carolina	4,919.3
50	North Dakota	2,288.1
26	Ohio	4,041.8
14	Oklahoma	4,558.6
11	Oregon	4,845.4
43	Pennsylvania	2,995.3
33	Rhode Island	3,476.4
5	South Carolina	5,221.4
49	South Dakota	2,319.8
10	Tennessee	4,890.2
8	Texas	4,955.5
18	Utah	4,476.1
44	Vermont	2,986.9
41	Virginia	3,028.1
7	Washington	5,105.6
47	West Virginia	2,602.8
37	Wisconsin	3,209.1
34	Wyoming	3,298.0

RANK ORDER

RANK	STATE	RATE
1	Arizona	5,829.5
2	Florida	5,694.7
3	New Mexico	5,518.9
4	Louisiana	5,422.8
5	South Carolina	5,221.4
6	Hawaii	5,198.9
7	Washington	5,105.6
8	Texas	4,955.5
9	North Carolina	4,919.3
10	Tennessee	4,890.2
11	Oregon	4,845.4
12	Maryland	4,816.1
13	Georgia	4,751.1
14	Oklahoma	4,558.6
15	Alabama	4,545.9
16	Missouri	4,527.8
17	Delaware	4,478.1
18	Utah	4,476.1
19	Kansas	4,408.8
20	Illinois	4,286.2
21	Nevada	4,268.6
22	Alaska	4,249.4
23	Arkansas	4,115.3
24	Michigan	4,109.9
25	Nebraska	4,095.5
26	Ohio	4,041.8
27	Mississippi	4,004.4
28	Colorado	3,982.6
29	Indiana	3,751.9
30	California	3,739.7
31	Montana	3,533.4
32	Minnesota	3,488.4
33	Rhode Island	3,476.4
34	Wyoming	3,298.0
35	Iowa	3,233.7
36	Connecticut	3,232.7
37	Wisconsin	3,209.1
38	Idaho	3,186.2
39	New Jersey	3,160.5
40	New York	3,099.6
41	Virginia	3,028.1
42	Massachusetts	3,026.1
43	Pennsylvania	2,995.3
44	Vermont	2,986.9
45	Kentucky	2,959.7
46	Maine	2,619.8
47	West Virginia	2,602.8
48	New Hampshire	2,433.1
49	South Dakota	2,319.8
50	North Dakota	2,288.1
	District of Columbia	7,276.5

Source: Federal Bureau of Investigation
"Crime in the United States 2000" (Uniform Crime Reports, October 22, 2001)
*Includes murder, rape, robbery, aggravated assault, burglary, larceny-theft and motor vehicle theft.

Percent Change in Crime Rate: 1999 to 2000

National Percent Change = 3.3% Decrease*

ALPHA ORDER

RANK	STATE	PERCENT CHANGE
4	Alabama	3.0
21	Alaska	(2.5)
14	Arizona	(1.1)
5	Arkansas	1.8
17	California	(1.7)
19	Colorado	(2.0)
31	Connecticut	(4.6)
41	Delaware	(7.4)
44	Florida	(8.2)
43	Georgia	(7.7)
1	Hawaii	7.5
6	Idaho	1.1
35	Illinois	(5.1)
12	Indiana	(0.4)
8	Iowa	0.3
13	Kansas	(0.7)
9	Kentucky	0.2
37	Louisiana	(5.6)
46	Maine	(8.9)
20	Maryland	(2.1)
40	Massachusetts	(7.2)
33	Michigan	(5.0)
25	Minnesota	(3.0)
38	Mississippi	(6.2)
14	Missouri	(1.1)
10	Montana	0.0
11	Nebraska	(0.3)
45	Nevada	(8.3)
NA	New Hampshire**	NA
39	New Jersey	(7.0)
41	New Mexico	(7.4)
36	New York	(5.5)
33	North Carolina	(5.0)
30	North Dakota	(4.4)
6	Ohio	1.1
23	Oklahoma	(2.7)
27	Oregon	(3.1)
28	Pennsylvania	(3.8)
25	Rhode Island	(3.0)
18	South Carolina	(1.9)
49	South Dakota	(12.3)
3	Tennessee	4.2
16	Texas	(1.5)
47	Utah	(10.1)
2	Vermont	6.0
48	Virginia	(10.2)
24	Washington	(2.8)
29	West Virginia	(4.3)
22	Wisconsin	(2.6)
31	Wyoming	(4.6)

RANK ORDER

RANK	STATE	PERCENT CHANGE
1	Hawaii	7.5
2	Vermont	6.0
3	Tennessee	4.2
4	Alabama	3.0
5	Arkansas	1.8
6	Idaho	1.1
6	Ohio	1.1
8	Iowa	0.3
9	Kentucky	0.2
10	Montana	0.0
11	Nebraska	(0.3)
12	Indiana	(0.4)
13	Kansas	(0.7)
14	Arizona	(1.1)
14	Missouri	(1.1)
16	Texas	(1.5)
17	California	(1.7)
18	South Carolina	(1.9)
19	Colorado	(2.0)
20	Maryland	(2.1)
21	Alaska	(2.5)
22	Wisconsin	(2.6)
23	Oklahoma	(2.7)
24	Washington	(2.8)
25	Minnesota	(3.0)
25	Rhode Island	(3.0)
27	Oregon	(3.1)
28	Pennsylvania	(3.8)
29	West Virginia	(4.3)
30	North Dakota	(4.4)
31	Connecticut	(4.6)
31	Wyoming	(4.6)
33	Michigan	(5.0)
33	North Carolina	(5.0)
35	Illinois	(5.1)
36	New York	(5.5)
37	Louisiana	(5.6)
38	Mississippi	(6.2)
39	New Jersey	(7.0)
40	Massachusetts	(7.2)
41	Delaware	(7.4)
41	New Mexico	(7.4)
43	Georgia	(7.7)
44	Florida	(8.2)
45	Nevada	(8.3)
46	Maine	(8.9)
47	Utah	(10.1)
48	Virginia	(10.2)
49	South Dakota	(12.3)
NA	New Hampshire**	NA
	District of Columbia	(9.8)

Source: Federal Bureau of Investigation
     "Crime in the United States 2000" (Uniform Crime Reports, October 22, 2001)
*Includes murder, rape, robbery, aggravated assault, burglary, larceny-theft and motor vehicle theft.
**Not available.

315

Violent Crimes in 2000

National Total = 1,424,289 Violent Crimes*

ALPHA ORDER

RANK	STATE	CRIMES	% of USA
20	Alabama	21,620	1.5%
40	Alaska	3,554	0.2%
18	Arizona	27,281	1.9%
29	Arkansas	11,904	0.8%
1	California	210,531	14.8%
24	Colorado	14,367	1.0%
31	Connecticut	11,058	0.8%
39	Delaware	5,363	0.4%
2	Florida	129,777	9.1%
9	Georgia	41,319	2.9%
43	Hawaii	2,954	0.2%
41	Idaho	3,267	0.2%
5	Illinois	81,567	5.7%
21	Indiana	21,230	1.5%
35	Iowa	7,796	0.5%
33	Kansas	10,470	0.7%
30	Kentucky	11,903	0.8%
15	Louisiana	30,440	2.1%
46	Maine	1,397	0.1%
8	Maryland	41,663	2.9%
16	Massachusetts	30,230	2.1%
6	Michigan	55,159	3.9%
25	Minnesota	13,813	1.0%
34	Mississippi	10,267	0.7%
17	Missouri	27,419	1.9%
44	Montana	2,171	0.2%
38	Nebraska	5,606	0.4%
32	Nevada	10,474	0.7%
45	New Hampshire	2,167	0.2%
13	New Jersey	32,298	2.3%
26	New Mexico	13,786	1.0%
4	New York	105,111	7.4%
11	North Carolina	40,051	2.8%
50	North Dakota	523	0.0%
12	Ohio	37,935	2.7%
23	Oklahoma	17,177	1.2%
28	Oregon	12,000	0.8%
7	Pennsylvania	51,584	3.6%
42	Rhode Island	3,121	0.2%
14	South Carolina	32,293	2.3%
48	South Dakota	1,259	0.1%
10	Tennessee	40,233	2.8%
3	Texas	113,653	8.0%
37	Utah	5,711	0.4%
49	Vermont	691	0.0%
22	Virginia	19,943	1.4%
19	Washington	21,788	1.5%
36	West Virginia	5,723	0.4%
27	Wisconsin	12,700	0.9%
47	Wyoming	1,316	0.1%

RANK ORDER

RANK	STATE	CRIMES	% of USA
1	California	210,531	14.8%
2	Florida	129,777	9.1%
3	Texas	113,653	8.0%
4	New York	105,111	7.4%
5	Illinois	81,567	5.7%
6	Michigan	55,159	3.9%
7	Pennsylvania	51,584	3.6%
8	Maryland	41,663	2.9%
9	Georgia	41,319	2.9%
10	Tennessee	40,233	2.8%
11	North Carolina	40,051	2.8%
12	Ohio	37,935	2.7%
13	New Jersey	32,298	2.3%
14	South Carolina	32,293	2.3%
15	Louisiana	30,440	2.1%
16	Massachusetts	30,230	2.1%
17	Missouri	27,419	1.9%
18	Arizona	27,281	1.9%
19	Washington	21,788	1.5%
20	Alabama	21,620	1.5%
21	Indiana	21,230	1.5%
22	Virginia	19,943	1.4%
23	Oklahoma	17,177	1.2%
24	Colorado	14,367	1.0%
25	Minnesota	13,813	1.0%
26	New Mexico	13,786	1.0%
27	Wisconsin	12,700	0.9%
28	Oregon	12,000	0.8%
29	Arkansas	11,904	0.8%
30	Kentucky	11,903	0.8%
31	Connecticut	11,058	0.8%
32	Nevada	10,474	0.7%
33	Kansas	10,470	0.7%
34	Mississippi	10,267	0.7%
35	Iowa	7,796	0.5%
36	West Virginia	5,723	0.4%
37	Utah	5,711	0.4%
38	Nebraska	5,606	0.4%
39	Delaware	5,363	0.4%
40	Alaska	3,554	0.2%
41	Idaho	3,267	0.2%
42	Rhode Island	3,121	0.2%
43	Hawaii	2,954	0.2%
44	Montana	2,171	0.2%
45	New Hampshire	2,167	0.2%
46	Maine	1,397	0.1%
47	Wyoming	1,316	0.1%
48	South Dakota	1,259	0.1%
49	Vermont	691	0.0%
50	North Dakota	523	0.0%
	District of Columbia	8,626	0.6%

Source: Federal Bureau of Investigation
"Crime in the United States 2000" (Uniform Crime Reports, October 22, 2001)
Violent crimes are offenses of murder, forcible rape, robbery and aggravated assault.

Average Time Between Violent Crimes in 2000

National Rate = A Violent Crime Occurs Every 22 Seconds*

ALPHA ORDER				RANK ORDER		
RANK	STATE	MINUTES.SECONDS		RANK	STATE	MINUTES.SECONDS
31	Alabama	24.19		1	North Dakota	1,004.58
11	Alaska	147.53		2	Vermont	760.38
33	Arizona	19.16		3	South Dakota	417.28
22	Arkansas	44.09		4	Wyoming	399.23
50	California	2.30		5	Maine	376.14
27	Colorado	36.35		6	New Hampshire	242.33
20	Connecticut	47.32		7	Montana	242.06
12	Delaware	98.00		8	Hawaii	177.56
49	Florida	4.03		9	Rhode Island	168.25
42	Georgia	12.43		10	Idaho	160.53
8	Hawaii	177.56		11	Alaska	147.53
10	Idaho	160.53		12	Delaware	98.00
46	Illinois	6.26		13	Nebraska	93.46
30	Indiana	24.46		14	Utah	92.02
16	Iowa	67.25		15	West Virginia	91.50
18	Kansas	50.12		16	Iowa	67.25
21	Kentucky	44.10		17	Mississippi	51.11
36	Louisiana	17.16		18	Kansas	50.12
5	Maine	376.14		19	Nevada	50.11
43	Maryland	12.37		20	Connecticut	47.32
35	Massachusetts	17.23		21	Kentucky	44.10
45	Michigan	9.32		22	Arkansas	44.09
26	Minnesota	38.03		23	Oregon	43.48
17	Mississippi	51.11		24	Wisconsin	41.23
34	Missouri	19.10		25	New Mexico	38.08
7	Montana	242.06		26	Minnesota	38.03
13	Nebraska	93.46		27	Colorado	36.35
19	Nevada	50.11		28	Oklahoma	30.36
6	New Hampshire	242.33		29	Virginia	26.22
38	New Jersey	16.16		30	Indiana	24.46
25	New Mexico	38.08		31	Alabama	24.19
47	New York	5.00		32	Washington	24.07
40	North Carolina	13.07		33	Arizona	19.16
1	North Dakota	1,004.58		34	Missouri	19.10
39	Ohio	13.52		35	Massachusetts	17.23
28	Oklahoma	30.36		36	Louisiana	17.16
23	Oregon	43.48		37	South Carolina	16.17
44	Pennsylvania	10.11		38	New Jersey	16.16
9	Rhode Island	168.25		39	Ohio	13.52
37	South Carolina	16.17		40	North Carolina	13.07
3	South Dakota	417.28		41	Tennessee	13.04
41	Tennessee	13.04		42	Georgia	12.43
48	Texas	4.37		43	Maryland	12.37
14	Utah	92.02		44	Pennsylvania	10.11
2	Vermont	760.38		45	Michigan	9.32
29	Virginia	26.22		46	Illinois	6.26
32	Washington	24.07		47	New York	5.00
15	West Virginia	91.50		48	Texas	4.37
24	Wisconsin	41.23		49	Florida	4.03
4	Wyoming	399.23		50	California	2.30
					District of Columbia	60.56

Source: Morgan Quitno Press using data from Federal Bureau of Investigation
   "Crime in the United States 2000" (Uniform Crime Reports, October 22, 2001)
*Violent crimes are offenses of murder, forcible rape, robbery and aggravated assault.

Violent Crimes per Square Mile in 2000

National Rate = 0.38 Violent Crimes per Square Mile*

RANK	STATE	RATE
23	Alabama	0.41
47	Alaska	0.01
28	Arizona	0.24
31	Arkansas	0.22
10	California	1.33
35	Colorado	0.14
7	Connecticut	1.99
5	Delaware	2.24
6	Florida	2.17
16	Georgia	0.70
21	Hawaii	0.46
44	Idaho	0.04
9	Illinois	1.41
18	Indiana	0.58
35	Iowa	0.14
37	Kansas	0.13
26	Kentucky	0.29
17	Louisiana	0.61
44	Maine	0.04
2	Maryland	3.39
3	Massachusetts	3.27
19	Michigan	0.57
34	Minnesota	0.16
32	Mississippi	0.21
24	Missouri	0.39
47	Montana	0.01
41	Nebraska	0.07
40	Nevada	0.09
30	New Hampshire	0.23
1	New Jersey	3.93
39	New Mexico	0.11
8	New York	1.95
15	North Carolina	0.76
47	North Dakota	0.01
14	Ohio	0.85
27	Oklahoma	0.25
38	Oregon	0.12
11	Pennsylvania	1.12
4	Rhode Island	2.54
12	South Carolina	1.04
46	South Dakota	0.02
13	Tennessee	0.95
22	Texas	0.43
41	Utah	0.07
41	Vermont	0.07
20	Virginia	0.47
25	Washington	0.31
28	West Virginia	0.24
33	Wisconsin	0.19
47	Wyoming	0.01

RANK ORDER

RANK	STATE	RATE
1	New Jersey	3.93
2	Maryland	3.39
3	Massachusetts	3.27
4	Rhode Island	2.54
5	Delaware	2.24
6	Florida	2.17
7	Connecticut	1.99
8	New York	1.95
9	Illinois	1.41
10	California	1.33
11	Pennsylvania	1.12
12	South Carolina	1.04
13	Tennessee	0.95
14	Ohio	0.85
15	North Carolina	0.76
16	Georgia	0.70
17	Louisiana	0.61
18	Indiana	0.58
19	Michigan	0.57
20	Virginia	0.47
21	Hawaii	0.46
22	Texas	0.43
23	Alabama	0.41
24	Missouri	0.39
25	Washington	0.31
26	Kentucky	0.29
27	Oklahoma	0.25
28	Arizona	0.24
28	West Virginia	0.24
30	New Hampshire	0.23
31	Arkansas	0.22
32	Mississippi	0.21
33	Wisconsin	0.19
34	Minnesota	0.16
35	Colorado	0.14
35	Iowa	0.14
37	Kansas	0.13
38	Oregon	0.12
39	New Mexico	0.11
40	Nevada	0.09
41	Nebraska	0.07
41	Utah	0.07
41	Vermont	0.07
44	Idaho	0.04
44	Maine	0.04
46	South Dakota	0.02
47	Alaska	0.01
47	Montana	0.01
47	North Dakota	0.01
47	Wyoming	0.01

District of Columbia 126.85

Source: Morgan Quitno Press using data from Federal Bureau of Investigation
"Crime in the United States 2000" (Uniform Crime Reports, October 22, 2001)
*Violent crimes are offenses of murder, forcible rape, robbery and aggravated assault. "Square miles" includes total land and water area.

Percent Change in Number of Violent Crimes: 1999 to 2000

National Percent Change = 0.1% Decrease*

ALPHA ORDER

RANK	STATE	PERCENT CHANGE
22	Alabama	0.9
46	Alaska	(9.1)
14	Arizona	3.6
4	Arkansas	9.7
20	California	1.3
12	Colorado	4.0
32	Connecticut	(2.5)
38	Delaware	(3.1)
24	Florida	0.6
28	Georgia	(0.6)
9	Hawaii	6.1
6	Idaho	6.6
32	Illinois	(2.5)
42	Indiana	(4.6)
37	Iowa	(3.0)
15	Kansas	3.1
32	Kentucky	(2.5)
43	Louisiana	(5.0)
27	Maine	(0.5)
5	Maryland	8.4
48	Massachusetts	(11.1)
35	Michigan	(2.7)
10	Minnesota	5.6
8	Mississippi	6.2
26	Missouri	0.2
13	Montana	3.9
49	Nebraska	(21.8)
19	Nevada	1.6
NA	New Hampshire**	NA
41	New Jersey	(3.7)
44	New Mexico	(5.1)
30	New York	(1.9)
39	North Carolina	(3.4)
1	North Dakota	23.3
7	Ohio	6.5
23	Oklahoma	0.7
40	Oregon	(3.5)
17	Pennsylvania	2.3
3	Rhode Island	9.9
30	South Carolina	(1.9)
16	South Dakota	2.6
10	Tennessee	5.6
21	Texas	1.2
35	Utah	(2.7)
18	Vermont	2.2
45	Virginia	(7.8)
25	Washington	0.3
47	West Virginia	(9.7)
29	Wisconsin	(1.6)
2	Wyoming	18.0

RANK ORDER

RANK	STATE	PERCENT CHANGE
1	North Dakota	23.3
2	Wyoming	18.0
3	Rhode Island	9.9
4	Arkansas	9.7
5	Maryland	8.4
6	Idaho	6.6
7	Ohio	6.5
8	Mississippi	6.2
9	Hawaii	6.1
10	Minnesota	5.6
10	Tennessee	5.6
12	Colorado	4.0
13	Montana	3.9
14	Arizona	3.6
15	Kansas	3.1
16	South Dakota	2.6
17	Pennsylvania	2.3
18	Vermont	2.2
19	Nevada	1.6
20	California	1.3
21	Texas	1.2
22	Alabama	0.9
23	Oklahoma	0.7
24	Florida	0.6
25	Washington	0.3
26	Missouri	0.2
27	Maine	(0.5)
28	Georgia	(0.6)
29	Wisconsin	(1.6)
30	New York	(1.9)
30	South Carolina	(1.9)
32	Connecticut	(2.5)
32	Illinois	(2.5)
32	Kentucky	(2.5)
35	Michigan	(2.7)
35	Utah	(2.7)
37	Iowa	(3.0)
38	Delaware	(3.1)
39	North Carolina	(3.4)
40	Oregon	(3.5)
41	New Jersey	(3.7)
42	Indiana	(4.6)
43	Louisiana	(5.0)
44	New Mexico	(5.1)
45	Virginia	(7.8)
46	Alaska	(9.1)
47	West Virginia	(9.7)
48	Massachusetts	(11.1)
49	Nebraska	(21.8)
NA	New Hampshire**	NA
	District of Columbia	2.1

Source: Federal Bureau of Investigation
"Crime in the United States 2000" (Uniform Crime Reports, October 22, 2001)
*Violent crimes are offenses of murder, forcible rape, robbery and aggravated assault.
**Not available.

319

Violent Crime Rate in 2000

National Rate = 506.1 Violent Crimes per 100,000 Population*

RANK	STATE	RATE
20	Alabama	486.2
10	Alaska	566.9
14	Arizona	531.7
22	Arkansas	445.3
9	California	621.6
31	Colorado	334.0
33	Connecticut	324.7
6	Delaware	684.4
1	Florida	812.0
16	Georgia	504.7
43	Hawaii	243.8
42	Idaho	252.5
8	Illinois	656.8
29	Indiana	349.1
40	Iowa	266.4
24	Kansas	389.4
36	Kentucky	294.5
7	Louisiana	681.1
49	Maine	109.6
3	Maryland	786.6
21	Massachusetts	476.1
11	Michigan	555.0
38	Minnesota	280.8
27	Mississippi	360.9
19	Missouri	490.0
44	Montana	240.6
32	Nebraska	327.6
15	Nevada	524.2
46	New Hampshire	175.4
25	New Jersey	383.8
4	New Mexico	757.9
12	New York	553.9
18	North Carolina	497.6
50	North Dakota	81.4
30	Ohio	334.1
17	Oklahoma	497.8
28	Oregon	350.7
23	Pennsylvania	420.0
35	Rhode Island	297.7
2	South Carolina	804.9
47	South Dakota	166.8
5	Tennessee	707.2
13	Texas	545.1
41	Utah	255.7
48	Vermont	113.5
37	Virginia	281.7
26	Washington	369.7
34	West Virginia	316.5
45	Wisconsin	236.8
39	Wyoming	266.5

RANK	STATE	RATE
1	Florida	812.0
2	South Carolina	804.9
3	Maryland	786.6
4	New Mexico	757.9
5	Tennessee	707.2
6	Delaware	684.4
7	Louisiana	681.1
8	Illinois	656.8
9	California	621.6
10	Alaska	566.9
11	Michigan	555.0
12	New York	553.9
13	Texas	545.1
14	Arizona	531.7
15	Nevada	524.2
16	Georgia	504.7
17	Oklahoma	497.8
18	North Carolina	497.6
19	Missouri	490.0
20	Alabama	486.2
21	Massachusetts	476.1
22	Arkansas	445.3
23	Pennsylvania	420.0
24	Kansas	389.4
25	New Jersey	383.8
26	Washington	369.7
27	Mississippi	360.9
28	Oregon	350.7
29	Indiana	349.1
30	Ohio	334.1
31	Colorado	334.0
32	Nebraska	327.6
33	Connecticut	324.7
34	West Virginia	316.5
35	Rhode Island	297.7
36	Kentucky	294.5
37	Virginia	281.7
38	Minnesota	280.8
39	Wyoming	266.5
40	Iowa	266.4
41	Utah	255.7
42	Idaho	252.5
43	Hawaii	243.8
44	Montana	240.6
45	Wisconsin	236.8
46	New Hampshire	175.4
47	South Dakota	166.8
48	Vermont	113.5
49	Maine	109.6
50	North Dakota	81.4
	District of Columbia	1,507.9

Source: Federal Bureau of Investigation
   "Crime in the United States 2000" (Uniform Crime Reports, October 22, 2001)
Violent crimes are offenses of murder, forcible rape, robbery and aggravated assault.

Percent Change in Violent Crime Rate: 1999 to 2000

National Percent Change = 3.2% Decrease*

ALPHA ORDER			RANK ORDER		
RANK	STATE	PERCENT CHANGE	RANK	STATE	PERCENT CHANGE
17	Alabama	(0.8)	1	North Dakota	21.7
46	Alaska	(10.1)	2	Wyoming	14.6
25	Arizona	(3.5)	3	Maryland	5.8
5	Arkansas	4.7	4	Ohio	5.6
18	California	(0.9)	5	Arkansas	4.7
19	Colorado	(1.9)	6	Rhode Island	3.9
35	Connecticut	(6.0)	7	Hawaii	3.8
37	Delaware	(6.8)	8	Mississippi	3.3
31	Florida	(4.9)	9	Idaho	3.1
33	Georgia	(5.5)	10	Minnesota	2.5
7	Hawaii	3.8	11	Tennessee	1.8
9	Idaho	3.1	12	Kansas	1.7
29	Illinois	(4.7)	13	Montana	1.6
37	Indiana	(6.8)	14	Pennsylvania	(0.1)
30	Iowa	(4.8)	15	South Dakota	(0.3)
12	Kansas	1.7	15	Vermont	(0.3)
28	Kentucky	(4.5)	17	Alabama	(0.8)
40	Louisiana	(7.0)	18	California	(0.9)
23	Maine	(2.2)	19	Colorado	(1.9)
3	Maryland	5.8	20	Missouri	(2.0)
48	Massachusetts	(13.6)	20	Washington	(2.0)
25	Michigan	(3.5)	22	Oklahoma	(2.1)
10	Minnesota	2.5	23	Maine	(2.2)
8	Mississippi	3.3	24	Texas	(2.7)
20	Missouri	(2.0)	25	Arizona	(3.5)
13	Montana	1.6	25	Michigan	(3.5)
49	Nebraska	(23.8)	27	Wisconsin	(3.7)
42	Nevada	(8.0)	28	Kentucky	(4.5)
NA	New Hampshire**	NA	29	Illinois	(4.7)
37	New Jersey	(6.8)	30	Iowa	(4.8)
44	New Mexico	(9.2)	31	Florida	(4.9)
34	New York	(5.9)	32	South Carolina	(5.0)
43	North Carolina	(8.2)	33	Georgia	(5.5)
1	North Dakota	21.7	34	New York	(5.9)
4	Ohio	5.6	35	Connecticut	(6.0)
22	Oklahoma	(2.1)	36	Oregon	(6.4)
36	Oregon	(6.4)	37	Delaware	(6.8)
14	Pennsylvania	(0.1)	37	Indiana	(6.8)
6	Rhode Island	3.9	37	New Jersey	(6.8)
32	South Carolina	(5.0)	40	Louisiana	(7.0)
15	South Dakota	(0.3)	41	Utah	(7.2)
11	Tennessee	1.8	42	Nevada	(8.0)
24	Texas	(2.7)	43	North Carolina	(8.2)
41	Utah	(7.2)	44	New Mexico	(9.2)
15	Vermont	(0.3)	45	West Virginia	(9.7)
47	Virginia	(10.5)	46	Alaska	(10.1)
20	Washington	(2.0)	47	Virginia	(10.5)
45	West Virginia	(9.7)	48	Massachusetts	(13.6)
27	Wisconsin	(3.7)	49	Nebraska	(23.8)
2	Wyoming	14.6	NA	New Hampshire**	NA
				District of Columbia	(7.4)

Source: Federal Bureau of Investigation
   "Crime in the United States 2000" (Uniform Crime Reports, October 22, 2001)
*Violent crimes are offenses of murder, forcible rape, robbery and aggravated assault.
**Not available.

Violent Crimes with Firearms in 2000

National Total = 267,386 Violent Crimes*

ALPHA ORDER

RANK	STATE	CRIMES	% of USA
14	Alabama	4,866	1.8%
37	Alaska	539	0.2%
11	Arizona	7,447	2.8%
22	Arkansas	2,731	1.0%
1	California	43,391	16.2%
25	Colorado	2,404	0.9%
28	Connecticut	1,958	0.7%
33	Delaware	1,028	0.4%
NA	Florida**	NA	NA
7	Georgia	10,961	4.1%
40	Hawaii	265	0.1%
36	Idaho	697	0.3%
NA	Illinois**	NA	NA
15	Indiana	4,168	1.6%
34	Iowa	767	0.3%
NA	Kansas**	NA	NA
30	Kentucky	1,513	0.6%
9	Louisiana	8,181	3.1%
45	Maine	81	0.0%
8	Maryland	9,192	3.4%
24	Massachusetts	2,462	0.9%
3	Michigan	14,297	5.3%
26	Minnesota	2,352	0.9%
31	Mississippi	1,261	0.5%
10	Missouri	7,594	2.8%
44	Montana	105	0.0%
32	Nebraska	1,240	0.5%
23	Nevada	2,683	1.0%
42	New Hampshire	139	0.1%
12	New Jersey	7,109	2.7%
21	New Mexico	2,744	1.0%
17	New York	3,843	1.4%
6	North Carolina	12,318	4.6%
47	North Dakota	29	0.0%
13	Ohio	6,906	2.6%
20	Oklahoma	3,221	1.2%
29	Oregon	1,693	0.6%
5	Pennsylvania	12,625	4.7%
39	Rhode Island	469	0.2%
27	South Carolina	2,140	0.8%
43	South Dakota	116	0.0%
4	Tennessee	13,230	4.9%
2	Texas	28,762	10.8%
35	Utah	712	0.3%
46	Vermont	59	0.0%
16	Virginia	3,854	1.4%
19	Washington	3,692	1.4%
38	West Virginia	516	0.2%
18	Wisconsin	3,716	1.4%
41	Wyoming	141	0.1%

RANK ORDER

RANK	STATE	CRIMES	% of USA
1	California	43,391	16.2%
2	Texas	28,762	10.8%
3	Michigan	14,297	5.3%
4	Tennessee	13,230	4.9%
5	Pennsylvania	12,625	4.7%
6	North Carolina	12,318	4.6%
7	Georgia	10,961	4.1%
8	Maryland	9,192	3.4%
9	Louisiana	8,181	3.1%
10	Missouri	7,594	2.8%
11	Arizona	7,447	2.8%
12	New Jersey	7,109	2.7%
13	Ohio	6,906	2.6%
14	Alabama	4,866	1.8%
15	Indiana	4,168	1.6%
16	Virginia	3,854	1.4%
17	New York	3,843	1.4%
18	Wisconsin	3,716	1.4%
19	Washington	3,692	1.4%
20	Oklahoma	3,221	1.2%
21	New Mexico	2,744	1.0%
22	Arkansas	2,731	1.0%
23	Nevada	2,683	1.0%
24	Massachusetts	2,462	0.9%
25	Colorado	2,404	0.9%
26	Minnesota	2,352	0.9%
27	South Carolina	2,140	0.8%
28	Connecticut	1,958	0.7%
29	Oregon	1,693	0.6%
30	Kentucky	1,513	0.6%
31	Mississippi	1,261	0.5%
32	Nebraska	1,240	0.5%
33	Delaware	1,028	0.4%
34	Iowa	767	0.3%
35	Utah	712	0.3%
36	Idaho	697	0.3%
37	Alaska	539	0.2%
38	West Virginia	516	0.2%
39	Rhode Island	469	0.2%
40	Hawaii	265	0.1%
41	Wyoming	141	0.1%
42	New Hampshire	139	0.1%
43	South Dakota	116	0.0%
44	Montana	105	0.0%
45	Maine	81	0.0%
46	Vermont	59	0.0%
47	North Dakota	29	0.0%
NA	Florida**	NA	NA
NA	Illinois**	NA	NA
NA	Kansas**	NA	NA
	District of Columbia**	NA	NA

Source: Morgan Quitno Press using data from Federal Bureau of Investigation
    "Crime in the United States 2000" (Uniform Crime Reports, October 22, 2001)
*Includes murder, robbery and aggravated assault. Does not include rape. National total reflects only those violent crimes for which the type of weapon was known and reported. There were an additional 288,955 violent crimes (excluding rape) for which the type of weapon was not reported to the F.B.I.
**Not available.

Violent Crime Rate with Firearms in 2000

National Rate = 124.4 Violent Crimes per 100,000 Population*

ALPHA ORDER

RANK ORDER

RANK	STATE	RATE
13	Alabama	149.6
23	Alaska	94.7
11	Arizona	160.0
18	Arkansas	111.6
16	California	128.4
29	Colorado	72.4
31	Connecticut	65.6
1	Delaware	260.2
NA	Florida**	NA
7	Georgia	179.7
42	Hawaii	21.9
33	Idaho	54.7
NA	Illinois**	NA
20	Indiana	101.2
40	Iowa	33.1
NA	Kansas**	NA
9	Kentucky	175.1
4	Louisiana	212.5
46	Maine	6.5
5	Maryland	206.1
36	Massachusetts	47.5
12	Michigan	159.0
35	Minnesota	50.7
22	Mississippi	96.6
10	Missouri	172.5
39	Montana	35.3
28	Nebraska	79.9
15	Nevada	134.3
44	New Hampshire	19.0
26	New Jersey	84.5
6	New Mexico	199.5
32	New York	55.0
8	North Carolina	177.8
47	North Dakota	5.1
19	Ohio	107.2
24	Oklahoma	93.3
34	Oregon	53.1
17	Pennsylvania	127.2
38	Rhode Island	44.8
3	South Carolina	222.0
43	South Dakota	19.4
2	Tennessee	246.3
14	Texas	139.9
37	Utah	45.7
45	Vermont	12.4
21	Virginia	98.1
30	Washington	68.9
25	West Virginia	84.9
27	Wisconsin	84.2
41	Wyoming	28.7

RANK	STATE	RATE
1	Delaware	260.2
2	Tennessee	246.3
3	South Carolina	222.0
4	Louisiana	212.5
5	Maryland	206.1
6	New Mexico	199.5
7	Georgia	179.7
8	North Carolina	177.8
9	Kentucky	175.1
10	Missouri	172.5
11	Arizona	160.0
12	Michigan	159.0
13	Alabama	149.6
14	Texas	139.9
15	Nevada	134.3
16	California	128.4
17	Pennsylvania	127.2
18	Arkansas	111.6
19	Ohio	107.2
20	Indiana	101.2
21	Virginia	98.1
22	Mississippi	96.6
23	Alaska	94.7
24	Oklahoma	93.3
25	West Virginia	84.9
26	New Jersey	84.5
27	Wisconsin	84.2
28	Nebraska	79.9
29	Colorado	72.4
30	Washington	68.9
31	Connecticut	65.6
32	New York	55.0
33	Idaho	54.7
34	Oregon	53.1
35	Minnesota	50.7
36	Massachusetts	47.5
37	Utah	45.7
38	Rhode Island	44.8
39	Montana	35.3
40	Iowa	33.1
41	Wyoming	28.7
42	Hawaii	21.9
43	South Dakota	19.4
44	New Hampshire	19.0
45	Vermont	12.4
46	Maine	6.5
47	North Dakota	5.1
NA	Florida**	NA
NA	Illinois**	NA
NA	Kansas**	NA
	District of Columbia**	NA

Source: Morgan Quitno Press using data from Federal Bureau of Investigation
    "Crime in the United States 2000" (Uniform Crime Reports, October 22, 2001)
*Based only on population of reporting jurisdictions. Includes murder, robbery and aggravated assault. Does not include rape. National rate reflects only those violent crimes for which the type of weapon was known and reported.
**Not available.

Percent of Violent Crimes Involving Firearms in 2000

National Percent = 25.6% of Violent Crimes*

ALPHA ORDER

RANK	STATE	PERCENT
5	Alabama	34.6
30	Alaska	21.0
10	Arizona	30.9
19	Arkansas	26.2
28	California	21.6
25	Colorado	24.2
29	Connecticut	21.1
21	Delaware	25.8
NA	Florida**	NA
2	Georgia	35.6
44	Hawaii	10.2
24	Idaho	24.4
NA	Illinois**	NA
17	Indiana	27.2
42	Iowa	12.0
NA	Kansas**	NA
9	Kentucky	31.3
6	Louisiana	33.5
47	Maine	7.6
18	Maryland	26.9
43	Massachusetts	10.8
11	Michigan	30.7
30	Minnesota	21.0
11	Mississippi	30.7
7	Missouri	32.4
45	Montana	9.5
23	Nebraska	24.7
14	Nevada	27.9
36	New Hampshire	17.9
27	New Jersey	23.0
20	New Mexico	26.1
35	New York	19.0
3	North Carolina	35.3
46	North Dakota	8.8
15	Ohio	27.7
33	Oklahoma	20.4
38	Oregon	16.6
13	Pennsylvania	29.6
37	Rhode Island	17.3
22	South Carolina	25.0
40	South Dakota	13.6
1	Tennessee	35.9
16	Texas	27.5
32	Utah	20.5
39	Vermont	14.5
8	Virginia	31.5
34	Washington	20.3
26	West Virginia	23.2
4	Wisconsin	34.8
41	Wyoming	12.3

RANK ORDER

RANK	STATE	PERCENT
1	Tennessee	35.9
2	Georgia	35.6
3	North Carolina	35.3
4	Wisconsin	34.8
5	Alabama	34.6
6	Louisiana	33.5
7	Missouri	32.4
8	Virginia	31.5
9	Kentucky	31.3
10	Arizona	30.9
11	Michigan	30.7
11	Mississippi	30.7
13	Pennsylvania	29.6
14	Nevada	27.9
15	Ohio	27.7
16	Texas	27.5
17	Indiana	27.2
18	Maryland	26.9
19	Arkansas	26.2
20	New Mexico	26.1
21	Delaware	25.8
22	South Carolina	25.0
23	Nebraska	24.7
24	Idaho	24.4
25	Colorado	24.2
26	West Virginia	23.2
27	New Jersey	23.0
28	California	21.6
29	Connecticut	21.1
30	Alaska	21.0
30	Minnesota	21.0
32	Utah	20.5
33	Oklahoma	20.4
34	Washington	20.3
35	New York	19.0
36	New Hampshire	17.9
37	Rhode Island	17.3
38	Oregon	16.6
39	Vermont	14.5
40	South Dakota	13.6
41	Wyoming	12.3
42	Iowa	12.0
43	Massachusetts	10.8
44	Hawaii	10.2
45	Montana	9.5
46	North Dakota	8.8
47	Maine	7.6
NA	Florida**	NA
NA	Illinois**	NA
NA	Kansas**	NA
	District of Columbia**	NA

Source: Morgan Quitno Press using data from Federal Bureau of Investigation
"Crime in the United States 2000" (Uniform Crime Reports, October 22, 2001)
*Includes murder, robbery and aggravated assault. Does not include rape. National percent reflects only those violent crimes for which the type of weapon was known and reported. There were an additional 288,955 violent crimes (excluding rape) for which the type of weapon was not reported to the F.B.I.
**Not available.

Murders in 2000

National Total = 15,517 Murders*

ALPHA ORDER

RANK	STATE	MURDERS	% of USA
18	Alabama	329	2.1%
41	Alaska	27	0.2%
15	Arizona	359	2.3%
27	Arkansas	168	1.1%
1	California	2,079	13.4%
30	Colorado	134	0.9%
33	Connecticut	98	0.6%
42	Delaware	25	0.2%
4	Florida	903	5.8%
7	Georgia	651	4.2%
40	Hawaii	35	0.2%
44	Idaho	16	0.1%
5	Illinois	891	5.7%
16	Indiana	352	2.3%
36	Iowa	46	0.3%
25	Kansas	169	1.1%
23	Kentucky	193	1.2%
9	Louisiana	560	3.6%
46	Maine	15	0.1%
11	Maryland	430	2.8%
32	Massachusetts	125	0.8%
6	Michigan	669	4.3%
28	Minnesota	151	1.0%
20	Mississippi	255	1.6%
17	Missouri	347	2.2%
44	Montana	16	0.1%
35	Nebraska	63	0.4%
31	Nevada	129	0.8%
43	New Hampshire	22	0.1%
19	New Jersey	289	1.9%
29	New Mexico	135	0.9%
3	New York	952	6.1%
9	North Carolina	560	3.6%
50	North Dakota	4	0.0%
12	Ohio	418	2.7%
24	Oklahoma	182	1.2%
34	Oregon	70	0.5%
8	Pennsylvania	602	3.9%
38	Rhode Island	45	0.3%
21	South Carolina	233	1.5%
49	South Dakota	7	0.0%
13	Tennessee	410	2.6%
2	Texas	1,238	8.0%
39	Utah	43	0.3%
48	Vermont	9	0.1%
14	Virginia	401	2.6%
22	Washington	196	1.3%
36	West Virginia	46	0.3%
25	Wisconsin	169	1.1%
47	Wyoming	12	0.1%

RANK ORDER

RANK	STATE	MURDERS	% of USA
1	California	2,079	13.4%
2	Texas	1,238	8.0%
3	New York	952	6.1%
4	Florida	903	5.8%
5	Illinois	891	5.7%
6	Michigan	669	4.3%
7	Georgia	651	4.2%
8	Pennsylvania	602	3.9%
9	Louisiana	560	3.6%
9	North Carolina	560	3.6%
11	Maryland	430	2.8%
12	Ohio	418	2.7%
13	Tennessee	410	2.6%
14	Virginia	401	2.6%
15	Arizona	359	2.3%
16	Indiana	352	2.3%
17	Missouri	347	2.2%
18	Alabama	329	2.1%
19	New Jersey	289	1.9%
20	Mississippi	255	1.6%
21	South Carolina	233	1.5%
22	Washington	196	1.3%
23	Kentucky	193	1.2%
24	Oklahoma	182	1.2%
25	Kansas	169	1.1%
25	Wisconsin	169	1.1%
27	Arkansas	168	1.1%
28	Minnesota	151	1.0%
29	New Mexico	135	0.9%
30	Colorado	134	0.9%
31	Nevada	129	0.8%
32	Massachusetts	125	0.8%
33	Connecticut	98	0.6%
34	Oregon	70	0.5%
35	Nebraska	63	0.4%
36	Iowa	46	0.3%
36	West Virginia	46	0.3%
38	Rhode Island	45	0.3%
39	Utah	43	0.3%
40	Hawaii	35	0.2%
41	Alaska	27	0.2%
42	Delaware	25	0.2%
43	New Hampshire	22	0.1%
44	Idaho	16	0.1%
44	Montana	16	0.1%
46	Maine	15	0.1%
47	Wyoming	12	0.1%
48	Vermont	9	0.1%
49	South Dakota	7	0.0%
50	North Dakota	4	0.0%
	District of Columbia	239	1.5%

Source: Federal Bureau of Investigation
"Crime in the United States 2000" (Uniform Crime Reports, October 22, 2001)
*Includes nonnegligent manslaughter.

Average Time Between Murders in 2000

National Rate = A Murder Occurs Every 34 Minutes*

ALPHA ORDER

RANK	STATE	HOURS.MINUTES
33	Alabama	26.38
10	Alaska	324.26
36	Arizona	24.24
24	Arkansas	52.08
50	California	4.13
21	Colorado	65.22
18	Connecticut	89.23
9	Delaware	350.24
47	Florida	9.42
44	Georgia	13.28
11	Hawaii	250.17
6	Idaho	547.30
46	Illinois	9.50
35	Indiana	24.53
14	Iowa	190.26
25	Kansas	51.50
28	Kentucky	45.23
41	Louisiana	15.38
5	Maine	584.00
40	Maryland	20.22
19	Massachusetts	70.05
45	Michigan	13.05
23	Minnesota	58.01
31	Mississippi	34.21
34	Missouri	25.15
6	Montana	547.30
16	Nebraska	139.03
20	Nevada	67.55
8	New Hampshire	398.11
32	New Jersey	30.19
22	New Mexico	64.53
48	New York	9.12
41	North Carolina	15.38
1	North Dakota	2,190.00
39	Ohio	20.58
27	Oklahoma	48.08
17	Oregon	125.08
43	Pennsylvania	14.33
13	Rhode Island	194.40
30	South Carolina	37.36
2	South Dakota	1,251.26
38	Tennessee	21.22
49	Texas	7.05
12	Utah	203.43
3	Vermont	973.20
37	Virginia	21.51
29	Washington	44.41
14	West Virginia	190.26
25	Wisconsin	51.50
4	Wyoming	730.00

RANK ORDER

RANK	STATE	HOURS.MINUTES
1	North Dakota	2,190.00
2	South Dakota	1,251.26
3	Vermont	973.20
4	Wyoming	730.00
5	Maine	584.00
6	Idaho	547.30
6	Montana	547.30
8	New Hampshire	398.11
9	Delaware	350.24
10	Alaska	324.26
11	Hawaii	250.17
12	Utah	203.43
13	Rhode Island	194.40
14	Iowa	190.26
14	West Virginia	190.26
16	Nebraska	139.03
17	Oregon	125.08
18	Connecticut	89.23
19	Massachusetts	70.05
20	Nevada	67.55
21	Colorado	65.22
22	New Mexico	64.53
23	Minnesota	58.01
24	Arkansas	52.08
25	Kansas	51.50
25	Wisconsin	51.50
27	Oklahoma	48.08
28	Kentucky	45.23
29	Washington	44.41
30	South Carolina	37.36
31	Mississippi	34.21
32	New Jersey	30.19
33	Alabama	26.38
34	Missouri	25.15
35	Indiana	24.53
36	Arizona	24.24
37	Virginia	21.51
38	Tennessee	21.22
39	Ohio	20.58
40	Maryland	20.22
41	Louisiana	15.38
41	North Carolina	15.38
43	Pennsylvania	14.33
44	Georgia	13.28
45	Michigan	13.05
46	Illinois	9.50
47	Florida	9.42
48	New York	9.12
49	Texas	7.05
50	California	4.13
	District of Columbia	36.39

Source: Morgan Quitno Press using data from Federal Bureau of Investigation
"Crime in the United States 2000" (Uniform Crime Reports, October 22, 2001)
*Includes nonnegligent manslaughter.

Percent Change in Number of Murders: 1999 to 2000

National Percent Change = 0.0% Change*

ALPHA ORDER

RANK	STATE	PERCENT CHANGE
27	Alabama	(4.6)
47	Alaska	(48.1)
31	Arizona	(6.5)
4	Arkansas	17.5
17	California	3.7
42	Colorado	(27.6)
33	Connecticut	(8.4)
16	Delaware	4.2
13	Florida	5.1
7	Georgia	11.7
36	Hawaii	(20.5)
43	Idaho	(36.0)
29	Illinois	(5.1)
35	Indiana	(10.0)
9	Iowa	7.0
10	Kansas	5.6
28	Kentucky	(4.9)
2	Louisiana	19.7
44	Maine	(40.0)
32	Maryland	(7.5)
18	Massachusetts	2.5
26	Michigan	(3.7)
6	Minnesota	12.7
2	Mississippi	19.7
25	Missouri	(3.3)
41	Montana	(27.3)
14	Nebraska	5.0
40	Nevada	(21.8)
NA	New Hampshire**	NA
23	New Jersey	0.7
38	New Mexico	(20.6)
11	New York	5.4
22	North Carolina	1.4
48	North Dakota	(60.0)
12	Ohio	5.3
39	Oklahoma	(21.2)
36	Oregon	(20.5)
20	Pennsylvania	1.7
1	Rhode Island	25.0
34	South Carolina	(9.7)
49	South Dakota	(61.1)
15	Tennessee	4.9
20	Texas	1.7
24	Utah	(2.3)
46	Vermont	(47.1)
19	Virginia	2.3
5	Washington	14.6
45	West Virginia	(41.8)
30	Wisconsin	(5.6)
8	Wyoming	9.1

RANK ORDER

RANK	STATE	PERCENT CHANGE
1	Rhode Island	25.0
2	Louisiana	19.7
2	Mississippi	19.7
4	Arkansas	17.5
5	Washington	14.6
6	Minnesota	12.7
7	Georgia	11.7
8	Wyoming	9.1
9	Iowa	7.0
10	Kansas	5.6
11	New York	5.4
12	Ohio	5.3
13	Florida	5.1
14	Nebraska	5.0
15	Tennessee	4.9
16	Delaware	4.2
17	California	3.7
18	Massachusetts	2.5
19	Virginia	2.3
20	Pennsylvania	1.7
20	Texas	1.7
22	North Carolina	1.4
23	New Jersey	0.7
24	Utah	(2.3)
25	Missouri	(3.3)
26	Michigan	(3.7)
27	Alabama	(4.6)
28	Kentucky	(4.9)
29	Illinois	(5.1)
30	Wisconsin	(5.6)
31	Arizona	(6.5)
32	Maryland	(7.5)
33	Connecticut	(8.4)
34	South Carolina	(9.7)
35	Indiana	(10.0)
36	Hawaii	(20.5)
36	Oregon	(20.5)
38	New Mexico	(20.6)
39	Oklahoma	(21.2)
40	Nevada	(21.8)
41	Montana	(27.3)
42	Colorado	(27.6)
43	Idaho	(36.0)
44	Maine	(40.0)
45	West Virginia	(41.8)
46	Vermont	(47.1)
47	Alaska	(48.1)
48	North Dakota	(60.0)
49	South Dakota	(61.1)
NA	New Hampshire**	NA
	District of Columbia	(0.8)

Source: Federal Bureau of Investigation
   "Crime in the United States 2000" (Uniform Crime Reports, October 22, 2001)
*Includes nonnegligent manslaughter.
**Not available.

Murder Rate in 2000

National Rate = 5.5 Murders per 100,000 Population*

RANK	STATE	RATE
5	Alabama	7.4
26	Alaska	4.3
9	Arizona	7.0
13	Arkansas	6.3
16	California	6.1
34	Colorado	3.1
36	Connecticut	2.9
32	Delaware	3.2
21	Florida	5.6
4	Georgia	8.0
36	Hawaii	2.9
47	Idaho	1.2
7	Illinois	7.2
18	Indiana	5.8
45	Iowa	1.6
13	Kansas	6.3
25	Kentucky	4.8
1	Louisiana	12.5
47	Maine	1.2
3	Maryland	8.1
40	Massachusetts	2.0
11	Michigan	6.7
34	Minnesota	3.1
2	Mississippi	9.0
15	Missouri	6.2
43	Montana	1.8
28	Nebraska	3.7
12	Nevada	6.5
43	New Hampshire	1.8
30	New Jersey	3.4
5	New Mexico	7.4
23	New York	5.0
9	North Carolina	7.0
50	North Dakota	0.6
28	Ohio	3.7
22	Oklahoma	5.3
40	Oregon	2.0
24	Pennsylvania	4.9
26	Rhode Island	4.3
18	South Carolina	5.8
49	South Dakota	0.9
7	Tennessee	7.2
17	Texas	5.9
42	Utah	1.9
46	Vermont	1.5
20	Virginia	5.7
31	Washington	3.3
38	West Virginia	2.5
32	Wisconsin	3.2
39	Wyoming	2.4

RANK ORDER

RANK	STATE	RATE
1	Louisiana	12.5
2	Mississippi	9.0
3	Maryland	8.1
4	Georgia	8.0
5	Alabama	7.4
5	New Mexico	7.4
7	Illinois	7.2
7	Tennessee	7.2
9	Arizona	7.0
9	North Carolina	7.0
11	Michigan	6.7
12	Nevada	6.5
13	Arkansas	6.3
13	Kansas	6.3
15	Missouri	6.2
16	California	6.1
17	Texas	5.9
18	Indiana	5.8
18	South Carolina	5.8
20	Virginia	5.7
21	Florida	5.6
22	Oklahoma	5.3
23	New York	5.0
24	Pennsylvania	4.9
25	Kentucky	4.8
26	Alaska	4.3
26	Rhode Island	4.3
28	Nebraska	3.7
28	Ohio	3.7
30	New Jersey	3.4
31	Washington	3.3
32	Delaware	3.2
32	Wisconsin	3.2
34	Colorado	3.1
34	Minnesota	3.1
36	Connecticut	2.9
36	Hawaii	2.9
38	West Virginia	2.5
39	Wyoming	2.4
40	Massachusetts	2.0
40	Oregon	2.0
42	Utah	1.9
43	Montana	1.8
43	New Hampshire	1.8
45	Iowa	1.6
46	Vermont	1.5
47	Idaho	1.2
47	Maine	1.2
49	South Dakota	0.9
50	North Dakota	0.6
	District of Columbia	41.8

Source: Federal Bureau of Investigation
   "Crime in the United States 2000" (Uniform Crime Reports, October 22, 2001)
*Includes nonnegligent manslaughter.

Percent Change in Murder Rate: 1999 to 2000

National Percent Change = 3.1% Decrease*

ALPHA ORDER

RANK ORDER

RANK	STATE	PERCENT CHANGE	RANK	STATE	PERCENT CHANGE
26	Alabama	(6.3)	1	Rhode Island	18.1
47	Alaska	(48.7)	2	Louisiana	17.1
35	Arizona	(12.9)	3	Mississippi	16.5
4	Arkansas	12.1	4	Arkansas	12.1
13	California	1.5	5	Washington	11.9
42	Colorado	(31.7)	6	Minnesota	9.4
32	Connecticut	(11.7)	7	Georgia	6.2
16	Delaware	0.2	8	Wyoming	6.0
18	Florida	(0.6)	9	Iowa	4.9
7	Georgia	6.2	10	Ohio	4.4
36	Hawaii	(22.2)	11	Kansas	4.3
43	Idaho	(38.1)	12	Nebraska	2.2
29	Illinois	(7.3)	13	California	1.5
33	Indiana	(12.0)	14	New York	1.1
9	Iowa	4.9	14	Tennessee	1.1
11	Kansas	4.3	16	Delaware	0.2
27	Kentucky	(6.8)	17	Massachusetts	(0.3)
2	Louisiana	17.1	18	Florida	(0.6)
44	Maine	(41.0)	19	Pennsylvania	(0.7)
31	Maryland	(9.7)	19	Virginia	(0.7)
17	Massachusetts	(0.3)	21	Texas	(2.2)
24	Michigan	(4.5)	22	New Jersey	(2.5)
6	Minnesota	9.4	23	North Carolina	(3.6)
3	Mississippi	16.5	24	Michigan	(4.5)
25	Missouri	(5.5)	25	Missouri	(5.5)
40	Montana	(28.8)	26	Alabama	(6.3)
12	Nebraska	2.2	27	Kentucky	(6.8)
41	Nevada	(29.2)	27	Utah	(6.8)
NA	New Hampshire**	NA	29	Illinois	(7.3)
22	New Jersey	(2.5)	30	Wisconsin	(7.6)
39	New Mexico	(24.0)	31	Maryland	(9.7)
14	New York	1.1	32	Connecticut	(11.7)
23	North Carolina	(3.6)	33	Indiana	(12.0)
48	North Dakota	(60.5)	34	South Carolina	(12.5)
10	Ohio	4.4	35	Arizona	(12.9)
38	Oklahoma	(23.3)	36	Hawaii	(22.2)
37	Oregon	(22.9)	37	Oregon	(22.9)
19	Pennsylvania	(0.7)	38	Oklahoma	(23.3)
1	Rhode Island	18.1	39	New Mexico	(24.0)
34	South Carolina	(12.5)	40	Montana	(28.8)
49	South Dakota	(62.2)	41	Nevada	(29.2)
14	Tennessee	1.1	42	Colorado	(31.7)
21	Texas	(2.2)	43	Idaho	(38.1)
27	Utah	(6.8)	44	Maine	(41.0)
46	Vermont	(48.4)	45	West Virginia	(41.8)
19	Virginia	(0.7)	46	Vermont	(48.4)
5	Washington	11.9	47	Alaska	(48.7)
45	West Virginia	(41.8)	48	North Dakota	(60.5)
30	Wisconsin	(7.6)	49	South Dakota	(62.2)
8	Wyoming	6.0	NA	New Hampshire**	NA
				District of Columbia	(10.0)

Source: Federal Bureau of Investigation
    "Crime in the United States 2000" (Uniform Crime Reports, October 22, 2001)
*Includes nonnegligent manslaughter.
**Not available.

Murders with Firearms in 2000

National Total = 8,493 Murders*

ALPHA ORDER

RANK	STATE	MURDERS	% of USA
17	Alabama	150	1.8%
40	Alaska	10	0.1%
12	Arizona	253	3.0%
24	Arkansas	105	1.2%
1	California	1,448	17.0%
27	Colorado	64	0.8%
29	Connecticut	62	0.7%
37	Delaware	12	0.1%
NA	Florida**	NA	NA
9	Georgia	340	4.0%
41	Hawaii	7	0.1%
39	Idaho	11	0.1%
6	Illinois*	411	4.8%
15	Indiana	206	2.4%
37	Iowa	12	0.1%
NA	Kansas**	NA	NA
31	Kentucky	47	0.6%
7	Louisiana	386	4.5%
42	Maine	6	0.1%
10	Maryland	296	3.5%
30	Massachusetts	56	0.7%
4	Michigan	474	5.6%
27	Minnesota	64	0.8%
20	Mississippi	111	1.3%
14	Missouri	227	2.7%
46	Montana	2	0.0%
35	Nebraska	18	0.2%
25	Nevada	89	1.0%
43	New Hampshire	5	0.1%
18	New Jersey	149	1.8%
26	New Mexico	67	0.8%
3	New York	563	6.6%
8	North Carolina	366	4.3%
48	North Dakota	0	0.0%
16	Ohio	181	2.1%
22	Oklahoma	108	1.3%
31	Oregon	47	0.6%
5	Pennsylvania	422	5.0%
33	Rhode Island	32	0.4%
19	South Carolina	130	1.5%
47	South Dakota	1	0.0%
11	Tennessee	283	3.3%
2	Texas	756	8.9%
36	Utah	15	0.2%
45	Vermont	4	0.0%
13	Virginia	251	3.0%
22	Washington	108	1.3%
34	West Virginia	23	0.3%
21	Wisconsin	110	1.3%
43	Wyoming	5	0.1%

RANK ORDER

RANK	STATE	MURDERS	% of USA
1	California	1,448	17.0%
2	Texas	756	8.9%
3	New York	563	6.6%
4	Michigan	474	5.6%
5	Pennsylvania	422	5.0%
6	Illinois*	411	4.8%
7	Louisiana	386	4.5%
8	North Carolina	366	4.3%
9	Georgia	340	4.0%
10	Maryland	296	3.5%
11	Tennessee	283	3.3%
12	Arizona	253	3.0%
13	Virginia	251	3.0%
14	Missouri	227	2.7%
15	Indiana	206	2.4%
16	Ohio	181	2.1%
17	Alabama	150	1.8%
18	New Jersey	149	1.8%
19	South Carolina	130	1.5%
20	Mississippi	111	1.3%
21	Wisconsin	110	1.3%
22	Oklahoma	108	1.3%
22	Washington	108	1.3%
24	Arkansas	105	1.2%
25	Nevada	89	1.0%
26	New Mexico	67	0.8%
27	Colorado	64	0.8%
27	Minnesota	64	0.8%
29	Connecticut	62	0.7%
30	Massachusetts	56	0.7%
31	Kentucky	47	0.6%
31	Oregon	47	0.6%
33	Rhode Island	32	0.4%
34	West Virginia	23	0.3%
35	Nebraska	18	0.2%
36	Utah	15	0.2%
37	Delaware	12	0.1%
37	Iowa	12	0.1%
39	Idaho	11	0.1%
40	Alaska	10	0.1%
41	Hawaii	7	0.1%
42	Maine	6	0.1%
43	New Hampshire	5	0.1%
43	Wyoming	5	0.1%
45	Vermont	4	0.0%
46	Montana	2	0.0%
47	South Dakota	1	0.0%
48	North Dakota	0	0.0%
NA	Florida**	NA	NA
NA	Kansas**	NA	NA
	District of Columbia**	NA	NA

Source: Federal Bureau of Investigation
    "Crime in the United States 2000" (Uniform Crime Reports, October 22, 2001)
*Of the 12,943 murders in 2000 for which supplemental data were received by the F.B.I. There were an additional 2,574 murders for which the type of murder weapon was not reported to the F.B.I. Includes nonnegligent manslaughter. Numbers are for reporting jurisdictions only. Illinois' figure is for Chicago only.
**Not available.

Murder Rate with Firearms in 2000

National Rate = 4.2 Murders per 100,000 Population*

ALPHA ORDER				RANK ORDER		
RANK	STATE	RATE		RANK	STATE	RATE
17	Alabama	4.6		1	Illinois*	14.3
32	Alaska	1.8		2	South Carolina	13.5
9	Arizona	5.4		3	Louisiana	10.0
19	Arkansas	4.3		4	Mississippi	8.5
19	California	4.3		5	New York	8.1
31	Colorado	1.9		6	Maryland	6.6
29	Connecticut	2.1		7	Virginia	6.4
26	Delaware	3.0		8	Georgia	5.6
NA	Florida**	NA		9	Arizona	5.4
8	Georgia	5.6		9	Kentucky	5.4
44	Hawaii	0.6		11	Michigan	5.3
40	Idaho	0.9		11	North Carolina	5.3
1	Illinois*	14.3		11	Tennessee	5.3
15	Indiana	5.0		14	Missouri	5.2
45	Iowa	0.5		15	Indiana	5.0
NA	Kansas**	NA		16	New Mexico	4.9
9	Kentucky	5.4		17	Alabama	4.6
3	Louisiana	10.0		18	Nevada	4.5
45	Maine	0.5		19	Arkansas	4.3
6	Maryland	6.6		19	California	4.3
37	Massachusetts	1.0		19	Pennsylvania	4.3
11	Michigan	5.3		22	West Virginia	3.8
35	Minnesota	1.4		23	Texas	3.7
4	Mississippi	8.5		24	Oklahoma	3.1
14	Missouri	5.2		24	Rhode Island	3.1
42	Montana	0.7		26	Delaware	3.0
36	Nebraska	1.2		27	Ohio	2.8
18	Nevada	4.5		28	Wisconsin	2.5
42	New Hampshire	0.7		29	Connecticut	2.1
32	New Jersey	1.8		30	Washington	2.0
16	New Mexico	4.9		31	Colorado	1.9
5	New York	8.1		32	Alaska	1.8
11	North Carolina	5.3		32	New Jersey	1.8
48	North Dakota	0.0		34	Oregon	1.5
27	Ohio	2.8		35	Minnesota	1.4
24	Oklahoma	3.1		36	Nebraska	1.2
34	Oregon	1.5		37	Massachusetts	1.0
19	Pennsylvania	4.3		37	Utah	1.0
24	Rhode Island	3.1		37	Wyoming	1.0
2	South Carolina	13.5		40	Idaho	0.9
47	South Dakota	0.2		41	Vermont	0.8
11	Tennessee	5.3		42	Montana	0.7
23	Texas	3.7		42	New Hampshire	0.7
37	Utah	1.0		44	Hawaii	0.6
41	Vermont	0.8		45	Iowa	0.5
7	Virginia	6.4		45	Maine	0.5
30	Washington	2.0		47	South Dakota	0.2
22	West Virginia	3.8		48	North Dakota	0.0
28	Wisconsin	2.5		NA	Florida**	NA
37	Wyoming	1.0		NA	Kansas**	NA
					District of Columbia**	NA

Source: Morgan Quitno Press using data from Federal Bureau of Investigation
  "Crime in the United States 2000" (Uniform Crime Reports, October 22, 2001)
*Of the 12,574 murders in 2000 for which supplemental data were received by the F.B.I. There were an additional
2,574 murders for which the type of murder weapon was not reported to the F.B.I. Includes nonnegligent
manslaughter. National and state rates based on population for reporting jurisdictions only. Illinois' rate is for
Chicago only. **Not available.

Percent of Murders Involving Firearms in 2000

National Percent = 65.6% of Murders*

ALPHA ORDER				RANK ORDER		
RANK	**STATE**	**PERCENT**		**RANK**	**STATE**	**PERCENT**
24	Alabama	64.4		1	Nebraska	75.0
39	Alaska	45.5		2	Louisiana	73.7
4	Arizona	71.5		3	Pennsylvania	73.3
17	Arkansas	68.2		4	Arizona	71.5
9	California	69.6		5	Rhode Island	71.1
33	Colorado	53.3		6	Maryland	71.0
23	Connecticut	65.3		6	Michigan	71.0
36	Delaware	50.0		8	Georgia	70.4
NA	Florida**	NA		9	California	69.6
8	Georgia	70.4		10	Missouri	69.4
46	Hawaii	21.2		11	Kentucky	69.1
14	Idaho	68.8		11	Oregon	69.1
21	Illinois*	65.8		13	Nevada	69.0
17	Indiana	68.2		14	Idaho	68.8
45	Iowa	29.3		15	Tennessee	68.7
NA	Kansas**	NA		16	Wisconsin	68.3
11	Kentucky	69.1		17	Arkansas	68.2
2	Louisiana	73.7		17	Indiana	68.2
41	Maine	40.0		19	Virginia	67.1
6	Maryland	71.0		20	North Carolina	67.0
38	Massachusetts	47.9		21	Illinois*	65.8
6	Michigan	71.0		22	Mississippi	65.7
29	Minnesota	59.3		23	Connecticut	65.3
22	Mississippi	65.7		24	Alabama	64.4
10	Missouri	69.4		24	South Carolina	64.4
36	Montana	50.0		26	Texas	61.4
1	Nebraska	75.0		27	New York	60.8
13	Nevada	69.0		28	Oklahoma	59.7
44	New Hampshire	35.7		29	Minnesota	59.3
35	New Jersey	51.6		30	West Virginia	59.0
31	New Mexico	57.3		31	New Mexico	57.3
27	New York	60.8		32	Washington	56.5
20	North Carolina	67.0		33	Colorado	53.3
48	North Dakota	0.0		34	Ohio	52.5
34	Ohio	52.5		35	New Jersey	51.6
28	Oklahoma	59.7		36	Delaware	50.0
11	Oregon	69.1		36	Montana	50.0
3	Pennsylvania	73.3		38	Massachusetts	47.9
5	Rhode Island	71.1		39	Alaska	45.5
24	South Carolina	64.4		40	Wyoming	41.7
47	South Dakota	16.7		41	Maine	40.0
15	Tennessee	68.7		41	Vermont	40.0
26	Texas	61.4		43	Utah	36.6
43	Utah	36.6		44	New Hampshire	35.7
41	Vermont	40.0		45	Iowa	29.3
19	Virginia	67.1		46	Hawaii	21.2
32	Washington	56.5		47	South Dakota	16.7
30	West Virginia	59.0		48	North Dakota	0.0
16	Wisconsin	68.3		NA	Florida**	NA
40	Wyoming	41.7		NA	Kansas**	NA
					District of Columbia**	NA

Source: Morgan Quitno Press using data from Federal Bureau of Investigation
    "Crime in the United States 2000" (Uniform Crime Reports, October 22, 2001)
*Of the 12,943 murders in 2000 for which supplemental data were received by the F.B.I. There were an additional 2,574 murders for which the type of murder weapon was not reported to the F.B.I. Murder includes nonnegligent manslaughter. Illinois' percentage is for Chicago only.
**Not available.

Murders with Handguns in 2000

National Total = 6,686 Murders*

RANK	STATE	MURDERS	% of USA
17	Alabama	129	1.9%
39	Alaska	7	0.1%
11	Arizona	221	3.3%
25	Arkansas	67	1.0%
1	California	1,247	18.7%
29	Colorado	44	0.7%
28	Connecticut	49	0.7%
37	Delaware	10	0.1%
NA	Florida**	NA	NA
7	Georgia	294	4.4%
42	Hawaii	4	0.1%
38	Idaho	8	0.1%
5	Illinois*	348	5.2%
13	Indiana	152	2.3%
39	Iowa	7	0.1%
NA	Kansas**	NA	NA
31	Kentucky	35	0.5%
6	Louisiana	329	4.9%
42	Maine	4	0.1%
8	Maryland	282	4.2%
30	Massachusetts	40	0.6%
10	Michigan	231	3.5%
27	Minnesota	51	0.8%
21	Mississippi	86	1.3%
14	Missouri	148	2.2%
46	Montana	2	0.0%
35	Nebraska	11	0.2%
24	Nevada	70	1.0%
44	New Hampshire	3	0.0%
16	New Jersey	133	2.0%
26	New Mexico	58	0.9%
3	New York	522	7.8%
9	North Carolina	279	4.2%
47	North Dakota	0	0.0%
15	Ohio	143	2.1%
23	Oklahoma	76	1.1%
32	Oregon	34	0.5%
4	Pennsylvania	400	6.0%
33	Rhode Island	28	0.4%
19	South Carolina	96	1.4%
47	South Dakota	0	0.0%
12	Tennessee	176	2.6%
2	Texas	539	8.1%
35	Utah	11	0.2%
44	Vermont	3	0.0%
18	Virginia	119	1.8%
22	Washington	77	1.2%
34	West Virginia	13	0.2%
20	Wisconsin	95	1.4%
41	Wyoming	5	0.1%

RANK	STATE	MURDERS	% of USA
1	California	1,247	18.7%
2	Texas	539	8.1%
3	New York	522	7.8%
4	Pennsylvania	400	6.0%
5	Illinois*	348	5.2%
6	Louisiana	329	4.9%
7	Georgia	294	4.4%
8	Maryland	282	4.2%
9	North Carolina	279	4.2%
10	Michigan	231	3.5%
11	Arizona	221	3.3%
12	Tennessee	176	2.6%
13	Indiana	152	2.3%
14	Missouri	148	2.2%
15	Ohio	143	2.1%
16	New Jersey	133	2.0%
17	Alabama	129	1.9%
18	Virginia	119	1.8%
19	South Carolina	96	1.4%
20	Wisconsin	95	1.4%
21	Mississippi	86	1.3%
22	Washington	77	1.2%
23	Oklahoma	76	1.1%
24	Nevada	70	1.0%
25	Arkansas	67	1.0%
26	New Mexico	58	0.9%
27	Minnesota	51	0.8%
28	Connecticut	49	0.7%
29	Colorado	44	0.7%
30	Massachusetts	40	0.6%
31	Kentucky	35	0.5%
32	Oregon	34	0.5%
33	Rhode Island	28	0.4%
34	West Virginia	13	0.2%
35	Nebraska	11	0.2%
35	Utah	11	0.2%
37	Delaware	10	0.1%
38	Idaho	8	0.1%
39	Alaska	7	0.1%
39	Iowa	7	0.1%
41	Wyoming	5	0.1%
42	Hawaii	4	0.1%
42	Maine	4	0.1%
44	New Hampshire	3	0.0%
44	Vermont	3	0.0%
46	Montana	2	0.0%
47	North Dakota	0	0.0%
47	South Dakota	0	0.0%
NA	Florida**	NA	NA
NA	Kansas**	NA	NA
	District of Columbia**	NA	NA

Source: Federal Bureau of Investigation
   "Crime in the United States 2000" (Uniform Crime Reports, October 22, 2001)
*Of the 12,943 murders in 2000 for which supplemental data were received by the F.B.I. There were an additional 2,574 murders for which the type of murder weapon was not reported to the F.B.I. There were also 943 murders that were reported as murders by "firearms, type unknown." Murder includes nonnegligent manslaughter. Numbers are for reporting jurisdictions only. Illinois' figure is for Chicago only. **Not available.

Murder Rate with Handguns in 2000

National Rate = 3.3 Murders per 100,000 Population*

ALPHA ORDER

RANK	STATE	RATE
11	Alabama	4.0
33	Alaska	1.2
8	Arizona	4.7
20	Arkansas	2.7
14	California	3.7
32	Colorado	1.3
29	Connecticut	1.6
24	Delaware	2.5
NA	Florida**	NA
7	Georgia	4.8
44	Hawaii	0.3
41	Idaho	0.6
1	Illinois*	12.1
14	Indiana	3.7
44	Iowa	0.3
NA	Kansas**	NA
10	Kentucky	4.1
3	Louisiana	8.5
44	Maine	0.3
6	Maryland	6.3
37	Massachusetts	0.7
22	Michigan	2.6
34	Minnesota	1.1
5	Mississippi	6.6
17	Missouri	3.4
37	Montana	0.7
37	Nebraska	0.7
16	Nevada	3.5
43	New Hampshire	0.4
29	New Jersey	1.6
9	New Mexico	4.2
4	New York	7.5
11	North Carolina	4.0
47	North Dakota	0.0
25	Ohio	2.2
25	Oklahoma	2.2
34	Oregon	1.1
11	Pennsylvania	4.0
20	Rhode Island	2.7
2	South Carolina	10.0
47	South Dakota	0.0
18	Tennessee	3.3
22	Texas	2.6
37	Utah	0.7
41	Vermont	0.6
19	Virginia	3.0
31	Washington	1.4
28	West Virginia	2.1
25	Wisconsin	2.2
36	Wyoming	1.0

RANK ORDER

RANK	STATE	RATE
1	Illinois*	12.1
2	South Carolina	10.0
3	Louisiana	8.5
4	New York	7.5
5	Mississippi	6.6
6	Maryland	6.3
7	Georgia	4.8
8	Arizona	4.7
9	New Mexico	4.2
10	Kentucky	4.1
11	Alabama	4.0
11	North Carolina	4.0
11	Pennsylvania	4.0
14	California	3.7
14	Indiana	3.7
16	Nevada	3.5
17	Missouri	3.4
18	Tennessee	3.3
19	Virginia	3.0
20	Arkansas	2.7
20	Rhode Island	2.7
22	Michigan	2.6
22	Texas	2.6
24	Delaware	2.5
25	Ohio	2.2
25	Oklahoma	2.2
25	Wisconsin	2.2
28	West Virginia	2.1
29	Connecticut	1.6
29	New Jersey	1.6
31	Washington	1.4
32	Colorado	1.3
33	Alaska	1.2
34	Minnesota	1.1
34	Oregon	1.1
36	Wyoming	1.0
37	Massachusetts	0.7
37	Montana	0.7
37	Nebraska	0.7
37	Utah	0.7
41	Idaho	0.6
41	Vermont	0.6
43	New Hampshire	0.4
44	Hawaii	0.3
44	Iowa	0.3
44	Maine	0.3
47	North Dakota	0.0
47	South Dakota	0.0
NA	Florida**	NA
NA	Kansas**	NA
	District of Columbia**	NA

Source: Morgan Quitno Press using data from Federal Bureau of Investigation
"Crime in the United States 2000" (Uniform Crime Reports, October 22, 2001)
*Of the 12,943 murders in 2000 for which supplemental data were received by the F.B.I. There were an additional 2,574 murders for which the type of murder weapon was not reported to the F.B.I. There were also 943 murders that were reported as murders by "firearms, type unknown." Murder includes nonnegligent manslaughter. Numbers are for reporting jurisdictions only. Illinois' figure is for Chicago only. **Not available.

334

Percent of Murders Involving Handguns in 2000

National Percent = 51.7% of Murders*

<table>
<tr><td colspan="3">ALPHA ORDER</td><td colspan="3">RANK ORDER</td></tr>
<tr><td>RANK</td><td>STATE</td><td>PERCENT</td><td>RANK</td><td>STATE</td><td>PERCENT</td></tr>
<tr><td>11</td><td>Alabama</td><td>55.4</td><td>1</td><td>Pennsylvania</td><td>69.4</td></tr>
<tr><td>39</td><td>Alaska</td><td>31.8</td><td>2</td><td>Maryland</td><td>67.6</td></tr>
<tr><td>4</td><td>Arizona</td><td>62.4</td><td>3</td><td>Louisiana</td><td>62.8</td></tr>
<tr><td>28</td><td>Arkansas</td><td>43.5</td><td>4</td><td>Arizona</td><td>62.4</td></tr>
<tr><td>7</td><td>California</td><td>59.9</td><td>5</td><td>Rhode Island</td><td>62.2</td></tr>
<tr><td>35</td><td>Colorado</td><td>36.7</td><td>6</td><td>Georgia</td><td>60.9</td></tr>
<tr><td>13</td><td>Connecticut</td><td>51.6</td><td>7</td><td>California</td><td>59.9</td></tr>
<tr><td>31</td><td>Delaware</td><td>41.7</td><td>8</td><td>Wisconsin</td><td>59.0</td></tr>
<tr><td>NA</td><td>Florida**</td><td>NA</td><td>9</td><td>New York</td><td>56.4</td></tr>
<tr><td>6</td><td>Georgia</td><td>60.9</td><td>10</td><td>Illinois*</td><td>55.7</td></tr>
<tr><td>46</td><td>Hawaii</td><td>12.1</td><td>11</td><td>Alabama</td><td>55.4</td></tr>
<tr><td>18</td><td>Idaho</td><td>50.0</td><td>12</td><td>Nevada</td><td>54.3</td></tr>
<tr><td>10</td><td>Illinois*</td><td>55.7</td><td>13</td><td>Connecticut</td><td>51.6</td></tr>
<tr><td>17</td><td>Indiana</td><td>50.3</td><td>14</td><td>Kentucky</td><td>51.5</td></tr>
<tr><td>45</td><td>Iowa</td><td>17.1</td><td>15</td><td>North Carolina</td><td>51.1</td></tr>
<tr><td>NA</td><td>Kansas**</td><td>NA</td><td>16</td><td>Mississippi</td><td>50.9</td></tr>
<tr><td>14</td><td>Kentucky</td><td>51.5</td><td>17</td><td>Indiana</td><td>50.3</td></tr>
<tr><td>3</td><td>Louisiana</td><td>62.8</td><td>18</td><td>Idaho</td><td>50.0</td></tr>
<tr><td>43</td><td>Maine</td><td>26.7</td><td>18</td><td>Montana</td><td>50.0</td></tr>
<tr><td>2</td><td>Maryland</td><td>67.6</td><td>18</td><td>Oregon</td><td>50.0</td></tr>
<tr><td>37</td><td>Massachusetts</td><td>34.2</td><td>21</td><td>New Mexico</td><td>49.6</td></tr>
<tr><td>36</td><td>Michigan</td><td>34.6</td><td>22</td><td>South Carolina</td><td>47.5</td></tr>
<tr><td>23</td><td>Minnesota</td><td>47.2</td><td>23</td><td>Minnesota</td><td>47.2</td></tr>
<tr><td>16</td><td>Mississippi</td><td>50.9</td><td>24</td><td>New Jersey</td><td>46.0</td></tr>
<tr><td>26</td><td>Missouri</td><td>45.3</td><td>25</td><td>Nebraska</td><td>45.8</td></tr>
<tr><td>18</td><td>Montana</td><td>50.0</td><td>26</td><td>Missouri</td><td>45.3</td></tr>
<tr><td>25</td><td>Nebraska</td><td>45.8</td><td>27</td><td>Texas</td><td>43.8</td></tr>
<tr><td>12</td><td>Nevada</td><td>54.3</td><td>28</td><td>Arkansas</td><td>43.5</td></tr>
<tr><td>44</td><td>New Hampshire</td><td>21.4</td><td>29</td><td>Tennessee</td><td>42.7</td></tr>
<tr><td>24</td><td>New Jersey</td><td>46.0</td><td>30</td><td>Oklahoma</td><td>42.0</td></tr>
<tr><td>21</td><td>New Mexico</td><td>49.6</td><td>31</td><td>Delaware</td><td>41.7</td></tr>
<tr><td>9</td><td>New York</td><td>56.4</td><td>31</td><td>Wyoming</td><td>41.7</td></tr>
<tr><td>15</td><td>North Carolina</td><td>51.1</td><td>33</td><td>Ohio</td><td>41.4</td></tr>
<tr><td>47</td><td>North Dakota</td><td>0.0</td><td>34</td><td>Washington</td><td>40.3</td></tr>
<tr><td>33</td><td>Ohio</td><td>41.4</td><td>35</td><td>Colorado</td><td>36.7</td></tr>
<tr><td>30</td><td>Oklahoma</td><td>42.0</td><td>36</td><td>Michigan</td><td>34.6</td></tr>
<tr><td>18</td><td>Oregon</td><td>50.0</td><td>37</td><td>Massachusetts</td><td>34.2</td></tr>
<tr><td>1</td><td>Pennsylvania</td><td>69.4</td><td>38</td><td>West Virginia</td><td>33.3</td></tr>
<tr><td>5</td><td>Rhode Island</td><td>62.2</td><td>39</td><td>Alaska</td><td>31.8</td></tr>
<tr><td>22</td><td>South Carolina</td><td>47.5</td><td>39</td><td>Virginia</td><td>31.8</td></tr>
<tr><td>47</td><td>South Dakota</td><td>0.0</td><td>41</td><td>Vermont</td><td>30.0</td></tr>
<tr><td>29</td><td>Tennessee</td><td>42.7</td><td>42</td><td>Utah</td><td>26.8</td></tr>
<tr><td>27</td><td>Texas</td><td>43.8</td><td>43</td><td>Maine</td><td>26.7</td></tr>
<tr><td>42</td><td>Utah</td><td>26.8</td><td>44</td><td>New Hampshire</td><td>21.4</td></tr>
<tr><td>41</td><td>Vermont</td><td>30.0</td><td>45</td><td>Iowa</td><td>17.1</td></tr>
<tr><td>39</td><td>Virginia</td><td>31.8</td><td>46</td><td>Hawaii</td><td>12.1</td></tr>
<tr><td>34</td><td>Washington</td><td>40.3</td><td>47</td><td>North Dakota</td><td>0.0</td></tr>
<tr><td>38</td><td>West Virginia</td><td>33.3</td><td>47</td><td>South Dakota</td><td>0.0</td></tr>
<tr><td>8</td><td>Wisconsin</td><td>59.0</td><td>NA</td><td>Florida**</td><td>NA</td></tr>
<tr><td>31</td><td>Wyoming</td><td>41.7</td><td>NA</td><td>Kansas**</td><td>NA</td></tr>
<tr><td></td><td></td><td></td><td></td><td>District of Columbia**</td><td>NA</td></tr>
</table>

Source: Morgan Quitno Press using data from Federal Bureau of Investigation
   "Crime in the United States 2000" (Uniform Crime Reports, October 22, 2001)
*Of the 12,943 murders in 2000 for which supplemental data were received by the F.B.I. There were an additional
2,574 murders for which the type of murder weapon was not reported to the F.B.I. There were also 943 murders that
were reported as murders by "firearms, type unknown." Murder includes nonnegligent manslaughter. Numbers are
for reporting jurisdictions only. Illinois' figure is for Chicago only. **Not available.

Murders with Rifles in 2000

National Total = 396 Murders*

ALPHA ORDER					RANK ORDER			
RANK	STATE	MURDERS	% of USA		RANK	STATE	MURDERS	% of USA
16	Alabama	8	2.0%		1	California	66	16.7%
29	Alaska	3	0.8%		2	Texas	47	11.9%
10	Arizona	13	3.3%		3	Louisiana	24	6.1%
21	Arkansas	5	1.3%		4	North Carolina	23	5.8%
1	California	66	16.7%		5	Michigan	18	4.5%
16	Colorado	8	2.0%		6	Oklahoma	17	4.3%
24	Connecticut	4	1.0%		7	Tennessee	16	4.0%
39	Delaware	0	0.0%		8	Mississippi	14	3.5%
NA	Florida**	NA	NA		8	Virginia	14	3.5%
14	Georgia	10	2.5%		10	Arizona	13	3.3%
39	Hawaii	0	0.0%		10	New York	13	3.3%
39	Idaho	0	0.0%		12	Washington	12	3.0%
32	Illinois*	2	0.5%		13	Pennsylvania	11	2.8%
29	Indiana	3	0.8%		14	Georgia	10	2.5%
32	Iowa	2	0.5%		15	Missouri	9	2.3%
NA	Kansas**	NA	NA		16	Alabama	8	2.0%
39	Kentucky	0	0.0%		16	Colorado	8	2.0%
3	Louisiana	24	6.1%		18	Ohio	7	1.8%
34	Maine	1	0.3%		18	Wisconsin	7	1.8%
34	Maryland	1	0.3%		20	South Carolina	6	1.5%
34	Massachusetts	1	0.3%		21	Arkansas	5	1.3%
5	Michigan	18	4.5%		21	Nevada	5	1.3%
24	Minnesota	4	1.0%		21	New Jersey	5	1.3%
8	Mississippi	14	3.5%		24	Connecticut	4	1.0%
15	Missouri	9	2.3%		24	Minnesota	4	1.0%
39	Montana	0	0.0%		24	Nebraska	4	1.0%
24	Nebraska	4	1.0%		24	New Mexico	4	1.0%
21	Nevada	5	1.3%		24	Oregon	4	1.0%
34	New Hampshire	1	0.3%		29	Alaska	3	0.8%
21	New Jersey	5	1.3%		29	Indiana	3	0.8%
24	New Mexico	4	1.0%		29	West Virginia	3	0.8%
10	New York	13	3.3%		32	Illinois*	2	0.5%
4	North Carolina	23	5.8%		32	Iowa	2	0.5%
39	North Dakota	0	0.0%		34	Maine	1	0.3%
18	Ohio	7	1.8%		34	Maryland	1	0.3%
6	Oklahoma	17	4.3%		34	Massachusetts	1	0.3%
24	Oregon	4	1.0%		34	New Hampshire	1	0.3%
13	Pennsylvania	11	2.8%		34	Vermont	1	0.3%
39	Rhode Island	0	0.0%		39	Delaware	0	0.0%
20	South Carolina	6	1.5%		39	Hawaii	0	0.0%
39	South Dakota	0	0.0%		39	Idaho	0	0.0%
7	Tennessee	16	4.0%		39	Kentucky	0	0.0%
2	Texas	47	11.9%		39	Montana	0	0.0%
39	Utah	0	0.0%		39	North Dakota	0	0.0%
34	Vermont	1	0.3%		39	Rhode Island	0	0.0%
8	Virginia	14	3.5%		39	South Dakota	0	0.0%
12	Washington	12	3.0%		39	Utah	0	0.0%
29	West Virginia	3	0.8%		39	Wyoming	0	0.0%
18	Wisconsin	7	1.8%		NA	Florida**	NA	NA
39	Wyoming	0	0.0%		NA	Kansas**	NA	NA
						District of Columbia**	NA	NA

Source: Federal Bureau of Investigation
   "Crime in the United States 2000" (Uniform Crime Reports, October 22, 2001)
*Of the 12,943 murders in 2000 for which supplemental data were received by the F.B.I. There were an additional 2,574 murders for which the type of murder weapon was not reported to the F.B.I. There were also 943 murders that were reported as murders by "firearms, type unknown." Murder includes nonnegligent manslaughter. Numbers are for reporting jurisdictions only. Illinois' figure is for Chicago only. **Not available.

Percent of Murders Involving Rifles in 2000

National Percent = 3.1% of Murders*

RANK	STATE	PERCENT
23	Alabama	3.4
2	Alaska	13.6
20	Arizona	3.7
25	Arkansas	3.2
25	California	3.2
8	Colorado	6.7
15	Connecticut	4.2
39	Delaware	0.0
NA	Florida**	NA
30	Georgia	2.1
39	Hawaii	0.0
39	Idaho	0.0
37	Illinois*	0.3
35	Indiana	1.0
12	Iowa	4.9
NA	Kansas**	NA
39	Kentucky	0.0
13	Louisiana	4.6
8	Maine	6.7
38	Maryland	0.2
36	Massachusetts	0.9
29	Michigan	2.7
20	Minnesota	3.7
5	Mississippi	8.3
28	Missouri	2.8
39	Montana	0.0
1	Nebraska	16.7
17	Nevada	3.9
7	New Hampshire	7.1
33	New Jersey	1.7
23	New Mexico	3.4
34	New York	1.4
15	North Carolina	4.2
39	North Dakota	0.0
31	Ohio	2.0
4	Oklahoma	9.4
11	Oregon	5.9
32	Pennsylvania	1.9
39	Rhode Island	0.0
27	South Carolina	3.0
39	South Dakota	0.0
17	Tennessee	3.9
19	Texas	3.8
39	Utah	0.0
3	Vermont	10.0
20	Virginia	3.7
10	Washington	6.3
6	West Virginia	7.7
14	Wisconsin	4.3
39	Wyoming	0.0

RANK	STATE	PERCENT
1	Nebraska	16.7
2	Alaska	13.6
3	Vermont	10.0
4	Oklahoma	9.4
5	Mississippi	8.3
6	West Virginia	7.7
7	New Hampshire	7.1
8	Colorado	6.7
8	Maine	6.7
10	Washington	6.3
11	Oregon	5.9
12	Iowa	4.9
13	Louisiana	4.6
14	Wisconsin	4.3
15	Connecticut	4.2
15	North Carolina	4.2
17	Nevada	3.9
17	Tennessee	3.9
19	Texas	3.8
20	Arizona	3.7
20	Minnesota	3.7
20	Virginia	3.7
23	Alabama	3.4
23	New Mexico	3.4
25	Arkansas	3.2
25	California	3.2
27	South Carolina	3.0
28	Missouri	2.8
29	Michigan	2.7
30	Georgia	2.1
31	Ohio	2.0
32	Pennsylvania	1.9
33	New Jersey	1.7
34	New York	1.4
35	Indiana	1.0
36	Massachusetts	0.9
37	Illinois*	0.3
38	Maryland	0.2
39	Delaware	0.0
39	Hawaii	0.0
39	Idaho	0.0
39	Kentucky	0.0
39	Montana	0.0
39	North Dakota	0.0
39	Rhode Island	0.0
39	South Dakota	0.0
39	Utah	0.0
39	Wyoming	0.0
NA	Florida**	NA
NA	Kansas**	NA
	District of Columbia**	NA

Source: Morgan Quitno Press using data from Federal Bureau of Investigation
   "Crime in the United States 2000" (Uniform Crime Reports, October 22, 2001)
*Of the 12,943 murders in 2000 for which supplemental data were received by the F.B.I. There were an additional
2,574 murders for which the type of murder weapon was not reported to the F.B.I. There were also 943 murders that
were reported as murders by "firearms, type unknown." Murder includes nonnegligent manslaughter. Numbers are
for reporting jurisdictions only. Illinois' figure is for Chicago only. **Not available.

Murders with Shotguns in 2000

National Total = 468 Murders*

	ALPHA ORDER				RANK ORDER		
RANK	STATE	MURDERS	% of USA	RANK	STATE	MURDERS	% of USA
12	Alabama	13	2.8%	1	Texas	65	13.9%
42	Alaska	0	0.0%	2	California	57	12.2%
15	Arizona	11	2.4%	3	North Carolina	33	7.1%
9	Arkansas	17	3.6%	4	New York	25	5.3%
2	California	57	12.2%	5	Georgia	24	5.1%
29	Colorado	2	0.4%	5	Michigan	24	5.1%
37	Connecticut	1	0.2%	5	Tennessee	24	5.1%
29	Delaware	2	0.4%	8	Louisiana	19	4.1%
NA	Florida**	NA	NA	9	Arkansas	17	3.6%
5	Georgia	24	5.1%	10	Virginia	16	3.4%
27	Hawaii	3	0.6%	11	Washington	14	3.0%
29	Idaho	2	0.4%	12	Alabama	13	2.8%
19	Illinois*	7	1.5%	12	Ohio	13	2.8%
23	Indiana	5	1.1%	14	South Carolina	12	2.6%
37	Iowa	1	0.2%	15	Arizona	11	2.4%
NA	Kansas**	NA	NA	15	Oklahoma	11	2.4%
27	Kentucky	3	0.6%	17	Missouri	10	2.1%
8	Louisiana	19	4.1%	18	Mississippi	8	1.7%
37	Maine	1	0.2%	19	Illinois*	7	1.5%
23	Maryland	5	1.1%	19	Minnesota	7	1.5%
29	Massachusetts	2	0.4%	21	Nevada	6	1.3%
5	Michigan	24	5.1%	21	New Jersey	6	1.3%
19	Minnesota	7	1.5%	23	Indiana	5	1.1%
18	Mississippi	8	1.7%	23	Maryland	5	1.1%
17	Missouri	10	2.1%	23	Pennsylvania	5	1.1%
42	Montana	0	0.0%	26	Wisconsin	4	0.9%
29	Nebraska	2	0.4%	27	Hawaii	3	0.6%
21	Nevada	6	1.3%	27	Kentucky	3	0.6%
37	New Hampshire	1	0.2%	29	Colorado	2	0.4%
21	New Jersey	6	1.3%	29	Delaware	2	0.4%
37	New Mexico	1	0.2%	29	Idaho	2	0.4%
4	New York	25	5.3%	29	Massachusetts	2	0.4%
3	North Carolina	33	7.1%	29	Nebraska	2	0.4%
42	North Dakota	0	0.0%	29	Oregon	2	0.4%
12	Ohio	13	2.8%	29	Utah	2	0.4%
15	Oklahoma	11	2.4%	29	West Virginia	2	0.4%
29	Oregon	2	0.4%	37	Connecticut	1	0.2%
23	Pennsylvania	5	1.1%	37	Iowa	1	0.2%
42	Rhode Island	0	0.0%	37	Maine	1	0.2%
14	South Carolina	12	2.6%	37	New Hampshire	1	0.2%
42	South Dakota	0	0.0%	37	New Mexico	1	0.2%
5	Tennessee	24	5.1%	42	Alaska	0	0.0%
1	Texas	65	13.9%	42	Montana	0	0.0%
29	Utah	2	0.4%	42	North Dakota	0	0.0%
42	Vermont	0	0.0%	42	Rhode Island	0	0.0%
10	Virginia	16	3.4%	42	South Dakota	0	0.0%
11	Washington	14	3.0%	42	Vermont	0	0.0%
29	West Virginia	2	0.4%	42	Wyoming	0	0.0%
26	Wisconsin	4	0.9%	NA	Florida**	NA	NA
42	Wyoming	0	0.0%	NA	Kansas**	NA	NA
					District of Columbia**	NA	NA

Source: Federal Bureau of Investigation
"Crime in the United States 2000" (Uniform Crime Reports, October 22, 2001)
*Of the 12,943 murders in 2000 for which supplemental data were received by the F.B.I. There were an additional 2,574 murders for which the type of murder weapon was not reported to the F.B.I. There were also 943 murders that were reported as murders by "firearms, type unknown." Murder includes nonnegligent manslaughter. Numbers are for reporting jurisdictions only. Illinois' figure is for Chicago only. **Not available.

Percent of Murders Involving Shotguns in 2000

National Percent = 3.6% of Murders*

ALPHA ORDER				RANK ORDER		
RANK	STATE	PERCENT		RANK	STATE	PERCENT
14	Alabama	5.6		1	Idaho	12.5
42	Alaska	0.0		2	Arkansas	11.0
26	Arizona	3.1		3	Hawaii	9.1
2	Arkansas	11.0		4	Delaware	8.3
29	California	2.7		4	Nebraska	8.3
34	Colorado	1.7		6	Washington	7.3
38	Connecticut	1.1		7	New Hampshire	7.1
4	Delaware	8.3		8	Maine	6.7
NA	Florida**	NA		9	Minnesota	6.5
17	Georgia	5.0		10	Oklahoma	6.1
3	Hawaii	9.1		11	North Carolina	6.0
1	Idaho	12.5		12	South Carolina	5.9
38	Illinois*	1.1		13	Tennessee	5.8
34	Indiana	1.7		14	Alabama	5.6
32	Iowa	2.4		15	Texas	5.3
NA	Kansas**	NA		16	West Virginia	5.1
21	Kentucky	4.4		17	Georgia	5.0
24	Louisiana	3.6		18	Utah	4.9
8	Maine	6.7		19	Mississippi	4.7
37	Maryland	1.2		19	Nevada	4.7
34	Massachusetts	1.7		21	Kentucky	4.4
24	Michigan	3.6		22	Virginia	4.3
9	Minnesota	6.5		23	Ohio	3.8
19	Mississippi	4.7		24	Louisiana	3.6
26	Missouri	3.1		24	Michigan	3.6
42	Montana	0.0		26	Arizona	3.1
4	Nebraska	8.3		26	Missouri	3.1
19	Nevada	4.7		28	Oregon	2.9
7	New Hampshire	7.1		29	California	2.7
33	New Jersey	2.1		29	New York	2.7
40	New Mexico	0.9		31	Wisconsin	2.5
29	New York	2.7		32	Iowa	2.4
11	North Carolina	6.0		33	New Jersey	2.1
42	North Dakota	0.0		34	Colorado	1.7
23	Ohio	3.8		34	Indiana	1.7
10	Oklahoma	6.1		34	Massachusetts	1.7
28	Oregon	2.9		37	Maryland	1.2
40	Pennsylvania	0.9		38	Connecticut	1.1
42	Rhode Island	0.0		38	Illinois*	1.1
12	South Carolina	5.9		40	New Mexico	0.9
42	South Dakota	0.0		40	Pennsylvania	0.9
13	Tennessee	5.8		42	Alaska	0.0
15	Texas	5.3		42	Montana	0.0
18	Utah	4.9		42	North Dakota	0.0
42	Vermont	0.0		42	Rhode Island	0.0
22	Virginia	4.3		42	South Dakota	0.0
6	Washington	7.3		42	Vermont	0.0
16	West Virginia	5.1		42	Wyoming	0.0
31	Wisconsin	2.5		NA	Florida**	NA
42	Wyoming	0.0		NA	Kansas**	NA
					District of Columbia**	NA

Source: Morgan Quitno Press using data from Federal Bureau of Investigation
   "Crime in the United States 2000" (Uniform Crime Reports, October 22, 2001)
*Of the 12,943 murders in 2000 for which supplemental data were received by the F.B.I. There were an additional 2,574 murders for which the type of murder weapon was not reported to the F.B.I. There were also 943 murders that were reported as murders by "firearms, type unknown." Murder includes nonnegligent manslaughter. Numbers are for reporting jurisdictions only. Illinois' figure is for Chicago only. **Not available.

Murders with Knives or Cutting Instruments in 2000

National Total = 1,743 Murders*

ALPHA ORDER

RANK	STATE	MURDERS	% of USA
18	Alabama	34	2.0%
42	Alaska	2	0.1%
13	Arizona	48	2.8%
25	Arkansas	23	1.3%
1	California	284	16.3%
24	Colorado	24	1.4%
29	Connecticut	16	0.9%
36	Delaware	6	0.3%
NA	Florida**	NA	NA
5	Georgia	58	3.3%
32	Hawaii	9	0.5%
39	Idaho	3	0.2%
9	Illinois*	54	3.1%
17	Indiana	36	2.1%
35	Iowa	7	0.4%
NA	Kansas**	NA	NA
32	Kentucky	9	0.5%
5	Louisiana	58	3.3%
42	Maine	2	0.1%
10	Maryland	51	2.9%
20	Massachusetts	31	1.8%
7	Michigan	56	3.2%
28	Minnesota	20	1.1%
26	Mississippi	22	1.3%
15	Missouri	40	2.3%
47	Montana	0	0.0%
38	Nebraska	4	0.2%
29	Nevada	16	0.9%
39	New Hampshire	3	0.2%
4	New Jersey	74	4.2%
23	New Mexico	25	1.4%
3	New York	164	9.4%
7	North Carolina	56	3.2%
45	North Dakota	1	0.1%
14	Ohio	46	2.6%
21	Oklahoma	30	1.7%
39	Oregon	3	0.2%
10	Pennsylvania	51	2.9%
34	Rhode Island	8	0.5%
22	South Carolina	27	1.5%
47	South Dakota	0	0.0%
12	Tennessee	49	2.8%
2	Texas	182	10.4%
31	Utah	11	0.6%
37	Vermont	5	0.3%
16	Virginia	39	2.2%
19	Washington	32	1.8%
42	West Virginia	2	0.1%
27	Wisconsin	21	1.2%
45	Wyoming	1	0.1%

RANK ORDER

RANK	STATE	MURDERS	% of USA
1	California	284	16.3%
2	Texas	182	10.4%
3	New York	164	9.4%
4	New Jersey	74	4.2%
5	Georgia	58	3.3%
5	Louisiana	58	3.3%
7	Michigan	56	3.2%
7	North Carolina	56	3.2%
9	Illinois*	54	3.1%
10	Maryland	51	2.9%
10	Pennsylvania	51	2.9%
12	Tennessee	49	2.8%
13	Arizona	48	2.8%
14	Ohio	46	2.6%
15	Missouri	40	2.3%
16	Virginia	39	2.2%
17	Indiana	36	2.1%
18	Alabama	34	2.0%
19	Washington	32	1.8%
20	Massachusetts	31	1.8%
21	Oklahoma	30	1.7%
22	South Carolina	27	1.5%
23	New Mexico	25	1.4%
24	Colorado	24	1.4%
25	Arkansas	23	1.3%
26	Mississippi	22	1.3%
27	Wisconsin	21	1.2%
28	Minnesota	20	1.1%
29	Connecticut	16	0.9%
29	Nevada	16	0.9%
31	Utah	11	0.6%
32	Hawaii	9	0.5%
32	Kentucky	9	0.5%
34	Rhode Island	8	0.5%
35	Iowa	7	0.4%
36	Delaware	6	0.3%
37	Vermont	5	0.3%
38	Nebraska	4	0.2%
39	Idaho	3	0.2%
39	New Hampshire	3	0.2%
39	Oregon	3	0.2%
42	Alaska	2	0.1%
42	Maine	2	0.1%
42	West Virginia	2	0.1%
45	North Dakota	1	0.1%
45	Wyoming	1	0.1%
47	Montana	0	0.0%
47	South Dakota	0	0.0%
NA	Florida**	NA	NA
NA	Kansas**	NA	NA
	District of Columbia**	NA	NA

Source: Federal Bureau of Investigation
    "Crime in the United States 2000" (Uniform Crime Reports, October 22, 2001)
*Of the 12,943 murders in 2000 for which supplemental data were received by the F.B.I. There were an additional
2,574 murders for which the type of murder weapon was not reported to the F.B.I. Includes nonnegligent
manslaughter. Numbers are for reporting jurisdictions only. Illinois' figure is for Chicago only.
**Not available.

Percent of Murders Involving Knives or Cutting Instruments in 2000

National Percent = 13.5% of Murders*

<table>
<tr><td colspan="3">ALPHA ORDER</td><td colspan="3">RANK ORDER</td></tr>
<tr><th>RANK</th><th>STATE</th><th>PERCENT</th><th>RANK</th><th>STATE</th><th>PERCENT</th></tr>
<tr><td>22</td><td>Alabama</td><td>14.6</td><td>1</td><td>Vermont</td><td>50.0</td></tr>
<tr><td>40</td><td>Alaska</td><td>9.1</td><td>2</td><td>North Dakota</td><td>33.3</td></tr>
<tr><td>23</td><td>Arizona</td><td>13.6</td><td>3</td><td>Hawaii</td><td>27.3</td></tr>
<tr><td>20</td><td>Arkansas</td><td>14.9</td><td>4</td><td>Utah</td><td>26.8</td></tr>
<tr><td>23</td><td>California</td><td>13.6</td><td>5</td><td>Massachusetts</td><td>26.5</td></tr>
<tr><td>10</td><td>Colorado</td><td>20.0</td><td>6</td><td>New Jersey</td><td>25.6</td></tr>
<tr><td>16</td><td>Connecticut</td><td>16.8</td><td>7</td><td>Delaware</td><td>25.0</td></tr>
<tr><td>7</td><td>Delaware</td><td>25.0</td><td>8</td><td>New Hampshire</td><td>21.4</td></tr>
<tr><td>NA</td><td>Florida**</td><td>NA</td><td>8</td><td>New Mexico</td><td>21.4</td></tr>
<tr><td>34</td><td>Georgia</td><td>12.0</td><td>10</td><td>Colorado</td><td>20.0</td></tr>
<tr><td>3</td><td>Hawaii</td><td>27.3</td><td>11</td><td>Idaho</td><td>18.8</td></tr>
<tr><td>11</td><td>Idaho</td><td>18.8</td><td>12</td><td>Minnesota</td><td>18.5</td></tr>
<tr><td>42</td><td>Illinois*</td><td>8.6</td><td>13</td><td>Rhode Island</td><td>17.8</td></tr>
<tr><td>35</td><td>Indiana</td><td>11.9</td><td>14</td><td>New York</td><td>17.7</td></tr>
<tr><td>15</td><td>Iowa</td><td>17.1</td><td>15</td><td>Iowa</td><td>17.1</td></tr>
<tr><td>NA</td><td>Kansas**</td><td>NA</td><td>16</td><td>Connecticut</td><td>16.8</td></tr>
<tr><td>28</td><td>Kentucky</td><td>13.2</td><td>16</td><td>Washington</td><td>16.8</td></tr>
<tr><td>37</td><td>Louisiana</td><td>11.1</td><td>18</td><td>Nebraska</td><td>16.7</td></tr>
<tr><td>26</td><td>Maine</td><td>13.3</td><td>19</td><td>Oklahoma</td><td>16.6</td></tr>
<tr><td>32</td><td>Maryland</td><td>12.2</td><td>20</td><td>Arkansas</td><td>14.9</td></tr>
<tr><td>5</td><td>Massachusetts</td><td>26.5</td><td>21</td><td>Texas</td><td>14.8</td></tr>
<tr><td>43</td><td>Michigan</td><td>8.4</td><td>22</td><td>Alabama</td><td>14.6</td></tr>
<tr><td>12</td><td>Minnesota</td><td>18.5</td><td>23</td><td>Arizona</td><td>13.6</td></tr>
<tr><td>29</td><td>Mississippi</td><td>13.0</td><td>23</td><td>California</td><td>13.6</td></tr>
<tr><td>32</td><td>Missouri</td><td>12.2</td><td>25</td><td>South Carolina</td><td>13.4</td></tr>
<tr><td>47</td><td>Montana</td><td>0.0</td><td>26</td><td>Maine</td><td>13.3</td></tr>
<tr><td>18</td><td>Nebraska</td><td>16.7</td><td>26</td><td>Ohio</td><td>13.3</td></tr>
<tr><td>31</td><td>Nevada</td><td>12.4</td><td>28</td><td>Kentucky</td><td>13.2</td></tr>
<tr><td>8</td><td>New Hampshire</td><td>21.4</td><td>29</td><td>Mississippi</td><td>13.0</td></tr>
<tr><td>6</td><td>New Jersey</td><td>25.6</td><td>29</td><td>Wisconsin</td><td>13.0</td></tr>
<tr><td>8</td><td>New Mexico</td><td>21.4</td><td>31</td><td>Nevada</td><td>12.4</td></tr>
<tr><td>14</td><td>New York</td><td>17.7</td><td>32</td><td>Maryland</td><td>12.2</td></tr>
<tr><td>39</td><td>North Carolina</td><td>10.3</td><td>32</td><td>Missouri</td><td>12.2</td></tr>
<tr><td>2</td><td>North Dakota</td><td>33.3</td><td>34</td><td>Georgia</td><td>12.0</td></tr>
<tr><td>26</td><td>Ohio</td><td>13.3</td><td>35</td><td>Indiana</td><td>11.9</td></tr>
<tr><td>19</td><td>Oklahoma</td><td>16.6</td><td>35</td><td>Tennessee</td><td>11.9</td></tr>
<tr><td>46</td><td>Oregon</td><td>4.4</td><td>37</td><td>Louisiana</td><td>11.1</td></tr>
<tr><td>41</td><td>Pennsylvania</td><td>8.9</td><td>38</td><td>Virginia</td><td>10.4</td></tr>
<tr><td>13</td><td>Rhode Island</td><td>17.8</td><td>39</td><td>North Carolina</td><td>10.3</td></tr>
<tr><td>25</td><td>South Carolina</td><td>13.4</td><td>40</td><td>Alaska</td><td>9.1</td></tr>
<tr><td>47</td><td>South Dakota</td><td>0.0</td><td>41</td><td>Pennsylvania</td><td>8.9</td></tr>
<tr><td>35</td><td>Tennessee</td><td>11.9</td><td>42</td><td>Illinois*</td><td>8.6</td></tr>
<tr><td>21</td><td>Texas</td><td>14.8</td><td>43</td><td>Michigan</td><td>8.4</td></tr>
<tr><td>4</td><td>Utah</td><td>26.8</td><td>44</td><td>Wyoming</td><td>8.3</td></tr>
<tr><td>1</td><td>Vermont</td><td>50.0</td><td>45</td><td>West Virginia</td><td>5.1</td></tr>
<tr><td>38</td><td>Virginia</td><td>10.4</td><td>46</td><td>Oregon</td><td>4.4</td></tr>
<tr><td>16</td><td>Washington</td><td>16.8</td><td>47</td><td>Montana</td><td>0.0</td></tr>
<tr><td>45</td><td>West Virginia</td><td>5.1</td><td>47</td><td>South Dakota</td><td>0.0</td></tr>
<tr><td>29</td><td>Wisconsin</td><td>13.0</td><td>NA</td><td>Florida**</td><td>NA</td></tr>
<tr><td>44</td><td>Wyoming</td><td>8.3</td><td>NA</td><td>Kansas**</td><td>NA</td></tr>
<tr><td></td><td></td><td></td><td></td><td>District of Columbia**</td><td>NA</td></tr>
</table>

Source: Morgan Quitno Press using data from Federal Bureau of Investigation
"Crime in the United States 2000" (Uniform Crime Reports, October 22, 2001)
*Of the 12,943 murders in 2000 for which supplemental data were received by the F.B.I. There were an additional 2,574 murders for which the type of murder weapon was not reported to the F.B.I. Includes nonnegligent manslaughter. Numbers are for reporting jurisdictions only. Illinois' percent is for Chicago only.
**Not available.

Murders by Hands, Fists or Feet in 2000

National Total = 900 Murders*

ALPHA ORDER

RANK	STATE	MURDERS	% of USA
16	Alabama	16	1.8%
37	Alaska	4	0.4%
16	Arizona	16	1.8%
27	Arkansas	9	1.0%
1	California	110	12.2%
16	Colorado	16	1.8%
29	Connecticut	8	0.9%
40	Delaware	3	0.3%
NA	Florida**	NA	NA
9	Georgia	31	3.4%
33	Hawaii	6	0.7%
46	Idaho	0	0.0%
4	Illinois*	49	5.4%
23	Indiana	11	1.2%
31	Iowa	7	0.8%
NA	Kansas**	NA	NA
31	Kentucky	7	0.8%
10	Louisiana	28	3.1%
37	Maine	4	0.4%
23	Maryland	11	1.2%
27	Massachusetts	9	1.0%
5	Michigan	48	5.3%
23	Minnesota	11	1.2%
19	Mississippi	13	1.4%
12	Missouri	22	2.4%
46	Montana	0	0.0%
46	Nebraska	0	0.0%
29	Nevada	8	0.9%
42	New Hampshire	2	0.2%
11	New Jersey	23	2.6%
23	New Mexico	11	1.2%
3	New York	75	8.3%
6	North Carolina	45	5.0%
43	North Dakota	1	0.1%
8	Ohio	40	4.4%
15	Oklahoma	18	2.0%
34	Oregon	5	0.6%
7	Pennsylvania	42	4.7%
40	Rhode Island	3	0.3%
19	South Carolina	13	1.4%
43	South Dakota	1	0.1%
14	Tennessee	19	2.1%
2	Texas	94	10.4%
34	Utah	5	0.6%
43	Vermont	1	0.1%
19	Virginia	13	1.4%
13	Washington	21	2.3%
34	West Virginia	5	0.6%
22	Wisconsin	12	1.3%
37	Wyoming	4	0.4%

RANK ORDER

RANK	STATE	MURDERS	% of USA
1	California	110	12.2%
2	Texas	94	10.4%
3	New York	75	8.3%
4	Illinois*	49	5.4%
5	Michigan	48	5.3%
6	North Carolina	45	5.0%
7	Pennsylvania	42	4.7%
8	Ohio	40	4.4%
9	Georgia	31	3.4%
10	Louisiana	28	3.1%
11	New Jersey	23	2.6%
12	Missouri	22	2.4%
13	Washington	21	2.3%
14	Tennessee	19	2.1%
15	Oklahoma	18	2.0%
16	Alabama	16	1.8%
16	Arizona	16	1.8%
16	Colorado	16	1.8%
19	Mississippi	13	1.4%
19	South Carolina	13	1.4%
19	Virginia	13	1.4%
22	Wisconsin	12	1.3%
23	Indiana	11	1.2%
23	Maryland	11	1.2%
23	Minnesota	11	1.2%
23	New Mexico	11	1.2%
27	Arkansas	9	1.0%
27	Massachusetts	9	1.0%
29	Connecticut	8	0.9%
29	Nevada	8	0.9%
31	Iowa	7	0.8%
31	Kentucky	7	0.8%
33	Hawaii	6	0.7%
34	Oregon	5	0.6%
34	Utah	5	0.6%
34	West Virginia	5	0.6%
37	Alaska	4	0.4%
37	Maine	4	0.4%
37	Wyoming	4	0.4%
40	Delaware	3	0.3%
40	Rhode Island	3	0.3%
42	New Hampshire	2	0.2%
43	North Dakota	1	0.1%
43	South Dakota	1	0.1%
43	Vermont	1	0.1%
46	Idaho	0	0.0%
46	Montana	0	0.0%
46	Nebraska	0	0.0%
NA	Florida**	NA	NA
NA	Kansas**	NA	NA
	District of Columbia**	NA	NA

Source: Federal Bureau of Investigation
    "Crime in the United States 2000" (Uniform Crime Reports, October 22, 2001)
Of the 12,943 murders in 2000 for which supplemental data were received by the F.B.I. There were an additional 2,574 murders for which the type of murder weapon was not reported to the F.B.I. Includes nonnegligent manslaughter. Numbers are for reporting jurisdictions only. Illinois' figure is for Chicago only.
**Not available.*

Percent of Murders Involving Hands, Fists or Feet in 2000

National Percent = 7.0% of Murders*

ALPHA ORDER

RANK	STATE	PERCENT
32	Alabama	6.9
4	Alaska	18.2
42	Arizona	4.5
38	Arkansas	5.8
39	California	5.3
9	Colorado	13.3
20	Connecticut	8.4
11	Delaware	12.5
NA	Florida**	NA
35	Georgia	6.4
4	Hawaii	18.2
46	Idaho	0.0
24	Illinois*	7.8
43	Indiana	3.6
6	Iowa	17.1
NA	Kansas**	NA
15	Kentucky	10.3
39	Louisiana	5.3
3	Maine	26.7
45	Maryland	2.6
25	Massachusetts	7.7
31	Michigan	7.2
16	Minnesota	10.2
25	Mississippi	7.7
33	Missouri	6.7
46	Montana	0.0
46	Nebraska	0.0
37	Nevada	6.2
8	New Hampshire	14.3
23	New Jersey	8.0
19	New Mexico	9.4
22	New York	8.1
21	North Carolina	8.2
1	North Dakota	33.3
13	Ohio	11.6
18	Oklahoma	9.9
29	Oregon	7.4
30	Pennsylvania	7.3
33	Rhode Island	6.7
35	South Carolina	6.4
7	South Dakota	16.7
41	Tennessee	4.6
27	Texas	7.6
12	Utah	12.2
17	Vermont	10.0
44	Virginia	3.5
14	Washington	11.0
10	West Virginia	12.8
28	Wisconsin	7.5
1	Wyoming	33.3

RANK ORDER

RANK	STATE	PERCENT
1	North Dakota	33.3
1	Wyoming	33.3
3	Maine	26.7
4	Alaska	18.2
4	Hawaii	18.2
6	Iowa	17.1
7	South Dakota	16.7
8	New Hampshire	14.3
9	Colorado	13.3
10	West Virginia	12.8
11	Delaware	12.5
12	Utah	12.2
13	Ohio	11.6
14	Washington	11.0
15	Kentucky	10.3
16	Minnesota	10.2
17	Vermont	10.0
18	Oklahoma	9.9
19	New Mexico	9.4
20	Connecticut	8.4
21	North Carolina	8.2
22	New York	8.1
23	New Jersey	8.0
24	Illinois*	7.8
25	Massachusetts	7.7
25	Mississippi	7.7
27	Texas	7.6
28	Wisconsin	7.5
29	Oregon	7.4
30	Pennsylvania	7.3
31	Michigan	7.2
32	Alabama	6.9
33	Missouri	6.7
33	Rhode Island	6.7
35	Georgia	6.4
35	South Carolina	6.4
37	Nevada	6.2
38	Arkansas	5.8
39	California	5.3
39	Louisiana	5.3
41	Tennessee	4.6
42	Arizona	4.5
43	Indiana	3.6
44	Virginia	3.5
45	Maryland	2.6
46	Idaho	0.0
46	Montana	0.0
46	Nebraska	0.0
NA	Florida**	NA
NA	Kansas**	NA
	District of Columbia**	NA

Source: Morgan Quitno Press using data from Federal Bureau of Investigation
"Crime in the United States 2000" (Uniform Crime Reports, October 22, 2001)
*Of the 12,943 murders in 2000 for which supplemental data were received by the F.B.I. There were an additional 2,574 murders for which the type of murder weapon was not reported to the F.B.I. Includes nonnegligent manslaughter. Numbers are for reporting jurisdictions only. Illinois' figure is for Chicago only.
**Not available.

343

Rapes in 2000

National Total = 90,186 Rapes*

ALPHA ORDER

RANK	STATE	RAPES	% of USA
22	Alabama	1,482	1.6%
38	Alaska	497	0.6%
18	Arizona	1,577	1.7%
34	Arkansas	848	0.9%
1	California	9,785	10.8%
14	Colorado	1,774	2.0%
35	Connecticut	678	0.8%
40	Delaware	424	0.5%
3	Florida	7,057	7.8%
13	Georgia	1,968	2.2%
43	Hawaii	346	0.4%
42	Idaho	384	0.4%
6	Illinois	4,090	4.5%
15	Indiana	1,759	2.0%
36	Iowa	676	0.7%
29	Kansas	1,022	1.1%
28	Kentucky	1,091	1.2%
21	Louisiana	1,497	1.7%
45	Maine	320	0.4%
19	Maryland	1,543	1.7%
16	Massachusetts	1,696	1.9%
4	Michigan	5,025	5.6%
10	Minnesota	2,240	2.5%
30	Mississippi	1,019	1.1%
25	Missouri	1,351	1.5%
47	Montana	301	0.3%
39	Nebraska	436	0.5%
33	Nevada	860	1.0%
37	New Hampshire	522	0.6%
24	New Jersey	1,357	1.5%
31	New Mexico	922	1.0%
7	New York	3,530	3.9%
12	North Carolina	2,181	2.4%
48	North Dakota	169	0.2%
5	Ohio	4,271	4.7%
23	Oklahoma	1,422	1.6%
26	Oregon	1,286	1.4%
8	Pennsylvania	3,247	3.6%
41	Rhode Island	412	0.5%
20	South Carolina	1,511	1.7%
46	South Dakota	305	0.3%
11	Tennessee	2,186	2.4%
2	Texas	7,856	8.7%
32	Utah	863	1.0%
50	Vermont	140	0.2%
17	Virginia	1,616	1.8%
9	Washington	2,737	3.0%
44	West Virginia	331	0.4%
27	Wisconsin	1,165	1.3%
49	Wyoming	160	0.2%

RANK ORDER

RANK	STATE	RAPES	% of USA
1	California	9,785	10.8%
2	Texas	7,856	8.7%
3	Florida	7,057	7.8%
4	Michigan	5,025	5.6%
5	Ohio	4,271	4.7%
6	Illinois	4,090	4.5%
7	New York	3,530	3.9%
8	Pennsylvania	3,247	3.6%
9	Washington	2,737	3.0%
10	Minnesota	2,240	2.5%
11	Tennessee	2,186	2.4%
12	North Carolina	2,181	2.4%
13	Georgia	1,968	2.2%
14	Colorado	1,774	2.0%
15	Indiana	1,759	2.0%
16	Massachusetts	1,696	1.9%
17	Virginia	1,616	1.8%
18	Arizona	1,577	1.7%
19	Maryland	1,543	1.7%
20	South Carolina	1,511	1.7%
21	Louisiana	1,497	1.7%
22	Alabama	1,482	1.6%
23	Oklahoma	1,422	1.6%
24	New Jersey	1,357	1.5%
25	Missouri	1,351	1.5%
26	Oregon	1,286	1.4%
27	Wisconsin	1,165	1.3%
28	Kentucky	1,091	1.2%
29	Kansas	1,022	1.1%
30	Mississippi	1,019	1.1%
31	New Mexico	922	1.0%
32	Utah	863	1.0%
33	Nevada	860	1.0%
34	Arkansas	848	0.9%
35	Connecticut	678	0.8%
36	Iowa	676	0.7%
37	New Hampshire	522	0.6%
38	Alaska	497	0.6%
39	Nebraska	436	0.5%
40	Delaware	424	0.5%
41	Rhode Island	412	0.5%
42	Idaho	384	0.4%
43	Hawaii	346	0.4%
44	West Virginia	331	0.4%
45	Maine	320	0.4%
46	South Dakota	305	0.3%
47	Montana	301	0.3%
48	North Dakota	169	0.2%
49	Wyoming	160	0.2%
50	Vermont	140	0.2%
	District of Columbia	251	0.3%

Source: Federal Bureau of Investigation
   "Crime in the United States 2000" (Uniform Crime Reports, October 22, 2001)
*Forcible rape is the carnal knowledge of a female forcibly and against her will. Assaults or attempts to commit rape by force or threat of force are included. However, statutory rape without force and other sex offenses are excluded.

Average Time Between Rapes in 2000

National Rate = A Rape Occurs Every 6 Minutes*

ALPHA ORDER				RANK ORDER		
RANK	STATE	HOURS.MINUTES		RANK	STATE	HOURS.MINUTES
29	Alabama	5.55		1	Vermont	62.34
13	Alaska	17.38		2	Wyoming	54.45
33	Arizona	5.33		3	North Dakota	51.50
17	Arkansas	10.20		4	Montana	29.06
50	California	0.54		5	South Dakota	28.43
37	Colorado	4.56		6	Maine	27.23
16	Connecticut	12.55		7	West Virginia	26.28
11	Delaware	20.40		8	Hawaii	25.19
48	Florida	1.14		9	Idaho	22.49
38	Georgia	4.27		10	Rhode Island	21.16
8	Hawaii	25.19		11	Delaware	20.40
9	Idaho	22.49		12	Nebraska	20.05
45	Illinois	2.08		13	Alaska	17.38
36	Indiana	4.59		14	New Hampshire	16.47
15	Iowa	12.58		15	Iowa	12.58
22	Kansas	8.34		16	Connecticut	12.55
23	Kentucky	8.02		17	Arkansas	10.20
30	Louisiana	5.51		18	Nevada	10.11
6	Maine	27.23		19	Utah	10.09
32	Maryland	5.41		20	New Mexico	9.30
35	Massachusetts	5.10		21	Mississippi	8.36
47	Michigan	1.44		22	Kansas	8.34
41	Minnesota	3.55		23	Kentucky	8.02
21	Mississippi	8.36		24	Wisconsin	7.31
26	Missouri	6.29		25	Oregon	6.49
4	Montana	29.06		26	Missouri	6.29
12	Nebraska	20.05		27	New Jersey	6.28
18	Nevada	10.11		28	Oklahoma	6.10
14	New Hampshire	16.47		29	Alabama	5.55
27	New Jersey	6.28		30	Louisiana	5.51
20	New Mexico	9.30		31	South Carolina	5.48
44	New York	2.29		32	Maryland	5.41
39	North Carolina	4.01		33	Arizona	5.33
3	North Dakota	51.50		34	Virginia	5.25
46	Ohio	2.03		35	Massachusetts	5.10
28	Oklahoma	6.10		36	Indiana	4.59
25	Oregon	6.49		37	Colorado	4.56
43	Pennsylvania	2.42		38	Georgia	4.27
10	Rhode Island	21.16		39	North Carolina	4.01
31	South Carolina	5.48		39	Tennessee	4.01
5	South Dakota	28.43		41	Minnesota	3.55
39	Tennessee	4.01		42	Washington	3.12
49	Texas	1.07		43	Pennsylvania	2.42
19	Utah	10.09		44	New York	2.29
1	Vermont	62.34		45	Illinois	2.08
34	Virginia	5.25		46	Ohio	2.03
42	Washington	3.12		47	Michigan	1.44
7	West Virginia	26.28		48	Florida	1.14
24	Wisconsin	7.31		49	Texas	1.07
2	Wyoming	54.45		50	California	0.54
					District of Columbia	34.54

Source: Morgan Quitno Press using data from Federal Bureau of Investigation
   "Crime in the United States 2000" (Uniform Crime Reports, October 22, 2001)
*Forcible rape is the carnal knowledge of a female forcibly and against her will. Assaults or attempts to commit rape by force or threat of force are included. However, statutory rape without force and other sex offenses are excluded.

Percent Change in Number of Rapes: 1999 to 2000

National Percent Change = 0.9% Increase*

ALPHA ORDER				RANK ORDER		
RANK	STATE	PERCENT CHANGE		RANK	STATE	PERCENT CHANGE
31	Alabama	(2.0)		1	Maine	33.9
35	Alaska	(3.9)		2	Arkansas	19.4
5	Arizona	14.0		3	North Dakota	19.0
2	Arkansas	19.4		4	Wyoming	16.8
14	California	4.5		5	Arizona	14.0
10	Colorado	5.7		6	Wisconsin	10.4
15	Connecticut	3.7		7	Minnesota	9.9
49	Delaware	(19.8)		8	Indiana	9.5
25	Florida	1.0		9	Utah	7.1
48	Georgia	(15.1)		10	Colorado	5.7
32	Hawaii	(2.3)		11	Oregon	5.5
42	Idaho	(7.9)		12	Rhode Island	5.4
37	Illinois	(4.8)		13	Nebraska	5.3
8	Indiana	9.5		14	California	4.5
47	Iowa	(13.3)		15	Connecticut	3.7
36	Kansas	(4.0)		16	Michigan	3.6
39	Kentucky	(5.0)		17	Louisiana	3.4
17	Louisiana	3.4		17	Ohio	3.4
1	Maine	33.9		17	Oklahoma	3.4
27	Maryland	(0.5)		20	Texas	3.2
23	Massachusetts	2.0		21	Vermont	2.9
16	Michigan	3.6		22	Montana	2.7
7	Minnesota	9.9		23	Massachusetts	2.0
46	Mississippi	(11.9)		24	North Carolina	1.2
41	Missouri	(6.1)		25	Florida	1.0
22	Montana	2.7		25	Washington	1.0
13	Nebraska	5.3		27	Maryland	(0.5)
43	Nevada	(8.8)		28	New York	(0.9)
NA	New Hampshire**	NA		29	Pennsylvania	(1.0)
34	New Jersey	(3.7)		30	West Virginia	(1.8)
32	New Mexico	(2.3)		31	Alabama	(2.0)
28	New York	(0.9)		32	Hawaii	(2.3)
24	North Carolina	1.2		32	New Mexico	(2.3)
3	North Dakota	19.0		34	New Jersey	(3.7)
17	Ohio	3.4		35	Alaska	(3.9)
17	Oklahoma	3.4		36	Kansas	(4.0)
11	Oregon	5.5		37	Illinois	(4.8)
29	Pennsylvania	(1.0)		37	South Carolina	(4.8)
12	Rhode Island	5.4		39	Kentucky	(5.0)
37	South Carolina	(4.8)		40	Virginia	(6.0)
44	South Dakota	(9.2)		41	Missouri	(6.1)
45	Tennessee	(9.5)		42	Idaho	(7.9)
20	Texas	3.2		43	Nevada	(8.8)
9	Utah	7.1		44	South Dakota	(9.2)
21	Vermont	2.9		45	Tennessee	(9.5)
40	Virginia	(6.0)		46	Mississippi	(11.9)
25	Washington	1.0		47	Iowa	(13.3)
30	West Virginia	(1.8)		48	Georgia	(15.1)
6	Wisconsin	10.4		49	Delaware	(19.8)
4	Wyoming	16.8		NA	New Hampshire**	NA
					District of Columbia	1.2

Source: Federal Bureau of Investigation
   "Crime in the United States 2000" (Uniform Crime Reports, October 22, 2001)
*Forcible rape is the carnal knowledge of a female forcibly and against her will. Assaults or attempts to commit rape by force or threat of force are included. However, statutory rape without force and other sex offenses are excluded.
**Not available.

Rape Rate in 2000

National Rate = 32.0 Rapes per 100,000 Population*

ALPHA ORDER

RANK	STATE	PERCENT CHANGE
24	Alabama	33.3
1	Alaska	79.3
28	Arizona	30.7
27	Arkansas	31.7
31	California	28.9
10	Colorado	41.2
47	Connecticut	19.9
2	Delaware	54.1
7	Florida	44.2
42	Georgia	24.0
33	Hawaii	28.6
29	Idaho	29.7
25	Illinois	32.9
31	Indiana	28.9
43	Iowa	23.1
16	Kansas	38.0
35	Kentucky	27.0
22	Louisiana	33.5
40	Maine	25.1
30	Maryland	29.1
36	Massachusetts	26.7
4	Michigan	50.6
6	Minnesota	45.5
21	Mississippi	35.8
41	Missouri	24.1
23	Montana	33.4
39	Nebraska	25.5
8	Nevada	43.0
9	New Hampshire	42.2
50	New Jersey	16.1
3	New Mexico	50.7
48	New York	18.6
34	North Carolina	27.1
38	North Dakota	26.3
19	Ohio	37.6
10	Oklahoma	41.2
19	Oregon	37.6
37	Pennsylvania	26.4
13	Rhode Island	39.3
17	South Carolina	37.7
12	South Dakota	40.4
15	Tennessee	38.4
17	Texas	37.7
14	Utah	38.6
44	Vermont	23.0
45	Virginia	22.8
5	Washington	46.4
49	West Virginia	18.3
46	Wisconsin	21.7
26	Wyoming	32.4

RANK ORDER

RANK	STATE	PERCENT CHANGE
1	Alaska	79.3
2	Delaware	54.1
3	New Mexico	50.7
4	Michigan	50.6
5	Washington	46.4
6	Minnesota	45.5
7	Florida	44.2
8	Nevada	43.0
9	New Hampshire	42.2
10	Colorado	41.2
10	Oklahoma	41.2
12	South Dakota	40.4
13	Rhode Island	39.3
14	Utah	38.6
15	Tennessee	38.4
16	Kansas	38.0
17	South Carolina	37.7
17	Texas	37.7
19	Ohio	37.6
19	Oregon	37.6
21	Mississippi	35.8
22	Louisiana	33.5
23	Montana	33.4
24	Alabama	33.3
25	Illinois	32.9
26	Wyoming	32.4
27	Arkansas	31.7
28	Arizona	30.7
29	Idaho	29.7
30	Maryland	29.1
31	California	28.9
31	Indiana	28.9
33	Hawaii	28.6
34	North Carolina	27.1
35	Kentucky	27.0
36	Massachusetts	26.7
37	Pennsylvania	26.4
38	North Dakota	26.3
39	Nebraska	25.5
40	Maine	25.1
41	Missouri	24.1
42	Georgia	24.0
43	Iowa	23.1
44	Vermont	23.0
45	Virginia	22.8
46	Wisconsin	21.7
47	Connecticut	19.9
48	New York	18.6
49	West Virginia	18.3
50	New Jersey	16.1
	District of Columbia	43.9

Source: Federal Bureau of Investigation
"Crime in the United States 2000" (Uniform Crime Reports, October 22, 2001)
Forcible rape is the carnal knowledge of a female forcibly and against her will. Assaults or attempts to commit rape by force or threat of force are included. However, statutory rape without force and other sex offenses are excluded.

Percent Change in Rape Rate: 1999 to 2000

National Percent Change = 2.3% Decrease*

ALPHA ORDER

RANK	STATE	PERCENT CHANGE
28	Alabama	(3.8)
32	Alaska	(5.0)
8	Arizona	6.2
3	Arkansas	14.0
12	California	2.3
20	Colorado	(0.4)
19	Connecticut	(0.1)
49	Delaware	(22.9)
31	Florida	(4.5)
48	Georgia	(19.3)
30	Hawaii	(4.4)
42	Idaho	(10.9)
38	Illinois	(7.0)
6	Indiana	7.0
46	Iowa	(15.0)
34	Kansas	(5.3)
37	Kentucky	(6.9)
15	Louisiana	1.1
1	Maine	31.6
26	Maryland	(2.9)
22	Massachusetts	(0.8)
9	Michigan	2.9
7	Minnesota	6.7
45	Mississippi	(14.2)
40	Missouri	(8.2)
17	Montana	0.5
11	Nebraska	2.5
47	Nevada	(17.4)
NA	New Hampshire**	NA
36	New Jersey	(6.8)
35	New Mexico	(6.6)
32	New York	(5.0)
28	North Carolina	(3.8)
2	North Dakota	17.4
10	Ohio	2.6
16	Oklahoma	0.6
12	Oregon	2.3
27	Pennsylvania	(3.3)
20	Rhode Island	(0.4)
39	South Carolina	(7.8)
43	South Dakota	(11.8)
44	Tennessee	(12.8)
22	Texas	(0.8)
14	Utah	2.1
18	Vermont	0.4
41	Virginia	(8.8)
24	Washington	(1.4)
25	West Virginia	(1.9)
5	Wisconsin	8.1
4	Wyoming	13.4

RANK ORDER

RANK	STATE	PERCENT CHANGE
1	Maine	31.6
2	North Dakota	17.4
3	Arkansas	14.0
4	Wyoming	13.4
5	Wisconsin	8.1
6	Indiana	7.0
7	Minnesota	6.7
8	Arizona	6.2
9	Michigan	2.9
10	Ohio	2.6
11	Nebraska	2.5
12	California	2.3
12	Oregon	2.3
14	Utah	2.1
15	Louisiana	1.1
16	Oklahoma	0.6
17	Montana	0.5
18	Vermont	0.4
19	Connecticut	(0.1)
20	Colorado	(0.4)
20	Rhode Island	(0.4)
22	Massachusetts	(0.8)
22	Texas	(0.8)
24	Washington	(1.4)
25	West Virginia	(1.9)
26	Maryland	(2.9)
27	Pennsylvania	(3.3)
28	Alabama	(3.8)
28	North Carolina	(3.8)
30	Hawaii	(4.4)
31	Florida	(4.5)
32	Alaska	(5.0)
32	New York	(5.0)
34	Kansas	(5.3)
35	New Mexico	(6.6)
36	New Jersey	(6.8)
37	Kentucky	(6.9)
38	Illinois	(7.0)
39	South Carolina	(7.8)
40	Missouri	(8.2)
41	Virginia	(8.8)
42	Idaho	(10.9)
43	South Dakota	(11.8)
44	Tennessee	(12.8)
45	Mississippi	(14.2)
46	Iowa	(15.0)
47	Nevada	(17.4)
48	Georgia	(19.3)
49	Delaware	(22.9)
NA	New Hampshire**	NA
	District of Columbia	(8.2)

Source: Federal Bureau of Investigation
   "Crime in the United States 2000" (Uniform Crime Reports, October 22, 2001)
*Forcible rape is the carnal knowledge of a female forcibly and against her will. Assaults or attempts to commit rape by force or threat of force are included. However, statutory rape without force and other sex offenses are excluded.
**Not available.

Rape Rate per 100,000 Female Population in 2000

National Rate = 62.9 Rapes per 100,000 Female Population*

ALPHA ORDER

RANK	STATE	RATE
26	Alabama	64.4
1	Alaska	164.1
28	Arizona	61.4
27	Arkansas	62.0
30	California	57.6
9	Colorado	83.1
47	Connecticut	38.6
2	Delaware	105.2
8	Florida	86.2
41	Georgia	47.3
31	Hawaii	57.4
29	Idaho	59.5
25	Illinois	64.5
32	Indiana	56.8
43	Iowa	45.3
15	Kansas	75.2
35	Kentucky	52.8
24	Louisiana	64.9
40	Maine	48.9
33	Maryland	56.3
37	Massachusetts	51.5
4	Michigan	99.2
6	Minnesota	90.2
21	Mississippi	69.3
42	Missouri	47.0
22	Montana	66.5
39	Nebraska	50.2
7	Nevada	87.7
9	New Hampshire	83.1
50	New Jersey	31.3
3	New Mexico	99.7
48	New York	35.9
34	North Carolina	53.1
36	North Dakota	52.5
20	Ohio	73.1
11	Oklahoma	81.0
18	Oregon	74.6
38	Pennsylvania	51.1
14	Rhode Island	75.6
19	South Carolina	73.2
12	South Dakota	80.2
16	Tennessee	74.9
17	Texas	74.8
13	Utah	77.5
44	Vermont	45.1
45	Virginia	44.8
5	Washington	92.5
49	West Virginia	35.6
46	Wisconsin	42.9
23	Wyoming	65.2

RANK ORDER

RANK	STATE	RATE
1	Alaska	164.1
2	Delaware	105.2
3	New Mexico	99.7
4	Michigan	99.2
5	Washington	92.5
6	Minnesota	90.2
7	Nevada	87.7
8	Florida	86.2
9	Colorado	83.1
9	New Hampshire	83.1
11	Oklahoma	81.0
12	South Dakota	80.2
13	Utah	77.5
14	Rhode Island	75.6
15	Kansas	75.2
16	Tennessee	74.9
17	Texas	74.8
18	Oregon	74.6
19	South Carolina	73.2
20	Ohio	73.1
21	Mississippi	69.3
22	Montana	66.5
23	Wyoming	65.2
24	Louisiana	64.9
25	Illinois	64.5
26	Alabama	64.4
27	Arkansas	62.0
28	Arizona	61.4
29	Idaho	59.5
30	California	57.6
31	Hawaii	57.4
32	Indiana	56.8
33	Maryland	56.3
34	North Carolina	53.1
35	Kentucky	52.8
36	North Dakota	52.5
37	Massachusetts	51.5
38	Pennsylvania	51.1
39	Nebraska	50.2
40	Maine	48.9
41	Georgia	47.3
42	Missouri	47.0
43	Iowa	45.3
44	Vermont	45.1
45	Virginia	44.8
46	Wisconsin	42.9
47	Connecticut	38.6
48	New York	35.9
49	West Virginia	35.6
50	New Jersey	31.3
	District of Columbia	82.9

Source: Morgan Quitno Press using data from Federal Bureau of Investigation
"Crime in the United States 2000" (Uniform Crime Reports, October 22, 2001)
*Forcible rape is the carnal knowledge of a female forcibly and against her will. Assaults or attempts to commit rape by force or threat of force are included. However, statutory rape without force and other sex offenses are excluded.

Robberies in 2000

National Total = 407,842 Robberies*

ALPHA ORDER

RANK	STATE	ROBBERIES	% of USA
22	Alabama	5,702	1.4%
42	Alaska	490	0.1%
16	Arizona	7,504	1.8%
34	Arkansas	2,001	0.5%
1	California	60,249	14.8%
28	Colorado	3,034	0.7%
25	Connecticut	3,832	0.9%
35	Delaware	1,394	0.3%
3	Florida	31,809	7.8%
11	Georgia	13,250	3.2%
38	Hawaii	1,123	0.3%
46	Idaho	223	0.1%
5	Illinois	25,758	6.3%
18	Indiana	6,282	1.5%
39	Iowa	1,071	0.3%
33	Kansas	2,048	0.5%
27	Kentucky	3,256	0.8%
15	Louisiana	7,532	1.8%
45	Maine	247	0.1%
9	Maryland	13,560	3.3%
20	Massachusetts	5,815	1.4%
8	Michigan	13,712	3.4%
26	Minnesota	3,713	0.9%
30	Mississippi	2,703	0.7%
14	Missouri	7,598	1.9%
44	Montana	249	0.1%
37	Nebraska	1,147	0.3%
23	Nevada	4,543	1.1%
43	New Hampshire	453	0.1%
10	New Jersey	13,553	3.3%
32	New Mexico	2,499	0.6%
2	New York	40,539	9.9%
12	North Carolina	12,595	3.1%
50	North Dakota	56	0.0%
7	Ohio	15,610	3.8%
31	Oklahoma	2,615	0.6%
29	Oregon	2,888	0.7%
6	Pennsylvania	18,155	4.5%
40	Rhode Island	922	0.2%
19	South Carolina	5,883	1.4%
47	South Dakota	131	0.0%
13	Tennessee	9,465	2.3%
4	Texas	30,257	7.4%
36	Utah	1,242	0.3%
48	Vermont	117	0.0%
17	Virginia	6,295	1.5%
21	Washington	5,812	1.4%
41	West Virginia	749	0.2%
24	Wisconsin	4,537	1.1%
49	Wyoming	70	0.0%

RANK ORDER

RANK	STATE	ROBBERIES	% of USA
1	California	60,249	14.8%
2	New York	40,539	9.9%
3	Florida	31,809	7.8%
4	Texas	30,257	7.4%
5	Illinois	25,758	6.3%
6	Pennsylvania	18,155	4.5%
7	Ohio	15,610	3.8%
8	Michigan	13,712	3.4%
9	Maryland	13,560	3.3%
10	New Jersey	13,553	3.3%
11	Georgia	13,250	3.2%
12	North Carolina	12,595	3.1%
13	Tennessee	9,465	2.3%
14	Missouri	7,598	1.9%
15	Louisiana	7,532	1.8%
16	Arizona	7,504	1.8%
17	Virginia	6,295	1.5%
18	Indiana	6,282	1.5%
19	South Carolina	5,883	1.4%
20	Massachusetts	5,815	1.4%
21	Washington	5,812	1.4%
22	Alabama	5,702	1.4%
23	Nevada	4,543	1.1%
24	Wisconsin	4,537	1.1%
25	Connecticut	3,832	0.9%
26	Minnesota	3,713	0.9%
27	Kentucky	3,256	0.8%
28	Colorado	3,034	0.7%
29	Oregon	2,888	0.7%
30	Mississippi	2,703	0.7%
31	Oklahoma	2,615	0.6%
32	New Mexico	2,499	0.6%
33	Kansas	2,048	0.5%
34	Arkansas	2,001	0.5%
35	Delaware	1,394	0.3%
36	Utah	1,242	0.3%
37	Nebraska	1,147	0.3%
38	Hawaii	1,123	0.3%
39	Iowa	1,071	0.3%
40	Rhode Island	922	0.2%
41	West Virginia	749	0.2%
42	Alaska	490	0.1%
43	New Hampshire	453	0.1%
44	Montana	249	0.1%
45	Maine	247	0.1%
46	Idaho	223	0.1%
47	South Dakota	131	0.0%
48	Vermont	117	0.0%
49	Wyoming	70	0.0%
50	North Dakota	56	0.0%
	District of Columbia	3,554	0.9%

Source: Federal Bureau of Investigation
    "Crime in the United States 2000" (Uniform Crime Reports, October 22, 2001)
*Robbery is the taking or attempting to take anything of value by force or threat of force.

Average Time Between Robberies in 2000

National Rate = A Robbery Occurs Every 1 Minute*

ALPHA ORDER

ALPHA ORDER

RANK ORDER

RANK	STATE	HOURS.MINUTES		RANK	STATE	HOURS.MINUTES
29	Alabama	1.32		1	North Dakota	156.26
9	Alaska	17.53		2	Wyoming	125.08
35	Arizona	1.10		3	Vermont	74.52
17	Arkansas	4.23		4	South Dakota	66.52
50	California	0.09		5	Idaho	39.17
23	Colorado	2.53		6	Maine	35.28
26	Connecticut	2.17		7	Montana	35.11
16	Delaware	6.17		8	New Hampshire	19.20
47	Florida	0.17		9	Alaska	17.53
40	Georgia	0.40		10	West Virginia	11.42
13	Hawaii	7.48		11	Rhode Island	9.30
5	Idaho	39.17		12	Iowa	8.11
46	Illinois	0.20		13	Hawaii	7.48
33	Indiana	1.23		14	Nebraska	7.38
12	Iowa	8.11		15	Utah	7.03
18	Kansas	4.17		16	Delaware	6.17
24	Kentucky	2.41		17	Arkansas	4.23
35	Louisiana	1.10		18	Kansas	4.17
6	Maine	35.28		19	New Mexico	3.31
41	Maryland	0.39		20	Oklahoma	3.21
30	Massachusetts	1.31		21	Mississippi	3.14
43	Michigan	0.38		22	Oregon	3.02
25	Minnesota	2.22		23	Colorado	2.53
21	Mississippi	3.14		24	Kentucky	2.41
37	Missouri	1.09		25	Minnesota	2.22
7	Montana	35.11		26	Connecticut	2.17
14	Nebraska	7.38		27	Nevada	1.56
27	Nevada	1.56		27	Wisconsin	1.56
8	New Hampshire	19.20		29	Alabama	1.32
41	New Jersey	0.39		30	Massachusetts	1.31
19	New Mexico	3.31		30	Washington	1.31
49	New York	0.13		32	South Carolina	1.29
39	North Carolina	0.42		33	Indiana	1.23
1	North Dakota	156.26		33	Virginia	1.23
44	Ohio	0.34		35	Arizona	1.10
20	Oklahoma	3.21		35	Louisiana	1.10
22	Oregon	3.02		37	Missouri	1.09
45	Pennsylvania	0.29		38	Tennessee	0.56
11	Rhode Island	9.30		39	North Carolina	0.42
32	South Carolina	1.29		40	Georgia	0.40
4	South Dakota	66.52		41	Maryland	0.39
38	Tennessee	0.56		41	New Jersey	0.39
47	Texas	0.17		43	Michigan	0.38
15	Utah	7.03		44	Ohio	0.34
3	Vermont	74.52		45	Pennsylvania	0.29
33	Virginia	1.23		46	Illinois	0.20
30	Washington	1.31		47	Florida	0.17
10	West Virginia	11.42		47	Texas	0.17
27	Wisconsin	1.56		49	New York	0.13
2	Wyoming	125.08		50	California	0.09

District of Columbia   2.28

Source: Morgan Quitno Press using data from Federal Bureau of Investigation
"Crime in the United States 2000" (Uniform Crime Reports, October 22, 2001)
*Robbery is the taking or attempting to take anything of value by force or threat of force.

Percent Change in Number of Robberies: 1999 to 2000

National Percent Change = 0.4% Decrease*

ALPHA ORDER

RANK	STATE	PERCENT CHANGE
8	Alabama	7.6
49	Alaska	(13.4)
15	Arizona	3.0
32	Arkansas	(1.1)
23	California	0.3
30	Colorado	(0.7)
42	Connecticut	(5.5)
44	Delaware	(6.6)
28	Florida	(0.5)
17	Georgia	2.2
8	Hawaii	7.6
25	Idaho	0.0
34	Illinois	(2.3)
38	Indiana	(3.3)
20	Iowa	1.9
25	Kansas	0.0
12	Kentucky	4.9
31	Louisiana	(0.8)
21	Maine	1.6
29	Maryland	(0.6)
33	Massachusetts	(2.0)
35	Michigan	(2.8)
40	Minnesota	(5.2)
48	Mississippi	(12.6)
11	Missouri	6.3
13	Montana	4.2
46	Nebraska	(9.3)
7	Nevada	7.9
NA	New Hampshire**	NA
39	New Jersey	(4.8)
37	New Mexico	(3.1)
45	New York	(7.5)
13	North Carolina	4.2
25	North Dakota	0.0
6	Ohio	8.4
43	Oklahoma	(6.1)
22	Oregon	1.0
35	Pennsylvania	(2.8)
3	Rhode Island	17.0
18	South Carolina	2.1
2	South Dakota	27.2
5	Tennessee	10.1
16	Texas	2.9
10	Utah	7.3
1	Vermont	80.0
47	Virginia	(9.4)
24	Washington	0.1
4	West Virginia	13.3
19	Wisconsin	2.0
41	Wyoming	(5.4)

RANK ORDER

RANK	STATE	PERCENT CHANGE
1	Vermont	80.0
2	South Dakota	27.2
3	Rhode Island	17.0
4	West Virginia	13.3
5	Tennessee	10.1
6	Ohio	8.4
7	Nevada	7.9
8	Alabama	7.6
8	Hawaii	7.6
10	Utah	7.3
11	Missouri	6.3
12	Kentucky	4.9
13	Montana	4.2
13	North Carolina	4.2
15	Arizona	3.0
16	Texas	2.9
17	Georgia	2.2
18	South Carolina	2.1
19	Wisconsin	2.0
20	Iowa	1.9
21	Maine	1.6
22	Oregon	1.0
23	California	0.3
24	Washington	0.1
25	Idaho	0.0
25	Kansas	0.0
25	North Dakota	0.0
28	Florida	(0.5)
29	Maryland	(0.6)
30	Colorado	(0.7)
31	Louisiana	(0.8)
32	Arkansas	(1.1)
33	Massachusetts	(2.0)
34	Illinois	(2.3)
35	Michigan	(2.8)
35	Pennsylvania	(2.8)
37	New Mexico	(3.1)
38	Indiana	(3.3)
39	New Jersey	(4.8)
40	Minnesota	(5.2)
41	Wyoming	(5.4)
42	Connecticut	(5.5)
43	Oklahoma	(6.1)
44	Delaware	(6.6)
45	New York	(7.5)
46	Nebraska	(9.3)
47	Virginia	(9.4)
48	Mississippi	(12.6)
49	Alaska	(13.4)
NA	New Hampshire**	NA
	District of Columbia	6.3

Source: Federal Bureau of Investigation
"Crime in the United States 2000" (Uniform Crime Reports, October 22, 2001)
*Robbery is the taking or attempting to take anything of value by force or threat of force.
**Not available.

Robbery Rate in 2000

National Rate = 144.9 Robberies per 100,000 Population*

RANK	STATE	RATE
21	Alabama	128.2
33	Alaska	78.2
15	Arizona	146.3
37	Arkansas	74.8
6	California	177.9
38	Colorado	70.5
22	Connecticut	112.5
6	Delaware	177.9
5	Florida	199.0
10	Georgia	161.9
26	Hawaii	92.7
48	Idaho	17.2
4	Illinois	207.4
23	Indiana	103.3
43	Iowa	36.6
34	Kansas	76.2
32	Kentucky	80.6
8	Louisiana	168.5
45	Maine	19.4
1	Maryland	256.0
27	Massachusetts	91.6
17	Michigan	138.0
36	Minnesota	75.5
25	Mississippi	95.0
20	Missouri	135.8
44	Montana	27.6
39	Nebraska	67.0
2	Nevada	227.3
42	New Hampshire	36.7
11	New Jersey	161.1
19	New Mexico	137.4
3	New York	213.6
12	North Carolina	156.5
50	North Dakota	8.7
18	Ohio	137.5
35	Oklahoma	75.8
31	Oregon	84.4
13	Pennsylvania	147.8
29	Rhode Island	88.0
14	South Carolina	146.6
47	South Dakota	17.4
9	Tennessee	166.4
16	Texas	145.1
40	Utah	55.6
46	Vermont	19.2
28	Virginia	88.9
24	Washington	98.6
41	West Virginia	41.4
30	Wisconsin	84.6
49	Wyoming	14.2

RANK	STATE	RATE
1	Maryland	256.0
2	Nevada	227.3
3	New York	213.6
4	Illinois	207.4
5	Florida	199.0
6	California	177.9
6	Delaware	177.9
8	Louisiana	168.5
9	Tennessee	166.4
10	Georgia	161.9
11	New Jersey	161.1
12	North Carolina	156.5
13	Pennsylvania	147.8
14	South Carolina	146.6
15	Arizona	146.3
16	Texas	145.1
17	Michigan	138.0
18	Ohio	137.5
19	New Mexico	137.4
20	Missouri	135.8
21	Alabama	128.2
22	Connecticut	112.5
23	Indiana	103.3
24	Washington	98.6
25	Mississippi	95.0
26	Hawaii	92.7
27	Massachusetts	91.6
28	Virginia	88.9
29	Rhode Island	88.0
30	Wisconsin	84.6
31	Oregon	84.4
32	Kentucky	80.6
33	Alaska	78.2
34	Kansas	76.2
35	Oklahoma	75.8
36	Minnesota	75.5
37	Arkansas	74.8
38	Colorado	70.5
39	Nebraska	67.0
40	Utah	55.6
41	West Virginia	41.4
42	New Hampshire	36.7
43	Iowa	36.6
44	Montana	27.6
45	Maine	19.4
46	Vermont	19.2
47	South Dakota	17.4
48	Idaho	17.2
49	Wyoming	14.2
50	North Dakota	8.7
	District of Columbia	621.3

Source: Federal Bureau of Investigation
"Crime in the United States 2000" (Uniform Crime Reports, October 22, 2001)
*Robbery is the taking or attempting to take anything of value by force or threat of force.

Percent Change in Robbery Rate: 1999 to 2000

National Percent Change = 3.5% Decrease*

ALPHA ORDER			RANK ORDER		
RANK	STATE	PERCENT CHANGE	RANK	STATE	PERCENT CHANGE
7	Alabama	5.8	1	Vermont	75.5
48	Alaska	(14.5)	2	South Dakota	23.5
30	Arizona	(4.1)	3	West Virginia	13.2
35	Arkansas	(5.6)	4	Rhode Island	10.6
21	California	(1.8)	5	Ohio	7.4
37	Colorado	(6.4)	6	Tennessee	6.1
43	Connecticut	(8.9)	7	Alabama	5.8
44	Delaware	(10.2)	8	Hawaii	5.3
36	Florida	(5.9)	9	Missouri	3.9
25	Georgia	(2.8)	10	Kentucky	2.8
8	Hawaii	5.3	11	Utah	2.3
28	Idaho	(3.3)	12	Montana	1.9
31	Illinois	(4.6)	13	Iowa	(0.1)
34	Indiana	(5.5)	13	Maine	(0.1)
13	Iowa	(0.1)	15	Wisconsin	(0.2)
19	Kansas	(1.2)	16	North Carolina	(1.0)
10	Kentucky	2.8	17	South Carolina	(1.1)
26	Louisiana	(2.9)	17	Texas	(1.1)
13	Maine	(0.1)	19	Kansas	(1.2)
26	Maryland	(2.9)	20	North Dakota	(1.3)
31	Massachusetts	(4.6)	21	California	(1.8)
29	Michigan	(3.5)	22	Oregon	(2.1)
40	Minnesota	(8.0)	23	Nevada	(2.3)
49	Mississippi	(14.9)	23	Washington	(2.3)
9	Missouri	3.9	25	Georgia	(2.8)
12	Montana	1.9	26	Louisiana	(2.9)
46	Nebraska	(11.7)	26	Maryland	(2.9)
23	Nevada	(2.3)	28	Idaho	(3.3)
NA	New Hampshire**	NA	29	Michigan	(3.5)
39	New Jersey	(7.9)	30	Arizona	(4.1)
38	New Mexico	(7.3)	31	Illinois	(4.6)
45	New York	(11.3)	31	Massachusetts	(4.6)
16	North Carolina	(1.0)	33	Pennsylvania	(5.0)
20	North Dakota	(1.3)	34	Indiana	(5.5)
5	Ohio	7.4	35	Arkansas	(5.6)
42	Oklahoma	(8.6)	36	Florida	(5.9)
22	Oregon	(2.1)	37	Colorado	(6.4)
33	Pennsylvania	(5.0)	38	New Mexico	(7.3)
4	Rhode Island	10.6	39	New Jersey	(7.9)
17	South Carolina	(1.1)	40	Minnesota	(8.0)
2	South Dakota	23.5	41	Wyoming	(8.1)
6	Tennessee	6.1	42	Oklahoma	(8.6)
17	Texas	(1.1)	43	Connecticut	(8.9)
11	Utah	2.3	44	Delaware	(10.2)
1	Vermont	75.5	45	New York	(11.3)
47	Virginia	(12.0)	46	Nebraska	(11.7)
23	Washington	(2.3)	47	Virginia	(12.0)
3	West Virginia	13.2	48	Alaska	(14.5)
15	Wisconsin	(0.2)	49	Mississippi	(14.9)
41	Wyoming	(8.1)	NA	New Hampshire**	NA
				District of Columbia	(3.6)

Source: Federal Bureau of Investigation
"Crime in the United States 2000" (Uniform Crime Reports, October 22, 2001)
*Robbery is the taking or attempting to take anything of value by force or threat of force.
**Not available.

Robberies with Firearms in 2000

National Total = 129,849 Robberies*

ALPHA ORDER

ALPHA ORDER

RANK	STATE	ROBBERIES	% of USA		RANK	STATE	ROBBERIES	% of USA
18	Alabama	2,255	1.7%		1	California	20,962	16.1%
39	Alaska	176	0.1%		2	Texas	13,140	10.1%
14	Arizona	3,091	2.4%		3	Florida	11,692	9.0%
28	Arkansas	939	0.7%		4	Pennsylvania	6,948	5.4%
1	California	20,962	16.1%		5	Michigan	6,276	4.8%
27	Colorado	950	0.7%		6	North Carolina	5,986	4.6%
22	Connecticut	1,286	1.0%		7	Georgia	5,837	4.5%
33	Delaware	508	0.4%		8	Maryland	5,566	4.3%
3	Florida	11,692	9.0%		9	Tennessee	5,130	4.0%
7	Georgia	5,837	4.5%		10	Ohio	4,555	3.5%
40	Hawaii	135	0.1%		11	New Jersey	4,538	3.5%
42	Idaho	62	0.0%		12	Louisiana	3,545	2.7%
NA	Illinois**	NA	NA		13	Missouri	3,321	2.6%
16	Indiana	2,478	1.9%		14	Arizona	3,091	2.4%
36	Iowa	276	0.2%		15	Wisconsin	2,502	1.9%
37	Kansas	246	0.2%		16	Indiana	2,478	1.9%
29	Kentucky	874	0.7%		17	Virginia	2,307	1.8%
12	Louisiana	3,545	2.7%		18	Alabama	2,255	1.7%
44	Maine	46	0.0%		19	New York	1,916	1.5%
8	Maryland	5,566	4.3%		20	Nevada	1,837	1.4%
23	Massachusetts	1,282	1.0%		21	Washington	1,496	1.2%
5	Michigan	6,276	4.8%		22	Connecticut	1,286	1.0%
24	Minnesota	1,063	0.8%		23	Massachusetts	1,282	1.0%
32	Mississippi	593	0.5%		24	Minnesota	1,063	0.8%
13	Missouri	3,321	2.6%		25	Oklahoma	1,035	0.8%
49	Montana	18	0.0%		26	New Mexico	952	0.7%
34	Nebraska	488	0.4%		27	Colorado	950	0.7%
20	Nevada	1,837	1.4%		28	Arkansas	939	0.7%
43	New Hampshire	47	0.0%		29	Kentucky	874	0.7%
11	New Jersey	4,538	3.5%		30	Oregon	798	0.6%
26	New Mexico	952	0.7%		31	South Carolina	627	0.5%
19	New York	1,916	1.5%		32	Mississippi	593	0.5%
6	North Carolina	5,986	4.6%		33	Delaware	508	0.4%
47	North Dakota	25	0.0%		34	Nebraska	488	0.4%
10	Ohio	4,555	3.5%		35	Utah	299	0.2%
25	Oklahoma	1,035	0.8%		36	Iowa	276	0.2%
30	Oregon	798	0.6%		37	Kansas	246	0.2%
4	Pennsylvania	6,948	5.4%		38	Rhode Island	220	0.2%
38	Rhode Island	220	0.2%		39	Alaska	176	0.1%
31	South Carolina	627	0.5%		40	Hawaii	135	0.1%
45	South Dakota	29	0.0%		41	West Virginia	81	0.1%
9	Tennessee	5,130	4.0%		42	Idaho	62	0.0%
2	Texas	13,140	10.1%		43	New Hampshire	47	0.0%
35	Utah	299	0.2%		44	Maine	46	0.0%
48	Vermont	21	0.0%		45	South Dakota	29	0.0%
17	Virginia	2,307	1.8%		45	Wyoming	29	0.0%
21	Washington	1,496	1.2%		47	North Dakota	25	0.0%
41	West Virginia	81	0.1%		48	Vermont	21	0.0%
15	Wisconsin	2,502	1.9%		49	Montana	18	0.0%
45	Wyoming	29	0.0%		NA	Illinois**	NA	NA
						District of Columbia	1,366	1.1%

RANK ORDER

Source: Federal Bureau of Investigation
      "Crime in the United States 2000" (Uniform Crime Reports, October 22, 2001)
*Of the 317,555 robberies in 2000 for which supplemental data were received by the F.B.I. There were an
additional 90,287 robberies for which the type of weapon was not reported to the F.B.I. Robbery is the taking or
attempting to take anything of value by force or threat of force. Numbers are for reporting jurisdictions only.
**Not available.

Robbery Rate with Firearms in 2000

National Rate = 60.2 Robberies per 100,000 Population*

ALPHA ORDER

RANK	STATE	RATE
15	Alabama	69.3
29	Alaska	30.9
17	Arizona	66.4
27	Arkansas	38.4
20	California	62.0
31	Colorado	28.6
26	Connecticut	43.1
1	Delaware	128.6
10	Florida	74.5
4	Georgia	95.7
41	Hawaii	11.1
45	Idaho	4.9
NA	Illinois**	NA
21	Indiana	60.2
40	Iowa	11.9
11	Kansas	72.4
3	Kentucky	101.2
6	Louisiana	92.1
49	Maine	3.7
2	Maryland	124.8
35	Massachusetts	23.6
14	Michigan	69.8
36	Minnesota	22.9
25	Mississippi	45.4
9	Missouri	75.4
44	Montana	5.2
28	Nebraska	31.4
7	Nevada	91.9
42	New Hampshire	6.4
24	New Jersey	53.9
16	New Mexico	69.2
33	New York	27.4
8	North Carolina	86.4
47	North Dakota	4.4
12	Ohio	70.7
30	Oklahoma	30.0
34	Oregon	25.0
13	Pennsylvania	70.0
37	Rhode Island	21.0
18	South Carolina	65.0
46	South Dakota	4.8
5	Tennessee	95.5
19	Texas	63.9
38	Utah	19.2
47	Vermont	4.4
22	Virginia	58.7
32	Washington	27.9
39	West Virginia	13.3
23	Wisconsin	56.7
43	Wyoming	5.9

RANK ORDER

RANK	STATE	RATE
1	Delaware	128.6
2	Maryland	124.8
3	Kentucky	101.2
4	Georgia	95.7
5	Tennessee	95.5
6	Louisiana	92.1
7	Nevada	91.9
8	North Carolina	86.4
9	Missouri	75.4
10	Florida	74.5
11	Kansas	72.4
12	Ohio	70.7
13	Pennsylvania	70.0
14	Michigan	69.8
15	Alabama	69.3
16	New Mexico	69.2
17	Arizona	66.4
18	South Carolina	65.0
19	Texas	63.9
20	California	62.0
21	Indiana	60.2
22	Virginia	58.7
23	Wisconsin	56.7
24	New Jersey	53.9
25	Mississippi	45.4
26	Connecticut	43.1
27	Arkansas	38.4
28	Nebraska	31.4
29	Alaska	30.9
30	Oklahoma	30.0
31	Colorado	28.6
32	Washington	27.9
33	New York	27.4
34	Oregon	25.0
35	Massachusetts	23.6
36	Minnesota	22.9
37	Rhode Island	21.0
38	Utah	19.2
39	West Virginia	13.3
40	Iowa	11.9
41	Hawaii	11.1
42	New Hampshire	6.4
43	Wyoming	5.9
44	Montana	5.2
45	Idaho	4.9
46	South Dakota	4.8
47	North Dakota	4.4
47	Vermont	4.4
49	Maine	3.7
NA	Illinois**	NA

	District of Columbia	238.8

Source: Morgan Quitno Press using data from Federal Bureau of Investigation
   "Crime in the United States 2000" (Uniform Crime Reports, October 22, 2001)
*Based only on population of reporting jurisdictions. Robbery is the taking or attempting to take anything of value by force or threat of force. National rate reflects only those robberies for which the type of weapon was known and reported.
**Not available.

Percent of Robberies Involving Firearms in 2000

National Percent = 40.9% of Robberies*

ALPHA ORDER				RANK ORDER		
RANK	STATE	PERCENT		RANK	STATE	PERCENT
2	Alabama	56.2		1	Louisiana	57.7
26	Alaska	39.9		2	Alabama	56.2
19	Arizona	42.1		3	Wisconsin	56.1
9	Arkansas	47.9		4	Georgia	55.1
33	California	34.8		5	Tennessee	54.9
31	Colorado	36.5		6	Virginia	51.4
28	Connecticut	38.4		7	North Carolina	51.0
15	Delaware	44.6		8	Michigan	48.5
30	Florida	37.2		9	Arkansas	47.9
4	Georgia	55.1		10	Indiana	47.7
49	Hawaii	12.0		11	South Carolina	46.5
40	Idaho	28.2		12	North Dakota	46.3
NA	Illinois**	NA		13	Maryland	46.0
10	Indiana	47.7		14	Missouri	45.4
41	Iowa	27.7		15	Delaware	44.6
23	Kansas	41.3		16	Kentucky	44.2
16	Kentucky	44.2		17	Texas	43.8
1	Louisiana	57.7		18	Nebraska	43.1
48	Maine	18.8		19	Arizona	42.1
13	Maryland	46.0		20	New Mexico	41.7
44	Massachusetts	24.5		20	Pennsylvania	41.7
8	Michigan	48.5		22	Wyoming	41.4
38	Minnesota	29.2		23	Kansas	41.3
24	Mississippi	40.5		24	Mississippi	40.5
14	Missouri	45.4		25	Nevada	40.4
41	Montana	27.7		26	Alaska	39.9
18	Nebraska	43.1		27	Oklahoma	39.6
25	Nevada	40.4		28	Connecticut	38.4
47	New Hampshire	20.0		29	Ohio	37.5
35	New Jersey	33.5		30	Florida	37.2
20	New Mexico	41.7		31	Colorado	36.5
36	New York	30.5		32	Vermont	35.0
7	North Carolina	51.0		33	California	34.8
12	North Dakota	46.3		33	West Virginia	34.8
29	Ohio	37.5		35	New Jersey	33.5
27	Oklahoma	39.6		36	New York	30.5
39	Oregon	28.5		37	Utah	29.5
20	Pennsylvania	41.7		38	Minnesota	29.2
45	Rhode Island	23.9		39	Oregon	28.5
11	South Carolina	46.5		40	Idaho	28.2
46	South Dakota	22.7		41	Iowa	27.7
5	Tennessee	54.9		41	Montana	27.7
17	Texas	43.8		43	Washington	26.9
37	Utah	29.5		44	Massachusetts	24.5
32	Vermont	35.0		45	Rhode Island	23.9
6	Virginia	51.4		46	South Dakota	22.7
43	Washington	26.9		47	New Hampshire	20.0
33	West Virginia	34.8		48	Maine	18.8
3	Wisconsin	56.1		49	Hawaii	12.0
22	Wyoming	41.4		NA	Illinois**	NA
					District of Columbia	38.4

Source: Morgan Quitno Press using data from Federal Bureau of Investigation
   "Crime in the United States 2000" (Uniform Crime Reports, October 22, 2001)
*Of the 317,555 robberies in 2000 for which supplemental data were received by the F.B.I. There were an
additional 90,287 robberies for which the type of weapon was not reported to the F.B.I. Robbery is the taking or
attempting to take anything of value by force or threat of force. Numbers are for reporting jurisdictions only.
**Not available.

Robberies with Knives or Cutting Instruments in 2000

National Total = 26,723 Robberies*

ALPHA ORDER

ALPHA ORDER

RANK	STATE	ROBBERIES	% of USA
26	Alabama	275	1.0%
39	Alaska	45	0.2%
8	Arizona	776	2.9%
30	Arkansas	142	0.5%
1	California	6,074	22.7%
22	Colorado	291	1.1%
21	Connecticut	323	1.2%
38	Delaware	75	0.3%
3	Florida	2,244	8.4%
14	Georgia	567	2.1%
37	Hawaii	78	0.3%
41	Idaho	32	0.1%
NA	Illinois**	NA	NA
19	Indiana	362	1.4%
34	Iowa	98	0.4%
40	Kansas	41	0.2%
29	Kentucky	149	0.6%
18	Louisiana	398	1.5%
42	Maine	31	0.1%
7	Maryland	954	3.6%
6	Massachusetts	1,030	3.9%
11	Michigan	718	2.7%
24	Minnesota	280	1.0%
35	Mississippi	94	0.4%
16	Missouri	530	2.0%
46	Montana	11	0.0%
36	Nebraska	91	0.3%
17	Nevada	427	1.6%
45	New Hampshire	18	0.1%
4	New Jersey	1,244	4.7%
20	New Mexico	324	1.2%
10	New York	721	2.7%
9	North Carolina	767	2.9%
49	North Dakota	2	0.0%
13	Ohio	595	2.2%
28	Oklahoma	225	0.8%
25	Oregon	276	1.0%
5	Pennsylvania	1,112	4.2%
31	Rhode Island	121	0.5%
33	South Carolina	108	0.4%
44	South Dakota	22	0.1%
12	Tennessee	683	2.6%
2	Texas	2,850	10.7%
31	Utah	121	0.5%
46	Vermont	11	0.0%
23	Virginia	288	1.1%
15	Washington	566	2.1%
43	West Virginia	29	0.1%
27	Wisconsin	263	1.0%
48	Wyoming	10	0.0%

RANK ORDER

RANK	STATE	ROBBERIES	% of USA
1	California	6,074	22.7%
2	Texas	2,850	10.7%
3	Florida	2,244	8.4%
4	New Jersey	1,244	4.7%
5	Pennsylvania	1,112	4.2%
6	Massachusetts	1,030	3.9%
7	Maryland	954	3.6%
8	Arizona	776	2.9%
9	North Carolina	767	2.9%
10	New York	721	2.7%
11	Michigan	718	2.7%
12	Tennessee	683	2.6%
13	Ohio	595	2.2%
14	Georgia	567	2.1%
15	Washington	566	2.1%
16	Missouri	530	2.0%
17	Nevada	427	1.6%
18	Louisiana	398	1.5%
19	Indiana	362	1.4%
20	New Mexico	324	1.2%
21	Connecticut	323	1.2%
22	Colorado	291	1.1%
23	Virginia	288	1.1%
24	Minnesota	280	1.0%
25	Oregon	276	1.0%
26	Alabama	275	1.0%
27	Wisconsin	263	1.0%
28	Oklahoma	225	0.8%
29	Kentucky	149	0.6%
30	Arkansas	142	0.5%
31	Rhode Island	121	0.5%
31	Utah	121	0.5%
33	South Carolina	108	0.4%
34	Iowa	98	0.4%
35	Mississippi	94	0.4%
36	Nebraska	91	0.3%
37	Hawaii	78	0.3%
38	Delaware	75	0.3%
39	Alaska	45	0.2%
40	Kansas	41	0.2%
41	Idaho	32	0.1%
42	Maine	31	0.1%
43	West Virginia	29	0.1%
44	South Dakota	22	0.1%
45	New Hampshire	18	0.1%
46	Montana	11	0.0%
46	Vermont	11	0.0%
48	Wyoming	10	0.0%
49	North Dakota	2	0.0%
NA	Illinois**	NA	NA
	District of Columbia	231	0.9%

Source: Federal Bureau of Investigation
"Crime in the United States 2000" (Uniform Crime Reports, October 22, 2001)
*Of the 317,555 robberies in 2000 for which supplemental data were received by the F.B.I. There were an additional 90,287 robberies for which the type of weapon was not reported to the F.B.I. Robbery is the taking or attempting to take anything of value by force or threat of force. Numbers are for reporting jurisdictions only.
**Not available.

Percent of Robberies Involving Knives or Cutting Instruments in 2000

National Percent = 8.4% of Robberies*

<table>
<tr><td colspan="3">ALPHA ORDER</td><td colspan="3">RANK ORDER</td></tr>
<tr><td>RANK</td><td>STATE</td><td>PERCENT</td><td>RANK</td><td>STATE</td><td>PERCENT</td></tr>
<tr><td>36</td><td>Alabama</td><td>6.9</td><td>1</td><td>Massachusetts</td><td>19.7</td></tr>
<tr><td>15</td><td>Alaska</td><td>10.2</td><td>2</td><td>Vermont</td><td>18.3</td></tr>
<tr><td>14</td><td>Arizona</td><td>10.6</td><td>3</td><td>South Dakota</td><td>17.2</td></tr>
<tr><td>32</td><td>Arkansas</td><td>7.2</td><td>4</td><td>Montana</td><td>16.9</td></tr>
<tr><td>17</td><td>California</td><td>10.1</td><td>5</td><td>Idaho</td><td>14.5</td></tr>
<tr><td>13</td><td>Colorado</td><td>11.2</td><td>6</td><td>Wyoming</td><td>14.3</td></tr>
<tr><td>20</td><td>Connecticut</td><td>9.6</td><td>7</td><td>New Mexico</td><td>14.2</td></tr>
<tr><td>40</td><td>Delaware</td><td>6.6</td><td>8</td><td>Rhode Island</td><td>13.1</td></tr>
<tr><td>34</td><td>Florida</td><td>7.1</td><td>9</td><td>Maine</td><td>12.7</td></tr>
<tr><td>47</td><td>Georgia</td><td>5.4</td><td>10</td><td>West Virginia</td><td>12.4</td></tr>
<tr><td>36</td><td>Hawaii</td><td>6.9</td><td>11</td><td>Utah</td><td>12.0</td></tr>
<tr><td>5</td><td>Idaho</td><td>14.5</td><td>12</td><td>New York</td><td>11.5</td></tr>
<tr><td>NA</td><td>Illinois**</td><td>NA</td><td>13</td><td>Colorado</td><td>11.2</td></tr>
<tr><td>35</td><td>Indiana</td><td>7.0</td><td>14</td><td>Arizona</td><td>10.6</td></tr>
<tr><td>19</td><td>Iowa</td><td>9.8</td><td>15</td><td>Alaska</td><td>10.2</td></tr>
<tr><td>36</td><td>Kansas</td><td>6.9</td><td>15</td><td>Washington</td><td>10.2</td></tr>
<tr><td>30</td><td>Kentucky</td><td>7.5</td><td>17</td><td>California</td><td>10.1</td></tr>
<tr><td>41</td><td>Louisiana</td><td>6.5</td><td>18</td><td>Oregon</td><td>9.9</td></tr>
<tr><td>9</td><td>Maine</td><td>12.7</td><td>19</td><td>Iowa</td><td>9.8</td></tr>
<tr><td>27</td><td>Maryland</td><td>7.9</td><td>20</td><td>Connecticut</td><td>9.6</td></tr>
<tr><td>1</td><td>Massachusetts</td><td>19.7</td><td>21</td><td>Texas</td><td>9.5</td></tr>
<tr><td>46</td><td>Michigan</td><td>5.6</td><td>22</td><td>Nevada</td><td>9.4</td></tr>
<tr><td>28</td><td>Minnesota</td><td>7.7</td><td>23</td><td>New Jersey</td><td>9.2</td></tr>
<tr><td>43</td><td>Mississippi</td><td>6.4</td><td>24</td><td>Oklahoma</td><td>8.6</td></tr>
<tr><td>32</td><td>Missouri</td><td>7.2</td><td>25</td><td>Nebraska</td><td>8.0</td></tr>
<tr><td>4</td><td>Montana</td><td>16.9</td><td>25</td><td>South Carolina</td><td>8.0</td></tr>
<tr><td>25</td><td>Nebraska</td><td>8.0</td><td>27</td><td>Maryland</td><td>7.9</td></tr>
<tr><td>22</td><td>Nevada</td><td>9.4</td><td>28</td><td>Minnesota</td><td>7.7</td></tr>
<tr><td>28</td><td>New Hampshire</td><td>7.7</td><td>28</td><td>New Hampshire</td><td>7.7</td></tr>
<tr><td>23</td><td>New Jersey</td><td>9.2</td><td>30</td><td>Kentucky</td><td>7.5</td></tr>
<tr><td>7</td><td>New Mexico</td><td>14.2</td><td>31</td><td>Tennessee</td><td>7.3</td></tr>
<tr><td>12</td><td>New York</td><td>11.5</td><td>32</td><td>Arkansas</td><td>7.2</td></tr>
<tr><td>41</td><td>North Carolina</td><td>6.5</td><td>32</td><td>Missouri</td><td>7.2</td></tr>
<tr><td>49</td><td>North Dakota</td><td>3.7</td><td>34</td><td>Florida</td><td>7.1</td></tr>
<tr><td>48</td><td>Ohio</td><td>4.9</td><td>35</td><td>Indiana</td><td>7.0</td></tr>
<tr><td>24</td><td>Oklahoma</td><td>8.6</td><td>36</td><td>Alabama</td><td>6.9</td></tr>
<tr><td>18</td><td>Oregon</td><td>9.9</td><td>36</td><td>Hawaii</td><td>6.9</td></tr>
<tr><td>39</td><td>Pennsylvania</td><td>6.7</td><td>36</td><td>Kansas</td><td>6.9</td></tr>
<tr><td>8</td><td>Rhode Island</td><td>13.1</td><td>39</td><td>Pennsylvania</td><td>6.7</td></tr>
<tr><td>25</td><td>South Carolina</td><td>8.0</td><td>40</td><td>Delaware</td><td>6.6</td></tr>
<tr><td>3</td><td>South Dakota</td><td>17.2</td><td>41</td><td>Louisiana</td><td>6.5</td></tr>
<tr><td>31</td><td>Tennessee</td><td>7.3</td><td>41</td><td>North Carolina</td><td>6.5</td></tr>
<tr><td>21</td><td>Texas</td><td>9.5</td><td>43</td><td>Mississippi</td><td>6.4</td></tr>
<tr><td>11</td><td>Utah</td><td>12.0</td><td>43</td><td>Virginia</td><td>6.4</td></tr>
<tr><td>2</td><td>Vermont</td><td>18.3</td><td>45</td><td>Wisconsin</td><td>5.9</td></tr>
<tr><td>43</td><td>Virginia</td><td>6.4</td><td>46</td><td>Michigan</td><td>5.6</td></tr>
<tr><td>15</td><td>Washington</td><td>10.2</td><td>47</td><td>Georgia</td><td>5.4</td></tr>
<tr><td>10</td><td>West Virginia</td><td>12.4</td><td>48</td><td>Ohio</td><td>4.9</td></tr>
<tr><td>45</td><td>Wisconsin</td><td>5.9</td><td>49</td><td>North Dakota</td><td>3.7</td></tr>
<tr><td>6</td><td>Wyoming</td><td>14.3</td><td>NA</td><td>Illinois**</td><td>NA</td></tr>
<tr><td></td><td></td><td></td><td></td><td>District of Columbia</td><td>6.5</td></tr>
</table>

Source: Morgan Quitno Press using data from Federal Bureau of Investigation
   "Crime in the United States 2000" (Uniform Crime Reports, October 22, 2001)
*Of the 317,555 robberies in 2000 for which supplemental data were received by the F.B.I. There were an
additional 90,287 robberies for which the type of weapon was not reported to the F.B.I. Robbery is the taking or
attempting to take anything of value by force or threat of force. Numbers are for reporting jurisdictions only.
**Not available.

Robberies with Blunt Objects and Other Dangerous Weapons in 2000

National Total = 32,760 Robberies*

RANK	STATE	ROBBERIES	% of USA
25	Alabama	311	0.9%
39	Alaska	39	0.1%
13	Arizona	789	2.4%
27	Arkansas	264	0.8%
1	California	5,608	17.1%
20	Colorado	370	1.1%
23	Connecticut	342	1.0%
35	Delaware	80	0.2%
2	Florida	3,427	10.5%
12	Georgia	968	3.0%
40	Hawaii	32	0.1%
45	Idaho	22	0.1%
NA	Illinois**	NA	NA
18	Indiana	421	1.3%
31	Iowa	152	0.5%
38	Kansas	67	0.2%
33	Kentucky	135	0.4%
19	Louisiana	414	1.3%
43	Maine	25	0.1%
6	Maryland	1,471	4.5%
16	Massachusetts	589	1.8%
4	Michigan	1,744	5.3%
22	Minnesota	350	1.1%
24	Mississippi	312	1.0%
15	Missouri	611	1.9%
46	Montana	11	0.0%
36	Nebraska	79	0.2%
21	Nevada	358	1.1%
41	New Hampshire	29	0.1%
9	New Jersey	1,137	3.5%
28	New Mexico	232	0.7%
17	New York	578	1.8%
7	North Carolina	1,403	4.3%
48	North Dakota	5	0.0%
5	Ohio	1,669	5.1%
30	Oklahoma	186	0.6%
29	Oregon	200	0.6%
11	Pennsylvania	1,057	3.2%
37	Rhode Island	76	0.2%
32	South Carolina	142	0.4%
41	South Dakota	29	0.1%
8	Tennessee	1,299	4.0%
3	Texas	3,144	9.6%
34	Utah	105	0.3%
47	Vermont	9	0.0%
14	Virginia	650	2.0%
10	Washington	1,111	3.4%
43	West Virginia	25	0.1%
26	Wisconsin	285	0.9%
49	Wyoming	4	0.0%

RANK	STATE	ROBBERIES	% of USA
1	California	5,608	17.1%
2	Florida	3,427	10.5%
3	Texas	3,144	9.6%
4	Michigan	1,744	5.3%
5	Ohio	1,669	5.1%
6	Maryland	1,471	4.5%
7	North Carolina	1,403	4.3%
8	Tennessee	1,299	4.0%
9	New Jersey	1,137	3.5%
10	Washington	1,111	3.4%
11	Pennsylvania	1,057	3.2%
12	Georgia	968	3.0%
13	Arizona	789	2.4%
14	Virginia	650	2.0%
15	Missouri	611	1.9%
16	Massachusetts	589	1.8%
17	New York	578	1.8%
18	Indiana	421	1.3%
19	Louisiana	414	1.3%
20	Colorado	370	1.1%
21	Nevada	358	1.1%
22	Minnesota	350	1.1%
23	Connecticut	342	1.0%
24	Mississippi	312	1.0%
25	Alabama	311	0.9%
26	Wisconsin	285	0.9%
27	Arkansas	264	0.8%
28	New Mexico	232	0.7%
29	Oregon	200	0.6%
30	Oklahoma	186	0.6%
31	Iowa	152	0.5%
32	South Carolina	142	0.4%
33	Kentucky	135	0.4%
34	Utah	105	0.3%
35	Delaware	80	0.2%
36	Nebraska	79	0.2%
37	Rhode Island	76	0.2%
38	Kansas	67	0.2%
39	Alaska	39	0.1%
40	Hawaii	32	0.1%
41	New Hampshire	29	0.1%
41	South Dakota	29	0.1%
43	Maine	25	0.1%
43	West Virginia	25	0.1%
45	Idaho	22	0.1%
46	Montana	11	0.0%
47	Vermont	9	0.0%
48	North Dakota	5	0.0%
49	Wyoming	4	0.0%
NA	Illinois**	NA	NA
	District of Columbia	394	1.2%

Source: Federal Bureau of Investigation
"Crime in the United States 2000" (Uniform Crime Reports, October 22, 2001)
*Of the 317,555 robberies in 2000 for which supplemental data were received by the F.B.I. There were an additional 90,287 robberies for which the type of weapon was not reported to the F.B.I. Robbery is the taking or attempting to take anything of value by force or threat of force. Numbers are for reporting jurisdictions only.
**Not available.

Percent of Robberies Involving Blunt Objects
And Other Dangerous Weapons in 2000
National Percent = 10.3% of Robberies*

ALPHA ORDER			RANK ORDER		
RANK	STATE	PERCENT	RANK	STATE	PERCENT
39	Alabama	7.7	1	South Dakota	22.7
33	Alaska	8.8	2	Mississippi	21.3
19	Arizona	10.7	3	Washington	20.0
11	Arkansas	13.5	4	Montana	16.9
29	California	9.3	5	Iowa	15.2
8	Colorado	14.2	6	Vermont	15.0
24	Connecticut	10.2	7	Virginia	14.5
42	Delaware	7.0	8	Colorado	14.2
18	Florida	10.9	9	Tennessee	13.9
32	Georgia	9.1	10	Ohio	13.7
49	Hawaii	2.8	11	Arkansas	13.5
27	Idaho	10.0	11	Michigan	13.5
NA	Illinois**	NA	13	New Hampshire	12.3
37	Indiana	8.1	14	Maryland	12.2
5	Iowa	15.2	15	North Carolina	11.9
16	Kansas	11.3	16	Kansas	11.3
44	Kentucky	6.8	16	Massachusetts	11.3
45	Louisiana	6.7	18	Florida	10.9
24	Maine	10.2	19	Arizona	10.7
14	Maryland	12.2	19	West Virginia	10.7
16	Massachusetts	11.3	21	South Carolina	10.5
11	Michigan	13.5	21	Texas	10.5
28	Minnesota	9.6	23	Utah	10.4
2	Mississippi	21.3	24	Connecticut	10.2
34	Missouri	8.4	24	Maine	10.2
4	Montana	16.9	24	New Mexico	10.2
42	Nebraska	7.0	27	Idaho	10.0
38	Nevada	7.9	28	Minnesota	9.6
13	New Hampshire	12.3	29	California	9.3
34	New Jersey	8.4	29	North Dakota	9.3
24	New Mexico	10.2	31	New York	9.2
31	New York	9.2	32	Georgia	9.1
15	North Carolina	11.9	33	Alaska	8.8
29	North Dakota	9.3	34	Missouri	8.4
10	Ohio	13.7	34	New Jersey	8.4
40	Oklahoma	7.1	36	Rhode Island	8.2
40	Oregon	7.1	37	Indiana	8.1
47	Pennsylvania	6.3	38	Nevada	7.9
36	Rhode Island	8.2	39	Alabama	7.7
21	South Carolina	10.5	40	Oklahoma	7.1
1	South Dakota	22.7	40	Oregon	7.1
9	Tennessee	13.9	42	Delaware	7.0
21	Texas	10.5	42	Nebraska	7.0
23	Utah	10.4	44	Kentucky	6.8
6	Vermont	15.0	45	Louisiana	6.7
7	Virginia	14.5	46	Wisconsin	6.4
3	Washington	20.0	47	Pennsylvania	6.3
19	West Virginia	10.7	48	Wyoming	5.7
46	Wisconsin	6.4	49	Hawaii	2.8
48	Wyoming	5.7	NA	Illinois**	NA
				District of Columbia	11.1

Source: Morgan Quitno Press using data from Federal Bureau of Investigation
   "Crime in the United States 2000" (Uniform Crime Reports, October 22, 2001)
*Of the 317,555 robberies in 2000 for which supplemental data were received by the F.B.I. There were an additional 90,287 robberies for which the type of weapon was not reported to the F.B.I. Robbery is the taking or attempting to take anything of value by force or threat of force. Numbers are for reporting jurisdictions only.
**Not available.

Robberies Committed with Hands, Fists or Feet in 2000

National Total = 128,223 Robberies*

ALPHA ORDER

RANK	STATE	ROBBERIES	% of USA
25	Alabama	1,172	0.9%
40	Alaska	181	0.1%
13	Arizona	2,690	2.1%
31	Arkansas	614	0.5%
1	California	27,566	21.5%
27	Colorado	994	0.8%
23	Connecticut	1,400	1.1%
34	Delaware	477	0.4%
2	Florida	14,029	10.9%
10	Georgia	3,217	2.5%
28	Hawaii	878	0.7%
43	Idaho	104	0.1%
NA	Illinois**	NA	NA
18	Indiana	1,937	1.5%
37	Iowa	471	0.4%
39	Kansas	241	0.2%
29	Kentucky	820	0.6%
20	Louisiana	1,787	1.4%
41	Maine	143	0.1%
8	Maryland	4,104	3.2%
15	Massachusetts	2,324	1.8%
7	Michigan	4,197	3.3%
17	Minnesota	1,951	1.5%
38	Mississippi	464	0.4%
12	Missouri	2,851	2.2%
47	Montana	25	0.0%
35	Nebraska	474	0.4%
19	Nevada	1,921	1.5%
42	New Hampshire	141	0.1%
5	New Jersey	6,634	5.2%
30	New Mexico	775	0.6%
11	New York	3,072	2.4%
9	North Carolina	3,590	2.8%
48	North Dakota	22	0.0%
6	Ohio	5,339	4.2%
26	Oklahoma	1,169	0.9%
21	Oregon	1,528	1.2%
4	Pennsylvania	7,543	5.9%
32	Rhode Island	505	0.4%
36	South Carolina	472	0.4%
45	South Dakota	48	0.0%
16	Tennessee	2,226	1.7%
3	Texas	10,889	8.5%
33	Utah	487	0.4%
49	Vermont	19	0.0%
24	Virginia	1,245	1.0%
14	Washington	2,390	1.9%
44	West Virginia	98	0.1%
22	Wisconsin	1,410	1.1%
46	Wyoming	27	0.0%

RANK ORDER

RANK	STATE	ROBBERIES	% of USA
1	California	27,566	21.5%
2	Florida	14,029	10.9%
3	Texas	10,889	8.5%
4	Pennsylvania	7,543	5.9%
5	New Jersey	6,634	5.2%
6	Ohio	5,339	4.2%
7	Michigan	4,197	3.3%
8	Maryland	4,104	3.2%
9	North Carolina	3,590	2.8%
10	Georgia	3,217	2.5%
11	New York	3,072	2.4%
12	Missouri	2,851	2.2%
13	Arizona	2,690	2.1%
14	Washington	2,390	1.9%
15	Massachusetts	2,324	1.8%
16	Tennessee	2,226	1.7%
17	Minnesota	1,951	1.5%
18	Indiana	1,937	1.5%
19	Nevada	1,921	1.5%
20	Louisiana	1,787	1.4%
21	Oregon	1,528	1.2%
22	Wisconsin	1,410	1.1%
23	Connecticut	1,400	1.1%
24	Virginia	1,245	1.0%
25	Alabama	1,172	0.9%
26	Oklahoma	1,169	0.9%
27	Colorado	994	0.8%
28	Hawaii	878	0.7%
29	Kentucky	820	0.6%
30	New Mexico	775	0.6%
31	Arkansas	614	0.5%
32	Rhode Island	505	0.4%
33	Utah	487	0.4%
34	Delaware	477	0.4%
35	Nebraska	474	0.4%
36	South Carolina	472	0.4%
37	Iowa	471	0.4%
38	Mississippi	464	0.4%
39	Kansas	241	0.2%
40	Alaska	181	0.1%
41	Maine	143	0.1%
42	New Hampshire	141	0.1%
43	Idaho	104	0.1%
44	West Virginia	98	0.1%
45	South Dakota	48	0.0%
46	Wyoming	27	0.0%
47	Montana	25	0.0%
48	North Dakota	22	0.0%
49	Vermont	19	0.0%
NA	Illinois**	NA	NA
	District of Columbia	1,562	1.2%

Source: Federal Bureau of Investigation
"Crime in the United States 2000" (Uniform Crime Reports, October 22, 2001)
*Also called strong-armed robberies. Of the 317,555 robberies in 2000 for which supplemental data were received by the F.B.I. There were an additional 90,287 robberies for which the type of weapon was not reported to the F.B.I. Robbery is the taking or attempting to take anything of value by force or threat of force. Numbers are for reporting jurisdictions only. **Not available.

Percent of Robberies Committed with Hands, Fists or Feet in 2000

National Percent = 40.4% of Robberies*

ALPHA ORDER

RANK	STATE	PERCENT
46	Alabama	29.2
25	Alaska	41.0
34	Arizona	36.6
43	Arkansas	31.3
12	California	45.8
31	Colorado	38.2
22	Connecticut	41.8
22	Delaware	41.8
14	Florida	44.7
45	Georgia	30.4
1	Hawaii	78.2
10	Idaho	47.3
NA	Illinois**	NA
33	Indiana	37.3
11	Iowa	47.2
27	Kansas	40.5
24	Kentucky	41.5
47	Louisiana	29.1
3	Maine	58.4
37	Maryland	33.9
16	Massachusetts	44.5
39	Michigan	32.4
6	Minnesota	53.5
40	Mississippi	31.7
28	Missouri	39.0
30	Montana	38.5
21	Nebraska	41.9
19	Nevada	42.3
2	New Hampshire	60.0
7	New Jersey	48.9
37	New Mexico	33.9
7	New York	48.9
44	North Carolina	30.6
26	North Dakota	40.7
17	Ohio	43.9
14	Oklahoma	44.7
5	Oregon	54.5
13	Pennsylvania	45.3
4	Rhode Island	54.8
36	South Carolina	35.0
32	South Dakota	37.5
49	Tennessee	23.8
35	Texas	36.3
9	Utah	48.1
40	Vermont	31.7
48	Virginia	27.7
18	Washington	43.0
20	West Virginia	42.1
42	Wisconsin	31.6
29	Wyoming	38.6

RANK ORDER

RANK	STATE	PERCENT
1	Hawaii	78.2
2	New Hampshire	60.0
3	Maine	58.4
4	Rhode Island	54.8
5	Oregon	54.5
6	Minnesota	53.5
7	New Jersey	48.9
7	New York	48.9
9	Utah	48.1
10	Idaho	47.3
11	Iowa	47.2
12	California	45.8
13	Pennsylvania	45.3
14	Florida	44.7
14	Oklahoma	44.7
16	Massachusetts	44.5
17	Ohio	43.9
18	Washington	43.0
19	Nevada	42.3
20	West Virginia	42.1
21	Nebraska	41.9
22	Connecticut	41.8
22	Delaware	41.8
24	Kentucky	41.5
25	Alaska	41.0
26	North Dakota	40.7
27	Kansas	40.5
28	Missouri	39.0
29	Wyoming	38.6
30	Montana	38.5
31	Colorado	38.2
32	South Dakota	37.5
33	Indiana	37.3
34	Arizona	36.6
35	Texas	36.3
36	South Carolina	35.0
37	Maryland	33.9
37	New Mexico	33.9
39	Michigan	32.4
40	Mississippi	31.7
40	Vermont	31.7
42	Wisconsin	31.6
43	Arkansas	31.3
44	North Carolina	30.6
45	Georgia	30.4
46	Alabama	29.2
47	Louisiana	29.1
48	Virginia	27.7
49	Tennessee	23.8
NA	Illinois**	NA
	District of Columbia	44.0

Source: Morgan Quitno Press using data from Federal Bureau of Investigation
"Crime in the United States 2000" (Uniform Crime Reports, October 22, 2001)
*Also called strong-armed robberies. Of the 317,555 robberies in 2000 for which supplemental data were received by the F.B.I. There were an additional 90,287 robberies for which the type of weapon was not reported to the F.B.I. Robbery is the taking or attempting to take anything of value by force or threat of force. Numbers are for reporting jurisdictions only. **Not available.

Bank Robberies in 2000

National Total = 7,116 Robberies*

	ALPHA ORDER				RANK ORDER		
RANK	STATE	ROBBERIES	% of USA	RANK	STATE	ROBBERIES	% of USA
27	Alabama	77	1.1%	1	California	1,279	18.0%
46	Alaska	3	0.0%	2	Florida	510	7.2%
10	Arizona	184	2.6%	3	Ohio	400	5.6%
38	Arkansas	18	0.3%	4	Pennsylvania	334	4.7%
1	California	1,279	18.0%	5	Texas	331	4.7%
17	Colorado	149	2.1%	6	Michigan	324	4.6%
39	Connecticut	16	0.2%	7	Washington	314	4.4%
36	Delaware	24	0.3%	8	New York	300	4.2%
2	Florida	510	7.2%	9	North Carolina	288	4.0%
13	Georgia	174	2.4%	10	Arizona	184	2.6%
35	Hawaii	37	0.5%	11	Illinois	180	2.5%
43	Idaho	12	0.2%	12	Nevada	178	2.5%
11	Illinois	180	2.5%	13	Georgia	174	2.4%
19	Indiana	137	1.9%	14	Maryland	167	2.3%
30	Iowa	50	0.7%	15	Massachusetts	153	2.2%
31	Kansas	48	0.7%	16	Oregon	150	2.1%
28	Kentucky	65	0.9%	17	Colorado	149	2.1%
26	Louisiana	86	1.2%	18	Virginia	148	2.1%
46	Maine	3	0.0%	19	Indiana	137	1.9%
14	Maryland	167	2.3%	20	New Jersey	136	1.9%
15	Massachusetts	153	2.2%	21	Tennessee	135	1.9%
6	Michigan	324	4.6%	22	South Carolina	121	1.7%
25	Minnesota	88	1.2%	23	Wisconsin	115	1.6%
29	Mississippi	63	0.9%	24	Missouri	93	1.3%
24	Missouri	93	1.3%	25	Minnesota	88	1.2%
45	Montana	4	0.1%	26	Louisiana	86	1.2%
34	Nebraska	44	0.6%	27	Alabama	77	1.1%
12	Nevada	178	2.5%	28	Kentucky	65	0.9%
40	New Hampshire	15	0.2%	29	Mississippi	63	0.9%
20	New Jersey	136	1.9%	30	Iowa	50	0.7%
33	New Mexico	45	0.6%	31	Kansas	48	0.7%
8	New York	300	4.2%	32	Utah	46	0.6%
9	North Carolina	288	4.0%	33	New Mexico	45	0.6%
49	North Dakota	1	0.0%	34	Nebraska	44	0.6%
3	Ohio	400	5.6%	35	Hawaii	37	0.5%
37	Oklahoma	23	0.3%	36	Delaware	24	0.3%
16	Oregon	150	2.1%	37	Oklahoma	23	0.3%
4	Pennsylvania	334	4.7%	38	Arkansas	18	0.3%
41	Rhode Island	13	0.2%	39	Connecticut	16	0.2%
22	South Carolina	121	1.7%	40	New Hampshire	15	0.2%
46	South Dakota	3	0.0%	41	Rhode Island	13	0.2%
21	Tennessee	135	1.9%	41	Vermont	13	0.2%
5	Texas	331	4.7%	43	Idaho	12	0.2%
32	Utah	46	0.6%	44	West Virginia	6	0.1%
41	Vermont	13	0.2%	45	Montana	4	0.1%
18	Virginia	148	2.1%	46	Alaska	3	0.0%
7	Washington	314	4.4%	46	Maine	3	0.0%
44	West Virginia	6	0.1%	46	South Dakota	3	0.0%
23	Wisconsin	115	1.6%	49	North Dakota	1	0.0%
49	Wyoming	1	0.0%	49	Wyoming	1	0.0%
					District of Columbia	12	0.2%

Source: Federal Bureau of Investigation
"Bank Crime Statistics, Federally Insured Financial Institutions, January 1, 2000 - December 31, 2000"
Does not include 11 robberies in Puerto Rico. In addition, there were 341 bank burglaries and 78 bank larcenies. Of these 7,546 bank crimes, loot valued at $78,011,622 was taken in 6,904 cases. Of this, $13,208,476 was recovered.

Aggravated Assaults in 2000

National Total = 910,744 Aggravated Assaults*

ALPHA ORDER

RANK	STATE	ASSAULTS	% of USA
19	Alabama	14,107	1.5%
41	Alaska	2,540	0.3%
16	Arizona	17,841	2.0%
26	Arkansas	8,887	1.0%
1	California	138,418	15.2%
25	Colorado	9,425	1.0%
32	Connecticut	6,450	0.7%
39	Delaware	3,520	0.4%
2	Florida	90,008	9.9%
10	Georgia	25,450	2.8%
44	Hawaii	1,450	0.2%
40	Idaho	2,644	0.3%
5	Illinois	50,828	5.6%
22	Indiana	12,837	1.4%
34	Iowa	6,003	0.7%
30	Kansas	7,231	0.8%
29	Kentucky	7,363	0.8%
14	Louisiana	20,851	2.3%
48	Maine	815	0.1%
9	Maryland	26,130	2.9%
13	Massachusetts	22,594	2.5%
6	Michigan	35,753	3.9%
28	Minnesota	7,709	0.8%
33	Mississippi	6,290	0.7%
15	Missouri	18,123	2.0%
43	Montana	1,605	0.2%
37	Nebraska	3,960	0.4%
35	Nevada	4,942	0.5%
45	New Hampshire	1,170	0.1%
18	New Jersey	17,099	1.9%
24	New Mexico	10,230	1.1%
4	New York	60,090	6.6%
11	North Carolina	24,715	2.7%
50	North Dakota	294	0.0%
17	Ohio	17,636	1.9%
21	Oklahoma	12,958	1.4%
27	Oregon	7,756	0.9%
7	Pennsylvania	29,580	3.2%
42	Rhode Island	1,742	0.2%
12	South Carolina	24,666	2.7%
47	South Dakota	816	0.1%
8	Tennessee	28,172	3.1%
3	Texas	74,302	8.2%
38	Utah	3,563	0.4%
49	Vermont	425	0.0%
23	Virginia	11,631	1.3%
20	Washington	13,043	1.4%
36	West Virginia	4,597	0.5%
31	Wisconsin	6,829	0.7%
46	Wyoming	1,074	0.1%

RANK ORDER

RANK	STATE	ASSAULTS	% of USA
1	California	138,418	15.2%
2	Florida	90,008	9.9%
3	Texas	74,302	8.2%
4	New York	60,090	6.6%
5	Illinois	50,828	5.6%
6	Michigan	35,753	3.9%
7	Pennsylvania	29,580	3.2%
8	Tennessee	28,172	3.1%
9	Maryland	26,130	2.9%
10	Georgia	25,450	2.8%
11	North Carolina	24,715	2.7%
12	South Carolina	24,666	2.7%
13	Massachusetts	22,594	2.5%
14	Louisiana	20,851	2.3%
15	Missouri	18,123	2.0%
16	Arizona	17,841	2.0%
17	Ohio	17,636	1.9%
18	New Jersey	17,099	1.9%
19	Alabama	14,107	1.5%
20	Washington	13,043	1.4%
21	Oklahoma	12,958	1.4%
22	Indiana	12,837	1.4%
23	Virginia	11,631	1.3%
24	New Mexico	10,230	1.1%
25	Colorado	9,425	1.0%
26	Arkansas	8,887	1.0%
27	Oregon	7,756	0.9%
28	Minnesota	7,709	0.8%
29	Kentucky	7,363	0.8%
30	Kansas	7,231	0.8%
31	Wisconsin	6,829	0.7%
32	Connecticut	6,450	0.7%
33	Mississippi	6,290	0.7%
34	Iowa	6,003	0.7%
35	Nevada	4,942	0.5%
36	West Virginia	4,597	0.5%
37	Nebraska	3,960	0.4%
38	Utah	3,563	0.4%
39	Delaware	3,520	0.4%
40	Idaho	2,644	0.3%
41	Alaska	2,540	0.3%
42	Rhode Island	1,742	0.2%
43	Montana	1,605	0.2%
44	Hawaii	1,450	0.2%
45	New Hampshire	1,170	0.1%
46	Wyoming	1,074	0.1%
47	South Dakota	816	0.1%
48	Maine	815	0.1%
49	Vermont	425	0.0%
50	North Dakota	294	0.0%
	District of Columbia	4,582	0.5%

Source: Federal Bureau of Investigation
   "Crime in the United States 2000" (Uniform Crime Reports, October 22, 2001)
*Aggravated assault is an attack for the purpose of inflicting severe bodily injury.

Average Time Between Aggravated Assaults in 2000

National Rate = An Aggravated Assault Occurs Every 35 Seconds*

RANK	STATE	MINUTES.SECONDS
32	Alabama	37.16
10	Alaska	206.56
35	Arizona	29.28
25	Arkansas	59.08
50	California	3.48
26	Colorado	55.46
19	Connecticut	81.29
12	Delaware	149.19
49	Florida	5.50
41	Georgia	20.39
7	Hawaii	362.29
11	Idaho	198.47
46	Illinois	10.20
29	Indiana	40.56
17	Iowa	87.34
21	Kansas	72.41
22	Kentucky	71.23
37	Louisiana	25.13
3	Maine	644.55
42	Maryland	20.07
38	Massachusetts	23.16
45	Michigan	14.42
23	Minnesota	68.11
18	Mississippi	83.34
36	Missouri	29.00
8	Montana	327.29
14	Nebraska	132.44
16	Nevada	106.21
6	New Hampshire	449.14
33	New Jersey	30.44
27	New Mexico	51.23
47	New York	8.45
40	North Carolina	21.16
1	North Dakota	1,787.46
34	Ohio	29.48
30	Oklahoma	40.34
24	Oregon	67.46
44	Pennsylvania	17.46
9	Rhode Island	301.43
39	South Carolina	21.19
4	South Dakota	644.07
43	Tennessee	18.40
48	Texas	7.04
13	Utah	147.31
2	Vermont	1,236.43
28	Virginia	45.11
31	Washington	40.18
15	West Virginia	114.20
20	Wisconsin	76.58
5	Wyoming	489.23

RANK	STATE	MINUTES.SECONDS
1	North Dakota	1,787.46
2	Vermont	1,236.43
3	Maine	644.55
4	South Dakota	644.07
5	Wyoming	489.23
6	New Hampshire	449.14
7	Hawaii	362.29
8	Montana	327.29
9	Rhode Island	301.43
10	Alaska	206.56
11	Idaho	198.47
12	Delaware	149.19
13	Utah	147.31
14	Nebraska	132.44
15	West Virginia	114.20
16	Nevada	106.21
17	Iowa	87.34
18	Mississippi	83.34
19	Connecticut	81.29
20	Wisconsin	76.58
21	Kansas	72.41
22	Kentucky	71.23
23	Minnesota	68.11
24	Oregon	67.46
25	Arkansas	59.08
26	Colorado	55.46
27	New Mexico	51.23
28	Virginia	45.11
29	Indiana	40.56
30	Oklahoma	40.34
31	Washington	40.18
32	Alabama	37.16
33	New Jersey	30.44
34	Ohio	29.48
35	Arizona	29.28
36	Missouri	29.00
37	Louisiana	25.13
38	Massachusetts	23.16
39	South Carolina	21.19
40	North Carolina	21.16
41	Georgia	20.39
42	Maryland	20.07
43	Tennessee	18.40
44	Pennsylvania	17.46
45	Michigan	14.42
46	Illinois	10.20
47	New York	8.45
48	Texas	7.04
49	Florida	5.50
50	California	3.48

| | District of Columbia | 114.43 |

Source: Morgan Quitno Press using data from Federal Bureau of Investigation
"Crime in the United States 2000" (Uniform Crime Reports, October 22, 2001)
*Aggravated assault is an attack for the purpose of inflicting severe bodily injury.

Percent Change in Number of Aggravated Assaults: 1999 to 2000

National Percent Change = 0.1% Decrease*

ALPHA ORDER				RANK ORDER		
RANK	STATE	PERCENT CHANGE		RANK	STATE	PERCENT CHANGE
26	Alabama	(1.1)		1	North Dakota	36.1
45	Alaska	(8.4)		2	Mississippi	20.7
17	Arizona	3.3		3	Wyoming	20.3
5	Arkansas	11.5		4	Maryland	14.6
20	California	1.4		5	Arkansas	11.5
11	Colorado	6.0		6	Minnesota	10.2
28	Connecticut	(1.2)		7	Idaho	10.1
21	Delaware	0.9		8	Hawaii	8.0
21	Florida	0.9		9	Rhode Island	7.2
26	Georgia	(1.1)		10	Pennsylvania	6.1
8	Hawaii	8.0		11	Colorado	6.0
7	Idaho	10.1		11	South Dakota	6.0
30	Illinois	(2.3)		13	Ohio	5.7
39	Indiana	(6.8)		14	Tennessee	5.5
31	Iowa	(2.5)		15	Kansas	5.0
15	Kansas	5.0		16	Montana	4.5
35	Kentucky	(5.1)		17	Arizona	3.3
41	Louisiana	(7.4)		18	Oklahoma	2.2
46	Maine	(9.1)		19	New York	2.1
4	Maryland	14.6		20	California	1.4
48	Massachusetts	(14.1)		21	Delaware	0.9
34	Michigan	(3.5)		21	Florida	0.9
6	Minnesota	10.2		23	Texas	0.3
2	Mississippi	20.7		24	Washington	0.1
29	Missouri	(1.5)		25	Nevada	(1.0)
16	Montana	4.5		26	Alabama	(1.1)
49	Nebraska	(27.1)		26	Georgia	(1.1)
25	Nevada	(1.0)		28	Connecticut	(1.2)
NA	New Hampshire**	NA		29	Missouri	(1.5)
33	New Jersey	(2.9)		30	Illinois	(2.3)
36	New Mexico	(5.5)		31	Iowa	(2.5)
19	New York	2.1		32	South Carolina	(2.6)
41	North Carolina	(7.4)		33	New Jersey	(2.9)
1	North Dakota	36.1		34	Michigan	(3.5)
13	Ohio	5.7		35	Kentucky	(5.1)
18	Oklahoma	2.2		36	New Mexico	(5.5)
38	Oregon	(6.2)		36	Wisconsin	(5.5)
10	Pennsylvania	6.1		38	Oregon	(6.2)
9	Rhode Island	7.2		39	Indiana	(6.8)
32	South Carolina	(2.6)		40	Vermont	(7.2)
11	South Dakota	6.0		41	Louisiana	(7.4)
14	Tennessee	5.5		41	North Carolina	(7.4)
23	Texas	0.3		41	Virginia	(7.4)
44	Utah	(7.7)		44	Utah	(7.7)
40	Vermont	(7.2)		45	Alaska	(8.4)
41	Virginia	(7.4)		46	Maine	(9.1)
24	Washington	0.1		47	West Virginia	(12.6)
47	West Virginia	(12.6)		48	Massachusetts	(14.1)
36	Wisconsin	(5.5)		49	Nebraska	(27.1)
3	Wyoming	20.3		NA	New Hampshire**	NA
					District of Columbia	(0.7)

Source: Federal Bureau of Investigation
   "Crime in the United States 2000" (Uniform Crime Reports, October 22, 2001)
Aggravated assault is an attack for the purpose of inflicting severe bodily injury.
**Not available.*

Aggravated Assault Rate in 2000

National Rate = 323.6 Aggravated Assaults per 100,000 Population*

ALPHA ORDER				RANK ORDER		
RANK	STATE	RATE		RANK	STATE	RATE
18	Alabama	317.2		1	South Carolina	614.8
10	Alaska	405.1		2	Florida	563.2
15	Arizona	347.7		3	New Mexico	562.4
16	Arkansas	332.4		4	Tennessee	495.2
9	California	408.7		5	Maryland	493.3
30	Colorado	219.1		6	Louisiana	466.6
36	Connecticut	189.4		7	Delaware	449.2
7	Delaware	449.2		8	Illinois	409.3
2	Florida	563.2		9	California	408.7
20	Georgia	310.9		10	Alaska	405.1
45	Hawaii	119.7		11	Oklahoma	375.5
34	Idaho	204.3		12	Michigan	359.7
8	Illinois	409.3		13	Texas	356.3
32	Indiana	211.1		14	Massachusetts	355.9
33	Iowa	205.1		15	Arizona	347.7
22	Kansas	269.0		16	Arkansas	332.4
37	Kentucky	182.2		17	Missouri	323.9
6	Louisiana	466.6		18	Alabama	317.2
49	Maine	63.9		19	New York	316.7
5	Maryland	493.3		20	Georgia	310.9
14	Massachusetts	355.9		21	North Carolina	307.0
12	Michigan	359.7		22	Kansas	269.0
42	Minnesota	156.7		23	West Virginia	254.2
29	Mississippi	221.1		24	Nevada	247.3
17	Missouri	323.9		25	Pennsylvania	240.9
38	Montana	177.9		26	Nebraska	231.4
26	Nebraska	231.4		27	Oregon	226.7
24	Nevada	247.3		28	Washington	221.3
47	New Hampshire	94.7		29	Mississippi	221.1
35	New Jersey	203.2		30	Colorado	219.1
3	New Mexico	562.4		31	Wyoming	217.5
19	New York	316.7		32	Indiana	211.1
21	North Carolina	307.0		33	Iowa	205.1
50	North Dakota	45.8		34	Idaho	204.3
43	Ohio	155.3		35	New Jersey	203.2
11	Oklahoma	375.5		36	Connecticut	189.4
27	Oregon	226.7		37	Kentucky	182.2
25	Pennsylvania	240.9		38	Montana	177.9
39	Rhode Island	166.2		39	Rhode Island	166.2
1	South Carolina	614.8		40	Virginia	164.3
46	South Dakota	108.1		41	Utah	159.5
4	Tennessee	495.2		42	Minnesota	156.7
13	Texas	356.3		43	Ohio	155.3
41	Utah	159.5		44	Wisconsin	127.3
48	Vermont	69.8		45	Hawaii	119.7
40	Virginia	164.3		46	South Dakota	108.1
28	Washington	221.3		47	New Hampshire	94.7
23	West Virginia	254.2		48	Vermont	69.8
44	Wisconsin	127.3		49	Maine	63.9
31	Wyoming	217.5		50	North Dakota	45.8
					District of Columbia	801.0

Source: Federal Bureau of Investigation
   "Crime in the United States 2000" (Uniform Crime Reports, October 22, 2001)
   *Aggravated assault is an attack for the purpose of inflicting severe bodily injury.

Percent Change in Aggravated Assault Rate: 1999 to 2000

National Percent Change = 3.2% Decrease*

ALPHA ORDER				RANK ORDER		
RANK	STATE	PERCENT CHANGE		RANK	STATE	PERCENT CHANGE
21	Alabama	(2.8)		1	North Dakota	34.3
39	Alaska	(9.5)		2	Mississippi	17.5
24	Arizona	(3.8)		3	Wyoming	16.8
7	Arkansas	6.4		4	Maryland	11.9
18	California	(0.7)		5	Minnesota	7.0
16	Colorado	0.0		6	Idaho	6.5
30	Connecticut	(4.8)		7	Arkansas	6.4
22	Delaware	(3.0)		8	Hawaii	5.6
28	Florida	(4.6)		9	Ohio	4.8
32	Georgia	(5.9)		10	Kansas	3.7
8	Hawaii	5.6		11	Pennsylvania	3.6
6	Idaho	6.5		12	South Dakota	2.9
28	Illinois	(4.6)		13	Montana	2.2
36	Indiana	(8.9)		14	Tennessee	1.7
27	Iowa	(4.4)		15	Rhode Island	1.3
10	Kansas	3.7		16	Colorado	0.0
34	Kentucky	(7.0)		17	Oklahoma	(0.5)
38	Louisiana	(9.4)		18	California	(0.7)
44	Maine	(10.7)		19	New York	(2.1)
4	Maryland	11.9		20	Washington	(2.2)
48	Massachusetts	(16.5)		21	Alabama	(2.8)
26	Michigan	(4.3)		22	Delaware	(3.0)
5	Minnesota	7.0		23	Texas	(3.6)
2	Mississippi	17.5		24	Arizona	(3.8)
24	Missouri	(3.8)		24	Missouri	(3.8)
13	Montana	2.2		26	Michigan	(4.3)
49	Nebraska	(29.0)		27	Iowa	(4.4)
43	Nevada	(10.4)		28	Florida	(4.6)
NA	New Hampshire**	NA		28	Illinois	(4.6)
33	New Jersey	(6.0)		30	Connecticut	(4.8)
41	New Mexico	(9.6)		31	South Carolina	(5.6)
19	New York	(2.1)		32	Georgia	(5.9)
45	North Carolina	(12.0)		33	New Jersey	(6.0)
1	North Dakota	34.3		34	Kentucky	(7.0)
9	Ohio	4.8		35	Wisconsin	(7.5)
17	Oklahoma	(0.5)		36	Indiana	(8.9)
37	Oregon	(9.1)		37	Oregon	(9.1)
11	Pennsylvania	3.6		38	Louisiana	(9.4)
15	Rhode Island	1.3		39	Alaska	(9.5)
31	South Carolina	(5.6)		39	Vermont	(9.5)
12	South Dakota	2.9		41	New Mexico	(9.6)
14	Tennessee	1.7		42	Virginia	(10.1)
23	Texas	(3.6)		43	Nevada	(10.4)
45	Utah	(12.0)		44	Maine	(10.7)
39	Vermont	(9.5)		45	North Carolina	(12.0)
42	Virginia	(10.1)		45	Utah	(12.0)
20	Washington	(2.2)		47	West Virginia	(12.7)
47	West Virginia	(12.7)		48	Massachusetts	(16.5)
35	Wisconsin	(7.5)		49	Nebraska	(29.0)
3	Wyoming	16.8		NA	New Hampshire**	NA
					District of Columbia	(9.9)

Source: Federal Bureau of Investigation
   "Crime in the United States 2000" (Uniform Crime Reports, October 22, 2001)
*Aggravated assault is an attack for the purpose of inflicting severe bodily injury.
**Not available.

369

Aggravated Assaults with Firearms in 2000

National Total = 129,044 Aggravated Assaults*

ALPHA ORDER					RANK ORDER			
RANK	STATE	ASSAULTS	% of USA		RANK	STATE	ASSAULTS	% of USA
13	Alabama	2,461	1.9%		1	California	20,981	16.3%
39	Alaska	353	0.3%		2	Texas	14,866	11.5%
10	Arizona	4,103	3.2%		3	Florida	12,416	9.6%
19	Arkansas	1,687	1.3%		4	Tennessee	7,817	6.1%
1	California	20,981	16.3%		5	Michigan	7,547	5.8%
21	Colorado	1,390	1.1%		6	North Carolina	5,966	4.6%
32	Connecticut	610	0.5%		7	Pennsylvania	5,255	4.1%
35	Delaware	508	0.4%		8	Georgia	4,784	3.7%
3	Florida	12,416	9.6%		9	Louisiana	4,250	3.3%
8	Georgia	4,784	3.7%		10	Arizona	4,103	3.2%
42	Hawaii	123	0.1%		11	Missouri	4,046	3.1%
31	Idaho	624	0.5%		12	Maryland	3,330	2.6%
NA	Illinois**	NA	NA		13	Alabama	2,461	1.9%
20	Indiana	1,484	1.1%		14	New Jersey	2,422	1.9%
36	Iowa	479	0.4%		15	Ohio	2,170	1.7%
40	Kansas	219	0.2%		16	Washington	2,088	1.6%
33	Kentucky	592	0.5%		17	Oklahoma	2,078	1.6%
9	Louisiana	4,250	3.3%		18	New Mexico	1,725	1.3%
48	Maine	29	0.0%		19	Arkansas	1,687	1.3%
12	Maryland	3,330	2.6%		20	Indiana	1,484	1.1%
26	Massachusetts	1,124	0.9%		21	Colorado	1,390	1.1%
5	Michigan	7,547	5.8%		22	South Carolina	1,383	1.1%
25	Minnesota	1,225	0.9%		23	New York	1,364	1.1%
34	Mississippi	557	0.4%		24	Virginia	1,296	1.0%
11	Missouri	4,046	3.1%		25	Minnesota	1,225	0.9%
46	Montana	85	0.1%		26	Massachusetts	1,124	0.9%
30	Nebraska	734	0.6%		27	Wisconsin	1,104	0.9%
29	Nevada	757	0.6%		28	Oregon	848	0.7%
44	New Hampshire	87	0.1%		29	Nevada	757	0.6%
14	New Jersey	2,422	1.9%		30	Nebraska	734	0.6%
18	New Mexico	1,725	1.3%		31	Idaho	624	0.5%
23	New York	1,364	1.1%		32	Connecticut	610	0.5%
6	North Carolina	5,966	4.6%		33	Kentucky	592	0.5%
49	North Dakota	4	0.0%		34	Mississippi	557	0.4%
15	Ohio	2,170	1.7%		35	Delaware	508	0.4%
17	Oklahoma	2,078	1.6%		36	Iowa	479	0.4%
28	Oregon	848	0.7%		37	West Virginia	412	0.3%
7	Pennsylvania	5,255	4.1%		38	Utah	398	0.3%
41	Rhode Island	217	0.2%		39	Alaska	353	0.3%
22	South Carolina	1,383	1.1%		40	Kansas	219	0.2%
45	South Dakota	86	0.1%		41	Rhode Island	217	0.2%
4	Tennessee	7,817	6.1%		42	Hawaii	123	0.1%
2	Texas	14,866	11.5%		43	Wyoming	107	0.1%
38	Utah	398	0.3%		44	New Hampshire	87	0.1%
47	Vermont	34	0.0%		45	South Dakota	86	0.1%
24	Virginia	1,296	1.0%		46	Montana	85	0.1%
16	Washington	2,088	1.6%		47	Vermont	34	0.0%
37	West Virginia	412	0.3%		48	Maine	29	0.0%
27	Wisconsin	1,104	0.9%		49	North Dakota	4	0.0%
43	Wyoming	107	0.1%		NA	Illinois**	NA	NA
						District of Columbia	819	0.6%

Source: Federal Bureau of Investigation
   "Crime in the United States 2000" (Uniform Crime Reports, October 22, 2001)
Of the 714,650 aggravated assaults in 2000 for which supplemental data were received by the F.B.I. There were
an additional 196,094 aggravated assaults for which the type of weapon was not reported to the F.B.I. Aggravated
assault is an attack for the purpose of inflicting severe bodily injury. Numbers are for reporting jurisdictions only.
**Not available.

Aggravated Assault Rate with Firearms in 2000

National Rate = 60.0 Aggravated Assaults per 100,000 Population*

ALPHA ORDER				RANK ORDER		
RANK	STATE	RATE		RANK	STATE	RATE
12	Alabama	75.7		1	Tennessee	145.5
20	Alaska	62.0		2	South Carolina	143.5
7	Arizona	88.2		3	Delaware	128.6
15	Arkansas	68.9		4	New Mexico	125.4
19	California	62.1		5	Louisiana	110.4
26	Colorado	41.9		6	Missouri	91.9
42	Connecticut	20.4		7	Arizona	88.2
3	Delaware	128.6		8	North Carolina	86.1
10	Florida	79.1		9	Michigan	83.9
11	Georgia	78.4		10	Florida	79.1
46	Hawaii	10.2		11	Georgia	78.4
23	Idaho	48.9		12	Alabama	75.7
NA	Illinois**	NA		13	Maryland	74.7
29	Indiana	36.0		14	Texas	72.3
40	Iowa	20.7		15	Arkansas	68.9
18	Kansas	64.4		16	Kentucky	68.5
16	Kentucky	68.5		17	West Virginia	67.8
5	Louisiana	110.4		18	Kansas	64.4
48	Maine	2.3		19	California	62.1
13	Maryland	74.7		20	Alaska	62.0
38	Massachusetts	22.9		21	Oklahoma	60.2
9	Michigan	83.9		22	Pennsylvania	52.9
35	Minnesota	26.4		23	Idaho	48.9
25	Mississippi	42.7		24	Nebraska	47.3
6	Missouri	91.9		25	Mississippi	42.7
32	Montana	29.4		26	Colorado	41.9
24	Nebraska	47.3		27	Washington	39.0
28	Nevada	37.9		28	Nevada	37.9
45	New Hampshire	11.9		29	Indiana	36.0
33	New Jersey	28.8		30	Ohio	33.7
4	New Mexico	125.4		31	Virginia	33.0
43	New York	19.5		32	Montana	29.4
8	North Carolina	86.1		33	New Jersey	28.8
49	North Dakota	0.7		34	Oregon	26.6
30	Ohio	33.7		35	Minnesota	26.4
21	Oklahoma	60.2		36	Utah	25.5
34	Oregon	26.6		37	Wisconsin	25.0
22	Pennsylvania	52.9		38	Massachusetts	22.9
40	Rhode Island	20.7		39	Wyoming	21.8
2	South Carolina	143.5		40	Iowa	20.7
44	South Dakota	14.4		40	Rhode Island	20.7
1	Tennessee	145.5		42	Connecticut	20.4
14	Texas	72.3		43	New York	19.5
36	Utah	25.5		44	South Dakota	14.4
47	Vermont	7.2		45	New Hampshire	11.9
31	Virginia	33.0		46	Hawaii	10.2
27	Washington	39.0		47	Vermont	7.2
17	West Virginia	67.8		48	Maine	2.3
37	Wisconsin	25.0		49	North Dakota	0.7
39	Wyoming	21.8		NA	Illinois**	NA
					District of Columbia	143.2

Source: Morgan Quitno Press using data from Federal Bureau of Investigation
    "Crime in the United States 2000" (Uniform Crime Reports, October 22, 2001)
*Based only on population of reporting jurisdictions. Aggravated assault is an attack for the purpose of inflicting severe bodily injury. National rate reflects only those robberies for which the type of weapon was known and reported.
**Not available.

Percent of Aggravated Assaults Involving Firearms in 2000

National Percent = 18.1% of Aggravated Assaults*

ALPHA ORDER

RANK	STATE	PERCENT
4	Alabama	25.1
25	Alaska	16.8
5	Arizona	25.0
15	Arkansas	20.3
33	California	15.2
18	Colorado	19.3
41	Connecticut	10.4
21	Delaware	18.0
36	Florida	14.0
6	Georgia	24.3
45	Hawaii	8.5
8	Idaho	23.8
NA	Illinois**	NA
34	Indiana	15.1
44	Iowa	9.0
24	Kansas	17.1
12	Kentucky	21.2
7	Louisiana	24.0
48	Maine	3.6
31	Maryland	15.4
47	Massachusetts	6.4
9	Michigan	22.9
27	Minnesota	16.5
10	Mississippi	22.5
3	Missouri	25.7
46	Montana	8.2
19	Nebraska	19.0
32	Nevada	15.3
27	New Hampshire	16.5
35	New Jersey	14.2
11	New Mexico	21.3
40	New York	10.5
2	North Carolina	26.4
49	North Dakota	1.5
23	Ohio	17.5
30	Oklahoma	16.0
39	Oregon	11.6
14	Pennsylvania	20.7
37	Rhode Island	12.5
17	South Carolina	19.8
38	South Dakota	11.9
1	Tennessee	28.9
16	Texas	20.2
27	Utah	16.5
42	Vermont	10.1
22	Virginia	17.6
25	Washington	16.8
13	West Virginia	21.1
20	Wisconsin	18.2
43	Wyoming	10.0

RANK ORDER

RANK	STATE	PERCENT
1	Tennessee	28.9
2	North Carolina	26.4
3	Missouri	25.7
4	Alabama	25.1
5	Arizona	25.0
6	Georgia	24.3
7	Louisiana	24.0
8	Idaho	23.8
9	Michigan	22.9
10	Mississippi	22.5
11	New Mexico	21.3
12	Kentucky	21.2
13	West Virginia	21.1
14	Pennsylvania	20.7
15	Arkansas	20.3
16	Texas	20.2
17	South Carolina	19.8
18	Colorado	19.3
19	Nebraska	19.0
20	Wisconsin	18.2
21	Delaware	18.0
22	Virginia	17.6
23	Ohio	17.5
24	Kansas	17.1
25	Alaska	16.8
25	Washington	16.8
27	Minnesota	16.5
27	New Hampshire	16.5
27	Utah	16.5
30	Oklahoma	16.0
31	Maryland	15.4
32	Nevada	15.3
33	California	15.2
34	Indiana	15.1
35	New Jersey	14.2
36	Florida	14.0
37	Rhode Island	12.5
38	South Dakota	11.9
39	Oregon	11.6
40	New York	10.5
41	Connecticut	10.4
42	Vermont	10.1
43	Wyoming	10.0
44	Iowa	9.0
45	Hawaii	8.5
46	Montana	8.2
47	Massachusetts	6.4
48	Maine	3.6
49	North Dakota	1.5
NA	Illinois**	NA

District of Columbia 17.9

Source: Morgan Quitno Press using data from Federal Bureau of Investigation
"Crime in the United States 2000" (Uniform Crime Reports, October 22, 2001)
*Of the 714,650 aggravated assaults in 2000 for which supplemental data were received by the F.B.I. There were an additional 196,094 aggravated assaults for which the type of weapon was not reported to the F.B.I. Aggravated assault is an attack for the purpose of inflicting severe bodily injury. Numbers are for reporting jurisdictions only.
**Not available.

Aggravated Assaults with Knives or Cutting Instruments in 2000

National Total = 128,687 Aggravated Assaults*

ALPHA ORDER

RANK ORDER

RANK	STATE	ASSAULTS	% of USA		RANK	STATE	ASSAULTS	% of USA
20	Alabama	1,690	1.3%		1	California	18,240	14.2%
37	Alaska	503	0.4%		2	Florida	16,542	12.9%
15	Arizona	2,404	1.9%		3	Texas	16,435	12.8%
24	Arkansas	1,312	1.0%		4	Michigan	6,708	5.2%
1	California	18,240	14.2%		5	Tennessee	5,444	4.2%
21	Colorado	1,628	1.3%		6	North Carolina	4,600	3.6%
30	Connecticut	893	0.7%		7	Maryland	4,495	3.5%
33	Delaware	645	0.5%		8	Georgia	3,875	3.0%
2	Florida	16,542	12.9%		9	Pennsylvania	3,768	2.9%
8	Georgia	3,875	3.0%		10	Louisiana	3,586	2.8%
43	Hawaii	176	0.1%		11	New Jersey	3,579	2.8%
34	Idaho	559	0.4%		12	Massachusetts	3,276	2.5%
NA	Illinois**	NA	NA		13	Missouri	2,639	2.1%
25	Indiana	1,306	1.0%		14	New York	2,607	2.0%
31	Iowa	855	0.7%		15	Arizona	2,404	1.9%
41	Kansas	227	0.2%		16	Washington	2,391	1.9%
36	Kentucky	506	0.4%		17	Ohio	2,070	1.6%
10	Louisiana	3,586	2.8%		18	Oklahoma	2,055	1.6%
47	Maine	99	0.1%		19	Minnesota	1,805	1.4%
7	Maryland	4,495	3.5%		20	Alabama	1,690	1.3%
12	Massachusetts	3,276	2.5%		21	Colorado	1,628	1.3%
4	Michigan	6,708	5.2%		22	New Mexico	1,502	1.2%
19	Minnesota	1,805	1.4%		23	Virginia	1,440	1.1%
38	Mississippi	476	0.4%		24	Arkansas	1,312	1.0%
13	Missouri	2,639	2.1%		25	Indiana	1,306	1.0%
46	Montana	121	0.1%		26	South Carolina	1,304	1.0%
32	Nebraska	665	0.5%		27	Nevada	1,163	0.9%
27	Nevada	1,163	0.9%		28	Oregon	1,090	0.8%
45	New Hampshire	155	0.1%		29	Wisconsin	1,002	0.8%
11	New Jersey	3,579	2.8%		30	Connecticut	893	0.7%
22	New Mexico	1,502	1.2%		31	Iowa	855	0.7%
14	New York	2,607	2.0%		32	Nebraska	665	0.5%
6	North Carolina	4,600	3.6%		33	Delaware	645	0.5%
49	North Dakota	39	0.0%		34	Idaho	559	0.4%
17	Ohio	2,070	1.6%		35	Utah	538	0.4%
18	Oklahoma	2,055	1.6%		36	Kentucky	506	0.4%
28	Oregon	1,090	0.8%		37	Alaska	503	0.4%
9	Pennsylvania	3,768	2.9%		38	Mississippi	476	0.4%
39	Rhode Island	412	0.3%		39	Rhode Island	412	0.3%
26	South Carolina	1,304	1.0%		40	West Virginia	244	0.2%
42	South Dakota	221	0.2%		41	Kansas	227	0.2%
5	Tennessee	5,444	4.2%		42	South Dakota	221	0.2%
3	Texas	16,435	12.8%		43	Hawaii	176	0.1%
35	Utah	538	0.4%		44	Wyoming	165	0.1%
48	Vermont	56	0.0%		45	New Hampshire	155	0.1%
23	Virginia	1,440	1.1%		46	Montana	121	0.1%
16	Washington	2,391	1.9%		47	Maine	99	0.1%
40	West Virginia	244	0.2%		48	Vermont	56	0.0%
29	Wisconsin	1,002	0.8%		49	North Dakota	39	0.0%
44	Wyoming	165	0.1%		NA	Illinois**	NA	NA
						District of Columbia	1,176	0.9%

Source: Federal Bureau of Investigation
    "Crime in the United States 2000" (Uniform Crime Reports, October 22, 2001)
*Of the 714,650 aggravated assaults in 2000 for which supplemental data were received by the F.B.I. There were
an additional 196,094 aggravated assaults for which the type of weapon was not reported to the F.B.I. Aggravated
assault is an attack for the purpose of inflicting severe bodily injury. Numbers are for reporting jurisdictions only.
**Not available.

Percent of Aggravated Assaults Involving Knives or Cutting Instruments in 2000

National Percent = 18.0% of Aggravated Assaults*

ALPHA ORDER

RANK	STATE	PERCENT
29	Alabama	17.2
4	Alaska	23.9
42	Arizona	14.6
37	Arkansas	15.8
45	California	13.2
8	Colorado	22.6
39	Connecticut	15.3
7	Delaware	22.8
24	Florida	18.6
19	Georgia	19.7
48	Hawaii	12.1
11	Idaho	21.4
NA	Illinois**	NA
44	Indiana	13.3
35	Iowa	16.0
28	Kansas	17.7
27	Kentucky	18.1
16	Louisiana	20.2
47	Maine	12.2
13	Maryland	20.7
23	Massachusetts	18.7
14	Michigan	20.4
3	Minnesota	24.3
22	Mississippi	19.2
31	Missouri	16.7
49	Montana	11.7
29	Nebraska	17.2
6	Nevada	23.5
2	New Hampshire	29.4
12	New Jersey	20.9
26	New Mexico	18.5
18	New York	20.0
15	North Carolina	20.3
43	North Dakota	14.4
31	Ohio	16.7
36	Oklahoma	15.9
40	Oregon	14.9
41	Pennsylvania	14.8
5	Rhode Island	23.7
24	South Carolina	18.6
1	South Dakota	30.7
17	Tennessee	20.1
9	Texas	22.4
10	Utah	22.2
33	Vermont	16.6
20	Virginia	19.5
21	Washington	19.3
46	West Virginia	12.5
34	Wisconsin	16.5
38	Wyoming	15.4

RANK ORDER

RANK	STATE	PERCENT
1	South Dakota	30.7
2	New Hampshire	29.4
3	Minnesota	24.3
4	Alaska	23.9
5	Rhode Island	23.7
6	Nevada	23.5
7	Delaware	22.8
8	Colorado	22.6
9	Texas	22.4
10	Utah	22.2
11	Idaho	21.4
12	New Jersey	20.9
13	Maryland	20.7
14	Michigan	20.4
15	North Carolina	20.3
16	Louisiana	20.2
17	Tennessee	20.1
18	New York	20.0
19	Georgia	19.7
20	Virginia	19.5
21	Washington	19.3
22	Mississippi	19.2
23	Massachusetts	18.7
24	Florida	18.6
24	South Carolina	18.6
26	New Mexico	18.5
27	Kentucky	18.1
28	Kansas	17.7
29	Alabama	17.2
29	Nebraska	17.2
31	Missouri	16.7
31	Ohio	16.7
33	Vermont	16.6
34	Wisconsin	16.5
35	Iowa	16.0
36	Oklahoma	15.9
37	Arkansas	15.8
38	Wyoming	15.4
39	Connecticut	15.3
40	Oregon	14.9
41	Pennsylvania	14.8
42	Arizona	14.6
43	North Dakota	14.4
44	Indiana	13.3
45	California	13.2
46	West Virginia	12.5
47	Maine	12.2
48	Hawaii	12.1
49	Montana	11.7
NA	Illinois**	NA

District of Columbia   25.7

Source: Morgan Quitno Press using data from Federal Bureau of Investigation
   "Crime in the United States 2000" (Uniform Crime Reports, October 22, 2001)
*Of the 714,650 aggravated assaults in 2000 for which supplemental data were received by the F.B.I. There were
an additional 196,094 aggravated assaults for which the type of weapon was not reported to the F.B.I. Aggravated
assault is an attack for the purpose of inflicting severe bodily injury. Numbers are for reporting jurisdictions only.
**Not available.

Aggravated Assaults with Blunt Objects and Other Dangerous Weapons in 2000

National Total = 256,782 Aggravated Assaults*

ALPHA ORDER					RANK ORDER			
RANK	STATE	ASSAULTS	% of USA		RANK	STATE	ASSAULTS	% of USA
20	Alabama	2,832	1.1%		1	California	43,562	17.0%
40	Alaska	578	0.2%		2	Florida	42,333	16.5%
15	Arizona	4,690	1.8%		3	Texas	28,452	11.1%
25	Arkansas	2,216	0.9%		4	Michigan	13,961	5.4%
1	California	43,562	17.0%		5	Tennessee	10,681	4.2%
24	Colorado	2,289	0.9%		6	Maryland	8,489	3.3%
26	Connecticut	2,214	0.9%		7	Massachusetts	7,805	3.0%
32	Delaware	1,362	0.5%		8	North Carolina	7,357	2.9%
2	Florida	42,333	16.5%		9	Pennsylvania	6,920	2.7%
10	Georgia	6,330	2.5%		10	Georgia	6,330	2.5%
42	Hawaii	365	0.1%		11	Missouri	5,896	2.3%
35	Idaho	956	0.4%		12	New Jersey	5,633	2.2%
NA	Illinois**	NA	NA		13	Louisiana	5,434	2.1%
19	Indiana	2,862	1.1%		14	Washington	5,006	1.9%
31	Iowa	1,551	0.6%		15	Arizona	4,690	1.8%
39	Kansas	670	0.3%		16	Oklahoma	4,663	1.8%
34	Kentucky	1,056	0.4%		17	New York	3,837	1.5%
13	Louisiana	5,434	2.1%		18	Ohio	3,811	1.5%
45	Maine	215	0.1%		19	Indiana	2,862	1.1%
6	Maryland	8,489	3.3%		20	Alabama	2,832	1.1%
7	Massachusetts	7,805	3.0%		21	New Mexico	2,536	1.0%
4	Michigan	13,961	5.4%		21	Oregon	2,536	1.0%
29	Minnesota	1,892	0.7%		23	Virginia	2,476	1.0%
36	Mississippi	855	0.3%		24	Colorado	2,289	0.9%
11	Missouri	5,896	2.3%		25	Arkansas	2,216	0.9%
41	Montana	481	0.2%		26	Connecticut	2,214	0.9%
30	Nebraska	1,753	0.7%		27	South Carolina	2,075	0.8%
28	Nevada	1,946	0.8%		28	Nevada	1,946	0.8%
47	New Hampshire	137	0.1%		29	Minnesota	1,892	0.7%
12	New Jersey	5,633	2.2%		30	Nebraska	1,753	0.7%
21	New Mexico	2,536	1.0%		31	Iowa	1,551	0.6%
17	New York	3,837	1.5%		32	Delaware	1,362	0.5%
8	North Carolina	7,357	2.9%		33	Wisconsin	1,343	0.5%
49	North Dakota	78	0.0%		34	Kentucky	1,056	0.4%
18	Ohio	3,811	1.5%		35	Idaho	956	0.4%
16	Oklahoma	4,663	1.8%		36	Mississippi	855	0.3%
21	Oregon	2,536	1.0%		37	Rhode Island	773	0.3%
9	Pennsylvania	6,920	2.7%		37	Utah	773	0.3%
37	Rhode Island	773	0.3%		39	Kansas	670	0.3%
27	South Carolina	2,075	0.8%		40	Alaska	578	0.2%
46	South Dakota	212	0.1%		41	Montana	481	0.2%
5	Tennessee	10,681	4.2%		42	Hawaii	365	0.1%
3	Texas	28,452	11.1%		43	West Virginia	357	0.1%
37	Utah	773	0.3%		44	Wyoming	324	0.1%
48	Vermont	88	0.0%		45	Maine	215	0.1%
23	Virginia	2,476	1.0%		46	South Dakota	212	0.1%
14	Washington	5,006	1.9%		47	New Hampshire	137	0.1%
43	West Virginia	357	0.1%		48	Vermont	88	0.0%
33	Wisconsin	1,343	0.5%		49	North Dakota	78	0.0%
44	Wyoming	324	0.1%		NA	Illinois**	NA	NA
						District of Columbia	2,121	0.8%

Source: Federal Bureau of Investigation
  "Crime in the United States 2000" (Uniform Crime Reports, October 22, 2001)
*Of the 714,650 aggravated assaults in 2000 for which supplemental data were received by the F.B.I. There were
an additional 196,094 aggravated assaults for which the type of weapon was not reported to the F.B.I. Aggravated
assault is an attack for the purpose of inflicting severe bodily injury. Numbers are for reporting jurisdictions only.
**Not available.

Percent of Aggravated Assaults Involving Blunt Objects
And Other Dangerous Weapons in 2000
National Percent = 35.9% of Aggravated Assaults*

ALPHA ORDER				RANK ORDER		
RANK	STATE	PERCENT		RANK	STATE	PERCENT
37	Alabama	28.9		1	Kansas	52.4
40	Alaska	27.5		2	Delaware	48.2
39	Arizona	28.6		3	Florida	47.7
42	Arkansas	26.6		4	Montana	46.4
27	California	31.5		5	Nebraska	45.3
26	Colorado	31.8		6	Massachusetts	44.6
14	Connecticut	37.9		7	Rhode Island	44.4
2	Delaware	48.2		8	Michigan	42.4
3	Florida	47.7		9	Washington	40.3
24	Georgia	32.1		10	Nevada	39.4
47	Hawaii	25.2		10	Tennessee	39.4
17	Idaho	36.5		12	Maryland	39.2
NA	Illinois**	NA		13	Texas	38.8
35	Indiana	29.1		14	Connecticut	37.9
35	Iowa	29.1		15	Kentucky	37.8
1	Kansas	52.4		16	Missouri	37.4
15	Kentucky	37.8		17	Idaho	36.5
30	Louisiana	30.6		18	Oklahoma	36.0
43	Maine	26.5		19	Mississippi	34.6
12	Maryland	39.2		19	Oregon	34.6
6	Massachusetts	44.6		21	Virginia	33.6
8	Michigan	42.4		22	New Jersey	32.9
46	Minnesota	25.5		23	North Carolina	32.5
19	Mississippi	34.6		24	Georgia	32.1
16	Missouri	37.4		25	Utah	32.0
4	Montana	46.4		26	Colorado	31.8
5	Nebraska	45.3		27	California	31.5
10	Nevada	39.4		28	New Mexico	31.3
45	New Hampshire	26.0		29	Ohio	30.8
22	New Jersey	32.9		30	Louisiana	30.6
28	New Mexico	31.3		31	Wyoming	30.3
33	New York	29.4		32	South Carolina	29.7
23	North Carolina	32.5		33	New York	29.4
38	North Dakota	28.8		33	South Dakota	29.4
29	Ohio	30.8		35	Indiana	29.1
18	Oklahoma	36.0		35	Iowa	29.1
19	Oregon	34.6		37	Alabama	28.9
41	Pennsylvania	27.3		38	North Dakota	28.8
7	Rhode Island	44.4		39	Arizona	28.6
32	South Carolina	29.7		40	Alaska	27.5
33	South Dakota	29.4		41	Pennsylvania	27.3
10	Tennessee	39.4		42	Arkansas	26.6
13	Texas	38.8		43	Maine	26.5
25	Utah	32.0		44	Vermont	26.1
44	Vermont	26.1		45	New Hampshire	26.0
21	Virginia	33.6		46	Minnesota	25.5
9	Washington	40.3		47	Hawaii	25.2
49	West Virginia	18.3		48	Wisconsin	22.2
48	Wisconsin	22.2		49	West Virginia	18.3
31	Wyoming	30.3		NA	Illinois**	NA
					District of Columbia	46.3

Source: Morgan Quitno Press using data from Federal Bureau of Investigation
   "Crime in the United States 2000" (Uniform Crime Reports, October 22, 2001)
*Of the 714,650 aggravated assaults in 2000 for which supplemental data were received by the F.B.I. There were
an additional 196,094 aggravated assaults for which the type of weapon was not reported to the F.B.I. Aggravated
assault is an attack for the purpose of inflicting severe bodily injury. Numbers are for reporting jurisdictions only.
**Not available.

Aggravated Assaults Committed with Hands, Fists or Feet in 2000

National Total = 200,137 Aggravated Assaults*

ALPHA ORDER

RANK	STATE	ASSAULTS	% of USA
22	Alabama	2,830	1.4%
36	Alaska	669	0.3%
9	Arizona	5,228	2.6%
19	Arkansas	3,107	1.6%
1	California	55,528	27.7%
30	Colorado	1,896	0.9%
29	Connecticut	2,123	1.1%
44	Delaware	313	0.2%
2	Florida	17,515	8.8%
10	Georgia	4,704	2.4%
33	Hawaii	786	0.4%
39	Idaho	478	0.2%
NA	Illinois**	NA	NA
15	Indiana	4,177	2.1%
25	Iowa	2,446	1.2%
46	Kansas	163	0.1%
37	Kentucky	636	0.3%
13	Louisiana	4,474	2.2%
41	Maine	467	0.2%
6	Maryland	5,363	2.7%
7	Massachusetts	5,301	2.6%
12	Michigan	4,679	2.3%
24	Minnesota	2,511	1.3%
38	Mississippi	585	0.3%
17	Missouri	3,188	1.6%
42	Montana	349	0.2%
34	Nebraska	715	0.4%
31	Nevada	1,076	0.5%
49	New Hampshire	148	0.1%
5	New Jersey	5,464	2.7%
26	New Mexico	2,335	1.2%
8	New York	5,242	2.6%
11	North Carolina	4,682	2.3%
48	North Dakota	150	0.1%
14	Ohio	4,340	2.2%
16	Oklahoma	4,162	2.1%
21	Oregon	2,854	1.4%
4	Pennsylvania	9,436	4.7%
43	Rhode Island	338	0.2%
27	South Carolina	2,234	1.1%
45	South Dakota	202	0.1%
18	Tennessee	3,138	1.6%
3	Texas	13,668	6.8%
35	Utah	710	0.4%
47	Vermont	159	0.1%
28	Virginia	2,154	1.1%
20	Washington	2,923	1.5%
32	West Virginia	940	0.5%
23	Wisconsin	2,612	1.3%
40	Wyoming	473	0.2%

RANK ORDER

RANK	STATE	ASSAULTS	% of USA
1	California	55,528	27.7%
2	Florida	17,515	8.8%
3	Texas	13,668	6.8%
4	Pennsylvania	9,436	4.7%
5	New Jersey	5,464	2.7%
6	Maryland	5,363	2.7%
7	Massachusetts	5,301	2.6%
8	New York	5,242	2.6%
9	Arizona	5,228	2.6%
10	Georgia	4,704	2.4%
11	North Carolina	4,682	2.3%
12	Michigan	4,679	2.3%
13	Louisiana	4,474	2.2%
14	Ohio	4,340	2.2%
15	Indiana	4,177	2.1%
16	Oklahoma	4,162	2.1%
17	Missouri	3,188	1.6%
18	Tennessee	3,138	1.6%
19	Arkansas	3,107	1.6%
20	Washington	2,923	1.5%
21	Oregon	2,854	1.4%
22	Alabama	2,830	1.4%
23	Wisconsin	2,612	1.3%
24	Minnesota	2,511	1.3%
25	Iowa	2,446	1.2%
26	New Mexico	2,335	1.2%
27	South Carolina	2,234	1.1%
28	Virginia	2,154	1.1%
29	Connecticut	2,123	1.1%
30	Colorado	1,896	0.9%
31	Nevada	1,076	0.5%
32	West Virginia	940	0.5%
33	Hawaii	786	0.4%
34	Nebraska	715	0.4%
35	Utah	710	0.4%
36	Alaska	669	0.3%
37	Kentucky	636	0.3%
38	Mississippi	585	0.3%
39	Idaho	478	0.2%
40	Wyoming	473	0.2%
41	Maine	467	0.2%
42	Montana	349	0.2%
43	Rhode Island	338	0.2%
44	Delaware	313	0.2%
45	South Dakota	202	0.1%
46	Kansas	163	0.1%
47	Vermont	159	0.1%
48	North Dakota	150	0.1%
49	New Hampshire	148	0.1%
NA	Illinois**	NA	NA
	District of Columbia	466	0.2%

Source: Federal Bureau of Investigation
"Crime in the United States 2000" (Uniform Crime Reports, October 22, 2001)
*Of the 714,650 aggravated assaults in 2000 for which supplemental data were received by the F.B.I. There were an additional 196,094 aggravated assaults for which the type of weapon was not reported to the F.B.I. Aggravated assault is an attack for the purpose of inflicting severe bodily injury. Numbers are for reporting jurisdictions only.
**Not available.

Percent of Aggravated Assaults Committed with Hands, Fists or Feet in 2000

National Percent = 28.0% of Aggravated Assaults*

ALPHA ORDER

RANK	STATE	PERCENT
27	Alabama	28.8
22	Alaska	31.8
22	Arizona	31.8
13	Arkansas	37.3
11	California	40.1
31	Colorado	26.3
15	Connecticut	36.4
49	Delaware	11.1
41	Florida	19.7
34	Georgia	23.9
3	Hawaii	54.2
45	Idaho	18.3
NA	Illinois**	NA
9	Indiana	42.5
6	Iowa	45.9
47	Kansas	12.7
37	Kentucky	22.8
32	Louisiana	25.2
1	Maine	57.7
33	Maryland	24.7
24	Massachusetts	30.3
46	Michigan	14.2
17	Minnesota	33.8
35	Mississippi	23.7
40	Missouri	20.2
18	Montana	33.7
44	Nebraska	18.5
38	Nevada	21.8
29	New Hampshire	28.1
20	New Jersey	32.0
27	New Mexico	28.8
10	New York	40.2
39	North Carolina	20.7
2	North Dakota	55.4
16	Ohio	35.0
19	Oklahoma	32.1
12	Oregon	38.9
14	Pennsylvania	37.2
42	Rhode Island	19.4
21	South Carolina	31.9
30	South Dakota	28.0
48	Tennessee	11.6
43	Texas	18.6
25	Utah	29.4
5	Vermont	47.2
26	Virginia	29.2
36	Washington	23.6
4	West Virginia	48.1
8	Wisconsin	43.1
7	Wyoming	44.2

RANK ORDER

RANK	STATE	PERCENT
1	Maine	57.7
2	North Dakota	55.4
3	Hawaii	54.2
4	West Virginia	48.1
5	Vermont	47.2
6	Iowa	45.9
7	Wyoming	44.2
8	Wisconsin	43.1
9	Indiana	42.5
10	New York	40.2
11	California	40.1
12	Oregon	38.9
13	Arkansas	37.3
14	Pennsylvania	37.2
15	Connecticut	36.4
16	Ohio	35.0
17	Minnesota	33.8
18	Montana	33.7
19	Oklahoma	32.1
20	New Jersey	32.0
21	South Carolina	31.9
22	Alaska	31.8
22	Arizona	31.8
24	Massachusetts	30.3
25	Utah	29.4
26	Virginia	29.2
27	Alabama	28.8
27	New Mexico	28.8
29	New Hampshire	28.1
30	South Dakota	28.0
31	Colorado	26.3
32	Louisiana	25.2
33	Maryland	24.7
34	Georgia	23.9
35	Mississippi	23.7
36	Washington	23.6
37	Kentucky	22.8
38	Nevada	21.8
39	North Carolina	20.7
40	Missouri	20.2
41	Florida	19.7
42	Rhode Island	19.4
43	Texas	18.6
44	Nebraska	18.5
45	Idaho	18.3
46	Michigan	14.2
47	Kansas	12.7
48	Tennessee	11.6
49	Delaware	11.1
NA	Illinois**	NA
	District of Columbia	10.2

Source: Morgan Quitno Press using data from Federal Bureau of Investigation
   "Crime in the United States 2000" (Uniform Crime Reports, October 22, 2001)
*Of the 714,650 aggravated assaults in 2000 for which supplemental data were received by the F.B.I. There were an additional 196,094 aggravated assaults for which the type of weapon was not reported to the F.B.I. Aggravated assault is an attack for the purpose of inflicting severe bodily injury. Numbers are for reporting jurisdictions only.
**Not available.

Property Crimes in 2000

National Total = 10,181,462 Property Crimes*

ALPHA ORDER				RANK ORDER			
RANK	STATE	CRIMES	% of USA	RANK	STATE	CRIMES	% of USA
20	Alabama	180,539	1.8%	1	California	1,056,183	10.4%
46	Alaska	23,087	0.2%	2	Texas	919,658	9.0%
12	Arizona	271,811	2.7%	3	Florida	780,377	7.7%
32	Arkansas	98,115	1.0%	4	New York	483,078	4.7%
1	California	1,056,183	10.4%	5	Illinois	450,748	4.4%
25	Colorado	156,937	1.5%	6	Ohio	420,939	4.1%
31	Connecticut	99,033	1.0%	7	North Carolina	355,921	3.5%
43	Delaware	29,727	0.3%	8	Michigan	353,297	3.5%
3	Florida	780,377	7.7%	9	Georgia	347,630	3.4%
9	Georgia	347,630	3.4%	10	Pennsylvania	316,274	3.1%
38	Hawaii	60,033	0.6%	11	Washington	279,144	2.7%
40	Idaho	37,961	0.4%	12	Arizona	271,811	2.7%
5	Illinois	450,748	4.4%	13	Tennessee	237,985	2.3%
18	Indiana	206,905	2.0%	14	New Jersey	233,637	2.3%
34	Iowa	86,834	0.9%	15	Missouri	225,919	2.2%
28	Kansas	108,057	1.1%	16	Maryland	213,422	2.1%
29	Kentucky	107,723	1.1%	17	Louisiana	211,904	2.1%
17	Louisiana	211,904	2.1%	18	Indiana	206,905	2.0%
42	Maine	32,003	0.3%	19	Virginia	194,405	1.9%
16	Maryland	213,422	2.1%	20	Alabama	180,539	1.8%
22	Massachusetts	161,901	1.6%	21	South Carolina	177,189	1.7%
8	Michigan	353,297	3.5%	22	Massachusetts	161,901	1.6%
24	Minnesota	157,798	1.5%	23	Wisconsin	159,424	1.6%
30	Mississippi	103,644	1.0%	24	Minnesota	157,798	1.5%
15	Missouri	225,919	2.2%	25	Colorado	156,937	1.5%
44	Montana	29,707	0.3%	26	Oregon	153,780	1.5%
37	Nebraska	64,479	0.6%	27	Oklahoma	140,125	1.4%
36	Nevada	74,823	0.7%	28	Kansas	108,057	1.1%
45	New Hampshire	27,901	0.3%	29	Kentucky	107,723	1.1%
14	New Jersey	233,637	2.3%	30	Mississippi	103,644	1.0%
35	New Mexico	86,605	0.9%	31	Connecticut	99,033	1.0%
4	New York	483,078	4.7%	32	Arkansas	98,115	1.0%
7	North Carolina	355,921	3.5%	33	Utah	94,247	0.9%
50	North Dakota	14,171	0.1%	34	Iowa	86,834	0.9%
6	Ohio	420,939	4.1%	35	New Mexico	86,605	0.9%
27	Oklahoma	140,125	1.4%	36	Nevada	74,823	0.7%
26	Oregon	153,780	1.5%	37	Nebraska	64,479	0.6%
10	Pennsylvania	316,274	3.1%	38	Hawaii	60,033	0.6%
41	Rhode Island	33,323	0.3%	39	West Virginia	41,344	0.4%
21	South Carolina	177,189	1.7%	40	Idaho	37,961	0.4%
48	South Dakota	16,252	0.2%	41	Rhode Island	33,323	0.3%
13	Tennessee	237,985	2.3%	42	Maine	32,003	0.3%
2	Texas	919,658	9.0%	43	Delaware	29,727	0.3%
33	Utah	94,247	0.9%	44	Montana	29,707	0.3%
47	Vermont	17,494	0.2%	45	New Hampshire	27,901	0.3%
19	Virginia	194,405	1.9%	46	Alaska	23,087	0.2%
11	Washington	279,144	2.7%	47	Vermont	17,494	0.2%
39	West Virginia	41,344	0.4%	48	South Dakota	16,252	0.2%
23	Wisconsin	159,424	1.6%	49	Wyoming	14,969	0.1%
49	Wyoming	14,969	0.1%	50	North Dakota	14,171	0.1%
					District of Columbia	33,000	0.3%

Source: Federal Bureau of Investigation
   "Crime in the United States 2000" (Uniform Crime Reports, October 22, 2001)
*Property crimes are offenses of burglary, larceny-theft and motor vehicle theft.

Average Time Between Property Crimes in 2000

National Rate = A Property Crime Occurs Every 3 Seconds*

ALPHA ORDER

RANK	STATE	MINUTES.SECONDS
31	Alabama	2.55
5	Alaska	22.46
39	Arizona	1.56
19	Arkansas	5.22
50	California	0.30
26	Colorado	3.21
20	Connecticut	5.19
7	Delaware	17.41
48	Florida	0.40
42	Georgia	1.31
13	Hawaii	8.46
11	Idaho	13.51
46	Illinois	1.10
33	Indiana	2.32
17	Iowa	6.03
23	Kansas	4.52
22	Kentucky	4.53
34	Louisiana	2.29
9	Maine	16.25
35	Maryland	2.28
29	Massachusetts	3.15
43	Michigan	1.29
27	Minnesota	3.20
21	Mississippi	5.04
36	Missouri	2.20
7	Montana	17.41
14	Nebraska	8.09
15	Nevada	7.01
6	New Hampshire	18.50
37	New Jersey	2.15
16	New Mexico	6.04
47	New York	1.05
43	North Carolina	1.29
1	North Dakota	37.05
45	Ohio	1.15
24	Oklahoma	3.45
25	Oregon	3.25
41	Pennsylvania	1.40
10	Rhode Island	15.46
30	South Carolina	2.58
3	South Dakota	32.20
38	Tennessee	2.13
49	Texas	0.34
18	Utah	5.35
4	Vermont	30.02
32	Virginia	2.42
40	Washington	1.53
12	West Virginia	12.43
28	Wisconsin	3.18
2	Wyoming	35.07

RANK ORDER

RANK	STATE	MINUTES.SECONDS
1	North Dakota	37.05
2	Wyoming	35.07
3	South Dakota	32.20
4	Vermont	30.02
5	Alaska	22.46
6	New Hampshire	18.50
7	Delaware	17.41
7	Montana	17.41
9	Maine	16.25
10	Rhode Island	15.46
11	Idaho	13.51
12	West Virginia	12.43
13	Hawaii	8.46
14	Nebraska	8.09
15	Nevada	7.01
16	New Mexico	6.04
17	Iowa	6.03
18	Utah	5.35
19	Arkansas	5.22
20	Connecticut	5.19
21	Mississippi	5.04
22	Kentucky	4.53
23	Kansas	4.52
24	Oklahoma	3.45
25	Oregon	3.25
26	Colorado	3.21
27	Minnesota	3.20
28	Wisconsin	3.18
29	Massachusetts	3.15
30	South Carolina	2.58
31	Alabama	2.55
32	Virginia	2.42
33	Indiana	2.32
34	Louisiana	2.29
35	Maryland	2.28
36	Missouri	2.20
37	New Jersey	2.15
38	Tennessee	2.13
39	Arizona	1.56
40	Washington	1.53
41	Pennsylvania	1.40
42	Georgia	1.31
43	Michigan	1.29
43	North Carolina	1.29
45	Ohio	1.15
46	Illinois	1.10
47	New York	1.05
48	Florida	0.40
49	Texas	0.34
50	California	0.30

District of Columbia   15.56

Source: Morgan Quitno Press using data from Federal Bureau of Investigation
"Crime in the United States 2000" (Uniform Crime Reports, October 22, 2001)
*Property crimes are offenses of burglary, larceny-theft and motor vehicle theft.

Property Crimes per Square Mile in 2000

National Rate = 2.7 Property Crimes per Square Mile*

RANK	STATE	RATE
23	Alabama	3.5
50	Alaska	0.0
28	Arizona	2.4
32	Arkansas	1.8
14	California	6.6
37	Colorado	1.5
3	Connecticut	17.9
7	Delaware	12.4
6	Florida	13.0
15	Georgia	5.9
9	Hawaii	9.3
45	Idaho	0.5
11	Illinois	7.8
16	Indiana	5.7
37	Iowa	1.5
39	Kansas	1.3
27	Kentucky	2.7
20	Louisiana	4.3
41	Maine	0.9
5	Maryland	17.4
4	Massachusetts	17.5
22	Michigan	3.7
32	Minnesota	1.8
30	Mississippi	2.1
25	Missouri	3.2
46	Montana	0.2
42	Nebraska	0.8
43	Nevada	0.7
26	New Hampshire	3.0
1	New Jersey	28.4
43	New Mexico	0.7
10	New York	8.9
13	North Carolina	6.8
46	North Dakota	0.2
8	Ohio	9.4
31	Oklahoma	2.0
36	Oregon	1.6
12	Pennsylvania	6.9
2	Rhode Island	27.1
16	South Carolina	5.7
46	South Dakota	0.2
18	Tennessee	5.6
24	Texas	3.4
40	Utah	1.1
32	Vermont	1.8
19	Virginia	4.6
21	Washington	4.0
35	West Virginia	1.7
28	Wisconsin	2.4
46	Wyoming	0.2

RANK	STATE	RATE
1	New Jersey	28.4
2	Rhode Island	27.1
3	Connecticut	17.9
4	Massachusetts	17.5
5	Maryland	17.4
6	Florida	13.0
7	Delaware	12.4
8	Ohio	9.4
9	Hawaii	9.3
10	New York	8.9
11	Illinois	7.8
12	Pennsylvania	6.9
13	North Carolina	6.8
14	California	6.6
15	Georgia	5.9
16	Indiana	5.7
16	South Carolina	5.7
18	Tennessee	5.6
19	Virginia	4.6
20	Louisiana	4.3
21	Washington	4.0
22	Michigan	3.7
23	Alabama	3.5
24	Texas	3.4
25	Missouri	3.2
26	New Hampshire	3.0
27	Kentucky	2.7
28	Arizona	2.4
28	Wisconsin	2.4
30	Mississippi	2.1
31	Oklahoma	2.0
32	Arkansas	1.8
32	Minnesota	1.8
32	Vermont	1.8
35	West Virginia	1.7
36	Oregon	1.6
37	Colorado	1.5
37	Iowa	1.5
39	Kansas	1.3
40	Utah	1.1
41	Maine	0.9
42	Nebraska	0.8
43	Nevada	0.7
43	New Mexico	0.7
45	Idaho	0.5
46	Montana	0.2
46	North Dakota	0.2
46	South Dakota	0.2
46	Wyoming	0.2
50	Alaska	0.0

| | District of Columbia | 485.3 |

Source: Morgan Quitno Press using data from Federal Bureau of Investigation
"Crime in the United States 2000" (Uniform Crime Reports, October 22, 2001)
*Property crimes are offenses of burglary, larceny-theft and motor vehicle theft. "Square miles" includes total land and water area.

Percent Change in Number of Property Crimes: 1999 to 2000

National Percent Change = 0.3% Decrease*

ALPHA ORDER			RANK ORDER		
RANK	STATE	PERCENT CHANGE	RANK	STATE	PERCENT CHANGE
6	Alabama	5.3	1	Hawaii	10.1
24	Alaska	(0.1)	2	Vermont	8.9
4	Arizona	6.4	3	Tennessee	8.5
5	Arkansas	6.3	4	Arizona	6.4
22	California	0.3	5	Arkansas	6.3
9	Colorado	3.9	6	Alabama	5.3
29	Connecticut	(0.9)	7	Nebraska	5.2
41	Delaware	(3.9)	8	Idaho	4.4
39	Florida	(3.5)	9	Colorado	3.9
36	Georgia	(3.3)	10	Iowa	2.8
1	Hawaii	10.1	10	Kentucky	2.8
8	Idaho	4.4	12	Indiana	2.7
33	Illinois	(2.8)	13	Texas	2.6
12	Indiana	2.7	14	Montana	2.1
10	Iowa	2.8	15	Rhode Island	2.0
20	Kansas	0.4	16	South Carolina	1.8
10	Kentucky	2.8	17	Ohio	1.6
36	Louisiana	(3.3)	18	Missouri	1.3
48	Maine	(7.6)	18	Nevada	1.3
30	Maryland	(1.2)	20	Kansas	0.4
36	Massachusetts	(3.3)	20	North Carolina	0.4
44	Michigan	(4.5)	22	California	0.3
27	Minnesota	(0.6)	23	Oregon	0.2
44	Mississippi	(4.5)	24	Alaska	(0.1)
18	Missouri	1.3	24	Oklahoma	(0.1)
14	Montana	2.1	26	Wisconsin	(0.5)
7	Nebraska	5.2	27	Minnesota	(0.6)
18	Nevada	1.3	27	Washington	(0.6)
NA	New Hampshire**	NA	29	Connecticut	(0.9)
43	New Jersey	(4.0)	30	Maryland	(1.2)
34	New Mexico	(2.9)	31	New York	(1.3)
31	New York	(1.3)	32	Pennsylvania	(2.1)
20	North Carolina	0.4	33	Illinois	(2.8)
41	North Dakota	(3.9)	34	New Mexico	(2.9)
17	Ohio	1.6	35	Wyoming	(3.2)
24	Oklahoma	(0.1)	36	Georgia	(3.3)
23	Oregon	0.2	36	Louisiana	(3.3)
32	Pennsylvania	(2.1)	36	Massachusetts	(3.3)
15	Rhode Island	2.0	39	Florida	(3.5)
16	South Carolina	1.8	39	West Virginia	(3.5)
49	South Dakota	(10.5)	41	Delaware	(3.9)
3	Tennessee	8.5	41	North Dakota	(3.9)
13	Texas	2.6	43	New Jersey	(4.0)
46	Utah	(5.9)	44	Michigan	(4.5)
2	Vermont	8.9	44	Mississippi	(4.5)
47	Virginia	(7.5)	46	Utah	(5.9)
27	Washington	(0.6)	47	Virginia	(7.5)
39	West Virginia	(3.5)	48	Maine	(7.6)
26	Wisconsin	(0.5)	49	South Dakota	(10.5)
35	Wyoming	(3.2)	NA	New Hampshire**	NA
				District of Columbia	(1.3)

Source: Federal Bureau of Investigation
   "Crime in the United States 2000" (Uniform Crime Reports, October 22, 2001)
*Property crimes are offenses of burglary, larceny-theft and motor vehicle theft.
**Not available.

Property Crime Rate in 2000

National Rate = 3,617.9 Property Crimes per 100,000 Population*

RANK	STATE	RATE		RANK	STATE	RATE
15	Alabama	4,059.7		1	Arizona	5,297.8
23	Alaska	3,682.5		2	Hawaii	4,955.1
1	Arizona	5,297.8		3	Florida	4,882.7
24	Arkansas	3,670.0		4	New Mexico	4,761.0
33	California	3,118.2		5	Louisiana	4,741.7
25	Colorado	3,648.6		6	Washington	4,736.0
38	Connecticut	2,908.0		7	Oregon	4,494.7
19	Delaware	3,793.6		8	North Carolina	4,421.8
3	Florida	4,882.7		9	South Carolina	4,416.5
11	Georgia	4,246.4		10	Texas	4,410.4
2	Hawaii	4,955.1		11	Georgia	4,246.4
37	Idaho	2,933.7		12	Utah	4,220.3
27	Illinois	3,629.4		13	Tennessee	4,183.0
29	Indiana	3,402.8		14	Oklahoma	4,060.8
36	Iowa	2,967.3		15	Alabama	4,059.7
18	Kansas	4,019.4		16	Missouri	4,037.7
42	Kentucky	2,665.2		17	Maryland	4,029.5
5	Louisiana	4,741.7		18	Kansas	4,019.4
46	Maine	2,510.2		19	Delaware	3,793.6
17	Maryland	4,029.5		20	Nebraska	3,767.9
44	Massachusetts	2,550.0		21	Nevada	3,744.4
28	Michigan	3,554.9		22	Ohio	3,707.7
31	Minnesota	3,207.6		23	Alaska	3,682.5
26	Mississippi	3,643.5		24	Arkansas	3,670.0
16	Missouri	4,037.7		25	Colorado	3,648.6
30	Montana	3,292.7		26	Mississippi	3,643.5
20	Nebraska	3,767.9		27	Illinois	3,629.4
21	Nevada	3,744.4		28	Michigan	3,554.9
48	New Hampshire	2,257.8		29	Indiana	3,402.8
40	New Jersey	2,776.6		30	Montana	3,292.7
4	New Mexico	4,761.0		31	Minnesota	3,207.6
45	New York	2,545.7		32	Rhode Island	3,178.7
8	North Carolina	4,421.8		33	California	3,118.2
49	North Dakota	2,206.6		34	Wyoming	3,031.5
22	Ohio	3,707.7		35	Wisconsin	2,972.3
14	Oklahoma	4,060.8		36	Iowa	2,967.3
7	Oregon	4,494.7		37	Idaho	2,933.7
43	Pennsylvania	2,575.3		38	Connecticut	2,908.0
32	Rhode Island	3,178.7		39	Vermont	2,873.4
9	South Carolina	4,416.5		40	New Jersey	2,776.6
50	South Dakota	2,153.0		41	Virginia	2,746.4
13	Tennessee	4,183.0		42	Kentucky	2,665.2
10	Texas	4,410.4		43	Pennsylvania	2,575.3
12	Utah	4,220.3		44	Massachusetts	2,550.0
39	Vermont	2,873.4		45	New York	2,545.7
41	Virginia	2,746.4		46	Maine	2,510.2
6	Washington	4,736.0		47	West Virginia	2,286.3
47	West Virginia	2,286.3		48	New Hampshire	2,257.8
35	Wisconsin	2,972.3		49	North Dakota	2,206.6
34	Wyoming	3,031.5		50	South Dakota	2,153.0
					District of Columbia	5,768.6

ALPHA ORDER

RANK ORDER

Source: Federal Bureau of Investigation
"*Crime in the United States 2000*" *(Uniform Crime Reports, October 22, 2001)*
Property crimes are offenses of burglary, larceny-theft and motor vehicle theft.

Percent Change in Property Crime Rate: 1999 to 2000

National Percent Change = 3.4% Decrease*

ALPHA ORDER

RANK	STATE	PERCENT CHANGE
4	Alabama	3.5
16	Alaska	(1.2)
13	Arizona	(0.9)
6	Arkansas	1.5
19	California	(1.9)
20	Colorado	(2.0)
30	Connecticut	(4.5)
42	Delaware	(7.6)
45	Florida	(8.8)
43	Georgia	(8.0)
1	Hawaii	7.7
7	Idaho	1.0
32	Illinois	(5.1)
11	Indiana	0.3
8	Iowa	0.8
13	Kansas	(0.9)
8	Kentucky	0.8
35	Louisiana	(5.4)
46	Maine	(9.1)
25	Maryland	(3.5)
37	Massachusetts	(6.0)
33	Michigan	(5.2)
25	Minnesota	(3.5)
39	Mississippi	(7.1)
15	Missouri	(1.0)
12	Montana	(0.1)
5	Nebraska	2.4
44	Nevada	(8.3)
NA	New Hampshire**	NA
39	New Jersey	(7.1)
41	New Mexico	(7.2)
35	New York	(5.4)
31	North Carolina	(4.6)
33	North Dakota	(5.2)
10	Ohio	0.7
22	Oklahoma	(2.7)
23	Oregon	(2.9)
29	Pennsylvania	(4.4)
28	Rhode Island	(3.6)
17	South Carolina	(1.4)
49	South Dakota	(13.1)
3	Tennessee	4.6
17	Texas	(1.4)
47	Utah	(10.2)
2	Vermont	6.2
47	Virginia	(10.2)
23	Washington	(2.9)
25	West Virginia	(3.5)
21	Wisconsin	(2.6)
37	Wyoming	(6.0)

RANK ORDER

RANK	STATE	PERCENT CHANGE
1	Hawaii	7.7
2	Vermont	6.2
3	Tennessee	4.6
4	Alabama	3.5
5	Nebraska	2.4
6	Arkansas	1.5
7	Idaho	1.0
8	Iowa	0.8
8	Kentucky	0.8
10	Ohio	0.7
11	Indiana	0.3
12	Montana	(0.1)
13	Arizona	(0.9)
13	Kansas	(0.9)
15	Missouri	(1.0)
16	Alaska	(1.2)
17	South Carolina	(1.4)
17	Texas	(1.4)
19	California	(1.9)
20	Colorado	(2.0)
21	Wisconsin	(2.6)
22	Oklahoma	(2.7)
23	Oregon	(2.9)
23	Washington	(2.9)
25	Maryland	(3.5)
25	Minnesota	(3.5)
25	West Virginia	(3.5)
28	Rhode Island	(3.6)
29	Pennsylvania	(4.4)
30	Connecticut	(4.5)
31	North Carolina	(4.6)
32	Illinois	(5.1)
33	Michigan	(5.2)
33	North Dakota	(5.2)
35	Louisiana	(5.4)
35	New York	(5.4)
37	Massachusetts	(6.0)
37	Wyoming	(6.0)
39	Mississippi	(7.1)
39	New Jersey	(7.1)
41	New Mexico	(7.2)
42	Delaware	(7.6)
43	Georgia	(8.0)
44	Nevada	(8.3)
45	Florida	(8.8)
46	Maine	(9.1)
47	Utah	(10.2)
47	Virginia	(10.2)
49	South Dakota	(13.1)
NA	New Hampshire**	NA
	District of Columbia	(10.4)

Source: Federal Bureau of Investigation
    "Crime in the United States 2000" (Uniform Crime Reports, October 22, 2001)
*Property crimes are offenses of burglary, larceny-theft and motor vehicle theft.
**Not available.

Burglaries in 2000

National Total = 2,049,946 Burglaries*

ALPHA ORDER

RANK ORDER

RANK	STATE	BURGLARIES	% of USA		RANK	STATE	BURGLARIES	% of USA
18	Alabama	40,331	2.0%		1	California	222,293	10.8%
46	Alaska	3,899	0.2%		2	Texas	188,975	9.2%
13	Arizona	51,902	2.5%		3	Florida	172,898	8.4%
31	Arkansas	21,443	1.0%		4	North Carolina	97,888	4.8%
1	California	222,293	10.8%		5	Ohio	88,636	4.3%
24	Colorado	27,133	1.3%		6	New York	87,946	4.3%
34	Connecticut	17,436	0.9%		7	Illinois	81,913	4.0%
43	Delaware	5,216	0.3%		8	Michigan	69,790	3.4%
3	Florida	172,898	8.4%		9	Georgia	68,488	3.3%
9	Georgia	68,488	3.3%		10	Tennessee	56,344	2.7%
37	Hawaii	10,665	0.5%		11	Pennsylvania	54,080	2.6%
40	Idaho	7,330	0.4%		12	Washington	53,476	2.6%
7	Illinois	81,913	4.0%		13	Arizona	51,902	2.5%
17	Indiana	41,108	2.0%		14	Louisiana	46,289	2.3%
35	Iowa	16,342	0.8%		15	New Jersey	43,924	2.1%
30	Kansas	21,484	1.0%		16	Missouri	41,685	2.0%
28	Kentucky	25,308	1.2%		17	Indiana	41,108	2.0%
14	Louisiana	46,289	2.3%		18	Alabama	40,331	2.0%
41	Maine	6,775	0.3%		19	Maryland	39,426	1.9%
19	Maryland	39,426	1.9%		20	South Carolina	38,888	1.9%
22	Massachusetts	30,600	1.5%		21	Oklahoma	31,661	1.5%
8	Michigan	69,790	3.4%		22	Massachusetts	30,600	1.5%
26	Minnesota	26,116	1.3%		23	Virginia	30,434	1.5%
25	Mississippi	26,918	1.3%		24	Colorado	27,133	1.3%
16	Missouri	41,685	2.0%		25	Mississippi	26,918	1.3%
45	Montana	3,946	0.2%		26	Minnesota	26,116	1.3%
38	Nebraska	10,131	0.5%		27	Oregon	25,618	1.2%
33	Nevada	17,526	0.9%		28	Kentucky	25,308	1.2%
44	New Hampshire	4,992	0.2%		29	Wisconsin	25,183	1.2%
15	New Jersey	43,924	2.1%		30	Kansas	21,484	1.0%
32	New Mexico	21,339	1.0%		31	Arkansas	21,443	1.0%
6	New York	87,946	4.3%		32	New Mexico	21,339	1.0%
4	North Carolina	97,888	4.8%		33	Nevada	17,526	0.9%
49	North Dakota	2,093	0.1%		34	Connecticut	17,436	0.9%
5	Ohio	88,636	4.3%		35	Iowa	16,342	0.8%
21	Oklahoma	31,661	1.5%		36	Utah	14,348	0.7%
27	Oregon	25,618	1.2%		37	Hawaii	10,665	0.5%
11	Pennsylvania	54,080	2.6%		38	Nebraska	10,131	0.5%
42	Rhode Island	6,620	0.3%		39	West Virginia	9,890	0.5%
20	South Carolina	38,888	1.9%		40	Idaho	7,330	0.4%
48	South Dakota	2,896	0.1%		41	Maine	6,775	0.3%
10	Tennessee	56,344	2.7%		42	Rhode Island	6,620	0.3%
2	Texas	188,975	9.2%		43	Delaware	5,216	0.3%
36	Utah	14,348	0.7%		44	New Hampshire	4,992	0.2%
47	Vermont	3,501	0.2%		45	Montana	3,946	0.2%
23	Virginia	30,434	1.5%		46	Alaska	3,899	0.2%
12	Washington	53,476	2.6%		47	Vermont	3,501	0.2%
39	West Virginia	9,890	0.5%		48	South Dakota	2,896	0.1%
29	Wisconsin	25,183	1.2%		49	North Dakota	2,093	0.1%
50	Wyoming	2,078	0.1%		50	Wyoming	2,078	0.1%
						District of Columbia	4,745	0.2%

Source: Federal Bureau of Investigation
    "Crime in the United States 2000" (Uniform Crime Reports, October 22, 2001)
*Burglary is the unlawful entry of a structure to commit a felony or theft. Attempts are included.

Average Time Between Burglaries in 2000

National Rate = A Burglary Occurs Every 15 Seconds*

<table>
<tr><td colspan="3">ALPHA ORDER</td><td colspan="3">RANK ORDER</td></tr>
<tr><td>RANK</td><td>STATE</td><td>MINUTES.SECONDS</td><td>RANK</td><td>STATE</td><td>MINUTES.SECONDS</td></tr>
<tr><td>33</td><td>Alabama</td><td>13.02</td><td>1</td><td>Wyoming</td><td>252.56</td></tr>
<tr><td>5</td><td>Alaska</td><td>134.48</td><td>2</td><td>North Dakota</td><td>251.07</td></tr>
<tr><td>38</td><td>Arizona</td><td>10.08</td><td>3</td><td>South Dakota</td><td>181.29</td></tr>
<tr><td>20</td><td>Arkansas</td><td>24.31</td><td>4</td><td>Vermont</td><td>150.08</td></tr>
<tr><td>50</td><td>California</td><td>2.22</td><td>5</td><td>Alaska</td><td>134.48</td></tr>
<tr><td>27</td><td>Colorado</td><td>19.22</td><td>6</td><td>Montana</td><td>133.12</td></tr>
<tr><td>17</td><td>Connecticut</td><td>30.08</td><td>7</td><td>New Hampshire</td><td>105.17</td></tr>
<tr><td>8</td><td>Delaware</td><td>100.46</td><td>8</td><td>Delaware</td><td>100.46</td></tr>
<tr><td>48</td><td>Florida</td><td>3.02</td><td>9</td><td>Rhode Island</td><td>79.24</td></tr>
<tr><td>42</td><td>Georgia</td><td>7.40</td><td>10</td><td>Maine</td><td>77.35</td></tr>
<tr><td>14</td><td>Hawaii</td><td>49.17</td><td>11</td><td>Idaho</td><td>71.43</td></tr>
<tr><td>11</td><td>Idaho</td><td>71.43</td><td>12</td><td>West Virginia</td><td>53.08</td></tr>
<tr><td>44</td><td>Illinois</td><td>6.25</td><td>13</td><td>Nebraska</td><td>51.53</td></tr>
<tr><td>34</td><td>Indiana</td><td>12.47</td><td>14</td><td>Hawaii</td><td>49.17</td></tr>
<tr><td>16</td><td>Iowa</td><td>32.10</td><td>15</td><td>Utah</td><td>36.38</td></tr>
<tr><td>21</td><td>Kansas</td><td>24.28</td><td>16</td><td>Iowa</td><td>32.10</td></tr>
<tr><td>23</td><td>Kentucky</td><td>20.46</td><td>17</td><td>Connecticut</td><td>30.08</td></tr>
<tr><td>37</td><td>Louisiana</td><td>11.21</td><td>18</td><td>Nevada</td><td>29.59</td></tr>
<tr><td>10</td><td>Maine</td><td>77.35</td><td>19</td><td>New Mexico</td><td>24.38</td></tr>
<tr><td>32</td><td>Maryland</td><td>13.20</td><td>20</td><td>Arkansas</td><td>24.31</td></tr>
<tr><td>29</td><td>Massachusetts</td><td>17.11</td><td>21</td><td>Kansas</td><td>24.28</td></tr>
<tr><td>43</td><td>Michigan</td><td>7.32</td><td>22</td><td>Wisconsin</td><td>20.52</td></tr>
<tr><td>25</td><td>Minnesota</td><td>20.08</td><td>23</td><td>Kentucky</td><td>20.46</td></tr>
<tr><td>26</td><td>Mississippi</td><td>19.32</td><td>24</td><td>Oregon</td><td>20.31</td></tr>
<tr><td>35</td><td>Missouri</td><td>12.37</td><td>25</td><td>Minnesota</td><td>20.08</td></tr>
<tr><td>6</td><td>Montana</td><td>133.12</td><td>26</td><td>Mississippi</td><td>19.32</td></tr>
<tr><td>13</td><td>Nebraska</td><td>51.53</td><td>27</td><td>Colorado</td><td>19.22</td></tr>
<tr><td>18</td><td>Nevada</td><td>29.59</td><td>28</td><td>Virginia</td><td>17.16</td></tr>
<tr><td>7</td><td>New Hampshire</td><td>105.17</td><td>29</td><td>Massachusetts</td><td>17.11</td></tr>
<tr><td>36</td><td>New Jersey</td><td>11.58</td><td>30</td><td>Oklahoma</td><td>16.36</td></tr>
<tr><td>19</td><td>New Mexico</td><td>24.38</td><td>31</td><td>South Carolina</td><td>13.31</td></tr>
<tr><td>45</td><td>New York</td><td>5.59</td><td>32</td><td>Maryland</td><td>13.20</td></tr>
<tr><td>47</td><td>North Carolina</td><td>5.22</td><td>33</td><td>Alabama</td><td>13.02</td></tr>
<tr><td>2</td><td>North Dakota</td><td>251.07</td><td>34</td><td>Indiana</td><td>12.47</td></tr>
<tr><td>46</td><td>Ohio</td><td>5.56</td><td>35</td><td>Missouri</td><td>12.37</td></tr>
<tr><td>30</td><td>Oklahoma</td><td>16.36</td><td>36</td><td>New Jersey</td><td>11.58</td></tr>
<tr><td>24</td><td>Oregon</td><td>20.31</td><td>37</td><td>Louisiana</td><td>11.21</td></tr>
<tr><td>40</td><td>Pennsylvania</td><td>9.43</td><td>38</td><td>Arizona</td><td>10.08</td></tr>
<tr><td>9</td><td>Rhode Island</td><td>79.24</td><td>39</td><td>Washington</td><td>9.50</td></tr>
<tr><td>31</td><td>South Carolina</td><td>13.31</td><td>40</td><td>Pennsylvania</td><td>9.43</td></tr>
<tr><td>3</td><td>South Dakota</td><td>181.29</td><td>41</td><td>Tennessee</td><td>9.20</td></tr>
<tr><td>41</td><td>Tennessee</td><td>9.20</td><td>42</td><td>Georgia</td><td>7.40</td></tr>
<tr><td>49</td><td>Texas</td><td>2.47</td><td>43</td><td>Michigan</td><td>7.32</td></tr>
<tr><td>15</td><td>Utah</td><td>36.38</td><td>44</td><td>Illinois</td><td>6.25</td></tr>
<tr><td>4</td><td>Vermont</td><td>150.08</td><td>45</td><td>New York</td><td>5.59</td></tr>
<tr><td>28</td><td>Virginia</td><td>17.16</td><td>46</td><td>Ohio</td><td>5.56</td></tr>
<tr><td>39</td><td>Washington</td><td>9.50</td><td>47</td><td>North Carolina</td><td>5.22</td></tr>
<tr><td>12</td><td>West Virginia</td><td>53.08</td><td>48</td><td>Florida</td><td>3.02</td></tr>
<tr><td>22</td><td>Wisconsin</td><td>20.52</td><td>49</td><td>Texas</td><td>2.47</td></tr>
<tr><td>1</td><td>Wyoming</td><td>252.56</td><td>50</td><td>California</td><td>2.22</td></tr>
<tr><td></td><td></td><td></td><td></td><td>District of Columbia</td><td>110.46</td></tr>
</table>

Source: Morgan Quitno Press using data from Federal Bureau of Investigation
"Crime in the United States 2000" (Uniform Crime Reports, October 22, 2001)
*Burglary is the unlawful entry of a structure to commit a felony or theft. Attempts are included.

Percent Change in Number of Burglaries: 1999 to 2000

National Percent Change = 2.4% Decrease*

ALPHA ORDER			RANK ORDER		
RANK	STATE	PERCENT CHANGE	RANK	STATE	PERCENT CHANGE
4	Alabama	4.4	1	Hawaii	13.2
6	Alaska	3.0	2	Tennessee	9.7
3	Arizona	5.0	3	Arizona	5.0
19	Arkansas	(1.1)	4	Alabama	4.4
15	California	(0.7)	4	Rhode Island	4.4
9	Colorado	0.6	6	Alaska	3.0
45	Connecticut	(9.6)	7	Ohio	1.9
13	Delaware	(0.6)	8	Montana	1.8
34	Florida	(4.7)	9	Colorado	0.6
31	Georgia	(4.1)	10	Kentucky	0.5
1	Hawaii	13.2	11	Nebraska	(0.3)
31	Idaho	(4.1)	12	Nevada	(0.5)
35	Illinois	(5.1)	13	Delaware	(0.6)
27	Indiana	(3.2)	13	North Carolina	(0.6)
29	Iowa	(3.9)	15	California	(0.7)
21	Kansas	(1.8)	15	New Mexico	(0.7)
10	Kentucky	0.5	15	Texas	(0.7)
26	Louisiana	(3.1)	18	Vermont	(1.0)
46	Maine	(10.1)	19	Arkansas	(1.1)
43	Maryland	(8.8)	20	Utah	(1.7)
40	Massachusetts	(7.2)	21	Kansas	(1.8)
44	Michigan	(9.1)	21	Wisconsin	(1.8)
36	Minnesota	(5.7)	23	Missouri	(1.9)
41	Mississippi	(7.5)	23	South Carolina	(1.9)
23	Missouri	(1.9)	25	Washington	(2.2)
8	Montana	1.8	26	Louisiana	(3.1)
11	Nebraska	(0.3)	27	Indiana	(3.2)
12	Nevada	(0.5)	28	Pennsylvania	(3.5)
NA	New Hampshire**	NA	29	Iowa	(3.9)
39	New Jersey	(6.5)	30	West Virginia	(4.0)
15	New Mexico	(0.7)	31	Georgia	(4.1)
36	New York	(5.7)	31	Idaho	(4.1)
13	North Carolina	(0.6)	33	Oregon	(4.2)
47	North Dakota	(10.4)	34	Florida	(4.7)
7	Ohio	1.9	35	Illinois	(5.1)
42	Oklahoma	(8.2)	36	Minnesota	(5.7)
33	Oregon	(4.2)	36	New York	(5.7)
28	Pennsylvania	(3.5)	38	Virginia	(6.1)
4	Rhode Island	4.4	39	New Jersey	(6.5)
23	South Carolina	(1.9)	40	Massachusetts	(7.2)
48	South Dakota	(11.0)	41	Mississippi	(7.5)
2	Tennessee	9.7	42	Oklahoma	(8.2)
15	Texas	(0.7)	43	Maryland	(8.8)
20	Utah	(1.7)	44	Michigan	(9.1)
18	Vermont	(1.0)	45	Connecticut	(9.6)
38	Virginia	(6.1)	46	Maine	(10.1)
25	Washington	(2.2)	47	North Dakota	(10.4)
30	West Virginia	(4.0)	48	South Dakota	(11.0)
21	Wisconsin	(1.8)	49	Wyoming	(11.5)
49	Wyoming	(11.5)	NA	New Hampshire**	NA
				District of Columbia	(6.4)

Source: Federal Bureau of Investigation
    "Crime in the United States 2000" (Uniform Crime Reports, October 22, 2001)
*Burglary is the unlawful entry of a structure to commit a felony or theft. Attempts are included.
**Not available.

Burglary Rate in 2000

National Rate = 728.4 Burglaries per 100,000 Population*

ALPHA ORDER

RANK	STATE	RATE
11	Alabama	906.9
31	Alaska	621.9
5	Arizona	1,011.6
16	Arkansas	802.1
26	California	656.3
29	Colorado	630.8
40	Connecticut	512.0
24	Delaware	665.6
3	Florida	1,081.8
15	Georgia	836.6
13	Hawaii	880.3
34	Idaho	566.5
25	Illinois	659.6
23	Indiana	676.1
35	Iowa	558.4
17	Kansas	799.1
30	Kentucky	626.2
4	Louisiana	1,035.8
37	Maine	531.4
21	Maryland	744.4
41	Massachusetts	482.0
22	Michigan	702.2
38	Minnesota	530.9
8	Mississippi	946.3
20	Missouri	745.0
45	Montana	437.4
32	Nebraska	592.0
14	Nevada	877.1
48	New Hampshire	404.0
39	New Jersey	522.0
2	New Mexico	1,173.1
43	New York	463.4
1	North Carolina	1,216.1
50	North Dakota	325.9
18	Ohio	780.7
9	Oklahoma	917.5
19	Oregon	748.8
44	Pennsylvania	440.4
28	Rhode Island	631.5
7	South Carolina	969.3
49	South Dakota	383.7
6	Tennessee	990.4
12	Texas	906.3
27	Utah	642.5
33	Vermont	575.0
46	Virginia	429.9
10	Washington	907.3
36	West Virginia	546.9
42	Wisconsin	469.5
47	Wyoming	420.8

RANK ORDER

RANK	STATE	RATE
1	North Carolina	1,216.1
2	New Mexico	1,173.1
3	Florida	1,081.8
4	Louisiana	1,035.8
5	Arizona	1,011.6
6	Tennessee	990.4
7	South Carolina	969.3
8	Mississippi	946.3
9	Oklahoma	917.5
10	Washington	907.3
11	Alabama	906.9
12	Texas	906.3
13	Hawaii	880.3
14	Nevada	877.1
15	Georgia	836.6
16	Arkansas	802.1
17	Kansas	799.1
18	Ohio	780.7
19	Oregon	748.8
20	Missouri	745.0
21	Maryland	744.4
22	Michigan	702.2
23	Indiana	676.1
24	Delaware	665.6
25	Illinois	659.6
26	California	656.3
27	Utah	642.5
28	Rhode Island	631.5
29	Colorado	630.8
30	Kentucky	626.2
31	Alaska	621.9
32	Nebraska	592.0
33	Vermont	575.0
34	Idaho	566.5
35	Iowa	558.4
36	West Virginia	546.9
37	Maine	531.4
38	Minnesota	530.9
39	New Jersey	522.0
40	Connecticut	512.0
41	Massachusetts	482.0
42	Wisconsin	469.5
43	New York	463.4
44	Pennsylvania	440.4
45	Montana	437.4
46	Virginia	429.9
47	Wyoming	420.8
48	New Hampshire	404.0
49	South Dakota	383.7
50	North Dakota	325.9
	District of Columbia	829.5

Source: Federal Bureau of Investigation
   "Crime in the United States 2000" (Uniform Crime Reports, October 22, 2001)
*Burglary is the unlawful entry of a structure to commit a felony or theft. Attempts are included.

Percent Change in Burglary Rate: 1999 to 2000

National Percent Change = 5.4% Decrease*

ALPHA ORDER

RANK	STATE	PERCENT CHANGE
3	Alabama	2.5
4	Alaska	1.7
9	Arizona	(2.2)
26	Arkansas	(5.7)
10	California	(2.8)
22	Colorado	(5.2)
47	Connecticut	(12.9)
17	Delaware	(4.4)
40	Florida	(9.9)
34	Georgia	(8.8)
1	Hawaii	10.8
30	Idaho	(7.2)
32	Illinois	(7.3)
24	Indiana	(5.4)
28	Iowa	(5.8)
12	Kansas	(3.0)
8	Kentucky	(1.5)
22	Louisiana	(5.2)
45	Maine	(11.6)
44	Maryland	(10.9)
38	Massachusetts	(9.7)
38	Michigan	(9.7)
33	Minnesota	(8.5)
42	Mississippi	(10.0)
15	Missouri	(4.1)
6	Montana	(0.4)
11	Nebraska	(2.9)
40	Nevada	(9.9)
NA	New Hampshire**	NA
37	New Jersey	(9.6)
20	New Mexico	(5.0)
36	New York	(9.5)
25	North Carolina	(5.5)
45	North Dakota	(11.6)
5	Ohio	1.0
43	Oklahoma	(10.6)
30	Oregon	(7.2)
26	Pennsylvania	(5.7)
7	Rhode Island	(1.3)
20	South Carolina	(5.0)
48	South Dakota	(13.6)
2	Tennessee	5.7
19	Texas	(4.6)
29	Utah	(6.2)
13	Vermont	(3.5)
34	Virginia	(8.8)
17	Washington	(4.4)
15	West Virginia	(4.1)
14	Wisconsin	(3.8)
49	Wyoming	(14.1)

RANK ORDER

RANK	STATE	PERCENT CHANGE
1	Hawaii	10.8
2	Tennessee	5.7
3	Alabama	2.5
4	Alaska	1.7
5	Ohio	1.0
6	Montana	(0.4)
7	Rhode Island	(1.3)
8	Kentucky	(1.5)
9	Arizona	(2.2)
10	California	(2.8)
11	Nebraska	(2.9)
12	Kansas	(3.0)
13	Vermont	(3.5)
14	Wisconsin	(3.8)
15	Missouri	(4.1)
15	West Virginia	(4.1)
17	Delaware	(4.4)
17	Washington	(4.4)
19	Texas	(4.6)
20	New Mexico	(5.0)
20	South Carolina	(5.0)
22	Colorado	(5.2)
22	Louisiana	(5.2)
24	Indiana	(5.4)
25	North Carolina	(5.5)
26	Arkansas	(5.7)
26	Pennsylvania	(5.7)
28	Iowa	(5.8)
29	Utah	(6.2)
30	Idaho	(7.2)
30	Oregon	(7.2)
32	Illinois	(7.3)
33	Minnesota	(8.5)
34	Georgia	(8.8)
34	Virginia	(8.8)
36	New York	(9.5)
37	New Jersey	(9.6)
38	Massachusetts	(9.7)
38	Michigan	(9.7)
40	Florida	(9.9)
40	Nevada	(9.9)
42	Mississippi	(10.0)
43	Oklahoma	(10.6)
44	Maryland	(10.9)
45	Maine	(11.6)
45	North Dakota	(11.6)
47	Connecticut	(12.9)
48	South Dakota	(13.6)
49	Wyoming	(14.1)
NA	New Hampshire**	NA
	District of Columbia	(15.0)

Source: Federal Bureau of Investigation
    "Crime in the United States 2000" (Uniform Crime Reports, October 22, 2001)
*Burglary is the unlawful entry of a structure to commit a felony or theft. Attempts are included.
**Not available.

Larcenies and Thefts in 2000

National Total = 6,965,957 Larcenies and Thefts*

RANK	STATE	THEFTS	% of USA
20	Alabama	127,399	1.8%
46	Alaska	16,838	0.2%
12	Arizona	176,705	2.5%
32	Arkansas	69,740	1.0%
1	California	651,855	9.4%
25	Colorado	112,843	1.6%
33	Connecticut	68,498	1.0%
44	Delaware	21,360	0.3%
3	Florida	518,298	7.4%
7	Georgia	240,440	3.5%
38	Hawaii	43,254	0.6%
39	Idaho	28,545	0.4%
5	Illinois	312,692	4.5%
18	Indiana	144,707	2.1%
34	Iowa	65,118	0.9%
28	Kansas	80,077	1.1%
30	Kentucky	73,141	1.0%
19	Louisiana	144,345	2.1%
41	Maine	23,906	0.3%
17	Maryland	145,423	2.1%
26	Massachusetts	105,425	1.5%
9	Michigan	227,783	3.3%
23	Minnesota	118,250	1.7%
31	Mississippi	69,758	1.0%
13	Missouri	159,539	2.3%
42	Montana	23,805	0.3%
36	Nebraska	49,118	0.7%
37	Nevada	44,125	0.6%
45	New Hampshire	20,761	0.3%
14	New Jersey	155,562	2.2%
35	New Mexico	57,925	0.8%
4	New York	340,901	4.9%
8	North Carolina	232,767	3.3%
50	North Dakota	11,092	0.2%
6	Ohio	293,277	4.2%
27	Oklahoma	96,116	1.4%
24	Oregon	114,230	1.6%
10	Pennsylvania	225,869	3.2%
43	Rhode Island	22,038	0.3%
21	South Carolina	123,094	1.8%
48	South Dakota	12,558	0.2%
15	Tennessee	154,111	2.2%
2	Texas	637,522	9.2%
29	Utah	73,438	1.1%
47	Vermont	13,184	0.2%
16	Virginia	146,158	2.1%
11	Washington	190,650	2.7%
40	West Virginia	28,139	0.4%
22	Wisconsin	119,605	1.7%
49	Wyoming	12,318	0.2%

RANK	STATE	THEFTS	% of USA
1	California	651,855	9.4%
2	Texas	637,522	9.2%
3	Florida	518,298	7.4%
4	New York	340,901	4.9%
5	Illinois	312,692	4.5%
6	Ohio	293,277	4.2%
7	Georgia	240,440	3.5%
8	North Carolina	232,767	3.3%
9	Michigan	227,783	3.3%
10	Pennsylvania	225,869	3.2%
11	Washington	190,650	2.7%
12	Arizona	176,705	2.5%
13	Missouri	159,539	2.3%
14	New Jersey	155,562	2.2%
15	Tennessee	154,111	2.2%
16	Virginia	146,158	2.1%
17	Maryland	145,423	2.1%
18	Indiana	144,707	2.1%
19	Louisiana	144,345	2.1%
20	Alabama	127,399	1.8%
21	South Carolina	123,094	1.8%
22	Wisconsin	119,605	1.7%
23	Minnesota	118,250	1.7%
24	Oregon	114,230	1.6%
25	Colorado	112,843	1.6%
26	Massachusetts	105,425	1.5%
27	Oklahoma	96,116	1.4%
28	Kansas	80,077	1.1%
29	Utah	73,438	1.1%
30	Kentucky	73,141	1.0%
31	Mississippi	69,758	1.0%
32	Arkansas	69,740	1.0%
33	Connecticut	68,498	1.0%
34	Iowa	65,118	0.9%
35	New Mexico	57,925	0.8%
36	Nebraska	49,118	0.7%
37	Nevada	44,125	0.6%
38	Hawaii	43,254	0.6%
39	Idaho	28,545	0.4%
40	West Virginia	28,139	0.4%
41	Maine	23,906	0.3%
42	Montana	23,805	0.3%
43	Rhode Island	22,038	0.3%
44	Delaware	21,360	0.3%
45	New Hampshire	20,761	0.3%
46	Alaska	16,838	0.2%
47	Vermont	13,184	0.2%
48	South Dakota	12,558	0.2%
49	Wyoming	12,318	0.2%
50	North Dakota	11,092	0.2%
	District of Columbia	21,655	0.3%

Source: Federal Bureau of Investigation

"Crime in the United States 2000" (Uniform Crime Reports, October 22, 2001)
Larceny and theft is the unlawful taking of property without use of force, violence or fraud. Attempts are included. Motor vehicle thefts are excluded.

Average Time Between Larcenies and Thefts in 2000

National Rate = A Larceny Occurs Every 5 Seconds*

<table>
<tr><td colspan="3">ALPHA ORDER</td><td colspan="3">RANK ORDER</td></tr>
<tr><th>RANK</th><th>STATE</th><th>MINUTES.SECONDS</th><th>RANK</th><th>STATE</th><th>MINUTES.SECONDS</th></tr>
<tr><td>31</td><td>Alabama</td><td>4.08</td><td>1</td><td>North Dakota</td><td>47.23</td></tr>
<tr><td>5</td><td>Alaska</td><td>31.13</td><td>2</td><td>Wyoming</td><td>42.40</td></tr>
<tr><td>39</td><td>Arizona</td><td>2.58</td><td>3</td><td>South Dakota</td><td>41.51</td></tr>
<tr><td>19</td><td>Arkansas</td><td>7.32</td><td>4</td><td>Vermont</td><td>39.52</td></tr>
<tr><td>49</td><td>California</td><td>0.49</td><td>5</td><td>Alaska</td><td>31.13</td></tr>
<tr><td>26</td><td>Colorado</td><td>4.40</td><td>6</td><td>New Hampshire</td><td>25.19</td></tr>
<tr><td>18</td><td>Connecticut</td><td>7.40</td><td>7</td><td>Delaware</td><td>24.37</td></tr>
<tr><td>7</td><td>Delaware</td><td>24.37</td><td>8</td><td>Rhode Island</td><td>23.51</td></tr>
<tr><td>48</td><td>Florida</td><td>1.01</td><td>9</td><td>Montana</td><td>22.05</td></tr>
<tr><td>44</td><td>Georgia</td><td>2.11</td><td>10</td><td>Maine</td><td>21.59</td></tr>
<tr><td>13</td><td>Hawaii</td><td>12.09</td><td>11</td><td>West Virginia</td><td>18.41</td></tr>
<tr><td>12</td><td>Idaho</td><td>18.25</td><td>12</td><td>Idaho</td><td>18.25</td></tr>
<tr><td>46</td><td>Illinois</td><td>1.41</td><td>13</td><td>Hawaii</td><td>12.09</td></tr>
<tr><td>32</td><td>Indiana</td><td>3.38</td><td>14</td><td>Nevada</td><td>11.55</td></tr>
<tr><td>17</td><td>Iowa</td><td>8.04</td><td>15</td><td>Nebraska</td><td>10.42</td></tr>
<tr><td>23</td><td>Kansas</td><td>6.34</td><td>16</td><td>New Mexico</td><td>9.04</td></tr>
<tr><td>21</td><td>Kentucky</td><td>7.11</td><td>17</td><td>Iowa</td><td>8.04</td></tr>
<tr><td>32</td><td>Louisiana</td><td>3.38</td><td>18</td><td>Connecticut</td><td>7.40</td></tr>
<tr><td>10</td><td>Maine</td><td>21.59</td><td>19</td><td>Arkansas</td><td>7.32</td></tr>
<tr><td>34</td><td>Maryland</td><td>3.37</td><td>19</td><td>Mississippi</td><td>7.32</td></tr>
<tr><td>25</td><td>Massachusetts</td><td>4.59</td><td>21</td><td>Kentucky</td><td>7.11</td></tr>
<tr><td>42</td><td>Michigan</td><td>2.19</td><td>22</td><td>Utah</td><td>7.10</td></tr>
<tr><td>28</td><td>Minnesota</td><td>4.26</td><td>23</td><td>Kansas</td><td>6.34</td></tr>
<tr><td>19</td><td>Mississippi</td><td>7.32</td><td>24</td><td>Oklahoma</td><td>5.28</td></tr>
<tr><td>38</td><td>Missouri</td><td>3.17</td><td>25</td><td>Massachusetts</td><td>4.59</td></tr>
<tr><td>9</td><td>Montana</td><td>22.05</td><td>26</td><td>Colorado</td><td>4.40</td></tr>
<tr><td>15</td><td>Nebraska</td><td>10.42</td><td>27</td><td>Oregon</td><td>4.36</td></tr>
<tr><td>14</td><td>Nevada</td><td>11.55</td><td>28</td><td>Minnesota</td><td>4.26</td></tr>
<tr><td>6</td><td>New Hampshire</td><td>25.19</td><td>29</td><td>Wisconsin</td><td>4.23</td></tr>
<tr><td>37</td><td>New Jersey</td><td>3.23</td><td>30</td><td>South Carolina</td><td>4.16</td></tr>
<tr><td>16</td><td>New Mexico</td><td>9.04</td><td>31</td><td>Alabama</td><td>4.08</td></tr>
<tr><td>47</td><td>New York</td><td>1.32</td><td>32</td><td>Indiana</td><td>3.38</td></tr>
<tr><td>43</td><td>North Carolina</td><td>2.16</td><td>32</td><td>Louisiana</td><td>3.38</td></tr>
<tr><td>1</td><td>North Dakota</td><td>47.23</td><td>34</td><td>Maryland</td><td>3.37</td></tr>
<tr><td>45</td><td>Ohio</td><td>1.47</td><td>35</td><td>Virginia</td><td>3.36</td></tr>
<tr><td>24</td><td>Oklahoma</td><td>5.28</td><td>36</td><td>Tennessee</td><td>3.25</td></tr>
<tr><td>27</td><td>Oregon</td><td>4.36</td><td>37</td><td>New Jersey</td><td>3.23</td></tr>
<tr><td>41</td><td>Pennsylvania</td><td>2.20</td><td>38</td><td>Missouri</td><td>3.17</td></tr>
<tr><td>8</td><td>Rhode Island</td><td>23.51</td><td>39</td><td>Arizona</td><td>2.58</td></tr>
<tr><td>30</td><td>South Carolina</td><td>4.16</td><td>40</td><td>Washington</td><td>2.46</td></tr>
<tr><td>3</td><td>South Dakota</td><td>41.51</td><td>41</td><td>Pennsylvania</td><td>2.20</td></tr>
<tr><td>36</td><td>Tennessee</td><td>3.25</td><td>42</td><td>Michigan</td><td>2.19</td></tr>
<tr><td>49</td><td>Texas</td><td>0.49</td><td>43</td><td>North Carolina</td><td>2.16</td></tr>
<tr><td>22</td><td>Utah</td><td>7.10</td><td>44</td><td>Georgia</td><td>2.11</td></tr>
<tr><td>4</td><td>Vermont</td><td>39.52</td><td>45</td><td>Ohio</td><td>1.47</td></tr>
<tr><td>35</td><td>Virginia</td><td>3.36</td><td>46</td><td>Illinois</td><td>1.41</td></tr>
<tr><td>40</td><td>Washington</td><td>2.46</td><td>47</td><td>New York</td><td>1.32</td></tr>
<tr><td>11</td><td>West Virginia</td><td>18.41</td><td>48</td><td>Florida</td><td>1.01</td></tr>
<tr><td>29</td><td>Wisconsin</td><td>4.23</td><td>49</td><td>California</td><td>0.49</td></tr>
<tr><td>2</td><td>Wyoming</td><td>42.40</td><td>49</td><td>Texas</td><td>0.49</td></tr>
<tr><td></td><td></td><td></td><td></td><td>District of Columbia</td><td>24.16</td></tr>
</table>

Source: Morgan Quitno Press using data from Federal Bureau of Investigation
    "Crime in the United States 2000" (Uniform Crime Reports, October 22, 2001)
*Larceny and theft is the unlawful taking of property without use of force, violence or fraud. Attempts are included.
Motor vehicle thefts are excluded.

Percent Change in Number of Larcenies and Thefts: 1999 to 2000

National Percent Change = 0.2% Increase*

RANK	STATE	PERCENT CHANGE		RANK	STATE	PERCENT CHANGE
	ALPHA ORDER				RANK ORDER	
6	Alabama	6.5		1	Vermont	13.6
21	Alaska	1.1		2	Arkansas	9.1
9	Arizona	5.4		3	Tennessee	8.0
2	Arkansas	9.1		4	Nebraska	7.5
33	California	(1.4)		5	Hawaii	6.9
14	Colorado	3.3		6	Alabama	6.5
31	Connecticut	(1.2)		7	Idaho	6.4
45	Delaware	(5.6)		8	Mississippi	5.8
39	Florida	(3.0)		9	Arizona	5.4
39	Georgia	(3.0)		10	Iowa	4.5
5	Hawaii	6.9		11	Indiana	4.3
7	Idaho	6.4		12	Texas	3.9
37	Illinois	(2.6)		13	Kentucky	3.4
11	Indiana	4.3		14	Colorado	3.3
10	Iowa	4.5		15	Oklahoma	2.7
25	Kansas	0.4		15	South Carolina	2.7
13	Kentucky	3.4		17	Nevada	2.2
43	Louisiana	(3.6)		18	Montana	1.9
46	Maine	(5.9)		19	Ohio	1.8
32	Maryland	(1.3)		20	Missouri	1.3
41	Massachusetts	(3.1)		21	Alaska	1.1
43	Michigan	(3.6)		22	North Carolina	1.0
25	Minnesota	0.4		22	Oregon	1.0
8	Mississippi	5.8		24	New York	0.8
20	Missouri	1.3		25	Kansas	0.4
18	Montana	1.9		25	Minnesota	0.4
4	Nebraska	7.5		27	Pennsylvania	(0.8)
17	Nevada	2.2		28	Washington	(0.9)
NA	New Hampshire**	NA		28	Wisconsin	(0.9)
42	New Jersey	(3.4)		30	Rhode Island	(1.1)
38	New Mexico	(2.8)		31	Connecticut	(1.2)
24	New York	0.8		32	Maryland	(1.3)
22	North Carolina	1.0		33	California	(1.4)
36	North Dakota	(2.5)		34	Wyoming	(1.6)
19	Ohio	1.8		35	West Virginia	(2.2)
15	Oklahoma	2.7		36	North Dakota	(2.5)
22	Oregon	1.0		37	Illinois	(2.6)
27	Pennsylvania	(0.8)		38	New Mexico	(2.8)
30	Rhode Island	(1.1)		39	Florida	(3.0)
15	South Carolina	2.7		39	Georgia	(3.0)
49	South Dakota	(10.6)		41	Massachusetts	(3.1)
3	Tennessee	8.0		42	New Jersey	(3.4)
12	Texas	3.9		43	Louisiana	(3.6)
47	Utah	(6.0)		43	Michigan	(3.6)
1	Vermont	13.6		45	Delaware	(5.6)
48	Virginia	(8.6)		46	Maine	(5.9)
28	Washington	(0.9)		47	Utah	(6.0)
35	West Virginia	(2.2)		48	Virginia	(8.6)
28	Wisconsin	(0.9)		49	South Dakota	(10.6)
34	Wyoming	(1.6)		NA	New Hampshire**	NA
					District of Columbia	(0.2)

Source: Federal Bureau of Investigation
   "Crime in the United States 2000" (Uniform Crime Reports, October 22, 2001)
Larceny and theft is the unlawful taking of property without use of force, violence or fraud. Attempts are included.
Motor vehicle thefts are excluded.
**Not available.*

Larceny and Theft Rate in 2000

National Rate = 2,475.3 Larcenies and Thefts per 100,000 Population*

RANK	STATE	RATE
15	Alabama	2,864.8
21	Alaska	2,685.8
2	Arizona	3,444.1
24	Arkansas	2,608.7
40	California	1,924.5
23	Colorado	2,623.5
39	Connecticut	2,011.4
19	Delaware	2,725.9
5	Florida	3,242.9
12	Georgia	2,937.0
1	Hawaii	3,570.2
35	Idaho	2,206.0
26	Illinois	2,517.8
30	Indiana	2,379.9
33	Iowa	2,225.2
11	Kansas	2,978.6
44	Kentucky	1,809.6
7	Louisiana	3,229.9
41	Maine	1,875.1
18	Maryland	2,745.7
49	Massachusetts	1,660.5
31	Michigan	2,291.9
29	Minnesota	2,403.7
28	Mississippi	2,452.2
16	Missouri	2,851.3
22	Montana	2,638.6
14	Nebraska	2,870.3
34	Nevada	2,208.2
47	New Hampshire	1,680.0
42	New Jersey	1,848.8
8	New Mexico	3,184.4
45	New York	1,796.4
13	North Carolina	2,891.8
46	North Dakota	1,727.2
25	Ohio	2,583.2
17	Oklahoma	2,785.4
3	Oregon	3,338.7
43	Pennsylvania	1,839.2
37	Rhode Island	2,102.2
9	South Carolina	3,068.1
48	South Dakota	1,663.7
20	Tennessee	2,708.8
10	Texas	3,057.4
4	Utah	3,288.5
36	Vermont	2,165.5
38	Virginia	2,064.8
6	Washington	3,234.6
50	West Virginia	1,556.1
32	Wisconsin	2,229.9
27	Wyoming	2,494.6

RANK	STATE	RATE
1	Hawaii	3,570.2
2	Arizona	3,444.1
3	Oregon	3,338.7
4	Utah	3,288.5
5	Florida	3,242.9
6	Washington	3,234.6
7	Louisiana	3,229.9
8	New Mexico	3,184.4
9	South Carolina	3,068.1
10	Texas	3,057.4
11	Kansas	2,978.6
12	Georgia	2,937.0
13	North Carolina	2,891.8
14	Nebraska	2,870.3
15	Alabama	2,864.8
16	Missouri	2,851.3
17	Oklahoma	2,785.4
18	Maryland	2,745.7
19	Delaware	2,725.9
20	Tennessee	2,708.8
21	Alaska	2,685.8
22	Montana	2,638.6
23	Colorado	2,623.5
24	Arkansas	2,608.7
25	Ohio	2,583.2
26	Illinois	2,517.8
27	Wyoming	2,494.6
28	Mississippi	2,452.2
29	Minnesota	2,403.7
30	Indiana	2,379.9
31	Michigan	2,291.9
32	Wisconsin	2,229.9
33	Iowa	2,225.2
34	Nevada	2,208.2
35	Idaho	2,206.0
36	Vermont	2,165.5
37	Rhode Island	2,102.2
38	Virginia	2,064.8
39	Connecticut	2,011.4
40	California	1,924.5
41	Maine	1,875.1
42	New Jersey	1,848.8
43	Pennsylvania	1,839.2
44	Kentucky	1,809.6
45	New York	1,796.4
46	North Dakota	1,727.2
47	New Hampshire	1,680.0
48	South Dakota	1,663.7
49	Massachusetts	1,660.5
50	West Virginia	1,556.1
	District of Columbia	3,785.4

Source: Federal Bureau of Investigation
  "Crime in the United States 2000" (Uniform Crime Reports, October 22, 2001)
*Larceny and theft is the unlawful taking of property without use of force, violence or fraud. Attempts are included.
Motor vehicle thefts are excluded.

Percent Change in Larceny and Theft Rate: 1999 to 2000

National Percent Change = 3.0% Decrease*

ALPHA ORDER			RANK ORDER		
RANK	STATE	PERCENT CHANGE	RANK	STATE	PERCENT CHANGE
2	Alabama	4.7	1	Vermont	10.7
13	Alaska	(0.1)	2	Alabama	4.7
20	Arizona	(1.9)	2	Nebraska	4.7
5	Arkansas	4.1	4	Hawaii	4.6
29	California	(3.5)	5	Arkansas	4.1
24	Colorado	(2.6)	5	Tennessee	4.1
35	Connecticut	(4.7)	7	Mississippi	3.0
46	Delaware	(9.2)	8	Idaho	2.9
45	Florida	(8.2)	9	Iowa	2.5
44	Georgia	(7.7)	10	Indiana	1.9
4	Hawaii	4.6	11	Kentucky	1.4
8	Idaho	2.9	12	Ohio	0.9
36	Illinois	(4.9)	13	Alaska	(0.1)
10	Indiana	1.9	13	Oklahoma	(0.1)
9	Iowa	2.5	15	Texas	(0.2)
18	Kansas	(0.8)	16	Montana	(0.3)
11	Kentucky	1.4	17	South Carolina	(0.6)
37	Louisiana	(5.7)	18	Kansas	(0.8)
43	Maine	(7.5)	19	Missouri	(1.0)
30	Maryland	(3.6)	20	Arizona	(1.9)
38	Massachusetts	(5.8)	21	Oregon	(2.1)
33	Michigan	(4.3)	22	West Virginia	(2.2)
23	Minnesota	(2.5)	23	Minnesota	(2.5)
7	Mississippi	3.0	24	Colorado	(2.6)
19	Missouri	(1.0)	25	Wisconsin	(3.0)
16	Montana	(0.3)	26	Pennsylvania	(3.1)
2	Nebraska	4.7	27	Washington	(3.2)
42	Nevada	(7.4)	28	New York	(3.3)
NA	New Hampshire**	NA	29	California	(3.5)
39	New Jersey	(6.5)	30	Maryland	(3.6)
41	New Mexico	(7.1)	31	North Dakota	(3.8)
28	New York	(3.3)	32	North Carolina	(4.0)
32	North Carolina	(4.0)	33	Michigan	(4.3)
31	North Dakota	(3.8)	34	Wyoming	(4.5)
12	Ohio	0.9	35	Connecticut	(4.7)
13	Oklahoma	(0.1)	36	Illinois	(4.9)
21	Oregon	(2.1)	37	Louisiana	(5.7)
26	Pennsylvania	(3.1)	38	Massachusetts	(5.8)
39	Rhode Island	(6.5)	39	New Jersey	(6.5)
17	South Carolina	(0.6)	39	Rhode Island	(6.5)
49	South Dakota	(13.1)	41	New Mexico	(7.1)
5	Tennessee	4.1	42	Nevada	(7.4)
15	Texas	(0.2)	43	Maine	(7.5)
47	Utah	(10.4)	44	Georgia	(7.7)
1	Vermont	10.7	45	Florida	(8.2)
48	Virginia	(11.2)	46	Delaware	(9.2)
27	Washington	(3.2)	47	Utah	(10.4)
22	West Virginia	(2.2)	48	Virginia	(11.2)
25	Wisconsin	(3.0)	49	South Dakota	(13.1)
34	Wyoming	(4.5)	NA	New Hampshire**	NA
				District of Columbia	(9.5)

Source: Federal Bureau of Investigation
"Crime in the United States 2000" (Uniform Crime Reports, October 22, 2001)
Larceny and theft is the unlawful taking of property without use of force, violence or fraud. Attempts are included. Motor vehicle thefts are excluded.
**Not available.*

Motor Vehicle Thefts in 2000

National Total = 1,165,559 Motor Vehicle Thefts*

ALPHA ORDER					RANK ORDER			
RANK	STATE		THEFTS	% of USA	RANK	STATE	THEFTS	% of USA
28	Alabama		12,809	1.1%	1	California	182,035	15.6%
42	Alaska		2,350	0.2%	2	Texas	93,161	8.0%
7	Arizona		43,204	3.7%	3	Florida	89,181	7.7%
33	Arkansas		6,932	0.6%	4	Illinois	56,143	4.8%
1	California		182,035	15.6%	5	Michigan	55,724	4.8%
21	Colorado		16,961	1.5%	6	New York	54,231	4.7%
27	Connecticut		13,099	1.1%	7	Arizona	43,204	3.7%
41	Delaware		3,151	0.3%	8	Ohio	39,026	3.3%
3	Florida		89,181	7.7%	9	Georgia	38,702	3.3%
9	Georgia		38,702	3.3%	10	Pennsylvania	36,325	3.1%
36	Hawaii		6,114	0.5%	11	Washington	35,018	3.0%
44	Idaho		2,086	0.2%	12	New Jersey	34,151	2.9%
4	Illinois		56,143	4.8%	13	Maryland	28,573	2.5%
19	Indiana		21,090	1.8%	14	Tennessee	27,530	2.4%
37	Iowa		5,374	0.5%	15	Massachusetts	25,876	2.2%
34	Kansas		6,496	0.6%	16	North Carolina	25,266	2.2%
30	Kentucky		9,274	0.8%	17	Missouri	24,695	2.1%
18	Louisiana		21,270	1.8%	18	Louisiana	21,270	1.8%
46	Maine		1,322	0.1%	19	Indiana	21,090	1.8%
13	Maryland		28,573	2.5%	20	Virginia	17,813	1.5%
15	Massachusetts		25,876	2.2%	21	Colorado	16,961	1.5%
5	Michigan		55,724	4.8%	22	South Carolina	15,207	1.3%
25	Minnesota		13,432	1.2%	23	Wisconsin	14,636	1.3%
32	Mississippi		6,968	0.6%	24	Oregon	13,932	1.2%
17	Missouri		24,695	2.1%	25	Minnesota	13,432	1.2%
45	Montana		1,956	0.2%	26	Nevada	13,172	1.1%
38	Nebraska		5,230	0.4%	27	Connecticut	13,099	1.1%
26	Nevada		13,172	1.1%	28	Alabama	12,809	1.1%
43	New Hampshire		2,148	0.2%	29	Oklahoma	12,348	1.1%
12	New Jersey		34,151	2.9%	30	Kentucky	9,274	0.8%
31	New Mexico		7,341	0.6%	31	New Mexico	7,341	0.6%
6	New York		54,231	4.7%	32	Mississippi	6,968	0.6%
16	North Carolina		25,266	2.2%	33	Arkansas	6,932	0.6%
47	North Dakota		986	0.1%	34	Kansas	6,496	0.6%
8	Ohio		39,026	3.3%	35	Utah	6,461	0.6%
29	Oklahoma		12,348	1.1%	36	Hawaii	6,114	0.5%
24	Oregon		13,932	1.2%	37	Iowa	5,374	0.5%
10	Pennsylvania		36,325	3.1%	38	Nebraska	5,230	0.4%
39	Rhode Island		4,665	0.4%	39	Rhode Island	4,665	0.4%
22	South Carolina		15,207	1.3%	40	West Virginia	3,315	0.3%
49	South Dakota		798	0.1%	41	Delaware	3,151	0.3%
14	Tennessee		27,530	2.4%	42	Alaska	2,350	0.2%
2	Texas		93,161	8.0%	43	New Hampshire	2,148	0.2%
35	Utah		6,461	0.6%	44	Idaho	2,086	0.2%
48	Vermont		809	0.1%	45	Montana	1,956	0.2%
20	Virginia		17,813	1.5%	46	Maine	1,322	0.1%
11	Washington		35,018	3.0%	47	North Dakota	986	0.1%
40	West Virginia		3,315	0.3%	48	Vermont	809	0.1%
23	Wisconsin		14,636	1.3%	49	South Dakota	798	0.1%
50	Wyoming		573	0.0%	50	Wyoming	573	0.0%
						District of Columbia	6,600	0.6%

Source: Federal Bureau of Investigation
   "Crime in the United States 2000" (Uniform Crime Reports, October 22, 2001)
*Includes the theft or attempted theft of a self-propelled vehicle. Excludes motorboats, construction equipment, airplanes and farming equipment.

Average Time Between Motor Vehicle Thefts in 2000

National Rate = A Motor Vehicle Theft Occurs Every 27 Seconds*

ALPHA ORDER

RANK	STATE	MINUTES.SECONDS
23	Alabama	41.02
9	Alaska	223.40
44	Arizona	12.10
18	Arkansas	75.49
50	California	2.53
30	Colorado	30.59
24	Connecticut	40.08
10	Delaware	166.48
48	Florida	5.53
42	Georgia	13.35
15	Hawaii	85.58
7	Idaho	251.58
47	Illinois	9.22
32	Indiana	24.55
14	Iowa	97.48
17	Kansas	80.55
21	Kentucky	56.40
33	Louisiana	24.43
5	Maine	397.35
38	Maryland	18.24
36	Massachusetts	20.19
46	Michigan	9.26
26	Minnesota	39.08
19	Mississippi	75.26
34	Missouri	21.17
6	Montana	268.43
13	Nebraska	100.30
25	Nevada	39.54
8	New Hampshire	244.41
39	New Jersey	15.23
20	New Mexico	71.36
45	New York	9.41
35	North Carolina	20.48
4	North Dakota	533.04
43	Ohio	13.28
22	Oklahoma	42.34
27	Oregon	37.44
41	Pennsylvania	14.28
12	Rhode Island	112.40
29	South Carolina	34.34
2	South Dakota	658.39
37	Tennessee	19.05
49	Texas	5.38
16	Utah	81.21
3	Vermont	649.41
31	Virginia	29.31
40	Washington	15.01
11	West Virginia	158.33
28	Wisconsin	35.55
1	Wyoming	917.17

RANK ORDER

RANK	STATE	MINUTES.SECONDS
1	Wyoming	917.17
2	South Dakota	658.39
3	Vermont	649.41
4	North Dakota	533.04
5	Maine	397.35
6	Montana	268.43
7	Idaho	251.58
8	New Hampshire	244.41
9	Alaska	223.40
10	Delaware	166.48
11	West Virginia	158.33
12	Rhode Island	112.40
13	Nebraska	100.30
14	Iowa	97.48
15	Hawaii	85.58
16	Utah	81.21
17	Kansas	80.55
18	Arkansas	75.49
19	Mississippi	75.26
20	New Mexico	71.36
21	Kentucky	56.40
22	Oklahoma	42.34
23	Alabama	41.02
24	Connecticut	40.08
25	Nevada	39.54
26	Minnesota	39.08
27	Oregon	37.44
28	Wisconsin	35.55
29	South Carolina	34.34
30	Colorado	30.59
31	Virginia	29.31
32	Indiana	24.55
33	Louisiana	24.43
34	Missouri	21.17
35	North Carolina	20.48
36	Massachusetts	20.19
37	Tennessee	19.05
38	Maryland	18.24
39	New Jersey	15.23
40	Washington	15.01
41	Pennsylvania	14.28
42	Georgia	13.35
43	Ohio	13.28
44	Arizona	12.10
45	New York	9.41
46	Michigan	9.26
47	Illinois	9.22
48	Florida	5.53
49	Texas	5.38
50	California	2.53
	District of Columbia	79.38

Source: Morgan Quitno Press using data from Federal Bureau of Investigation
   "Crime in the United States 2000" (Uniform Crime Reports, October 22, 2001)
*Includes the theft or attempted theft of a self-propelled vehicle. Excludes motorboats, construction equipment, airplanes and farming equipment.

Percent Change in Number of Motor Vehicle Thefts: 1999 to 2000

National Percent Change = 1.2% Increase*

ALPHA ORDER

RANK	STATE	PERCENT CHANGE
33	Alabama	(2.5)
45	Alaska	(11.6)
5	Arizona	13.0
17	Arkansas	4.0
9	California	8.0
4	Colorado	14.6
2	Connecticut	16.0
20	Delaware	3.5
38	Florida	(4.3)
35	Georgia	(3.5)
1	Hawaii	31.2
7	Idaho	9.9
29	Illinois	(0.9)
18	Indiana	3.9
14	Iowa	4.7
10	Kansas	7.4
15	Kentucky	4.6
32	Louisiana	(2.0)
48	Maine	(22.0)
6	Maryland	12.3
25	Massachusetts	1.0
31	Michigan	(1.9)
23	Minnesota	1.2
49	Mississippi	(48.5)
10	Missouri	7.4
16	Montana	4.4
36	Nebraska	(3.9)
NA	New Hampshire**	NA
34	New Jersey	(3.4)
43	New Mexico	(9.7)
40	New York	(6.9)
30	North Carolina	(1.2)
39	North Dakota	(4.8)
27	Ohio	(0.4)
22	Oklahoma	1.8
21	Oregon	2.2
42	Pennsylvania	(7.4)
3	Rhode Island	15.7
13	South Carolina	5.3
41	South Dakota	(7.3)
8	Tennessee	9.0
23	Texas	1.2
47	Utah	(12.5)
44	Vermont	(11.3)
28	Virginia	(0.8)
19	Washington	3.6
46	West Virginia	(11.9)
12	Wisconsin	5.9
36	Wyoming	(3.9)

RANK ORDER

RANK	STATE	PERCENT CHANGE
1	Hawaii	31.2
2	Connecticut	16.0
3	Rhode Island	15.7
4	Colorado	14.6
5	Arizona	13.0
6	Maryland	12.3
7	Idaho	9.9
8	Tennessee	9.0
9	California	8.0
10	Kansas	7.4
10	Missouri	7.4
12	Wisconsin	5.9
13	South Carolina	5.3
14	Iowa	4.7
15	Kentucky	4.6
16	Montana	4.4
17	Arkansas	4.0
18	Indiana	3.9
19	Washington	3.6
20	Delaware	3.5
21	Oregon	2.2
22	Oklahoma	1.8
23	Minnesota	1.2
23	Texas	1.2
25	Massachusetts	1.0
26	Nevada	0.6
27	Ohio	(0.4)
28	Virginia	(0.8)
29	Illinois	(0.9)
30	North Carolina	(1.2)
31	Michigan	(1.9)
32	Louisiana	(2.0)
33	Alabama	(2.5)
34	New Jersey	(3.4)
35	Georgia	(3.5)
36	Nebraska	(3.9)
36	Wyoming	(3.9)
38	Florida	(4.3)
39	North Dakota	(4.8)
40	New York	(6.9)
41	South Dakota	(7.3)
42	Pennsylvania	(7.4)
43	New Mexico	(9.7)
44	Vermont	(11.3)
45	Alaska	(11.6)
46	West Virginia	(11.9)
47	Utah	(12.5)
48	Maine	(22.0)
49	Mississippi	(48.5)
NA	New Hampshire**	NA
	District of Columbia	(0.8)

Source: Federal Bureau of Investigation
"Crime in the United States 2000" (Uniform Crime Reports, October 22, 2001)
Includes the theft or attempted theft of a self-propelled vehicle. Excludes motorboats, construction equipment, airplanes and farming equipment.
**Not available.*

Motor Vehicle Theft Rate in 2000

National Rate = 414.2 Motor Vehicle Thefts per 100,000 Population*

ALPHA ORDER				RANK ORDER		
RANK	STATE	RATE		RANK	STATE	RATE
32	Alabama	288.0		1	Arizona	842.1
24	Alaska	374.8		2	Nevada	659.2
1	Arizona	842.1		3	Washington	594.1
36	Arkansas	259.3		4	Michigan	560.7
7	California	537.4		5	Florida	558.0
21	Colorado	394.3		6	Maryland	539.5
22	Connecticut	384.6		7	California	537.4
20	Delaware	402.1		8	Hawaii	504.6
5	Florida	558.0		9	Tennessee	483.9
11	Georgia	472.8		10	Louisiana	475.9
8	Hawaii	504.6		11	Georgia	472.8
45	Idaho	161.2		12	Illinois	452.1
12	Illinois	452.1		13	Texas	446.8
26	Indiana	346.8		14	Rhode Island	445.0
42	Iowa	183.6		15	Missouri	441.4
39	Kansas	241.6		16	Massachusetts	407.6
40	Kentucky	229.5		17	Oregon	407.2
10	Louisiana	475.9		18	New Jersey	405.9
50	Maine	103.7		19	New Mexico	403.6
6	Maryland	539.5		20	Delaware	402.1
16	Massachusetts	407.6		21	Colorado	394.3
4	Michigan	560.7		22	Connecticut	384.6
34	Minnesota	273.0		23	South Carolina	379.0
38	Mississippi	245.0		24	Alaska	374.8
15	Missouri	441.4		25	Oklahoma	357.8
41	Montana	216.8		26	Indiana	346.8
29	Nebraska	305.6		27	Ohio	343.7
2	Nevada	659.2		28	North Carolina	313.9
44	New Hampshire	173.8		29	Nebraska	305.6
18	New Jersey	405.9		30	Pennsylvania	295.8
19	New Mexico	403.6		31	Utah	289.3
33	New York	285.8		32	Alabama	288.0
28	North Carolina	313.9		33	New York	285.8
46	North Dakota	153.5		34	Minnesota	273.0
27	Ohio	343.7		35	Wisconsin	272.9
25	Oklahoma	357.8		36	Arkansas	259.3
17	Oregon	407.2		37	Virginia	251.6
30	Pennsylvania	295.8		38	Mississippi	245.0
14	Rhode Island	445.0		39	Kansas	241.6
23	South Carolina	379.0		40	Kentucky	229.5
49	South Dakota	105.7		41	Montana	216.8
9	Tennessee	483.9		42	Iowa	183.6
13	Texas	446.8		43	West Virginia	183.3
31	Utah	289.3		44	New Hampshire	173.8
47	Vermont	132.9		45	Idaho	161.2
37	Virginia	251.6		46	North Dakota	153.5
3	Washington	594.1		47	Vermont	132.9
43	West Virginia	183.3		48	Wyoming	116.0
35	Wisconsin	272.9		49	South Dakota	105.7
48	Wyoming	116.0		50	Maine	103.7
					District of Columbia	1,153.7

Source: Federal Bureau of Investigation
"Crime in the United States 2000" (Uniform Crime Reports, October 22, 2001)
*Includes the theft or attempted theft of a self-propelled vehicle. Excludes motorboats, construction equipment, airplanes and farming equipment.

Percent Change in Motor Vehicle Theft Rate: 1999 to 2000

National Percent Change = 2.0% Decrease*

RANK	STATE	PERCENT CHANGE
31	Alabama	(4.2)
44	Alaska	(12.6)
9	Arizona	5.2
20	Arkansas	(0.7)
8	California	5.7
5	Colorado	8.1
2	Connecticut	11.7
19	Delaware	(0.4)
39	Florida	(9.5)
37	Georgia	(8.2)
1	Hawaii	28.4
6	Idaho	6.3
28	Illinois	(3.2)
17	Indiana	1.6
13	Iowa	2.6
7	Kansas	6.0
14	Kentucky	2.5
30	Louisiana	(4.1)
48	Maine	(23.3)
3	Maryland	9.6
24	Massachusetts	(1.8)
26	Michigan	(2.6)
24	Minnesota	(1.8)
49	Mississippi	(49.9)
11	Missouri	5.0
15	Montana	2.1
34	Nebraska	(6.4)
38	Nevada	(8.9)
NA	New Hampshire**	NA
35	New Jersey	(6.5)
46	New Mexico	(13.6)
42	New York	(10.7)
32	North Carolina	(6.1)
32	North Dakota	(6.1)
23	Ohio	(1.3)
21	Oklahoma	(1.0)
21	Oregon	(1.0)
40	Pennsylvania	(9.6)
4	Rhode Island	9.4
16	South Carolina	2.0
41	South Dakota	(10.0)
10	Tennessee	5.1
27	Texas	(2.7)
47	Utah	(16.5)
45	Vermont	(13.5)
29	Virginia	(3.7)
18	Washington	1.2
43	West Virginia	(12.0)
12	Wisconsin	3.7
36	Wyoming	(6.6)

RANK	STATE	PERCENT CHANGE
1	Hawaii	28.4
2	Connecticut	11.7
3	Maryland	9.6
4	Rhode Island	9.4
5	Colorado	8.1
6	Idaho	6.3
7	Kansas	6.0
8	California	5.7
9	Arizona	5.2
10	Tennessee	5.1
11	Missouri	5.0
12	Wisconsin	3.7
13	Iowa	2.6
14	Kentucky	2.5
15	Montana	2.1
16	South Carolina	2.0
17	Indiana	1.6
18	Washington	1.2
19	Delaware	(0.4)
20	Arkansas	(0.7)
21	Oklahoma	(1.0)
21	Oregon	(1.0)
23	Ohio	(1.3)
24	Massachusetts	(1.8)
24	Minnesota	(1.8)
26	Michigan	(2.6)
27	Texas	(2.7)
28	Illinois	(3.2)
29	Virginia	(3.7)
30	Louisiana	(4.1)
31	Alabama	(4.2)
32	North Carolina	(6.1)
32	North Dakota	(6.1)
34	Nebraska	(6.4)
35	New Jersey	(6.5)
36	Wyoming	(6.6)
37	Georgia	(8.2)
38	Nevada	(8.9)
39	Florida	(9.5)
40	Pennsylvania	(9.6)
41	South Dakota	(10.0)
42	New York	(10.7)
43	West Virginia	(12.0)
44	Alaska	(12.6)
45	Vermont	(13.5)
46	New Mexico	(13.6)
47	Utah	(16.5)
48	Maine	(23.3)
49	Mississippi	(49.9)
NA	New Hampshire**	NA
	District of Columbia	(10.0)

Source: Federal Bureau of Investigation
    "Crime in the United States 2000" (Uniform Crime Reports, October 22, 2001)
*Includes the theft or attempted theft of a self-propelled vehicle. Excludes motorboats, construction equipment, airplanes and farming equipment.
**Not available.

Crimes in Urban Areas in 2000

National Urban Total = 10,974,287 Crimes*

ALPHA ORDER

RANK	STATE	CRIMES	% of USA
19	Alabama	192,795	1.8%
41	Alaska	21,829	0.2%
10	Arizona	294,051	2.7%
28	Arkansas	97,449	0.9%
1	California	1,252,416	11.4%
22	Colorado	165,290	1.5%
27	Connecticut	102,161	0.9%
NA	Delaware**	NA	NA
3	Florida	881,079	8.0%
8	Georgia	350,352	3.2%
35	Hawaii	46,659	0.4%
38	Idaho	34,670	0.3%
NA	Illinois**	NA	NA
17	Indiana	205,694	1.9%
32	Iowa	87,547	0.8%
NA	Kansas**	NA	NA
NA	Kentucky**	NA	NA
16	Louisiana	225,277	2.1%
40	Maine	28,096	0.3%
14	Maryland	248,935	2.3%
20	Massachusetts	192,104	1.8%
6	Michigan	383,426	3.5%
24	Minnesota	156,347	1.4%
31	Mississippi	93,860	0.9%
15	Missouri	236,844	2.2%
NA	Montana**	NA	NA
34	Nebraska	64,060	0.6%
33	Nevada	80,383	0.7%
39	New Hampshire	29,368	0.3%
12	New Jersey	265,935	2.4%
29	New Mexico	94,984	0.9%
4	New York	573,150	5.2%
9	North Carolina	346,806	3.2%
45	North Dakota	12,788	0.1%
5	Ohio	435,385	4.0%
26	Oklahoma	147,804	1.3%
25	Oregon	155,540	1.4%
7	Pennsylvania	350,360	3.2%
36	Rhode Island	36,362	0.3%
21	South Carolina	175,033	1.6%
42	South Dakota	15,507	0.1%
13	Tennessee	255,283	2.3%
2	Texas	1,005,088	9.2%
30	Utah	94,846	0.9%
43	Vermont	14,231	0.1%
18	Virginia	197,258	1.8%
11	Washington	286,035	2.6%
37	West Virginia	34,845	0.3%
23	Wisconsin	157,807	1.4%
44	Wyoming	13,950	0.1%

RANK ORDER

RANK	STATE	CRIMES	% of USA
1	California	1,252,416	11.4%
2	Texas	1,005,088	9.2%
3	Florida	881,079	8.0%
4	New York	573,150	5.2%
5	Ohio	435,385	4.0%
6	Michigan	383,426	3.5%
7	Pennsylvania	350,360	3.2%
8	Georgia	350,352	3.2%
9	North Carolina	346,806	3.2%
10	Arizona	294,051	2.7%
11	Washington	286,035	2.6%
12	New Jersey	265,935	2.4%
13	Tennessee	255,283	2.3%
14	Maryland	248,935	2.3%
15	Missouri	236,844	2.2%
16	Louisiana	225,277	2.1%
17	Indiana	205,694	1.9%
18	Virginia	197,258	1.8%
19	Alabama	192,795	1.8%
20	Massachusetts	192,104	1.8%
21	South Carolina	175,033	1.6%
22	Colorado	165,290	1.5%
23	Wisconsin	157,807	1.4%
24	Minnesota	156,347	1.4%
25	Oregon	155,540	1.4%
26	Oklahoma	147,804	1.3%
27	Connecticut	102,161	0.9%
28	Arkansas	97,449	0.9%
29	New Mexico	94,984	0.9%
30	Utah	94,846	0.9%
31	Mississippi	93,860	0.9%
32	Iowa	87,547	0.8%
33	Nevada	80,383	0.7%
34	Nebraska	64,060	0.6%
35	Hawaii	46,659	0.4%
36	Rhode Island	36,362	0.3%
37	West Virginia	34,845	0.3%
38	Idaho	34,670	0.3%
39	New Hampshire	29,368	0.3%
40	Maine	28,096	0.3%
41	Alaska	21,829	0.2%
42	South Dakota	15,507	0.1%
43	Vermont	14,231	0.1%
44	Wyoming	13,950	0.1%
45	North Dakota	12,788	0.1%
NA	Delaware**	NA	NA
NA	Illinois**	NA	NA
NA	Kansas**	NA	NA
NA	Kentucky**	NA	NA
NA	Montana**	NA	NA

District of Columbia 41,626 0.4%

Source: Morgan Quitno Press using data from Federal Bureau of Investigation
   "Crime in the United States 2000" (Uniform Crime Reports, October 22, 2001)
*Estimated totals for urban areas, defined by the F.B.I. as Metropolitan Statistical Areas and other cities outside such areas. National total includes those states listed as not available. Includes murder, rape, robbery, aggravated assault, burglary, larceny-theft and motor vehicle theft.
**Not available.

Urban Crime Rate in 2000

National Urban Rate = 4,433.3 Crimes per 100,000 Population*

ALPHA ORDER				RANK ORDER		
RANK	STATE	RATE		RANK	STATE	RATE
16	Alabama	5,254.1		1	New Mexico	6,356.4
18	Alaska	5,055.4		2	Arizona	6,105.7
2	Arizona	6,105.7		3	Louisiana	6,013.2
12	Arkansas	5,334.9		4	Florida	5,832.0
32	California	3,768.7		5	Tennessee	5,598.8
26	Colorado	4,218.4		6	South Carolina	5,580.5
34	Connecticut	3,511.3		7	North Carolina	5,577.2
NA	Delaware**	NA		8	Mississippi	5,502.8
4	Florida	5,832.0		9	Missouri	5,463.0
13	Georgia	5,325.9		10	Washington	5,351.6
15	Hawaii	5,280.4		11	Oregon	5,347.3
28	Idaho	3,966.8		12	Arkansas	5,334.9
NA	Illinois**	NA		13	Georgia	5,325.9
27	Indiana	4,149.8		14	Oklahoma	5,298.3
25	Iowa	4,313.8		15	Hawaii	5,280.4
NA	Kansas**	NA		16	Alabama	5,254.1
NA	Kentucky**	NA		17	Texas	5,252.8
3	Louisiana	6,013.2		18	Alaska	5,055.4
42	Maine	3,084.8		19	Maryland	4,975.5
19	Maryland	4,975.5		20	Nebraska	4,918.4
43	Massachusetts	3,030.3		21	Utah	4,782.3
24	Michigan	4,359.6		22	Nevada	4,504.5
30	Minnesota	3,895.2		23	Ohio	4,361.6
8	Mississippi	5,502.8		24	Michigan	4,359.6
9	Missouri	5,463.0		25	Iowa	4,313.8
NA	Montana**	NA		26	Colorado	4,218.4
20	Nebraska	4,918.4		27	Indiana	4,149.8
22	Nevada	4,504.5		28	Idaho	3,966.8
45	New Hampshire	2,564.2		29	Vermont	3,907.9
40	New Jersey	3,160.5		30	Minnesota	3,895.2
1	New Mexico	6,356.4		31	Wyoming	3,871.6
39	New York	3,173.0		32	California	3,768.7
7	North Carolina	5,577.2		33	Wisconsin	3,631.8
44	North Dakota	2,999.9		34	Connecticut	3,511.3
23	Ohio	4,361.6		35	Rhode Island	3,468.6
14	Oklahoma	5,298.3		36	Virginia	3,302.9
11	Oregon	5,347.3		37	South Dakota	3,294.0
41	Pennsylvania	3,132.4		38	West Virginia	3,283.2
35	Rhode Island	3,468.6		39	New York	3,173.0
6	South Carolina	5,580.5		40	New Jersey	3,160.5
37	South Dakota	3,294.0		41	Pennsylvania	3,132.4
5	Tennessee	5,598.8		42	Maine	3,084.8
17	Texas	5,252.8		43	Massachusetts	3,030.3
21	Utah	4,782.3		44	North Dakota	2,999.9
29	Vermont	3,907.9		45	New Hampshire	2,564.2
36	Virginia	3,302.9		NA	Delaware**	NA
10	Washington	5,351.6		NA	Illinois**	NA
38	West Virginia	3,283.2		NA	Kansas**	NA
33	Wisconsin	3,631.8		NA	Kentucky**	NA
31	Wyoming	3,871.6		NA	Montana**	NA
					District of Columbia	7,276.5

Source: Morgan Quitno Press using data from Federal Bureau of Investigation
"Crime in the United States 2000" (Uniform Crime Reports, October 22, 2001)
*Estimated rates for urban areas, defined by the F.B.I. as Metropolitan Statistical Areas and other cities outside such areas. National rate includes those states listed as not available. Includes murder, rape, robbery, aggravated assault, burglary, larceny-theft and motor vehicle theft.
**Not available.

Percent of Crimes Occurring in Urban Areas in 2000

National Percent = 94.6% of Crimes*

ALPHA ORDER

RANK ORDER

RANK	STATE	PERCENT
12	Alabama	95.4
42	Alaska	81.9
5	Arizona	98.3
33	Arkansas	88.6
4	California	98.9
11	Colorado	96.5
24	Connecticut	92.8
NA	Delaware**	NA
10	Florida	96.8
32	Georgia	90.1
44	Hawaii	74.1
38	Idaho	84.1
NA	Illinois**	NA
31	Indiana	90.2
25	Iowa	92.5
NA	Kansas**	NA
NA	Kentucky**	NA
23	Louisiana	93.0
38	Maine	84.1
7	Maryland	97.6
1	Massachusetts	100.0
20	Michigan	93.9
30	Minnesota	91.1
41	Mississippi	82.4
22	Missouri	93.5
NA	Montana**	NA
29	Nebraska	91.4
18	Nevada	94.2
6	New Hampshire	97.7
1	New Jersey	100.0
17	New Mexico	94.6
8	New York	97.4
35	North Carolina	87.6
36	North Dakota	87.0
15	Ohio	94.9
19	Oklahoma	94.0
21	Oregon	93.8
13	Pennsylvania	95.2
3	Rhode Island	99.8
40	South Carolina	83.6
33	South Dakota	88.6
27	Tennessee	91.8
9	Texas	97.3
15	Utah	94.9
43	Vermont	78.3
26	Virginia	92.0
14	Washington	95.0
45	West Virginia	74.0
28	Wisconsin	91.7
37	Wyoming	85.7

RANK	STATE	PERCENT
1	Massachusetts	100.0
1	New Jersey	100.0
3	Rhode Island	99.8
4	California	98.9
5	Arizona	98.3
6	New Hampshire	97.7
7	Maryland	97.6
8	New York	97.4
9	Texas	97.3
10	Florida	96.8
11	Colorado	96.5
12	Alabama	95.4
13	Pennsylvania	95.2
14	Washington	95.0
15	Ohio	94.9
15	Utah	94.9
17	New Mexico	94.6
18	Nevada	94.2
19	Oklahoma	94.0
20	Michigan	93.9
21	Oregon	93.8
22	Missouri	93.5
23	Louisiana	93.0
24	Connecticut	92.8
25	Iowa	92.5
26	Virginia	92.0
27	Tennessee	91.8
28	Wisconsin	91.7
29	Nebraska	91.4
30	Minnesota	91.1
31	Indiana	90.2
32	Georgia	90.1
33	Arkansas	88.6
33	South Dakota	88.6
35	North Carolina	87.6
36	North Dakota	87.0
37	Wyoming	85.7
38	Idaho	84.1
38	Maine	84.1
40	South Carolina	83.6
41	Mississippi	82.4
42	Alaska	81.9
43	Vermont	78.3
44	Hawaii	74.1
45	West Virginia	74.0
NA	Delaware**	NA
NA	Illinois**	NA
NA	Kansas**	NA
NA	Kentucky**	NA
NA	Montana**	NA

District of Columbia   100.0

Source: Morgan Quitno Press using data from Federal Bureau of Investigation
"Crime in the United States 2000" (Uniform Crime Reports, October 22, 2001)
*Estimated percentages for urban areas, defined by the F.B.I. as Metropolitan Statistical Areas and other cities outside such areas. National percent includes those states listed as not available. Includes murder, rape, robbery, aggravated assault, burglary, larceny-theft and motor vehicle theft.
**Not available.

Crimes in Rural Areas in 2000

National Rural Total = 631,464 Crimes*

ALPHA ORDER					RANK ORDER			
RANK	STATE	CRIMES	% of USA		RANK	STATE	CRIMES	% of USA
25	Alabama	9,364	1.5%		1	North Carolina	49,166	7.8%
37	Alaska	4,812	0.8%		2	Georgia	38,597	6.1%
35	Arizona	5,041	0.8%		3	South Carolina	34,449	5.5%
21	Arkansas	12,570	2.0%		4	Florida	29,075	4.6%
20	California	14,298	2.3%		5	Texas	28,223	4.5%
31	Colorado	6,014	1.0%		6	Michigan	25,030	4.0%
26	Connecticut	7,930	1.3%		7	Ohio	23,489	3.7%
NA	Delaware**	NA	NA		8	Tennessee	22,935	3.6%
4	Florida	29,075	4.6%		9	Indiana	22,441	3.6%
2	Georgia	38,597	6.1%		10	Mississippi	20,051	3.2%
15	Hawaii	16,328	2.6%		11	Pennsylvania	17,498	2.8%
28	Idaho	6,558	1.0%		12	Virginia	17,090	2.7%
NA	Illinois**	NA	NA		13	Louisiana	17,067	2.7%
9	Indiana	22,441	3.6%		14	Missouri	16,494	2.6%
27	Iowa	7,083	1.1%		15	Hawaii	16,328	2.6%
NA	Kansas**	NA	NA		16	Minnesota	15,264	2.4%
NA	Kentucky**	NA	NA		17	New York	15,039	2.4%
13	Louisiana	17,067	2.7%		18	Washington	14,897	2.4%
33	Maine	5,304	0.8%		19	Wisconsin	14,317	2.3%
29	Maryland	6,150	1.0%		20	California	14,298	2.3%
44	Massachusetts	27	0.0%		21	Arkansas	12,570	2.0%
6	Michigan	25,030	4.0%		22	West Virginia	12,222	1.9%
16	Minnesota	15,264	2.4%		23	Oregon	10,240	1.6%
10	Mississippi	20,051	3.2%		24	Oklahoma	9,498	1.5%
14	Missouri	16,494	2.6%		25	Alabama	9,364	1.5%
NA	Montana**	NA	NA		26	Connecticut	7,930	1.3%
30	Nebraska	6,025	1.0%		27	Iowa	7,083	1.1%
36	Nevada	4,914	0.8%		28	Idaho	6,558	1.0%
42	New Hampshire	700	0.1%		29	Maryland	6,150	1.0%
45	New Jersey	0	0.0%		30	Nebraska	6,025	1.0%
32	New Mexico	5,407	0.9%		31	Colorado	6,014	1.0%
17	New York	15,039	2.4%		32	New Mexico	5,407	0.9%
1	North Carolina	49,166	7.8%		33	Maine	5,304	0.8%
41	North Dakota	1,906	0.3%		34	Utah	5,112	0.8%
7	Ohio	23,489	3.7%		35	Arizona	5,041	0.8%
24	Oklahoma	9,498	1.5%		36	Nevada	4,914	0.8%
23	Oregon	10,240	1.6%		37	Alaska	4,812	0.8%
11	Pennsylvania	17,498	2.8%		38	Vermont	3,954	0.6%
43	Rhode Island	82	0.0%		39	Wyoming	2,335	0.4%
3	South Carolina	34,449	5.5%		40	South Dakota	2,004	0.3%
40	South Dakota	2,004	0.3%		41	North Dakota	1,906	0.3%
8	Tennessee	22,935	3.6%		42	New Hampshire	700	0.1%
5	Texas	28,223	4.5%		43	Rhode Island	82	0.0%
34	Utah	5,112	0.8%		44	Massachusetts	27	0.0%
38	Vermont	3,954	0.6%		45	New Jersey	0	0.0%
12	Virginia	17,090	2.7%		NA	Delaware**	NA	NA
18	Washington	14,897	2.4%		NA	Illinois**	NA	NA
22	West Virginia	12,222	1.9%		NA	Kansas**	NA	NA
19	Wisconsin	14,317	2.3%		NA	Kentucky**	NA	NA
39	Wyoming	2,335	0.4%		NA	Montana**	NA	NA
						District of Columbia	0	0.0%

Source: Federal Bureau of Investigation
"Crime in the United States 2000" (Uniform Crime Reports, October 22, 2001)
*Estimated totals for rural areas, defined by the F.B.I. as other than Metropolitan Statistical Areas and other cities outside such areas. National total includes those states listed as not available. Includes murder, rape, robbery, aggravated assault, burglary, larceny-theft and motor vehicle theft.
**Not available.

Rural Crime Rate in 2000

National Rural Rate = 1,864.0 Crimes per 100,000 Population*

ALPHA ORDER				RANK ORDER		
RANK	STATE	RATE		RANK	STATE	RATE
38	Alabama	1,204.1		1	Hawaii	4,979.3
6	Alaska	2,465.9		2	South Carolina	3,934.7
26	Arizona	1,602.2		3	Florida	3,323.7
32	Arkansas	1,484.5		4	Washington	2,712.3
10	California	2,235.8		5	North Carolina	2,685.2
29	Colorado	1,570.6		6	Alaska	2,465.9
27	Connecticut	1,598.6		7	Georgia	2,400.0
NA	Delaware**	NA		8	Louisiana	2,361.9
3	Florida	3,323.7		9	Nevada	2,298.9
7	Georgia	2,400.0		10	California	2,235.8
1	Hawaii	4,979.3		11	Michigan	2,189.0
30	Idaho	1,561.6		12	Maryland	2,097.2
NA	Illinois**	NA		13	Utah	2,045.6
16	Indiana	1,996.9		14	Tennessee	2,030.2
40	Iowa	789.7		15	Oregon	1,997.6
NA	Kansas**	NA		16	Indiana	1,996.9
NA	Kentucky**	NA		17	Mississippi	1,760.4
8	Louisiana	2,361.9		18	Wyoming	1,749.5
34	Maine	1,456.6		19	Ohio	1,713.3
12	Maryland	2,097.2		20	Minnesota	1,685.5
43	Massachusetts	278.4		21	New Mexico	1,665.1
11	Michigan	2,189.0		22	New York	1,647.2
20	Minnesota	1,685.5		23	Texas	1,643.4
17	Mississippi	1,760.4		24	West Virginia	1,636.0
37	Missouri	1,309.3		25	Vermont	1,616.1
NA	Montana**	NA		26	Arizona	1,602.2
33	Nebraska	1,473.8		27	Connecticut	1,598.6
9	Nevada	2,298.9		28	Pennsylvania	1,596.4
41	New Hampshire	773.8		29	Colorado	1,570.6
44	New Jersey	0.0		30	Idaho	1,561.6
21	New Mexico	1,665.1		31	Virginia	1,544.9
22	New York	1,647.2		32	Arkansas	1,484.5
5	North Carolina	2,685.2		33	Nebraska	1,473.8
39	North Dakota	882.7		34	Maine	1,456.6
19	Ohio	1,713.3		35	Oklahoma	1,436.9
35	Oklahoma	1,436.9		36	Wisconsin	1,405.7
15	Oregon	1,997.6		37	Missouri	1,309.3
28	Pennsylvania	1,596.4		38	Alabama	1,204.1
44	Rhode Island	0.0		39	North Dakota	882.7
2	South Carolina	3,934.7		40	Iowa	789.7
42	South Dakota	705.5		41	New Hampshire	773.8
14	Tennessee	2,030.2		42	South Dakota	705.5
23	Texas	1,643.4		43	Massachusetts	278.4
13	Utah	2,045.6		44	New Jersey	0.0
25	Vermont	1,616.1		44	Rhode Island	0.0
31	Virginia	1,544.9		NA	Delaware**	NA
4	Washington	2,712.3		NA	Illinois**	NA
24	West Virginia	1,636.0		NA	Kansas**	NA
36	Wisconsin	1,405.7		NA	Kentucky**	NA
18	Wyoming	1,749.5		NA	Montana**	NA
					District of Columbia	0.0

Source: Morgan Quitno Press using data from Federal Bureau of Investigation
   "Crime in the United States 2000" (Uniform Crime Reports, October 22, 2001)
*Estimated rates for rural areas, defined by the F.B.I. as other than Metropolitan Statistical Areas and other cities outside such areas. National rate includes those states listed as not available. Includes murder, rape, robbery, aggravated assault, burglary, larceny-theft and motor vehicle theft.
**Not available.

Percent of Crimes Occurring in Rural Areas in 2000

National Percent = 5.4% of Crimes*

ALPHA ORDER

RANK	STATE	PERCENT
34	Alabama	4.6
4	Alaska	18.1
41	Arizona	1.7
12	Arkansas	11.4
42	California	1.1
35	Colorado	3.5
22	Connecticut	7.2
NA	Delaware**	NA
36	Florida	3.2
14	Georgia	9.9
2	Hawaii	25.9
7	Idaho	15.9
NA	Illinois**	NA
15	Indiana	9.8
21	Iowa	7.5
NA	Kansas**	NA
NA	Kentucky**	NA
23	Louisiana	7.0
7	Maine	15.9
39	Maryland	2.4
44	Massachusetts	0.0
26	Michigan	6.1
16	Minnesota	8.9
5	Mississippi	17.6
24	Missouri	6.5
NA	Montana**	NA
17	Nebraska	8.6
28	Nevada	5.8
40	New Hampshire	2.3
44	New Jersey	0.0
29	New Mexico	5.4
38	New York	2.6
11	North Carolina	12.4
10	North Dakota	13.0
30	Ohio	5.1
27	Oklahoma	6.0
25	Oregon	6.2
33	Pennsylvania	4.8
43	Rhode Island	0.2
6	South Carolina	16.4
12	South Dakota	11.4
19	Tennessee	8.2
37	Texas	2.7
30	Utah	5.1
3	Vermont	21.7
20	Virginia	8.0
32	Washington	5.0
1	West Virginia	26.0
18	Wisconsin	8.3
9	Wyoming	14.3

RANK ORDER

RANK	STATE	PERCENT
1	West Virginia	26.0
2	Hawaii	25.9
3	Vermont	21.7
4	Alaska	18.1
5	Mississippi	17.6
6	South Carolina	16.4
7	Idaho	15.9
7	Maine	15.9
9	Wyoming	14.3
10	North Dakota	13.0
11	North Carolina	12.4
12	Arkansas	11.4
12	South Dakota	11.4
14	Georgia	9.9
15	Indiana	9.8
16	Minnesota	8.9
17	Nebraska	8.6
18	Wisconsin	8.3
19	Tennessee	8.2
20	Virginia	8.0
21	Iowa	7.5
22	Connecticut	7.2
23	Louisiana	7.0
24	Missouri	6.5
25	Oregon	6.2
26	Michigan	6.1
27	Oklahoma	6.0
28	Nevada	5.8
29	New Mexico	5.4
30	Ohio	5.1
30	Utah	5.1
32	Washington	5.0
33	Pennsylvania	4.8
34	Alabama	4.6
35	Colorado	3.5
36	Florida	3.2
37	Texas	2.7
38	New York	2.6
39	Maryland	2.4
40	New Hampshire	2.3
41	Arizona	1.7
42	California	1.1
43	Rhode Island	0.2
44	Massachusetts	0.0
44	New Jersey	0.0
NA	Delaware**	NA
NA	Illinois**	NA
NA	Kansas**	NA
NA	Kentucky**	NA
NA	Montana**	NA
	District of Columbia	0.0

Source: Morgan Quitno Press using data from Federal Bureau of Investigation
  "Crime in the United States 2000" (Uniform Crime Reports, October 22, 2001)
*Estimated percentages for rural areas, defined by the F.B.I. as other than Metropolitan Statistical Areas and other cities outside such areas. National percent includes those states listed as not available. Includes murder, rape, robbery, aggravated assault, burglary, larceny-theft and motor vehicle theft.
**Not available.

Violent Crimes in Urban Areas in 2000

National Urban Total = 1,353,248 Violent Crimes*

ALPHA ORDER

RANK	STATE	CRIMES	% of USA
19	Alabama	20,545	1.5%
37	Alaska	2,943	0.2%
15	Arizona	26,491	2.0%
28	Arkansas	10,434	0.8%
1	California	208,738	15.4%
23	Colorado	13,879	1.0%
29	Connecticut	9,967	0.7%
NA	Delaware**	NA	NA
2	Florida	125,510	9.3%
8	Georgia	37,457	2.8%
39	Hawaii	2,302	0.2%
38	Idaho	2,572	0.2%
NA	Illinois**	NA	NA
20	Indiana	18,830	1.4%
31	Iowa	7,331	0.5%
NA	Kansas**	NA	NA
NA	Kentucky**	NA	NA
14	Louisiana	27,215	2.0%
41	Maine	1,213	0.1%
7	Maryland	40,676	3.0%
13	Massachusetts	30,224	2.2%
5	Michigan	52,564	3.9%
24	Minnesota	12,886	1.0%
32	Mississippi	6,926	0.5%
17	Missouri	25,326	1.9%
NA	Montana**	NA	NA
34	Nebraska	5,306	0.4%
30	Nevada	9,784	0.7%
40	New Hampshire	2,061	0.2%
12	New Jersey	32,298	2.4%
25	New Mexico	12,649	0.9%
4	New York	103,316	7.6%
11	North Carolina	35,528	2.6%
45	North Dakota	457	0.0%
10	Ohio	37,001	2.7%
22	Oklahoma	15,605	1.2%
27	Oregon	11,342	0.8%
6	Pennsylvania	49,866	3.7%
36	Rhode Island	3,092	0.2%
16	South Carolina	25,885	1.9%
42	South Dakota	1,067	0.1%
9	Tennessee	37,010	2.7%
3	Texas	110,032	8.1%
33	Utah	5,376	0.4%
44	Vermont	532	0.0%
21	Virginia	17,867	1.3%
18	Washington	20,926	1.5%
35	West Virginia	3,696	0.3%
26	Wisconsin	11,759	0.9%
43	Wyoming	1,010	0.1%

RANK ORDER

RANK	STATE	CRIMES	% of USA
1	California	208,738	15.4%
2	Florida	125,510	9.3%
3	Texas	110,032	8.1%
4	New York	103,316	7.6%
5	Michigan	52,564	3.9%
6	Pennsylvania	49,866	3.7%
7	Maryland	40,676	3.0%
8	Georgia	37,457	2.8%
9	Tennessee	37,010	2.7%
10	Ohio	37,001	2.7%
11	North Carolina	35,528	2.6%
12	New Jersey	32,298	2.4%
13	Massachusetts	30,224	2.2%
14	Louisiana	27,215	2.0%
15	Arizona	26,491	2.0%
16	South Carolina	25,885	1.9%
17	Missouri	25,326	1.9%
18	Washington	20,926	1.5%
19	Alabama	20,545	1.5%
20	Indiana	18,830	1.4%
21	Virginia	17,867	1.3%
22	Oklahoma	15,605	1.2%
23	Colorado	13,879	1.0%
24	Minnesota	12,886	1.0%
25	New Mexico	12,649	0.9%
26	Wisconsin	11,759	0.9%
27	Oregon	11,342	0.8%
28	Arkansas	10,434	0.8%
29	Connecticut	9,967	0.7%
30	Nevada	9,784	0.7%
31	Iowa	7,331	0.5%
32	Mississippi	6,926	0.5%
33	Utah	5,376	0.4%
34	Nebraska	5,306	0.4%
35	West Virginia	3,696	0.3%
36	Rhode Island	3,092	0.2%
37	Alaska	2,943	0.2%
38	Idaho	2,572	0.2%
39	Hawaii	2,302	0.2%
40	New Hampshire	2,061	0.2%
41	Maine	1,213	0.1%
42	South Dakota	1,067	0.1%
43	Wyoming	1,010	0.1%
44	Vermont	532	0.0%
45	North Dakota	457	0.0%
NA	Delaware**	NA	NA
NA	Illinois**	NA	NA
NA	Kansas**	NA	NA
NA	Kentucky**	NA	NA
NA	Montana**	NA	NA
	District of Columbia	8,626	0.6%

Source: Morgan Quitno Press using data from Federal Bureau of Investigation
"Crime in the United States 2000" (Uniform Crime Reports, October 22, 2001)
*Estimated totals for urban areas, defined by the F.B.I. as Metropolitan Statistical Areas and other cities outside such areas. National total includes those states listed as not available. Violent crimes are offenses of murder, forcible rape, robbery and aggravated assault.
**Not available.

Urban Violent Crime Rate in 2000

National Urban Rate = 546.7 Violent Crimes per 100,000 Population*

ALPHA ORDER

RANK ORDER

RANK	STATE	RATE
16	Alabama	559.9
7	Alaska	681.6
18	Arizona	550.1
14	Arkansas	571.2
8	California	628.1
30	Colorado	354.2
32	Connecticut	342.6
NA	Delaware**	NA
2	Florida	830.8
15	Georgia	569.4
40	Hawaii	260.5
36	Idaho	294.3
NA	Illinois**	NA
27	Indiana	379.9
29	Iowa	361.2
NA	Kansas**	NA
NA	Kentucky**	NA
6	Louisiana	726.4
44	Maine	133.2
4	Maryland	813.0
20	Massachusetts	476.8
9	Michigan	597.7
33	Minnesota	321.0
23	Mississippi	406.1
10	Missouri	584.2
NA	Montana**	NA
22	Nebraska	407.4
19	Nevada	548.3
42	New Hampshire	179.9
26	New Jersey	383.8
1	New Mexico	846.5
12	New York	572.0
13	North Carolina	571.3
45	North Dakota	107.2
28	Ohio	370.7
17	Oklahoma	559.4
25	Oregon	389.9
21	Pennsylvania	445.8
35	Rhode Island	294.9
3	South Carolina	825.3
41	South Dakota	226.6
5	Tennessee	811.7
11	Texas	575.0
38	Utah	271.1
43	Vermont	146.1
34	Virginia	299.2
24	Washington	391.5
31	West Virginia	348.3
39	Wisconsin	270.6
37	Wyoming	280.3

RANK	STATE	RATE
1	New Mexico	846.5
2	Florida	830.8
3	South Carolina	825.3
4	Maryland	813.0
5	Tennessee	811.7
6	Louisiana	726.4
7	Alaska	681.6
8	California	628.1
9	Michigan	597.7
10	Missouri	584.2
11	Texas	575.0
12	New York	572.0
13	North Carolina	571.3
14	Arkansas	571.2
15	Georgia	569.4
16	Alabama	559.9
17	Oklahoma	559.4
18	Arizona	550.1
19	Nevada	548.3
20	Massachusetts	476.8
21	Pennsylvania	445.8
22	Nebraska	407.4
23	Mississippi	406.1
24	Washington	391.5
25	Oregon	389.9
26	New Jersey	383.8
27	Indiana	379.9
28	Ohio	370.7
29	Iowa	361.2
30	Colorado	354.2
31	West Virginia	348.3
32	Connecticut	342.6
33	Minnesota	321.0
34	Virginia	299.2
35	Rhode Island	294.9
36	Idaho	294.3
37	Wyoming	280.3
38	Utah	271.1
39	Wisconsin	270.6
40	Hawaii	260.5
41	South Dakota	226.6
42	New Hampshire	179.9
43	Vermont	146.1
44	Maine	133.2
45	North Dakota	107.2
NA	Delaware**	NA
NA	Illinois**	NA
NA	Kansas**	NA
NA	Kentucky**	NA
NA	Montana**	NA

District of Columbia 1,507.9

Source: Morgan Quitno Press using data from Federal Bureau of Investigation
   "Crime in the United States 2000" (Uniform Crime Reports, October 22, 2001)
*Estimated rates for urban areas, defined by the F.B.I. as Metropolitan Statistical Areas and other cities outside such areas. National rate includes those states listed as not available. Violent crimes are offenses of murder, forcible rape, robbery and aggravated assault.
**Not available.

Percent of Violent Crimes Occurring in Urban Areas in 2000

National Percent = 95.0% of Violent Crimes*

<table>
<tr><td colspan="3">ALPHA ORDER</td><td colspan="3">RANK ORDER</td></tr>
<tr><td>RANK</td><td>STATE</td><td>PERCENT</td><td>RANK</td><td>STATE</td><td>PERCENT</td></tr>
<tr><td>16</td><td>Alabama</td><td>95.0</td><td>1</td><td>Massachusetts</td><td>100.0</td></tr>
<tr><td>38</td><td>Alaska</td><td>82.8</td><td>1</td><td>New Jersey</td><td>100.0</td></tr>
<tr><td>8</td><td>Arizona</td><td>97.1</td><td>3</td><td>California</td><td>99.1</td></tr>
<tr><td>34</td><td>Arkansas</td><td>87.7</td><td>3</td><td>Rhode Island</td><td>99.1</td></tr>
<tr><td>3</td><td>California</td><td>99.1</td><td>5</td><td>New York</td><td>98.3</td></tr>
<tr><td>12</td><td>Colorado</td><td>96.6</td><td>6</td><td>Maryland</td><td>97.6</td></tr>
<tr><td>29</td><td>Connecticut</td><td>90.1</td><td>7</td><td>Ohio</td><td>97.5</td></tr>
<tr><td>NA</td><td>Delaware**</td><td>NA</td><td>8</td><td>Arizona</td><td>97.1</td></tr>
<tr><td>10</td><td>Florida</td><td>96.7</td><td>9</td><td>Texas</td><td>96.8</td></tr>
<tr><td>28</td><td>Georgia</td><td>90.7</td><td>10</td><td>Florida</td><td>96.7</td></tr>
<tr><td>41</td><td>Hawaii</td><td>77.9</td><td>10</td><td>Pennsylvania</td><td>96.7</td></tr>
<tr><td>40</td><td>Idaho</td><td>78.7</td><td>12</td><td>Colorado</td><td>96.6</td></tr>
<tr><td>NA</td><td>Illinois**</td><td>NA</td><td>13</td><td>Washington</td><td>96.0</td></tr>
<tr><td>32</td><td>Indiana</td><td>88.7</td><td>14</td><td>Michigan</td><td>95.3</td></tr>
<tr><td>20</td><td>Iowa</td><td>94.0</td><td>15</td><td>New Hampshire</td><td>95.1</td></tr>
<tr><td>NA</td><td>Kansas**</td><td>NA</td><td>16</td><td>Alabama</td><td>95.0</td></tr>
<tr><td>NA</td><td>Kentucky**</td><td>NA</td><td>17</td><td>Nebraska</td><td>94.6</td></tr>
<tr><td>31</td><td>Louisiana</td><td>89.4</td><td>18</td><td>Oregon</td><td>94.5</td></tr>
<tr><td>36</td><td>Maine</td><td>86.8</td><td>19</td><td>Utah</td><td>94.1</td></tr>
<tr><td>6</td><td>Maryland</td><td>97.6</td><td>20</td><td>Iowa</td><td>94.0</td></tr>
<tr><td>1</td><td>Massachusetts</td><td>100.0</td><td>21</td><td>Nevada</td><td>93.4</td></tr>
<tr><td>14</td><td>Michigan</td><td>95.3</td><td>22</td><td>Minnesota</td><td>93.3</td></tr>
<tr><td>22</td><td>Minnesota</td><td>93.3</td><td>23</td><td>Wisconsin</td><td>92.6</td></tr>
<tr><td>44</td><td>Mississippi</td><td>67.5</td><td>24</td><td>Missouri</td><td>92.4</td></tr>
<tr><td>24</td><td>Missouri</td><td>92.4</td><td>25</td><td>Tennessee</td><td>92.0</td></tr>
<tr><td>NA</td><td>Montana**</td><td>NA</td><td>26</td><td>New Mexico</td><td>91.8</td></tr>
<tr><td>17</td><td>Nebraska</td><td>94.6</td><td>27</td><td>Oklahoma</td><td>90.8</td></tr>
<tr><td>21</td><td>Nevada</td><td>93.4</td><td>28</td><td>Georgia</td><td>90.7</td></tr>
<tr><td>15</td><td>New Hampshire</td><td>95.1</td><td>29</td><td>Connecticut</td><td>90.1</td></tr>
<tr><td>1</td><td>New Jersey</td><td>100.0</td><td>30</td><td>Virginia</td><td>89.6</td></tr>
<tr><td>26</td><td>New Mexico</td><td>91.8</td><td>31</td><td>Louisiana</td><td>89.4</td></tr>
<tr><td>5</td><td>New York</td><td>98.3</td><td>32</td><td>Indiana</td><td>88.7</td></tr>
<tr><td>32</td><td>North Carolina</td><td>88.7</td><td>32</td><td>North Carolina</td><td>88.7</td></tr>
<tr><td>35</td><td>North Dakota</td><td>87.4</td><td>34</td><td>Arkansas</td><td>87.7</td></tr>
<tr><td>7</td><td>Ohio</td><td>97.5</td><td>35</td><td>North Dakota</td><td>87.4</td></tr>
<tr><td>27</td><td>Oklahoma</td><td>90.8</td><td>36</td><td>Maine</td><td>86.8</td></tr>
<tr><td>18</td><td>Oregon</td><td>94.5</td><td>37</td><td>South Dakota</td><td>84.7</td></tr>
<tr><td>10</td><td>Pennsylvania</td><td>96.7</td><td>38</td><td>Alaska</td><td>82.8</td></tr>
<tr><td>3</td><td>Rhode Island</td><td>99.1</td><td>39</td><td>South Carolina</td><td>80.2</td></tr>
<tr><td>39</td><td>South Carolina</td><td>80.2</td><td>40</td><td>Idaho</td><td>78.7</td></tr>
<tr><td>37</td><td>South Dakota</td><td>84.7</td><td>41</td><td>Hawaii</td><td>77.9</td></tr>
<tr><td>25</td><td>Tennessee</td><td>92.0</td><td>42</td><td>Vermont</td><td>77.0</td></tr>
<tr><td>9</td><td>Texas</td><td>96.8</td><td>43</td><td>Wyoming</td><td>76.7</td></tr>
<tr><td>19</td><td>Utah</td><td>94.1</td><td>44</td><td>Mississippi</td><td>67.5</td></tr>
<tr><td>42</td><td>Vermont</td><td>77.0</td><td>45</td><td>West Virginia</td><td>64.6</td></tr>
<tr><td>30</td><td>Virginia</td><td>89.6</td><td>NA</td><td>Delaware**</td><td>NA</td></tr>
<tr><td>13</td><td>Washington</td><td>96.0</td><td>NA</td><td>Illinois**</td><td>NA</td></tr>
<tr><td>45</td><td>West Virginia</td><td>64.6</td><td>NA</td><td>Kansas**</td><td>NA</td></tr>
<tr><td>23</td><td>Wisconsin</td><td>92.6</td><td>NA</td><td>Kentucky**</td><td>NA</td></tr>
<tr><td>43</td><td>Wyoming</td><td>76.7</td><td>NA</td><td>Montana**</td><td>NA</td></tr>
<tr><td></td><td></td><td></td><td></td><td>District of Columbia</td><td>100.0</td></tr>
</table>

Source: Morgan Quitno Press using data from Federal Bureau of Investigation
"Crime in the United States 2000" (Uniform Crime Reports, October 22, 2001)
*Estimated percentages for urban areas, defined by the F.B.I. as Metropolitan Statistical Areas and other cities outside such areas. National percent includes those states listed as not available. Violent crimes are offenses of murder, forcible rape, robbery and aggravated assault.
**Not available.

Violent Crimes in Rural Areas in 2000

National Rural Total = 71,041 Violent Crimes*

ALPHA ORDER

RANK	STATE	CRIMES	% of USA
21	Alabama	1,075	1.5%
32	Alaska	611	0.9%
27	Arizona	790	1.1%
18	Arkansas	1,470	2.1%
15	California	1,793	2.5%
33	Colorado	488	0.7%
20	Connecticut	1,091	1.5%
NA	Delaware**	NA	NA
3	Florida	4,267	6.0%
4	Georgia	3,862	5.4%
31	Hawaii	652	0.9%
28	Idaho	695	1.0%
NA	Illinois**	NA	NA
10	Indiana	2,400	3.4%
34	Iowa	465	0.7%
NA	Kansas**	NA	NA
NA	Kentucky**	NA	NA
7	Louisiana	3,225	4.5%
39	Maine	184	0.3%
22	Maryland	987	1.4%
44	Massachusetts	6	0.0%
9	Michigan	2,595	3.7%
25	Minnesota	927	1.3%
6	Mississippi	3,341	4.7%
11	Missouri	2,093	2.9%
NA	Montana**	NA	NA
37	Nebraska	300	0.4%
29	Nevada	690	1.0%
41	New Hampshire	106	0.1%
45	New Jersey	0	0.0%
19	New Mexico	1,137	1.6%
14	New York	1,795	2.5%
2	North Carolina	4,523	6.4%
42	North Dakota	66	0.1%
24	Ohio	934	1.3%
17	Oklahoma	1,572	2.2%
30	Oregon	658	0.9%
16	Pennsylvania	1,718	2.4%
43	Rhode Island	29	0.0%
1	South Carolina	6,408	9.0%
38	South Dakota	192	0.3%
8	Tennessee	3,223	4.5%
5	Texas	3,621	5.1%
35	Utah	335	0.5%
40	Vermont	159	0.2%
12	Virginia	2,076	2.9%
26	Washington	862	1.2%
13	West Virginia	2,027	2.9%
23	Wisconsin	941	1.3%
36	Wyoming	306	0.4%

RANK ORDER

RANK	STATE	CRIMES	% of USA
1	South Carolina	6,408	9.0%
2	North Carolina	4,523	6.4%
3	Florida	4,267	6.0%
4	Georgia	3,862	5.4%
5	Texas	3,621	5.1%
6	Mississippi	3,341	4.7%
7	Louisiana	3,225	4.5%
8	Tennessee	3,223	4.5%
9	Michigan	2,595	3.7%
10	Indiana	2,400	3.4%
11	Missouri	2,093	2.9%
12	Virginia	2,076	2.9%
13	West Virginia	2,027	2.9%
14	New York	1,795	2.5%
15	California	1,793	2.5%
16	Pennsylvania	1,718	2.4%
17	Oklahoma	1,572	2.2%
18	Arkansas	1,470	2.1%
19	New Mexico	1,137	1.6%
20	Connecticut	1,091	1.5%
21	Alabama	1,075	1.5%
22	Maryland	987	1.4%
23	Wisconsin	941	1.3%
24	Ohio	934	1.3%
25	Minnesota	927	1.3%
26	Washington	862	1.2%
27	Arizona	790	1.1%
28	Idaho	695	1.0%
29	Nevada	690	1.0%
30	Oregon	658	0.9%
31	Hawaii	652	0.9%
32	Alaska	611	0.9%
33	Colorado	488	0.7%
34	Iowa	465	0.7%
35	Utah	335	0.5%
36	Wyoming	306	0.4%
37	Nebraska	300	0.4%
38	South Dakota	192	0.3%
39	Maine	184	0.3%
40	Vermont	159	0.2%
41	New Hampshire	106	0.1%
42	North Dakota	66	0.1%
43	Rhode Island	29	0.0%
44	Massachusetts	6	0.0%
45	New Jersey	0	0.0%
NA	Delaware**	NA	NA
NA	Illinois**	NA	NA
NA	Kansas**	NA	NA
NA	Kentucky**	NA	NA
NA	Montana**	NA	NA
	District of Columbia	0	0.0%

Source: Federal Bureau of Investigation
   "Crime in the United States 2000" (Uniform Crime Reports, October 22, 2001)
*Estimated totals for rural areas, defined by the F.B.I. as other than Metropolitan Statistical Areas and other cities outside such areas. National total includes those states listed as not available. Violent crimes are offenses of murder, forcible rape, robbery and aggravated assault.
**Not available.

Rural Violent Crime Rate in 2000

National Rural Rate = 209.7 Violent Crimes per 100,000 Population*

ALPHA ORDER

RANK	STATE	RATE
29	Alabama	138.2
7	Alaska	313.1
12	Arizona	251.1
24	Arkansas	173.6
10	California	280.4
32	Colorado	127.4
18	Connecticut	219.9
NA	Delaware**	NA
2	Florida	487.8
14	Georgia	240.1
21	Hawaii	198.8
26	Idaho	165.5
NA	Illinois**	NA
19	Indiana	213.6
41	Iowa	51.8
NA	Kansas**	NA
NA	Kentucky**	NA
3	Louisiana	446.3
42	Maine	50.5
5	Maryland	336.6
40	Massachusetts	61.9
17	Michigan	226.9
34	Minnesota	102.4
8	Mississippi	293.3
25	Missouri	166.1
NA	Montana**	NA
36	Nebraska	73.4
6	Nevada	322.8
33	New Hampshire	117.2
44	New Jersey	0.0
4	New Mexico	350.1
22	New York	196.6
13	North Carolina	247.0
43	North Dakota	30.6
37	Ohio	68.1
15	Oklahoma	237.8
31	Oregon	128.4
28	Pennsylvania	156.7
44	Rhode Island	0.0
1	South Carolina	731.9
38	South Dakota	67.6
9	Tennessee	285.3
20	Texas	210.8
30	Utah	134.0
39	Vermont	65.0
23	Virginia	187.7
27	Washington	156.9
11	West Virginia	271.3
35	Wisconsin	92.4
16	Wyoming	229.3

RANK ORDER

RANK	STATE	RATE
1	South Carolina	731.9
2	Florida	487.8
3	Louisiana	446.3
4	New Mexico	350.1
5	Maryland	336.6
6	Nevada	322.8
7	Alaska	313.1
8	Mississippi	293.3
9	Tennessee	285.3
10	California	280.4
11	West Virginia	271.3
12	Arizona	251.1
13	North Carolina	247.0
14	Georgia	240.1
15	Oklahoma	237.8
16	Wyoming	229.3
17	Michigan	226.9
18	Connecticut	219.9
19	Indiana	213.6
20	Texas	210.8
21	Hawaii	198.8
22	New York	196.6
23	Virginia	187.7
24	Arkansas	173.6
25	Missouri	166.1
26	Idaho	165.5
27	Washington	156.9
28	Pennsylvania	156.7
29	Alabama	138.2
30	Utah	134.0
31	Oregon	128.4
32	Colorado	127.4
33	New Hampshire	117.2
34	Minnesota	102.4
35	Wisconsin	92.4
36	Nebraska	73.4
37	Ohio	68.1
38	South Dakota	67.6
39	Vermont	65.0
40	Massachusetts	61.9
41	Iowa	51.8
42	Maine	50.5
43	North Dakota	30.6
44	New Jersey	0.0
44	Rhode Island	0.0
NA	Delaware**	NA
NA	Illinois**	NA
NA	Kansas**	NA
NA	Kentucky**	NA
NA	Montana**	NA
	District of Columbia	0.0

Source: Morgan Quitno Press using data from Federal Bureau of Investigation
   "Crime in the United States 2000" (Uniform Crime Reports, October 22, 2001)
*Estimated rates for rural areas, defined by the F.B.I. as other than Metropolitan Statistical Areas and other cities outside such areas. National rate includes those states listed as not available. Violent crimes are offenses of murder, forcible rape, robbery and aggravated assault.
**Not available.

Percent of Violent Crimes Occurring in Rural Areas in 2000

National Percent = 5.0% of Violent Crimes*

ALPHA ORDER

RANK	STATE	PERCENT
30	Alabama	5.0
8	Alaska	17.2
38	Arizona	2.9
12	Arkansas	12.3
42	California	0.9
34	Colorado	3.4
17	Connecticut	9.9
NA	Delaware**	NA
35	Florida	3.3
18	Georgia	9.3
5	Hawaii	22.1
6	Idaho	21.3
NA	Illinois**	NA
13	Indiana	11.3
26	Iowa	6.0
NA	Kansas**	NA
NA	Kentucky**	NA
15	Louisiana	10.6
10	Maine	13.2
40	Maryland	2.4
44	Massachusetts	0.0
32	Michigan	4.7
24	Minnesota	6.7
2	Mississippi	32.5
22	Missouri	7.6
NA	Montana**	NA
29	Nebraska	5.4
25	Nevada	6.6
31	New Hampshire	4.9
44	New Jersey	0.0
20	New Mexico	8.2
41	New York	1.7
13	North Carolina	11.3
11	North Dakota	12.6
39	Ohio	2.5
19	Oklahoma	9.2
28	Oregon	5.5
35	Pennsylvania	3.3
42	Rhode Island	0.9
7	South Carolina	19.8
9	South Dakota	15.3
21	Tennessee	8.0
37	Texas	3.2
27	Utah	5.9
4	Vermont	23.0
16	Virginia	10.4
33	Washington	4.0
1	West Virginia	35.4
23	Wisconsin	7.4
3	Wyoming	23.3

RANK ORDER

RANK	STATE	PERCENT
1	West Virginia	35.4
2	Mississippi	32.5
3	Wyoming	23.3
4	Vermont	23.0
5	Hawaii	22.1
6	Idaho	21.3
7	South Carolina	19.8
8	Alaska	17.2
9	South Dakota	15.3
10	Maine	13.2
11	North Dakota	12.6
12	Arkansas	12.3
13	Indiana	11.3
13	North Carolina	11.3
15	Louisiana	10.6
16	Virginia	10.4
17	Connecticut	9.9
18	Georgia	9.3
19	Oklahoma	9.2
20	New Mexico	8.2
21	Tennessee	8.0
22	Missouri	7.6
23	Wisconsin	7.4
24	Minnesota	6.7
25	Nevada	6.6
26	Iowa	6.0
27	Utah	5.9
28	Oregon	5.5
29	Nebraska	5.4
30	Alabama	5.0
31	New Hampshire	4.9
32	Michigan	4.7
33	Washington	4.0
34	Colorado	3.4
35	Florida	3.3
35	Pennsylvania	3.3
37	Texas	3.2
38	Arizona	2.9
39	Ohio	2.5
40	Maryland	2.4
41	New York	1.7
42	California	0.9
42	Rhode Island	0.9
44	Massachusetts	0.0
44	New Jersey	0.0
NA	Delaware**	NA
NA	Illinois**	NA
NA	Kansas**	NA
NA	Kentucky**	NA
NA	Montana**	NA

District of Columbia 0.0

Source: Morgan Quitno Press using data from Federal Bureau of Investigation
   "Crime in the United States 2000" (Uniform Crime Reports, October 22, 2001)
*Estimated percentages for rural areas, defined by the F.B.I. as other than Metropolitan Statistical Areas and other cities outside such areas. National percent includes those states listed as not available. Violent crimes are offenses of murder, forcible rape, robbery and aggravated assault.
**Not available.

Murders in Urban Areas in 2000

National Urban Total = 14,241 Murders*

ALPHA ORDER

RANK	STATE	MURDERS	% of USA
17	Alabama	307	2.2%
39	Alaska	16	0.1%
13	Arizona	358	2.5%
26	Arkansas	128	0.9%
1	California	2,052	14.4%
25	Colorado	129	0.9%
30	Connecticut	97	0.7%
37	Delaware	22	0.2%
4	Florida	862	6.1%
7	Georgia	567	4.0%
38	Hawaii	20	0.1%
42	Idaho	8	0.1%
NA	Illinois**	NA	NA
15	Indiana	323	2.3%
33	Iowa	45	0.3%
NA	Kansas**	NA	NA
NA	Kentucky**	NA	NA
8	Louisiana	503	3.5%
43	Maine	6	0.0%
10	Maryland	419	2.9%
27	Massachusetts	125	0.9%
5	Michigan	636	4.5%
24	Minnesota	133	0.9%
22	Mississippi	150	1.1%
15	Missouri	323	2.3%
NA	Montana**	NA	NA
32	Nebraska	54	0.4%
28	Nevada	123	0.9%
40	New Hampshire	14	0.1%
18	New Jersey	289	2.0%
29	New Mexico	115	0.8%
3	New York	934	6.6%
9	North Carolina	437	3.1%
45	North Dakota	4	0.0%
11	Ohio	383	2.7%
23	Oklahoma	142	1.0%
31	Oregon	59	0.4%
6	Pennsylvania	581	4.1%
34	Rhode Island	43	0.3%
19	South Carolina	179	1.3%
45	South Dakota	4	0.0%
12	Tennessee	365	2.6%
2	Texas	1,157	8.1%
35	Utah	41	0.3%
44	Vermont	5	0.0%
14	Virginia	329	2.3%
20	Washington	172	1.2%
36	West Virginia	34	0.2%
21	Wisconsin	151	1.1%
41	Wyoming	9	0.1%

RANK ORDER

RANK	STATE	MURDERS	% of USA
1	California	2,052	14.4%
2	Texas	1,157	8.1%
3	New York	934	6.6%
4	Florida	862	6.1%
5	Michigan	636	4.5%
6	Pennsylvania	581	4.1%
7	Georgia	567	4.0%
8	Louisiana	503	3.5%
9	North Carolina	437	3.1%
10	Maryland	419	2.9%
11	Ohio	383	2.7%
12	Tennessee	365	2.6%
13	Arizona	358	2.5%
14	Virginia	329	2.3%
15	Indiana	323	2.3%
15	Missouri	323	2.3%
17	Alabama	307	2.2%
18	New Jersey	289	2.0%
19	South Carolina	179	1.3%
20	Washington	172	1.2%
21	Wisconsin	151	1.1%
22	Mississippi	150	1.1%
23	Oklahoma	142	1.0%
24	Minnesota	133	0.9%
25	Colorado	129	0.9%
26	Arkansas	128	0.9%
27	Massachusetts	125	0.9%
28	Nevada	123	0.9%
29	New Mexico	115	0.8%
30	Connecticut	97	0.7%
31	Oregon	59	0.4%
32	Nebraska	54	0.4%
33	Iowa	45	0.3%
34	Rhode Island	43	0.3%
35	Utah	41	0.3%
36	West Virginia	34	0.2%
37	Delaware	22	0.2%
38	Hawaii	20	0.1%
39	Alaska	16	0.1%
40	New Hampshire	14	0.1%
41	Wyoming	9	0.1%
42	Idaho	8	0.1%
43	Maine	6	0.0%
44	Vermont	5	0.0%
45	North Dakota	4	0.0%
45	South Dakota	4	0.0%
NA	Illinois**	NA	NA
NA	Kansas**	NA	NA
NA	Kentucky**	NA	NA
NA	Montana**	NA	NA
	District of Columbia	239	1.7%

Source: Morgan Quitno Press using data from Federal Bureau of Investigation
"Crime in the United States 2000" (Uniform Crime Reports, October 22, 2001)
*Estimated totals for urban areas, defined by the F.B.I. as Metropolitan Statistical Areas and other cities outside such areas. National total includes those states listed as not available. Includes nonnegligent manslaughter.
**Not available.

Urban Murder Rate in 2000

National Urban Rate = 5.8 Murders per 100,000 Population*

ALPHA ORDER

RANK ORDER

RANK	STATE	RATE		RANK	STATE	RATE
4	Alabama	8.4		1	Louisiana	13.4
26	Alaska	3.7		2	Mississippi	8.8
9	Arizona	7.4		3	Georgia	8.6
11	Arkansas	7.0		4	Alabama	8.4
15	California	6.2		4	Maryland	8.4
29	Colorado	3.3		6	Tennessee	8.0
29	Connecticut	3.3		7	New Mexico	7.7
29	Delaware	3.3		8	Missouri	7.5
17	Florida	5.7		9	Arizona	7.4
3	Georgia	8.6		10	Michigan	7.2
36	Hawaii	2.3		11	Arkansas	7.0
43	Idaho	0.9		11	North Carolina	7.0
NA	Illinois**	NA		13	Nevada	6.9
14	Indiana	6.5		14	Indiana	6.5
37	Iowa	2.2		15	California	6.2
NA	Kansas**	NA		16	Texas	6.0
NA	Kentucky**	NA		17	Florida	5.7
1	Louisiana	13.4		17	South Carolina	5.7
46	Maine	0.7		19	Virginia	5.5
4	Maryland	8.4		20	New York	5.2
39	Massachusetts	2.0		20	Pennsylvania	5.2
10	Michigan	7.2		22	Oklahoma	5.1
29	Minnesota	3.3		23	Nebraska	4.1
2	Mississippi	8.8		23	Rhode Island	4.1
8	Missouri	7.5		25	Ohio	3.8
NA	Montana**	NA		26	Alaska	3.7
23	Nebraska	4.1		27	Wisconsin	3.5
13	Nevada	6.9		28	New Jersey	3.4
42	New Hampshire	1.2		29	Colorado	3.3
28	New Jersey	3.4		29	Connecticut	3.3
7	New Mexico	7.7		29	Delaware	3.3
20	New York	5.2		29	Minnesota	3.3
11	North Carolina	7.0		33	Washington	3.2
43	North Dakota	0.9		33	West Virginia	3.2
25	Ohio	3.8		35	Wyoming	2.5
22	Oklahoma	5.1		36	Hawaii	2.3
39	Oregon	2.0		37	Iowa	2.2
20	Pennsylvania	5.2		38	Utah	2.1
23	Rhode Island	4.1		39	Massachusetts	2.0
17	South Carolina	5.7		39	Oregon	2.0
45	South Dakota	0.8		41	Vermont	1.4
6	Tennessee	8.0		42	New Hampshire	1.2
16	Texas	6.0		43	Idaho	0.9
38	Utah	2.1		43	North Dakota	0.9
41	Vermont	1.4		45	South Dakota	0.8
19	Virginia	5.5		46	Maine	0.7
33	Washington	3.2		NA	Illinois**	NA
33	West Virginia	3.2		NA	Kansas**	NA
27	Wisconsin	3.5		NA	Kentucky**	NA
35	Wyoming	2.5		NA	Montana**	NA

District of Columbia   41.8

Source: Morgan Quitno Press using data from Federal Bureau of Investigation
   "Crime in the United States 2000" (Uniform Crime Reports, October 22, 2001)
*Estimated rates for urban areas, defined by the F.B.I. as Metropolitan Statistical Areas and other cities outside
such areas. National rate includes those states listed as not available. Includes nonnegligent manslaughter.
**Not available.

Percent of Murders Occurring in Urban Areas in 2000

National Percent = 91.8% of Murders*

ALPHA ORDER				RANK ORDER		
RANK	STATE	PERCENT		RANK	STATE	PERCENT
18	Alabama	93.3		1	Massachusetts	100.0
40	Alaska	59.3		1	New Jersey	100.0
4	Arizona	99.7		1	North Dakota	100.0
36	Arkansas	76.2		4	Arizona	99.7
6	California	98.7		5	Connecticut	99.0
11	Colorado	96.3		6	California	98.7
5	Connecticut	99.0		7	New York	98.1
26	Delaware	88.0		8	Iowa	97.8
13	Florida	95.5		9	Maryland	97.4
28	Georgia	87.1		10	Pennsylvania	96.5
42	Hawaii	57.1		11	Colorado	96.3
45	Idaho	50.0		12	Rhode Island	95.6
NA	Illinois**	NA		13	Florida	95.5
20	Indiana	91.8		14	Nevada	95.3
8	Iowa	97.8		14	Utah	95.3
NA	Kansas**	NA		16	Michigan	95.1
NA	Kentucky**	NA		17	Texas	93.5
22	Louisiana	89.8		18	Alabama	93.3
46	Maine	40.0		19	Missouri	93.1
9	Maryland	97.4		20	Indiana	91.8
1	Massachusetts	100.0		21	Ohio	91.6
16	Michigan	95.1		22	Louisiana	89.8
25	Minnesota	88.1		23	Wisconsin	89.3
41	Mississippi	58.8		24	Tennessee	89.0
19	Missouri	93.1		25	Minnesota	88.1
NA	Montana**	NA		26	Delaware	88.0
29	Nebraska	85.7		27	Washington	87.8
14	Nevada	95.3		28	Georgia	87.1
39	New Hampshire	63.6		29	Nebraska	85.7
1	New Jersey	100.0		30	New Mexico	85.2
30	New Mexico	85.2		31	Oregon	84.3
7	New York	98.1		32	Virginia	82.0
33	North Carolina	78.0		33	North Carolina	78.0
1	North Dakota	100.0		33	Oklahoma	78.0
21	Ohio	91.6		35	South Carolina	76.8
33	Oklahoma	78.0		36	Arkansas	76.2
31	Oregon	84.3		37	Wyoming	75.0
10	Pennsylvania	96.5		38	West Virginia	73.9
12	Rhode Island	95.6		39	New Hampshire	63.6
35	South Carolina	76.8		40	Alaska	59.3
42	South Dakota	57.1		41	Mississippi	58.8
24	Tennessee	89.0		42	Hawaii	57.1
17	Texas	93.5		42	South Dakota	57.1
14	Utah	95.3		44	Vermont	55.6
44	Vermont	55.6		45	Idaho	50.0
32	Virginia	82.0		46	Maine	40.0
27	Washington	87.8		NA	Illinois**	NA
38	West Virginia	73.9		NA	Kansas**	NA
23	Wisconsin	89.3		NA	Kentucky**	NA
37	Wyoming	75.0		NA	Montana**	NA
					District of Columbia	100.0

Source: Morgan Quitno Press using data from Federal Bureau of Investigation
   "Crime in the United States 2000" (Uniform Crime Reports, October 22, 2001)
*Estimated percentages for urban areas, defined by the F.B.I. as Metropolitan Statistical Areas and other cities outside such areas. National percent includes those states listed as not available. Includes nonnegligent manslaughter.
**Not available.

Murders in Rural Areas in 2000

National Rural Total = 1,276 Murders*

ALPHA ORDER   RANK ORDER

RANK	STATE	MURDERS	% of USA	RANK	STATE	MURDERS	% of USA
18	Alabama	22	1.7%	1	North Carolina	123	9.6%
26	Alaska	11	0.9%	2	Mississippi	105	8.2%
41	Arizona	1	0.1%	3	Georgia	84	6.6%
10	Arkansas	40	3.1%	4	Texas	81	6.3%
15	California	27	2.1%	5	Virginia	72	5.6%
34	Colorado	5	0.4%	6	Louisiana	57	4.5%
41	Connecticut	1	0.1%	7	South Carolina	54	4.2%
36	Delaware	3	0.2%	8	Tennessee	45	3.5%
9	Florida	41	3.2%	9	Florida	41	3.2%
3	Georgia	84	6.6%	10	Arkansas	40	3.1%
24	Hawaii	15	1.2%	10	Oklahoma	40	3.1%
31	Idaho	8	0.6%	12	Ohio	35	2.7%
NA	Illinois**	NA	NA	13	Michigan	33	2.6%
14	Indiana	29	2.3%	14	Indiana	29	2.3%
41	Iowa	1	0.1%	15	California	27	2.1%
NA	Kansas**	NA	NA	16	Missouri	24	1.9%
NA	Kentucky**	NA	NA	16	Washington	24	1.9%
6	Louisiana	57	4.5%	18	Alabama	22	1.7%
29	Maine	9	0.7%	19	Pennsylvania	21	1.6%
26	Maryland	11	0.9%	20	New Mexico	20	1.6%
44	Massachusetts	0	0.0%	21	Minnesota	18	1.4%
13	Michigan	33	2.6%	21	New York	18	1.4%
21	Minnesota	18	1.4%	21	Wisconsin	18	1.4%
2	Mississippi	105	8.2%	24	Hawaii	15	1.2%
16	Missouri	24	1.9%	25	West Virginia	12	0.9%
NA	Montana**	NA	NA	26	Alaska	11	0.9%
29	Nebraska	9	0.7%	26	Maryland	11	0.9%
33	Nevada	6	0.5%	26	Oregon	11	0.9%
31	New Hampshire	8	0.6%	29	Maine	9	0.7%
44	New Jersey	0	0.0%	29	Nebraska	9	0.7%
20	New Mexico	20	1.6%	31	Idaho	8	0.6%
21	New York	18	1.4%	31	New Hampshire	8	0.6%
1	North Carolina	123	9.6%	33	Nevada	6	0.5%
44	North Dakota	0	0.0%	34	Colorado	5	0.4%
12	Ohio	35	2.7%	35	Vermont	4	0.3%
10	Oklahoma	40	3.1%	36	Delaware	3	0.2%
26	Oregon	11	0.9%	36	South Dakota	3	0.2%
19	Pennsylvania	21	1.6%	36	Wyoming	3	0.2%
39	Rhode Island	2	0.2%	39	Rhode Island	2	0.2%
7	South Carolina	54	4.2%	39	Utah	2	0.2%
36	South Dakota	3	0.2%	41	Arizona	1	0.1%
8	Tennessee	45	3.5%	41	Connecticut	1	0.1%
4	Texas	81	6.3%	41	Iowa	1	0.1%
39	Utah	2	0.2%	44	Massachusetts	0	0.0%
35	Vermont	4	0.3%	44	New Jersey	0	0.0%
5	Virginia	72	5.6%	44	North Dakota	0	0.0%
16	Washington	24	1.9%	NA	Illinois**	NA	NA
25	West Virginia	12	0.9%	NA	Kansas**	NA	NA
21	Wisconsin	18	1.4%	NA	Kentucky**	NA	NA
36	Wyoming	3	0.2%	NA	Montana**	NA	NA
					District of Columbia	0	0.0%

Source: Federal Bureau of Investigation
   "Crime in the United States 2000" (Uniform Crime Reports, October 22, 2001)
*Estimated totals for rural areas, defined by the F.B.I. as other than Metropolitan Statistical Areas and other cities outside such areas. National total includes those states listed as not available. Includes nonnegligent manslaughter.
**Not available.

Rural Murder Rate in 2000

National Rural Rate = 3.8 Murders per 100,000 Population*

ALPHA ORDER

RANK	STATE	RATE
20	Alabama	2.8
9	Alaska	5.6
40	Arizona	0.3
11	Arkansas	4.7
16	California	4.2
37	Colorado	1.3
41	Connecticut	0.2
20	Delaware	2.8
11	Florida	4.7
10	Georgia	5.2
14	Hawaii	4.6
31	Idaho	1.9
NA	Illinois**	NA
23	Indiana	2.6
42	Iowa	0.1
NA	Kansas**	NA
NA	Kentucky**	NA
3	Louisiana	7.9
25	Maine	2.5
18	Maryland	3.8
43	Massachusetts	0.0
19	Michigan	2.9
29	Minnesota	2.0
1	Mississippi	9.2
31	Missouri	1.9
NA	Montana**	NA
26	Nebraska	2.2
20	Nevada	2.8
2	New Hampshire	8.8
43	New Jersey	0.0
6	New Mexico	6.2
29	New York	2.0
4	North Carolina	6.7
43	North Dakota	0.0
23	Ohio	2.6
8	Oklahoma	6.1
28	Oregon	2.1
31	Pennsylvania	1.9
43	Rhode Island	0.0
6	South Carolina	6.2
38	South Dakota	1.1
17	Tennessee	4.0
11	Texas	4.7
39	Utah	0.8
35	Vermont	1.6
5	Virginia	6.5
15	Washington	4.4
35	West Virginia	1.6
34	Wisconsin	1.8
26	Wyoming	2.2

RANK ORDER

RANK	STATE	RATE
1	Mississippi	9.2
2	New Hampshire	8.8
3	Louisiana	7.9
4	North Carolina	6.7
5	Virginia	6.5
6	New Mexico	6.2
6	South Carolina	6.2
8	Oklahoma	6.1
9	Alaska	5.6
10	Georgia	5.2
11	Arkansas	4.7
11	Florida	4.7
11	Texas	4.7
14	Hawaii	4.6
15	Washington	4.4
16	California	4.2
17	Tennessee	4.0
18	Maryland	3.8
19	Michigan	2.9
20	Alabama	2.8
20	Delaware	2.8
20	Nevada	2.8
23	Indiana	2.6
23	Ohio	2.6
25	Maine	2.5
26	Nebraska	2.2
26	Wyoming	2.2
28	Oregon	2.1
29	Minnesota	2.0
29	New York	2.0
31	Idaho	1.9
31	Missouri	1.9
31	Pennsylvania	1.9
34	Wisconsin	1.8
35	Vermont	1.6
35	West Virginia	1.6
37	Colorado	1.3
38	South Dakota	1.1
39	Utah	0.8
40	Arizona	0.3
41	Connecticut	0.2
42	Iowa	0.1
43	Massachusetts	0.0
43	New Jersey	0.0
43	North Dakota	0.0
43	Rhode Island	0.0
NA	Illinois**	NA
NA	Kansas**	NA
NA	Kentucky**	NA
NA	Montana**	NA
	District of Columbia	0.0

Source: Morgan Quitno Press using data from Federal Bureau of Investigation
    "Crime in the United States 2000" (Uniform Crime Reports, October 22, 2001)
*Estimated rates for rural areas, defined by the F.B.I. as other than Metropolitan Statistical Areas and other cities outside such areas. National rate includes those states listed as not available. Includes nonnegligent manslaughter.
**Not available.

Percent of Murders Occurring in Rural Areas in 2000

National Percent = 8.2% of Murders*

ALPHA ORDER				RANK ORDER		
RANK	STATE	PERCENT		RANK	STATE	PERCENT
29	Alabama	6.7		1	Maine	60.0
7	Alaska	40.7		2	Idaho	50.0
43	Arizona	0.3		3	Vermont	44.4
11	Arkansas	23.8		4	Hawaii	42.9
41	California	1.3		4	South Dakota	42.9
36	Colorado	3.7		6	Mississippi	41.2
42	Connecticut	1.0		7	Alaska	40.7
21	Delaware	12.0		8	New Hampshire	36.4
34	Florida	4.5		9	West Virginia	26.1
19	Georgia	12.9		10	Wyoming	25.0
4	Hawaii	42.9		11	Arkansas	23.8
2	Idaho	50.0		12	South Carolina	23.2
NA	Illinois**	NA		13	North Carolina	22.0
27	Indiana	8.2		13	Oklahoma	22.0
39	Iowa	2.2		15	Virginia	18.0
NA	Kansas**	NA		16	Oregon	15.7
NA	Kentucky**	NA		17	New Mexico	14.8
25	Louisiana	10.2		18	Nebraska	14.3
1	Maine	60.0		19	Georgia	12.9
38	Maryland	2.6		20	Washington	12.2
44	Massachusetts	0.0		21	Delaware	12.0
31	Michigan	4.9		22	Minnesota	11.9
22	Minnesota	11.9		23	Tennessee	11.0
6	Mississippi	41.2		24	Wisconsin	10.7
28	Missouri	6.9		25	Louisiana	10.2
NA	Montana**	NA		26	Ohio	8.4
18	Nebraska	14.3		27	Indiana	8.2
32	Nevada	4.7		28	Missouri	6.9
8	New Hampshire	36.4		29	Alabama	6.7
44	New Jersey	0.0		30	Texas	6.5
17	New Mexico	14.8		31	Michigan	4.9
40	New York	1.9		32	Nevada	4.7
13	North Carolina	22.0		32	Utah	4.7
44	North Dakota	0.0		34	Florida	4.5
26	Ohio	8.4		35	Rhode Island	4.4
13	Oklahoma	22.0		36	Colorado	3.7
16	Oregon	15.7		37	Pennsylvania	3.5
37	Pennsylvania	3.5		38	Maryland	2.6
35	Rhode Island	4.4		39	Iowa	2.2
12	South Carolina	23.2		40	New York	1.9
4	South Dakota	42.9		41	California	1.3
23	Tennessee	11.0		42	Connecticut	1.0
30	Texas	6.5		43	Arizona	0.3
32	Utah	4.7		44	Massachusetts	0.0
3	Vermont	44.4		44	New Jersey	0.0
15	Virginia	18.0		44	North Dakota	0.0
20	Washington	12.2		NA	Illinois**	NA
9	West Virginia	26.1		NA	Kansas**	NA
24	Wisconsin	10.7		NA	Kentucky**	NA
10	Wyoming	25.0		NA	Montana**	NA
					District of Columbia	0.0

Source: Morgan Quitno Press using data from Federal Bureau of Investigation
   "Crime in the United States 2000" (Uniform Crime Reports, October 22, 2001)
*Estimated percentages for rural areas, defined by the F.B.I. as other than Metropolitan Statistical Areas and other cities outside such areas. National percent includes those states listed as not available. Includes nonnegligent manslaughter.
**Not available.

Rapes in Urban Areas in 2000

National Urban Total = 82,673 Rapes*

RANK	STATE	RAPES	% of USA
19	Alabama	1,389	1.7%
37	Alaska	355	0.4%
15	Arizona	1,564	1.9%
31	Arkansas	756	0.9%
1	California	9,602	11.6%
13	Colorado	1,719	2.1%
33	Connecticut	616	0.7%
NA	Delaware**	NA	NA
3	Florida	6,719	8.1%
12	Georgia	1,773	2.1%
42	Hawaii	240	0.3%
38	Idaho	285	0.3%
NA	Illinois**	NA	NA
16	Indiana	1,543	1.9%
32	Iowa	635	0.8%
NA	Kansas**	NA	NA
NA	Kentucky**	NA	NA
21	Louisiana	1,355	1.6%
39	Maine	277	0.3%
17	Maryland	1,476	1.8%
14	Massachusetts	1,695	2.1%
4	Michigan	4,222	5.1%
10	Minnesota	1,921	2.3%
29	Mississippi	800	1.0%
24	Missouri	1,194	1.4%
NA	Montana**	NA	NA
36	Nebraska	389	0.5%
30	Nevada	787	1.0%
34	New Hampshire	481	0.6%
20	New Jersey	1,357	1.6%
28	New Mexico	808	1.0%
6	New York	3,416	4.1%
11	North Carolina	1,796	2.2%
43	North Dakota	150	0.2%
5	Ohio	4,079	4.9%
22	Oklahoma	1,306	1.6%
25	Oregon	1,151	1.4%
7	Pennsylvania	2,959	3.6%
35	Rhode Island	403	0.5%
23	South Carolina	1,214	1.5%
40	South Dakota	266	0.3%
9	Tennessee	2,028	2.5%
2	Texas	7,454	9.0%
27	Utah	811	1.0%
45	Vermont	106	0.1%
18	Virginia	1,427	1.7%
8	Washington	2,565	3.1%
41	West Virginia	250	0.3%
26	Wisconsin	1,005	1.2%
44	Wyoming	144	0.2%

RANK	STATE	RAPES	% of USA
1	California	9,602	11.6%
2	Texas	7,454	9.0%
3	Florida	6,719	8.1%
4	Michigan	4,222	5.1%
5	Ohio	4,079	4.9%
6	New York	3,416	4.1%
7	Pennsylvania	2,959	3.6%
8	Washington	2,565	3.1%
9	Tennessee	2,028	2.5%
10	Minnesota	1,921	2.3%
11	North Carolina	1,796	2.2%
12	Georgia	1,773	2.1%
13	Colorado	1,719	2.1%
14	Massachusetts	1,695	2.1%
15	Arizona	1,564	1.9%
16	Indiana	1,543	1.9%
17	Maryland	1,476	1.8%
18	Virginia	1,427	1.7%
19	Alabama	1,389	1.7%
20	New Jersey	1,357	1.6%
21	Louisiana	1,355	1.6%
22	Oklahoma	1,306	1.6%
23	South Carolina	1,214	1.5%
24	Missouri	1,194	1.4%
25	Oregon	1,151	1.4%
26	Wisconsin	1,005	1.2%
27	Utah	811	1.0%
28	New Mexico	808	1.0%
29	Mississippi	800	1.0%
30	Nevada	787	1.0%
31	Arkansas	756	0.9%
32	Iowa	635	0.8%
33	Connecticut	616	0.7%
34	New Hampshire	481	0.6%
35	Rhode Island	403	0.5%
36	Nebraska	389	0.5%
37	Alaska	355	0.4%
38	Idaho	285	0.3%
39	Maine	277	0.3%
40	South Dakota	266	0.3%
41	West Virginia	250	0.3%
42	Hawaii	240	0.3%
43	North Dakota	150	0.2%
44	Wyoming	144	0.2%
45	Vermont	106	0.1%
NA	Delaware**	NA	NA
NA	Illinois**	NA	NA
NA	Kansas**	NA	NA
NA	Kentucky**	NA	NA
NA	Montana**	NA	NA
	District of Columbia	251	0.3%

Source: Morgan Quitno Press using data from Federal Bureau of Investigation
"Crime in the United States 2000" (Uniform Crime Reports, October 22, 2001)
*Estimated totals for urban areas, defined by the F.B.I. as Metropolitan Statistical Areas and other cities outside such areas. National total includes those states listed as not available. Forcible rape is the carnal knowledge of a female forcibly and against her will. Attempts are included. However, statutory rape without force and other sex offenses are excluded. **Not available.

Urban Rape Rate in 2000

National Urban Rate = 33.4 Rapes per 100,000 Population*

ALPHA ORDER

RANK	STATE	RATE
22	Alabama	37.9
1	Alaska	82.2
26	Arizona	32.5
14	Arkansas	41.4
33	California	28.9
12	Colorado	43.9
43	Connecticut	21.2
NA	Delaware**	NA
9	Florida	44.5
37	Georgia	27.0
36	Hawaii	27.2
25	Idaho	32.6
NA	Illinois**	NA
28	Indiana	31.1
27	Iowa	31.3
NA	Kansas**	NA
NA	Kentucky**	NA
23	Louisiana	36.2
29	Maine	30.4
31	Maryland	29.5
38	Massachusetts	26.7
4	Michigan	48.0
6	Minnesota	47.9
7	Mississippi	46.9
35	Missouri	27.5
NA	Montana**	NA
30	Nebraska	29.9
11	Nevada	44.1
13	New Hampshire	42.0
45	New Jersey	16.1
3	New Mexico	54.1
44	New York	18.9
33	North Carolina	28.9
24	North Dakota	35.2
15	Ohio	40.9
8	Oklahoma	46.8
18	Oregon	39.6
39	Pennsylvania	26.5
21	Rhode Island	38.4
20	South Carolina	38.7
2	South Dakota	56.5
9	Tennessee	44.5
19	Texas	39.0
15	Utah	40.9
32	Vermont	29.1
40	Virginia	23.9
4	Washington	48.0
41	West Virginia	23.6
42	Wisconsin	23.1
17	Wyoming	40.0

RANK ORDER

RANK	STATE	RATE
1	Alaska	82.2
2	South Dakota	56.5
3	New Mexico	54.1
4	Michigan	48.0
4	Washington	48.0
6	Minnesota	47.9
7	Mississippi	46.9
8	Oklahoma	46.8
9	Florida	44.5
9	Tennessee	44.5
11	Nevada	44.1
12	Colorado	43.9
13	New Hampshire	42.0
14	Arkansas	41.4
15	Ohio	40.9
15	Utah	40.9
17	Wyoming	40.0
18	Oregon	39.6
19	Texas	39.0
20	South Carolina	38.7
21	Rhode Island	38.4
22	Alabama	37.9
23	Louisiana	36.2
24	North Dakota	35.2
25	Idaho	32.6
26	Arizona	32.5
27	Iowa	31.3
28	Indiana	31.1
29	Maine	30.4
30	Nebraska	29.9
31	Maryland	29.5
32	Vermont	29.1
33	California	28.9
33	North Carolina	28.9
35	Missouri	27.5
36	Hawaii	27.2
37	Georgia	27.0
38	Massachusetts	26.7
39	Pennsylvania	26.5
40	Virginia	23.9
41	West Virginia	23.6
42	Wisconsin	23.1
43	Connecticut	21.2
44	New York	18.9
45	New Jersey	16.1
NA	Delaware**	NA
NA	Illinois**	NA
NA	Kansas**	NA
NA	Kentucky**	NA
NA	Montana**	NA

District of Columbia 43.9

Source: Morgan Quitno Press using data from Federal Bureau of Investigation
"Crime in the United States 2000" (Uniform Crime Reports, October 22, 2001)
*Estimated rates for urban areas, defined by the F.B.I. as Metropolitan Statistical Areas and other cities outside such areas. National rate includes those states listed as not available. Forcible rape is the carnal knowledge of a female forcibly and against her will. Attempts are included. However, statutory rape without force and other sex offenses are excluded. **Not available.

Percent of Rapes Occurring in Urban Areas in 2000

National Percent = 91.7% of Rapes*

ALPHA ORDER				RANK ORDER		
RANK	STATE	PERCENT		RANK	STATE	PERCENT
14	Alabama	93.7		1	New Jersey	100.0
44	Alaska	71.4		2	Massachusetts	99.9
3	Arizona	99.2		3	Arizona	99.2
26	Arkansas	89.2		4	California	98.1
4	California	98.1		5	Rhode Island	97.8
6	Colorado	96.9		6	Colorado	96.9
21	Connecticut	90.9		7	New York	96.8
NA	Delaware**	NA		8	Maryland	95.7
10	Florida	95.2		9	Ohio	95.5
23	Georgia	90.1		10	Florida	95.2
45	Hawaii	69.4		11	Texas	94.9
43	Idaho	74.2		12	Utah	94.0
NA	Illinois**	NA		13	Iowa	93.9
31	Indiana	87.7		14	Alabama	93.7
13	Iowa	93.9		14	Washington	93.7
NA	Kansas**	NA		16	Tennessee	92.8
NA	Kentucky**	NA		17	New Hampshire	92.1
22	Louisiana	90.5		18	Oklahoma	91.8
34	Maine	86.6		19	Nevada	91.5
8	Maryland	95.7		20	Pennsylvania	91.1
2	Massachusetts	99.9		21	Connecticut	90.9
37	Michigan	84.0		22	Louisiana	90.5
36	Minnesota	85.8		23	Georgia	90.1
40	Mississippi	78.5		24	Wyoming	90.0
29	Missouri	88.4		25	Oregon	89.5
NA	Montana**	NA		26	Arkansas	89.2
26	Nebraska	89.2		26	Nebraska	89.2
19	Nevada	91.5		28	North Dakota	88.8
17	New Hampshire	92.1		29	Missouri	88.4
1	New Jersey	100.0		30	Virginia	88.3
32	New Mexico	87.6		31	Indiana	87.7
7	New York	96.8		32	New Mexico	87.6
38	North Carolina	82.3		33	South Dakota	87.2
28	North Dakota	88.8		34	Maine	86.6
9	Ohio	95.5		35	Wisconsin	86.3
18	Oklahoma	91.8		36	Minnesota	85.8
25	Oregon	89.5		37	Michigan	84.0
20	Pennsylvania	91.1		38	North Carolina	82.3
5	Rhode Island	97.8		39	South Carolina	80.3
39	South Carolina	80.3		40	Mississippi	78.5
33	South Dakota	87.2		41	Vermont	75.7
16	Tennessee	92.8		42	West Virginia	75.5
11	Texas	94.9		43	Idaho	74.2
12	Utah	94.0		44	Alaska	71.4
41	Vermont	75.7		45	Hawaii	69.4
30	Virginia	88.3		NA	Delaware**	NA
14	Washington	93.7		NA	Illinois**	NA
42	West Virginia	75.5		NA	Kansas**	NA
35	Wisconsin	86.3		NA	Kentucky**	NA
24	Wyoming	90.0		NA	Montana**	NA
					District of Columbia	100.0

Source: Morgan Quitno Press using data from Federal Bureau of Investigation
    "Crime in the United States 2000" (Uniform Crime Reports, October 22, 2001)
*Estimated percentages for urban areas, defined by the F.B.I. as Metropolitan Statistical Areas and other cities outside such areas. National percent includes those states listed as not available. Forcible rape is the carnal knowledge of a female forcibly and against her will. Attempts are included. However, statutory rape without force and other sex offenses are excluded. **Not available.

Rapes in Rural Areas in 2000

National Rural Total = 7,513 Rapes*

ALPHA ORDER

RANK	STATE	RAPES	% of USA
26	Alabama	93	1.2%
18	Alaska	142	1.9%
42	Arizona	13	0.2%
27	Arkansas	92	1.2%
13	California	183	2.4%
32	Colorado	55	0.7%
31	Connecticut	62	0.8%
NA	Delaware**	NA	NA
4	Florida	338	4.5%
10	Georgia	195	2.6%
24	Hawaii	106	1.4%
25	Idaho	99	1.3%
NA	Illinois**	NA	NA
9	Indiana	216	2.9%
36	Iowa	41	0.5%
NA	Kansas**	NA	NA
NA	Kentucky**	NA	NA
18	Louisiana	142	1.9%
35	Maine	43	0.6%
30	Maryland	67	0.9%
44	Massachusetts	1	0.0%
1	Michigan	803	10.7%
5	Minnesota	319	4.2%
8	Mississippi	219	2.9%
17	Missouri	157	2.1%
NA	Montana**	NA	NA
34	Nebraska	47	0.6%
29	Nevada	73	1.0%
36	New Hampshire	41	0.5%
45	New Jersey	0	0.0%
22	New Mexico	114	1.5%
22	New York	114	1.5%
3	North Carolina	385	5.1%
40	North Dakota	19	0.3%
11	Ohio	192	2.6%
21	Oklahoma	116	1.5%
20	Oregon	135	1.8%
7	Pennsylvania	288	3.8%
43	Rhode Island	9	0.1%
6	South Carolina	297	4.0%
38	South Dakota	39	0.5%
16	Tennessee	158	2.1%
2	Texas	402	5.4%
33	Utah	52	0.7%
39	Vermont	34	0.5%
12	Virginia	189	2.5%
14	Washington	172	2.3%
28	West Virginia	81	1.1%
15	Wisconsin	160	2.1%
41	Wyoming	16	0.2%

RANK ORDER

RANK	STATE	RAPES	% of USA
1	Michigan	803	10.7%
2	Texas	402	5.4%
3	North Carolina	385	5.1%
4	Florida	338	4.5%
5	Minnesota	319	4.2%
6	South Carolina	297	4.0%
7	Pennsylvania	288	3.8%
8	Mississippi	219	2.9%
9	Indiana	216	2.9%
10	Georgia	195	2.6%
11	Ohio	192	2.6%
12	Virginia	189	2.5%
13	California	183	2.4%
14	Washington	172	2.3%
15	Wisconsin	160	2.1%
16	Tennessee	158	2.1%
17	Missouri	157	2.1%
18	Alaska	142	1.9%
18	Louisiana	142	1.9%
20	Oregon	135	1.8%
21	Oklahoma	116	1.5%
22	New Mexico	114	1.5%
22	New York	114	1.5%
24	Hawaii	106	1.4%
25	Idaho	99	1.3%
26	Alabama	93	1.2%
27	Arkansas	92	1.2%
28	West Virginia	81	1.1%
29	Nevada	73	1.0%
30	Maryland	67	0.9%
31	Connecticut	62	0.8%
32	Colorado	55	0.7%
33	Utah	52	0.7%
34	Nebraska	47	0.6%
35	Maine	43	0.6%
36	Iowa	41	0.5%
36	New Hampshire	41	0.5%
38	South Dakota	39	0.5%
39	Vermont	34	0.5%
40	North Dakota	19	0.3%
41	Wyoming	16	0.2%
42	Arizona	13	0.2%
43	Rhode Island	9	0.1%
44	Massachusetts	1	0.0%
45	New Jersey	0	0.0%
NA	Delaware**	NA	NA
NA	Illinois**	NA	NA
NA	Kansas**	NA	NA
NA	Kentucky**	NA	NA
NA	Montana**	NA	NA
	District of Columbia	0	0.0%

Source: Federal Bureau of Investigation
   "Crime in the United States 2000" (Uniform Crime Reports, October 22, 2001)
*Estimated totals for rural areas, defined by the F.B.I. as other than Metropolitan Statistical Areas and other cities outside such areas. National total includes those states listed as not available. Forcible rape is the carnal knowledge of a female forcibly and against her will. Attempts are included. However, statutory rape without force and other sex offenses are excluded. **Not available.

Rural Rape Rate in 2000

National Rural Rate = 22.2 Rapes per 100,000 Population*

ALPHA ORDER

RANK	STATE	RATE
34	Alabama	12.0
1	Alaska	72.8
43	Arizona	4.1
38	Arkansas	10.9
11	California	28.6
25	Colorado	14.4
30	Connecticut	12.5
NA	Delaware**	NA
4	Florida	38.6
33	Georgia	12.1
9	Hawaii	32.3
14	Idaho	23.6
NA	Illinois**	NA
20	Indiana	19.2
42	Iowa	4.6
NA	Kansas**	NA
NA	Kentucky**	NA
19	Louisiana	19.7
36	Maine	11.8
16	Maryland	22.8
40	Massachusetts	10.3
2	Michigan	70.2
5	Minnesota	35.2
20	Mississippi	19.2
30	Missouri	12.5
NA	Montana**	NA
37	Nebraska	11.5
7	Nevada	34.2
3	New Hampshire	45.3
44	New Jersey	0.0
6	New Mexico	35.1
30	New York	12.5
17	North Carolina	21.0
41	North Dakota	8.8
26	Ohio	14.0
22	Oklahoma	17.5
12	Oregon	26.3
12	Pennsylvania	26.3
44	Rhode Island	0.0
8	South Carolina	33.9
29	South Dakota	13.7
26	Tennessee	14.0
15	Texas	23.4
18	Utah	20.8
28	Vermont	13.9
23	Virginia	17.1
10	Washington	31.3
39	West Virginia	10.8
24	Wisconsin	15.7
34	Wyoming	12.0

RANK ORDER

RANK	STATE	RATE
1	Alaska	72.8
2	Michigan	70.2
3	New Hampshire	45.3
4	Florida	38.6
5	Minnesota	35.2
6	New Mexico	35.1
7	Nevada	34.2
8	South Carolina	33.9
9	Hawaii	32.3
10	Washington	31.3
11	California	28.6
12	Oregon	26.3
12	Pennsylvania	26.3
14	Idaho	23.6
15	Texas	23.4
16	Maryland	22.8
17	North Carolina	21.0
18	Utah	20.8
19	Louisiana	19.7
20	Indiana	19.2
20	Mississippi	19.2
22	Oklahoma	17.5
23	Virginia	17.1
24	Wisconsin	15.7
25	Colorado	14.4
26	Ohio	14.0
26	Tennessee	14.0
28	Vermont	13.9
29	South Dakota	13.7
30	Connecticut	12.5
30	Missouri	12.5
30	New York	12.5
33	Georgia	12.1
34	Alabama	12.0
34	Wyoming	12.0
36	Maine	11.8
37	Nebraska	11.5
38	Arkansas	10.9
39	West Virginia	10.8
40	Massachusetts	10.3
41	North Dakota	8.8
42	Iowa	4.6
43	Arizona	4.1
44	New Jersey	0.0
44	Rhode Island	0.0
NA	Delaware**	NA
NA	Illinois**	NA
NA	Kansas**	NA
NA	Kentucky**	NA
NA	Montana**	NA

District of Columbia	0.0

Source: Morgan Quitno Press using data from Federal Bureau of Investigation
  "Crime in the United States 2000" (Uniform Crime Reports, October 22, 2001)
*Estimated rates for rural areas, defined by the F.B.I. as other than Metropolitan Statistical Areas and other cities outside such areas. National rate includes those states listed as not available. Forcible rape is the carnal knowledge of a female forcibly and against her will. Attempts are included. However, statutory rape without force and other sex offenses are excluded. **Not available.

Percent of Rapes Occurring in Rural Areas in 2000

National Percent = 8.3% of Rapes*

ALPHA ORDER				RANK ORDER		
RANK	STATE	PERCENT		RANK	STATE	PERCENT
31	Alabama	6.3		1	Hawaii	30.6
2	Alaska	28.6		2	Alaska	28.6
43	Arizona	0.8		3	Idaho	25.8
19	Arkansas	10.8		4	West Virginia	24.5
42	California	1.9		5	Vermont	24.3
40	Colorado	3.1		6	Mississippi	21.5
25	Connecticut	9.1		7	South Carolina	19.7
NA	Delaware**	NA		8	North Carolina	17.7
36	Florida	4.8		9	Michigan	16.0
23	Georgia	9.9		10	Minnesota	14.2
1	Hawaii	30.6		11	Wisconsin	13.7
3	Idaho	25.8		12	Maine	13.4
NA	Illinois**	NA		13	South Dakota	12.8
15	Indiana	12.3		14	New Mexico	12.4
33	Iowa	6.1		15	Indiana	12.3
NA	Kansas**	NA		16	Virginia	11.7
NA	Kentucky**	NA		17	Missouri	11.6
24	Louisiana	9.5		18	North Dakota	11.2
12	Maine	13.4		19	Arkansas	10.8
38	Maryland	4.3		19	Nebraska	10.8
44	Massachusetts	0.1		21	Oregon	10.5
9	Michigan	16.0		22	Wyoming	10.0
10	Minnesota	14.2		23	Georgia	9.9
6	Mississippi	21.5		24	Louisiana	9.5
17	Missouri	11.6		25	Connecticut	9.1
NA	Montana**	NA		26	Pennsylvania	8.9
19	Nebraska	10.8		27	Nevada	8.5
27	Nevada	8.5		28	Oklahoma	8.2
29	New Hampshire	7.9		29	New Hampshire	7.9
45	New Jersey	0.0		30	Tennessee	7.2
14	New Mexico	12.4		31	Alabama	6.3
39	New York	3.2		31	Washington	6.3
8	North Carolina	17.7		33	Iowa	6.1
18	North Dakota	11.2		34	Utah	6.0
37	Ohio	4.5		35	Texas	5.1
28	Oklahoma	8.2		36	Florida	4.8
21	Oregon	10.5		37	Ohio	4.5
26	Pennsylvania	8.9		38	Maryland	4.3
41	Rhode Island	2.2		39	New York	3.2
7	South Carolina	19.7		40	Colorado	3.1
13	South Dakota	12.8		41	Rhode Island	2.2
30	Tennessee	7.2		42	California	1.9
35	Texas	5.1		43	Arizona	0.8
34	Utah	6.0		44	Massachusetts	0.1
5	Vermont	24.3		45	New Jersey	0.0
16	Virginia	11.7		NA	Delaware**	NA
31	Washington	6.3		NA	Illinois**	NA
4	West Virginia	24.5		NA	Kansas**	NA
11	Wisconsin	13.7		NA	Kentucky**	NA
22	Wyoming	10.0		NA	Montana**	NA
					District of Columbia	0.0

Source: Morgan Quitno Press using data from Federal Bureau of Investigation
    "Crime in the United States 2000" (Uniform Crime Reports, October 22, 2001)
*Estimated percentages for rural areas, defined by the F.B.I. as other than Metropolitan Statistical Areas and other cities outside such areas. National percent includes those states listed as not available. Forcible rape is the carnal knowledge of a female forcibly and against her will. Attempts are included. However, statutory rape without force and other sex offenses are excluded. **Not available.

Robberies in Urban Areas in 2000

National Urban Total = 402,439 Robberies*

ALPHA ORDER

RANK	STATE	ROBBERIES	% of USA
20	Alabama	5,623	1.4%
39	Alaska	470	0.1%
14	Arizona	7,459	1.9%
31	Arkansas	1,905	0.5%
1	California	60,123	14.9%
26	Colorado	3,024	0.8%
24	Connecticut	3,753	0.9%
32	Delaware	1,346	0.3%
3	Florida	31,415	7.8%
10	Georgia	12,843	3.2%
36	Hawaii	984	0.2%
42	Idaho	204	0.1%
NA	Illinois**	NA	NA
16	Indiana	6,138	1.5%
35	Iowa	1,064	0.3%
NA	Kansas**	NA	NA
NA	Kentucky**	NA	NA
15	Louisiana	7,305	1.8%
41	Maine	230	0.1%
9	Maryland	13,491	3.4%
18	Massachusetts	5,815	1.4%
7	Michigan	13,635	3.4%
25	Minnesota	3,677	0.9%
30	Mississippi	2,339	0.6%
13	Missouri	7,549	1.9%
NA	Montana**	NA	NA
34	Nebraska	1,137	0.3%
23	Nevada	4,496	1.1%
40	New Hampshire	450	0.1%
8	New Jersey	13,553	3.4%
29	New Mexico	2,444	0.6%
2	New York	40,460	10.1%
11	North Carolina	11,877	3.0%
46	North Dakota	56	0.0%
6	Ohio	15,506	3.9%
28	Oklahoma	2,565	0.6%
27	Oregon	2,821	0.7%
5	Pennsylvania	18,013	4.5%
37	Rhode Island	922	0.2%
21	South Carolina	5,152	1.3%
43	South Dakota	129	0.0%
12	Tennessee	9,324	2.3%
4	Texas	30,067	7.5%
33	Utah	1,227	0.3%
44	Vermont	98	0.0%
17	Virginia	6,080	1.5%
19	Washington	5,744	1.4%
38	West Virginia	685	0.2%
22	Wisconsin	4,511	1.1%
45	Wyoming	66	0.0%

RANK ORDER

RANK	STATE	ROBBERIES	% of USA
1	California	60,123	14.9%
2	New York	40,460	10.1%
3	Florida	31,415	7.8%
4	Texas	30,067	7.5%
5	Pennsylvania	18,013	4.5%
6	Ohio	15,506	3.9%
7	Michigan	13,635	3.4%
8	New Jersey	13,553	3.4%
9	Maryland	13,491	3.4%
10	Georgia	12,843	3.2%
11	North Carolina	11,877	3.0%
12	Tennessee	9,324	2.3%
13	Missouri	7,549	1.9%
14	Arizona	7,459	1.9%
15	Louisiana	7,305	1.8%
16	Indiana	6,138	1.5%
17	Virginia	6,080	1.5%
18	Massachusetts	5,815	1.4%
19	Washington	5,744	1.4%
20	Alabama	5,623	1.4%
21	South Carolina	5,152	1.3%
22	Wisconsin	4,511	1.1%
23	Nevada	4,496	1.1%
24	Connecticut	3,753	0.9%
25	Minnesota	3,677	0.9%
26	Colorado	3,024	0.8%
27	Oregon	2,821	0.7%
28	Oklahoma	2,565	0.6%
29	New Mexico	2,444	0.6%
30	Mississippi	2,339	0.6%
31	Arkansas	1,905	0.5%
32	Delaware	1,346	0.3%
33	Utah	1,227	0.3%
34	Nebraska	1,137	0.3%
35	Iowa	1,064	0.3%
36	Hawaii	984	0.2%
37	Rhode Island	922	0.2%
38	West Virginia	685	0.2%
39	Alaska	470	0.1%
40	New Hampshire	450	0.1%
41	Maine	230	0.1%
42	Idaho	204	0.1%
43	South Dakota	129	0.0%
44	Vermont	98	0.0%
45	Wyoming	66	0.0%
46	North Dakota	56	0.0%
NA	Illinois**	NA	NA
NA	Kansas**	NA	NA
NA	Kentucky**	NA	NA
NA	Montana**	NA	NA
	District of Columbia	3,554	0.9%

Source: Morgan Quitno Press using data from Federal Bureau of Investigation
"Crime in the United States 2000" (Uniform Crime Reports, October 22, 2001)
*Estimated totals for urban areas, defined by the F.B.I. as Metropolitan Statistical Areas and other cities outside such areas. National total includes those states listed as not available. Robbery is the taking or attempting to take anything of value by force or threat of force.
**Not available.

Urban Robbery Rate in 2000

National Urban Rate = 162.6 Robberies per 100,000 Population*

ALPHA ORDER				RANK ORDER		
RANK	STATE	RATE		RANK	STATE	RATE
20	Alabama	153.2		1	Maryland	269.6
25	Alaska	108.8		2	Nevada	251.9
19	Arizona	154.9		3	New York	224.0
27	Arkansas	104.3		4	Florida	207.9
10	California	180.9		5	Tennessee	204.5
36	Colorado	77.2		6	Delaware	199.0
22	Connecticut	129.0		7	Georgia	195.2
6	Delaware	199.0		8	Louisiana	195.0
4	Florida	207.9		9	North Carolina	191.0
7	Georgia	195.2		10	California	180.9
24	Hawaii	111.4		11	Missouri	174.1
44	Idaho	23.3		12	South Carolina	164.3
NA	Illinois**	NA		13	New Mexico	163.6
23	Indiana	123.8		14	New Jersey	161.1
39	Iowa	52.4		15	Pennsylvania	161.0
NA	Kansas**	NA		16	Texas	157.1
NA	Kentucky**	NA		17	Ohio	155.3
8	Louisiana	195.0		18	Michigan	155.0
43	Maine	25.3		19	Arizona	154.9
1	Maryland	269.6		20	Alabama	153.2
32	Massachusetts	91.7		21	Mississippi	137.1
18	Michigan	155.0		22	Connecticut	129.0
33	Minnesota	91.6		23	Indiana	123.8
21	Mississippi	137.1		24	Hawaii	111.4
11	Missouri	174.1		25	Alaska	108.8
NA	Montana**	NA		26	Washington	107.5
35	Nebraska	87.3		27	Arkansas	104.3
2	Nevada	251.9		28	Wisconsin	103.8
40	New Hampshire	39.3		29	Virginia	101.8
14	New Jersey	161.1		30	Oregon	97.0
13	New Mexico	163.6		31	Oklahoma	91.9
3	New York	224.0		32	Massachusetts	91.7
9	North Carolina	191.0		33	Minnesota	91.6
46	North Dakota	13.1		34	Rhode Island	88.0
17	Ohio	155.3		35	Nebraska	87.3
31	Oklahoma	91.9		36	Colorado	77.2
30	Oregon	97.0		37	West Virginia	64.5
15	Pennsylvania	161.0		38	Utah	61.9
34	Rhode Island	88.0		39	Iowa	52.4
12	South Carolina	164.3		40	New Hampshire	39.3
41	South Dakota	27.4		41	South Dakota	27.4
5	Tennessee	204.5		42	Vermont	26.9
16	Texas	157.1		43	Maine	25.3
38	Utah	61.9		44	Idaho	23.3
42	Vermont	26.9		45	Wyoming	18.3
29	Virginia	101.8		46	North Dakota	13.1
26	Washington	107.5		NA	Illinois**	NA
37	West Virginia	64.5		NA	Kansas**	NA
28	Wisconsin	103.8		NA	Kentucky**	NA
45	Wyoming	18.3		NA	Montana**	NA
					District of Columbia	621.3

Source: Morgan Quitno Press using data from Federal Bureau of Investigation
"Crime in the United States 2000" (Uniform Crime Reports, October 22, 2001)
*Estimated rates for urban areas, defined by the F.B.I. as Metropolitan Statistical Areas and other cities outside such areas. National rate includes those states listed as not available. Robbery is the taking or attempting to take anything of value by force or threat of force.
**Not available.

Percent of Robberies Occurring in Urban Areas in 2000

National Percent = 98.7% of Robberies*

<table>
<tr><td colspan="3">ALPHA ORDER</td><td colspan="3">RANK ORDER</td></tr>
<tr><td>RANK</td><td>STATE</td><td>PERCENT</td><td>RANK</td><td>STATE</td><td>PERCENT</td></tr>
<tr><td>24</td><td>Alabama</td><td>98.6</td><td>1</td><td>Massachusetts</td><td>100.0</td></tr>
<tr><td>36</td><td>Alaska</td><td>95.9</td><td>1</td><td>New Jersey</td><td>100.0</td></tr>
<tr><td>9</td><td>Arizona</td><td>99.4</td><td>1</td><td>North Dakota</td><td>100.0</td></tr>
<tr><td>37</td><td>Arkansas</td><td>95.2</td><td>1</td><td>Rhode Island</td><td>100.0</td></tr>
<tr><td>5</td><td>California</td><td>99.8</td><td>5</td><td>California</td><td>99.8</td></tr>
<tr><td>7</td><td>Colorado</td><td>99.7</td><td>5</td><td>New York</td><td>99.8</td></tr>
<tr><td>28</td><td>Connecticut</td><td>97.9</td><td>7</td><td>Colorado</td><td>99.7</td></tr>
<tr><td>34</td><td>Delaware</td><td>96.6</td><td>8</td><td>Maryland</td><td>99.5</td></tr>
<tr><td>21</td><td>Florida</td><td>98.8</td><td>9</td><td>Arizona</td><td>99.4</td></tr>
<tr><td>33</td><td>Georgia</td><td>96.9</td><td>9</td><td>Michigan</td><td>99.4</td></tr>
<tr><td>43</td><td>Hawaii</td><td>87.6</td><td>9</td><td>Missouri</td><td>99.4</td></tr>
<tr><td>41</td><td>Idaho</td><td>91.5</td><td>9</td><td>Texas</td><td>99.4</td></tr>
<tr><td>NA</td><td>Illinois**</td><td>NA</td><td>9</td><td>Wisconsin</td><td>99.4</td></tr>
<tr><td>30</td><td>Indiana</td><td>97.7</td><td>14</td><td>Iowa</td><td>99.3</td></tr>
<tr><td>14</td><td>Iowa</td><td>99.3</td><td>14</td><td>New Hampshire</td><td>99.3</td></tr>
<tr><td>NA</td><td>Kansas**</td><td>NA</td><td>14</td><td>Ohio</td><td>99.3</td></tr>
<tr><td>NA</td><td>Kentucky**</td><td>NA</td><td>17</td><td>Pennsylvania</td><td>99.2</td></tr>
<tr><td>32</td><td>Louisiana</td><td>97.0</td><td>18</td><td>Nebraska</td><td>99.1</td></tr>
<tr><td>40</td><td>Maine</td><td>93.1</td><td>19</td><td>Minnesota</td><td>99.0</td></tr>
<tr><td>8</td><td>Maryland</td><td>99.5</td><td>19</td><td>Nevada</td><td>99.0</td></tr>
<tr><td>1</td><td>Massachusetts</td><td>100.0</td><td>21</td><td>Florida</td><td>98.8</td></tr>
<tr><td>9</td><td>Michigan</td><td>99.4</td><td>21</td><td>Utah</td><td>98.8</td></tr>
<tr><td>19</td><td>Minnesota</td><td>99.0</td><td>21</td><td>Washington</td><td>98.8</td></tr>
<tr><td>45</td><td>Mississippi</td><td>86.5</td><td>24</td><td>Alabama</td><td>98.6</td></tr>
<tr><td>9</td><td>Missouri</td><td>99.4</td><td>25</td><td>South Dakota</td><td>98.5</td></tr>
<tr><td>NA</td><td>Montana**</td><td>NA</td><td>25</td><td>Tennessee</td><td>98.5</td></tr>
<tr><td>18</td><td>Nebraska</td><td>99.1</td><td>27</td><td>Oklahoma</td><td>98.1</td></tr>
<tr><td>19</td><td>Nevada</td><td>99.0</td><td>28</td><td>Connecticut</td><td>97.9</td></tr>
<tr><td>14</td><td>New Hampshire</td><td>99.3</td><td>29</td><td>New Mexico</td><td>97.8</td></tr>
<tr><td>1</td><td>New Jersey</td><td>100.0</td><td>30</td><td>Indiana</td><td>97.7</td></tr>
<tr><td>29</td><td>New Mexico</td><td>97.8</td><td>30</td><td>Oregon</td><td>97.7</td></tr>
<tr><td>5</td><td>New York</td><td>99.8</td><td>32</td><td>Louisiana</td><td>97.0</td></tr>
<tr><td>38</td><td>North Carolina</td><td>94.3</td><td>33</td><td>Georgia</td><td>96.9</td></tr>
<tr><td>1</td><td>North Dakota</td><td>100.0</td><td>34</td><td>Delaware</td><td>96.6</td></tr>
<tr><td>14</td><td>Ohio</td><td>99.3</td><td>34</td><td>Virginia</td><td>96.6</td></tr>
<tr><td>27</td><td>Oklahoma</td><td>98.1</td><td>36</td><td>Alaska</td><td>95.9</td></tr>
<tr><td>30</td><td>Oregon</td><td>97.7</td><td>37</td><td>Arkansas</td><td>95.2</td></tr>
<tr><td>17</td><td>Pennsylvania</td><td>99.2</td><td>38</td><td>North Carolina</td><td>94.3</td></tr>
<tr><td>1</td><td>Rhode Island</td><td>100.0</td><td>38</td><td>Wyoming</td><td>94.3</td></tr>
<tr><td>43</td><td>South Carolina</td><td>87.6</td><td>40</td><td>Maine</td><td>93.1</td></tr>
<tr><td>25</td><td>South Dakota</td><td>98.5</td><td>41</td><td>Idaho</td><td>91.5</td></tr>
<tr><td>25</td><td>Tennessee</td><td>98.5</td><td>41</td><td>West Virginia</td><td>91.5</td></tr>
<tr><td>9</td><td>Texas</td><td>99.4</td><td>43</td><td>Hawaii</td><td>87.6</td></tr>
<tr><td>21</td><td>Utah</td><td>98.8</td><td>43</td><td>South Carolina</td><td>87.6</td></tr>
<tr><td>46</td><td>Vermont</td><td>83.8</td><td>45</td><td>Mississippi</td><td>86.5</td></tr>
<tr><td>34</td><td>Virginia</td><td>96.6</td><td>46</td><td>Vermont</td><td>83.8</td></tr>
<tr><td>21</td><td>Washington</td><td>98.8</td><td>NA</td><td>Illinois**</td><td>NA</td></tr>
<tr><td>41</td><td>West Virginia</td><td>91.5</td><td>NA</td><td>Kansas**</td><td>NA</td></tr>
<tr><td>9</td><td>Wisconsin</td><td>99.4</td><td>NA</td><td>Kentucky**</td><td>NA</td></tr>
<tr><td>38</td><td>Wyoming</td><td>94.3</td><td>NA</td><td>Montana**</td><td>NA</td></tr>
<tr><td></td><td></td><td></td><td></td><td>District of Columbia</td><td>100.0</td></tr>
</table>

Source: Morgan Quitno Press using data from Federal Bureau of Investigation
"Crime in the United States 2000" (Uniform Crime Reports, October 22, 2001)
*Estimated percentages for urban areas, defined by the F.B.I. as Metropolitan Statistical Areas and other cities outside such areas. National percent includes those states listed as not available. Robbery is the taking or attempting to take anything of value by force or threat of force.
**Not available.

Robberies in Rural Areas in 2000

National Rural Total = 5,403 Robberies*

ALPHA ORDER

RANK	STATE	ROBBERIES	% of USA
16	Alabama	79	1.5%
32	Alaska	20	0.4%
29	Arizona	45	0.8%
15	Arkansas	96	1.8%
13	California	126	2.3%
37	Colorado	10	0.2%
16	Connecticut	79	1.5%
27	Delaware	48	0.9%
4	Florida	394	7.3%
3	Georgia	407	7.5%
12	Hawaii	139	2.6%
33	Idaho	19	0.4%
NA	Illinois**	NA	NA
9	Indiana	144	2.7%
39	Iowa	7	0.1%
NA	Kansas**	NA	NA
NA	Kentucky**	NA	NA
6	Louisiana	227	4.2%
35	Maine	17	0.3%
20	Maryland	69	1.3%
43	Massachusetts	0	0.0%
19	Michigan	77	1.4%
30	Minnesota	36	0.7%
5	Mississippi	364	6.7%
26	Missouri	49	0.9%
NA	Montana**	NA	NA
37	Nebraska	10	0.2%
28	Nevada	47	0.9%
41	New Hampshire	3	0.1%
43	New Jersey	0	0.0%
24	New Mexico	55	1.0%
16	New York	79	1.5%
2	North Carolina	718	13.3%
43	North Dakota	0	0.0%
14	Ohio	104	1.9%
25	Oklahoma	50	0.9%
22	Oregon	67	1.2%
10	Pennsylvania	142	2.6%
43	Rhode Island	0	0.0%
1	South Carolina	731	13.5%
42	South Dakota	2	0.0%
11	Tennessee	141	2.6%
8	Texas	190	3.5%
36	Utah	15	0.3%
33	Vermont	19	0.4%
7	Virginia	215	4.0%
21	Washington	68	1.3%
23	West Virginia	64	1.2%
31	Wisconsin	26	0.5%
40	Wyoming	4	0.1%

RANK ORDER

RANK	STATE	ROBBERIES	% of USA
1	South Carolina	731	13.5%
2	North Carolina	718	13.3%
3	Georgia	407	7.5%
4	Florida	394	7.3%
5	Mississippi	364	6.7%
6	Louisiana	227	4.2%
7	Virginia	215	4.0%
8	Texas	190	3.5%
9	Indiana	144	2.7%
10	Pennsylvania	142	2.6%
11	Tennessee	141	2.6%
12	Hawaii	139	2.6%
13	California	126	2.3%
14	Ohio	104	1.9%
15	Arkansas	96	1.8%
16	Alabama	79	1.5%
16	Connecticut	79	1.5%
16	New York	79	1.5%
19	Michigan	77	1.4%
20	Maryland	69	1.3%
21	Washington	68	1.3%
22	Oregon	67	1.2%
23	West Virginia	64	1.2%
24	New Mexico	55	1.0%
25	Oklahoma	50	0.9%
26	Missouri	49	0.9%
27	Delaware	48	0.9%
28	Nevada	47	0.9%
29	Arizona	45	0.8%
30	Minnesota	36	0.7%
31	Wisconsin	26	0.5%
32	Alaska	20	0.4%
33	Idaho	19	0.4%
33	Vermont	19	0.4%
35	Maine	17	0.3%
36	Utah	15	0.3%
37	Colorado	10	0.2%
37	Nebraska	10	0.2%
39	Iowa	7	0.1%
40	Wyoming	4	0.1%
41	New Hampshire	3	0.1%
42	South Dakota	2	0.0%
43	Massachusetts	0	0.0%
43	New Jersey	0	0.0%
43	North Dakota	0	0.0%
43	Rhode Island	0	0.0%
NA	Illinois**	NA	NA
NA	Kansas**	NA	NA
NA	Kentucky**	NA	NA
NA	Montana**	NA	NA
	District of Columbia	0	0.0%

Source: Federal Bureau of Investigation
"Crime in the United States 2000" (Uniform Crime Reports, October 22, 2001)
*Estimated totals for rural areas, defined by the F.B.I. as other than Metropolitan Statistical Areas and other cities outside such areas. National total includes those states listed as not available. Robbery is the taking or attempting to take anything of value by force or threat of force.
**Not available.

Rural Robbery Rate in 2000

National Rural Rate = 15.9 Robberies per 100,000 Population*

ALPHA ORDER			RANK ORDER		
RANK	STATE	RATE	RANK	STATE	RATE
23	Alabama	10.2	1	South Carolina	83.5
23	Alaska	10.2	2	Florida	45.0
15	Arizona	14.3	3	Delaware	44.8
21	Arkansas	11.3	4	Hawaii	42.4
11	California	19.7	5	North Carolina	39.2
38	Colorado	2.6	6	Mississippi	32.0
14	Connecticut	15.9	7	Louisiana	31.4
3	Delaware	44.8	8	Georgia	25.3
2	Florida	45.0	9	Maryland	23.5
8	Georgia	25.3	10	Nevada	22.0
4	Hawaii	42.4	11	California	19.7
33	Idaho	4.5	12	Virginia	19.4
NA	Illinois**	NA	13	New Mexico	16.9
18	Indiana	12.8	14	Connecticut	15.9
41	Iowa	0.8	15	Arizona	14.3
NA	Kansas**	NA	16	Oregon	13.1
NA	Kentucky**	NA	17	Pennsylvania	13.0
7	Louisiana	31.4	18	Indiana	12.8
32	Maine	4.7	19	Tennessee	12.5
9	Maryland	23.5	20	Washington	12.4
43	Massachusetts	0.0	21	Arkansas	11.3
30	Michigan	6.7	22	Texas	11.1
34	Minnesota	4.0	23	Alabama	10.2
6	Mississippi	32.0	23	Alaska	10.2
35	Missouri	3.9	25	New York	8.7
NA	Montana**	NA	26	West Virginia	8.6
40	Nebraska	2.4	27	Vermont	7.8
10	Nevada	22.0	28	Ohio	7.6
36	New Hampshire	3.3	28	Oklahoma	7.6
43	New Jersey	0.0	30	Michigan	6.7
13	New Mexico	16.9	31	Utah	6.0
25	New York	8.7	32	Maine	4.7
5	North Carolina	39.2	33	Idaho	4.5
43	North Dakota	0.0	34	Minnesota	4.0
28	Ohio	7.6	35	Missouri	3.9
28	Oklahoma	7.6	36	New Hampshire	3.3
16	Oregon	13.1	37	Wyoming	3.0
17	Pennsylvania	13.0	38	Colorado	2.6
43	Rhode Island	0.0	38	Wisconsin	2.6
1	South Carolina	83.5	40	Nebraska	2.4
42	South Dakota	0.7	41	Iowa	0.8
19	Tennessee	12.5	42	South Dakota	0.7
22	Texas	11.1	43	Massachusetts	0.0
31	Utah	6.0	43	New Jersey	0.0
27	Vermont	7.8	43	North Dakota	0.0
12	Virginia	19.4	43	Rhode Island	0.0
20	Washington	12.4	NA	Illinois**	NA
26	West Virginia	8.6	NA	Kansas**	NA
38	Wisconsin	2.6	NA	Kentucky**	NA
37	Wyoming	3.0	NA	Montana**	NA
				District of Columbia	0.0

Source: Morgan Quitno Press using data from Federal Bureau of Investigation
  "Crime in the United States 2000" (Uniform Crime Reports, October 22, 2001)
*Estimated rates for rural areas, defined by the F.B.I. as other than Metropolitan Statistical Areas and other cities outside such areas. National rate includes those states listed as not available. Robbery is the taking or attempting to take anything of value by force or threat of force.
**Not available.

Percent of Robberies Occurring in Rural Areas in 2000

National Percent = 1.3% of Robberies*

ALPHA ORDER				RANK ORDER		
RANK	STATE	PERCENT		RANK	STATE	PERCENT
23	Alabama	1.4		1	Vermont	16.2
11	Alaska	4.1		2	Mississippi	13.5
34	Arizona	0.6		3	Hawaii	12.4
10	Arkansas	4.8		3	South Carolina	12.4
41	California	0.2		5	Idaho	8.5
40	Colorado	0.3		5	West Virginia	8.5
19	Connecticut	2.1		7	Maine	6.9
12	Delaware	3.4		8	North Carolina	5.7
24	Florida	1.2		8	Wyoming	5.7
14	Georgia	3.1		10	Arkansas	4.8
3	Hawaii	12.4		11	Alaska	4.1
5	Idaho	8.5		12	Delaware	3.4
NA	Illinois**	NA		12	Virginia	3.4
16	Indiana	2.3		14	Georgia	3.1
31	Iowa	0.7		15	Louisiana	3.0
NA	Kansas**	NA		16	Indiana	2.3
NA	Kentucky**	NA		16	Oregon	2.3
15	Louisiana	3.0		18	New Mexico	2.2
7	Maine	6.9		19	Connecticut	2.1
39	Maryland	0.5		20	Oklahoma	1.9
43	Massachusetts	0.0		21	South Dakota	1.5
34	Michigan	0.6		21	Tennessee	1.5
27	Minnesota	1.0		23	Alabama	1.4
2	Mississippi	13.5		24	Florida	1.2
34	Missouri	0.6		24	Utah	1.2
NA	Montana**	NA		24	Washington	1.2
29	Nebraska	0.9		27	Minnesota	1.0
27	Nevada	1.0		27	Nevada	1.0
31	New Hampshire	0.7		29	Nebraska	0.9
43	New Jersey	0.0		30	Pennsylvania	0.8
18	New Mexico	2.2		31	Iowa	0.7
41	New York	0.2		31	New Hampshire	0.7
8	North Carolina	5.7		31	Ohio	0.7
43	North Dakota	0.0		34	Arizona	0.6
31	Ohio	0.7		34	Michigan	0.6
20	Oklahoma	1.9		34	Missouri	0.6
16	Oregon	2.3		34	Texas	0.6
30	Pennsylvania	0.8		34	Wisconsin	0.6
43	Rhode Island	0.0		39	Maryland	0.5
3	South Carolina	12.4		40	Colorado	0.3
21	South Dakota	1.5		41	California	0.2
21	Tennessee	1.5		41	New York	0.2
34	Texas	0.6		43	Massachusetts	0.0
24	Utah	1.2		43	New Jersey	0.0
1	Vermont	16.2		43	North Dakota	0.0
12	Virginia	3.4		43	Rhode Island	0.0
24	Washington	1.2		NA	Illinois**	NA
5	West Virginia	8.5		NA	Kansas**	NA
34	Wisconsin	0.6		NA	Kentucky**	NA
8	Wyoming	5.7		NA	Montana**	NA
					District of Columbia	0.0

Source: Morgan Quitno Press using data from Federal Bureau of Investigation
   "Crime in the United States 2000" (Uniform Crime Reports, October 22, 2001)
*Estimated percentages for rural areas, defined by the F.B.I. as other than Metropolitan Statistical Areas and other cities outside such areas. National percent includes those states listed as not available. Robbery is the taking or attempting to take anything of value by force or threat of force.
**Not available.

Aggravated Assaults in Urban Areas in 2000

National Urban Total = 853,895 Aggravated Assaults*

ALPHA ORDER

RANK	STATE	ASSAULTS	% of USA
18	Alabama	13,226	1.5%
37	Alaska	2,102	0.2%
14	Arizona	17,110	2.0%
25	Arkansas	7,645	0.9%
1	California	136,961	16.0%
24	Colorado	9,007	1.1%
30	Connecticut	5,501	0.6%
35	Delaware	3,012	0.4%
2	Florida	86,514	10.1%
10	Georgia	22,274	2.6%
41	Hawaii	1,058	0.1%
38	Idaho	2,075	0.2%
NA	Illinois**	NA	NA
21	Indiana	10,826	1.3%
29	Iowa	5,587	0.7%
NA	Kansas**	NA	NA
NA	Kentucky**	NA	NA
13	Louisiana	18,052	2.1%
43	Maine	700	0.1%
8	Maryland	25,290	3.0%
9	Massachusetts	22,589	2.6%
5	Michigan	34,071	4.0%
27	Minnesota	7,155	0.8%
33	Mississippi	3,637	0.4%
17	Missouri	16,260	1.9%
NA	Montana**	NA	NA
32	Nebraska	3,726	0.4%
31	Nevada	4,378	0.5%
40	New Hampshire	1,116	0.1%
15	New Jersey	17,099	2.0%
23	New Mexico	9,282	1.1%
4	New York	58,506	6.9%
11	North Carolina	21,418	2.5%
46	North Dakota	247	0.0%
16	Ohio	17,033	2.0%
20	Oklahoma	11,592	1.4%
26	Oregon	7,311	0.9%
6	Pennsylvania	28,313	3.3%
39	Rhode Island	1,724	0.2%
12	South Carolina	19,340	2.3%
44	South Dakota	668	0.1%
7	Tennessee	25,293	3.0%
3	Texas	71,354	8.4%
34	Utah	3,297	0.4%
45	Vermont	323	0.0%
22	Virginia	10,031	1.2%
19	Washington	12,445	1.5%
36	West Virginia	2,727	0.3%
28	Wisconsin	6,092	0.7%
42	Wyoming	791	0.1%

RANK ORDER

RANK	STATE	ASSAULTS	% of USA
1	California	136,961	16.0%
2	Florida	86,514	10.1%
3	Texas	71,354	8.4%
4	New York	58,506	6.9%
5	Michigan	34,071	4.0%
6	Pennsylvania	28,313	3.3%
7	Tennessee	25,293	3.0%
8	Maryland	25,290	3.0%
9	Massachusetts	22,589	2.6%
10	Georgia	22,274	2.6%
11	North Carolina	21,418	2.5%
12	South Carolina	19,340	2.3%
13	Louisiana	18,052	2.1%
14	Arizona	17,110	2.0%
15	New Jersey	17,099	2.0%
16	Ohio	17,033	2.0%
17	Missouri	16,260	1.9%
18	Alabama	13,226	1.5%
19	Washington	12,445	1.5%
20	Oklahoma	11,592	1.4%
21	Indiana	10,826	1.3%
22	Virginia	10,031	1.2%
23	New Mexico	9,282	1.1%
24	Colorado	9,007	1.1%
25	Arkansas	7,645	0.9%
26	Oregon	7,311	0.9%
27	Minnesota	7,155	0.8%
28	Wisconsin	6,092	0.7%
29	Iowa	5,587	0.7%
30	Connecticut	5,501	0.6%
31	Nevada	4,378	0.5%
32	Nebraska	3,726	0.4%
33	Mississippi	3,637	0.4%
34	Utah	3,297	0.4%
35	Delaware	3,012	0.4%
36	West Virginia	2,727	0.3%
37	Alaska	2,102	0.2%
38	Idaho	2,075	0.2%
39	Rhode Island	1,724	0.2%
40	New Hampshire	1,116	0.1%
41	Hawaii	1,058	0.1%
42	Wyoming	791	0.1%
43	Maine	700	0.1%
44	South Dakota	668	0.1%
45	Vermont	323	0.0%
46	North Dakota	247	0.0%
NA	Illinois**	NA	NA
NA	Kansas**	NA	NA
NA	Kentucky**	NA	NA
NA	Montana**	NA	NA
	District of Columbia	4,582	0.5%

Source: Morgan Quitno Press using data from Federal Bureau of Investigation
   "Crime in the United States 2000" (Uniform Crime Reports, October 22, 2001)
*Estimated totals for urban areas, defined by the F.B.I. as Metropolitan Statistical Areas and other cities outside such areas. National total includes those states listed as not available. Aggravated assault is an attack for the purpose of inflicting severe bodily injury.
**Not available.

Urban Aggravated Assault Rate in 2000

National Urban Rate = 344.9 Aggravated Assaults per 100,000 Population*

<u>ALPHA ORDER</u>

<u>RANK ORDER</u>

RANK	STATE	RATE		RANK	STATE	RATE
15	Alabama	360.4		1	New Mexico	621.2
6	Alaska	486.8		2	South Carolina	616.6
17	Arizona	355.3		3	Florida	572.7
9	Arkansas	418.5		4	Tennessee	554.7
11	California	412.1		5	Maryland	505.5
29	Colorado	229.9		6	Alaska	486.8
34	Connecticut	189.1		7	Louisiana	481.9
8	Delaware	445.3		8	Delaware	445.3
3	Florida	572.7		9	Arkansas	418.5
19	Georgia	338.6		10	Oklahoma	415.5
42	Hawaii	119.7		11	California	412.1
27	Idaho	237.4		12	Michigan	387.4
NA	Illinois**	NA		13	Missouri	375.0
31	Indiana	218.4		14	Texas	372.9
22	Iowa	275.3		15	Alabama	360.4
NA	Kansas**	NA		16	Massachusetts	356.3
NA	Kentucky**	NA		17	Arizona	355.3
7	Louisiana	481.9		18	North Carolina	344.4
45	Maine	76.9		19	Georgia	338.6
5	Maryland	505.5		20	New York	323.9
16	Massachusetts	356.3		21	Nebraska	286.1
12	Michigan	387.4		22	Iowa	275.3
35	Minnesota	178.3		23	West Virginia	256.9
32	Mississippi	213.2		24	Pennsylvania	253.1
13	Missouri	375.0		25	Oregon	251.3
NA	Montana**	NA		26	Nevada	245.3
21	Nebraska	286.1		27	Idaho	237.4
26	Nevada	245.3		28	Washington	232.8
43	New Hampshire	97.4		29	Colorado	229.9
33	New Jersey	203.2		30	Wyoming	219.5
1	New Mexico	621.2		31	Indiana	218.4
20	New York	323.9		32	Mississippi	213.2
18	North Carolina	344.4		33	New Jersey	203.2
46	North Dakota	57.9		34	Connecticut	189.1
36	Ohio	170.6		35	Minnesota	178.3
10	Oklahoma	415.5		36	Ohio	170.6
25	Oregon	251.3		37	Virginia	168.0
24	Pennsylvania	253.1		38	Utah	166.2
39	Rhode Island	164.5		39	Rhode Island	164.5
2	South Carolina	616.6		40	South Dakota	141.9
40	South Dakota	141.9		41	Wisconsin	140.2
4	Tennessee	554.7		42	Hawaii	119.7
14	Texas	372.9		43	New Hampshire	97.4
38	Utah	166.2		44	Vermont	88.7
44	Vermont	88.7		45	Maine	76.9
37	Virginia	168.0		46	North Dakota	57.9
28	Washington	232.8		NA	Illinois**	NA
23	West Virginia	256.9		NA	Kansas**	NA
41	Wisconsin	140.2		NA	Kentucky**	NA
30	Wyoming	219.5		NA	Montana**	NA

District of Columbia   801.0

Source: Morgan Quitno Press using data from Federal Bureau of Investigation
   "Crime in the United States 2000" (Uniform Crime Reports, October 22, 2001)
*Estimated rates for urban areas, defined by the F.B.I. as Metropolitan Statistical Areas and other cities outside such areas. National rate includes those states listed as not available. Aggravated assault is an attack for the purpose of inflicting severe bodily injury.
**Not available.

Percent of Aggravated Assaults Occurring in Urban Areas in 2000

National Percent = 93.8% of Aggravated Assaults*

ALPHA ORDER				RANK ORDER		
RANK	STATE	PERCENT		RANK	STATE	PERCENT
18	Alabama	93.8		1	Massachusetts	100.0
38	Alaska	82.8		1	New Jersey	100.0
10	Arizona	95.9		3	Rhode Island	99.0
32	Arkansas	86.0		4	California	98.9
4	California	98.9		5	New York	97.4
12	Colorado	95.6		6	Maryland	96.8
35	Connecticut	85.3		7	Ohio	96.6
34	Delaware	85.6		8	Florida	96.1
8	Florida	96.1		9	Texas	96.0
28	Georgia	87.5		10	Arizona	95.9
44	Hawaii	73.0		11	Pennsylvania	95.7
40	Idaho	78.5		12	Colorado	95.6
NA	Illinois**	NA		13	New Hampshire	95.4
36	Indiana	84.3		13	Washington	95.4
19	Iowa	93.1		15	Michigan	95.3
NA	Kansas**	NA		16	Oregon	94.3
NA	Kentucky**	NA		17	Nebraska	94.1
30	Louisiana	86.6		18	Alabama	93.8
33	Maine	85.9		19	Iowa	93.1
6	Maryland	96.8		20	Minnesota	92.8
1	Massachusetts	100.0		21	Utah	92.5
15	Michigan	95.3		22	New Mexico	90.7
20	Minnesota	92.8		23	Tennessee	89.8
46	Mississippi	57.8		24	Missouri	89.7
24	Missouri	89.7		25	Oklahoma	89.5
NA	Montana**	NA		26	Wisconsin	89.2
17	Nebraska	94.1		27	Nevada	88.6
27	Nevada	88.6		28	Georgia	87.5
13	New Hampshire	95.4		29	North Carolina	86.7
1	New Jersey	100.0		30	Louisiana	86.6
22	New Mexico	90.7		31	Virginia	86.2
5	New York	97.4		32	Arkansas	86.0
29	North Carolina	86.7		33	Maine	85.9
37	North Dakota	84.0		34	Delaware	85.6
7	Ohio	96.6		35	Connecticut	85.3
25	Oklahoma	89.5		36	Indiana	84.3
16	Oregon	94.3		37	North Dakota	84.0
11	Pennsylvania	95.7		38	Alaska	82.8
3	Rhode Island	99.0		39	South Dakota	81.9
41	South Carolina	78.4		40	Idaho	78.5
39	South Dakota	81.9		41	South Carolina	78.4
23	Tennessee	89.8		42	Vermont	76.0
9	Texas	96.0		43	Wyoming	73.6
21	Utah	92.5		44	Hawaii	73.0
42	Vermont	76.0		45	West Virginia	59.3
31	Virginia	86.2		46	Mississippi	57.8
13	Washington	95.4		NA	Illinois**	NA
45	West Virginia	59.3		NA	Kansas**	NA
26	Wisconsin	89.2		NA	Kentucky**	NA
43	Wyoming	73.6		NA	Montana**	NA
				District of Columbia		100.0

Source: Morgan Quitno Press using data from Federal Bureau of Investigation
   "Crime in the United States 2000" (Uniform Crime Reports, October 22, 2001)
*Estimated percentages for urban areas, defined by the F.B.I. as Metropolitan Statistical Areas and other cities
outside such areas. National percent includes those states listed as not available. Aggravated assault is an
attack for the purpose of inflicting severe bodily injury.
**Not available.

Aggravated Assaults in Rural Areas in 2000

National Rural Total = 56,849 Aggravated Assaults*

ALPHA ORDER					RANK ORDER			
RANK	STATE		ASSAULTS	% of USA	RANK	STATE	ASSAULTS	% of USA
21	Alabama		881	1.5%	1	South Carolina	5,326	9.4%
32	Alaska		438	0.8%	2	Florida	3,494	6.1%
24	Arizona		731	1.3%	3	North Carolina	3,297	5.8%
18	Arkansas		1,242	2.2%	4	Georgia	3,176	5.6%
15	California		1,457	2.6%	5	Texas	2,948	5.2%
33	Colorado		418	0.7%	6	Tennessee	2,879	5.1%
19	Connecticut		949	1.7%	7	Louisiana	2,799	4.9%
30	Delaware		508	0.9%	8	Mississippi	2,653	4.7%
2	Florida		3,494	6.1%	9	Indiana	2,011	3.5%
4	Georgia		3,176	5.6%	10	West Virginia	1,870	3.3%
35	Hawaii		392	0.7%	11	Missouri	1,863	3.3%
27	Idaho		569	1.0%	12	Michigan	1,682	3.0%
NA	Illinois**		NA	NA	13	Virginia	1,600	2.8%
9	Indiana		2,011	3.5%	14	New York	1,584	2.8%
34	Iowa		416	0.7%	15	California	1,457	2.6%
NA	Kansas**		NA	NA	16	Oklahoma	1,366	2.4%
NA	Kentucky**		NA	NA	17	Pennsylvania	1,267	2.2%
7	Louisiana		2,799	4.9%	18	Arkansas	1,242	2.2%
40	Maine		115	0.2%	19	Connecticut	949	1.7%
22	Maryland		840	1.5%	20	New Mexico	948	1.7%
45	Massachusetts		5	0.0%	21	Alabama	881	1.5%
12	Michigan		1,682	3.0%	22	Maryland	840	1.5%
29	Minnesota		554	1.0%	23	Wisconsin	737	1.3%
8	Mississippi		2,653	4.7%	24	Arizona	731	1.3%
11	Missouri		1,863	3.3%	25	Ohio	603	1.1%
NA	Montana**		NA	NA	26	Washington	598	1.1%
38	Nebraska		234	0.4%	27	Idaho	569	1.0%
28	Nevada		564	1.0%	28	Nevada	564	1.0%
42	New Hampshire		54	0.1%	29	Minnesota	554	1.0%
46	New Jersey		0	0.0%	30	Delaware	508	0.9%
20	New Mexico		948	1.7%	31	Oregon	445	0.8%
14	New York		1,584	2.8%	32	Alaska	438	0.8%
3	North Carolina		3,297	5.8%	33	Colorado	418	0.7%
43	North Dakota		47	0.1%	34	Iowa	416	0.7%
25	Ohio		603	1.1%	35	Hawaii	392	0.7%
16	Oklahoma		1,366	2.4%	36	Wyoming	283	0.5%
31	Oregon		445	0.8%	37	Utah	266	0.5%
17	Pennsylvania		1,267	2.2%	38	Nebraska	234	0.4%
44	Rhode Island		18	0.0%	39	South Dakota	148	0.3%
1	South Carolina		5,326	9.4%	40	Maine	115	0.2%
39	South Dakota		148	0.3%	41	Vermont	102	0.2%
6	Tennessee		2,879	5.1%	42	New Hampshire	54	0.1%
5	Texas		2,948	5.2%	43	North Dakota	47	0.1%
37	Utah		266	0.5%	44	Rhode Island	18	0.0%
41	Vermont		102	0.2%	45	Massachusetts	5	0.0%
13	Virginia		1,600	2.8%	46	New Jersey	0	0.0%
26	Washington		598	1.1%	NA	Illinois**	NA	NA
10	West Virginia		1,870	3.3%	NA	Kansas**	NA	NA
23	Wisconsin		737	1.3%	NA	Kentucky**	NA	NA
36	Wyoming		283	0.5%	NA	Montana**	NA	NA
						District of Columbia	0	0.0%

Source: Federal Bureau of Investigation
   "Crime in the United States 2000" (Uniform Crime Reports, October 22, 2001)
*Estimated totals for rural areas, defined by the F.B.I. as other than Metropolitan Statistical Areas and other cities
outside such areas. National total includes those states listed as not available. Aggravated assault is an attack
for the purpose of inflicting severe bodily injury.
**Not available.

Rural Aggravated Assault Rate in 2000

National Rural Rate = 167.8 Aggravated Assaults per 100,000 Population*

ALPHA ORDER

RANK	STATE	RATE
29	Alabama	113.3
13	Alaska	224.5
11	Arizona	232.3
24	Arkansas	146.7
12	California	227.8
30	Colorado	109.2
17	Connecticut	191.3
2	Delaware	473.8
3	Florida	399.4
16	Georgia	197.5
27	Hawaii	119.5
26	Idaho	135.5
NA	Illinois**	NA
19	Indiana	178.9
40	Iowa	46.4
NA	Kansas**	NA
NA	Kentucky**	NA
4	Louisiana	387.3
43	Maine	31.6
6	Maryland	286.4
39	Massachusetts	51.6
23	Michigan	147.1
35	Minnesota	61.2
10	Mississippi	232.9
22	Missouri	147.9
NA	Montana**	NA
37	Nebraska	57.2
7	Nevada	263.8
36	New Hampshire	59.7
45	New Jersey	0.0
5	New Mexico	291.9
20	New York	173.5
18	North Carolina	180.1
44	North Dakota	21.8
41	Ohio	44.0
15	Oklahoma	206.6
33	Oregon	86.8
28	Pennsylvania	115.6
45	Rhode Island	0.0
1	South Carolina	608.3
38	South Dakota	52.1
8	Tennessee	254.9
21	Texas	171.7
32	Utah	106.4
42	Vermont	41.7
25	Virginia	144.6
31	Washington	108.9
9	West Virginia	250.3
34	Wisconsin	72.4
14	Wyoming	212.0

RANK ORDER

RANK	STATE	RATE
1	South Carolina	608.3
2	Delaware	473.8
3	Florida	399.4
4	Louisiana	387.3
5	New Mexico	291.9
6	Maryland	286.4
7	Nevada	263.8
8	Tennessee	254.9
9	West Virginia	250.3
10	Mississippi	232.9
11	Arizona	232.3
12	California	227.8
13	Alaska	224.5
14	Wyoming	212.0
15	Oklahoma	206.6
16	Georgia	197.5
17	Connecticut	191.3
18	North Carolina	180.1
19	Indiana	178.9
20	New York	173.5
21	Texas	171.7
22	Missouri	147.9
23	Michigan	147.1
24	Arkansas	146.7
25	Virginia	144.6
26	Idaho	135.5
27	Hawaii	119.5
28	Pennsylvania	115.6
29	Alabama	113.3
30	Colorado	109.2
31	Washington	108.9
32	Utah	106.4
33	Oregon	86.8
34	Wisconsin	72.4
35	Minnesota	61.2
36	New Hampshire	59.7
37	Nebraska	57.2
38	South Dakota	52.1
39	Massachusetts	51.6
40	Iowa	46.4
41	Ohio	44.0
42	Vermont	41.7
43	Maine	31.6
44	North Dakota	21.8
45	New Jersey	0.0
45	Rhode Island	0.0
NA	Illinois**	NA
NA	Kansas**	NA
NA	Kentucky**	NA
NA	Montana**	NA
	District of Columbia	0.0

Source: Morgan Quitno Press using data from Federal Bureau of Investigation
"Crime in the United States 2000" (Uniform Crime Reports, October 22, 2001)
*Estimated rates for rural areas, defined by the F.B.I. as other than Metropolitan Statistical Areas and other cities outside such areas. National rate includes those states listed as not available. Aggravated assault is an attack for the purpose of inflicting severe bodily injury.
**Not available.

Percent of Aggravated Assaults Occurring in Rural Areas in 2000

National Percent = 6.2% of Aggravated Assaults*

ALPHA ORDER

RANK	STATE	PERCENT
29	Alabama	6.2
9	Alaska	17.2
37	Arizona	4.1
15	Arkansas	14.0
43	California	1.1
35	Colorado	4.4
12	Connecticut	14.7
13	Delaware	14.4
39	Florida	3.9
19	Georgia	12.5
3	Hawaii	27.0
7	Idaho	21.5
NA	Illinois**	NA
11	Indiana	15.7
28	Iowa	6.9
NA	Kansas**	NA
NA	Kentucky**	NA
17	Louisiana	13.4
14	Maine	14.1
41	Maryland	3.2
45	Massachusetts	0.0
32	Michigan	4.7
27	Minnesota	7.2
1	Mississippi	42.2
23	Missouri	10.3
NA	Montana**	NA
30	Nebraska	5.9
20	Nevada	11.4
33	New Hampshire	4.6
45	New Jersey	0.0
25	New Mexico	9.3
42	New York	2.6
18	North Carolina	13.3
10	North Dakota	16.0
40	Ohio	3.4
22	Oklahoma	10.5
31	Oregon	5.7
36	Pennsylvania	4.3
44	Rhode Island	1.0
6	South Carolina	21.6
8	South Dakota	18.1
24	Tennessee	10.2
38	Texas	4.0
26	Utah	7.5
5	Vermont	24.0
16	Virginia	13.8
33	Washington	4.6
2	West Virginia	40.7
21	Wisconsin	10.8
4	Wyoming	26.4

RANK ORDER

RANK	STATE	PERCENT
1	Mississippi	42.2
2	West Virginia	40.7
3	Hawaii	27.0
4	Wyoming	26.4
5	Vermont	24.0
6	South Carolina	21.6
7	Idaho	21.5
8	South Dakota	18.1
9	Alaska	17.2
10	North Dakota	16.0
11	Indiana	15.7
12	Connecticut	14.7
13	Delaware	14.4
14	Maine	14.1
15	Arkansas	14.0
16	Virginia	13.8
17	Louisiana	13.4
18	North Carolina	13.3
19	Georgia	12.5
20	Nevada	11.4
21	Wisconsin	10.8
22	Oklahoma	10.5
23	Missouri	10.3
24	Tennessee	10.2
25	New Mexico	9.3
26	Utah	7.5
27	Minnesota	7.2
28	Iowa	6.9
29	Alabama	6.2
30	Nebraska	5.9
31	Oregon	5.7
32	Michigan	4.7
33	New Hampshire	4.6
33	Washington	4.6
35	Colorado	4.4
36	Pennsylvania	4.3
37	Arizona	4.1
38	Texas	4.0
39	Florida	3.9
40	Ohio	3.4
41	Maryland	3.2
42	New York	2.6
43	California	1.1
44	Rhode Island	1.0
45	Massachusetts	0.0
45	New Jersey	0.0
NA	Illinois**	NA
NA	Kansas**	NA
NA	Kentucky**	NA
NA	Montana**	NA
	District of Columbia	0.0

Source: Morgan Quitno Press using data from Federal Bureau of Investigation
  "Crime in the United States 2000" (Uniform Crime Reports, October 22, 2001)
*Estimated percentages for rural areas, defined by the F.B.I. as other than Metropolitan Statistical Areas and other cities outside such areas. National percent includes those states listed as not available. Aggravated assault is an attack for the purpose of inflicting severe bodily injury.
**Not available.

Property Crimes in Urban Areas in 2000

National Urban Total = 9,621,039 Property Crimes*

ALPHA ORDER					RANK ORDER			
RANK	STATE	CRIMES	% of USA		RANK	STATE	CRIMES	% of USA
19	Alabama	172,250	1.8%		1	California	1,043,678	10.8%
42	Alaska	18,886	0.2%		2	Texas	895,056	9.3%
10	Arizona	267,560	2.8%		3	Florida	755,569	7.9%
29	Arkansas	87,015	0.9%		4	New York	469,834	4.9%
1	California	1,043,678	10.8%		5	Ohio	398,384	4.1%
21	Colorado	151,411	1.6%		6	Michigan	330,862	3.4%
27	Connecticut	92,194	1.0%		7	Georgia	312,895	3.3%
39	Delaware	27,321	0.3%		8	North Carolina	311,278	3.2%
3	Florida	755,569	7.9%		9	Pennsylvania	300,494	3.1%
7	Georgia	312,895	3.3%		10	Arizona	267,560	2.8%
35	Hawaii	44,357	0.5%		11	Washington	265,109	2.8%
37	Idaho	32,098	0.3%		12	New Jersey	233,637	2.4%
NA	Illinois**	NA	NA		13	Tennessee	218,273	2.3%
17	Indiana	186,864	1.9%		14	Missouri	211,518	2.2%
32	Iowa	80,216	0.8%		15	Maryland	208,259	2.2%
NA	Kansas**	NA	NA		16	Louisiana	198,062	2.1%
NA	Kentucky**	NA	NA		17	Indiana	186,864	1.9%
16	Louisiana	198,062	2.1%		18	Virginia	179,391	1.9%
41	Maine	26,883	0.3%		19	Alabama	172,250	1.8%
15	Maryland	208,259	2.2%		20	Massachusetts	161,880	1.7%
20	Massachusetts	161,880	1.7%		21	Colorado	151,411	1.6%
6	Michigan	330,862	3.4%		22	South Carolina	149,148	1.6%
25	Minnesota	143,461	1.5%		23	Wisconsin	146,048	1.5%
30	Mississippi	86,934	0.9%		24	Oregon	144,198	1.5%
14	Missouri	211,518	2.2%		25	Minnesota	143,461	1.5%
NA	Montana**	NA	NA		26	Oklahoma	132,199	1.4%
34	Nebraska	58,754	0.6%		27	Connecticut	92,194	1.0%
33	Nevada	70,599	0.7%		28	Utah	89,470	0.9%
40	New Hampshire	27,307	0.3%		29	Arkansas	87,015	0.9%
12	New Jersey	233,637	2.4%		30	Mississippi	86,934	0.9%
31	New Mexico	82,335	0.9%		31	New Mexico	82,335	0.9%
4	New York	469,834	4.9%		32	Iowa	80,216	0.8%
8	North Carolina	311,278	3.2%		33	Nevada	70,599	0.7%
46	North Dakota	12,331	0.1%		34	Nebraska	58,754	0.6%
5	Ohio	398,384	4.1%		35	Hawaii	44,357	0.5%
26	Oklahoma	132,199	1.4%		36	Rhode Island	33,270	0.3%
24	Oregon	144,198	1.5%		37	Idaho	32,098	0.3%
9	Pennsylvania	300,494	3.1%		38	West Virginia	31,149	0.3%
36	Rhode Island	33,270	0.3%		39	Delaware	27,321	0.3%
22	South Carolina	149,148	1.6%		40	New Hampshire	27,307	0.3%
43	South Dakota	14,440	0.2%		41	Maine	26,883	0.3%
13	Tennessee	218,273	2.3%		42	Alaska	18,886	0.2%
2	Texas	895,056	9.3%		43	South Dakota	14,440	0.2%
28	Utah	89,470	0.9%		44	Vermont	13,699	0.1%
44	Vermont	13,699	0.1%		45	Wyoming	12,940	0.1%
18	Virginia	179,391	1.9%		46	North Dakota	12,331	0.1%
11	Washington	265,109	2.8%		NA	Illinois**	NA	NA
38	West Virginia	31,149	0.3%		NA	Kansas**	NA	NA
23	Wisconsin	146,048	1.5%		NA	Kentucky**	NA	NA
45	Wyoming	12,940	0.1%		NA	Montana**	NA	NA
						District of Columbia	33,000	0.3%

Source: Morgan Quitno Press using data from Federal Bureau of Investigation
"Crime in the United States 2000" (Uniform Crime Reports, October 22, 2001)
*Estimated totals for urban areas, defined by the F.B.I. as Metropolitan Statistical Areas and other cities outside such areas. National total includes those states listed as not available. Property crimes are offenses of burglary, larceny-theft and motor vehicle theft.
**Not available.

Urban Property Crime Rate in 2000

National Urban Rate = 3,886.6 Property Crimes per 100,000 Population*

ALPHA ORDER

RANK	STATE	RATE
16	Alabama	4,694.2
20	Alaska	4,373.9
1	Arizona	5,555.7
12	Arkansas	4,763.7
36	California	3,140.6
26	Colorado	3,864.1
35	Connecticut	3,168.7
22	Delaware	4,039.3
7	Florida	5,001.2
13	Georgia	4,756.5
5	Hawaii	5,019.9
30	Idaho	3,672.6
NA	Illinois**	NA
27	Indiana	3,769.9
25	Iowa	3,952.6
NA	Kansas**	NA
NA	Kentucky**	NA
3	Louisiana	5,286.8
39	Maine	2,951.6
21	Maryland	4,162.5
45	Massachusetts	2,553.6
28	Michigan	3,761.9
32	Minnesota	3,574.1
4	Mississippi	5,096.8
10	Missouri	4,878.8
NA	Montana**	NA
19	Nebraska	4,511.1
24	Nevada	3,956.2
46	New Hampshire	2,384.2
42	New Jersey	2,776.6
2	New Mexico	5,509.9
44	New York	2,601.0
6	North Carolina	5,005.9
41	North Dakota	2,892.7
23	Ohio	3,991.0
15	Oklahoma	4,739.0
9	Oregon	4,957.3
43	Pennsylvania	2,686.6
34	Rhode Island	3,173.7
14	South Carolina	4,755.3
37	South Dakota	3,067.3
11	Tennessee	4,787.1
17	Texas	4,677.7
18	Utah	4,511.3
29	Vermont	3,761.8
38	Virginia	3,003.7
8	Washington	4,960.1
40	West Virginia	2,935.0
33	Wisconsin	3,361.2
31	Wyoming	3,591.3

RANK ORDER

RANK	STATE	RATE
1	Arizona	5,555.7
2	New Mexico	5,509.9
3	Louisiana	5,286.8
4	Mississippi	5,096.8
5	Hawaii	5,019.9
6	North Carolina	5,005.9
7	Florida	5,001.2
8	Washington	4,960.1
9	Oregon	4,957.3
10	Missouri	4,878.8
11	Tennessee	4,787.1
12	Arkansas	4,763.7
13	Georgia	4,756.5
14	South Carolina	4,755.3
15	Oklahoma	4,739.0
16	Alabama	4,694.2
17	Texas	4,677.7
18	Utah	4,511.3
19	Nebraska	4,511.1
20	Alaska	4,373.9
21	Maryland	4,162.5
22	Delaware	4,039.3
23	Ohio	3,991.0
24	Nevada	3,956.2
25	Iowa	3,952.6
26	Colorado	3,864.1
27	Indiana	3,769.9
28	Michigan	3,761.9
29	Vermont	3,761.8
30	Idaho	3,672.6
31	Wyoming	3,591.3
32	Minnesota	3,574.1
33	Wisconsin	3,361.2
34	Rhode Island	3,173.7
35	Connecticut	3,168.7
36	California	3,140.6
37	South Dakota	3,067.3
38	Virginia	3,003.7
39	Maine	2,951.6
40	West Virginia	2,935.0
41	North Dakota	2,892.7
42	New Jersey	2,776.6
43	Pennsylvania	2,686.6
44	New York	2,601.0
45	Massachusetts	2,553.6
46	New Hampshire	2,384.2
NA	Illinois**	NA
NA	Kansas**	NA
NA	Kentucky**	NA
NA	Montana**	NA

District of Columbia   5,768.6

Source: Morgan Quitno Press using data from Federal Bureau of Investigation
   "Crime in the United States 2000" (Uniform Crime Reports, October 22, 2001)
*Estimated rates for urban areas, defined by the F.B.I. as Metropolitan Statistical Areas and other cities outside such areas. National rate includes those states listed as not available. Property crimes are offenses of burglary, larceny-theft and motor vehicle theft.
**Not available.

Percent of Property Crimes Occurring in Urban Areas in 2000

National Percent = 94.5% of Property Crimes*

ALPHA ORDER

RANK	STATE	PERCENT
12	Alabama	95.4
43	Alaska	81.8
5	Arizona	98.4
35	Arkansas	88.7
4	California	98.8
11	Colorado	96.5
24	Connecticut	93.1
27	Delaware	91.9
10	Florida	96.8
33	Georgia	90.0
46	Hawaii	73.9
39	Idaho	84.6
NA	Illinois**	NA
32	Indiana	90.3
25	Iowa	92.4
NA	Kansas**	NA
NA	Kentucky**	NA
23	Louisiana	93.5
41	Maine	84.0
7	Maryland	97.6
1	Massachusetts	100.0
21	Michigan	93.6
31	Minnesota	90.9
42	Mississippi	83.9
21	Missouri	93.6
NA	Montana**	NA
30	Nebraska	91.1
18	Nevada	94.4
6	New Hampshire	97.9
1	New Jersey	100.0
13	New Mexico	95.1
8	New York	97.3
36	North Carolina	87.5
37	North Dakota	87.0
17	Ohio	94.6
19	Oklahoma	94.3
20	Oregon	93.8
14	Pennsylvania	95.0
3	Rhode Island	99.8
40	South Carolina	84.2
34	South Dakota	88.9
28	Tennessee	91.7
8	Texas	97.3
16	Utah	94.9
44	Vermont	78.3
26	Virginia	92.3
14	Washington	95.0
45	West Virginia	75.3
29	Wisconsin	91.6
38	Wyoming	86.4

RANK ORDER

RANK	STATE	PERCENT
1	Massachusetts	100.0
1	New Jersey	100.0
3	Rhode Island	99.8
4	California	98.8
5	Arizona	98.4
6	New Hampshire	97.9
7	Maryland	97.6
8	New York	97.3
8	Texas	97.3
10	Florida	96.8
11	Colorado	96.5
12	Alabama	95.4
13	New Mexico	95.1
14	Pennsylvania	95.0
14	Washington	95.0
16	Utah	94.9
17	Ohio	94.6
18	Nevada	94.4
19	Oklahoma	94.3
20	Oregon	93.8
21	Michigan	93.6
21	Missouri	93.6
23	Louisiana	93.5
24	Connecticut	93.1
25	Iowa	92.4
26	Virginia	92.3
27	Delaware	91.9
28	Tennessee	91.7
29	Wisconsin	91.6
30	Nebraska	91.1
31	Minnesota	90.9
32	Indiana	90.3
33	Georgia	90.0
34	South Dakota	88.9
35	Arkansas	88.7
36	North Carolina	87.5
37	North Dakota	87.0
38	Wyoming	86.4
39	Idaho	84.6
40	South Carolina	84.2
41	Maine	84.0
42	Mississippi	83.9
43	Alaska	81.8
44	Vermont	78.3
45	West Virginia	75.3
46	Hawaii	73.9
NA	Illinois**	NA
NA	Kansas**	NA
NA	Kentucky**	NA
NA	Montana**	NA

District of Columbia   100.0

Source: Morgan Quitno Press using data from Federal Bureau of Investigation
    "Crime in the United States 2000" (Uniform Crime Reports, October 22, 2001)
*Estimated percentages for urban areas, defined by the F.B.I. as Metropolitan Statistical Areas and other cities
outside such areas. National percent includes those states listed as not available. Property crimes are offenses of
burglary, larceny-theft and motor vehicle theft.
**Not available.

438

Property Crimes in Rural Areas in 2000

National Rural Total = 560,423 Property Crimes*

ALPHA ORDER

RANK	STATE	CRIMES	% of USA
24	Alabama	8,289	1.5%
37	Alaska	4,201	0.7%
35	Arizona	4,251	0.8%
21	Arkansas	11,100	2.0%
20	California	12,505	2.2%
30	Colorado	5,526	1.0%
26	Connecticut	6,839	1.2%
39	Delaware	2,406	0.4%
4	Florida	24,808	4.4%
2	Georgia	34,735	6.2%
12	Hawaii	15,676	2.8%
28	Idaho	5,863	1.0%
NA	Illinois**	NA	NA
8	Indiana	20,041	3.6%
27	Iowa	6,618	1.2%
NA	Kansas**	NA	NA
NA	Kentucky**	NA	NA
17	Louisiana	13,842	2.5%
32	Maine	5,120	0.9%
31	Maryland	5,163	0.9%
45	Massachusetts	21	0.0%
7	Michigan	22,435	4.0%
15	Minnesota	14,337	2.6%
10	Mississippi	16,710	3.0%
14	Missouri	14,401	2.6%
NA	Montana**	NA	NA
29	Nebraska	5,725	1.0%
36	Nevada	4,224	0.8%
43	New Hampshire	594	0.1%
46	New Jersey	0	0.0%
34	New Mexico	4,270	0.8%
19	New York	13,244	2.4%
1	North Carolina	44,643	8.0%
41	North Dakota	1,840	0.3%
6	Ohio	22,555	4.0%
25	Oklahoma	7,926	1.4%
23	Oregon	9,582	1.7%
11	Pennsylvania	15,780	2.8%
44	Rhode Island	53	0.0%
3	South Carolina	28,041	5.0%
42	South Dakota	1,812	0.3%
9	Tennessee	19,712	3.5%
5	Texas	24,602	4.4%
33	Utah	4,777	0.9%
38	Vermont	3,795	0.7%
13	Virginia	15,014	2.7%
16	Washington	14,035	2.5%
22	West Virginia	10,195	1.8%
18	Wisconsin	13,376	2.4%
40	Wyoming	2,029	0.4%

RANK ORDER

RANK	STATE	CRIMES	% of USA
1	North Carolina	44,643	8.0%
2	Georgia	34,735	6.2%
3	South Carolina	28,041	5.0%
4	Florida	24,808	4.4%
5	Texas	24,602	4.4%
6	Ohio	22,555	4.0%
7	Michigan	22,435	4.0%
8	Indiana	20,041	3.6%
9	Tennessee	19,712	3.5%
10	Mississippi	16,710	3.0%
11	Pennsylvania	15,780	2.8%
12	Hawaii	15,676	2.8%
13	Virginia	15,014	2.7%
14	Missouri	14,401	2.6%
15	Minnesota	14,337	2.6%
16	Washington	14,035	2.5%
17	Louisiana	13,842	2.5%
18	Wisconsin	13,376	2.4%
19	New York	13,244	2.4%
20	California	12,505	2.2%
21	Arkansas	11,100	2.0%
22	West Virginia	10,195	1.8%
23	Oregon	9,582	1.7%
24	Alabama	8,289	1.5%
25	Oklahoma	7,926	1.4%
26	Connecticut	6,839	1.2%
27	Iowa	6,618	1.2%
28	Idaho	5,863	1.0%
29	Nebraska	5,725	1.0%
30	Colorado	5,526	1.0%
31	Maryland	5,163	0.9%
32	Maine	5,120	0.9%
33	Utah	4,777	0.9%
34	New Mexico	4,270	0.8%
35	Arizona	4,251	0.8%
36	Nevada	4,224	0.8%
37	Alaska	4,201	0.7%
38	Vermont	3,795	0.7%
39	Delaware	2,406	0.4%
40	Wyoming	2,029	0.4%
41	North Dakota	1,840	0.3%
42	South Dakota	1,812	0.3%
43	New Hampshire	594	0.1%
44	Rhode Island	53	0.0%
45	Massachusetts	21	0.0%
46	New Jersey	0	0.0%
NA	Illinois**	NA	NA
NA	Kansas**	NA	NA
NA	Kentucky**	NA	NA
NA	Montana**	NA	NA
	District of Columbia	0	0.0%

Source: Federal Bureau of Investigation
    "Crime in the United States 2000" (Uniform Crime Reports, October 22, 2001)
*Estimated totals for rural areas, defined by the F.B.I. as other than Metropolitan Statistical Areas and other cities outside such areas. National total includes those states listed as not available. Property crimes are offenses of burglary, larceny-theft and motor vehicle theft.
**Not available.

Rural Property Crime Rate in 2000

National Rural Rate = 1,654.3 Property Crimes per 100,000 Population*

ALPHA ORDER			RANK ORDER		
RANK	STATE	RATE	RANK	STATE	RATE
39	Alabama	1,065.9	1	Hawaii	4,780.5
8	Alaska	2,152.8	2	South Carolina	3,202.8
33	Arizona	1,351.1	3	Florida	2,836.0
36	Arkansas	1,310.9	4	Washington	2,555.4
11	California	1,955.4	5	North Carolina	2,438.1
24	Colorado	1,443.2	6	Delaware	2,243.9
30	Connecticut	1,378.7	7	Georgia	2,159.9
6	Delaware	2,243.9	8	Alaska	2,152.8
3	Florida	2,836.0	9	Nevada	1,976.1
7	Georgia	2,159.9	10	Michigan	1,962.0
1	Hawaii	4,780.5	11	California	1,955.4
29	Idaho	1,396.1	12	Louisiana	1,915.6
NA	Illinois**	NA	13	Utah	1,911.5
15	Indiana	1,783.3	14	Oregon	1,869.2
41	Iowa	737.9	15	Indiana	1,783.3
NA	Kansas**	NA	16	Maryland	1,760.6
NA	Kentucky**	NA	17	Tennessee	1,744.9
12	Louisiana	1,915.6	18	Ohio	1,645.1
27	Maine	1,406.1	19	Minnesota	1,583.1
16	Maryland	1,760.6	20	Vermont	1,551.1
44	Massachusetts	216.6	21	Wyoming	1,520.2
10	Michigan	1,962.0	22	Mississippi	1,467.1
19	Minnesota	1,583.1	23	New York	1,450.6
22	Mississippi	1,467.1	24	Colorado	1,443.2
38	Missouri	1,143.1	25	Pennsylvania	1,439.7
NA	Montana**	NA	26	Texas	1,432.6
28	Nebraska	1,400.4	27	Maine	1,406.1
9	Nevada	1,976.1	28	Nebraska	1,400.4
42	New Hampshire	656.7	29	Idaho	1,396.1
45	New Jersey	0.0	30	Connecticut	1,378.7
34	New Mexico	1,314.9	31	West Virginia	1,364.7
23	New York	1,450.6	32	Virginia	1,357.2
5	North Carolina	2,438.1	33	Arizona	1,351.1
40	North Dakota	852.2	34	New Mexico	1,314.9
18	Ohio	1,645.1	35	Wisconsin	1,313.3
37	Oklahoma	1,199.0	36	Arkansas	1,310.9
14	Oregon	1,869.2	37	Oklahoma	1,199.0
25	Pennsylvania	1,439.7	38	Missouri	1,143.1
45	Rhode Island	0.0	39	Alabama	1,065.9
2	South Carolina	3,202.8	40	North Dakota	852.2
43	South Dakota	637.9	41	Iowa	737.9
17	Tennessee	1,744.9	42	New Hampshire	656.7
26	Texas	1,432.6	43	South Dakota	637.9
13	Utah	1,911.5	44	Massachusetts	216.6
20	Vermont	1,551.1	45	New Jersey	0.0
32	Virginia	1,357.2	45	Rhode Island	0.0
4	Washington	2,555.4	NA	Illinois**	NA
31	West Virginia	1,364.7	NA	Kansas**	NA
35	Wisconsin	1,313.3	NA	Kentucky**	NA
21	Wyoming	1,520.2	NA	Montana**	NA
				District of Columbia	0.0

Source: Morgan Quitno Press using data from Federal Bureau of Investigation
    "Crime in the United States 2000" (Uniform Crime Reports, October 22, 2001)
*Estimated rates for rural areas, defined by the F.B.I. as other than Metropolitan Statistical Areas and other cities outside such areas. National rate includes those states listed as not available. Property crimes are offenses of burglary, larceny-theft and motor vehicle theft.
**Not available.

Percent of Property Crimes Occurring in Rural Areas in 2000

National Percent = 5.5% of Property Crimes*

ALPHA ORDER

RANK	STATE	PERCENT
35	Alabama	4.6
4	Alaska	18.2
42	Arizona	1.6
12	Arkansas	11.3
43	California	1.2
36	Colorado	3.5
23	Connecticut	6.9
20	Delaware	8.1
37	Florida	3.2
14	Georgia	10.0
1	Hawaii	26.1
8	Idaho	15.4
NA	Illinois**	NA
15	Indiana	9.7
22	Iowa	7.6
NA	Kansas**	NA
NA	Kentucky**	NA
24	Louisiana	6.5
6	Maine	16.0
40	Maryland	2.4
45	Massachusetts	0.0
25	Michigan	6.4
16	Minnesota	9.1
5	Mississippi	16.1
25	Missouri	6.4
NA	Montana**	NA
17	Nebraska	8.9
29	Nevada	5.6
41	New Hampshire	2.1
45	New Jersey	0.0
34	New Mexico	4.9
38	New York	2.7
11	North Carolina	12.5
10	North Dakota	13.0
30	Ohio	5.4
28	Oklahoma	5.7
27	Oregon	6.2
32	Pennsylvania	5.0
44	Rhode Island	0.2
7	South Carolina	15.8
13	South Dakota	11.1
19	Tennessee	8.3
38	Texas	2.7
31	Utah	5.1
3	Vermont	21.7
21	Virginia	7.7
32	Washington	5.0
2	West Virginia	24.7
18	Wisconsin	8.4
9	Wyoming	13.6

RANK ORDER

RANK	STATE	PERCENT
1	Hawaii	26.1
2	West Virginia	24.7
3	Vermont	21.7
4	Alaska	18.2
5	Mississippi	16.1
6	Maine	16.0
7	South Carolina	15.8
8	Idaho	15.4
9	Wyoming	13.6
10	North Dakota	13.0
11	North Carolina	12.5
12	Arkansas	11.3
13	South Dakota	11.1
14	Georgia	10.0
15	Indiana	9.7
16	Minnesota	9.1
17	Nebraska	8.9
18	Wisconsin	8.4
19	Tennessee	8.3
20	Delaware	8.1
21	Virginia	7.7
22	Iowa	7.6
23	Connecticut	6.9
24	Louisiana	6.5
25	Michigan	6.4
25	Missouri	6.4
27	Oregon	6.2
28	Oklahoma	5.7
29	Nevada	5.6
30	Ohio	5.4
31	Utah	5.1
32	Pennsylvania	5.0
32	Washington	5.0
34	New Mexico	4.9
35	Alabama	4.6
36	Colorado	3.5
37	Florida	3.2
38	New York	2.7
38	Texas	2.7
40	Maryland	2.4
41	New Hampshire	2.1
42	Arizona	1.6
43	California	1.2
44	Rhode Island	0.2
45	Massachusetts	0.0
45	New Jersey	0.0
NA	Illinois**	NA
NA	Kansas**	NA
NA	Kentucky**	NA
NA	Montana**	NA

	District of Columbia	0.0

Source: Morgan Quitno Press using data from Federal Bureau of Investigation
"Crime in the United States 2000" (Uniform Crime Reports, October 22, 2001)
*Estimated percentages for rural areas, defined by the F.B.I. as other than Metropolitan Statistical Areas and other cities outside such areas. National percent includes those states listed as not available. Property crimes are offenses of burglary, larceny-theft and motor vehicle theft.
**Not available.

Burglaries in Urban Areas in 2000

National Urban Total = 1,869,626 Burglaries*

ALPHA ORDER

RANK	STATE	BURGLARIES	% of USA
16	Alabama	37,249	2.0%
42	Alaska	2,579	0.1%
9	Arizona	50,684	2.7%
29	Arkansas	17,689	0.9%
1	California	217,410	11.6%
23	Colorado	26,041	1.4%
31	Connecticut	15,524	0.8%
41	Delaware	4,486	0.2%
3	Florida	165,038	8.8%
8	Georgia	59,268	3.2%
35	Hawaii	6,946	0.4%
38	Idaho	5,847	0.3%
NA	Illinois**	NA	NA
18	Indiana	35,592	1.9%
32	Iowa	14,138	0.8%
NA	Kansas**	NA	NA
NA	Kentucky**	NA	NA
14	Louisiana	41,929	2.2%
39	Maine	4,824	0.3%
15	Maryland	37,914	2.0%
19	Massachusetts	30,595	1.6%
7	Michigan	62,625	3.3%
25	Minnesota	21,606	1.2%
28	Mississippi	19,728	1.1%
17	Missouri	36,347	1.9%
NA	Montana**	NA	NA
34	Nebraska	8,591	0.5%
30	Nevada	16,346	0.9%
40	New Hampshire	4,747	0.3%
13	New Jersey	43,924	2.3%
27	New Mexico	19,782	1.1%
4	New York	83,865	4.5%
6	North Carolina	79,123	4.2%
46	North Dakota	1,564	0.1%
5	Ohio	82,055	4.4%
21	Oklahoma	28,502	1.5%
24	Oregon	22,936	1.2%
11	Pennsylvania	49,153	2.6%
37	Rhode Island	6,606	0.4%
20	South Carolina	30,451	1.6%
43	South Dakota	2,288	0.1%
10	Tennessee	49,460	2.6%
2	Texas	179,398	9.6%
33	Utah	13,239	0.7%
44	Vermont	2,180	0.1%
22	Virginia	26,641	1.4%
12	Washington	48,906	2.6%
36	West Virginia	6,813	0.4%
26	Wisconsin	21,294	1.1%
45	Wyoming	1,650	0.1%

RANK ORDER

RANK	STATE	BURGLARIES	% of USA
1	California	217,410	11.6%
2	Texas	179,398	9.6%
3	Florida	165,038	8.8%
4	New York	83,865	4.5%
5	Ohio	82,055	4.4%
6	North Carolina	79,123	4.2%
7	Michigan	62,625	3.3%
8	Georgia	59,268	3.2%
9	Arizona	50,684	2.7%
10	Tennessee	49,460	2.6%
11	Pennsylvania	49,153	2.6%
12	Washington	48,906	2.6%
13	New Jersey	43,924	2.3%
14	Louisiana	41,929	2.2%
15	Maryland	37,914	2.0%
16	Alabama	37,249	2.0%
17	Missouri	36,347	1.9%
18	Indiana	35,592	1.9%
19	Massachusetts	30,595	1.6%
20	South Carolina	30,451	1.6%
21	Oklahoma	28,502	1.5%
22	Virginia	26,641	1.4%
23	Colorado	26,041	1.4%
24	Oregon	22,936	1.2%
25	Minnesota	21,606	1.2%
26	Wisconsin	21,294	1.1%
27	New Mexico	19,782	1.1%
28	Mississippi	19,728	1.1%
29	Arkansas	17,689	0.9%
30	Nevada	16,346	0.9%
31	Connecticut	15,524	0.8%
32	Iowa	14,138	0.8%
33	Utah	13,239	0.7%
34	Nebraska	8,591	0.5%
35	Hawaii	6,946	0.4%
36	West Virginia	6,813	0.4%
37	Rhode Island	6,606	0.4%
38	Idaho	5,847	0.3%
39	Maine	4,824	0.3%
40	New Hampshire	4,747	0.3%
41	Delaware	4,486	0.2%
42	Alaska	2,579	0.1%
43	South Dakota	2,288	0.1%
44	Vermont	2,180	0.1%
45	Wyoming	1,650	0.1%
46	North Dakota	1,564	0.1%
NA	Illinois**	NA	NA
NA	Kansas**	NA	NA
NA	Kentucky**	NA	NA
NA	Montana**	NA	NA
	District of Columbia	4,745	0.3%

Source: Morgan Quitno Press using data from Federal Bureau of Investigation
    "Crime in the United States 2000" (Uniform Crime Reports, October 22, 2001)
*Estimated totals for urban areas, defined by the F.B.I. as Metropolitan Statistical Areas and other cities outside
such areas. National total includes those states listed as not available. Burglary is the unlawful entry of a
structure to commit a felony or theft. Attempts are included.
**Not available.

Urban Burglary Rate in 2000

National Urban Rate = 755.3 Burglaries per 100,000 Population*

RANK	STATE	RATE		RANK	STATE	RATE
9	Alabama	1,015.1		1	New Mexico	1,323.8
33	Alaska	597.3		2	North Carolina	1,272.4
7	Arizona	1,052.4		3	Mississippi	1,156.6
11	Arkansas	968.4		4	Louisiana	1,119.2
29	California	654.2		5	Florida	1,092.4
26	Colorado	664.6		6	Tennessee	1,084.7
35	Connecticut	533.6		7	Arizona	1,052.4
27	Delaware	663.2		8	Oklahoma	1,021.7
5	Florida	1,092.4		9	Alabama	1,015.1
15	Georgia	901.0		10	South Carolina	970.9
19	Hawaii	786.1		11	Arkansas	968.4
24	Idaho	669.0		12	Texas	937.6
NA	Illinois**	NA		13	Nevada	916.0
21	Indiana	718.1		14	Washington	915.0
23	Iowa	696.6		15	Georgia	901.0
NA	Kansas**	NA		16	Missouri	838.4
NA	Kentucky**	NA		17	Ohio	822.0
4	Louisiana	1,119.2		18	Oregon	788.5
36	Maine	529.7		19	Hawaii	786.1
20	Maryland	757.8		20	Maryland	757.8
40	Massachusetts	482.6		21	Indiana	718.1
22	Michigan	712.1		22	Michigan	712.1
34	Minnesota	538.3		23	Iowa	696.6
3	Mississippi	1,156.6		24	Idaho	669.0
16	Missouri	838.4		25	Utah	667.5
NA	Montana**	NA		26	Colorado	664.6
28	Nebraska	659.6		27	Delaware	663.2
13	Nevada	916.0		28	Nebraska	659.6
45	New Hampshire	414.5		29	California	654.2
37	New Jersey	522.0		30	West Virginia	642.0
1	New Mexico	1,323.8		31	Rhode Island	630.2
41	New York	464.3		32	Vermont	598.6
2	North Carolina	1,272.4		33	Alaska	597.3
46	North Dakota	366.9		34	Minnesota	538.3
17	Ohio	822.0		35	Connecticut	533.6
8	Oklahoma	1,021.7		36	Maine	529.7
18	Oregon	788.5		37	New Jersey	522.0
44	Pennsylvania	439.5		38	Wisconsin	490.1
31	Rhode Island	630.2		39	South Dakota	486.0
10	South Carolina	970.9		40	Massachusetts	482.6
39	South Dakota	486.0		41	New York	464.3
6	Tennessee	1,084.7		42	Wyoming	457.9
12	Texas	937.6		43	Virginia	446.1
25	Utah	667.5		44	Pennsylvania	439.5
32	Vermont	598.6		45	New Hampshire	414.5
43	Virginia	446.1		46	North Dakota	366.9
14	Washington	915.0		NA	Illinois**	NA
30	West Virginia	642.0		NA	Kansas**	NA
38	Wisconsin	490.1		NA	Kentucky**	NA
42	Wyoming	457.9		NA	Montana**	NA

| | District of Columbia | 829.5 |

Source: Morgan Quitno Press using data from Federal Bureau of Investigation
   "Crime in the United States 2000" (Uniform Crime Reports, October 22, 2001)
*Estimated rates for urban areas, defined by the F.B.I. as Metropolitan Statistical Areas and other cities outside such areas. National rate includes those states listed as not available. Burglary is the unlawful entry of a structure to commit a felony or theft. Attempts are included.
**Not available.

Percent of Burglaries Occurring in Urban Areas in 2000

National Percent = 91.2% of Burglaries*

ALPHA ORDER

RANK	STATE	PERCENT
15	Alabama	92.4
44	Alaska	66.1
5	Arizona	97.7
34	Arkansas	82.5
4	California	97.8
7	Colorado	96.0
23	Connecticut	89.0
30	Delaware	86.0
8	Florida	95.5
28	Georgia	86.5
45	Hawaii	65.1
36	Idaho	79.8
NA	Illinois**	NA
27	Indiana	86.6
28	Iowa	86.5
NA	Kansas**	NA
NA	Kentucky**	NA
19	Louisiana	90.6
42	Maine	71.2
6	Maryland	96.2
1	Massachusetts	100.0
21	Michigan	89.7
33	Minnesota	82.7
41	Mississippi	73.3
26	Missouri	87.2
NA	Montana**	NA
31	Nebraska	84.8
12	Nevada	93.3
10	New Hampshire	95.1
1	New Jersey	100.0
13	New Mexico	92.7
9	New York	95.4
35	North Carolina	80.8
40	North Dakota	74.7
14	Ohio	92.6
20	Oklahoma	90.0
22	Oregon	89.5
18	Pennsylvania	90.9
3	Rhode Island	99.8
39	South Carolina	78.3
38	South Dakota	79.0
24	Tennessee	87.8
11	Texas	94.9
16	Utah	92.3
46	Vermont	62.3
25	Virginia	87.5
17	Washington	91.5
43	West Virginia	68.9
32	Wisconsin	84.6
37	Wyoming	79.4

RANK ORDER

RANK	STATE	PERCENT
1	Massachusetts	100.0
1	New Jersey	100.0
3	Rhode Island	99.8
4	California	97.8
5	Arizona	97.7
6	Maryland	96.2
7	Colorado	96.0
8	Florida	95.5
9	New York	95.4
10	New Hampshire	95.1
11	Texas	94.9
12	Nevada	93.3
13	New Mexico	92.7
14	Ohio	92.6
15	Alabama	92.4
16	Utah	92.3
17	Washington	91.5
18	Pennsylvania	90.9
19	Louisiana	90.6
20	Oklahoma	90.0
21	Michigan	89.7
22	Oregon	89.5
23	Connecticut	89.0
24	Tennessee	87.8
25	Virginia	87.5
26	Missouri	87.2
27	Indiana	86.6
28	Georgia	86.5
28	Iowa	86.5
30	Delaware	86.0
31	Nebraska	84.8
32	Wisconsin	84.6
33	Minnesota	82.7
34	Arkansas	82.5
35	North Carolina	80.8
36	Idaho	79.8
37	Wyoming	79.4
38	South Dakota	79.0
39	South Carolina	78.3
40	North Dakota	74.7
41	Mississippi	73.3
42	Maine	71.2
43	West Virginia	68.9
44	Alaska	66.1
45	Hawaii	65.1
46	Vermont	62.3
NA	Illinois**	NA
NA	Kansas**	NA
NA	Kentucky**	NA
NA	Montana**	NA
	District of Columbia	100.0

Source: Morgan Quitno Press using data from Federal Bureau of Investigation
    "Crime in the United States 2000" (Uniform Crime Reports, October 22, 2001)
*Estimated percentages for urban areas, defined by the F.B.I. as Metropolitan Statistical Areas and other cities outside such areas. National percent includes those states listed as not available. Burglary is the unlawful entry of a structure to commit a felony or theft. Attempts are included.
**Not available.

444

Burglaries in Rural Areas in 2000

National Rural Total = 180,320 Burglaries*

ALPHA ORDER

RANK	STATE	BURGLARIES	% of USA
23	Alabama	3,082	1.7%
34	Alaska	1,320	0.7%
35	Arizona	1,218	0.7%
20	Arkansas	3,754	2.1%
13	California	4,883	2.7%
38	Colorado	1,092	0.6%
28	Connecticut	1,912	1.1%
39	Delaware	730	0.4%
5	Florida	7,860	4.4%
3	Georgia	9,220	5.1%
21	Hawaii	3,719	2.1%
32	Idaho	1,483	0.8%
NA	Illinois**	NA	NA
10	Indiana	5,516	3.1%
26	Iowa	2,204	1.2%
NA	Kansas**	NA	NA
NA	Kentucky**	NA	NA
16	Louisiana	4,360	2.4%
27	Maine	1,951	1.1%
31	Maryland	1,512	0.8%
45	Massachusetts	5	0.0%
7	Michigan	7,165	4.0%
15	Minnesota	4,510	2.5%
6	Mississippi	7,190	4.0%
11	Missouri	5,338	3.0%
NA	Montana**	NA	NA
30	Nebraska	1,540	0.9%
36	Nevada	1,180	0.7%
43	New Hampshire	245	0.1%
46	New Jersey	0	0.0%
29	New Mexico	1,557	0.9%
17	New York	4,081	2.3%
1	North Carolina	18,765	10.4%
41	North Dakota	529	0.3%
9	Ohio	6,581	3.6%
22	Oklahoma	3,159	1.8%
25	Oregon	2,682	1.5%
12	Pennsylvania	4,927	2.7%
44	Rhode Island	14	0.0%
4	South Carolina	8,437	4.7%
40	South Dakota	608	0.3%
8	Tennessee	6,884	3.8%
2	Texas	9,577	5.3%
37	Utah	1,109	0.6%
33	Vermont	1,321	0.7%
19	Virginia	3,793	2.1%
14	Washington	4,570	2.5%
24	West Virginia	3,077	1.7%
18	Wisconsin	3,889	2.2%
42	Wyoming	428	0.2%

RANK ORDER

RANK	STATE	BURGLARIES	% of USA
1	North Carolina	18,765	10.4%
2	Texas	9,577	5.3%
3	Georgia	9,220	5.1%
4	South Carolina	8,437	4.7%
5	Florida	7,860	4.4%
6	Mississippi	7,190	4.0%
7	Michigan	7,165	4.0%
8	Tennessee	6,884	3.8%
9	Ohio	6,581	3.6%
10	Indiana	5,516	3.1%
11	Missouri	5,338	3.0%
12	Pennsylvania	4,927	2.7%
13	California	4,883	2.7%
14	Washington	4,570	2.5%
15	Minnesota	4,510	2.5%
16	Louisiana	4,360	2.4%
17	New York	4,081	2.3%
18	Wisconsin	3,889	2.2%
19	Virginia	3,793	2.1%
20	Arkansas	3,754	2.1%
21	Hawaii	3,719	2.1%
22	Oklahoma	3,159	1.8%
23	Alabama	3,082	1.7%
24	West Virginia	3,077	1.7%
25	Oregon	2,682	1.5%
26	Iowa	2,204	1.2%
27	Maine	1,951	1.1%
28	Connecticut	1,912	1.1%
29	New Mexico	1,557	0.9%
30	Nebraska	1,540	0.9%
31	Maryland	1,512	0.8%
32	Idaho	1,483	0.8%
33	Vermont	1,321	0.7%
34	Alaska	1,320	0.7%
35	Arizona	1,218	0.7%
36	Nevada	1,180	0.7%
37	Utah	1,109	0.6%
38	Colorado	1,092	0.6%
39	Delaware	730	0.4%
40	South Dakota	608	0.3%
41	North Dakota	529	0.3%
42	Wyoming	428	0.2%
43	New Hampshire	245	0.1%
44	Rhode Island	14	0.0%
45	Massachusetts	5	0.0%
46	New Jersey	0	0.0%
NA	Illinois**	NA	NA
NA	Kansas**	NA	NA
NA	Kentucky**	NA	NA
NA	Montana**	NA	NA
	District of Columbia	0	0.0%

Source: Federal Bureau of Investigation
   "Crime in the United States 2000" (Uniform Crime Reports, October 22, 2001)
*Estimated totals for rural areas, defined by the F.B.I. as other than Metropolitan Statistical Areas and other cities outside such areas. National total includes those states listed as not available. Burglary is the unlawful entry of a structure to commit a felony or theft. Attempts are included.
**Not available.

Rural Burglary Rate in 2000

National Rural Rate = 532.3 Burglaries per 100,000 Population*

ALPHA ORDER

RANK	STATE	RATE
31	Alabama	396.3
8	Alaska	676.4
32	Arizona	387.1
28	Arkansas	443.3
6	California	763.6
39	Colorado	285.2
33	Connecticut	385.4
7	Delaware	680.8
4	Florida	898.5
13	Georgia	573.3
1	Hawaii	1,134.1
36	Idaho	353.1
NA	Illinois**	NA
21	Indiana	490.8
41	Iowa	245.7
NA	Kansas**	NA
NA	Kentucky**	NA
12	Louisiana	603.4
17	Maine	535.8
19	Maryland	515.6
44	Massachusetts	51.6
10	Michigan	626.6
20	Minnesota	498.0
9	Mississippi	631.3
29	Missouri	423.7
NA	Montana**	NA
35	Nebraska	376.7
15	Nevada	552.0
40	New Hampshire	270.8
45	New Jersey	0.0
23	New Mexico	479.5
26	New York	447.0
2	North Carolina	1,024.8
42	North Dakota	245.0
22	Ohio	480.0
24	Oklahoma	477.9
18	Oregon	523.2
25	Pennsylvania	449.5
45	Rhode Island	0.0
3	South Carolina	963.7
43	South Dakota	214.0
11	Tennessee	609.4
14	Texas	557.7
27	Utah	443.8
16	Vermont	539.9
37	Virginia	342.9
5	Washington	832.1
30	West Virginia	411.9
34	Wisconsin	381.8
38	Wyoming	320.7

RANK ORDER

RANK	STATE	RATE
1	Hawaii	1,134.1
2	North Carolina	1,024.8
3	South Carolina	963.7
4	Florida	898.5
5	Washington	832.1
6	California	763.6
7	Delaware	680.8
8	Alaska	676.4
9	Mississippi	631.3
10	Michigan	626.6
11	Tennessee	609.4
12	Louisiana	603.4
13	Georgia	573.3
14	Texas	557.7
15	Nevada	552.0
16	Vermont	539.9
17	Maine	535.8
18	Oregon	523.2
19	Maryland	515.6
20	Minnesota	498.0
21	Indiana	490.8
22	Ohio	480.0
23	New Mexico	479.5
24	Oklahoma	477.9
25	Pennsylvania	449.5
26	New York	447.0
27	Utah	443.8
28	Arkansas	443.3
29	Missouri	423.7
30	West Virginia	411.9
31	Alabama	396.3
32	Arizona	387.1
33	Connecticut	385.4
34	Wisconsin	381.8
35	Nebraska	376.7
36	Idaho	353.1
37	Virginia	342.9
38	Wyoming	320.7
39	Colorado	285.2
40	New Hampshire	270.8
41	Iowa	245.7
42	North Dakota	245.0
43	South Dakota	214.0
44	Massachusetts	51.6
45	New Jersey	0.0
45	Rhode Island	0.0
NA	Illinois**	NA
NA	Kansas**	NA
NA	Kentucky**	NA
NA	Montana**	NA
	District of Columbia	0.0

Source: Morgan Quitno Press using data from Federal Bureau of Investigation
   "Crime in the United States 2000" (Uniform Crime Reports, October 22, 2001)
*Estimated rates for rural areas, defined by the F.B.I. as other than Metropolitan Statistical Areas and other cities outside such areas. National rate includes those states listed as not available. Burglary is the unlawful entry of a structure to commit a felony or theft. Attempts are included.
**Not available.

Percent of Burglaries Occurring in Rural Areas in 2000

National Percent = 8.8% of Burglaries*

ALPHA ORDER					RANK ORDER		
RANK	**STATE**	**PERCENT**			**RANK**	**STATE**	**PERCENT**
32	Alabama	7.6			1	Vermont	37.7
3	Alaska	33.9			2	Hawaii	34.9
42	Arizona	2.3			3	Alaska	33.9
13	Arkansas	17.5			4	West Virginia	31.1
43	California	2.2			5	Maine	28.8
40	Colorado	4.0			6	Mississippi	26.7
24	Connecticut	11.0			7	North Dakota	25.3
17	Delaware	14.0			8	South Carolina	21.7
39	Florida	4.5			9	South Dakota	21.0
18	Georgia	13.5			10	Wyoming	20.6
2	Hawaii	34.9			11	Idaho	20.2
11	Idaho	20.2			12	North Carolina	19.2
NA	Illinois**	NA			13	Arkansas	17.5
20	Indiana	13.4			14	Minnesota	17.3
18	Iowa	13.5			15	Wisconsin	15.4
NA	Kansas**	NA			16	Nebraska	15.2
NA	Kentucky**	NA			17	Delaware	14.0
28	Louisiana	9.4			18	Georgia	13.5
5	Maine	28.8			18	Iowa	13.5
41	Maryland	3.8			20	Indiana	13.4
45	Massachusetts	0.0			21	Missouri	12.8
26	Michigan	10.3			22	Virginia	12.5
14	Minnesota	17.3			23	Tennessee	12.2
6	Mississippi	26.7			24	Connecticut	11.0
21	Missouri	12.8			25	Oregon	10.5
NA	Montana**	NA			26	Michigan	10.3
16	Nebraska	15.2			27	Oklahoma	10.0
35	Nevada	6.7			28	Louisiana	9.4
37	New Hampshire	4.9			29	Pennsylvania	9.1
45	New Jersey	0.0			30	Washington	8.5
34	New Mexico	7.3			31	Utah	7.7
38	New York	4.6			32	Alabama	7.6
12	North Carolina	19.2			33	Ohio	7.4
7	North Dakota	25.3			34	New Mexico	7.3
33	Ohio	7.4			35	Nevada	6.7
27	Oklahoma	10.0			36	Texas	5.1
25	Oregon	10.5			37	New Hampshire	4.9
29	Pennsylvania	9.1			38	New York	4.6
44	Rhode Island	0.2			39	Florida	4.5
8	South Carolina	21.7			40	Colorado	4.0
9	South Dakota	21.0			41	Maryland	3.8
23	Tennessee	12.2			42	Arizona	2.3
36	Texas	5.1			43	California	2.2
31	Utah	7.7			44	Rhode Island	0.2
1	Vermont	37.7			45	Massachusetts	0.0
22	Virginia	12.5			45	New Jersey	0.0
30	Washington	8.5			NA	Illinois**	NA
4	West Virginia	31.1			NA	Kansas**	NA
15	Wisconsin	15.4			NA	Kentucky**	NA
10	Wyoming	20.6			NA	Montana**	NA
						District of Columbia	0.0

Source: Morgan Quitno Press using data from Federal Bureau of Investigation
  "Crime in the United States 2000" (Uniform Crime Reports, October 22, 2001)
*Estimated percentages for rural areas, defined by the F.B.I. as other than Metropolitan Statistical Areas and other cities outside such areas. National percent includes those states listed as not available. Burglary is the unlawful entry of a structure to commit a felony or theft. Attempts are included.
**Not available.

Larcenies and Thefts in Urban Areas in 2000

National Urban Total = 6,627,289 Larcenies and Thefts*

ALPHA ORDER

RANK ORDER

RANK	STATE	THEFTS	% of USA	RANK	STATE	THEFTS	% of USA
19	Alabama	122,937	1.9%	1	California	645,492	9.7%
42	Alaska	14,454	0.2%	2	Texas	624,267	9.4%
11	Arizona	174,141	2.6%	3	Florida	503,001	7.6%
29	Arkansas	63,336	1.0%	4	New York	332,186	5.0%
1	California	645,492	9.7%	5	Ohio	278,789	4.2%
22	Colorado	108,758	1.6%	6	Georgia	217,591	3.3%
28	Connecticut	64,196	1.0%	7	Pennsylvania	216,265	3.3%
41	Delaware	19,782	0.3%	8	Michigan	213,888	3.2%
3	Florida	503,001	7.6%	9	North Carolina	210,084	3.2%
6	Georgia	217,591	3.3%	10	Washington	182,087	2.7%
35	Hawaii	32,197	0.5%	11	Arizona	174,141	2.6%
36	Idaho	24,614	0.4%	12	New Jersey	155,562	2.3%
NA	Illinois**	NA	NA	13	Missouri	151,285	2.3%
18	Indiana	132,020	2.0%	14	Tennessee	143,294	2.2%
31	Iowa	61,176	0.9%	15	Maryland	142,030	2.1%
NA	Kansas**	NA	NA	16	Virginia	136,117	2.1%
NA	Kentucky**	NA	NA	17	Louisiana	135,508	2.0%
17	Louisiana	135,508	2.0%	18	Indiana	132,020	2.0%
39	Maine	21,064	0.3%	19	Alabama	122,937	1.9%
15	Maryland	142,030	2.1%	20	Wisconsin	111,027	1.7%
25	Massachusetts	105,414	1.6%	21	Minnesota	109,615	1.7%
8	Michigan	213,888	3.2%	22	Colorado	108,758	1.6%
21	Minnesota	109,615	1.7%	23	Oregon	108,073	1.6%
30	Mississippi	61,448	0.9%	24	South Carolina	106,012	1.6%
13	Missouri	151,285	2.3%	25	Massachusetts	105,414	1.6%
NA	Montana**	NA	NA	26	Oklahoma	92,179	1.4%
33	Nebraska	45,212	0.7%	27	Utah	70,035	1.1%
34	Nevada	41,364	0.6%	28	Connecticut	64,196	1.0%
40	New Hampshire	20,444	0.3%	29	Arkansas	63,336	1.0%
12	New Jersey	155,562	2.3%	30	Mississippi	61,448	0.9%
32	New Mexico	55,444	0.8%	31	Iowa	61,176	0.9%
4	New York	332,186	5.0%	32	New Mexico	55,444	0.8%
9	North Carolina	210,084	3.2%	33	Nebraska	45,212	0.7%
46	North Dakota	9,928	0.1%	34	Nevada	41,364	0.6%
5	Ohio	278,789	4.2%	35	Hawaii	32,197	0.5%
26	Oklahoma	92,179	1.4%	36	Idaho	24,614	0.4%
23	Oregon	108,073	1.6%	37	Rhode Island	22,001	0.3%
7	Pennsylvania	216,265	3.3%	38	West Virginia	21,965	0.3%
37	Rhode Island	22,001	0.3%	39	Maine	21,064	0.3%
24	South Carolina	106,012	1.6%	40	New Hampshire	20,444	0.3%
43	South Dakota	11,474	0.2%	41	Delaware	19,782	0.3%
14	Tennessee	143,294	2.2%	42	Alaska	14,454	0.2%
2	Texas	624,267	9.4%	43	South Dakota	11,474	0.2%
27	Utah	70,035	1.1%	44	Vermont	10,970	0.2%
44	Vermont	10,970	0.2%	45	Wyoming	10,833	0.2%
16	Virginia	136,117	2.1%	46	North Dakota	9,928	0.1%
10	Washington	182,087	2.7%	NA	Illinois**	NA	NA
38	West Virginia	21,965	0.3%	NA	Kansas**	NA	NA
20	Wisconsin	111,027	1.7%	NA	Kentucky**	NA	NA
45	Wyoming	10,833	0.2%	NA	Montana**	NA	NA
					District of Columbia	21,655	0.3%

Source: Morgan Quitno Press using data from Federal Bureau of Investigation
   "Crime in the United States 2000" (Uniform Crime Reports, October 22, 2001)
*Estimated totals for urban areas, defined by the F.B.I. as Metropolitan Statistical Areas and other cities outside
such areas. National total includes those states listed as not available. Larceny and theft is the unlawful taking of
property without use of force, violence or fraud. Attempts are included. Motor vehicle thefts are excluded.
**Not available.

Urban Larceny and Theft Rate in 2000

National Urban Rate = 2,677.2 Larcenies and Thefts per 100,000 Population*

ALPHA ORDER

RANK ORDER

RANK	STATE	RATE		RANK	STATE	RATE
14	Alabama	3,350.3		1	Oregon	3,715.4
15	Alaska	3,347.4		2	New Mexico	3,710.3
5	Arizona	3,615.9		3	Hawaii	3,643.8
10	Arkansas	3,467.4		4	Louisiana	3,617.1
41	California	1,942.4		5	Arizona	3,615.9
28	Colorado	2,775.6		6	Mississippi	3,602.6
38	Connecticut	2,206.4		7	Utah	3,531.3
24	Delaware	2,924.7		8	Missouri	3,489.5
16	Florida	3,329.5		9	Nebraska	3,471.3
17	Georgia	3,307.7		10	Arkansas	3,467.4
3	Hawaii	3,643.8		11	Washington	3,406.8
26	Idaho	2,816.3		12	South Carolina	3,380.0
NA	Illinois**	NA		13	North Carolina	3,378.5
30	Indiana	2,663.5		14	Alabama	3,350.3
21	Iowa	3,014.4		15	Alaska	3,347.4
NA	Kansas**	NA		16	Florida	3,329.5
NA	Kentucky**	NA		17	Georgia	3,307.7
4	Louisiana	3,617.1		18	Oklahoma	3,304.3
36	Maine	2,312.7		19	Texas	3,262.5
25	Maryland	2,838.8		20	Tennessee	3,142.7
46	Massachusetts	1,662.8		21	Iowa	3,014.4
33	Michigan	2,431.9		22	Vermont	3,012.4
29	Minnesota	2,730.9		23	Wyoming	3,006.6
6	Mississippi	3,602.6		24	Delaware	2,924.7
8	Missouri	3,489.5		25	Maryland	2,838.8
NA	Montana**	NA		26	Idaho	2,816.3
9	Nebraska	3,471.3		27	Ohio	2,792.9
35	Nevada	2,318.0		28	Colorado	2,775.6
45	New Hampshire	1,785.0		29	Minnesota	2,730.9
43	New Jersey	1,848.8		30	Indiana	2,663.5
2	New Mexico	3,710.3		31	Wisconsin	2,555.2
44	New York	1,839.0		32	South Dakota	2,437.3
13	North Carolina	3,378.5		33	Michigan	2,431.9
34	North Dakota	2,329.0		34	North Dakota	2,329.0
27	Ohio	2,792.9		35	Nevada	2,318.0
18	Oklahoma	3,304.3		36	Maine	2,312.7
1	Oregon	3,715.4		37	Virginia	2,279.1
42	Pennsylvania	1,933.5		38	Connecticut	2,206.4
39	Rhode Island	2,098.7		39	Rhode Island	2,098.7
12	South Carolina	3,380.0		40	West Virginia	2,069.6
32	South Dakota	2,437.3		41	California	1,942.4
20	Tennessee	3,142.7		42	Pennsylvania	1,933.5
19	Texas	3,262.5		43	New Jersey	1,848.8
7	Utah	3,531.3		44	New York	1,839.0
22	Vermont	3,012.4		45	New Hampshire	1,785.0
37	Virginia	2,279.1		46	Massachusetts	1,662.8
11	Washington	3,406.8		NA	Illinois**	NA
40	West Virginia	2,069.6		NA	Kansas**	NA
31	Wisconsin	2,555.2		NA	Kentucky**	NA
23	Wyoming	3,006.6		NA	Montana**	NA

District of Columbia 3,785.4

Source: Morgan Quitno Press using data from Federal Bureau of Investigation
    "Crime in the United States 2000" (Uniform Crime Reports, October 22, 2001)
*Estimated rates for urban areas, defined by the F.B.I. as Metropolitan Statistical Areas and other cities outside such areas. National rate includes those states listed as not available. Larceny and theft is the unlawful taking of property without use of force, violence or fraud. Attempts are included. Motor vehicle thefts are excluded.
**Not available.

Percent of Larcenies and Thefts Occurring in Urban Areas in 2000

National Percent = 95.1% of Larcenies and Thefts*

RANK	STATE	PERCENT
11	Alabama	96.5
43	Alaska	85.8
5	Arizona	98.5
34	Arkansas	90.8
4	California	99.0
12	Colorado	96.4
24	Connecticut	93.7
30	Delaware	92.6
10	Florida	97.0
35	Georgia	90.5
46	Hawaii	74.4
41	Idaho	86.2
NA	Illinois**	NA
33	Indiana	91.2
21	Iowa	93.9
NA	Kansas**	NA
NA	Kentucky**	NA
21	Louisiana	93.9
38	Maine	88.1
8	Maryland	97.7
1	Massachusetts	100.0
21	Michigan	93.9
29	Minnesota	92.7
38	Mississippi	88.1
19	Missouri	94.8
NA	Montana**	NA
31	Nebraska	92.0
24	Nevada	93.7
5	New Hampshire	98.5
1	New Jersey	100.0
14	New Mexico	95.7
9	New York	97.4
36	North Carolina	90.3
37	North Dakota	89.5
18	Ohio	95.1
13	Oklahoma	95.9
20	Oregon	94.6
14	Pennsylvania	95.7
3	Rhode Island	99.8
42	South Carolina	86.1
32	South Dakota	91.4
27	Tennessee	93.0
7	Texas	97.9
17	Utah	95.4
44	Vermont	83.2
26	Virginia	93.1
16	Washington	95.5
45	West Virginia	78.1
28	Wisconsin	92.8
40	Wyoming	87.9

RANK	STATE	PERCENT
1	Massachusetts	100.0
1	New Jersey	100.0
3	Rhode Island	99.8
4	California	99.0
5	Arizona	98.5
5	New Hampshire	98.5
7	Texas	97.9
8	Maryland	97.7
9	New York	97.4
10	Florida	97.0
11	Alabama	96.5
12	Colorado	96.4
13	Oklahoma	95.9
14	New Mexico	95.7
14	Pennsylvania	95.7
16	Washington	95.5
17	Utah	95.4
18	Ohio	95.1
19	Missouri	94.8
20	Oregon	94.6
21	Iowa	93.9
21	Louisiana	93.9
21	Michigan	93.9
24	Connecticut	93.7
24	Nevada	93.7
26	Virginia	93.1
27	Tennessee	93.0
28	Wisconsin	92.8
29	Minnesota	92.7
30	Delaware	92.6
31	Nebraska	92.0
32	South Dakota	91.4
33	Indiana	91.2
34	Arkansas	90.8
35	Georgia	90.5
36	North Carolina	90.3
37	North Dakota	89.5
38	Maine	88.1
38	Mississippi	88.1
40	Wyoming	87.9
41	Idaho	86.2
42	South Carolina	86.1
43	Alaska	85.8
44	Vermont	83.2
45	West Virginia	78.1
46	Hawaii	74.4
NA	Illinois**	NA
NA	Kansas**	NA
NA	Kentucky**	NA
NA	Montana**	NA
	District of Columbia	100.0

Source: Morgan Quitno Press using data from Federal Bureau of Investigation
  "Crime in the United States 2000" (Uniform Crime Reports, October 22, 2001)
Estimated percentages for urban areas, defined by the F.B.I. as Metropolitan Statistical Areas and other cities outside such areas. National percent includes those states listed as not available. Larceny and theft is the unlawful taking of property without use of force, violence or fraud. Attempts are included. Motor vehicle thefts are excluded.
**Not available.*

Larcenies and Thefts in Rural Areas in 2000

National Rural Total = 338,688 Larcenies and Thefts*

ALPHA ORDER

RANK	STATE	THEFTS	% of USA
24	Alabama	4,462	1.3%
37	Alaska	2,384	0.7%
35	Arizona	2,564	0.8%
20	Arkansas	6,404	1.9%
21	California	6,363	1.9%
26	Colorado	4,085	1.2%
25	Connecticut	4,302	1.3%
39	Delaware	1,578	0.5%
4	Florida	15,297	4.5%
1	Georgia	22,849	6.7%
9	Hawaii	11,057	3.3%
29	Idaho	3,931	1.2%
NA	Illinois**	NA	NA
8	Indiana	12,687	3.7%
27	Iowa	3,942	1.2%
NA	Kansas**	NA	NA
NA	Kentucky**	NA	NA
13	Louisiana	8,837	2.6%
33	Maine	2,842	0.8%
32	Maryland	3,393	1.0%
45	Massachusetts	11	0.0%
6	Michigan	13,895	4.1%
15	Minnesota	8,635	2.5%
18	Mississippi	8,310	2.5%
19	Missouri	8,254	2.4%
NA	Montana**	NA	NA
30	Nebraska	3,906	1.2%
34	Nevada	2,761	0.8%
43	New Hampshire	317	0.1%
46	New Jersey	0	0.0%
36	New Mexico	2,481	0.7%
14	New York	8,715	2.6%
2	North Carolina	22,683	6.7%
41	North Dakota	1,164	0.3%
5	Ohio	14,488	4.3%
28	Oklahoma	3,937	1.2%
23	Oregon	6,157	1.8%
12	Pennsylvania	9,604	2.8%
44	Rhode Island	37	0.0%
3	South Carolina	17,082	5.0%
42	South Dakota	1,084	0.3%
10	Tennessee	10,817	3.2%
7	Texas	13,255	3.9%
31	Utah	3,403	1.0%
38	Vermont	2,214	0.7%
11	Virginia	10,041	3.0%
17	Washington	8,563	2.5%
22	West Virginia	6,174	1.8%
16	Wisconsin	8,578	2.5%
40	Wyoming	1,485	0.4%

RANK ORDER

RANK	STATE	THEFTS	% of USA
1	Georgia	22,849	6.7%
2	North Carolina	22,683	6.7%
3	South Carolina	17,082	5.0%
4	Florida	15,297	4.5%
5	Ohio	14,488	4.3%
6	Michigan	13,895	4.1%
7	Texas	13,255	3.9%
8	Indiana	12,687	3.7%
9	Hawaii	11,057	3.3%
10	Tennessee	10,817	3.2%
11	Virginia	10,041	3.0%
12	Pennsylvania	9,604	2.8%
13	Louisiana	8,837	2.6%
14	New York	8,715	2.6%
15	Minnesota	8,635	2.5%
16	Wisconsin	8,578	2.5%
17	Washington	8,563	2.5%
18	Mississippi	8,310	2.5%
19	Missouri	8,254	2.4%
20	Arkansas	6,404	1.9%
21	California	6,363	1.9%
22	West Virginia	6,174	1.8%
23	Oregon	6,157	1.8%
24	Alabama	4,462	1.3%
25	Connecticut	4,302	1.3%
26	Colorado	4,085	1.2%
27	Iowa	3,942	1.2%
28	Oklahoma	3,937	1.2%
29	Idaho	3,931	1.2%
30	Nebraska	3,906	1.2%
31	Utah	3,403	1.0%
32	Maryland	3,393	1.0%
33	Maine	2,842	0.8%
34	Nevada	2,761	0.8%
35	Arizona	2,564	0.8%
36	New Mexico	2,481	0.7%
37	Alaska	2,384	0.7%
38	Vermont	2,214	0.7%
39	Delaware	1,578	0.5%
40	Wyoming	1,485	0.4%
41	North Dakota	1,164	0.3%
42	South Dakota	1,084	0.3%
43	New Hampshire	317	0.1%
44	Rhode Island	37	0.0%
45	Massachusetts	11	0.0%
46	New Jersey	0	0.0%
NA	Illinois**	NA	NA
NA	Kansas**	NA	NA
NA	Kentucky**	NA	NA
NA	Montana**	NA	NA
	District of Columbia	0	0.0%

Source: Federal Bureau of Investigation
   "Crime in the United States 2000" (Uniform Crime Reports, October 22, 2001)
*Estimated totals for rural areas, defined by the F.B.I. as other than Metropolitan Statistical Areas and other cities outside such areas. National total includes those states listed as not available. Larceny and theft is the unlawful taking of property without use of force, violence or fraud. Attempts are included. Motor vehicle thefts are excluded.
**Not available.

Rural Larceny and Theft Rate in 2000

National Rural Rate = 999.7 Larcenies and Thefts per 100,000 Population*

RANK	STATE	RATE
39	Alabama	573.8
11	Alaska	1,221.7
31	Arizona	814.9
35	Arkansas	756.3
19	California	995.0
17	Colorado	1,066.8
28	Connecticut	867.2
5	Delaware	1,471.7
3	Florida	1,748.7
6	Georgia	1,420.8
1	Hawaii	3,371.9
24	Idaho	936.0
NA	Illinois**	NA
15	Indiana	1,129.0
41	Iowa	439.5
NA	Kansas**	NA
NA	Kentucky**	NA
10	Louisiana	1,222.9
32	Maine	780.5
14	Maryland	1,157.0
44	Massachusetts	113.4
12	Michigan	1,215.2
23	Minnesota	953.5
36	Mississippi	729.6
37	Missouri	655.2
NA	Montana**	NA
21	Nebraska	955.4
8	Nevada	1,291.6
43	New Hampshire	350.4
45	New Jersey	0.0
34	New Mexico	764.0
22	New York	954.6
9	North Carolina	1,238.8
40	North Dakota	539.1
18	Ohio	1,056.7
38	Oklahoma	595.6
13	Oregon	1,201.1
27	Pennsylvania	876.2
45	Rhode Island	0.0
2	South Carolina	1,951.1
42	South Dakota	381.6
20	Tennessee	957.5
33	Texas	771.8
7	Utah	1,361.7
26	Vermont	904.9
25	Virginia	907.7
4	Washington	1,559.1
30	West Virginia	826.5
29	Wisconsin	842.2
16	Wyoming	1,112.6

RANK	STATE	RATE
1	Hawaii	3,371.9
2	South Carolina	1,951.1
3	Florida	1,748.7
4	Washington	1,559.1
5	Delaware	1,471.7
6	Georgia	1,420.8
7	Utah	1,361.7
8	Nevada	1,291.6
9	North Carolina	1,238.8
10	Louisiana	1,222.9
11	Alaska	1,221.7
12	Michigan	1,215.2
13	Oregon	1,201.1
14	Maryland	1,157.0
15	Indiana	1,129.0
16	Wyoming	1,112.6
17	Colorado	1,066.8
18	Ohio	1,056.7
19	California	995.0
20	Tennessee	957.5
21	Nebraska	955.4
22	New York	954.6
23	Minnesota	953.5
24	Idaho	936.0
25	Virginia	907.7
26	Vermont	904.9
27	Pennsylvania	876.2
28	Connecticut	867.2
29	Wisconsin	842.2
30	West Virginia	826.5
31	Arizona	814.9
32	Maine	780.5
33	Texas	771.8
34	New Mexico	764.0
35	Arkansas	756.3
36	Mississippi	729.6
37	Missouri	655.2
38	Oklahoma	595.6
39	Alabama	573.8
40	North Dakota	539.1
41	Iowa	439.5
42	South Dakota	381.6
43	New Hampshire	350.4
44	Massachusetts	113.4
45	New Jersey	0.0
45	Rhode Island	0.0
NA	Illinois**	NA
NA	Kansas**	NA
NA	Kentucky**	NA
NA	Montana**	NA

District of Columbia   0.0

Source: Morgan Quitno Press using data from Federal Bureau of Investigation
"Crime in the United States 2000" (Uniform Crime Reports, October 22, 2001)
*Estimated rates for rural areas, defined by the F.B.I. as other than Metropolitan Statistical Areas and other cities outside such areas. National rate includes those states listed as not available. Larceny and theft is the unlawful taking of property without use of force, violence or fraud. Attempts are included. Motor vehicle thefts are excluded.
**Not available.

Percent of Larcenies and Thefts Occurring in Rural Areas in 2000

National Percent = 4.9% of Larcenies and Thefts*

RANK	STATE	PERCENT
36	Alabama	3.5
4	Alaska	14.2
41	Arizona	1.5
13	Arkansas	9.2
43	California	1.0
35	Colorado	3.6
22	Connecticut	6.3
17	Delaware	7.4
37	Florida	3.0
12	Georgia	9.5
1	Hawaii	25.6
6	Idaho	13.8
NA	Illinois**	NA
14	Indiana	8.8
24	Iowa	6.1
NA	Kansas**	NA
NA	Kentucky**	NA
24	Louisiana	6.1
8	Maine	11.9
39	Maryland	2.3
45	Massachusetts	0.0
24	Michigan	6.1
18	Minnesota	7.3
8	Mississippi	11.9
28	Missouri	5.2
NA	Montana**	NA
16	Nebraska	8.0
22	Nevada	6.3
41	New Hampshire	1.5
45	New Jersey	0.0
32	New Mexico	4.3
38	New York	2.6
11	North Carolina	9.7
10	North Dakota	10.5
29	Ohio	4.9
34	Oklahoma	4.1
27	Oregon	5.4
32	Pennsylvania	4.3
44	Rhode Island	0.2
5	South Carolina	13.9
15	South Dakota	8.6
20	Tennessee	7.0
40	Texas	2.1
30	Utah	4.6
3	Vermont	16.8
21	Virginia	6.9
31	Washington	4.5
2	West Virginia	21.9
19	Wisconsin	7.2
7	Wyoming	12.1

RANK	STATE	PERCENT
1	Hawaii	25.6
2	West Virginia	21.9
3	Vermont	16.8
4	Alaska	14.2
5	South Carolina	13.9
6	Idaho	13.8
7	Wyoming	12.1
8	Maine	11.9
8	Mississippi	11.9
10	North Dakota	10.5
11	North Carolina	9.7
12	Georgia	9.5
13	Arkansas	9.2
14	Indiana	8.8
15	South Dakota	8.6
16	Nebraska	8.0
17	Delaware	7.4
18	Minnesota	7.3
19	Wisconsin	7.2
20	Tennessee	7.0
21	Virginia	6.9
22	Connecticut	6.3
22	Nevada	6.3
24	Iowa	6.1
24	Louisiana	6.1
24	Michigan	6.1
27	Oregon	5.4
28	Missouri	5.2
29	Ohio	4.9
30	Utah	4.6
31	Washington	4.5
32	New Mexico	4.3
32	Pennsylvania	4.3
34	Oklahoma	4.1
35	Colorado	3.6
36	Alabama	3.5
37	Florida	3.0
38	New York	2.6
39	Maryland	2.3
40	Texas	2.1
41	Arizona	1.5
41	New Hampshire	1.5
43	California	1.0
44	Rhode Island	0.2
45	Massachusetts	0.0
45	New Jersey	0.0
NA	Illinois**	NA
NA	Kansas**	NA
NA	Kentucky**	NA
NA	Montana**	NA
	District of Columbia	0.0

Source: Morgan Quitno Press using data from Federal Bureau of Investigation
 "Crime in the United States 2000" (Uniform Crime Reports, October 22, 2001)
*Estimated percentages for rural areas, defined by the F.B.I. as other than Metropolitan Statistical Areas and other cities outside such areas. National percent includes those states listed as not available. Larceny and theft is the unlawful taking of property without use of force, violence or fraud. Attempts are included. Motor vehicle thefts are excluded. **Not available.

Motor Vehicle Thefts in Urban Areas in 2000

National Urban Total = 1,124,124 Motor Vehicle Thefts*

ALPHA ORDER

RANK	STATE	THEFTS	% of USA
27	Alabama	12,064	1.1%
40	Alaska	1,853	0.2%
6	Arizona	42,735	3.8%
31	Arkansas	5,990	0.5%
1	California	180,776	16.1%
20	Colorado	16,612	1.5%
25	Connecticut	12,474	1.1%
37	Delaware	3,053	0.3%
3	Florida	87,530	7.8%
8	Georgia	36,036	3.2%
33	Hawaii	5,214	0.5%
41	Idaho	1,637	0.1%
NA	Illinois**	NA	NA
18	Indiana	19,252	1.7%
35	Iowa	4,902	0.4%
NA	Kansas**	NA	NA
NA	Kentucky**	NA	NA
17	Louisiana	20,625	1.8%
42	Maine	995	0.1%
12	Maryland	28,315	2.5%
13	Massachusetts	25,871	2.3%
4	Michigan	54,349	4.8%
26	Minnesota	12,240	1.1%
32	Mississippi	5,758	0.5%
15	Missouri	23,886	2.1%
NA	Montana**	NA	NA
34	Nebraska	4,951	0.4%
23	Nevada	12,889	1.1%
39	New Hampshire	2,116	0.2%
10	New Jersey	34,151	3.0%
29	New Mexico	7,109	0.6%
5	New York	53,783	4.8%
16	North Carolina	22,071	2.0%
43	North Dakota	839	0.1%
7	Ohio	37,540	3.3%
28	Oklahoma	11,518	1.0%
22	Oregon	13,189	1.2%
9	Pennsylvania	35,076	3.1%
36	Rhode Island	4,663	0.4%
24	South Carolina	12,685	1.1%
44	South Dakota	678	0.1%
14	Tennessee	25,519	2.3%
2	Texas	91,391	8.1%
30	Utah	6,196	0.6%
45	Vermont	549	0.0%
19	Virginia	16,633	1.5%
11	Washington	34,116	3.0%
38	West Virginia	2,371	0.2%
21	Wisconsin	13,727	1.2%
46	Wyoming	457	0.0%

RANK ORDER

RANK	STATE	THEFTS	% of USA
1	California	180,776	16.1%
2	Texas	91,391	8.1%
3	Florida	87,530	7.8%
4	Michigan	54,349	4.8%
5	New York	53,783	4.8%
6	Arizona	42,735	3.8%
7	Ohio	37,540	3.3%
8	Georgia	36,036	3.2%
9	Pennsylvania	35,076	3.1%
10	New Jersey	34,151	3.0%
11	Washington	34,116	3.0%
12	Maryland	28,315	2.5%
13	Massachusetts	25,871	2.3%
14	Tennessee	25,519	2.3%
15	Missouri	23,886	2.1%
16	North Carolina	22,071	2.0%
17	Louisiana	20,625	1.8%
18	Indiana	19,252	1.7%
19	Virginia	16,633	1.5%
20	Colorado	16,612	1.5%
21	Wisconsin	13,727	1.2%
22	Oregon	13,189	1.2%
23	Nevada	12,889	1.1%
24	South Carolina	12,685	1.1%
25	Connecticut	12,474	1.1%
26	Minnesota	12,240	1.1%
27	Alabama	12,064	1.1%
28	Oklahoma	11,518	1.0%
29	New Mexico	7,109	0.6%
30	Utah	6,196	0.6%
31	Arkansas	5,990	0.5%
32	Mississippi	5,758	0.5%
33	Hawaii	5,214	0.5%
34	Nebraska	4,951	0.4%
35	Iowa	4,902	0.4%
36	Rhode Island	4,663	0.4%
37	Delaware	3,053	0.3%
38	West Virginia	2,371	0.2%
39	New Hampshire	2,116	0.2%
40	Alaska	1,853	0.2%
41	Idaho	1,637	0.1%
42	Maine	995	0.1%
43	North Dakota	839	0.1%
44	South Dakota	678	0.1%
45	Vermont	549	0.0%
46	Wyoming	457	0.0%
NA	Illinois**	NA	NA
NA	Kansas**	NA	NA
NA	Kentucky**	NA	NA
NA	Montana**	NA	NA
	District of Columbia	6,600	0.6%

*Source: Morgan Quitno Press using data from Federal Bureau of Investigation
"Crime in the United States 2000" (Uniform Crime Reports, October 22, 2001)
*Estimated totals for urban areas, defined by the F.B.I. as Metropolitan Statistical Areas and other cities outside such areas. National total includes those states listed as not available. Motor vehicle theft includes the theft or attempted theft of a self-propelled vehicle. Excludes motorboats, construction equipment, airplanes and farming equipment. **Not available.*

Urban Motor Vehicle Theft Rate in 2000

National Urban Rate = 454.1 Motor Vehicle Thefts per 100,000 Population*

ALPHA ORDER

RANK	STATE	RATE
30	Alabama	328.8
18	Alaska	429.1
1	Arizona	887.4
31	Arkansas	327.9
12	California	544.0
20	Colorado	424.0
19	Connecticut	428.7
16	Delaware	451.4
6	Florida	579.4
11	Georgia	547.8
5	Hawaii	590.1
41	Idaho	187.3
NA	Illinois**	NA
25	Indiana	388.4
38	Iowa	241.5
NA	Kansas**	NA
NA	Kentucky**	NA
10	Louisiana	550.5
46	Maine	109.2
7	Maryland	565.9
22	Massachusetts	408.1
4	Michigan	618.0
35	Minnesota	304.9
29	Mississippi	337.6
9	Missouri	550.9
NA	Montana**	NA
26	Nebraska	380.1
2	Nevada	722.3
42	New Hampshire	184.8
23	New Jersey	405.9
14	New Mexico	475.7
36	New York	297.7
28	North Carolina	354.9
40	North Dakota	196.8
27	Ohio	376.1
21	Oklahoma	412.9
15	Oregon	453.4
33	Pennsylvania	313.6
17	Rhode Island	444.8
24	South Carolina	404.4
44	South Dakota	144.0
8	Tennessee	559.7
13	Texas	477.6
34	Utah	312.4
43	Vermont	150.8
37	Virginia	278.5
3	Washington	638.3
39	West Virginia	223.4
32	Wisconsin	315.9
45	Wyoming	126.8

RANK ORDER

RANK	STATE	RATE
1	Arizona	887.4
2	Nevada	722.3
3	Washington	638.3
4	Michigan	618.0
5	Hawaii	590.1
6	Florida	579.4
7	Maryland	565.9
8	Tennessee	559.7
9	Missouri	550.9
10	Louisiana	550.5
11	Georgia	547.8
12	California	544.0
13	Texas	477.6
14	New Mexico	475.7
15	Oregon	453.4
16	Delaware	451.4
17	Rhode Island	444.8
18	Alaska	429.1
19	Connecticut	428.7
20	Colorado	424.0
21	Oklahoma	412.9
22	Massachusetts	408.1
23	New Jersey	405.9
24	South Carolina	404.4
25	Indiana	388.4
26	Nebraska	380.1
27	Ohio	376.1
28	North Carolina	354.9
29	Mississippi	337.6
30	Alabama	328.8
31	Arkansas	327.9
32	Wisconsin	315.9
33	Pennsylvania	313.6
34	Utah	312.4
35	Minnesota	304.9
36	New York	297.7
37	Virginia	278.5
38	Iowa	241.5
39	West Virginia	223.4
40	North Dakota	196.8
41	Idaho	187.3
42	New Hampshire	184.8
43	Vermont	150.8
44	South Dakota	144.0
45	Wyoming	126.8
46	Maine	109.2
NA	Illinois**	NA
NA	Kansas**	NA
NA	Kentucky**	NA
NA	Montana**	NA

District of Columbia   1,153.7

Source: Morgan Quitno Press using data from Federal Bureau of Investigation
    "Crime in the United States 2000" (Uniform Crime Reports, October 22, 2001)
*Estimated rates for urban areas, defined by the F.B.I. as Metropolitan Statistical Areas and other cities outside such areas. National rate includes those states listed as not available. Motor vehicle theft includes the theft or attempted theft of a self-propelled vehicle. Excludes motorboats, construction equipment, airplanes and farming equipment. **Not available.

Percent of Motor Vehicle Thefts Occurring in Urban Areas in 2000

National Percent = 96.4% of Motor Vehicle Thefts*

ALPHA ORDER

RANK	STATE	PERCENT
25	Alabama	94.2
42	Alaska	78.9
7	Arizona	98.9
35	Arkansas	86.4
4	California	99.3
11	Colorado	97.9
22	Connecticut	95.2
16	Delaware	96.9
9	Florida	98.1
29	Georgia	93.1
36	Hawaii	85.3
43	Idaho	78.5
NA	Illinois**	NA
31	Indiana	91.3
32	Iowa	91.2
NA	Kansas**	NA
NA	Kentucky**	NA
15	Louisiana	97.0
44	Maine	75.3
6	Maryland	99.1
1	Massachusetts	100.0
13	Michigan	97.5
33	Minnesota	91.1
40	Mississippi	82.6
18	Missouri	96.7
NA	Montana**	NA
23	Nebraska	94.7
11	Nevada	97.9
8	New Hampshire	98.5
1	New Jersey	100.0
17	New Mexico	96.8
5	New York	99.2
34	North Carolina	87.4
37	North Dakota	85.1
20	Ohio	96.2
28	Oklahoma	93.3
23	Oregon	94.7
19	Pennsylvania	96.6
1	Rhode Island	100.0
39	South Carolina	83.4
38	South Dakota	85.0
30	Tennessee	92.7
9	Texas	98.1
21	Utah	95.9
46	Vermont	67.9
27	Virginia	93.4
14	Washington	97.4
45	West Virginia	71.5
26	Wisconsin	93.8
41	Wyoming	79.8

RANK ORDER

RANK	STATE	PERCENT
1	Massachusetts	100.0
1	New Jersey	100.0
1	Rhode Island	100.0
4	California	99.3
5	New York	99.2
6	Maryland	99.1
7	Arizona	98.9
8	New Hampshire	98.5
9	Florida	98.1
9	Texas	98.1
11	Colorado	97.9
11	Nevada	97.9
13	Michigan	97.5
14	Washington	97.4
15	Louisiana	97.0
16	Delaware	96.9
17	New Mexico	96.8
18	Missouri	96.7
19	Pennsylvania	96.6
20	Ohio	96.2
21	Utah	95.9
22	Connecticut	95.2
23	Nebraska	94.7
23	Oregon	94.7
25	Alabama	94.2
26	Wisconsin	93.8
27	Virginia	93.4
28	Oklahoma	93.3
29	Georgia	93.1
30	Tennessee	92.7
31	Indiana	91.3
32	Iowa	91.2
33	Minnesota	91.1
34	North Carolina	87.4
35	Arkansas	86.4
36	Hawaii	85.3
37	North Dakota	85.1
38	South Dakota	85.0
39	South Carolina	83.4
40	Mississippi	82.6
41	Wyoming	79.8
42	Alaska	78.9
43	Idaho	78.5
44	Maine	75.3
45	West Virginia	71.5
46	Vermont	67.9
NA	Illinois**	NA
NA	Kansas**	NA
NA	Kentucky**	NA
NA	Montana**	NA
	District of Columbia	100.0

Source: Morgan Quitno Press using data from Federal Bureau of Investigation
  "Crime in the United States 2000" (Uniform Crime Reports, October 22, 2001)
*Estimated percentages for urban areas, defined by the F.B.I. as Metropolitan Statistical Areas and other cities outside such areas. National percent includes those states listed as not available. Motor vehicle theft includes the theft or attempted theft of a self-propelled vehicle. Excludes motorboats, construction equipment, airplanes and farming equipment. **Not available.

Motor Vehicle Thefts in Rural Areas in 2000

National Rural Total = 41,435 Motor Vehicle Thefts*

ALPHA ORDER				
RANK	STATE		THEFTS	% of USA
22	Alabama		745	1.8%
26	Alaska		497	1.2%
28	Arizona		469	1.1%
16	Arkansas		942	2.3%
10	California		1,259	3.0%
31	Colorado		349	0.8%
25	Connecticut		625	1.5%
42	Delaware		98	0.2%
7	Florida		1,651	4.0%
2	Georgia		2,666	6.4%
19	Hawaii		900	2.2%
29	Idaho		449	1.1%
NA	Illinois**		NA	NA
5	Indiana		1,838	4.4%
27	Iowa		472	1.1%
NA	Kansas**		NA	NA
NA	Kentucky**		NA	NA
24	Louisiana		645	1.6%
32	Maine		327	0.8%
37	Maryland		258	0.6%
44	Massachusetts		5	0.0%
9	Michigan		1,375	3.3%
13	Minnesota		1,192	2.9%
12	Mississippi		1,210	2.9%
21	Missouri		809	2.0%
NA	Montana**		NA	NA
34	Nebraska		279	0.7%
33	Nevada		283	0.7%
43	New Hampshire		32	0.1%
46	New Jersey		0	0.0%
38	New Mexico		232	0.6%
30	New York		448	1.1%
1	North Carolina		3,195	7.7%
39	North Dakota		147	0.4%
8	Ohio		1,486	3.6%
20	Oklahoma		830	2.0%
23	Oregon		743	1.8%
11	Pennsylvania		1,249	3.0%
45	Rhode Island		2	0.0%
3	South Carolina		2,522	6.1%
40	South Dakota		120	0.3%
4	Tennessee		2,011	4.9%
6	Texas		1,770	4.3%
35	Utah		265	0.6%
36	Vermont		260	0.6%
14	Virginia		1,180	2.8%
18	Washington		902	2.2%
15	West Virginia		944	2.3%
17	Wisconsin		909	2.2%
41	Wyoming		116	0.3%

RANK ORDER				
RANK	STATE		THEFTS	% of USA
1	North Carolina		3,195	7.7%
2	Georgia		2,666	6.4%
3	South Carolina		2,522	6.1%
4	Tennessee		2,011	4.9%
5	Indiana		1,838	4.4%
6	Texas		1,770	4.3%
7	Florida		1,651	4.0%
8	Ohio		1,486	3.6%
9	Michigan		1,375	3.3%
10	California		1,259	3.0%
11	Pennsylvania		1,249	3.0%
12	Mississippi		1,210	2.9%
13	Minnesota		1,192	2.9%
14	Virginia		1,180	2.8%
15	West Virginia		944	2.3%
16	Arkansas		942	2.3%
17	Wisconsin		909	2.2%
18	Washington		902	2.2%
19	Hawaii		900	2.2%
20	Oklahoma		830	2.0%
21	Missouri		809	2.0%
22	Alabama		745	1.8%
23	Oregon		743	1.8%
24	Louisiana		645	1.6%
25	Connecticut		625	1.5%
26	Alaska		497	1.2%
27	Iowa		472	1.1%
28	Arizona		469	1.1%
29	Idaho		449	1.1%
30	New York		448	1.1%
31	Colorado		349	0.8%
32	Maine		327	0.8%
33	Nevada		283	0.7%
34	Nebraska		279	0.7%
35	Utah		265	0.6%
36	Vermont		260	0.6%
37	Maryland		258	0.6%
38	New Mexico		232	0.6%
39	North Dakota		147	0.4%
40	South Dakota		120	0.3%
41	Wyoming		116	0.3%
42	Delaware		98	0.2%
43	New Hampshire		32	0.1%
44	Massachusetts		5	0.0%
45	Rhode Island		2	0.0%
46	New Jersey		0	0.0%
NA	Illinois**		NA	NA
NA	Kansas**		NA	NA
NA	Kentucky**		NA	NA
NA	Montana**		NA	NA
	District of Columbia		0	0.0%

Source: Federal Bureau of Investigation
    "Crime in the United States 2000" (Uniform Crime Reports, October 22, 2001)
*Estimated totals for rural areas, defined by the F.B.I. as other than Metropolitan Statistical Areas and other cities outside such areas. National total includes those states listed as not available. Motor vehicle theft includes the theft or attempted theft of a self-propelled vehicle. Excludes motorboats, construction equipment, airplanes and farming equipment. **Not available.*

Rural Motor Vehicle Theft Rate in 2000

National Rural Rate = 122.3 Motor Vehicle Thefts per 100,000 Population*

ALPHA ORDER

RANK	STATE	RATE
28	Alabama	95.8
3	Alaska	254.7
11	Arizona	149.1
20	Arkansas	111.2
4	California	196.9
30	Colorado	91.1
16	Connecticut	126.0
29	Delaware	91.4
5	Florida	188.7
8	Georgia	165.8
2	Hawaii	274.5
22	Idaho	106.9
NA	Illinois**	NA
10	Indiana	163.6
40	Iowa	52.6
NA	Kansas**	NA
NA	Kentucky**	NA
32	Louisiana	89.3
31	Maine	89.8
34	Maryland	88.0
41	Massachusetts	51.6
18	Michigan	120.2
14	Minnesota	131.6
25	Mississippi	106.2
39	Missouri	64.2
NA	Montana**	NA
37	Nebraska	68.2
13	Nevada	132.4
44	New Hampshire	35.4
45	New Jersey	0.0
36	New Mexico	71.4
42	New York	49.1
7	North Carolina	174.5
38	North Dakota	68.1
21	Ohio	108.4
17	Oklahoma	125.6
12	Oregon	144.9
19	Pennsylvania	114.0
45	Rhode Island	0.0
1	South Carolina	288.1
43	South Dakota	42.2
6	Tennessee	178.0
27	Texas	103.1
26	Utah	106.0
24	Vermont	106.3
23	Virginia	106.7
9	Washington	164.2
15	West Virginia	126.4
33	Wisconsin	89.2
35	Wyoming	86.9

RANK ORDER

RANK	STATE	RATE
1	South Carolina	288.1
2	Hawaii	274.5
3	Alaska	254.7
4	California	196.9
5	Florida	188.7
6	Tennessee	178.0
7	North Carolina	174.5
8	Georgia	165.8
9	Washington	164.2
10	Indiana	163.6
11	Arizona	149.1
12	Oregon	144.9
13	Nevada	132.4
14	Minnesota	131.6
15	West Virginia	126.4
16	Connecticut	126.0
17	Oklahoma	125.6
18	Michigan	120.2
19	Pennsylvania	114.0
20	Arkansas	111.2
21	Ohio	108.4
22	Idaho	106.9
23	Virginia	106.7
24	Vermont	106.3
25	Mississippi	106.2
26	Utah	106.0
27	Texas	103.1
28	Alabama	95.8
29	Delaware	91.4
30	Colorado	91.1
31	Maine	89.8
32	Louisiana	89.3
33	Wisconsin	89.2
34	Maryland	88.0
35	Wyoming	86.9
36	New Mexico	71.4
37	Nebraska	68.2
38	North Dakota	68.1
39	Missouri	64.2
40	Iowa	52.6
41	Massachusetts	51.6
42	New York	49.1
43	South Dakota	42.2
44	New Hampshire	35.4
45	New Jersey	0.0
45	Rhode Island	0.0
NA	Illinois**	NA
NA	Kansas**	NA
NA	Kentucky**	NA
NA	Montana**	NA
	District of Columbia	0.0

Source: Morgan Quitno Press using data from Federal Bureau of Investigation
   "Crime in the United States 2000" (Uniform Crime Reports, October 22, 2001)
*Estimated rates for rural areas, defined by the F.B.I. as other than Metropolitan Statistical Areas and other cities outside such areas. National rate includes those states listed as not available. Motor vehicle theft includes the theft or attempted theft of a self-propelled vehicle. Excludes motorboats, construction equipment, airplanes and farming equipment. **Not available.

Percent of Motor Vehicle Thefts Occurring in Rural Areas in 2000

National Percent = 3.6% of Motor Vehicle Thefts*

ALPHA ORDER

RANK	STATE	PERCENT
22	Alabama	5.8
5	Alaska	21.1
40	Arizona	1.1
12	Arkansas	13.6
43	California	0.7
35	Colorado	2.1
25	Connecticut	4.8
31	Delaware	3.1
37	Florida	1.9
18	Georgia	6.9
11	Hawaii	14.7
4	Idaho	21.5
NA	Illinois**	NA
16	Indiana	8.7
15	Iowa	8.8
NA	Kansas**	NA
NA	Kentucky**	NA
32	Louisiana	3.0
3	Maine	24.7
41	Maryland	0.9
44	Massachusetts	0.0
34	Michigan	2.5
14	Minnesota	8.9
7	Mississippi	17.4
29	Missouri	3.3
NA	Montana**	NA
23	Nebraska	5.3
35	Nevada	2.1
39	New Hampshire	1.5
44	New Jersey	0.0
30	New Mexico	3.2
42	New York	0.8
13	North Carolina	12.6
10	North Dakota	14.9
27	Ohio	3.8
19	Oklahoma	6.7
23	Oregon	5.3
28	Pennsylvania	3.4
44	Rhode Island	0.0
8	South Carolina	16.6
9	South Dakota	15.0
17	Tennessee	7.3
37	Texas	1.9
26	Utah	4.1
1	Vermont	32.1
20	Virginia	6.6
33	Washington	2.6
2	West Virginia	28.5
21	Wisconsin	6.2
6	Wyoming	20.2

RANK ORDER

RANK	STATE	PERCENT
1	Vermont	32.1
2	West Virginia	28.5
3	Maine	24.7
4	Idaho	21.5
5	Alaska	21.1
6	Wyoming	20.2
7	Mississippi	17.4
8	South Carolina	16.6
9	South Dakota	15.0
10	North Dakota	14.9
11	Hawaii	14.7
12	Arkansas	13.6
13	North Carolina	12.6
14	Minnesota	8.9
15	Iowa	8.8
16	Indiana	8.7
17	Tennessee	7.3
18	Georgia	6.9
19	Oklahoma	6.7
20	Virginia	6.6
21	Wisconsin	6.2
22	Alabama	5.8
23	Nebraska	5.3
23	Oregon	5.3
25	Connecticut	4.8
26	Utah	4.1
27	Ohio	3.8
28	Pennsylvania	3.4
29	Missouri	3.3
30	New Mexico	3.2
31	Delaware	3.1
32	Louisiana	3.0
33	Washington	2.6
34	Michigan	2.5
35	Colorado	2.1
35	Nevada	2.1
37	Florida	1.9
37	Texas	1.9
39	New Hampshire	1.5
40	Arizona	1.1
41	Maryland	0.9
42	New York	0.8
43	California	0.7
44	Massachusetts	0.0
44	New Jersey	0.0
44	Rhode Island	0.0
NA	Illinois**	NA
NA	Kansas**	NA
NA	Kentucky**	NA
NA	Montana**	NA

| | District of Columbia | 0.0 |

Source: Morgan Quitno Press using data from Federal Bureau of Investigation
   "Crime in the United States 2000" (Uniform Crime Reports, October 22, 2001)
*Estimated percentages for rural areas, defined by the F.B.I. as other than Metropolitan Statistical Areas and other cities outside such areas. National percent includes those states listed as not available. Motor vehicle theft includes the theft or attempted theft of a self-propelled vehicle. Excludes motorboats, construction equipment, airplanes and farming equipment. **Not available.

Crimes Reported at Universities and Colleges in 2000

National Total = 95,500 Reported Crimes*

ALPHA ORDER

RANK	STATE	CRIMES	% of USA
22	Alabama	1,432	1.5%
38	Alaska	164	0.2%
10	Arizona	2,916	3.1%
29	Arkansas	993	1.0%
1	California	12,798	13.4%
16	Colorado	2,088	2.2%
24	Connecticut	1,271	1.3%
34	Delaware	591	0.6%
8	Florida	4,115	4.3%
4	Georgia	4,909	5.1%
NA	Hawaii**	NA	NA
NA	Idaho**	NA	NA
NA	Illinois**	NA	NA
15	Indiana	2,634	2.8%
30	Iowa	879	0.9%
NA	Kansas**	NA	NA
NA	Kentucky**	NA	NA
12	Louisiana	2,852	3.0%
37	Maine	331	0.3%
14	Maryland	2,658	2.8%
9	Massachusetts	3,567	3.7%
3	Michigan	5,204	5.4%
31	Minnesota	873	0.9%
27	Mississippi	1,102	1.2%
28	Missouri	1,091	1.1%
NA	Montana**	NA	NA
32	Nebraska	604	0.6%
33	Nevada	598	0.6%
NA	New Hampshire**	NA	NA
13	New Jersey	2,702	2.8%
23	New Mexico	1,330	1.4%
6	New York	4,616	4.8%
7	North Carolina	4,371	4.6%
36	North Dakota	355	0.4%
5	Ohio	4,864	5.1%
25	Oklahoma	1,231	1.3%
NA	Oregon**	NA	NA
20	Pennsylvania	1,678	1.8%
35	Rhode Island	581	0.6%
26	South Carolina	1,209	1.3%
NA	South Dakota**	NA	NA
11	Tennessee	2,911	3.0%
2	Texas	8,872	9.3%
21	Utah	1,510	1.6%
NA	Vermont**	NA	NA
17	Virginia	1,926	2.0%
18	Washington	1,745	1.8%
40	West Virginia	96	0.1%
19	Wisconsin	1,696	1.8%
39	Wyoming	137	0.1%

RANK ORDER

RANK	STATE	CRIMES	% of USA
1	California	12,798	13.4%
2	Texas	8,872	9.3%
3	Michigan	5,204	5.4%
4	Georgia	4,909	5.1%
5	Ohio	4,864	5.1%
6	New York	4,616	4.8%
7	North Carolina	4,371	4.6%
8	Florida	4,115	4.3%
9	Massachusetts	3,567	3.7%
10	Arizona	2,916	3.1%
11	Tennessee	2,911	3.0%
12	Louisiana	2,852	3.0%
13	New Jersey	2,702	2.8%
14	Maryland	2,658	2.8%
15	Indiana	2,634	2.8%
16	Colorado	2,088	2.2%
17	Virginia	1,926	2.0%
18	Washington	1,745	1.8%
19	Wisconsin	1,696	1.8%
20	Pennsylvania	1,678	1.8%
21	Utah	1,510	1.6%
22	Alabama	1,432	1.5%
23	New Mexico	1,330	1.4%
24	Connecticut	1,271	1.3%
25	Oklahoma	1,231	1.3%
26	South Carolina	1,209	1.3%
27	Mississippi	1,102	1.2%
28	Missouri	1,091	1.1%
29	Arkansas	993	1.0%
30	Iowa	879	0.9%
31	Minnesota	873	0.9%
32	Nebraska	604	0.6%
33	Nevada	598	0.6%
34	Delaware	591	0.6%
35	Rhode Island	581	0.6%
36	North Dakota	355	0.4%
37	Maine	331	0.3%
38	Alaska	164	0.2%
39	Wyoming	137	0.1%
40	West Virginia	96	0.1%
NA	Hawaii**	NA	NA
NA	Idaho**	NA	NA
NA	Illinois**	NA	NA
NA	Kansas**	NA	NA
NA	Kentucky**	NA	NA
NA	Montana**	NA	NA
NA	New Hampshire**	NA	NA
NA	Oregon**	NA	NA
NA	South Dakota**	NA	NA
NA	Vermont**	NA	NA
	District of Columbia**	NA	NA

Source: Morgan Quitno Press using data from Federal Bureau of Investigation
 "Crime in the United States 2000" (Uniform Crime Reports, October 22, 2001)
*Includes murder, rape, robbery, aggravated assault, burglary, larceny-theft and motor vehicle theft. Total is only for states shown separately. Many states had incomplete reports.
**Not available.

Crimes Reported at Universities and Colleges as a Percent of All Crimes in 2000

National Percent = 0.91% of Crimes*

ALPHA ORDER

RANK ORDER

RANK	STATE	PERCENT
31	Alabama	0.74
33	Alaska	0.61
16	Arizona	1.04
21	Arkansas	0.96
18	California	1.01
7	Colorado	1.27
11	Connecticut	1.14
4	Delaware	1.62
38	Florida	0.44
8	Georgia	1.22
NA	Hawaii**	NA
NA	Idaho**	NA
NA	Illinois**	NA
10	Indiana	1.18
22	Iowa	0.95
NA	Kansas**	NA
NA	Kentucky**	NA
11	Louisiana	1.14
24	Maine	0.92
16	Maryland	1.04
2	Massachusetts	1.77
8	Michigan	1.22
36	Minnesota	0.51
23	Mississippi	0.93
38	Missouri	0.44
NA	Montana**	NA
25	Nebraska	0.88
32	Nevada	0.71
NA	New Hampshire**	NA
19	New Jersey	0.98
6	New Mexico	1.28
30	New York	0.77
14	North Carolina	1.10
1	North Dakota	2.34
15	Ohio	1.08
29	Oklahoma	0.78
NA	Oregon**	NA
37	Pennsylvania	0.45
3	Rhode Island	1.64
34	South Carolina	0.58
NA	South Dakota**	NA
13	Tennessee	1.13
25	Texas	0.88
5	Utah	1.42
NA	Vermont**	NA
27	Virginia	0.83
34	Washington	0.58
40	West Virginia	0.20
19	Wisconsin	0.98
27	Wyoming	0.83

RANK	STATE	PERCENT
1	North Dakota	2.34
2	Massachusetts	1.77
3	Rhode Island	1.64
4	Delaware	1.62
5	Utah	1.42
6	New Mexico	1.28
7	Colorado	1.27
8	Georgia	1.22
8	Michigan	1.22
10	Indiana	1.18
11	Connecticut	1.14
11	Louisiana	1.14
13	Tennessee	1.13
14	North Carolina	1.10
15	Ohio	1.08
16	Arizona	1.04
16	Maryland	1.04
18	California	1.01
19	New Jersey	0.98
19	Wisconsin	0.98
21	Arkansas	0.96
22	Iowa	0.95
23	Mississippi	0.93
24	Maine	0.92
25	Nebraska	0.88
25	Texas	0.88
27	Virginia	0.83
27	Wyoming	0.83
29	Oklahoma	0.78
30	New York	0.77
31	Alabama	0.74
32	Nevada	0.71
33	Alaska	0.61
34	South Carolina	0.58
34	Washington	0.58
36	Minnesota	0.51
37	Pennsylvania	0.45
38	Florida	0.44
38	Missouri	0.44
40	West Virginia	0.20
NA	Hawaii**	NA
NA	Idaho**	NA
NA	Illinois**	NA
NA	Kansas**	NA
NA	Kentucky**	NA
NA	Montana**	NA
NA	New Hampshire**	NA
NA	Oregon**	NA
NA	South Dakota**	NA
NA	Vermont**	NA
	District of Columbia**	NA

Source: Morgan Quitno Press using data from Federal Bureau of Investigation
   "Crime in the United States 2000" (Uniform Crime Reports, October 22, 2001)
*Includes murder, rape, robbery, aggravated assault, burglary, larceny-theft and motor vehicle theft. National
percent is only for states shown separately. Many states had incomplete reports.
**Not available.

Violent Crimes Reported at Universities and Colleges in 2000

National Total = 2,297 Reported Violent Crimes*

ALPHA ORDER					RANK ORDER			
RANK	STATE		CRIMES	% of USA	RANK	STATE	CRIMES	% of USA
25	Alabama		24	1.0%	1	California	293	12.8%
35	Alaska		5	0.2%	2	Texas	200	8.7%
15	Arizona		66	2.9%	3	Massachusetts	166	7.2%
27	Arkansas		21	0.9%	4	Louisiana	133	5.8%
1	California		293	12.8%	5	Florida	126	5.5%
21	Colorado		33	1.4%	6	Ohio	111	4.8%
27	Connecticut		21	0.9%	7	New York	104	4.5%
40	Delaware		0	0.0%	8	North Carolina	102	4.4%
5	Florida		126	5.5%	9	Maryland	97	4.2%
13	Georgia		75	3.3%	10	Michigan	88	3.8%
NA	Hawaii**		NA	NA	11	New Jersey	85	3.7%
NA	Idaho**		NA	NA	12	Tennessee	84	3.7%
NA	Illinois**		NA	NA	13	Georgia	75	3.3%
17	Indiana		45	2.0%	14	Virginia	67	2.9%
29	Iowa		20	0.9%	15	Arizona	66	2.9%
NA	Kansas**		NA	NA	16	Pennsylvania	48	2.1%
NA	Kentucky**		NA	NA	17	Indiana	45	2.0%
4	Louisiana		133	5.8%	18	Wisconsin	39	1.7%
36	Maine		4	0.2%	19	Oklahoma	38	1.7%
9	Maryland		97	4.2%	20	Washington	35	1.5%
3	Massachusetts		166	7.2%	21	Colorado	33	1.4%
10	Michigan		88	3.8%	22	New Mexico	30	1.3%
24	Minnesota		25	1.1%	23	Nevada	28	1.2%
30	Mississippi		14	0.6%	24	Minnesota	25	1.1%
31	Missouri		12	0.5%	25	Alabama	24	1.0%
NA	Montana**		NA	NA	26	South Carolina	22	1.0%
38	Nebraska		3	0.1%	27	Arkansas	21	0.9%
23	Nevada		28	1.2%	27	Connecticut	21	0.9%
NA	New Hampshire**		NA	NA	29	Iowa	20	0.9%
11	New Jersey		85	3.7%	30	Mississippi	14	0.6%
22	New Mexico		30	1.3%	31	Missouri	12	0.5%
7	New York		104	4.5%	31	Utah	12	0.5%
8	North Carolina		102	4.4%	33	Rhode Island	10	0.4%
34	North Dakota		6	0.3%	34	North Dakota	6	0.3%
6	Ohio		111	4.8%	35	Alaska	5	0.2%
19	Oklahoma		38	1.7%	36	Maine	4	0.2%
NA	Oregon**		NA	NA	36	West Virginia	4	0.2%
16	Pennsylvania		48	2.1%	38	Nebraska	3	0.1%
33	Rhode Island		10	0.4%	39	Wyoming	1	0.0%
26	South Carolina		22	1.0%	40	Delaware	0	0.0%
NA	South Dakota**		NA	NA	NA	Hawaii**	NA	NA
12	Tennessee		84	3.7%	NA	Idaho**	NA	NA
2	Texas		200	8.7%	NA	Illinois**	NA	NA
31	Utah		12	0.5%	NA	Kansas**	NA	NA
NA	Vermont**		NA	NA	NA	Kentucky**	NA	NA
14	Virginia		67	2.9%	NA	Montana**	NA	NA
20	Washington		35	1.5%	NA	New Hampshire**	NA	NA
36	West Virginia		4	0.2%	NA	Oregon**	NA	NA
18	Wisconsin		39	1.7%	NA	South Dakota**	NA	NA
39	Wyoming		1	0.0%	NA	Vermont**	NA	NA
						District of Columbia**	NA	NA

Source: Morgan Quitno Press using data from Federal Bureau of Investigation
   "Crime in the United States 2000" (Uniform Crime Reports, October 22, 2001)
*Includes murder, rape, robbery and aggravated assault. Total is only for states shown separately. Many states
had incomplete reports.
**Not available.

Violent Crimes Reported at Universities and Colleges
As a Percent of All Violent Crimes in 2000
National Percent = 0.18% of Violent Crimes*

ALPHA ORDER

RANK	STATE	PERCENT
31	Alabama	0.11
28	Alaska	0.14
13	Arizona	0.24
22	Arkansas	0.18
28	California	0.14
14	Colorado	0.23
21	Connecticut	0.19
40	Delaware	0.00
32	Florida	0.10
22	Georgia	0.18
NA	Hawaii**	NA
NA	Idaho**	NA
NA	Illinois**	NA
18	Indiana	0.21
10	Iowa	0.26
NA	Kansas**	NA
NA	Kentucky**	NA
3	Louisiana	0.44
7	Maine	0.29
14	Maryland	0.23
2	Massachusetts	0.55
26	Michigan	0.16
22	Minnesota	0.18
28	Mississippi	0.14
39	Missouri	0.04
NA	Montana**	NA
38	Nebraska	0.05
9	Nevada	0.27
NA	New Hampshire**	NA
10	New Jersey	0.26
16	New Mexico	0.22
32	New York	0.10
12	North Carolina	0.25
1	North Dakota	1.15
7	Ohio	0.29
16	Oklahoma	0.22
NA	Oregon**	NA
34	Pennsylvania	0.09
5	Rhode Island	0.32
36	South Carolina	0.07
NA	South Dakota**	NA
18	Tennessee	0.21
22	Texas	0.18
18	Utah	0.21
NA	Vermont**	NA
4	Virginia	0.34
26	Washington	0.16
36	West Virginia	0.07
6	Wisconsin	0.31
35	Wyoming	0.08

RANK ORDER

RANK	STATE	PERCENT
1	North Dakota	1.15
2	Massachusetts	0.55
3	Louisiana	0.44
4	Virginia	0.34
5	Rhode Island	0.32
6	Wisconsin	0.31
7	Maine	0.29
7	Ohio	0.29
9	Nevada	0.27
10	Iowa	0.26
10	New Jersey	0.26
12	North Carolina	0.25
13	Arizona	0.24
14	Colorado	0.23
14	Maryland	0.23
16	New Mexico	0.22
16	Oklahoma	0.22
18	Indiana	0.21
18	Tennessee	0.21
18	Utah	0.21
21	Connecticut	0.19
22	Arkansas	0.18
22	Georgia	0.18
22	Minnesota	0.18
22	Texas	0.18
26	Michigan	0.16
26	Washington	0.16
28	Alaska	0.14
28	California	0.14
28	Mississippi	0.14
31	Alabama	0.11
32	Florida	0.10
32	New York	0.10
34	Pennsylvania	0.09
35	Wyoming	0.08
36	South Carolina	0.07
36	West Virginia	0.07
38	Nebraska	0.05
39	Missouri	0.04
40	Delaware	0.00
NA	Hawaii**	NA
NA	Idaho**	NA
NA	Illinois**	NA
NA	Kansas**	NA
NA	Kentucky**	NA
NA	Montana**	NA
NA	New Hampshire**	NA
NA	Oregon**	NA
NA	South Dakota**	NA
NA	Vermont**	NA
	District of Columbia**	NA

Source: Morgan Quitno Press using data from Federal Bureau of Investigation
    "Crime in the United States 2000" (Uniform Crime Reports, October 22, 2001)
Includes murder, rape, robbery, aggravated assault, burglary, larceny-theft and motor vehicle theft. National percent is only for states shown separately. Many states had incomplete reports.
**Not available.*

Property Crimes Reported at Universities and Colleges in 2000

National Total = 93,203 Reported Property Crimes*

ALPHA ORDER

RANK	STATE	CRIMES	% of USA
22	Alabama	1,408	1.5%
38	Alaska	159	0.2%
10	Arizona	2,850	3.1%
29	Arkansas	972	1.0%
1	California	12,505	13.4%
16	Colorado	2,055	2.2%
24	Connecticut	1,250	1.3%
33	Delaware	591	0.6%
8	Florida	3,989	4.3%
4	Georgia	4,834	5.2%
NA	Hawaii**	NA	NA
NA	Idaho**	NA	NA
NA	Illinois**	NA	NA
14	Indiana	2,589	2.8%
30	Iowa	859	0.9%
NA	Kansas**	NA	NA
NA	Kentucky**	NA	NA
12	Louisiana	2,719	2.9%
37	Maine	327	0.4%
15	Maryland	2,561	2.7%
9	Massachusetts	3,401	3.6%
3	Michigan	5,116	5.5%
31	Minnesota	848	0.9%
27	Mississippi	1,088	1.2%
28	Missouri	1,079	1.2%
NA	Montana**	NA	NA
32	Nebraska	601	0.6%
35	Nevada	570	0.6%
NA	New Hampshire**	NA	NA
13	New Jersey	2,617	2.8%
23	New Mexico	1,300	1.4%
6	New York	4,512	4.8%
7	North Carolina	4,269	4.6%
36	North Dakota	349	0.4%
5	Ohio	4,753	5.1%
25	Oklahoma	1,193	1.3%
NA	Oregon**	NA	NA
20	Pennsylvania	1,630	1.7%
34	Rhode Island	571	0.6%
26	South Carolina	1,187	1.3%
NA	South Dakota**	NA	NA
11	Tennessee	2,827	3.0%
2	Texas	8,672	9.3%
21	Utah	1,498	1.6%
NA	Vermont**	NA	NA
17	Virginia	1,859	2.0%
18	Washington	1,710	1.8%
40	West Virginia	92	0.1%
19	Wisconsin	1,657	1.8%
39	Wyoming	136	0.1%

RANK ORDER

RANK	STATE	CRIMES	% of USA
1	California	12,505	13.4%
2	Texas	8,672	9.3%
3	Michigan	5,116	5.5%
4	Georgia	4,834	5.2%
5	Ohio	4,753	5.1%
6	New York	4,512	4.8%
7	North Carolina	4,269	4.6%
8	Florida	3,989	4.3%
9	Massachusetts	3,401	3.6%
10	Arizona	2,850	3.1%
11	Tennessee	2,827	3.0%
12	Louisiana	2,719	2.9%
13	New Jersey	2,617	2.8%
14	Indiana	2,589	2.8%
15	Maryland	2,561	2.7%
16	Colorado	2,055	2.2%
17	Virginia	1,859	2.0%
18	Washington	1,710	1.8%
19	Wisconsin	1,657	1.8%
20	Pennsylvania	1,630	1.7%
21	Utah	1,498	1.6%
22	Alabama	1,408	1.5%
23	New Mexico	1,300	1.4%
24	Connecticut	1,250	1.3%
25	Oklahoma	1,193	1.3%
26	South Carolina	1,187	1.3%
27	Mississippi	1,088	1.2%
28	Missouri	1,079	1.2%
29	Arkansas	972	1.0%
30	Iowa	859	0.9%
31	Minnesota	848	0.9%
32	Nebraska	601	0.6%
33	Delaware	591	0.6%
34	Rhode Island	571	0.6%
35	Nevada	570	0.6%
36	North Dakota	349	0.4%
37	Maine	327	0.4%
38	Alaska	159	0.2%
39	Wyoming	136	0.1%
40	West Virginia	92	0.1%
NA	Hawaii**	NA	NA
NA	Idaho**	NA	NA
NA	Illinois**	NA	NA
NA	Kansas**	NA	NA
NA	Kentucky**	NA	NA
NA	Montana**	NA	NA
NA	New Hampshire**	NA	NA
NA	Oregon**	NA	NA
NA	South Dakota**	NA	NA
NA	Vermont**	NA	NA
NA	District of Columbia**	NA	NA

Source: Morgan Quitno Press using data from Federal Bureau of Investigation
    "Crime in the United States 2000" (Uniform Crime Reports, October 22, 2001)
*Includes burglary, larceny-theft and motor vehicle theft. Total is only for states shown separately. Many states had incomplete reports.
**Not available.

Property Crimes at Universities and Colleges
As a Percent of All Property Crimes in 2000
National Percent = 1.02% of Property Crimes*

ALPHA ORDER

RANK	STATE	PERCENT
31	Alabama	0.78
33	Alaska	0.69
19	Arizona	1.05
23	Arkansas	0.99
16	California	1.18
9	Colorado	1.31
11	Connecticut	1.26
3	Delaware	1.99
38	Florida	0.51
8	Georgia	1.39
NA	Hawaii**	NA
NA	Idaho**	NA
NA	Illinois**	NA
12	Indiana	1.25
23	Iowa	0.99
NA	Kansas**	NA
NA	Kentucky**	NA
10	Louisiana	1.28
22	Maine	1.02
13	Maryland	1.20
2	Massachusetts	2.10
7	Michigan	1.45
36	Minnesota	0.54
19	Mississippi	1.05
39	Missouri	0.48
NA	Montana**	NA
27	Nebraska	0.93
32	Nevada	0.76
NA	New Hampshire**	NA
18	New Jersey	1.12
6	New Mexico	1.50
27	New York	0.93
13	North Carolina	1.20
1	North Dakota	2.46
17	Ohio	1.13
30	Oklahoma	0.85
NA	Oregon**	NA
37	Pennsylvania	0.52
4	Rhode Island	1.71
34	South Carolina	0.67
NA	South Dakota**	NA
15	Tennessee	1.19
26	Texas	0.94
5	Utah	1.59
NA	Vermont**	NA
25	Virginia	0.96
35	Washington	0.61
40	West Virginia	0.22
21	Wisconsin	1.04
29	Wyoming	0.91

RANK ORDER

RANK	STATE	PERCENT
1	North Dakota	2.46
2	Massachusetts	2.10
3	Delaware	1.99
4	Rhode Island	1.71
5	Utah	1.59
6	New Mexico	1.50
7	Michigan	1.45
8	Georgia	1.39
9	Colorado	1.31
10	Louisiana	1.28
11	Connecticut	1.26
12	Indiana	1.25
13	Maryland	1.20
13	North Carolina	1.20
15	Tennessee	1.19
16	California	1.18
17	Ohio	1.13
18	New Jersey	1.12
19	Arizona	1.05
19	Mississippi	1.05
21	Wisconsin	1.04
22	Maine	1.02
23	Arkansas	0.99
23	Iowa	0.99
25	Virginia	0.96
26	Texas	0.94
27	Nebraska	0.93
27	New York	0.93
29	Wyoming	0.91
30	Oklahoma	0.85
31	Alabama	0.78
32	Nevada	0.76
33	Alaska	0.69
34	South Carolina	0.67
35	Washington	0.61
36	Minnesota	0.54
37	Pennsylvania	0.52
38	Florida	0.51
39	Missouri	0.48
40	West Virginia	0.22
NA	Hawaii**	NA
NA	Idaho**	NA
NA	Illinois**	NA
NA	Kansas**	NA
NA	Kentucky**	NA
NA	Montana**	NA
NA	New Hampshire**	NA
NA	Oregon**	NA
NA	South Dakota**	NA
NA	Vermont**	NA
	District of Columbia**	NA

Source: Morgan Quitno Press using data from Federal Bureau of Investigation
   "Crime in the United States 2000" (Uniform Crime Reports, October 22, 2001)
*Includes burglary, larceny-theft and motor vehicle theft. Total is only for states shown separately. Many states had incomplete reports.
**Not available.

Crimes in 1996

National Total = 13,493,863 Crimes*

ALPHA ORDER

RANK ORDER

RANK	STATE	CRIMES	% of USA	RANK	STATE	CRIMES	% of USA
23	Alabama	205,962	1.5%	1	California	1,660,131	12.3%
45	Alaska	33,084	0.2%	2	Texas	1,092,002	8.1%
13	Arizona	312,927	2.3%	3	Florida	1,079,623	8.0%
33	Arkansas	117,951	0.9%	4	New York	751,456	5.6%
1	California	1,660,131	12.3%	5	Illinois	630,259	4.7%
25	Colorado	195,681	1.5%	6	Ohio	497,831	3.7%
28	Connecticut	138,414	1.0%	7	Michigan	490,971	3.6%
44	Delaware	35,488	0.3%	8	Georgia	463,952	3.4%
3	Florida	1,079,623	8.0%	9	Pennsylvania	428,756	3.2%
8	Georgia	463,952	3.4%	10	North Carolina	404,684	3.0%
37	Hawaii	77,961	0.6%	11	New Jersey	346,116	2.6%
39	Idaho	47,709	0.4%	12	Washington	326,968	2.4%
5	Illinois	630,259	4.7%	13	Arizona	312,927	2.3%
19	Indiana	262,742	1.9%	14	Maryland	307,461	2.3%
35	Iowa	104,067	0.8%	15	Louisiana	297,556	2.2%
31	Kansas	120,414	0.9%	16	Tennessee	289,904	2.1%
29	Kentucky	122,979	0.9%	17	Missouri	272,450	2.0%
15	Louisiana	297,556	2.2%	18	Virginia	264,882	2.0%
41	Maine	42,189	0.3%	19	Indiana	262,742	1.9%
14	Maryland	307,461	2.3%	20	Massachusetts	233,758	1.7%
20	Massachusetts	233,758	1.7%	21	South Carolina	229,861	1.7%
7	Michigan	490,971	3.6%	22	Minnesota	207,891	1.5%
22	Minnesota	207,891	1.5%	23	Alabama	205,962	1.5%
30	Mississippi	122,842	0.9%	24	Wisconsin	197,182	1.5%
17	Missouri	272,450	2.0%	25	Colorado	195,681	1.5%
43	Montana	39,499	0.3%	26	Oregon	192,132	1.4%
38	Nebraska	73,292	0.5%	27	Oklahoma	186,602	1.4%
36	Nevada	96,052	0.7%	28	Connecticut	138,414	1.0%
46	New Hampshire	32,809	0.2%	29	Kentucky	122,979	0.9%
11	New Jersey	346,116	2.6%	30	Mississippi	122,842	0.9%
34	New Mexico	113,097	0.8%	31	Kansas	120,414	0.9%
4	New York	751,456	5.6%	32	Utah	119,717	0.9%
10	North Carolina	404,684	3.0%	33	Arkansas	117,951	0.9%
50	North Dakota	17,189	0.1%	34	New Mexico	113,097	0.8%
6	Ohio	497,831	3.7%	35	Iowa	104,067	0.8%
27	Oklahoma	186,602	1.4%	36	Nevada	96,052	0.7%
26	Oregon	192,132	1.4%	37	Hawaii	77,961	0.6%
9	Pennsylvania	428,756	3.2%	38	Nebraska	73,292	0.5%
42	Rhode Island	39,536	0.3%	39	Idaho	47,709	0.4%
21	South Carolina	229,861	1.7%	40	West Virginia	45,346	0.3%
47	South Dakota	21,740	0.2%	41	Maine	42,189	0.3%
16	Tennessee	289,904	2.1%	42	Rhode Island	39,536	0.3%
2	Texas	1,092,002	8.1%	43	Montana	39,499	0.3%
32	Utah	119,717	0.9%	44	Delaware	35,488	0.3%
49	Vermont	17,687	0.1%	45	Alaska	33,084	0.2%
18	Virginia	264,882	2.0%	46	New Hampshire	32,809	0.2%
12	Washington	326,968	2.4%	47	South Dakota	21,740	0.2%
40	West Virginia	45,346	0.3%	48	Wyoming	20,462	0.2%
24	Wisconsin	197,182	1.5%	49	Vermont	17,687	0.1%
48	Wyoming	20,462	0.2%	50	North Dakota	17,189	0.1%
					District of Columbia	64,599	0.5%

Source: Federal Bureau of Investigation
   "Crime in the United States 1997" (Uniform Crime Reports, November 22, 1998)
*Revised figures. Includes murder, rape, robbery, aggravated assault, burglary, larceny-theft and motor vehicle theft.

Percent Change in Number of Crimes: 1996 to 2000

National Percent Change = 14.0% Decrease*

RANK	STATE	PERCENT CHANGE
4	Alabama	(1.8)
41	Alaska	(19.5)
8	Arizona	(4.4)
11	Arkansas	(6.7)
48	California	(23.7)
21	Colorado	(12.5)
44	Connecticut	(20.5)
2	Delaware	(1.1)
29	Florida	(15.7)
31	Georgia	(16.2)
39	Hawaii	(19.2)
24	Idaho	(13.6)
28	Illinois	(15.5)
23	Indiana	(13.2)
18	Iowa	(9.1)
3	Kansas	(1.6)
6	Kentucky	(2.7)
37	Louisiana	(18.6)
45	Maine	(20.8)
34	Maryland	(17.0)
36	Massachusetts	(17.8)
33	Michigan	(16.8)
35	Minnesota	(17.5)
13	Mississippi	(7.3)
12	Missouri	(7.0)
40	Montana	(19.3)
8	Nebraska	(4.4)
19	Nevada	(11.2)
NA	New Hampshire**	NA
47	New Jersey	(23.2)
19	New Mexico	(11.2)
46	New York	(21.7)
5	North Carolina	(2.2)
27	North Dakota	(14.5)
14	Ohio	(7.8)
29	Oklahoma	(15.7)
25	Oregon	(13.7)
26	Pennsylvania	(14.2)
14	Rhode Island	(7.8)
17	South Carolina	(8.9)
41	South Dakota	(19.5)
7	Tennessee	(4.0)
10	Texas	(5.4)
32	Utah	(16.5)
1	Vermont	2.8
38	Virginia	(19.1)
16	Washington	(8.0)
NA	West Virginia**	NA
22	Wisconsin	(12.7)
43	Wyoming	(20.4)

RANK	STATE	PERCENT CHANGE
1	Vermont	2.8
2	Delaware	(1.1)
3	Kansas	(1.6)
4	Alabama	(1.8)
5	North Carolina	(2.2)
6	Kentucky	(2.7)
7	Tennessee	(4.0)
8	Arizona	(4.4)
8	Nebraska	(4.4)
10	Texas	(5.4)
11	Arkansas	(6.7)
12	Missouri	(7.0)
13	Mississippi	(7.3)
14	Ohio	(7.8)
14	Rhode Island	(7.8)
16	Washington	(8.0)
17	South Carolina	(8.9)
18	Iowa	(9.1)
19	Nevada	(11.2)
19	New Mexico	(11.2)
21	Colorado	(12.5)
22	Wisconsin	(12.7)
23	Indiana	(13.2)
24	Idaho	(13.6)
25	Oregon	(13.7)
26	Pennsylvania	(14.2)
27	North Dakota	(14.5)
28	Illinois	(15.5)
29	Florida	(15.7)
29	Oklahoma	(15.7)
31	Georgia	(16.2)
32	Utah	(16.5)
33	Michigan	(16.8)
34	Maryland	(17.0)
35	Minnesota	(17.5)
36	Massachusetts	(17.8)
37	Louisiana	(18.6)
38	Virginia	(19.1)
39	Hawaii	(19.2)
40	Montana	(19.3)
41	Alaska	(19.5)
41	South Dakota	(19.5)
43	Wyoming	(20.4)
44	Connecticut	(20.5)
45	Maine	(20.8)
46	New York	(21.7)
47	New Jersey	(23.2)
48	California	(23.7)
NA	New Hampshire**	NA
NA	West Virginia**	NA

District of Columbia   (35.6)

Source: Morgan Quitno Press using data from Federal Bureau of Investigation
    "Crime in the United States" (Uniform Crime Reports, 1997 and 2000 editions)
*Includes murder, rape, robbery, aggravated assault, burglary, larceny-theft and motor vehicle theft.
**Not comparable.

Crime Rate in 1996

National Rate = 5,086.6 Crimes per 100,000 Population*

<table>
<tr><td colspan="3">ALPHA ORDER</td><td colspan="3">RANK ORDER</td></tr>
<tr><td>RANK</td><td>STATE</td><td>RATE</td><td>RANK</td><td>STATE</td><td>RATE</td></tr>
<tr><td>24</td><td>Alabama</td><td>4,820.1</td><td>1</td><td>Florida</td><td>7,497.4</td></tr>
<tr><td>16</td><td>Alaska</td><td>5,450.4</td><td>2</td><td>Arizona</td><td>7,067.0</td></tr>
<tr><td>2</td><td>Arizona</td><td>7,067.0</td><td>3</td><td>Louisiana</td><td>6,838.8</td></tr>
<tr><td>25</td><td>Arkansas</td><td>4,699.2</td><td>4</td><td>New Mexico</td><td>6,602.3</td></tr>
<tr><td>19</td><td>California</td><td>5,207.8</td><td>5</td><td>Hawaii</td><td>6,584.5</td></tr>
<tr><td>20</td><td>Colorado</td><td>5,118.5</td><td>6</td><td>Georgia</td><td>6,309.7</td></tr>
<tr><td>35</td><td>Connecticut</td><td>4,227.7</td><td>7</td><td>South Carolina</td><td>6,214.1</td></tr>
<tr><td>23</td><td>Delaware</td><td>4,894.9</td><td>8</td><td>Maryland</td><td>6,061.9</td></tr>
<tr><td>1</td><td>Florida</td><td>7,497.4</td><td>9</td><td>Oregon</td><td>5,996.6</td></tr>
<tr><td>6</td><td>Georgia</td><td>6,309.7</td><td>10</td><td>Nevada</td><td>5,992.0</td></tr>
<tr><td>5</td><td>Hawaii</td><td>6,584.5</td><td>11</td><td>Utah</td><td>5,985.9</td></tr>
<tr><td>37</td><td>Idaho</td><td>4,012.5</td><td>12</td><td>Washington</td><td>5,909.4</td></tr>
<tr><td>18</td><td>Illinois</td><td>5,320.0</td><td>13</td><td>Texas</td><td>5,708.9</td></tr>
<tr><td>28</td><td>Indiana</td><td>4,498.2</td><td>14</td><td>Oklahoma</td><td>5,652.9</td></tr>
<tr><td>42</td><td>Iowa</td><td>3,648.9</td><td>15</td><td>North Carolina</td><td>5,526.2</td></tr>
<tr><td>26</td><td>Kansas</td><td>4,681.7</td><td>16</td><td>Alaska</td><td>5,450.4</td></tr>
<tr><td>45</td><td>Kentucky</td><td>3,166.3</td><td>17</td><td>Tennessee</td><td>5,449.3</td></tr>
<tr><td>3</td><td>Louisiana</td><td>6,838.8</td><td>18</td><td>Illinois</td><td>5,320.0</td></tr>
<tr><td>44</td><td>Maine</td><td>3,394.1</td><td>19</td><td>California</td><td>5,207.8</td></tr>
<tr><td>8</td><td>Maryland</td><td>6,061.9</td><td>20</td><td>Colorado</td><td>5,118.5</td></tr>
<tr><td>40</td><td>Massachusetts</td><td>3,837.1</td><td>21</td><td>Michigan</td><td>5,117.5</td></tr>
<tr><td>21</td><td>Michigan</td><td>5,117.5</td><td>22</td><td>Missouri</td><td>5,084.0</td></tr>
<tr><td>30</td><td>Minnesota</td><td>4,463.1</td><td>23</td><td>Delaware</td><td>4,894.9</td></tr>
<tr><td>27</td><td>Mississippi</td><td>4,522.9</td><td>24</td><td>Alabama</td><td>4,820.1</td></tr>
<tr><td>22</td><td>Missouri</td><td>5,084.0</td><td>25</td><td>Arkansas</td><td>4,699.2</td></tr>
<tr><td>29</td><td>Montana</td><td>4,493.6</td><td>26</td><td>Kansas</td><td>4,681.7</td></tr>
<tr><td>32</td><td>Nebraska</td><td>4,436.6</td><td>27</td><td>Mississippi</td><td>4,522.9</td></tr>
<tr><td>10</td><td>Nevada</td><td>5,992.0</td><td>28</td><td>Indiana</td><td>4,498.2</td></tr>
<tr><td>48</td><td>New Hampshire</td><td>2,823.5</td><td>29</td><td>Montana</td><td>4,493.6</td></tr>
<tr><td>33</td><td>New Jersey</td><td>4,332.9</td><td>30</td><td>Minnesota</td><td>4,463.1</td></tr>
<tr><td>4</td><td>New Mexico</td><td>6,602.3</td><td>31</td><td>Ohio</td><td>4,455.7</td></tr>
<tr><td>36</td><td>New York</td><td>4,132.3</td><td>32</td><td>Nebraska</td><td>4,436.6</td></tr>
<tr><td>15</td><td>North Carolina</td><td>5,526.2</td><td>33</td><td>New Jersey</td><td>4,332.9</td></tr>
<tr><td>49</td><td>North Dakota</td><td>2,669.1</td><td>34</td><td>Wyoming</td><td>4,254.1</td></tr>
<tr><td>31</td><td>Ohio</td><td>4,455.7</td><td>35</td><td>Connecticut</td><td>4,227.7</td></tr>
<tr><td>14</td><td>Oklahoma</td><td>5,652.9</td><td>36</td><td>New York</td><td>4,132.3</td></tr>
<tr><td>9</td><td>Oregon</td><td>5,996.6</td><td>37</td><td>Idaho</td><td>4,012.5</td></tr>
<tr><td>43</td><td>Pennsylvania</td><td>3,556.4</td><td>38</td><td>Rhode Island</td><td>3,993.5</td></tr>
<tr><td>38</td><td>Rhode Island</td><td>3,993.5</td><td>39</td><td>Virginia</td><td>3,968.3</td></tr>
<tr><td>7</td><td>South Carolina</td><td>6,214.1</td><td>40</td><td>Massachusetts</td><td>3,837.1</td></tr>
<tr><td>47</td><td>South Dakota</td><td>2,969.9</td><td>41</td><td>Wisconsin</td><td>3,821.4</td></tr>
<tr><td>17</td><td>Tennessee</td><td>5,449.3</td><td>42</td><td>Iowa</td><td>3,648.9</td></tr>
<tr><td>13</td><td>Texas</td><td>5,708.9</td><td>43</td><td>Pennsylvania</td><td>3,556.4</td></tr>
<tr><td>11</td><td>Utah</td><td>5,985.9</td><td>44</td><td>Maine</td><td>3,394.1</td></tr>
<tr><td>46</td><td>Vermont</td><td>3,002.9</td><td>45</td><td>Kentucky</td><td>3,166.3</td></tr>
<tr><td>39</td><td>Virginia</td><td>3,968.3</td><td>46</td><td>Vermont</td><td>3,002.9</td></tr>
<tr><td>12</td><td>Washington</td><td>5,909.4</td><td>47</td><td>South Dakota</td><td>2,969.9</td></tr>
<tr><td>50</td><td>West Virginia</td><td>2,483.4</td><td>48</td><td>New Hampshire</td><td>2,823.5</td></tr>
<tr><td>41</td><td>Wisconsin</td><td>3,821.4</td><td>49</td><td>North Dakota</td><td>2,669.1</td></tr>
<tr><td>34</td><td>Wyoming</td><td>4,254.1</td><td>50</td><td>West Virginia</td><td>2,483.4</td></tr>
<tr><td></td><td></td><td></td><td></td><td>District of Columbia</td><td>11,896.7</td></tr>
</table>

Source: Federal Bureau of Investigation
    "Crime in the United States 1997" (Uniform Crime Reports, November 22, 1998)
*Revised figures. Includes murder, rape, robbery, aggravated assault, burglary, larceny-theft and motor vehicle theft.

Percent Change in Crime Rate: 1996 to 2000

National Percent Change = 18.9% Decrease*

ALPHA ORDER			RANK ORDER		
RANK	**STATE**	**PERCENT CHANGE**	**RANK**	**STATE**	**PERCENT CHANGE**
2	Alabama	(5.7)	1	Vermont	(0.5)
36	Alaska	(22.0)	2	Alabama	(5.7)
23	Arizona	(17.5)	3	Kansas	(5.8)
13	Arkansas	(12.4)	4	Kentucky	(6.5)
47	California	(28.2)	5	Nebraska	(7.7)
37	Colorado	(22.2)	6	Delaware	(8.5)
40	Connecticut	(23.5)	7	Ohio	(9.3)
6	Delaware	(8.5)	8	Tennessee	(10.3)
42	Florida	(24.0)	9	Missouri	(10.9)
43	Georgia	(24.7)	10	North Carolina	(11.0)
31	Hawaii	(21.0)	11	Iowa	(11.4)
28	Idaho	(20.6)	12	Mississippi	(11.5)
25	Illinois	(19.4)	13	Arkansas	(12.4)
22	Indiana	(16.6)	14	Rhode Island	(12.9)
11	Iowa	(11.4)	15	Texas	(13.2)
3	Kansas	(5.8)	16	Washington	(13.6)
4	Kentucky	(6.5)	17	North Dakota	(14.3)
30	Louisiana	(20.7)	18	Pennsylvania	(15.8)
39	Maine	(22.8)	19	South Carolina	(16.0)
28	Maryland	(20.6)	19	Wisconsin	(16.0)
32	Massachusetts	(21.1)	21	New Mexico	(16.4)
27	Michigan	(19.7)	22	Indiana	(16.6)
34	Minnesota	(21.8)	23	Arizona	(17.5)
12	Mississippi	(11.5)	24	Oregon	(19.2)
9	Missouri	(10.9)	25	Illinois	(19.4)
33	Montana	(21.4)	25	Oklahoma	(19.4)
5	Nebraska	(7.7)	27	Michigan	(19.7)
48	Nevada	(28.8)	28	Idaho	(20.6)
NA	New Hampshire**	NA	28	Maryland	(20.6)
46	New Jersey	(27.1)	30	Louisiana	(20.7)
21	New Mexico	(16.4)	31	Hawaii	(21.0)
44	New York	(25.0)	32	Massachusetts	(21.1)
10	North Carolina	(11.0)	33	Montana	(21.4)
17	North Dakota	(14.3)	34	Minnesota	(21.8)
7	Ohio	(9.3)	35	South Dakota	(21.9)
25	Oklahoma	(19.4)	36	Alaska	(22.0)
24	Oregon	(19.2)	37	Colorado	(22.2)
18	Pennsylvania	(15.8)	38	Wyoming	(22.5)
14	Rhode Island	(12.9)	39	Maine	(22.8)
19	South Carolina	(16.0)	40	Connecticut	(23.5)
35	South Dakota	(21.9)	41	Virginia	(23.7)
8	Tennessee	(10.3)	42	Florida	(24.0)
15	Texas	(13.2)	43	Georgia	(24.7)
45	Utah	(25.2)	44	New York	(25.0)
1	Vermont	(0.5)	45	Utah	(25.2)
41	Virginia	(23.7)	46	New Jersey	(27.1)
16	Washington	(13.6)	47	California	(28.2)
NA	West Virginia**	NA	48	Nevada	(28.8)
19	Wisconsin	(16.0)	NA	New Hampshire**	NA
38	Wyoming	(22.5)	NA	West Virginia**	NA
				District of Columbia	(38.8)

Source: Morgan Quitno Press using data from Federal Bureau of Investigation
"Crime in the United States" (Uniform Crime Reports, 1997 and 2000 editions)
*Includes murder, rape, robbery, aggravated assault, burglary, larceny-theft and motor vehicle theft.
**Not comparable.

Violent Crimes in 1996

National Total = 1,688,540 Violent Crimes*

ALPHA ORDER

RANK ORDER

RANK	STATE	CRIMES	% of USA		RANK	STATE	CRIMES	% of USA
20	Alabama	24,159	1.4%		1	California	274,996	16.3%
39	Alaska	4,417	0.3%		2	Florida	151,350	9.0%
19	Arizona	27,963	1.7%		3	New York	132,206	7.8%
30	Arkansas	13,161	0.8%		4	Texas	123,270	7.3%
1	California	274,996	16.3%		5	Illinois	105,482	6.2%
25	Colorado	15,463	0.9%		6	Michigan	60,951	3.6%
28	Connecticut	13,490	0.8%		7	Pennsylvania	57,905	3.4%
38	Delaware	4,845	0.3%		8	Ohio	47,896	2.8%
2	Florida	151,350	9.0%		9	Maryland	47,230	2.8%
10	Georgia	46,966	2.8%		10	Georgia	46,966	2.8%
42	Hawaii	3,322	0.2%		11	North Carolina	43,068	2.6%
43	Idaho	3,177	0.2%		12	New Jersey	42,459	2.5%
5	Illinois	105,482	6.2%		13	Tennessee	41,175	2.4%
18	Indiana	31,366	1.9%		14	Louisiana	40,426	2.4%
35	Iowa	7,771	0.5%		15	Massachusetts	39,122	2.3%
34	Kansas	10,642	0.6%		16	South Carolina	36,875	2.2%
33	Kentucky	12,448	0.7%		17	Missouri	31,669	1.9%
14	Louisiana	40,426	2.4%		18	Indiana	31,366	1.9%
44	Maine	1,553	0.1%		19	Arizona	27,963	1.7%
9	Maryland	47,230	2.8%		20	Alabama	24,159	1.4%
15	Massachusetts	39,122	2.3%		21	Washington	23,857	1.4%
6	Michigan	60,951	3.6%		22	Virginia	22,782	1.3%
24	Minnesota	15,782	0.9%		23	Oklahoma	19,710	1.2%
29	Mississippi	13,261	0.8%		24	Minnesota	15,782	0.9%
17	Missouri	31,669	1.9%		25	Colorado	15,463	0.9%
45	Montana	1,415	0.1%		26	Oregon	14,837	0.9%
36	Nebraska	7,182	0.4%		27	New Mexico	14,399	0.9%
32	Nevada	13,005	0.8%		28	Connecticut	13,490	0.8%
46	New Hampshire	1,373	0.1%		29	Mississippi	13,261	0.8%
12	New Jersey	42,459	2.5%		30	Arkansas	13,161	0.8%
27	New Mexico	14,399	0.9%		31	Wisconsin	13,039	0.8%
3	New York	132,206	7.8%		32	Nevada	13,005	0.8%
11	North Carolina	43,068	2.6%		33	Kentucky	12,448	0.7%
50	North Dakota	541	0.0%		34	Kansas	10,642	0.6%
8	Ohio	47,896	2.8%		35	Iowa	7,771	0.5%
23	Oklahoma	19,710	1.2%		36	Nebraska	7,182	0.4%
26	Oregon	14,837	0.9%		37	Utah	6,638	0.4%
7	Pennsylvania	57,905	3.4%		38	Delaware	4,845	0.3%
41	Rhode Island	3,437	0.2%		39	Alaska	4,417	0.3%
16	South Carolina	36,875	2.2%		40	West Virginia	3,836	0.2%
47	South Dakota	1,297	0.1%		41	Rhode Island	3,437	0.2%
13	Tennessee	41,175	2.4%		42	Hawaii	3,322	0.2%
4	Texas	123,270	7.3%		43	Idaho	3,177	0.2%
37	Utah	6,638	0.4%		44	Maine	1,553	0.1%
49	Vermont	714	0.0%		45	Montana	1,415	0.1%
22	Virginia	22,782	1.3%		46	New Hampshire	1,373	0.1%
21	Washington	23,857	1.4%		47	South Dakota	1,297	0.1%
40	West Virginia	3,836	0.2%		48	Wyoming	1,201	0.1%
31	Wisconsin	13,039	0.8%		49	Vermont	714	0.0%
48	Wyoming	1,201	0.1%		50	North Dakota	541	0.0%
						District of Columbia	13,411	0.8%

Source: Federal Bureau of Investigation
   "Crime in the United States 1997" (Uniform Crime Reports, November 22, 1998)
*Revised figures. Violent crimes are offenses of murder, forcible rape, robbery and aggravated assault.

Percent Change in Number of Violent Crimes: 1996 to 2000

National Percent Change = 15.6% Decrease*

RANK	STATE	PERCENT CHANGE
23	Alabama	(10.5)
37	Alaska	(19.5)
8	Arizona	(2.4)
21	Arkansas	(9.6)
45	California	(23.4)
16	Colorado	(7.1)
35	Connecticut	(18.0)
2	Delaware	10.7
34	Florida	(14.3)
27	Georgia	(12.0)
25	Hawaii	(11.1)
4	Idaho	2.8
43	Illinois	(22.7)
48	Indiana	(32.3)
5	Iowa	0.3
6	Kansas	(1.6)
14	Kentucky	(4.4)
47	Louisiana	(24.7)
22	Maine	(10.0)
26	Maryland	(11.8)
43	Massachusetts	(22.7)
20	Michigan	(9.5)
29	Minnesota	(12.5)
42	Mississippi	(22.6)
32	Missouri	(13.4)
1	Montana	53.4
41	Nebraska	(21.9)
37	Nevada	(19.5)
NA	New Hampshire**	NA
46	New Jersey	(23.9)
13	New Mexico	(4.3)
39	New York	(20.5)
15	North Carolina	(7.0)
12	North Dakota	(3.3)
40	Ohio	(20.8)
31	Oklahoma	(12.9)
36	Oregon	(19.1)
24	Pennsylvania	(10.9)
19	Rhode Island	(9.2)
28	South Carolina	(12.4)
10	South Dakota	(2.9)
7	Tennessee	(2.3)
17	Texas	(7.8)
33	Utah	(14.0)
11	Vermont	(3.2)
29	Virginia	(12.5)
18	Washington	(8.7)
NA	West Virginia**	NA
9	Wisconsin	(2.6)
3	Wyoming	9.6

RANK	STATE	PERCENT CHANGE
1	Montana	53.4
2	Delaware	10.7
3	Wyoming	9.6
4	Idaho	2.8
5	Iowa	0.3
6	Kansas	(1.6)
7	Tennessee	(2.3)
8	Arizona	(2.4)
9	Wisconsin	(2.6)
10	South Dakota	(2.9)
11	Vermont	(3.2)
12	North Dakota	(3.3)
13	New Mexico	(4.3)
14	Kentucky	(4.4)
15	North Carolina	(7.0)
16	Colorado	(7.1)
17	Texas	(7.8)
18	Washington	(8.7)
19	Rhode Island	(9.2)
20	Michigan	(9.5)
21	Arkansas	(9.6)
22	Maine	(10.0)
23	Alabama	(10.5)
24	Pennsylvania	(10.9)
25	Hawaii	(11.1)
26	Maryland	(11.8)
27	Georgia	(12.0)
28	South Carolina	(12.4)
29	Minnesota	(12.5)
29	Virginia	(12.5)
31	Oklahoma	(12.9)
32	Missouri	(13.4)
33	Utah	(14.0)
34	Florida	(14.3)
35	Connecticut	(18.0)
36	Oregon	(19.1)
37	Alaska	(19.5)
37	Nevada	(19.5)
39	New York	(20.5)
40	Ohio	(20.8)
41	Nebraska	(21.9)
42	Mississippi	(22.6)
43	Illinois	(22.7)
43	Massachusetts	(22.7)
45	California	(23.4)
46	New Jersey	(23.9)
47	Louisiana	(24.7)
48	Indiana	(32.3)
NA	New Hampshire**	NA
NA	West Virginia**	NA

District of Columbia (35.7)

Source: Morgan Quitno Press using data from Federal Bureau of Investigation
   "Crime in the United States" (Uniform Crime Reports, 1997 and 2000 editions)
*Violent crimes are offenses of murder, forcible rape, robbery and aggravated assault.
**Not comparable.

Violent Crime Rate in 1996

National Rate = 636.5 Violent Crimes per 100,000 Population*

ALPHA ORDER

RANK	STATE	RATE
21	Alabama	565.4
10	Alaska	727.7
17	Arizona	631.5
24	Arkansas	524.3
6	California	862.7
33	Colorado	404.5
32	Connecticut	412.0
12	Delaware	668.3
1	Florida	1,051.0
15	Georgia	638.7
39	Hawaii	280.6
41	Idaho	267.2
5	Illinois	890.4
22	Indiana	537.0
40	Iowa	272.5
31	Kansas	413.8
38	Kentucky	320.5
4	Louisiana	929.1
47	Maine	124.9
3	Maryland	931.2
14	Massachusetts	642.2
16	Michigan	635.3
36	Minnesota	338.8
25	Mississippi	488.3
19	Missouri	590.9
46	Montana	161.0
28	Nebraska	434.7
8	Nevada	811.3
49	New Hampshire	118.2
23	New Jersey	531.5
7	New Mexico	840.6
11	New York	727.0
20	North Carolina	588.1
50	North Dakota	84.0
30	Ohio	428.7
18	Oklahoma	597.1
27	Oregon	463.1
26	Pennsylvania	480.3
34	Rhode Island	347.2
2	South Carolina	996.9
45	South Dakota	177.2
9	Tennessee	774.0
13	Texas	644.4
37	Utah	331.9
48	Vermont	121.2
35	Virginia	341.3
29	Washington	431.2
44	West Virginia	210.1
42	Wisconsin	252.7
43	Wyoming	249.7

RANK ORDER

RANK	STATE	RATE
1	Florida	1,051.0
2	South Carolina	996.9
3	Maryland	931.2
4	Louisiana	929.1
5	Illinois	890.4
6	California	862.7
7	New Mexico	840.6
8	Nevada	811.3
9	Tennessee	774.0
10	Alaska	727.7
11	New York	727.0
12	Delaware	668.3
13	Texas	644.4
14	Massachusetts	642.2
15	Georgia	638.7
16	Michigan	635.3
17	Arizona	631.5
18	Oklahoma	597.1
19	Missouri	590.9
20	North Carolina	588.1
21	Alabama	565.4
22	Indiana	537.0
23	New Jersey	531.5
24	Arkansas	524.3
25	Mississippi	488.3
26	Pennsylvania	480.3
27	Oregon	463.1
28	Nebraska	434.7
29	Washington	431.2
30	Ohio	428.7
31	Kansas	413.8
32	Connecticut	412.0
33	Colorado	404.5
34	Rhode Island	347.2
35	Virginia	341.3
36	Minnesota	338.8
37	Utah	331.9
38	Kentucky	320.5
39	Hawaii	280.6
40	Iowa	272.5
41	Idaho	267.2
42	Wisconsin	252.7
43	Wyoming	249.7
44	West Virginia	210.1
45	South Dakota	177.2
46	Montana	161.0
47	Maine	124.9
48	Vermont	121.2
49	New Hampshire	118.2
50	North Dakota	84.0
	District of Columbia	2,469.8

Source: Federal Bureau of Investigation
   "Crime in the United States 1997" (Uniform Crime Reports, November 22, 1998)
*Revised figures. Violent crimes are offenses of murder, forcible rape, robbery and aggravated assault.

Percent Change in Violent Crime Rate: 1996 to 2000

National Percent Change = 20.5% Decrease*

ALPHA ORDER				RANK ORDER		
RANK	STATE	PERCENT CHANGE		RANK	STATE	PERCENT CHANGE
18	Alabama	(14.0)		1	Montana	49.4
34	Alaska	(22.1)		2	Wyoming	6.7
25	Arizona	(15.8)		3	Delaware	2.4
21	Arkansas	(15.1)		4	Iowa	(2.2)
46	California	(27.9)		5	North Dakota	(3.1)
29	Colorado	(17.4)		6	Idaho	(5.5)
33	Connecticut	(21.2)		7	Kansas	(5.9)
3	Delaware	2.4		7	South Dakota	(5.9)
36	Florida	(22.7)		9	Wisconsin	(6.3)
32	Georgia	(21.0)		10	Vermont	(6.4)
17	Hawaii	(13.1)		11	Kentucky	(8.1)
6	Idaho	(5.5)		12	Tennessee	(8.6)
43	Illinois	(26.2)		13	New Mexico	(9.8)
47	Indiana	(35.0)		14	Maine	(12.2)
4	Iowa	(2.2)		15	Michigan	(12.6)
7	Kansas	(5.9)		15	Pennsylvania	(12.6)
11	Kentucky	(8.1)		17	Hawaii	(13.1)
44	Louisiana	(26.7)		18	Alabama	(14.0)
14	Maine	(12.2)		19	Rhode Island	(14.3)
24	Maryland	(15.5)		19	Washington	(14.3)
41	Massachusetts	(25.9)		21	Arkansas	(15.1)
15	Michigan	(12.6)		22	North Carolina	(15.4)
27	Minnesota	(17.1)		22	Texas	(15.4)
42	Mississippi	(26.1)		24	Maryland	(15.5)
27	Missouri	(17.1)		25	Arizona	(15.8)
1	Montana	49.4		26	Oklahoma	(16.6)
40	Nebraska	(24.6)		27	Minnesota	(17.1)
48	Nevada	(35.4)		27	Missouri	(17.1)
NA	New Hampshire**	NA		29	Colorado	(17.4)
45	New Jersey	(27.8)		30	Virginia	(17.5)
13	New Mexico	(9.8)		31	South Carolina	(19.3)
38	New York	(23.8)		32	Georgia	(21.0)
22	North Carolina	(15.4)		33	Connecticut	(21.2)
5	North Dakota	(3.1)		34	Alaska	(22.1)
34	Ohio	(22.1)		34	Ohio	(22.1)
26	Oklahoma	(16.6)		36	Florida	(22.7)
39	Oregon	(24.3)		37	Utah	(23.0)
15	Pennsylvania	(12.6)		38	New York	(23.8)
19	Rhode Island	(14.3)		39	Oregon	(24.3)
31	South Carolina	(19.3)		40	Nebraska	(24.6)
7	South Dakota	(5.9)		41	Massachusetts	(25.9)
12	Tennessee	(8.6)		42	Mississippi	(26.1)
22	Texas	(15.4)		43	Illinois	(26.2)
37	Utah	(23.0)		44	Louisiana	(26.7)
10	Vermont	(6.4)		45	New Jersey	(27.8)
30	Virginia	(17.5)		46	California	(27.9)
19	Washington	(14.3)		47	Indiana	(35.0)
NA	West Virginia**	NA		48	Nevada	(35.4)
9	Wisconsin	(6.3)		NA	New Hampshire**	NA
2	Wyoming	6.7		NA	West Virginia**	NA
					District of Columbia	(38.9)

Source: Morgan Quitno Press using data from Federal Bureau of Investigation
    "Crime in the United States" (Uniform Crime Reports, 1997 and 2000 editions)
*Violent crimes are offenses of murder, forcible rape, robbery and aggravated assault.
**Not comparable.

Murders in 1996

National Total = 19,645 Murders*

ALPHA ORDER

RANK	STATE	MURDERS	% of USA
15	Alabama	444	2.3%
39	Alaska	45	0.2%
18	Arizona	377	1.9%
26	Arkansas	219	1.1%
1	California	2,916	14.8%
29	Colorado	180	0.9%
32	Connecticut	158	0.8%
43	Delaware	31	0.2%
5	Florida	1,077	5.5%
9	Georgia	630	3.2%
41	Hawaii	40	0.2%
40	Idaho	43	0.2%
4	Illinois	1,179	6.0%
17	Indiana	420	2.1%
37	Iowa	53	0.3%
30	Kansas	170	0.9%
23	Kentucky	228	1.2%
6	Louisiana	762	3.9%
44	Maine	25	0.1%
11	Maryland	588	3.0%
33	Massachusetts	157	0.8%
7	Michigan	722	3.7%
31	Minnesota	167	0.9%
21	Mississippi	301	1.5%
16	Missouri	433	2.2%
42	Montana	34	0.2%
38	Nebraska	48	0.2%
25	Nevada	220	1.1%
46	New Hampshire	20	0.1%
19	New Jersey	338	1.7%
28	New Mexico	197	1.0%
3	New York	1,353	6.9%
10	North Carolina	619	3.2%
48	North Dakota	14	0.1%
12	Ohio	538	2.7%
24	Oklahoma	223	1.1%
34	Oregon	129	0.7%
8	Pennsylvania	686	3.5%
44	Rhode Island	25	0.1%
20	South Carolina	332	1.7%
50	South Dakota	9	0.0%
13	Tennessee	503	2.6%
2	Texas	1,477	7.5%
36	Utah	63	0.3%
49	Vermont	11	0.1%
14	Virginia	500	2.5%
22	Washington	255	1.3%
35	West Virginia	69	0.4%
27	Wisconsin	204	1.0%
47	Wyoming	16	0.1%

RANK ORDER

RANK	STATE	MURDERS	% of USA
1	California	2,916	14.8%
2	Texas	1,477	7.5%
3	New York	1,353	6.9%
4	Illinois	1,179	6.0%
5	Florida	1,077	5.5%
6	Louisiana	762	3.9%
7	Michigan	722	3.7%
8	Pennsylvania	686	3.5%
9	Georgia	630	3.2%
10	North Carolina	619	3.2%
11	Maryland	588	3.0%
12	Ohio	538	2.7%
13	Tennessee	503	2.6%
14	Virginia	500	2.5%
15	Alabama	444	2.3%
16	Missouri	433	2.2%
17	Indiana	420	2.1%
18	Arizona	377	1.9%
19	New Jersey	338	1.7%
20	South Carolina	332	1.7%
21	Mississippi	301	1.5%
22	Washington	255	1.3%
23	Kentucky	228	1.2%
24	Oklahoma	223	1.1%
25	Nevada	220	1.1%
26	Arkansas	219	1.1%
27	Wisconsin	204	1.0%
28	New Mexico	197	1.0%
29	Colorado	180	0.9%
30	Kansas	170	0.9%
31	Minnesota	167	0.9%
32	Connecticut	158	0.8%
33	Massachusetts	157	0.8%
34	Oregon	129	0.7%
35	West Virginia	69	0.4%
36	Utah	63	0.3%
37	Iowa	53	0.3%
38	Nebraska	48	0.2%
39	Alaska	45	0.2%
40	Idaho	43	0.2%
41	Hawaii	40	0.2%
42	Montana	34	0.2%
43	Delaware	31	0.2%
44	Maine	25	0.1%
44	Rhode Island	25	0.1%
46	New Hampshire	20	0.1%
47	Wyoming	16	0.1%
48	North Dakota	14	0.1%
49	Vermont	11	0.1%
50	South Dakota	9	0.0%
	District of Columbia	397	2.0%

Source: Federal Bureau of Investigation
"Crime in the United States 1997" (Uniform Crime Reports, November 22, 1998)
*Revised figures. Includes nonnegligent manslaughter.

Percent Change in Number of Murders: 1996 to 2000

National Percent Change = 21.0% Decrease

ALPHA ORDER

RANK	STATE	PERCENT CHANGE
33	Alabama	(25.9)
42	Alaska	(40.0)
5	Arizona	(4.8)
29	Arkansas	(23.3)
36	California	(28.7)
32	Colorado	(25.6)
41	Connecticut	(38.0)
22	Delaware	(19.4)
15	Florida	(16.2)
3	Georgia	3.3
10	Hawaii	(12.5)
47	Idaho	(62.8)
30	Illinois	(24.4)
15	Indiana	(16.2)
11	Iowa	(13.2)
4	Kansas	(0.6)
14	Kentucky	(15.4)
34	Louisiana	(26.5)
42	Maine	(40.0)
35	Maryland	(26.9)
25	Massachusetts	(20.4)
6	Michigan	(7.3)
8	Minnesota	(9.6)
13	Mississippi	(15.3)
24	Missouri	(19.9)
46	Montana	(52.9)
2	Nebraska	31.3
44	Nevada	(41.4)
NA	New Hampshire**	NA
12	New Jersey	(14.5)
39	New Mexico	(31.5)
37	New York	(29.6)
7	North Carolina	(9.5)
48	North Dakota	(71.4)
27	Ohio	(22.3)
20	Oklahoma	(18.4)
45	Oregon	(45.7)
9	Pennsylvania	(12.2)
1	Rhode Island	80.0
38	South Carolina	(29.8)
26	South Dakota	(22.2)
21	Tennessee	(18.5)
15	Texas	(16.2)
40	Utah	(31.7)
19	Vermont	(18.2)
23	Virginia	(19.8)
28	Washington	(23.1)
NA	West Virginia**	NA
18	Wisconsin	(17.2)
31	Wyoming	(25.0)

RANK ORDER

RANK	STATE	PERCENT CHANGE
1	Rhode Island	80.0
2	Nebraska	31.3
3	Georgia	3.3
4	Kansas	(0.6)
5	Arizona	(4.8)
6	Michigan	(7.3)
7	North Carolina	(9.5)
8	Minnesota	(9.6)
9	Pennsylvania	(12.2)
10	Hawaii	(12.5)
11	Iowa	(13.2)
12	New Jersey	(14.5)
13	Mississippi	(15.3)
14	Kentucky	(15.4)
15	Florida	(16.2)
15	Indiana	(16.2)
15	Texas	(16.2)
18	Wisconsin	(17.2)
19	Vermont	(18.2)
20	Oklahoma	(18.4)
21	Tennessee	(18.5)
22	Delaware	(19.4)
23	Virginia	(19.8)
24	Missouri	(19.9)
25	Massachusetts	(20.4)
26	South Dakota	(22.2)
27	Ohio	(22.3)
28	Washington	(23.1)
29	Arkansas	(23.3)
30	Illinois	(24.4)
31	Wyoming	(25.0)
32	Colorado	(25.6)
33	Alabama	(25.9)
34	Louisiana	(26.5)
35	Maryland	(26.9)
36	California	(28.7)
37	New York	(29.6)
38	South Carolina	(29.8)
39	New Mexico	(31.5)
40	Utah	(31.7)
41	Connecticut	(38.0)
42	Alaska	(40.0)
42	Maine	(40.0)
44	Nevada	(41.4)
45	Oregon	(45.7)
46	Montana	(52.9)
47	Idaho	(62.8)
48	North Dakota	(71.4)
NA	New Hampshire**	NA
NA	West Virginia**	NA
	District of Columbia	(39.8)

Source: Morgan Quitno Press using data from Federal Bureau of Investigation
   "Crime in the United States" (Uniform Crime Reports, 1997 and 2000 editions)
*Includes nonnegligent manslaughter.

Murder Rate in 1996

National Rate = 7.4 Murders per 100,000 Population*

RANK	STATE	RATE		RANK	STATE	RATE
6	Alabama	10.4		1	Louisiana	17.5
20	Alaska	7.4		2	Nevada	13.7
13	Arizona	8.5		3	Maryland	11.6
11	Arkansas	8.7		4	New Mexico	11.5
9	California	9.1		5	Mississippi	11.1
29	Colorado	4.7		6	Alabama	10.4
27	Connecticut	4.8		7	Illinois	10.0
31	Delaware	4.3		8	Tennessee	9.5
17	Florida	7.5		9	California	9.1
12	Georgia	8.6		10	South Carolina	9.0
39	Hawaii	3.4		11	Arkansas	8.7
37	Idaho	3.6		12	Georgia	8.6
7	Illinois	10.0		13	Arizona	8.5
22	Indiana	7.2		13	North Carolina	8.5
47	Iowa	1.9		15	Missouri	8.1
24	Kansas	6.6		16	Texas	7.7
25	Kentucky	5.9		17	Florida	7.5
1	Louisiana	17.5		17	Michigan	7.5
46	Maine	2.0		17	Virginia	7.5
3	Maryland	11.6		20	Alaska	7.4
43	Massachusetts	2.6		20	New York	7.4
17	Michigan	7.5		22	Indiana	7.2
37	Minnesota	3.6		23	Oklahoma	6.8
5	Mississippi	11.1		24	Kansas	6.6
15	Missouri	8.1		25	Kentucky	5.9
35	Montana	3.9		26	Pennsylvania	5.7
42	Nebraska	2.9		27	Connecticut	4.8
2	Nevada	13.7		27	Ohio	4.8
49	New Hampshire	1.7		29	Colorado	4.7
32	New Jersey	4.2		30	Washington	4.6
4	New Mexico	11.5		31	Delaware	4.3
20	New York	7.4		32	New Jersey	4.2
13	North Carolina	8.5		33	Oregon	4.0
45	North Dakota	2.2		33	Wisconsin	4.0
27	Ohio	4.8		35	Montana	3.9
23	Oklahoma	6.8		36	West Virginia	3.8
33	Oregon	4.0		37	Idaho	3.6
26	Pennsylvania	5.7		37	Minnesota	3.6
44	Rhode Island	2.5		39	Hawaii	3.4
10	South Carolina	9.0		40	Wyoming	3.3
50	South Dakota	1.2		41	Utah	3.2
8	Tennessee	9.5		42	Nebraska	2.9
16	Texas	7.7		43	Massachusetts	2.6
41	Utah	3.2		44	Rhode Island	2.5
47	Vermont	1.9		45	North Dakota	2.2
17	Virginia	7.5		46	Maine	2.0
30	Washington	4.6		47	Iowa	1.9
36	West Virginia	3.8		47	Vermont	1.9
33	Wisconsin	4.0		49	New Hampshire	1.7
40	Wyoming	3.3		50	South Dakota	1.2
					District of Columbia	73.1

ALPHA ORDER (left)   RANK ORDER (right)

Source: Federal Bureau of Investigation
   "Crime in the United States 1997" (Uniform Crime Reports, November 22, 1998)
*Revised figures. Includes nonnegligent manslaughter.

476

Percent Change in Murder Rate: 1996 to 2000

National Percent Change = 25.7% Decrease*

ALPHA ORDER

RANK	STATE	PERCENT CHANGE
33	Alabama	(28.8)
43	Alaska	(41.9)
10	Arizona	(17.6)
29	Arkansas	(27.6)
36	California	(33.0)
37	Colorado	(34.0)
40	Connecticut	(39.6)
27	Delaware	(25.6)
26	Florida	(25.3)
4	Georgia	(7.0)
8	Hawaii	(14.7)
47	Idaho	(66.7)
30	Illinois	(28.0)
15	Indiana	(19.4)
9	Iowa	(15.8)
3	Kansas	(4.5)
12	Kentucky	(18.6)
32	Louisiana	(28.6)
41	Maine	(40.0)
34	Maryland	(30.2)
20	Massachusetts	(23.1)
5	Michigan	(10.7)
6	Minnesota	(13.9)
13	Mississippi	(18.9)
22	Missouri	(23.5)
46	Montana	(53.8)
2	Nebraska	27.6
45	Nevada	(52.6)
NA	New Hampshire**	NA
14	New Jersey	(19.0)
39	New Mexico	(35.7)
35	New York	(32.4)
10	North Carolina	(17.6)
48	North Dakota	(72.7)
19	Ohio	(22.9)
18	Oklahoma	(22.1)
44	Oregon	(50.0)
7	Pennsylvania	(14.0)
1	Rhode Island	72.0
38	South Carolina	(35.6)
25	South Dakota	(25.0)
24	Tennessee	(24.2)
21	Texas	(23.4)
42	Utah	(40.6)
17	Vermont	(21.1)
23	Virginia	(24.0)
31	Washington	(28.3)
NA	West Virginia**	NA
16	Wisconsin	(20.0)
28	Wyoming	(27.3)

RANK ORDER

RANK	STATE	PERCENT CHANGE
1	Rhode Island	72.0
2	Nebraska	27.6
3	Kansas	(4.5)
4	Georgia	(7.0)
5	Michigan	(10.7)
6	Minnesota	(13.9)
7	Pennsylvania	(14.0)
8	Hawaii	(14.7)
9	Iowa	(15.8)
10	Arizona	(17.6)
10	North Carolina	(17.6)
12	Kentucky	(18.6)
13	Mississippi	(18.9)
14	New Jersey	(19.0)
15	Indiana	(19.4)
16	Wisconsin	(20.0)
17	Vermont	(21.1)
18	Oklahoma	(22.1)
19	Ohio	(22.9)
20	Massachusetts	(23.1)
21	Texas	(23.4)
22	Missouri	(23.5)
23	Virginia	(24.0)
24	Tennessee	(24.2)
25	South Dakota	(25.0)
26	Florida	(25.3)
27	Delaware	(25.6)
28	Wyoming	(27.3)
29	Arkansas	(27.6)
30	Illinois	(28.0)
31	Washington	(28.3)
32	Louisiana	(28.6)
33	Alabama	(28.8)
34	Maryland	(30.2)
35	New York	(32.4)
36	California	(33.0)
37	Colorado	(34.0)
38	South Carolina	(35.6)
39	New Mexico	(35.7)
40	Connecticut	(39.6)
41	Maine	(40.0)
42	Utah	(40.6)
43	Alaska	(41.9)
44	Oregon	(50.0)
45	Nevada	(52.6)
46	Montana	(53.8)
47	Idaho	(66.7)
48	North Dakota	(72.7)
NA	New Hampshire**	NA
NA	West Virginia**	NA
	District of Columbia	(42.8)

Source: Morgan Quitno Press using data from Federal Bureau of Investigation
  "Crime in the United States" (Uniform Crime Reports, 1997 and 2000 editions)
*Includes nonnegligent manslaughter.
**Not comparable.

Rapes in 1996

National Total = 96,252 Rapes*

ALPHA ORDER

RANK	STATE	RAPES	% of USA
24	Alabama	1,397	1.5%
40	Alaska	398	0.4%
25	Arizona	1,381	1.4%
31	Arkansas	1,046	1.1%
1	California	10,244	10.6%
21	Colorado	1,765	1.8%
35	Connecticut	755	0.8%
37	Delaware	454	0.5%
3	Florida	7,508	7.8%
11	Georgia	2,357	2.4%
42	Hawaii	326	0.3%
43	Idaho	313	0.3%
6	Illinois	4,548	4.7%
14	Indiana	1,992	2.1%
36	Iowa	561	0.6%
28	Kansas	1,096	1.1%
27	Kentucky	1,230	1.3%
18	Louisiana	1,805	1.9%
46	Maine	260	0.3%
16	Maryland	1,905	2.0%
20	Massachusetts	1,767	1.8%
4	Michigan	5,466	5.7%
12	Minnesota	2,327	2.4%
32	Mississippi	981	1.0%
22	Missouri	1,566	1.6%
47	Montana	238	0.2%
38	Nebraska	447	0.5%
33	Nevada	856	0.9%
39	New Hampshire	404	0.4%
15	New Jersey	1,976	2.1%
29	New Mexico	1,088	1.1%
7	New York	4,174	4.3%
13	North Carolina	2,289	2.4%
49	North Dakota	155	0.2%
5	Ohio	4,617	4.8%
23	Oklahoma	1,545	1.6%
26	Oregon	1,272	1.3%
8	Pennsylvania	3,034	3.2%
45	Rhode Island	287	0.3%
17	South Carolina	1,821	1.9%
44	South Dakota	300	0.3%
10	Tennessee	2,475	2.6%
2	Texas	8,376	8.7%
34	Utah	836	0.9%
48	Vermont	159	0.2%
19	Virginia	1,783	1.9%
9	Washington	2,828	2.9%
41	West Virginia	358	0.4%
30	Wisconsin	1,086	1.1%
50	Wyoming	140	0.1%

RANK ORDER

RANK	STATE	RAPES	% of USA
1	California	10,244	10.6%
2	Texas	8,376	8.7%
3	Florida	7,508	7.8%
4	Michigan	5,466	5.7%
5	Ohio	4,617	4.8%
6	Illinois	4,548	4.7%
7	New York	4,174	4.3%
8	Pennsylvania	3,034	3.2%
9	Washington	2,828	2.9%
10	Tennessee	2,475	2.6%
11	Georgia	2,357	2.4%
12	Minnesota	2,327	2.4%
13	North Carolina	2,289	2.4%
14	Indiana	1,992	2.1%
15	New Jersey	1,976	2.1%
16	Maryland	1,905	2.0%
17	South Carolina	1,821	1.9%
18	Louisiana	1,805	1.9%
19	Virginia	1,783	1.9%
20	Massachusetts	1,767	1.8%
21	Colorado	1,765	1.8%
22	Missouri	1,566	1.6%
23	Oklahoma	1,545	1.6%
24	Alabama	1,397	1.5%
25	Arizona	1,381	1.4%
26	Oregon	1,272	1.3%
27	Kentucky	1,230	1.3%
28	Kansas	1,096	1.1%
29	New Mexico	1,088	1.1%
30	Wisconsin	1,086	1.1%
31	Arkansas	1,046	1.1%
32	Mississippi	981	1.0%
33	Nevada	856	0.9%
34	Utah	836	0.9%
35	Connecticut	755	0.8%
36	Iowa	561	0.6%
37	Delaware	454	0.5%
38	Nebraska	447	0.5%
39	New Hampshire	404	0.4%
40	Alaska	398	0.4%
41	West Virginia	358	0.4%
42	Hawaii	326	0.3%
43	Idaho	313	0.3%
44	South Dakota	300	0.3%
45	Rhode Island	287	0.3%
46	Maine	260	0.3%
47	Montana	238	0.2%
48	Vermont	159	0.2%
49	North Dakota	155	0.2%
50	Wyoming	140	0.1%
	District of Columbia	260	0.3%

Source: Federal Bureau of Investigation
   "Crime in the United States 1997" (Uniform Crime Reports, November 22, 1998)
*Revised figures. Forcible rape is the carnal knowledge of a female forcibly and against her will. Assaults or attempts to commit rape by force or threat of force are included. However, statutory rape without force and other sex offenses are excluded.

Percent Change in Number of Rapes: 1996 to 2000

National Percent Change = 6.3% Decrease*

ALPHA ORDER

RANK	STATE	PERCENT CHANGE
12	Alabama	6.1
3	Alaska	24.9
8	Arizona	14.2
46	Arkansas	(18.9)
24	California	(4.5)
18	Colorado	0.5
35	Connecticut	(10.2)
28	Delaware	(6.6)
26	Florida	(6.0)
43	Georgia	(16.5)
12	Hawaii	6.1
5	Idaho	22.7
34	Illinois	(10.1)
37	Indiana	(11.7)
6	Iowa	20.5
29	Kansas	(6.8)
36	Kentucky	(11.3)
45	Louisiana	(17.1)
4	Maine	23.1
47	Maryland	(19.0)
23	Massachusetts	(4.0)
32	Michigan	(8.1)
22	Minnesota	(3.7)
14	Mississippi	3.9
40	Missouri	(13.7)
2	Montana	26.5
20	Nebraska	(2.5)
18	Nevada	0.5
NA	New Hampshire**	NA
48	New Jersey	(31.3)
41	New Mexico	(15.3)
42	New York	(15.4)
25	North Carolina	(4.7)
9	North Dakota	9.0
30	Ohio	(7.5)
31	Oklahoma	(8.0)
17	Oregon	1.1
11	Pennsylvania	7.0
1	Rhode Island	43.6
44	South Carolina	(17.0)
16	South Dakota	1.7
37	Tennessee	(11.7)
27	Texas	(6.2)
15	Utah	3.2
39	Vermont	(11.9)
33	Virginia	(9.4)
21	Washington	(3.2)
NA	West Virginia**	NA
10	Wisconsin	7.3
7	Wyoming	14.3

RANK ORDER

RANK	STATE	PERCENT CHANGE
1	Rhode Island	43.6
2	Montana	26.5
3	Alaska	24.9
4	Maine	23.1
5	Idaho	22.7
6	Iowa	20.5
7	Wyoming	14.3
8	Arizona	14.2
9	North Dakota	9.0
10	Wisconsin	7.3
11	Pennsylvania	7.0
12	Alabama	6.1
12	Hawaii	6.1
14	Mississippi	3.9
15	Utah	3.2
16	South Dakota	1.7
17	Oregon	1.1
18	Colorado	0.5
18	Nevada	0.5
20	Nebraska	(2.5)
21	Washington	(3.2)
22	Minnesota	(3.7)
23	Massachusetts	(4.0)
24	California	(4.5)
25	North Carolina	(4.7)
26	Florida	(6.0)
27	Texas	(6.2)
28	Delaware	(6.6)
29	Kansas	(6.8)
30	Ohio	(7.5)
31	Oklahoma	(8.0)
32	Michigan	(8.1)
33	Virginia	(9.4)
34	Illinois	(10.1)
35	Connecticut	(10.2)
36	Kentucky	(11.3)
37	Indiana	(11.7)
37	Tennessee	(11.7)
39	Vermont	(11.9)
40	Missouri	(13.7)
41	New Mexico	(15.3)
42	New York	(15.4)
43	Georgia	(16.5)
44	South Carolina	(17.0)
45	Louisiana	(17.1)
46	Arkansas	(18.9)
47	Maryland	(19.0)
48	New Jersey	(31.3)
NA	New Hampshire**	NA
NA	West Virginia**	NA
	District of Columbia	(3.5)

Source: Morgan Quitno Press using data from Federal Bureau of Investigation
   "Crime in the United States" (Uniform Crime Reports, 1997 and 2000 editions)
*Forcible rape is the carnal knowledge of a female forcibly and against her will. Assaults or attempts to commit rape by force or threat of force are included. However, statutory rape without force and other sex offenses are excluded.
**Not comparable

Rape Rate in 1996

National Rate = 36.3 Rapes per 100,000 Population*

ALPHA ORDER

RANK	STATE	RATE
26	Alabama	32.7
1	Alaska	65.6
31	Arizona	31.2
16	Arkansas	41.7
27	California	32.1
12	Colorado	46.2
45	Connecticut	23.1
3	Delaware	62.6
6	Florida	52.1
27	Georgia	32.1
36	Hawaii	27.5
41	Idaho	26.3
21	Illinois	38.4
25	Indiana	34.1
49	Iowa	19.7
14	Kansas	42.6
29	Kentucky	31.7
17	Louisiana	41.5
48	Maine	20.9
22	Maryland	37.6
34	Massachusetts	29.0
4	Michigan	57.0
8	Minnesota	50.0
23	Mississippi	36.1
32	Missouri	29.2
37	Montana	27.1
37	Nebraska	27.1
5	Nevada	53.4
24	New Hampshire	34.8
43	New Jersey	24.7
2	New Mexico	63.5
46	New York	23.0
30	North Carolina	31.3
44	North Dakota	24.1
18	Ohio	41.3
10	Oklahoma	46.8
20	Oregon	39.7
42	Pennsylvania	25.2
34	Rhode Island	29.0
9	South Carolina	49.2
19	South Dakota	41.0
11	Tennessee	46.5
13	Texas	43.8
15	Utah	41.8
39	Vermont	27.0
40	Virginia	26.7
7	Washington	51.1
50	West Virginia	19.6
47	Wisconsin	21.0
33	Wyoming	29.1

RANK ORDER

RANK	STATE	RATE
1	Alaska	65.6
2	New Mexico	63.5
3	Delaware	62.6
4	Michigan	57.0
5	Nevada	53.4
6	Florida	52.1
7	Washington	51.1
8	Minnesota	50.0
9	South Carolina	49.2
10	Oklahoma	46.8
11	Tennessee	46.5
12	Colorado	46.2
13	Texas	43.8
14	Kansas	42.6
15	Utah	41.8
16	Arkansas	41.7
17	Louisiana	41.5
18	Ohio	41.3
19	South Dakota	41.0
20	Oregon	39.7
21	Illinois	38.4
22	Maryland	37.6
23	Mississippi	36.1
24	New Hampshire	34.8
25	Indiana	34.1
26	Alabama	32.7
27	California	32.1
27	Georgia	32.1
29	Kentucky	31.7
30	North Carolina	31.3
31	Arizona	31.2
32	Missouri	29.2
33	Wyoming	29.1
34	Massachusetts	29.0
34	Rhode Island	29.0
36	Hawaii	27.5
37	Montana	27.1
37	Nebraska	27.1
39	Vermont	27.0
40	Virginia	26.7
41	Idaho	26.3
42	Pennsylvania	25.2
43	New Jersey	24.7
44	North Dakota	24.1
45	Connecticut	23.1
46	New York	23.0
47	Wisconsin	21.0
48	Maine	20.9
49	Iowa	19.7
50	West Virginia	19.6
	District of Columbia	47.9

Source: Federal Bureau of Investigation
   "Crime in the United States 1997" (Uniform Crime Reports, November 22, 1998)
*Revised figures. Forcible rape is the carnal knowledge of a female forcibly and against her will. Assaults or attempts to commit rape by force or threat of force are included. However, statutory rape without force and other sex offenses are excluded.

Percent Change in Rape Rate: 1996 to 2000

National Percent Change = 11.8% Decrease*

ALPHA ORDER				RANK ORDER		
RANK	STATE	PERCENT CHANGE		RANK	STATE	PERCENT CHANGE
12	Alabama	1.8		1	Rhode Island	35.5
3	Alaska	20.9		2	Montana	23.2
15	Arizona	(1.6)		3	Alaska	20.9
46	Arkansas	(24.0)		4	Maine	20.1
23	California	(10.0)		5	Iowa	17.3
24	Colorado	(10.8)		6	Idaho	12.9
30	Connecticut	(13.9)		7	Wyoming	11.3
29	Delaware	(13.6)		8	North Dakota	9.1
36	Florida	(15.2)		9	Pennsylvania	4.8
47	Georgia	(25.2)		10	Hawaii	4.0
10	Hawaii	4.0		11	Wisconsin	3.3
6	Idaho	12.9		12	Alabama	1.8
32	Illinois	(14.3)		13	Mississippi	(0.8)
36	Indiana	(15.2)		14	South Dakota	(1.5)
5	Iowa	17.3		15	Arizona	(1.6)
24	Kansas	(10.8)		16	Oregon	(5.3)
34	Kentucky	(14.8)		17	Nebraska	(5.9)
41	Louisiana	(19.3)		18	Utah	(7.7)
4	Maine	20.1		19	Massachusetts	(7.9)
44	Maryland	(22.6)		20	Minnesota	(9.0)
19	Massachusetts	(7.9)		20	Ohio	(9.0)
26	Michigan	(11.2)		22	Washington	(9.2)
20	Minnesota	(9.0)		23	California	(10.0)
13	Mississippi	(0.8)		24	Colorado	(10.8)
39	Missouri	(17.5)		24	Kansas	(10.8)
2	Montana	23.2		26	Michigan	(11.2)
17	Nebraska	(5.9)		27	Oklahoma	(12.0)
42	Nevada	(19.5)		28	North Carolina	(13.4)
NA	New Hampshire**	NA		29	Delaware	(13.6)
48	New Jersey	(34.8)		30	Connecticut	(13.9)
43	New Mexico	(20.2)		30	Texas	(13.9)
40	New York	(19.1)		32	Illinois	(14.3)
28	North Carolina	(13.4)		33	Virginia	(14.6)
8	North Dakota	9.1		34	Kentucky	(14.8)
20	Ohio	(9.0)		34	Vermont	(14.8)
27	Oklahoma	(12.0)		36	Florida	(15.2)
16	Oregon	(5.3)		36	Indiana	(15.2)
9	Pennsylvania	4.8		38	Tennessee	(17.4)
1	Rhode Island	35.5		39	Missouri	(17.5)
45	South Carolina	(23.4)		40	New York	(19.1)
14	South Dakota	(1.5)		41	Louisiana	(19.3)
38	Tennessee	(17.4)		42	Nevada	(19.5)
30	Texas	(13.9)		43	New Mexico	(20.2)
18	Utah	(7.7)		44	Maryland	(22.6)
34	Vermont	(14.8)		45	South Carolina	(23.4)
33	Virginia	(14.6)		46	Arkansas	(24.0)
22	Washington	(9.2)		47	Georgia	(25.2)
NA	West Virginia**	NA		48	New Jersey	(34.8)
11	Wisconsin	3.3		NA	New Hampshire**	NA
7	Wyoming	11.3		NA	West Virginia**	NA
					District of Columbia	(8.4)

Source: Morgan Quitno Press using data from Federal Bureau of Investigation
"Crime in the United States" (Uniform Crime Reports, 1997 and 2000 editions)
*Forcible rape is the carnal knowledge of a female forcibly and against her will. Assaults or attempts to commit rape by force or threat of force are included. However, statutory rape without force and other sex offenses are excluded.
**Not comparable.

481

Robberies in 1996

National Total = 535,594 Robberies*

ALPHA ORDER

RANK	STATE	ROBBERIES	% of USA
20	Alabama	7,124	1.3%
42	Alaska	710	0.1%
18	Arizona	7,429	1.4%
32	Arkansas	2,864	0.5%
1	California	94,222	17.6%
28	Colorado	3,755	0.7%
23	Connecticut	5,552	1.0%
37	Delaware	1,304	0.2%
3	Florida	41,643	7.8%
11	Georgia	15,100	2.8%
35	Hawaii	1,606	0.3%
46	Idaho	241	0.0%
4	Illinois	33,106	6.2%
19	Indiana	7,249	1.4%
38	Iowa	1,286	0.2%
34	Kansas	2,476	0.5%
30	Kentucky	3,643	0.7%
12	Louisiana	12,036	2.2%
44	Maine	292	0.1%
7	Maryland	19,944	3.7%
17	Massachusetts	7,778	1.5%
10	Michigan	16,907	3.2%
24	Minnesota	5,385	1.0%
29	Mississippi	3,646	0.7%
15	Missouri	9,142	1.7%
45	Montana	261	0.0%
39	Nebraska	1,052	0.2%
26	Nevada	4,931	0.9%
43	New Hampshire	317	0.1%
8	New Jersey	18,838	3.5%
33	New Mexico	2,782	0.5%
2	New York	61,822	11.5%
13	North Carolina	12,001	2.2%
50	North Dakota	71	0.0%
9	Ohio	18,336	3.4%
31	Oklahoma	3,519	0.7%
27	Oregon	3,914	0.7%
6	Pennsylvania	22,784	4.3%
40	Rhode Island	824	0.2%
22	South Carolina	6,361	1.2%
47	South Dakota	138	0.0%
14	Tennessee	11,902	2.2%
5	Texas	32,804	6.1%
36	Utah	1,377	0.3%
49	Vermont	91	0.0%
16	Virginia	8,181	1.5%
21	Washington	6,587	1.2%
41	West Virginia	737	0.1%
25	Wisconsin	4,982	0.9%
48	Wyoming	98	0.0%

RANK ORDER

RANK	STATE	ROBBERIES	% of USA
1	California	94,222	17.6%
2	New York	61,822	11.5%
3	Florida	41,643	7.8%
4	Illinois	33,106	6.2%
5	Texas	32,804	6.1%
6	Pennsylvania	22,784	4.3%
7	Maryland	19,944	3.7%
8	New Jersey	18,838	3.5%
9	Ohio	18,336	3.4%
10	Michigan	16,907	3.2%
11	Georgia	15,100	2.8%
12	Louisiana	12,036	2.2%
13	North Carolina	12,001	2.2%
14	Tennessee	11,902	2.2%
15	Missouri	9,142	1.7%
16	Virginia	8,181	1.5%
17	Massachusetts	7,778	1.5%
18	Arizona	7,429	1.4%
19	Indiana	7,249	1.4%
20	Alabama	7,124	1.3%
21	Washington	6,587	1.2%
22	South Carolina	6,361	1.2%
23	Connecticut	5,552	1.0%
24	Minnesota	5,385	1.0%
25	Wisconsin	4,982	0.9%
26	Nevada	4,931	0.9%
27	Oregon	3,914	0.7%
28	Colorado	3,755	0.7%
29	Mississippi	3,646	0.7%
30	Kentucky	3,643	0.7%
31	Oklahoma	3,519	0.7%
32	Arkansas	2,864	0.5%
33	New Mexico	2,782	0.5%
34	Kansas	2,476	0.5%
35	Hawaii	1,606	0.3%
36	Utah	1,377	0.3%
37	Delaware	1,304	0.2%
38	Iowa	1,286	0.2%
39	Nebraska	1,052	0.2%
40	Rhode Island	824	0.2%
41	West Virginia	737	0.1%
42	Alaska	710	0.1%
43	New Hampshire	317	0.1%
44	Maine	292	0.1%
45	Montana	261	0.0%
46	Idaho	241	0.0%
47	South Dakota	138	0.0%
48	Wyoming	98	0.0%
49	Vermont	91	0.0%
50	North Dakota	71	0.0%
	District of Columbia	6,444	1.2%

Source: Federal Bureau of Investigation
"Crime in the United States 1997" (Uniform Crime Reports, November 22, 1998)
*Revised figures. Robbery is the taking or attempting to take anything of value by force or threat of force.

Percent Change in Number of Robberies: 1996 to 2000

National Percent Change = 23.9% Decrease*

ALPHA ORDER

RANK	STATE	PERCENT CHANGE
27	Alabama	(20.0)
42	Alaska	(31.0)
6	Arizona	1.0
40	Arkansas	(30.1)
47	California	(36.1)
26	Colorado	(19.2)
42	Connecticut	(31.0)
4	Delaware	6.9
33	Florida	(23.6)
18	Georgia	(12.3)
40	Hawaii	(30.1)
9	Idaho	(7.5)
31	Illinois	(22.2)
19	Indiana	(13.3)
22	Iowa	(16.7)
24	Kansas	(17.3)
16	Kentucky	(10.6)
48	Louisiana	(37.4)
21	Maine	(15.4)
45	Maryland	(32.0)
34	Massachusetts	(25.2)
25	Michigan	(18.9)
42	Minnesota	(31.0)
36	Mississippi	(25.9)
23	Missouri	(16.9)
7	Montana	(4.6)
3	Nebraska	9.0
12	Nevada	(7.9)
NA	New Hampshire**	NA
38	New Jersey	(28.1)
15	New Mexico	(10.2)
46	New York	(34.4)
5	North Carolina	4.9
30	North Dakota	(21.1)
20	Ohio	(14.9)
35	Oklahoma	(25.7)
37	Oregon	(26.2)
28	Pennsylvania	(20.3)
2	Rhode Island	11.9
9	South Carolina	(7.5)
8	South Dakota	(5.1)
29	Tennessee	(20.5)
11	Texas	(7.8)
14	Utah	(9.8)
1	Vermont	28.6
32	Virginia	(23.1)
17	Washington	(11.8)
NA	West Virginia**	NA
13	Wisconsin	(8.9)
39	Wyoming	(28.6)

RANK ORDER

RANK	STATE	PERCENT CHANGE
1	Vermont	28.6
2	Rhode Island	11.9
3	Nebraska	9.0
4	Delaware	6.9
5	North Carolina	4.9
6	Arizona	1.0
7	Montana	(4.6)
8	South Dakota	(5.1)
9	Idaho	(7.5)
9	South Carolina	(7.5)
11	Texas	(7.8)
12	Nevada	(7.9)
13	Wisconsin	(8.9)
14	Utah	(9.8)
15	New Mexico	(10.2)
16	Kentucky	(10.6)
17	Washington	(11.8)
18	Georgia	(12.3)
19	Indiana	(13.3)
20	Ohio	(14.9)
21	Maine	(15.4)
22	Iowa	(16.7)
23	Missouri	(16.9)
24	Kansas	(17.3)
25	Michigan	(18.9)
26	Colorado	(19.2)
27	Alabama	(20.0)
28	Pennsylvania	(20.3)
29	Tennessee	(20.5)
30	North Dakota	(21.1)
31	Illinois	(22.2)
32	Virginia	(23.1)
33	Florida	(23.6)
34	Massachusetts	(25.2)
35	Oklahoma	(25.7)
36	Mississippi	(25.9)
37	Oregon	(26.2)
38	New Jersey	(28.1)
39	Wyoming	(28.6)
40	Arkansas	(30.1)
40	Hawaii	(30.1)
42	Alaska	(31.0)
42	Connecticut	(31.0)
42	Minnesota	(31.0)
45	Maryland	(32.0)
46	New York	(34.4)
47	California	(36.1)
48	Louisiana	(37.4)
NA	New Hampshire**	NA
NA	West Virginia**	NA
	District of Columbia	(44.8)

Source: Morgan Quitno Press using data from Federal Bureau of Investigation
  "Crime in the United States" (Uniform Crime Reports, 1997 and 2000 editions)
*Robbery is the taking or attempting to take anything of value by force or threat of force.
**Not comparable.

Robbery Rate in 1996

National Rate = 201.9 Robberies per 100,000 Population*

RANK	STATE	RATE
19	Alabama	166.7
30	Alaska	117.0
18	Arizona	167.8
32	Arkansas	114.1
4	California	295.6
34	Colorado	98.2
17	Connecticut	169.6
12	Delaware	179.9
5	Florida	289.2
10	Georgia	205.4
23	Hawaii	135.6
47	Idaho	20.3
6	Illinois	279.4
26	Indiana	124.1
41	Iowa	45.1
36	Kansas	96.3
37	Kentucky	93.8
7	Louisiana	276.6
45	Maine	23.5
1	Maryland	393.2
25	Massachusetts	127.7
13	Michigan	176.2
31	Minnesota	115.6
24	Mississippi	134.2
16	Missouri	170.6
43	Montana	29.7
40	Nebraska	63.7
3	Nevada	307.6
44	New Hampshire	27.3
8	New Jersey	235.8
22	New Mexico	162.4
2	New York	340.0
21	North Carolina	163.9
50	North Dakota	11.0
20	Ohio	164.1
33	Oklahoma	106.6
28	Oregon	122.2
11	Pennsylvania	189.0
38	Rhode Island	83.2
14	South Carolina	172.0
48	South Dakota	18.9
9	Tennessee	223.7
15	Texas	171.5
39	Utah	68.9
49	Vermont	15.4
27	Virginia	122.6
29	Washington	119.0
42	West Virginia	40.4
35	Wisconsin	96.6
46	Wyoming	20.4

RANK	STATE	RATE
1	Maryland	393.2
2	New York	340.0
3	Nevada	307.6
4	California	295.6
5	Florida	289.2
6	Illinois	279.4
7	Louisiana	276.6
8	New Jersey	235.8
9	Tennessee	223.7
10	Georgia	205.4
11	Pennsylvania	189.0
12	Delaware	179.9
13	Michigan	176.2
14	South Carolina	172.0
15	Texas	171.5
16	Missouri	170.6
17	Connecticut	169.6
18	Arizona	167.8
19	Alabama	166.7
20	Ohio	164.1
21	North Carolina	163.9
22	New Mexico	162.4
23	Hawaii	135.6
24	Mississippi	134.2
25	Massachusetts	127.7
26	Indiana	124.1
27	Virginia	122.6
28	Oregon	122.2
29	Washington	119.0
30	Alaska	117.0
31	Minnesota	115.6
32	Arkansas	114.1
33	Oklahoma	106.6
34	Colorado	98.2
35	Wisconsin	96.6
36	Kansas	96.3
37	Kentucky	93.8
38	Rhode Island	83.2
39	Utah	68.9
40	Nebraska	63.7
41	Iowa	45.1
42	West Virginia	40.4
43	Montana	29.7
44	New Hampshire	27.3
45	Maine	23.5
46	Wyoming	20.4
47	Idaho	20.3
48	South Dakota	18.9
49	Vermont	15.4
50	North Dakota	11.0
	District of Columbia	1,186.7

Source: Federal Bureau of Investigation
"Crime in the United States 1997" (Uniform Crime Reports, November 22, 1998)
*Revised figures. Robbery is the taking or attempting to take anything of value by force or threat of force.

Percent Change in Robbery Rate: 1996 to 2000

National Percent Change = 28.2% Decrease*

ALPHA ORDER

RANK	STATE	PERCENT CHANGE
27	Alabama	(23.1)
41	Alaska	(33.2)
9	Arizona	(12.8)
43	Arkansas	(34.4)
48	California	(39.8)
32	Colorado	(28.2)
42	Connecticut	(33.7)
4	Delaware	(1.1)
38	Florida	(31.2)
24	Georgia	(21.2)
39	Hawaii	(31.6)
12	Idaho	(15.3)
29	Illinois	(25.8)
16	Indiana	(16.8)
19	Iowa	(18.8)
22	Kansas	(20.9)
10	Kentucky	(14.1)
47	Louisiana	(39.1)
18	Maine	(17.4)
45	Maryland	(34.9)
33	Massachusetts	(28.3)
25	Michigan	(21.7)
44	Minnesota	(34.7)
35	Mississippi	(29.2)
21	Missouri	(20.4)
6	Montana	(7.1)
3	Nebraska	5.2
30	Nevada	(26.1)
NA	New Hampshire**	NA
40	New Jersey	(31.7)
13	New Mexico	(15.4)
46	New York	(37.2)
5	North Carolina	(4.5)
22	North Dakota	(20.9)
15	Ohio	(16.2)
34	Oklahoma	(28.9)
37	Oregon	(30.9)
26	Pennsylvania	(21.8)
2	Rhode Island	5.8
11	South Carolina	(14.8)
7	South Dakota	(7.9)
28	Tennessee	(25.6)
13	Texas	(15.4)
20	Utah	(19.3)
1	Vermont	24.7
31	Virginia	(27.5)
17	Washington	(17.1)
NA	West Virginia**	NA
8	Wisconsin	(12.4)
36	Wyoming	(30.4)

RANK ORDER

RANK	STATE	PERCENT CHANGE
1	Vermont	24.7
2	Rhode Island	5.8
3	Nebraska	5.2
4	Delaware	(1.1)
5	North Carolina	(4.5)
6	Montana	(7.1)
7	South Dakota	(7.9)
8	Wisconsin	(12.4)
9	Arizona	(12.8)
10	Kentucky	(14.1)
11	South Carolina	(14.8)
12	Idaho	(15.3)
13	New Mexico	(15.4)
13	Texas	(15.4)
15	Ohio	(16.2)
16	Indiana	(16.8)
17	Washington	(17.1)
18	Maine	(17.4)
19	Iowa	(18.8)
20	Utah	(19.3)
21	Missouri	(20.4)
22	Kansas	(20.9)
22	North Dakota	(20.9)
24	Georgia	(21.2)
25	Michigan	(21.7)
26	Pennsylvania	(21.8)
27	Alabama	(23.1)
28	Tennessee	(25.6)
29	Illinois	(25.8)
30	Nevada	(26.1)
31	Virginia	(27.5)
32	Colorado	(28.2)
33	Massachusetts	(28.3)
34	Oklahoma	(28.9)
35	Mississippi	(29.2)
36	Wyoming	(30.4)
37	Oregon	(30.9)
38	Florida	(31.2)
39	Hawaii	(31.6)
40	New Jersey	(31.7)
41	Alaska	(33.2)
42	Connecticut	(33.7)
43	Arkansas	(34.4)
44	Minnesota	(34.7)
45	Maryland	(34.9)
46	New York	(37.2)
47	Louisiana	(39.1)
48	California	(39.8)
NA	New Hampshire**	NA
NA	West Virginia**	NA
	District of Columbia	(47.6)

Source: Morgan Quitno Press using data from Federal Bureau of Investigation
   "Crime in the United States" (Uniform Crime Reports, 1997 and 2000 editions)
*Robbery is the taking or attempting to take anything of value by force or threat of force.
**Not comparable.

Aggravated Assaults in 1996

National Total = 1,037,049 Aggravated Assaults*

ALPHA ORDER

RANK	STATE	ASSAULTS	% of USA
20	Alabama	15,194	1.5%
38	Alaska	3,264	0.3%
19	Arizona	18,776	1.8%
27	Arkansas	9,032	0.9%
1	California	167,614	16.2%
25	Colorado	9,763	0.9%
31	Connecticut	7,025	0.7%
39	Delaware	3,056	0.3%
2	Florida	101,122	9.8%
9	Georgia	28,879	2.8%
43	Hawaii	1,350	0.1%
41	Idaho	2,580	0.2%
4	Illinois	66,649	6.4%
16	Indiana	21,705	2.1%
35	Iowa	5,871	0.6%
33	Kansas	6,900	0.7%
30	Kentucky	7,347	0.7%
13	Louisiana	25,823	2.5%
44	Maine	976	0.1%
14	Maryland	24,793	2.4%
8	Massachusetts	29,420	2.8%
6	Michigan	37,856	3.7%
29	Minnesota	7,903	0.8%
28	Mississippi	8,333	0.8%
18	Missouri	20,528	2.0%
46	Montana	882	0.1%
36	Nebraska	5,635	0.5%
32	Nevada	6,998	0.7%
48	New Hampshire	632	0.1%
17	New Jersey	21,307	2.1%
24	New Mexico	10,332	1.0%
5	New York	64,857	6.3%
11	North Carolina	28,159	2.7%
50	North Dakota	301	0.0%
15	Ohio	24,405	2.4%
21	Oklahoma	14,423	1.4%
26	Oregon	9,522	0.9%
7	Pennsylvania	31,401	3.0%
42	Rhode Island	2,301	0.2%
10	South Carolina	28,361	2.7%
47	South Dakota	850	0.1%
12	Tennessee	26,295	2.5%
3	Texas	80,613	7.8%
37	Utah	4,362	0.4%
49	Vermont	453	0.0%
23	Virginia	12,318	1.2%
22	Washington	14,187	1.4%
40	West Virginia	2,672	0.3%
34	Wisconsin	6,767	0.7%
45	Wyoming	947	0.1%

RANK ORDER

RANK	STATE	ASSAULTS	% of USA
1	California	167,614	16.2%
2	Florida	101,122	9.8%
3	Texas	80,613	7.8%
4	Illinois	66,649	6.4%
5	New York	64,857	6.3%
6	Michigan	37,856	3.7%
7	Pennsylvania	31,401	3.0%
8	Massachusetts	29,420	2.8%
9	Georgia	28,879	2.8%
10	South Carolina	28,361	2.7%
11	North Carolina	28,159	2.7%
12	Tennessee	26,295	2.5%
13	Louisiana	25,823	2.5%
14	Maryland	24,793	2.4%
15	Ohio	24,405	2.4%
16	Indiana	21,705	2.1%
17	New Jersey	21,307	2.1%
18	Missouri	20,528	2.0%
19	Arizona	18,776	1.8%
20	Alabama	15,194	1.5%
21	Oklahoma	14,423	1.4%
22	Washington	14,187	1.4%
23	Virginia	12,318	1.2%
24	New Mexico	10,332	1.0%
25	Colorado	9,763	0.9%
26	Oregon	9,522	0.9%
27	Arkansas	9,032	0.9%
28	Mississippi	8,333	0.8%
29	Minnesota	7,903	0.8%
30	Kentucky	7,347	0.7%
31	Connecticut	7,025	0.7%
32	Nevada	6,998	0.7%
33	Kansas	6,900	0.7%
34	Wisconsin	6,767	0.7%
35	Iowa	5,871	0.6%
36	Nebraska	5,635	0.5%
37	Utah	4,362	0.4%
38	Alaska	3,264	0.3%
39	Delaware	3,056	0.3%
40	West Virginia	2,672	0.3%
41	Idaho	2,580	0.2%
42	Rhode Island	2,301	0.2%
43	Hawaii	1,350	0.1%
44	Maine	976	0.1%
45	Wyoming	947	0.1%
46	Montana	882	0.1%
47	South Dakota	850	0.1%
48	New Hampshire	632	0.1%
49	Vermont	453	0.0%
50	North Dakota	301	0.0%
	District of Columbia	6,310	0.6%

Source: Federal Bureau of Investigation
   "Crime in the United States 1997" (Uniform Crime Reports, November 22, 1998)
*Revised figures. Aggravated assault is an attack for the purpose of inflicting severe bodily injury.

Percent Change in Number of Aggravated Assaults: 1996 to 2000

National Percent Change = 12.2% Decrease*

ALPHA ORDER

RANK	STATE	PERCENT CHANGE
23	Alabama	(7.2)
40	Alaska	(22.2)
18	Arizona	(5.0)
13	Arkansas	(1.6)
35	California	(17.4)
16	Colorado	(3.5)
27	Connecticut	(8.2)
2	Delaware	15.2
29	Florida	(11.0)
31	Georgia	(11.9)
4	Hawaii	7.4
8	Idaho	2.5
42	Illinois	(23.7)
48	Indiana	(40.9)
9	Iowa	2.2
7	Kansas	4.8
11	Kentucky	0.2
38	Louisiana	(19.3)
34	Maine	(16.5)
6	Maryland	5.4
41	Massachusetts	(23.2)
19	Michigan	(5.6)
15	Minnesota	(2.5)
44	Mississippi	(24.5)
30	Missouri	(11.7)
1	Montana	82.0
47	Nebraska	(29.7)
46	Nevada	(29.4)
NA	New Hampshire**	NA
39	New Jersey	(19.7)
12	New Mexico	(1.0)
24	New York	(7.4)
32	North Carolina	(12.2)
14	North Dakota	(2.3)
45	Ohio	(27.7)
28	Oklahoma	(10.2)
37	Oregon	(18.5)
21	Pennsylvania	(5.8)
43	Rhode Island	(24.3)
33	South Carolina	(13.0)
17	South Dakota	(4.0)
5	Tennessee	7.1
25	Texas	(7.8)
36	Utah	(18.3)
22	Vermont	(6.2)
19	Virginia	(5.6)
26	Washington	(8.1)
NA	West Virginia**	NA
10	Wisconsin	0.9
3	Wyoming	13.4

RANK ORDER

RANK	STATE	PERCENT CHANGE
1	Montana	82.0
2	Delaware	15.2
3	Wyoming	13.4
4	Hawaii	7.4
5	Tennessee	7.1
6	Maryland	5.4
7	Kansas	4.8
8	Idaho	2.5
9	Iowa	2.2
10	Wisconsin	0.9
11	Kentucky	0.2
12	New Mexico	(1.0)
13	Arkansas	(1.6)
14	North Dakota	(2.3)
15	Minnesota	(2.5)
16	Colorado	(3.5)
17	South Dakota	(4.0)
18	Arizona	(5.0)
19	Michigan	(5.6)
19	Virginia	(5.6)
21	Pennsylvania	(5.8)
22	Vermont	(6.2)
23	Alabama	(7.2)
24	New York	(7.4)
25	Texas	(7.8)
26	Washington	(8.1)
27	Connecticut	(8.2)
28	Oklahoma	(10.2)
29	Florida	(11.0)
30	Missouri	(11.7)
31	Georgia	(11.9)
32	North Carolina	(12.2)
33	South Carolina	(13.0)
34	Maine	(16.5)
35	California	(17.4)
36	Utah	(18.3)
37	Oregon	(18.5)
38	Louisiana	(19.3)
39	New Jersey	(19.7)
40	Alaska	(22.2)
41	Massachusetts	(23.2)
42	Illinois	(23.7)
43	Rhode Island	(24.3)
44	Mississippi	(24.5)
45	Ohio	(27.7)
46	Nevada	(29.4)
47	Nebraska	(29.7)
48	Indiana	(40.9)
NA	New Hampshire**	NA
NA	West Virginia**	NA

District of Columbia (27.4)

Source: Morgan Quitno Press using data from Federal Bureau of Investigation
    "Crime in the United States" (Uniform Crime Reports, 1997 and 2000 editions)
*Aggravated assault is an attack for the purpose of inflicting severe bodily injury.
**Not comparable.

Aggravated Assault Rate in 1996

National Rate = 390.9 Aggravated Assaults per 100,000 Population*

RANK	STATE	RATE
23	Alabama	355.6
6	Alaska	537.7
13	Arizona	424.0
21	Arkansas	359.8
7	California	525.8
31	Colorado	255.4
36	Connecticut	214.6
14	Delaware	421.5
2	Florida	702.2
17	Georgia	392.8
45	Hawaii	114.0
35	Idaho	217.0
5	Illinois	562.6
20	Indiana	371.6
37	Iowa	205.9
27	Kansas	268.3
39	Kentucky	189.2
4	Louisiana	593.5
47	Maine	78.5
9	Maryland	488.8
10	Massachusetts	482.9
16	Michigan	394.6
41	Minnesota	169.7
25	Mississippi	306.8
19	Missouri	383.1
46	Montana	100.3
24	Nebraska	341.1
12	Nevada	436.6
49	New Hampshire	54.4
28	New Jersey	266.7
3	New Mexico	603.2
22	New York	356.7
18	North Carolina	384.5
50	North Dakota	46.7
33	Ohio	218.4
11	Oklahoma	436.9
26	Oregon	297.2
29	Pennsylvania	260.5
32	Rhode Island	232.4
1	South Carolina	766.7
44	South Dakota	116.1
8	Tennessee	494.3
15	Texas	421.4
34	Utah	218.1
48	Vermont	76.9
40	Virginia	184.5
30	Washington	256.4
42	West Virginia	146.3
43	Wisconsin	131.1
38	Wyoming	196.9

RANK	STATE	RATE
1	South Carolina	766.7
2	Florida	702.2
3	New Mexico	603.2
4	Louisiana	593.5
5	Illinois	562.6
6	Alaska	537.7
7	California	525.8
8	Tennessee	494.3
9	Maryland	488.8
10	Massachusetts	482.9
11	Oklahoma	436.9
12	Nevada	436.6
13	Arizona	424.0
14	Delaware	421.5
15	Texas	421.4
16	Michigan	394.6
17	Georgia	392.8
18	North Carolina	384.5
19	Missouri	383.1
20	Indiana	371.6
21	Arkansas	359.8
22	New York	356.7
23	Alabama	355.6
24	Nebraska	341.1
25	Mississippi	306.8
26	Oregon	297.2
27	Kansas	268.3
28	New Jersey	266.7
29	Pennsylvania	260.5
30	Washington	256.4
31	Colorado	255.4
32	Rhode Island	232.4
33	Ohio	218.4
34	Utah	218.1
35	Idaho	217.0
36	Connecticut	214.6
37	Iowa	205.9
38	Wyoming	196.9
39	Kentucky	189.2
40	Virginia	184.5
41	Minnesota	169.7
42	West Virginia	146.3
43	Wisconsin	131.1
44	South Dakota	116.1
45	Hawaii	114.0
46	Montana	100.3
47	Maine	78.5
48	Vermont	76.9
49	New Hampshire	54.4
50	North Dakota	46.7
	District of Columbia	1,162.1

Source: Federal Bureau of Investigation
"Crime in the United States 1997" (Uniform Crime Reports, November 22, 1998)
*Revised figures. Aggravated assault is an attack for the purpose of inflicting severe bodily injury.

Percent Change in Aggravated Assault Rate: 1996 to 2000

National Percent Change = 17.2% Decrease*

ALPHA ORDER			RANK ORDER		
RANK	STATE	PERCENT CHANGE	RANK	STATE	PERCENT CHANGE
20	Alabama	(10.8)	1	Montana	77.4
39	Alaska	(24.7)	2	Wyoming	10.5
29	Arizona	(18.0)	3	Delaware	6.6
16	Arkansas	(7.6)	4	Hawaii	5.0
36	California	(22.3)	5	Maryland	0.9
26	Colorado	(14.2)	6	Kansas	0.3
23	Connecticut	(11.7)	7	Tennessee	0.2
3	Delaware	6.6	8	Iowa	(0.4)
31	Florida	(19.8)	9	North Dakota	(1.9)
34	Georgia	(20.9)	10	Wisconsin	(2.9)
4	Hawaii	5.0	11	Kentucky	(3.7)
12	Idaho	(5.9)	12	Idaho	(5.9)
42	Illinois	(27.2)	13	New Mexico	(6.8)
47	Indiana	(43.2)	14	South Dakota	(6.9)
8	Iowa	(0.4)	15	Pennsylvania	(7.5)
6	Kansas	0.3	16	Arkansas	(7.6)
11	Kentucky	(3.7)	17	Minnesota	(7.7)
35	Louisiana	(21.4)	18	Michigan	(8.8)
30	Maine	(18.6)	19	Vermont	(9.2)
5	Maryland	0.9	20	Alabama	(10.8)
40	Massachusetts	(26.3)	21	Virginia	(10.9)
18	Michigan	(8.8)	22	New York	(11.2)
17	Minnesota	(7.7)	23	Connecticut	(11.7)
43	Mississippi	(27.9)	24	Washington	(13.7)
28	Missouri	(15.5)	25	Oklahoma	(14.1)
1	Montana	77.4	26	Colorado	(14.2)
46	Nebraska	(32.2)	27	Texas	(15.4)
48	Nevada	(43.4)	28	Missouri	(15.5)
NA	New Hampshire**	NA	29	Arizona	(18.0)
38	New Jersey	(23.8)	30	Maine	(18.6)
13	New Mexico	(6.8)	31	Florida	(19.8)
22	New York	(11.2)	31	South Carolina	(19.8)
33	North Carolina	(20.2)	33	North Carolina	(20.2)
9	North Dakota	(1.9)	34	Georgia	(20.9)
45	Ohio	(28.9)	35	Louisiana	(21.4)
25	Oklahoma	(14.1)	36	California	(22.3)
37	Oregon	(23.7)	37	Oregon	(23.7)
15	Pennsylvania	(7.5)	38	New Jersey	(23.8)
44	Rhode Island	(28.5)	39	Alaska	(24.7)
31	South Carolina	(19.8)	40	Massachusetts	(26.3)
14	South Dakota	(6.9)	41	Utah	(26.9)
7	Tennessee	0.2	42	Illinois	(27.2)
27	Texas	(15.4)	43	Mississippi	(27.9)
41	Utah	(26.9)	44	Rhode Island	(28.5)
19	Vermont	(9.2)	45	Ohio	(28.9)
21	Virginia	(10.9)	46	Nebraska	(32.2)
24	Washington	(13.7)	47	Indiana	(43.2)
NA	West Virginia**	NA	48	Nevada	(43.4)
10	Wisconsin	(2.9)	NA	New Hampshire**	NA
2	Wyoming	10.5	NA	West Virginia**	NA
				District of Columbia	(31.1)

Source: Morgan Quitno Press using data from Federal Bureau of Investigation
"Crime in the United States" (Uniform Crime Reports, 1997 and 2000 editions)
*Aggravated assault is an attack for the purpose of inflicting severe bodily injury.
**Not comparable.

Property Crimes in 1996

National Total = 11,805,323 Property Crimes*

RANK	STATE	CRIMES	% of USA
24	Alabama	181,803	1.5%
46	Alaska	28,667	0.2%
13	Arizona	284,964	2.4%
33	Arkansas	104,790	0.9%
1	California	1,385,135	11.7%
25	Colorado	180,218	1.5%
28	Connecticut	124,924	1.1%
45	Delaware	30,643	0.3%
3	Florida	928,273	7.9%
8	Georgia	416,986	3.5%
37	Hawaii	74,639	0.6%
39	Idaho	44,532	0.4%
5	Illinois	524,777	4.4%
19	Indiana	231,376	2.0%
35	Iowa	96,296	0.8%
31	Kansas	109,772	0.9%
30	Kentucky	110,531	0.9%
15	Louisiana	257,130	2.2%
41	Maine	40,636	0.3%
14	Maryland	260,231	2.2%
20	Massachusetts	194,636	1.6%
7	Michigan	430,020	3.6%
22	Minnesota	192,109	1.6%
32	Mississippi	109,581	0.9%
18	Missouri	240,781	2.0%
42	Montana	38,084	0.3%
38	Nebraska	66,110	0.6%
36	Nevada	83,047	0.7%
44	New Hampshire	31,436	0.3%
11	New Jersey	303,657	2.6%
34	New Mexico	98,698	0.8%
4	New York	619,250	5.2%
10	North Carolina	361,616	3.1%
50	North Dakota	16,648	0.1%
6	Ohio	449,935	3.8%
27	Oklahoma	166,892	1.4%
26	Oregon	177,295	1.5%
9	Pennsylvania	370,851	3.1%
43	Rhode Island	36,099	0.3%
21	South Carolina	192,986	1.6%
47	South Dakota	20,443	0.2%
16	Tennessee	248,729	2.1%
2	Texas	968,732	8.2%
29	Utah	113,079	1.0%
49	Vermont	16,973	0.1%
17	Virginia	242,100	2.1%
12	Washington	303,111	2.6%
40	West Virginia	41,510	0.4%
23	Wisconsin	184,143	1.6%
48	Wyoming	19,261	0.2%

RANK	STATE	CRIMES	% of USA
1	California	1,385,135	11.7%
2	Texas	968,732	8.2%
3	Florida	928,273	7.9%
4	New York	619,250	5.2%
5	Illinois	524,777	4.4%
6	Ohio	449,935	3.8%
7	Michigan	430,020	3.6%
8	Georgia	416,986	3.5%
9	Pennsylvania	370,851	3.1%
10	North Carolina	361,616	3.1%
11	New Jersey	303,657	2.6%
12	Washington	303,111	2.6%
13	Arizona	284,964	2.4%
14	Maryland	260,231	2.2%
15	Louisiana	257,130	2.2%
16	Tennessee	248,729	2.1%
17	Virginia	242,100	2.1%
18	Missouri	240,781	2.0%
19	Indiana	231,376	2.0%
20	Massachusetts	194,636	1.6%
21	South Carolina	192,986	1.6%
22	Minnesota	192,109	1.6%
23	Wisconsin	184,143	1.6%
24	Alabama	181,803	1.5%
25	Colorado	180,218	1.5%
26	Oregon	177,295	1.5%
27	Oklahoma	166,892	1.4%
28	Connecticut	124,924	1.1%
29	Utah	113,079	1.0%
30	Kentucky	110,531	0.9%
31	Kansas	109,772	0.9%
32	Mississippi	109,581	0.9%
33	Arkansas	104,790	0.9%
34	New Mexico	98,698	0.8%
35	Iowa	96,296	0.8%
36	Nevada	83,047	0.7%
37	Hawaii	74,639	0.6%
38	Nebraska	66,110	0.6%
39	Idaho	44,532	0.4%
40	West Virginia	41,510	0.4%
41	Maine	40,636	0.3%
42	Montana	38,084	0.3%
43	Rhode Island	36,099	0.3%
44	New Hampshire	31,436	0.3%
45	Delaware	30,643	0.3%
46	Alaska	28,667	0.2%
47	South Dakota	20,443	0.2%
48	Wyoming	19,261	0.2%
49	Vermont	16,973	0.1%
50	North Dakota	16,648	0.1%
	District of Columbia	51,188	0.4%

Source: Federal Bureau of Investigation
"Crime in the United States 1997" (Uniform Crime Reports, November 22, 1998)
*Revised figures. Property crimes are offenses of burglary, larceny-theft and motor vehicle theft.

Percent Change in Number of Property Crimes: 1996 to 2000

National Percent Change = 13.8% Decrease*

ALPHA ORDER

RANK	STATE	PERCENT CHANGE
2	Alabama	(0.7)
38	Alaska	(19.5)
9	Arizona	(4.6)
13	Arkansas	(6.4)
48	California	(23.7)
22	Colorado	(12.9)
42	Connecticut	(20.7)
7	Delaware	(3.0)
29	Florida	(15.9)
31	Georgia	(16.6)
39	Hawaii	(19.6)
27	Idaho	(14.8)
25	Illinois	(14.1)
20	Indiana	(10.6)
18	Iowa	(9.8)
3	Kansas	(1.6)
5	Kentucky	(2.5)
34	Louisiana	(17.6)
43	Maine	(21.2)
37	Maryland	(18.0)
33	Massachusetts	(16.8)
35	Michigan	(17.8)
36	Minnesota	(17.9)
11	Mississippi	(5.4)
12	Missouri	(6.2)
44	Montana	(22.0)
5	Nebraska	(2.5)
19	Nevada	(9.9)
NA	New Hampshire**	NA
47	New Jersey	(23.1)
21	New Mexico	(12.3)
44	New York	(22.0)
3	North Carolina	(1.6)
28	North Dakota	(14.9)
13	Ohio	(6.4)
30	Oklahoma	(16.0)
23	Oregon	(13.3)
26	Pennsylvania	(14.7)
15	Rhode Island	(7.7)
17	South Carolina	(8.2)
41	South Dakota	(20.5)
8	Tennessee	(4.3)
10	Texas	(5.1)
32	Utah	(16.7)
1	Vermont	3.1
40	Virginia	(19.7)
16	Washington	(7.9)
NA	West Virginia**	NA
24	Wisconsin	(13.4)
46	Wyoming	(22.3)

RANK ORDER

RANK	STATE	PERCENT CHANGE
1	Vermont	3.1
2	Alabama	(0.7)
3	Kansas	(1.6)
3	North Carolina	(1.6)
5	Kentucky	(2.5)
5	Nebraska	(2.5)
7	Delaware	(3.0)
8	Tennessee	(4.3)
9	Arizona	(4.6)
10	Texas	(5.1)
11	Mississippi	(5.4)
12	Missouri	(6.2)
13	Arkansas	(6.4)
13	Ohio	(6.4)
15	Rhode Island	(7.7)
16	Washington	(7.9)
17	South Carolina	(8.2)
18	Iowa	(9.8)
19	Nevada	(9.9)
20	Indiana	(10.6)
21	New Mexico	(12.3)
22	Colorado	(12.9)
23	Oregon	(13.3)
24	Wisconsin	(13.4)
25	Illinois	(14.1)
26	Pennsylvania	(14.7)
27	Idaho	(14.8)
28	North Dakota	(14.9)
29	Florida	(15.9)
30	Oklahoma	(16.0)
31	Georgia	(16.6)
32	Utah	(16.7)
33	Massachusetts	(16.8)
34	Louisiana	(17.6)
35	Michigan	(17.8)
36	Minnesota	(17.9)
37	Maryland	(18.0)
38	Alaska	(19.5)
39	Hawaii	(19.6)
40	Virginia	(19.7)
41	South Dakota	(20.5)
42	Connecticut	(20.7)
43	Maine	(21.2)
44	Montana	(22.0)
44	New York	(22.0)
46	Wyoming	(22.3)
47	New Jersey	(23.1)
48	California	(23.7)
NA	New Hampshire**	NA
NA	West Virginia**	NA
	District of Columbia	(35.5)

Source: Morgan Quitno Press using data from Federal Bureau of Investigation
   "Crime in the United States" (Uniform Crime Reports, 1997 and 2000 editions)
*Property crimes are offenses of burglary, larceny-theft and motor vehicle theft.
**Not comparable.

Property Crime Rate in 1996

National Rate = 4,450.1 Property Crimes per 100,000 Population*

ALPHA ORDER			RANK ORDER		
RANK	STATE	RATE	RANK	STATE	RATE
25	Alabama	4,254.7	1	Florida	6,446.3
16	Alaska	4,722.7	2	Arizona	6,435.5
2	Arizona	6,435.5	3	Hawaii	6,304.0
27	Arkansas	4,174.9	4	Louisiana	5,909.7
22	California	4,345.1	5	New Mexico	5,761.7
17	Colorado	4,714.0	6	Georgia	5,671.0
34	Connecticut	3,815.6	7	Utah	5,654.0
26	Delaware	4,226.6	8	Oregon	5,533.6
1	Florida	6,446.3	9	Washington	5,478.2
6	Georgia	5,671.0	10	South Carolina	5,217.2
3	Hawaii	6,304.0	11	Nevada	5,180.7
36	Idaho	3,745.3	12	Maryland	5,130.7
21	Illinois	4,429.6	13	Texas	5,064.5
33	Indiana	3,961.2	14	Oklahoma	5,055.8
41	Iowa	3,376.4	15	North Carolina	4,938.1
24	Kansas	4,268.0	16	Alaska	4,722.7
46	Kentucky	2,845.8	17	Colorado	4,714.0
4	Louisiana	5,909.7	18	Tennessee	4,675.4
42	Maine	3,269.2	19	Missouri	4,493.0
12	Maryland	5,130.7	20	Michigan	4,482.2
43	Massachusetts	3,194.9	21	Illinois	4,429.6
20	Michigan	4,482.2	22	California	4,345.1
28	Minnesota	4,124.3	23	Montana	4,332.7
29	Mississippi	4,034.6	24	Kansas	4,268.0
19	Missouri	4,493.0	25	Alabama	4,254.7
23	Montana	4,332.7	26	Delaware	4,226.6
32	Nebraska	4,001.8	27	Arkansas	4,174.9
11	Nevada	5,180.7	28	Minnesota	4,124.3
48	New Hampshire	2,705.3	29	Mississippi	4,034.6
35	New Jersey	3,801.4	30	Ohio	4,027.0
5	New Mexico	5,761.7	31	Wyoming	4,004.4
40	New York	3,405.3	32	Nebraska	4,001.8
15	North Carolina	4,938.1	33	Indiana	3,961.2
49	North Dakota	2,585.1	34	Connecticut	3,815.6
30	Ohio	4,027.0	35	New Jersey	3,801.4
14	Oklahoma	5,055.8	36	Idaho	3,745.3
8	Oregon	5,533.6	37	Rhode Island	3,646.4
44	Pennsylvania	3,076.1	38	Virginia	3,627.0
37	Rhode Island	3,646.4	39	Wisconsin	3,568.7
10	South Carolina	5,217.2	40	New York	3,405.3
47	South Dakota	2,792.8	41	Iowa	3,376.4
18	Tennessee	4,675.4	42	Maine	3,269.2
13	Texas	5,064.5	43	Massachusetts	3,194.9
7	Utah	5,654.0	44	Pennsylvania	3,076.1
45	Vermont	2,881.7	45	Vermont	2,881.7
38	Virginia	3,627.0	46	Kentucky	2,845.8
9	Washington	5,478.2	47	South Dakota	2,792.8
50	West Virginia	2,273.3	48	New Hampshire	2,705.3
39	Wisconsin	3,568.7	49	North Dakota	2,585.1
31	Wyoming	4,004.4	50	West Virginia	2,273.3
				District of Columbia	9,426.9

Source: Federal Bureau of Investigation
 "Crime in the United States 1997" (Uniform Crime Reports, November 22, 1998)
*Revised figures. Property crimes are offenses of burglary, larceny-theft and motor vehicle theft.

Percent Change in Property Crime Rate: 1996 to 2000

National Percent Change = 18.7% Decrease*

ALPHA ORDER

RANK	STATE	PERCENT CHANGE
2	Alabama	(4.6)
33	Alaska	(22.0)
23	Arizona	(17.7)
12	Arkansas	(12.1)
48	California	(28.2)
35	Colorado	(22.6)
38	Connecticut	(23.8)
9	Delaware	(10.2)
40	Florida	(24.3)
43	Georgia	(25.1)
30	Hawaii	(21.4)
32	Idaho	(21.7)
24	Illinois	(18.1)
17	Indiana	(14.1)
12	Iowa	(12.1)
3	Kansas	(5.8)
5	Kentucky	(6.3)
27	Louisiana	(19.8)
37	Maine	(23.2)
31	Maryland	(21.5)
28	Massachusetts	(20.2)
29	Michigan	(20.7)
34	Minnesota	(22.2)
7	Mississippi	(9.7)
8	Missouri	(10.1)
39	Montana	(24.0)
3	Nebraska	(5.8)
47	Nevada	(27.7)
NA	New Hampshire**	NA
46	New Jersey	(27.0)
22	New Mexico	(17.4)
44	New York	(25.2)
10	North Carolina	(10.5)
18	North Dakota	(14.6)
6	Ohio	(7.9)
26	Oklahoma	(19.7)
25	Oregon	(18.8)
20	Pennsylvania	(16.3)
14	Rhode Island	(12.8)
19	South Carolina	(15.3)
36	South Dakota	(22.9)
10	Tennessee	(10.5)
15	Texas	(12.9)
45	Utah	(25.4)
1	Vermont	(0.3)
40	Virginia	(24.3)
16	Washington	(13.5)
NA	West Virginia**	NA
21	Wisconsin	(16.7)
40	Wyoming	(24.3)

RANK ORDER

RANK	STATE	PERCENT CHANGE
1	Vermont	(0.3)
2	Alabama	(4.6)
3	Kansas	(5.8)
3	Nebraska	(5.8)
5	Kentucky	(6.3)
6	Ohio	(7.9)
7	Mississippi	(9.7)
8	Missouri	(10.1)
9	Delaware	(10.2)
10	North Carolina	(10.5)
10	Tennessee	(10.5)
12	Arkansas	(12.1)
12	Iowa	(12.1)
14	Rhode Island	(12.8)
15	Texas	(12.9)
16	Washington	(13.5)
17	Indiana	(14.1)
18	North Dakota	(14.6)
19	South Carolina	(15.3)
20	Pennsylvania	(16.3)
21	Wisconsin	(16.7)
22	New Mexico	(17.4)
23	Arizona	(17.7)
24	Illinois	(18.1)
25	Oregon	(18.8)
26	Oklahoma	(19.7)
27	Louisiana	(19.8)
28	Massachusetts	(20.2)
29	Michigan	(20.7)
30	Hawaii	(21.4)
31	Maryland	(21.5)
32	Idaho	(21.7)
33	Alaska	(22.0)
34	Minnesota	(22.2)
35	Colorado	(22.6)
36	South Dakota	(22.9)
37	Maine	(23.2)
38	Connecticut	(23.8)
39	Montana	(24.0)
40	Florida	(24.3)
40	Virginia	(24.3)
40	Wyoming	(24.3)
43	Georgia	(25.1)
44	New York	(25.2)
45	Utah	(25.4)
46	New Jersey	(27.0)
47	Nevada	(27.7)
48	California	(28.2)
NA	New Hampshire**	NA
NA	West Virginia**	NA

District of Columbia   (38.8)

Source: Morgan Quitno Press using data from Federal Bureau of Investigation
   "Crime in the United States" (Uniform Crime Reports, 1997 and 2000 editions)
*Property crimes are offenses of burglary, larceny-theft and motor vehicle theft.
**Not comparable.

Burglaries in 1996

National Total = 2,506,400 Burglaries*

ALPHA ORDER					RANK ORDER				
RANK	STATE		BURGLARIES	% of USA	RANK	STATE		BURGLARIES	% of USA
21	Alabama		42,821	1.7%	1	California		312,212	12.5%
44	Alaska		5,118	0.2%	2	Florida		219,056	8.7%
15	Arizona		55,630	2.2%	3	Texas		204,390	8.2%
32	Arkansas		23,925	1.0%	4	New York		129,828	5.2%
1	California		312,212	12.5%	5	Illinois		108,185	4.3%
25	Colorado		34,436	1.4%	6	North Carolina		98,539	3.9%
29	Connecticut		27,574	1.1%	7	Ohio		93,336	3.7%
43	Delaware		5,830	0.2%	8	Michigan		85,908	3.4%
2	Florida		219,056	8.7%	9	Georgia		81,968	3.3%
9	Georgia		81,968	3.3%	10	Pennsylvania		71,357	2.8%
37	Hawaii		12,781	0.5%	11	New Jersey		63,259	2.5%
41	Idaho		8,431	0.3%	12	Tennessee		61,896	2.5%
5	Illinois		108,185	4.3%	13	Washington		58,512	2.3%
19	Indiana		45,782	1.8%	14	Louisiana		56,379	2.2%
35	Iowa		18,954	0.8%	15	Arizona		55,630	2.2%
31	Kansas		25,239	1.0%	16	Maryland		50,331	2.0%
30	Kentucky		26,736	1.1%	17	Missouri		47,919	1.9%
14	Louisiana		56,379	2.2%	18	South Carolina		47,487	1.9%
40	Maine		9,303	0.4%	19	Indiana		45,782	1.8%
16	Maryland		50,331	2.0%	20	Massachusetts		42,896	1.7%
20	Massachusetts		42,896	1.7%	21	Alabama		42,821	1.7%
8	Michigan		85,908	3.4%	22	Oklahoma		41,447	1.7%
24	Minnesota		35,515	1.4%	23	Virginia		39,255	1.6%
27	Mississippi		30,755	1.2%	24	Minnesota		35,515	1.4%
17	Missouri		47,919	1.9%	25	Colorado		34,436	1.4%
46	Montana		4,908	0.2%	26	Oregon		31,664	1.3%
38	Nebraska		10,152	0.4%	27	Mississippi		30,755	1.2%
34	Nevada		19,558	0.8%	28	Wisconsin		30,356	1.2%
45	New Hampshire		5,063	0.2%	29	Connecticut		27,574	1.1%
11	New Jersey		63,259	2.5%	30	Kentucky		26,736	1.1%
33	New Mexico		23,586	0.9%	31	Kansas		25,239	1.0%
4	New York		129,828	5.2%	32	Arkansas		23,925	1.0%
6	North Carolina		98,539	3.9%	33	New Mexico		23,586	0.9%
50	North Dakota		1,991	0.1%	34	Nevada		19,558	0.8%
7	Ohio		93,336	3.7%	35	Iowa		18,954	0.8%
22	Oklahoma		41,447	1.7%	36	Utah		16,965	0.7%
26	Oregon		31,664	1.3%	37	Hawaii		12,781	0.5%
10	Pennsylvania		71,357	2.8%	38	Nebraska		10,152	0.4%
42	Rhode Island		8,135	0.3%	39	West Virginia		9,979	0.4%
18	South Carolina		47,487	1.9%	40	Maine		9,303	0.4%
47	South Dakota		4,077	0.2%	41	Idaho		8,431	0.3%
12	Tennessee		61,896	2.5%	42	Rhode Island		8,135	0.3%
3	Texas		204,390	8.2%	43	Delaware		5,830	0.2%
36	Utah		16,965	0.7%	44	Alaska		5,118	0.2%
48	Vermont		3,964	0.2%	45	New Hampshire		5,063	0.2%
23	Virginia		39,255	1.6%	46	Montana		4,908	0.2%
13	Washington		58,512	2.3%	47	South Dakota		4,077	0.2%
39	West Virginia		9,979	0.4%	48	Vermont		3,964	0.2%
28	Wisconsin		30,356	1.2%	49	Wyoming		3,184	0.1%
49	Wyoming		3,184	0.1%	50	North Dakota		1,991	0.1%
						District of Columbia		9,828	0.4%

Source: Federal Bureau of Investigation
"Crime in the United States 1997" (Uniform Crime Reports, November 22, 1998)
*Revised figures. Burglary is the unlawful entry of a structure to commit a felony or theft. Attempts are included.

Percent Change in Number of Burglaries: 1996 to 2000

National Percent Change = 18.2% Decrease*

ALPHA ORDER

RANK ORDER

RANK	STATE	PERCENT CHANGE
6	Alabama	(5.8)
37	Alaska	(23.8)
7	Arizona	(6.7)
13	Arkansas	(10.4)
43	California	(28.8)
33	Colorado	(21.2)
48	Connecticut	(36.8)
15	Delaware	(10.5)
32	Florida	(21.1)
23	Georgia	(16.4)
24	Hawaii	(16.6)
19	Idaho	(13.1)
39	Illinois	(24.3)
12	Indiana	(10.2)
20	Iowa	(13.8)
21	Kansas	(14.9)
5	Kentucky	(5.3)
26	Louisiana	(17.9)
41	Maine	(27.2)
34	Maryland	(21.7)
42	Massachusetts	(28.7)
29	Michigan	(18.8)
40	Minnesota	(26.5)
17	Mississippi	(12.5)
18	Missouri	(13.0)
31	Montana	(19.6)
2	Nebraska	(0.2)
13	Nevada	(10.4)
NA	New Hampshire**	NA
45	New Jersey	(30.6)
11	New Mexico	(9.5)
46	New York	(32.3)
3	North Carolina	(0.7)
1	North Dakota	5.1
4	Ohio	(5.0)
36	Oklahoma	(23.6)
30	Oregon	(19.1)
38	Pennsylvania	(24.2)
28	Rhode Island	(18.6)
27	South Carolina	(18.1)
44	South Dakota	(29.0)
10	Tennessee	(9.0)
8	Texas	(7.5)
22	Utah	(15.4)
16	Vermont	(11.7)
35	Virginia	(22.5)
9	Washington	(8.6)
NA	West Virginia**	NA
25	Wisconsin	(17.0)
47	Wyoming	(34.7)

RANK	STATE	PERCENT CHANGE
1	North Dakota	5.1
2	Nebraska	(0.2)
3	North Carolina	(0.7)
4	Ohio	(5.0)
5	Kentucky	(5.3)
6	Alabama	(5.8)
7	Arizona	(6.7)
8	Texas	(7.5)
9	Washington	(8.6)
10	Tennessee	(9.0)
11	New Mexico	(9.5)
12	Indiana	(10.2)
13	Arkansas	(10.4)
13	Nevada	(10.4)
15	Delaware	(10.5)
16	Vermont	(11.7)
17	Mississippi	(12.5)
18	Missouri	(13.0)
19	Idaho	(13.1)
20	Iowa	(13.8)
21	Kansas	(14.9)
22	Utah	(15.4)
23	Georgia	(16.4)
24	Hawaii	(16.6)
25	Wisconsin	(17.0)
26	Louisiana	(17.9)
27	South Carolina	(18.1)
28	Rhode Island	(18.6)
29	Michigan	(18.8)
30	Oregon	(19.1)
31	Montana	(19.6)
32	Florida	(21.1)
33	Colorado	(21.2)
34	Maryland	(21.7)
35	Virginia	(22.5)
36	Oklahoma	(23.6)
37	Alaska	(23.8)
38	Pennsylvania	(24.2)
39	Illinois	(24.3)
40	Minnesota	(26.5)
41	Maine	(27.2)
42	Massachusetts	(28.7)
43	California	(28.8)
44	South Dakota	(29.0)
45	New Jersey	(30.6)
46	New York	(32.3)
47	Wyoming	(34.7)
48	Connecticut	(36.8)
NA	New Hampshire**	NA
NA	West Virginia**	NA
	District of Columbia	(51.7)

Source: Morgan Quitno Press using data from Federal Bureau of Investigation
   "Crime in the United States" (Uniform Crime Reports, 1997 and 2000 editions)
*Burglary is the unlawful entry of a structure to commit a felony or theft. Attempts are included.
**Not comparable.

Burglary Rate in 1996

National Rate = 944.8 Burglaries per 100,000 Population*

ALPHA ORDER

RANK	STATE	RATE
15	Alabama	1,002.1
26	Alaska	843.2
6	Arizona	1,256.3
20	Arkansas	953.2
19	California	979.4
22	Colorado	900.8
27	Connecticut	842.2
30	Delaware	804.1
1	Florida	1,521.2
11	Georgia	1,114.8
12	Hawaii	1,079.5
36	Idaho	709.1
21	Illinois	913.2
32	Indiana	783.8
40	Iowa	664.6
18	Kansas	981.3
38	Kentucky	688.4
4	Louisiana	1,295.8
34	Maine	748.4
16	Maryland	992.3
37	Massachusetts	704.1
23	Michigan	895.4
33	Minnesota	762.5
10	Mississippi	1,132.4
24	Missouri	894.2
46	Montana	558.4
42	Nebraska	614.5
8	Nevada	1,220.1
49	New Hampshire	435.7
31	New Jersey	791.9
2	New Mexico	1,376.9
35	New York	713.9
3	North Carolina	1,345.6
50	North Dakota	309.2
28	Ohio	835.4
7	Oklahoma	1,255.6
17	Oregon	988.3
43	Pennsylvania	591.9
29	Rhode Island	821.7
5	South Carolina	1,283.8
47	South Dakota	557.0
9	Tennessee	1,163.5
13	Texas	1,068.5
25	Utah	848.3
39	Vermont	673.0
45	Virginia	588.1
14	Washington	1,057.5
48	West Virginia	546.5
44	Wisconsin	588.3
41	Wyoming	662.0

RANK ORDER

RANK	STATE	RATE
1	Florida	1,521.2
2	New Mexico	1,376.9
3	North Carolina	1,345.6
4	Louisiana	1,295.8
5	South Carolina	1,283.8
6	Arizona	1,256.3
7	Oklahoma	1,255.6
8	Nevada	1,220.1
9	Tennessee	1,163.5
10	Mississippi	1,132.4
11	Georgia	1,114.8
12	Hawaii	1,079.5
13	Texas	1,068.5
14	Washington	1,057.5
15	Alabama	1,002.1
16	Maryland	992.3
17	Oregon	988.3
18	Kansas	981.3
19	California	979.4
20	Arkansas	953.2
21	Illinois	913.2
22	Colorado	900.8
23	Michigan	895.4
24	Missouri	894.2
25	Utah	848.3
26	Alaska	843.2
27	Connecticut	842.2
28	Ohio	835.4
29	Rhode Island	821.7
30	Delaware	804.1
31	New Jersey	791.9
32	Indiana	783.8
33	Minnesota	762.5
34	Maine	748.4
35	New York	713.9
36	Idaho	709.1
37	Massachusetts	704.1
38	Kentucky	688.4
39	Vermont	673.0
40	Iowa	664.6
41	Wyoming	662.0
42	Nebraska	614.5
43	Pennsylvania	591.9
44	Wisconsin	588.3
45	Virginia	588.1
46	Montana	558.4
47	South Dakota	557.0
48	West Virginia	546.5
49	New Hampshire	435.7
50	North Dakota	309.2
	District of Columbia	1,809.9

Source: Federal Bureau of Investigation
"Crime in the United States 1997" (Uniform Crime Reports, November 22, 1998)
*Revised figures. Burglary is the unlawful entry of a structure to commit a felony or theft. Attempts are included.

Percent Change in Burglary Rate: 1996 to 2000

National Percent Change = 22.9% Decrease*

ALPHA ORDER				RANK ORDER		
RANK	STATE	PERCENT CHANGE		RANK	STATE	PERCENT CHANGE
5	Alabama	(9.5)		1	North Dakota	5.4
33	Alaska	(26.2)		2	Nebraska	(3.7)
20	Arizona	(19.5)		3	Ohio	(6.5)
13	Arkansas	(15.9)		4	Kentucky	(9.0)
44	California	(33.0)		5	Alabama	(9.5)
40	Colorado	(30.0)		6	North Carolina	(9.6)
48	Connecticut	(39.2)		7	Indiana	(13.7)
17	Delaware	(17.2)		8	Washington	(14.2)
38	Florida	(28.9)		9	Vermont	(14.6)
30	Georgia	(25.0)		10	New Mexico	(14.8)
18	Hawaii	(18.5)		11	Tennessee	(14.9)
21	Idaho	(20.1)		12	Texas	(15.2)
36	Illinois	(27.8)		13	Arkansas	(15.9)
7	Indiana	(13.7)		14	Iowa	(16.0)
14	Iowa	(16.0)		15	Mississippi	(16.4)
19	Kansas	(18.6)		16	Missouri	(16.7)
4	Kentucky	(9.0)		17	Delaware	(17.2)
21	Louisiana	(20.1)		18	Hawaii	(18.5)
39	Maine	(29.0)		19	Kansas	(18.6)
30	Maryland	(25.0)		20	Arizona	(19.5)
43	Massachusetts	(31.5)		21	Idaho	(20.1)
24	Michigan	(21.6)		21	Louisiana	(20.1)
41	Minnesota	(30.4)		23	Wisconsin	(20.2)
15	Mississippi	(16.4)		24	Michigan	(21.6)
16	Missouri	(16.7)		25	Montana	(21.7)
25	Montana	(21.7)		26	Rhode Island	(23.1)
2	Nebraska	(3.7)		27	Oregon	(24.2)
37	Nevada	(28.1)		28	Utah	(24.3)
NA	New Hampshire**	NA		29	South Carolina	(24.5)
45	New Jersey	(34.1)		30	Georgia	(25.0)
10	New Mexico	(14.8)		30	Maryland	(25.0)
46	New York	(35.1)		32	Pennsylvania	(25.6)
6	North Carolina	(9.6)		33	Alaska	(26.2)
1	North Dakota	5.4		34	Oklahoma	(26.9)
3	Ohio	(6.5)		34	Virginia	(26.9)
34	Oklahoma	(26.9)		36	Illinois	(27.8)
27	Oregon	(24.2)		37	Nevada	(28.1)
32	Pennsylvania	(25.6)		38	Florida	(28.9)
26	Rhode Island	(23.1)		39	Maine	(29.0)
29	South Carolina	(24.5)		40	Colorado	(30.0)
42	South Dakota	(31.1)		41	Minnesota	(30.4)
11	Tennessee	(14.9)		42	South Dakota	(31.1)
12	Texas	(15.2)		43	Massachusetts	(31.5)
28	Utah	(24.3)		44	California	(33.0)
9	Vermont	(14.6)		45	New Jersey	(34.1)
34	Virginia	(26.9)		46	New York	(35.1)
8	Washington	(14.2)		47	Wyoming	(36.4)
NA	West Virginia**	NA		48	Connecticut	(39.2)
23	Wisconsin	(20.2)		NA	New Hampshire**	NA
47	Wyoming	(36.4)		NA	West Virginia**	NA
					District of Columbia	(54.2)

Source: Morgan Quitno Press using data from Federal Bureau of Investigation
    "Crime in the United States" (Uniform Crime Reports, 1997 and 2000 editions)
*Burglary is the unlawful entry of a structure to commit a felony or theft. Attempts are included.
**Not comparable.

Larcenies and Thefts in 1996

National Total = 7,904,685 Larcenies and Thefts*

RANK	STATE	THEFTS	% of USA
25	Alabama	123,350	1.6%
46	Alaska	20,557	0.3%
13	Arizona	188,300	2.4%
32	Arkansas	73,010	0.9%
1	California	830,457	10.5%
22	Colorado	130,576	1.7%
29	Connecticut	81,328	1.0%
45	Delaware	21,665	0.3%
3	Florida	605,448	7.7%
7	Georgia	288,803	3.7%
36	Hawaii	54,701	0.7%
39	Idaho	33,872	0.4%
5	Illinois	358,515	4.5%
18	Indiana	160,777	2.0%
33	Iowa	71,893	0.9%
30	Kansas	78,145	1.0%
31	Kentucky	73,653	0.9%
16	Louisiana	173,271	2.2%
41	Maine	29,557	0.4%
15	Maryland	173,817	2.2%
26	Massachusetts	119,562	1.5%
8	Michigan	276,909	3.5%
20	Minnesota	138,671	1.8%
34	Mississippi	69,299	0.9%
17	Missouri	168,870	2.1%
40	Montana	30,928	0.4%
38	Nebraska	50,315	0.6%
37	Nevada	52,295	0.7%
43	New Hampshire	24,611	0.3%
12	New Jersey	193,961	2.5%
35	New Mexico	65,139	0.8%
4	New York	399,522	5.1%
10	North Carolina	238,511	3.0%
49	North Dakota	13,433	0.2%
6	Ohio	311,071	3.9%
27	Oklahoma	109,506	1.4%
24	Oregon	128,618	1.6%
9	Pennsylvania	250,758	3.2%
44	Rhode Island	23,367	0.3%
23	South Carolina	129,650	1.6%
47	South Dakota	15,532	0.2%
19	Tennessee	152,405	1.9%
2	Texas	659,414	8.3%
28	Utah	87,542	1.1%
50	Vermont	12,124	0.2%
14	Virginia	184,237	2.3%
11	Washington	215,706	2.7%
42	West Virginia	28,300	0.4%
21	Wisconsin	135,941	1.7%
48	Wyoming	15,408	0.2%

RANK	STATE	THEFTS	% of USA
1	California	830,457	10.5%
2	Texas	659,414	8.3%
3	Florida	605,448	7.7%
4	New York	399,522	5.1%
5	Illinois	358,515	4.5%
6	Ohio	311,071	3.9%
7	Georgia	288,803	3.7%
8	Michigan	276,909	3.5%
9	Pennsylvania	250,758	3.2%
10	North Carolina	238,511	3.0%
11	Washington	215,706	2.7%
12	New Jersey	193,961	2.5%
13	Arizona	188,300	2.4%
14	Virginia	184,237	2.3%
15	Maryland	173,817	2.2%
16	Louisiana	173,271	2.2%
17	Missouri	168,870	2.1%
18	Indiana	160,777	2.0%
19	Tennessee	152,405	1.9%
20	Minnesota	138,671	1.8%
21	Wisconsin	135,941	1.7%
22	Colorado	130,576	1.7%
23	South Carolina	129,650	1.6%
24	Oregon	128,618	1.6%
25	Alabama	123,350	1.6%
26	Massachusetts	119,562	1.5%
27	Oklahoma	109,506	1.4%
28	Utah	87,542	1.1%
29	Connecticut	81,328	1.0%
30	Kansas	78,145	1.0%
31	Kentucky	73,653	0.9%
32	Arkansas	73,010	0.9%
33	Iowa	71,893	0.9%
34	Mississippi	69,299	0.9%
35	New Mexico	65,139	0.8%
36	Hawaii	54,701	0.7%
37	Nevada	52,295	0.7%
38	Nebraska	50,315	0.6%
39	Idaho	33,872	0.4%
40	Montana	30,928	0.4%
41	Maine	29,557	0.4%
42	West Virginia	28,300	0.4%
43	New Hampshire	24,611	0.3%
44	Rhode Island	23,367	0.3%
45	Delaware	21,665	0.3%
46	Alaska	20,557	0.3%
47	South Dakota	15,532	0.2%
48	Wyoming	15,408	0.2%
49	North Dakota	13,433	0.2%
50	Vermont	12,124	0.2%
	District of Columbia	31,385	0.4%

Source: Federal Bureau of Investigation
"Crime in the United States 1997" (Uniform Crime Reports, November 22, 1998)
*Revised figures. Larceny and theft is the unlawful taking of property without use of force, violence or fraud. Attempts are included. Motor vehicle thefts are excluded.

Percent Change in Number of Larcenies and Thefts: 1996 to 2000

National Percent Change = 11.9% Decrease*

ALPHA ORDER

RANK	STATE	PERCENT CHANGE
2	Alabama	3.3
40	Alaska	(18.1)
16	Arizona	(6.2)
11	Arkansas	(4.5)
47	California	(21.5)
27	Colorado	(13.6)
33	Connecticut	(15.8)
7	Delaware	(1.4)
28	Florida	(14.4)
36	Georgia	(16.7)
46	Hawaii	(20.9)
32	Idaho	(15.7)
26	Illinois	(12.8)
19	Indiana	(10.0)
17	Iowa	(9.4)
3	Kansas	2.5
6	Kentucky	(0.7)
36	Louisiana	(16.7)
41	Maine	(19.1)
35	Maryland	(16.3)
23	Massachusetts	(11.8)
39	Michigan	(17.7)
29	Minnesota	(14.7)
5	Mississippi	0.7
13	Missouri	(5.5)
48	Montana	(23.0)
8	Nebraska	(2.4)
31	Nevada	(15.6)
NA	New Hampshire**	NA
43	New Jersey	(19.8)
20	New Mexico	(11.1)
29	New York	(14.7)
8	North Carolina	(2.4)
38	North Dakota	(17.4)
14	Ohio	(5.7)
25	Oklahoma	(12.2)
21	Oregon	(11.2)
18	Pennsylvania	(9.9)
14	Rhode Island	(5.7)
12	South Carolina	(5.1)
41	South Dakota	(19.1)
4	Tennessee	1.1
10	Texas	(3.3)
34	Utah	(16.1)
1	Vermont	8.7
45	Virginia	(20.7)
22	Washington	(11.6)
NA	West Virginia**	NA
24	Wisconsin	(12.0)
44	Wyoming	(20.1)

RANK ORDER

RANK	STATE	PERCENT CHANGE
1	Vermont	8.7
2	Alabama	3.3
3	Kansas	2.5
4	Tennessee	1.1
5	Mississippi	0.7
6	Kentucky	(0.7)
7	Delaware	(1.4)
8	Nebraska	(2.4)
8	North Carolina	(2.4)
10	Texas	(3.3)
11	Arkansas	(4.5)
12	South Carolina	(5.1)
13	Missouri	(5.5)
14	Ohio	(5.7)
14	Rhode Island	(5.7)
16	Arizona	(6.2)
17	Iowa	(9.4)
18	Pennsylvania	(9.9)
19	Indiana	(10.0)
20	New Mexico	(11.1)
21	Oregon	(11.2)
22	Washington	(11.6)
23	Massachusetts	(11.8)
24	Wisconsin	(12.0)
25	Oklahoma	(12.2)
26	Illinois	(12.8)
27	Colorado	(13.6)
28	Florida	(14.4)
29	Minnesota	(14.7)
29	New York	(14.7)
31	Nevada	(15.6)
32	Idaho	(15.7)
33	Connecticut	(15.8)
34	Utah	(16.1)
35	Maryland	(16.3)
36	Georgia	(16.7)
36	Louisiana	(16.7)
38	North Dakota	(17.4)
39	Michigan	(17.7)
40	Alaska	(18.1)
41	Maine	(19.1)
41	South Dakota	(19.1)
43	New Jersey	(19.8)
44	Wyoming	(20.1)
45	Virginia	(20.7)
46	Hawaii	(20.9)
47	California	(21.5)
48	Montana	(23.0)
NA	New Hampshire**	NA
NA	West Virginia**	NA
	District of Columbia	(31.0)

Source: Morgan Quitno Press using data from Federal Bureau of Investigation
"Crime in the United States" (Uniform Crime Reports, 1997 and 2000 editions)
*Larceny and theft is the unlawful taking of property without use of force, violence or fraud. Attempts are included.
Motor vehicle thefts are excluded.
**Not comparable.

Larceny and Theft Rate in 1996

National Rate = 2,979.7 Larcenies and Thefts per 100,000 Population*

ALPHA ORDER

RANK	STATE	RATE
27	Alabama	2,886.7
15	Alaska	3,386.7
3	Arizona	4,252.5
26	Arkansas	2,908.8
35	California	2,605.1
14	Colorado	3,415.5
38	Connecticut	2,484.1
24	Delaware	2,988.3
4	Florida	4,204.5
7	Georgia	3,927.7
1	Hawaii	4,620.0
30	Idaho	2,848.8
23	Illinois	3,026.2
33	Indiana	2,752.6
37	Iowa	2,520.8
22	Kansas	3,038.3
49	Kentucky	1,896.3
6	Louisiana	3,982.3
40	Maine	2,377.9
13	Maryland	3,427.0
48	Massachusetts	1,962.6
28	Michigan	2,886.3
25	Minnesota	2,977.1
36	Mississippi	2,551.5
20	Missouri	3,151.1
10	Montana	3,518.5
21	Nebraska	3,045.7
17	Nevada	3,262.3
44	New Hampshire	2,118.0
39	New Jersey	2,428.2
9	New Mexico	3,802.6
42	New York	2,197.0
18	North Carolina	3,257.0
45	North Dakota	2,085.9
31	Ohio	2,784.1
16	Oklahoma	3,317.4
5	Oregon	4,014.3
46	Pennsylvania	2,079.9
41	Rhode Island	2,360.3
11	South Carolina	3,505.0
43	South Dakota	2,121.9
29	Tennessee	2,864.8
12	Texas	3,447.4
2	Utah	4,377.1
47	Vermont	2,058.4
32	Virginia	2,760.1
8	Washington	3,898.5
50	West Virginia	1,549.8
34	Wisconsin	2,634.5
19	Wyoming	3,203.3

RANK ORDER

RANK	STATE	RATE
1	Hawaii	4,620.0
2	Utah	4,377.1
3	Arizona	4,252.5
4	Florida	4,204.5
5	Oregon	4,014.3
6	Louisiana	3,982.3
7	Georgia	3,927.7
8	Washington	3,898.5
9	New Mexico	3,802.6
10	Montana	3,518.5
11	South Carolina	3,505.0
12	Texas	3,447.4
13	Maryland	3,427.0
14	Colorado	3,415.5
15	Alaska	3,386.7
16	Oklahoma	3,317.4
17	Nevada	3,262.3
18	North Carolina	3,257.0
19	Wyoming	3,203.3
20	Missouri	3,151.1
21	Nebraska	3,045.7
22	Kansas	3,038.3
23	Illinois	3,026.2
24	Delaware	2,988.3
25	Minnesota	2,977.1
26	Arkansas	2,908.8
27	Alabama	2,886.7
28	Michigan	2,886.3
29	Tennessee	2,864.8
30	Idaho	2,848.8
31	Ohio	2,784.1
32	Virginia	2,760.1
33	Indiana	2,752.6
34	Wisconsin	2,634.5
35	California	2,605.1
36	Mississippi	2,551.5
37	Iowa	2,520.8
38	Connecticut	2,484.1
39	New Jersey	2,428.2
40	Maine	2,377.9
41	Rhode Island	2,360.3
42	New York	2,197.0
43	South Dakota	2,121.9
44	New Hampshire	2,118.0
45	North Dakota	2,085.9
46	Pennsylvania	2,079.9
47	Vermont	2,058.4
48	Massachusetts	1,962.6
49	Kentucky	1,896.3
50	West Virginia	1,549.8
	District of Columbia	5,779.9

Source: Federal Bureau of Investigation
    "Crime in the United States 1997" (Uniform Crime Reports, November 22, 1998)
*Revised figures. Larceny and theft is the unlawful taking of property without use of force, violence or fraud.
Attempts are included. Motor vehicle thefts are excluded.

Percent Change in Larceny and Theft Rate: 1996 to 2000

National Percent Change = 16.9% Decrease*

ALPHA ORDER

RANK	STATE	PERCENT CHANGE
2	Alabama	(0.8)
34	Alaska	(20.7)
29	Arizona	(19.0)
11	Arkansas	(10.3)
47	California	(26.1)
41	Colorado	(23.2)
29	Connecticut	(19.0)
9	Delaware	(8.8)
40	Florida	(22.9)
45	Georgia	(25.2)
39	Hawaii	(22.7)
38	Idaho	(22.6)
23	Illinois	(16.8)
18	Indiana	(13.5)
16	Iowa	(11.7)
3	Kansas	(2.0)
5	Kentucky	(4.6)
28	Louisiana	(18.9)
35	Maine	(21.1)
32	Maryland	(19.9)
19	Massachusetts	(15.4)
33	Michigan	(20.6)
31	Minnesota	(19.3)
4	Mississippi	(3.9)
10	Missouri	(9.5)
44	Montana	(25.0)
7	Nebraska	(5.8)
48	Nevada	(32.3)
NA	New Hampshire**	NA
42	New Jersey	(23.9)
22	New Mexico	(16.3)
27	New York	(18.2)
13	North Carolina	(11.2)
26	North Dakota	(17.2)
8	Ohio	(7.2)
21	Oklahoma	(16.0)
23	Oregon	(16.8)
15	Pennsylvania	(11.6)
12	Rhode Island	(10.9)
17	South Carolina	(12.5)
36	South Dakota	(21.6)
6	Tennessee	(5.4)
14	Texas	(11.3)
43	Utah	(24.9)
1	Vermont	5.2
45	Virginia	(25.2)
25	Washington	(17.0)
NA	West Virginia**	NA
19	Wisconsin	(15.4)
37	Wyoming	(22.1)

RANK ORDER

RANK	STATE	PERCENT CHANGE
1	Vermont	5.2
2	Alabama	(0.8)
3	Kansas	(2.0)
4	Mississippi	(3.9)
5	Kentucky	(4.6)
6	Tennessee	(5.4)
7	Nebraska	(5.8)
8	Ohio	(7.2)
9	Delaware	(8.8)
10	Missouri	(9.5)
11	Arkansas	(10.3)
12	Rhode Island	(10.9)
13	North Carolina	(11.2)
14	Texas	(11.3)
15	Pennsylvania	(11.6)
16	Iowa	(11.7)
17	South Carolina	(12.5)
18	Indiana	(13.5)
19	Massachusetts	(15.4)
19	Wisconsin	(15.4)
21	Oklahoma	(16.0)
22	New Mexico	(16.3)
23	Illinois	(16.8)
23	Oregon	(16.8)
25	Washington	(17.0)
26	North Dakota	(17.2)
27	New York	(18.2)
28	Louisiana	(18.9)
29	Arizona	(19.0)
29	Connecticut	(19.0)
31	Minnesota	(19.3)
32	Maryland	(19.9)
33	Michigan	(20.6)
34	Alaska	(20.7)
35	Maine	(21.1)
36	South Dakota	(21.6)
37	Wyoming	(22.1)
38	Idaho	(22.6)
39	Hawaii	(22.7)
40	Florida	(22.9)
41	Colorado	(23.2)
42	New Jersey	(23.9)
43	Utah	(24.9)
44	Montana	(25.0)
45	Georgia	(25.2)
45	Virginia	(25.2)
47	California	(26.1)
48	Nevada	(32.3)
NA	New Hampshire**	NA
NA	West Virginia**	NA
	District of Columbia	(34.5)

Source: Morgan Quitno Press using data from Federal Bureau of Investigation
   "Crime in the United States" (Uniform Crime Reports, 1997 and 2000 editions)
*Larceny and theft is the unlawful taking of property without use of force, violence or fraud. Attempts are included.
Motor vehicle thefts are excluded.
**Not comparable.

Motor Vehicle Thefts in 1996

National Total = 1,394,238 Motor Vehicle Thefts*

ALPHA ORDER

RANK	STATE	THEFTS	% of USA
27	Alabama	15,632	1.1%
42	Alaska	2,992	0.2%
11	Arizona	41,034	2.9%
34	Arkansas	7,855	0.6%
1	California	242,466	17.4%
28	Colorado	15,206	1.1%
24	Connecticut	16,022	1.1%
41	Delaware	3,148	0.2%
3	Florida	103,769	7.4%
9	Georgia	46,215	3.3%
35	Hawaii	7,157	0.5%
44	Idaho	2,229	0.2%
6	Illinois	58,077	4.2%
17	Indiana	24,817	1.8%
38	Iowa	5,449	0.4%
36	Kansas	6,388	0.5%
30	Kentucky	10,142	0.7%
16	Louisiana	27,480	2.0%
45	Maine	1,776	0.1%
12	Maryland	36,083	2.6%
14	Massachusetts	32,178	2.3%
5	Michigan	67,203	4.8%
21	Minnesota	17,923	1.3%
32	Mississippi	9,527	0.7%
19	Missouri	23,992	1.7%
43	Montana	2,248	0.2%
37	Nebraska	5,643	0.4%
29	Nevada	11,194	0.8%
46	New Hampshire	1,762	0.1%
8	New Jersey	46,437	3.3%
31	New Mexico	9,973	0.7%
4	New York	89,900	6.4%
18	North Carolina	24,566	1.8%
47	North Dakota	1,224	0.1%
10	Ohio	45,528	3.3%
25	Oklahoma	15,939	1.1%
23	Oregon	17,013	1.2%
7	Pennsylvania	48,736	3.5%
39	Rhode Island	4,597	0.3%
26	South Carolina	15,849	1.1%
49	South Dakota	834	0.1%
13	Tennessee	34,428	2.5%
2	Texas	104,928	7.5%
33	Utah	8,572	0.6%
48	Vermont	885	0.1%
20	Virginia	18,608	1.3%
15	Washington	28,893	2.1%
40	West Virginia	3,231	0.2%
22	Wisconsin	17,846	1.3%
50	Wyoming	669	0.0%

RANK ORDER

RANK	STATE	THEFTS	% of USA
1	California	242,466	17.4%
2	Texas	104,928	7.5%
3	Florida	103,769	7.4%
4	New York	89,900	6.4%
5	Michigan	67,203	4.8%
6	Illinois	58,077	4.2%
7	Pennsylvania	48,736	3.5%
8	New Jersey	46,437	3.3%
9	Georgia	46,215	3.3%
10	Ohio	45,528	3.3%
11	Arizona	41,034	2.9%
12	Maryland	36,083	2.6%
13	Tennessee	34,428	2.5%
14	Massachusetts	32,178	2.3%
15	Washington	28,893	2.1%
16	Louisiana	27,480	2.0%
17	Indiana	24,817	1.8%
18	North Carolina	24,566	1.8%
19	Missouri	23,992	1.7%
20	Virginia	18,608	1.3%
21	Minnesota	17,923	1.3%
22	Wisconsin	17,846	1.3%
23	Oregon	17,013	1.2%
24	Connecticut	16,022	1.1%
25	Oklahoma	15,939	1.1%
26	South Carolina	15,849	1.1%
27	Alabama	15,632	1.1%
28	Colorado	15,206	1.1%
29	Nevada	11,194	0.8%
30	Kentucky	10,142	0.7%
31	New Mexico	9,973	0.7%
32	Mississippi	9,527	0.7%
33	Utah	8,572	0.6%
34	Arkansas	7,855	0.6%
35	Hawaii	7,157	0.5%
36	Kansas	6,388	0.5%
37	Nebraska	5,643	0.4%
38	Iowa	5,449	0.4%
39	Rhode Island	4,597	0.3%
40	West Virginia	3,231	0.2%
41	Delaware	3,148	0.2%
42	Alaska	2,992	0.2%
43	Montana	2,248	0.2%
44	Idaho	2,229	0.2%
45	Maine	1,776	0.1%
46	New Hampshire	1,762	0.1%
47	North Dakota	1,224	0.1%
48	Vermont	885	0.1%
49	South Dakota	834	0.1%
50	Wyoming	669	0.0%
	District of Columbia	9,975	0.7%

Source: Federal Bureau of Investigation
"Crime in the United States 1997" (Uniform Crime Reports, November 22, 1998)
Revised figures. Includes the theft or attempted theft of a self-propelled vehicle. Excludes motorboats, construction equipment, airplanes and farming equipment.

Percent Change in Number of Motor Vehicle Thefts: 1996 to 2000

National Percent Change = 16.4% Decrease*

ALPHA ORDER				RANK ORDER		
RANK	STATE	PERCENT CHANGE		RANK	STATE	PERCENT CHANGE
30	Alabama	(18.1)		1	Washington	21.2
37	Alaska	(21.5)		2	Nevada	17.7
4	Arizona	5.3		3	Colorado	11.5
20	Arkansas	(11.8)		4	Arizona	5.3
41	California	(24.9)		5	Missouri	2.9
3	Colorado	11.5		6	North Carolina	2.8
32	Connecticut	(18.2)		7	Kansas	1.7
9	Delaware	0.1		8	Rhode Island	1.5
22	Florida	(14.1)		9	Delaware	0.1
27	Georgia	(16.3)		10	Iowa	(1.4)
25	Hawaii	(14.6)		11	Illinois	(3.3)
15	Idaho	(6.4)		12	South Carolina	(4.1)
11	Illinois	(3.3)		13	South Dakota	(4.3)
26	Indiana	(15.0)		13	Virginia	(4.3)
10	Iowa	(1.4)		15	Idaho	(6.4)
7	Kansas	1.7		16	Nebraska	(7.3)
17	Kentucky	(8.6)		17	Kentucky	(8.6)
39	Louisiana	(22.6)		17	Vermont	(8.6)
44	Maine	(25.6)		19	Texas	(11.2)
36	Maryland	(20.8)		20	Arkansas	(11.8)
34	Massachusetts	(19.6)		21	Montana	(13.0)
28	Michigan	(17.1)		22	Florida	(14.1)
42	Minnesota	(25.1)		23	Ohio	(14.3)
47	Mississippi	(26.9)		23	Wyoming	(14.3)
5	Missouri	2.9		25	Hawaii	(14.6)
21	Montana	(13.0)		26	Indiana	(15.0)
16	Nebraska	(7.3)		27	Georgia	(16.3)
2	Nevada	17.7		28	Michigan	(17.1)
NA	New Hampshire**	NA		29	Wisconsin	(18.0)
46	New Jersey	(26.5)		30	Alabama	(18.1)
45	New Mexico	(26.4)		30	Oregon	(18.1)
48	New York	(39.7)		32	Connecticut	(18.2)
6	North Carolina	2.8		33	North Dakota	(19.4)
33	North Dakota	(19.4)		34	Massachusetts	(19.6)
23	Ohio	(14.3)		35	Tennessee	(20.0)
38	Oklahoma	(22.5)		36	Maryland	(20.8)
30	Oregon	(18.1)		37	Alaska	(21.5)
43	Pennsylvania	(25.5)		38	Oklahoma	(22.5)
8	Rhode Island	1.5		39	Louisiana	(22.6)
12	South Carolina	(4.1)		40	Utah	(24.6)
13	South Dakota	(4.3)		41	California	(24.9)
35	Tennessee	(20.0)		42	Minnesota	(25.1)
19	Texas	(11.2)		43	Pennsylvania	(25.5)
40	Utah	(24.6)		44	Maine	(25.6)
17	Vermont	(8.6)		45	New Mexico	(26.4)
13	Virginia	(4.3)		46	New Jersey	(26.5)
1	Washington	21.2		47	Mississippi	(26.9)
NA	West Virginia**	NA		48	New York	(39.7)
29	Wisconsin	(18.0)		NA	New Hampshire**	NA
23	Wyoming	(14.3)		NA	West Virginia**	NA
					District of Columbia	(33.8)

Source: Morgan Quitno Press using data from Federal Bureau of Investigation
   "Crime in the United States" (Uniform Crime Reports, 1997 and 2000 editions)
*Includes the theft or attempted theft of a self-propelled vehicle. Excludes motorboats, construction equipment, airplanes and farming equipment.
**Not comparable.

Motor Vehicle Theft Rate in 1996

National Rate = 525.6 Motor Vehicle Thefts per 100,000 Population*

ALPHA ORDER

RANK	STATE	RATE
32	Alabama	365.8
18	Alaska	492.9
1	Arizona	926.7
37	Arkansas	312.9
2	California	760.6
30	Colorado	397.8
20	Connecticut	489.4
24	Delaware	434.2
3	Florida	720.6
9	Georgia	628.5
10	Hawaii	604.5
44	Idaho	187.5
19	Illinois	490.2
27	Indiana	424.9
42	Iowa	191.1
41	Kansas	248.4
39	Kentucky	261.1
8	Louisiana	631.6
48	Maine	142.9
4	Maryland	711.4
15	Massachusetts	528.2
5	Michigan	700.5
31	Minnesota	384.8
33	Mississippi	350.8
23	Missouri	447.7
40	Montana	255.7
35	Nebraska	341.6
6	Nevada	698.3
46	New Hampshire	151.6
12	New Jersey	581.3
11	New Mexico	582.2
17	New York	494.4
36	North Carolina	335.5
43	North Dakota	190.1
29	Ohio	407.5
21	Oklahoma	482.9
14	Oregon	531.0
28	Pennsylvania	412.2
22	Rhode Island	464.3
26	South Carolina	428.5
50	South Dakota	113.9
7	Tennessee	647.1
13	Texas	548.6
25	Utah	428.6
47	Vermont	150.3
38	Virginia	278.8
16	Washington	522.2
45	West Virginia	176.9
34	Wisconsin	345.9
49	Wyoming	139.1

RANK ORDER

RANK	STATE	RATE
1	Arizona	926.7
2	California	760.6
3	Florida	720.6
4	Maryland	711.4
5	Michigan	700.5
6	Nevada	698.3
7	Tennessee	647.1
8	Louisiana	631.6
9	Georgia	628.5
10	Hawaii	604.5
11	New Mexico	582.2
12	New Jersey	581.3
13	Texas	548.6
14	Oregon	531.0
15	Massachusetts	528.2
16	Washington	522.2
17	New York	494.4
18	Alaska	492.9
19	Illinois	490.2
20	Connecticut	489.4
21	Oklahoma	482.9
22	Rhode Island	464.3
23	Missouri	447.7
24	Delaware	434.2
25	Utah	428.6
26	South Carolina	428.5
27	Indiana	424.9
28	Pennsylvania	412.2
29	Ohio	407.5
30	Colorado	397.8
31	Minnesota	384.8
32	Alabama	365.8
33	Mississippi	350.8
34	Wisconsin	345.9
35	Nebraska	341.6
36	North Carolina	335.5
37	Arkansas	312.9
38	Virginia	278.8
39	Kentucky	261.1
40	Montana	255.7
41	Kansas	248.4
42	Iowa	191.1
43	North Dakota	190.1
44	Idaho	187.5
45	West Virginia	176.9
46	New Hampshire	151.6
47	Vermont	150.3
48	Maine	142.9
49	Wyoming	139.1
50	South Dakota	113.9

District of Columbia   1,837.0

Source: Federal Bureau of Investigation
   "Crime in the United States 1997" (Uniform Crime Reports, November 22, 1998)
*Revised figures. Includes the theft or attempted theft of a self-propelled vehicle. Excludes motorboats, construction equipment, airplanes and farming equipment.

Percent Change in Motor Vehicle Theft Rate: 1996 to 2000

National Percent Change = 21.2% Decrease*

ALPHA ORDER

RANK	STATE	PERCENT CHANGE
29	Alabama	(21.3)
34	Alaska	(24.0)
12	Arizona	(9.1)
23	Arkansas	(17.1)
43	California	(29.3)
2	Colorado	(0.9)
30	Connecticut	(21.4)
10	Delaware	(7.4)
31	Florida	(22.6)
37	Georgia	(24.8)
21	Hawaii	(16.5)
18	Idaho	(14.0)
11	Illinois	(7.8)
24	Indiana	(18.4)
5	Iowa	(3.9)
4	Kansas	(2.7)
17	Kentucky	(12.1)
36	Louisiana	(24.7)
40	Maine	(27.4)
35	Maryland	(24.2)
32	Massachusetts	(22.8)
27	Michigan	(20.0)
42	Minnesota	(29.1)
44	Mississippi	(30.2)
3	Missouri	(1.4)
19	Montana	(15.2)
14	Nebraska	(10.5)
7	Nevada	(5.6)
NA	New Hampshire**	NA
44	New Jersey	(30.2)
46	New Mexico	(30.7)
48	New York	(42.2)
8	North Carolina	(6.4)
26	North Dakota	(19.3)
20	Ohio	(15.7)
39	Oklahoma	(25.9)
33	Oregon	(23.3)
41	Pennsylvania	(28.2)
6	Rhode Island	(4.2)
15	South Carolina	(11.6)
9	South Dakota	(7.2)
38	Tennessee	(25.2)
25	Texas	(18.6)
47	Utah	(32.5)
15	Vermont	(11.6)
13	Virginia	(9.8)
1	Washington	13.8
NA	West Virginia**	NA
28	Wisconsin	(21.1)
22	Wyoming	(16.6)

RANK ORDER

RANK	STATE	PERCENT CHANGE
1	Washington	13.8
2	Colorado	(0.9)
3	Missouri	(1.4)
4	Kansas	(2.7)
5	Iowa	(3.9)
6	Rhode Island	(4.2)
7	Nevada	(5.6)
8	North Carolina	(6.4)
9	South Dakota	(7.2)
10	Delaware	(7.4)
11	Illinois	(7.8)
12	Arizona	(9.1)
13	Virginia	(9.8)
14	Nebraska	(10.5)
15	South Carolina	(11.6)
15	Vermont	(11.6)
17	Kentucky	(12.1)
18	Idaho	(14.0)
19	Montana	(15.2)
20	Ohio	(15.7)
21	Hawaii	(16.5)
22	Wyoming	(16.6)
23	Arkansas	(17.1)
24	Indiana	(18.4)
25	Texas	(18.6)
26	North Dakota	(19.3)
27	Michigan	(20.0)
28	Wisconsin	(21.1)
29	Alabama	(21.3)
30	Connecticut	(21.4)
31	Florida	(22.6)
32	Massachusetts	(22.8)
33	Oregon	(23.3)
34	Alaska	(24.0)
35	Maryland	(24.2)
36	Louisiana	(24.7)
37	Georgia	(24.8)
38	Tennessee	(25.2)
39	Oklahoma	(25.9)
40	Maine	(27.4)
41	Pennsylvania	(28.2)
42	Minnesota	(29.1)
43	California	(29.3)
44	Mississippi	(30.2)
44	New Jersey	(30.2)
46	New Mexico	(30.7)
47	Utah	(32.5)
48	New York	(42.2)
NA	New Hampshire**	NA
NA	West Virginia**	NA
	District of Columbia	(37.2)

Source: Morgan Quitno Press using data from Federal Bureau of Investigation
    "Crime in the United States" (Uniform Crime Reports, 1997 and 2000 editions)
*Includes the theft or attempted theft of a self-propelled vehicle. Excludes motorboats, construction equipment, airplanes and farming equipment.
**Not comparable.

Hate Crimes in 2000

National Total = 9,430 Reported Hate Crimes*

ALPHA ORDER

RANK	STATE	HATE CRIMES	% of USA
NA	Alabama**	NA	NA
45	Alaska	5	0.1%
9	Arizona	338	3.6%
47	Arkansas	4	0.0%
1	California	2,264	24.0%
19	Colorado	136	1.4%
15	Connecticut	204	2.2%
35	Delaware	37	0.4%
10	Florida	268	2.8%
36	Georgia	36	0.4%
NA	Hawaii**	NA	NA
28	Idaho	59	0.6%
14	Illinois	213	2.3%
20	Indiana	131	1.4%
34	Iowa	38	0.4%
29	Kansas	50	0.5%
25	Kentucky	89	0.9%
42	Louisiana	13	0.1%
37	Maine	29	0.3%
13	Maryland	225	2.4%
4	Massachusetts	526	5.6%
5	Michigan	500	5.3%
16	Minnesota	198	2.1%
48	Mississippi	2	0.0%
23	Missouri	93	1.0%
38	Montana	24	0.3%
41	Nebraska	19	0.2%
21	Nevada	115	1.2%
32	New Hampshire	39	0.4%
2	New Jersey	702	7.4%
38	New Mexico	24	0.3%
3	New York	617	6.5%
31	North Carolina	42	0.4%
45	North Dakota	5	0.1%
11	Ohio	261	2.8%
22	Oklahoma	96	1.0%
18	Oregon	166	1.8%
17	Pennsylvania	171	1.8%
29	Rhode Island	50	0.5%
32	South Carolina	39	0.4%
44	South Dakota	7	0.1%
12	Tennessee	260	2.8%
8	Texas	340	3.6%
24	Utah	92	1.0%
40	Vermont	20	0.2%
6	Virginia	383	4.1%
7	Washington	348	3.7%
26	West Virginia	75	0.8%
27	Wisconsin	60	0.6%
43	Wyoming	12	0.1%

RANK ORDER

RANK	STATE	HATE CRIMES	% of USA
1	California	2,264	24.0%
2	New Jersey	702	7.4%
3	New York	617	6.5%
4	Massachusetts	526	5.6%
5	Michigan	500	5.3%
6	Virginia	383	4.1%
7	Washington	348	3.7%
8	Texas	340	3.6%
9	Arizona	338	3.6%
10	Florida	268	2.8%
11	Ohio	261	2.8%
12	Tennessee	260	2.8%
13	Maryland	225	2.4%
14	Illinois	213	2.3%
15	Connecticut	204	2.2%
16	Minnesota	198	2.1%
17	Pennsylvania	171	1.8%
18	Oregon	166	1.8%
19	Colorado	136	1.4%
20	Indiana	131	1.4%
21	Nevada	115	1.2%
22	Oklahoma	96	1.0%
23	Missouri	93	1.0%
24	Utah	92	1.0%
25	Kentucky	89	0.9%
26	West Virginia	75	0.8%
27	Wisconsin	60	0.6%
28	Idaho	59	0.6%
29	Kansas	50	0.5%
29	Rhode Island	50	0.5%
31	North Carolina	42	0.4%
32	New Hampshire	39	0.4%
32	South Carolina	39	0.4%
34	Iowa	38	0.4%
35	Delaware	37	0.4%
36	Georgia	36	0.4%
37	Maine	29	0.3%
38	Montana	24	0.3%
38	New Mexico	24	0.3%
40	Vermont	20	0.2%
41	Nebraska	19	0.2%
42	Louisiana	13	0.1%
43	Wyoming	12	0.1%
44	South Dakota	7	0.1%
45	Alaska	5	0.1%
45	North Dakota	5	0.1%
47	Arkansas	4	0.0%
48	Mississippi	2	0.0%
NA	Alabama**	NA	NA
NA	Hawaii**	NA	NA
	District of Columbia	5	0.1%

Source: Federal Bureau of Investigation
"Hate Crimes Statistics 2000" (Uniform Crime Reports, November 19, 2001)
*Figures are for reporting law enforcement agencies. Participating agencies covered 84.2 percent of the U.S. population. Fifty-four percent of the incidents were motivated by racial bias; 18.3 percent by religious bias; 16.1 percent by sexual-orientation bias; and 11.3 percent by ethnicity/national origin bias.
**Not available.

Rate of Hate Crimes in 2000

National Rate = 3.4 Hate Crimes per 100,000 Population*

ALPHA ORDER

RANK	STATE	RATE
NA	Alabama**	NA
42	Alaska	0.8
4	Arizona	6.5
47	Arkansas	0.1
3	California	6.7
21	Colorado	3.1
5	Connecticut	6.0
12	Delaware	4.7
31	Florida	1.7
45	Georgia	0.4
NA	Hawaii**	NA
14	Idaho	4.5
31	Illinois	1.7
28	Indiana	2.2
36	Iowa	1.3
30	Kansas	1.9
28	Kentucky	2.2
46	Louisiana	0.3
26	Maine	2.3
15	Maryland	4.2
1	Massachusetts	8.3
9	Michigan	5.0
18	Minnesota	4.0
47	Mississippi	0.1
31	Missouri	1.7
24	Montana	2.7
38	Nebraska	1.1
7	Nevada	5.7
21	New Hampshire	3.1
1	New Jersey	8.3
36	New Mexico	1.3
20	New York	3.2
44	North Carolina	0.5
42	North Dakota	0.8
26	Ohio	2.3
23	Oklahoma	2.8
10	Oregon	4.8
35	Pennsylvania	1.4
10	Rhode Island	4.8
40	South Carolina	1.0
41	South Dakota	0.9
13	Tennessee	4.6
34	Texas	1.6
17	Utah	4.1
19	Vermont	3.3
8	Virginia	5.4
6	Washington	5.9
15	West Virginia	4.2
38	Wisconsin	1.1
25	Wyoming	2.4

RANK ORDER

RANK	STATE	RATE
1	Massachusetts	8.3
1	New Jersey	8.3
3	California	6.7
4	Arizona	6.5
5	Connecticut	6.0
6	Washington	5.9
7	Nevada	5.7
8	Virginia	5.4
9	Michigan	5.0
10	Oregon	4.8
10	Rhode Island	4.8
12	Delaware	4.7
13	Tennessee	4.6
14	Idaho	4.5
15	Maryland	4.2
15	West Virginia	4.2
17	Utah	4.1
18	Minnesota	4.0
19	Vermont	3.3
20	New York	3.2
21	Colorado	3.1
21	New Hampshire	3.1
23	Oklahoma	2.8
24	Montana	2.7
25	Wyoming	2.4
26	Maine	2.3
26	Ohio	2.3
28	Indiana	2.2
28	Kentucky	2.2
30	Kansas	1.9
31	Florida	1.7
31	Illinois	1.7
31	Missouri	1.7
34	Texas	1.6
35	Pennsylvania	1.4
36	Iowa	1.3
36	New Mexico	1.3
38	Nebraska	1.1
38	Wisconsin	1.1
40	South Carolina	1.0
41	South Dakota	0.9
42	Alaska	0.8
42	North Dakota	0.8
44	North Carolina	0.5
45	Georgia	0.4
46	Louisiana	0.3
47	Arkansas	0.1
47	Mississippi	0.1
NA	Alabama**	NA
NA	Hawaii**	NA

District of Columbia — 0.9

Source: Morgan Quitno Press using data from Federal Bureau of Investigation
   "Hate Crimes Statistics 2000" (Uniform Crime Reports, November 19, 2001)
*Figures are for reporting law enforcement agencies. Participating agencies covered 84.2 percent of the U.S.
population. Fifty-four percent of the incidents were motivated by racial bias; 18.3 percent by religious bias; 16.1
percent by sexual-orientation bias; and 11.3 percent by ethnicity/national origin bias.
**Not available.

Criminal Victimization in 2000

Each year the Bureau of Justice Statistics conducts the National Criminal Victimization Survey (NCVS). Unlike the FBI's Uniform Crime Reports, which collects crime data from law enforcement agencies, the NCVS information is obtained through interviews with victims of crime.

Type of Crime	Number of Victimizations	Victimization Rates*
All crimes	25,893	NA
Personal crimes	6,597	29.1
Crimes of violence	6,323	27.9
Completed violence**	2,044	9.0
Attempted/threatened violence	4,279	18.9
Rape/Sexual Assault	261	1.2
Rape/attempted rape	147	0.6
Rape	92	0.4
Attempted rape	55	0.2
Sexual assault	114	0.5
Robbery	732	3.2
Completed/property taken	520	2.3
With injury	160	0.7
Without injury	360	1.6
Attempted to take property	212	0.9
With injury	66	0.3
Without injury	146	0.6
Assault	5,330	23.5
Aggravated	1,293	5.7
With injury	346	1.5
Threatened with weapon	946	4.2
Simple	4,038	17.8
With minor injury	989	4.4
Without injury	3,048	13.4
Personal theft**	274	1.2
Property crimes	19,297	178.1
Household burglary	3,444	31.8
Completed	2,909	26.9
Forcible entry	1,038	9.6
Unlawful entry without force	1,872	17.3
Attempted forcible entry	534	4.9
Motor vehicle theft	937	8.6
Completed	642	5.9
Attempted	295	2.7
Theft	14,916	137.7
Completed**	14,300	132.0
Less than $50	4,707	43.4
$50-$249	5,297	48.9
$250 or more	3,177	29.3
Attempted	616	5.7

Source: U.S. Department of Justice, Bureau of Justice Statistics
    "Criminal Victimization 2000: Changes 1999-2000 with Trends 1993-2000" (Bulletin, June 2001, NCJ-187007)
*Rates are per 1,000 persons age 12 or older or per 1,000 households. In 2000, there were 226,804,610 persons age 12 or older and 108,352,960 households. **Completed violent crimes include rape, sexual assault, robbery with or without injury, aggravated assault with injury, and simple assault with minor injury. The NCVS is based on interviews with victims and thus cannot measure murder. Personal theft includes pick pocketing, purse snatching and attempted purse snatching not shown separately. Completed theft includes thefts with unknown losses.

VII. APPENDIX

Population in 2001

National Total = 284,796,887*

ALPHA ORDER

RANK	STATE	POPULATION	% of USA
23	Alabama	4,464,356	1.6%
47	Alaska	634,892	0.2%
20	Arizona	5,307,331	1.9%
33	Arkansas	2,692,090	0.9%
1	California	34,501,130	12.1%
24	Colorado	4,417,714	1.6%
29	Connecticut	3,425,074	1.2%
45	Delaware	796,165	0.3%
4	Florida	16,396,515	5.8%
10	Georgia	8,383,915	2.9%
42	Hawaii	1,224,398	0.4%
39	Idaho	1,321,006	0.5%
5	Illinois	12,482,301	4.4%
14	Indiana	6,114,745	2.1%
30	Iowa	2,923,179	1.0%
32	Kansas	2,694,641	0.9%
25	Kentucky	4,065,556	1.4%
22	Louisiana	4,465,430	1.6%
40	Maine	1,286,670	0.5%
19	Maryland	5,375,156	1.9%
13	Massachusetts	6,379,304	2.2%
8	Michigan	9,990,817	3.5%
21	Minnesota	4,972,294	1.7%
31	Mississippi	2,858,029	1.0%
17	Missouri	5,629,707	2.0%
44	Montana	904,433	0.3%
38	Nebraska	1,713,235	0.6%
35	Nevada	2,106,074	0.7%
41	New Hampshire	1,259,181	0.4%
9	New Jersey	8,484,431	3.0%
36	New Mexico	1,829,146	0.6%
3	New York	19,011,378	6.7%
11	North Carolina	8,186,268	2.9%
48	North Dakota	634,448	0.2%
7	Ohio	11,373,541	4.0%
28	Oklahoma	3,460,097	1.2%
27	Oregon	3,472,867	1.2%
6	Pennsylvania	12,287,150	4.3%
43	Rhode Island	1,058,920	0.4%
26	South Carolina	4,063,011	1.4%
46	South Dakota	756,600	0.3%
16	Tennessee	5,740,021	2.0%
2	Texas	21,325,018	7.5%
34	Utah	2,269,789	0.8%
49	Vermont	613,090	0.2%
12	Virginia	7,187,734	2.5%
15	Washington	5,987,973	2.1%
37	West Virginia	1,801,916	0.6%
18	Wisconsin	5,401,906	1.9%
50	Wyoming	494,423	0.2%

RANK ORDER

RANK	STATE	POPULATION	% of USA
1	California	34,501,130	12.1%
2	Texas	21,325,018	7.5%
3	New York	19,011,378	6.7%
4	Florida	16,396,515	5.8%
5	Illinois	12,482,301	4.4%
6	Pennsylvania	12,287,150	4.3%
7	Ohio	11,373,541	4.0%
8	Michigan	9,990,817	3.5%
9	New Jersey	8,484,431	3.0%
10	Georgia	8,383,915	2.9%
11	North Carolina	8,186,268	2.9%
12	Virginia	7,187,734	2.5%
13	Massachusetts	6,379,304	2.2%
14	Indiana	6,114,745	2.1%
15	Washington	5,987,973	2.1%
16	Tennessee	5,740,021	2.0%
17	Missouri	5,629,707	2.0%
18	Wisconsin	5,401,906	1.9%
19	Maryland	5,375,156	1.9%
20	Arizona	5,307,331	1.9%
21	Minnesota	4,972,294	1.7%
22	Louisiana	4,465,430	1.6%
23	Alabama	4,464,356	1.6%
24	Colorado	4,417,714	1.6%
25	Kentucky	4,065,556	1.4%
26	South Carolina	4,063,011	1.4%
27	Oregon	3,472,867	1.2%
28	Oklahoma	3,460,097	1.2%
29	Connecticut	3,425,074	1.2%
30	Iowa	2,923,179	1.0%
31	Mississippi	2,858,029	1.0%
32	Kansas	2,694,641	0.9%
33	Arkansas	2,692,090	0.9%
34	Utah	2,269,789	0.8%
35	Nevada	2,106,074	0.7%
36	New Mexico	1,829,146	0.6%
37	West Virginia	1,801,916	0.6%
38	Nebraska	1,713,235	0.6%
39	Idaho	1,321,006	0.5%
40	Maine	1,286,670	0.5%
41	New Hampshire	1,259,181	0.4%
42	Hawaii	1,224,398	0.4%
43	Rhode Island	1,058,920	0.4%
44	Montana	904,433	0.3%
45	Delaware	796,165	0.3%
46	South Dakota	756,600	0.3%
47	Alaska	634,892	0.2%
48	North Dakota	634,448	0.2%
49	Vermont	613,090	0.2%
50	Wyoming	494,423	0.2%
	District of Columbia	571,822	0.2%

Source: U.S. Bureau of the Census
"States" (December 27, 2001, http://eire.census.gov/popest/data/states.php)
*Resident population.

Population in 2000

National Total = 284,796,887*

ALPHA ORDER

RANK	STATE	POPULATION	% of USA
23	Alabama	4,451,493	1.6%
48	Alaska	627,601	0.2%
20	Arizona	5,165,274	1.8%
33	Arkansas	2,678,030	0.9%
1	California	34,000,446	12.1%
24	Colorado	4,323,410	1.5%
29	Connecticut	3,410,079	1.2%
45	Delaware	786,234	0.3%
4	Florida	16,054,328	5.7%
10	Georgia	8,229,823	2.9%
42	Hawaii	1,212,281	0.4%
39	Idaho	1,299,258	0.5%
5	Illinois	12,435,970	4.4%
14	Indiana	6,089,950	2.2%
30	Iowa	2,927,509	1.0%
32	Kansas	2,691,750	1.0%
25	Kentucky	4,047,424	1.4%
22	Louisiana	4,469,970	1.6%
40	Maine	1,276,961	0.5%
19	Maryland	5,310,908	1.9%
13	Massachusetts	6,357,072	2.3%
8	Michigan	9,952,006	3.5%
21	Minnesota	4,931,093	1.7%
31	Mississippi	2,849,100	1.0%
17	Missouri	5,603,553	2.0%
44	Montana	903,157	0.3%
38	Nebraska	1,712,577	0.6%
35	Nevada	2,018,723	0.7%
41	New Hampshire	1,239,881	0.4%
9	New Jersey	8,429,007	3.0%
36	New Mexico	1,821,282	0.6%
3	New York	18,989,332	6.7%
11	North Carolina	8,077,367	2.9%
47	North Dakota	640,919	0.2%
7	Ohio	11,359,955	4.0%
27	Oklahoma	3,453,250	1.2%
28	Oregon	3,429,293	1.2%
6	Pennsylvania	12,282,591	4.4%
43	Rhode Island	1,050,236	0.4%
26	South Carolina	4,023,438	1.4%
46	South Dakota	755,509	0.3%
16	Tennessee	5,702,027	2.0%
2	Texas	20,946,503	7.4%
34	Utah	2,241,555	0.8%
49	Vermont	609,709	0.2%
12	Virginia	7,104,016	2.5%
15	Washington	5,908,372	2.1%
37	West Virginia	1,807,099	0.6%
18	Wisconsin	5,372,243	1.9%
50	Wyoming	494,001	0.2%

RANK ORDER

RANK	STATE	POPULATION	% of USA
1	California	34,000,446	12.1%
2	Texas	20,946,503	7.4%
3	New York	18,989,332	6.7%
4	Florida	16,054,328	5.7%
5	Illinois	12,435,970	4.4%
6	Pennsylvania	12,282,591	4.4%
7	Ohio	11,359,955	4.0%
8	Michigan	9,952,006	3.5%
9	New Jersey	8,429,007	3.0%
10	Georgia	8,229,823	2.9%
11	North Carolina	8,077,367	2.9%
12	Virginia	7,104,016	2.5%
13	Massachusetts	6,357,072	2.3%
14	Indiana	6,089,950	2.2%
15	Washington	5,908,372	2.1%
16	Tennessee	5,702,027	2.0%
17	Missouri	5,603,553	2.0%
18	Wisconsin	5,372,243	1.9%
19	Maryland	5,310,908	1.9%
20	Arizona	5,165,274	1.8%
21	Minnesota	4,931,093	1.7%
22	Louisiana	4,469,970	1.6%
23	Alabama	4,451,493	1.6%
24	Colorado	4,323,410	1.5%
25	Kentucky	4,047,424	1.4%
26	South Carolina	4,023,438	1.4%
27	Oklahoma	3,453,250	1.2%
28	Oregon	3,429,293	1.2%
29	Connecticut	3,410,079	1.2%
30	Iowa	2,927,509	1.0%
31	Mississippi	2,849,100	1.0%
32	Kansas	2,691,750	1.0%
33	Arkansas	2,678,030	0.9%
34	Utah	2,241,555	0.8%
35	Nevada	2,018,723	0.7%
36	New Mexico	1,821,282	0.6%
37	West Virginia	1,807,099	0.6%
38	Nebraska	1,712,577	0.6%
39	Idaho	1,299,258	0.5%
40	Maine	1,276,961	0.5%
41	New Hampshire	1,239,881	0.4%
42	Hawaii	1,212,281	0.4%
43	Rhode Island	1,050,236	0.4%
44	Montana	903,157	0.3%
45	Delaware	786,234	0.3%
46	South Dakota	755,509	0.3%
47	North Dakota	640,919	0.2%
48	Alaska	627,601	0.2%
49	Vermont	609,709	0.2%
50	Wyoming	494,001	0.2%
	District of Columbia	571,066	0.2%

Source: U.S. Bureau of the Census
   "States" (December 27, 2001, http://eire.census.gov/popest/data/states.php)
*Resident population as of July 1.

Population in 1996

National Total = 265,228,572*

ALPHA ORDER

ALPHA ORDER

RANK	STATE	POPULATION	% of USA
23	Alabama	4,290,403	1.6%
48	Alaska	604,918	0.2%
21	Arizona	4,432,308	1.7%
33	Arkansas	2,504,858	0.9%
1	California	31,780,829	12.0%
25	Colorado	3,812,716	1.4%
28	Connecticut	3,267,030	1.2%
46	Delaware	727,090	0.3%
4	Florida	14,426,911	5.4%
10	Georgia	7,332,225	2.8%
41	Hawaii	1,184,434	0.4%
40	Idaho	1,187,706	0.4%
6	Illinois	11,953,003	4.5%
14	Indiana	5,834,908	2.2%
30	Iowa	2,848,473	1.1%
32	Kansas	2,598,266	1.0%
24	Kentucky	3,881,051	1.5%
22	Louisiana	4,338,763	1.6%
39	Maine	1,241,436	0.5%
19	Maryland	5,057,142	1.9%
13	Massachusetts	6,085,393	2.3%
8	Michigan	9,739,184	3.7%
20	Minnesota	4,647,723	1.8%
31	Mississippi	2,709,925	1.0%
16	Missouri	5,367,888	2.0%
44	Montana	876,656	0.3%
37	Nebraska	1,647,657	0.6%
38	Nevada	1,596,476	0.6%
42	New Hampshire	1,160,768	0.4%
9	New Jersey	8,009,624	3.0%
36	New Mexico	1,706,151	0.6%
3	New York	18,143,805	6.8%
11	North Carolina	7,307,658	2.8%
47	North Dakota	642,858	0.2%
7	Ohio	11,187,032	4.2%
27	Oklahoma	3,289,634	1.2%
29	Oregon	3,195,087	1.2%
5	Pennsylvania	12,038,008	4.5%
43	Rhode Island	987,858	0.4%
26	South Carolina	3,738,974	1.4%
45	South Dakota	730,699	0.3%
17	Tennessee	5,313,576	2.0%
2	Texas	19,006,240	7.2%
34	Utah	2,022,253	0.8%
49	Vermont	586,352	0.2%
12	Virginia	6,665,491	2.5%
15	Washington	5,509,963	2.1%
35	West Virginia	1,818,983	0.7%
18	Wisconsin	5,173,828	2.0%
50	Wyoming	480,085	0.2%

RANK ORDER

RANK	STATE	POPULATION	% of USA
1	California	31,780,829	12.0%
2	Texas	19,006,240	7.2%
3	New York	18,143,805	6.8%
4	Florida	14,426,911	5.4%
5	Pennsylvania	12,038,008	4.5%
6	Illinois	11,953,003	4.5%
7	Ohio	11,187,032	4.2%
8	Michigan	9,739,184	3.7%
9	New Jersey	8,009,624	3.0%
10	Georgia	7,332,225	2.8%
11	North Carolina	7,307,658	2.8%
12	Virginia	6,665,491	2.5%
13	Massachusetts	6,085,393	2.3%
14	Indiana	5,834,908	2.2%
15	Washington	5,509,963	2.1%
16	Missouri	5,367,888	2.0%
17	Tennessee	5,313,576	2.0%
18	Wisconsin	5,173,828	2.0%
19	Maryland	5,057,142	1.9%
20	Minnesota	4,647,723	1.8%
21	Arizona	4,432,308	1.7%
22	Louisiana	4,338,763	1.6%
23	Alabama	4,290,403	1.6%
24	Kentucky	3,881,051	1.5%
25	Colorado	3,812,716	1.4%
26	South Carolina	3,738,974	1.4%
27	Oklahoma	3,289,634	1.2%
28	Connecticut	3,267,030	1.2%
29	Oregon	3,195,087	1.2%
30	Iowa	2,848,473	1.1%
31	Mississippi	2,709,925	1.0%
32	Kansas	2,598,266	1.0%
33	Arkansas	2,504,858	0.9%
34	Utah	2,022,253	0.8%
35	West Virginia	1,818,983	0.7%
36	New Mexico	1,706,151	0.6%
37	Nebraska	1,647,657	0.6%
38	Nevada	1,596,476	0.6%
39	Maine	1,241,436	0.5%
40	Idaho	1,187,706	0.4%
41	Hawaii	1,184,434	0.4%
42	New Hampshire	1,160,768	0.4%
43	Rhode Island	987,858	0.4%
44	Montana	876,656	0.3%
45	South Dakota	730,699	0.3%
46	Delaware	727,090	0.3%
47	North Dakota	642,858	0.2%
48	Alaska	604,918	0.2%
49	Vermont	586,352	0.2%
50	Wyoming	480,085	0.2%
	District of Columbia	538,273	0.2%

Source: U.S. Bureau of the Census
"State Population Estimates" (December 29, 1999, http://www.census.gov/population/estimates/state/st-99-3.txt)
*Includes armed forces residing in each state.

Urban Population in 2000

National Total = 247,544,180 Urban Population*

ALPHA ORDER

RANK	STATE	POPULATION	% of USA
23	Alabama	3,669,414	1.5%
43	Alaska	431,792	0.2%
16	Arizona	4,815,998	1.9%
30	Arkansas	1,826,626	0.7%
1	California	33,232,149	13.4%
21	Colorado	3,918,354	1.6%
25	Connecticut	2,909,510	1.2%
41	Delaware	676,375	0.3%
4	Florida	15,107,611	6.1%
9	Georgia	6,578,268	2.7%
39	Hawaii	883,621	0.4%
40	Idaho	873,995	0.4%
NA	Illinois**	NA	NA
15	Indiana	4,956,698	2.0%
28	Iowa	2,029,454	0.8%
NA	Kansas**	NA	NA
NA	Kentucky**	NA	NA
22	Louisiana	3,746,365	1.5%
38	Maine	910,783	0.4%
14	Maryland	5,003,234	2.0%
10	Massachusetts	6,339,400	2.6%
7	Michigan	8,794,977	3.6%
20	Minnesota	4,013,863	1.6%
32	Mississippi	1,705,673	0.7%
19	Missouri	4,335,431	1.8%
NA	Montana**	NA	NA
34	Nebraska	1,302,446	0.5%
31	Nevada	1,784,499	0.7%
35	New Hampshire	1,145,329	0.5%
8	New Jersey	8,414,350	3.4%
33	New Mexico	1,494,312	0.6%
3	New York	18,063,476	7.3%
11	North Carolina	6,218,280	2.5%
44	North Dakota	426,281	0.2%
6	Ohio	9,982,134	4.0%
27	Oklahoma	2,789,626	1.1%
26	Oregon	2,908,776	1.2%
5	Pennsylvania	11,184,985	4.5%
37	Rhode Island	1,048,319	0.4%
24	South Carolina	3,136,490	1.3%
42	South Dakota	470,772	0.2%
17	Tennessee	4,559,616	1.8%
2	Texas	19,134,472	7.7%
29	Utah	1,983,262	0.8%
45	Vermont	364,161	0.1%
12	Virginia	5,972,296	2.4%
13	Washington	5,344,885	2.2%
36	West Virginia	1,061,296	0.4%
18	Wisconsin	4,345,168	1.8%
46	Wyoming	360,313	0.1%

RANK ORDER

RANK	STATE	POPULATION	% of USA
1	California	33,232,149	13.4%
2	Texas	19,134,472	7.7%
3	New York	18,063,476	7.3%
4	Florida	15,107,611	6.1%
5	Pennsylvania	11,184,985	4.5%
6	Ohio	9,982,134	4.0%
7	Michigan	8,794,977	3.6%
8	New Jersey	8,414,350	3.4%
9	Georgia	6,578,268	2.7%
10	Massachusetts	6,339,400	2.6%
11	North Carolina	6,218,280	2.5%
12	Virginia	5,972,296	2.4%
13	Washington	5,344,885	2.2%
14	Maryland	5,003,234	2.0%
15	Indiana	4,956,698	2.0%
16	Arizona	4,815,998	1.9%
17	Tennessee	4,559,616	1.8%
18	Wisconsin	4,345,168	1.8%
19	Missouri	4,335,431	1.8%
20	Minnesota	4,013,863	1.6%
21	Colorado	3,918,354	1.6%
22	Louisiana	3,746,365	1.5%
23	Alabama	3,669,414	1.5%
24	South Carolina	3,136,490	1.3%
25	Connecticut	2,909,510	1.2%
26	Oregon	2,908,776	1.2%
27	Oklahoma	2,789,626	1.1%
28	Iowa	2,029,454	0.8%
29	Utah	1,983,262	0.8%
30	Arkansas	1,826,626	0.7%
31	Nevada	1,784,499	0.7%
32	Mississippi	1,705,673	0.7%
33	New Mexico	1,494,312	0.6%
34	Nebraska	1,302,446	0.5%
35	New Hampshire	1,145,329	0.5%
36	West Virginia	1,061,296	0.4%
37	Rhode Island	1,048,319	0.4%
38	Maine	910,783	0.4%
39	Hawaii	883,621	0.4%
40	Idaho	873,995	0.4%
41	Delaware	676,375	0.3%
42	South Dakota	470,772	0.2%
43	Alaska	431,792	0.2%
44	North Dakota	426,281	0.2%
45	Vermont	364,161	0.1%
46	Wyoming	360,313	0.1%
NA	Illinois**	NA	NA
NA	Kansas**	NA	NA
NA	Kentucky**	NA	NA
NA	Montana**	NA	NA
	District of Columbia	572,059	0.2%

Source: Morgan Quitno Press using data from Federal Bureau of Investigation
   "Crime in the United States 2000" (Uniform Crime Reports, October 22, 2001)
*Estimated totals for urban areas, defined by the F.B.I. as Metropolitan Statistical Areas and other cities outside such areas. National total includes states not shown separately.
**Not available.

Rural Population in 2000

National Total = 33,877,726 Rural Population*

ALPHA ORDER

RANK	STATE	POPULATION	% of USA
19	Alabama	777,686	2.3%
40	Alaska	195,140	0.6%
33	Arizona	314,634	0.9%
18	Arkansas	846,774	2.5%
23	California	639,499	1.9%
29	Colorado	382,907	1.1%
26	Connecticut	496,055	1.5%
42	Delaware	107,225	0.3%
17	Florida	874,767	2.6%
3	Georgia	1,608,185	4.7%
31	Hawaii	327,916	1.0%
27	Idaho	419,958	1.2%
NA	Illinois**	NA	NA
9	Indiana	1,123,787	3.3%
15	Iowa	896,870	2.6%
NA	Kansas**	NA	NA
NA	Kentucky**	NA	NA
21	Louisiana	722,611	2.1%
30	Maine	364,140	1.1%
34	Maryland	293,252	0.9%
44	Massachusetts	9,697	0.0%
6	Michigan	1,143,467	3.4%
14	Minnesota	905,616	2.7%
7	Mississippi	1,138,985	3.4%
5	Missouri	1,259,780	3.7%
NA	Montana**	NA	NA
28	Nebraska	408,817	1.2%
39	Nevada	213,758	0.6%
43	New Hampshire	90,457	0.3%
45	New Jersey	0	0.0%
32	New Mexico	324,734	1.0%
13	New York	912,981	2.7%
1	North Carolina	1,831,033	5.4%
38	North Dakota	215,919	0.6%
4	Ohio	1,371,006	4.0%
22	Oklahoma	661,028	2.0%
25	Oregon	512,623	1.5%
11	Pennsylvania	1,096,069	3.2%
45	Rhode Island	0	0.0%
16	South Carolina	875,522	2.6%
35	South Dakota	284,072	0.8%
8	Tennessee	1,129,667	3.3%
2	Texas	1,717,348	5.1%
36	Utah	249,907	0.7%
37	Vermont	244,666	0.7%
10	Virginia	1,106,219	3.3%
24	Washington	549,236	1.6%
20	West Virginia	747,048	2.2%
12	Wisconsin	1,018,507	3.0%
41	Wyoming	133,469	0.4%

RANK ORDER

RANK	STATE	POPULATION	% of USA
1	North Carolina	1,831,033	5.4%
2	Texas	1,717,348	5.1%
3	Georgia	1,608,185	4.7%
4	Ohio	1,371,006	4.0%
5	Missouri	1,259,780	3.7%
6	Michigan	1,143,467	3.4%
7	Mississippi	1,138,985	3.4%
8	Tennessee	1,129,667	3.3%
9	Indiana	1,123,787	3.3%
10	Virginia	1,106,219	3.3%
11	Pennsylvania	1,096,069	3.2%
12	Wisconsin	1,018,507	3.0%
13	New York	912,981	2.7%
14	Minnesota	905,616	2.7%
15	Iowa	896,870	2.6%
16	South Carolina	875,522	2.6%
17	Florida	874,767	2.6%
18	Arkansas	846,774	2.5%
19	Alabama	777,686	2.3%
20	West Virginia	747,048	2.2%
21	Louisiana	722,611	2.1%
22	Oklahoma	661,028	2.0%
23	California	639,499	1.9%
24	Washington	549,236	1.6%
25	Oregon	512,623	1.5%
26	Connecticut	496,055	1.5%
27	Idaho	419,958	1.2%
28	Nebraska	408,817	1.2%
29	Colorado	382,907	1.1%
30	Maine	364,140	1.1%
31	Hawaii	327,916	1.0%
32	New Mexico	324,734	1.0%
33	Arizona	314,634	0.9%
34	Maryland	293,252	0.9%
35	South Dakota	284,072	0.8%
36	Utah	249,907	0.7%
37	Vermont	244,666	0.7%
38	North Dakota	215,919	0.6%
39	Nevada	213,758	0.6%
40	Alaska	195,140	0.6%
41	Wyoming	133,469	0.4%
42	Delaware	107,225	0.3%
43	New Hampshire	90,457	0.3%
44	Massachusetts	9,697	0.0%
45	New Jersey	0	0.0%
45	Rhode Island	0	0.0%
NA	Illinois**	NA	NA
NA	Kansas**	NA	NA
NA	Kentucky**	NA	NA
NA	Montana**	NA	NA
	District of Columbia	0	0.0%

Source: Morgan Quitno Press using data from Federal Bureau of Investigation
"Crime in the United States 2000" (Uniform Crime Reports, October 22, 2001)
*Estimated totals for rural areas, defined by the F.B.I. as other than Metropolitan Statistical Areas and other cities outside such areas. National total includes states not shown separately.
**Not available.

Population 10 to 17 Years Old in 2000

National Total = 32,568,509

ALPHA ORDER

RANK	STATE	POPULATION	% of USA
23	Alabama	512,085	1.6%
46	Alaska	89,355	0.3%
21	Arizona	594,692	1.8%
34	Arkansas	311,560	1.0%
1	California	4,036,968	12.4%
24	Colorado	494,862	1.5%
29	Connecticut	374,200	1.1%
47	Delaware	87,243	0.3%
4	Florida	1,668,799	5.1%
9	Georgia	958,500	2.9%
42	Hawaii	132,624	0.4%
39	Idaho	170,631	0.5%
5	Illinois	1,439,044	4.4%
13	Indiana	707,908	2.2%
31	Iowa	342,622	1.1%
32	Kansas	328,711	1.0%
26	Kentucky	449,659	1.4%
22	Louisiana	565,627	1.7%
40	Maine	147,490	0.5%
19	Maryland	611,461	1.9%
15	Massachusetts	671,935	2.1%
8	Michigan	1,178,581	3.6%
20	Minnesota	601,406	1.8%
30	Mississippi	353,903	1.1%
16	Missouri	658,896	2.0%
43	Montana	113,230	0.3%
37	Nebraska	209,749	0.6%
36	Nevada	216,660	0.7%
41	New Hampshire	145,340	0.4%
10	New Jersey	919,244	2.8%
35	New Mexico	236,775	0.7%
3	New York	2,098,833	6.4%
11	North Carolina	861,985	2.6%
48	North Dakota	78,467	0.2%
7	Ohio	1,317,063	4.0%
27	Oklahoma	411,482	1.3%
28	Oregon	389,047	1.2%
6	Pennsylvania	1,366,472	4.2%
44	Rhode Island	112,021	0.3%
25	South Carolina	459,719	1.4%
45	South Dakota	97,094	0.3%
18	Tennessee	627,828	1.9%
2	Texas	2,607,947	8.0%
33	Utah	316,287	1.0%
49	Vermont	72,433	0.2%
12	Virginia	781,196	2.4%
14	Washington	693,628	2.1%
38	West Virginia	189,438	0.6%
17	Wisconsin	646,932	2.0%
50	Wyoming	63,806	0.2%

RANK ORDER

RANK	STATE	POPULATION	% of USA
1	California	4,036,968	12.4%
2	Texas	2,607,947	8.0%
3	New York	2,098,833	6.4%
4	Florida	1,668,799	5.1%
5	Illinois	1,439,044	4.4%
6	Pennsylvania	1,366,472	4.2%
7	Ohio	1,317,063	4.0%
8	Michigan	1,178,581	3.6%
9	Georgia	958,500	2.9%
10	New Jersey	919,244	2.8%
11	North Carolina	861,985	2.6%
12	Virginia	781,196	2.4%
13	Indiana	707,908	2.2%
14	Washington	693,628	2.1%
15	Massachusetts	671,935	2.1%
16	Missouri	658,896	2.0%
17	Wisconsin	646,932	2.0%
18	Tennessee	627,828	1.9%
19	Maryland	611,461	1.9%
20	Minnesota	601,406	1.8%
21	Arizona	594,692	1.8%
22	Louisiana	565,627	1.7%
23	Alabama	512,085	1.6%
24	Colorado	494,862	1.5%
25	South Carolina	459,719	1.4%
26	Kentucky	449,659	1.4%
27	Oklahoma	411,482	1.3%
28	Oregon	389,047	1.2%
29	Connecticut	374,200	1.1%
30	Mississippi	353,903	1.1%
31	Iowa	342,622	1.1%
32	Kansas	328,711	1.0%
33	Utah	316,287	1.0%
34	Arkansas	311,560	1.0%
35	New Mexico	236,775	0.7%
36	Nevada	216,660	0.7%
37	Nebraska	209,749	0.6%
38	West Virginia	189,438	0.6%
39	Idaho	170,631	0.5%
40	Maine	147,490	0.5%
41	New Hampshire	145,340	0.4%
42	Hawaii	132,624	0.4%
43	Montana	113,230	0.3%
44	Rhode Island	112,021	0.3%
45	South Dakota	97,094	0.3%
46	Alaska	89,355	0.3%
47	Delaware	87,243	0.3%
48	North Dakota	78,467	0.2%
49	Vermont	72,433	0.2%
50	Wyoming	63,806	0.2%
	District of Columbia	47,071	0.1%

Source: U.S. Bureau of the Census
"Census 2000 Summary File 1"

Total Area of States in Square Miles in 2001

National Total = 3,717,796 Square Miles*

ALPHA ORDER

RANK	STATE	MILES	% of USA
30	Alabama	52,237	1.4%
1	Alaska	615,230	16.6%
6	Arizona	114,006	3.1%
28	Arkansas	53,182	1.4%
3	California	158,869	4.3%
8	Colorado	104,100	2.8%
48	Connecticut	5,544	0.2%
49	Delaware	2,396	0.1%
23	Florida	59,928	1.6%
24	Georgia	58,977	1.6%
47	Hawaii	6,459	0.2%
14	Idaho	83,574	2.3%
25	Illinois	57,918	1.6%
38	Indiana	36,420	1.0%
26	Iowa	56,276	1.5%
15	Kansas	82,282	2.2%
37	Kentucky	40,411	1.1%
31	Louisiana	49,651	1.3%
39	Maine	33,741	0.9%
42	Maryland	12,297	0.3%
45	Massachusetts	9,241	0.3%
11	Michigan	96,705	2.6%
12	Minnesota	86,943	2.3%
32	Mississippi	48,286	1.3%
21	Missouri	69,709	1.9%
4	Montana	147,046	4.0%
16	Nebraska	77,358	2.1%
7	Nevada	110,567	3.0%
44	New Hampshire	9,283	0.3%
46	New Jersey	8,215	0.2%
5	New Mexico	121,598	3.3%
27	New York	53,989	1.5%
29	North Carolina	52,672	1.4%
18	North Dakota	70,704	1.9%
34	Ohio	44,828	1.2%
20	Oklahoma	69,903	1.9%
10	Oregon	97,132	2.6%
33	Pennsylvania	46,058	1.2%
50	Rhode Island	1,231	0.0%
40	South Carolina	31,189	0.8%
17	South Dakota	77,121	2.1%
36	Tennessee	42,146	1.1%
2	Texas	267,277	7.2%
13	Utah	84,904	2.3%
43	Vermont	9,615	0.3%
35	Virginia	42,326	1.1%
19	Washington	70,637	1.9%
41	West Virginia	24,231	0.7%
22	Wisconsin	65,499	1.8%
9	Wyoming	97,818	2.6%

RANK ORDER

RANK	STATE	MILES	% of USA
1	Alaska	615,230	16.6%
2	Texas	267,277	7.2%
3	California	158,869	4.3%
4	Montana	147,046	4.0%
5	New Mexico	121,598	3.3%
6	Arizona	114,006	3.1%
7	Nevada	110,567	3.0%
8	Colorado	104,100	2.8%
9	Wyoming	97,818	2.6%
10	Oregon	97,132	2.6%
11	Michigan	96,705	2.6%
12	Minnesota	86,943	2.3%
13	Utah	84,904	2.3%
14	Idaho	83,574	2.3%
15	Kansas	82,282	2.2%
16	Nebraska	77,358	2.1%
17	South Dakota	77,121	2.1%
18	North Dakota	70,704	1.9%
19	Washington	70,637	1.9%
20	Oklahoma	69,903	1.9%
21	Missouri	69,709	1.9%
22	Wisconsin	65,499	1.8%
23	Florida	59,928	1.6%
24	Georgia	58,977	1.6%
25	Illinois	57,918	1.6%
26	Iowa	56,276	1.5%
27	New York	53,989	1.5%
28	Arkansas	53,182	1.4%
29	North Carolina	52,672	1.4%
30	Alabama	52,237	1.4%
31	Louisiana	49,651	1.3%
32	Mississippi	48,286	1.3%
33	Pennsylvania	46,058	1.2%
34	Ohio	44,828	1.2%
35	Virginia	42,326	1.1%
36	Tennessee	42,146	1.1%
37	Kentucky	40,411	1.1%
38	Indiana	36,420	1.0%
39	Maine	33,741	0.9%
40	South Carolina	31,189	0.8%
41	West Virginia	24,231	0.7%
42	Maryland	12,297	0.3%
43	Vermont	9,615	0.3%
44	New Hampshire	9,283	0.3%
45	Massachusetts	9,241	0.3%
46	New Jersey	8,215	0.2%
47	Hawaii	6,459	0.2%
48	Connecticut	5,544	0.2%
49	Delaware	2,396	0.1%
50	Rhode Island	1,231	0.0%
	District of Columbia	68	0.0%

Source: U.S. Bureau of the Census
 "1990 Census of Population and Housing" (Series CPH-1)
*Total of land and water area.

IX. SOURCES

Administrative Office of the U.S. Courts
Statistics Division
One Columbus Circle, NE
Washington, DC 20544
202-502-2600
www.uscourts.gov

Bureau of the Census
4700 Silver Hill Road
Suitland, MD 20746
301-457-2800
www.census.gov

Bureau of Justice Assistance
810 Seventh Street, NW
4th Floor
Washington DC 20531
202-616-6500
www.ojp.usdoj.gov/BJA/

Bureau of Justice Statistics Clearinghouse
810 Seventh Street, NW
Washington, DC 20531
202-307-0765
www.ojp.usdoj.gov/bjs/

Children's Bureau
Administration for Children & Familes; HHS
370 L'Enfant Promenade, SW
Washington, DC 20447
202-401-9215
www.acf.dhhs.gov

Drugs and Crime Clearinghouse of the Office of National Drug Control Policy
Box 6000
Rockville, MD 20849-6000
800-666-3332
www.whitehousedrugpolicy.gov

Federal Bureau of Investigation
J. Edgar Hoover FBI Building
935 Pennsylvania Avenue, NW
Washington, DC 20535-0001
202-324-3000
Internet: http://www.fbi.gov

Juvenile Justice Clearinghouse
Box 6000
Rockville, MD 20849-6000
800-638-8736
www.ojjdp.ncjrs.org

National Archive of Crime and Justice Programs
Inter-University Consortium for Political
  and Social Research
P.O. Box 1248
Ann Arbor, MI 48106
800-999-0960
www.icpsr.umich.edu/NACJD/home.html

National Association of State Alcohol and Drug Abuse Directors, Inc.
808 17th Street, NW
Suite 410
Washington, DC 20006
202-293-0090
www.nasadad.org

National Center for State Courts
300 Newport Avenue
Williamsburg, VA 23185
757-253-2000
www.ncsconline.org/

National Institute of Justice
810 Seventh Street, NW.
Washington, DC 20531
202-307-2942
www.ojp.usdoj.gov/nij

National Clearinghouse on Child Abuse and Neglect
330 C Street, SW
Washington, DC 20447
800-394-3366
www.calib.com/nccanch/

National Criminal Justice Reference Service (NCJRS)
Box 6000
Rockville, MD 20849-6000
800-851-3420
www.ncjrs.org

Substance Abuse and Mental Health Services Administration
U.S. Department of Health and Human Services
5600 Fishers Lane
Rockville, MD 20857
301-443-8956
www.samhsa.gov

Victims of Crime Resource Center
810 Seventh Street, NW.
Washington, DC 20531
800-627-6872
www.ojp.usdoj.gov/ovc/

X. INDEX

X. INDEX (continued)

X. INDEX (continued)

X. INDEX (continued)

CHAPTER INDEX

Arrests

Corrections

Drugs and Alcohol

Finance

Juveniles

Law Enforcement

Offenses

HOW TO USE THIS INDEX

Place left thumb on the outer edge of this page. To locate the desired entry, fold back the remaining page edges and align the index edge mark with the appropriate page edge mark.

Other books by Morgan Quitno Press:

- *State Statistical Trends (monthly journal)*
- *State Rankings 2002 ($54.95)*
- *Health Care State Rankings 2002 ($54.95)*
- *City Crime Rankings, 8th Edition ($42.95)*

Call toll free: 1-800-457-0742 or
visit us at www.statestats.com